ABNORMAL PSYCHOLOGY
Patterns, Issues, Interventions

FRANK COSTIN
University of Illinois at Urbana–Champaign

JURIS G. DRAGUNS
The Pennsylvania State University

John Wiley & Sons
New York · Chichester · Brisbane · Toronto · Singapore

Aquisitions Editor, Deborah Moore
Managing Editor, Joan Kalkut
Production Supervisor, Dawn Reitz
Editorial Supervisor, Priscilla Todd
Manufacturing Manager, Robin Garmise
Photo Research Manager, Stella Kupferburg

Text and Cover Design: Michael Jung

Library of Congress Cataloging in Publication Data:

Costin, Frank.
  Abnormal psychology.

  References p. R1–R51
  1. Psychology, Pathological.   I. Draguns, Juris G.,
1932–   . II. Title.
RC454.C67 1989   616.89   88-28087
ISBN 0-471-60610-3

Printed in the United States of America

10 9 8 7 6 5 4 3 2 1

To the memory of my parents, Jennie and Samuel
F. C.

To my wife, Marie, and our children, Julie and George
J. G. D.

About the Authors

Frank Costin received his Ph.D. degree from the University of Chicago. He is now Professor Emeritus of Psychology at the University of Illinois, Urbana-Champaign, where he continues in his scholarly work. He has served in United States Air Force hospital programs, the Chicago State Hospital, and the University of Illinois Counseling Center. He has been an Honorary Visiting Scholar at the University of London's Institute of Education, Visiting Professor at the University of Oregon, and a consultant and guest lecturer at colleges and universities in the United States, Great Britain, Ireland, and West Germany.

Professor Costin is a Fellow of the American Psychological Association and a past president of the Division on the Teaching of Psychology. His current research has focused on social and psychological analyses of myths about rape. In addition to his publications in professional journals and books, Professor Costin has served in various editorial positions, including editor of the Methods and Techniques Department of *Teaching of Psychology*.

His teaching career has encompassed undergraduate and graduate courses in abnormal, clinical, developmental, educational, and personality psychology; televised programs for introductory psychology; and courses in the teaching of psychology. He is a founder of the University of Illinois Annual Institute on the Teaching of Psychology. Professor Costin is a recipient of the University of Illinois College of Liberal Arts Award for Distinguished Teaching and the Alpha Lambda Delta Award for Excellence in Freshmen Instruction.

Juris G. Draguns earned his Ph.D. degree from the University of Rochester. Trained as a clinical psychologist, he held a succession of professional and research positions at the Rochester State Hospital in Rochester, New York, and Worcester State Hospital in Worcester, Massachusetts. Concurrently, he taught courses at the University of Rochester, Clark University, and Leicester Junior College. Since 1967 he has been on the faculty of The Pennsylvania State University where he is now Professor of psychology.

Professor Draguns has taught undergraduate and graduate courses in abnormal psychology and related fields for the past 28 years. He has held visiting appointments at the Johannes Gutenberg University in Mainz, West Germany; the East–West Center in Honolulu, Hawaii; Flinders University of South Australia; and National Taiwan University in Taipei.

In connection with his research on cultural influences on psychopathology, he has traveled widely in North and South America, Europe, Australia, and Asia. For two years, he was Director of the Clinical Psychology Graduate Program at Penn State. Dr. Draguns is the author of numerous journal articles and book chapters in the psychological, psychiatric, and anthropological literature. He is the co-editor of *Handbook of Cross-Cultural Psychology: Psychopathology* (Vol. 6) and of three editions of *Counseling Across Cultures* as well as of *Roots of Perception* and *Psychological Processes in Cognition and Personality*.

For as long as civilization has existed, the phenomena that we now study as abnormal psychology have generated curiosity, puzzlement, and concern. Great minds of the remote and recent past have addressed themselves to issues of abnormal behavior and experience through poetry, prose, the pictorial and plastic arts, and philosophy. At various points in the book, we illustrate how the humanities, especially literature, have contributed to an understanding of abnormality.

Although humanistic studies have provided many brilliant personal vistas of abnormal psychology, cumulative progress in knowledge has had to wait for the development of various scientific disciplines. Today, we study problems of abnormal behavior and experience at multiple levels of inquiry and with different scientific methods. It is the shared concern of clinical psychology, social work, psychiatry, neurology, psychiatric nursing, and pharmocology. These approaches range from the investigation of biological and physical deficits in the development of abnormality to studies of social and cultural influences.

This book reflects such spans of knowledge. In addition, we draw information from the fields of law and history when it has bearing on the problems of abnormal behavior and experience. We believe that the inclusion of all these areas is highly appropriate, not only for students who enroll in abnormal psychology courses as part of their general education but also for students whose undergraduate concentration is psychology.

History

We are fully committed to using historical knowledge for understanding contemporary abnormal psychology. More than 2000 years ago, Marcus Tullius Cicero, the great Roman statesman, orator, and author, declared, "To be ignorant of what occurred before you were born is to remain always a child." It is in the spirit of this aphorism that we consider throughout the book historical facts, theories, and issues and their influence on modern concepts of abnormality. We do this in the contexts in which they have direct relevance rather than following the more conventional practice of confining the history of abnormal psychology to an isolated chapter.

In Chapter 2, we show that the origins of classifying mental disorders go back to ancient days. In *The Sacred Disease*, Hippocrates (ca. 460–377 B.C.) argued that mental disorders were not caused by divine intervention, as was commonly believed, but were due to disturbances in the brain. Thus, in a rudimentary fashion, his beliefs foreshadowed modern concepts of psychological disability.

In Chapter 10, we discuss disorders of mood, including alternating periods of abnormal depression and excitement. This condition, known today as bipolar mood disorder, was apparently recognized in ancient days. For example, the biblical story of King Saul tells how he suffered from episodes of extreme melancholy followed by outbursts of extremely excited behavior.

The insanity plea as a legal defense in criminal cases has in recent years evoked a great deal of debate among both mental health professionals and legal experts. The idea that insanity should be a mitigating factor in crime has evolved from a long series of legal opinions, going back to the Talmud. In 1813, British law established a specific set of criteria to be used in trials involving the insanity defense. In Chapter 21, we describe how all this came about and discuss its significance for understanding problems of mental disorder in today's legal world.

These are but a few examples of how history is used in this book. Our purpose is not only to expand the understanding of current problems of abnormal behavior and experiences but also to show how the attainment of such understanding represents a continuous intellectual search from one generation to the next.

Culture

Throughout the book, we emphasize the social and cultural significance of abnormal behavior. For example, we discuss rape not simply as a sexual disorder, along with voyeurism, exhibitionism, and other so-called sexual deviations, but as criminal sexual exploitation in which the rapist may or may not be suffering from a specific mental disorder.

Similarly, in dealing with senile disorders, we examine the social and psychological problems of old age and the effects of social attitudes and policies on the development and manifestations of mental disorders during that period of life.

In recent years, gender issues have become increasingly important in the study of abnormal psychology. Thus, we examine such problems as the influence of gender roles on the development of mental disorders and the question of gender bias in diagnosing such disorders.

Controversy

In explaining how abnormality can be understood from a variety of theoretical and practical positions, we have tried to avoid proving that a particular approach is "superior." This does not mean that we hold to a sterile neutrality. When we conclude that the weight of evidence favors a particular view or explanation of abnormal behavior, we also present relevant counterarguments. In this way, we hope to promote thoughtful reflection and discussion of the issues.

Organization

The book is divided into three major parts. Part 1 (Chapters 1–4) deals with various approaches to understanding abnormal behavior and experience. In Chapter 1, we discuss criteria for defining and recognizing abnormality, the roles of mental health professionals, and concepts of positive mental health. In Chapter 2, we introduce basic concepts and principles involved in the diagnosis, classification, and assessment of mental disorders. In Chapters 3 and 4, we discuss biomedical, psychodynamic, social learning, humanistic, and cultural approaches to understanding mental disorders.

Part 2 (Chapters 5–17) deals with patterns of mental disorders, their etiology, and how people suffering from such disorders can be helped. For purposes of organization and terminology, we follow the classification system of the American Psychiatric Association's *Diagnostic and Statistical Manual of Mental Disorders*, revised edition (DSM-III-R), published in 1987. The fact that the classification system we use was developed under the auspices of the psychiatric profession by no means commits us to an exclusively biomedical view of abnormality. Throughout the book, we consider a variety of theoretical and practical approaches to understanding mental disorders. Furthermore, we maintain a critical attitude toward DSM-III-R, evaluating its negative as well as positive features.

Part 3 (Chapters 18–21) examines on a broad scale various approaches to the treatment of mental disorders: biomedical, psychodynamic, humanistic, behavioral, and cognitive. Here we consider both individual and group methods of psychotherapy and their effectiveness. In the final chapter, we deal with legal issues of abnormality and problems of community mental health.

Acknowledgments

We thank the following colleagues for their helpful comments in reviewing the manuscript at various stages of its development:

Jack Adams, University of Illinois, Urbana–Champaign

Deborah Balogh, Ball State University

Patricia Barker, Schenectady County Community College

Michael Coles, University of Illinois, Urbana–Champaign

Joan DiGiovanni, Western New England College

Robert Emery, University of Virginia

Polly Gillette, Northern Virginia Community College, Annandale

William Greenough, University of Illinois, Urbana–Champaign

Daniel Klein, State University of New York at Stony Brook

Gerald Peterson, Saginaw Valley State College

Glenn Shean, College of William and Mary

Paul Wachtel, CUNY; City College

We acknowledge with appreciation the support of Emanuel Donchin, Head of the Department of Psychology at the University of Illinois, Urbana–Champaign, and the valuable help we received from the library resources of our universities. We are especially grateful to the following librarians at the University of Illinois: Karen Bingham, Education and Social Science; Helen Watson and Patricia Donahoe–Petrie, Susan Stout Memorial Library, Department of Psychology; and the staff of the Health Sciences, Law, and Rare Book Library. We also thank Eileen Place, Jane Baldwin, and Fae Kiifner–Jackson of the University of Illinois for their efficient work in processing the manuscript.

We are grateful for the understanding and expertise of the John Wiley editorial and production staff, and in particular for the contributions of the Psychology Editor, Deborah Moore, and those of Jo-Anne Naples, Kathleen Shankman, Stella Kupferberg, Joan

Kalkut, and Dawn Reitz. We also thank Warren Abraham for his early encouragement of our project.

To a significant extent, this book grew out of our many years of teaching undergraduate courses in abnormal psychology. The stimulation we received from our students in no small measure made this book possible.

Frank Costin

January 1989   Juris G. Draguns

In writing this book, we have included a number of features designed to help you study its content and profit from doing so.

1. We begin each chapter with an outline and conclude each chapter with a comprehensive summary of the main points. We suggest that you read the outline first, then the summary, next the chapter itself, and after that the summary again. The preliminary reading should stimulate your interest and help you understand the more detailed information. The second reading of the summary will refresh your memory of the more detailed material in the chapter.

2. Special boxes are used at various points in the text to amplify and enrich the main narrative. They include a photographic essay showing highlights of Freud's professional career and personal life and another on sculptured images from ancient Mexican civilization to illustrate how depression was perceived. Throughout the book, the boxes are integrated with the main narrative. To avoid having them perceived merely as extras, we refer to each box at the point in the text where it is most relevant to the topic under discussion. In this way, we increase their enrichment value and usefulness.

3. Every field of study has its special technical language. Depending on your previous knowledge of psychology, you may already be familiar with some of the terminology in this book. When a technical term first appears, it is defined and usually illustrated. In addition, many of these are defined in a glossary at the end of the book. We suggest that you look closely at the context in which the terms occur, because it can help you understand the concepts that they represent. After all, technical terminology is simply a shorthand way of communicating those concepts.

4. References are cited in the text by the authors' last names and dates of publication, as in these examples: Adler, 1964; Arieti & Bemporad, 1980. In some instances, a citation in the text has two dates — for example, Freud, 1940/1949. The first is the original publication date; the second locates the citation in the complete reference list at the back of the book. This method of citation is used when the material is an English translation of a book or article published at an earlier date or when it has been reprinted from another source. Here is the full reference for the Freud citation: Freud, S. (1949). *An outline of psychoanalysis* (J. Strachey, Trans.). New York: Norton. (Original work published 1940). The reference list not only documents the various sources of information cited in the text but is also useful for consultation when pursuing particular topics in more detail.

5. There are two indexes. One contains the names of all individuals mentioned in the book and the numbers of the pages on which they are referred to. The other is for the subject matter of the book. Since a particular topic or concept may be discussed in a variety of contexts, the subject index can be especially helpful for locating those contexts.

6. A Study Guide accompanies the textbook. It contains many helpful exercises and suggestions for studying to promote learning.

Contents

part

I

Approaches to Understanding Abnormality

There are a number of basic approaches to describing and explaining abnormal behavior and experience. Chapter 1 focuses on statistical and psychosocial abnormality, criteria of mental disorders and positive mental health, and the roles of mental health professionals. Chapter 2 considers various approaches to classifying mental disorders, the meaning and use of diagnosis, and methods of assessing mental disorders. Chapter 3 deals with biomedical and psychodynamic viewpoints. Biomedical approaches emphasize the importance of underlying biological factors in the development and expression of mental disorders; psychodynamic concepts focus on unconscious motivation, anxiety, and conflict. Chapter 4 considers how principles of learning, the social and cultural environment, and humanistic concepts of thought and behavior can all contribute to an understanding of abnormal behavior and experience. Throughout Part 1 the primary emphasis is on the contribution each of these approaches makes to understanding abnormality. Each chapter begins with an outline of the major topics and ends with a summary.

1

Basic Characteristics of Abnormality

Nature reveals some of her deeper
secrets through the abnormal.

EDUARD C. LINDEMAN
Quoted in *Contemporary Psychology* (1967)

He complained primarily of an inability to walk around in public and when he attempted to leave his home unaccompanied he experienced a severe fear reaction, which he described as a feeling that "something dreadful was about to happen" to him. . . . The bodily reactions that accompanied these subjective feelings of apprehension included breathlessness, palpitations, and feelings of weakness that forced him to support himself against the nearest wall. . . . In practice, [this] meant that whenever he walked outside his home for any distance he was obliged to creep alongside a wall, touching it as he proceeded. (Rachman, 1978, p. 141)

Mr. and Mrs. A. are an attractive, gregarious couple, married for 15 years . . . [They are] in the midst of a crisis over their sexual problems. . . . Mrs. A. . . . reports that throughout their entire marriage she has become extremely frustrated because sex has "always been hopeless for us." She is now seriously considering leaving her husband.

The difficulty is in the husband's rapid ejaculation. Whenever any lovemaking is attempted, Mr. A. becomes anxious, moves quickly toward intercourse, and reaches orgasm either immediately upon entering his wife's vagina or within one or two strokes. . . . He has severe feelings of inadequacy and guilt, and she experiences a mixture of frustration and resentment toward his "ineptness and lack of concern." Recently they have developed a pattern of avoiding sex which leaves them both frustrated, but which keeps overt hostility to a minimum. (Spitzer, Skodol, Gibbon, & Williams, 1981, p. 108)

[Sylvia] Frumkin talked for one hour, non-stop, to some of the other patients, to some of their visitors, to the therapy aides, to the cleaner, to laundry workers and diningroom employees and other people who passed through the ward, and to herself. . . . "Hitler did a good job. He cleaned up the streets. He invented the Volkswagen. I love Darth Vader. I am Darth Vader. I figured out that Mayor Koch is Charles Nelson Reilly. Adolph Hitler is forgiven. He invented methadone and the Mercedes Benz. It was all a price war. I'm Tania and I have the biggest house in the country. Bess Myers was originally the Statue of Liberty. I married Neil Diamond a long time ago." (Sheehan, 1982, p. 60)

The first case illustrates an anxiety disorder known as **agoraphobia** — an irrational fear of leaving home or venturing into public places (Chapter 5). Mr. A's problem is premature ejaculation, a form of sexual dysfunction (Chapter 9). The case of Sylvia Frumkin reveals a psychological disturbance far more devastating than the other two, schizophrenia, one of the most disabling of all mental disorders (Chapter 11).

Although these examples differ, they all illustrate two basic approaches to defining abnormality, the statistical approach and the psychosocial approach. The first focuses on the relative *infrequency* of abnormal behavior and experience. The second emphasizes the *content* of those events — their psychological and social characteristics. Both approaches are essential for defining abnormality.

Statistical Abnormality

From a statistical viewpoint, abnormality is a quantitative deviation from the average — the normal. *Abnormal* events are the events that happen least often; *normal* events, those that occur most often. Consider, for example, the plight of Sylvia Frumkin. Her thinking and behavior were so impaired that she required treatment in a mental hospital. Statistically, however, her behavior was abnormal not because it was highly disorganized but because its occurrence in the general population is relatively infrequent. Most people are not schizophrenic. The patterns of abnormality described in the other two cases are also statistically abnormal, not because of the obvious distress they reveal but because they happen less often than patterns of behavior and thinking that are relatively free of such sexual frustration and irrational fear.

Although the concept of statistical infrequency is essential for defining abnormal behavior and experience, its exclusive use can be highly misleading. For example, consider the matter of intelligence. Table 1.1 shows the distribution of test scores (IQs) obtained by administering the revised Wechsler Adult Intelligence Test (WAIS-R) to a representative sample of 1800 people in the United States whose ages ranged from 16 to 74 (Wechsler, 1981, p. 29). The WAIS-R is widely used to help determine the extent to which abnormal behavior and experiences might involve a deficit in intellectual ability. As the table shows, most of the individuals (about 49 percent) have scores between 90 and 109, the average range. The small group with scores of 130 or above is classified as very superior. At the other extreme, the group scoring 69 or below is classified as mentally retarded. Both groups are statistically abnormal, since their scores deviate sharply from the average range. They also differ considerably in the psychological characteristics that the WAIS-R measures, such as reasoning, memory, and fluency in the use of words (Wechsler, 1981, p. 8). Although abnormal psychology deals with problems related to relatively low intellectual ability (mental retardation), it is not particularly concerned with the other extreme, very high intelligence (see Chapter 17).

Statistical concepts are important for defining abnormality, but they are not sufficient. One must also consider the *quality* of events in determining their abnormality. Abnormal psychology deals with the statistically abnormal patterns of behavior and experience that reflect inadequacy rather than competence, failure rather than success, impairment rather than effectiveness. Not all statistically deviant behavior and experiences are abnormal, in the sense in which we use that term. However, all abnormal behavior and experiences *are* statistically deviant.

Table 1.1 Classification of Intelligence According to IQ scores Obtained with the Wechsler Adult Intelligence Scale – Revised (WAIS-R)		
IQ	**Classification**	**Percent Included**
130 and above	Very superior	2.6
120–129	Superior	6.9
110–119	High average	16.6
90–109	Average	49.1
80–89	Low average	16.1
70–79	Borderline	6.4
69 and below	Mentally retarded	2.3

Source: Wechsler, 1981, p. 28.

Psychosocial Abnormality

The second basic approach to defining abnormality focuses directly on the characteristics of experience and behavior that reveal psychological and social impairment. Sylvia Frumkin's behavior is clearly abnormal in a psychosocial sense because it reflects her inability to think and speak coherently and to interact effectively with her social environment. By the same token, the frustration and fear shown in the other two cases also indicate impaired relationships to the environment, so we classify them as abnormal also.

A central feature of psychosocial impairment is its *maladaptive* nature. Although **maladaptive behavior**, thinking, and feeling may take many specific forms, they all tend to reflect two fundamental disabilities: a persistent failure to respond effectively to environmental demands and an inability to reach desired goals. Furthermore, maladaptive behavior often interferes with other people's responses to environmental demands and their attempts to reach their goals. It is frequently accompanied by such disabling feelings as anxiety, conflict, depression, guilt, and alienation from others.

Maladaptive behavior and experiences range from responses to environmental demands that are only slightly inadequate to those that barely meet the minimal requirements of effective daily living. Even serious patterns of abnormality may show noticeably different degrees of severity. For example, the sexual problem of Mr. A. is sufficiently distressing to cause personal misery and perhaps lead to a break-up of his marriage, but it is significantly less severe than the destruction of personality reflected in Sylvia Frumkin's schizophrenic behavior. Although the problem of agoraphobia is certainly incapacitating, its degree of severity falls somewhere between the other two patterns of abnormality.

"Correct me if I'm wrong, but hasn't the fine line between sanity and madness gotten finer?"

Edgar Allan Poe.

Sylvia Plath.

Gustave Mahler.

Abraham Lincoln.

Maladaptive behavior and experience can exist together with great achievements, as in the case of these famous persons.

People may show maladaptive behavior in some aspects of their lives and still be highly successful in other areas. To cite just a few notable examples:

■ The American authors Edgar Allan Poe and Sylvia Plath experienced recurring episodes of severe depression (Allen, 1934, pp. 670–675; O'Connor, 1988, p. 19).

■ Gustav Mahler, the brilliant Austrian composer and conductor, was tortured by conflict, anxiety, and depression until his untimely death at the age of 51. He would sometimes comment about his anguish on the musical scores he was composing (Crandall, 1981; Henahan, 1984; Mahler, 1968).

■ "Abraham Lincoln suffered from severe spells of deep depression and self-doubt. During one such episode, which occurred shortly after he broke his engagement to Mary Todd, Lincoln wrote his partner Stuart: 'I am now the most miserable man living. If what I feel were equally distributed to the whole human family, there would not be one cheerful face on the earth'" (Sandburg, 1926, p. 261).

The fact that maladaptive behavior and experiences can exist together with positive strengths and accomplishments does not minimize the seriousness of psychosocial disorder. Rather, it testifies to the resilience that some very troubled people may still have and to their ability to succeed in certain areas despite mental disturbance.

Certain criteria are highly useful for recognizing and describing the basic characteristics of psychological and social abnormality. We consider these criteria under four broad and somewhat overlapping subject areas: (a) gross departures from social standards, (b) poor contact with reality, (c) intellectual and social inefficiency, and (d) personal distress.

Gross Departures from Social Standards

Social Deviance

All societies maintain certain standards and rules that define the tolerable limits of acceptable (normal) social behavior. The criteria for such behavior may be quite explicit, as in local ordinances and other laws, or they may be taken for granted, "go without saying," as some sociologists put it (Scheff, 1984, pp. 37–38). Behavior that departs markedly from acceptable limits — **social deviance** — is especially likely to be perceived as abnormal when it interferes with other people's activities and goals or offends them in other socially significant ways.

"The Scream" by Edvard Munch.

BOX 1.1 Can Genius and Mental Disorder Coexist?

The Norwegian artist Edvard Munch was a pioneer of the modern Expressionist movement. When he was only five, Munch watched his mother suffer from tuberculosis and die of a hemorrhage. After that he was raised by a strict and hostile father. As Munch later wrote, his father would become almost insane in his punishments. Until he was 45, Munch tried to overcome developing signs of psychotic disorder by painting images of a troubled past. An outstanding characteristic of his work was the use of straight or wavy parallel lines, often centering around a bizarre figure. According to some art critics, this represented his fear of being overwhelmed by a cruel world. Beginning with his 45th year, Munch became increasingly psychotic. He replaced the world he so feared with that of his paintings. He called them his children. When he did not like a painting, he would sometimes beat it with a whip, saying that this harsh treatment improved its character. Apparently he was reflecting his father's treatment of him when he was a child.

Source: Adapted from Wilson, 1969, p. 150.

Deviations from social standards take many forms. Among those that are regarded as grossly abnormal in a wide range of cultural settings are chronic alcoholism and other types of severe substance abuse; sexual abuse, such as rape, incest, and the seduction of children by adults; and the persistent antisocial behavior of individuals whose irresponsibility and low level of conscience characterize all of their interpersonal relations. Mental health professionals label people who consistently display this latter pattern as psychopathic personalities, sociopathic personalities, and, most recently, "antisocial personalities" (see Chapter 12). The following excerpt from a case study illustrates some of the basic characteristics of the antisocial personality.

> One of . . . 23 children in the first grade [of a rural school], Benny was known as a "mean kid." He had only one friend, whom he abused, stole from, and frequently deserted. Through the next five years, he became a petty thief. . . . At 13 he was referred to the mental health center, [where a diagnosis] of character disorder, antisocial type was made. . . . [Placement. . . . in a [foster] home or juvenile training center was recommended. The parents successfully resisted both alternatives. . . . [More] crime quickly followed [and] he was placed on probation. At 18 he was arrested on charges of drug [possession] and car theft. The Court . . . referred him again to the mental health center. This time he said, "This town is too small for me; they all have it in for me. I'll go into the Service and start over again if you can help me." He lasted six weeks, went AWOL, was discharged and moved to a large city. For the next [several] years he came home for money, clothes, or refuge. He served a short sentence for assault. At age 22, Benny was killed . . . in a drug-related incident. His parents said, "We knew it would happen. It was just a matter of when and where." (Reid, 1978, p. 69)

Cultural Relativism

The concept of **cultural relativism** is crucial for evaluating abnormality as a departure from social standards of behavior, for what is maladaptive social behavior in one cultural setting may not be judged so in another. Judgments of such abnormality may also vary within a given society, depending on the particular situation in which the behavior occurs.

In many communities the night club act of a male impersonating a female is perceived to be within the tolerable limits of social normality, but a man's consistent attempts to pass as a woman in public are likely to be viewed as abnormal. Chapter 4 discusses in detail the implications of cultural relativism for defining and understanding abnormality.

Poor Contact with Reality

One of the most serious manifestations of abnormal behavior and experiences is poor contact with reality. Common signs are distorted perceptions and thoughts, disorientation, and inappropriate physical activity.

Distorted Perceptions and Thoughts

Among the more peculiar aspects of poor contact with reality are the abnormal perceptions called **hallucinations**. These experiences may involve any of the senses, but, unlike normal sensory perceptions, they occur in the absence of identifiable external stimuli. Nevertheless, they may appear so real to the person experiencing them that they stimulate maladaptive behavior. This interplay between abnormal perception and behavior is illustrated in the following case.

> A 20-year old in boot camp began hearing several people in his barracks discussing his homosexuality and debating with his father (thousands of miles away) the best way to kill him. These "conversations" were clear and persistent, finally forcing [him] to flee camp in hopes of escaping his tormentors. (Taylor & Heiser, 1971, p. 485)

Illusions, which are perceptual misinterpretations of actual external stimuli, also reveal poor contact with reality. For example, the ticking of a clock might be perceived as voices delivering insulting messages; the gentle swaying of trees might be perceived as a secret warning of some impending disaster.

Not all illusions indicate poor contact with reality. For example, almost all naive observers misperceive the visual designs in Figure 1.1 at first. Illusions that denote serious loss of contact with reality do not easily yield to contradictory objective evidence.

Yet another sign of poor contact with reality is **delusions**, false beliefs that persist in spite of contradictory evidence readily available in the immediate environment. Confronting deluded individuals with that evidence has little or no effect in correcting their false beliefs. Delusions may take a variety of forms and directions.

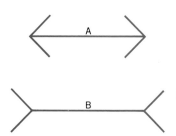

Figure 1.1

The Müller-Lyer illusion. Is line B really longer than line A?

■ **Delusions of grandeur** center around the individual's exaggerated beliefs in his or her power and importance.

■ **Delusions of control** are false beliefs that other people have immense power over one's thoughts and behavior and that one is constantly being manipulated by that power.

■ **Delusions of reference** are false beliefs that people's motives and behavior are always being directed toward oneself.

■ **Paranoid delusions** are typified by an unrealistic and persistent suspicion of other people's intentions and behavior.

■ **Paranoid delusions** often help support **delusions of persecution**, false beliefs that one is constantly being harmed by others.

In the following excerpt from a case study, paranoid delusions seem to dominate, intermingled at times with delusions of persecution and control. It is interesting to note how Carlos uses hallucinations to support some of his false beliefs:

> Carlos stated that . . . he had to be constantly on the alert so he would not be cheated or hurt by others. Carlos said that his parents and his brothers and sisters were against him too, and they could hurt him also if they had the opportunity to do so. . . . [Carlos] reported that he could hear voices laughing at him and telling him to do evil things. . . . Many times he became enraged by the voices he heard, and before he knew it, he was involved in a physical dispute with someone. Carlos indicated that the voices seemed to bother him more when he was in his home environment than when he was confined in a hospital. [He] revealed that he also had special powers that made it possible for him to hear what other persons were thinking about him. He said that he knew some of the doctors were trying to kill him. (Leon, 1974, pp. 266–267)

Abnormal thinking may also be manifested through various forms of distorted communication. One idea may run into another in such a bizarre and disorganized fashion as to convey little meaning by ordinary standards of discourse: "A psychotic patient was asked how long she had been in the hospital. She answered: 'Oh, three weeks — since different statements are made — because it is hot — Mr. Smith is a cheap guy — French — how goes about it?'" (Kolb & Brodie, 1982, p. 128).

Distorted communication is not always so obscure. Sometimes the language is fairly close to commonly accepted meaning but involves a pattern peculiar enough to puzzle the listener. However, if one has some knowledge of the individual's personal problems and habitual verbal mannerisms, it is possible to translate the language, as in the following case.

> A patient states that he is alive, "Because you really live physically because you have menu three times a day. That's the physical." (*What else is there besides the physical?*) "Then you're alive mostly to serve a work from the standpoint of methodical business." A knowledge of the patient's habitual idiom and his preoccupation with serving the world makes this translation possible: "You live physically because you have three meals a day and you live to perform a service in your daily routines." The use of such personal idiom, even without other disorganization, is in effect to cut the patient off from the interpersonal relations that he needs. Neither his family nor the other patients were willing to make the constant effort which was necessary to communicate with this man. He himself gave the impression of not caring whether he communicated with anyone or not. (Cameron, 1963, p. 612)

Disorientation

Inadequate contact with reality may also be revealed by signs of **disorientation**. For example, disoriented persons may not know the season of the year or the calendar year. They may not understand where they are or recognize familiar people and places. Disorientation is most often caused by biophysical factors, such as traumatic brain injury, drugs, or infectious diseases; however, it may also occur in the absence of any known organic disability. The following excerpt from a case study illustrates the serious state of disorientation in a middle-aged man who had been drinking heavily for many years: "On examination, the patient alternates between apprehension and chatty, superficial warmth. He is quite keyed up and talks almost constantly. At times he recognizes the doctor, but at other times he thinks the doctor is his older brother. Twice during the examination he calls the doctor by his older brother's name and asks when he arrived, evidently having lost track entirely of the interview up to that point. . . . He is disoriented for time, and thinks that he is in a supermarket parking lot rather than in a hospital" (Spitzer, Skodol, Gibbon, & Williams, 1981, p. 105).

Inappropriate Physical Activity

Individuals may sometimes reveal inadequate contact with reality through their excessive outbursts of physical activity. Such attacks may vary from inappropriate elation (*euphoria*) to equally inappropriate violence. Symptoms such as these are typical of manic episodes, a form of mood disorder (Chapter 10). The following example describes the behavior of a man in the midst of a highly maladaptive display of exuberance. His disorder was diagnosed as hypomania, a relatively mild level of a manic disorder.

> A wealthy executive, forty-eight years of age, was brought to the hospital by a business associate. . . . Questioning revealed that for the preceding four months the patient had been working intensely but erratically, making quick business decisions that sometimes produced brilliant results, but as often proved unsound and unprofitable. Moreover, his social behavior had become impulsive and unpredictable; for instance, he had twice abruptly adjourned business conferences in the midst of serious work with a sudden invitation to everyone present "to quit, have a drink, and come play golf at my club." . . . While he was driving them to the golf course the patient suddenly expanded his invitation to include a complete weekend for everyone at his country home two hundred miles away. . . . In his executive capacities he continued with similar impetuosity to arrange unnecessary trips and conferences and to propose extravagant promotional schemes; similarly, in his entertainments for the firm's customers, his restlessness, unnecessary lavishness, excessive drinking, and forced gaiety had been increasingly embarrassing to his friends. These insisted, however, that the patient had previously been a sober, stable, and rather undemonstrative individual. (Masserman, 1973, p. 153)

In contrast to excessive physical activity, some individuals may reveal inadequate contact with reality through too little or highly bizarre physical activity. For example, they may become absorbed for long periods of time in stereotyped posturing, such as standing rigidly with arms raised. Or they may lie in bed and refuse to move or speak, seemingly unaware of any surrounding activity. (Chapter 11 discusses such behavior as a form of schizophrenic disorder.)

Intellectual and Social Inefficiency

A third general class of criteria for determining the presence of abnormality is inefficiency in intellectual performance and social interaction. In applying these criteria we need to consider two central questions. How do people's achievements compare with objective measures of their intellectual abilities? How do their abilities and achievements relate to the requirements of their social roles?

To answer the first question we can compare how well individuals are able to handle their everyday intellectual tasks with various assessments of intellectual ability, such as standardized intelligence tests. If their actual accomplishments are markedly less than their test performance would predict, we can begin to suspect that emotional problems are preventing them from applying their abilities more efficiently. Similarly, when measures of intelligence reveal a much lower performance than we would expect from the individual's previous educational and vocational achievements, emotional problems may be interfering with efficient performance on the intelligence test. Procedures such as these are commonly used in psychological and psychiatric clinics to estimate inefficiency (see Chapter 2).

In answering the second question — how do abilities and achievements relate to the requirements of social roles? — it is essential to realize that those roles vary considerably in the degree of efficiency they demand. Whether the discrepancy between an individual's high ability and low accomplishment is perceived as a sign of abnormality depends to a great extent on that person's social roles and the expectations they arouse in other people. That is one reason people who suffer from serious emotional disturbances sometimes drift into menial jobs that require very little of their intellectual abilities and educational background. In such jobs the gap between their current accomplishments and their abilities may attract little attention. Indeed, it may actually support their abnormality, especially if they wish to withdraw from contact with other people and from challenges of the environment (Costin, 1976, p. 9).

The more complex a person's social role, the more likely inefficiency will be perceived as a sign of abnormality. Suppose a top executive in a construction firm persists in suggesting ideas that will certainly cause great financial loss to the firm if they are carried out. The individual's associates are likely to regard the person as abnormal or mentally ill, since such behavior is at great variance with the social role of an executive. On the other hand, if an unskilled laborer in the same firm proposes some equally strange ideas about running the business, fellow workers might simply laugh and dismiss the behavior, because it does not conflict with their expectations of social roles.

Personal Distress

People often seek the help of mental health professionals because of distress such as physical discomfort, anxiety, phobias, obsessions and compulsions, and depression. Their distress may be so intense that they become thoroughly *demoralized* and thus feel alienated from others.

Physical Discomfort

Among the most common complaints of physical discomfort are pain, nausea, and fatigue. Before concluding that these complaints arise from psychosocial factors, it is crucial to rule out the possibility of organic disease. That is not a simple matter, for the borderline is not always clear-cut between physical discomfort of psychological and social origins and that which stems from organic disease. For instance, symptoms of psychosocial origin may mimic neurological disorders, such as paralysis, deafness, or blindness. Furthermore, psychological and social conflict can be an important factor in producing or aggravating physical illnesses such as ulcers and digestive disorders (see Chapters 6 and 7).

Anxiety

Another complaint of personal distress that may reveal psychosocial abnormality is anxiety. Although mental health practitioners can sometimes infer the presence of anxiety by observing the behavior of an individual independently of any expressed complaint, more often it is the person's description of anxiety that furnishes the main clues.

Everyone, of course, experiences anxiety at one time or another. In many instances it is adaptive — appropriate to the situation or event that produced it. For example, it is normal to worry about the results of an important school examination or to be apprehen-

People often seek the help of
mental health professionals
because of intense anxiety.

sive about the outcome of a loved one's illness. Indeed, moderate amounts of anxiety can
be highly productive, as actors, lecturers, athletes, and other public performers well
known. However, anxiety may be maladaptive—unrelated to a particular event or
situation or highly disproportionate to the seriousness of the situation. It also may persist
long after the initial reasons for it have vanished.

Sometimes maladaptive anxiety is unfocused. That is, a person may be extremely
apprehensive but unable to say just what the anxiety is about. Sigmund Freud, whose
theories we discuss in Chapter 3, called that condition free-floating anxiety. Long before
Freud's time, however, as far back as biblical days, there was knowledge of such vague
anxiety. An incisive description of it occurs in Leviticus when this threat of punishment for
disobeying God is pronounced: "and ye shall flee when none pursueth you."

Phobias

Disabling anxiety may be highly focused rather than vague, as in the persistent, irrational
fears known as **phobias.** The irrationality of phobias is usually obvious not only to the
objective observer but to the victim as well. Nevertheless, phobias may be uncontrollable.
This unhappy state of affairs is portrayed in the autobiography of William Ellery Leonard,
poet and professor at the University of Wisconsin. For much of his life, Leonard suffered
from agoraphobia: "I always knew the terror was without sufficient motivation. I could
only say: as soon as I get a certain distance from home—a distance varying back and
forth from yards to miles in the past fifteen years—I am overwhelmed with a feeling of
insecurity, or terror of the seizure of terror; and I fear the seizure at a given distance"
(Leonard, 1928, p. 321).

Obsessions and Compulsions

A more subtle form of anxiety is reflected in obsessive compulsive disorders. These disturbances are marked by distressing preoccupations with certain thoughts (obsessions) and uncontrollable repetition of certain acts (compulsions). The purpose of the compulsions is to reduce anxiety, which often stems from unwanted but intrusive thoughts. Although obsessions and compulsive behavior may help control deeper anxieties that the individual dares not face consciously, the ultimate effect can be highly maladaptive. Not only do obsessions and compulsions perpetuate discomfort for the victim but they also have negative effects on interpersonal relationships. The following example illustrates these problems.

> A boy, aged seventeen years, . . . had developed a highly elaborate ritual based upon the cardinal points of the compass. He could not sit down until he had identified the north, south, east, and west sides of the room that he had entered. When he had done so, he touched each wall in that order and then relaxed and was capable of conducting conversation on other topics. According to his parents, he would now refuse to eat his breakfast until he had been assured that food from each compass direction was on the table. Thus breakfast cereal from the North, orange juice from the South, and so forth were provided and eaten in the correct order. (Maher, 1966, p. 200)

Along with the kinds of vague maladaptive anxiety described earlier, phobias, obsessions, and compulsive behavior have traditionally been called neurotic disorders. Since they all involve anxiety of some sort, whether obvious or subtle, the current practice is to classify them under the general label anxiety disorders. Chapter 5 discusses in detail the various forms of these disorders, their causes, and methods of alleviating them.

Depression

As in the case of anxiety, phobias, and obsessive compulsive behavior, one can sometimes infer abnormal depression simply by observing overt behavior. For example, crying, facial expressions of sadness, slowness in bodily movements, withdrawal from social activities, severe reduction in work — all these can serve as important clues. In addition, verbal complaints of distress may reveal depression even more directly, especially complaints of hopelessness, worthlessness, and apathy. Such reactions are apparent in this patient's recall of episodes of depression:

> The symptoms: unprovoked tears plummeting down my cheek at odd times and for long spells. . . . I [dreaded] being with people. Social life was painful.
>
> I avoided going to my office. . . . I was sure I was the living example of the Peter Principle: I had overreached the top level of my capabilities, which, it seemed, was anybody else's lowest level. After all, wasn't I completely worthless? Everyone was better than I. I'd marvel at the efficiency of the people who did even the simplest of jobs. . . . Everyone was so content and capable. (Kline, 1975, p. 117)

Normal depression merges gradually into abnormal depression. Determining where one ends and the other begins is often a matter for skilled professional judgments. In general, the same criteria of abnormality that apply to anxiety hold true for depression: It is abnormal when it appears unrelated to particular events or situations, is highly inappropriate to the situation, or persists far beyond the original situation that led to it. For example, it is obviously normal for us to feel depressed as we mourn the loss of someone who has been close to us. During this period it is again normal to be less efficient in our daily tasks and to suffer some impairment in relating to other people. When similar kinds of losses initiate abnormal depression, the mourning, inefficiency, and impairment in personal relations are much more severe and they last far beyond what we would reasonably expect. The depressed person seems to lack the ability to bounce back that is typical of normal depression. Chapter 10 discusses in more detail the various criteria that can be used to differentiate normal, adaptive depression from abnormal, maladaptive depression.

Demoralization and Alienation

In an address before the Society for the Psychological Study of Social Issues, Jerome D. Frank (1972) observed that people reveal diverse kinds of personal distress when seeking help, but one basic condition underlies all of them: demoralization. Demoralization typically occurs when people are unable to cope with situations that they and others about them think they should handle. As a result, their lives become highly constricted. For example, they are self-absorbed and preoccupied with trying to cope with threats from their environment. They often experience depression, self-blame, guilt, and shame. In the face of what they perceive as a menacing environment, they begin to resent people who they think should help them "but who seem unable or unwilling to do so, and who, in addition, are often aggravated by [their] behavior" (Frank, 1972, p. 33). Consequently, they become alienated from others.

Frank also points out that the distress people reveal to a psychotherapist may interact with demoralization both directly and indirectly. For example, complaints of anxiety and depression directly reflect a state of demoralization. In more indirect or symbolic forms, complaints of migraine headaches may be expressed in an emotional context of hopelessness and a feeling that one lacks self-control. Similarly, complaints of stomach pains may occur in a context of feeling helpless.

Frank argues that what ultimately impels people to seek psychotherapy is not simply their specific symptoms of distress but their demoralization. He concludes, therefore, that "whatever else psychotherapy does, it fails if it does not restore the patient's morale" (Frank, 1972, p. 34).

Roles of Mental Health Professionals

Mental health professionals have developed a number of ways to help people overcome their psychological and social disabilities and acquire more adaptive ways of living. These methods include psychotherapy, changing the social and physical environment, and biomedical treatment, such as the use of drugs to reduce anxiety and depression or to help an individual regain adequate contact with reality.

Although the professional training of mental health professionals differs, their roles often overlap. This commonality is most apparent in their use of **psychotherapy** — the use of psychological techniques to bring about positive changes in thinking, feeling, and acting. The central goal of psychotherapy is to help troubled people move away from maladaptive ways of living and develop more adaptive ways. In succeeding chapters — especially Chapters 18, 19, and 20 — we consider in detail how mental health professionals help people with their problems through psychotherapy and other means. We also consider various ethical issues that arise in such practices and some of the criteria consumers should use in choosing a practitioner. For the present, we simply state briefly who these practitioners are.

■ **Clinical psychologists** usually earn a doctoral degree in psychology, but for some positions a master's degree may be acceptable. They carry out diagnosis, psychotherapy, and research and often teach in universities and colleges.

■ *Counseling psychologists* most often work to help people with their educational and vocational problems, or with relatively normal problems of living.

■ The training and work of *school psychologists* resembles that of clinical and counseling psychologists. These psychologists also complete courses in education to help them work with students and their problems and to understand the school system and the nature of learning in school.

■ Prior to their advanced training in mental disorders, *psychiatrists* earn a medical degree. They diagnose and treat mental disorders, and they are the only mental health professionals who can legally prescribe and use drugs and other medical methods.

■ *Psychiatric nurses* have increasingly engaged in direct treatment in hospital settings, especially in their work with group therapy. Advanced training leads to the specialty of *nurse practitioner.*

■ *Psychoanalysts* derive their principles and methods of psychotherapy from Freudian theory and its modifications (Chapter 3). They usually obtain their initial training in medicine and then complete advanced training in special psychoanalytic institutes. In recent years other mental health professionals have obtained such advanced training.

■ *Clinical social workers* typically obtain a master of social work degree (M.S.W.), although degrees at the doctoral level may also be earned. Clinical social workers emphasize the relationship between psychological problems and the social conditions that contribute to them. They conduct psychotherapy in mental health agencies and also engage in independent practice.

■ *School social workers* help students with personal problems. They also work with classroom teachers to help them understand the kinds of problems students face and how those problems are related to life in school.

■ Some mental health professionals specialize in *marital and family problems.* They come from various professional backgrounds: clinical and counseling psychology, psychiatry, and clinical social work, as well as special graduate programs developed specifically to treat problems of marriage and family life.

■ *Pastoral counselors* complete special programs in schools of theology that include courses in psychology, psychiatry, and social work. They help individuals solve religious conflicts and related psychosocial problems, often collaborating with other mental health professionals in their counseling activities.

Positive Mental Health

All mental health professionals share two main goals: to help people overcome their abnormal patterns of thinking and acting and to help them move toward more positive mental health. They are also concerned with preventing mental and behavioral disabilities. Such prevention depends not only on understanding the causes of abnormality — whether they be biological, social, or psychological — but also on helping people develop and maintain mental health throughout their lives.

How should we define *positive mental health?* To begin with, it is not simply the absence of abnormality. There are so many ways of being mentally healthy that a definitive list of criteria is not feasible; various voluntary and government agencies provide some useful practical guides for the general public. A widely distributed statement is published by the Mental Health Association (MHA). One of the nation's largest voluntary citizens' organizations, the main purpose of the MHA is to combat mental illness and promote mental health. The MHA's brochure, *Mental Health is 1, 2, 3*, includes the following criteria for calling people mentally healthy.

1. **They feel comfortable about themselves.** For example, they are not bowled over by their emotions, they neither underestimate nor overestimate their abilities, they have self-respect, and they feel able to deal with most situations that come their way.

2. **They feel right about other people.** For example, they are able to give love and to consider the interests of others, they have personal relationships that are satisfying and lasting, and they respect the many differences they find in people.

3. **They are able to meet the demands of life.** For example, they accept their responsibilities, they shape their environment whenever possible and adjust to it whenever necessary, and they welcome new experiences and new ideas.

A Note on Terminology

Mental health professionals use a variety of terms in referring to abnormal behavior and experience that are sufficiently disturbing to warrant their attention. Most common are *mental disorder, behavior disorder, mental illness, emotional disorder, emotional disturbance,* and *psychopathology.* We use these terms more or less interchangeably. However, some mental health professionals do differ in their preferences. Their choices reflect a variety of influences: the particular kinds of professional education and training they received, their personal and social values, the settings in which they work, and the theories they hold about the causes and development of abnormal behavior and experiences (see Chapters 2, 3, and 4).

Mental retardation is also a term often encountered in professional writings on abnormality. It refers to individuals whose intellectual development and functioning are noticeably retarded at birth or soon afterwards, or become so during early childhood. However, many people who have experienced a serious loss in emotional functioning also suffer deficits in their intellectual abilities. Such people are *not* considered mentally retarded if they have at one time shown adequate intellectual functioning. Mental retardation need not involve emotional disturbance, although it often does, especially when the intellectual deficit is relatively severe. In Chapter 17 we discuss the nature and causes of mental retardation and its possible prevention as well as programs for helping mentally retarded people acquire more adaptive ways of responding to environmental demands.

Insanity is still another term found in writings on abnormality. For many years it was used in psychiatry as well as in popular speech to refer to severe forms of abnormality. Its proper use today is as a legal term rather than a psychiatric or psychological one. Insane persons are those who have been judged in a court of law to be so psychologically disabled that they are not responsible for their criminal behavior and therefore should not be subject to the usual rules of criminal justice and penalties. Concepts of legal insanity are encountered most often when individuals are on trial for crimes such as murder and other acts of extreme violence and are defended on the plea that they be found not guilty by reason of insanity. To a great extent this plea relies on the testimony of expert witnesses, usually psychiatrists or psychologists, whose main function is to present evidence that will help establish whether the accused is suffering from a psychotic disorder. **Psychotic disorders** typically involve serious impairment of an individual's ability to recognize and deal with reality, to communicate meaningfully with others, and to maintain an adequate degree of emotional stability. The witnesses themselves do not render an opinion of insanity; that is a legal matter to be decided by the court. Instead, under the direction of attorneys and the presiding judge, they answer questions that help the court apply its particular test of insanity, a test of criminal responsibility. The various tests that have emerged over the years have relied increasingly on the use of psychological and biomedical knowledge of abnormality. Chapter 21 presents a history of how these tests have developed and discusses their implications for an individual's civil rights.

Nervous breakdown is a general label that mental health professionals sometimes use informally. Often encountered in popular writings and speech, it is a catch-all term applied to many forms of abnormal behavior and experiences. It is sometimes used as a way of avoiding the stigma that may be associated with receiving professional help because of serious psychological disturbances, particularly if the disorders were serious enough to result in confinement to a mental hospital. For some people, *nervous breakdown* has a softer or less demeaning effect than *mental illness, emotional illness,* and *mental disorder.* In Chapter 4 we discuss the stigma sometimes attached to a person who has been a patient in a mental hospital.

Summary

1. Two basic methods of defining abnormal behavior and experience are the statistical approach and the psychosocial approach.

2. From a statistical viewpoint, abnormality is a quantitative deviation from the average (normal). Abnormality occurs least often; normality occurs most often. Although statistical infrequency is essential for defining abnormality, it has limitations. For example, one group of individuals may have an extremely high level of intellectual ability; another group may have an extremely low level. Both groups are statistically abnormal, but from a psychosocial viewpoint they are very different.

3. The psychosocial approach to defining abnormality focuses on characteristics of behavior and experience that reveal psychological and social impairment. A fundamental feature of this impairment is a persistent failure to respond adaptively to demands of the environment and a persistent inability to reach desired goals. Abnormal psychology deals with statistically abnormal patterns of experience and behavior that reflect these kinds of impairment.

4. A number of basic criteria are useful for recognizing and describing psychological and social abnormality. They include (a) gross departures from socially acceptable standards, (b) poor contact with reality, (c) intellectual and social inefficiency, and (d) personal distress. How these criteria are applied may vary, depending on the social and cultural environment in which the behavior and experiences occur.

5. Mental health practitioners and researchers have developed various ways to help people overcome their psychological and social impairment and acquire more adaptive ways of living. Among the methods used to accomplish those goals of positive mental health are psychotherapy, changes in the social and physical environment, and biomedical treatment — for example, the use of therapeutic drugs.

6. Mental health professionals come from a variety of academic backgrounds and types of training. Most widely recognized are clinical and counseling psychologists; psychoanalysts, psychiatrists, and psychiatric nurses; clinical and school social workers;

marriage and family therapists; and pastoral counselors. The roles of these professionals sometimes overlap, especially in the area of psychotherapy.

7. Mental health professionals use a variety of terms in referring to psychosocial abnormality. Most common are *mental disorder, behavior disorder, psychopathology, mental illness, emotional disorder,* and *emotional disturbance.* We will use these terms interchangeably, although some mental health professionals have their special preferences.

8. Insanity is a legal term applied to individuals who in a court of law are judged not responsible for their criminal behavior because they were psychologically disabled.

2

Mental Disorders: Diagnosis, Classification, and Assessment

Order and simplification are the first steps
toward the mastery of a subject — the actual
enemy is the unknown.

THOMAS MANN
The Magic Mountain **(1939)**

At the very outset of helping people, the mental health professional must discover how they perceive their problems: their hopes, doubts, and worries; the significant events of their lives; their sources of gratification and frustration; and a host of other personal details. Significant information about their problems can often be gained from family members, friends, or others who know them well. It is also important to obtain knowledge about the physical health of these troubled people, since psychological disorders sometimes stem from abnormal organic conditions — for example, brain malfunction caused by drug abuse, physical trauma, or infections (see Chapter 13). This entire process is called **assessment**.

Assessment is most prominent during the early phases of treatment, but it is actually a continuous process. As treatment progresses, the therapist reappraises the situation, fits treatment to the unique circumstances of the troubled individual, and then judges the effectiveness of those efforts.

Assessment of the mental status of a person accused of a crime can be crucial in determining whether that individual is competent to stand trial or appreciates the criminality of the act. Assessment is also important in deciding whether an individual should be involuntarily confined to an institution for treatment (see Chapter 21).

In the first part of this chapter we consider two basic and highly related processes in the assessment of psychological disorders: diagnosis and classification. We then examine specific methods of diagnostic assessment.

Diagnosis and Classification

Diagnosis is the art and science of determining the nature of a disorder and differentiating it from other disorders (*Dorland's Illustrated Medical Dictionary*, 1988). During the 1940s and 1950s, mental health professionals criticized psychiatric diagnosis on the grounds that it ignored individual variation and had a dehumanizing effect; however, since the 1960s, interest in the diagnosis and classification of mental disorders has increased, emphasizing that these activities should grow out of directly observing abnormal behavior and understanding the developmental history of the disorder (Robins & Helzer, 1986).

The main objectives of diagnosis are

- To gather information that will help explain the causes (etiology) of the disorder.

- To predict the progress and probable outcome of the disorder (prognosis).

- To plan the most appropriate methods of helping individuals overcome their disorder (treatment).

As a rule, the most immediate and practical objective of diagnosis is to develop a program of treatment — for example, psychotherapy, social intervention, or biological therapy. Ideally, diagnosis should be the key to treatment, but the relationship is not usually that direct (Phillips & Draguns, 1971; Price, 1978; Woodruff, Goodwin, & Guze, 1974). Nevertheless, mental health practitioners generally expect that diagnosis will at least provide some clues for carrying out treatment.

In diagnosing psychological disorders it is customary to assign the individual to a qualitative category that represents a particular pattern of disturbance. For example, a person may be diagnosed as having an anxiety disorder, a major depression, or a schizophrenic disorder, to name only a few of the many diagnostic classifications in current use among the various kinds of mental health professionals. (See Chapters 1 and 19 for a discussion of these professional roles.)

In assigning individuals to diagnostic categories, clinicians emphasize **symptoms** and patterns of symptoms, which are called **syndromes.** Symptoms that an individual reveals directly are known as **complaints** ("I have a lot of trouble sleeping"). Symptoms that the clinician observes without the individual representing them directly are called **signs.** For example, abnormal slowness of speech may provide a clue to depression. Clues to a disorder may also be revealed in various abnormal physical findings—for example, an infection of the brain (see Chapter 13).

Ideally, all persons assigned to a particular category in a diagnostic classification system should have certain characteristics that distinguish them from persons in other categories (Swets, 1988, p. 1285). Of course, human behavior is too flexible for such rigid demands to be completely met. Characteristics are bound to overlap from one diagnostic category to another. However, as we will discuss later, modern methods of classifying mental disorders aim to reduce that difficulty by developing precise criteria for assigning individuals to the various categories.

Historical Background of Classifications

Influence of Hippocrates

Hippocrates, the "father of Greek medicine," described with remarkable accuracy his extensive observations of mental disorders.

The science of classifying abnormal patterns of behavior and experience is called **nosology.** Its roots can be traced to the days of Hippocrates (ca. 460–377 B.C.), the father of Greek medicine. In *The Sacred Disease*, Hippocrates described with remarkable accuracy his many observations of mental disorders and disputed some of the current theories about their origin. He argued that, contrary to popular thought, epilepsy, like all mental disorders, was not of sacred origin but could be explained on the basis of natural causes. The natural cause of mental disorders, Hippocrates wrote, was an unhealthy brain, "which makes us mad or delirious, inspires us with dread and fear . . . brings sleeplessness . . . aimless anxieties and acts that are contrary to habit" (Jones, 1923, p. 175).

The observations that Hippocrates recorded in his daily practice of medicine became in large measure the cornerstone for a system of classifying abnormal behavior and experiences that remained influential throughout ancient Greece and Rome. Among the diagnostic categories developed were **mania,** an "acute disturbance without fever"; **melancholia,** a term that embraced all chronic mental disorders, including long-lasting depression; and **hysteria,** a disorder believed to occur only in women and marked with agitation, pain, and convulsions. According to ancient Greek knowledge, hysteria was caused by a wandering uterus (*hysterikos*) that eventually reached the woman's throat, thus causing severe symptoms of mental and physical discomfort (Zilboorg & Henry, 1941, pp. 47–48).

Renaissance Period

The science of nosology languished during the Middle Ages; but with the Renaissance, interest among medical practitioners was rekindled. One of the most outstanding classifiers of that period was the Swiss physician Theophrastus Bombastus Von Hohenheim

During the 16th century, Paracelsus, a Swiss physician, expanded the classification system for mental disorders developed in ancient Greece and Rome.

During the late nineteenth and early twentieth centuries, the German psychiatrist Emil Kraepelin synthesized earlier work on the classification of mental disorders.

(1493–1541), more commonly known as Paracelsus. He expanded the system used during the days of Greece and Rome, adding the new diagnostic category **insanity**, which included mental disorders whose appearance was influenced by the phases of the moon.

19th and Early 20th Century

During the first half of the 19th century, the German psychiatrist Wilhelm Griesinger (1817–1868) developed a classification system that was greatly influenced by Hippocrates's theory that all mental disorders could be traced to faulty conditions in the brain. At the same time, the French psychiatrist Benedict Augustin Morel (1809–1873) grouped mental disorders according to their etiology and prognosis. He emphasized in his classification manual a disorder he named **dementia praecox**, meaning precocious mental deterioration. Morel thought that dementia praecox occurred only during youth (hence praecox) and inevitably progressed to a fatal end.

Karl Ludwig Kahlbaum (1828–1899), a German psychiatrist, expanded Morel's ideas and developed an extensive classification of mental disorders based on descriptions of their etiology, course, and typical outcome. Emil Kraepelin (1855–1925), another German psychiatrist, synthesized the work on classification by combining the organic approach of Griesinger, who had arranged disorders according to the kinds of bodily defects involved, with the developmental approaches of Morel and Kahlbaum, who had grouped disorders according to their origin, progression, and expected outcome.

Like Morel, Kraepelin emphasized dementia praecox, but he went beyond Morel's efforts by bringing together many other kinds of disturbances under that one label (Kraepelin, 1915/1923). However, he agreed with Morel's pessimistic view of the disorder and indeed expanded on it. Kraepelin believed that dementia praecox was caused by defective sex glands, resulting in chemical imbalances in the nervous system. The disease always began early in life, claimed Kraepelin, because puberty was a crucial time in sexual development. Like Morel, he believed that inevitably the disorder progressed to an incurable intellectual deterioration **(dementia)**.

Adolph Meyer and American Psychiatry

Adolph Meyer (1866–1950), who emigrated from Zurich in 1892 and became a professor of psychiatry at Johns Hopkins University, introduced Kraepelin's classification system to American psychiatry. Meyer believed that Kraepelin had exaggerated the role of

Psychiatrist Adolph Meyer emigrated to the United States from Zurich in 1892. In his view, which was called "psychobiology," psychological as well as organic factors must be considered in explaining mental disorders.

Swiss psychiatrist Eugen Bleuler revised Kraepelin's views of "dementia praecox." He coined the term "schizophrenia" as a better label.

organic defects in the development of mental disorders and had seriously neglected psychological influences. Throughout his career Meyer continually emphasized that psychological as well as organic factors must be considered in explaining the nature of mental disorders. Meyer's wife, Mary, worked with him by visiting the homes of patients to learn more about how their backgrounds may have contributed to their psychological problems (Hilgard, 1987, p. 627; Meyer, 1934, 1935; Rutter, 1986). Meyer's concept, known as **psychobiology**, has been an important influence on modern studies of abnormal behavior and experiences, in both the United States and other countries.

Contributions of Bleuler

The Swiss psychiatrist Eugen Bleuler (1857–1939), a contemporary of Meyer, shared Meyer's views on the dual importance of biological and psychological factors in the development of mental disorders. Bleuler was especially critical of Kraepelin's concept of dementia praecox, observing that the disorder did *not* necessarily begin in youth and did not inevitably lead to an incurable state of mental deterioration. However, Bleuler was not just critical. He developed a new theory emphasizing that what Kraepelin had named dementia praecox represented disorders of thought — a group of disorders in which intellectual functions and emotional functions were no longer integrated. For example, a patient might relate that her parents were killed but not show emotions appropriate to the narrative. To emphasize this disintegration, Bleuler renamed the group of disorders **schizophrenias**, a label he derived from the Greek *schizein* ("to divide") and *phren* "mind") (Bleuler, 1911/1950). We discuss Bleuler's theories and their influence on current views of schizophrenic disorders in Chapter 11.

Criticisms and Defense of Diagnostic Classification

Diagnostic Categories

Various objections to diagnostic classification systems have emerged over the years (Klerman, 1986, pp. 12–13). Some critics argue that the use of specific diagnostic categories cannot possibly encompass all the richness and complexity, or convey the uniqueness of the individual so diagnosed. For many years the distinguished American psychiatrist Karl Menninger has been one of the principal proponents of this view. That a specific diagnostic label tells considerably less than we need to know about an individual is obvious. What is controversial about Menninger's criticism is his remedy: Abandon the use of diagnostic categories and describe people only as they are, on the basis of their personal problems, circumstances, and difficulties (Menninger, Mayman, & Pruyser, 1963).

Consistent with Menninger's views, other critics of diagnostic labeling claim that it stands in the way of understanding and humanely helping the individual who has been labeled. There are two aspects of this criticism. First of all, the argument goes, a specific diagnostic category becomes a self-fulfilling prophecy. Through a series of complex social pressures, people are made to behave in accordance with how they have been labeled (Scheff, 1984, pp. 62–74). Moreover, the label, once assigned, is difficult to remove. Consequently, we continue to focus on the label and neglect environmental conditions that may be contributing to the person's problems (Rothblum, Solomon, & Albee, 1986, p. 178).

A second aspect of the claim that diagnostic labeling interferes with understanding the individual goes like this: The use of specific diagnostic categories creates a gulf between the person so labeled and other people, including those who are supposed to be helping that person. The diagnostic category becomes a screen through which we view the behavior of the labeled person. All too easily, we come to regard the individual as a paranoid, a schizophrenic, a hypochondriac, an antisocial personality, and so forth, rather than as a person with a variety of troubled social roles. It is a short step, the argument continues, to regarding that person as nothing but a schizophrenic, a perception all too often accompanied by social rejection and stigma (Laing, 1967; Szasz, 1974).

Some critics emphasize that assigning a diagnostic category to an individual does not help the clinician make decisions about treatment, even though that is a prime purpose of diagnosis. For example, people who are placed in identical diagnostic categories not only require different kinds of therapeutic intervention but also differ markedly in their prospects for improvement (Ullmann & Krasner, 1975).

Hans J. Eysenck, a British psychologist, advocates discarding traditional psychiatric categories and replacing them with a limited number of dimensions on which people would vary quantitatively.

Continuity of Psychological Disorder

Still another argument against dividing abnormal behavior and thinking into a discrete number of diagnostic categories is that psychological disorders represent a continuum of disturbance. They may vary from slight to intense on a number of dimensions and thus defy being broken up into qualitatively distinct units. Hans Eysenck, a British psychologist, advocates discarding traditional psychiatric categories and replacing them with a limited number of dimensions on which people would vary quantitatively (1986). On the basis of his research, Eysenck suggests a minimum set of three major dimensions — psychoticism, neuroticism, and extraversion–introversion. However, he points out that as research proceeds in applying these three to diagnosis, further dimensions "cannot be ruled out" (p. 90).

In Defense of Diagnostic Classification

Although they are aware of the limitations and potential misuse of diagnostic categories, the vast majority of mental health professionals accept, at least implicitly, the necessity for a system of diagnostic classification. They attempt to apply it in their daily work so as to maximize its helpful aspects and minimize its harmful effects. The defenders of diagnostic classification as a legitimate, helpful, and humane activity contend that the disadvantages we reviewed are not inevitable (American Psychiatric Association, 1980a, 1987; Kendell, 1973). For example, the tendency of psychiatric labels to remain with an individual is a possible consequence that can be monitored and prevented. Furthermore, the claim that the label creates the disorder has been shown to be highly exaggerated (Gove, 1970, 1975; Rosenberg, 1970).

Supporters of diagnostic classification also point out that a diagnostic category is simply a convenient shorthand way of communicating with the mental health profession. It can also serve as a practical way of communicating with patients, provided it does not become a substitute for factual information. The issue of practicality is especially important today because practitioners are required to describe disorders with a standard vocabulary in order to be reimbursed by insurance companies for their treatment procedures.

DSM-III-R: Basic Characteristics

Developmental Background

The consensus among most mental health professionals today is that the structure and use of diagnostic classifications need to be improved rather than abandoned. The *Diagnostic and Statistical Manual of Mental Disorders* (DSM-III-R) (American Psychiatric Association, 1987) represents the most recent efforts to make the enterprise more objective, reliable, and useful. DSM-III-R is a revised version of the third edition of the manual, known as DSM-III (American Psychiatric Association, 1980a). The first edition of DSM, published in 1952, was the first official diagnostic manual to contain a glossary of the terms used in describing diagnostic categories. Reflecting the influence of Adolph Meyer's psychobiological interpretations of mental disorders, the 1952 edition described the various diagnostic categories in terms of the individual's reactions to psychological, social, and biological factors. The second edition (DSM-II), published in 1968, based its classification on the 1968 edition of the World Health Organization's *International Classification of Diseases* (ICD-8). The term *reaction* was dropped, and except for *neuroses* the new classification did not reflect any specific framework for interpreting nonorganic mental disorders (American Psychiatric Association, 1987, pp. xviii–xix).

Structure of DSM-III-R

Although they provided a concise description of mental disorders, neither of the first two editions of DSM contained sufficient material to serve as guides in making reliable diagnoses; but DSM-III was an improvement. The present revision, DSM-III-R, is a further refinement and clarification and contains several new features. DSM-III-R is the standard reference in the United States for the diagnostic classification of mental disorders (see Box 2.1).

> ## BOX 2.1 Classification of Mental Disorders: DSM-III-R Axis I and II categories
>
> The following classification is a condensed version. (NOS stands for not otherwise specified.) Axis I includes all the primary clinical syndromes of mental disorders except for developmental disorders and personality disorders. These are listed on Axis II. In addition, Axis I includes the V Codes: Conditions Not Attributable to a Mental Disorder That Are a Focus of Attention or Treatment. The clinician may specify the current severity of a disorder by stating one of the following after the diagnosis: *mild, moderate,* or *severe* (currently meets diagnostic criteria); *in partial remission; in complete remission.* Multiple diagnoses are made when it is necessary to describe the person's present condition more extensively. In that case the clinician also indicates the *principal diagnosis*—the diagnosis chiefly responsible for evaluating or treating the person.
>
> Each specific diagnosis is accompanied by a code number, not shown here. To facilitate communication among mental health professionals—for example, in re-

ports to federal agencies — the codes used in DSM-III-R are compatible with those for mental disorders listed in the ninth revision of the *International Classification of Diseases, Clinical Modification* (ICD-9-CM). The ICD-9-CM was developed in the United States and is more extensive and specific than the mental disorders section of ICD-9.

Disorders Usually First Evident in Infancy or Childhood

Developmental Disorders (Axis II)

Mental Retardation: Mild; moderate; severe; profound; unspecified
Pervasive Developmental Disorders: Autistic disorder; pervasive developmental disorder NOS
Specific Developmental Disorders: Academic skills disorders; language and speech disorders; motor skills disorders
Other Developmental Disorders: Developmental disorder NOS

Disruptive Behavior Disorders: Attention-deficit hyperactivity disorder; conduct disorder; oppositional defiant disorder
Anxiety Disorders of Childhood or Adolescence: Separation anxiety disorder; avoidant disorder of childhood or adolescence; overanxious disorder
Eating Disorders: Anorexia nervosa; bulimia nervosa; pica; rumination disorder of infancy; eating disorder NOS
Gender Identity Disorders: Gender identity disorder of childhood; transsexualism; gender identity disorder of adolescence or adulthood, nontranssexual type; gender identity disorder NOS
Tic Disorders: Tourette's disorder; chronic motor or vocal tic; transient tic disorder; tic disorder NOS
Elimination Disorders: Functional encopresis; functional enuresis
Speech Disorders Not Elsewhere Classified: Cluttering; stuttering
Other Disorders of Infancy, Childhood, or Adolescence: Elective mutism; identity disorder; reactive attachment disorder of infancy or early childhood; stereotopy/habit disorder; undifferentiated attention-deficit disorder

Organic Mental Disorders

Dementias Arising in the Senium and Presenium: Primary degenerative dementia of the Alzheimer type, senile onset; primary degenerative dementia of the Alzheimer type, presenile onset; multi-infarct dementia; senile dementia NOS; presenile dementia NOS
Psychoactive Substance – Induced Organic Mental Disorders: Alcohol; amphetamine; caffeine; cannabis; cocaine; hallucinogen; inhalant; nicotine; opioid; phencyclidine (PCP); sedative, hypnotic, or anxiolytic; other or unspecified psychoactive substance
Organic Mental Disorders Associated with Axis III Physical Disorders or Conditions or Whose Etiology Is Unknown: Delirium; dementia; amnestic disorder; organic delusional disorder; organic hallucinosis; organic mood disorder; organic anxiety disorder; organic personality disorder; organic mental disorder NOS.

Psychoactive Substance Use Disorders

Except for caffeine, any of the drugs listed above may be included in a diagnosis of substance dependence or abuse. The diagnosis of polysubstance dependence is used when several of these substances are involved.

Schizophrenia

Catatonic; disorganized; paranoid; undifferentiated; residual

Delusional (Paranoid) Disorder

Erotomanic; grandiose; jealous; persecutory; somatic; unspecified

Psychotic Disorders Not Elsewhere Classified

Brief reactive psychosis; schizophreniform disorder; schizoaffective disorder; induced psychotic disorder; psychotic disorder NOS (atypical psychosis)

Mood Disorders

Bipolar disorders: Bipolar disorder (mixed, manic, depressed); cyclothymia; bipolar disorder NOS
Depressive Disorders: Major depression (single episode, recurrent); dysthymia (or depressive neurosis); depressive disorder NOS

Anxiety Disorders (or Anxiety or Phobic Neuroses)

Panic disorder (with agoraphobia; without agoraphobia); agoraphobia without history of panic disorder; social phobia; simple phobia; obsessive compulsive disorder (or obsessive compulsive neurosis); post-traumatic stress disorder; generalized anxiety disorder; anxiety disorder NOS

Somatoform Disorders

Body dysmorphic disorder; conversion disorder (or hysterical neurosis, conversion type); hypochondriasis (or hypochondriacal neurosis); somatization disorder; somatoform pain disorder; undifferentiated somatoform disorder; somatoform disorder NOS.

Dissociative Disorders (or Hysterical Neuroses, Dissociative Type)

Multiple personality disorder; psychogenic fugue; psychogenic amnesia; depersonalization disorder (or depersonalization neurosis); dissociative disorder NOS

Sexual Disorders

Paraphilias: Exhibitionism; fetishism; frotteurism; pedophilia; sexual masochism; sexual sadism; transvestic fetishism; voyeurism; paraphilia NOS (for example, zoophilia)
Sexual Dysfunctions: Sexual desire disorders; sexual arousal disorders; orgasm disorders; sexual pain disorders; sexual dysfunction NOS
Other Sexual Disorders: Sexual disorder NOS

Sleep Disorders

Dyssomnias: Insomnia disorder; sleep-wake schedule disorder; other dyssomnias; dyssomnia NOS
Parasomnias: Dream anxiety disorder (nightmare disorder); sleep terror disorder; sleepwalking disorder; parasomnia NOS

Factitious Disorders

With physical symptoms; with psychological symptoms; factitious disorder NOS

Impulse Control Disorders Not Elsewhere Classified

Intermittent explosive disorder; kleptomania; pathological gambling; pyromania; trichotillomania; impulse control disorder NOS

Adjustment Disorder

With anxious mood; depressed mood; disturbance of conduct; mixed disturbance of emotions and conduct; mixed emotional features; physical complaints; withdrawal; work (or academic) inhibition; adjustment disorder NOS

Psychological Factors Affecting Physical Condition

Physical condition is specified on Axis III

Personality Disorders (Axis II)

Cluster A: Paranoid; schizoid; schizotypal
Cluster B: Antisocial; borderline; histrionic; narcissistic
Cluster C: Avoidant; dependent; obsessive compulsive; passive aggressive; personality disorder NOS

Conditions Not Attributable to a Mental Disorder That Are a Focus of Attention or Treatment (V codes — i.e., code numbers are preceded by *V*)

Academic problem; adult antisocial behavior; (borderline intellectual functioning, coded on Axis II); childhood or adolescent antisocial behavior; malingering; marital problem; noncompliance with medical treatment; occupational problem; parent-child; other interpersonal problem; other specified family circumstances; phase of life problem or other life circumstance problem; uncomplicated bereavement

Additional Codes

Unspecified mental disorder (nonpsychotic)
No diagnoses or conditions on Axis I
Diagnoses or condition deferred on Axis I

No diagnoses or conditions on Axis II
Diagnoses or conditions deferred on Axis II

Multiaxial System

Axis I.   Clinical Syndromes and V Codes
Axis II. Developmental Disorders; Personality Disorders
Axis III. Physical Disorders and Conditions
Axis IV. Severity of Psychosocial Stressors
Axis V.   Global Assessment of Functioning

Source: Adapted from American Psychiatric Association, 1987, pp. 3–17, 433–434.

These paintings by mentally ill patients were selected from a large collection reproduced in Edward Adamson's *Art as Healing*. A well-known British artist, Mr. Adamson established a studio in 1946 at the Netherne Hospital, London, where he remained as art director for many years. Here, through their artistic creations, patients could express the suffering and alienation that many were not able to communicate in other ways. Their art helped them work toward a positive reconstruction of their lives.

My Head Is Going Round and Round." The thinking of highly disturbed people is frequently confused.

People who suffer from abnormal feeling
persecution often imagine that eyes are
from everywhere.

Nightmare. The young man who did this
painting dreamed repeatedly that he was
being smothered by an enormous black
beetle.

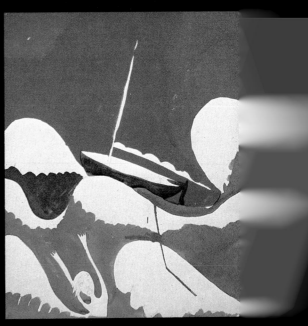

"I'm Being Persecuted." This painting
reflects a theme common in the delusions of
paranoid patients.

Drowning. In this patient's painting of a
dream, drowning represents feelings of
helplessness and hopelessness.

This picture shows the distorted image of a young man, as he saw himself. The two colors of the face cut it into halves, a feature often found in the paintings of those who have departed from reality.

A patient depicted his depression by painting this weeping eye, like the flower of a growing plant. He actually labeled this picture "self-portrait."

The Embrace. In the hospital, with loved ones absent, the need to give and receive affection is all the more powerful.

The Tear. The man who painted this picture was deeply concerned about the effect of his illness on his marriage. A female eye is weeping a tear that is itself an eye.

"All I want to do is to give my doctor flowers . . ."

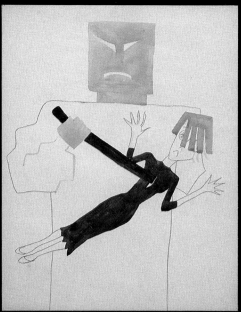

Here the patient is expressing her need for acceptance by her therapist and her fear that instead he does not understand her and is rejecting her (". . . *but all he does is to dig out my heart!*").

Retaliation. The doctor shown here is a large creature with X-ray eyes. The patient is a tiny scorpion who tries defiantly to retaliate with her own eyeball.

Goals

A general objective of both the 1980 and 1987 editions of the DSM was to improve meaningful communication among mental health professionals. More specifically, the following goals guided the development of diagnostic categories (American Psychiatric Association, 1987, pp. xix – xx).

1. Usefulness for treatment and management decisions in a variety of clinical settings.
2. Reliability of diagnostic categories.
3. Acceptance by clinicians and researchers of different theoretical orientations.
4. Usefulness for educating mental health professionals.
5. Maintenance of compatibility with ICD-9-CM codes.
6. Avoidance of new terminology and concepts that depart from tradition except when clearly needed.
7. Achievement of consensus on diagnostic terms that have been used inconsistently and avoidance of terms that have outlived their usefulness.
8. Consistency with research data on the validity of diagnostic categories.
9. Responsiveness to critiques from clinicians and researchers.

Diagnostic Criteria and Related Information

Building upon the precedent set in DSM-III, the revised version emphasizes highly specific descriptions of the characteristics necessary for diagnosing a particular mental disorder. We will refer to such criteria in future chapters in our discussions of mental disorders.

In addition to diagnostic criteria, the descriptions of mental disorders contain a wide variety of other information. The organization of this material is similar to that used in DSM-III. For example, it includes age of onset, sex ratio, prevalence, familial pattern, and predisposing factors.

Multiaxial System

The DSM-III-R retains the multiaxial (multidimensional) approach to evaluation begun in DSM-III. In delineating five different axes (dimensions) for making clinical decisions, DSM-III and its revision expand on pioneering work carried out some years earlier (Phillips, 1968). This system of diagnosing psychological disorders is based on isolated symptoms and symptoms in association with precipitating circumstances as well as on the individual's social competence. Social competence includes the highest educational level that has been attained, occupation, and the nature of interpersonal relationships. In the following summary of the DSM-III-R axes, the first three axes present the official diagnostic assessment — that is, the disorders themselves. The other two axes are refinements to help clarify the other diagnoses and make them more meaningful.

Axis I includes the majority of clinical syndromes comprising DSM-III-R. These are the most obvious and serious mental disorders currently troubling the individual (see Box 2.1). Axis I also includes various conditions not attributable to a mental disorder but that nevertheless may be a focus of attention or treatment. These conditions are listed in the manual as V codes, since the code number for each kind of problem carries a prefix of V. Examples are malingering, marital problems, and parent – child problems (American Psychiatric Association, 1987, pp. 359 – 362).

Axis II includes long-term developmental and personality disorders that have probably been in existence for many years. They are listed in Box 2.1. The purpose of separating Axis I from Axis II is to ensure that the clinician will consider the possible presence of these disorders, which are frequently overlooked when attention is directed to the more obvious and striking Axis I disorders. Axis II disorders generally begin in childhood or adolescence and persist into adulthood. The Axis I – Axis II distinction is also helpful in evaluating children's disorders, since it emphasizes the importance of paying attention to abnormal development of cognitive, social, and motor skills (American Psychiatric Association, 1987, p. 16).

Axis III, which covers physical disorders and conditions, gives the clinician an opportunity to record a current physical problem that may be related to the person's psychological disorder. For example, a neurological abnormality may be associated with dementia (loss of intellectual functioning). Also, the physical ailment may be potentially relevant to a better understanding of the person and to plans for managing care.

Axis IV deals with the severity of psychosocial stressors. This axis gives the clinician an opportunity to rate stressors that may have had a significant influence on the development and manifestation of the mental disorder. Axis IV is analogous to Phillips's concept of precipitating circumstances. We mentioned Phillips's (1968) pioneering multidimensional approach to diagnosis earlier. Understanding the severity of psychosocial stressors may help in planning treatment, including attempts to reduce the stressors or help the individual cope with them. DSM-III-R shows the codes, terms, and examples that serve as guides in rating the severity of psychosocial stressors.

Axis V refers to the *global assessment of functioning*. DSM-III referred to this axis as the highest level of adaptive functioning. Axis V parallels Phillips's (1968) concept of social competence that we discussed earlier. Its purpose is to help clinicians make an overall judgment of the individual's psychological, social, and occupational functioning on a continuum from mental health to illness (American Psychiatric Association, 1987, p. 12). Ratings are based on current functioning (at the time of evaluation) and on the highest level of functioning during the past year. This information can be helpful in prognosis, since individuals often return to their previous level of functioning after an episode of mental disorder. Table 2.1 shows examples from the guide provided in DSM-III-R, which also includes more detailed information on how the scale should be used.

Table 2.1 Global Assessment of Functioning Scale (GAF Scale)

Code

90 | 81	Absent or minimal symptoms (e.g., mild anxiety before an exam), good functioning in all areas, interested and involved in a wide range of activities, socially effective, generally satisfied with life, no more than everyday problems or concerns (e.g., an occasional argument with family members).
70 | 61	Some mild symptoms (e.g., depressed mood and mild insomnia) or some difficulty in social, occupational, or school functioning (e.g., occasional truancy or theft within the household), but generally functioning pretty well, has some meaningful interpersonal relationships.
50 41	Serious symptoms (e.g., suicidal ideation, severe obsessional rituals, frequent shoplifting) or any serious impairment in social, occupational, or school functioning (e.g., no friends, unable to keep a job).
30 | 21	Behavior is considerably influenced by delusions or hallucinations or serious impairment in communication or judgment (e.g., sometimes incoherent, acts grossly inappropriately, suicidal preoccupation) or inability to function in almost all areas (e.g., stays in bed all day no job, home, or friends).
10 1	Persistent danger of severely hurting self or others (e.g., recurrent violence) or persistent inability to maintain minimal personal hygiene or serious suicidal act with clear expectation of death.

The GAF Scale in DSM-III-R (Axis V) is a guide for helping the clinician rate the individual's psychological, social, and occupational functioning on a hypothetical continuum of mental health – illness. The scale codes range from 1 to 90. For purposes of illustration we have listed examples of functioning at five different code ranges. The scale itself contains examples for nine such code ranges.

Source: Adapted from American Psychiatric Association, 1987, p. 12.

New Controversial Disorders

Three new diagnostic categories were proposed during the development of DSM-III-R: sadistic personality disorder, self-defeating personality disorder, and late luteal phase dysphoric disorder. However, the proposal aroused a storm of controversy, so these categories were relegated to an appendix "to facilitate further systematic study and research" (American Psychiatric Association, 1987, p. 367). Whether or not they will or should become a part of Axis I or Axis II in a future revision of the DSM is highly debatable. Since we deal with the first two personality disorders in some detail in Chapter 12, we will confine our present discussion to late luteal phase dysphoric disorder, more commonly called *premenstrual stress* or *premenstrual tension*. In the original proposal for DSM-III-R the label used was *premenstrual dysphoric disorder* (*dysphoric* refers to an emotional state of discomfort or general malaise). It was changed to the present terminology as being "technically more accurate" (Boffey, 1986, p. 11). DSM-III-R offers the following rationale for including the "disorder."

> Many females report a variety of physical and emotional changes associated with specific phases of the menstrual cycle. For most of these females, these changes are not severe, cause little distress, and have no effect on social or occupational functioning. In contrast, the essential feature of Late Luteal Phase Dysphoric Disorder is a pattern of clinically significant emotional and behavioral symptoms that occur during the last week of the luteal phase and remit within a few days after the onset of the follicular phase. In most females these symptoms occur in the week before, and remit within a few days of the onset of menses. (American Psychiatric Association, 1987, p. 367)

Diagnostic criteria include the following (a) marked changes in mood; (b) persistent and marked anger or irritability; (c) marked anxiety, tension, or feeling on edge; (d) feelings of hopelessness or self-abasement; (e) decreased interest in usual activities; (f) fatigue or marked lack of energy; (g) difficulty in concentrating; (h) marked change in appetite, overeating, or specific cravings for food; (i) insomnia or hypersomnia; and (j) physical symptoms such as breast tenderness or swelling, headaches, joint or muscle pain; sensations of bloating, or weight gain. To justify the diagnosis, at least five of these symptoms must be present for most of the time during each luteal phase, and at least one of the symptoms must be among the first four listed. Furthermore, the symptoms must interfere seriously with work or social relationships. The condition is confirmed by the woman's daily ratings of her symptoms during at least two menstrual cycles.

As these diagnostic criteria indicate, specific physiological changes in the menstrual cycle set off the "disorder," but only certain women show abnormal psychological reactions to these premenstrual changes in hormonal activity. Various clinical psychologists and psychiatrists, as well as other mental health professionals who share a feminist perspective, argue that the diagnosis stigmatizes women with menstrual problems as being mentally ill or psychiatrically disturbed when their problems might well be more biological than psychological. These professionals acknowledge the reality of premenstrual tension among some women, but they repudiate the notion that it needs to be included in the DSM as a form of mental disorder. Supporters of the diagnostic category claim that without it, the relatively few women who suffer from the disorder may go untreated if it is uncomplicated by other mental disorders. Admittedly, the argument continues, the scientific evidence to support such a diagnosis is still not strong enough to warrant its inclusion in the main body of DSM-III-R. Nevertheless, advocates of the diagnosis conclude that it is of sufficient clinical importance to justify its placement in an appendix of the manual for purposes of further study and research (Fisher, 1986a, 1986b; Holden, 1986c; Landers, 1986a).

Conclusions

DSM-III-R promises to be a powerful aid in the development of explicit rules that link symptoms, observations, recording of data, and diagnostic judgment. Like DSM-III, it rejects tying diagnosis to a single label and supports the capture of pertinent information on adaptation and maladaptation through a multidimensional approach. It now represents a blend of sophistication in methodology and traditional concepts of diagnosis and classification.

Writing from the standpoint of clinical psychology, Theodore Millon (1986, pp. 62–67) has developed a number of suggestions for future revisions of DSM. Although these suggestions were based on an intensive analysis of DSM-III, the ones we have listed apply as well to DSM-III-R.

1. Although a number of individual psychologists and social workers have been involved in DSM revisions, the American Psychological Association and the National Association of Social Workers should be included as part of the official planning group for DSM-IV.

2. The interpersonal style that individuals use to achieve their goals and solve their conflicts should be recognized more explicitly.

3. Introduction of new diagnostic categories and revisions of older ones should take greater advantage of research findings.

4. More attention should be paid to etiological factors in the development and expression of disorders.

5. Wherever feasible, diagnostic categories should indicate the effects of various therapeutic approaches to disorders.

Technical Issues in Diagnosis

Reliability

Like any other assessment of behavior, the diagnosis of mental disorders should be free from personal bias. Ideally, the diagnostic judgments reached by several psychiatrists, psychologists, or other mental health professionals concerning a particular person should be interchangeable — that is, perfectly reliable. In practice, of course, this goal is seldom met. Some researchers have reported that agreement among diagnosticians is at best only moderate and often quite low. Other analysts, however, using the same evidence, have come to more optimistic findings. They conclude that the unreliability of diagnoses is exaggerated and in some instances completely unjustified (Kendell, 1975; Spitzer & Fleiss, 1974). It is crucial to know, then, what circumstances are likely to increase reliability and what conditions are likely to decrease it. A number of researchers have come to the following conclusions (Blashfield & Draguns, 1976a; Buss, 1966; Kendell, 1973; Phillips & Draguns, 1971).

1. Psychotic conditions — for example, schizophrenic disorders — are diagnosed more reliably than neuroses such as anxiety, somatoform, and dissociative disorders.

2. The more general the category, the more reliable the diagnosis. For example, it is easier to differentiate neurotic disorders from psychotic conditions than it is to distinguish among the specific subcategories within each of those broad groups of disorders.

3. The more disturbed the behavior, the more reliable the diagnosis. Thus, schizophrenia is diagnosed more reliably than are the milder forms of mental disorder. This finding is especially important, since the more severe a disorder, the more immediate the attention it usually demands.

4. Too great or too little emotional distance between the diagnostician and the patient lowers reliability.

5. Social and cultural distance also decreases reliability. It is easier to diagnose members of one's own group correctly than to diagnose persons of different circumstances.

6. Reliability increases when the rules governing assignment to diagnostic categories are clear and explicit. (For this reason DSM-III-R should produce more reliable diagnoses than its predecessors.)

Descriptive Validity

The term **descriptive validity** as applied to the diagnosis of mental disorders refers to the homogeneity of people within a diagnostic category. The basic question here is: To what extent do people who have been placed within a particular diagnostic category actually reveal similar behavior? In the past, lack of homogeneity has been one of the most frequent criticisms leveled at traditional systems of clarifying mental disorders. Edward Zigler and Leslie Phillips (1961) conducted a particularly important study of descriptive validity. They studied the records of almost 800 patients admitted to the Worcester State Hospital from 1945 to 1957. They found that the behavior that was characteristic of the diagnostic category to which a patient had been assigned did not necessarily correspond to the behavior actually observed in the patient. Furthermore, certain symptoms overlapped significantly, so one could not always conclude that a specific symptom corresponded to a specific diagnosis. Zigler and Phillips concluded that even though there was some relationship between the expression of certain symptoms and the diagnostic classification of the individual, the correspondence was often slight. In fact, it was so irregular that knowing a patient's diagnostic category transmitted only a very small amount of knowledge about the specific symptoms the person had displayed.

In interpreting their findings, Zigler and Phillips suggested that single symptoms do not differentiate categories as well as one might want, but patterns of symptoms (i.e., syndromes) do much better. Their conclusion bolsters the contention of many clinicians that attempts to match specific symptoms with specific categories is misleading. Diagnosticians usually do not depend merely on discrete symptoms to reach a diagnostic decision. Rather, they look for patterns (Spitzer, 1976). Thus, as Zigler and Phillips found, one would expect reasonably good agreement between such patterns of behavior and diagnostic categories.

Most criticisms concerning the lack of descriptive validity in the diagnoses of mental disorders have been based on classifications prior to DSM-III. The new, more stringent rules of diagnostic assignment in DSM-III-R should increase homogeneity within diagnostic categories and thus increase descriptive validity.

Predictive Validity

The crucial issue of **predictive validity** in diagnosing psychological disorders revolves around such questions as the following: How helpful is the diagnosis for enabling the mental health professional to (a) choose among available courses of treatment, (b) predict how well the patient will respond to such intervention, and (c) maximize the chances of successful treatment and minimize chances of failure? Although no clinician claims that diagnostic systems accomplish these goals perfectly, many argue that diagnosis is far from useless. They emphasize that, within limits, knowing the diagnostic category to which an individual has been assigned enhances the predictive validity of diagnosis (Draguns & Phillips, 1971; Kendell, 1975; Robins & Helzer, 1986, p. 430; Woodruff, Goodwin, & Guze, 1974). This is especially true with the more explicit statements of symptoms and symptom patterns in DSM-III-R. Despite improvements, reliability and validity will continue to pose problems, so a careful clinician will seek information over and above the diagnostic label in formulating and implementing a treatment plan. As progress in developing DSM-IV continues, however, a greater shift toward reliability and validity seems promising (Millon & Klerman, 1986).

Coverage

The concept of coverage has only recently been introduced as a criterion for evaluating the diagnosis of mental disorders. Unlike reliability and validity, which focus on specific diagnostic categories, coverage pertains to the entire diagnostic system. In determining the degree of coverage, questions such as the following are asked: How inclusive is the diagnostic system? Does it leave out any patterns of abnormal behavior? The official diagnostic system in the United States, as represented by DSM-III-R, includes all manifestations of abnormal behavior.

Two kinds of costs are associated with such complete coverage. For one thing, wastebasket categories develop to accommodate the heterogeneous array of cases that defy placement in any of the other slots — for example, "psychotic disorder NOS" (not otherwise specified) in DSM-III-R. For another, aspiring to perfect coverage tends to reduce reliability (Blashfield & Draguns, 1976a). Because the various wastebasket categories have vague boundaries, they contribute more than their share of diagnostic disagreements. In general, the larger the number of categories to which an individual can be assigned, the higher the chance for disagreement or error and the lower the reliability of the assignment.

Errors in Clinical Judgment in Diagnosis

In his insightful analysis of diagnostic procedures, clinical psychologist Paul Meehl (1986, p. 223) points to the interesting work of a "brilliant diagnostician," T. A. Peppard, who practiced internal medicine in Minneapolis for many years. Peppard (1949) carried out a

Paul Meehl, long-time professor of psychology at the University of Minnesota, has made extensive and insightful analyses of the procedures for diagnosing mental disorders.

statistical study of the diagnostic mistakes he had made over a number of years. Consistent with what is now generally known in medical practice, he found that his errors of omission were more common than his errors of commission. These omissions occurred for various reasons. Prominent among them were failure to look for something, looking for the right things but not giving them adequate weight, and making errors in "judgment calls." Although Peppard's diagnostic errors were made in the context of internal medicine, it seems reasonable to conclude that similar kinds of errors may also occur in the diagnosis of psychological disorders.

Social Issues in Diagnosis

Rosenhan's Demonstration

Certain critics allege that the use of diagnostic categories (labels) to describe mental disorders is open to contamination through various social factors. To support this contention they cite the well-publicized study by David Rosenhan (1973). Rosenhan sent eight individuals with no history of psychological disturbance, treatment, or hospitalization to psychiatric hospitals in different regions of the United States. Each complained of hearing voices. Except for this symptom and their occupations (several held or were training for positions in psychology and psychiatry), they gave truthful personal histories. All eight volunteers were admitted to psychiatric hospitals. With only one exception, they were diagnosed as schizophrenic.

Once they were admitted, they stopped complaining of hearing voices and acted in their customary normal manner. The disappearance of their sole symptom did not lead to their prompt release. Instead, their average stay in their respective institutions amounted to 19 days, with a range of 7 to 52. Moreover, psychiatrists and nurses tended to record whatever the pseudopatients did in light of their alleged illness. If they wrote, this was recorded as "writing behavior," presumably related to their disturbance. If they sat back and waited, they were described as passive. If they inquired about their prospects for release, they were seen as demanding. Paradoxically, some of the real patients sensed that the pseudopatients were different from them and made remarks to that effect. Even upon discharge, the typical diagnosis was schizophrenia in remission. Several days of perfectly normal behavior were not enough to offset one symptom!

Rosenhan concluded that psychiatric diagnosis was more a matter of the social setting in which it took place than the behavior that was actually exhibited. According to Rosenhan, there was a definite time lag between the disappearance of psychiatric symptoms and the recognition of that fact by the hospital staff. Indeed, even when staff members noted the absence of the symptoms, they still labeled the pseudopatients mentally ill.

Rosenhan's dramatic demonstration and conclusions provoked a storm of criticism (Crown, 1975; Kety, 1974; Millon, 1975; Spitzer, 1976; Weinger, 1975). As Spitzer (1976) argued, the psychiatrists were right in taking both the symptoms (hearing voices) and subsequent normal behavior into account for their later diagnosis of schizophrenia in remission. All that Rosenhan had demonstrated was that psychiatrists can be temporarily fooled by the faked expression of an atypical psychiatric symptom — a rather trivial conclusion, in no way related to the actual validity of diagnostic concepts and practices in psychiatry.

One may well debate whether Rosenhan or his critics have made the more compelling argument. However, one fact remains. Under the experimental conditions imposed by Rosenhan, psychiatrists were unable to tell pseudopatients from the real ones, although at least a few of the real patients accomplished that feat.

**Abuses of
Psychiatric Diagnosis**

Rosenhan's conclusions concerning the weakness of psychiatric diagnosis and diagnostic labeling are debatable. Nevertheless, his study clearly shows that psychiatrists, clinical psychologists, and other members of the clinical mental health team are fallible. Although that is not a startling discovery, there is another, more alarming body of evidence that some mental health professionals are politically and morally corrupt. This corruption involves the deliberate misuse of psychiatric diagnosis, sanctioned at the highest levels of government, to maintain the political power of the state.

A case in point is the evidence that psychiatric hospitalization in the Soviet Union is used to remove social and political dissidents. Some of these people are placed in general psychiatric institutions and others in special psychiatric hospitals operated by the central police agency and restricted to individuals accused or convicted of crimes. The official diagnostic system of the Soviet Union recognizes the category "sluggish schizophrenia," a label often imposed on political, religious, or other dissidents (Faraone, 1982; Merskey & Shafran, 1986). Cooperating Soviet psychiatrists routinely regard dissatisfaction with the existing political system and the wish to reform it as symptoms of this novel disorder, even in the absence of any of the traditional signs of schizophrenia. Cure or remission is deemed to take place when patients renounce their defiant attitudes and beliefs. Before this goal is attained, the patients are often treated with high dosages of antipsychotic drugs or tranquilizers that produce a variety of unpleasant and frightening side effects. No measures are taken to counteract these side effects (Barringer, 1987; Keller, 1987; Rosenhan, 1983, pp. 112–114).

The question arises as to whether some or all of the people so diagnosed may be politically deviant *and* psychologically disturbed. The Soviet psychiatrists engaged in these treatment practices, and apologists for them in the West, have maintained for years that this is indeed the case. However, after an exhaustive study of the available evidence, Bloch and Reddaway (1977) concluded that the dissidents were normal and symptom-free. By that time, several of the former inmates of special psychiatric institutions were in the West and voluntarily submitted to independent psychiatric examinations. They were found to be free of psychiatric disturbance. In Bloch and Reddaway's words (1977, p. 254): "Many of the dissenters who were interned and later emigrated have adapted quickly and successfully to life in their new homes. Among those we have met, Rips and Volpin were, in 1976, teaching mathematics at universities, Feigin was a trade-union official, Medvedev was a research biologist and writer, Plyushch was preparing to become a mathematics teacher, and Gorbanevskaya was a writer and editor." The assembly of the World Psychiatric Association in Honolulu in 1977 officially took note of the evidence of systematic abuse of psychiatry for political purposes in the Soviet Union and condemned those practices.

The abuse of psychiatric diagnosis for political or personal ends has also occurred in nontotalitarian countries, including the United States. For example, influential citizens with the cooperation of psychiatrists have sometimes succeeded in pushing inconvenient or difficult people out of the way by confining them to mental hospitals (Rosenhan, 1983). Although such abuse must be condemned and rectified, it is not official policy, deliberately designed to help governments maintain their political power. (See Chapter 21 for the historical development and current status of laws protecting the rights of mentally ill persons, especially in the United States.)

Early in 1988 the official Soviet news agency, Tass, announced that the Soviet Union was adopting a new set of legal rights for mental patients (Keller, 1988). The statutes are the first fundamental revision of Soviet regulations concerning psychiatry in 27 years. They not only make it a crime to "lock up a perfectly healthy person" in a mental hospital but they give patients and their families the right to sue for release. They also give the

Health Ministry final authority over the notorious "special" hospitals used to incarcerate political dissidents. Formerly these hospitals were under the jurisdiction of the Interior Ministry (the central police agency). Interestingly, although the Soviet press has not openly criticized the psychiatric abuse of political dissidents, it has recently begun to discuss corruption and incompetence in the psychiatric profession itself.

Specialists in Soviet affairs have welcomed these legal changes, especially the ones concerned with human rights. However, some have voiced skepticism about whether the laws will be translated into action. They conclude that the situation certainly merits close watch and that, at least from a legal point of view, the changes are a promising sign (Holden, 1988; Keller, 1988, p. 1).

Methods of Psychological Assessment

Interviews

Interviews are the most basic and frequently used method of assessing psychological disorders. Not only do they yield valuable diagnostic information about a person's abnormal behavior and thinking, but they also disclose background factors that may have contributed to such disturbances. For example, knowledge concerning family history can be used for reaching a diagnosis or estimating the possibility of a genetic basis for a disorder. Obtaining a family history of psychological problems may also reveal significant life experiences that can in part explain the development of disorders (Andreasen, Rice, Endicott, Reich, & Coryell, 1986; Rosenthal & Akiskal, 1985; Turner & Hersen, 1985; Weissman, Merikangas, John, Wickramaratne, Prusoff, & Kidd, 1986). Interviews can also be a first step in establishing a therapeutic relationship, even in the case of such severe disturbances as schizophrenia (Szymanski & Keill, 1985, p. 129).

Basic Approaches

Interviews vary considerably in how they are conducted, especially in the degree of structure they impose. **Structured interviews** follow rigid and specific rules; **semistructured interviews** are more flexible, using suggestive guidelines rather than rules.

In structured interviews the clinician asks specific questions, designed in advance to determine the nature of the person's problems. These questions usually follow an exact sequence and wording and include well-defined rules for recording and judging responses. Thus, two different interviewers following a structured procedure should be able to obtain highly similar information (Edelbrock & Costello, 1984; Kendell, 1975; Spiker & Ehler, 1984; Spitzer & Williams, 1980).

In semistructured interviews the interchange between clinician and client (patient) is more free-flowing. The interviewer's judgment plays a greater role in determining what is asked. In addition to asking specific questions, the clinician makes broad suggestions for discussing possible problem areas. Since these areas often develop as the interview proceeds, semistructured interviews give people an opportunity to reveal problems in their own way.

Each approach has certain advantages. Structured procedures minimize the interviewer's bias and erroneous judgments, thus yielding more objective information. Semistructured interviews tend to elicit more spontaneous reactions from the client, and thus may capture information that ordinarily would not emerge during highly structured interviews. Clinicians often combine structured and semistructured techniques within the same assessment interview. At the beginning of the interview the structure may be open-ended, designed to put the client at ease and permit a flexible exploration of problems. As the interview proceeds, the structure can then become more directive, enabling the clinician to reach a more definitive assessment of the client's condition.

Interview Schedules

A practical way of lending structure to assessment interviews is the use of **interview schedules**, a number of which have been developed in recent years (Spiker & Ehler, 1984).

1. **The Present State Examination (PSE)**, developed in Britain by Wing, Cooper, and Sartorius (1974), consists of 145 items covering a wide variety of symptoms. Most of the items involve highly specific and probing questions. However, there is also opportunity for the interviewer to ask broader questions to amplify the specific information. Each symptom included in the schedule is rated as present or absent. The degree of severity of a present symptom is also rated. A computer program is available to classify the various symptoms into patterns (syndromes). These syndromes can be converted into broad descriptive categories of mental disorders according to the system employed in the *International Classification of Diseases* (ICD). As we pointed out earlier in the chapter, the ICD is highly compatible with the DSM-III-R classification. Research with the PSE indicates that it has high reliability. The instrument is especially popular with European mental health professionals.

2. **The Schedule for Affective Disorders and Schizophrenia (SADS)** is a semistructured approach to diagnosis, using both highly specific questions and more flexible, open-ended probes (Endicott & Spitzer, 1978). It is divided into two sections. The first section deals with the present, the second with the persons's past history of mental disorders. The SADS is widely used in the United States and is reported to have good reliability (Spiker & Ehler, 1984, p. 297).

3. **The Diagnostic Interview Schedule (DIS)** is a highly structured schedule originally developed for use in epidemiological research surveys by the National Institute of Mental Health. The primary purpose of such surveys is to determine the frequency of mental disorders in different regions of the United States. Reliability studies show good agreement among interviewers (Spiker & Ehler, 1984, p. 297).

In recent years a number of interview schedules for assessing mental disorders have been developed for use with children and adolescents (Edelbrock & Costello, 1984). The following examples illustrate some of their main features.

1. **The Kiddie-SADS** is a semistructured schedule for children and adolescents (Puig-Antich & Chambers, 1978). It is modeled after SADS. In addition to items related to affective and schizophrenic disorders, the Kiddie-SADS includes items dealing with other disorders of childhood and adolescence — for example, separation anxiety, phobias, and obsessive compulsive disturbances. In using the schedule, the interviewer gathers information not only from the child or adolescent but also from the parents, carefully noting discrepancies and attempting to resolve them through further questioning.

The reliability of the Kiddie-SADS is not as high as that of the adult version. This lower reliability probably represents the greater difficulty in assessing childhood psychopathology (Chambers et al., 1986).

2. **The Child Assessment Schedule (CAS)** is a semistructured interview schedule for children ages 7 through 12 (Hodges, Kline, Stern, Cytryn, & McKnew, 1982; Hodges,

McKnew, Cytryn, Stern, & Kline, 1982). It contains questions about a wide range of topics, such as the child's school experiences, friends, family, fears and worries, self-image, and mood. It also includes specific items dealing with symptom complexes, such as separation anxiety, depression, attention deficits, and hyperactivity. Clinical judgment is used in administering the schedule and interpreting its results. For instance, the clinician decides the order in which to explore topics and specific items as well as the range of content. Responses to questions are tabulated as yes or no, or, when more appropriate, as ambiguous, not applicable, or no response. The schedule yields total scores for each content area and symptom complex, as well as an overall score.

3. **The Diagnostic Interview Schedule for Children (DISC)** is a highly structured schedule covering a broad range of mental disorders (Costello, Edelbrock, Kalas, Kessler, & Klaric, 1982). The DISC is basically a modification of the Diagnostic Interview Schedule (DIS) for adults. Both were designed by the National Institute of Mental Health primarily for use in epidemiological studies.

Computer Interviews

In recent years the use of computers to "interview" patients has gained a great deal of momentum (Erdman, Klein, & Greist, 1985). The potential advantages of this approach include the reliability of the information and an increased ability to obtain specific data concerning the patient. However, some mental health professionals say that the procedures are too impersonal and rely mainly on highly structured verbal information. Thus, computer interviews may miss subtle aspects of the patient's problems since they cannot adapt the wording of questions from one patient to another.

Currently, the most promising use of computer interviewing is in highly focused evaluations of specific problem areas — for example, the risk of suicide in depressed patients, drug and alcohol abuse, and various sexual disorders. Computer interviewing may prove valuable for self-help programs in the treatment of phobic disorders (irrational fears) and mild depression. These kinds of programs could reach a large number of individuals who might otherwise receive little professional help. Concurrently with self-help programs, computer interviews may be used to educate patients concerning the nature and treatment of psychological disorders (Erdman, Klein, & Greist, 1985).

Intelligence Tests

Clinical Purpose

As Chapter 1 pointed out, impaired intellectual functioning is an important criterion in the assessment of mental disorder. To some extent, the kinds of interviews we have discussed can reveal such impairment, but more precise information can usually be obtained through the use of individual intelligence tests — tests administered to one person at a time. These clinical tests of intelligence are basically standardized interviews that focus on the assessment of cognitive skills.

Clinical intelligence tests can furnish clues to mental disorders in a number of ways. A discrepancy between test performance and a person's education, occupation, and intellectual accomplishments suggests the presence of emotional problems. Of course, other possible psychosocial influences, such as the lack of opportunity or motivation for intellectual achievement, must also be considered. Then again, the results of intelligence tests might be quite consistent with previous intellectual accomplishments, and this consistency could help confirm a diagnosis of **mental retardation**: the abnormal deficiency of cognitive skills that begins very early in life (see Chapter 17).

Diagnostic clinical interviews may vary from having a high degree of structure to being flexible and open-ended.

Historical Background

Although crude attempts to develop objective assessments of mental abilities can be traced to the 16th century, it was not until the 19th century that more scientific methods of measuring intelligence began to emerge. Outstanding among these pioneering efforts was the work of the British scientist Sir Francis Galton (1822–1911) and the American psychologist James McKeen Cattell (1860–1944). Cattell spent several postdoctoral years working with Galton in his Anthrometric Laboratory in London (Hale, 1983; Sattler, 1982, pp. 29–31). The Galton–Cattell tests assumed that highly intelligent people show a fine sensory discrimination of stimuli and a quickness of mind. Accordingly, the tests involved such laboratory tasks as discriminating weights, sizes, tones, colors, and rhythms. They also included various tests of memory. Subsequently, the British psychologist and logician Charles E. Spearman (1863–1945), using more refined methods of statistical

Sir Francis Galton, eminent British scientist of the 19th century. He was a pioneer in the development of concepts and methods for objectively measuring intelligence.

James McKeen Cattell, an American psychologist, spent several postdoctoral years working with Galton and was greatly influenced by his approach to measuring intelligence.

French psychologist Alfred Binet, working with Psychiatrist Théophile Simon, developed the first practical appraisal of general intelligence, the Binet-Simon test.

In 1916, Lewis Terman, Professor of Psychology at Stanford University, published a revision of the Binet test which he named the Stanford-Binet Intelligence Scale. This test and its descendents have greatly influenced the measurement of intelligence in the United States.

analysis, showed that the kinds of tasks used by Galton and Cattell were not only intercorrelated but also positively correlated with schoolchildren's marks. Spearman concluded that these findings were consistent with his concept of intelligence as a general factor (g) that runs through many kinds of mental tasks (Cattell, 1890; Galton, 1883; Hilgard, 1987, pp. 459–461; Jensen, 1980, pp. 138–139; Sattler, 1982, pp. 30–31; Spearman, 1904).

The first practical appraisal of general intelligence was developed in France by Alfred Binet (1867–1911), a psychologist, and Théophile Simon (1873–1961), a psychiatrist. Their task, in response to the charge of a 1904 commission appointed by the French Minister of Education, was to find ways of distinguishing between mentally retarded and normal children, so those who were mentally retarded could be given special education. Especially important in the test was the emphasis on complex intellectual processes such as judgment, which Binet and Simon believed to be the essence of general intelligence (Binet & Simon, 1905, 1916; Thorndike, Hagen, & Sattler, 1986, p. 1).

Binet and Simon developed a series of tasks that they administered to children of various ages. They analyzed the responses to see which test items on the average were passed at each age level and selected items so that each group of tasks corresponded to that passed at a given age.

The test items were then administered individually in an interview fashion. Intelligence was determined by how high on the scale (that is, the age level) the child could reach before failing the tasks at the next highest age level. The highest level achieved was called **mental age (MA)**. The MA indicated only the absolute level of intellectual functioning, not the relative level. For example, an 8-year-old child, a 6-year-old, and a 4-year-old might all score an MA of six. However, the first would be below average in intellectual ability, the second average, and the third above average.

Stanford – Binet Intelligence Scale

By 1910 a number of American psychologists had translated the Binet – Simon test into English. In 1916 Lewis Terman of Stanford University published a revision. Appropriately named the Stanford – Binet Intelligence Scale, this test and its descendants became the best-known versions of the Binet – Simon tests to be used in the United States (Terman & Merrill, 1937, 1960, 1973; Thorndike, Hagen, & Sattler, 1986). Although the original purpose of the scale was to identify mentally retarded children, in its successive editions it became a measure of general intelligence for use in a wide variety of situations where knowledge of children's cognitive functioning was required.

Several years before the publication of the 1st edition of the Stanford – Binet Scale in

This five-year-old is completing one of the tasks on the Stanford–Binet Intelligence Scale.

1916, the German psychologist William Stern (1871–1938) had suggested that a relative index of intelligence could be obtained by dividing the mental age (MA) derived from the Binet test by the individual's chronological age (CA). Terman adopted this procedure, defining Stern's ratio as an **intelligence quotient (IQ)**. To avoid decimals Terman multiplied the quotient by 100, as in the following formula: $IQ = 100 \times MA/CA$. Thus, if the person's MA and CA are the same, the IQ is 100, exactly average. Because the arithmetical concept of IQ was easily understood, it became established in successive revisions of the Stanford–Binet (Hilgard, 1987, p. 464; Stern, 1914).

As the use of the Stanford–Binet became more widespread, it became evident that the Stern–Terman formula for estimating intelligence posed serious problems. The central difficulty was the erroneous assumption that mental age did not increase beyond age 16. Consider, for example, a bright child of 12 who scores the maximum MA of 16 on the Stanford–Binet. The resulting IQ would be 133, considerably above average. If the child takes the test four years later at the age of 16 and scores the maximum again, the IQ drops to 100, an obviously peculiar circumstance. The test posed similar problems when it was administered to adults. Suppose an adult of 32 scored an MA of 16. the resulting IQ would be 50. Thus, even though the person made the highest MA score possible, the IQ would be very much below average; indeed, it would indicate serious mental retardation.

To overcome the problem of an insufficiently high ceiling for the MA, Terman and his colleagues revised the scale so that the IQ was no longer computed according to the Stern IQ formula. Instead, it became a **deviation IQ**. This index, calculated from specially prepared tables, related an individual's score on the test to age-mates in the standardization sample. The distribution of IQs was based on the reasonable assumption that they are normally (symmetrically) distributed in the general population. As Figure 2.1 shows, the areas under the curve (in percentages) are divided into standard deviation units. The midpoint of the distribution has a standard deviation of zero and is arbitrarily designated as an IQ of 100. The various other IQ scores shown under the curve correspond to cutoff

Figure 2.1

Relationship of normal curve to IQs for the Stanford–Binet Intelligence Scale (3rd edition) and the Wechsler Adult Intelligence Scale–Revised (WAIS-R). (Adapted from Sattler, 1982, p. 16; Terman & Merrill, 1973; Wechsler, 1981, p. 27.)

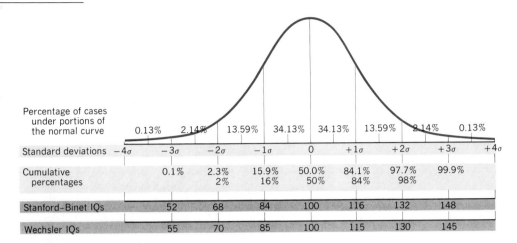

points that range from three standard deviations below the mean IQ of 100 to three standard deviations above it. Each standard deviation above or below the mean represents 16 IQ points. As the curve indicates, approximately 2 percent of the population is at the IQ level of 68 or below, and 2 percent is at the IQ level of 132 or above.

The 4th edition of the Stanford–Binet Intelligence Scale (1986) has been thoroughly revised, reflecting the many social and cultural changes that have occurred in the United States since the previous edition. The scale is constructed to appraise cognitive development from ages 2 to 23. The new edition groups the various tasks according to four areas of intellectual ability: verbal reasoning, quantitative reasoning, abstract/visual reasoning, and short-term memory. Indices of performance are obtained for each specific test within those areas, for each area, and for the scale as a whole (composite score). IQs are no longer used to indicate relative performance. Instead, raw scores are converted into standard age scores (SAS), which correspond closely to the statistical properties of IQs used in the previous editions. For example, the SAS for each of the four cognitive ability areas as well as the composite SAS have a mean of 100 and a standard deviation of 16. This procedure was adopted to make the new scale statistically comparable to the previous edition of the Stanford–Binet. The change in terminology from IQ to SAS reflects more accurately the meaning of the index of intelligence (Anastasi, 1988, pp. 241–246; Thorndike, Hagen, & Sattler, 1986).

Wechsler Adult Intelligence Scale

The development of what is now known as the Wechsler Adult Intelligence Scale–Revised (WAIS-R) began while David Wechsler was chief psychologist at the Bellevue Psychiatric Hospital in New York City. The earliest versions appeared in 1939 and 1942 and were called the Wechsler–Bellevue Intelligence Scales I and II. They were succeeded by the 1st edition of the Wechsler Adult Intelligence Scale in 1955. Wechsler also developed an intelligence scale for children (WISC), constructed on the same principles as the scale for adults. The revised versions of these scales (WAIS-R and WISC-R) are widely used in the appraisal of general intelligence for a variety of educational purposes and in the clinical diagnosis of mental disorders (Wechsler, 1974, 1981). We focus here on the adult scale.

WAIS-R uses a deviation IQ as an index of intellectual ability. Deviation IQs derived from the WAIS-R are calculated from tables that convert the raw test scores to standard scores that compare the person taking the test with age-mates. The distribution of IQs thus obtained is based on the theoretical normal curve shown in Figure 2.1. As the curve indicates, the midpoint of the IQ distribution is set at 100. The other IQ scores shown correspond to cutoff points ranging from three standard deviations below the midpoint (the

David Wechsler was for many years chief psychologist at the Bellevue Psychiatric Hospital in New York. He developed a series of individual tests for adults and children that provide not only an appraisal of general intelligence but also clues to the diagnosis of mental disorder.

Administering the revised Wechsler Adult Intelligence Scale (WAIS-R). The woman is carrying out one of the performance (nonverbal) tests of the scale.

A 12-year-old performing the picture arrangement task on the revised Wechsler Intelligence Scale for Children (WISC-R).

mean IQ of 100) to three standard deviations above. Each standard deviation represents 15 IQ points.

The WAIS-R was standardized on an equal number of females and males and on individuals whose ages ranged from 16 to 74. The standardization sample included a wide range of occupational and educational levels and nonwhite and white individuals. The scale yields three IQs: Verbal Performance, and Full Scale (Verbal plus Performance). Box 2.2 shows the various types of tasks involved, and Table 2.2 shows the classification of total IQs. As the table indicates, they correspond closely to the standard age scores of the Stanford–Binet scale (4th edition).

The WAIS-R can play an important part in educational applications, such as planning educational programs, and in the diagnosis of mental disorders. Sharp discrepancies among the various tasks (subtests) may disclose certain patterns of maladaptive thinking and behavior. For example, very low scores on the block design test or digit span task (Box 2.2), together with otherwise normal or superior scores on other tests, may suggest the possibility of brain damage. Test results may help establish whether people suffering from a psychotic disorder marked by a significant break with reality reveal a deterioration of intellectual functioning only in specific areas or whether the decline is more general. Test results can furnish clues concerning the presence of abnormal anxiety, especially when scores on such verbal tasks as vocabulary are relatively unimpaired, and scores on various problem-solving tasks are significantly lower. Furthermore, the tests can provide samples of problem-solving ability in a variety of situations, thus revealing the extent to which emotional disturbance is interfering with that ability. Tests may also reveal how the person approaches the solving of problems. For example, is there a strong tendency to guess wildly or, conversely, to be overly cautious? Like other individual (clinical) intelligence tests, the WAIS-R can yield more information about a person's intellectual ability than can a simple quantitative index such as the IQ.

BOX 2.2 Wechsler Adult Intelligence Scale—Revised (WAIS-R)

The *Wechsler Adult Intelligence Scale—Revised* (*WAIS-R*) consists of 6 verbal and 5 performance tests. Three separate IQs can be derived from these tests: Verbal, Performance, and Full Scale (all 11 tests). The type of task involved in each test is shown here. The numbers preceding the tests show the order in which they occur in the WAIS-R manual for examiners. Although this sequence is usually followed in administering the scales, examiners are advised that they may depart from the standard sequence if the person being tested is not comfortable with the regular alteration of Verbal and Performance tests (Wechsler, 1981, p. 53).

Verbal Tests

1.	Information	General knowledge in a variety of fields of graded difficulty—the kind of information acquired in school and by keeping up with current events.
3.	Digit span	Repeating numbers as given and backward; tests attention and rote memory.
5.	Vocabulary	Defining the meaning of words.
7.	Arithmetic	Computational problems of graded difficulty; no knowledge beyond basic arithmetic operations required.
9.	Comprehension	Understanding appropriate responses to a variety of social situations; tests practical knowledge.
11.	Similarities	Identifying the basic similarity of two objects (for example, wood and coal); tests abstract thinking.

Performance Tests

2.	Picture completion	Identifying an important or essential part that is missing from each picture; tests visual alertness and visual memory.
4.	Picture arrangement	Rearranging a series of pictures so that they tell a meaningful story from beginning to end; tests understanding of social situations.
6.	Block design	Copying designs of increasing complexity with four or nine blocks in red, white, and red-and-white; tests ability to perceive patterns.
8.	Object assembly	Putting together a number of pieces so that they represent a complete object; tests ability to deal with part-whole relationships.
10.	Digit symbol	Applying a code in which each symbol stands for a different digit; tests speed of learning and recording.

Source: Wechsler, 1981, pp. 59–86.

Table 2.2 Ability Classifications: Stanford–Binet Intelligence Scale (4th Edition) and Wechsler Adult Intelligence Scale–Revised (WAIS-R)

Stanford–Binet (4th edition) Composite Standard Age Score	Wechsler Adult Intelligence Scale–Revised (WAIS-R) IQ	Classification	Percent Included (approximate)
132 and above	130 and above	Very superior	2
121–131	120–129	Superior	7
111–120	110–119	High average	16
89–110	90–109	Average	50
79–88	80–89	Low average	16
68–78	70–79	Slow learner (borderline)	7
67 and below	69 and below	Mentally retarded	2

The 4th edition of the Stanford–Binet Intelligence Scale uses a numerical index called the standard age score (SAS) rather than IQ to designate level of intellectual ability. However, the SAS distribution corresponds closely to the IQ distribution of the 3rd edition and to IQs derived from such individual tests as the Wechsler Adult Intelligence Scale–Revised (WAIS-R) and the revised Wechsler Intelligence Scale for Children (WISC-R).

Source: Thorndike, Hagen, & Sattler, 1986, pp. 127–129; Wechsler, 1981, p. 28.

Personality Inventories

Basic Characteristics

Mental health professionals use various kinds of **personality inventories** in assessing mental disorders. Inventories, a highly objective approach to personality assessment, consist of printed questions or statements about a person's behavior and feelings that require either a very limited response, such as yes–no or true–false, or a more refined gradation—for example, from strongly agree to strongly disagree. In some inventories a response such as cannot say is an option. Since this format is basically a way of describing oneself, personality inventories are often known as self-report instruments.

Some personality inventories measure a single dimension, such as anxiety. More often, they are *multidimensional*, measuring various aspects of the individual's personal characteristics. In addition, inventories may be designed to assess only the individual's present state without assuming that the reported characteristics are relatively enduring ones. Other inventories attempt to measure basic **personality traits:** more deeply embedded characteristics that the individual has had for some time.

Over the years there have been many definitions of *personality traits* (Allport, 1937; Hall & Lindzey, 1978, pp. 7–9; Hilgard, 1987, pp. 497–500; Levy, 1983, pp. 125–126). One of the most straightforward and useful ones is that offered by J. P. Guilford, who defined *personality traits* as distinguishable, relatively enduring ways in which an individual differs from others. These traits, Guilford pointed out, may range from highly general characteristics, such as self-confidence, to narrow and specific habits (Guilford, 1959, p. 6).

The Minnesota Multiphasic Personality Inventory

Literally hundreds of personality inventories have been published and subjected to critical review during the last decade (Buros, 1978). Some focus on the assessment of abnormal personality patterns and related aspects of psychopathology. Others are designed for more normal situations and practices, such as educational guidance and counseling; social, organizational, and industrial problems; and research into the nature of normal personality development and expression. Our concern here is with the inventory approach to diagnosing and classifying mental disorders and their relationship to normal personality patterns and behavior. To illustrate, we focus on the most widely used inventory for such purposes: the **Minnesota Multiphasic Personality Inventory (MMPI)**. It was first developed in 1940 by Starke R. Hathaway, a psychologist, and J. Charnley McKinley, a psychiatrist, both at the University of Minnesota, and it was published in 1943. Since then there have been many modifications in interpreting scores as well as the development of special scales derived from the inventory. These are designed to measure more specific aspects of abnormal personality. The entire inventory is currently undergoing a complete revision.

Hathaway and McKinley's basic approach to constructing the MMPI was empirical. They first collected more than 1000 items from a variety of sources, including case studies of psychologically disturbed individuals, textbooks, and previously published inventories. They then reduced the number of items considerably and administered the remaining pool to two different groups: the **criterion group**, patients who had been diagnosed by clinicians as having various kinds of psychological disturbances, and a **control group** of normal individuals, consisting mainly of visitors to the University of Minnesota Hospital who had not been under any kind of medical care. Later, when the MMPI would be used for purposes of clinical assessment, this procedure would allow a comparison to be made to see whether responses were more like those of the criterion group or the control group (Butcher & Finn, 1983; Butcher & Keller, 1984; Hathaway & McKinley, 1943; Hilgard, 1987, p. 513).

After various refinements the MMPI eventually came to consist of 550 different items. As a reliability check 16 items appear twice. Responses to the items are scored and coded for 10 clinical scales (patterns of psychological disturbances) and 4 validity scales. Table 2.4 lists the 14 scales and some of the typical characteristics associated with high scores. Responses to items on the validity scales help to interpret the clinical scales. For example, if individuals consistently omit many items (high scores on the cannot say scale) or place themselves in an overly favorable light (high scores on the lie scale), their scores on the clinical scale should be regarded with a great deal of caution, and perhaps considered invalid.

Unlike many other personality inventories, the MMPI includes some items that on the face of it appear to be much less relevant to psychological disturbance than other items. For example, "I like to attend lectures on serious subjects" appears to be considerably more innocuous than "The future seems hopeless to me." Nevertheless, the decision to retain an item was based on its ability to discriminate between psychologically disturbed individuals and normal persons on a particular dimension, regardless of the content of the item.

Although computing scores for the various scales is a relatively straightforward task, interpreting is far more complex, because it requires an understanding of the complex interrelationships among scores on all the scales. Highly extensive code books have been developed for that purpose, as well as sophisticated computer technology that furnishes an assessment of the person's personality patterns in narrative form (see Box 2.3).

The MMPI is undergoing an extension revision, including new standardization, to reflect changes in the social and cultural scene since the original development of the inventory (Butcher & Keller, 1984). Among the main goals of the revision are the following.

1. Maintaining the integrity of the validity and clinical scales.

BOX 2.3 Sample MMPI Automated Interpretive Report

THE MINNESOTA REPORT©*   Page 1

for the Minnesota Multiphasic Personality Inventory©: Adult System

By James N. Butcher, Ph.D.

Client No. 98765432101   Gender: Female
Setting: Medical   Age: 40
Report Date: 1-Nov-83
ISS Code Number: 00021987 002 0002

Profile Validity This is a valid MMPI profile. The client's responses to the MMPI validity items suggest that she cooperated with the evaluation enough to provide useful interpretive information. The resulting clinical profile is an adequate indication of her present personality functioning.

Symptomatic Pattern Individuals with this MMPI profile tend to be chronically maladjusted. Narcissistic and rather self-indulgent, the client is somewhat dependent and demands attention from others. She appears to be rather hostile and irritable and tends to resent others.

She has great trouble showing anger and may express it in passive–aggressive ways. She may have a problem with acting-out behavior and may have experienced difficulty with her sexual behavior in the past. She tends to blame her own difficulties on others and refuses to accept responsibility for her own problems.

Her response content also suggests that she may feel somewhat estranged from people—somewhat alienated and concerned over the actions of others—and may blame others for her negative frame of mind. She views the world as a threatening place, sees herself as having been unjustly blamed for others' problems, and feels that she is getting a raw deal out of life. These characteristics are reflected in the content of her responses. The items she endorsed include content suggesting that her thinking is confused and bizarre. She feels that others do not understand her and are trying to control her. She is also tending toward withdrawal into a world of fantasy.

Interpersonal Relations She is experiencing great difficulty in her social relationships, and feels that others do not understand her and do not give her enough sympathy. She is somewhat aloof, cold, non-giving, and uncompromising, and attempts to advance herself at the expense of others. Her lack of trust may prevent her from developing warm, close relationships.

Behavioral Stability This profile reflects a pattern of long-standing poor adjustment. Her anger may produce periods of intense interpersonal difficulty.

Diagnostic Considerations An individual with this profile is usually viewed as having a Personality Disorder, such as a Passive–Aggressive or Paranoid Personality. The possibility of a Paranoid Disorder should be considered, however.

Treatment Considerations Individuals with this profile tend not to seek psychological treatment on their own, and they are usually not good candidates for psychotherapy. They resist psychological interpretation, argue, and tend to rationalize and to blame others for their problems. In addition, they frequently leave therapy prematurely.

NOTE: This MMPI interpretation can serve as a useful source of hypotheses about clients. This report is based on objectively derived scale indexes and scale interpretations that have been developed in diverse groups of patients. The personality descriptions, inferences and recommendations contained herein need to be verified by other sources of clinical information since individual clients may not fully match the prototype. The information in this report should most appropriately be used by a trained, qualified test interpreter. The information contained in this report should be considered confidential.

MINNESOTA MULTIPHASIC PERSONALITY INVENTORY
Copyright THE UNIVERSITY OF MINNESOTA
1943, Renewed 1970. This Report 1982. All rights reserved.
Scored and Distributed Exclusively by NCS INTERPRETIVE SCORING SYSTEMS
Under License from The University of Minnesota

*"The Minnesota Report" and "Minnesota Multiphasic Personality Inventory" are trademarks owned by the University Press of The University of Minnesota.

Source: Butcher & Keller, 1984, pp. 319–320.

Table 2.3 Validity and Clinical Scales of the Minnesota Multiphasic Personality Inventory (MMPI)

MMPI Scales	Characteristics Associated with High Scores
Validity Scales	
Cannot Say (?)	Evasiveness; noncooperativeness.
Lie (L)	Tendency to place self in overly favorable light.
Infrequency ("Fake bad") (F)	Tendency to claim unusual attributes; may reflect careless responses.
Defensiveness (K)	Unwillingness to disclose personal information.
Clinical Scales	
Hypochondriasia (Hs)	Numerous vague physical problems.
Depression (D)	Depressed mood; low self-esteem.
Hysteria (Hy)	Neurotic defenses — for example, excessive use of denial and repression in coping with stress.
Psychopathic deviate (Pd)	Antisocial behavior.
Masculinity – femininity (Mf)	Males: sensitive, aesthetic, passive, conflicts over heterosexuality.
	Females: aggressive, self-confident, insensitive.
Paranoia (Pa)	Suspicious, aloof, hostile, angry.
Psychasthenia (Pt)	Anxious, obsessive, compulsive, phobic.
Schizophrenia (Sc)	Alienated life-style, withdrawn, bizarre thinking.
Mania (Ma)	Impatient, grandiose, impulsive, overly optimistic.
Social introversion (Si)	Excessively shy, prone to guilt feelings.

The masculinity-femininity scale, obviously outdated and sexist, is a good example of why the MMPI needed to be revised. The abbreviations in parentheses are for coding scores in analyzing patterns of responses.
Source: Butcher & Finn, 1983, pp. 337–338; Butcher & Keller, 1984, p. 311.

2. Broadening the item pool to include such personality variables as treatment compliance, willingness to change, and problems of interpersonal relationships.

3. Revising or deleting scales and the language of items that are out-of-date, awkwardly phrased, or sexist (for example, the masculinity–feminity scale).

4. Developing new and up-to-date norms on a nationwide basis.

5. Developing separate forms of the MMPI for adults and adolescents. New items will be included for the adolescent form that are especially germane to typical problems of adolescence.

Projective Tests

Self-report personality tests assume that the people who take the tests can describe their feelings, problems, and other aspects of their personalities objectively. But many people may not understand themselves that well, or they may be unduly inhibited, and thus reluctant to reveal themselves for a variety of reasons. Although devices have been developed to detect such hesitations, as in the validity scales of the MMPI, they do not substitute for what the person has not revealed. Some psychologists have therefore argued that we need personality tests that do not depend on self-report — that is, tests that get at personality traits and related psychological problems more indirectly and subtly. This argument has supported the development and clinical use of projective tests.

In contrast to inventories, **projective tests** have a more ambiguous structure. For example, respondents may be asked to describe what they see in an inkblot or to tell a story about a picture depicting a social scene. Thus, projective tests are open to a greater variety of responses. The underlying assumption is that in responding to ambiguous stimuli, individuals will reveal (project onto the stimuli) certain personality characteristics, including those of which they may not be conscious. Advocates of projective tests claim that they can elicit information about an individual's personality patterns that is more deeply revealing than that obtained from inventories.

Inkblot Methods

Inkblots were one of the earliest forms of projective techniques for assessing personality. Typically, individuals are shown a series of inkblots and asked to describe what they see in each blot. The technique was developed by Hermann Rorschach (1884–1922), a Swiss psychiatrist. It is said that Rorschach got the idea of using inkblots as a personality test during a ride in the country with his two children. As they described what they saw in clouds, he concluded that their perceptions reflected various aspects of their personalities (Davison & Neale, 1986, p. 17). Interestingly, the notion that clouds (like inkblots) can elicit a variety of images appeared in classical literature long before the time of Rorschach — for example, in these lines from *The Clouds* by Aristophanes (ca. 450–385 B.C.):

> Haven't you sometimes seen a cloud
>   that looked like a centaur;
> Or a leopard perhaps? Or a wolf?
>   Or a bull?

This is one of the ten inkblots used in the Rorschach test. According to the theory of the tests when people tell what they perceive in the inkblots, they project into the description their own personality characteristics.

The original inkblots, first published more than 65 years ago (Rorschach, 1921a, 1921b), are still widely used in the clinical assessment of personality, although various

Swiss psychiatrist Hermann Rorschach was not the first to use inkblots in studying psychological processes. However, the test he invented to measure personality was more systematic and broader in scope and theory than previous efforts.

Administering the Rorschach test: a 13-year-old reacts to one of the inkblots.

methods of scoring and interpreting responses have emerged. The stimuli consist of 10 inkblots similar to those shown in the photo — 4 in color and 6 in black and white, with varying degrees of shading. Traditionally, the test is carried out in two phases. In the first part the examiner asks the individual to describe what the inkblots look like and records the responses to each one. In the second phase the examiner goes back to each blot and asks why the responses were made — that is, why the blot was perceived in those ways.

There are several prominent systems for scoring and interpreting responses to the inkblots, including those pioneered by Samuel Beck and Bruno Klopfer, as well as more recent methods developed by John Exner (Beck, 1944, 1945, 1952; Beck, Beck, Levitt, & Molish, 1961; Beck & Molish, 1967; Exner, 1974, 1978, 1980; Klopfer, Ainsworth, Klopfer, & Holt, 1954, 1956; Klopfer & Kelley, 1942; Klopfer, Meyer, & Brawer, 1970). Essentially these systems deal with three main kinds of variables: location, determinants, and content of responses.

■ **Location** refers to the part of the blot that the individual describes. For example, the individual may respond to the blot as a whole. In some systems of analysis this reflects the tendency to organize and relate concepts. The person may emphasize obvious details, perhaps reflecting in this way a tendency to think concretely. Some individuals may mix these patterns.

■ **Determinants** of responses include such aspects of the blot as its form (shape) and color. Responses to form usually indicate the extent to which the individual perceives the environment realistically. This is an especially important variable in diagnosing psychotic thinking such as schizophrenia. Color responses are often analyzed in relation to form. For example, emotionality may be interpreted as uncontrolled when many color responses are combined with poor, unrealistic form responses.

■ **Content** is recorded and interpreted according to the things people perceive in the blots — for example, human figures and parts of the body, inanimate objects, animals, and so forth. Content may also be scored according to the frequency with which such responses occur among people in general. For example, a very ordinary number of content responses may reflect a mundane or unimaginative way of perceiving the environment. On the other hand, overwhelmingly unusual responses may reflect seriously disturbed ways of perceiving the environment that are out of touch with reality and thus psychotic.

One of the main difficulties with the Rorschach test is that the number and kinds of responses are so variable and complex that scoring and interpreting them are subject to a great deal of disagreement from one examiner to another. In an attempt to overcome some of these problems, psychologist Wayne Holtzman has developed a technique that attempts to meet the more rigorous standards of personality inventories — tests that can be scored objectively. It has supplemented but not replaced the Rorschach in clinical assessment.

The Holtzman inkblot technique is a streamlined version of the Rorschach test. It consists of 45 inkblots instead of 10, elicits only one response per blot, and has two parallel forms. Thus, it permits the examiner to assess reliability by comparing a person's performance on each form. The Holtzman method obtains scores for 22 variables, including some of the same elements scored in the Rorschach tests, such as form, location, and determinants. In addition, scores for anxiety, hostility, and abnormal verbalizing are obtained (Holtzman, Thorpe, Swartz, & Herron, 1961). Although in some instances the reliability of responses obtained with the Holtzman technique improves on the more traditional Rorschach test, the method has not been as promising as its authors had expected, especially with respect to its usefulness in the diagnosis of psychological abnormality (Zubin, 1972).

In recent years a number of researchers, building on the pioneering work of Samuel Beck and Bruno Klopfer, have developed approaches to analysis that promise to improve the usefulness of inkblot methods (Erdberg & Exner, 1984). They take an eclectic view rather than adopting a single theoretical perspective. Box 2.4 illustrates that such an approach can use basic questions about personality and behavior and relate them to various elements of the person's response to the inkblots. In general, this approach does not focus on predicting highly specific behaviors — for example, whether the marriage of a recovered schizophrenic will survive over the next 10 years or whether a juvenile delinquent will turn against members of his gang and assault one of his peers. Rather, the emphasis is on obtaining clues to such factors as the person's subjective life, motives, preoccupations, coping style, and stability of personality structure. Such data can be helpful in diagnosing psychological disturbances and recommending treatment.

Thematic Apperception Test

Another projective method in the clinical assessment of personality is to present individuals with a series of pictures and ask them to tell a story about each one. The pictures are ambiguous enough to allow all sorts of stories to be told. Henry Murray and his associates at Harvard University developed the original picture story test, called the **Thematic Apperception Test (TAT)** (Murray, 1938, 1943). Like the inkblot method, the TAT is a widely used technique for the clinical assessment of personality. Some of the pictures

BOX 2.4 Diagnostic Questions in the Analysis of Rorschach Responses

A frequent use of Rorschach data is to help mental health professionals establish a diagnosis and develop a plan of treatment for psychologically disturbed individuals. As a guide to this process, Philip Erdberg and John E. Exner, Jr. (1984), have related various elements of Rorschach responses to the kinds of questions they claim the Rorschach test can deal with. These relationships are based on an extensive review of research. For example, answering the first question listed here, dealing with coping style, Erdberg and Exner point to research findings that suggest the following relationships: a preponderance of human movement responses suggests the person's emphasis on using inner resources to cope; a preponderance of color responses suggests an emphasis on interacting with the environment as a way of coping. Here are the specific questions that Erdberg and Exner relate in detail to Rorschach responses.

1. What is the person's typical style of coping with his or her needs and stressful situations?
2. How likely is the person's coping style to work? What kinds of problems will it encounter?
3. How likely is the person to function realistically and objectively?
4. How mature is the person's psychological functioning?
5. What is the extent and quality of the person's concept of self?
6. What is the quality of the person's reality testing?
7. What is the frequency and efficiency with which the person attempts to organize the environment?
8. With what balance of activity and passivity does the person interact with the world?
9. How does the person respond to the affective aspects of his or her surroundings?
10. Is it likely that the person is schizophrenic?
11. Is it likely that the person is suicidal?

Henry Murray, for many years a professor at Harvard University, developed with his colleagues the original picture story test: the Thematic Appreciation Test (TAT).

are designed for females, some for males, and others for both sexes. As a rule no more than 20 of the pictures are administered to a single person. Some clinicians select even fewer, depending on the specific purpose for which they are using the test. The pictures show people in a variety of situations — alone, in couples, or in groups — and in a variety of settings. The object of the test is to elicit stories about the scenes that go beyond mere description. The individual is asked to tell a story with a beginning, a middle, and an end and to include what led to the situation and what its outcome will be. The testee is also encouraged to tell about the thoughts and feelings of the people in the story.

Many variations of the TAT have appeared since Murray's original development of the test. Some are specifically designed for children, others are for different racial or ethnic groups, and still others are designed to assess problems of old age (Bellak & Bellak, 1973; Murstein, 1973).

A young man taking the Thematic Appreciation Test (TAT). His task is to tell a story about each picture presented.

A number of methods of analyzing the stories have been developed. In general, they focus on answering these kinds of questions.

- What kinds of personal relationships are revealed in the stories?
- With whom does the storyteller seem to identify?
- What kinds of motives are revealed by the characters?
- What basic outlook on life seems to dominate?

Presumably, these variables reflect a projection into the stories of the individual's needs, motives, attitudes, and other personality characteristics. In addition, analyses usually examine the basic themes of the various stories. Do they deal with conflict? Love? Dependency? The clinician also tries to discover how the storyteller perceives the social and physical environment. For instance, is it threatening or benign?

Many other variables can be analyzed. Some psychologists use a checklist that contains a wide variety of factors. No one story is sufficient for a clinical assessment of personality characteristics; the clinician looks for trends and relationships between one story and another. For example, does the testee express conflict consistently from one story to another, no matter what the content of the picture?

Research with the TAT suggests that the relationship between the story content and its expression in actual behavior is complex and cannot be predicted with certainty. The motives revealed through the TAT will not inevitably be expressed in real-life actions, but we need not assume that they will be completely independent of behavior. What such motives are, regardless of their behavioral outlets, may well be worth knowing clinically, since they may furnish clues to the diagnosis of psychological problems (Murstein, 1973).

Reliability and Validity

In comparison with self-report personality tests such as the MMPI, projective tests have less reliability and validity. In self-report tests the scoring of responses is direct and objective, so that agreement among scorers is high. In projective tests the scoring of responses may vary according to the particular system used. The problem of reliability has been reduced by the development of structured scoring systems that enable examinees to reach a higher degree of agreement. The more perplexing problem is that of validity. What do the responses mean? How useful are they in assessing the individual's personality patterns and psychological problems? Although self-report tests are not free of these problems, their objective nature allows for greater validity.

Although studies have generally shown significant disagreement among clinicians who interpret projective devices, some researchers argue that their validity should not be gauged in the same way as self-report personality tests (Exner, 1980; Schwartz & Lazar, 1979; Shaffer, Duszynski, & Thomas, 1981). For example, they question whether projective techniques require a high degree of structure for interpreting the content of responses. Since responses are unique to an individual, how they are generated becomes more important than their specific content. In accordance with this principle, Erdberg and Exner (1984) have related various elements of responses on the Rorschach test to the kinds of questions these responses can answer (see Box 2.4). Contemporary research on the usefulness of projective techniques, especially the Rorschach test, are continuing in that direction.

Traditionally, the goal of projective tests has been an overall assessment of personality and psychological functioning. However, these variables are far too diverse and complicated for any one assessment instrument to measure them comprehensively and successfully. If used as clues to the assessment of mental disorders, projective tests can furnish valuable hypotheses about such conditions. Results need to be balanced against information from other assessment procedures in diagnosing mental disorders and recommending treatment. Actually the same principle applies to any assessment procedure, even though one may be more reliable and valid than another.

Neuropsychological Assessment

A special problem in the assessment of mental disorders is the diagnosis of brain damage and related abnormalities (Goldstein, 1984; Hamsher, 1984; Jones & Butters, 1983; Taylor, Fletcher, & Satz, 1984). A variety of tests have demonstrated their sensitivity to pathology of the central nervous system. The Rorschach test and the WAIS-R can provide some useful clues for this purpose. More often, however, neuropsychological problems are diagnosed through devices specifically designed for that purpose: psychological tests (which we examine in this section), electroencephalogram (EEG) measures of brain functions, and the newer brain scan techniques (see Chapter 14 for a discussion of latter methods).

The Visual Motor Gestalt Test

A valuable psychological instrument for the appraisal of possible brain damage is the **Visual Motor Gestalt test**, commonly known as the Bender Gestalt Test (Bender, 1938). It consists of a series of cards with geometric designs on them (see Figure 2.2). The testee's task is to copy these designs. The clinician notes characteristics of performance and compares them to the established patterns of performance of brain-injured individuals and those free of such injury. The Bender Gestalt Test is also used as a measure of perceptual-motor development in children (Koppitz, 1964).

Figure 2.2

Pattern similar to one used in the Visual Motor Gestalt Test. (Adapted from Bender, 1938.)

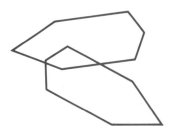

Halstead – Reitan Battery

A much more ambitious and complete assessment of brain damage and related neuropsychological abnormalities is represented by the **Halstead – Reitan Neuropsychological Battery (HRB)** (Jones & Butters, 1983, pp. 384–386; Reitan & Wolfson, 1985). Originally designed as an instrument for research in evaluating brain–behavior relationships, the HRB has been highly successful in diagnosing the presence of brain damage, with 70 percent to 90 percent accuracy (Anthony, Heaton, & Lehman, 1980; Boll, 1981). Although the HRB is widely used, it is not without its critics. Among the disadvantages cited are its length (from six to eight hours), the lack of specificity with respect to establishing the source of the brain impairment, and an insufficient examination of general memory functions (Goldstein, 1984, pp. 197–200).

The Luria – Nebraska Battery

The basis for the **Luria – Nebraska Neuropsychological Battery** is over 40 years of clinical experience and experimentation by Alexander Luria (1902–1977), the distinguished Russian neuropsychologist. The battery has been standardized and validated for use in this country with children as well as adults (Golden, 1981; Golden, Hammeke, & Purisch, 1978, 1980). Like the Halstead–Reitan Battery, it taps a large variety of functions: rhythmic, acoustic, tactile, visual, speech comprehension, speech production, writing, reading, arithmetic, memory, and problem solving. The general feature of the multitude of tasks included on the battery is that they are performed with ease by a person of normal ability whose brain is intact. They present difficulties, and often insurmountable problems to people with brain dysfunction. In addition to differentiating between persons with and without brain damage, the battery provides information on the extent and site of brain damage and identifies the functions that are lost or impaired. It thus points a way toward rehabilitation—how a skill that has been affected can be reacquired or replaced by other skills.

In its present form, the Luria–Nebraska Battery is relatively new. Much work remains to be done to fully identify its potential and its limitations. Critics argue that Luria's name should be removed from the title, because the battery does not really represent his thinking about neuropsychological problems—a charge that has been strongly denied (Adams, 1980; Golden, 1980). Critics also state that the scoring is too subjective. On the other hand, many clinicians support the battery, pointing to the increasing amount of positive evidence for its reliability and validity (Goldstein, 1984, pp. 200–206; Jones & Butters, 1983, pp. 387–388).

Observations of Nonverbal Behavior

Although most of the assessment procedures we have discussed so far require verbal responses to stimuli, nonverbal behavior may also be involved. For example, neither the Visual Motor Gestalt Test nor the performance subtests of the Wechsler Adult Intelligence

Scale (WAIS) require words to complete the tasks. Furthermore, in administering the WAIS the examiner not only obtains a quantitative measure of intellectual abilities but also records observations of the person's general test-taking behavior, such as anxiety, fearfulness, carelessness, or disorganization.

Observations of nonverbal behavior during diagnostic interviews can also furnish clues for assessing psychological disorders. Indeed, this may occur at the very outset of the interview. Consider, for instance, the following notes of a clinician observing a student who had come to a university health clinic: "When he signed his name on the admission form, his hands were visibly tremulous. He generally appeared uneasy, and glanced furtively around the room, paying special attention to electrical outlets, air-conditioning vents, and most especially to the camera, although he had been assured that it was not in use" (Rosenthal & Akiskal, 1985, p. 28). According to the therapist, the student's general appearance suggested diagnostic hypotheses that helped focus the interview on such possibilities as a delusional disorder or a psychotic condition induced by drugs.

Observations of nonverbal behavior during diagnostic interviews can be especially critical in the assessment of children's psychological disturbances. Clinicians who work with children are well aware that they often become easily tired or inattentive during an interview and therefore may retreat from verbally expressing their thoughts and feelings. The following exchange illustrates how a therapist observed the nonverbal responses of a 9-year-old child referred to a clinic because of problems possibly related to depression. Notice how the interviewer also used nonverbal behavior in attempting to clarify the child's problems (Kovacs, 1986, p. 449).

Interviewer: "One of the feelings that kids can have is feeling sad, unhappy, down in the dumps. Have you been feeling sad, unhappy?"

Child: "Yeah."

Interviewer: "Have you been feeling sad all the time? Or many times? Or once in a while?"

Child: "Kind of — uhm — many times."

Interviewer: "Can other people tell when you are sad?"

Child: (Nods)

Interviewer: "How can other people tell when you are sad? How do you look?"

Child: (Makes a distinctly angry face)

Interviewer: "Tell me about the last time you were sad. What happened?"

Child: "Well, it's like — like my sister always takes away my books and yells and gets me real mad."

Interviewer: "Now, this is going to be a hard question. See if you can help me with it." "When your sister takes . . . the feeling you have, is it *sad* (interviewer makes appropriate facial expression) or *mad* (interviewer makes facial expression). Or, is it like two feelings?"

Child: "Uhm — it's more like mad."

Behavior therapists, whose methods we discuss in detail in Chapter 20, have been especially active in developing techniques for assessing maladaptive nonverbal behavior. Such observations can then be used as a guide for planning treatment of the disorder. Consider the following example from a checklist designed to measure performance anxiety in people who must deliver a speech in public. Raters are trained to observe the speaker every 30 seconds and record the presence or absence of such specific behaviors as trembling in knees, arms held rigidly, tremors of hands, lack of eye contact, lip moistening, voice quivering, and speech blocks or stammers (Paul, 1966).

Checklists of nonverbal and verbal problem behavior have also been developed for making ratings based on past observations rather than present ones. These lists can be helpful in assessing psychological disturbances, since it is not always feasible to observe current behavior directly. This is especially so for parents' and teachers' ratings of children. Unfortunately, retrospective ratings can be subject to faulty memory, or the behavior may no longer be present in the person being rated. Nevertheless, they can still provide information for further inquiry (Ollendick & Meador, 1984, pp. 356–357, 362–363).

Naturalistic Observation

The systematic monitoring and recording of behavior in a person's natural (real-life) environment is **naturalistic observation**. This type of observation may be made of parent–child interactions in the home, the behavior of patients in a hospital ward, and the behavior of children in the classroom and playground (Haynes, 1983). As a rule, individuals monitoring and recording the behavior have undergone special training for the task.

Naturalistic observation: David Elkind, child psychologist at Tufts University, observing children in a kindergarten.

Although the method of naturalistic observation has been known for many years to psychologists, anthropologists, and other social scientists, behavioral therapists have emphasized its use in the assessment of psychological disorder in recent years. This way of acquiring information reflects an immediate interaction with the environment that is consistent with their therapeutic approach. By observing problem behavior in its natural setting the therapist is in a better position to decide what target behaviors need to be modified. These observations can also be helpful for a later assessment of therapeutic effects.

It is not always feasible to observe behavior in its natural setting, so **analogue observations** are sometimes used. These are contrived situations that simulate natural settings. For example, parent–child interaction can be structured in role-playing in a clinic room, drinking behavior can be observed in an artificially structured bar, and social skills can be observed in a structured situation designed to elicit those kinds of responses (Haynes, 1983, pp. 407–410).

Cognitive Behavior and Assessment

A relatively new and vigorous approach of behavior therapy capitalizes on the importance of cognitive factors in the assessment of psychological disturbances. This emphasis also includes the relationship of self-control and self-reinforcement to such behavior. Consequently, current practitioners of cognitive behavior therapy (Chapter 20) are developing techniques for the recording of self-statements (what we say about ourselves), self-reinforcements (how we reward ourselves), and problem-solving strategies (the steps we covertly take as we tackle personal problems). In general, cognitive behaviorists are interested in more than just observing overt abnormal behavior directly and objectively recording it. They also wish to obtain information concerning the private, subjectively experienced events that precede, accompany, or follow disturbed behavior. This information can then be related to methods of intervention designed to change that behavior (Haaga & Davison, 1986; Kanfer & Gaelick, 1986; Meichenbaum, 1977, 1986).

Summary

1. The assessment of mental disorders is a complex process. It includes a history of the individual's problems, the person's current perceptions of problems as well as how others may perceive them, the clinician's observations of behavior, and information concerning the individual's physical health. Such knowledge forms the basis for reaching a diagnosis.

2. The main objectives of a diagnosis are to gather information that can help explain the causes (etiology) of the person's disorder, to predict its progress and probable outcome (prognosis), and to plan a program of treatment.

3. In reaching a diagnosis the clinician usually assigns the individual to a qualitative diagnostic category (for example, major depression) that represents a particular pattern of mental disorder. This process is called diagnostic classification.

4. Diagnostic classification involves knowledge of the person's symptoms and syndromes. Symptoms that the individual reveals directly ("I worry all the time") are called complaints. Symptoms that the clinician can observe without the person telling about them are called signs (for example, abnormal slowness of speech,

suggesting deep depression). Other clues to diagnostic classification can be gained from physical examinations and laboratory tests of various bodily functions.

5. The science of classifying mental disorders (nosology) can be traced to the days of Hippocrates and his treatise *The Sacred Disease*. In this work he denied the divine origin of mental illness and attributed the symptoms to disturbances in the brain. His classification of mental disorders included such categories as mania, melancholia, and hysteria, concepts that influenced the science of nosology for centuries to come.

6. The classification of mental disorders declined during the Middle Ages but revived during the Renaissance, especially with the work of the Swiss psychiatrist Paracelsus. During the 19th century, nosology expanded considerably with the contributions of German psychiatrists Wilhelm Griesinger, Karl Kahlbaum, and Emil Kraepelin, as well as the French psychiatrist Augustin Morel.

7. Kraepelin's system of classification was introduced to the psychiatric profession in the United States by Adolph Meyer, a Swiss psychiatrist who had emigrated from Zurich and whose views became highly influential. Because of its emphasis on psychological as well as biological factors, Meyer's approach to understanding mental disorder was known as psychobiology. During the same period the Swiss psychiatrist Eugen Bleuler also influenced the development of knowledge about mental disorders, especially with his concept of schizophrenia. Bleuler invented the term *schizophrenia* to indicate a split between the patient's emotional and cognitive life.

8. Over the years a number of objections to diagnostic classification systems appeared. Among them were the arguments that diagnostic labels (for example, schizophrenia) tell us very little about the complexities of the individual's mental disorder and indeed may become derogatory terms. Furthermore, diagnostic labels can create a gulf between the patient and other people. Finally, the arguments go, emphasis on developing a finite number of diagnostic categories ignores the fact that mental disorders represent a continuum, ranging from slight to highly intense dimensions.

9. Admitting that diagnostic classification can be misused by reliance on labels as a substitute for clear descriptions and explanations of mental disorders, defenders of classification point out that labels are simply convenient, shorthand ways of communicating. It is not the label as such that is the problem. Rather, it is the derogatory attitudes toward mental illness that some people hold — attitudes that need to be changed.

10. The most widely used system of classification in the United States is the revised 3rd edition (1987) of the *Diagnostic and Statistical Manual of Mental Disorders* (DSM-III-R), developed by the American Psychiatric Association. It is a refinement and improvement of three previous editions, the first published in 1952. Among its improvements is the more explicit description of criteria to be used in reaching a diagnosis and the further development of a multiaxial (multidimensional) system. The various axes (dimensions) include the syndromes of mental disorders, physical disorders, and conditions that may be related to psychological disorders, the severity of psychosocial stressors that are involved in the person's disorder, and a rating of the individual's overall adaptive functioning. A number of new controversial and tentative diagnostic categories have also been introduced.

11. Already under way are detailed plans for developing DSM-IV. Among the changes that have been proposed are a greater emphasis on causes of mental disorders and inclusion of the American Psychological Association and the National Association of Social Workers in the official planning group.

12. Technical issues in diagnosis involve problems of reliability, predictive validity, and coverage of diagnostic categories, as well as various errors in clinical judgment.

13. The diagnosis of mental disorders involves a number of social issues. Chief among them are the social effects of incorrect diagnoses and the political abuse of psychiatric power.

14. Methods of psychological assessment and their role in diagnosing mental disorders include interviews, intelligence and personality tests, measures of psychophysiological functioning, and direct observations of nonverbal behavior in various situations.

15. Interviews can range from highly structured to relatively unstructured (open-ended) approaches. A number of interview schedules have been developed to guide the clinician in carrying out interviews, especially in supplying structure.

16. Personality tests include personality inventories (self-report instruments) and projective devices. The latter consist of more ambiguous stimuli, such as inkblots.

17. The assessment of neuropsychological functioning can reveal brain damage and related abnormalities that contribute to mental disorders. A variety of diagnostic procedures have been developed to measure such malfunctioning. They include psychological tests, laboratory measures of brain waves, and brain scan techniques.

18. Direct observations of nonverbal behavior may also provide clues in the assessment of mental disorders. This information can be obtained during the administration of individual intelligence tests and projective devices and during interviews, including those with children.

19. Observations of both verbal and nonverbal behavior may be carried out in more natural situations. Examples are parent-child interactions in the home, behavior of patients in a hospital ward, and behavior of children in the schoolroom or on the playground.

20. A relatively new approach in assessment emphasizes the importance of cognitive factors in diagnosing psychological disorders. This approach includes the relationship of self-control and self-reinforcement (how we reward ourselves) to such disturbances, as well as the problem-solving strategies the individual may use. In addition, cognitive approaches obtain information concerning people's highly private appraisal of their experiences.

3

Biomedical and Psychodynamic Viewpoints

A disease known is half cured.
THOMAS FULLER, M.D.
Gnomologia (1732)

In this chapter we deal with two broad approaches to understanding abnormal behavior and experience: biomedical and psychodynamic. The biomedical approach focuses on the specific physical disturbances that contribute to the origin, development, and expression of mental disorders. The psychodynamic approach emphasizes that the basic causes of mental disorders lie in unconscious motives and conflicts. Thus, to understand an individual's psychological problems, it is necessary to bring to consciousness the nature of those motives and conflicts and the events that have contributed to them.

Biomedical Viewpoints

The belief that mental disorders have their origin in biological disturbances can be traced to ancient days. More than 2000 years ago, Hippocrates wrote: "From the brain, and from the brain only, arise our pleasures, joys, laughter and jests, as well as our sorrows, pains, griefs and tears. . . . It is the same thing which makes us mad or delirious, inspires us with dread and fear, . . . brings sleeplessness, inopportune mistakes, aimless anxieties, absentmindedness, and acts that are contrary to habit. These things that we suffer all come from the brain, when it is not healthy" (Jones, 1923, p. 175).

Modern biomedical explanations of the cause and development of mental disorders also emphasize that most, if not all, such disorders can ultimately be traced to biological and physical disturbances in the body. Furthermore, the brain and nervous system remain the focus of attention. This does not mean, of course, that factors such as psychological stress and adverse social conditions are unimportant. Nevertheless, the most fundamental goal of the biomedical approach to understanding abnormality is the discovery of biological and physical factors that help explain its origin and development.

In recent years the biomedical approach has been greatly strengthened by rapid developments in **neuroscience**. This broad field of knowledge integrates a number of disciplines whose common goal is to discover how the structures and functions of the brain are related to behavior and experience. Neuroscience addresses a number of questions — for example, the nature of brain structures and diseases caused by their abnormalities; the effect of drugs on brain processes; the relationship between chemical processes and brain functions; the relationship between brain structures and such mental functions as memory, reasoning, and emotion; and the relationship between brain and glandular functions (Andreasen, 1984a, p. 27; Axelrod, 1984; Snyder, 1984).

Physical Disease and Psychopathology: Some Parallel Concepts

Traditional biomedical concepts of mental disorder parallel those of physical disease. As defined medically, *physical disease* is a morbid (abnormal) process having a characteristic train of symptoms. The disease may affect the whole body or any of its parts, and its pathology may or may not be known (*Dorland's Illustrated Medical Dictionary*, 1988).

Pathology refers to the underlying nature of the disease process, such as abnormal changes in the structure or function of bodily cells and tissues. Although the term *mental disorder* is now preferred to *mental disease*, the parallel with physical disease remains. Thus, mental disorders are often referred to as forms of **psychopathology** (*psycho* means "mind," and *pathology* means "disease"), or mental illness.

Symptoms, Syndromes, and Diagnosis

As with physical illnesses, the various behavioral and physical manifestations of mental disorders are their symptoms, and the patterns of symptoms that distinguish one disorder from another are called syndromes. The identification of symptoms and syndromes is necessary in reaching a diagnosis.

Diagnosis is a crucial element in biomedical thinking. Ideally, a program of treatment is based on the diagnosis. Furthermore, a diagnosis is necessary for establishing the causes (etiology) of the illness and for predicting its probable outcomes. However, biomedical approaches must make allowances for situations in which the diagnosis is uncertain or the causes of the abnormal condition are unknown, yet the patient requires immediate help. Under such circumstances, it is common for therapy to be based on the empirical evidence that it helped patients who had shown similar symptoms in the past.

Three broad categories of physical disease have analogues in biomedical concepts of behavior and mental disorders: infectious disease, systemic disease, and noninfectious trauma (Buss, 1966; Costin, 1976).

Infectious Disease

The basic causes of infectious disease are parasitic organisms, such as bacteria, protozoa, and viruses. But it is not simply the organisms that must be considered in determining the etiology of an infectious disease. Their interaction with various characteristics of the person whose body has been invaded is also important. Some individuals may have a greater ability to resist the invasion, perhaps because they are naturally immune, or have been vaccinated against the disease, or enjoy a general state of good health.

Certain forms of psychopathology also stem from infectious disease. Encephalitis (inflammation of the brain) results from the invasion of infectious organisms, producing such symptoms of dementia as impaired memory, judgment, and abstract thinking. The idea that infections of the body could be related to psychopathology gained great impetus from a long series of discoveries that eventually linked syphilitic infection of the nervous system with a psychological disorder originally called **general paralysis**, or **general paresis**. Among the specific symptoms of this disorder are a deterioration in judgment and other intellectual functions, a gross decline in personal habits, and delusions of grandeur.

The eventual establishment of a connection between general paresis and syphilitic infection of the brain was an outstanding biomedical achievement (see Box 3.1), which led many biomedical researchers to believe that practically all mental disorders would eventually be traced to infectious disease. We now know, however, that infectious disease accounts for a relatively small proportion of mental disorders. (We discuss these disturbances in Chapter 13).

Systemic Disease

Physical disorders that are not caused by infectious organisms but whose symptoms indicate malfunctioning of a bodily organ or system of organs are called systemic diseases. The term *functional* is sometimes used to differentiate this type of disorder from infectious disease.

BOX 3.1 Syphilis and Paresis: Some Historical Landmarks

The psychotic behavior that can result from syphilis of the brain has variously been called *paresis*, *dementia paralytica*, and *general paralysis*. Present knowledge concerning its origin and effects has emerged from a series of landmark attempts of biomedical researchers to link psychological disability with organic disease.

1798 The English physician John Haslam (1764–1844) first clearly described paresis on observing in certain patients in Bethlehem Hospital an association among delusions of grandeur, deterioration of intellectual functions, and progressive paralysis. In his remarkable treatise, *Observations of Madness and Melancholy*, Haslam pointed with great accuracy to certain outstanding characteristics of the paretic patient: "Speech is defective, . . . arms and legs are more or less deprived of their voluntary movements, and in the majority of patients, memory is materially weakened. These patients, as a rule, fail to recognize their condition. So weak that they can scarcely keep on their legs, they still maintain they are extremely strong and capable of the greatest deeds" (quoted in Zilboorg & Henry, 1941, p. 527).

1805 The French psychiatrist Jean Etienne Dominique Esquirol (1772–1840) observed that patients with symptoms of paresis never recover. Although Esquirol failed to recognize that paresis is a distinct entity and not a complication of various forms of mental disorder, he influenced his pupil A. L. Bayle (1799–1858) to search in that direction.

1826 After studying more than 100 cases, Bayle presented a definitive report of his view that paresis is a separate disorder, not a complication of several diseases. He described the deterioration of the intellect, delusions of grandeur, and the general paralysis that characterize the disorder (Zilboorg & Henry, 1941, pp. 529–530).

1857 The German physician Johann von Esmarch (1823–1908) concluded from case studies that syphilis is the cause of paresis.

1869 The Scottish ophthalmologist Douglas Argyll-Robertson (1837–1909) observed abnormal pupillary reflexes in paretic patients. The pupils failed to accommodate to light but did accommodate to distance. Thus, he established an important diagnostic sign of paresis.

1894 Jean Alfred Fournier (1832–1914), a French physician, reported that a history of syphilis occurs in 65 percent of patients diagnosed as paretic, compared to only 10 percent of patients with other kinds of mental disorders. He hypothesized that paresis originates in syphilitic infection, which, even though it seems to be cured, invades the tissues of the brain. He also developed a test for detecting *ataxia*, an unsteady gait that often occurs when syphilis invades the central nervous system.

1905 Fritz Richard Schaudinn (1871–1906), a German bacteriologist, found the spirochete *Treponema pallidum* in skin lesions of syphilitic patients.

1913 Hideyo Noguchi (1876–1928), a Japanese-born American bacteriologist, demonstrated that the spirochete *Treponema pallidum* causes the brain damage in paresis. He observed the organism during postmortem examinations of the brains of patients who had been diagnosed with paresis. Thus, after more than a century of clinical observation and research, the essential link between syphilis and paresis was finally established beyond doubt (Zilboorg & Henry, 1941, pp. 545–546.).

Treponema pallidum, the spirochete that causes syphilis. Notice the paleness (pallidum) and spiral shape (spirochete) of the organism.

French psychiatrist Jean E. D. Esquirol recognized almost 200 years ago that patients suffering from paresis never recover.

Sources: *Dorland's Illustrated Medical Dictionary*, 1988; Garrison, 1924; Hinsie & Campbell, 1977; Zilboorg & Henry, 1941.

The causes of systemic disease may often be only partially known, as in various forms of diabetes — diseases involving faulty metabolism of carbohydrates. There are also systemic diseases whose causes are either not known or only superficially understood. A common example is **hypertension,** an abnormal and persistent elevation of arterial blood pressure that occurs in the absence of organic disabilities known to contribute to hypertension — for example, certain kidney disorders. *Essential* is a medical term indicating that the physical causes of the disease are still problematic.

The systemic disease approach to understanding the origins of abnormal behavior and experience has been applied extensively in studies of the brain and nervous system and of heredity. Work in these areas has focused especially on depression and schizophrenia. Since we examine the biomedical research on those disorders in detail in Chapters 10 and 11, we will at this time discuss only briefly a number of studies to illustrate how the concept of systemic disease is related to psychopathology.

Depression. A great deal of research has been carried out on biochemical factors in the development and expression of abnormal depression, concentrating on the faulty metabolism of certain chemical compounds in the brain and nervous system called **biogenic amines.** The term *biogenic* is used for these amines because of the important part they play in various biological functions.

Studies of the biochemistry of depression have focused on two biogenic amines: **norepinephrine** and **serotonin.** Both occur naturally in various parts of the brain, and both are **neurotransmitters** — that is, they transmit impulses from one neuron (nerve cell) to another (McGeer & McGeer, 1980; van Praag, 1977, p. 17; Wetzel, 1984, pp. 243–244). Various studies suggest that abnormal depression is associated with a deficiency of norepinephrine at certain sites of the brain that act as receivers of nerve impulses (Kaplan & Sadock, 1985, p. 242; Schildkraut, 1965, 1969, 1975, 1977). Whether such deficiency is a necessary or sufficient condition for abnormal depression remains an open question, since other neurotransmitters may also be associated with the disorder. Some researchers have found abnormally low levels of serotonin in the cerebrospinal fluid of deeply depressed patients, but a number of studies have failed to distinguish between one biogenic amine and another as a specific cause of abnormal depression (Akiskal & McKinney, 1975; Schuyler, 1974). Furthermore, some researchers believe that the biochemical deficiencies found in depressed individuals may actually be secondary reactions triggered by still other, unidentified biochemical substances (Mendels, 1970, 1975).

Studies have been carried out to discover the possible role of heredity in the etiology of depression. In a critical analysis of such investigations, Mendels (1970) concluded that although heredity probably plays a part, it is not "a sufficient cause in itself" (p. 93).

Schizophrenic Disorders. Various researchers have found that by stimulating certain areas of the brain they can produce symptoms that resemble those often found in **schizophrenic disorders.** Electrical stimulation of various parts of the limbic system (see Figure 3.1) produces hallucinations and delusions (Paul, 1977, p. 376; Torrey & Peterson, 1974). Stimulant drugs such as amphetamines (speed) create abnormal activity in the limbic area, resulting in symptoms similar to those that occur when the area is stimulated electrically. These results suggest that one of the factors contributing to the development of at least some symptoms of schizophrenic disorders may well be an abnormal biochemical activity in the brain (Buchsbaum & Haier, 1983; Snyder, 1972, 1973).

Researchers have also found abnormal amounts of hormones, enzymes, and other biochemical substances in the blood or urine of schizophrenic patients — abnormalities

Figure 3.1

Medial view of the limbic system of the human brain. (Adapted from Kimble, 1988, p. 80.)

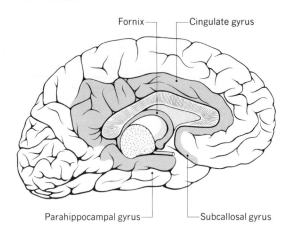

Fornix — Cingulate gyrus

Parahippocampal gyrus — Subcallosal gyrus

that do not usually appear in nonschizophrenic patients (Neale & Oltmanns, 1980, pp. 217–252; Shean, 1978). It may be that an excess of these substances triggers abnormal functioning of the brain and nervous system, thus producing symptoms of schizophrenia; however, a direct cause-and-effect relationship has not been demonstrated. Perhaps the schizophrenic disorder itself, in a manner yet unknown, produces the biochemical abnormalities, or a third unknown variable may be responsible. In criticizing studies based simply on the correlation between a diagnosis of schizophrenia and the presence of a strange substance in the body, van Praag (1977) succinctly pointed to the faulty logic that operates: "Strange people, strange substances" (p. 403).

A more recent development in biochemical research on schizophrenia is the discovery of substances in the brain called *endorphins*. These are opiate-like biochemicals that may play an important part in producing schizophrenic disorders. However, research has not yet determined the extent to which they do so. Some evidence suggests that under certain circumstances endorphins may actually reduce psychotic symptoms. In fact, a number of drugs used to treat schizophrenic disorders have a biochemical structure similar to naturally occurring endorphin in the brain (Bowers, 1981). (See Chapter 11 for a more detailed discussion of endorphins and schizophrenia.)

As in the case of abnormal depression, biomedical researchers have actively attempted to discover a genetic basis of schizophrenic disorders. This work frequently overlaps with the biochemical research just described, since genetic defects may contribute to biochemical malfunctioning. Indeed, evidence that genetic factors are involved in the transmission of schizophrenic disorders may be the strongest support for the view that biochemical factors operate in their development. An increasing amount of evidence now points to the importance of heredity in the etiology of schizophrenic disorders (Kessler, 1981; Kety, 1969, 1975; Rosenthal, 1968, 1970, 1971; van Praag, 1977, p. 177). Three different lines of research support the role of heredity in the development of schizophrenia.

1. Family studies show that schizophrenia occurs frequently among close relatives than in the population at large.

2. Studies of twins show that the probability of identical twins developing schizophrenia is greater than that for fraternal twins.

3. Studies of the children born to schizophrenic parents but reared in foster families show that the incidence of schizophrenic disorders is higher for those children than for the natural children of the foster parents.

The genetically identical Genain quadruplets. All as young women suffered breakdowns and were diagnosed as being schizophrenic, a startling phenomenon supporting the view that heredity is an important factor in the etiology of schizophrenic disorders. (D. Rosenthal ed. 1963. *Genain Quadruplets.* New York, Basic Books.)

Although these findings are impressive, they do not in themselves demonstrate that heredity is an inevitable factor in the etiology of schizophrenic disorders. The disorders may sometimes run in families because of a social and psychological environment that is especially favorable to their development. Furthermore, the greater probability of schizophrenia occurring in identical as opposed to fraternal twins may also be due to the well-known psychological closeness of identical twins. (We consider these and related issues in more detail in Chapter 11.)

Noninfectious Trauma

A third category of physical disease with a counterpart in biomedical views of psychopathology is a malfunctioning of the body resulting from aversive environmental intrusions. Physical forces, such as a blow on the head, or bodily injury, and the ingestion of various chemical substances can damage bodily functions. Such noninfectious trauma can lead to **syndrome**, a mental disorder involving a sharp decrease in the clarity with which a person perceives and understands environmental events. Delirious people have much trouble in paying attention to external stimuli. Their thinking becomes disorganized, and their memory may be severely impaired. They may experience illusions, such as perceiving a stain on the wall as a frightening animal, or they may have hallucinations, such as seeing objects in their environment that do not exist as external stimuli (see Chapter 13).

Some mental health researchers and practitioners have extended biomedical concepts of noninfectious trauma to include psychological events. Although the concept *psychologi-*

cal trauma originated in psychoanalytic theory, many mental health professionals, including those of a biomedical persuasion, accept it. Psychologically traumatic events occur in a variety of ways. Consider, for example, the following description by a 19-year-old college student, whose fears remained with her long after a sexual assault, during which the rapist threatened to kill her: "I'm walking around on guard 24 hours a day. . . . I can't walk down the street by myself without looking behind me every five minutes. I get this frozen feeling when some man honks his horn when I'm walking down the street, even in the middle of the day; if I pass strange men on the street, I want to run. I'm really scared so much of the time, and that's kind of where it's left me now, a year later" (Groth & Birnbaum, 1981, p. 80).

Critical Reactions to the Illness Parallel

Many mental health professionals who do not have a biomedical orientation routinely use such concepts as *psychopathology* and *mental illness*, even though they may not accept all of the biomedical parallels between physical disease and mental disorder. Some, however, strongly object to such language and the implications they believe it has for understanding abnormal behavior and experience. For example, psychologist George Albee (1977, p. 721) points out that many people have emotional problems in living that are produced by the problems inherent in an industrial civilization; therefore, their difficulties should not be regarded as forms of mental illness.

Furthermore, the argument goes, overemphasis on the importance of organic sources of abnormal behavior and experience leads to undue reliance on purely medical procedures — that is, biological and physical methods — for helping people with their problems of living. Other approaches, such as psychotherapy, reeducation, and changes in the social environment, may not be applied sufficiently. By using such terms as *problems of living* and *behavior disorder*, critics try to avoid the assumption that biological disturbances underlie most, if not all, psychological abnormality (Albee, 1977; Szasz, 1970). However, they are sometimes willing to use such terms as *mental disorder* and even *psychopathology*, although the latter is problematic because it suggests an analogy between psychological abnormality and physical pathology.

Most of the objections to illness concepts of psychological disorders come from mental health professionals who are not medically trained. An interesting exception is Thomas Szasz, for many years a professor of psychiatry at the Upstate Medical Center of the State University of New York. He consistently argues that because only a relatively small proportion of so-called mental illnesses have their direct origin in physical disease, the use of that term to designate the many forms of abnormal behavior and experience (that is, mental disorders) is highly inappropriate. He prefers the term *problems of living*, declaring that mental illness is a myth (Szasz, 1960, 1963, 1970, 1974). Responses to Szasz usually argue that one can accept an illness concept of psychological disorders without necessarily subscribing to the belief that biological and physical abnormalities are the only contributing factors (Thorne, 1966).

In recent years, controversy over the illness concept of mental disorders has subsided, especially as biomedically oriented workers in the field of psychopathology have increasingly recognized the importance of social and cultural influences on the development and expression of abnormal behavior and experience. Indeed, Szasz himself has gone beyond the myth of mental illness as such, and his concerns have extended to such issues as the illegitimate use of psychiatric power in the involuntary commitment of patients to mental hospitals, the wrongfulness of legal tests of insanity, and suicide prevention (Szasz, 1970, 1977a, 1986). (We discuss these issues in Chapter 21, where we deal with community problems of mental health.)

Thomas Szasz, long-time professor of psychiatry at the Upstate Medical Center of the State University of New York. Szasz has been a persistent critic of the concept of "mental illness." He prefers to use the term "problems of living."

Body — Environment Interaction and Mental Disorders

Behavior — Genetic Analysis

David Rosenthal, biomedical researcher and exponent of the behavior-genetic view that heredity interacts with the environment in their influence on behavior.

Modern biomedical researchers on the etiology of abnormal behavior and experience emphasize the interaction between an individual's environment and internal organic abnormalities. Thus, they deny that their only goal is to trace the causes of mental disorder to biological factors while ignoring the importance of social and psychological determinants (van Praag, 1977). This position is clearly reflected in the discipline of behavior-genetic analysis, the study of individual differences in behavior that can be traced, at least in part, to differences in genetic makeup (Hirsch, 1967, 1986; Hirsch, McGuire, & Vetta, 1980; Loehlin, Willerman, & Horn, 1988).

Consistent with modern behavior-genetic analysis, David Rosenthal (1971) points to certain misconceptions about the relationship between behavior and heredity. Some people seem to believe, says Rosenthal, that "heredity is synonymous with . . . inevitability and immutability. [That] is . . . not so, especially with regard to behavior. What heredity [does] is to restrict the range . . . of responses . . . or to make some responses more probable than others" (pp. 158–159).

Biomedical researcher James Shields (1968) supports this view of the relationship between genetic factors and the development of psychopathology. He points out that even if genetic variables were found to be paramount in the manifestation of schizophrenic disorders, it would still be no less important to identify the kinds of psychological and sociological factors that facilitate or prevent schizophrenia in individuals who are genetically vulnerable. According to Shields, "any line of investigation is to be encouraged that will enable the genetic-environmental interaction to be better understood and rational prophylactic measures to be adopted" (p. 123).

These applications of behavior–genetic analysis represent a basic approach to understanding body–environment interaction in the development of mental disorders. This approach is known as the **diathesis–stress** concept. *Diathesis* refers to the predisposition toward a disorder—for example, a genetic error. The term *stress* refers to the conditions in one's environment, as well as one's feelings and attitudes that contribute more immediately to the onset of a disorder.

Individuals with a similar biological predisposition toward psychopathology may differ significantly in the extent to which they reveal abnormality because of differences in the particular environmental events they encounter (Goldstein, 1988, pp. 284–285).

Pathogenesis: An Integrated Biomedical View

In his historical survey of psychology, Ernest R. Hilgard (1987) points out that the most basic problems in psychology, existing at least since the days of Plato, revolve around how to conceptualize the relationship between mind and body. In current psychological language, the problem is the relationship between mind and brain. Although far from solved, the search for answers has advanced our understanding of the nature of neural processes and their relationship to "thought, emotion, and action" (p. 424).

In applying the mind and brain problem to psychopathology, the biomedical researcher Herman M. van Praag (1977) has developed an integrated viewpoint that he calls *pathogenesis*. As he summarizes this concept: "Every state of behavior . . . is dependent on a given functional state of the brain. . . . [T]here is no disturbed behavior without corresponding cerebral substrate [an underlying condition of the brain]. . . . [P]athogenic influences—[whether] psychological, environmental, or somatic—affect mental life. . . . indirectly, via changes in cerebral organization. . . . [T]he brain [is] . . . an intermediary agent" (p. 13). To illustrate further his concept of pathogenesis, van Praag

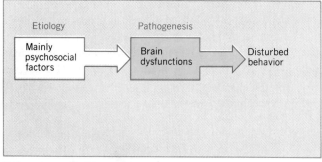
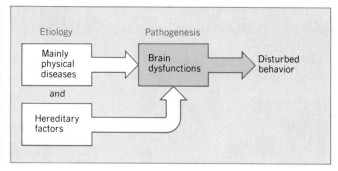

Figure 3.2

How psychosocial and biological factors contribute to the development of behavior disorders. (Adapted from van Praag, 1977, p. 14.)

cites an often-asked but spurious question: Is behavior disorder a psychosocial or a biochemical disturbance? If one must propose some sort of dichotomy, he argues, it is more proper to make the following kind of distinction (van Praag, 1977, p. 14)

1. Behavior disorders in which psychological and social factors contribute to an important degree to the development of the cerebral dysfunctions that generate these disorders.

2. Behavior disorders based on cerebral dysfunctions that to an important extent must be ascribed to factors other than psychosocial factors — for example, acquired physical diseases that involve damage to the brain, or hereditary factors involving a deficiency in a fundamental enzyme.

Figure 3.2 illustrates this dichotomy. Notice that van Praag uses the term *etiology* for the underlying conditions that ultimately may lead to disturbed behavior, whereas *pathogenesis* refers to the more immediate forerunners of the disturbed behavior — brain dysfunctions. Thus, the brain acts as an intermediary agent.

From this viewpoint, then, in all psychopathology the brain and nervous system must be malfunctioning in response to environmental demands. The crucial questions are how the malfunctioning comes about and what can be done about it. In some instances, as Figure 3.2 shows, the initial (etiological) factors that produced the brain dysfunctions (pathogenesis) can be traced mainly to psychosocial conditions, such as environmental pressures, anxiety, and conflict. On the other hand, the brain dysfunction may arise mainly from physical diseases and hereditary factors. Essentially this viewpoint is a variation of the diathesis – stress concept.

Methods of treating the disturbed person do not always have to correspond directly to the main etiological factors. For example, psychotherapy and changes in the physical and social environment can be extremely helpful even in cases where the source of difficulty lies mainly in organic disabilities, such as brain deterioration in old age, traumatic injury to the brain, or infectious disease. Furthermore, as we discuss in detail in Chapter 18, drugs may be useful for reducing brain dysfunctions even when the etiology can be traced to psychosocial factors.

Pervasiveness of Biomedical Viewpoints

Biomedical viewpoints have had a significant influence on the thinking of mental health professionals trained in other fields of study besides medicine, such as clinical psychologists and social workers, especially if they work in a medical setting. In addition, biomedical viewpoints are often reflected in popular writings on psychological problems. Consider, for example, a parent who wrote to "Dear Abby" about her son, who had been peeping into neighbors' windows. The parent did not want to consult a "doctor" because of the humiliation it would cause the family. Abby's response clearly reflects traditional biomedical views. Pointing out that "window peeping" is usually a symptom of a deeper emotional problem, Abby encouraged the parent to consult a "doctor." If the son had a "kink" in his back, said Abby, there would be no question of seeing a doctor. What he had instead was a "kink" in his "thinking" (Van Buren, 1978).

Biomedical concepts also play an important part in the messages that many voluntary mental health agencies, such as the Mental Health Association, aim toward the general public. Frequent use of the term *mental illness* reflects the pervasiveness and influence of the biomedical parallel between concepts of physical disease and mental disorder. In *How to Deal with Your Tensions* (n.d.), the Mental Health Association says: "Mental and emotional illness are terms used to describe several different disorders of the mind, each affecting the way the person thinks, feels, behaves. . . . The important thing to remember about mental illness is that it *is* an illness. . . . If emotional disturbances become too distressing to the person or to others, we should recognize and deal with them as mental illnesses requiring professional treatment."

Statements in some other publications of the association, however, agree with views of critics of the illness concept of mental disorders. Such statements focus on the importance of the social environment in the development of mental disorders and the relationship between personal stress and the social system. Nevertheless, critics may argue that because the statements appear in the presence of illness language, the total message may still convey the view that abnormal physical and biological conditions underlie most, if not all, psychological disorders.

Psychodynamic Viewpoints

Psychodynamic approaches to understanding abnormality focus on unconscious motives and conflicts as the basic source of mental disorders. We begin our discussion with **psychoanalysis**, the bedrock of psychodynamic theory and practice.

Psychoanalytic thought and practice have developed in a number of different directions, so current viewpoints disagree in certain respects. Nevertheless, they all owe their origin to the work of Sigmund Freud, founder of psychoanalysis (see Box 3.2). Although Freud speculated from time to time about specific biological abnormalities that might underlie mental disorders, especially in his early writings, his interest centered on the analysis of psychological events (Parisi, 1987). Therefore, he gave the name *psycho-analysis* to his theories of personality and behavior and to the methods of therapy he developed to help people overcome their psychological disabilities.

Like the biomedical viewpoints, psychoanalysis assumes that abnormal behavior and experience can ultimately be traced to internal causes. However, psychoanalysis focuses on **intrapsychic events** — events that occur within the mind — rather than on physical and biochemical processes. Thus, psychoanalytic theory is psychodynamic, since it deals with such internal forces of the mind as conflicting motives and desires. Psychoanalysts do not deny the influences of physical and biochemical abnormalities on psychological disorders, but such explanations lie outside the scope of their professional activities.

We turn now to basic viewpoints of Freudian psychoanalysis, also known as classical or orthodox psychoanalysis. Following that, we consider some of the modifications in psychoanalysis that have been made since Freud's day, as well as other psychodynamic approaches.

A. Freud's birthplace.

B. Freud and his family.

BOX 3.2 Scenes from Sigmund Freud's Life: A Photographic Essay

It has been said that Freudian psychoanalytic doctrine is Freud's autobiography (Henry, 1967). Although the statement is an exaggeration, there is more than a grain of truth to it, as the following scenes from Freud's life illustrate.

Sigmund Freud was born in 1865 in Frieberg, Moravia, now part of Czechoslovakia (a). His father was a wool merchant. When Sigmund was about 3 years old, the family moved to Leipzig, and soon after that to Vienna. A famous family portrait (b) shows Freud as a young man, surrounded by his mother, father, and other children in the family. Freud's father, who was old enough to be his grandfather, had been married before. He had a son, Phillip, by this first marriage. Phillip, who is not shown in this picture, was 20 years older than Sigmund, and Sigmund resented him. Years later, when Freud carried out a self-analysis, he recalled that as a small child he had believed Phillip to be his father. Freud concluded that his jealousy of Phillip's relationship to their mother had caused his hostility. Freud was convinced that this self-observation fitted what he observed in his patients as they talked about their family life and rivalries.

In 1885 Freud studied in Paris under the famous neurologist Jean-Martin Charcot, who had attracted attention across Europe because of his use of hypnosis in treating mental disorders. Freud so admired Charcot's work that he later hung a lithograph in his office of

C. Jean-Martin Charcot, a French neurologist, demonstrates "hysterical paralysis."

D. Freud marries Martha Bernays after a long engagement.

E. Freud's consulting room in Vienna.

Charcot demonstrating to his intrigued colleagues a woman who was paralyzed, not neurologically but psychologically (c). She suffered from a hysterical disorder—the first kind of disorder that Freud treated. Charcot claimed much success in using hypnosis to relieve symptoms such as these. When Freud returned to Vienna, he emulated Charcot's methods, but he later became convinced that it was not sufficient to relieve symptoms—one had to get at causes as well.

In 1886 Freud married Martha Bernays after a four-year engagement (d). To afford to get married he had to give up a career in physiological research and prepare for private practice as a neurologist. Freud spent the entire four years of his engagement getting the necessary clinical experience in neurology. Although he later earned his living and achieved fame as a psychoanalyst, he never abandoned his interest in biological determinants of behavior (Gay, 1988, p. 122; Sulloway, 1979).

Freud's consulting room was in a second-floor flat at 19 Berggasse in Vienna, where he and his family lived for many years. Featured in the room were rugs on the wall, many art objects, and, of course, the now-famous couch (e). "Princesses, poets, and philosophers came to lie on his plush couch and unfold their dreams, fantasies, and memories" (Wilson, 1969, p. 96). On May 6, 1954, the World Health Organization placed a tablet on the door of 19 Berggasse, bearing this inscription: "Here lived and worked Professor Sigmund Freud in the years 1891–1938, the creator and founder of psychoanalysis" (Jones, 1957, p. 227). The house is now a museum honoring Freud.

F. Freud and his colleagues during his visit to the United States.

A high point in Freud's career was his visit to the United States in 1909. A photograph taken during the trip shows Freud with a group of American and European psychologists and psychoanalysts at Clark University (f). Freud is in the front at the extreme left. Next to him is G. Stanley Hall, pioneer of child psychology in the United States. He was president of Clark University at the time. At the right is C. G. Jung, who broke away from the Freudian movement and founded his own school of psychoanalytic thought and practice. In the rear, left to right, are A. A. Brill, Ernest Jones, and Sandor Ferenci, all loyal disciples of Freud. Jones, an English psychoanalyst, eventually wrote a definitive biography of Freud.

After the Nazi takeover of Austria in 1938, Freud's life

was in great danger because he was a Jew. During that year the Nazi police raided his apartment, confiscating passports and seizing money. The Gestapo arrested his daughter, Anna, but then released her. As they did to many other houses in Vienna, the Nazi's draped Freud's place with a swastika (g).

That same year a huge ransom was paid to the Nazis for

them to allow Freud to leave the country. In June 1939, Freud, with his wife, Martha, and daughter, Anna, departed for London. Marie Bonaparte, who had been his patient, financed the ransom. With the help of William Bullitt, United States ambassador to France, she escorted the 82-year-old Freud to the safety of London (h). Here he lived until his death at 20 Maresfield Gardens, with his daughter, also a psychoanalyst. The house is now a museum containing many of the possessions Freud was able to bring from Vienna.

In London, Freud worked on the manuscript of his last major book, *An Outline of Psychoanalysis*, which summarized his basic viewpoints (i). It was not published until after his death. Freud had suffered for years from cancer of the jaw and the agony of some 33 operations to alleviate the disease. He was in much pain during the last month of his life but refused pain-killing drugs. "I prefer," he once said, "to think in torment than not to be able to think clearly" (Jones, 1957, p. 245). He died just after midnight on September 23, 1939. His body was cremated at the Golders Green Cemetery, London, and his ashes repose there in one of his favorite Grecian urns. His longtime friend and colleague Ernest Jones concluded the funeral oration with this eulogy: "And so we take leave of a man whose like we shall not know again. From our heart we thank you for having lived; for having done; and for having loved" (Jones, 1957, p. 248).

G. The Nazis mark Freud's house with a swastika.

H. Freud flees from the Nazi to London.

I. Freud works on the manuscript of his last major book, *An Outline of Psychoanalysis*, published posthumously.

Freudian Psychoanalysis

Intrapsychic Process: Motivation and Conflict and Anxiety

Freud's observations of his patients convinced him that their neurotic symptoms could be traced to internal psychological (intrapsychic) processes. We consider here three central and interrelated aspects of those intrapsychic processes: *motivation, conflict,* and *anxiety.*

A central assumption of Freudian psychoanalysis, and indeed all psychodynamic theories, is that behavior is motivated, purposive, and goal-directed. Such theories also assume that individuals are often not aware of the true motives that influence their thoughts and behavior. The motives, thoughts, and feelings that are the subject matter of psychoanalysis must be inferred from behavior.

Freud concluded that behavior is motivated not only from what his patients said but also from what they did not say. He was constantly impressed by the fact that his patients had forgotten events in their lives that proved to be crucial in the development of their psychopathology. Freud reasoned that because such memories were too painful to tolerate, they had been **repressed**—pushed from the conscious into the **unconscious**. Symptoms of psychopathology persisted because, distressing as they were, they nevertheless helped maintain this state of repression.

In his earlier theories, Freud considered the stages of consciousness and unconsciousness to be more or less independent. Later, however, he emphasized that their relationship was continuous and fluid. Not only could conscious conflicts in motives and the memories surrounding them became unconscious through repression, but they could also emerge again into consciousness, thus creating more anxiety. As he thought more deeply about the matter, Freud proposed an intermediate state that he called the **preconscious**. The preconscious can become unconscious rather easily, but transforming the unconscious to consciousness can be accomplished only with great difficulty, requiring a considerable expenditure of effort. Indeed, said Freud, it may never become conscious at all (Freud, 1933/1965, p. 71).

Freud believed that the internal conflict producing symptoms of psychopathology stemmed mainly from the inborn drives of sex and aggression. He theorized that these biological forces often conflict with the moral standards that the individual has incorporated from parents or other authority figures in society. Conflict also arises because of the restraints society inevitably imposes on the overt expression of sex and aggression. These conflicts and the anxiety they arouse show their presence in various symptoms of psychopathology. However, the individual does not recognize the actual source of the symptoms and attributes them to other, more plausible causes.

Freud distinguished between realistic anxiety and neurotic (maladaptive) anxiety. **Realistic anxiety**, he said, is a response to a known, real danger in the external world. In contrast, **neurotic anxiety** is a response to nonobjective danger, or, as Freud said, "to a danger we do not know." The source of this danger, he proposed, was in the biological drives of sex and aggression, forces that might threaten the individual. It was also possible, said Freud, for the danger to be known, but the anxiety related to it to be greater than it should be (Freud, 1936, p. 113).

Freud proposed a third form of anxiety, which he called moral anxiety (literally, conscience anxiety, *Gewissensangst*). **Moral anxiety** occurs as the result of the conscience incorporating the threats of punishment that parents or other authority figures make early in the child's life—threats intended to prevent the child from transgressing moral rules. These threats arouse anxiety because the child often perceives them as a danger of losing parental love. As the conscience develops and the child emerges into adolescence and adulthood, anxiety may arise whenever the commands of conscience are violated, just as earlier in life it resulted from actual threats of parental punishment (Freud, 1933/1965, p. 62).

In Freud's thinking, the relationship between normal behavior and experience and psychopathology is a continuous one. He regarded the intrapsychic conflicts his patients disclosed as exaggerated versions of the kinds of conflict and anxieties that normal individuals show in their everyday lives. In a book that brought him early fame, *The Psychopathology of Everyday Life*, Freud described how anxiety, conflict, and the forces of repression are revealed not only in individuals so disturbed that they seek help through psychoanalysis but also in everyday behavior. For example, forgetting names and places, making slips of the tongue and in writing, breaking or losing objects — all these common mistakes can be clues to unconscious conflict and anxiety (Freud, 1901/1960).

Structures of Personality and Psychopathology

To account for how the intrapsychic processes of motivation, conflict, and anxiety function, Freud proposed certain structures of personality that he called agencies of mental life. As translated from his original works in German, these agencies are generally known as the id, the ego, and the superego.

The Id. Psychological development begins with the **id**, a Latin word that translators of Freud rendered from *das Es* (the it). According to Freud, *das Es* contains "everything that is inherited, that is present at birth, . . . above all, therefore, the instincts" (Freud, 1940/1949, p. 14). Freud chose the term *Es* for those inborn biological forces at the suggestion of George Groddeck (1923/1961), a German physician whose ideas attracted Freud. In turn, Groddeck had been influenced by the German philosopher Friedrich Nietzsche, who used *Es* to describe whatever in nature was impersonal. To Freud, the label was highly appropriate for his own concept of *das Es*, since it represented to him the most primitive and biologically fixed agent of the mind (Freud, 1933/1965, p. 72).

Translators of Freud chose the term *instinct* to represent *trieb* (Freud, 1940/1949, p. 14), but *trieb* is better translated into English as **drive**. Not only does that term come closer to modern concepts of human biological motivation as a state of excitement or tension, but it is also preferred by contemporary followers of Freudian theory (Bettelheim, 1982, pp. 87–91).

For Freud two drives formed the main components of the id: **Eros**, named after the Greek god of love, and the **destructive (or death) drive**. The latter drive became well known as Thanatos, after the god of death in Greek legend. Wilhelm Stekel, a colleague with whom Freud quarreled, was the first to use Thanatos as a designation for the death wish. However, Freud himself never used the term in his writings, supposedly because of an intense dislike of Stekel (Gay, 1988, pp. 213–214; Jones, 1957, p. 273; Roazen, 1975, p. 218).

According to Freud, Eros uses a special form of energy called **libido**. Freud emphasized that libido is more than sexual energy; it is the source of all pleasurable behavior. Thus, Eros obeys the pleasure principle. In his later writings Freud ascribed an even broader role to Eros; it produces not only pleasurable activity but all constructive activity. Therefore, he considered Eros and libido as sources of all the energy that promotes life (Freud, 1940/1949).

In contrast to the constructive life force of Eros, the aim of the destructive drive is to "undo conditions . . . to reduce living things to an inorganic state" (Freud, 1940/1949, p. 20). Freud used *aggression* rather than *death* in referring to the general nature of the destructive drive, a term that is more acceptable to modern psychoanalysis. He pointed out that aggression can be directed not only toward the external world but also toward oneself. An individual may prefer to direct aggression toward someone else but is prevented by the dictates of conscience (Freud, 1940/1949, pp. 22–23). Contemporary followers of Freud maintain this difference between inward and outward aggression, commonly accepting that abnormal depression, guilt, and other self-destructive feelings and behavior represent the turning of the aggressive drive toward oneself (Fancher, 1973, pp. 207–210). Freud also pointed out that the constructive drive of Eros and the aggressive drive could work with as well as against each other. For example, "the act of eating is a destruction of the object with the final aim of incorporating it, and the sexual act is an act of aggression having as its purpose the most intimate union" (Freud, 1940/1949, p. 21).

The Ego. Very early in life, under the influence of the external world, a new mental agency arises from within the id. Freud named it *das Ich* (the I), a term that translators have rendered into the Latin equivalent, **ego**. Although *ego* has been thoroughly established in English translations of Freud's writings, some interpreters of psychoanalysis believe that it is important to keep in mind the English meaning of *das Ich*. As Paul Wachtel (1977) has pointed out, "Thinking of *das Ich* as the I . . . highlights the view of the ego as an organization of psychological processes including, and strongly infused with, the feeling of self" (p. 33). According to Freud, the ego (das Ich) is an intermediary between the id and external reality. The ego controls all voluntary actions. It reacts to the external world by storing experiences in the memory, and by learning to modify the external world in appropriate ways. The ego relates to the internal stimuli from the id by controlling those demands. The ego must decide "whether they shall be allowed to obtain satisfaction" and learns to postpone such satisfaction "to times and circumstances favorable in the outside world." In some instances the ego must suppress the excitement from the id completely (Freud, 1940/1949, pp. 15–16). Thus, Freud perceived the ego as the intellectual agency of the personality. The ego reasons, criticizes, makes decisions, and defends itself against internal conflict and external danger.

In his metaphorical way, Freud compared the ego's relations to the id with that of a rider to a horse. The horse supplies the locomotive energy, and the rider decides on the goal and how to guide the powerful animal's movement. But, said Freud, "only too often there arises between the ego and the id the . . . situation of the rider being obliged to guide the horse along the path by which it itself wants to go (Freud, 1933/1965, p. 77).

The ego, then, must be sufficiently strong to reconcile the demands of the id and external reality — demands that are often in conflict. Freud was generally pessimistic about how well the ego could attain such strength. Nevertheless, as he stated in *The Future of an Illusion*: "The voice of the intellect is a soft one, but it does not rest until it has gained a hearing. Finally, after a countless succession of rebuffs, it succeeds" (Freud, 1927/1961, p. 53).

The Superego. As the ego continues to develop throughout childhood, a new structure of personality emerges, which Freud called the *Uber-Ich*, above or over the I. In English writings Freud's compound noun is known as the **superego** (Bettelheim, 1982).

The superego includes two components: conscience and ideals. The conscience represents the ideals and the moral rights and wrongs that are gradually absorbed from parents (or parent surrogates) during the long period of childhood dependence. In addition, the superego gradually incorporates various "contributions from later successors and substitutes of [one's] parents, such as teachers, admired figures in public life, or high social ideals" (Freud, 1940/1949, p. 17).

In executing its functions, the superego "observes the ego, gives it orders, corrects it and threatens it with punishment, exactly like the parents whose place it has taken" (Freud, 1940/1949, p. 121). If the demands of the superego are violated, the ego experiences guilt. Ordinarily, this guilt occurs when the ego admits into its consciousness those sexual or aggressive drives that the superego has forbidden. The superego creates a new task for the ego: The ego must not only interact with external reality but at the same time it must balance its demands with those of the superego and the id (Freud, 1940/1949, p. 21).

Psychopathology. According to Freud, the symptoms of mental disorder (psychopathology) reflect the inability of the ego to handle adequately the often conflicting demands of the id, superego, and external reality. The healthy individual, he said, develops a strong ego and a reasonable superego — a superego that is not overly severe. The neurotic, abnormally anxious ego is weak and is no longer able to fulfill the tasks set to it by the external world (Freud, 1940/1949, p. 76).

Freud observed that in spite of a weakened ego unable to balance intrapsychic conflicts satisfactorily, most neurotic individuals are able to maintain their position in real life. That is, they do not reveal the loss of contact with reality that characterizes psychotic individuals (see Chapter 1). For the latter, the demands of the id are so intense, and the claims of the superego so remorseless, that they loosen the organization of the ego. It is no longer able to deal adequately with reality. Indeed, Freud concluded that the psychotic ego was so divorced from reality that the techniques of psychoanalysis, which he devised for treating neuroses, were not suitable for psychotic patients (Freud, 1940/1949, p. 64). Not all of Freud's colleagues agreed that psychoanalysis should be limited to neurotics, or, in more current language, people suffering from anxiety disorders (see Chapter 5). Even today, there is some disagreement on the issue, although most orthodox analysts continue to follow Freud's tradition (Malcolm, 1981, pp. 128–134).

Psychosexual Development

To explain how an inadequate ego comes about, Freud constructed an extensive theory of *psychosexual development*. A weak ego can result from traumatic events and from the failure to complete satisfactorily the tasks of a particular phase of development.

Freud's theory of psychosexual development describes a series of phases centering around the erotic zones of the body: the mouth, anus, and genitals. The child's reactions to sexual stimuli from those zones inevitably reflect parental attitudes, control, and even censure. A crucial task for the child at each phase of psychosexual development is to cope with the feelings of anxiety and frustration that result from such parental concerns. How the child manages this anxiety and frustration at one phase has a significant effect on the ability to resolve conflict and frustration at succeeding phases, and thus has a powerful influence on personality development and behavior (see Table 3.1).

Oral – Dependent Phase. Freud challenged the Victorian attitudes of his time by stating boldly that sexual life does not begin at puberty but is clearly manifested soon after birth. "The baby's obstinate persistence in sucking," he asserted, "originates from and is stimulated by the taking of nourishment. . . . [N]evertheless [it] seeks to obtain pleasure independently of nourishment. . . . [F]or that reason [it] should be described as 'sexual'" (Freud, 1940/1949, p. 28). To attain this satisfaction, the baby must be completely dependent on another person, usually the mother (or mother surrogate). Thus, during the **oral – dependent phase** of psychosexual development, composing about the first year of life, the child learns to associate sexual and nutritional satisfaction with being dependent.

Freud pointed out that frustration and conflict are bound to arise as the baby seeks to gain oral satisfaction. Any threat to this satisfaction, such as prolonged absence of the

Table 3.1 Phases of Psychosexual Development: Freudian Concepts	
Age Period	**Psychosexual Phase**
First 6 months	Oral – dependent
6 months to end of 2nd year	Anal – sadistic
3 – 6 years	Phallic: Oedipus complex and Electra complex
6 – 12 years	Latency
Adolescence and adulthood	Genital

Age periods are convenient approximations, not rigid time limits.
Source: Adapted from Freud, 1940/1949, pp. 25 – 32.

mother, arouses anxiety. If this threat is continuous and extreme, the baby may grow up to become overdependent, not only on the mother but on other people as well. Threats to this dependence resurrect the original anxiety. The term *overdependent character* has been applied to this pattern of personality. According to Freudian theory, in its more extreme forms such excessive dependence can become a disabling psychological disorder, affecting the individual in sexual and other interpersonal relationships that require a reasonable balance between self-reliance and dependence.

Anal – Sadistic Phase. Between the ages of 1 and 3 the child discovers that sexual satisfaction can be gained from anal functions. Freud emphasized that this satisfaction is only a forerunner to later, more mature sexual pleasure, but he insisted that it represented an advance over the more rudimentary sexual satisfaction of the oral phase.

As children progress through the anal phase, they begin to combine their anal pleasure with aggressiveness. This fusion of sex and aggression led Freud to give the name **anal – sadistic** to this phase of psychosexual development. One of the most important ways in which the child accomplishes the fusion is to attempt to control parents (or other parental figures) during the toilet-training period. By letting go or holding on they can use their anal functions to please or displease their parents. In this manner children can begin to develop a primitive form of independence and self-assertion (Abraham, 1924/1948).

Normally, said Freud, the interest of children in anal functions develops into a "group of traits that are familiar to us as parsimony, a sense of order and cleanliness . . . qualities which though valuable and welcome in themselves, may be intensified till they become markedly dominant and produce . . . the anal character" (Freud, 1930/1962, pp. 43 – 44). For example, if children become fixated on their anal sensations, they may as adults develop miserly or abnormally obstinate character traits, rather than simply being parsimonious. Or they may become so obsessed with order and cleanliness that their compulsive behavior interferes with normal interpersonal relationships. Thus, in Freud's view, fixation on the anal – sadistic phase of psychosexual development paved the way for neurotic symptoms, especially those of obsessive compulsive disorders (Freud, 1917/1955; 1913/1958; 1908/1959). (See Chapter 5 for a discussion of these disorders.)

When Freud first presented his ideas about anal eroticism, in 1908, members of the psychiatric establishment greeted them with jeers. As Freud's biographer Ernest Jones (1955, pp. 295 – 296) described it, associating such a "lowly part of the body as the anus" with "character" appeared to Freud's professional contemporaries as the most outrageous thing he had yet done. However, by 1923, Freud's fellow psychoanalysts had firmly accepted the concept of anal–sadistic sexuality and its implications for personality development and abnormality.

Phallic Latency and Phases. With the **phallic phase**, boys and girls develop along different paths. This phase, which extends from approximately ages 3 to 6, obtains its name from the Greek word *phallos*, meaning "penis." Freud thought that *phallic* was an appropriate label because of the sexual excitement the boy begins to gain from his penis. The girl derives sexual excitement from the clitoris rather than the vagina, but Freud applied the term *phallic* to girls because the clitoris is anatomically analogous to the penis.

The central feature of the phallic phase for the boy is the **Oedipus complex**, the onset of which Freud described explicitly in sexual terms. As the boy begins to feel pleasurable sensations in his penis and learns to obtain them by manual stimulation, he becomes "his mother's lover," and "tries to seduce her by showing her the male organ of which he is the proud owner." Hitherto he has envied his father because of his physical strength and his authority. Now, however, his father becomes a rival for his mother's love. This feeling of rivalry is intensified whenever he is able to "share his mother's bed" during his father's absence (Freud, 1940/1949, p. 91).

In giving the name *Oedipus complex* to the boy's psychosexual involvement with his mother, Freud borrowed from Greek legend and Sophocles's famous tragedy *Oedipus Rex*. Oedipus, who was abandoned in infancy, kills a stranger during a roadside argument, not knowing that the victim is actually his father. Later, Oedipus marries his father's widow, without realizing that she is his own mother.

As a sexual rival the boy identifies with his father, taking on his masculine qualities. But "under the conditions of our society," said Freud, the Oedipus complex is "invariably doomed to a terrible end" (1940/1949, p. 91). What is this terrible end? The boy's mother knows full well that his sexual excitement is directed toward her. She feels that this is wrong and forbids him to manipulate his genitals. In order to make the order more forceful, she says she will tell the father, and he will cut the penis off. The boy's fearful reaction to this threat constitutes the **castration complex** (Freud, 1940/1949, pp. 91–92). Ordinarily, the boy terminates his Oedipus complex and enters the **latency phase** of psychosexual development, which extends from about ages 6 to 12. He ceases his overt sexual rivalry with his father and represses his sexual desire for his mother. He continues, however, to strengthen his identification with his father, incorporating his father's conscience and ideals into his own developing superego.

In Freud's view, the phallic phase of psychosexual development and the subsequent latency phase are crucial for the development of a masculine character, which depends on the boy identifying with the father. If the father is not a sufficiently masculine rival, or he is absent and there is no adequate father substitute, the boy may not engage in sexual rivalry or identify with masculinity. Under such conditions, the boy's superego development may be impaired. He may also identify almost exclusively with his mother, and thus develop a feminine rather than a masculine character. In extreme instances, this overidentification with femininity may result in homosexuality as the boy emerges into an adult sex role (see Chapter 9). Even if adequate male identification does occur, the threat of castration may be so severe that the boy develops abnormal fears of a male sexual role, leading to avoidance or fear of women during adulthood.

The girl's psychosexual development during the phallic phase follows a different sequence. To begin with, the girl discovers that she lacks a penis and thus begins to envy boys. Indeed, said Freud, "her whole development may be said to take place under the influence of her envy for the penis" (1940/1949, p. 97). At first she tries to imitate boys but soon realizes that the lack of a penis prevents this. She may attempt to gain sexual pleasure by manipulating her genitals but often fails to obtain sufficient gratification. Thus, her feelings of inferiority about having a "stunted penis" may extend to her whole self.

Inevitably the girl must search for an explanation as to why she lacks a penis. She fixes the blame on her mother for sending her into the world "so insufficiently equipped," as Freud put it. As a result of this blame, she turns from the dependent affection she has for her mother to an identification with her, taking on her feminine qualities. By identifying with her mother, the girl can now compete with her for her father's sexual affection. The affection may begin as a wish to have his penis at her command, and thus compensate for her own lack of one. This desire gives way to another wish — to have a baby from him as a gift (Freud, 1940/1949, p. 99; 1924/1961a, pp. 178–179; 1925/1961).

The girl's identification and sexual rivalry with her mother constitute the **Electra complex**, a term that Freud borrowed from Greek legend and the dramas of Sophocles. Electra hates her mother, Clytemnestra, because she helped kill Electra's father, Agamemnon. Seven years later, Electra, plotting with her brother Orestes, murders her mother out of revenge.

The Oedipus complex and the Electra complex involve deep-seated emotions concerning the penis, but in quite opposite ways. According to Freud, the threat of castration during the phallic phase terminates the boy's Oedipus complex. For the girl, it is the lack of a penis, and consequent envy of the boy, that brings her Electra complex to an end.

The Electra complex is crucial for the girl's development of a feminine character. She must give up her wish to have her father as a sexual partner, thus terminating the phallic phase of psychosexual development and entering the latency phase. However, she continues to strengthen her femininity and superego through identification with her mother. If the girl fails to resolve her Electra complex, thus retaining her penis envy and early desire to be a boy, she may in extreme cases end as a homosexual (Freud, 1940/1949, p. 99).

In explaining why girls proceed through the phallic phase differently from boys, Freud emphasized that the physical distinction is bound to find its expression in differences of psychological development. "Anatomy is destiny," said Freud, varying a saying of Napoleon's (Freud, 1924/1961a, p. 178). Perhaps nothing in classical psychoanalytic theory has aroused more opposition than Freud's concept of penis envy and its role in the development of femininity.

Genital Phases: Adolescence and Adulthood. With the onset of puberty, boys and girls enter the **genital phase** and initiation into future adult sex roles. Freud emphasized that psychosexual development during adolescence depends to a great extent on how successfully earlier phases were completed.

Adulthood is a continuation of the genital phase of psychosexual development, the fruition of sexual maturity. It represents a consolidation of all the psychosexual tasks accomplished during previous phases of development.

Criticisms of Freudian Psychoanalytic Theory

The following sections discuss some of the more common critical reactions to Freud's work. The focus is on broad fundamentals rather than specific details (Hall & Lindzey, 1978, pp. 66–70).

Overemphasis on Biological Drives

Freud emphasized the biological basis of sex and aggression (the id) to such an extent that he consistently disregarded social and cultural influences on the expression of these biological drives. Although he indicated at times that one does learn through the ego how to behave aggressively and sexually, the overriding emphasis is on instincts (biological drives) rather than social learning. Freud assumed that the Oedipus complex and the Electra complex were universal and that the basic conflict always derived from sexual (biological) drives.

Many contemporary psychologists (and some psychoanalysts as well) do not agree with the literal way that Freud described these complexes. Some psychoanalysts interpret the Oedipus complex as a struggle for power. The specific sexual aspects may or may not be present.

Penis Envy

Critics have reacted strongly to Freud's concept of penis envy. This group includes various activists in the women's movement, such as historian Kate Millett (1970) and anthropologist Margaret Mead (1979), as well as some psychoanalysts. The pioneering neo-Freudian Karen Horney made this observation: "It would require tremendous evidence to make it plausible that women, physically built for specifically female functions, should be physically determined by a wish for attributes of the other sex. But actually the data presented for this contention are scant" (Horney, 1939, p. 104–105).

Weaknesses in Data

Freud relied mainly on what adults told him about their childhoods in forming conclusions about the kinds of conflicts, anxieties, and frustrations that determined personality development and psychopathology. Obviously, there are pitfalls in this retrospective method, since such data may not necessarily reflect what actually happened during childhood. Those psychoanalysts who have worked directly with children claim in some instances to have verified certain of Freud's concepts, but in other cases they have not been able to do so. Among the most outstanding of these psychoanalysts is Freud's daughter, Anna Freud, who founded the Hampstead Child-Therapy Clinic in London shortly after World War II. The clinic's staff includes mostly nonmedical mental health professionals engaged in the study and treatment of children.

Weaknesses in Methodology

A common criticism of Freud is that his method of testing hypotheses was dubious, since his observations were not sufficiently controlled. For example, he did not keep verbatim notes on what he and his patients talked about during psychoanalytic sessions. He wrote his case descriptions hours after the sessions had concluded. His recall may therefore have been influenced by what he wanted to have happen. Furthermore, it is not always clear what data Freud based his conclusions on. Sometimes he made them explicit, but sometimes he did not. For that reason many of his observations could not be repeated. Under such conditions it was practically impossible to compare his conclusions to data gathered by other psychoanalysts.

Empirical Tests of Freudian Theory

Freud's theories can be tested empirically provided one separates global explanations from the more specific psychoanalytic propositions derived from them. In turn, various hypotheses, capable of being tested empirically, can be deduced from the specific psychoanalytic propositions (Kline, 1972, 1981). The following illustrates how such a hypothesis can be derived.

1. **Global theory:** The Oedipus complex, and its termination, involves such psychological and biological dynamics as the boy's libidinal attachment to his mother, his identification with his father, and conflict arising from the fear of castration.

2. **Specific psychoanalytic proposition:** The solution of the Oedipus complex is a crucial determinant of personality.

3. **Hypothesis:** Around the age of 4, boys perceive their fathers as rivals and model their fathers' behavior.

The strategy of reducing global theory to (testable) hypotheses was used in the various analyses we now consider.

Kline's Analysis

After critically reviewing hundreds of studies dealing with Freudian theory, Kline (1972, 1981) concluded that much of the broad theory is unscientific in that it cannot be tested empirically. However, specific hypotheses derived from Freudian theory could be tested. Analysis of such empirical tests led Kline to decide that there was indirect support for a number of psychoanalytic concepts and propositions, especially those related to depression and the Oedipus complex. However, he emphasized that aspects of the theory should be retained only if objective research has demonstrated their validity. Otherwise, the theory should be modified. Kline also pointed to various directions future studies should take in attempting to establish the soundness of Freudian concepts.

Eysenck – Wilson Analysis

Hans Eysenck and Glenn Wilson (1973) analyzed some of the same studies that Kline reviewed—in particular, those dealing with psychosexual development during the oral and anal phases, the Oedipus and castration complexes, and the nature of neurosis and psychosis. In general, Eysenck and Wilson reached negative conclusions about the studies. They emphasized the failure of researchers to discuss alternate hypotheses, the lack of statistical sophistication, and the fact that there was "hardly any attempt to replicate findings" (p. 389).

Fisher – Greenberg Analysis

The comprehensive survey of studies that Fisher and Greenberg (1977) conducted uncovered methodological weaknesses as well as some support for a number of concepts and hypotheses.

In the case of the Oedipus and castration complexes, Fisher and Greenberg concluded that the theory can help explain normal and abnormal personality development provided it is not always interpreted as literally as Freud did. For example, the boy's identification with his father during the Oedipal period may develop more out of the father's warmth and nurturance in persuading his son to be like him (masculine) than out of specific sexual competition for the mother's affection. This persuasion may well involve elements of rivalry and anxiety for the boy.

The boy's castration anxiety may not be so much a force that impels him to increase his identification with his father after terminating the Oedipus complex (as Freud believed) as a barrier between him and his father that interferes with identification. However, if the father has a nurturant attitude, he can reduce the boy's castration anxieties and convince him that it is safe to be close to his father. Thus, identification with his father can be strengthened (Fisher & Greenberg, 1977, p. 405).

One factor in the development of homosexuality may be the failure of the boy to identify with his father and the girl with her mother, but not all instances of homosexuality stem from such failure. (We discuss alternate factors in Chapter 9.)

Silverman Research Program

In a series of intriguing laboratory studies carried out over a period of some 15 years, Lloyd Silverman and his co-workers at the Research Center for Mental Health of New York University (Silverman, 1976; Silverman & Weinberger, 1985) have tested various hypotheses stemming from the general Freudian proposition that abnormal behavior can be increased by the stimulation of conflicts related to unconscious sexual and aggressive wishes.

The Silverman group used a procedure called **subliminal psychodynamic activation**. Individuals were shown pictures and printed phrases by means of a tachistoscope, an instrument that allows very rapid exposure of a stimulus — in this case, 0.004 seconds. The exposure is so brief that the subjects cannot consciously recognize the stimulus. However, various studies have concluded that it may nevertheless affect their feelings and behavior (Dixon, 1971). This phenomenon is known as subliminal perception.

One series of experiments centered around the psychoanalytic proposition that depression is a result of turning unconscious aggressive feelings toward others onto oneself. If this is true, the experimenters reasoned, depressed individuals should increase their depression when unconscious oral–aggressive motives are aroused. To test this hypothesis, researchers presented subjects who had definite symptoms of serious depression with aggressive pictures, such as a man holding a dagger, or aggressive messages, such as the phrase *CANNIBAL EATS PERSON*. The individuals rated their feelings before and after the exposures. In a different session, they were shown, subliminally, various nonaggressive pictures or verbal messages — for example, a person reading a newspaper, or the words *PEOPLE ARE WALKING*. Again, they were asked to rate their feelings before and after. The investigators found that depression increased when the subjects viewed aggressive stimuli, but no change occurred when they viewed the neutral content. To demonstrate that unconscious motivation was at work, researchers showed similar messages to subjects so that they could actually see them. There was no effect on the patient's symptoms of depression. These results, the experimenters concluded, supported the concept of unconscious motivation.

The Silverman research has aroused a great deal of interest, since presumably it supports the psychoanalytic theory of the unconscious. Unfortunately, recent and vigorous criticism has cast serious doubt on the results of that research (Balay & Shevrin, 1988). Critics point not only to certain methodological weaknesses but also to the fact that other investigators using the same techniques as Silverman and his colleagues have been unable to replicate the original findings. Until those problems are overcome, the Silverman studies represent thought-provoking hypotheses rather than firm conclusions.

Basic Contributions of Freudian Theory

Although many of Freud's specific conclusions are debatable, a number of fundamental concepts that have emerged from his work have greatly influenced modern psychology.

Freud established the concept of *determinism* — a basic assumption that psychologists generally accept today, although they may formulate it differently. Behavior is determined — there are reasons for what we do. Indeed, Freud emphasized that behavior is overdetermined — that is, its causes are complex. Any given act may have a number of different causes.

Freud pioneered the concept of **unconscious motivation** — the proposition that the residue from earlier experiences affects later behavior even though one may not be aware of that influence. Although contemporary psychologists debate the precise nature of unconscious processes, they continue to seek new ways of thinking about and investigating them.

Even psychologists who reject Freud's specific formulation of the Oedipus complex, the Electra complex, and the development of the superego have been influenced by his identification concepts in seeking to understand personality development and behavior. Although interpretations of the process often differ from Freud's, few current explanations of normal and abnormal personality development fail to consider how boys and girls identify with their parents (or parent substitutes) and how the modeling of parental behavior affects the development of conscience, ideals, and adult sex roles.

Modern psychology takes for granted the *continuity of development* — that is, the idea that new ways of thinking and behaving often develop out of old patterns. This idea was far from commonplace in Freud's day. Not only was he a pioneer in emphasizing and demonstrating it, but he also studied how people's attempts to resolve their conflicts, frustrations, and anxieties can affect the continuity of their personality development.

We have presented only a sample of the kinds of contributions Freud made toward understanding normal and abnormal personality and behavior. In balancing them against criticisms, we might well consider James Joyce's comment in *Ulysses*, intended for Shakespeare but quite appropriate for Freud: "A man of genius makes no mistakes. His errors are . . . the portals of discovery" (Joyce, 1961, p. 190).

Ego Psychology and Defense Mechanisms

In spite of his belief in the great importance of the id, Freud did assert that one must understand the nature of the ego and its defenses in order to understand how it handles conflict and anxiety. He pointed out that the ego often distorts or even denies the true meaning of its conflicts and anxieties. He called these distortions and denials **defense mechanisms** and thus laid the groundwork for a psychoanalytic movement that came to be known as ego psychology.

Ego psychology clarifies and extends classical Freudian psychoanalysis. During the 1940s and 1950s certain followers of Freud began to expand his concepts of the ego and its defenses — in particular, Freud's daughter, Anna Freud (1946, 1966); Heinz Hartmann (1958, 1964), the leading theoretician of the movement; David Rapaport (1951, 1967); and Erik Erikson (1963, 1964, 1968). They did not abandon the idea that biological drives play an important part in motivating behavior, but they shifted from Freud's emphasis on the primacy of the id to a greater recognition of the ego's role in determining human actions.

A central principle of ego psychology is that the ego is autonomous. Hartmann insisted that the ego does not emerge from the id, as Freud theorized, but develops as an independent mental agency. Thus, the operations of the ego and its defenses are not just a matter of resolving conflicts stemming from id impulses. The ego may also be concerned with how to solve a problem or make choices that involve conflicts completely within itself. At times the ego may resolve its conflicts by considering only the external reality and

Anna Freud, pioneer exponent of ego psychology. She elaborated and refined the theory of ego defense mechanisms.

Erik Erikson, prolific writer and developer of ego psychology. Erikson endowed the ego with such characteristics as autonomy, will, identity, industry, competence, and integrity.

superego restraints. Therefore, biological drives do not always have to be the primary sources of the ego's conflicts and anxieties.

As ego psychology became more influential, psychoanalysts elaborated on the autonomous functions of the ego and attributed to it various qualities that went considerably beyond Freud's original conceptions. In his *theory of psychosocial development*, Erik Erikson endowed the ego with such characteristics as trust and hope, autonomy and will, identity and fidelity, industry and competence, intimacy and love, and integrity (Erikson, 1963, pp. 247–274).

We now consider one of the most important developments in ego psychology — the systematic study of the ego's defenses against conflict, anxiety, and stress. Such knowledge has had a great influence on the thinking of contemporary psychoanalysts, and other mental health professionals have found it useful as well (Vaillant, 1986).

Repression

A central function of repression is to expel from consciousness the impulses of sex and aggression that conflict with the superego and thus evoke intolerable anxiety. Repression may also be set into motion by the ego's fear of retaliation if it responds to such impulses. In addition, the ego may use repression to forget various events associated with anxiety and fear, thus preventing those memories from arousing painful emotions.

In their pioneering work on interpreting repression as a learned phenomenon, Dollard and Miller (1950) pointed out that the persistent use of repression as a way of adapting to conflict and anxiety is eventually self-defeating. It prevents individuals from facing directly what they fear, and thus prevents them from learning through experience how to deal with the anxiety realistically, or learning that the anxiety is no longer justified.

Denial

A basic process that theoretically is involved in all defense mechanisms, **denial** is most often applied to situations in which the ego undergoes a great deal of conflict and anxiety because external reality does not permit it to express impulses from the id, or express motives residing within the ego itself. The ego may therefore deny, often in subtle and indirect ways, that the reality actually exists. For example, the ego may engage in fantasy, creating imaginary and sometimes symbolic situations to replace those that it fears to confront.

Denial can also take a form that Ernest Jones, a disciple and biographer of Freud, called **rationalization** (Jones, 1923). The ego invents intellectually reasonable excuses for the way it handles feelings of anxiety, conflict, and guilt, especially if it wishes to engage in behavior forbidden by the superego.

Regression

The ego may reduce or avoid conflict and anxiety by resuming earlier, less mature forms of thought and behavior. Such **regression** may involve deep feelings of helplessness, dependence, and self-centeredness. Or it may be revealed in immature ways of expressing sexual and aggressive impulses. For example, a man may revive his strong libidinal attachment to his mother as a way of avoiding the conflict and anxiety he experiences when trying to establish mature sexual relationships with women.

Reaction Formation

In using the defense mechanism of **reaction formation**, the ego avoids conflicting and anxiety-producing demands of the id, superego, or external reality by expressing the opposite of the demands. For example, aggressive wishes may be changed into overly affectionate behavior. Sexual desire aimed toward a particular person may arouse so much anxiety, conflict, or guilt that the desire is transformed into opposite feelings, such as disgust. A major clue for inferring the mechanism of reaction formation lies in the typically exaggerated nature of the defensive behavior itself.

Undoing

The mechanism of **undoing**, which is closely related to reaction formation, involves a shift of feelings from one extreme to another, so that the second attitude contradicts the first. Undoing extends the contradiction, since it is an action, real or imaginary, that is directly opposite to a previous action or thought. The second action undoes the first.

Undoing is a form of "magical" thought and behavior that in many circumstances is quite normal; we all use it at one time or another. For example, parents will often indulge in magic when they kiss their child's bruises, making the pain go away. The magic of love has undone the pain.

In its abnormal mode, undoing may occur in compulsive and obsessive disorders (see Chapter 5). Consider the case of a man who harbored destructive (albeit unconscious) wishes toward his mother. "An irreligious patient who obsessively had to pray for the health of his sick mother had the further compulsion of slapping his mouth lightly after having said the prayer. This was an undoing of the warding-off symptom, a return of the warded-off death wish toward the mother which meant: 'I am putting the words of prayer back into my mouth'" (Fenichel, 1945, p. 154).

Displacement

In using the defense mechanism of **displacement** the ego shifts various id impulses or demands of the superego and external reality from one situation to another. For example, an employee may not dare to express aggression toward an employer, but instead displaces the aggression onto other persons whose retaliation is not feared, such as subordinates on the job or a spouse and children at home.

Projection

The ego may defend itself against conflict, anxiety, and guilt by ascribing to others **(projecting)** motives and feelings that the superego has forbidden. For example, a person may deny persistent aggressive or sexual impulses by constantly perceiving them in other people's behavior.

Although projection may be used in a normal, adaptive manner, its persistent use as a defense often indicates psychopathology, especially in paranoid disorders. Such disturbances are characterized by abnormally excessive suspiciousness and hostility, often expressed in delusions of persecution (see Chapter 11). According to some psychoanalytic interpretations, this suspicion is often an inversion of the paranoid person's own hostility; "It is not I who hates and wants to hurt this fellow; it is he who hates and wants to hurt me. Hence I have to defend myself" (Menninger, Mayman, & Pruyser, 1963, p. 224).

Introjection and Identification

As the boy identifies with his father and the girl with her mother, they begin to **introject** (assimilate) values and beliefs that they did not formerly possess. These processes can also serve the ego as defenses against conflict and anxiety. For example, to handle its own frustrated needs and goals, the ego may identify with other individuals who have been highly successful in achieving their goals. Thus, the ego may ascribe to itself (introject) their values and beliefs.

The ego may also defend itself by **identifying** with something it actually dreads, a defense that Anna Freud (1946) called identification with the aggressor. Psychoanalyst Bruno Bettelheim (1943) noted an especially grim example in writing about his experiences in the Nazi concentration camps of Dachau and Buchenwald. Some of the older prisoners of the camp managed to survive by gradually changing their personalities so as to accept as their own some of the values of the Gestapo, even glorying in obtaining pieces of Gestapo uniforms.

Isolation

The ego separates an idea, motive, or act of behavior from its emotional component with the process of **isolation**. For example, if the ego violates the superego by engaging in forbidden sexual activities or entertains ideas of doing so, it may defend itself by repressing the emotional aspect of the situation and concentrating only on the intellectual content. This isolation permits the ego to tolerate the memory of the forbidden act or continue to engage in it. Thus, inventing excuses for the forbidden thoughts and behavior, as in rationalization, is not necessary. The process of isolation can be seen in the following revelations of a prostitute describing her descent from a high-priced call girl to an ordinary streetwalker.

> At the beginning I was very excited. But in order to continue I had to turn myself off. I had to dissociate who I was from what I was doing. It's a process of numbing yourself. . . . When I turned myself off, I was numb—emotionally, sexually numb. . . . As a call girl, I pretended to enjoy it sexually. You have to act as if you had an orgasm. As a streetwalker, I didn't. I used to lie there with my hands behind my back and do mathematic equations in my head or memorize the keyboard typewriter. . . . Here's all these guys slobbering over you all night long. . . . I'm lying there, doing math or conjugations of Spanish poetry in my head. (Laughs.) (Terkel, 1974, pp. 60, 62, 65).

As this frank and insightful narrative shows, for a time isolation as a defense mechanism may be adaptive, enabling one to endure an otherwise intolerable situation. However, its continual use may lead to more desperate patterns of behavior. In the case of the prostitute, drugs eventually became a more numbing defense.

Neo-Freudian Psychoanalysis

The term *neo-Freudian* has been applied rather broadly to various psychoanalysts who retained many of Freud's basic concepts but who also developed certain corrective measures. In a sense, the growth of ego psychology within traditional psychoanalysis and its focus on the autonomy of the ego is a kind of neo-Freudian movement. However, we have reserved the term *neo-Freudian psychoanalysis* for psychoanalysts who not only emphasize the ego more than biological drives but who also focus more than ego psychologists on the influence of the social and cultural environment in determining both normal and abnormal behavior. (See Chapter 19 for neo-Freudian therapy.)

Among the pioneers in the neo-Freudian movement were Erich Fromm (1947, 1955), Karen Horney (1937, 1939, 1945, 1946, 1967, 1970), and Harry Stack Sullivan (1953a, 1953b). More recently, Heinz Kohut (1971, 1977), of the Chicago Institute of Psychoanalysis, has emerged as a creative and influential neo-Freudian. Although the neo-Freudians do not deny the importance of understanding the biological roots of motivation, they point to the necessity for considering nonbiological factors as well. They argue that the ego's defense system is not only a way of responding to biological drives but also a way of dealing with the frustrations, conflicts, and anxieties that grow out of social and cultural expectations as to how such drives are to be expressed.

Like classical psychoanalysts, neo-Freudians focus on the nature of neurotic disorders and ways of overcoming them rather than on psychotic disturbances. They also subscribe to basic concepts of the unconscious and defense mechanisms. They depart from classical theory in their emphasis on interpersonal relationships, the nature of the society in which an individual lives, and the ways that society contributes to the frustration of our needs and the development of anxiety. Neo-Freudians emphasize that ego defenses arise out of the failure to satisfy certain social needs and achieve positive interpersonal relations. This failure is often more dominant in producing mental disorders than are the frustrated demands of biological urges. Partly as a result of their attention to the social aspects of psychopathology, neo-Freudians emphasize current happenings in a person's life. They do not, however, ignore the importance of an individual's past history. Thus, their thought is an extension of Freudian theory rather than a transformation. Freud himself pointed to the importance of external reality as one of the forces the ego must struggle with in handling conflict and anxiety. Neo-Freudians argue that he did not sufficiently consider how different kinds of social and cultural realities can influence this struggle.

Defectors from the Freudian Circle

Although ego psychologists and neo-Freudians modified many of Freud's ideas, they still considered themselves to be psychoanalysts. In contrast, a number of psychotherapists who at one time were part of Freud's inner circle eventually broke with him personally as well as professionally, founding their own systems of psychodynamic thought and practice. Among them were Carl Gustav Jung (1875–1961) and Alfred Adler (1870–1937). Mental health professionals as well as popular writers on the subject of abnormal psychology and psychiatry often refer to them as psychoanalysts. They themselves, however, regarded their views as a rejection of the psychoanalytic movement founded by Freud, and so distinct from it that they felt impelled to coin new terms for their approaches. Jung called his system **analytical psychology**, and Adler named his **individual psychology**.

Many of Jung's concepts of psychopathology involve his theory of the **collective unconscious**, which contains the ancestral roots of an individual's culture — that is, the original patterns or models of cultural ideas and beliefs. According to Jung, the symptoms of psychopathology, and especially of neurotic anxiety, represent clues as to what is missing in the troubled person's life — that is, an alienation from the collective unconscious. For individuals to gain true understanding of their psychological problems, they must get in touch with the collective unconscious through special methods of psychotherapy (Jung, 1928/1953; 1936/1959).

Adler's theory of the unconscious and its role in psychopathology is tied to his concepts of overcompensation and inferiority. According to Adler, neurotic individuals tend to be overwhelmed with feelings of helplessness and inferiority. To avoid facing those feelings, they relegate them to the unconscious and overcompensate by striving for unrealistic goals. Thus, the unconscious becomes a vehicle for avoiding one's responsibility to face one's problems and shortcomings. Adlerian therapy aims to uncover those devices and enable the individual to assume a more realistic approach to life (Adler, 1964; Ellenberger, 1970).

In certain respects, advocates of women's rights have found Adler's approach to understanding abnormality more acceptable than Freud's. As we pointed out earlier in the chapter, Freud argued that women feel inferior because they envy men their possession of a penis. Adler, on the other hand, concluded that women may well feel inferior, but they have such a feeling because of our culture, which historically has undervalued them (Mosak, 1984). Although Adler coined the term *masculine protest* in describing how some women protest against their social role, he assigned the blame not to biology but to culture. As the following assertion shows, he departed strongly from Freud in a direction more consistent with modern knowledge and changing times: "This attitude on the part of the woman, of protest against her social role[,] . . . springs from a sexual role which has already been regarded in the family as subordinate. But it is essentially encouraged by our imperfect civilization, which strives both secretly and openly to assign an inferior position to women" (Adler, 1964, p. 64).

In Chapter 19, where we deal with psychodynamic approaches to psychotherapy, we elaborate on Jungian and Adlerian concepts of psychopathology and their application to helping people solve their problems of maladaptive behavior and thinking.

Summary

1. Biomedical explanations of mental disorders, which trace their origin to the writings of Hippocrates, emphasize that ultimately the causes can be found in disturbed bodily functions, including abnormal processes in the brain and nervous system. However, biomedical views also take account of other factors, such as psychosocial stress and adverse social conditions, in the contribution to mental disorders.

2. In recent years, advances in neuroscience have bolstered biomedical views of mental disorders. Neuroscience is a field of study that integrates knowledge concerning the structures and functions of the brain and nervous system and their relationship to behavior and experience.

3. Traditional biomedical concepts of mental disorder parallel concepts of physical disease. Thus, mental disorders are regarded as forms of psychopathology or mental illness, and descriptions of mental disorders use such concepts as symptoms, syndromes, and diagnosis.

4. Three traditional types of physical pathology underscore the parallels between biomedical views of physical disease and mental disorder: infectious disease, systemic disease, and noninfectious trauma. For example, certain forms of psychopathology may stem from such infectious diseases as syphilis and encephalitis. The systemic approach to understanding abnormal behavior and experience has been applied in studies of the brain and nervous system and of genetic influences, especially as they are involved in schizophrenia and major depression. The concept of trauma, originally referring to physical damage, has been applied to psychological effects, such as the personal distress resulting from rape.

5. Modern biomedical research on the etiology of mental disorders emphasizes the interaction between internal organic abnormality and psychosocial factors. For example, behavior–genetic analysis rejects the idea that genetic factors inevitably lead to fixed patterns of behavior, arguing that environmental influences and psychological states can modify the expression of genetic possibilities. This view is expressed in the concept of diathesis–stress. *Diathesis* is the biological predisposition for acquiring a disorder; *stress* refers to events and conditions in the environment as well as inner feelings and attitudes that can contribute more immediately to the onset of a disorder.

6. A concept similar to diathesis–stress is *pathogenesis*. This integrated biomedical view holds that the brain and nervous system must be malfunctioning in all forms of psychopathology; however, psychosocial conditions can be important contributors to this malfunctioning. Thus, psychotherapy and changes in the physical and social environment can be helpful even in situations where the source of the disorder can be traced to organic disabilities, such as traumatic injuries and infectious disease.

7. The influence of biomedical viewpoints on the work of mental health professionals is not confined to those whose background is in medicine but extends to others, such as clinical psychologists and social workers. In addition, biomedical concepts are reflected in the popular media and in the many messages that voluntary mental health agencies aim toward the general public.

8. Psychodynamic approaches to understanding abnormality focus on unconscious motives and conflicts. The basic foundation of these approaches is the theory and practice of psychoanalysis. Psychoanalytic thought and practice have developed in a variety of directions. However, they can all be traced to the founder of psychoanalysis, Sigmund Freud.

9. Like biomedical viewpoints, psychoanalysis assumes that abnormal behavior and experience can ultimately be traced to disturbed internal processes. However, these disturbed conditions are intrapsychic — occurring within the mind. Thus, psychoanalysis is a psychodynamic approach because it deals with internal forces of the mind, such as unconscious and conflicting motives.

10. Freudian (orthodox) psychoanalysis emphasizes three central aspects of intrapsychic events: the motivation of behavior, conflict in motives and desires, and anxiety. The concept of motivation focuses on the unconscious, the repository of motives and memories that the individual does not want to face openly. Instead, they are repressed — buried in the unconscious. Conflict and anxiety stem mainly from the inborn drives of sex and aggression. The inability to handle conflict and anxiety is expressed in symptoms of psychopathology.

11. In explaining how an inadequate ego comes about, Freud constructed an elaborate theory of psychosexual development. Failure to progress adequately through the various phases of this development results in a weak ego and psychopathology. In

the oral–dependent phase, which begins soon after birth, the baby obtains not only nutritional satisfaction from feeding but sexual pleasure as well. During the anal–sadistic phase (ages 1 to 3), the child experiences a rudimentary form of sexual satisfaction through anal functions and develops an aggressive (sadistic) desire to control parents by holding on or letting go during toilet training. The phallic phase (ages 3 to 6) is dominated by the Oedipus complex for the boy and the Electra complex for the girl. The boy develops a sexual attraction to his mother and in doing so competes with the father. This competition leads to an identification with the father. Similarly, the girl is sexually attracted to the father, competes with the mother, and thus identifies with her.

12. During the phallic phase, the boy experiences the castration complex: threats from the mother and father that he will lose his penis if he continues his sexual overtures toward the mother. This threat forces him into the latency phase, a period of sexual quiet. In contrast, the girl suffers from penis envy, desiring to possess that organ. She gives up that desire, identifying with her mother and her feminine qualities and accepting her lack of a penis.

13. With the genital phase (adolescence and adulthood) the boy and girl enter sexual maturity. How well they fare depends on how satisfactorily they proceeded through the previous phases of psychosexual development.

14. A number of criticisms have been directed toward Freud's concepts and theories. They include his overemphasis on sex and aggression as biologically determined drives, the concept of penis envy and thus the "inferiority" of women, the fact that his data were based mainly on the memories of adults but were generalized to children, and weaknesses in methodology.

15. Various empirical studies have tested Freud's concepts and theories indirectly. Results of some were highly negative, but others found support for such theories as the Oedipus complex and castration anxiety, provided they are interpreted not only sexually but as a problem of power. In addition, the theory of unconscious motivation and related unconscious perceptions has been tested through laboratory experiments but their findings are contradictory.

16. Freud's lasting contributions to modern psychology include the principles of determinism, unconscious motivation, identification, and the continuity of development.

17. Ego psychology is a clarification and extension of orthodox Freudian psychoanalysis rather than a radical departure from it. Among its developers were Anna Freud, Heinz Hartmann, David Rapaport, and Erik Erikson. They emphasized that the ego is autonomous and develops independently, rather than emerging from the id as Freud stated. Ego psychology extended in great detail Freud's concepts of defense mechanisms—how the ego defends itself against anxiety and conflict.

18. Neo-Freudian psychoanalysts retained many of Freud's basic concepts, such as unconscious motivation and intrapsychic conflict, but developed certain corrective measures. In particular, neo-Freudians place less emphasis on biological drives and focus more on cultural and social determinants of conflicts, frustration, and mental disorders. Among the pioneers in the neo-Freudian movement were Erich Fromm, Karen Horney, and Harry Stack Sullivan. More recently, Heinz Kohut has been an influential neo-Freudian.

19. Several of Freud's inner circle went well beyond modification and founded new movements that rejected much of his approach. Prominent among those defectors were Carl Gustav Jung and Alfred Adler. Jung called his system *analytical* *psychology*, and Adler named his *individual psychology*. Jung believed that psychopathology resulted from the individual's alienation from the collective unconscious —the ancestral roots of the person's cultural background. Adler focused on the role of unconscious feelings of inferiority and the tendency to overcompensate for those feelings.

4

Social Learning, Cultural, and Humanistic Viewpoints

To be fond of learning is to be near to knowledge.

TZE-SZE
The Doctrine of the Mean (5th century B.C.)

Culture is not a biologically transmitted complex.

RUTH BENEDICT
Patterns of Culture (1934)

No problem of human destiny is beyond human beings.

JOHN F. KENNEDY
Address at American University (1963)

In recent years mental health researchers and practitioners have turned increasingly to principles of learning as a way of understanding abnormal behavior and experience. They have been greatly influenced by the work of sociologists and anthropologists who emphasize that abnormality is a departure from the rules and customs of a particular society or culture. We begin this chapter, therefore, by examining how principles of learning can help explain patterns of abnormality and how they can be used to help people overcome maladaptive ways of living. We also consider how social and cultural influences interact with learning to help shape psychological disorders. We examine the concept of social deviance to see how it is used to stigmatize the mentally ill and the effects of social prejudice and discrimination on the development and expression of abnormality. We then turn to a cross-cultural analysis of psychopathology, focusing on such questions as: How do patterns of abnormality vary from one culture to another? Are there certain concepts of abnormality that different societies and cultures have in common? What are the limits to the social and cultural influences that help shape patterns of abnormality? Finally, we discuss humanistic concepts of abnormal behavior and experience. This approach emphasizes how we can become alienated from our potentialities for psychological growth and positive mental health. The philosophy of existentialism has greatly influenced humanistic viewpoints, especially its insistence that we are free to make choices about the direction of our lives.

Classical Conditioning

Long before the modern era of laboratory experiments on learning, certain literary figures were clearly aware of a learning process now called **classical conditioning.** Consider, for example, the following translation of a story from Lope de Vega's play *El Capellan* (*The Chaplain of the Virgin*), written about 1615.

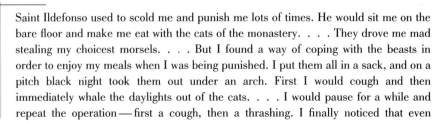

Saint Ildefonso used to scold me and punish me lots of times. He would sit me on the bare floor and make me eat with the cats of the monastery. . . . They drove me mad stealing my choicest morsels. . . . But I found a way of coping with the beasts in order to enjoy my meals when I was being punished. I put them all in a sack, and on a pitch black night took them out under an arch. First I would cough and then immediately whale the daylights out of the cats. . . . I would pause for a while and repeat the operation—first a cough, then a thrashing. I finally noticed that even

> without beating them, the beasts moaned and yelped like the very devil whenever I coughed. I then let them loose. Thereafter, . . . [i]f an animal approached my food, all I had to do was to cough, and how that cat did scat! (Bousfield, 1955, p. 828)

Although far from being a scientific experiment, this story illustrates an important principle of learning that centuries later was demonstrated more precisely in the laboratory. It states that fear can become attached to a formerly neutral stimulus by the association of that stimulus with a painful experience.

The Pavlovian Paradigm

Historical Background

Classical conditioning was first demonstrated experimentally by the Russian physiologist Ivan Petrovich Pavlov (1849–1936). Pavlov carried out extensive investigations on the digestive and nervous systems, for which he was awarded the Nobel prize in 1904. After many years of experiments on the nature of conditioning as a learning process, Pavlov described the results in what have now become classics in the history of research on learning: *Conditioned Reflexes* (1927) and *Lectures on Conditioned Reflexes* (1928). The term *conditioned reflex* is a translation from the Russian. Some learning theorists have pointed out that a better rendering would have been *conditional reflex*, since it occurs only under special conditions (Hilgard & Bower, 1966). *Conditioned* has become the common usage, but *reflex* has been broadened to *response*, since Pavlovian conditioning can produce behavior that is more complex than a single, isolated reflex. Thus, the consequence of Pavlovian (classical) conditioning is now called a **conditioned response.**

Pavlov was 75 years old by the time he completed his two books on conditioning. Nevertheless, he expanded his work to the study of psychiatry, spending the rest of his life observing patients in mental hospitals. His aim was to discover how the principles of conditioning that he had demonstrated in the laboratory with dogs could be used to understand the abnormal behavior he observed in hospitals.

Pavlov's Pioneering Experiments

Classical conditioned was first demonstrated in the laboratory by the Russian physiologist Ivan Petrovich Pavlov, whose work on the digestive system won him a Nobel prize.

Pavlov became attracted to the idea of a conditioned reflex when he noticed in his experiments that a dog salivated not only as a reaction to food in its mouth but also at the sight or smell of food or the food dish or even at hearing the footsteps of the laboratory assistant who brought the food. These latter reactions were not biologically determined — that is, the food had not stimulated the salivary glands directly. Pavlov became curious about the nature of the phenomenon that activated salivation in this indirect manner. At first he called the dog's reaction *psychic secretions*, to distinguish them from the secretions that occurred when food was placed directly in the dog's mouth. Later he called them *conditioned reflexes*, to indicate that some form of learning had taken place under special conditions. This discovery led Pavlov to his many years of systematic investigation on the conditioned reflex.

In his most famous series of experiments, Pavlov sounded a bell and gave a dog meat powder shortly thereafter. The two stimuli were then paired repeatedly, and eventually the sound of the bell alone was sufficient to elicit salivation. Figure 4.1 shows the laboratory arrangement that Pavlov used. The conditioned response of salivation was not identical with the original response to food. For example, the salivation was often less obvious. In general, this kind of relationship between an original response and a conditioned one is characteristic of classical conditioning.

Pavlov demonstrated that a conditioned response gradually diminishes if the conditioned stimulus is repeated alone. This process is called **extinction.** However, by

Figure 4.1
Pavlov's laboratory arrangement
for studying the conditioned
response of salivation. (From
Yerkes & Morgulis, 1909, p.
280.)

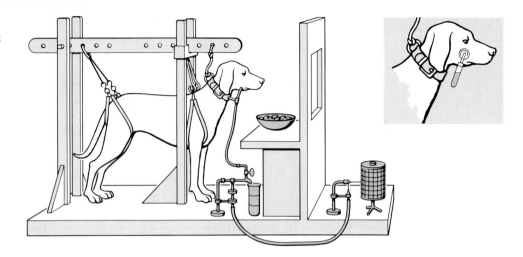

occasionally pairing again the **unconditioned stimulus** (food) with the **conditioned stimulus** (bell), Pavlov found that the conditioned response could be reestablished. Conditioned responses in everyday life are not rapidly extinguished, because the occasional pairing of the unconditioned and the conditioned stimulus helps maintain the response.

Pavlov also found that simply pairing two stimuli did not automatically ensure that conditioning would occur. Disturbances in the environment of the laboratory and the dog's internal motivational state interfered with the conditioning process. If the dog had been well fed before the conditioning procedures began, they were much less effective than when it was hungry.

Conditioned Emotional Responses

Pavlov's Work

Pavlov was able to produce what he called pathological conditioning in dogs. First he trained a dog to associate food with a luminous circle. Then he conditioned it to differentiate between the circle and a luminous ellipse by pairing food with the circle but not with the ellipse. His next step was gradually to make the ellipse look more like the circle. Eventually the dog reached a point where it was no longer able to differentiate, and it began to show signs of conflict: "The whole behaviour of the animal underwent an abrupt change. The hitherto quiet dog began to squeal on its stand, kept wriggling . . . and bit through the tubes connecting the animal's room with the observer, a behaviour which had never happened before. On being taken [again] into the experimental room the dog barked violently, which was also contrary to its usual custom; in short it presented all the symptoms of a condition of acute neurosis" (Pavlov, 1927, p. 291). Although it is a simplification to trace neurotic disorders only to the kind of conditioning produced in the dog, Pavlov's experiment does suggest at least one way in which unresolved emotional conflict can initiate maladaptive behavior.

Watson – Rayner Study of Little Albert

Since Pavlov's classic work, other experiments have used a variety of stimuli to demonstrate how emotional responses can be conditioned. One of the earliest studies was carried

John B. Watson, an American psychologist and founder of the behaviorist movement in psychology. Building on the work of Pavlov, Watson demonstrated that classical conditioning can play an important part in acquiring fear.

out more than 65 years ago by John B. Watson (1913), founder of the behaviorist movement in psychology, and his colleague Rosalie Rayner. The central figure in the experiment was an 11-month-old boy named Albert, now immortalized in the research literature as little Albert.

Watson and Rayner knew prior to the experiment that Albert would react with signs of fear to sudden loud noises. However, he definitely was not afraid of a tame white rat; indeed, he enjoyed playing with it. The experimental procedure went like this: First the experimenters gave the rat to Albert; then they made a loud noise by striking a steel bar with a hammer. After seven representations of this joint stimulation, as Watson and Rayner described it, they showed the rat alone to Albert and noted the following reactions: "The instant the rat was shown the baby began to cry. Almost instantly he turned sharply to the left, fell over on his left side, raised himself on all fours and began to crawl away so rapidly that he was caught with difficulty before reaching the edge of the table" (Watson & Rayner, 1920, p. 5). Watson and Rayner concluded that the experiment was "as convincing a case of a completely conditioned fear response as could have been theoretically pictured" (p. 5).

The experiments were also able to produce a phenomenon that Pavlov had previously demonstrated, **generalization** of a conditioned response. Pavlov had shown that after a conditioned response to a particular musical tone had been established, variations in the pitch would also elicit that response. As a rule, the closer the similarity between the original conditioned stimulus and the later stimuli, the more likely that generalization would occur. Watson and Rayner reported that 5 days after little Albert had been conditioned to fear the white rat he also showed strong fear reactions when presented with a rabbit, dog, and sealskin coat. Other stimuli that resembled the rat less closely, such as cotton, a bearded Santa Claus mask, and Watson's hair, evoked some fear but not as much as the rat. After 31 days had elapsed, the generalization effect had weakened but was still present. Although Albert began to touch the coat and the rabbit, he showed evidence of conflict in doing so (Watson & Rayner, 1920, p. 10). At this point the experiment ended.

For many years, various psychologists cited Watson and Rayner's experiment with Albert as a pioneering model for explaining how phobias are acquired. **Phobias** are irrational fears that persist in spite of objective evidence that the feared situation is not harmful (see Chapter 5). Recently, however, Ben Harris (1979) has cast serious doubt on whether the study actually did demonstrate that classical conditioning in itself can account for the development of a phobic disorder. Harris pointed out that although Albert still showed some signs of fear a month after the conditioning procedures had ended, the fear lacked the strength usually associated with a true phobia. Furthermore, Harris observed, a phobia not only involves an irrational fear of a situation but also persistent attempts to avoid it. He concluded that the Watson–Rayner experiment did not provide clear-cut evidence that little Albert had indeed learned such avoidance behavior, and had thus developed a phobia.

Although Watson and Rayner's experiment did not show that classical conditioning alone produces phobic disorders, it did suggest that such conditioning can play a partial role. The conditioning may be a crucial initial stage; however, persistence of the fear — an important characteristic of phobic disorders — depends on other forms of learning. For example, the person learns that by actively avoiding a situation, the anxiety it produces can also be avoided. It is the avoidance behavior that especially contributes to the difficulties in everyday living that are usually associated with a firmly established phobic disorder. Later in the chapter we discuss how such avoidance behavior is acquired and maintained.

**Conditioned
Emotional Responses
in Everyday Life**

Many psychologists assume that the development of emotionally conditioned responses in everyday life is based on the same principles that govern experimental procedures in the laboratory. Obviously, in the everyday environment the pairing of stimuli is more subject to chance. Thus, it is frequently much more difficult — indeed, at times impossible — to discover the stimuli that are involved in producing the conditioned emotional responses one acquires throughout life.

Operant Conditioning

Principles of operant conditioning have been extensively demonstrated in the laboratory by B. F. Skinner, professor emeritus at Harvard University. Skinner's work was influenced by the earlier experiments of Thorndike.

Classical conditioning does not produce a new kind of behavior. Prior to conditioning, Pavlov's dogs could already salivate when presented with food. As a result of the conditioning procedures, they responded in a similar manner to a stimulus that had not previously elicited salivation — the sound of a bell. Little Albert's fear responses were also in his repertoire of behavior prior to conditioning. Thus, one can think of classical conditioning as an old response to a new stimulus situation. We now examine **operant conditioning**, which does produce new behavior.

Principles of operant conditioning have been studied most extensively by B. F. Skinner (1904–   ), professor emeritus of psychology at Harvard University. Skinner's work was greatly influenced by the earlier experiments of Edward Lee Thorndike (1874–1949), professor of educational psychology at Teachers College, Columbia University. Thorndike was a pioneer in demonstrating experimentally that rewards strengthen learning (Thorndike, 1898, 1935). Skinner himself prefers the term *reinforcer* rather than *reward*. A reinforcer is an environmental stimulus or situation that the learner operates on and that makes it more likely that the behavior (operation) will be repeated. The role of reinforcers in learning is central to Skinner's theory of operant conditioning.

Skinner's concepts and principles of operant conditioning originated in his laboratory studies of animal learning (1938/1966). Since then he has expanded and applied them to human learning, to the technology of teaching, to problems of social and cultural change, to abnormal behavior, and to methods of psychotherapy (Skinner, 1953, 1968, 1974, 1975). To understand these principles and their practical applications, it is important to consider Skinner's philosophy of behaviorism.

Methodological versus Radical Behaviorism

Earlier behaviorists, such as Watson, insisted that private experiences could not be the concern of the psychologist because they were unobservable. For example, we cannot measure sensations and perceptions as such; we can measure only a person's ability to distinguish one sensation or perception from another by directly observing that person's overt behavior. Watson rejected learning about people's experiences through self-report —that is, through their descriptions of thoughts and other introspections (Kessen & Cahan, 1986).

Skinner differentiates between the position of **methodological behaviorism,** which rejects the study of private events, and his own position of **radical behaviorism** (Skinner, 1987, pp. 781–782). He accepts the usefulness of studying psychological events that take place "in the private world within the skin," provided they can be "translated into behavior" (Skinner, 1974, pp. 16–17). Furthermore, he argues that in avoiding the problems that go with trying to study "mental, private events," methodological behaviorism ignores much important evidence: "What about the power of mind over matter   in   psychosomatic   medicine? . . . What   about . . . intrapsychic   processes . . . in which feelings produce or suppress other feelings and memories evoke or mask other memories? What about the cognitive processes said to explain perception, thinking, the construction of sentences, and artistic creation? Must all this be ignored because it cannot be studied objectively?" (1974, pp. 15–16). Skinner answers his questions with his view of radical behaviorism: "Radical behaviorism . . . does not deny the possibility of self-observation . . . or its possible usefulness. . . . It . . . can therefore consider events taking place in the private world within the skin. . . . It simply questions the nature of the object observed and the reliability of the observation" (Skinner, 1974, pp. 16–17).

More recently, Skinner has insisted even more strongly on the true role of psychology as a science: the experimental analysis of behavior that is directly observable. He argues that cognitive and humanistic psychology, as well as many forms of psychotherapy, are obstacles to this role, since they deal with the mind and other internal, nonobservable events, without always translating them into what can be observed directly (Skinner, 1987). Although many psychologists, including some who consider themselves to be behaviorists, would not agree with Skinner's position, the principles of learning that have developed from his experimental analysis of behavior remain highly influential. This is especially true of *operant conditioning*.

Principles and Applications of Operant Conditioning

Respondent versus Operant Behavior

Skinner distinguishes between two kinds of behavior: respondent and operant. **Respondent behavior** is involuntary, elicited directly by a stimulus, as when food in the mouth causes salivation. *Respondent conditioning* is Skinner's term for classical conditioning. As we have pointed out, this kind of learning does not produce new behavior; instead an old response is transferred to a new stimulus situation.

Operant behavior is voluntary and spontaneous. In Skinner's words, it is *emitted behavior*. It is called operant behavior because it operates on the environment to produce changes that may lead to new patterns of behavior — for example, verbal and motor skills. This process of learning is called operant conditioning. Some psychologists call it instrumental conditioning or instrumental learning, because what the learner does is instrumental in changing the environment. In turn, changes in the environment help produce changes in behavior — that is, they influence learning.

Reinforcement and Punishment

Initially, operant behavior may be random, not focused consistently on specific environmental stimuli. However, if the consequences of an operant act are favorable — that is, if it results in reaching a goal or reducing tension — then the behavior is more likely to be emitted again. Further association of the behavior with such consequences tends to increase that likelihood. The environmental stimuli that the learner operates on and that increase the probability that the behavior will be repeated are called *reinforcers*. Their occurrence during operant behavior is called **reinforcement,** defined as any event whose occurrence after a response increases the probability of that response.

Skinner also distinguishes between positive and negative reinforcers, a practice now common in analyzing the functional relationship of reinforcement to operant behavior and learning. A **positive reinforcer** strengthens the behavior that produces it. For example, a glass of water is a positive reinforcer when we are thirsty. If we drink the water, the probability increases that we will do so again on similar occasions. In contrast, a **negative reinforcer** strengthens the behavior that reduces or terminates it. For instance, if we take off a shoe that is too tight, terminating the painful pressure on our foot is negatively reinforcing. Thus, we are more likely to repeat that behavior when the shoe pinches again (Skinner, 1974, p. 46).

Many psychologists, even those who in general agree with Skinner's concepts of learning, continue to use the term *reward* as a synonym for a positive reinforcer. However, Skinner regards the term as less precise and objective than *positive reinforcer.*

Skinner also emphasizes the difference between his concept of punishment and negative reinforcement. The purpose of **punishment** is to remove behavior; negative reinforcement is designed to generate or strengthen behavior. Thus, in Skinner's view, punishment is the reverse of reinforcement (Skinner, 1974, p. 62). Skinner has consistently opposed the use of punishment in teaching desirable behavior. He maintains that although it may work immediately, it does not produce long-term positive results (Goleman, 1987).

Shaping and Discriminative Stimuli

An experimenter, teacher, parent, or therapist can **shape** operant behavior by positively reinforcing a response when it first resembles the desired behavior and continuing to do so as the behavior comes closer to the goal.

Some environmental stimuli act as signals to indicate when and where operant behavior is likely to be reinforced. These are called **discriminative stimuli.** Their influence on operant learning begins early in life. For example, small children quickly discover that to obtain **primary reinforcers** from their parents, such as food, water, and bodily comfort, they must first get their parents' attention. This attention may involve a smile, nod, or other sign of positive recognition. As children succeed in gaining primary reinforcement in the presence of attention-giving signals, the signals become discriminative stimuli, indicating the time and place when primary reinforcement is most likely to occur. These discriminative stimuli then serve as **learned reinforcers,** promoting further kinds of operant behavior. Before long, the child seeks nods and smiles for their own reinforcing

By repeatedly smiling at her baby, the mother *reinforces* (strengthens) the baby's smiling behavior. Positive reinforcement is a central principle of operant conditioning.

value, independent of primary reinforcement. Thus, parental attention gradually becomes a **generalized reinforcer** for the child, helping to develop and maintain a wide variety of operant behaviors.

Discriminative stimuli and learned reinforcers are important controllers of operant behavior and learning. Since the social and physical environment contains so many stimuli, people must be taught which ones serve best for obtaining reinforcement. Some people may behave abnormally (maladaptively) because they have not learned which discriminative stimuli can serve as clues for reinforcing adaptive behavior. An important function of psychotherapy, and especially behavior therapy, is to help people learn how to seek reinforcement in an appropriate manner (see Chapter 20).

Intermittent Reinforcement

Once an act of operant behavior has been established, it may become extinguished if reinforcement stops. However, reinforcement need not be continual for the behavior to persist, especially if the behavior has been learned on an intermittent schedule — that is, reinforced only occasionally. The principle of **intermittent reinforcement** (also called partial reinforcement) can help explain why certain kinds of behavior may persist even though reinforcement has become very infrequent. Consider the case of pathological gambling, a chronic pattern of maladaptive behavior that DSM-III-R classifies as a disorder of impulse control (see Chapter 12). Pathological gamblers may regularly lose large amounts of money, but they continue to gamble because their behavior is positively reinforced once in a while. The desire to keep on gambling is especially likely to continue if significant amounts of money were won early in the development of the behavior pattern. Then, even though drastic losses begin to appear with regularity, only an occasional reinforcement (winning) is necessary for the gambling (and losing) behavior to be maintained. Even if the chronic gambler has not had much personal experience with winning, seeing or hearing about other people winning can also be reinforcing. In human learning, simply observing the reinforcing experiences of others often becomes an effec-

Positive reinforcement need not be continuous to encourage behavior. Gamblers may regularly lose money but continue to gamble because they win once in a while. This reinforcement is called intermittent.

tive reinforcement of behavior. Other people, then, can serve as models of learning (Bandura, 1977). This is called **vicarious reinforcement.**

Models of Behavior and Vicarious Reinforcement

Albert Bandura, a former president of the American Psychological Association, has demonstrated experimentally that observing reinforcing experiences of other people helps the observer to behave similarly. This modeling is called *vicarious* reinforcement.

Bandura, Blanchard, and Ritter (1968) demonstrated the importance of learning through observation and vicarious reinforcement in a pioneering experiment. The subjects were volunteers who wanted to overcome their fear of snakes. They were tested before the treatment procedures began to determine their willingness to enter a room that contained a live, four-foot-long king snake, a nonpoisonous species. The highest scorers, those who were willing to handle the snake with a gloved hand, were eliminated, and the remaining subjects were divided into four groups, each receiving a different form of treatment.

1. The first group underwent **systematic desensitization,** a form of treatment that paired muscular relaxation with a graded series of imagined snakes. The subjects began by imagining mildly fearful situations and progressed to extremely frightening ones. The main principle at work is that relaxation is incompatible with fear. This therapeutic method can reduce the tendency to avoid feared situations and eventually eliminate the fear (see Chapter 20).

2. Symbolic modeling was used to treat the second group of subjects. They watched a film of people handling snakes; the scenes ranged from the handling of plastic snakes to those in which a live snake crawled over the demonstrator's body.

3. Live modeling with participation was the mode of treatment for the third group. The subjects observed a model handling a snake in various situations while showing no fear; gradually, the observers were led into handling the snake themselves.

4. The *fourth group* was a *control* group and received no treatment at all.

At the end of the experiment, all subjects were given the same test they had taken at the beginning. Figure 4.2 illustrates the results. The control group did not change, but all the other groups became more willing to approach and handle the snakes. The greatest increase was in the third group, which had been treated with live modeling with participa-

Figure 4.2

Observation of fearless models can reduce fear, as is shown by the mean number of approach responses made by subjects before and after receiving their respective treatments. (From Bandura, 1969, p. 186.)

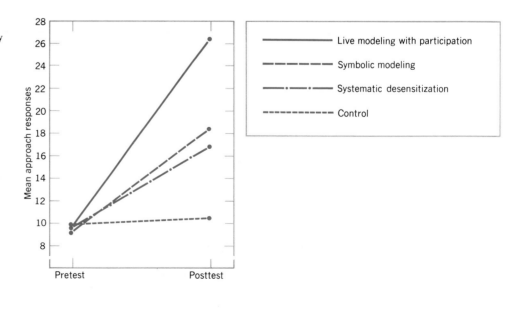

tion. The second group, which had only observed a film of people handling snakes (symbolic modeling), decreased its fear of snakes almost as much as the first group, which had undergone systematic desensitization. Thus, vicarious reinforcement was effective in reducing fears.

In a follow-up study, the experimenters found that 47 percent of the subjects had encountered snakes in one way or another since the first study. In each instance, the subjects stated that the reduction in fear they had achieved in treatment generalized to naturalistic situations. Some subjects were able to visit reptile exhibits and look at pictures of snakes. Others were able to participate in such recreational activities as picnicking, camping, hunting, and hiking without being afraid of encountering snakes. Formerly, they had avoided those kinds of activities (Bandura, 1969, pp. 188–189).

How Respondent and Operant Conditioning Work Together

Controlled Situations. So far we have described respondent (classical) conditioning and operant (instrumental) conditioning as if they were completely independent processes of learning. However, they usually work together, even in many highly controlled situations that focus directly on pairing stimuli in the classical manner. Consider, for example, the use of conditioning procedures for helping people overcome alcoholism. Repeatedly pairing the pleasurable taste of alcohol with an aversive stimulus eventually imparts a negative meaning to the pleasurable stimulus similar to that associated with the aversive stimulus. Some therapists have used electric shock and harsh drugs as the aversive stimuli, but that procedure has been criticized as inhumane (Lazarus, 1971). Furthermore, studies have shown that even though 50 to 60 percent of individuals who stayed with this harsh treatment were able to abstain from drinking, the dropout rate was extremely high. Other therapists have used less physically punishing stimuli, such as having the individual imagine an unpleasant scene (for example, vomiting) in association with the imagined act of drinking. Only about 40 percent of the individuals treated in this manner achieved complete abstinence; however, the dropout rate was considerably lower than for treatments using physically aversive stimuli (Miller & Hester, 1980).

Although the success of such treatments seems to be based solely on classical conditioning, operant behavior actually plays an important part (Kanfer & Phillips, 1970, pp. 96–99). When the individual carries out instructions to raise a glass of alcoholic beverage and take a sip (actual or imaginary), the aversive stimulus that follows (actual or imaginary) becomes associated with a complex of operant behaviors—tasting, smelling, seeing, and thinking about alcohol. Thus, the individual's behavior is instrumental in forging an association between alcohol and aversive stimuli.

Many other behavioral methods besides aversive conditioning have been used to help the problem drinker abstain or learn how to drink more moderately. Among these are teaching the individual various social skills that can be used as alternatives to drinking, using operant conditioning to reinforce abstinence or a significant reduction in drinking, and teaching various forms of self-control. The latter may include formal classroom instruction and the assignment of appropriate readings concerning problem drinking and how it can be handled (Miller, 1978; Miller & Hester, 1980). In addition, positive reinforcement plays a crucial role in the efforts of such organizations as Alcoholics Anonymous (AA). In Chapter 14 we discuss the AA program and its claim that for problem drinkers the goal must be abstinence rather than learning to drink more moderately.

Conditioning in Everyday Life. Although it is more difficult to detect the intertwining of respondent and operant conditioning in family life, their interdependence goes on. For example, children may learn to become proficient readers by listening to instructions, watching models, practicing, and being reinforced positively for all these acts of operant behavior. But in carrying them out, the consequences of their behavior may also become associated, in a respondent manner, with the sight and thought of books, libraries, magazines, and similar kinds of stimuli. Thus, not only do the children learn through operant conditioning to be literate, but they also learn, through respondent (classical) conditioning, to feel good merely upon contact with the symbols and institutions of that literacy.

Conversely, some children may encounter mostly punishment in learning to read. For example, they may experience aversive stimuli or have positive reinforcers withdrawn when they fail to read properly. Under those circumstances they not only may fail to read properly but may also associate the mere sight of books and libraries with strong feelings of aversion.

The principle that respondent and operant conditioning are interdependent can also explain how certain forms of maladaptive behavior, such as irrational anxieties and fears, may have their source in respondent conditioning but be maintained through operant conditioning. For example, an initial fear of speaking in public can be classically conditioned through the association of a classroom recitation with some highly frightening experience. Later, even though the original aversive stimulus is no longer present, the fear may be maintained because the individual has learned through operant behavior to avoid situations in which the fear may arise. Thus, there is no opportunity for the fear to be extinguished. In Chapter 20 we explain in detail how classical conditioning, operant conditioning, and modeling can be used to help individuals reduce or eliminate their maladaptive anxieties and fears.

Cognitive Psychology and Learning

Cognition and Conditioning

As we pointed out earlier in the chapter, Pavlov noticed that when his dogs were satiated with food it became more difficult to condition them if food was the unconditioned stimulus. Nevertheless, he and other early experimenters who adopted his method continued to concentrate on external stimuli, with little regard for the influence of internal motivational states. As the behaviorist movement in the psychology of learning developed, internal cognitive processes, such as thinking, were considered irrelevant for understanding conditioned responses. It is true that in his view of radical behaviorism, B. F. Skinner (1974) departed from tradition in his statement that internal, private events should not be dismissed in studying learning as long as they could be tied to observable behavior. Nevertheless, Skinner has not been concerned with cognition in his experimental work on respondent and operant conditioning.

As a way of comparing traditional behaviorist views of conditioning with a cognitive approach, consider Pavlov's demonstration of the conditioned response of salivation. Traditional behaviorism regarded the conditioned response (CR) simply as the result of **contiguity** — the close association in time of the conditioned stimulus and the neutral, unconditioned stimulus (UCS). Although a congitive interpretation does not ignore the importance of contiguity, it emphasizes that the conditioned stimulus (CS — the bell) acts as a signal to the dog that the unconditioned stimulus (food) is forthcoming. The conditioned stimulus takes on the meaning of the unconditioned stimulus. The conditioned response, therefore, is an anticipatory response — an expectation. Thus, conditioning involves a cognitive process, not merely a mechanical connection of two stimuli (Rescorla,

1988, p. 153). As Albert Bandura, (1974) has put it in a discussion of human conditioning:

> Contrary to popular belief, the fabled reflexive conditioning in humans is largely a myth. *Conditioning* is simply a descriptive term for learning through paired experiences, not an explanation of how the changes come about. Originally, conditioning was assumed to occur automatically. On closer examination it turned out to be cognitively mediated. People do not learn despite repetitive paired experiences unless they recognize that events are correlated. . . . The critical factor . . . is not that events occur in time, but that people learn to predict them and to summon up appropriate anticipatory reactions. (p. 859)

Bandura's remarks concerning the importance of correlated events and anticipatory reactions apply not only to classical conditioning but to operant conditioning (instrumental learning) as well. Reinforcers in the environment do not facilitate learning simply because they are there; rather, the learner must anticipate that manipulating the reinforcers will help reach a goal. This anticipation is a cognitive process. As learning becomes more complex and goals more difficult to reach, the importance of cognition increases. Reasoning, problem solving, the sudden attainment of insight — all may be involved. **Cognition,** then, is the processing of information: acquiring, storing, and applying knowledge. Cognitive psychologists are concerned with how individuals select, code, and use such information (Baars, 1986; Glass & Holyoak, 1986; "Special Issue," 1980; Wood, 1983).

Cognition and Introspection

Cognition is an internal, covert process. Much of what goes on must be inferred from overt behavior rather than observed directly. In human learning **introspection** — the self-description of one's cognition — can aid the discovery and use of such covert activities. The early behaviorists, especially those who followed the philosophy and methods of John B. Watson (1913, 1924), believed that introspection was too unreliable for a science of learning, since studying such content of the mind depended too much on the ambiguities of verbal communication (Pribram, 1986, p. 507). Today, however, introspection plays a part not only in basic research on human learning but also in changing abnormal behavior. In fact, introspection is involved in a flourishing movement that combines principles of cognitive psychology with classical and operant conditioning in the treatment of mental disorders (Kendall & Kriss, 1983). We discuss those approaches in Chapter 20.

Social and Cultural Influences on Behavior

The importance of learning in the development of abnormal behavior and experience can be more fully understood if one considers the social and cultural context in which it occurs. The acquisition of particular patterns of behavior, thought, and feeling and the judgment as to whether those patterns are abnormal may vary significantly from one society to another. Such judgments depend a great deal on the rules and reinforcers that prevail in a given culture and society. By **culture** we mean the total way of life of a people — their ways of thinking, feeling, and believing. Thus, culture is a broader and more abstract concept than **society,** which refers to a group of people who are related to each other in specific ways.

Social and cultural approaches to understanding abnormality are especially important in showing how the interpersonal and social systems to which people belong can shape psychopathology. To change maladaptive behavior, it is often necessary to make changes in the systems themselves. Sociologists and cultural anthropologists as well as community psychologists and certain behavior therapists have emphasized this viewpoint (see Chapters 20 and 21). The interpersonal and social systems they have studied include family, friendship, and occupational groups; social and economic classes; religious and ethnic affiliations; educational institutions; and various social agencies, such as mental hospitals and mental health clinics (Paul & Lentz, 1977; Rappaport & Seidman, 1983; Scheff, 1984; Townsend, 1978).

Abnormality as Socially Deviant Behavior

From a purely statistical perspective, **deviant behavior** is a departure from some numerical average, regardless of whether it is desirable or undesirable. However, sociologists and anthropologists emphasize that the concept of deviance is applied to acts and situations that not only violate social norms but also bring a strong negative reaction from others. Furthermore, the deviants in a society not only depart from certain standards and expectations, they may also be stigmatized for their deviance and be perceived as fundamentally different from others (Scheff, 1984, p. 20).

This theme of being different is part of a larger stigmatizing identity that people ascribe to the mentally ill. The stigma, argues Scheff, implies that, like all deviants, mentally ill people may well "belong to a fundamentally different class of human beings, or perhaps even to a different species" (1984, p. 61).

Rule Breaking and Residual Deviance

According to Scheff's analysis of social and cultural deviance, mental illness falls into a special category of rule breaking. There are many standards of behavior for which social agreement is so great that members of a society take them for granted. For example, the typical rules that govern what is decent or what is real go without saying, and violating them is unthinkable. These are the residual rules of a society, and breaking them constitutes **residual deviance.** Many of the common symptoms of mental illness, especially those that lead to hospitalization, are examples of residual deviance. For instance, in ordinary society a person engaged in conversation is expected to face those involved, and not look away or stare preoccupied into empty space. Other people would interpret the violation of such social expectations not as a simple matter of being ill-bred (violation of an explicit rule) but as "strange, bizarre, and frightening," and would perhaps label the person "mentally ill" (Scheff, 1984, pp. 36 – 38).

Erving Goffman makes a similar point in his analysis of withdrawing behavior, which he calls *away behavior.* It is socially acceptable to engage in reverie by sunbathing on the beach, an activity that shields one's away behavior. However, on such occasions one is expected to follow certain customs and rituals that proclaim to observers that one is a sunbather, not simply engaged in reverie. The rule that governs such behavior is a

This woman's reverie fits within "residual" rules of social behavior, that is, standards of behavior so universally accepted that they are taken for granted. But had she indulged in a similar withdrawal at a dinner party, she would be violating "residual" rules and might be perceived as mentally ill.

residual one. It is taken for granted that if one engages in reverie in a public place, one must do it in certain socially acceptable ways. Similarly, in an airplane or train, it is socially acceptable to spend long periods of time gazing in reverie out a window. But doing so at a dinner party is a violation of residual rules and might well be interpreted as a sign of mental illness (Goffman, 1963, pp. 58–59).

Social Roles as Reinforcers of Mental Illness

The deviant who has embarked on a career of mental illness has accepted a role that society prescribes. Family members, friends, occupational organizations, and even the very institutions that purport to alleviate the disturbances may reinforce that acceptance (Scheff, 1984). Therapists, other members of the staff, and even other patients may contribute to the reinforcement. The following scene from a meeting of patients in a women's ward of a hospital shows how this can occur.

New Patient: "I don't belong here. I don't like all these crazy people. When can I talk to the doctor? I've been here four days and I haven't seen the doctor. I'm not crazy."

Another Patient: "She says she's not crazy." (Laughter from patients.)

Another Patient: "Honey, what I'd like to know is, if you're not crazy, how did you get your ass in this hospital?"

New Patient: "It's complicated, but I can explain. My husband and I . . ."

First Patient: "That's what they all say." (General laughter.) (Scheff, 1984, p. 66)

In a study of patients in German and American mental hospitals, Townsend (1978) found the social systems of such hospitals to be so counterproductive as to warrant their being abolished, or at least significantly transformed. In Chapter 21 we discuss in detail various social issues involved in the hospitalization of mentally ill patients.

Stereotyping of mental illness may also be reinforced through the mass media. For example, newspaper accounts of violent acts may indicate that the perpetrator was once a mental patient. Assuming that the information is accurate, the highly selective nature of such reporting is apt to convey that people treated for mental illness commit acts of violence more often than the general population. In fact, the opposite is true; but in persistently linking mental illness and violence, newspaper stories strengthen fears and prejudices concerning the mentally ill (Holden, 1986a). To illustrate the negative bias of such reporting, Scheff (1984) formulated a hypothetical newspaper announcement: "Mrs. Ralph Jones, an ex-mental patient, was elected president of the Fairview Home and Garden Society at their meeting last Thursday." Scheff then noted that for such an item to appear would be "almost inconceivable" (p. 58).

Sex Differences in Mental Disorders

Various sociological studies in the United States have concluded that mental disorders tend to occur more often in women than in men (Chesler, 1972; Gove & Tudor, 1973, 1977; Tudor, Tudor, & Gove, 1977). Data from psychiatric facilities in Britain have also shown higher rates for women than for men (Smart, 1977). These findings are based mainly on diagnoses of (1) neurotic disorders, in which maladaptive anxiety and conflicts are central features; and (2) certain psychotic disorders that do not involve specific brain damage—for example, major depression. Various hypotheses have been advanced to explain this phenomenon (Al-Issa, 1980, 1982; Broverman, Broverman, Clarkson, Rosenkrantz, & Vogel, 1970; Johnson, 1987; Nathanson, 1975; Sarbin & Juhasz, 1978). The next five sections will discuss the most prominent of these hypotheses.

Cultural Acceptability

A study by Phillips (1963) supports the hypothesis that it is more culturally acceptable for women to express symptoms of mental disorder than it is for men. Phillips reported that men were more strongly rejected than women when both sexes revealed identical behavior and consulted the same sources of help, such as a member of the clergy, a physician, a psychiatrist, and a mental hospital. A later study, however, failed to confirm those findings (Clancy & Gove, 1975). Since the two studies were published 12 years apart, a shift toward greater equality in cultural attitudes toward women may help explain the difference in results.

Role Responsibilities

It is possible that some women's role obligations give them more time than men to consult mental health professionals; therefore, they are diagnosed more often as mentally ill. A number of studies found that reports of mental illness were lower for married women than for women who were single. The researchers concluded that the more demanding requirements of marriage made it more difficult for married women to seek professional help and to assume the sick role (Nathanson, 1975). In support of that hypothesis, another study found that women with young children or with a job outside the home tended to have a relatively low rate of contact with mental health professionals (Brown, Bhrolchain, & Harris, 1975). As women's work responsibilities outside the home grow, future studies might show a decreasing difference between reported mental illness in women and men. Furthermore, it may not be the role per se that is the important variable but how women perceive the importance of that role.

**Power and
Social Roles**

A number of sociological studies have pointed out that because conventional attitudes tend to view men's social roles as more powerful than women's, women are more likely to be diagnosed as mentally ill when their behavior conflicts with certain social norms (Sarbin & Juhasz, 1978). For example, Linn (1961) found that women living with their spouses or parents were more likely to be hospitalized for mental illness than men in the same living situations whose behavior was similar. He also found that in severely strained relationships on the job, men were more likely to be dismissed, and women were more often thought to be mentally disturbed (weak) and therefore in need of hospitalization.

**Stress and
Social Roles**

Some researchers have proposed that women's social roles are more stressful than those of men, thus resulting in more frequent diagnoses of mental illness. The central argument underlying this hypothesis is that the disadvantaged social and economic position that women often occupy in American society in comparison with men predisposes them toward a greater degree of frustration, dissatisfaction, and emotional turmoil. Thus, they may be especially vulnerable to psychological disorders in which social conflict plays a central part, such as the dilemma of advancing in a career versus staying home to rear children (Gove & Tudor, 1973, pp. 52–54; Wetzel, 1984, pp. 105–108).

The stress hypothesis was first advanced to explain the rise of mental illness in women after World War II. However, Dohrenwend and Dohrenwend (1974, 1976) have pointed out that the increase could be the result of a broader definition of *mental illness* by American psychiatrists after World War II, as well as changes in methods of research by the investigators who reported such increases.

Bias of Diagnosticians

Various researchers have hypothesized that mental illness may be diagnosed more often in women than in men because clinicians are biased. This hypothesis finds indirect support in a widely cited study of sex-role stereotypes and their relationship to judgments of mental health (Broverman, Broverman, Clarkson, Rosenkrantz, & Vogel, 1970). Female and male mental health professionals actively engaged in clinical work (psychologists, psychiatrists, and social workers) were asked to make judgments concerning the characteristics of positive mental health in adults. The results showed that they generally used a double standard in making these judgments. Socially desirable characteristics were ascribed more often to healthy men, socially undesirable characteristics to healthy women. Healthy women were thought to be more submissive, less independent, more easily influenced, less aggressive, more excitable in minor crises, more likely to have their feelings hurt, more emotional, more conceited about their appearance, and less objective. "This constellation," the researchers pointed out, "seems a most unusual way of describing any mature, healthy individual" (p. 5). They concluded that the clinicians, female as well as male, reflected a sex-role stereotype dominant in our society, and thus helped to perpetuate it.

Although suggestive, this study does not show directly that clinicians are likely to diagnose mental illness more often in women than in men. Nevertheless, the issue of sexism in diagnostic criteria is important and sensitive, deserving further study (Widiger & Nietzel, 1984). To examine this issue more directly we recorded the frequency of diagnoses for adult men and women as listed in DSM-III-R (American Psychiatric Association, 1987). Consistent with several previous studies based on DSM-III (Kaplan, 1983a; Kass, Spitzer, & Williams, 1983; Oakes, 1984; Williams & Spitzer, 1983), our analysis showed that men are diagnosed more often with certain disorders and women with others. Schizophrenic disorders, hypochondriasis (hypochondriacal neurosis), and obsessive compulsive disorder (obsessive compulsive neurosis) are as common in men as in women. However, major depression, generalized anxiety disorder (excessive or unrealistic apprehensions about various life circumstances), and multiple personality (a rare form of hysterical neurosis) are diagnosed more often in women.

Other examples that illustrate the complexity of the relationship between sex differences and diagnosis can be inferred from the following.

More Common in Women	**More Common in Men**
Somatization disorder: recurrent bodily complaints not caused by physical ailment	*Alcohol hallucinosis:* vivid and unpleasant hallucinations caused by excessive alcohol ingestion
Inhibited orgasm	*Transsexualism:* persistent wish to have genitals of other sex
Functional dyspareunia: recurrent genital pain during intercourse	*Transvestism:* persistent cross-dressing to obtain sexual excitement
Histrionic disorder: Overly dramatic behavior leading to adverse interpersonal relationships	*Paranoid personality disorder:* pervasive and unwarranted suspicion and mistrust of others
Dependent personality disorder: abnormal passive submission to others and lack of self-responsibility	*Antisocial personality disorder:* chronic antisocial behavior in which rights of others are violated

These findings do not as a whole support a claim of consistent bias against women in the diagnosis of mental disorders. However, some of the differences may well reflect stereotyped and other biased expectations concerning social roles, held not only by mental health professionals but also by those who come for help (Kaplan, 1983a, 1983b; Oakes, 1984; Wakefield, 1987). For example, our society has traditionally expected complaints about bodily ailments and sexual disturbances from women and antisocial behavior from men. Since attitudes toward sex roles in our society are becoming more flexible, the kinds of differences we have discussed may decline considerably in the future.

Effects of Racism

Failure to understand and accept cultural differences among racial and ethnic groups may lead to a misperception of mental and behavior disorders. That is especially likely in a society where certain minority groups are the targets of prejudice and discrimination so great and persistent as to place many of their members in a chronic state of social and economic disadvantage.

Black psychiatrists William H. Grier and Price M. Cobbs (1969) studied paranoid thinking and behavior among blacks in the United States. As a prelude to their analysis they pointed out that although other groups have suffered prejudice and discrimination that placed them at a social, economic, and psychological disadvantage, the situation of blacks has been more severe. Brought to this country by force, blacks were completely cut off from their past and robbed of their culture. The impact has been so great that, in many instances, blacks have had little, if any, knowledge of their cultural past.

Grier and Cobbs found that, like paranoid people in general, black paranoid individuals consistently perceive dangers that do not exist. However, on a more realistic level, they also tend to be especially sensitive to the motives of people around them. In part, their

Psychiatrist Price M. Cobbs, who is co-author of *Black Rage* with fellow psychiatrist William H. Grier. The two men studied the paranoid behavior of black patients and concluded that, although paranoid fears as such are maladaptive, sensitivity to prejudice and discrimination can have adaptive value provided suspicions do not impair a person's grasp on reality.

Ruth Benedict, for many years a distinguished professor of social anthropology at Columbia University, pioneered the now classic theory of "cultural relativism." According to this theory, psychopathology must be interpreted in the context of the particular cultural setting in which it occurs.

paranoid condition as well as their more realistic sensitivity stems from and is intensified by their marginal social status and a history of exploitation by whites that robbed them of their cultural heritage. Indeed, it is often difficult for outsiders to discern the difference between paranoid symptoms and a realistic sensitivity to potential sources of prejudice and discrimination. Nevertheless, Grier and Cobbs assert, this intense but realistic sensitivity can have adaptive value. Although blacks may at times find that survival depends on maintaining suspicion toward whites, they must not allow that suspicion to impair their grasp of reality. Grier and Cobbs conclude that this adaptation is a demanding requirement, one that not everyone can manage with grace (1969, p. 135).

Cultural Relativism and Abnormality

Classical Theory

Modern research dealing with cultural influences on abnormal behavior and experience stems largely from the classical theory of **cultural relativism.** According to this theory, psychopathology has meaning only when considered in the context of a particular social and cultural setting. Thus, what is abnormal in one culture may be normal in another. The theory originated primarily in the influential work of Ruth Benedict (1887–1948), for many years a professor of social anthropology at Columbia University. Her concept of abnormality flows logically from her relativistic view of culture: "Culture may value . . . even highly unstable human types. . . . Those who function inadequately in any society are not those with fixed 'abnormal' traits, but may well be those whose responses have received no support in the institutions of their culture" (Benedict, 1934/1950, pp. 249–250).

Limitations of Cultural Relativism

In recent years there has been a critical reaction to the extreme position of cultural relativism, directed especially to relativistic interpretations of psychotic disorders. The central feature of such disturbances is inadequate contact with reality—for example, delusions, hallucinations, distorted communication, and various signs of disorientation. Some researchers have argued that serious loss of contact with reality should be regarded as abnormal wherever it occurs. As Arnold Buss (1966) points out, in every society some members lose contact with reality. Although societies may indeed vary in the extent to which they value or tolerate these deviations, that does not make them normal. Buss concludes, "Reality, in the sense of recognizing the physical world around us, is a universal issue, and failure to be in contact with reality must be considered universally abnormal" (p. 12).

Extensive cross-cultural studies of psychopathology have supported Buss's position. Ari Kiev (1972) concluded that serious departures from reality have roots in the individual's biological characteristics. However, the particular content of such psychotic symptoms may vary, depending on cultural factors. H. Warren Dunham (1976) reached similar conclusions, but in doing so he pointed to the danger of not recognizing cultural differences in how psychopathology may be expressed. Failure to recognize such differences sometimes results in people being diagnosed as mentally ill mainly because they happen to be living in a culture radically different from their own. Thus, others may view them as mentally ill when they simply are behaving in ways that are appropriate to the culture they know best.

During the last decade a number of other cross-cultural studies of psychopathology have indicated the limitations of following cultural relativism too strictly. Many of the basic forms of psychopathology, such as schizophrenia and major depression, occur across a wide spectrum of cultures; however, the specific ways in which individuals manifest those disorders may well differ from one society to another (Al-Issa, 1982; Dohrenwend & Dohrenwend, 1974; Engelsmann, 1982; Kennedy, 1973; King, 1978; Murphy, 1976; Triandis & Draguns, 1980; Triandis, Malpass, & Davidson, 1973). To illustrate this limitation of cultural relativism, we will examine some of the commonalities and differences in patterns of psychopathology as revealed by various cross-cultural studies.

Psychopathology across Cultures

Cultural Acceptance and Abnormality

In her studies of Eskimos living on an island in the Bering Sea, Jane Murphy (1976) found that the Eskimos made a clear distinction between the shaman (priest-healer) who acts out delusions while treating illnesses and an ordinary person who shows similar kinds of delusions. In the following instance the shaman had deluded herself into believing that she was possessed by the spirit of an animal, a belief that was an essential part of her curing rite.

> The seance is opened by singing and drumming. After a time the shamaness falls down very hard on the floor. In a while, the tapping of her fingers and toes is heard on the walrus skin floor. Slowly she gets up, and already she is thought to "look awful, like a dog, very scary." She crawls back and forth across the floor making growling sounds. In this state she begins to carry out the various rites which Eskimos believe will cure sickness, such as sucking the illness out of the body and blowing it into the air. Following this the shamaness falls to the floor again and the seance is over. (Murphy, 1976, p. 1022)

Murphy compared this instance with one reported by another anthropologist about a member of the Baffin Island Eskimos. The second instance involving the delusion of being an animal was not associated with the role of shaman; rather, it was a continuous and fixed belief: "She barked herself hoarse, tried to claw her husband, thought her feet were turning into fox paws, believed that the fox was moving up in her body so that she could feel its hair in her mouth, lost control of her bowels at times, and finally became so excited that she was tied up and put into a coffin-like box with an opening at the head through which she could be fed" (Murphy, 1976, p. 1022).

The Baffin Island woman was thought to be crazy, but the behavior of the shaman was perceived as quite appropriate to her work, and definitely not crazy. Delusions in Eskimo society may or may not be labeled as signs of mental illness. The distinction depends on the degree to which the delusions "are controlled and utilized for a specific social function. The inability to control these processes is what is meant by a 'mind out of order'" (Murphy, 1976, p. 1022).

Murphy's interpretation of the shaman's professional role and its relevance for understanding delusions is highly consistent with conclusions that Wittkower (1969) reached in an earlier study of societies in West Africa and the Caribbean: "According to native healers and the native population at large, a person is considered insane if his perceptions and beliefs go beyond those that are culturally shared, if they give rise to psychological suffering and inability to function effectively, and if the behavior displayed has a disturbing effect on others. Hence the native healers and the native population are usually quite capable of making a distinction between acceptable beliefs in magic and witchcraft and what we would call paranoid ideas" (p. 813).

Murphy also compared signs of serious psychopathology in the Eskimos with those in the Yorubas, an African agricultural society. She found a remarkable similarity between what the two cultures regarded as mental illness. In addition, both cultures revealed patterns that Westernized mental health professionals generally regard as abnormal. The following signs of mental illness reported by Murphy are based on information supplied by native healers, by members of the society identified by village herdsmen as being "crazy," and by actual patients in the custody of native healers.

Eskimos	Yorubas
Talking to oneself	Hearing voices and trying to get other people to see their source, though none can be seen
Screaming at someone who does not exist	
Believing that a child or husband was murdered by witchcraft when nobody else believes it	Laughing when there is nothing to laugh at
Refusing to eat for fear eating will kill one	Talking all the time or not talking at all
Refusing to talk	Asking oneself questions and then answering them
Running away	Picking up sticks and leaves for no purpose except to put them in a pile
Getting lost	
Hiding in strange places	Throwing away food because it is thought to contain *juju* (magic)
Making strange grimaces	
Drinking urine	Tearing off one's clothes
Becoming strong and violent	Setting fires
Killing dogs	Defecating in public and then mushing around in the feces
Threatening people	Taking up a weapon and suddenly hitting someone with it

A comparison of the two columns shows that they reflect certain basic commonalities of psychopathology, such as bizarre physical activity, distorted communication, hallucinations, and delusions — all of which represent a decided break with reality.

Other Commonalities and Differences

Symptoms of major depression have been compared in African and European patients (Binitie, 1975). Certain commonalities were observed, most notably the loss of interest in work and the social environment. However, African patients placed a great deal of emphasis on bodily complaints but little on feelings of guilt and ideas of suicide. Among the Europeans the emphasis was just the opposite.

Another cross-cultural study of major depression sent questionnaires to more than 60 psychiatrists in 30 countries of Europe, Asia, and Africa (Murphy, Wittkower, & Chance, 1967, 1970). Using a standard rating form, the psychiatrists reported their impressions of the occurrence of four basic symptoms of major depressive illness in their cultures: (a) a mood of depression or dejection, (b) mood changes from day to day, (c) insomnia with early morning awakening, and (d) decrease of interest in the social environment. In addition, the psychiatrists were asked to report on the frequency of more specific symptoms of depression, such as loss of appetite, self-accusation, loss of sexual interest, self-neglect, and retarded thinking. The four basic symptoms were almost universally chosen as the core of depressive disorders, but the more specific symptoms varied from one culture to another. Although this study is open to criticism because it relied on subjective impressions of depression rather than examination of patients' records, the results are consistent with Binitie's findings for African and European patients suffering from depression.

In his cross-cultural analysis of schizophrenia, H. B. M. Murphy (1982) found that although the disorder occurred in a wide variety of cultures, the degree of disability that the process produced varied greatly. He attributed this variation to social and cultural conditions. Such conditions, he concluded, "can determine whether the symptoms invite acceptance or rejection of the patient by society, and they probably influence whether or not predisposed persons develop the disease" (1982, p. 247). For example, certain cultural influences may interfere with information processing, and thereby increase the risk of developing a schizophrenic reaction. In support of this possibility, Murphy points to a study of the Hutterite society—a North American minority—and to his own studies of island peoples in the South Pacific. The low rate of hospitalization for schizophrenia was consistent with a cultural pattern that provided for community decisions and clear-cut paths of action for individuals who apparently were predisposed to schizophrenia. In contrast, he found that the Irish have a complex style of communication that makes it difficult for the individual to distinguish reality from fantasy. This pattern may help explain the prevalence of a high risk for schizophrenia in that society. Earlier studies, which are summarized in Table 4.1, are consistent with Murphy's findings.

Viewpoints of Humanistic Psychology

In common with the humanities, **humanistic psychology** focuses on human values, for both the individual and the group. Traditionally, psychology has confined itself to studying how people react to humanistic areas of experience and to the values held by others in those areas. Humanistic psychology holds that psychology itself is not a value-free science (Hilgard, 1987, pp. 791–792) and, in fact, takes a further step, consciously allowing values inherent in the humanities to be explicit guides for its activities. Accordingly, humanistic psychology strives to understand people's needs and goals and the gap that may persist between their potentialities and the fulfillment of those needs and goals. That gap can become an important source of serious psychological problems.

Table 4.1 Cross-cultural Comparisons of Schizophrenic Disorders: Commonalities and Differences

Investigators	Method	Results
Carpenter, Strauss, and Bartko, 1973	The diagnoses of schizophrenic disorders in nine countries were studied.	Seven signs of schizophrenia common to the diagnoses in all nine countries were identified: restricted affect, poor insight, thinking aloud, poor rapport, incoherent speech, unrealistic information, and bizarre delusions.
Cooper and Sartorius, 1977	The source of major differences between Great Britain and the United States in the incidence of schizophrenia as reported in national health statistics of these countries was traced.	Once diagnostic practices were standardized, the apparent differences in the proportion of schizophrenics disappeared.
Kitano, 1970	Parents, siblings, and spouses of schizophrenic Japanese patients in Los Angeles, Hawaii, Tokyo, and Okinawa were asked how the patients acted during the year before hospitalization, the events that led up to hospitalization, and how the patients got along in the family.	Almost all of the patients were lonely, isolated people. Their loneliness was a long-term condition, not merely an isolation resulting from the decision to have them hospitalized. The most immediate event that led to hospitalization was the patient's disruption of family life.
Seifert, Draguns, and Caudill, 1971	Symptoms of schizophrenia were observed in hospitalized psychiatric patients in Japan. Symptoms often included hallucinations and delusions.	Symptoms were similar to those found in the United States. However, the particular style in which the symptoms were organized often differed from one country to another.
World Health Organization, 1973	Comparisons were made between patterns of symptoms displayed by psychiatric patients free of organic pathology who sought services at residential psychiatric facilities in nine countries: Colombia, Czechoslovakia, Denmark, India, Nigeria, Taiwan, the Soviet Union, the United Kingdom, and the United States.	Similar clusters of symptoms were noted in all of the facilities, especially in the case of schizophrenic disorders. A core group of individuals diagnosed as schizophrenic was identified in each of the nine countries.

Historical Development

In its early development, leaders of the humanistic psychology movement referred to it as a third force, one that went beyond the mainstream approaches of American psychology —behaviorism, experimental psychology, and psychodynamic approaches. To implement that force, the *Journal of Humanistic Psychology* was founded in 1961, and two years later the American Association of Humanistic Psychology was organized. In 1972, the

Abraham H. Maslow, paramount leader in the development of humanistic psychology. Maslow developed a hierarchy of human needs, ranging from biological motives for survival at the bottom to the need for fulfilling one's potentialities at the top.

movement became an official part of the American Psychological Association with the establishment of the Division of Humanistic Psychology (Hilgard, 1987, p. 788).

The chief leader in the development of humanistic psychology was Abraham H. Maslow (1908–1970), who spent most of his academic career as a professor of psychology at Brooklyn College and Brandeis University. In his landmark book, *Motivation and Personality* (1954), Maslow proposed a hierarchy of human needs that placed biological motives of physical survival at the bottom of the hierarchy and the realization of one's potentialities for psychological and social development at the top. This ultimate level he called self-actualization.

Another leader in the establishment of humanistic psychology was Carl Rogers (1902–1987), whose theories and practice of person-centered psychotherapy we discuss in Chapter 19. Rogers emphasized the importance of self-actualization as a goal in healthy human development and in psychotherapy. He also stressed the importance of having people who come for help with their psychological problems realize that they can make choices in determining their future. This concept of free choice did not, of course, begin with humanistic psychology. For centuries, it has been discussed and debated among philosophers. Consider this statement by the Greek philosopher Epictetus (ca. 55–135 A.D.): "The good or ill of man lies within his own will" (Tripp, 1970, p. 1048).

In his historical analysis of humanistic psychology as a movement within American psychology, Hilgard (1987, p. 849) points out that although it emphasizes human values, the movement does not represent a rapprochement—a bringing together—of psychology and the humanities as usually defined.

Approaches to Understanding Abnormality

As we discussed in Chapter 3, psychodynamic theories emphasize unconscious motives and conflicts as major sources of psychological disorders. Humanistic approaches reject that view as too narrow. They do not deny that unconscious conflicts exist and that they may be of great importance in understanding the mainsprings of maladjustment and frustration. Yet, they believe that the image of the person that results is less than completely human. An important human characteristic is the tendency toward growth and self-actualization—the fulfillment of one's potential. As human beings we strive toward imposing meaning on our lives and on the world we live in. Humanistic psychology claims that these basic human characteristics, and the consequences of their frustration, are not actively incorporated into either the psychodynamic or the behaviorist approach to understanding abnormality. Thus, the argument goes, they are incomplete even though they may make a contribution to this understanding. It is necessary for humanistic psychology to fill that gap.

Humanistic concepts of abnormal behavior and experience are closely tied to the existentialist movement in philosophy and psychology (Smith, 1982). **Existentialism** focuses on the current existence of individuals and their present motives, self-perceptions, and psychological problems. The origin of the term itself is an important clue to the essence of existentialist views, for *existence* comes from the Latin root *existere*, meaning "to stand out, emerge." Existentialism emphasizes the human being as an emerging individual, a person who is constantly becoming, who makes choices, and who is not simply the victim of blind forces or desires. To Jean-Paul Sartre (1905–1980), the eminent exponent of existentialist philosophy, we are nothing but what we make of ourselves. That, said Sartre, is the first principle of existentialism (Sartre, 1947, p. 18). In

Jean-Paul Sartre, eminent developer of existential philosophy. Sartre believed that people make choices rather than being unknowing victims of blind forces and their desires.

Rollo May, existentialist psychologist and therapist, was greatly influenced by Kierkegaard's concepts of anxiety. May's book, *The Meaning of Anxiety*, has become a classic.

reacting to Sartre's dictum that we are what we choose, psychologist and therapist Rollo May (1969) adds the proviso: "within the limits of our given world." May comments further: "We are all born of woman, struggle through stages of growth the best we can, and ultimately die; and what we think about it will not change those brute facts. *It will*, however vastly change *how* we negotiate this threescore and ten" (p. 13).

In developing his views on existentialism and their relationship to psychological disorder, May introduced to American psychologists the ideas of Søren Kierkegaard (1813–1855), a Danish philosopher and theologian. One of Kierkegaard's central concepts had been translated as "dread" (Kierkegaard, 1844/1944). May (1977, pp. 36–37) interpreted that term to mean "anxiety," especially when it related to motivation and mental disorder. (We discuss May's views of anxiety in Chapter 5.) May was also greatly influenced by the American theologian Paul Johannes Tillich (1886–1965), with whom he had studied. Tillich's book *The Courage to Be* (1952) served as a clear and fundamental introduction to existentialism for American psychologists (Hilgard, 1987, p. 504).

Humanistic and existentialist views play a prominent part in a number of systems of psychotherapy. They are central to person-centered therapy as developed by Carl Rogers, whose views we discussed earlier. In addition, existentialist philosophy greatly influenced the development of Gestalt therapy by Frederick and Laura Perls. We consider these views in Chapter 19.

Summary

1. The earliest form of learning to be studied extensively in the laboratory was classical conditioning. Stemming from the pioneering experiments of the Russian physiologist Ivan Pavlov, classical conditioning may be defined as an old response to a new stimulus situation.

2. The conditioned response results from the pairing of two stimuli: an unconditioned stimulus and a conditioned stimulus. Pavlov found that if he presented food (an unconditioned stimulus) to a hungry dog, the dog would salivate — an unconditioned response. If the unconditioned stimulus was repeatedly paired with a new stimulus, the sound of a bell, eventually the dog would salivate when the bell was sounded in the absence of food — a conditioned response.

3. The conditioned response is not as automatic as it may appear. Pavlov found that if the dog was not hungry it was difficult, and sometimes impossible, to establish a conditioned response. This idea of readiness can be applied to human conditioning as well.

4. Pavlov discovered that a conditioned response could generalize to stimuli similar to the conditioned stimulus. He also found that a conditioned response could be extinguished unless the conditioned stimulus (bell) was occasionally paired again with the unconditioned stimulus (food). A cognitive explanation of this phenomenon is that the conditioned stimulus creates an expectancy — food is coming. If food does not eventually appear, the expectancy, and therefore the conditioned response (salivation), disappears.

5. In the United States an early leader in the experimental work on the process of establishing conditioned responses was John B. Watson, a pioneering behaviorist in the psychology of learning. Watson and Rosalie Rayner used classical conditioning procedures to establish a fear response in an 11-month-old child, Albert. The experiment was initially cited as demonstrating how phobias (irrational fears) can be acquired; but later, some psychologists doubted that Albert developed a true phobia. In any case, it is clear that classical conditioning outside the laboratory is more complex. It may be very difficult at times to discover the actual stimuli involved in producing the conditioned response. Nevertheless, it is reasonable to conclude that conditioned responses do occur in everyday life, and that in certain instances they may at least partially explain some forms of abnormal as well as normal behavior.

6. B. F. Skinner, one of the most influential psychologists today, distinguishes between classical conditioning (he calls it respondent conditioning) and operant conditioning. Respondent conditioning is based on involuntary, elicited behavior, as when food in the mouth produces salivation. Operant conditioning is based on voluntary, spontaneous behavior. It is emitted rather than elicited. Such behavior operates on the environment.

7. Whereas respondent (classical) conditioning is an old response to a new stimulus, operant conditioning produces new behavior. This process is also called instrumental learning, because what the learner does is instrumental in changing the environment (operating on it). In turn, changes in the environment help produce changes in behavior, thus influencing the learning of new responses.

8. Initially, operant behavior may be random; but if the consequences of the behavior are favorable, the behavior is likely to be emitted again. The environmental stimuli

that the learner operates on and that increase the probability that such behavior will be repeated are called reinforcers. Their occurrence during operant behavior is called reinforcement.

9. Skinner distinguishes between positive and negative reinforcers. A positive reinforcer strengthens the behavior that produces it. A negative reinforcer strengthens the behavior that reduces or terminates it. Punishment is often confused with negative reinforcement. The purpose of punishment is to remove behavior, whereas negative reinforcement is designed to strengthen or generate behavior. Thus, punishment is the reverse of reinforcement. Skinner opposes punishment as a way of teaching desirable behavior.

10. Some environmental stimuli act as signals to indicate where and when operant behavior is likely to be reinforced. They are called discriminative stimuli, and they begin to influence the learning of both normal and abnormal behavior early in life.

11. An experimenter, teacher, parent, or therapist can shape operant behavior by reinforcing positively any response that at first resembles the desired behavior. Shaping has been used extensively in the treatment of mental disorders.

12. Reinforcement need not be continual for behavior to persist. Intermittent (partial) reinforcement, in which behavior is reinforced only some of the time, can be effective in establishing and prolonging behavior.

13. Vicarious reinforcements — observing models of desired behavior — can be effective. This approach has been used in various forms of therapy designed to reduce anxiety.

14. Cognitive psychologists emphasize that learning often depends a great deal on the learner's expectations. Reinforcers in the environment do not facilitate learning just because they are there. The learner must *anticipate* that manipulating the reinforcers will help in reaching a goal. This anticipation is a *cognitive* process. Reasoning, problem solving, and the sudden attainment of insight may all be involved. Such processes involve the acquiring, storing, and applying of knowledge. Cognitive psychologists, especially in their study of learning, are concerned with how individuals select, code, and use such information. Unlike traditional behaviorists, cognitive psychologists do not reject introspection as an important factor in studying how learning occurs. Introspection — the self-description of one's cognition — is currently part of an active movement that combines cognitive psychology with principles of classical and operant conditioning in the treatment of mental disorders.

15. Although learning takes place according to basic principles common to all societies and cultures, what one learns and whether the behavior that learning produces is regarded as normal or abnormal may vary considerably from one society to another.

16. Sociologists and anthropologists have studied the concept of deviance in relation to abnormality. This concept is applied to behavior that not only violates social norms but also brings strong negative reactions from others. Individuals are often stigmatized because of their social deviance, especially the mentally ill.

17. Mental illness falls into a special form of rule breaking, called residual deviance, which involves breaking social rules of behavior so taken for granted that violating them is unthinkable. Mental illness and people's reactions to those who are diagnosed as mentally ill reflect such residual deviance.

18. Affected by the reactions of family members, friends, occupational organizations, and other social institutions, mentally ill people may reinforce their illness by

accepting the social role of being mentally ill and embarking on a career of mental illness.

19. Various sociological studies have concluded that mental disorders occur more often in women than in men. Among the reasons given for this disparity are: (a) women are more willing to express symptoms of mental disorder because our culture is more accepting of that willingness, (b) the sick role is more compatible with women's traditional responsibilities and social expectations, (c) women's social roles are less powerful than those of men, (d) women's social roles are more stressful, and (e) clinicians are more likely to diagnose mental illness in women than in men.

20. Although some evidence supports these conclusions, they are still debatable. Furthermore, the conclusion that women have a higher frequency of mental illness than men does not necessarily apply across the board. In the case of certain disorders, the frequency for men is greater than for women.

21. Failure to understand and accept cultural differences among racial and ethnic groups may lead to misperceptions of mental disorders. According to black psychiatrists Grier and Cobbs, the survival tactics of some blacks in being highly suspicious of white people's motives and behavior appear to be paranoid but may well be realistically defensive.

22. The classical theory of cultural relativism states that the meaning of abnormality depends on the context of a particular society or culture. Although in general this is true, an extreme version of it is misleading. Certain patterns of abnormality, such as inadequate contact with reality (psychosis) are considered to be abnormal in virtually all societies.

23. A large number of cross-cultural studies of psychopathology support a less extreme application of the position of cultural relativism in the description of abnormality. Certain kinds of disorders, such as major depression and schizophrenia, occur across a wide spectrum of cultures. However, the particular content of those disorders and the specific ways in which they are manifested differ from one society to another.

24. The views of humanistic psychology emerged about 30 years ago as a third force to fill a void between the experimental psychology of behaviorism and psychodynamic approaches. Among the sustaining leaders in this movement were Abraham Maslow and Carl Rogers. Maslow emphasized a hierarchy of human motives, with self-actualization as the pinnacle. Rogers, the founder of person-centered psychotherapy, also emphasized self-actualization and the freedom of choosing one's goals. Much of their thinking can be traced to the philosophy of existentialism, which emphasizes that the human being is an emerging individual — one who is constantly making choices rather than being the victim of blind forces and drives. Following the work of the French philosopher Jean-Paul Sartre, the American psychotherapist Rollo May, along with Rogers, has been a leader in applying existentialism to an understanding of abnormality and psychotherapy.

Patterns
of Disorders

In Part 1 (Chapters 1 – 4) we considered the basic characteristics of abnormal behavior and experience and various approaches to understanding them. That appraisal included the
classification of mental disorders widely used in the United
States today and found in the *Diagnostic and Statistical
Manual of Mental Disorders* – Revised, published in 1987
and commonly known as DSM-III-R. In Part 2 (Chapters
5 – 17) we examine in more detail the specific nature of those
disorders — their central features, historical background, etiology, and treatment. We also discuss how such disturbances
can be interpreted from different theoretical and practical
viewpoints.

Outline of Topics

My apprehensions come in crowds;
I dread the rustling of the grass;
The very shadows of the clouds
Have power to shake me as they pass;
I question things and do not find
One that will answer to my mind:
And all the world appears unkind.

WILLIAM WORDSWORTH
"The Affliction of Margaret" (1904)

In his portrayal of Margaret's affliction, Wordsworth depicted a pattern of apprehension, fear, and self-doubt similar to contemporary descriptions of anxiety disorders. Traditionally, mental health professionals have considered such disorders to be forms of neuroses. In DSM-II neuroses (a concept originating in psychoanalytic theory) are a major diagnostic category (American Psychiatric Association, 1968). DSM-III and DSM-III-R (American Psychiatric Association, 1980a, 1987), which aimed to classify mental disorders on the basis of observable behavior rather than theories, retained some of the specific patterns of symptoms formerly listed under neuroses but classified them as anxiety disorders.

In discussing anxiety disorders we will continue to use the traditional term *neurosis*. It is so entrenched in the writings and speech of mental health professionals and the general public that to ignore it would be impractical and confusing (Trimble, 1985, pp. 5–6). Indeed, as a link with tradition, both DSM-III and DSM-III-R include it as an acceptable alternative in their labeling of certain anxiety disorders. Furthermore, its retention is compatible with the mental disorders section of the *International Classification of Diseases* (ICD), developed under the auspices of the World Health Organization. (See Chapter 2 for a discussion of the ICD.)

Basic Concepts of Anxiety

Before examining in detail the various patterns of anxiety disorders, we will consider some fundamental concepts of anxiety itself. With this knowledge we will be in a better position to understand the role of anxiety in psychological disturbances.

Components of Anxiety

Anxiety—a convenient shorthand term for highly complex and varied patterns of experience and behavior—includes three basic components: subjective reactions, such as apprehension and self-doubt; overt behavior—for example, trembling and restlessness; and physiological reactions, such as increased heart rate and respiration.

Subjective Reactions

Cognitive (thinking) reactions are probably the most prominent characteristics of subjective anxiety (Lehrer & Woolfolk, 1982). They are often accompanied by various degrees of **affect** (feeling tone). For example, thoughts of self-doubt may be accompanied by feelings of uneasiness and tension. Cognitive reactions may also interact with physiological components of anxiety, as when worry about a future event increases heart rate. In turn, awareness of bodily changes can heighten the worry.

Subjective anxiety is necessarily assessed indirectly. Typically, individuals are asked to describe their thoughts, feelings, and behavior. These data may be obtained through ordinary conversation or, more formally and systematically, through structured interviews and psychological tests. The individual usually reports anxiety reactions by responding to a set of printed questions or statements. These items may inquire into the person's usual condition of anxiety (**trait anxiety**), or they may focus on anxiety in response to specific situations (**state anxiety**). Items in anxiety tests tend to be quite brief and straightforward. Responses are usually of the yes–no or agree–disagree type. A variety of such tests has been developed for a wide range of ages. One of the most frequently used tests is the Children's Manifest Anxiety Scale (Reynolds & Paget, 1981). (See Chapter 2 for a detailed description of self-report tests in assessing psychological abnormality.)

Overt Behavior

The second major component of anxiety — disturbed overt behavior — can be observed directly, and these observations can also be compared with self-reported behavior. The anxious individual may show a wide variety of changes in behavior, such as grimacing, eye blinking, and stuttering. Tremors, restlessness, and overactivity are often present. Sudden noises and bright lights may cause the anxious person to respond overquickly. Expressions of irritability or other emotional outbursts are common. These as well as other changes in overt behavior can provide clues to affective aspects of anxiety — feelings that may not have been fully revealed in self-report assessments.

Physiological Reactions

The third component of anxiety — physiological reactions — involves primarily the **sympathetic division** of the autonomic nervous system (see Figure 5.1). This division controls increases in heart rate, dilation of the arteries of the skeletal muscles and heart, and increase in perspiration — to cite a few of the possible changes. Although the sympathetic division is usually engaged during anxiety and fear, in extreme cases the **parasympathetic division** (see Figure 5.1) may also become activated. For example, severe anxiety may produce an involuntary discharge of the bladder or bowels, whose actions are controlled by the parasympathetic division.

Self-reports of physiological reactions can be helpful in assessing an individual's anxiety. For greater accuracy, however, especially in research, it is desirable to measure physiological arousal with special instruments that record such changes more objectively and precisely.

Adaptive and Maladaptive Anxiety

Anxiety may range from highly adaptive (normal) to highly maladaptive (abnormal) reactions. **Adaptive anxiety** is appropriate to the situation and can even enhance efficiency and achievement. In contrast, **maladaptive anxiety** is self-defeating; it tends to interfere with efficiency and achievement. For example, excessive anxiety can increase errors on various tasks. It can also result in overly cautious behavior, such as delaying appropriate responses and decision (Eisdorfer, 1977).

One can experience moderate levels of anxiety and still perform effectively. Indeed, under certain circumstances moderate anxiety can be motivating and constructive. A study of anticipatory anxiety prior to major surgery illustrates this point (Janis, 1971). Patients who had expressed a moderate degree of anxiety prior to the operation faired better in

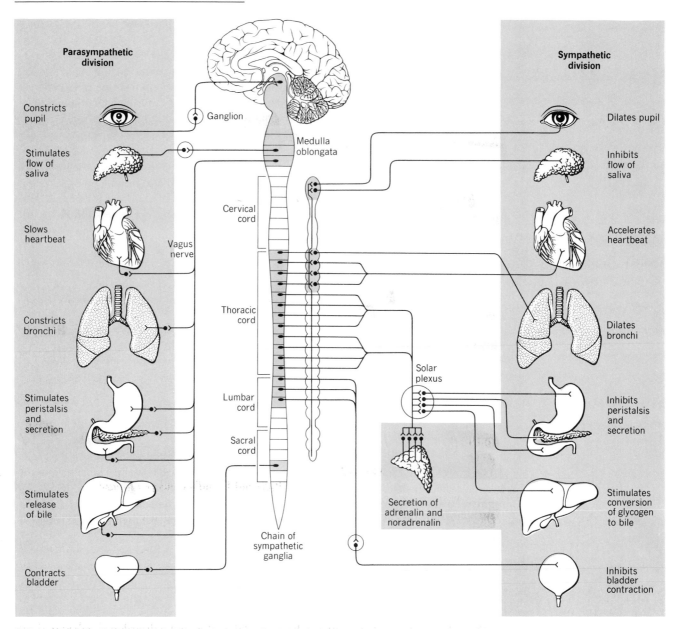

Parasympathetic division

Constricts pupil

Stimulates flow of saliva

Slows heartbeat

Vagus nerve

Constricts bronchi

Stimulates peristalsis and secretion

Stimulates release of bile

Contracts bladder

Ganglion

Medulla oblongata

Cervical cord

Thoracic cord

Lumbar cord

Sacral cord

Chain of sympathetic ganglia

Solar plexus

Secretion of adrenalin and noradrenalin

Sympathetic division

Dilates pupil

Inhibits flow of saliva

Accelerates heartbeat

Dilates bronchi

Inhibits peristalsis and secretion

Stimulates conversion of glycogen to bile

Inhibits bladder contraction

Figure 5.1

The autonomic nervous system. (From Atkinson, Atkinson, & Hilgard, 1983, p. 51.)

their postoperative adjustment than those who had shown either a very low or a very high level of preoperative anxiety. This particular investigation was carried out by means of intensive interviews and inspection of observational notes made by doctors and nurses. In a follow-up study, college students who had undergone major surgery completed questionnaires concerning their preoperative and postoperative feelings about their ordeal (Janis, 1971, pp. 96–97). A similar relationship was found between anticipatory anxiety and postoperative adjustment. As Figure 5.2 shows, students who were moderately afraid prior to the operation tended to have a more satisfactory postoperative adjustment than those whose preoperative fears were either very low or very high.

These results not only illustrate the disruptive effects of excessive anticipatory anxiety but also contradict the popular notion that people who remain extremely calm about an

Figure 5.2

Relationship between fear prior to major surgery and postoperative adjustment. (Adapted from Janis, 1971, p. 97.)

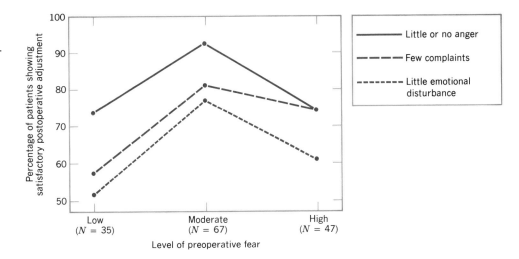

impending ordeal will be much less disturbed when they handle the subsequent stress than people who show some anxiety. Indeed, the findings suggest that when people are exposed to severe stress, those who are most confident about their invulnerability at the beginning may well be the most likely to be highly disturbed when they actually undergo the stressful events. Furthermore, a moderate degree of anxiety and fear about realistic danger can be constructively motivating, helping the individual develop effective inner defenses for coping with the danger (Janis, 1971, p. 97; May, 1977, pp. 374–380).

Psychodynamics of Anxiety

Freudian Concepts

Freud's concept of *angst*, variously translated as anxiety, morbid anxiety, and dread, owes much to the earlier writings of Søren Kierkegaard, 19th-century Danish philosopher.

The use of the term *anxiety* in psychological research and practice, especially in the area of abnormal psychology, owes much to Sigmund Freud's concept of *angst*, which has no direct English equivalent. Some interpreters of Freud's works have translated *angst* as "*morbid anxiety*"; others have simply called it "anxiety" (Freud, 1936; Jones, 1955, pp. 223–224; McReynolds, 1976). The term was not new with Freud. Years before his time, the Danish philosopher Søren Kierkegaard (1813–1855), whose influence on existentialism was discussed in Chapter 4, used *angst* in his writings on disturbed psychological states. Early translators called it "dread"; more recently, however, it has been interpreted as "anxiety," thus coming closer to Freud's concept (Kierkegaard, 1844/1944; May, 1977, pp. 36–37).

Freud viewed anxiety (*angst*) as a basic condition of neurotic disorders. He emphasized the difference between realistic or objective anxiety and neurotic anxiety. **Objective anxiety** is experienced in the face of a real danger in the environment, one that the individual anticipates and is fully aware of. **Neurotic anxiety** has its source in the unconscious. The difference between the two kinds of anxiety is not always clear-cut, however. One may correctly appraise a dangerous situation and be anxious about it, but the anxiety may be greatly out of proportion to what the situation realistically demands. Such exaggerated anxiety would also be neurotic (Freud, 1936, p. 113).

According to Freudian psychoanalytic theory, neurotic anxiety is an expression of **intrapsychic conflict.** Such conflict may arise when biological impulses of sex and aggression (the id) oppose the demands of conscience and ideals (the superego). Conflict and the arousal of anxiety may also occur when the internal demands of the id oppose the external demands of the environment (see Chapter 3).

Consider an adult who is highly anxious about sexual or aggressive desires. These desires are threatening because to express them would conflict with moral rules acquired during childhood. Anxious about the possibility of losing parental love and protection, the child conforms to the rules and incorporates them into the superego. At this point the child's anxiety is morally realistic, for it forms the basis of the moral guilt so necessary to civilization (Freud, 1933/1965, p. 62). However, as the child's superego develops, moral anxiety and feelings of guilt may become unrealistically severe. Thus, adults may experience anxiety whenever they experience desires contrary to earlier moral teachings. This may happen even though the individual realizes that the desires are not socially unacceptable and that parental punishment is no longer an actual physical danger. However, the moral lessons of childhood may have been fixed too inflexibly, so that anxiety associated with threats of punishment and loss of love persist in the unconscious, and neurotic anxiety becomes established.

How do neurotic conflict and anxiety become transformed into the symptoms of neurotic disorders? According to Freudian theory, the ego plays a central role. When intrapsychic conflict and anxiety become too painful, the ego attempts to block them from consciousness through the defense mechanism of repression — pushing awareness of the conflict and its source into the unconscious. To maintain this repression, the ego may employ a variety of defense mechanisms. For example, it may project id impulses into external reality. That is, individuals may deny their own strong and persistent aggressive or sexual desires by constantly seeing them in other people. They can then cope with these attributed impulses instead of dealing directly with the conflict and anxiety aroused by their own desires. (See Chapter 3 for a detailed discussion of defense mechanisms and the role of the ego.)

Although defense mechanisms can be used successfully without any abnormal effects, conflict and anxiety may become so intense and unbearable that they arouse an extreme and self-defeating use of ego defenses. This abnormal (maladaptive) use of defenses represents in large part the symptoms of neurotic (anxiety) disorders.

Other Psychodynamic Viewpoints

Like traditional Freudian theorists, neo-Freudians (see Chapter 3) assume that the symptoms of neuroses (anxiety disorders) represent unconscious defenses against conflict and anxiety too painful to admit to consciousness. However, they emphasize that the source of neurotic conflict and anxiety may lie more in the demands and frustrations that arise from social and interpersonal relationships than from biological drives of aggression and sex. Neo-Freudians such as Karen Horney and her followers stress that neurotic anxiety originates in the failure during early childhood to satisfy needs for love and affection, reliable care, and regard for one's helplessness (Horney, 1937, 1939, 1945, 1946, 1970; Kelman, 1965). Later, childhood neurotic anxiety may be strengthened by failure to satisfy needs for understanding, respect, and self-esteem. Continual frustration of such needs early in life forms the core of neurosis — basic anxiety. This anxiety is revealed in such neurotic symptoms as exaggerated and inappropriate feelings of helplessness, loneliness, and hostility.

As we pointed out in Chapter 3, Alfred Adler and his followers dissented strongly from Freudian theory. They emphasized that neuroses stem from the individual's overcompensation for deep-seated feelings of inferiority. Thus, they claimed, abnormal anxiety is often the result of an inability to make decisions because one's feelings of inferiority are too great. Self-doubt becomes the driving force of neurotic anxiety. However, it is difficult to face this truth consciously. The symptoms of anxiety neuroses become ways of warding off that truth (Adler, 1929/1964, pp. 2–4).

Abnormal Anxiety and Learning

In contrast to Freudian psychoanalytic theory and other psychodynamic perspectives, traditional learning theory focuses on the problem behavior itself. One of the earliest and most vigorous statements of this position is that of Eysenck and Rachman (1965), whose views stem from the learning theories of Pavlov, Watson, and Skinner (see Chapter 4). They emphasize that "Freudian theory regards neurotic symptoms as adaptive mechanisms which are evidence of repression; they are 'the visible upshot of unconscious causes.' Learning theory does not postulate any such 'unconscious causes.' It regards neurotic symptoms as simply learned habits; there is no neurosis underlying the symptom, but merely the symptom itself. *Get rid of the symptom (skeletal and autonomic) and you have eliminated the neurosis*" (pp. 9–10). Admitting that they have oversimplified their basic position, Eysenck and Rachman go on to emphasize the essence of treatment from a learning theory point of view: "In the case of *surplus* conditioned responses (i.e., undesirable behavior) treatment should consist in the extinction of these responses; in the case of *deficient* conditioned responses (desirable behavior) treatment should consist in the building up of the missing stimulus–response connections" (p. 10).

In more recent years, the application of learning theory to the understanding and treatment of anxiety disorders has become more flexible. Notwithstanding the rejection of psychoanalytic views of intrapsychic conflict, the learning theory perspective does not deny the role of inference about internal cognitive and emotional events, provided the events can be directly linked to observable stimuli and behavior. In this sense, then, behavior theory and therapy look for underlying causes just as psychoanalysis does, except that the causes are interpreted differently (Bandura, 1969, 1974, 1977). "Behavior therapists are often effective," according to Paul Wachtel (1977), "precisely because they are *not* behavioristic in any narrowly construed way. In their clinical work they find it necessary to make inferences and to concern themselves with what their patients want and feel as well as what they do" (p. 8).

Even within the flexible framework that modern exponents of learning theory have adopted, the fundamental position is still that anxiety disorders are maladaptive patterns of thought and behavior acquired according to the same basic principles of learning that govern the acquisition of adaptive patterns. (See Chapter 4 for a discussion of those principles.)

Patterns and Origins of Anxiety Disorders

DSM-III-R Classification

DSM-III-R classifies anxiety disorders into these broad patterns: panic disorders, phobic disorders (or phobic neuroses), generalized anxiety disorder, obsessive compulsive disorder (or obsessive compulsive neurosis), and posttraumatic stress disorder.

■ **Panic disorders** are marked by recurrent attacks of panic anxiety. These attacks are apparently unrelated to any kind of life-threatening situation.

■ The central characteristic of **phobic disorders** is an irrational fear and consequent avoidance of situations. The phobic individual usually realizes that the fear is unreasonable but nevertheless suffers anxiety either when anticipating the feared situation or when actually in it.

The recurrent attacks of panic
anxiety suffered in panic
disorders are apparently unrelated
to a specific life-threatening
situation.

■ **Generalized anxiety disorder** is marked by a chronic state of vague apprehension, such as worrying that something terrible is about to happen even though there is no objective evidence to support that belief.

■ The essential features of **obsessive compulsive disorder** are (a) the constant recurrence of persistent but unwanted ideas, thoughts, and impulses (obsessions); and (b) repetitive, stereotyped actions that the individual recognizes as senseless but cannot resist doing (compulsions).

■ The central characteristic of **posttraumatic stress disorder** is repeated attacks of anxiety that follow severe, emotionally damaging experiences. Nightmares and flashbacks —reliving the painful experiences—may occur.

Some individuals display symptoms that overlap from one type of anxiety disorder to another. For example, hyperactivity of the autonomic nervous system (see Figure 5.1) is common not only in generalized anxiety disorder but also in panic disorder. It is often manifested by sweating, pounding of the heart, upset stomach, hot flashes or chills, and shortness of breath (American Psychiatric Association, 1987, pp. 238, 253).

Such panic reactions may also occur in a phobic disorder, especially when the person is forced to think about, approach, or actually participate in the feared situation. The clinician must therefore focus on the total pattern of an anxiety disorder, not just on a few isolated characteristics, when distinguishing it from another disorder.

Although anxiety disorders are maladaptive, they do not involve the gross disorganization and loss of contact with reality so typical of psychotic disorders (which we discuss in later chapters). Furthermore, people who suffer from anxiety disorders usually recognize that their behavior is maladaptive, even though they may have little understanding of why they are disturbed. Such recognition is often absent in psychotic individuals.

The causes and expression of anxiety disorders, like many other forms of psychopathology, depend on a host of interacting factors. Among them are the individual's conflicts, frustrations, and defense mechanisms; the environment in which the disturbed behavior occurs; the learning history of that behavior and the reinforcers that currently maintain it; and various personality characteristics that have developed over the years and are entrenched in the individual's life-style. Therefore, even if all the individuals in a particular group reveal symptoms sufficiently similar to justify classifying them in the same diagnostic category, they may differ significantly in various nuances of feeling, thought, and behavior that reflect such disorders.

Panic Disorder

Imagine yourself riding on a crowded bus on the way to work. Suddenly, out of the clear blue, your heart starts to pound, you can't catch your breath, you feel dizzy, disoriented, nauseated and panicky. You think you're going to die or go crazy.

Though your legs have turned to rubber, as soon as the bus stops you push your way out onto the street and start running, anywhere just to get away from the crowds. This is the third time in a month this has happened on your way to work. You're terrified to think what might be wrong with you. One thing you do know is that you'll never take the bus to work again — if you dare to go to work at all. (Brody, 1984, p. 18)

The scene you are being asked to imagine is a typical example of a panic disorder. As described in DSM-III-R, its essential features include recurrent panic (anxiety) attacks that (a) happen at unexpected times and (b) are not set off by situations in which the individual is the focus of others' attention (American Psychiatric Association, 1987, pp. 235–236). The diagnosis of panic disorder also depends on the frequency with which the panic attacks occur (at least four within a four-week period) and the absence of any physical or other mental disorder that may account for such attacks. Various somatic symptoms similar to those found in panic disorder may be caused by an abnormally low level of glucose in the blood (**hypoglycemia**) or excessive activity of the thyroid gland (**hyperthyroidism**).

Among the most common somatic symptoms of panic disorder are difficulty in breathing, unusually rapid heartbeat, chest pain or other discomfort in that region, choking and smothering sensations, dizziness or sensations of revolving in space, faintness, abnormal sensations of burning or prickling, hot and cold flashes, profuse sweating, and trembling or shaking. Not every individual undergoing an attack of panic will necessarily experience all of these bodily changes (Rachman, 1988).

Panic disorder may also be manifested by the sudden onset of apprehension, fearfulness, and even terror. Some individuals are seized with a fear of dying, as in the following example.

A 25-year-old married insurance salesman is admitted to the medical service of a hospital by his internist when he arrives at the emergency room, for the fourth time in a month, insisting that he is having a heart attack. The cardiologist's work-up is completely negative.

The patient states that his "heart problem" started six months ago when he had a sudden episode of terror, chest pain, palpitations, sweating, and shortness of breath while driving across a bridge on his way to visit a prospective client. His father and uncle had both had heart problems, and the patient was sure he was developing a similar illness. Not wanting to alarm his wife and family, he initially said nothing; but when the attacks began to recur several times a month, he consulted his internist. The internist found nothing wrong and told him he should try to relax, take more time off from work, and develop some leisure interests. In spite of his attempts to follow this advice the attacks recurred with increasing intensity and frequency.

The patient claims that he believes the doctors who say there is nothing wrong with his heart, but during an attack he still becomes concerned that he is having a heart attack and will die. (Spitzer, Skodol, Gibbon, & Williams, 1981, p. 35)

Panic disorder frequently begins in late adolescence or early adulthood, but it may occur during middle age as well. The disorder is fairly common (American Psychiatric Association, 1987, pp. 236–237).

Phobic Disorders

A phobia is the channeling of fear and anxiety toward a particular object, person, or situation. The word *phobia* comes from the Greek *phobos*, meaning "panic–fear," "terror," "flight." Phobos was also the name of the ancient Greek deity who instilled fear and panic in enemies. As Paul Errera (1962, p. 326) points out, Phobos was included in

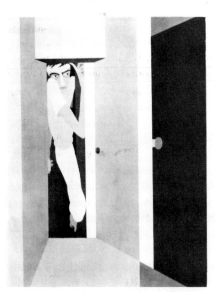  

Phobias, which are irrational fears of objects or situations, can take many directions. These stylized scenes by John Vassos illustrate (a) fear of small enclosed places, (b) fear of storms, and (c) fear of sleep.

the family of Gods. One of the oldest forms on the fear-mask, Phobos was also depicted often on weapons and shields.

It has been estimated that from 2 to 4 percent of the population in the United States suffer at one time or another from a phobic disorder. However, data from various outpatient clinics suggest that although phobic disorders can be devastating they constitute less than 5 percent of all types of neurotic disorders seen in people over 18 years of age (Kaplan & Sadock, 1985, p. 321).

Phobic individuals usually recognize that what they fear presents no real danger; nevertheless, they cannot control their irrational feelings. Although they sometimes try to resist this irrationality and approach the feared situation, the anxiety their attempts arouse usually becomes so intense that they retreat to avoidance behavior. They may assert that such behavior is rational because they know they will be overwhelmed with anxiety if they do approach the feared stimuli. However, they usually admit that the anxiety itself is not rational.

Not all irrational fears necessarily represent phobic disorders. Much depends on the extent to which one's daily life is disrupted by the avoidance of the feared situation. Some people may have highly circumscribed phobias that cause little, if any, disability. They therefore feel no need to seek help for such irrational fears, or they try to reduce them on their own. Differences in the extent to which phobias can be disruptive are well illustrated in a study of 325 randomly selected residents of Burlington, Vermont (Agras, Sylvester, & Oliveau, 1969). Interviews with these individuals revealed that the most common fear was of snakes; 39 percent expressed mild fear and 25 percent intense fear, though this is a region with few harmful snakes. The fear of snakes created no seriously disabling phobias because it lacked functional significance in that particular community. Disabling phobic disorders were much less prevalent than common fears. About 8 percent of the individuals surveyed had mildly disabling phobias, and less than 1 percent suffered from severely disabling phobias. *Severely disabling* was defined as being absent from work or unable to manage common household tasks because of a phobia. Among the most devastating phobias were irrational fears of illness and injury, being in a public place, or traveling alone.

Classifying Patterns of Phobias

At one time it was customary for writers of textbooks on psychiatry and abnormal psychology to compile long lists of specific phobias, each bearing a label derived from Greek or Latin — for example, acarophobia — the fear of mites, ticks, and small insects; mysophobia — the fear of dirt and germs; and even phobophobia — the fear of being afraid.

Labeling phobias may make interesting reading, but it has little scientific or professional value. However, classifying patterns of phobias can be helpful, especially in research. For example, on the basis of clinical observation, Marks (1969) concluded that phobias can be conveniently divided into two main classes: those whose stimuli are external to the individual (Class I) and those whose stimuli are internal to the individual (Class II). Class I includes various forms of agoraphobia (fear of being in a public place), social phobias (fear of social gatherings), animal phobias, and miscellaneous specific phobias, such as fear of thunderstorms. Class II can be divided into two main subtypes: phobias related to fears of illness — for example, the fear that any heart palpitation must mean heart disease in spite of objective evidence to the contrary — and obsessive phobias, such as the fear that one will kill one's own child. Marks cautions that the distinction between Class I and Class II sometimes breaks down. For example, agoraphobia (Class I) may be accompanied by an irrational fear of dying (Class II). In the case of an obsessive fear that one will kill one's own child (Class II), an individual may hide all knives to avoid being tempted by such external stimuli (Class I). Marks also emphasizes that most research on phobias has been carried out on Class I phobias, since they are easier to discern and study than Class II phobias.

The DSM-III-R classification of phobic disorders reflects in part the work of Marks. It consists of three major categories: agoraphobia, social phobia, and simple phobia. In addition, anxiety related to separation from major attachment figures, such as parents, often takes the form of phobic reactions. Children may fear being away from home or even being in a room by themselves; they may be afraid to go to bed alone or refuse to go to school for fear of being separated from their more familiar surroundings. These kinds of reactions are classified in DSM-III-R as characteristics of **separation anxiety disorder** (American Psychiatric Association, 1987, pp. 58–60; Morris & Kratochwill, 1983, p. 44). We discuss separation anxiety in Chapter 17, where we deal with various psychological disorders of childhood and adolescence.

Agoraphobia

Agora is a Greek word meaning "place of assembly" or "marketplace." Thus, **agoraphobia** can be translated as "fear of public places." However, in modern clinical usage the term has a broader meaning. DSM-III-R cites the following situations as common in agoraphobic disorders: being outside one's home alone, being in a crowd or standing in a line, being on a bridge, and traveling in a train, bus, or car (American Psychiatric Association, 1987, p. 240).

The initial phase of agoraphobia often consists of recurrent attacks of panic. The individual learns to anticipate attacks and becomes reluctant to be alone or to be in situations that have become associated with them. For example, the perception of panic as a heart attack rather than as an anxiety disorder could result in an exaggerated fear of having subsequent episodes of panic. This fear could then increase the tendency to avoid various situations that the individual believes would precipitate further experiences of panic (Breier, Charney, & Heninger, 1986, p. 1035). In some instances, there seems to be no previous history of panic attacks associated with being alone or leaving home. In either case, the agoraphobia may become so severe that the individual is eventually housebound.

Prevalence and Patterns. Agoraphobia with episodes of panic is the most prevalent and severe form of phobic disorders. In its various manifestations it constitutes the main complaint of the majority of people who seek treatment for their phobias (Frampton, 1974; Marks, 1969; 1978).

Typically, agoraphobia begins in young adulthood, between ages 18 and 35. It rarely occurs in childhood and rarely begins after age 40. Agoraphobia with panic is diagnosed more frequently in women than in men (American Psychiatric Association, 1987, p. 237; Turns, 1985). This does not necessarily mean that it is actually more prevalent among women. More women than men may be willing to seek help, or women may experience more social pressure to do so.

Victims of agoraphobia vary widely in the way they express their fear and anxiety and in the extent to which they are handicapped in everyday life. The British psychotherapist Muriel Frampton, who has made a special study of agoraphobia, supplies the following examples from her practice.

■ One patient is unable to leave the house at all. As soon as she gets outside the garden gate she feels dizzy and faint. Her legs seem just like jelly, and she retreats in panic to her front door and shuts herself in once more. . . .

■ A young mother had told how for a time she really felt safe only *in bed*, and in fact spent the major part of her day in the bedroom. . . .

■ Recently one man spoke to me of his wife's dilemma. "She appears to be a perfectly normal person," he said. "You'd never think there was anything wrong with her. But she cannot walk across the street alone. Yet she can *drive* anywhere. . . .

■ A young man came to me for help with the opposite problem: he goes out and about fairly freely, but feels quite unsafe when driving his car, especially on a broad, straight road like a motorway. (Frampton, 1974, pp. 16–17)

Self-perceived Causes. How do individuals suffering from agoraphobia perceive the causes of their irrational fears? To answer this question, Ost and Hugdahl (1983) administered a questionnaire to 80 agoraphobic patients of both sexes whose ages ranged from 22 to 68 years. Items dealing with various possible causes were constructed so as to be relevant for conditioning experiences, vicarious events, and the learning of negative information. The large majority (81 percent) ascribed the origin of their phobias to conditioning experiences, 9 percent recalled vicarious experiences, and none stated the learning of negative information. The remaining 10 percent could not recall any specific circumstances that would explain the acquisition of their phobia (Ost & Hugdahl, 1983).

Social Phobia

Convinced she was a "total flop" when it came to crowds, Susan dreaded speaking before more than one person at a time. Even Tupperware parties unnerved her; she gasped and trembled at introductions.

Her lifelong terror worsened over time, especially after she learned that her job for a large Pittsburgh corporation required her to show films to employees.

"It was this fear of getting up and talking. I'd sometimes feel faint, I'd gasp for air, I'd be all choked up. I'd be awake all night for days ahead of time," said Susan, 33, who asked that her real name not be revealed.

She tried hypnosis, relaxation classes, dream therapy. She considered resigning. Nothing helped until she contacted Western Psychiatric Institute and Clinic, where she learned that what she had thought was only severe shyness was in fact a debilitating disorder known as social phobia. (Dunn, 1984, p. B–7)

The central feature of **social phobia** is a persistent, irrational fear of and desire to avoid situations in which the individual may be exposed to scrutiny by others (American Psychiatric Association, 1987, p. 227). Among the most common social phobias are fears of public speaking, carrying on an extended conversation, blushing in front of others, eating or drinking in public, and using public lavatories. Victims of social phobias realize that their disturbance is unreasonable and disabling but nevertheless succumb to it.

Social phobias usually begin soon after puberty, although their onset may be as late as age 30. Researchers generally agree that these disorders occur less often than agoraphobia. As in all phobias, whether an individual's particular social fear is sufficiently disabling to be considered a phobic disorder depends not only on the severity of the fear itself but also on the extent to which the anxiety and the avoidance behavior it provokes interfere with daily activities and goals. Some people may be noticeably fearful of making public speeches or dread carrying on conversations in the midst of a large social group. However, they may choose occupations and social routines that enable them to avoid such anxiety-producing situations but at the same time achieve a reasonable degree of personal satisfaction. Although they may occasionally wish they could engage in the feared activities, their disappointment may be only minimally distressful to themselves or to those with whom they must interact.

Simple Phobia

As defined in DSM-III-R, the essential feature of **simple phobia** is a persistent fear of an object or situation "other than fear of having a panic attack (as in Panic Disorder), or of humiliation or embarrassment in certain social situations (Social Phobia)" (American Psychiatric Association, 1987, p. 244). Simple phobia is generally less complex than agoraphobia or social phobia and therefore is often labeled *specific phobia*. Among the more common simple phobias are fear of animals, especially reptiles, insects, and rodents; fear of high places (acrophobia); and fear of enclosed places such as elevators, tunnels, narrow streets, and small rooms (claustrophobia).

The degree of impairment imposed by simple phobias may vary considerably, depending on the individual's life circumstances. For example, an intense and irrational fear of flying may be of minor consequence for people whose travel habits are naturally circumscribed. On the other hand, such a phobia would obviously be seriously disruptive for individuals whose occupations required them to travel long distances in a short time.

Freudian View of Phobias

According to traditional Freudian theory, the symptoms of phobic disorders represent the ego's defense against fears and anxieties that arise from threatening impulses of sex and aggression—biological drives that were previously repressed but have now filtered into consciousness. To avoid the pain of consciously acknowledging the true source of such fears and anxieties, the ego displaces the internal danger by substituting an external threat—one that can readily be perceived in the environment.

Freud's celebrated case of little Hans, first published in 1909, has served as a prototype of the view that a phobic disorder involves the displacement of internal danger. When Hans was 5 years old, he developed an irrational fear of being bitten by a horse. The fear intensified to the point where Hans was extremely anxious about leaving his home because he might encounter a horse. Freud interpreted this phobia as a symbolic fear of Hans's father, a fear that had its roots in Hans's Oedipus complex and castration anxiety—sexual impulses toward his mother, rivalry with his father for the mother's love, and the resulting fear that his father would punish him by destroying his penis (see Chapter 3). To avoid that fear and the anxiety it produced, Hans transferred the fear to a symbol of his father—a horse. Thus, he not only avoided castration anxiety but also reduced (maladaptively) his ambivalent feelings about his father, for he both loved and feared him (Freud, 1909/1955).

Although displacement is a central concept in psychoanalytic interpretations of phobic disorders, it may sometimes be secondary to other ego defenses. In his later writings on anxiety, Freud (1936) cited the case of a young man whose agoraphobia was shown upon analysis to be a defense against admitting into consciousness an even more painful source of anxiety—conflict between his erotic desire for prostitutes and his fear of acquiring syphilis as a punishment. But the dynamics of the agoraphobia involved more than a displacement of current fears. To yield to the temptation would not simply arouse fear of contracting a disease but would also cause him to regress to painful conflicts experienced during the phallic phase of childhood. According to Freud, on a deeper level the young man's phobia represented a defense against the revival of fear experienced during the

Oedipal phase of psychosexual development, when the threat of castration frightened him into abandoning his overt sexual desire for his mother (Freud, 1936, p. 63).

Phobias and Self-doubt

Another interpretation of phobias is that they may often stem from feelings of personal inadequacy. Consider the individual who fears making a speech in public and consequently avoids all such situations. Of course, the fear and avoidance behavior may arise in part because of the realization that communication skills are poor. A more fundamental source, however, may lie in deeply held feelings of inferiority — self-doubt that one may not be fully aware of or be willing to deal with directly.

O. H. Mowrer used the phenomenon of stage fright to illustrate how phobias can stem from unresolved doubts about one's general feelings of insecurity and inadequacy, especially with respect to conflicts of conscience.

> If a somewhat insecure person is afraid of being "seen through," what more vulnerable or threatening situation than that of being before an audience with all eyes upon him? He is being watched, scrutinized, "examined," in a way that otherwise rarely occurs; and if there are guilty secrets in a person's life, such a situation is obviously precarious. Eyes (with their implications of watchfulness, inquiry, attention) are a proverbial symbol of *conscience*; and if one is on bad terms with this part of his personality and is trying not to "think about" what it is that conscience has "against" him, an audience, with its concentrated gaze, is a powerful reminder of his moral vulnerability. (Mowrer, 1965, p. 198)

Phobias and Conditioning

Explanations of phobic disorders based on principles of classical conditioning (see Chapter 4) do not require a search for unconscious inner conflicts or hidden self-doubts. Rather, they emphasize that phobias are initiated by the same basic processes of conditioning that account for the acquisition of normal fears. For example, a child who previously had no fear of dogs may suffer a painful bite from a dog. In classical conditioning language the bite is an unconditioned stimulus and the pain an unconditioned response — a response that did not require any previous experience or learning. However, the pain now becomes associated with the sight of the dog — a conditioned stimulus. Upon seeing the dog again, the child, now expecting pain, reacts with fear — a conditioned response. Indeed, even the anticipation of seeing the dog and thus experiencing pain may produce anxiety and avoidance. The conditioned response of fear and subsequent avoidance behavior may then be generalized to similar objects or situations, such as other dogs or animals that resemble dogs. Eventually, their presence may also elicit fear and avoidance even though the child had no painful experience with them. Thus, the phobia takes on an irrational aspect.

Assuming that a particular phobia has been acquired through classical conditioning, the question arises as to why the fear and avoidance of the situation are maintained. Ordinarily, conditioned responses that have been established in the laboratory become weakened and in time extinguished if the pairing of the conditioned and unconditioned stimuli is not occasionally repeated. There are several reasons that this laboratory paradigm may not necessarily apply to conditioning in everyday life

1. Additional frightening experiences may become associated with the feared object through other information. For example, the child who first learned to fear dogs because of a painful bite may later be warned about the danger of meeting strange dogs or may hear stories of dangerous encounters with them or other animals. Thus the connection between dogs and fear is strengthened, even though encounters with them were carefully avoided.

2. Fears that have been acquired through classical conditioning may be maintained through operant conditioning (see Chapter 4). The phobic individual learns that avoidance of a feared object or situation prevents the fear and anxiety from arising. Thus, the phobia is reinforced. Furthermore, the avoidance behavior prevents any future opportunity for learning that the fear is groundless. For example, there is no opportunity to learn that not all dogs bite and that, indeed, encountering them can have positive rather than negative consequences. As long as the feared object or situation is avoided, positive reinforcement cannot occur.

3. Avoidance of the feared situation may have positive consequences in that the phobic individual gains rewards that otherwise would not have been obtainable. For example, the child who develops a phobia for school may use the fear to gain favors at home that formerly would not have been granted. However, this reason has very limited value, for many phobic individuals undergo so much anxiety about their fear that it seems unlikely they would often use it to gain positive reinforcement.

4. By definition, phobias are irrational. This irrationality in itself is a powerful force that helps maintain the phobia. Simply telling someone that a phobia is nonsense is seldom effective in eliminating the fear. Thus, special techniques have been developed to recondition the phobic individual. For example, the phobic stimulus is repeatedly paired with relaxation, so that, eventually, confronting those stimuli does not elicit anxiety and avoidance (see Chapter 20).

Limitations of Classical Conditioning of Phobias

Although many learning psychologists have accepted the laboratory model of classical conditioning as a way of explaining how phobias are acquired in everyday life, three persuasive arguments have demonstrated its limitations.

1. Failure of repeated frightening experiences to produce phobias. Rachman points out that during World War II the great majority of civilians who endured repeated air raids did not acquire long-term fears or phobias. Short-lived fears, of course, were common; but they did not show the persistent quality of phobias. The absence of conditioned phobic responses was contrary to what classical conditioning theory would predict (Rachman, 1978, p. 187; 1979, p. 379).

2. Aversive conditioning in infants. Among the earliest studies in the classical conditioning of fear in infants was the famous experiment by Watson and Rayner (1920) in which little Albert was conditioned to be afraid of a white rat associated with a loud, disagreeable noise (see Chapter 4). The result of this experiment has often been accepted as evidence that fears and therefore phobias are acquired mainly through classical conditioning. However, a number of other classical conditioning experiments with infants have failed to establish fear reactions. English (1929) repeatedly paired a startling noise with a wooden duck but was unable to establish a conditioned response of fear of the duck. Bregman (1934) attempted to condition 15 infants to fear wooden and cloth objects by pairing them with an aversive conditioned stimulus — the startling sound of an electric bell. Repeated pairings failed to establish any fear reactions.

Frightening experiences do not necessarily produce phobias. During World War II the great majority of civilians in London endured repeated air raids without developing long-term fears or phobias. Their resistance was strengthened through mutual emotional support.

3. Aversive conditioning in adults. More recently, researchers working with adult volunteers attempted to establish phobic reactions to a neutral stimulus (a complex geometric design) by pairing it with a painful but tolerable electric shock delivered by means of an electrode attached to a shin. Although there was evidence that a conditioned response of fear occurred, it did not involve the disturbed physiological reactions that genuine phobic disorders typically do (Hallam & Rachman, 1976). In a series of experiments involving aversion therapy, chronic alcoholics who volunteered to receive such therapy were compared with another group of alcoholics who did not undergo that kind of treatment (Hallam, Rachman, & Falkowski, 1972). The aversion therapy consisted of pairing electric shock with fantasies of drinking and with the taste, smell, and sight of several preferred alcoholic beverages. Although the alcoholics who were subjected to shock acquired a distaste for alcohol, they did not show any increase in the kinds of fears, anxieties, and physiological reactions characteristic of phobic disorders. Indeed, distaste for alcohol was the only response after conditioning that consistently distinguished them from the group of alcoholics that had not received aversion therapy.

These studies show that laboratory classical conditioning methods may sometimes fail to produce phobias that are analogous both psychologically and physiologically to those seen in everyday life. Thus, the question arises as to whether phobic disorders are inevitably acquired through classical conditioning.

Equipotentiality

Traditional views of classical conditioning usually assume that environmental events are all equally capable of being conditioned stimuli of fear (Eysenck & Rachman, 1965). This assumption, which has come to be known as the **equipotentiality premise of conditioning** (Rachman, 1978) can be traced to Pavlov (1928), who said: "Any natural phenomenon chosen at will may be converted into a conditioned stimulus. . . . Any visual stimulus, any desired sound, any odor, and the stimulation of any part of the skin" (p. 86).

Various critics have challenged the assumption that all environmental events have an equal potential for being conditioned fear stimuli. One line of evidence against the equipotentiality premise is based on epidemiological studies of common fears. As we noted earlier in the chapter, a survey of fears in a Vermont city (Agras, Sylvester, & Oliveau, 1969) found that the prevalence of fear of snakes was far greater than fear of the dentist, although contacts with the latter were much more frequent. Indeed, in this particular locality, the chance of encountering snakes in one's everyday routine was minimal. Thus, classical conditioning alone could not account for the difference in this distribution of fears.

Biological Readiness

A more central argument against the equipotentiality premise is that some fears are more easily acquired through classical conditioning than others because the organism is readier to respond with fear to certain conditioned stimuli. This preparedness, as Martin Seligman calls it, is especially true for conditioned responses that have survival value. Drawing upon animal studies to bolster his position, Seligman (1970, 1971) cites various experiments to demonstrate that animals can be conditioned to fear some stimuli more readily than others because of their greater significance for survival. For example, rats can be conditioned to associate fear with taste in just one trial, even when there is a delay of several hours between tasting and becoming ill. On the other hand, experiments in which a light was paired with foot shock found that several trials were required before rats could be conditioned to fear the light. Even then, the interval between the light and the shock had to be very short, a matter of a few seconds.

Extending the concept of preparedness to human fears, Seligman argues that it helps explain why certain phobias are more common than others. For example, irrational fears of the dark, of heights, and of leaving the safety of one's home to venture into public places are far more common than "pajama phobias, grass phobias, electric-outlet phobias, and hammer phobias" (Seligman, 1971, p. 312). That is because the first set of fears is the kind that has had survival value in the long evolutionary history of the human species. Thus, biological preparedness not only helps explain why we do not become conditioned to all potential fear stimuli but also why fears can be acquired in just one conditioning trial and why they are so persistent.

Seligman's preparedness hypothesis proposes not only that fears rooted in our biological heritage are those most likely to be acquired through classical conditioning but also that such fears will be especially resistant to extinction. Partial support for this idea comes from the work of Ohman, Erixon, and Lofberg (1975). The subjects of their study were young men and women at Uppsala University (Sweden) who volunteered for the experiments and were paid for their participation. Phobic stimuli (pictures of snakes) and neutral stimuli (pictures of houses or human faces) were paired with the unconditioned stimulus of shock delivered to fingers of the right hand. Conditioned responses, as measured by skin conductance, were established for the neutral as well as the phobic stimuli, but responses to the latter were more resistant to extinction.

Although Seligman emphasizes the biological, noncognitive nature of preparedness, he does not claim that it is crucial in the classical conditioning of all phobias: "It is not argued that no phobia about objects of modern technology exists, or that all phobias are noncognitive. People sometimes talk themselves into phobias. There are airplane phobias and fears of electric shock. The preparedness view is not disconfirmed by isolated examples: it points to the fact that the great majority of phobias are about objects of natural importance to the survival of the species. It does not deny that other phobias are possible, it only claims that they should be less frequent, since they are less prepared" (Seligman, 1971, p. 316).

It is essential to understand the context in which Seligman's argument occurs. Saying that biological preparedness is a crucial element in the classical conditioning of fears and phobias does not exclude their being learned in other ways as well. Two additional processes must be considered: the role of vicarious experiences, such as observing the behavior of others; and the direct transmission of information, including beliefs and attitudes. These social learning processes may operate independently of conditioning or in combination with it (McNally, 1987; Rachman, 1978).

Generalized Anxiety Disorder

A central characteristic of generalized anxiety disorder is an intense but vague apprehension. The individual persistently worries that something terrible is about to happen but is unable to state specifically the actual nature of the impending disaster—a condition that Freud called free-floating anxiety. It is especially this free-floating quality that differentiates generalized anxiety disorder from phobic and panic disorders. The pervasive but nameless anxiety is vividly portrayed in the opening scene of Edgar Allen Poe's short story *The Fall of the House of Usher* (1839/1978).

> During the whole of a dull, dark, and soundless day in the autumn of the year, when the clouds hung oppressively low in the heavens, I had been passing alone, on horseback, through a singularly dreary tract of country, and at length found myself, as the shades of the evening drew on, within view of the melancholy House of Usher. I know not how it was—but, with the first glimpse of the building, a sense of insufferable gloom pervaded my spirit. . . . I looked upon the scene before me with an utter depression of soul. . . . There was an iciness, a sinking, a sickening of the heart—an unredeemed dreariness of thought. . . . What was it—I paused to think—what was it so unnerved me in the contemplation of the House of Usher? It was a mystery all insoluble; nor could I grapple with the shadowy fancies that crowded upon me as I wondered. (pp. 397–398)

The circumstances of this cartoon contrast well with the shadowy fancies plaguing the horseback rider in *The Fall of the House of Usher*.

"WHAT A RELIEF. NOW I CAN FOCUS MY FREE-FLOATING ANXIETY ON TO SOMETHING SPECIFIC."

In addition to the vague apprehension of free-floating anxiety, motor symptoms such as tremors, restlessness, and jumpiness may occur. There may also be various signs of autonomic hyperactivity, such as sweating, heart pounding, dizziness, and stomach discomfort. These bodily reactions are similar to those in a panic attack but are usually milder. Other typical symptoms include extreme vigilance and scanning of the environment — overattention to what is occurring. As a result there may be a persistent pattern of irritability, impatience, and the feeling of being on edge.

Obsessive Compulsive Disorder

The presence of either obsessions or compulsions is sufficient for a diagnosis of obsessive compulsive disorder. (Obsessive compulsive neurosis is listed as an acceptable alternative label in DSM-III-R.) The essential features of obsessions are recurrent and persistent ideas, thoughts, images, or impulses that the individual experiences as intrusive and unwanted. To cope with this intrusion the victim attempts to suppress them or to neutralize them with other thoughts or acts. Compulsions are repetitive patterns of behavior carried out in stereotyped fashion according to certain inflexible rules. Their purpose is to ward off or neutralize some feared event. Generally, the behavior has no realistic relationship to the dreaded event or is performed to an excessive degree. The individual realizes that the actions are unreasonable but nevertheless feels compelled to complete them (American Psychiatric Association, 1987, p. 245).

Although anxiety is a crucial component of obsessive compulsive disorder, its role is less obvious than in other anxiety disorders, such as phobias, panic disorder, and generalized anxiety. For example, abnormal compulsions are not usually attempts to avoid

"...AND FLAIR SOAP HAS A SPECIAL OFFER FOR ALL YOU OBSESSIVE-COMPULSIVES WHO WASH YOUR HANDS BETWEEN 30 AND 50 TIMES A DAY..."

situations, as is the case in phobic behavior. Rather, their main purpose is to prevent, in a magiclike way, the occurrence of situations that arouse anxiety. Also, compulsive behavior may be used to undo the negative effects of contact with an anxiety-producing situation. Thus, repeated washing of one's hands throughout the day may serve to dispel a fear of being contaminated with germs, even when that possibility is remote. It is when the ritual cannot be carried out that obvious signs of anxiety may appear.

For purposes of diagnosis it is useful to differentiate between obsessions and compulsions. In practice, however, the two overlap considerably. People with obsessive ideas often show compulsive behavior, and vice versa. Thus, it is appropriate for these two components to be linked as a single diagnostic category. However, the symptoms themselves may take many forms and directions. The most common manifestations of obsessions are recurrent and uncontrollable thoughts of violence, guilt, contamination, and self-doubt. Compulsions often take the form of ritualistic counting, touching, checking, and handwashing.

One of the earliest descriptions of the elaborate ritualistic behavior sometimes found in obsessive compulsive disorder is in Freud's paper "The Neuropsychoses of Defense" (1894/1962). The title is a curious one, perhaps reflecting Freud's early interest in the neurological basis of mental disorders. In this paper Freud described an 11-year-old boy who followed an obsessive ceremonial before going to bed. First he told his mother in the greatest detail all the events of the day. There must be no scraps of paper or rubbish on the carpet of the bedroom, the bed must be pushed right to the wall, three chairs must stand by it, and the pillows must lie in a particular way. In order to get to sleep he must first kick out a certain number of times with both legs and then lie on his side (p. 172).

Differential Diagnosis   It is important to distinguish between obsessive compulsive disorder and other kinds of maladaptive thoughts and actions that are often labeled obsessive or compulsive but whose functional significance is quite different. For example, one may engage in excessive brooding, such as persistently dwelling on certain unpleasant circumstances or events, without perceiving this obsession as an involuntary invasion of consciousness. In addition, certain instances of excessive eating, drinking, gambling, and various sexual activities are sometimes referred to as compulsive behavior. These compulsions often become a focus of discussion in the popular press, in such articles as "Compulsive Gambling — Disease Affects Many Lives" (Slavin, 1976) and "Are You a Workaholic?" (Rosenbaum, 1979). However, these kinds of excesses are inherently pleasurable. The individual who engages in them may indeed wish to resist doing so, but only because of their secondary negative consequences. They do not have the involuntary quality found in a true obsessive compulsive disorder. Some of these maladaptive patterns are classified in DSM-III-R as disorders of impulse control (which we discuss in Chapter 12).

The ritualistic acts often found in obsessive compulsive disorder sometimes resemble the bizarre behavior in certain forms of psychosis, especially schizophrenia (see Chapter 11). However, their functional significance is quite different. Individuals suffering from an obsessive compulsive disorder maintain adequate contact with reality and are painfully aware of the absurdity of their thinking and behavior. They may be extremely preoccupied with their obsessions and compulsions, but, unlike psychotic individuals, they do not withdraw from people. Furthermore, they can separate their inner thoughts from external reality. Indeed, their highly structured obsessions and compulsions may well help protect them from the extreme personality disorganization of psychotic states (Nemiah, 1973, 1985a, p. 905).

Normal versus Abnormal Patterns

What everyday language may label an obsession or compulsion does not necessarily represent an obsessive compulsive disorder. All of us have been preoccupied with a harmless obsession, such as repeatedly dwelling on a trivial jingle. Ordinarily, this does not arouse intense anxiety or permanently interfere with the tasks of work and home, and it usually fades away in a short time.

In the same vein, certain forms of compulsive behavior are usually considered to be normal aspects of personality. For example, some people are extremely meticulous, but this attention to neatness does not necessarily interfere with their everyday functioning. In certain cultural settings it may even be considered a virtue. Some forms of compulsive behavior may be highly constructive — for example, an airline pilot's methodical inspection of instruments before takeoff, an accountant's extreme preoccupation with accurately recording various financial details, and a proofreader's intense concern with checking every word in a manuscript.

Obsessive thoughts and compulsive acts often occur as part of the normal development of children (Marks, 1978, pp. 143–144). Many a young child tries to ward off some imaginary impending disaster by compulsively engaging in certain magic rituals, such as carefully avoiding stepping on sidewalk cracks or touching every other picket in a fence. The normality of such behavior is delightfully portrayed in A. A. Milne's *When We Were Very Young* (1924/1961).

Whenever I walk in a London Street,
I'm ever so careful to watch my feet;
    And I keep in the squares,
    And the masses of bears,
Who wait at the corners all ready to eat
The sillies who tread on the lines of the street.
    Go back to their lairs
    And I say to them, "Bears,

Just look how I'm walking in all of the squares."
And the little bears growl to each other, "He's mine.
As soon as he's silly and steps on a line." (p. 14)

Role of Anxiety

Anxiety plays a multifaceted role in obsessive compulsive disorder. The intrusion of obsessions and compulsions produces anxiety, for not only do the victims perceive the intrusion as beyond their control but they also realize that it interferes with their everyday lives. Furthermore, they often find it increasingly difficult to shield their peculiar ritualistic behavior from other people, who are apt to view it as undesirable and attempt to discourage it. This disapproval tends to add to their anxiety and misery. However, if they attempt to resist carrying out their compulsive behavior, their anxiety and misery increase even more. Thus, the defense they have acquired to counteract dangerous and anxiety provoking obsession is ultimately self-defeating.

The central role of compulsive rituals in controlling obsessive anxiety can be seen in the following case of an 11-year-old boy whose alienation from his parents led him to place all his love and trust in his aged grandfather. The boy realized this was a fragile alliance, and the thought of his grandfather dying aroused a great deal of anxiety.

Peter began to be visited by anxious thoughts which seemed to force themselves into his mind. He had images of the house catching fire; he was afraid it would be struck by lightning or shattered in a high wind. He thought of various ways in which harm might come to his grandfather, and then he began to develop . . . magical acts designed to prevent this catastrophe. If the thought crossed his mind that the house might burn, he felt compelled to touch something in order to avert the danger. If he had such a thought while stepping on a crack he had to step on the crack again to cancel the thought. Soon he needed to perform extra touchings for good measure, and sometimes he would spend nearly an hour going through one of these operations. When people began to notice his peculiar behavior, he developed a technique for discharging all of the unlucky thoughts of the day in the privacy of his bedroom at night. If he pointed four times (a lucky number) to the southwest (a lucky direction), he would counteract the danger. But he never felt satisfied. He had to point $4 \times 4 \times 4 \times 4$ times, 256 times, and this took half an hour. He invented short cuts like stamping his foot to stand for groups of numbers, but in the end no time was saved. If the ritual could not be completed, he felt absolutely miserable. He was at the mercy of *obsessive thoughts* and *compulsive actions*, all of which had the significance of *undoing* the harm contained in a destructive thought. (White & Watt, 1973, pp. 218–219)

Ritualistic behavior as a way of controlling obsessive anxiety may also consist of constantly repeating acts that initially were constructive and reassuring but now become a matter of anxious doubt. For example, after leaving for the day a merchant may so doubt that the store was locked properly that the compulsion to return becomes overwhelming. However, a single check is not sufficient to allay anxiety. Repeated returns and repeated inspections become necessary. As a result, the journey home may be considerably delayed, accompanied by lingering doubts and worries as to whether the inspections were adequate. The inefficiency of such obsessive compulsive behavior is obvious.

Although anxiety plays a central role in both obsessive compulsive and phobic disorders, its function differs in certain respects. In phobias, anxiety and fear serve to motivate the individuals to avoid contact with a particular object or situation. As long as this avoidance can be maintained, the anxiety is controlled. In contrast, the obsessive compulsive individual, especially one who engages in compulsive ritualistic behavior, is not so much concerned with avoiding certain situations as with the consequences of coming in contact with them. For example, some compulsive individuals constantly worry about the consequences of touching contaminated or dirty objects and need to perform elaborate rituals of washing after doing so. In many instances, however, they do not actively avoid the sources of contamination as long as they know they will be free afterward to wash away the dirt. This way of controlling anxiety is different from that of phobic individuals, who usually so fear the situation evoking anxiety that they persistently avoid it and can be persuaded to approach it only with great difficulty (Marks, 1978, pp. 157–158).

Another difference between the function of anxiety in obsessive compulsive disorder and its role in phobias has to do with the various rituals obsessive compulsive individuals often develop around their anxieties. For instance, if they know they have an opportunity to wash thoroughly after contacting a contaminated object, they will approach it more readily than otherwise. As one woman described her reactions to being contaminated with dirt: "That's the funny thing about it — it's not all that bad. My first feeling is panic, and my first thought is that I want to die . . . but I know you can't die just by wishing it, so then I've got to wash with a special procedure which is so long and drawn out it never seems to come to an end — have to wash the top and round the top before washing my hands" (Marks, 1978, p. 158).

Posttraumatic Stress Disorder

The repeated occurrence of acute anxiety following severe and aversive emotional experiences is involved in posttraumatic stress disorder. Among the events that can induce this disorder are military combat, natural disasters (earthquakes, tornadoes, and floods), serious accidents, cruelty inflicted on humans by humans, torture or unusual confinement, and sexual assault. Individuals suffering from posttraumatic stress disorder may show such signs of anxiety as abnormal sensitivity to light and sound, impaired memory, and an inability to concentrate. Nightmares are common. When the traumatic experience is so severe as to result in the death of others, survivors may have feelings of guilt about their escape: Why was I the only one? Flashbacks — a reliving of the painful experience that initiated the disorder — may occur from time to time (American Psychiatric Association, 1980a, pp. 236–238; Cummings, 1987; Figley, 1985).

Posttraumatic stress disorder is a relatively new diagnostic label; however, the disorder has been known for many years under different names (Trimble, 1985). The chronic anxiety brought on by recurrent battle experiences during World War I was called shell shock. With World War II the term was softened to combat fatigue. Indeed, one writer has claimed that posttraumatic stress disorder is a new name for a condition as old as war (Turkington, 1982, p. 15).

Symptoms of posttraumatic stress disorder may persist long after exposure to the life-threatening situation has ended. A study of 135 randomly selected Holocaust survivors living in Montreal 33 years later found that in comparison with a control group they showed significantly more signs of psychiatric disturbances. This was true regardless of the age at which they had first been confined in a concentration camp (Eaton, Sigal, & Weinfeld, 1982).

A single traumatic event may also have far-reaching effects. For example, the health and performance of officers and crew of the USS *Belknap* following a collision at sea was

Some Vietnam war veterans developed posttraumatic stress disorder not only because of their traumatic experiences in battle but also because they had been engaged in an unpopular war lacking the public support given to earlier wars.

compared with that of officers and crew of the USS *Yarnell*, which had not been involved in any accident. Comparisons over a three-year period found that significantly more members of the *Belknap* were hospitalized during that period because of neurotic anxiety and related symptoms (Hoiberg & McCaughey, 1984).

Posttraumatic anxiety reactions may also vary with the particular nature of the threatening experiences. Anxiety reactions in Vietnam veterans resulted not only from the combat experiences themselves but also from the social and political nature of the war and the quality of social support the veterans received upon returning home (Roberts, 1988; Stretch, 1985). As one writer has summarized the matter

The Vietnam veteran was sent to Southeast Asia at a very young age to fight an unpopular war he did not understand. . . . Even as his friends were killed beside him, he was never able to find a reason for the destruction of which he was a part.

He fought in the wet jungles of America's first guerrilla war in a constant state of uncertainty. Virtual teenagers, these vets spent a year in an alien environment during a crucial period of the development of their adult personalities. At a time when peers at home were exploring moral and ethical responsibility, the Vietnam soldier concentrated only on survival. This disruption caused problems later in life which have never been resolved.

When the veteran returned home alone, there was no victory parade waiting for him. There was only an increasing feeling at home that the war — and therefore his part in it — was morally wrong. People didn't want to hear about the war. Worse, many blamed the veteran for his part in it.

In previous wars, the country shared in the collective guilt of a returning veteran who may have committed atrocities as part of the war effort. In Vietnam, the country refused to accept this collective guilt, blamed the veteran for the violence and left him to shoulder the burden alone. (Turkington, 1982, p. 15)

In addition to such symptoms of posttraumatic stress disorder as nightmares and survival guilt, feelings of cultural alienation and even criminal behavior have been prominent (Foy, Sipprelle, Rueger, & Carroll, 1984; Margolick, 1985; Shatan, 1978). The alienation has led some veterans to seek a life of extreme social isolation. In a number of instances they have retreated to the wilderness, where they follow an existence resembling that of 19th century mountain men. Among this group are trip-wire veterans, a term used by American servicemen for the deadly unseen traps the Vietcong laid along trails followed by GI patrols. The term also applies to soldiers who were especially talented in finding and dismantling the traps. One of these veterans expressed his alienation this way: "There's a lot the public don't know, and probably will never know, about what happened in 'Nam.' . . . The only job skills I have are those that might be useful to a hit man for the Mafia." He said he avoided all human contact, because "I couldn't stand to be touched," and that he suffered from paranoia and nightmares. He was finally persuaded to enter a counseling program sponsored by the state. ("U.S. Wilds Hide Scars of Vietnam," 1983).

Similar words of alienation were spoken by another trip-wire veteran, who sought refuge in the woods because of his recurring nightmares. However, the isolation became too much, and he also emerged to seek counseling. "I became afraid of everything," he said; "I had to get out." As he began to recover, he made trips into the woods to find other trip-wire veterans and persuade them to enter counseling ("U.S. Wilds," 1983).

Just as the social and political implications of the Vietnam War contributed to the development of posttraumatic stress disorder, so may another kind of violation of personal integrity — sexual assault. Victims often suffer not only from the traumatic effects of the physical assault itself but also from what they perceive as a degradation of their personal worth and dignity (Janoff-Bulman, 1985, pp. 21–22; Steketee & Foa, 1987). Consider, for example, this 19-year-old college student. Although she did not experience such common symptoms of posttraumatic stress disorder as nightmares, disruption of eating habits, or excessive crying spells, her anxiety reactions were in some ways even more threatening: "I'm really scared so much of the time. I can't walk down the street by myself without looking behind me every five minutes. . . . If I pass a strange man on the street I want to run . . . and that's kind of where it's left me now, a year later. It made me realize, and I can't express this enough, how unfair it is to be a woman and of not being able to sustain my independence, not being able to walk around freely if I just want to take a walk. . . . I feel threatened so much of the time." (Groth & Birnbaum, 1981, pp. 80–81).

Treatment of Anxiety Disorders

Psychodynamic Approaches

Traditional psychoanalytic approaches to the treatment of anxiety disorders are based on the assumption that the symptoms themselves are only indicators of deeper problems. Thus, the causes of the symptoms must be discovered, their dynamics understood by the patient, and the deeper unrecognized problems brought to consciousness and resolved. Obviously, all this takes a great deal of time. Although more rapid and flexible psychodynamic methods have been developed that shortcut some of the more extended procedures of traditional psychoanalytic therapy, the basic assumption remains (see Chapter 19). For that reason, people who need to solve their anxiety problems more rapidly so that they can resume a normal life as soon as possible have turned increasingly to therapies with a more direct, behavioral orientation.

In some instances psychodynamic approaches to anxiety disorders may focus on the individual's maladaptive feelings of guilt and their interference with daily living. This is an especially important problem in many individuals suffering from posttraumatic stress disorder. Such guilt may be a prominent feature even though the individual was clearly a victim of a violent act and not to blame. For example, in cases of sexual assault, myths about rape may turn the victim into someone who is at fault. Thus, therapy aims not only at reducing the more obvious symptoms of anxiety but also at working through feelings of guilt to reduce self-blame (Cohen & Roth, 1987; Roth, Dye, & Lebowitz, 1988).

In other instances, victims of rape attempt to mask their emotional reactions by assuming a calm affect to isolate themselves from the traumatic event (Burgess & Holmstrom, 1977, p. 319). This reaction may also become an important aspect of psychodynamic therapy. In Chapter 21 we discuss in more detail the dynamics and social-psychological views of rape.

Cognitive – Behavior Therapy and Related Approaches

Since its inception and development into a prominent method of treatment, behavior therapy has focused increasingly on ways of helping people overcome phobic patterns of disorder (Wolpe, 1975, 1978, 1985). Conditioning techniques such as systematic desensitization have been widely used. People suffering from phobias are taught to associate the feared situation with an incompatible but positive response such as deep relaxation. Gradually, the bond is strengthened between the positive feeling and the stimuli that arouse anxiety and fear.

Over the years, behavior therapy for anxiety disorders has become more flexible. Eliminating symptoms of anxiety is often combined with helping the individual achieve insight into the nature of the anxiety disorder. Methods of self-control are taught, and the teaching includes frequent homework assignments designed to help the individual overcome anxiety reactions. The methods tend to focus on the avoidance behavior typical of anxiety disorders and the disruption of daily living that behavior brings about. By means of operant conditioning the anxious individual learns to develop constructive behaviors to replace maladaptive ones. Here the emphasis is on the positive reinforcement of the desired behavior, including methods of **cognitive structuring,** in which the anxious person learns to develop new ways of thinking about the problem. In Chapter 20 we discuss these and related approaches in more detail.

Group therapy, which we examine in Chapter 20, is another technique behavior therapists use to treat anxiety disorders. Some studies suggest that improvement is enhanced when therapy involves anxious individuals and others who play significant roles in their lives. Homebound agoraphobic women have been treated in groups that included their spouses. The therapy emphasized cognitive restructuring and gradual exposure to situations outside the home. Improvement was greater for these women than for other women who followed the same therapy procedures but did not have their husbands present. Although other variables, not fully understood, may well have contributed to the greater success of the couples groups, the researchers concluded that the participation of spouses in the therapy was a definite advantage (Barlow, O'Brien, & Last, 1984).

Behavior therapists have also extended their approach to relate anxiety disorders to physical factors that may be contributing to them. A study of agoraphobic individuals in a psychiatric clinic in the Netherlands found that 60 percent suffered from hyperventilation syndrome (HVS), which is manifested by abnormally rapid, prolonged, and deep breathing (overbreathing). Most of them mentioned that the fear of having an attack of HVS was an important factor in their disorder. The researchers concluded that the treatment of HVS should reduce agoraphobia, and thus could be an efficient approach to the treatment of anxiety disorders involving panic. Later reports of HVS therapy have supported that conclusion (Bonn, Readhead, & Timmons, 1984; Ley, 1987).

Biomedical Treatment

Prior to the 1950s the most widely used drugs for the treatment of anxiety disorders were the **barbiturates,** a group of sedatives that have a calming effect in relatively low doses. As the dosage increases, this effect increases, eventually approximating ordinary sleep. Still higher doses induce even deeper sleep, an anesthetic effect. Continuous use of barbiturates raises the user's level of tolerance, thus inviting higher doses and subsequent addiction (see Chapter 15).

Because barbiturates so readily become addictive and create serious possibilities of overdoses, their use in the treatment of anxiety disorders has steadily declined. In the past several decades they have generally been displaced by less dangerous drugs, but these too are still subject to abuse and can cause addiction. Among them are **meprobamate** (Equanil, Miltown) and the benzodiazepines (Librium, Valium). Meprobamate is especially effective in alleviating panic attacks; the benzodiazepines are particularly useful when anxiety makes sleep a serious problem. More recently some researchers have found that **imipramine,** a drug ordinarily used in the treatment of severe depression (see Chapter

10), is surprisingly effective in alleviating symptoms of anxiety disorder (Kahn et al., 1986). However, further studies need to be done to confirm those provisional results. In Chapter 18 we discuss in more detail the use and limitations of various drugs in treating anxiety disorders.

Summary

1. *Anxiety* is a convenient shorthand term for complex and varied patterns of feelings and behavior. These patterns include three main components: subjective reactions, such as feelings of apprehension; overt behavior, such as trembling and restlessness; and internal physiological reactions, such as increased heart rate.

2. Anxiety may range from highly adaptive (normal) to highly maladaptive (abnormal) feelings and behavior. Adaptive anxiety is appropriate to a situation; maladaptive anxiety is inappropriate and self-defeating.

3. Freud viewed anxiety as a basic condition of neurotic disorders. He distinguished between realistic anxiety and neurotic anxiety. In realistic anxiety the person is faced with a real or objective danger; neurotic anxiety has its source in unconscious motives and conflicts. It may also be exaggerated and therefore inappropriate version of realistic anxiety. Neurotic anxiety most often arises from intrapsychic conflicts, when sexual and aggressive desires (the id) oppose the demands of conscience and ideals (the superego). Neurotic anxiety may also result from the opposing demands of the id and the external environment.

4. Neo-Freudians agree that the symptoms of neurotic disorders (anxiety disorders) represent unconscious defenses against conflict and anxiety too painful to face openly. However, they deny that the sources of such anxiety and conflict are confined to biological drives of sex and aggression. Anxiety may sometimes stem more from the demands and frustrations involved in social circumstances and interpersonal relationships.

5. Explanations of anxiety disorders based on traditional learning theory reject the psychodynamic assumption that the symptoms of anxiety disorders are only indicators of deeper unresolved problems stemming from unconscious motives. The focus of inquiry is on the problem behavior itself. A basic rule is that anxiety disorders are learned according to the same principles that govern the learning of normal behavior. In recent years the application of learning theory to the understanding of anxiety disorders have become more flexible under the influence of cognitive psychology. Although they still reject psychoanalytic concepts of intrapsychic conflict, cognitively oriented behavior theories of learning accept the usefulness of inferences about experiences not open to direct observation. However, it must be possible to link these inferences to observable stimuli and behavior.

6. DSM-III-R classifies anxiety disorders into panic disorders, phobic disorders (or phobic neuroses), generalized anxiety disorder, obsessive compulsive disorder (or obsessive compulsive neurosis), and posttraumatic stress disorder.

7. Panic disorder is marked by recurrent seizures of panic anxiety in the absence of any life-threatening situation. They frequently begin in late adolescence or early adulthood, but they may develop during middle age as well.

8. Phobic disorders channel fear and anxiety toward a particular object, person, or situation. The fears are irrational, in that victims realize that what they fear presents no real danger.

9. The three main patterns of phobic disorders are: (a) agoraphobia, the fear of being outside one's home, traveling, or being in other public places; (b) simple phobias, such as fear of high or enclosed places; and (c) social phobias, such as fear of making a speech in public.

10. Explanations of phobias include theories of conditioning, psychodynamic theories, and theories that emphasize a person's feelings of self-doubt and inferiority. All of these theories have been subject to critical scrutiny and enjoy various degrees of acceptance among mental health professionals.

11. An important aspect of conditioning theories for explaining phobias is the concept of preparedness. Seligman and his associates have proposed that whether or not conditioning produces phobias depends on whether the stimulus has biological survival value for the individual.

12. A central characteristic of generalized anxiety disorder is an intense but inexplicable apprehension, which Freud called free-floating anxiety. Bodily symptoms such as tremor, restlessness, sweating, and dizziness may also be present.

13. The persistence of either obsessions or compulsions is sufficient to justify a diagnosis of obsessive compulsive disorder. Obsessive symptoms include recurrent and persistent ideas, thoughts, images, or impulses that are unwanted but that cannot be controlled by voluntarily expelling or ignoring them. Compulsions are repetitive patterns of stereotyped behavior carried out to ward off or to neutralize some feared event. Usually the behavior has no realistic relationship to the perceived danger.

14. Anxiety is a crucial but subtle component of obsessive compulsive disorder. The compulsions are attempts not to avoid situations but to prevent in a magiclike way the occurrence of situations that arouse anxiety. Although obsessions and compulsions can be distinguished, the two are often intertwined; hence the diagnostic concept of obsessive compulsive disorder.

15. It is important to distinguish abnormal compulsive behavior from routine acts that have the air of compulsions but are adaptive, such as the inspection of aircraft functions before takeoff.

16. Posttraumatic stress disorder involves the repeated occurrence of acute anxiety following severe and aversive emotional experiences. Among such experiences are military combat, natural disasters such as earthquakes and floods, serious accidents, torture or unusual confinement, and sexual assault. Individuals suffering from posttraumatic stress disorder may show such symptoms of anxiety disorder as an abnormal sensitivity to light and sound, inability to concentrate, nightmares, and feelings of guilt at having escaped the traumatic situation while others did not. Flashbacks may also occur.

17. Symptoms of posttraumatic stress may persist long after the initial experience. The anxiety reactions of Vietnam veterans persisted years after they had returned home.

18. The treatment of anxiety disorders may follow a variety of procedures. In psychoanalytic and other psychodynamic approaches, the central goal is to enable the person to achieve insight into the causes of the disorder. These causes, of course, are subject to the interpretations of the therapist, which may vary depending on the particular psychodynamic approach favored.

19. Cognitive – behavior approaches to the treatment of anxiety disorders often use conditioning techniques combined with helping the individual achieve insight into the nature and origin of the problem.

20. Therapeutic drugs, such as antianxiety medications, may also be used in the treatment of anxiety disorders. However, some of them are addictive and are used less than they were before.

6

Dissociative and Somatoform Disorders

We may with advantage at
times forget what we know.
                    PUBLILIUS SYRUS
Moral Sayings, Maxim 234 (first century A.D.)

He will be the slave of many
masters who is his body's slave.
                            SENECA
        Letters of Lucilius (first century A.D.)

A curly-haired blond youth walked out of the Atlantic Ocean onto a deserted beach in Key West one week ago and he does not remember his name, his family, where he is from or how he got here. . . . He speaks quietly and has a slight stammer when he is excited. His eyes show signs of strain when he tries to recall his past.

"It was like waking up and opening my eyes," he said. "I felt rain on my head and it was dark. I was drifting or floating. I can get back to that point, in the water, and I can't get back any farther. I don't know who I am." . . .

He had no money and no personal papers. The youth says he has no recollection of anyone having been with him or being in a boat, but there were marks on his shoulders, he says, "like I was carrying some scuba diving gear." (Memory Is a Blank," 1972).

The news story did not venture a diagnosis of the young man's condition. However, the description strongly suggests psychogenic amnesia, one of the several forms of **dissociative disorders** we discuss in this chapter. Their central feature is a sudden alteration in the normal integration of consciousness, identity, and behavior in the absence of any organic disease that can explain the alteration.

Somatoform disorders, the other major diagnostic category we examine in this chapter, involve somatic (bodily) symptoms that take the form of physical disease, but they cannot be traced to actual organic disability and there are strong indications that the complaints are related to psychological factors. Among the common somatic symptoms are recurring and persistent headaches, loss of sensation in various parts of the body, and various aches and pains.

Historical Background

Many of the symptoms now classified in DSM-III-R under dissociative and somatoform disorders have traditionally been labeled hysteria, or hysterical neuroses. Observations of what medical historians believe may well have been hysterical disorders can be found in ancient writings, especially those involving physical disabilities. Throughout the ages, such disorders have been thought to be a female disease (Chodoff, 1982). Fragments of the *Kahun Papyrus*, a medical treatise written about 2000 B.C., describe such cases as "a woman aching in all her limbs with pain to the sockets of her eyes," a "woman pained in her teeth and jaws [who] knows not how to open her mouth," and a woman "ill in seeing" and suffering from pains in the neck (Veith, 1977, p. 11). According to Egyptian physicians, these symptoms were caused by an upward dislocation of the uterus that severely crowded other organs of the body.

It was not until the teachings of Hippocrates (ca. 460–377 B.C.) that the term **hysteria** actually came into use. It was derived from the Greek word *hystera*, meaning "uterus." Hippocrates described various hysterical disorders that he thought occurred solely in women deprived of sexual relations. He claimed that this deprivation caused the uterus to become displaced, resulting in anxiety, choking sensations, and vomiting. Hippocrates also thought that dislocation of the uterus could result in palpitations, excessive perspiration, and convulsions resembling epileptic seizures. Accordingly, he said that to treat hysteria the uterus should be pushed into place. In another prescription Hippocrates stated that "when a woman suffers from hysteria . . . an attack of sneezing is beneficial" (Jones, W., 1923, p. 167). The sneezing is supposed to restore the uterus to its proper position.

The idea that symptoms of hysteria are caused by abnormalities of the uterus had been abandoned by the time Freud began his studies of neurotic disorders. However, the idea of a relationship between sexuality and hysterical symptoms persisted. There is no evidence that Freud and his followers were directly influenced by Hippocrates's theory; nevertheless, they believed that frustration and conflict arising from sexual impulses played a crucial role in the origin of hysterical neuroses. From this perspective, the symptoms of hysteria are unusual but often dramatic defenses against conflict and anxiety that the individual does not openly recognize.

Freud was greatly influenced in his views of hysterical neurosis by an older colleague, Joseph Breuer, with whom he wrote the now classic *Studies in Hysteria*. Although Breuer later became less certain about the sexual origin of these disorders, in his pioneering work with Freud he expressed the conviction that marriage often brings new sexual traumas that may well lead to symptoms of hysteria. To emphasize his point even more, he added, "I do not think I exaggerate when I assert that the great majority of severe neuroses in women originate in the marriage bed" (Breuer & Freud, 1893/1936, p. 185; Veith 1977, pp. 82–84). This notion was consistent with the sexual views of the Victorian period, which emphasized the inherent sexual passivity of women.

As followers of psychoanalytic theory began to explore new directions and the influence of learning theory and sociological studies grew, many researchers and practitioners in psychopathology broadened their interpretations of hysterical disorders. Increasingly, they perceive such disorders as maladaptive ways of adjusting to conflict, frustration, and anxiety that may arise from a variety of sources, especially the social environment, not simply from inborn sexual drives. They also tend to agree that, regardless of the source, one of the main functions of hysterical symptoms is to help the individual avoid the intolerable stress that would occur if conflict and frustration were openly recognized or dealt with directly.

The Austrian physician Joseph Breuer, an older colleague of Sigmund Freud, had a great influence on Freud's views of neurotic disorders, especially "hysteria." In DSM-III-R language, hysteria is a "conversion" disorder in which psychological conflict is transferred into physical symptoms.

Patterns of Dissociative Disorders

In DSM-II, dissociative disorders were subsumed under the diagnostic category hysterical neuroses, dissociative type (American Psychiatric Association, 1968, p. 40). With the publication of DSM-III and DSM-III-R (American Psychiatric Association, 1980a, 1987), the use of such traditional terms as *hysterical* and *neurosis* became less prominent. Thus, hysterical neurosis, dissociative type gave way to dissociative disorders. However, to maintain a link with tradition, both DSM-III and its revision list the older label as a secondary but acceptable alternative.

Dissociative disorders are classified into four main categories: psychogenic amnesia, psychogenic fugue, multiple personality, and depersonalization disorder. DSM-III-R also includes a residual category, dissociative disorder not otherwise classified (NOS). This category is reserved for those who appear to have symptoms of a dissociative disorder but do not satisfy the criteria for any of the more specific patterns. Among the disturbances likely to be classified as NOS are states of dissociation resulting from brainwashing and other forms of stressful indoctrination under captive circumstances — for example, the conversion of prisoners of war to the enemy's way of thinking.

Sleepwalking, also known as **somnambulism** (from the Latin *somnus*, "sleep," and *ambulare*, "to walk"), is another form of dissociative disorder. DSM-III-R classifies it under the general diagnostic category of sleep disorders (American Psychiatric Association, 1987, pp. 311–313). However, we think it is appropriate to deal with sleepwalking in this chapter, along with other patterns of dissociative disorders.

Psychogenic Amnesia

The central feature of **psychogenic amnesia** is a sudden and serious loss of memory. This loss goes considerably beyond ordinary forgetfulness and cannot be accounted for on the basis of an organic disability. The amnesia involves the failure to recall important personal information that in some cases has been stored in the memory for many years. It may even extend to a complete loss of identity. Occasionally, the victim of psychogenic amnesia wanders about aimlessly in a highly confused state, as in the following case.

> Barbara M. has had a loss of memory since 12 noon today. The patient [was] brought in [at 7:00 P.M.] by the police, who apparently found her wandering around in the area of Winthrop Beach. She is able to account for her actions today until 12 noon, i.e., she arose late in the morning and took her baby son to a girlfriend's so that she could go to the doctor to get pills for her "kidney trouble." She recalls getting on the Charlestown bus, but nothing more until finding herself on the police stretcher in the ambulance. She claims she lives in Chelsea, but can't remember the address. (Nemiah, 1985b, p. 945)

There are four main types of psychogenic amnesia: localized, selective, generalized, and continuous (American Psychiatric Association, 1980a, p. 253). Most common is **localized amnesia**. Here the individual fails to recall events that occurred during a relatively brief period. It may be for only a few hours and usually is not longer than several days. Barbara M's episode is an example of this type, for she began to emerge from her amnesic state shortly after entering the hospital. Localized amnesia often follows a highly traumatic incident. For example, the uninjured survivor of an automobile accident in which all other members of the immediate family were killed may not be able to recall any of the events that happened during the time of the accident and even several days later.

Somewhat less often, the period of amnesia may be brief, as in the localized type, but more **selective**. For instance, the uninjured survivor just mentioned might recall the arrangements that were made for the funeral and details of the service, but not any of the discussions with relatives and friends during the same period.

Generalized amnesia and continuous amnesia are the least common types of psychogenic memory loss. In **generalized amnesia**, the loss of memory is for an individual's entire past life. The loss of memory in **continuous amnesia** is more restrictive, since the individual still remembers certain events that occurred before the onset of the amnesia. Thus, continuous amnesia is similar to localized amnesia, except that the memory loss is for a longer period of time.

Psychogenic amnesia occurs most often in adolescents and young adults. It is seldom found in elderly people. The cause of amnesia in the elderly is generally organic rather than psychological (see Chapter 13).

The onset of psychogenic amnesia is sudden, usually following severe psychosocial stress that frequently involves highly traumatic events. Among them are serious automobile accidents and other encounters with possible death — for example, those occurring in wartime or during natural disasters such as floods, earthquakes, and fires. Even when there is no physical danger, psychosocial stress can be sufficiently severe to induce an amnesic episode. For instance, it may occur in situations that the individual perceives as a great threat to self-esteem, such as being deserted by a loved one or failing to achieve some crucial goal.

In contrast to the often permanent memory loss in amnesia that is caused by organic disease, psychogenic amnesia is usually temporary, and recovery is fairly rapid. Furthermore, the memory loss that may occur in organic disorders is confined mainly to recent events, but in psychogenic amnesia it varies from recent events to those covering many years in the past.

An especially vexing problem that arises in diagnosing psychogenic amnesia is the possibility of malingering, especially where the claim of lost memory may serve to excuse the individual from charges of criminal behavior. One way of detecting malingerers is to question them carefully while they are under hypnosis. A condition similar to that of hypnosis may sometimes be induced through the use of certain drugs, including sedative-hypnotics such as amobarbital (Amytal) and various nonbarbiturate hypnotics (Hilgard, 1973; Honigfeld & Howard, 1978, p. 48). Hypnosis and drugs, together with psychotherapy, can also be used to help victims of psychogenic amnesia overcome their memory loss and work through the problems of psychosocial stress that led to the amnesic episode.

Psychogenic Fugue

A complex variation of psychogenic amnesia is **psychogenic fugue** (flight). The central characteristic that distinguishes it from psychogenic amnesia is the abrupt onset of traveling away from home or place of work and the taking on of a completely or partly new identity without recalling the previous one. As in psychogenic amnesia, the memory loss in psychogenic fugue is of psychological origin. The distinction is important, since such memory loss may also result from organic disability, as in the case of alcohol or other drug intoxication and traumatic injuries to the head. Unlike psychogenic amnesia, where aimless and confused wandering sometimes accompanies the loss of personal identity, the traveling in psychogenic fugue is more purposeful. Victims of a fugue may find themselves in a strange place far from home, not knowing how they got there or where they are from. Nevertheless, the way in which they go about their travels would not appear to the ordinary observer as confused wandering.

The extent to which a new identity is adopted during a fugue may vary considerably. In some cases it is quite fragmented, and social contacts are minimal or avoided. In other instances the change is more elaborate. The individual begins a new life with no memory of any previous identity. During this time the person may engage in complex social activities, perhaps marrying, even unknowingly committing bigamy. Ostensibly the behavior in this role does not suggest any form of psychopathology. Indeed, when amnesic

In this scene from the classic Hitchcock film *Spellbound*, Gregory Peck tries to recall who he really is. Although the story interprets his loss of memory in a narrow psychodynamic fashion, the film's point that a highly traumatic event can precipitate a psychogenic fugue is consistent with DSM-III-R explanations.

victims recover, people who knew them in the new life may be quite perplexed to discover that they were suffering from a psychological disorder.

Psychogenic fugue typically occurs after some kind of severe psychosocial stress — for example, marital discord, personal rejection, loss of self-esteem, or, most often, anxiety and conflict arising from wartime or natural disasters. Most fugues are relatively brief, with a restricted amount of travel. In some instances, however, they may involve a great deal of wandering, sometimes even thousands of miles.

Psychodynamic and social learning theories agree that a basic goal of the dissociative process in psychogenic amnesia and fugue is to avoid the distress involved in conflict and frustration, regardless of the source. The dissociation serves as a maladaptive way of handling conflict, frustration, and anxiety that in the past the individual has been unable to deal with adequately. The victim separates from conscious awareness the memory of past events related to that inadequacy. In social learning terms, taking on a new identity, or at least forgetting the old one, is reinforced (rewarded) because it helps the individual avoid dealing directly with painful problems. Unfortunately, the avoidance is only a temporary solution; upon recovering, the victim of the fugue must still encounter the frustration, conflict, and anxiety that initiated the dissociation.

The view that a fugue represents an attempt to escape problems is consistent with observations that the new identity assumed during a fugue is often marked by more gregarious and uninhibited traits than were present before flight. Usually, the individual had been rather quiet and ordinary (American Psychiatric Association, 1987, p. 272). The victim of a fugue seldom, if ever, has any kind of positive identification. Presumably this omission is purposeful, though not consciously so, since immediate identification would defeat the purpose of the fugue.

Multiple Personality Disorder

Contrary to popular opinion, **multiple personality disorder** is rare, although its dramatic appeal cannot be denied. DSM-III-R lists the following criteria: "A. The existence within the individual of two or more distinct personalities . . . each with its own relatively enduring pattern of perceiving, relating to, and thinking about the environment and self. B. Each of these personality states recurrently takes full control of the individual's behavior" (American Psychiatric Association, 1987, p. 269).

In popular speech and writings, multiple personality is often called split personality; however, that term is more suitable for schizophrenia, a group of psychotic disorders marked by a serious split (from the Greek *schizo*) between thought and emotion (see Chapter 11). For example, a schizophrenic person may describe a tragic event with a remarkable lack of emotion or highly inappropriate emotion, such as laughter. Although the patterns of personality, or roles, that the individual reveals in multiple personality disorder are dissociated and coexist independently, the behavior is appropriate for the role that is dominant at the time. Furthermore, with each role there is adequate contact with reality and little, if any, evidence of psychotic symptoms (Benner & Joscelyne, 1984; Greaves, 1980).

Multiple Personality in Fiction

Robert Louis Stevenson's *The Strange Case of Dr. Jekyll and Mr. Hyde* (1886/1974) is probably the most famous fictional portrayal of what we now call multiple personality. First published in 1886 and reprinted many times since, the story is remarkable for its insight into the nature of dissociation. In the following scene toward the end of the story,

In this scene from a film based on Robert L. Stevenson's *The Strange Case of Dr. Jekyll and Mr. Hyde*, Dr. Jekyll (played by Frederic March) sees his evil personality, Mr. Hyde, emerging. Stevenson's story was a remarkably accurate portrayal, in symbolic fashion, of the phenomenon known today as "multiple personality," a form of dissociation.

Dr. Jekyll thinks he has conquered his evil personality, Mr. Hyde, whose constant reappearance and murderous behavior have escaped Dr. Jekyll's controlling medications.

> It was a fine, clear January day, . . . and the Regent's Park was full of winter chirrupings and sweet with spring odours. I sat in the sun on a bench; the animal within me licking the chops of memory; the spiritual side a little drowsed, promising subsequent penitence, but not yet moved to begin. After all, I reflected, I was like my neighbours; and then I smiled, comparing myself with other men, comparing my active goodwill with the lazy cruelty of their neglect. And at the very moment of that vainglorious thought, a qualm came over me. . . . I began to be aware of a change in the temper of my thoughts, a greater boldness, a contempt of danger, a dissolution of the bonds of obligation. I looked down; my clothes hung formlessly on my shrunken limbs; the hand that lay on my knee was corded and hairy. I was once more Edward Hyde. A moment before I had been safe of all men's respect, wealthy, beloved— . . . and now I was the common quarry of mankind, hunted, houseless, a known murderer, thrall to the gallows. (pp. 141–142)

The Classic Case of Miss Beauchamp

One of the earliest and best known descriptions of multiple personality to be fully reported in the professional literature on psychopathology is Morton Prince's case of Miss Beauchamp (1908). Miss Beauchamp had three alternating personalities. Prince named them the Saint, characterized by extreme piety and religious scruples; the Child (Sally), mischievous and carefree; and the Woman (or Realist), strong, resolute, self-reliant, and intolerant of saintliness.

> Miss Christine L. Beauchamp (pronounced *Beecham*), the subject of this study, is a person in whom several personalities have become developed; that is to say, she may change her personality from time to time, often from hour to hour, and with each change her character becomes transformed and her memories altered. In addition to the real, original or normal self, the self that was born and which she was intended by nature to be, she may be any one of three different persons. . . . Each varies . . . from the other two, and from the original Miss Beauchamp. Two of the personalities have no knowledge of each other or of the third, excepting such information as may be obtained by inference or second hand. . . . Of a sudden one of the two wakes up to find herself, she knows not where, and ignorant of what she has said or done a moment before. Only one of the three has knowledge of the lives of the others, and this one presents such a bizarre character, so far removed from the others in individuality, that the transformation from one of the other personalities to herself is one of the most striking and dramatic features of the case. The personalities come and go in kaleidoscopic succession, many changes often being made in the course of twenty-four hours. And so it happens that Miss Beauchamp, if I may use the name to designate several distinct people, at one moment says and does and plans and arranges something to which a short time before she most strongly objected, indulges tastes which a moment before would have been abhorrent to her ideals, and undoes or destroys what she had just laboriously planned and arranged. (pp. 1–2)

In a later analysis of the case, Prince (1939) concluded that Miss Beauchamp's personalities represented abnormal exaggerations of three long-standing and conflicting sets of attitudes and strivings, all of which had existed prior to her dissociated states. Early in life she had been torn between being a dutiful, prim child and having a rebellious, playful fantasy life. The conflicting memories served as a basis for her later development of the three dissociated personalities. Miss Beauchamp eventually was able to integrate her separate personalities into a complete, normal personality that remained durable (Prince, 1939, p. 268).

In a critical appraisal of the case of Miss Beauchamp, McCurdy (1941) was especially concerned with how the therapist can contribute to a patient's multiple personality. He pointed out that Dr. Prince was the center of Miss Beauchamp's life for several years during treatment. The very methods of treatment he used, such as relying heavily on hypnosis to stimulate her memories, may well have encouraged the emergence and persistence of her different selves, or at least enriched them.

McCurdy's conclusion that hypnosis encouraged Miss Beauchamp's dissociation is consistent with recent reports that patients who have symptoms of multiple personality also make excellent hypnotic subjects. These findings are based on clinical observations as well as standard tests of hypnotic susceptibility (Bliss, 1984; Bliss & Jeppsen, 1985).

The Three Faces of Eve

One of the best-known and most thoroughly researched cases of multiple personality since the days of Prince's Miss Beauchamp is that of Eve. During her therapy sessions she disclosed three distinct and conflicting patterns of personality: Eve White, Eve Black, and Jane. As the therapist noted her behavior at various times, Eve White was "neat, demure,

Joanne Woodward won an Oscar for her portrayal of multiple personality in *The Three Faces of Eve*. In the famous case study reported by Thigpen and Cleckley, the "three faces" represented the three personalities that Eve experienced: Eve White, neat and demure; Eve Black, playful and provocative; and Jane, mature and competent. In this scene Ms. Woodward is playing the role of Eve Black.

and poised"; Eve Black was "playful," "provocative," and had a "quick, reckless" smile; and Jane showed "maturity," "competence," and "vitality," and had a "fresh and lovely" smile (Thigpen & Cleckley, 1954; 1957, pp. 9, 24, 125–126).

In an independent analysis of Eve's dissociation, Charles Osgood and Zella Luria (1954) found that an objective measure of personality revealed her three different patterns of personality. Each personality gave different responses to the test, and these responses corresponded to the therapist's observations. In commenting on the phenomenon of multiple personality, Luria and Osgood (1976) observed

> It is easy in reading about and writing about cases of multiple personality to forget that we are dealing with a single human being with a single brain. Is it possible that in cases of multiple personality we are dealing with an exaggerated form of role playing? All of us have somewhat different personalities in different social situations, but for most of us there is no dissociation . . . when we are at home with the family we do not forget what we said and did at the office. But even in clinical cases of multiple personality, . . . it appears there is a real personality that is aware of all its roles. It is only the roles that are dissociative with respect to each other, presumably because, affectively, they are deeply incongruent with each other. (p. 286)

A Cautionary Note

The rarity of multiple personality is in startling contrast to its dramatic appeal. In a review of the professional literature most available to American psychologists, Taylor and Martin (1944) could find only 76 cases during the previous 100 years. Writing in 1972, Horton and Miller claimed they had found less than a dozen reported cases of multiple personality

In 1975 Chris Sizemore revealed that she was the famous Eve depicted in the case study and film *Three Faces of Eve*. She stated that after her treatment by Thigpen and Cleckley she had experienced other personalities, but that she was now recovered. (Sizemore & Pittillo, 1977).

in the last 50 years. They also observed that the therapists, not the patients, often provided the names of the alternative selves. Furthermore, the fact that hypnosis was frequently used suggests that the therapy itself encouraged the emergence of the different selves. The therapists may have been so willing to accept the patients' beliefs about having several different personalities that the conviction was reinforced (Kampman, 1976).

From time to time, spectacular accounts of people said to have many different personalities have appeared in the popular press. One of the more lurid reports in recent years was that of a campus rapist whose defense was that he had 10 personalities. It was the rapist personality, he claimed, that committed the sexual assaults, not his normal self (Van, 1978). On the basis of testimony by psychiatrists, he was found not guilty by reason of insanity. This was an unusual verdict for the kind of disorder he professed to have, and it was contrary to most legal interpretations of the insanity plea. As a rule, such pleas require some evidence of a psychotic disorder—for example, schizophrenia or an organic brain disorder. (See Chapter 21 for a discussion of these issues.) Considering the dubious nature of the rapist's defense and considering the questions we have posed about the nature of multiple personality, it is wise to remain scientifically skeptical about claims of abundant selves (Ludolph, 1985; Thigpen & Cleckley, 1984).

Depersonalization Disorder

The central feature of depersonalization is a drastic change in self-perceptions so that one's ordinary experiences are temporarily lost or greatly distorted. Depersonalization may involve sensations of unreality. For example, one may perceive oneself from a distance, as if one is another person, or feel that one is in a dream. Some individuals

This scene suggests the disorder known as "depersonalization." The person feels as though in a dream or in a world without reality.

undergoing depersonalization have strange perceptions of their bodies — for example, they feel that their arms or legs have changed considerably in size. They may also perceive other people as mechanical or dead (American Psychiatric Association, 1987, p. 276).

Occasional symptoms of depersonalization do not necessarily mean that the individual is suffering from a **depersonalization disorder**. The symptoms must be sufficiently severe to result in social or occupational impairment. It has been estimated that mild symptoms of depersonalization, without social or occupational impairment, occur at some time in many young adults. Studies of college students found that as many as 50 percent experienced slight transient episodes (Meyers & Grant, 1972; Nemiah, 1985b, p. 953). Symptoms of depersonalization may appear as secondary disturbances in such disorders as drug intoxication, major depression, schizophrenia, and anxiety disorders. In those instances a diagnosis of depersonalization disorder would not be appropriate.

Historical Background

The syndrome of depersonalization in the American Psychiatric Association's classification of mental disorders was first mentioned in the 1968 DSM-II. However, clinical reports depicting symptoms of depersonalization appeared more than 100 years ago. In 1873 the French psychiatrist M. Krishaber described in his treatise *De la néuropathie cérébro-cardiaque* various disturbances he had observed in 38 patients. Among the symptoms he noted were anxiety, fatigue, depression, and strange self-perceptions. He gave the name "*cérébro-cardiaque*" to this mixture of symptoms because they involved not only mental disturbances but also abnormal physiological reactions, such as palpitations and difficulty in breathing. About one-third of the patients revealed alterations in perception that today would likely be diagnosed as symptoms of depersonalization. Here are some of the patients' descriptions of their abnormal experiences: "I experience one self that thinks, another self that acts. At such times I lose the feeling of the reality of the world. I feel I am plunged into a deep dream. . . . I feel as if I was almost entirely separated from the world, as if there was some barriers between me and it. . . . [I]t often seems to me that I am not a part of the world. My voice sounds strange to me, and when I see my fellow patients I say to myself: 'They are figures in a dream'" (Krishaber, 1873, cited in Nemiah, 1985, p. 952).

Unfortunately, Krishaber's work had little influence on his medical colleagues. Almost 40 years after his observations, the French philosopher Laurent Dugas and his colleague F. Moutier, a clinician, reviewed Krishaber's treatise and added new cases of depersonalization, a term that Dugas coined (Dugas & Moutier, 1911). However, it was not until the 1930s that specialists in psychopathology paid much attention to the phenomenon. By 1950 it was well on its way to being recognized as a syndrome in its own right (Nemiah, 1985b, p. 952; Taylor, 1982).

Although the phenomenon of depersonalization has been widely recognized by mental health professionals, some have questioned whether it is actually a form of dissociation, since there is no particular disturbance in memory. Nevertheless, it is classified as such in DSM-III-R because an important component of identity — the perception of one's reality — is lost.

Onset, Etiology, and Therapy

The onset of depersonalization disorder is usually during adolescence; rarely does it begin after age 40. Symptoms appear suddenly, and they tend to be chronic, with recovery often followed by recurring episodes. A number of factors may contribute to the development of the disorder. Among them are fatigue, anxiety, depression, intense physical pain, and such traumatic experiences as automobile accidents, military combat, and confinement in a concentration camp. There is no reliable information concerning the prevalence of the disorder or whether it occurs at different rates in males and females (American Psychiatric Association, 1987, p. 276; Cohen, 1954).

From a psychodynamic perspective, the fact that depersonalization typically begins during adolescence suggests that it may be linked with the kinds of identity crises adolescents frequently experience. In Erik Erikson's terms (1959, 1963, 1968), the central conflict of adolescence is identity versus role confusion. Adolescents in Western culture are often met with a bewildering array of choices concerning education, career, marriage, and moral values. Conflicts in making decisions about these complex issues may well be expressed in strong doubts about social identity and roles. When the doubts are extreme, they may be revealed in some form of depersonalization. If sufficiently severe, the reaction may warrant a diagnosis of depersonalization disorder. In such instances the symptoms can serve to deny conflict or to escape from it.

A variety of approaches have been used to help individuals suffering from depersonalization disorder (Nemiah, 1985b, p. 956). Some therapists may prescribe sedatives, especially if anxiety is a strong component. This treatment is often accompanied by psychotherapy, or psychotherapy alone may be used. Psychotherapy may emphasize the gaining of insight into the underlying causes of symptoms, or it may focus more directly on the disordered behavior itself, helping the individual learn how to acquire more productive techniques for handling symptoms. Suggesting changes in the environmental factors that contribute to the disorder may also be an important component of the more behavioral approaches to treatment. Of course, more than one method of psychotherapy can be used. Indeed, some therapists prefer to combine the attainment of insight with the more active learning methods (see Chapters 19 and 20).

Sleepwalking

It is difficult to determine the prevalence of sleepwalking, although most evidence indicates that it is more common in children than in adults. Some studies report that approximately 15 percent of all children between the ages of 5 and 12 have at least one episode, and its occurrence in the general population has been estimated from 1 to 6 percent.

Sleepwalking in Children

Although some clinicians believe that any form of sleepwalking is potentially a highly disturbing and even dangerous condition, it usually has no serious or lasting consequences, especially in children. Indeed, studies of children who were sleepwalkers have shown that almost all of them outgrew the behavior after several years. This suggests that a predisposing factor is a delay in the maturation of the central nervous system. In contrast, sleepwalking in adults is more apt to be associated with serious psychological problems (Kaplan & Sadock, 1985, pp. 571–572).

Traditional views of sleepwalking regard it as an acting out of dreams. According to modern laboratory research, however, it occurs exclusively during the stage of sleep when no dreaming takes place, as shown by the absence of rapid eye movements (REMs). Such movements are known to be reliable indicators of dreaming. The stage of sleep without rapid eye movements is called NREM sleep, and it occurs most frequently during the first third of the night. Several studies have compared the nightly sleep patterns of sleepwalking children with a normal group of children. Recordings of brain wave patterns showed that except for the interruptions, the sleep patterns and the percentages of time spent in both REM and NREM sleep were the same. Furthermore, the brain wave patterns that occurred during sleepwalking were more like those that occur during sleep than during wakefulness (Jacobson, Kales, & Kales, 1969). This latter finding suggests that sleepwalking is indeed an appropriate term for this kind of disorder. The following description is typical of the kinds of sleepwalking episodes that occurred in these laboratory studies.

> The 9-year-old male sleepwalker was put to be at 9 PM. At 10:35 PM, while in Stage 4 (NREM) sleep, he abruptly sat up in bed [with] staring eyes and a blank expression on his face. He made some fumbling repetitive movements with the blanket and then climbed out of bed. He walked rather unsteadily around the laboratory, at times mumbling or speaking mostly incoherently. While able to negotiate the maze of laboratory equipment and furniture, he nevertheless appeared to be in a decreased state of awareness, moving clumsily though occasionally rapidly. He seemed internally preoccupied and would not answer if spoken to, but on one occasion answered monosyllabically. He walked to the laboratory door and fumbled repetitively with the lock. Having no success, he returned to his bed spontaneously. The episode lasted seven minutes. Later during the same night, he called "help" and "mother" while [the] [recording of brain waves] showed Stage 4 sleep without apparent awakening. (Jacobson, Kales, & Kales, 1969, pp. 113–114)

Sleepwalking incidents at home may go on for longer periods of time, sometimes as much as 40 minutes. In some instances the behavior has a more bizarre quality and may involve crying, screaming, and inability to control urinary functions. About one-third of such episodes end with the child awakening. Almost always there is complete amnesia for the sleepwalking episode, even if the child is questioned immediately afterwards.

The treatment of sleepwalking in children consists mainly of cautioning parents to eliminate things that may be hazardous, to lock windows where the child is apt to be walking, and if possible to arrange for the child to sleep on the first floor (Freedman, Kaplan, & Sadock, 1976, p. 71). These suggestions rest on the assumption that sleepwalking is something a child is highly likely to outgrow. Since parents sometimes report that their children's sleepwalking happens most often after periods of stress, undue excitement, or marked environmental change, extra caution may be appropriate when such conditions occur.

Sleepwalking in Adults

Sleepwalking in adults usually is a more serious disorder. As a rule it reflects a greater degree of anxiety, conflict, and frustration. During sleepwalking the individual may engage in what appears to be highly purposive behavior involving repetitive rituals that seem to have an important meaning to the sleepwalker. Such behavior is insightfully portrayed in Shakespeare's great tragedy *Macbeth*. In the following scene Lady Macbeth acts out during sleepwalking her secret conflict and guilt after her husband had murdered King Duncan and had murderers kill Banquo and Lady Macduff and her son. (Act 5, Scene 1).

> **Doctor:** You see, her eyes are open.
>
> **Gentlewoman:** Ay, but their sense is shut.
>
> **Doctor:** What is it she does now? Look, how she rubs her hands.
>
> **Gentlewoman:** It is an accustomed action with her, to seem thus washing her hands: I have known her to continue in this a quarter of an hour.
>
> **Lady Macbeth:** Yet here's a spot.

During sleepwalking the person may engage in repetitive rituals reflecting conflict and anxiety, a point that Shakespeare evidently understood. In this scene from *Macbeth*, Lady Macbeth during sleepwalking indicates the guilt she connects to her hands after her husband had murdered King Duncan and ordered murderers to kill others.

Doctor: Hark! she speaks: I will set down what comes from her, to satisfy my remembrance the more strongly.

Lady Macbeth: Out, damned spot! out, I say! One: two: why, then 'tis time to do 't. Hell is murky. Fie, my lord, fie! a soldier, and afeard? What need we fear who knows it, when none can call our power to account? Yet who would have thought the old man to have had so much blood in him?

Doctor: Do you mark that?

Lady Macbeth: The thane of Fife had a wife; where is she now? What, will these hands ne'er be clean?

Patterns of Somatoform Disorders

As we indicated at the beginning of the chapter, somatoform disorders involve somatic (bodily) symptoms that take the form of (suggest) physical disease but in the absence of organic etiology. The most common patterns are somatization disorder, conversion disorder, somatoform pain disorder, and hypochondriasis (American Psychiatric Association, 1987, pp. 255–267).

Somatization Disorder

The main symptoms of **somatization disorder** are chronic and multiple complaints of bodily discomfort, such as recurring headaches, fatigue, bowel trouble, nausea, and abdominal pain. These complaints persist even though repeated medical examinations reveal no evidence of any underlying physical disease. Traditionally these kinds of symptoms have been regarded as a form of hysterical neurosis, and more specifically as Briquet's syndrome (Rubin, Zorumski, & Guze, 1986). The latter designation comes from the work of Paul Briquet (1797–1881), a French psychiatrist who wrote a lengthy book on hysteria (1859).

Complaints of bodily ailments occur in other psychological disorders, but a diagnosis of somatization disorder reflects the total pattern of symptoms. This pattern includes the style and development of complaints, such as their dramatic and vague nature, their complicated medical history, and the extent to which the various complaints occur in combination. These complaints are of several years' duration, usually beginning before the age of 30.

As a guide for understanding the full clinical picture of somatization disorder, DSM-III-R describes six groups of symptoms. Each group contains from 4 to 12 specific complaints. At least 13 complaints must be present to warrant a diagnosis of somatization disorder. In applying these criteria, it is also crucial for the clinician to rule out the possibility of physical disease as an explanation of the complaints. Samples of complaints for each of the six groups of symptoms follow (American Psychiatric Association, 1987, pp. 263–264).

1. Gastrointestinal. The individual complains of abdominal pain or spells of vomiting.

2. Pain. There are complaints of various kinds of pain, such as back pain, pain in the extremities, or pain in the genital area (other than during intercourse).

3. Cardiopulmonary. Complaints may include shortness of breath, palpitations, chest pain, and dizziness.

4. Pseudoneurological. Among the symptoms are loss of sensation, inability to speak or being able to speak only in a whisper, difficulty in walking, paralysis, blindness, convulsions, deafness, double vision, and fainting spells.

5. Psychosexual. The individual complains of a long-standing lack of interest in sexual activities, or a lack of pleasure during intercourse, or pain during intercourse.

6. Female reproductive symptoms. Complaints include excessively painful menstruation or menstrual irregularity, such as excessive bleeding or abnormal stoppage of menstrual flow.

Somatization disorder is diagnosed much more often in women then in men. It has been estimated that from 1 to 2 percent of women suffer from the disorder at some time in their lives. Only rarely, however, is the disorder diagnosed in men (American Psychiatric Association, 1987, p. 260; Corywell, 1980). The fact that more women than men are diagnosed as having a somatization disorder may be influenced by certain social and cultural factors. Stereotyped attitudes that reinforce the belief that women are naturally weaker may be so persuasive that women are more willing than men to admit to bodily aches and pains. Also, these stereotypes may influence the diagnosticians themselves. (See Chapter 4 for a more detailed discussion of such issues.)

There is some evidence that somatization disorder occurs more often among family members than in the general population (Nemiah, 1985c, p. 925), suggesting that genetic factors play a role in its development. However, another factor to consider is the important influence family members have on one another. For example, a child may be consistently rewarded for physical complaints, no matter how trivial. Furthermore, parents who magnify the importance of their own physical ailments may serve as models for the development of somatization symptoms in their children.

The various impairments that result from somatization disorder can be complex. The physical ailments themselves may interfere with carrying out a productive life. Individuals may undergo repeated and sometimes unnecessary surgery. The medications they constantly seek and often acquire expose them to the possibility of drug addiction. For example, they may become unduly dependent on tranquilizers, barbiturates, or other habit-forming sedative-hypnotics (Chapter 15). The depressive effects of the medication are often coupled with serious depression over the illness. As a result, suicidal thoughts and even attempts may occur (Corywell, 1981).

The symptoms of somatization disorder rarely disappear spontaneously. As a result, the individual continues year after year to seek medical help for the ailment. However, unless that help includes some form of psychotherapy aimed at changing the sick behavior rather than simply alleviating symptoms temporarily with medication, the prognosis is more negative than positive. Such psychotherapy may involve a number of different approaches: helping the person gain insight into the reasons for the complaints, applying behavior modification techniques, and helping the individual make changes in environmental circumstances that may be reinforcing the sick behavior. (See Chapters 19 and 20 for a detailed discussion of such methods.)

Conversion Disorder

The central feature of **conversion disorder** (hysterical neurosis, conversion type) is a loss of or alteration in physical functioning that suggests a physical disorder but is actually an expression of psychological conflict (American Psychiatric Association, 1987, p. 257; Rubin, Zorumski, & Guze, 1986, p. 522). The concept of conversion disorder can be traced to Freud's early practice of psychoanalysis. Freud theorized that in certain forms of hysteria the individual's neurotic anxiety is converted into sensory-motor channels. As a result, the normal functioning of an organ or organ system becomes blocked (Freud, 1894/1962, pp. 45–51).

The most obvious symptoms of conversion disorder are those that resemble neurological disabilities. Among them are paralysis of arms or legs, loss of speech (aphonia), convulsive seizures, blindness, loss of the sense of smell (anosmia), loss of feeling or sensation (anesthesia), and various other abnormalities of sensation, such as burning or prickling (paresthesia). It has long been known that hypnosis or even strong suggestion can induce these kinds of symptoms. Indeed, people who develop conversion reactions tend to be highly suggestible and have difficulty separating fact from fantasy (Kolb & Brodie, 1982, p. 503).

Much of the professional literature on conversion disorder has emphasized the phenomenon of *la belle indifférence*—an apparent lack of concern about one's symptoms that is highly inappropriate in view of their disabling effects (Kaplan & Sadock, 1985, p. 169). However, some clinical researchers have argued that this indifference may not be as crucial in diagnosing conversion disorder as traditional practice has held. For example, a study of patients at the Henry Phipps Psychiatric Clinic of Johns Hopkins Hospital found that only 32 percent of those who had conversion symptoms showed any evidence of *la belle indifférence* (Stephens & Kamp, 1962). Other clinical observations have also raised doubts about the usefulness of *la belle indifférence* as an important diagnostic clue, pointing out that it is often absent in individuals who display other symptoms of a conversion disorder (Lazare, 1981). Furthermore, medical patients who are seriously ill with a physical disease but remain stoic about their disability sometimes reveal this so-called indifference (American Psychiatric Association, 1987, p. 257).

Conversion Disorder versus Organic Disease

In reaching a diagnosis of conversion disorder, it is crucial to rule out the possibility that organic pathology may be producing the symptoms. A clue for differentiating certain forms of conversion disorder from organic disease is the highly restricted and anatomically improbable symptoms that conversion patients display. For instance, isolated bands of skin may lose sensation or a motor paralysis of the arm may terminate exactly at the shoulder. In such cases the loss of function does not correspond to the physical structure of the affected organ or organ system. A classic example of this discrepancy is glove anesthesia, in which an individual reports complete loss of sensation in the hand but no impairment in the arm. Many years ago the eminent French neurologist Jean-Martin Charcot (1825–1893) recognized the phenomenon of glove anesthesia. He called it neurological nonsense, since the sensory nerves that serve the hand also run through the arm. Charcot concluded that such symptoms were of psychological rather than organic origin and defined them as forms of hysteria.

Pierre Janet (1859–1947), who studied under Charcot, elaborated on his teacher's demonstrations of conversion hysteria. In his classic *The Major Symptoms of Hysteria* (1907), he described in detail the various ways in which hysterical symptoms, such as paralysis and anesthesias, failed to correspond to anatomical reality.

> The hysteric patient . . . seems to attend to the popular conception of the organ rather than to its anatomic conception. . . . For the common people, the hand terminates at the wrist. They don't care if all the principal muscles that animate the hand and fingers are lodged beyond in the fore-arm. She stops her anesthesia at the wrist, as would the vulgar, who, in their ignorance, say that if the hand does not move, it is because the hand is diseased. Now this popular conception of the limbs is formed by old ideas we have about our limbs, which we all keep in spite of our anatomic notions. So these hysteric anesthesias seem again to have something mental, intellectual, in them. (pp. 157–158)

Janet did point out that in certain limited cases—for example, alcoholic intoxication—one might develop a restricted anesthesia. However, he added that in 9 cases out of 10 the diagnostician would be safe in suspecting hysterical anesthesia (Janet, 1907, pp. 153–158).

Prevalence and Sex Differences

Although symptoms of conversion disorder were quite common in the time of Freud, Charcot, and Janet, they occur much less often now. Changes in education and cultural expectations probably account for much of the difference. Essentially, people are more sophisticated about psychological and medical subjects today.

Several studies have found that conversion disorders are diagnosed more often for women than for men, especially women of relatively low educational and economic status. One interpretation of these findings has been that women have less control over their environments and thus are apt to express their problems as bodily symptoms rather than as psychological conflicts (Al-Issa, 1982; Mechanic, 1974b).

Onset and Interpretation of Symptoms

The symptoms of conversion disorder begin suddenly and in a situation of extreme psychological stress, usually during adolescence or early adulthood but occasionally during middle age or even later.

Just as the symptoms usually begin abruptly, they also disappear suddenly, especially if the individual is removed from the stressful situation that contributed to the onset of the symptoms. For example, a soldier might develop a paralyzed arm as a way of resolving his conflict over firing a gun in battle. However, shortly after being removed from combat, he may recover the use of the arm quite rapidly. The diagnosis of conversion disorder in this instance assumes that the soldier may have been consciously aware of his conflict over firing his gun but not aware that the conflict was related to his symptoms.

This example shows how conversion symptoms can be used to avoid a threatening situation. Psychodynamic clinicians refer to this defense mechanism as **secondary gain**. They also point out that the symptoms are used for **primary gain** — that is, they help the individual repress the underlying conflicts aroused by the situation. The following case illustrates this maladaptive use of conversion symptoms: "A married man of twenty-eight was in a motor accident. He sustained minor scratches and was otherwise apparently unhurt, but he emerged from the accident completely blind. The absence of any injury that could be responsible for loss of vision led to a diagnosis of hysteria. It was discovered that the accident occurred while he was driving to the maternity hospital to see his wife and first-born child. His first remark to the psychiatrist was that he could not tie his wife down to a blind man and would now divorce her" (White & Watt, 1981, p. 214).

Behavioral and social learning theorists also interpret conversion symptoms as a means of avoiding conflict. However, they focus on the environmental situations that stimulated the conversion responses rather than on such psychodynamic processes as repression (Jones, 1980).

Outcome

Conversion disorder can be quite disabling. Since it often prevents the individual from carrying out expected daily activities, treatment should begin as soon as possible. In addition to psychotherapy, the individual may require significant changes in the environmental situation that triggered the symptoms or that helps sustain them. If help is not forthcoming, the loss of physical function itself can have drastic consequences. For example, prolonged paralysis of an arm or leg may result in atrophy of the muscles. Persistence of symptoms over a long period of time can also reinforce the development of a chronic sick role.

Somatoform Pain Disorder

The central feature of **somatoform pain disorder** is a preoccupation with pain that persists for at least six months in the absence of any organic pathology that could help account for it. Even if some degree of organic pathology is involved, somatoform pain disorder is suspected when the complaints of pain or resulting social or occupational impairment far exceed what one would normally expect from the physical findings

(American Psychiatric Association, 1987, p. 264–266). In DSM-III this disorder was called *psychogenic pain disorder*, to emphasize that the cause presumably was psychological. Although that same view underlies the DSM-III-R classification, the term *somatoform* is used to indicate its relationship to other somatoform disorders—that is, physical symptoms that suggest a physical disorder, but in the absence of demonstrable organic findings.

Symptoms of somatoform pain disorder are usually not as dramatic as those that occur in conversion disorder, and they are probably much more common. Indeed, some clinicians believe that it may be the most common pattern of somatoform disorder (Kaplan & Sadock, 1985, pp. 348–349).

Onset and Development

Although somatoform pain disorder can begin at almost any age, its first occurrence is usually during early childhood or adolescence. The symptoms generally appear suddenly, precipitated by severe psychosocial stress. The pain may lessen if the stressful situation improves or if appropriate treatment helps the individual come to terms with the stress. Without proper intervention the pain may persist for months or even years. The degree of impairment varies considerably, depending on the duration and intensity of the pain. In some instances the pain may be tolerated, often with the aid of medication, and social and occupational life may be only slightly disturbed. At the other end of the spectrum, the pain may become so severe that the person needs to be hospitalized.

Somatoform pain is sometimes so unusual that it quickly arouses the suspicion that it is not related to a physical disease. The pain may also be an exaggeration of some minor physical disturbance. Many troublesome stimuli occur in the body from time to time. Ordinarily we ignore them, but we would probably perceive them as painful if we continually focused attention on them. This persistent focus can contribute significantly to a chronic course of pain disorder.

It is interesting to note that relatives of persons diagnosed with somatoform pain disorder have had more painful injuries and illnesses than occur in the general population (American Psychiatric Association, 1987, p. 265). This fact suggests that at least some individuals who develop the disorder have become sensitized to pain by observing it in family members.

Treatment

Traditional approaches to treatment, such as psychodynamic therapies, emphasize the importance of helping individuals gain insight into the anxieties and conflicts that underlie their pain. Behavioral therapies focus on the direct control of the pain behavior and associated feelings, as well as on the antecedents that seem to trigger the pain response. Some therapists seek to combine elements of insight therapy with behavior modification techniques. (See Chapters 19 and 20 for a detailed discussion of these methods.)

Cautela (1977) developed a procedure of covert conditioning that he used successfully to modify pain behavior. Although in this instance the patient suffered from arthritic pain, the basic principles of the method could be applied to somatoform pain as well. The main procedures used were as follows (p. 50).

1. She was taught relaxation as a self-control procedure to reduce general stress and to reduce the pain.

2. She was told to shout "stop" to herself, relax all over with special emphasis on her wrists, knees, and toes, and then to imagine a pleasant scene whenever she became especially aware of pain and when there was an intensification of it.

3. She was taught to . . . reduce pain in situations such as getting in and out of chairs, walking, writing, typing, turning door knobs, and unscrewing lids. The scenes involved imagining that she was in one of these situations, but experiencing no pain, and then imagining a reinforcing scene. She was asked to do this five times a day for each situation experience.

4. She was told not to complain to anyone about her pain experience.

5. Her husband and children were asked to ignore her whenever she complained.

The woman reported that after one week of following these procedures her pain was minimal. At the time of Cautela's report, eight weeks after the beginning of treatment, she said that improvement was maintained. Cautela (1977, p. 50) emphasized that his purpose in presenting the case was not to prove that his method was necessarily the best way of helping people modify their pain. Rather, he aimed to illustrate a theoretical model and a methodology that could help expand the available tools for such treatment.

Hypochondriasis

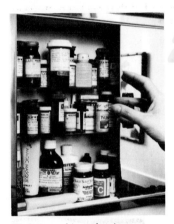

Medicine cabinet showing a multitude of medications, including prescription drugs. Because of an exaggerated concern with supposed bodily ills, the hypochondriac often becomes a slave to excessive and unnecessary medication.

The main features of **hypochondriais** (also called *hypochondriacal neurosis*) are an exaggerated concern with bodily sensations and functions, coupled with a chronic fear that one has a serious undetected physical disease (American Psychiatric Association, 1987, p. 259–261; Barsky, Wyshak, & Klerman, 1986). (See Box 6.1 for the criteria used in diagnosing this disorder.) The term *hypochondriasis* comes from the Greek words *hypo*, "below," and *chondros*, "cartilage of the breastbone." It reflects the ancient belief that the upper abdominal area, especially the spleen, is the seat of morbid depression about one's health. Although that notion has long since been discarded, the terms *hypochondriasis* and *hypochondriacal* remain in use.

Unlike conversion disorder, hypochondriasis does not involve any actual loss or distortion of bodily functions. It also differs from somatization disorder in that the central preoccupation is on bodily symptoms and an unrealistic fear of having a disease; in somatization disorder there is a concentration on the symptoms themselves rather than the fear of disease.

The irrational beliefs of the hypochondriacal individual remain in spite of repeated physical examinations and professional reassurances that no disease is present. However, the fears are not delusional, as is often the case in psychotically depressed individuals who may be convinced that various internal organs have been destroyed or altered in some bizarre manner (see Chapter 10). Although the concerns of the hypochondriacal individual are ill-founded and maladaptive, they are far more plausible than those found in major depression. Nevertheless, the unrealistic fears and beliefs are usually strong enough to cause a significant impairment in social or occupational pursuits.

Most often, the symptoms of hypochondriasis first appear during adolescence. However, it is not unusual for their onset to be in the 30s or 40s. The disorder is diagnosed as frequently in men as in women.

The daily life of hypochondriacal individuals often becomes almost completely centered on their intense preoccupation with bodily functions. As some clinicians have observed, such individuals are "exquisitely attuned to every facet of their normal physiology and are markedly concerned with minor changes in bodily functioning" (Millon & Millon, 1974, p. 304). They often keep a complete record of their bodily functions, describing them in detail not only to the professionals whom they repeatedly consult but also to family

---

BOX 6.1 Criteria for the Diagnosis of Hypochondriasis

The following criteria for hypochondriasis are derived from DSM-III and various clinical surveys. They are also consistent with descriptions of the disorder in DSM-III-R. All eight criteria taken together represent the most severe form of hypochondriasis. The number of symptoms necessary to diagnose lesser degrees of severity might well vary from one clinician to another.

1. Disease conviction. The individual believes he or she has a serious disease that remains undetected.

2. Disease fear. The person is constantly worried and apprehensive about contracting one or more diseases and so responds with great alarm at the slightest hint of illness.

3. Bodily preoccupation. The individual is preoccupied with personal physiological functions, bodily appearance, and health in general.

4. Somatic symptoms. There are many complaints of aversive physical sensations, disturbing bodily functions, or changes in bodily structure that suggest some kind of physical disease.

5. Illness and sick role behavior. The person acts as if she or he has a chronic physical disease and lives as an invalid.

6. Disability. The individual is socially and occupationally disabled by the symptoms.

7. Absence of medical disease. There is little, if any, evidence of an organic disease to account for the person's complaints, or if some physical illness is present, the complaints are clearly disproportionate to its extent and severity.

Source: Criteria from Barsky, Wyshak, & Klerman, 1986, p. 495.

---

members, friends, and co-workers. It is not unusual for them to go from one physician to another, always dissatisfied with any failure to discover the nature of the physical disease they are convinced they have. Some will magnify a particular symptom, such as an occasional cough, into a serious disease, in spite of professional opinion to the contrary. Others express their fears concerning a variety of organs or organ systems, moving from one to another at different times. Still others may be preoccupied with a particular organ, such as the fear of heart disease, in spite of the lack of medical evidence.

Interpreting Hypochondriacal Symptoms

The intense preoccupation of hypochondriacal individuals with bodily functions enables them to avoid facing deeper fears. Traditional psychoanalytic theory relates this defense reaction to the loss of libidinal (sexual) energy. This deficit, so goes the theory, stems from unconscious feelings of anxiety and guilt about sexual drives. According to Freud's classic explanation, the hypochondriac withdraws sexual energy from the objects of the external world and diverts it by concentrating on various internal organs. In this way the actual source of anxiety can be denied. However, the ultimate effect is damaging. Just as organic disease has a debilitating effect on libidinal energy, so does preoccupation with bodily organs and fear of disease. Thus, the limited libidinal energy of the hypochondriac is reduced even more (Freud, 1914/1957).

A broader approach to understanding hypochondriasis combines elements of existentialist self theory, psychodynamics, and social learning. Here the view is that hypochondriacal symptoms originate in deep-seated feelings of inadequacy reflected in low self-esteem, doubts about one's ability to accept responsibility, and poor relationships with other people. These deficits are not openly admitted or even recognized on a conscious level, so the pain of admitting them directly is avoided. Instead of saying, "I am worthless," the individual can complain, "I am ill"—a more socially acceptable assertion. Furthermore, hypochondriacal symptoms bring secondary gains—positive reinforcement in social learning terms. For example, preoccupation with bodily processes and complaints about fears of illness may gain attention, sympathy, and the reassurance that in spite of inadequacies, the person is wanted and loved. A person may also use hypochondriacal fears and complaints to control other people's behavior, thus expressing more subtly an aggression the individual dares not display openly (Kenyon, 1976; McCranie, 1979).

The sociocultural environment affects the translation of psychological distress into bodily symptoms. Such use of bodily symptoms tends to be stronger among people of less education and lower socioeconomic status. Cultures also differ in the extent to which they encourage the expression of bodily discomfort and the value or stigma they attach to the seeking of medical help for such ailments. Thus, the frequency of hypochondriacal complaints can vary significantly from one sociocultural environment to another (Kenyon, 1976; Barsky & Klerman, 1983).

Treatment

As in all psychological disorders involving physical complaints, it is important to rule out organic pathology as a cause of the symptoms. Unfortunately, however, the tendency of many hypochondriacal individuals to go from one physician to another may result in excessive repetition of diagnostic procedures, such as exploratory surgery, and their attendant risks. Thus, the earlier the victim of hypochondriasis can be guided into some kind of mental health care, once organic pathology has been ruled out, the more likely that excessive diagnostic procedures will be avoided.

The great majority of hypochondriacal individuals are seen in general medical settings, where the focus is usually on demonstrable evidence of physical pathology (disease) rather than the patient's perceptions of that illness (Barsky & Klerman, 1983). Furthermore, even when the medical practitioner is sensitive to the psychological implications of hypochondriacal complaints, it is often very difficult to convince the patient to seek mental health services. That is to be expected, since the patient is so often convinced that the problem is purely physical (American Psychiatric Association, 1987, p. 260).

Successful treatment of hypochondriacal individuals may combine a variety of approaches, from types of psychotherapy to the use of medication. Kellner (1982) has described how a large number of patients, 17 to 60 years old, were helped considerably through an integrated approach that focused on (a) offering accurate information about the psychological and physiological processes involved in hypochondriacal disorder, (b) helping the individual become aware of how selective attention was playing a part in exaggerating bodily ailments, (c) repeating physical examinations when such reassurance seemed appropriate, (d) providing emotional support with sympathetic understanding, and (e) prescribing antianxiety medication when necessary.

Some clinicians have pointed to a special problem psychotherapists often face in working with hypochondriacal individuals and with others who suffer from somatoform disorders. Although it is important to convey a sympathetic understanding of the hypochondriacal complaints, therapists must be careful not to reinforce the sick role that has been developed as a way of coping with problems and lessening social responsibilities (Nowlin & Busse, 1977; Stone & Neale, 1981).

Summary

1. The central feature of dissociative disorders is a sudden alteration in the normal integration of consciousness, identity, and behavior. Somatoform disorders involve bodily (somatic) symptoms that take the form of physical disease; however, the symptoms cannot be traced to any organic disability.

2. DSM-III-R classifies dissociative disorders into four main categories: psychogenic amnesia, psychogenic fugue, multiple personality, and depersonalization disorder.

3. The central feature of psychogenic amnesia is a sudden and severe loss of memory. The amnesia involves failure to recall important personal information and may extend to a complete loss of identity. These disabilities cannot be accounted for on the basis of any organic findings. The most common form of psychogenic amnesia is localized; the individual fails to recall events that occurred during a relatively brief period. Psychogenic amnesia occurs most often in adolescents and young adults. Its onset is sudden, usually following highly traumatic events.

4. Psychogenic fugue is a more complex variation of psychogenic amnesia. Individuals travel abruptly away from home or work, forget their identity, and take on a new one. As in psychogenic amnesia, these fugues occur in the absence of organic disabilities.

5. Psychogenic amnesia and fugue represent maladaptive ways of escaping from problems of conflict and frustration. Psychodynamic interpretations emphasize that the source of these conflicts and frustrations resides in the unconscious. Social learning theory emphasizes that the amnesia and fugue are reinforced, since they help the individual avoid dealing directly with painful problems. The two viewpoints are not necessarily contradictory.

6. Contrary to popular opinion and despite the increased attention to the disorder in recent years, multiple personality is rare. DSM-III-R includes these criteria; the individual has two or more distinct and relatively enduring patterns of personality; and each of these patterns recurrently takes full control of the individual's behavior. Multiple personality should not be confused with the concept of split personality. There is some evidence that a therapist can contribute to a patient's multiple personality.

7. The research of psychologists Charles Osgood and Zella Luria has supported the authenticity of multiple personality states. Using objective measures of personality, the researchers detected distinctly different patterns of personality in two different cases. However, they also pointed out that multiple personality may be an exaggerated and abnormal instance of the role playing all of us manifest under different social situations.

8. Depersonalization disorder, another form of dissociation, is characterized by a severe change in self-perception. Ordinary experiences of one's self are temporarily lost or greatly disturbed. The disorder includes distorted perceptions of one's body and perceptions of other people as being mechanical or dead.

9. Depersonalization disorder usually begins in adolescence and rarely after age 40. The onset is sudden. From a psychodynamic viewpoint, it may be an identity crisis.

10. A variety of methods have been used in the treatment of depersonalization disorder. They include medication, various techniques of behavior therapy, and psychother-

apy that emphasizes the gaining of insight into one's problems and their relationship to the disorder.

11. Sleepwalking, also known as somnambulism, is another form of dissociation. DSM-III-R classifies it under the general diagnostic category of sleep disorders; however, it fits certain criteria of dissociative disorders. Various estimates of the prevalence of sleepwalking indicate that it is more common in children than in adults.

12. Traditional views of sleepwalking have regarded it as an acting out of dreams. However, laboratory studies of eye movements during sleep show that sleepwalking occurs during the stages of sleep when no dreaming takes place.

13. The treatment of sleepwalking in children consists mainly of eliminating obstacles in the house. Studies of sleepwalking show that most children outgrow the disorder, suggesting the nervous system needs a longer period to mature. In contrast, sleepwalking in adults indicate serious psychological problems.

14. Somatoform disorders involve bodily symptoms that take the form of physical disease, but they cannot be traced to actual organic disability. The most common patterns of somatoform disorders are somatization disorder, conversion disorder, somatoform pain disorder, and hypochondriasis.

15. The main symptoms of somatization disorder are chronic and multiple complaints of bodily discomfort — for example, fatigue, bowel trouble, headaches, nausea, and abdominal pain. These complaints continue even though repeated medical examinations show no evidence of any underlying physical disease.

16. There is some evidence that somatization disorder occurs more often among family members than in the general population. Although this suggests that genetic factors play a role, family members might also promote the disorder through their influence on one another.

17. Somatization disorder can interfere significantly with the individual's carrying on a productive life. Furthermore, frequent going to the doctor may result in overmedication and even addiction. Unnecessary surgery is another hazard. Unlike dissociative disorders, the symptoms of somatization rarely disappear spontaneously. Thus, psychotherapy and helping the individual change conditions in the environment that may be contributing to the disorder should be initiated as soon as possible.

18. The main characteristic of conversion disorder (also called hysterical neurosis, conversion type) is a loss or an alteration in physical functioning that suggests a physical disorder but instead is an expression of psychological conflict. That is, the conflict is converted into physical symptoms.

19. The most obvious symptoms of conversion disorder are those that resemble neurological disabilities, such as paralysis of arms or legs, loss of speech, and loss of sensation. These symptoms can be induced through hypnosis, and people who develop conversion symptoms are often highly suggestible, similar to those who respond well to hypnotic suggestion.

20. A symptom often mentioned in the clinical literature is *la belle indifférence* — an apparent lack of concern about one's disability that is highly inappropriate, given such states as a supposed paralysis or loss of sensation. However, some clinicians doubt that *la belle indifférence* is as frequent as is sometimes thought.

21. In reaching a diagnosis of conversion disorder, it is crucial to rule out the presence of organic factors. In his classic study of hysteria, the French psychiatrist Pierre

Janet demonstrated that a clue to conversion disorder could be found in the fact that patients displayed symptoms that failed to correspond to what would actually occur in an organically induced disorder. For example, the patient might report anesthesia in the hand ending abruptly at the wrist. The condition would extend to the arm if the paralysis had a neurological basis.

22. Symptoms of conversion disorder are less common now than they were some years ago because people are more educated and sophisticated about medical and psychological matters.

23. Conversion disorders have been diagnosed more often in women than in men. One interpretation is that women have less control over their social and economic environments than men; thus, they are more likely to express frustrations through bodily symptoms. Furthermore, there may be a sex bias in diagnosis.

24. Symptoms of conversion disorder often begin abruptly and end suddenly. They seem to begin in situations of psychological stress, conflict, and frustration.

25. Conversion symptoms need to be treated as soon as possible. Not only do they prevent the individual from carrying out everyday tasks, but they may also have physical consequences.

26. The main characteristic of somatoform pain disorder is a preoccupation with pain that lasts for at least six months in the absence of any organic disability that could explain it. Even if organic pathology is involved, the complaints of pain are far greater than one would expect from the nature of the organic problem.

27. Although symptoms of somatoform pain disorder are less dramatic than those of conversion disorder, they are more common. They can begin at any age, although the first complaints are usually during early childhood or adolescence. Relatives of persons diagnosed with somatoform pain disorder have often had more painful injuries and physical illnesses than occur in the general population. This fact suggests that some victims of somatoform pain disorder become overly sensitive to pain by observing it in family members.

28. The psychodynamic approach to treating somatoform pain disorder emphasizes gaining insight into one's anxieties, conflicts, and frustrations. Behavioral therapists focus more directly on developing methods of controlling the pain, but they may include insight therapy in this program. Biomedical approaches, such as biofeedback, attempt to teach the individual how to control pain.

29. The main features of hypochondriasis (also called hypochondriacal neurosis) are an exaggerated concern with one's bodily sensations, together with a chronic and unreasonable fear that one has a serious, undetected physical disease.

30. Unlike conversion disorder, hypochondriasis does not involve any actual loss of bodily functions. However, the irrational beliefs of the hypochondriacal individual remain, in spite of repeated physical examinations and professional judgments that no physical disease is present. Symptoms of hypochondriasis appear most often during adolescence, although it is not unusual for the onset to occur in the 20s or 40s.

31. The life-style of hypochondriacal individuals may become almost completely centered around their intense preoccupation with bodily functions, which often prevents them from reaching many social and occupational goals. The psychodynamic viewpoint holds that this intense preoccupation helps such individuals avoid deeper fears stemming from unconscious conflicts. Traditional psychoanalytic theory focuses on sexual conflicts; a broader approach combines elements of existential self theory, social learning, and psychodynamic concepts. In the broader view, hypochondriacal symptoms originate in deep-seated feelings of inadequacy, low self-esteem, doubts about one's ability to accept responsibility, and poor relationships with other people. These deficits are not openly admitted; the focus on the body helps people avoid psychological pain. It may also bring secondary gain, or, in social learning terms, be reinforcing.

32. In treating hypochondriacal disorders, the clinician must first rule out the possibility that organic factors are producing a physical illness. Various forms of psychotherapy can then be carried out. These methods may, under certain circumstances, be combined with medication to allay intense anxieties and enable the person to profit better from psychotherapy.

7

**Psychosomatic
Disorders:
Interaction of
Psychosocial and
Biophysical
Conditions**

If the mind, which rules the body, ever forgets itself so far as to trample upon its slave, the slave is never generous enough to forgive the injury; but will rise and smite its oppressor.

HENRY WADSWORTH LONGFELLOW
Hyperion **(1839)**

"I am woken in the early hours of the morning by an intense pain behind my left eye, as if someone was sticking a red hot needle into it. I get out of bed to find my nose feels blocked and the left eye is watering. When I look in the mirror, the eye is red. The attack lasts half an hour and goes as quickly as it came. The extraordinary thing is that the attack occurs every night at 2 or 3 A.M. and this has been going on for nearly three weeks" (Rose & Gawel, 1979, p. 9). The man who described his symptoms so vividly suffered from a type of headache called *migrainous neuralgia*, more commonly known as **migraine.** A Sumerian poet first described migraine almost 5000 years ago. It affects more men than women, and it has tormented such famous people as Thomas Jefferson, Leo Tolstoy, Charles Dickens, Virginia Woolf, Edgar Allan Poe, and Peter Ilich Tchaikovsky (Adams, Feuerstein, & Fowler, 1980; Lyons, 1983, p. 19). Migraine is just one of the many abnormal biophysical conditions that for many years have been labeled psychosomatic disorders.

Historical Background

The term *psychosomatic* is derived from the Greek words *psyche* ("mind") and *soma* ("body"). Literally, psychosomatic refers to mind–body relationships. As traditionally defined, **psychosomatic disorders** are physical illnesses whose development and expression have been significantly influenced by psychological factors. That definition has now been expanded to include the influence of psychosocial and cultural factors as well (Lipowski, 1984).

Concepts of psychosomatic disorders can be traced at least to the origins of Western medicine in ancient Greece. Hippocrates (ca. 460–377 B.C.) set forth certain opinions about mind–body relationships that are consistent with modern views. Mental states, he said, can produce profound physical changes in the individual. Furthermore, in both health and disease, a person must be understood as a whole, not as a collection of separate units (Zilboorg & Henry, 1941, pp. 46, 50).

The German physician Johann Christian August Heinroth (1773–1843) introduced the term *psychosomatic* into Western medicine. In his dissertation *De Morborum Animi et Pathematum Animi Differentia* (*On the Difference between Emotions and Mental Disorders*), Heinroth emphasized the importance of psychological and social factors in the development of physical disease. He also pointed to the need for humanistic and religious convictions in treating patients. Love and compassion, he said, are essential in the relationship between physician and patient (Heinroth, 1818/1975; Lipowski, 1984; Mora, 1975; Wittkower, 1977).

More than a century earlier, another eminent physician, George Ernest Stahl (1660–1734), was already exploring in some detail various concepts of what later were called psychosomatic disorders. For many years a professor of medicine at the University of Halle, Stahl noted the "stupendous, sudden and quick effect of the so-called passions on

Walter B. Cannon, American physiologist. In his work on bodily changes in emotional reactions, Cannon helped usher in the modern scientific study of psychosomatic disorders.

the body." In his observations of psychological reactions to physical disease, Stahl anticipated modern views by expressing the belief that certain emotions could interfere with a patient's recovery (Zilboorg & Henry, 1941, p. 279).

In the 19th and early 20th centuries, Freud's investigations into the dynamics of unconscious emotional conflict (see Chapter 3). Pavlov's discoveries concerning the nature of conditioned physiological responses (see Chapter 4), and the work of the American physiologist Walter Bradford Cannon (1871–1945) on bodily changes in emotional reactions (1915, 1963) all helped usher in the modern scientific study of psychosomatic disorders and methods of alleviating them.

In succeeding decades, a number of publications stimulated the developing field of psychosomatic research. Helen Flanders Dunbar (1935, 1938, 1943, 1946) wrote extensively on relationships between emotion and physical disease. In 1939, the journal *Psychosomatic Medicine* was established under her editorship. The board of editors represented a broad spectrum of disciplines: psychoanalysis, internal medicine, neurology, psychiatry, psychology, comparative physiology, and pediatrics. The journal continues to be a world leader in the field (Jenkins, 1985). Another landmark was James L. Halliday's *Psychosocial Medicine*, published in 1948. The book reflects Halliday's credo that every personal problem is also a communal problem. Other notable publications during this period were Edward Weiss and O. Spurgeon English's *Psychosomatic Medicine* (1943, 1949), psychoanalyst Franz Alexander's text of the same title (1950), and *Psychosomatic Research* by Roy Grinker (1953).

Diagnostic Considerations

DSM Classification

Psychosomatic disorders were classified as *psychophysiologic disorders* in DSM-II (American Psychiatric Association, 1968). DSM-III and DSM-III-R replaced that term with the diagnostic category *psychological factors affecting physical condition*. This category covers any physical condition to which psychological factors seem to be contributing significantly, and it is used to describe disorders that previous editions of the manual referred to as psychosomatic or psychophysiologic.

The DSM concept that psychological factors contribute to abnormal biophysical conditions has broad applications. These factors may play a part in initiating such conditions and may also intensify them. Furthermore, psychological factors include the meanings an individual gives to environmental stimuli, especially social situations, although the individual may not be fully aware of those meanings or their relationship to the physical disorder (American Psychiatric Association, 1987, pp. 333–334). Thus, the contributory factors that DSM-III and DSM-III-R call psychological should be expanded to include social and cultural variables.

Although the DSM classification no longer uses psychosomatic as a diagnostic category, the term has become so firmly embedded in the research and professional literature and in popular writings that we have retained it. However, a literal interpretation of the word *psychosomatic* is misleading, since it does not imply the broader view we emphasize. By *psychosomatic disorders*, we mean patterns of abnormal biophysical conditions whose onset or intensification is strongly influenced by their interaction with psychological, social, and cultural factors. This meaning is consistent with the holistic view of health and illness that is increasingly reflected in the current practice and research of various mental health professionals, both medical and nonmedical (Everly, 1986; Gentry, 1984; Lipowski, 1984; Mostofsky, 1985).

Psychosomatic versus Somatoform Disorders

It is essential to distinguish between psychosomatic disorders and somatoform disorders. As we discussed in Chapter 6, the symptoms of somatoform disorders often resemble physical illness superficially; however, they are not caused by organic damage to the body. In contrast, the symptoms in psychosomatic disorders can be traced to actual organic pathology. The presence of organic pathology distinguishes psychosomatic disorders from somatoform disorders. There are two other crucial differences as well.

1. In certain instance of somatoform disorders, complaints of physical discomfort or the apparent existence of physical disability may serve to reduce anxiety or help the individual avoid deep-seated conflicts not consciously recognized. The symptoms of psychosomatic disorders, however, rarely alleviate anxiety; indeed, they usually increase it.

2. The symptoms in somatoform disorders tend to be diffuse, typically involving more than one organ or organ system. In psychosomatic disorders the symptoms tend to focus on a single organ or organ system.

Although it is always necessary for nonmedical psychotherapists to work cooperatively with physicians when a patient's problems include complaints of physical discomfort, such consultation is especially important in the case of psychosomatic disorders (American Psychological Association, 1985). Although psychotherapy may help individuals deal constructively with the psychological and sociocultural problems that contributed to their disability, the physical illness itself requires medical assessment and treatment.

Patterns of Psychosomatic Disorders

Psychosomatic disorders involve a wide range of organs and organ systems. A common and highly disabling pattern of disorder is *migraine*, a severe one-sided headache often accompanied by nausea and disturbed vision.

Table 7.1 describes some of the more common patterns of psychosomatic disorders. These disorders may resemble biophysical diseases whose onset and progress are not especially related to psychosocial factors. For example, hypertension (abnormally high blood pressure) may be initiated or aggravated not only by emotional events but also by a diseased kidney.

Unfortunately, psychosomatic disorders are often viewed less seriously than they should be. As Bakal (1979) points out: "Many people have believed that a physical symptom induced by psychological factors cannot really be serious—certainly not as serious as the same symptom induced by physical factors. For example, the belief that emotionally triggered asthma is 'fake asthma' has been found among both the relatives and physicians of patients suffering from this disorder. . . . A family practitioner . . . referred a patient suffering from asthma to a psychiatrist on the basis that 'it can't really be serious since everybody knows this patient's asthma is all psychic'" (p. 9).

Since psychological and sociocultural factors can play a role in all physical illnesses, one could logically argue that every physical disorder is psychosomatic to some extent. Indeed, research has demonstrated that emotional distress and adverse life events can affect the immune system of the body, making an individual more vulnerable to physical disease (Ader & Cohen, 1984). Some researchers have suggested that this loss of immunity may even be involved in such diseases as cancer and diabetes, although their position is highly controversial (Ader, 1981; Bammer & Newberry, 1981; Cooper, 1984;

Table 7.1 Examples of Organs or Organ Systems That May Be Involved in Psychosomatic Disorders	
Organ or Organ System	**Examples of Disorder**
Skin	Pruritis: chronic itching
	Neurodermatitis: chronic inflammation and discharge of fluid
Musculoskeletal	Chronic backache, muscle cramps, tension headache
Cardiovascular	Hypertension: persistent abnormal elevation of blood pressure
	Paroxysmal tachycardia: sudden attacks of abnormally rapid heartbeat
	Arrhythmia: irregular heartbeat
	Migraine: severe one-sided headache, usually accompanied by nausea and disturbed vision
	Angina pectoris: spasmodic pain in the chest, often accompanied by a feeling of suffocation and impending death
Respiratory	Bronchial asthma: Spasmodic contractions of air passages in lungs and difficulty in breathing
	Hyperventilation: Overbreathing associated with a sudden reduction of carbon dioxide in the blood (common symptoms include faintness, light-headedness, tingling sensations in limbs, and feeling unable to get sufficient air)
Gastrointestinal	Gastric and duodenal ulcers: peptic ulcers found in the mucous membranes of the stomach or the duodenal area of the small intestine, caused by acidic action of gastric juice
	Gastritis: inflammation of the stomach
	Colitis: inflammation of the colon
	Pylorospasm: spasm of the pylorus or pyloric portion of the stomach — an opening through which the contents of the stomach are emptied into the duodenum
	Anorexia nervosa: severe decrease in food intake, resulting in emaciation (occurs most often in adolescent girls and young women — see Chapter 16)
Endocrine	Hyperthyroidism: Overactivity of the thyroid gland
Genitourinary	Menstrual disturbances
	Micturation abnormalities, including painful or abnormally frequent urination

Source: Kaplan & Sadock, 1985, pp. 488–543.

Greer, 1979; Hall, 1983; Holden, 1978; Surwit, Feinglos, & Scovern, 1983; Tache, Selye, & Day, 1979; Turkington, 1985; Wasylenki & Freeman, 1980). For example, stress may inhibit the immune system by producing elevated levels of adrenal corticoid hormones in the blood plasma. The excess of hormones can result in a decrease in leukocytes (white blood cells or corpuscles). This is a cancerous condition known as leukocytopenia, meaning a poverty of leukocytes.

The inclusion of psychological and sociocultural influences in a wider range of abnormal physical conditions does not mean we should abandon the concept of psychosomatic disorders. Rather, the problem is to recognize the role played by a wide range of life events and situations and to study systematically various aspects of those roles. The ultimate goal is "to develop more effective preventive, therapeutic, and rehabilitative techniques" (Lipowski, 1977, pp. xv–xvi).

Psychosomatic Disorders and Stress

Somatic Weakness

According to the theory of **somatic weakness,** a psychosomatic disorder is most likely to occur in a bodily organ or organ system that was already biologically vulnerable. The weakness may be genetic, or it may be the result of a previous physical illness or injury (Lachman, 1972, p. 57). For example, the person with an oversensitive digestive tract who develops a psychosomatic disorder is likely to have ulcers; the individual who already had a physical disability that interfered with breathing is likely to develop asthma.

A study that seems to support the somatic weakness theory, found that 80 percent of asthma patients had suffered from prior respiratory infections. Presumably the infections had weakened the respiratory system, making it more vulnerable to psychosocial stress (Rees, 1964). Unfortunately, few studies of this sort have been carried out, since it is difficult to demonstrate a clear-cut connection between a prior physical illness and a subsequent psychosomatic disturbance. Furthermore, the conclusion that the site of the psychosomatic disorder was determined by the prior somatic weakness relies mainly on ex post facto reasoning: "The organ broke down, therefore it was weak" (Ullmann & Krasner, 1975, p. 214).

Another approach to the somatic weakness theory emphasizes the role of the autonomic nervous system (see Figure 5.1). A biological predisposition to develop ulcers has been linked to excessive levels of pepsinogen, an enzyme whose production is controlled in part by the autonomic nervous system. Pepsinogen is secreted by gastric glands; converted into pepsin, it aids in the digestion of proteins. However, excessive amounts of pepsin can have an irritating effect on tissues. In a study at a U.S. Army training base, people who already had high serum levels of pepsinogen were compared with those who had low levels. Although both groups were exposed to the same environment, the high-pepsinogen group developed peptic ulcers far more frequently. A biological predisposition to ulcers may have interacted with stress to produce the disorder (Wasylenki & Freeman, 1980).

Selye's Theory of Stress

Stress and Stressors

One of the most influential approaches to understanding the role of stress in psychosomatic disorders is the comprehensive theory developed by Hans Selye (1950, 1956, 1976, 1980, 1982). Selye defines *stress* very broadly as "the *nonspecific* (that is, common) *result of any demand upon the body,* be the effect mental or somatic" (1982, p. 7). Selye observes that "a variety of dissimilar situations — emotional arousal, effort, fatigue, pain, fear, concentration, humiliation, loss of blood, and even great and unexpected success — are capable of producing stress; hence, no single factor can, in itself, be pinpointed as the cause of the reaction as such. . . . Medical research has shown that while people may face quite different problems, in some respects their bodies respond in a stereotyped pattern; identical biochemical changes enable us to cope with any type of increased demand on vital activity" (pp. 7–8). Selye coined the term **stressors** for the various situations that may produce stress. Strictly speaking, any demand on the body, including demands necessary to maintain life, may act as a stressor. However, Selye points out that certain stressors may be particularly threatening, and these have the

Highly threatening stressors can play a crucial role in the development of psychosomatic disorders.

greatest implications for psychosomatic disorders. Among such stressors are infectious organisms that invade the body, traumatic injuries, great extremes in temperature, unfamiliar or sudden stimuli, and emotionally arousing situations.

The body reacts to threatening stressors by mobilizing its physiological resources. Under ordinary circumstances, these emergency reactions do not last long. However, if the stressful situations continue over a long period of time, the emergency reactions are likely to become exhausted and various psychosomatic symptoms may emerge.

**General Adaptation
Syndrome**

Selye (1976, 1982) has given the name **general adaptation syndrome (GAS)** to the various stressors in life and one's reactions to them. There are three stages to the GAS: alarm reaction, resistance, and exhaustion.

The **alarm reaction** is the initial emergency stage and involves a rapid mobilization of the body's resources for action. The adrenal cortex (situated near the kidney) produces additional amounts of hormones that help various parts of the body meet the emergency —for example, the liver, which releases glycogen (carbohydrates). The sympathetic division of the autonomic nervous system is stimulated. This increases heart activity, facilitates the secretion of epinephrine (adrenaline), inhibits intestinal activity, and dilates the pupils of the iris. All of these changes are highly adaptive. They prepare the organism for sudden and extensive activity and great expenditures of energy if they are necessary for the body to defend or protect itself.

However, as Seyle observes, "no living organism can be maintained continuously in a state of alarm" (1976, p. 37). Continuous exposure to highly damaging stressors is incompatible with life. However, if the organism survives, the alarm reaction is followed by the second stage of the GAS—the resistance stage.

In the **resistance stage,** the adrenal cortex enlarges and defensive reactions approach their limits of adaptation. If exposure to noxious stressors continues and the resistance to them is prolonged excessively, body resources become depleted and resistance can no longer be maintained. **Exhaustion** occurs, and possibly death. According to Selye, the psychosomatic symptoms that may occur because of prolonged defensive reactions to aversive stressors represent **diseases of adaptation.** For example, blood pressure rises during the alarm reaction stage as an adaptive measure. However, if this reaction continues too long, a chronic pattern of high blood pressure (hypertension) may become established and persist even in the absence of the stressors that first contributed to it.

Implications of Selye's Theory

Selye's theory of stress is especially valuable in its emphasis on the possible adverse effects of prolonged stress. It can help us understand the relationship between physiological stress and the onset of psychosomatic disorders. However, the theory has certain limitations. It does not explain why one person develops a disease of adaptation and another does not, even though both have encountered the same stressors. Nor does it explain why one person develops a particular kind of adaptation syndrome (for example, hypertension) while another develops a quite different reaction (for example, colitis). The somatic weakness theory provides a possible reason for such differences. Individuals vary in their vulnerability to stressors because of a preexisting weakness in a particular organ or organ system. Thus, when they are exposed to prolonged stress, the weak organ is most likely to be affected.

Diathesis—Stress: An Integrative Approach

The **diathesis—stress theory** of psychosomatic disorders considers not only the effects of biological vulnerability and the impact of environmental stressors but also how individuals perceive those stressors and cope with them. Thus, the theory deals with psychosocial as well as biophysical stress. Individuals possess a predisposition (diathesis) to develop certain biophysical disorders, such as hypertension, ulcers, and tension headaches. Given this predisposition and the presence of appropriate stressors in the environment, the individual reacts with various physiological and psychological defenses. However, physiological stress is most likely to occur when the individual not only perceives environmental stressors as serious threats to physical or psychological well-being but also feels unable to cope adequately with them. Physiological stress may be manifested in a variety of ways — for example, through muscle tension, increased heart rate, skin reactions, and the release of hormones from the adrenal glands. If these reactions become too prolonged and intense, they may act as powerful antecedents to physical disease or aggravate already existing disease (Bakal, 1979, p. 74; Baum, Singer, & Baum, 1981).

Like Selye's theory of stress, the diathesis—stress theory does not predict what particular psychosomatic disorder will develop in a given individual. It points instead to the tremendous differences that exist in people's vulnerability to psychosomatic disorders. Given the same set of environmental stressors, variations in biological predispositions and perceptions of threat may produce psychosomatic illness in some individuals but not in others.

Stress and Type A Behavior

More than two decades ago, Meyer Friedman and Ray Rosenman (1959, 1960) began to identify a pattern of behavior that they believed to be significantly correlated with coronary heart disease, the single largest cause of death in the United States. They called this

A chronic sense of urgency is one of the various facets of a coronary-prone pattern of behavior that Friedman and Rosenman have identified and called Type A.

pattern *coronary-prone behavior*, or **Type A behavior.** This behavior includes extreme competitiveness, hostility, and a pervasive sense of time urgency. In contrast, people exhibiting *noncoronary-prone behavior* (**Type B behavior**) tend to be more relaxed and less hostile and impatient.

Type A individuals have a strong need to maintain personal control over all life events, even when this may be inappropriate and cause undue stress: "Meeting deadlines, waiting in traffic, receiving favors, and bureaucratic red tape are just a few of the daily instances where our freedom to behave as we choose is threatened. Perhaps attempts at maintaining control in such situations by individuals with high expectations or concerns for control (perhaps Type As) result in a cumulatively more stressful existence than for people without such concerns" (Rhodewalt & Comer, 1982, p. 157).

Researchers at the University of London found that students who revealed Type A behavior also had unrealistically high internal standards and unrealistically high expectations of success. Thus, they tended to suffer more disappointment and self-doubt than did Type B students, who assessed their capabilities more realistically (Furnham, Borovoy, & Henley, 1986).

Assessment of Type A Behavior

The principal methods for assessing patterns of Type A behavior include structured interviews and self-report inventories (questionnaires). Most of the research with these instruments has focused on middle-aged men, since that group is at highest risk for cardiovascular disease. However, an approach that combines both instruments has proved to be successful in identifying Type A behavior in female and male adolescents (Rosenman, 1978; Siegel & Leitch, 1981; Wright, 1988, pp. 9–14).

One of the most widely known self-report methods, used by practitioners as well as researchers, is the Jenkins Activity Survey (JAS). It is designed to duplicate in a shorter time the basic kinds of assessments that are made through structured interviews (Appels, Jenkins, & Rosenman, 1982; Jenkins, Rosenman, & Friedman, 1967; Jenkins, Zyzanski, & Rosenman, 1971, 1979; Rosenman, 1978; Rosenman & Chesney, 1982). For each question in the JAS, the respondent is asked to choose the answer that "is true for you." The following items illustrate the general nature of the questions:

- How often do you actually "put words in the person's mouth" in order to speed things up?
  A. Frequently
  B. Occasionally
  C. Almost never

- How often do you find yourself hurrying to get places when there is plenty of time?
  A. Frequently
  B. Occasionally
  C. Almost never

- Would people you know well agree that you tend to get irritated easily?
  A. Definitely yes
  B. Probably yes
  C. Probably no
  D. Definitely no

Type A Behavior and Physical Disorders

A large body of research has accumulated to support the conclusion that Type A behavior may in some instances contribute to coronary heart disease as much as or even more than such risk factors as abnormally high levels of serum cholesterol, obesity, cigarette smoking, and hypertension. Indeed, these factors may interact with Type A behavior to increase the individual's vulnerability. For example, Type A behavior is related to high blood pressure, which in turn increases the probability of heart disease. Studies have also demonstrated a relationship between Type A behavior and **atherosclerosis,** a circulatory disease in which deposits of yellowish plaque containing cholesterol and other fatty substances are deposited in arteries, causing the arterial walls to thicken and lose elasticity. In Type A individuals, atherosclerosis is not limited to coronary arteries (Blumenthal, Williams, Kong, Schanberg, & Thompson, 1978; Glass, Contrada, & Snow, 1980; Harrell, 1980; Kahn et al., 1982; Matthews, 1982; Rosenman & Chesney, 1982; Stevens, Turner, Rhodewalt, & Talbot, 1984).

Although most of the research on Type A behavior has focused on its relationship to coronary heart disease, a number of studies have related it to other abnormal biophysical conditions as well. One investigation found that Type A behavior was associated with a greater frequency of migraine headaches involving contractions of the blood vessels and headache pain caused by muscular tension (Woods, Morgan, Day, Jefferson, & Harris, 1984).

Type A Behavior and Psychosocial Stress

Several recent studies have failed to find significant relationships between Type A behavior and deaths from coronary heart disease (Ragland & Brand, 1988). It may well be that certain components of Type A behavior, such as hostility, are more important risk factors than others. Thus, if one considers Type A behavior only as a total pattern, the factors that predict heart disease may in some instances be masked by those that do not. A finer analysis of Type A behavior, in which subtypes are used as predictors of disease, is needed to resolve this question.

A number of recent studies move in this direction by examining the relationship between Type A behavior and specific aspects of psychosocial stress (Ivancevich & Matteson, 1988; Krantz, Contrada, Hill, & Friedler, 1988). Type A behavior often places an individual in highly stressful social circumstances, thus increasing the risk of heart disease (Byrne & Rosenman, 1986). We do not know how the interaction of Type A behavior and psychosocial stress actually leads to physical disorders. A reasonable hypothesis is that both activate the autonomic nervous system. If this activation is extreme and occurs repeatedly, the adverse effects may produce cardiovascular symptoms (Krantz, Glass, Schaeffer, & Davis, 1982). A study of Type A university administrators found that those who perceived their jobs as highly stressful or had many undesirable and uncontrollable life experiences were more likely to have cardiovascular problems than those whose perceptions were more benign and who felt more in control (Rhodewalt, Hays, Chemers, & Wysocki, 1984).

Vickers, Hervig, Rahe, and Rosenman (1981) studied 550 middle-aged men to see how coping skills and the use of defense mechanisms were related to Type A behavior. Coping skills included objectivity in evaluating ideas and events, logical thinking, tolerance of ambiguity, ability to take another person's viewpoint (empathy), and ability to concentrate without undue distraction. Defense mechanisms included rationalization, projection, and denial (see Chapter 3). Type A behavior was measured with the Jenkins Activity Scale. The individuals who were deficient in coping skills and who used defense mechanisms excessively were especially prone to Type A behavior. Presumably, poor coping and maladaptive use of defense mechanisms increase stress. Thus, one could conclude that the risk of heart disease increases for Type A individuals who experience stress because of their inability to cope successfully and their excessive use of defenses against conflict and frustration (Krantz & Manuck, 1984).

Changing Type A Behavior

One of the most ambitious attempts to change Type A behavior involved more than 1000 predominantly male volunteers in the San Francisco Bay area. None smoked, and all had suffered serious damage to heart muscle tissue resulting from a blocking of circulation (Powell, Friedman, Thoresen, Gill, & Ulmer, 1984). A total of 862 individuals were randomly assigned to either an experimental section receiving a combination of cardiac and Type A counseling or to a control section receiving cardiac counseling only. The remaining 150 persons agreed to undergo a yearly physical examination and behavioral assessment but did not receive any counseling. The purpose of the third group was to allow the researchers to assess the kinds of changes in behavior that might occur without special counseling. Throughout the study, all individuals continued to be seen by their own physicians.

Counseling was carried out in small groups. Cardiologists conducted the cardiac counseling, which emphasized information about the nature of myocardial infarction and how physical risk factors, such as diet and hypertension, may contribute to cardiovascular problems. Psychologists and psychiatrists conducted the Type A counseling. It was based on a cognitive–social learning model that helped the participants understand the psychosocial nature of the behavior that had contributed to their cardiovascular problems and how to change it.

After 24 months, the individuals who received both cardiac counseling and Type A counseling showed significantly less Type A behavior than the other two groups. In addition, they had a significantly lower recurrence of cardiovascular problems than the group that had received no counseling.

Psychoanalytic Explanations of Psychosomatic Disorders

Various psychoanalytic practitioners and researchers have proposed that certain psychosomatic disorders can be differentiated according to the patterns of conflict and frustration an individual experienced during childhood. The disorders most often explained on this basis involve the digestive system (see Figure 7.1) and the respiratory system.

Peptic Ulcers

In their work at the Chicago Institute of Psychoanalysis, which for many years has pioneered in developing innovative approaches to psychoanalysis, Franz Alexander and his colleagues reported that the occurrence of **peptic ulcers** in the stomach was closely related to conflicts and frustrations arising from dependence needs (Alexander, 1950;

Figure 7.1

The digestive system. (From Hassett, 1978, p. 75.)

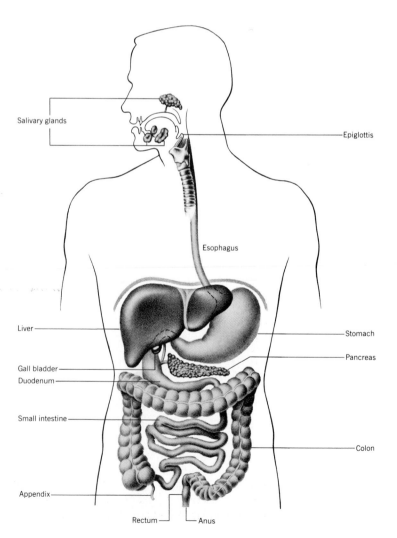

Salivary glands

Epiglottis

Esophagus

Liver

Stomach

Pancreas

Gall bladder

Duodenum

Small intestine

Colon

Appendix

Rectum — Anus

Alexander, French, & Pollack, 1968). These conflicts are expressed mainly through denial that the needs actually exist or through an exaggerated submissiveness to them.

Individuals who deny dependence are usually very ambitious, assertive, driving, and hard-hitting. They make it a point not to admit they need help and take all kinds of heavy responsibilities independently. According to Alexander (1950), they are responding to an extreme but unconscious need for dependence by utilizing the defense mechanism of reaction formation (see Chapter 3). Although their need for parental love is long-standing, they have repressed their awareness of it. Recognition of this need would create undue anxiety because it would conflict with their current aspirations for complete independence. However, repression does not solve their problem, for it becomes the unconscious psychological stimulus for overactivity of the parasympathetic nervous system and an oversecretion of stomach fluids. Persistent oversecretion may eventually lead to peptic ulcers.

> The stomach responds continuously as if food were being taken in. . . . The patient wants food as a symbol of love and help rather than as satiation of a physiological need. . . . [T]his permanent chronic emotional stimulation of the stomach is similar to that which occurs temporarily during the ingestion of food with a resultant chronic hypermobility and hypersecretion. The empty stomach is thus constantly exposed to the same physiological stimulus to which it is exposed only periodically, under normal conditions, when it contains or is about to receive food. (pp. 105 – 106)

The second type of ulcer patient Alexander describes is the person who submits excessively to dependence needs. This kind of individual tends to be clinging and demanding, playing a child's role even as an adult. Such behavior is apt to be met with considerable disapproval and rejection, thus producing chronic frustration, conflict, and anxiety. In turn, these reactions lead to overactivity of the parasympathetic nervous system, oversecretion of acidic gastric juices, and eventually ulcers.

Colitis

According to some psychoanalytic explanations, **colitis (inflammation of the colon)** often originates during toilet training as the result of excessive parental expectations for consistent bowel control. The child reacts to this strict training by wishing to punish the overcontrolling parents or parental surrogates. But since they are more powerful, the child's hostility is directed inward toward the offending organ — the bowel. Colitis during adulthood may then represent a regression to inward anger that developed during childhood. More broadly, it reflects the frustration of the desire to meet one's obligations and accomplish particular tasks (Lachman, 1972).

Bronchial Asthma

Various psychoanalytic theorists have proposed that **bronchial asthma** originates in early childhood experiences related to needs for dependence and love. If a parent is cold and rejecting, the child is likely to develop strong feelings of hostility. Reluctant to express this anger directly for fear of being abandoned, the child complains indirectly by wheezing and whining: "Sounds accompanying the breathing difficulties of asthma resemble such wheezing and whining and presumably relate to similar lung activity. The asthmatic reaction may then be conceived as a partially suppressed plaintive cry" (Lachman, 1972, p. 61). The asthmatic reaction may persist all during childhood and into adulthood, becoming especially severe whenever feelings of anger are aroused toward parents, other authority figures, or anyone who withholds wanted love.

Evaluation of Psychoanalytic Explanations

Theories concerning the relationship between personality characteristics and specific psychosomatic disorders have been derived mainly from the psychoanalysis of adults. Necessarily, then, the data to support those theories are retrospective, based on how such individuals describe their earlier life experiences and the psychoanalyst's interpretation and reconstruction of those experiences.

Recognizing the possibility of bias in such procedures, Alexander and his colleagues carried out an extensive study that they hoped would provide more objective evidence (Alexander, French, & Pollack, 1968). Their goal was to determine whether psychoanalysts who were familiar with theories of psychosomatic specificity could differentiate certain physical disorders correctly on the basis of data from clinical interviews. The study involved 83 patients, each previously diagnosed with one of seven psychosomatic diseases. The psychoanalysts knew what the diseases were but did not know the diagnoses for the individual patients. Their task was to make correct diagnoses based on the clinical interview data they were given concerning the patients' conflicts and frustrations.

Three of the psychosomatic disorders were those we have discussed: peptic ulcer, colitis, and bronchial asthma. The other four disorders, and the kind of conflict and frustration that supposedly contributed to their development, were as follows.

Disorder	Conflict and Frustration
Rheumatoid arthritis: chronic inflammation in joints for which no specific organic cause can be determined	Difficulty in handling hostile impulses; conflict resolved by combining self-control with benevolent tyranny
Essential hypertension: chronic abnormal elevation of blood pressure for which no specific organic cause is known	Continuous struggle against asserting oneself; fear of losing affection leads to overcontrol of aggressive impulses
Neurodermatitis: inflammation of the skin, such as is found in eczema	Conflict and guilt over desire to show one's body as a means of obtaining physical love from others
Hyperthyroidism: a disease condition resulting from overactivity of the thyroid gland	Constant struggle against fears concerning the physical integrity of the body, especially the fear of death; attempts to master the fears are expressed by denying them and seeking dangerous situations

Since the study involved seven psychosomatic disorders, the odds of a psychoanalyst making a correct diagnosis for a given patient simply by chance were approximately 14 percent (1/7). The diagnosticians did better than chance, but they made correct judgments usually less than 50 percent of the time. Such evidence is not very strong support for the general theory that a single specific factor — for example, conflict and frustration during childhood — is responsible for a particular psychosomatic disorder. Other studies and reviews of research have cast serious doubt on the theory (Bakal, 1979; Luborsky, Docherty, & Penick, 1973; Stein, 1986; Viney, 1985).

Psychosomatic Disorders and the Sociocultural Environment

Research and practice in the field of psychosomatic disorders have become increasingly concerned with relationships between physical disease and highly stressful sociocultural stimuli. Such stressors vary greatly within a given society and from one culture to another (Guthrie, Verstraete, Deines, & Stern, 1975; Pearlin, 1982). Especially crucial are those that derive from the growing complexity of the environment. For example, population density and overcrowding may produce sensory overload and excessive social stimulation. These stressors may in turn evoke psychological and physiological reactions that make one more susceptible to physical disorders (Baum, Singer, & Baum, 1981; Goldberger, 1982; Kaminoff & Proshansky, 1982; Lipowski, 1973). Other social factors are economic insecurity and adverse working conditions (Holt, 1982; Wittkower, 1974, 1977). Indeed, the very act of getting to work, especially in crowded urban areas, may play an important role. A study of transportation and stress found that the blood pressure of commuters who had to drive in congested traffic rose the faster they drove and the longer they traveled (Novaco, Stokols, Campbell, & Stokols, 1979).

Environmental stimuli are a matter not merely of the information that individuals receive from their surroundings but also how they evaluate that information: "The 'more unhealthy' members of every group that we have studied have consistently evaluated their life situations as depriving, threatening, conflict-producing, or over-demanding, while the 'more healthy' have not, even though in many cases, the 'unhealthy' have lived in a social and interpersonal milieu that other observers regarded as 'objectively no different' from that of the healthy" (Hinkle, 1961, p. 293).

Noise and Psychosomatic Disorders

Researchers dealing with the effects of noise on physical and mental health usually distinguish between sound and noise. *Sound* is changes in air pressure that the ear can detect. *Noise* is sound that a listener finds undesirable.

The intensity of sound is ordinarily measured in decibels (dB). The sound of light traffic is approximately 55 dB; a jet airliner takeoff at 200 feet is approximately 120 dB (Cohen & Weinstein, 1981, p. 37). Long-term exposure to high-intensity levels of sound can damage sensitive cells in the cochlea of the ear, resulting in serious hearing loss.

Experiencing sound as noise does not necessarily depend directly on the intensity of the sound (Borsky, 1980; Cohen, 1980; Cohen, Glass, & Phillips, 1979; Cohen & Weinstein, 1981). A devoted fan of hard rock may find listening to the music at 110 dB quite pleasurable; a not-so-enchanted neighbor might well find the same decibel level highly offensive. The sound of whispering students during a lecture may register at a very low decibel level, but to the lecturer the noise may be quite annoying. Usually, however, the kinds of noise that contribute to psychosomatic disorders are at higher rather than lower decibel levels.

When extreme, the physical and psychological stress that noise produces can alter bodily functions, and these changes may lead to physical damage. Although the overall evidence is inconsistent, it does suggest that intensive long-term exposure to noise can

This engineer in a noisy plant is trying to carry on a conversation by telephone. Some studies show that chronic exposure to aversive noise can alter bodily functions, which in turn may cause physical damage to the body.

increase one's susceptibility to disease and thus contribute to the development of psychosomatic disorders. If people exposed to noise can become habituated to it, they can reduce its adverse effects, but some people are more vulnerable than others (Cohen & Weinstein, 1981; Glass & Singer, 1972; Jansen, 1969; Kryter, 1970; McLean & Tarnopolsky, 1977; Tarnopolsky, Watkins, & Hand, 1980).

Effects of Overcrowding

Some studies have shown that an extremely high concentration of people in residential areas is associated with an increase in the rate of stress-related disorders requiring psychiatric hospitalization (Freedman, Heshka, & Levy, 1975). One explanation for this increase is that emotional problems and stress limit one's effectiveness in interpersonal relations, thus making one less likely to cooperate with other family members in crowded conditions. As a result, the family may attempt to solve the conflict through hospitalization.

More direct evidence concerning the effects of overcrowding on the development of psychosomatic disorders comes from studies of living conditions in prisons. Prisoners sharing a dormitory cell suffered more physical illnesses than prisoners in single cells. For example, systolic and diastolic blood pressure were higher (D'Atri, 1975; McCain, Cox, & Paulus, 1976). Other studies have confirmed the relationship between crowding in prison and high blood pressure and have found that the greater the crowding, the higher the death rate and the larger the number of inmates who develop mental disorders (Applebome, 1988; Paulus, McCain, & Cox, 1978).

The effects of overcrowding on stress and physical illness may not be so much a function of the crowding itself as the lack of control over one's behavior that such conditions impose. This lack can lead to considerable frustration, conflict, and stress, which in turn can contribute to the development of psychosomatic disorders. A number of studies have shown that the negative effects of crowded residential areas on one's physical and mental state can be reduced if the conditions allow for some degree of control over

A number of studies on overcrowding in prisons have shown that prisoners who shared a dormitory cell suffered more physical illness, such as high blood pressure, than did prisoners living singly in one-person cells.

one's behavior and cooperation with others in achieving this control. This relationship between control, cooperation, and the effects of overcrowding has also been demonstrated in various laboratory experiments (Epstein, 1981).

Other Effects of Sensory Overload

Persistent noise, crowding, and other negative aspects of increased urbanization may contribute not only to the development of physical disorders but also to intellectual and emotional disturbances. Sensory overload may impair one's ability to perform intellectual

In daily life the stress and physical illness brought on by overcrowded conditions may not be simply a function of the overcrowding. The lack of control a person has over his or her behavior in the face of the imposed conditions can add considerably to frustration, conflict, and stress.

tasks, or it may lead to social alienation and personal disorganization. In an experiment designed to test this possibility, female and male volunteers were subjected for some 40 minutes to a rapid succession of intense auditory and visual stimuli that dealt with a wide variety of themes — birth, death, violence, eroticism, outer space, surgical procedures, and others. The subjects revealed an increase in hostile thoughts and feelings of estrangement from other people. Furthermore, their speech showed signs of disorganization, reflected in the inability to complete sentences and in the use of disconnected phrases (Gottschalk, Haer, & Bates, 1972).

Psychosomatic Disorders and Learning

Classical and Operant Conditioning

Laboratory experiments have demonstrated that certain forms of emotional responses, such as fear and anger, can be established, at least in part, through classical conditioning (in Skinnerian terms, respondent conditioning — see Chapter 4). Various physiological functions may also undergo classical conditioning, which in turn may lead to psychosomatic disorders. That is, an individual may learn to associate an emotionally stressful situation with the responses of a particular organ or organ system. Subsequently, other stressful situations, similar to the original one, may arouse the same organ. If the conditioned arousal occurs sufficiently often and with sufficient intensity, malfunctioning and even structural damage to the organ or organ system may result. The following example illustrates the critical role such learning can play in the development of a psychosomatic disorder — in this case, ulcers.

> Suppose [an individual] suffers a major frustration and reacts with a profound physiological arousal of anger that manifests itself in part in gastrointestinal pain. . . . [The] . . . arousal and [pain] . . . may become associated with the people, the circumstances, the place, and the time of the original occurrence, as well as with any other aspect of the provoking situation. . . . [F]uture encounters with those people, that place, and stimuli relating to or similar to the frustration situation [and thinking about them] may lead to emotional arousal . . . increased gastric secretion and decreased gastrointestinal mobility . . . and eventually to duodenal ulcers. (Lachman, 1972, p. 58)

Psychosomatic disorders may also develop, or be aggravated, though operant conditioning, a process of learning discussed in Chapter 4. The physiological reactions that eventually lead to organ malfunctioning may persist because they are reinforced: "In response to an emotional situation [a man] develops vigorous cardiac contractions and as a consequence reports pain and other uncomfortable stimulation from within the upper thoracic region; should that symptom be rewarded [reinforced] by compassionate attention and by diminished family or vocational responsibilities. . . . vigorous cardiac contraction and subsequent pain could become a well established reaction to stressful situations, which might also lead in time to cardiac damage (Lachman, 1972, p. 58).

Classical and operant conditioning often work together in producing or intensifying psychosomatic disorders. Potentially harmful physiological responses to certain stressful situations may originally be established through classical conditioning. However, they may persist and eventually produce physical damage because certain experiences, such as sympathetic attention, reinforce those responses. This reinforcement makes it more likely that whenever such stressful situations are encountered, the same adverse physiological responses will occur.

Operant Conditioning and Biofeedback

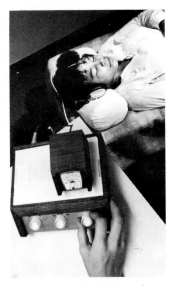

This woman is learning to relax by listening to clicks that signal every time she contracts the muscles in her forehead. The monitoring clicks are the instrumental part of *biofeedback,* which teaches the person how to control stress and related bodily functions.

Laboratory studies have demonstrated that various responses controlled by the autonomic nervous system can be self-regulated to an appreciable extent through operant conditioning. Individuals have learned to lower their heart rate and blood pressure and to alter skin temperature as a way of reducing the throbbing pain of tension headaches. Learning to control such autonomic functions has been accomplished through various kinds of verbal reinforcement and the use of monitoring equipment that provides individuals with information concerning their progress toward self-regulation. Sufferers from asthma have been able to decrease the resistance of their airways to normal breathing by observing a visual display that continually informs them of their respiratory functions (Feldman, 1976; Reed, Katkin, & Goldband, 1986, pp. 381–383).

The discovery that responses of the autonomic nervous system can be self-regulated through operant conditioning stems largely from the pioneering work of Neal Miller (1969). Such operant procedures, now known as **biofeedback,** constitute one of the central tools of **behavioral medicine,** a rapidly expanding field of therapy that applies a variety of behavioral techniques to the treatment of psychosomatic disorders (Agras, 1984; Basmajian, 1979; Fuller, 1978; Hassett, 1978; Melzack, 1975; Miller, 1978; Sargent, 1977; Shapiro, 1981).

Fuller (1978) has summarized the rationale and use of biofeedback procedures as follows.

> Biofeedback is the use of instrumentation to mirror psychophysiological processes of which the individual is not normally aware and which may be brought under voluntary control. . . . The receipt of this feedback enables the individual to become a more active participant in the process of his or her own health maintenance. Measured from electrodes or sensors on the appropriate portions of the body, the information is . . . displayed by the instrumentation. . . . [W]ith the instruments, the individual may learn to recognize the relationship between psychological and physical changes and more objectively relate them to tension and realization in the environment. . . . [T]hese concepts have direct application to psychotherapy in that the psychotherapist becomes an element or part of the biofeedback loop. (p. 39)

It is difficult to know the extent to which the biofeedback procedures themselves are responsible for changing physiological responses during therapy. The changes might be influenced by other factors inherent in the learning situation—for example, the therapist's suggestions that treatment will be effective, the state of relaxation induced by such expectations, and the distraction from the physiological disturbance that the treatment provides. Such factors, called **placebo effects,** have been known in professional circles for many years, although they are often disregarded in evaluating the effectiveness of a particular kind of therapy (Shapiro & Morris, 1978). In the words of one medical specialist, placebo effects have been the "great secret of doctors," since many things get better by themselves (Thomas, 1974).

A number of authorities in the field of psychosomatic research and practice have been concerned with the lack of controlled clinical studies on the effectiveness of biofeedback procedures (Blanchard & Young, 1974; Melzack, 1975; Miller, 1974; Miller & Dworkin, 1977; Sargent, 1977). In particular, Melzack (1975) warned against the belief that biofeedback methods are a cure-all, a belief that has received support in much popular writing and advertising. Melzack emphasizes that before clinicians introduce a particular biofeedback procedure into regular therapeutic practice, experimental evidence should demonstrate that the following events have occurred (p. 19).

1. The effect of the procedure is greater than the placebo effect alone.

2. The changes that are produced are great enough to be of clinical significance.

3. The success of the procedures in the laboratory can be transferred to normal, everyday situations.

4. The benefits of the procedures last long enough to be meaningful.

According to Melzack, very few studies purporting to show the effectiveness of biofeedback have included all four criteria. He concludes: "There is no evidence so far that biofeedback is the panacea promised by best-selling books. It is time to stop the exhilarating speculations and to carry out well-controlled research instead" (p. 81).

Since Melzack's warning, other biofeedback researchers and practitioners have agreed that the early enthusiasm over biofeedback as therapy was excessive. However, they point out that its usefulness is growing as the result of better-controlled studies using more sophisticated methods and instruments. The promise, they say, lies in using biofeedback selectively, rather than applying it indiscriminately. Independent of what the final verdict may be, the fact that biofeedback procedures encourage the patient to take an active part is in itself a potentially valuable contribution to the therapy (Green & Shellenberger, 1986; Hassett, 1978, p. 147; Norris, 1986; Reed, Katkin, & Goldband, 1986, pp. 423–424; Roberts, 1985, 1986; White & Tursky, 1986). The extent to which the promise of biofeedback is fully realized depends a great deal on whether it will be integrated with other approaches designed to reach a particular therapeutic goal (Norris, 1986; Roberts, 1985, 1986).

Psychosomatic Disorders and Psychotherapy

Individuals who suffer from a psychosomatic disorder may have great difficulty in verbalizing their feelings. Instead, they communicate their emotional distress through physical symptoms. Thus, a useful approach to psychotherapy is to help individuals become aware of the relationship between stress and the onset or aggravation of their physical disorder. This awareness may then help them learn how to deal more adaptively with stress and may hasten their recovery.

The particular mode of psychotherapy used to accomplish such goals may vary considerably (Luborsky, Singer, & Luborsky, 1975). In some instances, psychoanalysis can help, especially the modified forms that emphasize current situations (see Chapters 3 and 19). In other instances, behavioral methods, such as biofeedback and other reinforcement techniques, can be useful. For example, relaxation therapy has been successful in helping individuals learn to reduce blood pressure (Southam, Agras, Taylor, & Kraemer, 1982).

It is important for psychotherapists to work closely with the physicians who are primarily responsible for the medical care of the patient. In some instances, the physician can play a supportive psychotherapeutic role by helping the patient understand how psychosocial factors are intimately related to the physical illness. Like the psychotherapist, the physician can help educate the patient about mind–body relationships (Taylor, 1980). Critical reviews of the research on physical illness and psychological stress suggest that psychotherapy has a beneficial effect on physical illness. In addition, it may improve the psychological adjustment of individuals who are at high risk for developing psychosomatic disorders. At the same time, however, the importance of psychological factors in physical illness should not be exaggerated. Further research is needed to establish more firmly the extent to which psychological distress is related to physical illness and the usefulness of psychological intervention (Friedman & Booth-Kewley, 1987).

Summary

1. Psychosomatic disorders have traditionally been defined as physical illnesses whose onset and expression are significantly influenced by psychological factors. Concepts of psychosomatic disorders can be traced at least to the origins of Western medicine in ancient Greece.

2. The German physician Heinroth introduced the term *psychosomatic* into Western medicine. In 1818 he published a dissertation that emphasized the importance of psychological and social factors in the development of physical disease.

3. In the 19th and 20th centuries, the work of Freud, Pavlov, and the physiologist Walter Cannon helped usher in the modern scientific study of psychosomatic disorders. In succeeding years, the writings of Helen Flanders Dunbar became highly influential.

4. DSM-III-R no longer uses the term *psychosomatic* in its diagnostic classification system, but the concept is included in the broad diagnostic category *psychological factors affecting physical conditions*. Our own use of the term goes beyond DSM-III-R. We defined *psychosomatic disorders* in a holistic fashion: patterns of biophysical abnormalities whose onset or intensification is strongly influenced by their interaction with psychological, social, and cultural factors.

5. The symptoms of somatoform disorders often bear a superficial resemblance to physical illness, but they are not caused by organic damage to the body. In contrast, the symptoms of psychosomatic disorders do involve organic pathology. Patterns of psychosomatic disorders may involve practically any organ or organ system.

6. There is some evidence that psychological and sociocultural factors can affect the immune system of the body, making the individual more vulnerable to physical disease.

7. Various theories have emerged to explain the relationship between stress and psychosomatic disorders. According to the somatic weakness theory, a psychosomatic disorder is most likely to occur in a particular organ or organ system that is already biologically weak. However, this theory has been criticized as being overly simplistic and failing to take into account other contributing factors, especially the complex nature of stress.

8. A broader and more influential theory is Hans Selye's concept of the general adaptation syndrome, which has three stages: alarm reaction, resistance, and exhaustion. Prolonged stress at any of these stages, especially resistance and exhaustion, can lead to various psychosomatic disorders.

9. The diathesis–stress theory of psychosomatic disorders incorporates features of the somatic weakness theory and the general adaptation syndrome in a more comprehensive explanation. This approach considers not only the effects of an individual's vulnerability and the environmental stressors that increase that vulnerability but also how the individual perceives those stressors and copes with them. An individual may have a biological or psychosocial predisposition to develop a psychosomatic disorder. Given this predisposition (diathesis), and the presence of appropriate stressors in the environment, the individual reacts with various psychological and physical defenses. When the person perceives stressors as serious threats to those defenses and to general well-being and also feels unable to cope adequately with them, physiological signs of stress begin to appear. Prolongation of those states help produce psychosomatic disorders.

10. Some of the most extensive empirical studies of psychosomatic disorders and stress concern the relationship between Type A behavior and coronary heart disease. According to Friedman and Rosenman, pioneers in this research, Type A behavior includes extreme competitiveness, hostility, and a sense of time urgency. A number of methods have been developed for measuring specific aspects of Type A behavior. They include structured interviews and self-report inventories. One of the best-known inventories is the Jenkins Activity Survey.

11. A large body of research has accumulated to support the conclusion that Type A behavior can contribute to heart disease as much as or even more than such well-known risk factors as obesity, cigarette smoking, hypertension, and abnormally high levels of cholesterol. These factors may interact with Type A behavior to further increase the individual's vulnerability.

12. Among the most successful programs of psychotherapy developed to reduce Type A behavior are those involving a cognitive-social learning model. A central goal of this approach is to help individuals understand the psychological and social nature of their behavior, how it contributes to their psychosomatic problems, and how that behavior can be modified.

13. Several recent studies have questioned the relationship between Type A behavior and heart disease. Some failed to confirm earlier results; others found methodological weaknesses in previous work. One reason for the contradictory results may be that certain aspects of Type A behavior are more harmful than others.

14. Psychoanalytic explanations of psychosomatic disorders propose that certain disorders — in particular, people ulcers, colitis, and bronchial asthma — can be differentiated according to the nature of the conflicts and frustrations an individual experienced during childhood.

15. Psychoanalysts propose that the conflicts and frustrations leading to peptic ulcers are expressed through denying the unmet dependence needs of childhood or through being overly submissive to them.

16. Psychoanalytic explanations of colitis claim that the disorder originates in excessive parental expectations for bowel control during the child's toilet training. The child develops hostile feelings toward the parents over this excessive control but directs it toward the offending organ — the bowel.

17. Various psychoanalytic theorists propose that bronchial asthma stems from frustrated needs for dependence and love early in life. Reluctant to express frustration directly, the child complains by wheezing and whining. This asthmatic reaction may persist and become especially severe later in life whenever feelings of anger are aroused toward authority figures or others who withhold love.

18. Various studies have evaluated psychoanalytic theories of psychosomatic disorders. The evidence that any one factor is sufficient to explain a particular psychosomatic disorder is weak.

19. Research has found that sociocultural factors such as noise and overcrowding can produce sensory overload and excessive social stimulation. These, in turn, can be important in the etiology of psychosomatic disorders.

20. Laboratory experiments have demonstrated that certain forms of emotional responses can be learned through classical and operant conditioning. If these responses occur at highly intense levels and over long periods of time, they can contribute to the development of psychosomatic disorders.

21. Laboratory techniques have been developed for teaching individuals how to control tension headaches, abnormally high blood pressure, and other abnormal reactions mediated by the autonomic nervous system. Prominent among these methods is biofeedback, a technique based on operant conditioning. Although various studies have reported success in using biofeedback, some critics argue that better-controlled methods of evaluation are needed to establish its success rate more firmly. Furthermore, it should not be considered a panacea for all psychosomatic disorders but should be used selectively as a part of a total treatment package.

22. Whatever the form of psychotherapy selected to treat a psychosomatic disorder, it is important for the psychotherapist to work closely with the physician who is primarily responsible for the medical care of the patient.

8

Gender Identity Disorders and Paraphilias

The omnipresent process of sex, as it is
woven into the whole texture of our man's
or woman's body, is the pattern of all the
process of our life.

HAVELOCK ELLIS
The New Spirit (1891)

This patient, in her 20s, appears to be a beautiful woman. . . . [S]he is a fashion
model who no one in the fashion world knows to be a biologically normal male. . . .
As far back as memory goes, she recalls being feminine and wishing she were
biologically female. . . . [She] hates her male body, wants it changed to female, but
does not deny it is male. (Stoller, 1976(b), p. 148)

[The patient] requested consultation because of irresistible urges to exhibit his naked
penis to female strangers. . . . At age 18 . . . he first experienced an overwhelm-
ing desire to engage in the sexual activity for which he now sought consultation. . . .
He felt guilty and ashamed after exhibiting himself and vowed never to repeat it.
Nevertheless . . . the behavior recurred frequently, usually at periods of tension.
(Spitzer, Skodol, Gibbon, & Williams, 1981, p. 13)

Always the same age group, six to eleven; no younger and no older; outside those
limits don't appeal to me at all. Playing about with them with my hands under their
skirts, tickling their bottoms. . . . Five, ten minutes at the outside, then I got my
ejaculation and that was it. (Parker, 1972, pp. 27–28)

These case excerpts illustrate only a few of the patterns of psychosexual disturbances
discussed in this chapter. The first is an example of transsexualism, a form of gender
identity disorder. This pattern of abnormality involves conflict, anxiety, and discomfort
concerning one's anatomic sex and the gender role one identifies with.

The second and third excerpts illustrate paraphilias. The man who could not resist
displaying his penis to strangers was diagnosed as suffering from exhibitionism. The man
who felt sexually drawn only to children suffered from pedophilia.

Gender Identity Disorders

Deep feelings of frustration and discomfort that arise from a persistent conflict between
biological sex and gender role mark gender identity disorders (Stoller, 1985). Before
discussing the nature and causes of these disorders, we will clarify our use of the terms
sex, gender, gender identity, and *gender role*.

■ **Sex** refers to the biological characteristics that differentiate females from males.
Among these characteristics are the external genitalia (the clitoris and penis, for example),
the internal genitalia (the uterus and prostate, for example), the gonads (the ovaries and
testes), the hormonal states, and the various secondary sex characteristics (breast structure and distribution of body hair, for example).

Gender roles have become more flexible. The fact that this young girl is engaging in a sport traditionally considered to be a male activity need not imply that she has problems of gender identity.

■ **Gender** is a psychological and cultural concept rather than a biological one. "If the proper terms for sex are 'male and female,' the corresponding terms for gender are 'masculine' and 'feminine'; these latter may be quite independent of [biological] sex. Gender is the amount of masculinity or femininity in a person and, obviously, while there are mixtures of both in many humans, the normal male has a preponderance of masculinity and the normal female a preponderance of femininity" (Stoller, 1974, pp. 9–10).

■ **Gender identity** is the sense of belonging to one biological sex and not to the other. As personality develops, the matter of gender identity can become complex. For example, one may perceive oneself to be not only a man but a "masculine man" or an "effeminate man" or a man who has fantasies about being a woman (Stoller, 1974, p. 10).

■ **Gender role** refers to the social behavior individuals display in accordance with gender identity. Such behavior reveals how people evaluate that identity and how they want others to evaluate it. Thus, "gender identity is the private experience of gender role, and gender role is the public expression of gender identity" (Money & Ehrhardt, 1972, p. 4).

Biological Abnormality and Gender Identity

In rare instances, faulty development during the prenatal period results in a baby being born with anatomical characteristics of both sexes. This condition is known as **intersexuality** (Green, 1975; Money & Ehrhardt, 1972; Stoller, 1974, 1976a, 1985). For example, an individual may be born with ovaries as well as testes. This form of intersexuality is called **true hermaphroditism**. The external genitalia of the hermaphrodite are often incompletely female or male and may resemble one or the other more closely. In other instances of hermaphroditism, the independent development of ovaries and testes may result in obvious incongruities between the appearance of secondary sex characteristics and external genitalia. A true hermaphrodite, for example, can have breast development like that of a female but external genitalia that are definitely male.

In another form of intersexuality, **pseudohermaphroditism**, the appearance of the genitalia is ambiguous even though the gonads are of one sex. Illustrative of this condition is the case of a child whose external genitalia at birth were apparently those of a normal girl and who was reared as a girl until adolescence. A medical examination at that time revealed that chromosomally she was a male with an erectile penis of clitoris size, a urethra that opened on the underside of the penis (hypospadias), undescended testicles, a scrotal sac that resembled labia, and a normal prostate (Stoller, 1974, pp. 67–72).

Unless such problems are corrected early through chromosomal tests to determine the genetic sex and sex reassignment surgery to remedy the ambiguous appearance of the external genitalia, serious gender identity conflict can develop. This conflict may be worsened if the parents have ambivalent attitudes about the sex they want their child to be.

Transsexualism

People with the disorder of **transsexualism** feel a deep sense of discomfort with their sexual anatomy. They have a strong and persistent desire to be rid of their inappropriate genitals and an equally persistent wish to assume the gender role of the other sex and to live as a member of the other sex. (Masters, Johnson, & Kolodny, 1988, p. 292).

Transsexualism has been known for many years, but only in the last several decades has it received much systematic and scientific study. The term itself was coined in 1923 by the German sexologist Magnus Hirschfeld (1868–1935), although cases describing various aspects of the disorder had been reported much earlier (Bullough, 1987).

Although transsexualism is usually considered to be rare, various estimates indicate that its prevalence in the general population is greater than was once supposed. It occurs over three times more frequently in males than females: 1 case in 30,000 versus 1 case in 100,000 (American Psychiatric Association, 1987, p. 75). Whether transsexualism has actually increased in recent years is debatable. It may well be that more permissive attitudes about sexual matters and the rapid increase in professional interest in problems of gender identity, especially through clinics devoted to such problems, have encouraged a greater number of transsexuals to seek help.

Transsexualism in Childhood

The full syndrome of transsexualism does not usually appear until adolescence or early adulthood. Similar behavior does occur in childhood, although less often (Metcalf & Williams, 1977). The central feature of the disorder in children is a deep and persistent feeling of discomfort about their sexual anatomy. This feeling goes far beyond the temporary rejection of conventional gender role behavior. It is a deeply experienced disturbance of the normal sense of maleness or femaleness. Transsexual boys and girls persistently and strongly express a desire to be of the other sex, and sometimes even insist they are (American Psychiatric Association, 1987, p. 74).

The repudiation of sexual anatomy has a different significance for children than for adults because children lack the biological maturity that in adulthood adds considerably to the intensity of the conflict. Nevertheless, children who reject their sexual anatomy and identify strongly with the other sex often come into serious conflict with the social expectations of family and peers. Such problems can create much misery and lay the foundation for conflict over gender identity and role in adulthood. A number of studies have concluded that young boys with normal male physical characteristics who persistently reveal feminine role behavior and who openly verbalize a desire to be of the other sex are high risks for developing adult gender disturbances, such as transsexualism (Davenport, 1986; Green, 1975; Lebovitz, 1972; Stoller, 1976a, 1976b, 1985).

In the early 1950s surgical sex reassignment became highly publicized when the media reported that a Danish plastic surgeon had transformed the American ex-Marine George Jorgensen into Christine Jorgensen. Shown here is Ms. Jorgensen some 27 years after her operation.

Transsexualism and Surgical Reassignment

The basic dilemma facing transsexuals is the intolerable fact of their sexual anatomy, a condition they regard as abnormal. A biological male who wants to be female often feels that his femininity is trapped in a male body alien to his real nature. This conflict between gender identity and sexual anatomy may be so distressing that it impels transsexuals not only to dress and attempt to live permanently as members of the other sex but also to seek surgical and hormonal treatment that will alter their sexual anatomy to conform to their gender identity and desired gender role.

The first published report of surgery for a transsexual patient came from Germany in 1931. In the early 1950s, surgical sex reassignment became highly publicized when the Danish plastic surgeon Paul Fogh-Anderson transformed George Jorgensen, an American ex-Marine, into Christine Jorgensen (Masters, Johnson, & Kolodny, 1988; Pauly & Edgerton, 1986). In 1966, the first medical center for performing sexual reassignment operations opened at Johns Hopkins University, and several other centers were established subsequently.

The operation is a drastic one. In the male-to-female transformation, the penis is excised and the testes removed. The external genitalia are then reconstructed, and an artificial vagina is created. Breasts are created through plastic surgery and hormone treatment. After complete healing, the individual is able to have sexual intercourse with a man in the same manner (at least physically) as if she had been a biological woman.

Female-to-male operations occur less often and are less satisfactory technically. Breasts must be removed, a hysterectomy performed, testicles constructed, and a penis formed. A prosthetic device implanted in a sleevelike structure can be used to give the artificial penis more rigidity.

Because surgical reassignment is so drastic, it is not ordinarily carried out unless the individual is so intolerably miserable, so identified with the other sex and gender role, and so unable to gain from psychotherapy that no alternate solution seems feasible. It is indeed a measure of last resort (Kirkpatrick & Friedmann, 1976; Lothstein & Levine, 1981).

Transsexuals who have undergone surgical reassignment have the full range of reactions — positive, negative, and mixed. In recent years, a number of medical research centers discontinued transsexual operations, claiming that there is insufficient evidence for their psychological benefits (Abramowitz, 1986; Eber, 1980; Lindemalm, Körlin, & Uddenberg, 1986; Lothstein, 1980, 1982; Masters, Johnson, & Kolodny, 1986, p. 209; Pauly & Edgerton, 1986).

Paraphilias

Paraphilias involve intense sexual urges and fantasies centering on at least one of the following: (a) nonhuman objects; (b) real or pretended suffering or humiliation, either by oneself or with one's sexual partner; (c) children or other nonconsenting people. The individual repeatedly acts on these urges or is highly distressed by them (American Psychiatric Association, 1987, p. 279). Obviously, the behavior resulting from such urges violates widely held social standards of sexual conduct and indeed sometimes results in legal difficulties for the offenders.

Almost all of the paraphilias described in DSM-III and DSM-III-R were classified in the 1968 edition (DSM-II) as sexual deviations. The current label was adopted to emphasize that the deviation (*para*) centers on the particular object or situation the individual is attracted to (*philia*). Paraphilias include the following specific patterns (which will be discussed individually in this chapter): pedophilia, exhibitionism, voyeurism, sexual sadism, sexual masochism, fetishism, transvestism, zoophilia, and frotteurism.

In addition to these disorders, DSM-III-R includes a residual diagnostic category — "not otherwise specified (NOS)" — for individuals with paraphilia disturbances that do not fit the more usual ones. In this category are **coprophilia** (sexual pleasure associated with defecating on one's sex partner, being defecated on, or handling and eating feces), **urolagnia** (sexual gratification associated with urinating on a partner or being urinated on), **necrophilia** (sexual arousal at the sight of a corpse — and in more extreme cases, sexual intercourse with a corpse), and **telephone scatologia** (preoccupation with sexual arousal through making obscene phone calls).

Pedophilia

The most common form of paraphilia for which people suffer legal sanctions is pedophilia (Meyer, 1985). The central feature of **pedophilia** (literally, love of children) is the persistent attempt of an adult or late adolescent to obtain sexual excitement and satisfaction through contact with children — usually, but not necessarily, children of the opposite sex. In specifying the criteria for diagnosing pedophilia, DSM-III-R defines the age of children as 13 or younger, the age of the perpetrator as 16 or older, and the difference in age as five years or more (American Psychiatric Association, 1987, pp. 284–285). Pedophilia is almost exclusively a male disorder. The majority of individuals so diagnosed are middle aged, although their ages extend over a wide range (Bell & Hall, 1976).

The pedophile may sometimes confine himself to simply watching children while he engages in fantasies of sexual activity. Closer contact usually involves fondling various parts of a child's body, including the genital area. Less often he induces the child to reciprocate his touching, which may involve manipulating his penis, perhaps masturbating him to orgasm. In more extreme cases he may persuade the child to perform fellatio — that is, taking the penis into the mouth. There are also pedophiles who like to carry out fellatio themselves, or perform oral–genital acts on female children (cunnilingus). Less often they may attempt anal or vaginal intercourse.

Pedophilia is a habitual pattern of maladaptive sexual behavior. The diagnosis is not appropriate for isolated sexual acts with children. Although clearly exploitive and contrary to widely held social norms, such isolated behavior has less serious consequences for both the perpetrator and the victim than the behavior of the confirmed pedophile who repeatedly has sexual contacts with children.

Pedophilia and Sexual Abuse

Professional mental health workers and the popular press often refer to pedophiles as child molesters or sexual abusers of children. Such terms are exceedingly broad, for they encompass the habitual acts of pedophiles as well as the acts of individuals who have sexual contact with children only on isolated occasions. Although the behavior of this latter group violates socially acceptable standards, it does not indicate pedophilia and indeed may occur in the absence of any well-defined mental disorder. True pedophiles probably represent no more than 5 to 10 percent of the men who commit sex offenses against children (Gagnon, 1977).

The popular image of the child molester is of a stranger picking up children on street corners. Some molesters are predatory, but many more of them, including pedophiles, are among the child's family, friends, and neighbors (Kempe & Kempe, 1984, p. 32; Masters, Johnson, & Kolodny, 1986, p. 386). In his study of more than 4000 women who reported their preadolescent sexual contacts with adult males, Kinsey and his colleagues found that most repeated experiences had occurred with a male relative who lived in the same household (Kinsey, Pomeroy, Martin, & Gebhard, 1953/1965). Since the offender is often a family member or friend of the family, the child may offer little or no resistance to his sexual advances. This compliance is apt to be reinforced by the guilt the child feels about the sexual experience. Sometimes other members of the family know about the activity of the child molester, but they ignore it because of the shame and conflict it arouses, especially if he is a member of the household. (Costin, 1979, p. 450; Costin & Rapp, 1984, pp. 291–292; Lanyon, 1986).

The term *phsyical child abuse* is often used to include sexual abuse. However, a child may be abused sexually without physical violence. The motivation for sexual abuse is sexual gratification, whereas those who practice physical child abuse seem intent mainly on hurting the child, whether or not some kind of sexual activity is involved (Luther & Price, 1980).

Most individuals who practice pedophilia are nonviolent sexual abusers, since they usually do not try to inflict physical harm on their victims. They sometimes try to bribe children into sexual acts, but even if they use more threatening means to gain the child's acquiescence, the central motivation is sexual desire rather than the need to inflict physical damage.

Etiology and Dynamics

Various explanations of the pedophile's development and behavior stress sexual inadequacy and immaturity. The kinds of childhood events and family relationships that may lead to this failure are illustrated in Bell and Hall's (1976) analysis of Norman.

Norman had been confined several times in mental hospitals, mainly because of his pedophiliac behavior. Attempts to cure him, which included electroshock therapy, had been unsuccessful. Norman had spent some time in the U.S. Army and had completed several years of college, with the ambition of being a writer. As a child, Norman was a loner, and his painful experiences with other children caused him to retreat to his family. When Norman was 4, his father forced him to suck his (the father's) penis. "The size of his erection frightened me. I had never been approached like that before by my father. In fact, I can't recall having sexual thoughts prior to that time. All I can remember is my father's hypnotic stare as I tried to push his penis away from my face. . . . I feared for my life. I felt drawn by my father's almost hypnotic force" (Bell & Hall, 1976, p. 194).

The incestuous behavior continued until the father was forced to leave the family, never to return. According to Bell and Hall, these sexual encounters contributed greatly to Norman's failure to develop a strong, mature masculine role. Instead, Norman fixated at a primitive, infantile level. Although his initial reaction was fear, his comments suggest that he came to enjoy the sexual contact with his father, in spite of the ambivalence he felt about it. His father's behavior also served as a model for him to try similar kinds of immature sexual activities, although he did so nonaggressively.

The work of Bell and Hall and that of other researchers suggest the following conclusions about the etiology and dynamics of pedophiliac behavior (Kaplan & Sadock, 1985, pp. 450–451; McCary, 1979; Sadoff, 1976).

■ The pedophiliac individual fears failure in normal interpersonal relationships, especially those involving sexual relationships with an experienced woman. He avoids this anticipated failure by engaging sexually (through fantasy or in actuality) with children because their immaturity does not challenge his self-esteem.

■ He has a narcissistic self-image, a self-love retained from childhood. According to this interpretation, the child he sexually desires represents to some extent the child in him that he has failed to outgrow.

■ As a child, the pedophile has had poor models from whom to learn adequate interpersonal relationships, especially with respect to sexual behavior. Indeed, the models may well set an example that the child eventually adopts.

Exhibitionism

The compulsive desire to obtain sexual stimulation and gratification by exposing one's sexual organs to an unsuspecting stranger is **exhibitionism.** There is no attempt to continue with any other sexual contact. Exhibitionism rarely, if ever, occurs among women. It is apparently confined to men, who typically expose themselves to female adults or children (Groth, Hobson, & Gary, 1982).

Exhibitionism generally occurs in public places. As a result, the exhibitionist is especially vulnerable to arrest. It has been estimated that approximately one-third of the individuals apprehended for sexual offenses are charged with exhibitionism. They are usually in their middle 20s; very few are past 40 (Evans, 1970; pp. 563–564; Masters, Johnson, & Kolodny, 1986, pp. 380–382).

Many specialists in paraphiliac disorders emphasize that exhibitionists usually have a poor relationship with a sexual partner. Unsure of themselves sexually, they are usually immature and undemanding in their gender role. Nevertheless sexual tension seems to drive them to make some impact on the sexuality of women. This unsureness and unresolved tension leads them to shock women, thus displaying a sexual power they cannot express in a more normal, socially acceptable way. Indeed, for many exhibitionists the shock effect of displaying their penis is a crucial aspect of the act. Any strong reaction of the victim, such as fear, disgust, or embarrassment, is taken as a compliment to their virility (Chesser, 1971; Storr, 1974; Trimmer, 1978). The need to shock the victim is well illustrated in this narrative of an exhibitionist: "No, it's not a prelude to a sex assault, there's never anything like that in my mind. Just to shock; if a woman looks disgusted and turns away, then I'm satisfied. A woman smiled at me once and came towards me instead; I ran away from her as hard as I could" (Parker, 1972, pp. 218–219).

Exhibitionism is the compulsive desire of a male to obtain sexual gratification by exposing his genitals to unsuspecting females. An important goal is to shock the viewers. Obviously, the exhibitionist in the cartoon did not achieve his goal.

"You don't often see a real silk lining, these days..."
© Punch—Spencer/Rothco

Psychoanalytic Interpretations

Orthodox psychoanalytic theory claims that exhibitionism is a way of denying castration fears that originated during the Oedipal stage of psychosexual development (see Chapter 3). During this period the boy competes with his father for the mother's affection and comes to fear that castration will result from his strong feelings of sexual desire. According to Freudian theory, the exhibitionist has fixated on this aspect of psychosexual development. He still fears castration unconsciously. By displaying his penis to women, he can reassure himself that he is powerful and has nothing to fear. The shock effect he seeks helps bolster this reassurance, proving that he can dominate women. As the psychoanalyst Fenichel (1945) has put it, the exhibitionist is saying to his victim: "Reassure me that I have a penis by reacting to the sight of it. . . . Reassure me that you are afraid of my penis, that is, that you fear me; then I do not need to be afraid myself" (p. 345).

Some psychoanalytic interpretations minimize the element of castration and focus on a childish need to dominate women, a need that may have developed from various kinds of childhood experiences. For example, the exhibitionist may be unconsciously defying a mother whose excessive domineering prevented his achieving a more mature sex life (Witzig, 1970).

Explanations Based on Learning Theory

In reviewing various behavioral explanations of exhibitionism, Tollison and Adams (1979) point out that many exhibitionists describe the event that seemed to start their abnormal pattern as accidental. Some report that urinating or masturbating in an inappropriate place was an important factor. Although their initial reaction to being discovered was embarrassment and anxiety, cognitive replaying of the event led to sexual arousal. Thus, a chain of conditioning began.

Although some experimental evidence supports this cognitive learning interpretation of exhibitionism, the results are far from conclusive (Evans, 1970). One must also consider the possibility that previous sexual problems predisposed the individual to acquire exhibitionist behavior. This information is important because it can help us understand why one individual becomes conditioned to exhibitionism and another does not, even though both experience the same kind of erotic surprise.

Voyeurism

The central feature of **voyeurism** (from the French *voir*, "to see") is the compulsive desire to gain sexual satisfaction by viewing the sexual organs or sexual acts of others, especially unsuspecting strangers. Looking at unsuspecting women in various stages of undress (peeping) or watching them engage in sexual activity is often accompanied by sexual excitement to the point of orgasm. The excitement and orgasm may also occur after the peeping episode, when the voyeur recalls the scene.

In most Westernized cultures there are various socially acceptable places and ways of viewing nude or seminude women in public places: in topless bars, at striptease shows, and, to a milder degree, on the beach. Although such looking is often called voyeuristic, especially in popular writings and movies, it does not in itself necessarily represent a sexual disorder. Voyeurism involves one or more of these elements: (a) the viewing and the sexual excitement it creates become preferred to all other ways of gaining sexual satisfaction, (b) the person who is viewed usually has not consented, and (c) the viewer risks serious legal consequences if he is detected.

Psychodynamic Interpretations

According to psychoanalytic theory, the child's desire to observe genitals is a normal aspect of psychosexual development, especially during the phallic phase (ages 3 to 6). The adult male's voyeuristic behavior is generally interpreted as a fixation of that normal desire — a result of unresolved Oedipal conflict from the phallic phase (Brenner, 1973, p. 27; Fenichel, 1945, pp. 347–349; Freud, 1940/1949, pp. 90–91). Psychoanalysts explain the occurrence of this fixation and its consequences in various ways. Among the most common theories is that the voyeur has never really abandoned his early sexual desire for his mother, although social taboos and the development of the superego have forced him to repress that desire. Peeping at women in various stages of undress represents unconsciously an indirect but safe way of obtaining the sexual excitement once associated with the mother.

Traditional psychoanalytic theory often bolsters this general explanation with the concept of castration anxiety. The voyeur's behavior is a safe way of obtaining sexual excitement because it avoids the persistent fear of castration — a threat from his parents that ended his overt sexual advances to his mother during the phallic stage. Castration anxiety is strengthened during the Oedipal period by his observation that girls do not have a penis; thus, he fears the loss could happen to him (Fancher, 1973, pp. 212–213; Fenichel, 1945, pp. 74–83; Freud, 1940/1949, p. 92) As a voyeur, however, he can express his unconscious desire for his mother without fear of castration. Viewing female genitals at a safe distance not only reduces that fear but also reassures him that he does have a penis. In this way, his sense of manhood is strengthened. Why is it that this sense of manhood cannot be supported through actual sexual intercourse with a woman? The orthodox psychoanalytic answer is that the voyeur unconsciously equates the vagina with the mouth and with dangerous teeth. Inserting the penis into the vagina might result in castration, — that is, the penis might be bitten off (Fenichel, 1945, p. 78).

Over the years, various psychodynamic practitioners and researchers have become more flexible in their interpretation of Oedipal competition (see Chapter 3). Some psychodynamic interpret the Oedipal conflict as a struggle for power; sexual motivation may or may not be a central part of the struggle. Furthermore, the boy's fear of castration need not be taken as literally as Freud described it. General fears concerning one's adequacy in relationships with women rather than a literal fear of castration might be more relevant in explaining voyeurism. For example, voyeurism may be an attempt to compensate for shyness. Looking is safer than direct engagement; it satisfies curiosity without the danger of rejection and damage to self-esteem. It may also help compensate for feelings of inferiority arising out of childhood and adolescent experiences with women.

In this vein, Alfred Adler, whose concepts and principles were discussed in Chapter 3, interpreted voyeurism as a function of the looker's timidity in solving problems of sexuality. "There are many men," he said, "who are too cowardly to strive for a real solution of the life-problem of sex and who, looking for a relief or substitute, stop short at some practical manifestations of sexuality. If they are visual types, and their vision is not transferred to other objects, they become voyeurs or exhibitionists" (Adler, 1964, p. 143). Except for the use of the term *cowardly*, Adler's explanation is consistent with the underlying theme of many other psychodynamic explanations of voyeurism that avoid an explicit emphasis on castration fear.

Learning to Be a Voyeur

From a social learning viewpoint, voyeurism represents a behavioral deficit in the usual repertory of adult sexual functions. For most adults, sexual functions ordinarily range from various forms of initial arousal to the more intense stages of lovemaking. Although it is normal for individuals to engage in only parts of the continuum on various occasions, the chronic voyeur ignores most aspects of it, concentrating on looking as a means of obtaining ultimate sexual satisfaction—a pattern of behavior that becomes selectively reinforced over a period of time. Although he usually obtains orgasm through masturbation while looking or soon afterwards, the looking itself serves as the main motivation for his sexual behavior.

Positive variables that can strengthen voyeurism include not only masturbation and the achievement of orgasm in association with the peeping but also the attainment of sexual pleasure through recalling the experience. Frequent repetition of these sequences strengthens the voyeuristic behavior further.

Negative variables also help strengthen voyeuristic patterns. For example, puritanical family attitudes about sexual relationships or personality characteristics, such as excessive shyness, may inhibit the potential voyeur from learning how to relate sexually in normal social situations and may cause him to fear sexual relationships. Still highly curious about female sexuality, the potential voyeur may turn to peeping to gain sexual satisfaction. Gradually, he discovers that he can achieve satisfaction in a way that poses no threat.

In some instances, the voyeur may seek to overcome the fear of sexual relationships by marrying. However, if the voyeuristic patterns have become ingrained, or if the man is disappointed in the marital relationship, he may continue his pattern of peeping, since it provides the most satisfactory reduction of sexual tension.

Sexual Sadism

In its broadest sense, sadism refers to pleasure gained from inflicting pain or abuse on others. The term *sadism* is derived from Donatien-Alphonse-François Sade (1740–1814), better known as Marquis de Sade. In his writings, Sade depicted characters who gained sexual pleasure by treating others with extreme cruelty. Although sadistic behavior occurs in nonsexual encounters, our discussion will be confined to the disorder that DSM-III-R calls sexual sadism.

The essential characteristic of **sexual sadism** is the habitual desire to obtain sexual arousal and gratification by abusing the sexual partner. It may involve not only physically painful acts but also verbal humiliation. Sexual sadism is more common among men, especially those under the age of 35. Sadistic fantasies alone are not sufficient to warrant a diagnosis of sexual sadism. Crucial elements are the acting out of those fantasies or marked distress at having them (American Psychiatric Association, 1987, p. 287).

Theories of Sadism

Sexual sadism is the habitual desire to obtain sexual arousal and satisfaction by abusing the sexual partner. The term *sadism* is derived from the name of the Marquis de Sade, who described in his writings various characters who gained sexual pleasure by treating others with extreme cruelty.

Several clinical studies have shown that certain neurological disabilities, including damage to the temporal lobe of the brain, are accompanied by sadistic-type behavior, not always in a sexual direction. This observation has led to the theory that sexual sadism itself may have an organic basis. However, in only a very few instances has any direct connection been established between neurological impairment and sexual sadism. The bulk of research deals with psychodynamic and social learning hypotheses rather than organic ones (Tollison & Adams, 1979, pp. 291–294).

Traditional psychoanalytic theory views sexual sadism as a way of reducing anxiety in the seeking of sexual satisfaction. This anxiety stems from unconscious fears associated with the attempt to gain sexual pleasure during childhood. According to Fenichel (1945), the starting point in the sexual sadist's defense against such anxiety is this unconsciously held idea: "Before I can enjoy sexuality, I must convince myself that I am powerful." That belief leads to a more sadistic idea: "I get sexual pleasure through torturing other persons." Thus, by threatening the objects of their sexuality, sadists avoid facing the fear that they themselves are threatened by sexual urges (p. 354).

Fenichel also has proposed that some sadists are reacting not only to unconscious anxiety over sexual fears but also to self-destructive tendencies (1945, p. 355). Once these tendencies are established, sadists attempt to resist them by turning their destructive impulses outward, toward sexual objects.

As in other psychoanalytic theories of paraphilias, these views of sadism are based mainly on highly selected clinical studies of adults who sought psychoanalytic treatment. Although in some cases such explanations may seem plausible, the theories themselves lack sufficient evidence to be generalized as broadly as some psychoanalysts claim.

Hypotheses based on learning theory propose that sexual sadism develops as the result of sexual excitement and orgasm being associated with the witnessing of painful situations or the inflicting of pain on someone else. Such associations might well occur more or less accidentally. Although little direct evidence supports such hypotheses, certain experiments with animals and humans imply that they are plausible. Several studies have shown that if aggressive behavior is rewarded, it is likely to increase. Thus, if aggression coincides with sexually rewarding experiences, it may come to be a necessary component of sexual activity (Dryer & Church, 1970; Geen & Pigg, 1970). Social and psychological reinforcers of sexually sadistic behavior may begin quite early in life, before the individual has reached sexual maturity. If the sequence of reinforcing events is not interrupted, the sadistic behavior may grow increasingly violent and destructive.

Some researchers with a learning theory perspective point out that many societies equate pride and self-esteem with masculinity. By demonstrating sexual power through the inflicting of pain, males can dominate and show their superior status (Fesbach, 1971; Johnson, 1972). It may well be that a significant number of sexual sadists have equated masculinity with sexual power to an abnormal degree — an equation that also exists to a lesser and more controlled extent among other men in their society.

Sexual Sadism and Rape

Sexual sadism may involve either a consenting or a nonconsenting partner. Among the most extreme instances of nonconsent are those in which rape is necessary for the sadist to become sexually aroused or to maintain sexual excitement. We begin our discussion of this relationship by examining certain legal definitions of rape.

Legal tradition considers **forcible rape** to be one of the most extreme forms of violation of the self, second only to homicide (Davis, 1980, p. 101). The term itself may seem redundant, since *rape* implies the use of force. However, there is a legal distinction between forcible rape and **statutory rape**. The latter refers to situations in which an adult has sexual relations with a minor, even if that person consents. The legal definitions of *forcible* rape vary from state to state (Loh, 1981). For purposes of our discussion on the relationship between rape and sadism, we will use the term *rape* in its broad social meaning to include all sexual acts in which an individual is forced to participate against her or his will.

Regardless of the degree of their brutality, most rapists are not necessarily manifesting the disorder of sexual sadism. Indeed, some rapists are unable to maintain sexual excitement during the assault. Most importantly, however, the majority of rapists do not require the infliction of physical or psychological suffering on another person in order to achieve sexual desire and excitement. Rather, violent sex for them is primarily a way of debasing, humiliating, and rendering powerless the victims of their assault. The gaining of sexual satisfaction, in the physical sense, is secondary (Amir, 1971; Brownmiller, 1975; Geis, 1977; Groth & Birnbaum, 1981; Hilberman, 1976; Holstrom, & Burgess, 1980; Koerper, 1980). On the other hand, sexual sadists who rape may torture and even murder their victims in order to gain sexual satisfaction.

Although rape may sometimes involve sexual sadism, it does not in itself represent a type of paraphilia. We will therefore defer the detailed consideration of psychological and sociocultural aspects of sexual assault to Chapter 21, where we deal with legal issues of abnormality and problems of community mental health.

Sexual Masochism

The term *masochism* is derived from the surname of Leopold von Sacher Masoch (1836–1895), an Austrian novelist who portrayed characters gaining sexual pleasure from cruel treatment. The term has been broadened to include the experiencing of

The central feature of sexual masochism is the habitual desire to obtain sexual arousal and satisfaction by being mistreated, physically or verbally. The term *masochism* is derived from the surname of Leopold von Sacher-Masoch, an Austrian novelist whose characters gained sexual pleasure through the cruel treatment from their partners.

pleasure from many other kinds of suffering, such as hardships and self-denial. Our discussion, however, is confined to masochism as a sexual disorder.

The central feature of **sexual masochism** is the habitual desire to obtain sexual excitement and gratification by being mistreated. This mistreatment may involve physical acts of violence inflicted by the masochist's sexual partner or it may be restricted to psychological abasement — for example, verbal humiliation. As a guide for recognizing sexual masochism, DSM-III-R lists the following diagnostic criteria: (a) the individual is preoccupied with sexual urges and fantasies involving humiliation, physical pain, or other forms of suffering; (b) the individual repeatedly gives in to these urges or is highly distressed by them (American Psychiatric Association, 1987, pp. 286–287).

The active expression of sexual masochism usually begins in early adulthood, although fantasies about it may have been present during childhood. Some people engage in masochistic fantasies to enhance their normal sexual relations. A diagnosis of sexual masochism is not appropriate unless the individual habitually performs masochistic acts. Furthermore, masochism as a sexual disorder should not be confused with the mildly rough play some individuals enjoy during sex.

A number of studies (Kinsey, Pomeroy, Martin, & Gebhard, 1953/1965) have found that women are more likely than men to seek masochistic sexual activities. This difference is not surprising given the prominence of cultural stereotypes that place women in a sexually submissive role and ascribe to men the role of sexual aggressor. The commercia-

Although women as well as men may seek masochistic sexual activity, its commercialization is aimed mainly at men. Some houses of prostitution cater to masochistic men by providing them with various forms of "bondage."

lization of sexual masochism, however, is aimed primarily at men. Some houses of prostitution cater especially to masochistic men.

From a traditional psychoanalytic viewpoint, sexual masochism seems to contradict a basic principle of human motivation: We seek pleasure and avoid pain. According to psychoanalytic theory, this apparent contradiction can be resolved when one realizes that, like many other human sensations, pain may be a source of sexual excitement. This fusion of pain with sexual pleasure is rooted in biological drives that are an inherent part of human nature (see Chapter 3). Sexual masochism develops when the erogenous effects of pain become fixated in an extreme fashion and persist during adult sexual development. The origin of the fixation, according to psychoanalytic theory, can be traced to childhood feelings of guilt and fear of punishment concerning sexual behavior—for example, masturbation. The fixation of masochism represents an inward turning of hostility that one unconsciously feels toward authority figures who in earlier years forbade those sexual activities. Through self-punishment the masochist avoids guilt feelings and the fear of retribution, while at the same time enjoying the sexual pleasure that had been forbidden (Fenichel, 1945, pp. 358–365; Freud, 1924/1961b).

A broader psychodynamic perspective proposes that parental neglect or rejection of a child's basic need for love and affection can play an important part in the development of sexual masochism. If a parent's relationship to a child was dominated by punishing behavior, the child may eventually come to perceive that experiencing pain in close interpersonal relationships is a way of receiving attention that otherwise might not be forthcoming. Later in life, masochism may be expressed in various intimate relationships, including sexual activities, as a way of gaining acceptance. As Karen Horney has analyzed the matter, the lack of self-confidence characteristic of masochistic individuals contributes to their conviction that appealing to pity through suffering is the only way to win affection. This basic orientation pervades many of the masochist's life activities, including sexual behavior (Horney, 1967, p. 228). Horney focused mainly on masochistic behavior and feelings in women; however, her theory can be applied to men as well.

Although experiments with animals have shown that they can learn to endure punishment in order to become sexually aroused, the application of this finding to the development of sexual masochism is problematic (Rachman & Hodgson, 1968). Most explanations of sexual masochism derived from learning theory involve interpretations of individual case studies rather than experiments. A basic conclusion of such investigations is that in the early learning history of the sexual masochist, sexual stimulation and satisfaction come to be associated with pain. For example, a parent may spank a child but afterwards, perhaps because of guilt feelings, apply a soothing lotion to the child's anal region. Since this area is sexually receptive, the child may form an association between pain and sexual pleasure. Repetition can then strengthen the connection, so that the child learns to expect sexual pleasure as a consequence of being hurt.

For the most part, the various theories must remain speculative, at least in their general application. It may well be that for some masochistic individuals a psychodynamic explanation is valid and for others a learning approach is more appropriate.

Fetishism

The main feature of **fetishism** is the use of nonliving objects as the preferred or even exclusive mode of sexual arousal and satisfaction. In relatively rare instances, the fetish is some part of the human body, such as the foot or hair. The diagnosis of fetishism does not usually apply to situations in which an object is used as a direct source of sexual stimulation because of its inherent physical properties (an example of which is the regular use of a vibrator) (American Psychiatric Association, 1987, p. 282). When fetishistic activity is limited to cross-dressing, the disorder is classified as transvestism, which we consider in the next section.

Specialists in psychopathology generally agree that most, if not all, fetishists are male (Gagnon, 1977; Gebhard, 1976; Kolb & Brodie, 1982; McCary, 1979). Their sexual activity is often directed primarily toward the fetishistic object itself, such as masturbating into a woman's shoe, boot, or undergarment. In other instances, the fetish may be an essential part of sexual activity with a human partner, such as requiring that certain objects be present or worn in order for sexual arousal and satisfaction to occur. However, such behavior needs to be distinguished from the more conventional uses some men make of erotic paraphernalia to enhance their sexual pleasure. As Gagnon (1977) has pointed out: "The husband who likes his wife in sexy underwear or stockings before or during sex, but who also enjoys sex without the accoutrements, is not quite a fetishist. The fetish begins to emerge when the underwear is required for him to perform or when the underwear becomes a separate object of arousal" (p. 332).

Although the most common fetishistic items are those that are part of everyday life, such as underwear, boots, and shoes, many pornographic shops display merchandise designed to appeal to certain hard-core fetishists, especially those with sadistic or masochistic tendencies. This merchandise may include fancy leather whips and thongs. The promotion of such items may also be found in underground publications that form part of the communication network among various fetishists.

Psychoanalytic Views of Fetishism

Orthodox psychoanalytic theory postulates two factors basic to fetishism: the castration complex and the defense mechanism of denial (see Chapter 3). The fetishistic object is associated with the penis, often symbolically, and is used by the fetishist to deny his fear of castration (Fenichel, 1945; 1940/1949). This fear is a residue from the castration anxiety experienced during the Oedipal phase of psychosexual development — anxiety that intensified when the person perceived that females had no penis. Although the fetishist has repressed those memories, they return later in life when he is faced with the possibility of engaging in sexual relations with women. He wishes to believe they do have a penis so as to assure himself that he will not be castrated. However, he does not have the courage to assert that he really has seen a woman with a penis. He chooses another solution, one that still denies reality but less obviously. He attributes to a part of the body or to some other object the role of the penis that he cannot do without. It is usually something that he actually saw at a time when he saw a woman's genitals, or it is a symbolic substitute for the penis (Freud, 1940/1949, pp. 116–117).

This psychoanalytic theory of fetishism applies to males only, since the emphasis on penis substitution or symbolism could not enable a female to maintain the belief that she possessed a penis. The theory fits the fact that practically all fetishists are males, but it does not prove the theory, for almost all the paraphilias involve males rather than females. Indeed, little, if any, empirical evidence supports the theory directly, although a number of studies have corroborated indirectly the occurrence of castration anxiety itself, provided castration is not interpreted too literally. There is some empirical evidence that certain erotic stimuli arouse anxiety in some males and increase their concern about body damage (castration anxiety), and that such anxiety is higher in males than females (Fisher & Greenberg, 1977; Kline, 1972, 1981).

A number of other psychoanalytic explanations of fetishism have been offered over the years, all highly speculative. It has been suggested that the fetishist views his entire body as phallic and therefore inserts himself into hollow objects, shoes, coats, gloves, and so forth—all of these being symbols of female genitalia. Other interpretations are that fetishism is symbolic masturbation, a symbolic attempt to return to a mother figure, or a gross disturbance of body image originating in early life experiences (Caprio. 1961).

Fetishism and Cultural Diversity

In his analysis of fetishism, Gebhard (1976) points out that even though psychoanalytic explanations lack sufficient empirical evidence, their basic assumption that the fetishistic object has symbolic sexual value is sound. Fetishism seems to be confined to well-developed, highly complex cultures. Its virtual absence in preliterate societies may mean that the disorder can develop only in a culture that emphasizes from infancy on the use of verbal, written, and other symbols. This idea is reinforced, Gebhard concludes, "by the fact that fetishism seems largely confined to literate people taught to be imaginative and to make extensive use of symbolism in verbal and written communication and hence in their thought processes" (Gebhard, 1976, p. 162).

Fetishism and Conditioning

At least some fetishism may be acquired initially through classical conditioning and then maintained through subsequent reinforcement of operant behavior. (See Chapter 4 for a detailed discussion of these learning processes.) For example, an adolescent may masturbate regularly while looking at pictures of women clad only in high boots. After repeated experiences of this kind, he eventually associates sexual stimulation and gratification with boots and wishes to masturbate in their presence, or he may find it necessary to have them present in order to be adequately stimulated in sexual activity with a woman. Repetition of the behavior and of the subsequent orgasmic pleasure reinforces the fetishism.

Explanations of fetishism based on learning theory are difficult to verify because most of the information clinicians have about it comes from anecdotal evidence. It is difficult to know whether such retrospective data can account for fetishistic behavior in the absence of other corroborating observations, which are obviously not likely to be obtained.

Transvestism

The central feature of **transvestism** is habitual cross-dressing by a heterosexual male to achieve sexual arousal or satisfaction. DSM-III-R labels this disorder *transvestic fetishism* because of the focus on women's clothing as a sexual stimulus. We prefer *transvestism*, since it is more generally used by mental health professionals and the mass media. The term is derived from the Latin *trans* ("across") and *vestire* ("to clothe"). Authorities generally agree that transvestism is exclusively a male disorder (American Psychiatric Association, 1987, p. 288; Money & Ehrhardt, 1972; Stoller, 1985).

Although transvestites obtain genital excitement from dressing like women and experience great distress if this behavior is interfered with, their cross-dressing and cross-gender identification are transitory. Unlike transsexuals, transvestites regard themselves as male when not cross-dressing and may even do so when dressed as women; and they do not repudiate their sexual anatomy. Although they sometimes cross-dress in public and attempt to pass as women, they usually have little desire to do so and prefer to cross-dress in private. In such circumstances, the wearing of female clothing may be accompanied by masturbation, or it may be a necessary part of sexual relations with women (Green, 1975; Tripp, 1976).

The central activity of transvestism is habitual cross-dressing by a heterosexual male to obtain sexual gratification. Although the cross-dressing is sometimes carried out in public, as in this photograph, more often it is done in private, whether as a solitary practice or as a necessary part of sexual relations with a woman.

Danny La Rue, world-famous female impersonator, is shown here displaying one of the many costumes he wore in *Hello Dolly*. Men whose entire professional careers are spent impersonating women may well be reflecting a degree of ambivalence about their gender identity and role, but whatever conflict may be present is usually minimal and need not reflect the presence of a psychosexual disorder.

Patterns and Significance of Cross-dressing

Transvestites vary widely in their behavior patterns. Some wear female clothing only on special occasions and in complete privacy. Others cross-dress compulsively on a regular schedule, sometimes in cooperation with their wives or lovers. Still others use their cross-dressing mainly in public to pass temporarily as women. Some transvestites become highly involved in their own subculture. They communicate with one another through the personals columns of certain erotically oriented magazines and through their own publication, *Transvestia*; they also form clubs and hold conventions (Pomeroy, 1972).

Individuals who wish to pass as women in public are probably more seriously disturbed than those who practice other forms of transvestism (Stoller, 1974). Cross-dressing in public also is much more likely to encounter strong social censure, including legal sanctions, than is cross-dressing in private or on special occasions in the company of other transvestites. The threat of social conflict is apt to intensify the anxiety and discomfort the transvestite is already experiencing.

Some transvestites are able to pursue their cross-dressing without feeling unduly guilty. Others experience a great deal of anxiety, conflict, and shame, especially if they need feminine attire to become genitally aroused in sexual intercourse. Although their sexual partners (usually women) may object to this, some transvestites find that they cannot perform successfully unless they cross-dress. Consequently, their sexual activities with women may be quite limited. Furthermore, they may become so preoccupied with fantasies of cross-dressing and the accompanying genital excitement that their more general interpersonal relations are hampered as well. Their obsession with cross-dressing, even if confined within the family, can seriously impair their relationships with their wives and other family members.

A pattern of cross-dressing that is often confused with transvestism is one that occurs in certain instances of male homosexuality. A minority of homosexual males habitually cross-dress. Although their gender identity tends to be in the direction of women, it is often colored by hostility toward them. A specialist in psychosexual disorders interprets the effeminate role that these homosexual individuals adopt as a "caricature of femininity, a subtle angry mimicry" (Stoller, 1977, p. 37, 1985, p. 1039). It is important for them to have an audience, to amuse and baffle onlookers. In addition, their cross-dressing may serve to attract certain men. However, unlike transvestites, they do not usually experience genital arousal from cross-dressing; nor, as in the case of male transsexualism, do they believe they actually belong to the female sex. Throughout their cross-dressing, and in spite of their tendency to identify with femininity and with the superficial aspects of that gender role, they consider themselves to be biological men who are sexually attracted to other men.

Under certain circumstances, cross-dressing may occur without any special implication of psychosexual abnormality. Children often put on clothes and makeup in imitation of the

Dustin Hoffman's cross-dressing in *Tootsie* was described in some film reviews as transvestism. However, the cross-dressing was a temporary expedient for getting a job, and was not done to gain sexual arousal.

other sex as part of their early and playful experimentation with gender roles. Casual cross-dressing may also occur in various forms of entertainment without any abnormal significance, as in stage shows where male actors adopt the role of the other sex for purposes of a particular performance. Individuals who especially like engaging in this kind of cross-dressing may well be reflecting a certain amount of ambivalence about their gender identity and role; however, whatever conflict is present is usually quite mild and certainly need not reflect the presence of a psychosexual disorder. Of course, professional female impersonators may be effeminate homosexual men, or transvestites who enjoy posing temporarily as women, or even men with a transsexual orientation. Their skill may provide them with a socially acceptable and productive means of acting out their psychosexual preference without experiencing undue anxiety and conflict.

Etiological Factors in Transvestism

There is no firm evidence that transvestism has a specific genetic basis or stems from any kind of biological abnormality, such as hormonal imbalance. Biological factors may some day be discovered to play an important role, but for the present one must look primarily to psychosocial influences.

Parents can play a disturbing role in the development of transvestism. Stoller (1974, pp. 183–184) claims there is one outstanding element in the histories of all adult transvestites: the unconscious need of their mother (or another powerful woman) to feminize them, stemming from a strong envy of and hostility toward males. The mother wants to humiliate her boy, so she makes a girl out of him by occasionally dressing him like a girl and suggesting in other ways that he should identify mainly with females. At the same time, however, she conveys that she realizes he is a male and has a penis. Thus, she transfers two conflicting messages: He is indeed a male, but he should act as much as possible like a female.

The typical father of the transvestite, according to Stoller, is a coconspirator, since he makes little attempt to stop the mother from dressing the boy as a girl and encouraging him to act like one. Often such fathers are not home much of the time, and when they are, they tend to be passive about the cross-dressing. Fathers may also play a more direct role in reinforcing cross-dressing: As the result of their own conflict about what is going on, they may punish the boy for his cross-dressing by forcing him to continue doing so. According to Stoller, many of his transvestite patients have been able to date their cross-dressing from such incidents.

The way that parents or parental figures can reinforce transvestite behavior early in life is well illustrated in the following revelation of a transvestite adult. His mother dressed him as a girl when he was a small boy. Then, between the ages of 10 and 17, his cross-dressing became firmly established under the influence of his aunt.

> I would spend every summer at her ranch. The first thing she would do was to give me a pixie haircut. . . . The next day, dressed as a girl, I would accompany her to town and we would shop for a new dress for me. To everyone she met, she would introduce me as her "niece."
>
> This went on every year until I was thirteen years old. . . . When I arrived . . . there laid out on the bed was a girdle, a garter belt and bra, size 32AA, and my first pair of nylons. She then took me over to the new dressing table she had bought me and slid back the top to reveal my very own makeup kit. I was thrilled to death. . . .
>
> The next morning . . . I remember I stuffed by bra with cotton, put on my garter belt, and slipped on my nylons with no effort. . . . My aunt applied my lipstick

because I was so excited I couldn't get it on straight. Then off to town we went, aunt and "niece." What a wonderful day. I shall never forget it. (Stoller, 1967, p. 335)

Zoophilia

The central characteristic of **zoophilia** (also known as bestiality) is the habitual desire for sexual arousal and gratification mainly or exclusively through physical contact with animals, even when opportunities for human relationships are readily available. (Zoophilia should not be confused with the occasional use of animals for sexual purposes.) Most reported cases of zoophilia involve males (Tollison & Adams, 1979, pp. 364–365). In some instances, the sexual contact may include anal or vaginal coitus with the animal, or the animal may be induced to lick or rub against the genitals of the human partner. The confirmed zoophiliac may also become sexually excited merely by fantasizing sexual activity with an animal.

Zoophilia is a relatively rare form of paraphilia. The Kinsey surveys of sexual behavior, which after many years remain the most comprehensive studies of their kind, found that coitus with animals had the lowest frequency of all sources of sexual outlet. About 6 percent of males had some kind of sexual contact with animals after the onset of adolescence, although it was seldom habitual; the comparable frequency for females was about 3 percent (Kinsey, Pomeroy, & Martin, 1948; Kinsey, Pomeroy, Martin, & Gebhard, 1953/1965). The majority of these encounters took place among boys on farms. The surveys showed that as adolescents emerge into adulthood the frequency of sexual contacts with animals drops substantially. Among unmarried males over 20 years of age, 1 percent engaged in casual or repeated sexual activity with an animal. However, there is the relatively rare male who, after a considerable amount of sexual activity with animals, may become so conditioned that he finds himself aroused merely by thinking about it, perhaps years after he has stopped having actual contact (Kinsey, Pomeroy, & Martin, 1948). Such men are likely candidates for a diagnosis of zoophilia.

The Kinsey surveys also found that sexual activity with animals was much rarer among female adults than among male adults. Of almost 6000 women interviewed, only 25 revealed that they had used an animal for sexual excitement, and only 13 of these women had engaged in this practice more than three times (Kinsey, Pomeroy, Martin, & Gebhard, 1953/1965, p. 506). These data are consistent with the fact that almost all zoophiliacs are males.

The taboo against human sexual contact with animals is widespread in spite of many sex researchers' arguments that its occasional occurrence, especially as youthful experimentation, is probably harmless. Indeed, having sexual intercourse with an animal is illegal in most of the United States, involving such charges as crime against nature and sodomy. As in the case of much legal terminology about deviant sexual acts, the terms are not particularly precise, since they are often used in connection with anal intercourse among humans, still a crime in certain localities even between consenting partners. However, unless sexual acts with animals are so flagrant as to be publicly offensive, the legal prohibitions are not apt to interfere much with the habitual zoophiliac's behavior. More disturbing consequences are the feelings of guilt and social isolation experienced because of the overwhelming preoccupation with this form of sexual activity. The alienation it imposes is not only from human sexual relationships but from other aspects of normal interpersonal experiences as well.

Frotteurism

The practice of **frotteurism** is probably more common than mental health professionals have thought. In DSM-III, it was classified in the residual diagnostic category "atypical paraphilias". However, in DSM-III-R, it is listed with the other specific paraphilias. The frotteur (one who touches) is habitually compelled to become sexually aroused by touching or rubbing against a nonconsenting person, usually a stranger in a public place. Almost always a male, the frotteur usually confines his activities to touching or rubbing against a woman's breasts, buttocks, or thighs in public conveyances, where he can take advantage of impersonal and crowded conditions. Because of such conditions the victim may not notice the frotteur's deviant behavior (Sadoff, 1976).

Treatment of Paraphilias

**Psychodynamic
Approaches**

A basic assumption of psychodynamic therapies is that paraphiliac individuals must gain insight into the origin and dynamics of their deviant feelings and behavior in order to overcome them. The specific methods used to help them attain that goal depend on the particular theories the therapist holds concerning the causes of the deviant feelings and behavior and the nature of the psychological forces (dynamics) within the individual that help maintain the deviance (see Chapters 3 and 19). However, all psychodynamic approaches assume that the individual is not consciously aware of those forces. Therefore, therapy must be directed toward bringing them into consciousness so they can be dealt with constructively.

Most of the published accounts of psychotherapy with paraphiliac individuals have dealt with psychoanalytic methods. Various individual case reports state that psychoanalysis can be successful in reducing paraphiliac behavior. However, few studies indicate how the effectiveness of psychoanalysis compares with that of other psychodynamic approaches or with nonpsychodynamic methods, such as behavior therapy. Furthermore, few psychoanalytic studies have been controlled to determine the extent to which the techniques themselves brought about the changes and the extent to which other factors, such as the personality of the therapist, may have been the dominant influences (Luborsky & Spence, 1978).

Behavior Therapy

In its early days behavior therapy tended to discount the gaining of insight in the treatment of psychological disorders and concentrated on directly changing the undesirable behavior. Although the emphasis today is still on changing behavior, therapists also attempt to help the individual understand the nature of the problem and how it developed so as to facilitate attempts to change the deviant behavior more directly.

One of the earliest methods behavior therapists used to treat paraphiliac disorders was aversion therapy. In this procedure, an unpleasant stimulus is paired with the undesirable behavior. For example, a person whose problem is sexual sadism may be directed to fantasize about sadistic behavior and then will receive a shock as soon as he reports the fantasy. An exhibitionist might receive a shock paired with a verbal description of peeping behavior. A transvestite may receive an aversive stimulus while cross-dressing.

All of these techniques are based on principles of classical conditioning (Chapter 4). In recent years, objections that such aversive stimuli as electric shock are inhumane have resulted in the use of less harsh stimuli, such as the inhalation of ammonia. In addition, directing the individual to imagine aversive stimuli has been used as a substitute (Marks, 1978a).

The recent trend in behavior therapy for paraphilias has been away from the use of aversive conditioning and toward the development of positive behavior as an alternative to the negative, paraphiliac behavior. A variety of techniques (which we will discuss in detail in Chapter 20) may be used. They include classical conditioning, the direct teaching of social skills, and the development of self-regulated behavior. For example, the therapist may direct the individual to fantasize images of positive sexual behavior as an alternative to paraphiliac behavior. The exhibitionist who regularly seeks sexual excitement by displaying his penis to an unsuspecting stranger will be guided toward more acceptable sexual behavior by being told to masturbate while viewing images of heterosexual intercourse. At the same time he can be taught through direct training methods to be more assertive in relating to others in social situations so that his exhibitionism need not be a substitute for that lack.

Assessing the effectiveness of behavior therapy for the treatment of paraphilias is difficult, especially because of the lack of well-controlled studies. In a comprehensive survey of behavior therapy in the treatment of paraphilias, Emmelkamp (1986, pp. 425–427) found that a number of procedures were apparently successful but that various methodological flaws precluded the drawing of firm conclusions.

Summary

1. Gender identity disorders are marked by frustration and discomfort arising from a persistent conflict between the individual's biological sex and gender role. Gender identity refers to the sense of belonging, psychologically and culturally, to one biological sex and not to the other. Gender role refers to the social behavior an individual displays in accordance with gender identity. This behavior reveals how the person evaluates that identity and wants others to evaluate it.

2. In relatively rare circumstances, faulty development during the prenatal period may result in a baby being born with certain anatomical characteristics of the other sex. Unless corrected early in life, this condition, called hermaphroditism, can contribute to gender identity conflict.

3. Transsexualism is a gender identity disorder in which the individual wishes to have the anatomic characteristics of the other sex, to assume the gender role, and to live as a member of that sex. Transsexualism occurs more often in males than in females. It is less rare than was once thought. It can occur in childhood, but it occurs more often in adulthood. Surgical reassignment, involving changes in the sexual anatomy of the individual and hormonal treatment, is a last resort mode of therapy.

4. Paraphilias are more common than transsexualism. They involve a recurrent preoccupation with intense sexual urges and fantasies that require at least one of these conditions: (a) nonhuman objects; (b) real or pretended suffering or humiliation on the part of oneself or one's sexual partner; (c) children or other nonconsenting persons.

5. Pedophilia is the most common paraphilia among individuals who have been legally apprehended because of their sexual behavior. Its central feature is the persistent attempt by an adult to gain sexual excitement and satisfaction through contact with

children. As with other paraphilias, pedophilia is almost exclusively a male disorder. A common emphasis in various explanations of the etiology of pedophilia is the importance of negative childhood events and family relationships that contribute to inadequate and immature sexual development and behavior. There is also some evidence that pedophiles harbor feelings of hostility toward women, have a narcissistic self-image, and have had poor models of sexual behavior in their developmental years.

6. Exhibitionism involves repeated attempts to gain sexual stimulation and satisfaction by exposing one's sexual organs to an unsuspecting stranger. There is no attempt to follow the exhibition with any other kind of sexual contact. The behavior usually occurs in public places, thus increasing the likelihood that the offender will be apprehended. Orthodox psychoanalytic theory claims that exhibitionism is a way of denying castration fears that originated during the Oedipal phase of psychosexual development. The exhibitionist still fears castration, but by displaying his penis he can reassure himself that he is powerful and need have no fear. The shock effect he seeks bolsters this reassurance. Explanations of exhibitionism based on learning theory state that the initial act of sexual exposure may have been accidental. However, cognitive replaying led to sexual arousal, and thus a chain of conditioning was established that eventually developed into exhibitionism. Although some evidence supports this explanation, the results are not conclusive. Other etiological factors to be considered are previous sexual problems that could predispose the individual to exhibitionist behavior.

7. The central feature of voyeurism is the compulsive desire to gain sexual satisfaction by viewing the sexual organs or sexual acts of others, usually by looking at unsuspecting women in various stages of undress or sexual activity. Traditional psychoanalytic theory traces voyeurism to the male child's normal desire to observe genitals during the phallic phase. However, in conjunction with those normal desires, the boy may not abandon his early sexual desire for his mother. Peeping at women represents an unconscious but safe way of obtaining the sexual excitement he once associated with his mother. Other psychodynamic interpretations of voyeurism not tied to psychoanalytic theory interpret the disorder as a function of the peeper's timidity in solving problems of sexuality. From a social learning viewpoint, voyeurism is a maladaptive pattern of behavior that has been selectively reinforced over a long period of time so that the usual range of socially acceptable forms of sexual arousal and fulfillment become greatly narrowed.

8. The central characteristic of sexual sadism is the habitual desire to obtain sexual arousal and satisfaction by inflicting suffering on others. This may include not only physical abuse but verbal humiliation as well. Sadistic desire, for example through fantasy, is not sufficient to warrant a diagnosis of sexual sadism. The individual must also act out the desire. Some theories have speculated that sexual sadism may be due to neurological disabilities. However, evidence to support this idea is extremely scant. Traditional psychoanalytic theory views sexual sadism as a way of reducing anxiety in seeking sexual satisfaction. Hypotheses based on learning theory have proposed that sexual sadism develops as the result of the association of sexual excitement and orgasm with the witnessing of painful situations or the administering of pain to others at one time or another.

9. Although sexual sadism may be a factor in rape, the act itself is more often carried out by individuals who are not diagnosed as sexual sadists. Basically, rape is a criminal act designed to display dominance. The majority of rapists do not require

the infliction of pain on another person in order to carry out the act. Furthermore, the gaining of sexual satisfaction is secondary. The primary motives in most instances are to humiliate, debase, and render powerless the victims of the sexual assault.

10. The central characteristic of sexual masochism is the habitual desire to obtain sexual excitement and gratification by being mistreated. This mistreatment may involve physical acts of violence inflicted by a sexual partner or psychological humiliation, such as verbal abuse. A number of studies have found that somewhat more women than men tend to seek gratification through sexual masochism. However, the commercialization of sexual masochism is aimed primarily at men. Psychoanalytic theorists trace sexual masochism to childhood feelings of guilt and fear of punishment concerning sexual behavior — for example, masturbation. Through self-punishment the masochist avoids guilt feelings and fear of retribution while at the same time enjoying the sexual pleasures that had been forbidden during childhood. A broader psychodynamic perspective proposes that sexual sadism stems from parents' rejection of a child's basic needs for love and affection. Eventually the child may come to believe that such a rejection, perhaps reinforced with harsh punishment, is a normal part of human relationships.

11. The main feature of fetishism is the use of nonliving objects as the preferred or even exclusive way of gaining sexual arousal and satisfaction. Most, if not all, fetishists are male. Orthodox psychoanalytic theory proposes two factors basic to fetishism: the castration complex and the defense mechanism of denial. Cultural analyses have pointed out that even though psychoanalytic explanations of fetishism based on variations of the castration complex lack sufficient empirical evidence, their basic assumption that the fetishistic object is a sexual symbol is reasonable. Learning theorists emphasize that fetishism can initially develop through classical conditioning and then continue through the reinforcement of operant behavior.

12. The main characteristic of transvestism is the habitual cross-dressing by a heterosexual male in order to achieve sexual arousal or satisfaction. Unlike transsexuals, transvestites regard themselves as male when not cross-dressing and may even do so when dressed as women. The most seriously disturbed pattern of cross-dressing behavior is when the individual habitually wishes to pass as a woman in public. A pattern of cross-dressing often confused with transvestism occurs in certain instances of male homosexual behavior. Parents can play a prominent role in the development of transvestism. Some researchers have claimed that an outstanding element in the histories of adult transvestites is the unconscious need of their mothers to feminize them. The father tends to be passive about the mother's behavior. Parents or parental figures can also reinforce transvestism by encouraging cross-dressing during childhood.

13. The central feature of zoophilia is the habitual desire for sexual gratification mainly or exclusively through physical contact with animals.

14. Frotteurism involves the habitual desire of an individual to become sexually aroused by touching or rubbing against a nonconsenting person — usually a stranger — in a public place.

15. Methods that have been used in the treatment of paraphilias include psychodynamic approaches, which emphasize the gaining of insight into the nature and causes of the abnormal behavior, and behavior therapy. In recent years, behavior therapists have combined their direct approach to changing behavior with the goal of helping the person gain insight into the maladaptive behavior.

9

Unconventional Sexual Preference and Sexual Dysfunction

My own view, for what it's worth, is
that sexuality is lovely, there cannot
be too much of it, it is self-limiting
if it is satisfactory, and satisfaction
diminishes tension and clears the mind
for attention and learning.

PAUL GOODMAN
Compulsory Miseducation (1964)

In this chapter we continue our discussion of sexuality but focus on very different kinds of problems from those considered in Chapter 8. We begin with an analysis of **unconventional sexual preference,** which we define as sexual relationships between mutually consenting members of the same sex. We then turn to problems of **sexual dysfunctions** — disorders that involve disturbances in the psychological and physiological functions of normal sexual responses.

Unconventional Sexual Preference

DSM Classification of Homosexuality

The fact that homosexuality as such is not listed in DSM-III-R (American Psychiatric Association, 1987) represents a historic departure from traditional psychiatric thinking. In December 1973, the board of trustees of the American Psychiatric Association decided that the diagnostic category "homosexuality" should be removed from DSM-II, where it was classified as a sexual deviation, along with fetishism, voyeurism, exhibitionism, and pedophilia (American Psychiatric Association, 1968). (See Chapter 8.) A new diagnostic category, **sexual orientation disturbance,** was substituted. It was to be used for homosexuals who were in conflict about their sexual orientation and wanted to change it or learn how to live with it.

Whether or not homosexuality should be considered a mental disorder had been the subject of a great deal of debate prior to the 1973 decision; the debate had been accelerated by the organized homosexual community, which protested that the classification of their sexual preference as a mental illness was an act of prejudice ("Homosexuality Dropped," 1974). Though a number of psychiatrists deplored the social prejudice against homosexuals, they still regarded homosexuality as a form of psychopathology. The declaration was later put to a vote before the entire membership of the American Psychiatric Association. The majority upheld the decision, but there was a significant amount of dissent.

The American Psychiatric Association's Task Force on Nomenclature and Statistics implicitly endorsed the position that homosexuality is a minority life-style that some individuals are able to follow without any more psychological or social conflict and personal distress than heterosexuals experience. The task force also pointed out, however, that "modern methods of treatment enable a significant proportion of homosexuals who wish to change their sexual orientation to do so. At the same time, homosexuals who are bothered by or in conflict with their sexual feelings, but who are either uninterested in changing, or unable to change their sexual orientation, can be helped to accept themselves as they are and to rid themselves of self-hatred (Spitzer, 1973, p. 2).

DSM-III (American Psychiatric Association, 1980a) replaced *sexual orientation disturbance* with **ego-dystonic homosexuality.** The new category no longer endorsed the idea that therapists should help troubled homosexuals accept themselves as they are and rid themselves of self-hatred when they do not want to change their sexual orientation. Indeed, a central characteristic of ego-dystonic homosexuality was the desire to acquire or increase heterosexual relations (Bayer & Spitzer, 1982; Spitzer, 1981).

DSM-III-R strengthens the view that homosexuality per se is not a mental disorder. It eliminates the diagnosis ego-dystonic homosexuality, but problems of homosexuality can still be noted under the diagnostic heading "Sexual Disorders Not Otherwise Specified." At the discretion of the clinician, this diagnosis can be applied in cases where there is marked distress about sexual orientation (American Psychiatric Association, 1987, p. 296).

The succession of changes is consistent with the more understanding attitudes toward homosexuality of the last decade. Nevertheless, many individual and public practices continue to stigmatize and discriminate against homosexuals, particularly those who openly reveal their sexual preference. Such practices and the attitudes behind them promote psychological and social problems among people who have chosen a homosexual way of life or who contemplate doing so — problems analogous to those of other minority groups who encounter prejudice and discrimination.

From a psychosocial perspective, homosexuality can be regarded as a life-style that some people follow adaptively; but for others it may create distressing conflicts and maladaptive ways of coping with them.

Homosexual Development and Behavior

Kinsey Surveys and Related Studies

The Kinsey surveys of human sexual behavior have been criticized for various methodological weaknesses, but they remain the most comprehensive, systematic, and widely quoted studies of their kind (Kinsey, Pomeroy, & Martin, 1948; Kinsey, Pomeroy, Martin, & Gebhard, 1953/1965). The surveys were carried out under the auspices of the Institute for Sex Research at Indiana University and were directed by the founder of the institute, Alfred C. Kinsey (1894–1956). Data were gathered from some 12,000 individuals through highly structured personal interviews. More than 300 items involving these major areas were covered: social and economic status, marital history, sex education, physical and physiological data, nocturnal sex dreams, masturbation, animal contacts, heterosexual history, and homosexual history. Our concern here is with the last two areas.

The extent to which individuals said they engaged in heterosexual or homosexual behavior was rated on a scale from 0 (entirely heterosexual) to 6 (entirely homosexual). Figure 9.1 shows the scale and the definitions for each point on it. The concept of

Figure 9.1

Heterosexual–homosexual rating scale. (From Kinsey, Pomeroy, & Martin, 1948, p. 638.)

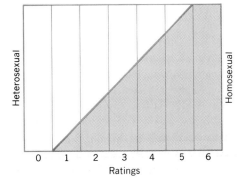

0 = entirely heterosexual
1 = largely heterosexual, but with incidental homosexual history
2 = largely heterosexual, but with distinct homosexual history
3 = equally heterosexual and homosexual
4 = largely homosexual, but with a distinct heterosexual history
5 = largely homosexual, but with incidental heterosexual history
6 = entirely homosexual

The Kinsey surveys remain the
most comprehensive and
systematic studies of human
sexual behavior. Here Dr. Kinsey
is interviewing one of the many
persons who volunteered to take
part in the surveys.

continuity of sexual orientation rather than an either – or choice is widely accepted today
among professionals in the field of sexual research as well as among significant segments
of the educated public. That was not so much the case in the late 1930s and early 1940s,
when Kinsey and his associates first collected their data.

On the basis of some 5300 case histories, the survey of men estimated that about 4
percent of white men in the United States were exclusively homosexual, 10 percent had
been almost entirely homosexual for at least three years, and 37 percent had experienced
homosexual orgasm at some time since the beginning of adolescence. The frequency of
homosexual behavior for some 5900 white women was noticeably less. Only about 3
percent had been entirely or largely homosexual at any age period, and only 13 percent
had experienced homosexual orgasm after the onset of adolescence.

These data must be regarded with caution. First of all, the subjects of the surveys were
volunteers. Thus, the findings were based exclusively on information about individuals
who were willing to reveal their sexual preferences and activities. The survey team was
aware of the bias that this situation introduced and attempted to overcome it by obtaining a
100 percent agreement to be interviewed from all the groups it solicited at various
meetings of social and civic clubs, student and professional organizations, and other
groups. However, not all members attended the recruitment meetings, and some, of
course, refused to participate even though they were present. All in all, about 26 percent
of the men and 15 percent of the women came from 100 percent groups (Kinsey,
Pomeroy, & Martin, 1948, p. 95; Kinsey, Pomeroy, Martin, & Gebhard, 1953/1965,
p. 30).

Second, the homosexual activity that the Kinsey team reported is difficult to interpret,
since for the most part the survey data are not concerned with what the sexual experiences

meant to the respondents. This was especially true for men. All interpretations of the reported homosexual activities must necessarily be based completely on statistical frequencies, which may or may not correspond significantly to the attitudes and feelings associated with the behavior. For example, did the respondents view such sexual relationships as being positive or negative? What kinds of conflicts did they have? Such variables are important, perhaps even crucial, for understanding the meaning of homosexual behavior in an individual's life and the extent to which the behavior is adaptive or maladaptive. The situation was somewhat better for the data on women, since the research team added a number of questions to the interview schedule that dealt with how the women felt about their sexual behavior. Nevertheless, statistical frequencies of sexual acts remained the major source of interpretation for both heterosexual and homosexual behavior.

Also, the report dealt only with white individuals. To what extent the findings can be applied to nonwhites is conjectural. Although nonwhites were interviewed, the research team decided not to include them in the analysis because the number was too small to permit comparisons of subgroups, such as different age and occupational groups. For example, only 934 case histories of nonwhite women were available, compared with 5940 case histories of white women (Kinsey, Pomeroy, Martin, & Gebhard, 1953/1965, p. 22).

In spite of methodological shortcomings, the surveys have had a tremendous influence on the development of more understanding attitudes about the nature of homosexuality and the recognition that not all such behavior is maladaptive. The Kinsey reports have been especially influential on recent thinking about female homosexuality. One of the most interesting findings was that women are much less promiscuous in their homosexual relationships than men. The difference may be due partially to the greater importance that male homosexuals place on achieving orgasm. Of course, orgasm is also a common goal in lesbian relationships; however, some research findings suggest that lesbians focus more strongly on the importance of caring and feelings of attachment as an integral part of their sexual life. Various surveys in which male and female members of homosexual groups described their sexual relationships have found that men placed more importance on explicit genital experiences and their enjoyment of one-night stands. In contrast, women were less explicit in describing the genital aspects of their sexual relationships and expressed a greater preference for long-term relationships rather than single encounters (Bell, Weinberg, & Hammersmith, 1981; Gagnon & Simon, 1973; Saghir & Robins, 1969; Saghir, Robins, & Walbran, 1969).

Laud Humphreys (1975) has examined the "tearoom" activities of homosexual men whose desire for instant and impersonal sex was in some respects consistent with the differences between male and female homosexuality just described. (*Tearoom* is a euphemism certain homosexual males use for public toilets where fast and anonymous sexual encounters can take place.) Humphreys's analysis of the interviews revealed that men who were the least involved in tearoom activities were the most likely to use the vocabulary of conventional heterosexual marriage. They seemed more at ease with their homosexual orientation than did the more frequent users of tearooms. Although they engaged in tearoom encounters occasionally, they did not consider them the primary focus of their sexual activities.

It may be that the greater promiscuity and less concern with close and permanent relationships that many homosexual men show in comparison with lesbians reflect differences between male and female sexuality in general. This possibility is supported by data from the Kinsey report: "The male's greater inclination to be promiscuous shows up in the record of his petting experience, his experience in pre-marital coitus, extra-marital coitus, and in homosexual relationships. In all of these types of relationships, few females have anywhere near the number of partners that many a promiscuous male may have" (Kinsey, Pomeroy, Martin, & Gebhard, 1953/1965, p. 683).

In interpreting these findings, Kinsey and his colleagues emphasized that in both heterosexual and homosexual relationships, men's promiscuity was related to the anticipation of variations in the genital anatomy of their sexual partners and the different techniques they might use during sexual contacts. Although women did not ignore such factors, they tended to find them less significant.

Whether Kinsey's conclusions are as appropriate today as when he and his colleagues carried out their studies is problematic. However, more recent data, gathered mainly from members of the National Organization for Women (NOW), revealed that women placed greater emphasis than men on closeness and sharing and less emphasis on sheer genital contact. This was true for both heterosexual and homosexual relationships (Hite, 1976).

Biological Theories of Homosexuality

Over the years, a number of biological theories have attempted to explain homosexuality. Some claim that it has a genetic basis, but the scanty data that exist either fail to support that proposition or are inconclusive (Eckert, Bouchard, Bohlen, & Heston, 1986; Rosenthal, 1971). Other studies report that homosexuality may stem, at least in part, from imbalances in sex hormones. One group of investigators found that the urine of homosexual men contained less testosterone (a male sex hormone) than did the urine of heterosexual men, and that lesbians excreted less estrogen (a female sex hormone) than did heterosexual women (Loraine, Adamopoulos, Kirkham, Ismail, & Dove, 1971). In a similar study, Kolodny, Masters, Hendrix, and Toro (1971) reported that 35 men who claimed to be exclusively homosexual had lower amounts of testosterone in the blood than one expect to find in heterosexual males.

Although of interest, findings such as these do not demonstrate conclusively that hormonal imbalance is a cause of homosexuality, for it is conceivable that sustained homosexual behavior may itself lead to decreases in testosterone. In fact, Kolodny and his co-workers suggested that possibility as another way of interpreting their findings. Barry and Barry (1972) argued that the intensive life-style of some homosexuals might explain the results of the Kolodny study. They pointed out that many homosexuals who cruise a great deal during the night may average less than four hours of sleep. Since testosterone levels usually decrease during the day and presumably are restored during sleeping hours (they return to high levels in early morning), Barry and Barry concluded that the deficits in testosterone could actually result from lack of sleep. Furthermore, Birk, Williams, Chasin, and Rose (1973), who studied 66 male homosexual patients undergoing psychotherapy, found no correlation between the serum testosterone levels and the ratings of homosexual activity based on Kinsey's rating scale. In fact, as a group these patients had normal testosterone levels.

In general, recent critical analyses of studies aimed at discovering biological influences in the development of homosexuality have concluded that homosexuality is not directly the result of hormonal abnormalities. However, the analyses have also concluded that abnormal hormonal development during the prenatal period, in combination with postnatal social and psychological factors, may facilitate the development of a homosexual orientation (Ellis & Ames, 1987; Masters, Johnson, & Kolodny, 1986, pp. 348–349; Money, 1987, p. 398).

Psychoanalytic Views of Homosexuality

As we pointed out in Chapter 3, orthodox Freudian theory states that male homosexuality stems from failure of the boy during the Oedipal period of psychosexual development to identify adequately with his father. Consequently, he fails to acquire a masculine gender

Using information obtained from psychoanalysts, Irving Bieber and his associates concluded that male homosexual patients had experienced fewer opportunities to identify with their father than had heterosexual male patients.

role. The difficulty may be compounded by overidentification with his mother. If, during the Oedipal stage, the girl does not overcome her penis envy and identify with her mother, she too may develop a homosexual character. This specific formulation of the role of identification in the development of homosexuality has been widely criticized as being too culture-bound, especially since Freud's concepts of masculinity and femininity are narrow when judged by current knowledge of gender differences (see Box 9.1).

The importance of identification in the development of homosexuality has also been examined within a broader psychoanalytic framework, as illustrated in the comprehensive empirical study directed by Irving Bieber (Bieber et al., 1962). The data were furnished by a large number of cooperating psychoanalysts who completed an extensive questionnaire concerning their male patients. Of these patients, 106 were homosexual and 100 were heterosexual. The responses showed that the lack of opportunity to identify adequately with one's father, or rejection of the opportunity (aided by the mother), was a more important factor in the life of the homosexual patients than in the life of the heterosexual patients.

The Bieber study is open to a number of criticisms. To begin with, the data were based only on homosexual individuals who were sufficiently troubled to seek help. Obviously, parental relationships for homosexuals who were not so troubled might well have been different. A second criticism is that the ratings of past histories were all completed by psychoanalysts whose theoretical biases could seriously influence those ratings. A third important objection is that, like all such studies, the data were retrospective and thus subject to errors of faulty memory or other biases.

Although the criticisms just cited are important ones, the results of these studies still suggest some support for psychoanalytically oriented theory of how homosexuality may develop. Furthermore, some of the major findings have also been obtained in a study by Evans (1969), who attacked the problem in a different manner. Evans adapted Bieber's questionnaire and gave it to male homosexuals and heterosexuals who had been recruited from a nonpatient population. The homosexuals were all members of a gay organization. The fact that the findings of the Evans and Bieber studies were similar lends at least some support to the importance of identification in the development of homosexual attitudes and behavior. Of course, one can accept the empirical results without necessarily subscribing to the Freudian theory of how identification occurs.

A more recent study partially supports the Evans research. Johanna Millic and Douglas Crowne (1986) administered a parent–child relations questionnaire to young male adults recruited from a homosexual organization in Canada and to a group of heterosexual students at a Canadian college. Subjects rated their parents' childrearing practices on five dimensions: loving, demanding, attention, rejecting, and casual. The "rejecting" ratings of the homosexual group were significantly higher for both parents than were the ratings of the heterosexual group. The researchers also pointed out that the rejection may have been initiated by the parents' suspicion of their sons' movement toward a homosexual orientation. This rejection could then further influence the homosexual development. More research is needed to explore this possibility. One approach would be to obtain recollections of childrearing practices from the parents of homosexual and heterosexual males (Millic & Crowne, 1986, p. 245).

Modeling and Reinforcement

The extent to which parental figures act as models of homosexual or heterosexual attitudes and behavior and the extent to which the child's modeling of those attitudes and behavior are reinforced may have an important influence on the early development of sexual orientation. If the child's modeling of the parents' attitudes and behavior is positively reinforced (rewarded), the attitudes and behavior are likely to become part of the child's

BOX 9.1 Freud Writes to an American Mother about Homosexuality

Given Freud's theories of homosexuality, one might not suspect that he personally was compassionate in his attitude toward homosexuals. He anticipated by some 40 years the 1973 decision of the American Psychiatric Association to reject homosexuality per se as a mental disorder.

The following letter by Freud was written late in his life, just four years before his death. It was a reply to an American woman who was deeply troubled by her son's homosexuality. She sent a copy of Freud's letter to Alfred Kinsey with this anonymous note: "Herewith I enclose a letter from a great and good man which you may retain. From a Grateful Mother." In turn, Kinsey sent Freud's letter to the *American Journal of Psychiatry*, where it was published ("Historical Notes: A Letter from Freud," 1951).

April 9, 1935

Dear Mrs. ———:

I gather from your letter that your son is a homosexual. I am most impressed by the fact that you do not mention this term yourself in your information about him. May I question you, why you avoid it? Homosexuality is assuredly no advantage but it is nothing to be ashamed of, no vice, no degradation, it cannot be classified as an illness; we consider it to be a variation of the sexual function produced by a certain arrest of sexual development. Many highly respectable individuals of ancient and modern times have been homosexuals, several of the greatest men among them. (Plato, Michelangelo, Leonardo da Vinci etc.). It is a great injustice to persecute homosexuality as a crime and a cruelty too. If you do not believe me, read the books of Havelock Ellis.

By asking me if I can help, you mean, I suppose, if I can abolish homosexuality and make normal heterosexuality take its place. The answer is, in a general way we cannot promise to achieve it. In a certain number of cases we succeed in developing the blighted germs of heterosexual tendencies which are present in every homosexual, in the majority of cases it is no more possible. It is a question of the quality and the age of the individual. The result of treatment cannot be predicted.

What analysis can do for your son runs in a different line. If he is unhappy, neurotic, torn by conflicts, inhibited in his social life, analysis may bring him harmony, peace of mind, full efficiency, whether he remains a homosexual or gets changed. If you make up your mind he should have analysis with me — I don't expect you will — he has to come over to Vienna. I have no intention of leaving here. However, don't neglect to give me your answer.

Sincerely yours with kind wishes,

FREUD

P.S. I did not find it difficult to read your handwriting. Hope you will not find my writing and my English a harder task.

repertoire. If the modeling is ignored, they are less likely to become part of the repertoire. Positive reinforcement may be direct, as when children try out what they have observed and are rewarded for doing so. It may also be vicarious — that is, it may occur through the child's observation of the attitudes and behavior that parents reward in other individuals (Bandura, 1969, 1977).

Punishment

The consistent use of punishment in child rearing may also be effective in helping to produce a homosexual pattern. For example, a child may be consistently punished by a parent for expressing erotic interest or actually engaging in sex play with children of the other sex but not warned specifically against such activities with children of the same sex. Indeed, some parents may not realize that such behavior is likely to occur. Thus, the child may learn to avoid heterosexual explorations and seek homosexual contacts instead, since they are less likely to be suspected and thus may go unnoticed. Consequently, greater opportunities for homosexual gratification may develop and be reinforced, setting a pattern for later sexual preferences.

Alienation

Constant alienation from peers of the other sex may also play a part in the development of homosexuality. For example, extreme feminine behavior may isolate some boys from normal masculine acceptance and approval. To end this isolation, they may become involved in homosexual relations, thus obtaining the approval and affection from male peers that were denied them earlier. Similar events may in some instances influence the development of lesbian relationships (Millon & Millon, 1974).

Consistent with this alienation hypothesis are the results of a 15-year study by Richard Green (1986), which found that 33 out of 44 extremely effeminate boys matured into adulthood as homosexuals or bisexuals. By effeminate Green meant that these boys were indifferent to the typical interests usually found in boyhood. In a comparison group of boys who were much more masculine in their interests and behavior, only one became a bisexual adult and none were exclusively homosexual. Interpreting these findings, Green concluded that the indifference of the homosexuals to typical boyhood interests and behavior alienated them from their male peers and often from their fathers. These boys may then have become starved for the affection of males, motivating them to seek love from men rather than women during adolescence and adulthood. Green also pointed out that such psychosocial influences may well interact with genetic factors.

Modeling, reinforcement, punishment, and alienation from peers are only some of the psychosocial factors that may influence the development and expression of homosexual attitudes and behavior. The events that lead to their establishment are diverse, complex, and sometimes unpredictable. It may well be that accidents of life contribute more toward the development of homosexuality than systematic research is able to reveal.

Homosexuality and Discrimination

A significant segment of the general public still holds negative attitudes toward homosexuals. Indeed, such attitudes may well have increased in recent years, especially in view of the wide publicity given to the spread of AIDS (acquired immune deficiency syndrome) among homosexual men (Barnes, 1986; Eckholm, 1986; Landers, 1986b; Masters, Johnson, & Kolodny, 1986, pp. 543–548; Nordheimer, 1987). Nevertheless, the overall shift in recent years has been in a more positive or at least a more open direction.

Many of the gains homosexuals have achieved in reducing discrimination have come through their militancy and use of political and economic pressures.

Much of the gain in reducing discrimination has been achieved through the militancy of gay and lesbian organizations and their use of political and economic power, especially in large urban centers. In many instances, these groups have argued for their civil and economic rights on the same basis that various ethnic, religious, and racial minorities have for many years used against discriminatory practices. On some occasions, gay and lesbian organizations have joined forces with groups that represent a broad spectrum of women fighting against discrimination in educational opportunities and employment practices.

A historic step in reducing discrimination against homosexuals was the July 1975 decision of the United States Civil Service Commission that homosexuals may not arbitrarily be denied federal jobs. The guidelines also stipulate that before a person can be dismissed from a position on the basis of homosexuality, a rational connection must be made between that person's homosexual conduct and failure to perform the job. The rules state that, for each case in which sexual conduct is an issue, the same standard must be applied as in evaluating heterosexual behavior and no employee can be disqualified solely on the basis of homosexual conduct. Obviously, the decision is of crucial importance, since the commission controls the employment and working conditions of millions of federal employees. Notable exceptions to the decision are such special categories as the Federal Bureau of Investigation, the Central Intelligence Agency, and foreign service specialists at the State Department.

Another landmark in attempts to reduce discrimination against homosexuals has been the publication of a handbook by the American Civil Liberties Union delineating the legal rights of homosexuals and how those rights can be protected (Boggan, Haft, Lister, & Rupp, 1975). This handbook is one in a series dealing with the rights of such groups as mental patients, prisoners, teachers, students, women, and the poor.

Maintaining a Homosexual Life-style

Although some homosexuals are able to maintain their life-style with little or no social conflict or personal distress, others cannot. What are some of the factors that contribute to such problems? A basic principle is that homosexuals are inherently just as able to deal with everyday problems as are heterosexuals, but society's adverse attitudes present them with more than the average number of problems. Among them are the following.

■ Feelings of alienation from a society that disapproves of their sexual orientation. The adverse attitudes homosexuals meet resemble those that have been directed against others who did not fit the expectations of the dominant society (certain immigrants, for example).

■ Legal threats may play a role in creating a heightened sensitivity in some homosexuals and even in creating a paranoid orientation toward heterosexuals.

■ Although sexual relationships in Western society have become more permissive, they are still sufficiently structured to create problems for those who live outside these norms. As a result the homosexual may suffer especially from feelings of inferiority and guilt.

■ Because of the stigma they may face, many homosexuals do not reveal their sexual preference even to their families. Consequently, they may feel a great deal of conflict and strain in relating to family members, even if they are no longer living at home. To some extent, other relationships at home can carry the same burden. For example, closet homosexuals may fear to let heterosexual friends know about their sexual preferences, thus creating the need for secrecy and resulting feelings of guilt.

■ Self-doubt may become intensified: "If I accept my homosexuality, why do I keep it a secret?" The recent emphasis in homosexual circles on coming out of the closet could well be an antidote to this doubt and guilt.

Given these kinds of problems, why do some homosexuals experience much distress and conflict while others do not? One important reason may be that many have developed problems that are relatively independent of their sexual orientation. They might well have become disturbed even if they had not made a homosexual choice. The conflict that arises because of that choice may intensify other problems.

Perhaps even more crucial is the social situation in which homosexuals live. Some, because they live in communities where there is strong mutual support, may have no greater personal problems than do heterosexuals. Those who live in communities providing less support are more likely to feel guilt, conflict, and alienation. Consequently, they are more apt to succumb to maladaptive patterns of interpersonal relationships.

Homosexuality and Psychotherapy

Homosexuals who feel troubled about their life-style and who want help have two main options: to learn how to change their orientation or to learn how to accept it and become more fulfilled. Psychoanalysts have usually assumed that it is good for the homosexual to become heterosexual; thus, they accept patients with the understanding that change is the goal. Other therapists, however, argue that the choice of whether or not to change is up to the homosexual client who comes voluntarily for treatment. Going further, Davison (1976, 1978) argues that therapists should stop trying to change homosexuals. Given the negative social attitudes they face, homosexuals who do come to therapists in order to change are not really doing so in an atmosphere of freedom and voluntary choice. Therapists would do better, Davison claims, to help homosexuals learn how to accept their sexual preference, if that is what they want to do, and to solve problems they may have that are independent of their particular sexual orientation.

Sexual Dysfunctions

> Tony was a 55 year old restaurant owner . . . married for five years. . . . He was obese, always had a cigar in his mouth, and was carelessly dressed. Teresa, on the other hand, was slim and carefully groomed. . . . This was the second marriage for both. He had been divorced, and she had been a widow. . . .
>
> Teresa complained that Tony had no sexual interest in her. He admitted this, and attributed it to the pressure of business. The couple had intercourse approximately once a month, during which time he tended to climax rapidly. Teresa was increasingly agitated and depressed about this situation. Tony's medical history was negative, and he reported that he had had a "strong sex drive" in his first marriage. (Kaplan, 1979, p. 105)

This case excerpt illustrates just a few of the many kinds of problems that DSM-III-R classifies as sexual dysfunctions. They involve conflict and distress caused by disturbances in the psychophysiological changes that normally occur during the sexual response cycle.

Sexual Response Cycle

Over a 12-year period, the research team of William Masters and Virginia Johnson (1966) observed the psychophysiological responses of some 700 women and men who had volunteered to engage in such sexual activities as masturbation and intercourse in Masters and Johnson's laboratory. Prior to this research, Alfred Kinsey and his associates at the Kinsey Institute for Sex Research had made some films showing the overt behavior of men and women during masturbation and intercourse. The researchers incorporated some of these observations into the institute's comprehensive report on female sexual behavior, but they did not reveal the specific ways in which the data were obtained. This omission may have reflected their opinion that attitudes toward sex research in the 1950s were not sufficiently positive to risk such disclosure (Kinsey, Pomeroy, Martin, & Gebhard, 1953/1965; Pomeroy, 1972).

Masters and Johnson were not the first to study human sexual response by actually observing men and women engaging in various forms of sexual activity. However, they were pioneers in that the observations they made included not only overt sexual behavior but also a wide range of psychophysiological changes. For example, the women volunteers were asked to masturbate after inserting into their vaginas a clear plastic device shaped like a penis and containing a light and a camera. This enabled Masters and Johnson to film the various physical changes in sex organs that occur internally during sexual activity. They also measured changes in the external genitalia of both female and male subjects as well as heart rate, blood pressure, respiration, and skin reactions. They supplemented this kind of information with data obtained through detailed interviews.

As a way of organizing their observations of psychophysiological changes, Masters and Johnson divided the **sexual response cycle** into four stages: excitement (labeled arousal in DSM-III-R), the beginning of psychophysiological arousal; plateau, a more intense continuation of excitement; orgasm, the climax and release of sexual tension; and resolution, a return to the unaroused state (Masters & Johnson, 1966; Masters, Johnson, & Kolodny, 1986, pp. 57–76). These stages occur in masturbation as well as in sexual activities involving partners. Their onset and timing are influenced by psychological and social factors, such as the nature of the sex act and how participants feel about it, the

William Masters and Virginia Johnson developed new laboratory methods for studying the human sexual response cycle and its dysfunctions.

environment in which the sexual activity occurs, the attitudes an individual has learned with regard to sexuality, and how sex partners feel about each other.

In her analysis of the sexual response cycle, Helen Singer Kaplan (1979) concentrated on only two of the stages (she prefers the term *phases*) that Masters and Johnson described: excitement and orgasm. However, she also added a preliminary phase that they did not explicitly consider: desire. The DSM-III-R classification of sexual dysfunctions is based mainly on the research of Masters, Johnson, and Kaplan.

Diagnostic Classification of Sexual Dysfunctions

DSM-III-R classifies sexual dysfunctions as follows (American Psychiatric Association, 1987, pp. 290–296): sexual desire disorders, sexual arousal disorders, inhibited male or female orgasm, premature ejaculation, dyspareunia, vaginismus, and sexual dysfunction NOS. (The last category is reserved for dysfunctions not otherwise specified—that is, dysfunctions that do not fit any of the specific diagnostic categories. One example is the habitual absence of erotic sensation during the excitement and orgasm phase, even though the physiological changes are normal.) The dysfunctions enumerated here will be discussed in detail in this chapter.

A diagnosis of sexual dysfunction implies that psychosocial factors play a central role in the etiology of the disorder. Thus, the diagnosis should not be used if the sexual disturbance is caused exclusively by organic factors. Prominent among organic factors are various physical diseases, medications, and recreational drugs such as alcohol, cocaine, and heroin ("Drugs That Cause Sexual Dysfunction," 1983). In some instances, organic factors may account partly for the sexual problem although psychological and social factors also contribute to it. In such circumstances, the clinician makes two diagnoses: one for the organic condition that helps explain the origin of the sexual disability and the other for the sexual dysfunction itself. Sometimes, another mental disorder is the primary cause of the sexual problem. For example, sexual disability can stem from severe depression. A diagnosis of sexual dysfunction is not appropriate unless the clinician has evidence that the sexual problem preceded the other disorder or was significantly influenced by other psychosocial factors (American Psychiatric Association, 1987, pp. 292–293).

This approach to the diagnosis of sexual dysfunctions can be an important guide for therapy. For example, if an abnormal physical condition appears to be mostly responsible for the sexual disability, treating that condition directly might be sufficient to alleviate the sexual problem. However, if the dysfunction is only partly the result of an abnormal physical condition, then greater attention to the sexual problem is appropriate.

Patterns and Etiology of Sexual Dysfunctions

Disorders of Sexual Desire

Sexual desire (in psychoanalytic language, the libido) is an appetite or drive that is activated by specific nerve centers in the brain. The various sensations that result are the primary motivation for seeking sexual experiences. The secretion of certain hormones, especially testosterone, enhances motivation; the sexual drive is also greatly influenced by the individual's past learning, present attitudes and moods, and a host of environmental circumstances.

Sexual desire disorders are among the most common forms of sexual dysfunction. The central feature is a persistent and pervasive lack of sexual desire or, in some instances, an extreme aversion to any kind of genital contact (American Psychiatric Association, 1987, p. 293). Such conditions contribute significantly to the individual's conflict and distress or to the distress of a partner. A diagnosis of sexual desire disorder must rule out the possibility that the disturbance is caused exclusively by an organic factor or another mental disorder. Other factors to be considered are the individual's age, the frequency of sexual desire, the degree of dissatisfaction, and the circumstances that surround the lack of desire. Assessing their relevance can be difficult. Consider the matter of frequency of sexual activity. Is every two weeks normal for a busy executive in her 30s, or is it a sign of inhibition? How does one apply the concept of normality to an equally busy man in his 50s who desires sexual activity only once a month? Frequency of desire as a criterion of sexual dysfunction must be considered in the broader context of the person's daily life (Kaplan, 1977; 1979, pp. 59, 79–82; 1983, pp. 242–245; Lief, 1977; Masters & Johnson, 1982; Renshaw, 1982).

Individuals may experience little desire but still engage in regular sexual activity. They may do so from a sense of duty, out of fear that the partner will leave, in consideration of the partner's well-being, to reassure themselves that they can still perform sexually, or simply for financial gain, as in prostitution. Usually, however, the chronic lack of sexual desire eventually tends to decrease sexual activity, and it often leads to serious conflict with a sex partner.

Loss of sexual desire may be global or situational. In global loss, the individual experiences little sexual desire and does not even have erotic fantasies. In certain instances, this deficit may involve an intense fear of sex, as is common in women who have been victims of sexual assault (Becker, Skinner, Abel, & Cichon, 1986; Stuart, Hammond, & Pett, 1987).

Situational loss of sexual desire is more common than global loss. Here the individual experiences desire only in sexual situations that are psychologically safe. For example, a man who has strong doubts about his self-worth and social status may seek sexual activity only with women from a lower social class than his.

Traditional psychoanalytic interpretations of sexual desire disorders stem from Freud's concept of the libido. As we discussed in Chapter 3, the libido is the sexual energy of Eros, which Freud postulated as the instinct (drive) containing all of the individual's constructive forces. Libidinal energy is originally determined by the development of chemical processes in the body and inherited constitutional factors. However, the libido is not static. It is affected by environmental circumstances and can be suppressed or enhanced by the ego. In its early development, the ego's expression of libidinal energy is narcissistic, centering on the self. As the individual becomes more mature, the ego increasingly directs this sexual energy toward others, a direction that Freud called object libido. When one is completely in love, said Freud, the ego transfers the main quantity of libido from the self to another person (1940/1949, p. 24).

Although orthodox psychoanalytic explanations assume a biological deficit in libidinal energy, they also emphasize that the lack of desire is often a defense against unconscious anxiety and conflict. These first develop during the Oedipal period of psychosexual development. According to psychoanalytic theory, when a man who has not resolved the Oedipal conflict begins to encounter sexual situations, the original anxiety that occurred during the Oedipal period is renewed and directed toward the sexual partner. Sexual desire becomes repressed because the person may unconsciously perceive his spouse as the parent with whom sex is forbidden. The absence of sexual desire serves as a defense against incestuous wishes.

A social learning and cultural approach to understanding sexual desire disorders also emphasizes the importance of early family influences. Negative attitudes about sex may be so pervasive in certain families that the child learns to inhibit the expression of sexual interest and to feel guilty about it.

Helen Singer Kaplan (1979, 1983) postulates that disorders of sexual desire may involve different levels of conflict. At a deep, unconscious level, the lack of sexual desire may indeed stem from Oedipal kinds of conflicts. At a more conscious level, the deficit may stem from negative attitudes toward sex learned during childhood and reinforced through later experiences. The individual may have serious doubts about becoming committed to one partner and fear becoming too intimate as the price for gaining pleasure. Continuing anger of one partner toward the other may also contribute significantly to the disorder.

Inaccurate ways of thinking and perceiving may contribute to problems of sexual desire. Rook and Hammen (1977) have suggested that sexual desire can be affected by how one perceives internal and external cues associated with being aroused, how one labels sensations and stimuli as being erotic, and what one expects from being sexually aroused. In applying these concepts to therapy, L. LoPiccolo (1980) has concluded that some individuals with deficits in sexual desire do reveal patterns that are consistent with Rook and Hammen's formulation:

1. They have not learned to perceive accurately their levels of physiological sexual arousal. They either diminish or mislabel their sensations.

2. They have not learned how to facilitate their arousal.

3. They use a limited number of cues in defining a situation as sexual or defining their own sexual arousal.

4. They have limited expectations for their ability to be sexually aroused.

5. On the basis of these ways of perceiving and thinking, they usually regard themselves as not being very sexual.

Helen Singer Kaplan, author, researcher, and therapist, has made significant contributions to the understanding of sexual dysfunctions.

Sexual Arousal Disorder in Women

Sexual arousal disorder is the recurrent and persistent failure to obtain or maintain the psychophysiological changes of arousal (excitement). The most prominent physiological characteristic of inadequate sexual arousal in women is the partial or complete failure to attain the lubrication and swelling of external genitalia and expansion of the vagina normally associated with the excitement phase of the sexual response cycle. Often accompanying this lack of physiological response is an absence of erotic feeling during sexual activity and a negative emotional reaction. As a result, an increasing tendency to avoid sexual relations may develop.

Inadequate sexual arousal in women is also known as frigidity. Although the term often occurs in clinical as well as popular writings, it is an unfortunate choice. The label is confusing because it has traditionally been used more broadly to include other sexual dysfunctions, such as disorders of desire and orgasm. Especially undesirable is the disparaging nature of the term, since it implies that women who suffer from disorders of sexual excitement are necessarily cold and hostile to men. On the contrary, they may be warm and responsive individuals who are troubled about their sexual problems and would like to overcome them (Andersen, 1983, p. 106).

Orthodox psychoanalytic theory proposes that sexual conflicts originating during the phallic phase of psychosexual development are the principal contributors to inhibited sexual arousal in adult women. During this early period (roughly between the ages of 3 and 5) the girl has libidinal desires for her father and desires to eliminate her mother as a sexual rival. Freud called this the Electra complex (see Chapter 3). Since such incestuous wishes are forbidden and threatened with punishment if openly acknowledged, the girl must repress them. In addition to fear of punishment, she fears the loss of love from her mother because of those incestuous wishes. If she is unable to resolve this conflict by giving up her sexual wishes for her father, she develops problems of inhibited sexual arousal, seeing in men the forbidden father.

Behavioral explanations of deficits in sexual arousal in women look for environmental events that helped the woman associate negative emotional reactions with sex. Such conditioning may result from psychological and physical trauma, such as sexual assault or other forms of sexual abuse (Becker & Skinner, 1983), or it may originate in unusual pain suffered during early attempts at sexual intercourse. The experience of pain may have been exacerbated by inept partners whose lack of consideration prevented adequate arousal. Lazarus (1971) has pointed out that lack of sexual arousal in women can often be traced to early "formative encounters with insensitive men who provided crudeness and vulgarity in place of tenderness and consideration" (p. 144).

Certain kinds of experience in early childhood may also inhibit sexual excitement in women. For example, the young girl may misinterpret scenes of sexual relations between her parents, perceiving cries of passion as evidence of harm being done to the mother. Indeed, the father may actually be brutal, causing obvious distress to the mother. Thus, the child may experience negative modeling of sexual relations that contribute to distorted notions of sexual activity. In turn, parental warnings about sex as a duty may reinforce these notions. Thus, although she may later experience periods of desire, her fears of being hurt may prevent their fulfillment.

Sexual Arousal Disorder in Men

The central physiological characteristic of sexual arousal disorders in men is the complete or partial failure to have an erection or to maintain it until completion of the sexual act. This problem is commonly known as *impotence*, a term used in both clinical and popular writings. The label is inappropriate, since it implies a general lack of sexual potency. In spite of their particular difficulty, so-called impotent men may have strong sexual desires. Thus, **erectile disorder** is a more accurate diagnostic term (American Psychiatric Association, 1987, p. 294).

In most cultures, male self-esteem is equated with the ability to maintain an erection during sexual activity. Failure to do so may well be one of the most humiliating sexual dysfunctions that men experience. Consider how this man perceived his problem of erectile failure when his therapist asked him what he wanted to gain from therapy: "I want to feel like a whole man again. If I could just function normally at least some of the time

when I'm with a woman, that would do it. . . . I'm not going to feel good about myself until I can get a good hard-on and use it. I feel so useless when that thing just hangs limp between my legs" (Zilbergeld, 1978, p. 239). Social pressure to be sexually powerful is much greater for men than for women, and women do not perceive a lack of sexual arousal to be as debasing as men do (Tollison & Adams, 1979, p. 136).

Traditional psychoanalytic views of erectile disorder emphasize the influence of traumatic childhood experiences, especially those associated with the Oedipus complex (see Chapter 3). If the Oedipus conflict is not resolved, a man may unconsciously associate his sexual excitement with childhood feelings of guilt and the fear of being castrated for his incestuous desires. His failure to achieve an erection becomes a defense against the anxiety of making himself vulnerable to castration — that is, exposing his penis to danger by inserting it into the vagina (Fenichel, 1945, p. 170).

Behavioral explanations of erectile dysfunction also cite the importance of anxiety. However, they emphasize that the anxiety results from the man's excessive concern with how well he will perform sexually rather than from childhood feelings of guilt and fear of punishment for sexual desires. Performance anxiety may be learned in a variety of ways. For example, it may arise from a series of failures to become adequately aroused because of stressful environmental circumstances surrounding the sexual activity. Where the stress is especially intense, a single failure may be sufficient to initiate erectile dysfunction. As anxiety about the ability to achieve an erection increases, the man often begins to monitor his performance constantly, becoming a spectator rather than a spontaneous participant in the sexual activity (Masters, Johnson, & Kolodny, 1983, p. 464). In addition, his sex partner's criticism of his inadequacy may reinforce his concern about his performance. As a result he may develop an even deeper conviction of his inferiority.

Another problem sometimes related to erectile dysfunction is the concern some men have that their penis is too small to give their sex partner adequate pleasure. The myth that a large penis is more likely to impart sexual pleasure than a relatively small one reflects the importance men generally ascribe to sexual power. In fact, however, the size of a penis is irrelevant to the giving and receiving of sexual excitement. The vagina is a muscular organ that can accommodate a wide range of penis sizes. Furthermore, there is only a moderate relationship between the size of the penis when flaccid and its size when erect (Karafin, 1982; Rowan, 1982).

Inhibited Female Orgasm

The central feature of **inhibited female orgasm** is the persistent absence or delay of orgasm following a normal phase of sexual excitement (American Psychiatric Association, 1987, p. 294). The orgasmic threshold is distributed along a continuum, ranging from ease in experiencing orgasm with a minimum of stimulation to complete failure to have an orgasm under any circumstance. The following list illustrates the nature of the continuum. Clinicians who practice sex therapy generally agree that the first three items represent normal variations of the female sexual response and the last two indicate abnormal response patterns that warrant professional treatment (Kaplan, 1983, pp. 203–203).

1. At one extreme are those few women who can experience an orgasm without coitus or any other physical contact with the clitoral area. For example, erotic fantasies, kissing, or stimulation of the breasts may be sufficient.

2. The next segment on the continuum includes women who are able to have an orgasm through coitus without direct clitoral stimulation. Vaginal contact seems to be the central focus of their excitement. Perhaps 20 to 30 percent of women fit this part of the continuum.

3. Next on the continuum, and more frequent, are those women who can reach orgasm during coitus but only if it involves some form of clitoral stimulation, direct or indirect. In some instances the clitoral stimulation that triggers the orgasm may occur shortly after coitus is concluded.

4. The next segment of the distribution includes women who are unable to climax in the presence of a partner. However, they can stimulate themselves to orgasm when they are alone, especially with the aid of erotic fantasies.

5. The last segment of the continuum includes women who cannot have an orgasm under any condition. A common clinical label for such inability is **primary orgasmic dysfunction.** Recent estimates suggest that from 7 to 10 percent of women in the United States fall into this segment of the orgasmic continuum (Andersen, 1983). However, as we indicate in the following discussion, more recent criteria of orgasmic dysfunction suggest that this estimate should be as low as 1 percent (Wakefield, 1987).

Recurrent and persistent absence of orgasm does not in itself mean that the woman suffers from a sexual dysfunction. As indicated earlier, the diagnosis of inhibited orgasm is made only if orgasm is not achieved after a normal phase of sexual arousal. The diagnosis is not appropriate if the excitement was inadequate in focus, intensity, or duration (American Psychiatric Association, 1987, p. 294). This inadequacy may occur for a number of reasons. Especially important is the possibility that the woman's sex partner is not stimulating her properly. Some men may not engage in sufficient lovemaking prior to intercourse or may not be aware of the importance of stimulating the clitoral area during coitus and the most effective ways of doing that. Some men are not able to maintain penile intromission long enough for the woman to be adequately stimulated ("Duration of Penile Intromission," 1982). Inadequacy of focus, intensity, or duration of sexual arousal may also be influenced by the attitude of the woman's sex partner toward the significance of orgasm. For example, a man may view the woman's orgasm as essential every time they engage in sexual relations. This psychological pressure may add to the inability of the woman to become sufficiently excited to attain orgasm, especially if the man considers vaginal penetration to be the only way of helping her do so (Bess & Warren, 1982).

It is also important to consider the extent to which the woman's failure to reach orgasm contributes significantly to personal distress or to conflict with her sex partner. For example, erotic feelings and close physical intimacy with a sex partner may be sufficient for some women even though the sexual activity rarely culminates in an orgasm. As long as this pattern is also acceptable to the partner, a diagnosis of inhibited female orgasm is usually not warranted. Furthermore, some women cannot achieve orgasm regularly during coitus, but can do so shortly afterward with clitoral stimulation. This may occur through masturbation or through manual stimulation by the partner. Again, if such a pattern is mutually satisfying, one need not conclude that the woman has a sexual dysfunction.

Inhibited Male Orgasm

The central feature of **inhibited male orgasm** is the recurrent and persistent delay in or absence of ejaculation following an adequate phase of sexual arousal (American Psychiatric Association, 1987, p. 295). This sexual dysfunction has also been called retarded ejaculation (Kaplan, 1983) and ejaculatory incompetence (Masters and Johnson, 1970; Masters, Johnson, & Kolodny, 1986, pp. 467–469). The requirement that a diagnosis of inhibited male orgasm should be made only if the problem follows an adequate phase of sexual excitement is consistent with clinical evidence. This evidence shows that in most instances of retarded ejaculation the man's sexual arousal is not impaired, and he has little or no difficulty in achieving and maintaining an erection (Masters & Johnson, 1970, p. 116; Tollison & Adams, 1979, p. 125). The following case illustrates how the discrepancy between the ability to become sexually aroused and the inability to reach an orgasm during coitus can contribute to interpersonal conflict and distress.

A 33-year-old college professor . . . [complained] that he had never been able to ejaculate while making love. He had no trouble in attaining and maintaining an erection and no difficulties in stimulating his partner to her orgasm, but he could never be stimulated himself to ejaculation and would finally give up in boredom. He had always been able to reach ejaculation by masturbation, which he does twice a week; but he has never been willing to allow a partner to masturbate him to orgasm. . . .

The patient's current relationship is in jeopardy because his [partner] is eager to marry and have children. He has never wanted to have children and is reluctant to become a father, but the pressures from [his lover] have forced him to seek therapy. Throughout the interview his attitude toward the problem is one of distance and disdain. He describes the problem as though he were a neutral observer, with little apparent feeling. (Spitzer, Skodol, Gibbon, & Williams, 1981, p. 48)

Inhibited male orgasm may range from mild delays in ejaculation that happen only in certain stressful situations to the total absence of orgasm under any circumstance. The latter condition is rare, occurring in only 1 or 2 percent of men who seek therapy for problems of sexual dysfunction (Apfelbaum, 1980, p. 284).

Premature Ejaculation

The recurrent and persistent absence of reasonable control of ejaculation during sexual activity is **premature ejaculation.** Although men differ in how they phrase their complaints of premature ejaculation, they usually agree that they lack voluntary control over the ejaculation process and that the lack is contrary to what they want.

Some clinical definitions of premature ejaculation include a specific minimum time that the individual should be able to control the stimulation of his penis before ejaculating. In criticizing such statements, Masters and Johnson offer an alternate definition of *premature ejaculation* that takes into consideration the requirements of the sexual partners rather than arbitrary and fixed minimum periods of time: "the Foundation considers a man a premature ejaculator if he cannot control his ejaculatory process for a sufficient length of time during intravaginal containment to satisfy his partner in at least 50 percent of their coital connections. If the female partner is persistently nonorgasmic for reasons other than rapidity of the man's ejaculatory process, there is no validity to the definition. At least this definition does move away from the 'stopwatch' concept" (Masters & Johnson, 1970, p. 72).

Although this definition does indeed avoid the stopwatch concept, it is still limited. One could argue that the criterion of 50 percent is itself too arbitrary. Furthermore, the definition is confined to intravaginal sexual activity. A man might also become distressed because he cannot control his ejaculation when receiving penis stimulation from his partner orally or manually. Nevertheless, lack of control in that kind of situation is less likely to create conflict with the sex partner than is premature ejaculation during intravaginal activity.

Inability to control ejaculation need not necessarily become a disruptive problem. Some men who ejaculate very rapidly during intravaginal activity may still be able to maintain a satisfactory sexual relationship by bringing their partner to orgasm before inserting the penis or doing so shortly after ejaculating through manual or oral stimulation. How well this pattern succeeds depends a great deal on the partners' mutual acceptance of the situation. In some instances, however, the woman may interpret her partner's rapid ejaculation as disregard for her pleasure and therefore feel rejected and even hostile. This is especially apt to occur if she believes that vaginal penetration is the only right way to achieve orgasm with her partner. Her reaction to frustration may in turn reinforce her partner's belief that he is a sexual failure, thus causing him to feel even more pressure to perform well. Unfortunately, this pressure is likely to hinder rather than to help him (Kaplan, 1983, pp. 221–222).

Psychoanalytic interpretations of premature ejaculation have generally been based on two related hypotheses — that the man's prematurity is an act of hostility designed to punish the woman and that the hostility stems from early fears of castration during the Oedipal period. By ejaculating rapidly and thus depriving his sex partner of pleasure, the man punishes the woman (symbolically the mother) for having created the castration anxiety. Furthermore, by focusing on the premature ejaculation as his sexual problem, he is able to keep out of consciousness the true origins of the problem: fear of castration and hostility toward women (Abraham, 1917/1927; Fenichel, 1945, pp. 69, 173).

In evaluating psychoanalytic theories of premature ejaculation, Helen Singer Kaplan (1974, 1983) agrees that in some instances deep-seated hostility toward women plays an important role. However, it does not necessarily stem from unresolved Oedipus conflicts and castration anxiety. Furthermore, according to Kaplan, hostility is not a constant feature in problems of premature ejaculation. Therefore, "the psychodynamics and relationship system of each patient must be carefully and individually evaluated" (Kaplan, 1983, p. 224).

Early failure to control ejaculation adequately may occur in different individuals under a variety of circumstances. However, the effect could be quite similar, predisposing the individual to anticipate rapid ejaculation in future sexual relationships. Each sexual encounter then becomes infused with anxious self-doubt. Since this performance anxiety may well hasten premature ejaculation, a self-fulfilling prophecy is established, with anxiety over the possibility of future failures helping to ensure their occurrence.

In her therapeutic work with premature ejaculators, Kaplan (1974, 1983) finds that many of her male patients are not adequately aware of the state of their sexual excitement and their level of tension. Thus, they have not learned to control them. They focus obsessively on trying to control their ejaculation; but as their excitement mounts, they remain unaware of the sensory cues of an approaching orgasm. If this focus is coupled with anxiety over their performance, their inability to be in touch with these sensory cues is increased even more.

A number of therapists and researchers who specialize in psychosexual dysfunctions have theorized that some men learn to ejaculate prematurely as the result of early experiences that required rapid completion of sexual activity. The pioneering work of Masters and Johnson (1970) represents a significant contribution to that theory. They found that the early sexual experiences of premature ejaculators tended to have a common theme: the experiences occurred under hurried conditions. Some men had habitually resorted to withdrawal as a contraceptive measure. Masters and Johnson point out that this conditions a rapid ejaculatory response accompanied by the belief that the vagina is to be used only fleetingly as a stimulant for male ejaculatory pleasure (1970, p. 95).

For many older men, Masters and Johnson found a different pattern. Early sexual experiences had often been with prostitutes, who encouraged the men to finish as fast as they could. Although that is a reasonable economic strategy for prostitutes, it could well help condition their clients to develop premature ejaculation.

Dyspareunia

Painful sexual intercourse or coital discomfort is **dyspareunia** (from the Greek *dyspareunos*, meaning "badly mated"). The causes of dyspareunia may be physical, psychosocial, or both. The DSM-III-R criterion for diagnosing this disorder is recurrent or persistent genital pain in a male or female before, during, or after sexual intercourse that is not caused exclusively by lack of lubrication or by vaginal spasms (American Psychiatric Association, 1987, p. 295).

Among the most common physical factors contributing to dyspareunia in women are infections of the vagina and the cervix (the neck of the uterus, which protrudes into the vagina). Atrophic vaginitis is a form of vaginal inflammation that may occur in women with low levels of estrogen, a condition that most often occurs during the postmenopausal period.

Although clinical reports of dyspareunia usually focus on women, it is not as unusual in men as those reports sometimes imply. Physical problems that can contribute to the dyspareunia include a tight, nonretractable foreskin and inflammatory conditions in the genital system (Abarbanel, 1978; Bancroft, 1983, p. 215; Reckler, 1983; Roen, 1983).

Traditional psychoanalytic explanations of coital pain regard it as a symbolic expression of unconscious sexual conflicts. Guilt and ambivalence about sex are converted into pain, which can then be used as defense against engaging in sexual activity.

From a broader perspective, Lazarus (1980, pp. 148–149) considers the psychosocial causes of dyspareunia to fall into three main classes: developmental, traumatic, and relational. Developmental causes involve the individual's early learning experiences, especially within the family. Early feelings of guilt and shame about sex, ingrained religious taboos that create ambivalence and confusion, misinformation about sex that promotes anxiety and fear — these are some of the developmental factors that can contribute to dyspareunia. Among the traumatic factors that can influence the onset of the disorders, especially in women, are sexual assault and painful first attempts at sexual intercourse. Relational factors are fears of being overheard or seen during coitus and similar kinds of situational events. A more central factor, however, is how the sex partners feel about each other. For example, if the relationship is one of hostility and distrust, or lacks meaningful communication, resentment toward a partner may take the form of dyspareunia (Offir, 1982, p. 195).

Vaginismus

In the disorder of **vaginismus,** recurrent and persistent muscular spasms of the outer third of the vagina interfere seriously with coitus. The spasms are involuntary, reflexive reactions to the fear that the vagina may be penetrated. Ordinarily, during arousal, the vaginal muscles and the opening to the vagina relax. In vaginismus, however, the muscles may contract so tightly when coitus is attempted that entry becomes virtually impossible. In some instances, when spasms are less severe, penetration may be accomplished forcibly, but the experience for the woman is very painful. Vaginismus may occur even in

women whose vaginas become lubricated during arousal and who are also able to have orgasm through manual or oral stimulation (Kaplan, 1983, p. 260; Offir, 1982, p. 295).

In the DSM-III-R classification of sexual dysfunctions, a diagnosis of vaginismus requires that the disturbance not be caused exclusively (some clinicians would prefer the word *mainly*) by a physical disorder (American Psychiatric Association, 1987, p. 295). Vaginal spasms may have had their origin in fear of pain associated with such disorders as vaginitis, genital herpes, or surgical injuries. DSM-III-R also stipulates that a diagnosis of functional vaginismus should not be made if the vaginal spasms are a manifestation of another Axis I disorder. For example, the spasms might occur as part of a phobia that involves an irrational fear of any close sexual contact (see Chapter 6).

The diagnosis of functional vaginismus requires not only the patient's own description of her problem, and sometimes related information from her sex partner, but also a thorough pelvic examination. During the examination, attempts at a vaginal exploration often elicit spasms similar to those that occur when the patient's sex partner attempts vaginal penetration. The gynecological examination is also important for determining the extent to which physical disorders may be contributing to the vaginismus (Bancroft, 1983, p. 292; Masters, Johnson, & Kolodny, 1986, pp. 470–471).

Traditional psychoanalytic theory holds that vaginismus is a symbolic expression of unconscious hostility toward men (Fenichel, 1945). The vaginal spasms represent an unconscious wish to castrate men by denying them sexual pleasure. Presumably this wish grows out of the little girl's failure to resolve her penis envy during the phallic phase of psychosexual development (see Chapter 3).

Little evidence has emerged from clinical studies to support the psychoanalytic theory of vaginismus (Tollison & Adams, 1979). This does not mean, however, that anger may not be important in the psychodynamics of vaginismus. Kaplan (1974) has observed that some women with vaginismus show a great deal of hostility toward their husband. This anger need not be interpreted as a reaction to penis envy. It may arise from a variety of negative experiences with men, often during adulthood. Kaplan also points out that some women who seek help for the problem of vaginismus show little hostility toward their sex partners. In fact, they are often relieved and elated when they are able to overcome their dysfunction, have sexual intercourse without fear, and increase their partner's pleasure (p. 416).

A variety of other psychosocial factors can contribute to the development of functional vaginismus — for example, conflict and guilt over sexual pleasure or painful memories of unhappy attempts at sexual intercourse. Highly traumatic experiences, such as sexual assault, may also be central etiological factors (Masters & Johnson, 1970, pp. 256–257).

Psychosocial Treatment of Sexual Dysfunctions

Until the 1970s, medical and mental health professionals treated people for problems of sexual dysfunction as only part of their practice. Since then, sex therapy has become a specialty in its own right (Offir, 1982, p. 277).

As we pointed out earlier, sexual dysfunctions may be caused primarily by organic factors, such as physical disease, by psychological and social factors, or by a combination of these influences. In the following discussion, we focus on approaches to treatment where the sources of the dysfunctions are mainly or exclusively psychosocial.

Psychoanalytic Therapy

Psychoanalytic approaches to the treatment of sexual dysfunctions all share the belief that the symptoms stem from unconscious conflicts and anxieties. To overcome the dysfunction, the individual must understand the nature and origin of those dynamic forces. The sexual difficulty that an individual first presents in therapy is only a sign of deeper problems not yet recognized. By understanding the problems, the individual will be able to overcome the sexual dysfunction itself. Psychoanalytic approaches assume that the unconscious conflicts and anxieties that underlie the dysfunction originated in childhood problems of sexuality. The techniques used in the psychoanalytic treatment of sexual dysfunctions focus on interpreting the patient's free associations and dreams. (See Chapter 19 for a detailed discussion of the goals and methods of psychoanalytic therapy.)

Over the years, various modifications of classical psychoanalytic theory have appeared — for example, those developed by the neo-Freudian and ego psychologists (Chapter 3). These theories tend to focus much more on conflicts and anxieties stemming from current interpersonal relationships than on childhood experiences in the etiology of sexual dysfunctions. Nevertheless, they still assume that the sexual problem an individual presents to the therapist is only a symptom of a more fundamental problem not yet recognized. This view is illustrated in the following remarks of neo-Freudian Harry Stack Sullivan: "See if you can't find something besides the sexual problem in the strangers that come to you for help. Quite frequently it is no trick at all to find something very much more serious than the sexual difficulty; and quite often the sexual difficulty is remedied in the process of dealing with the other problems" (Sullivan, 1953a, p. 296).

Critical reviews of research show little evidence that psychoanalysis, at least in its traditional forms, is an effective and practical way of treating sexual dysfunctions (Goldberg, 1983; Heiman, LoPiccolo, & LoPiccolo, 1981; Hogan, 1978; Kilmann & Auerbach, 1979; Luborsky & Spence, 1978; Reynolds, 1977; Wright, Perrault, & Mathieu, 1977). For one thing, psychoanalytic therapy usually focuses on the reconstruction of personality and character rather than on specific changes in behavior. Thus, even when reports on psychoanalytic treatment of sexual dysfunctions seem to be favorable, it is difficult to know whether the treatment actually alleviated the specific sexual problems themselves. Furthermore, psychoanalysis can be a long and expensive procedure, sometimes lasting for several years. Even in its modified, shorter forms, the treatment may go on for many months. As a result, more practical methods based on experimental studies of learning and cognition have been developed.

Cognitive – Behavioral Approaches

During the 1950s and 1960s, cognitive and behavioral methods of treating sexual dysfunctions became increasingly prominent. These approaches emphasized the nature of the dysfunction itself and the attitudes and thinking that seemed to contribute to it. The concern of cognitive – behavioral approaches was chiefly with present symptoms rather than the remote past. Various direct methods of treatment were developed that many sex therapists still use today. They include reducing anxiety about sex through the use of conditioning and other learning procedures, providing information to help overcome ignorance about sexual matters, helping individuals learn to be more open and assertive about their sexuality, and teaching specific sexual and social skills (Ellis, 1980; Lazarus, 1963; Wolpe, 1969).

Building on the earlier work of cognitive and behavioral therapists, Masters and Johnson (1970) developed techniques that emphasized even more a direct approach to remedying the symptoms of sexual dysfunctions and teaching appropriate sexual behavior. Other sex therapists have amplified their pioneering methods (Bancroft, 1983;

Kaplan, 1974, 1975, 1979, 1983, 1987; L. LoPiccolo, 1980; LoPiccolo & Miller, 1975), and some have combined these direct methods with treatment aimed at helping the person gain insight into the nature of the sexual problems. This insight often involves the dynamics of conflicts and interpersonal relationships whose meaning and significance have not been apparent to the individual (Sollod & Kaplan, 1976).

The work of Helen Singer Kaplan reflects the blending of dynamic and cognitive–behavioral approaches in sex therapy. In comparing the new sex therapy with more traditional modes of psychotherapy, such as psychoanalysis, Kaplan points out that the older approaches consider the reconstruction of personality to be essential even when the sexual problem is highly specific. In contrast, the aim of the new sex therapy, which relies more on direct behavioral–cognitive techniques, is more limited. Nevertheless, it may still at times include attention to internal psychological conflicts, or, in more psychoanalytic language, intrapsychic conflicts.

A number of basic cognitive–behavioral procedures are common to most therapists (Goldberg, 1983; Heiman, LoPiccolo, & LoPiccolo, 1981; Kaplan, 1979, pp. 40–53; Lazarus, 1980; Masters & Johnson, 1970; Redd, Porterfield, & Andersen, 1979, pp. 302–306).

1. Typically, the program of therapy involves a couple rather than a single individual, even if the complaint comes from only one of the sex partners. Thus, the sexual problem becomes a mutual responsibility.

2. In some instances an individual seeking help for a sexual dysfunction may not have a sex partner available at that time, or the partner may not be willing to participate in the treatment. A number of therapy programs have been developed on the basis of techniques of couple-centered sex therapy but modified to lessen the necessity of a partner (Barbach, 1975; Goldberg, 1983; Heinrich & Price, 1977; Lobitz & Baker, 1979; Price, Reynolds, Cohen, Anderson, and Schochet, 1981; Zilbergeld, 1975, 1980).

3. Following the practice established by Masters and Johnson, many sex therapy clinics routinely use cotherapists when working with a heterosexual couple. Usually one therapist is a woman and the other a man. The assumption is that no man can ever fully understand the woman's sexual experience and no woman can fully understand the man's. However, there is no convincing evidence that the procedure is really necessary for successful sex therapy. The use of cotherapists does allow an experienced therapist to teach an inexperienced one various therapy skills. Nevertheless, it is questionable whether the extra cost justifies whatever advantage there may be (LoPiccolo, Heiman, Hogan, & Roberts, 1985; Mehlman, Baucom, & Anderson, 1983; Redd, Porterfield, & Andersen, 1979, p. 303).

4. Attitudes toward sex are discussed. The goal is to modify attitudes that may be hindering sexual relationships. For example, excessive prudishness about sex or the attitude that sex is a necessary evil may be important problems to resolve. Attitudes of hostility or undue dominance may also interfere with sexual feelings and relationships and need to be explored.

5. When appropriate, the therapist guides the couple (or individual) in acquiring helpful information about sexual behavior and feelings through reading, discussion, and direct instruction.

6. Graded exercises are assigned to help overcome problems of sexual performance. Some go on in the therapist's office as well as in the privacy of the couple's home. They include sensate focus, the stop-start and squeeze technique, and directed masturbation.

Many sex therapists regard **sensate focus** (pleasuring) as a key exercise in reducing anxiety about sexual contact. The partners learn to caress in the nude and to discover what pleases the other without any immediate expectation or demand to carry the experience to completion, such as engaging in coitus or having an orgasm (Kaplan, 1987).

The effectiveness of sensate focus in overcoming psychosexual dysfunctions has been reported mainly in clinical studies that did not involve comparisons with other forms of treatment (Andersen, 1983). Nevertheless, the findings have been impressive. For example, Masters and Johnson (1970) found an overall success rate of 82 percent for 193 cases of primary orgasmic dysfunction in which the treatment relied strongly on the use of sensate focus. Other therapists have reported similar success with the technique, especially where anxiety concerning sexual performance is a key factor (Andersen, 1983).

It is not clear what specific mechanisms contribute to the effectiveness of sensate focus. On the basis of clinical observations, Helen Kaplan (1975, p. 33–34) has offered an explanation that combines learning theory with the dynamics of psychological defenses. She points out that sensate focus is a learning experience that reinforces pleasurable behavior and experiences and reduces sexual anxiety because it removes the fear of failure.

The stop–start technique, first developed by James Semans (1956), and the squeeze technique, originated by Masters and Johnson (1970), are used for overcoming premature ejaculation. As a preliminary step, the therapist instructs the couple to practice a number of limited sexual activities, or they may begin with more direct genital stimulation. As soon as the man reaches the point where he feels he must ejaculate he tells his partner, who then applies the stop–start or the squeeze technique.

In the **start–stop technique,** the woman halts all contact with her partner's genitals until his urge to ejaculate diminishes. She then resumes stimulation. Gradually, the number of stops required to delay ejaculation decreases as the man acquires the ability to be stimulated for longer periods of time without ejaculating.

In the **squeeze technique,** as soon as the man signals that he has the urge to ejaculate, the woman squeezes his penis firmly for about 3 to 4 seconds. She then releases the pressure and waits for 15 to 30 seconds before stimulating the penis again. When her partner again indicates he is ready to ejaculate, she repeats the procedure. A recent variation of this technique is the basilar squeeze (Masters, Johnson, & Kolodny, 1986, p. 493). In this method, the squeeze is applied at the base of the penis by either the man or the woman while the penis is inside the vagina. Ordinarily the basilar squeeze is used after the man has improved his ejaculatory control through the earlier technique. The couple goes through these exercises three to four times during a session before permitting ejaculation to take place. With succeeding sessions, the man's ability to control ejaculation for longer periods of time increases (Heiman, LoPiccolo, & LoPiccolo, 1981, pp. 613–614; Jacobson & Bussod, 1983, p. 622).

Directed masturbation is a relatively recent innovation in the treatment of such dysfunctions as inhibited sexual excitement and chronic failure to experience orgasm (Andersen, 1983; Heiman, LoPiccolo, & LoPiccolo, 1976; LoPiccolo & Stock, 1986). It has been especially successful for women who have never had an orgasm (primary orgasmic dysfunction).

Andersen (1983) has reviewed a wide range of reports from 15 therapists on the use of directed masturbation for 150 women. She concluded that it is an effective method for helping such women learn to achieve orgasms and suggested a number of reasons for its success. First of all, it is more likely to produce orgasm than is coital activity. Over 30 years ago, Kinsey and his co-workers (1953/1965) found that the average woman could achieve orgasm about 95 percent of the time during masturbation but only 75 percent of the time during intercourse. Furthermore, in directed masturbation, the nature and intensity of the stimulation is completely under the woman's control. Thus, she can learn to focus on her own physical sensations and sexual feelings apart from any anxiety about succeeding with a partner. As her ability to reach an orgasm on her own increases, it becomes more likely that she can learn to do so with a sex partner.

Summary

1. Homosexuality is no longer listed in the DSM classification as a specific mental disorder. In 1980, the former diagnosis of sexual orientation disturbance was replaced with ego-dystonic homosexuality, a term reserved for homosexuals who experienced a great deal of personal conflict and distress. That diagnosis was dropped in the 1987 edition, DSM-III-R. However, problems of homosexuality can still be referred to under the broad diagnostic category "sexual disorder not otherwise specified." That label allows clinicians to note when individuals experience marked distress because of their sexual orientation.

2. From a psychosocial perspective, homosexuality is a life-style that some people follow in an adaptive manner. For others, however, this style may create distressing conflicts and maladaptive ways of coping with them.

3. Data derived from the Kinsey surveys revealed many important facts about homosexuality. Homosexual behavior is part of a continuum of sexual behavior ranging from entirely homosexual to entirely heterosexual. In addition, female homosexuals are less promiscuous than male homosexuals.

4. Various theories have attempted to establish a biological basis for homosexuality. Chief among the factors investigated are hormonal imbalances and heredity. Critical analyses of these studies suggest that abnormal hormonal development during the prenatal period, in conjunction with psychosocial influences, may possibly facilitate the acquiring of a homosexual orientation.

5. Psychoanalytic views of homosexuality emphasize that it stems from failure, during the Oedipal or Electra phase of psychosexual development, to identity with the parent of the same sex. Although some evidence seems to support that theory, this failure in identification is not necessarily the sole or even the paramount factor. Other early experiences must also be considered. Children may become alienated from their same-sex peer groups, or they may be punished when they engage in heterosexual activity while homosexual activity goes unsuspected.

6. A significant segment of the general public holds negative attitudes toward homosexuality. The AIDS epidemic has helped aggravate those feelings. Especially when they result in discrimination, such attitudes can increase the conflict and distress of homosexuals. During the last decade, attitudes toward homosexuality have moved in a more positive and open direction, and in some instances a less discriminating one.

7. Maintaining a homosexual way of life without undue stress or other serious psychological problems depends to a great extent on the absence of negative public attitudes. When such attitudes are present, one can expect conflict, self-doubt, and other psychological problems to continue among individuals choosing a homosexual way of life.

8. The use of psychotherapy to help homosexuals resolve their conflicts or change their orientation is a highly controversial issue. One extreme position is that psychotherapy should be carried out only when the homosexual wants to become

heterosexual. The opposite position holds that psychotherapy should not attempt to change homosexuals in a heterosexual direction but rather should help them accept in a more adaptive manner their present homosexual preference. A more flexible position is that homosexuals who come for psychotherapy should be left to choose their own goals with respect to their sexual orientation. This may involve changing to heterosexuality or developing an acceptance of their homosexuality.

9. Sexual dysfunctions involve conflict and distress caused by disturbances in the psychophysiological changes that normally occur during the sexual response cycle. This cycle includes sexual desire, excitement (arousal), plateau (a continuation of arousal), orgasm, and resolution (a general sense of relaxation, relief of muscular tension, and well-being). These phases of the sexual response cycle were investigated in the pioneering research of Masters and Johnson and Helen Kaplan.

10. DSM-III-R classifies sexual dysfunctions according to the stage in the sexual response cycle where the dysfunction occurs. These dysfunctions include sexual desire disorder (in males it is called erectile disorder), inhibited male and female orgasm, premature ejaculation, dyspareunia (genital pain associated with intercourse, and vaginismus (recurrent and involuntary vaginal spasms that interfere with intercourse).

11. A diagnosis of sexual dysfunction implies that psychosocial factors play a central role in the etiology of the disorder. Therefore the diagnosis should not be used if the sexual disturbance is caused exclusively by organic factors such as physical disease, medications, and excessive use of recreational drugs. In some cases, organic factors may account partly for the problem, but psychosocial factors are also highly influential.

12. Until the 1970s, most professionals who treated people with problems of sexual dysfunction did so as only part of their practice. Today sex therapy has become a specialty in its own right.

13. Psychoanalytic treatment of sexual dysfunctions assumes that the sexual difficulty the patient describes is only a sign of deeper problems. A central goal of the therapy is to help the person gain insight into those problems. By doing so the individual will be able to remedy the sexual dysfunction itself.

14. Modifiers of psychoanalysis, such as the neo-Freudians, tend to focus more on current conflicts and anxieties that could be contributing to the sexual dysfunction. Nevertheless, they retain the assumption that the dysfunction is a symptom of some deeper problem that must be solved first.

15. Critical reviews of research reveal little evidence that psychoanalysis, at least in its traditional form, is an effective and practical way of treating sexual dysfunctions. Even when it produces positive results, the process is usually lengthy and expensive.

16. Cognitive–behavioral therapy, which attacks problems of sexual dysfunction more directly than psychodynamic approaches, also appears to be more effective. This therapy often combines a direct approach to changing behavior and ways of thinking with helping the individual achieve insight into the nature and causes of the disorder. These attempts may or may not assume that unconscious motivation is involved. In any case, modern cognitive–behavioral methods often find a blend of insight-oriented therapy and direct behavioral techniques to be especially effective.

17. Among the cognitive–behavioral techniques are graded exercises designed to sensitize the individuals to the problems of dysfunction they experience and to gradually improve their sexual performance. These exercises include such methods as sensate focus and directed masturbation.

10

Disorders of Mood

There is not a string attuned to mirth
But has its chord in melancholy.

THOMAS HOOD
Ode to Melancholy **(1827)**

ABC, a professional man in his mid-30's, was admitted to the hospital in a state of excitement and hyperactivity. . . . This was his fifth manic illness in 20 years. It had been preceded by a period of some concern over his relatively unsuccessful practice, but he had not manifested any marked degree of worry or depression.

On this admission to the hospital he was examined by the female doctor serving as admitting officer that day. When he was prepared for the physical examination, his gown was removed and a sheet placed over the lower part of his body. He immediately discarded the sheet, looked at the physician in a sly way, and asked whether it disturbed her to examine him in the nude. . . . He was irritable, sarcastic, and boastful. As the doctor was leaving the room, he asked, "What did you say your name is?" She replied, "Dr. D." He asked three more times and each time she said, "D." He then said, "I hope you get the significance and moral of this story. Freud just sent me a message about this. When I was in professional school, one of the professors taught me at least one thing — when someone asks your name, reply "John Jones," not Mr. Jones." What is your name?" She replied "D" once more and left. (Freedman, Kaplan, & Sadock, 1976, pp. 500–501)

Mary Preston was . . . hospitalized because of an overwhelming . . . depression. She expressed the belief that all her efforts were futile and there was no purpose in living. . . . Mrs. Preston complained that she had difficulty sleeping, she usually woke up early in the morning and then could not fall back asleep again. She also stated that she has been extremely upset and confused over the past few months and she wrung her hands and cried as she related this information to the interviewer. (Leon, 1974, p. 278)

In this chapter we consider the disturbances that are classified in DSM-III-R under the broad category of **mood disorders** (American Psychiatric Association, 1987, p. 213). They may range from abnormal excitement and elation, as in the case of ABC, to the kind of maladaptive depression that Mary Preston experienced.

Disorders of mood are also known as *affective disorders*. The term *affective* comes from the psychological concept of affect, meaning the feeling tone (mood) of an emotion apart from its other components: physiological changes, thinking, and overt behavior. However, the separation is arbitrary, since mood is inevitably reflected in those other components, just as they, in turn, influence mood. Thus, the study of affective disorders deals not only with disturbances of mood but also with the maladaptive changes in bodily processes, thinking, and overt behavior that accompany those moods.

As classified in DSM-III-R, mood disorders do not include affective abnormalities resulting primarily from such physical illnesses as deterioration of brain tissue, traumatic injuries, or infections. Nor do they include abnormal shifts in mood caused mainly by medications or other drugs — for example, alcohol and narcotics. This does not mean, however, that abnormal biochemical processes may not be important in the development of mood disorders. There is growing evidence that in addition to psychological and sociocultural influences, biochemical imbalances in the brain can be significant factors.

In recent years the popular media as well as mental health researchers and practitioners have paid increasing attention to mood disorders, especially depression (Holden, 1986a, 1986b; Morris, 1986). In commenting on this trend, psychiatrist Gerald Klerman suggests that just as the decades before World War II were called the age of anxiety, so a new age of melancholia may have emerged. Ecological destruction, the ever-present spectre of nuclear war, the growing discrepancy between expectations and fulfillment — all of these play a role in the growing attention to depression. In addition, there is a more understanding and accepting attitude toward people who suffer from mood disorders (Klerman, 1980, p. 1305).

Historical Background

Even in ancient days it was known that some people suffered from recurring attacks of incapacitating depression or from sudden changes in mood dominated by abnormal excitement, unrealistic optimism, or superficial feelings of well-being — in today's clinical language, manic episodes. For the most part, evidence of such disorders comes from written records, but some ancient works of art depict various human disturbances that today we would probably call mood disorders (see Box 10.1).

Biblical Sources

One of the earliest accounts of mood disorders occurs in the biblical story of King Saul, who apparently had periodic episodes of deep depression. We are told that Saul's servants sought a "cunning player on a harp" to drive out Saul's "evil spirit." As the story goes, whenever the evil spirit (depression) visited Saul, the shepherd David played on his harp and Saul became refreshed and well (1 Sam. 16; King James Version).

Evidently, Saul suffered from a bipolar mood disorder, for attacks of abnormal excitement often followed his depression. During one of those periods of excitement he even tried to kill David, whose music had been so successful in bringing him out of depression. Saul eventually committed suicide while in a state of depression (Whitwell, 1936).

Greek and Roman Era

Hippocrates (ca. 460–377 B.C.) was so impressed by the frequency with which abnormal excitement and depression occurred that he classified all mental disorders into three groups: mania (abnormal excitement), melancholia (abnormal depression), and phrenitis, which corresponds roughly to modern concepts of schizophrenic disorders (which we will discuss in Chapter 11). His earliest writings, *Prognostics* and *Predictions*, were based on complaints of illness inscribed on the walls of Aesculapian temples — special places of healing dedicated to the Greek god of medicine, Aesculapius. These writings, together with some of Hippocrates's later works, bear a remarkable resemblance to some modern clinical observations of mental disorders (Lewis, 1934; Zilboorg & Henry, 1941).

Hippocrates believed that melancholia stemmed from an overabundance of black bile flowing to the brain and that mania was caused by a predominance of heat and dampness

BOX 10.1 Depression as Revealed
by Pre-Columbian Art

Ceramic and stone figures from the pre-Columbian cultures of Mexico suggest that depressive disorders were definitely known. Psychiatrists Juan Ramon de la Fuente and Donato Alarcon-Segovia (1980) have selected 150 figures that they believe represent various forms of physical illness and pathological states of mind. These pieces are housed in the Museo Nacional de Antropologia and in private collections in Mexico. The three figures reproduced here illustrate signs of serious depression. Figure a, from the shaft–tomb cultures of Western Mexico (100 B.C.–A.D. 250), represents an example of postpartum depression, a dejected state following childbirth. The figure is distinguished by the appearance of great sadness and an expression of hopelessness. Figure b, from the late classical period of Mayan culture (A.D. 600–900), depicts an old woman biting her fingers. De la Fuente and Alarcon-Segovia interpret this piece as portraying a state of agitated depression. Figure c is from the late classical Gulf Coast culture of central Veracruz (A.D. 550–950). It shows an elderly man whose bland expression, dropping lip, lowered glance, and presumed silence are interpreted by de la Fuente and Alarcon-Segovia as revealing signs of deep melancholy.

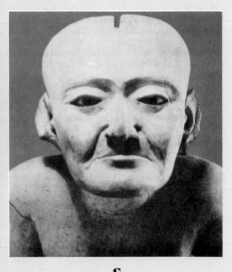

a   b   c

Source: de la Fuente & Alarcon-Segovia, 1980, pp. 1095–1098.

in the brain. Especially violent episodes of mania, which he called *furor*, resulted from an excess of normal blood arriving at the brain, producing a state similar to alcoholic intoxication (Whitwell, 1936). In spite of his erroneous explanations, Hippocrates anticipated modern biochemical theories of manic and depressive episodes by focusing on the importance of brain functions.

During the first and second centuries, a number of Roman physicians became increasingly aware that abnormal excitement (mania) might be related to abnormal depression (melancholia). The most outstanding of these physicians was Aretaeus of Cappadocia (A.D. 120–180), who proposed that mania and melancholia were the expression of a single illness. Melancholia, he said, was the forerunner of mania. With remarkable insight for this time, Aretaeus qualified his views by observing that "mania . . . is not always . . . the offspring of melancholy . . . since it often begins originally without any presenting melancholy" (Zilboorg & Henry, 1941, p. 74). The idea that mania and depression are related, and that one could follow the other, eventually became established in modern psychiatry with the concept of manic–depressive psychosis, and most recently, the concept of bipolar disorders (American Psychiatric Association, 1987, p. 225.)

The belief that mania and melancholia can alternate in the same individual was elaborated some centuries later by the Roman physician Alexander Trallianus (525–605), who described various symptoms in detail. For example, he described the plight of a woman who in her manic state believed that her middle finger held the entire world in her power. However, she then became very depressed, said Trallianus, because she feared that if she bent her finger the whole world would be destroyed (Whitwell, 1936).

Later Writings

During the 17th century, the French physician Théophile Bonet (1620–1689) reiterated the ancient idea that mania and melancholia were part of a single disorder. He called it manic-depressive insanity. Eventually, that label was adopted by Emil Kraepelin (1855–1926), the eminent German psychiatrist whose synthesis of diagnostic systems has had a lasting influence on the classification of mental disorders (see Chapter 2). Kraepelin's use of the term *manic–depressive insanity* first appeared in the sixth edition (1899) of his *Textbook of Psychiatry* (translated by Defendorf, 1902). In the following years, Kraepelin became firmly committed to the belief that manic–depressive insanity was a single disease process with many complex variations (Kraepelin, 1915/1923, 1921/1977).

Modern scientific evidence does not support the theory that manic and depressive disturbances always reflect a single disorder. However, the now well-established fact that some individuals undergo both manic and depressive episodes (bipolar disorders) was anticipated in the ideas of earlier centuries.

Classification and Patterns of Mood Disorders

DSM-III-R classifies mood disorders into two broad categories: bipolar disorders and depressive disorders. Each of these categories is further classified into more specific syndromes (American Psychiatric Association, 1987, pp. 213–214).

Bipolar disorders include four distinct patterns: mixed, manic, depressed, and cyclothymia. **Bipolar disorder, mixed,** refers to syndromes in which manic and major depressive episodes are intermingled or alternate rapidly every few days. **Bipolar disorder, manic,** applies to the syndrome in which individuals currently are experiencing only a manic episode. **Bipolar disorder, depressed,** includes the syndrome of individuals who are undergoing a major depressive episode and who in the past have experienced one of more manic episodes. Most people experiencing a manic episode eventually have one or more major depressive episodes. **Cyclothymia** refers to mood disturbances involving numerous periods of depression and maniclike behavior (hypomania) that are considerably less severe and that do not last as long as full-fledged manic and major depressive episodes.

Depressive disorders are disorders of people who have experienced one or more major depressive episodes but who have no history of manic syndromes. Some clinicians refer to these disorders as unipolar depression. There are three diagnostic subcategories of depressive disorders. **Major depression, single episode,** is the disorder of individuals who are undergoing a major depressive episode for the first time. **Major depression, recurrent,** is the disorder of those who previously have had one or more major depressive episodes. **Dysthymia** is a chronic disturbance whose central feature is periods of depressed mood. It is considerably less severe than major depression and its episodes are of shorter duration.

Manic and Major Depressive Episodes

Manic and major depressive episodes may involve relatively moderate personal and social impairment, or they may involve experiences and behavior that reveal gross departures from reality and thus are psychotic. The inflated feelings of self-esteem that typically occur during a manic episode may for some individuals be a matter of uncritical self-confidence that results in reckless decisions. In other instances, however, inflated feelings of self-worth may assume delusional proportions. An individual may claim to have a special relationship with some famous person (or even a deity) that will ensure success in all ventures. In a similar manner, the mood in a major depressive episode may vary from moderate feelings of sadness and hopelessness to a point where the individual wants to commit suicide because of a deep conviction of utter unworthiness. This irrational feeling of despair may be combined with unjustified suspicions and self-accusations, such as the delusion that one is being persecuted because of having committed some great sin.

"EVER HAVE ONE OF THOSE GREAT DAYS WHEN YOU'RE JUST BETWEEN MANIC AND DEPRESSIVE?"

Major depressive episodes may range from relatively moderate personal and social impairment to extreme sadness, hopelessness, and withdrawal from others, as in the case of this young woman.

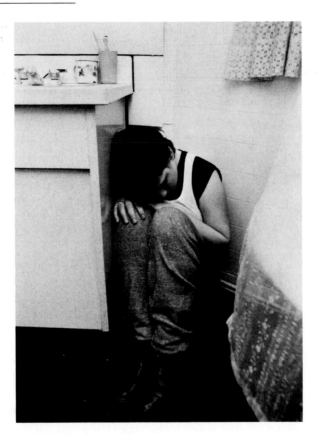

Patterns of Manic Episodes

Typically, people undergoing a manic episode display inappropriate and uncontrollable states of elation and expansiveness (euphoria), often accompanied by an extreme acceleration of motor and verbal behavior. For example, manic individuals often become unusually loud and boisterous. They may talk incessantly, sometimes to the point where their speech is highly irrelevant and even incoherent. They frequently are unable to concentrate on one subject for a reasonable length of time and shift rapidly from one topic to another. Their hyperactivity is usually accompanied by a decreased need for sleep. In extreme instances, they may go for several days without sleep, showing no signs of fatigue and continuing to express unrealistic feelings of well-being (Cancro, 1985, p. 767).

The tremendous energy that can be expended during a manic episode is well illustrated in the following excerpt from *A Mind That Found Itself*, the autobiography of Clifford Beers, who was hospitalized because of recurring manic and depressive episodes. After his recovery, Beers founded the National Committee for Mental Hygiene, now called the Mental Health Association.

During the latter part of that first week I wrote many letters, so many, indeed, that I soon exhausted a liberal supply of stationery. . . . It was now at my own suggestion that the supervisor gave me large sheets of manila wrapping paper. These I proceeded to cut into strips a foot wide. One such strip, four feet long, would suffice for a mere *billet-doux*; but a real letter usually required several such strips pasted together. More than once letters twenty or thirty feet long were written; and on one occasion the accumulation of two or three days of excessive productivity, when spread upon the floor, reached from one end of the corridor to the other — a distance of about one hundred feet. My hourly output was something like twelve feet, with an average of one hundred and fifty words to the foot. Despite my speed my letters were not incoherent. They were simply digressive, which was to be expected, as elation befogs one's "goal idea." (Beers, 1908/1937, pp. 95–96)

Social judgment during a manic episode may become seriously impaired, often leading to indiscreet public behavior. The conventional social and sexual restraints that individuals normally observe may be reduced considerably. People may appear in public outlandishly dressed and wearing unusual makeup. They may approach strangers in the street, distributing food, money, or advice at will. Their great lack of judgment, coupled with an abnormally inflated sense of self-esteem, may extend to such inappropriate acts as suddenly calling friends and acquaintances at all hours of the night, going on buying sprees, and making foolish financial investments.

Not all of these characteristics necessarily pertain to every manic individual. Manic episodes can range from relatively mild levels of disturbance to those that are clearly psychotic. Some individuals grow steadily worse during the course of an episode, especially in its earlier stages or in the absence of therapy. Others maintain a fairly constant level throughout the episode.

As a guide to the symptoms of manic episodes, DSM-III-R includes a detailed set of diagnostic criteria. These criteria are useful not only for purposes of diagnosis but also to help clinicians decide how individuals should be helped. For example, they can serve as a guide for deciding the extent to which drugs or other forms of therapy should be used and whether hospitalization is necessary.

The mean age at which manic episodes first appear is in the early 20s. However, a significant number of new cases appear after age 50 (American Psychiatric Association, 1987, p. 216). The onset is sudden, with manic mood and behavior increasing rapidly within a few days. As a rule, manic episodes also end abruptly, more abruptly than major depressive episodes.

For some persons the duration of a manic episode is only a matter of days; for others an episode may extend over weeks or months. It has been estimated that the uninterrupted natural course of a manic episode averages about two months. However, it is often difficult to know precisely how long the natural course would be, since it is desirable to initiate therapy as early as possible. The use of lithium carbonate to normalize (rather than simply sedate) manic moods and behavior has been highly effective. Such therapy may begin just as soon as the diagnosis is reasonably sure (see Chapter 18 for a detailed discussion of how lithium and other drugs are used to treat manic disorders).

The frequency with which an individual experiences manic episodes is highly variable. Some people have only one episode in their entire lives. Others suffer recurring episodes separated by many years. Still others undergo a cluster of episodes, one following another rather closely (American Psychiatric Association, 1987, p. 229).

As one would expect, the residual effects of manic episodes are likely to be most serious when there have been a number of recurrences, especially at frequent intervals. Such lingering effects may take the form of occasional inability to concentrate adequately, brief but abnormal spells of elation or irritability, and other short-lasting but inappropriate elevations of mood. Although not nearly as impairing as the manic episodes themselves, these aberrations may interfere significantly with the individual's social and personal life. The possibility of such residual damage has important implications for helping those who experience manic episodes. Even if drug therapy rapidly alleviates the symptoms of an episode, other forms of intervention, especially psychotherapy and manipulation of the environment, are necessary. They are important not only for recovery from symptoms but also for posttherapy adjustment and future prevention.

Patterns of Major Depressive Episodes

Normal and abnormal depression are on a continuum, one merging into the other. Although in most instances the extreme ends of the continuum are obvious, where normality ends and abnormality begins is often difficult to determine. To a great extent, such judgment depends not only on skilled clinical observations but also on the criteria of depression used and how they are shaped by the values of a particular society and culture. (See Chapter 4 for a discussion of cultural relativity and abnormality.) Although the following list of differences between normal and abnormal depression is not exhaustive, it can serve as a useful orientation to an understanding of major depression.

1. It is certainly normal for one to mourn the loss of a loved one or to feel depressed about losing an important position or a cherished possession. Indeed, such mourning and depression may often be extremely important for helping one work through a period of loss while forming a bridge from the past to the future. It is appropriate for these feelings to produce a temporary inefficiency in one's daily life and a temporary impairment in one's interaction with other people. Although personal loss may also initiate abnormal depression, the mourning, inefficiency, and impaired interpersonal relations that occur are much more severe and long-lasting. The abnormally depressed person seems to lack the resiliency that one finds in the normally depressed individual (Arieti & Bemporad, 1980, p. 1365; Costin, 1976, p. 9).

2. Prolonged abnormal depression usually occurs in response to events that would ordinarily produce only a brief state of dejection in normal people. This discrepancy is due partially to the fact that the abnormally depressed individual has not learned how to tolerate frustration effectively. Indeed, external events that stimulate inappropriate depression sometimes represent clues to frustration experienced earlier in life that the individual never learned to handle adequately.

3. Conflict, anxiety, and guilt are usually more deeply embedded in abnormal depression. Consider, for example, the paradoxical phenomenon of success depression. An individual may become deeply depressed just after receiving an eagerly sought promotion. The new job and higher social status may now require activities that the individual had previously been anxious about but not faced openly, such as the use of authority, or new forms of interpersonal relationships. The resulting depression could then be a reaction to the possibility of confronting the conflict, and thus suffering even more anxiety and guilt (Berglas, 1986; Miller, Rosellini, & Seligman, 1977).

4. Abnormally depressed individuals are more likely to use their symptoms (not necessarily consciously) to achieve what psychodynamically oriented clinicians call secondary gains. In terms of learning theory, these gains correspond to the reinforcement of symptoms (see Chapter 4). For example, self-abasement, dejection, and withdrawal represent a surrender to frustration and conflict. However, depressed individuals may also use these reactions to gain attention and sympathy and thus some assurance of self-worth. As they succeed in doing so, the symptoms become reinforced.

People who undergo a major depressive episode typically experience a pervasive loss of interest and pleasure in life. Most individuals who are severely depressed feel lonely and unworthy. They usually show a great deal of self-pity, complaining that all the pleasure has gone out of their lives. They often feel discouraged, helpless, and overburdened. They tend to be highly pessimistic about the future. This pattern of depression is illustrated in the following sample statements from a questionnaire administered at a psychiatric clinic (Hunt, Singer, & Cobb, 1967). Depressed individuals who came to the clinic usually agreed with such statements. The labels in parentheses refer to the dimensions of depression that the statements represent: I feel unwanted (social isolation); I feel as though nothing I do is really any good (low self-esteem); I am my own worst enemy (hopelessness); people ask too much of me (burdened). Responses to more recently developed questionnaires have revealed similar patterns of self-perceived depression (Beck, 1978; Beck, Steer, & Garbin, 1988; Zimmerman, Coryell, Corenthal, & Wilson, 1986).

People undergoing depressive episodes may also express their dejected mood through abnormal motor behavior. They may find it hard to move about and speak, or their depression may be coupled with restlessness, so that it becomes difficult for them to sleep. Their facial expression may be extremely sad, reflecting their depressed mood.

At a more extreme level, episodes of depression may involve delusions and hallucinations, especially those concerned with self-accusation and guilt. For example, individuals may be convinced they have committed some terrible crime that cannot (indeed, should not) be forgiven, and they may hear voices that support their false belief. Delusions sometimes involve bizarre notions about bodily changes, such as the belief that one's intestines are disintegrating or that the brain is decaying.

Clearly, then, no single particular symptom is always characteristic of a major depressive episode. As Martin Seligman (1975) has pointed out: "Depressives often feel sad, but sadness need not be present to diagnose depression; if a patient doesn't feel sad, but is verbally and motorically retarded, cries a lot, has lost twenty pounds in the last month, and the onset of symptoms can be traced to his wife's death, then depression is the appropriate diagnosis. Motor retardation also is not necessary, for a depressive can be quite agitated" (pp. 80–81).

Depression in elderly people often stems from or is intensified by some great personal loss, as in the death of a loved one. Such depression may be quite normal.

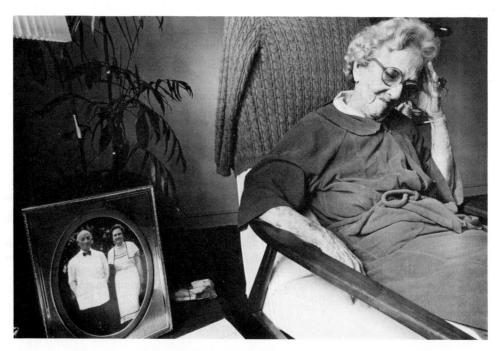

Prevalence and Onset. Studies of adult populations in the United States, England, and continental Europe have estimated that from 18 to 23 percent of women and 8 to 12 percent of men have suffered at least one major depressive episode. For about 6 percent of the women and 3 percent of the men, the attacks were sufficiently severe to require hospitalization. In contrast to manic episodes, which typically begin during young adulthood, major depressive episodes may first occur at almost any age during adulthood, as well as in childhood and adolescence (American Psychiatric Association, 1987, p. 220; Bemporad, 1978; Kovacs, Feinberg, Crouse-Novak, Paulauskas, Pollock, & Feinstein, 1984; Malmquist, 1983; Sturt, Kumakura, & Der, 1984).

Why is major depression more frequent in women than in men? After reviewing various theories and the evidence for them, Susan Nolen-Hoeksema (1987) concluded that depressed men are more likely to engage in a variety of distracting behaviors that tend to counteract their mood. In contrast, women are more likely to amplify their depressed mood by ruminating about its causes. It may well be, as Nolen-Hoeksema suggests, that the former pattern is more adaptive. However, it may also be that women in our society have fewer opportunities than men to engage in the range of distracting activities that can help alleviate a depressed mood.

Rate of Development and Frequency. As in manic episodes, the onset of a major depressive episode is sometimes abrupt, especially if the individual has been subjected to a great deal of psychosocial stress. Often, however, the depression develops gradually over a period of days or even weeks.

Some people experience depressive episodes infrequently, perhaps only a single episode. Others suffer one or more recurrences, separated by many years of normal living. Still others may undergo a cluster of depressive episodes (closely spaced attacks), recover, and then later experience another cluster. In general, the danger of recurring depressive episodes tends to increase with age.

Outcome and Therapy. After recovering from a major depressive episode, some individuals return to about the same level of social and personal functioning as before the attack (American Psychiatric Association, 1987, pp. 228–229). However, vulnerability to future depression may be a significant residual effect, especially if there has been a succession of depressive episodes over a short period of time. Furthermore, as such episodes recur, the likelihood increases that a manic episode will eventually appear, thus signaling the advent of a bipolar disorder. In the usual bipolar pattern, a manic episode appears before a depressive one. However, the possibility that recurrent depressive episodes will lead to the emergence of a bipolar disorder should not be ignored.

Since repeated episodes of depression are likely to increase a person's vulnerability to even more such attacks, it is essential that programs be employed after recovery to help prevent recurrence. Such prophylactic methods may require that psychotherapy continue, that environmental changes be made, and that antidepressant drugs be used for a time.

Age and Depression. Although the central theme of dejection and loss of pleasure in living is typical of major depressive episodes at any age, certain other features are associated more with one age period than another (American Psychiatric Association, 1987, p. 220; Arieti & Bemporad, 1978, pp. 77–82). Depressive episodes during childhood are often connected with separation anxiety. Usually such anxiety is expressed by refusal to attend school and the fear that parents will disappear or suddenly die. (See Chapter 16 for a discussion of separation anxiety and depression in children.) As in the case of adults, abnormal depression during childhood often involves feelings of low

Episodes of depression in
adolescents are often coupled
with the feeling that people don't
understand them, especially
parents.

self-esteem. Illustrative of such feelings are the following statements made by children
during interviews at the National Institute of Mental Health (Yahraes, 1978, p. 1). These
children made high depression scores on scales designed to measure abnormal moods and
related symptoms. "'I am the biggest troublemaker in my family,' said a worried-looking
10-year-old girl. 'I cry a lot and feel weird a lot.' Between spells of crying, a 12-year-old
boy said, 'I think I am the stupidest kid in class. . . . I never really try to kill myself, but
sometimes I think to drown myself.' A dejected 8-year-old girl declared: 'I feel ugly and
like a dumbbell. . . . Sometimes I would like to kill my friends or my own stomach or
arm. . . . Friends make fun of me all the time.'"

Episodes of depression during adolescence are sometimes associated with restlessness,
negative attitudes, and even antisocial behavior. The desire to run away from home is
often coupled with the feeling that no one understands. Adolescents may also reveal their
depression by withdrawing from family life and spending (or wanting to spend) most of
their time alone. This withdrawal may be carried over to school activities. Since major
depressive episodes are apt to breed future ones, especially if prolonged, it is important
for parents and other authority figures in the adolescent's life to pay attention to such
clues of depression and to differentiate them from normal adolescent rebellion and
withdrawal or normal forms of depression. This is no easy task. One general guide is to
observe whether the depression is acted out in relation to parents and other adults only or
toward peers as well. The latter instance is more typical of a major depressive disorder.

As in the case of younger adults, major depressive episodes in elderly people may in large measure stem from or be intensified by some great personal loss — the death of a loved one, the loss of money or other highly prized possession, or forced retirement from a valued position, for example. However, in contrast to the losses of younger people, the kinds of losses that help induce depression in older people tend to be irretrievable. In a sense, their depression may be more appropriate and therefore less abnormal than younger people's depressive reactions to personal losses.

Endogenous versus Exogenous Depression. Practitioners and researchers in psychopathology sometimes distinguish between endogenous and exogenous episodes of depression. The onset of **endogenous depression** is relatively independent of a precipitating life experience. **Exogenous depression** (sometimes called *reactive depression*) is more likely to be precipitated by stressful environmental events and personal experiences.

DSM-III-R does not distinguish between endogenous and exogenous depression. This is consistent with the observations of various clinicians that some episodes of major depression presumed to be exogenous have actually been preceded by stressful experiences (Nelson & Charney, 1981). Clinicians who continue to use the distinction do so mainly as a way of emphasizing different approaches in the treatment of major depressive disorders. Martin Seligman (1975) points out: "In endogenous depressions, mood often cycles with regularity. In reactive depressions, mood is self-limiting, and it is therapeutically important for depressed patients to know their despair will lift if they wait long enough" (1975, p. 88).

In actual clinical practice, it is difficult to make a sharp separation between endogenous and exogenous depression. As Eugene Paykel (1975, p. 67) has concluded: "The consensus of . . . recent studies is that, while predominantly unprecipitated depressions do occur, they are related only weakly to any particular symptom patterns of clinical classification. Moreover, the separation between unprecipitated and precipitated depression is not clear cut. One grades into the other without any clear cut-off point."

Cross-cultural Differences in Depression. Some years ago, a number of anthropological studies concluded that the frequency of depressive disorders varies from culture to culture. Observers of East African societies reported that, in contrast to Western cultures, depression seemed to be relatively rare, although manic disorders were quite common (Mendels, 1970). The difference was ascribed to the strong protection that African culture offered against depression — including open expressions of mourning, the extended family with its network of group support, and a tribal superego that reduced the burden of individual guilt. Strong family ties and an emphasis on the group as opposed to the individual may also help explain why the frequency of depression in Japan is far less than in Western countries, especially among people over 65 (Hasegawa, 1985).

In a comprehensive and critical review of cross-cultural research, Anthony Marsella (1980) came to a number of general conclusions that summarize cultural similarities and differences in depressive disorders.

1. Apparently there is no universal conception of depression. Many non-Western cultures have concepts of depression that differ very much from those held by Western mental health professionals. Nevertheless, certain characteristics of depressive disorders in non-Western cultures resemble those in Western societies, although they may not be perceived in those cultures as depression.

2. Methodological limitations in gathering cross-cultural data make it difficult to arrive at firm conclusions concerning differences in the epidemiology (rate of distribution) of depressive disorders around the world. Within those limitations, however, it does seem that depression is less common in non-Western cultures. Even when it does appear in non-Western societies, it is often manifested quite differently.

3. The more Westernized a culture tends to be, the more one finds both somatic (bodily) and psychological components of depression.

4. Manifestations of depression in non-Western societies seem to involve less expression of guilt and self-abasement. This lack is consistent with the observation that attempts at suicide and suicidal wishes are relatively rare.

Bipolar Disorders

As we stated earlier in our discussion of the DSM-III-R classification of mood disorders, bipolar disorders may take a number of directions. Symptoms of manic and major depressive episodes may be intermingled or alternate rapidly every few days (bipolar disorder, mixed). The current disturbance may also consist only of manic symptoms, with or without a history of previous manic or depressive episodes (bipolar disorder, manic). An individual may be currently undergoing a major depressive episode, having experienced sometime in the past one or more manic episodes (bipolar disorder, depressed).

Although people may experience manic episodes without ever having a major depressive episode, most manic individuals eventually do undergo at least one depressive episode (Weissman & Boyd, 1985, p. 764). The change from a manic episode to depression, or vice versa, may take place gradually over a number of days, with a normal period intervening. However, the switching process can also occur much more rapidly, within hours or even minutes, and with little or no normal transition (American Psychiatric Association, 1987, p. 216). The dramatic way in which this switching can take place is illustrated in the following description of a woman who changed with astonishing rapidity from severe depression to highly disruptive manic behavior.

> For 4 months Mrs. S. had spent most of her time lying in bed. . . . She expresses many feelings of hopelessness and worthlessness and has difficulty concentrating. . . . Suddenly, one day, her mood seems to be remarkably better. She is pleasant, verbalizes more, and appears somewhat cheerful. The following evening, however, she goes to sleep and wakes up at 2:45 am. The rate of her speech is increased, she is moving rapidly, and over a matter of a few hours she develops paranoid thinking, becomes provocative, shows a flight of ideas, is intrusive and into everyone's activities. Over a couple of days this activity increases to the point where she is psychotic, unable to control her actions, and attempts to break the furniture. (Krasner & Isenstein, 1977, p. 1)

Bipolar disorders occur in about 1 percent of the adult population of the United States. In contrast, the prevalence of major depression ranges from 10 to 15 percent. Furthermore, epidemiological studies in the United States have found that the frequency of bipolar disorders is approximately the same for women as for men, whereas major depression is more common in women (American Psychiatric Association, 1987, p. 225; Rush & Fulton, 1982, p. 431). It is not clear why there are gender differences in the frequency of major depression but not of bipolar disorders. One reason may be that bipolar disorders are more subject to biological influences, whereas major depression reflects a greater degree of social and cultural influence, and this affects women and men differently.

Cyclothymia and Dysthymia

Less severe than manic and major depressive episodes, but nevertheless quite distressing, are the patterns of abnormal mood that DSM-III-R classifies as cyclothymia and dysthymia. Their symptoms parallel to some extent those found in manic and major depressive episodes, but as a whole they are considerably less disruptive. For example, they do not involve psychotic perceptions and thinking, such as the hallucinations and delusions that may occur in bipolar and major depressive disorders.

Cyclothymia

The central feature of cyclothymia is a chronic disturbance in mood that lasts at least two years. It involves numerous periods of depression and hypomania, but they are not of sufficient severity and duration to meet the criteria for a major depressive or manic episode (American Psychiatric Association, 1987, pp. 226–228). The term **hypomania** (below mania) is used to indicate abnormalities of mood and behavior that fall somewhere between normal elation and the extreme euphoria found in full-fledged manic episodes. Depressive and hypomanic periods may be separated by intervals of normal mood and behavior lasting for months at a time. Symptoms may be intermixed or alternate rapidly.

Depressive periods are characterized by a mood of general dejection and a loss of interest or pleasure in everyday activities. During hypomanic periods the mood is abnormally elevated and expansive. The following symptoms show the contrast in more detail. Not every depressive or hypomanic symptom listed would necessarily occur in every person.

Depressive Periods	**Hypomanic Periods**
Inability to sleep or abnormally prolonged sleep	Decreased need for sleep
Feelings of inadequacy (low self-esteem)	Inflated self-esteem
Chronic fatigue or other signs of low energy	More energetic than usual
Diminished productivity or effectiveness	Increased productivity, unusual and self-imposed work hours
Inability to concentrate or think clearly	Increase in creative thinking
Withdrawal from social life	Extreme gregariousness
Loss of interest in sexual activity	Unusual increase in sexual activity, without realization of possible negative consequences
Diminished interest in pleasurable activity, feelings of guilt over previous pleasurable activities	Excessive involvement in pleasurable activities without regard for possible negative consequences (e.g., buying sprees)

Dysthymia

Also called depressive neurosis, dysthymia is a chronic depressed mood occurring in people who have no history of a major depressive, manic, or hypomanic episode. The person often talks about feeling low and appears to be sad much of the time. Although the symptoms of dysthymia resemble to some extent those found in major depressive episodes, the periods of depression are much less severe, do not last as long, and in other ways do not meet the criteria of major depressive episodes. For adults, a diagnosis of dysthymic disorder is made only when periods of depression have occurred over a span of at least two years. For children and adolescents, the periods should have appeared during at least one year. Periods of dysthymic depression are often separated by normal moods that last from a few days to a few weeks (American Psychiatric Association, 1987, p. 230).

In some instances, the depressed mood in a dysthymic disorder may not be obvious, since it can be masked by complaints that overshadow it, such as bodily ailments, insomnia, and other symptoms of physical discomfort. Furthermore, a significant number of individuals who have been diagnosed as suffering from a dysthymic disorder may actually be showing the residual effects of a previous major depressive episode that was inadequately recognized or poorly treated (Kielholz, 1973; Klerman, 1980).

As these characteristics indicate, dysthymia is a complex disorder and may take a variety of directions. DSM-III-R classifies the disorder into two subtypes. The primary subtype includes the cases in which the mood disturbance is not related to a preexisting chronic, nonmood, Axis I disorder (for example, anxiety disorder) or to a physical disorder (Axis III). The secondary subtype includes cases where the mood disturbance is related to such conditions. (See Chapter 2 for a discussion of Axis I and Axis III.) In addition, the clinician specifies whether the onset of dysthymia is early (before age 21) or late (after that age) (American Psychiatric Association, 1987, pp. 230, 233; Klein, Taylor, Dickstein, & Harding, 1988, in press).

There are a number of crucial differences between dysthymia and episodes of major depression.

1. The distortions of reality sometimes found in major depressive episodes, such as hallucinations and delusions, are by definition not characteristic of dysthymia. This is one of the main qualitative differences between the two kinds of depression (Lewinsohn, 1975).

2. Major depressive episodes are more severe and reflect a greater degree of helplessness than dysthymia. Thus, the two kinds of depression differ quantitatively.

3. Dysthymia is more often reactive. Typically, it is initiated by environmental events, such as stress, frustration, some personal loss, or a fear of rejection. Although stressful events can also precipitate major depressive episodes, the episodes often occur relatively independently. This observation lends support to the theory that biological disturbances play a more important role in major depressive episodes.

4. Although suicide is always a possibility in all forms of depression, it is less a danger in dysthymia than in major depression. Beck (1970) and his colleagues at the Philadelphia General Hospital found that suicidal wishes were present to a significant extent in some 40 percent of psychotically depressed patients but in only 14 percent of those who were dysthymic.

Despite the significant differences between dysthymia and major depression, recent research has suggested the strong possibility of a genetic link between the two disorders. Increased rates of dysthymia have been found in the relatives of patients diagnosed with a major depressive disorder (Klein, Clark, Dansky, & Margolis, 1988; Klein, Taylor, Dickstein, & Harding, 1988; Rosenthal, Akiskal, Scott-Strauss, Rosenthal, & David, 1981). These data indicate that at least some forms of dysthymia may represent milder manifestations of a genetic predisposition toward major depressive disorder. Similarly, relatives of patients with bipolar mood disorder show increased rates of cyclothymia

(Klein, Depue, & Slater, 1986). Given findings such as these, it is all the more important to treat dysthymia and cyclothymia as early as possible, and thus attempt to reduce the risk of more disabling mood disorders.

Biochemical Factors in Mood Disorders
Biogenic Amines

One of the most active areas of biochemical research on mood disorders, especially manic and major depressive episodes, involves certain organic compounds in the body known as **biogenic amines**. They include two main classes: catecholamines and indoleamines. The most important catecholamines are epinephrine (adrenaline), norepinephrine (noradrenaline), and dopamine. Among the indoleamines, serotonin has been the chief focus of research. **Catecholamines** are derived from the amino acid tyrosine. Although widely distributed in the body, they are produced primarily in the adrenal glands, the brain, and the sympathetic division of the autonomic nervous system.

The creative experiments of Walter Bradford Cannon (1871–1943) and his colleagues at the Harvard Physiological Laboratory foreshadowed the importance of catecholamines for understanding biochemical changes in mood disorders. The researchers found that animals secreted epinephrine whenever they showed signs of anger or fear (Cannon, 1915, 1963). Since Cannon's pioneering work, a great deal of research has demonstrated the important role of epinephrine in human and animal emotion. Epinephrine has a powerful effect on bodily processes controlled by the sympathetic division of the autonomic nervous system. It stimulates contractions of capillaries and arteries, increases blood pressure, stimulates the heart muscle, and accelerates the heart rate. It also hastens the release of glucose into the bloodstream. In short, epinephrine is a potent hormone that gets the body ready for sudden expenditures of energy—a crucial requirement in the arousal of strong, active emotions.

Norepinephrine is similar in biochemical composition to epinephrine. It is produced mainly in the adrenal glands, brain, and nervous system. Because it occurs in the brain in significantly greater amounts than epinephrine (Julien, 1981, pp. 238–239), it has had much more attention in biochemical research on mood disorders.

Serotonin is another name for the biochemical compound 5–hydroxytryptamine (5HT). Page (1954) and his co-workers coined the term *serotonin* for a substance they discovered in the blood that acted as a powerful constrictor of blood vessels. The substance turned out to be 5HT, a derivative of the amino acid tryptophan (Green & Costain, 1979). Serotonin is also present in many other parts of the body besides the bloodstream, including the gastrointestinal tract, the brain, and the autonomic nervous system.

Norepinephrine, dopamine, and serotonin are **neurotransmitters**—substances that transmit electrochemical impulses from one neuron (nerve cell) to another (McGeer & McGeer, 1980). Neurotransmitters are part of an intricate electrochemical network that enables the brain to process changes in the stimulation and response of the nervous system, especially changes that regulate moods and other aspects of emotional experience and behavior. During the last several decades, various lines of inquiry have produced a vast literature on the relationship between neurotransmitters and mood disorders. In the following discussion, we examine the main findings of that research and the strategies that were used to obtain them.

The Catecholamine Hypothesis

The early work of Joseph Schildkraut and his colleagues at the National Institute of Mental Health provided a strong impetus to research on the relationship between biogenic amines and mood disorders (Bunney & Davis, 1965; Schildkraut, 1965, 1969, 1975, 1977; Schildkraut & Kety, 1967). The original **catecholamine hypothesis** was that "some, if not all, depressions are associated with an absolute or relative deficiency of catecholamines, particularly norepinephrine, at functionally significant adrenergic receptor sites in the brain. Elation conversely may be associated with an excess of such amines" (Schildkraut, 1965, p. 509). Adrenergic receptor sites are the nerve fibers in the brain that liberate norepinephrine when they transmit electrochemical impulses from one neuron to another.

A crucial problem with testing the catecholamine hypothesis is that we cannot determine directly the level of amine activity in the living human brain because we obviously cannot remove and examine living brain tissues (Schuyler, 1974). An alternative has been to examine the quantity of amines in the urine to see if it is related to the occurrence of affective disorders. The assumption is that, since some of the amines from the brain will appear in the urine, their presence can be used as an index to the level of amine activity in the brain. A number of studies employing this strategy have found that in bipolar disorders the level of norepinephrine and dopamine in the urine was lower during episodes of depression than after recovery or during manic episodes. Furthermore, in some instances, an abnormal increase in those amines preceded the switch from depressive to manic episodes by just a day (Schildkraut, 1977).

Although these results are consistent with the catecholamine hypothesis, they must be regarded with caution. For one thing, catecholamines in the urine can come from many areas of the body beside the brain. Furthermore, it is difficult for catecholamines in the brain to pass to other areas of the body and be taken up in the urine. Thus, only a very small portion of the urinary amines actually reflects the presence of brain amines (Ciaranello & Patrick, 1977, p. 19). Indeed, Schildkraut (1977) himself concluded that the level of catecholamines in the urine provided only a partial and indirect index of amine activity in the brain.

Metabolites of Biogenic Amines

Another approach to discovering the relationship between biogenic amines and mood disorders is to examine the products that result from the metabolism of amines—the biochemical changes they undergo in maintaining bodily processes. These products of metabolism are called **metabolites**. Some evidence suggests that metabolites of amines, especially those of norepinephrine and dopamine, occur in fewer areas of the body outside the brain than do the mother substances themselves. In addition, the metabolites pass more readily from the brain. Thus, their presence in the body outside the brain may be a reasonably good index of actual brain amine activity (Arieti & Bemporad, 1978, p. 51; Schildkraut, 1975).

MHPG. A metabolite of norepinephrine that has received particular attention is the acidic compound MHPG, 3–methoxy–4–hydroxy–phenylethyleneglycol. Some investigators have estimated that from 30 to 50 percent of the MHPG found in the urine is derived from norepinephrine metabolism in the brain (Akiskal & McKinney, 1975; Andreasen, 1984a, pp. 183–184; Schildkraut, 1977).

A number of studies have found abnormally low levels of MHPG in the urine of depressed patients (Fawcett, Maas, & Dekirmenjian, 1972; Rosenbaum et al., 1983).

Other studies have reported similar results and have detected elevated levels of MHPG in the urine of patients undergoing manic episodes (Bond, Jenner, & Sampson, 1972; Greenspan, Schildkraut, Gordon, Baer, Arnoff, & Durell, 1970). However, the overall evidence is not clear-cut, since other investigators have reported that some depressed individuals excrete normal levels of MHPG in their urine. This discrepancy has led several researchers to conclude that low levels of MHPG may represent a particular subgroup of biochemical abnormalities associated with depression and may not be characteristic of other subgroups. (Kolb & Brodie, 1982, p. 410; Maas, 1975; Wolpert, 1980, pp. 1321–1322).

Research has also been carried out on levels of MHPG in the cerebrospinal fluid of depressed patients. Although some investigators have found it to be within the normal range, others have reported abnormally low levels. The data are also contradictory for manic disorders. Some studies have found high levels of MHPG in the cerebrospinal fluid of persons diagnosed with manic episodes; others have reported no abnormal elevations (Mendels, Stern, & Frazer, 1976; Post, Gordon, Goodwin, & Bunney, 1973). These differences may stem from a variety of reasons: differences in the procedures used in obtaining spinal fluid, the unreliability of assaying the MHPG itself, and differences in how individuals handle norepinephrine metabolism.

Several studies suggest that the low levels of MHPG found in depressed individuals could be the result of reduced psychomotor activity and lack of exercise, a typical concomitant of depression. Some researchers have reported that MHPG levels in depressed patients rose to normal when the patients were persuaded to increase their general physical activity (Post, Kotin, Goodwin, & Gordon, 1973). It may be that depletion of MHPG is a factor in only certain patterns of depression, such as those especially marked by abnormal decrease in general activity (Akiskal & McKinney, 1975).

Research on MHPG does not conclusively support the hypothesis that norepinephrine plays a direct role in the development of depressive or manic disorders. However, it may well play a secondary role, or it may interact with other biochemical factors yet to be discovered. There is also the possibility that norepinephrine has its most significant influence in bipolar disorders. Some studies have shown a marked shift in the MHPG level in the cerebrospinal fluid according to the direction of the patient's switch in mood: a high level during manic episodes and a low level during depression (Shopsin, Wilk, Sathananthan, Gershon, & Davis, 1974). Although the results were not obtained for every patient, they were fairly consistent. In general, they agree with data from previous investigations that indicate that catecholamines may be more significantly involved in the switch process of bipolar disorder than in mood disorders where only depressive episodes occur (Murphy, Goodwin, & Bunney, 1975).

5 – HIAA. Various studies on biochemical changes in mood disorders have involved the compound *5 – HIAA*, 5 – hydroxyindoleacetic acid, the principal metabolite of serotonin. Early research on 5 – HIAA centered on its occurrence in the urine, with conflicting results. Some investigations reported a low level of 5 – HIAA in depressed patients and a high level in manic patients. This finding was consistent with the catecholamine hypothesis. Other studies, however, found no significant relationship between the level of 5 – HIAA and affective disorders (Robins & Hartman, 1972; van Praag, 1977).

A different line of research has concentrated on the presence of 5 – HIAA in the cerebrospinal fluid, with more consistent results. The most consistent finding has been that severely depressed patients have a reduced level of 5 – HIAA in their cerebrospinal fluid (Mendels, 1975; Schildkraut, Green, & Mooney, 1985, p. 772). However, a major problem in interpreting these results is the difficulty of knowing whether a significant percentage of 5–HIAA was actually metabolized in the brain, since nerve endings that secrete serotonin are also present in the spinal cord. Nevertheless, it is likely that enough 5–HIAA originated in the brain to support the hypothesis that a deficiency in brain serotonin may play an important role in the development and expression of depressive episodes (Van Praag, 1977).

The results of studies involving metabolites of biogenic amines need to be interpreted cautiously because of various methodological problems. Since the metabolites derived from the brain become mixed with those already present in peripheral areas of the body, it is difficult to determine in any precise way the proportion of metabolites actually produced in the brain. Methods that attempt to do this have been developed, but the results are not always reliable. The problem is especially perplexing in the case of urine. Some researchers therefore place more reliance on results obtained from examining cerebrospinal fluid, because the fluid has passed through various parts of the brain into the spinal column.

Even when the accuracy of measuring biogenic amines is satisfactory, there are other problems that are difficult to control. Diet, exercise, fears related to hospitalization, physical disease, the particular characteristics of the affective disorder itself—all can influence the chemical content of the specimen that is being examined. The handling of such methodological problems demands a degree of precision that has not always been met. Nevertheless, in spite of potential pitfalls and conflicting results, the studies on metabolites of biogenic amines have provided helpful clues for understanding the biological aspects of affective disorders and have furnished promising leads for future research (Maas et al., 1987).

Drug Treatment of Mood Disorders

Other efforts to obtain evidence concerning the role of biogenic amines in affective disorders have involved drugs that alleviate episodes of depression. The drugs most often used in the United States are the *tricyclics*, such as imipramine (Tofanil) and amitriptyline (Elavil) (Bakal, 1979; Honigfeld & Howard, 1978; Klerman, 1982). These drugs increase the production of norepinephrine in the brain, thus suggesting a link between deficiencies in catecholamines and depression. However, tricyclics are slow-acting drugs, requiring two to four weeks before their beneficial effects are noticeable (Honigfeld & Howard, 1978). Although initially they tend to increase norepinephrine in the brain, their continuous use can actually decrease its production. Evidently, the sites in the brain that produce biogenic amines lose their sensitivity to tricyclics when they are administered continuously (Becker, 1977; Berger & Barchas, 1977; Frazer, 1975). During long-term treatment, the individual may actually lose norepinephrine even though symptoms of depression have been alleviated. These paradoxical effects raise doubts as to whether one can rely on the therapeutic usefulness of tricyclics to demonstrate that deficits in brain amines are crucial factors in the etiology of depressive episodes.

Another group of drugs used to treat major depressive episodes are the **monoamine oxidase inhibitors (MAOIs)**. As the name implies, MAOIs block the production of monoamine oxidase (MAO), a brain enzyme that reduces the availability of biogenic amines. Consequently, MAOIs can increase the concentration of norepinephrine, dopamine, and serotonin in the brain (Julien, 1981, pp. 87–88). The success of MAOIs in alleviating depression, especially when it is marked by severely retarded motor behavior and thought processes, has been used to support the hypothesis that a deficiency in brain amines can induce depression. Like the tricyclics, however, MAOIs require several weeks of continuous use before improvement becomes apparent, and their early effect is to increase brain amines while long-term use reduces them. Thus, the fact that MAOIs can eventually relieve depression does not in itself demonstrate that deficiencies in norepinephrine, dopamine, or serotonin are necessarily involved in the etiology of depression.

In spite of inconsistencies, the weight of evidence favors the influence of biogenic amines on mood disorders, but the relationship is far more complex than was once thought, and certainly not a direct cause-and-effect phenomenon. Depression does seem to be associated with an abnormal decrease in the availability of serotonin in the brain and of such catecholamines as dopamine and norepinephrine. Furthermore, the relationship between biogenic amines and depression is probably most important for the endogenous pattern, in which environmental events do not seem to be crucial factors.

The evidence from biochemical studies supports the conclusion that manic or depressive episodes are not homogeneous disorders, either biochemically or psychologically. Even when the symptoms seem to be similar in a given group of individuals, the underlying biochemical factors may not necessarily be the same. Such differences can help account for the contradictory findings in studies on the biochemistry of mood disorders. Since these studies report their findings in terms of averages, individual differences become masked but may still contribute to the discrepancy in results from one study to another. Future research on mood disorders, then, must concentrate on the analysis of individual differences in biochemical disturbances rather than relying solely on group differences.

Even where the evidence is positive, it is unlikely that an imbalance in brain amines alone can account for the complex kinds of behavior and experience found in mood disorders. Imbalances in other systems of neurotransmitters, whose functions are not yet clearly understood, may also be involved, especially in bipolar disorders (Berger & Barchas, 1977; Zis & Goodman, 1982, p. 186).

Mood Disorders and Heredity

Various studies have suggested that genetics may play an important part in the origin and expression of manic and major depressive episodes (Kolata, 1986; Snyder, 1980, p. 18; Wender, Kety, Rosenthal, Schulsinger, Ortmann, & Lunde, 1986). Some researchers have come to this conclusion without relating it specifically to abnormal biochemical changes in brain amines. Others, however, have hypothesized that these biochemical disturbances themselves have a genetic basis (Akiskal & McKinney, 1975; Cadoret & Tanna, 1977; Goldstein, 1988; Mendels, 1974; Rosenthal, 1971; Schuyler, 1974).

Research on Families

The rate of mood disorders in the general population has been compared with the rate of first-degree relatives of patients diagnosed with an affective disorder. (First-degree relatives include parents, siblings, and children.) These studies showed that, on the average, the risk of developing a mood disorder was 10 times higher for the relatives than it was for the general population (Cardoret & Winokur, 1975, p. 335). Although the studies were based on reasonably sound statistical data, there is a crucial difficulty in interpreting the results. The studies did not correct for the effect of environmental influences. An outstanding exception is a pioneering study by Stenstedt (1952) of families living in a rural area of Sweden. Stenstedt found that the overall rate of manic and major depressive episodes was greater in the families of patients with affective disorders than it was in the general population of the area in which those families lived. However, he also found that family members with unfavorable childhoods had a greater risk of developing an affective disorder than family members with favorable childhoods. Thus, environmental as well as genetic influences were important.

Studies of Twins

The strongest evidence for genetic influences in the development of mood disorders comes from studies that compared identical twins with fraternal twins. Identical twins are monozygotic (MZ), because they come from the same fertilized ovum (zygote) and thus have the same genetic characteristics. Fraternal twins are dizygotic (DZ), since they come from two different ova; thus their genetic similarity is like that of ordinary siblings. Because MZ twins have the same genetic endowment, evidence for the effects of heredity on mood disorder can be obtained by comparing their concordance rate (the percentage of pairs who develop the disorder) with the concordance rate of DZ twins.

Various investigators have reported that the concordance rate for MZ twins is considerably higher than for DZ pairs (Nurnberger & Gershon, 1982, pp. 9–10). In a more recent study of the concordance rates of MZ twins, Torgersen (1986) concluded that genetic factors are important in the development of bipolar and major depressive disorders but not of dysthymic disorder.

Stress and Conflict in Mood Disorders

Although it may not always be obvious, especially to the casual observer, stressful life events can be crucial factors in the onset and development of manic and major depressive episodes (Coyne, Aldwin, & Lazarus, 1981; Coyne, Kahn, & Gotlib, 1987; Kennedy, Thompson, Stancer, Roy, & Persad, 1983; Klerman, 1980; Lloyd, 1980; Paykel, 1979a, 1979b, 1982; Wetzel, 1984, ch. 4). The conflict associated with such stress often builds up gradually over a long period of time. Then, when an individual experiences an apparently minor stressful event shortly before the onset of a manic or depressive episode, observers may have great difficulty in understanding why the incident had such grave consequences. The presumably minor happening may simply be the last link in a chain of stressful experiences. Depressed or manic individuals may themselves be puzzled about their reactions. They may therefore exaggerate the effect of the precipitating event so as to avoid recognizing the earlier conflicts and frustrations that led to their current stress. Since these events appear to be trivial, there is always the danger that they will be dismissed as unimportant. It then becomes easier to ascribe the disorder almost exclusively to biological influences and to fail to see how such influences can interact with psychosocial and cultural events.

On the other hand, even when the events that immediately precede a manic or depressive episode are major, predisposing factors must also be considered (Paykel, 1975, 1979b, 1982). These include previous patterns of learning and personality development, the social and cultural milieu in which the individual lives, and biological abnormalities.

Psychodynamic Concepts

Manic Episodes

In many respects, manic episodes represent reactions to stress, frustration, and conflict that normal people also have, but in a more exaggerated and less adaptive manner. It is not unusual for some people to become involved in a flurry of more or less trivial activity to avoid particularly threatening situations or memories. However, there is a fundamental difference between that kind of reaction and the frantic behavior of manic individuals.

In normal (adaptive) increases in activity, there is usually an adequate degree of control and contact with reality. In contrast, manic excitement involves a loss of control and often an open break with reality. Furthermore, normally excited people do not as a rule perceive their newly acquired activity as a desirable state to maintain for prolonged periods of time. Indeed, they may return to their more ordinary, everyday behavior actually refreshed from the change in pace, able to face their personal problems more constructively because of the temporary distraction from them (Costin, 1976, p. 104). In contrast, truly manic individuals are alienated and self-defeating; they seldom perceive their disturbed episodes as beneficial. Although their recovery usually marks a return to normal premanic behavior, the manic episode itself is not particularly helpful in improving their postmanic behavior.

Many practitioners and researchers in the field of psychopathology and mental health, especially those with a psychodynamic orientation, believe that manic behavior is often a defense against an underlying depression, or threat of depression. Clinical observation supports this belief, as is illustrated in the case of a man who was brought to the hospital by a business associate because his behavior had become highly impulsive and unpredictable.

After being admitted to the hospital, the man went about singing and whistling, told "pointless, off-color stories," flirted crudely with the female patients and nurses, neglected his meals, and was immodest and careless about his appearance. But in the midst of all this, having been rebuked for a particularly irresponsible act, he suddenly broke down, cried, and said to the physician: "For God's sake, Doc, let me be. Can't you see that I've just got to act happy?" Later interviews revealed that for some time he had been suffering from a combination of highly stressful events. His much younger second wife, whom he prized as a symbol of his "renewed youth," had been unfaithful to him; and the top-level position he held was constantly being threatened by "younger, more energetic, and better trained men" (Masserman, 1973, p. 154).

A number of studies have found that some people who are especially susceptible to manic episodes have a deep fear of relying on others. They may only partially admit this fear or may not be consciously aware of it at all. As a way of compensating for the problem, they may play the manic game—a game in which they are highly proficient at making other people uncomfortable (Janowsky, El-Yousef, & Davis, 1974). They become experts at discovering vulnerable points in other people and focus on those areas to bolster their own self-esteem. They become alienated from their victims because of the discomfort they thrust on them, and this alienation reinforces their manic behavior.

Depressive Episodes

Psychodynamic explanations of depression have several features in common (Stricker, 1983a).

Defense against Loss. In contrast to the irritability and obvious hostility that manic individuals often display, depressed people show little overt hostility. Freud provided the classical psychoanalytic interpretation of this common observation in his famous essay *Mourning and Melancholia* (1917/1957). In Freud's view, depression represents a reaction to the loss of a love object. The loss may be symbolic—for example, when a person unconsciously perceives rejection to be a total deprivation of love. The loss makes the individual angry, but the anger is not expressed outwardly because its source is no longer present or, on a more symbolic level, is not consciously recognized. Consequently, the hostility is turned inward (introjected), resulting in depression, self-hatred, and, in extreme cases, suicidal wishes.

Freud pointed out that abnormal depression (melancholia) and the normal state of mourning share certain characteristics, such as dejection over a loss, lack of interest in one's surroundings, and the slowing down of activity. However, there are crucial differences. Melancholia involves self-reproach over one's failings, a loss of self-esteem, and an irrational need to be punished. Even when the melancholia is initiated by the loss of an object of love, the individual often does not recognize that the loss is related to the introjected hostility (Freud, 1917/1957, p. 245).

Intrapsychic Conflict.   Freud later revised his theory about abnormal depression in the context of his newly developed concepts of personality structure and the death instinct (or aggressive instinct, as he also called it). In *The Ego and the Id* (1923/1962), Freud proposed that melancholia results from an extreme conflict between an overly harsh superego (conscience and ideals) and the ego (the rational, intellectual self). (See Chapter 3 for a discussion of Freud's theory of personality structure.) The depressed person fears the loss of love, a fear that resides in the superego as the legacy of parents and other parental figures. Thus, Freud retained the concept of loss, but tied it more specifically to the aggressive impulses that have invaded the superego and helped transform it into an overly harsh master. This invasion helps explain why the severely depressed individual may take the step of self-destruction (suicide).

In spite of Freud's later thinking on the subject, many followers of psychoanalysis take his earlier explanation in *Mourning and Melancholia* as his final statement on the origin of depression (Arieti & Bemporad, 1978, p. 24). The reason for this may be that his later theorizing is relatively brief and less explicit, especially with respect to why destructive instincts should invade the superego. Another reason for minimizing his later theory may be that the concept of the death instinct fell into disrepute among many psychoanalysts (see Chapter 3).

Childhood Frustrations and Traumatic Experiences.   Karl Abraham (1877–1925), the first psychoanalyst in Germany, is generally credited with the initial psychoanalytic investigation of depression (1911/1960), preceding Freud's *Mourning and Melancholia*. His views must have stimulated Freud's theorizing, and he later incorporated some of Freud's ideas into his own work. Abraham emphasized such factors as conflict and frustration, early childhood disappointments, and the idea that depression in adulthood could be a revival of the traumatic experiences of childhood. Under the influence of Freud's concept of introjected hostility, Abraham concluded that abnormally depressed people introject and devour the love object from whom they have suffered unbearable disappointment. In this way they achieve a melancholic form of identification with that love object. Their desire for vengeance against the source of their disappointment (the love object) is now turned inward, finding satisfaction in tormenting the ego—an activity that in part is pleasurable (Abraham, 1924/1948).

Low Self-esteem.   Following the lines of ego psychology (Chapter 3), various psychoanalytic theorists have emphasized that highly depressed people suffer from experiencing a discrepancy between their actual self and their idealized self. In Edith Jacobson's view (1975), abnormal depression originates in the frustration of needs, leading to hostile attacks to overcome that frustration. If the blocking of needs continues, the hostility is then directed toward the ego's self-image. The result is a lowering of self-esteem and an increasing discrepancy between the actual self and the desired (ideal) self. The depressed individual may then turn to manic activity as a defense against the depression, or seek a new love object. If these defenses fail, an even greater depression of psychotic proportion may result. The ego withdraws from the outer world and retreats into complete surrender.

Karen Horney and Harry Stack Sullivan also have associated depression with low self-esteem and a discrepancy between the ideal self and the real self. We discussed their psychoanalytic theories of interpersonal relationships in Chapter 3, and we will deal with their approaches to psychotherapy in Chapter 19.

Learned Helplessness and Depression

Seligman's Original Theory

Martin Seligman (1974, 1975) criticized the Freudian view that abnormally depressed individuals have turned inward the hostility that they bear toward others. Seligman cited evidence that, contrary to what Freudian theory would predict, "the dreams of depressives, like their waking life, are drained of hostility. Even in dreams, they see themselves as passive victims and losers" (1975, p. 89). Seligman proposed a theory of **learned helplessness** to explain how such depression can develop. As the result of his early experiments with dogs, he concluded that "organisms, when exposed to uncontrollable events, learn that responding is futile" (1975, p. 74). If these uncontrollable events become traumatic, the individual's initial fear and anxiety give way to depression. Seligman and his co-workers integrated their theory and data with the experimental and clinical work of other researchers and found increasing support for the concept of learned helplessness and implications for developing ways of helping people recover from depression (Seligman, 1974, 1975; Hiroto & Seligman, 1975; Miller & Seligman, 1975; Price, Tryon, & Raps, 1978).

Seligman's Reformulated Theory

As a result of their further work and that of other researchers, Seligman and his colleagues revised and extended their original theory of learned helplessness (Abramson, Garber, & Seligman, 1980; Abramson, Seligman, Teasdale, 1978; Seligman, Abramson, Semmel, & von Baeyer, 1979; Wortman & Dintzer, 1978). The essential ingredients of this reformulation are as follows.

1. Depression includes four classes of deficits: motivational, cognitive, self-esteem, and affective. The first three deficits are the result of being unable to control events. Affective deficits stem from the expectation that bad outcomes will occur.

2. When individuals believe that highly desirable outcomes are improbable and that nothing in their repertoire of responses can change that, then helplessness and depression will follow.

3. How general the depression becomes depends on how global the individual's self-attribution of helplessness is. How chronic the depression becomes depends on the stability of that self-attribution.

4. Whether self-esteem is lowered during depression depends on the extent to which individuals internalize their self-attribution of helplessness—that is, believe they cause

According to Seligman's theory of learned helplessness, exposure to uncontrollable and devastating events (for example, drought), may lead to feelings of helplessness and depression. This is especially likely to occur if the victims feel that nothing in their repertoire of responses could possibly alleviate the situation.

their helplessness and failure. A predisposition to make unstable, specific, and external attributions about the causes of good outcomes may also lead to depression.

5. The intensity of the deficits in depression (motivational, cognitive, self-esteem, and affective) depends on how strong or certain the individual's expectation of uncontrollability is. In addition, expectations of uncontrollability interact with the importance the individual attaches to the outcome of an event: The more important the outcome, the more an expectation of uncontrollability is likely to lower self-esteem and produce sadness.

A number of studies since the reformulation of Seligman's theory support the view that feelings of uncontrollability are an important factor in the development of depression. Warren and McEachren (1983), for example, found that women who felt they had little or no control over their lives were much more likely to experience episodes of depressive disorder than women who did not have this self-perception.

Seligman and his colleagues have applied their reformulated theory of learned helplessness to psychotherapy with depressed individuals. The basic goal is to reduce ways of thinking that involve beliefs of helplessness and to increase productive ways of thinking about one's self and one's relationship to others. More specifically, therapeutic goals include (a) reducing the individual's estimates as to how frequently uncontrollable events will occur; (b) increasing expectations that a significant number of events can be controlled; (c) changing unrealistic attributions for failure or success — for example, always blaming oneself for failure and attributing success simply to luck; and (d) increasing self-esteem.

The following statements illustrate how a therapist might help an individual move from an unrealistic, self-blaming attribution for failure to a more realistic, externally focused attribution; and how an individual might be helped to move from an unrealistic externally directed attribution for success to a more realistic internal attribution. "*For failure* (change from internal to external attribution): 'The system minimized the opportunities of women. It is not that you are incompetent.' *For success* (change from external to internal attribution): 'He loves you because you are nurturant not because he is insecure'" (Abramson, Seligman, & Teasdale, 1978, p. 69). In addition to such verbal methods, therapy aimed at reducing helplessness may involve the assignment of structured tasks to increase positive experiences of self-confidence and readings that deal with how that can be achieved (Steinmetz, Lewinsohn, & Antonuccio, 1983).

Cognitive Theory of Depression

Closely related to learned helplessness is the theory that people become abnormally depressed because of basic errors in thinking. Various psychotherapists ascribe such errors to a lack of social skills, and therefore direct their therapeutic efforts toward helping the individual remedy those deficiencies (Bellack, Hersen, & Himmelhoch, 1981; Ellis, 1987a, 1987b).

Aaron T. Beck (1970) originated much of the research centering around the theory that erroneous ways of thinking influence the development of depressive disorders. In his early work, Beck found that depressed patients tended to interpret their unfortunate experiences as being their own fault, or they magnified the extent to which their own deficiencies contributed to those unfortunate experiences. Beck concluded that these depressed patients were committing a number of errors in thinking that greatly influenced their depression. Their interpretations were based on insufficient evidence, they magnified slight deficiencies in themselves that others would probably overlook, and they minimized achievements that other people would probably view as highly worthy.

More recently, Beck and his co-workers have expanded this cognitive approach to explaining depression. It now includes three major components: the cognitive triad, schemas, and faulty information processing (Beck & Young, 1985).

The Cognitive Triad

Three self-defeating ways of thinking form the **cognitive triad:** (a) negative ways of perceiving oneself—for example, as defective, inadequate, or deprived; (b) the tendency to perceive current experiences in a negative way, such as feeling that the world makes unreasonable demands and presents insuperable obstacles to reaching life goals; and (c) a negative view of the future—for example, anticipating that current difficulties will continue indefinitely.

Schemas

The concept of schemas explains why depressed people often maintain their self-defeating and pain-inducing attitudes even though one can point to positive factors in their lives. **Schemas** are the cognitive patterns with which individuals select and interpret the many different stimuli that impinge on them each day. The kinds of schemas individuals use will determine how they structure their experiences. A chief problem for depressed individuals is that they persist in distorting their interpretations of specific situations to fit schemas that in the past were dysfunctional (maladaptive). This prevents them from being flexible and matching particular stimuli with appropriate schemas. Thus, depressed individuals lose much of their voluntary control over their cognitive processes and cannot adaptively use the schemas that are more appropriate for changing situations. As the depression worsens, the fixed schemas dominate thinking increasingly, so that logical connections between actual situations and negative interpretations of those situations are loosened. As a result, it become increasingly difficult for depressed individuals to see that their continuous negative interpretation of events may be erroneous and that they need not be continually depressed by those events.

Faulty Information Processing

In Beck's cognitive model of depression, **faulty information processing** consists of systematic errors in thinking that help maintain the individual's belief in the truth of negative concepts in spite of objective evidence to the contrary. These errors in thinking include the following (Beck, Rush, Shaw, & Emery, 1979, p. 14; Hewitt & Dyck, 1986).

- **Arbitrary reference:** drawing a specific conclusion in the absence of evidence that supports the conclusion or when the evidence is directly contrary to that conclusion.

- **Selective abstraction:** focusing on details taken out of context and ignoring more relevant features of the situation.

- **Overgeneralization:** coming to a general conclusion based on one or more isolated incidents, and then applying that conclusion to a wide variety of unrelated situations. Although Beck and his colleagues do not make it explicit, this kind of erroneous thinking also operates in certain forms of social prejudice — an interesting parallel.

- **Magnification:** gross distortions in evaluating the significance of an event — for example, exaggerating the importance of negative occurrences and minimizing the importance of positive ones.

- **Personalization:** the tendency to relate external events to oneself when there is little or no basis for doing so.

- **Absolutistic thinking:** the tendency to put all experiences in one of two opposite sets — for example, things are perfect or defective, immaculate or filthy; and people are saints or sinners.

Applications to Therapy

Beck and his colleagues have developed a highly detailed set of procedures for the treatment of depression — **cognitive therapy.** The methods are aimed at correcting the errors in thinking involved in the basic components we have described: the cognitive triad, schemas, and faulty information processing. The specific techniques include verbal methods as well as behavioral strategies. For example, patients are taught (a) to monitor their negative, automatic thoughts; (b) to recognize relationships among their thoughts, behavior, and feelings; (c) to examine the evidence that supports or contradicts their automatic negative thinking; (d) to substitute more reality-oriented interpretations for their biased cognitions; and (e) to identify and alter the maladaptive beliefs that lead to their distorted ways of thinking (Beck, Rush, Shaw, & Emery, 1979, p. 4).

Studies comparing the effectiveness of different methods of therapy in treating major depressive disorders show various results. Some favor either psychotherapy or drug treatment; others report that a combination of these is most effective; still others find that psychotherapy and drug therapy are equally effective (Beckman, 1984; Board on Mental Health and Behavioral Medicine, 1985; Mervis, 1986; Smith, Glass, & Miller, 1980; Steinbrueck, Maxwell, & Howard, 1983). The effectiveness of the various approaches to treating depression depends largely on the particular situation and the person involved. Not all depressed individuals respond positively to medication. Some refuse it because of personal objections, or they develop side effects that cause them to terminate treatment. Furthermore, the prolonged use of drugs may in some instances undermine the individual's psychological resources for dealing with depression by reinforcing the loss of self-control (Steinbrueck, Maxwell, & Howard, 1983).

On the other hand, the severity of the depression may necessitate the use of drugs to at least start the individual toward recovery, even though psychotherapy will also be used. Indeed, some clinicians argue that negative effects of drugs are often not crucial and that antidepressant medication may actually facilitate psychotherapy by improving the cognitive clarity of the patient. Furthermore, where the depression is bipolar, the use of medication becomes even more appropriate, since biochemical influences are more likely to be at work (Beckman, 1984).

Depression and Suicide

A constant danger in major depressive episodes is the possibility of suicide (Hamilton, 1982; National Institute of Mental Health, 1983). In recent years, both the mass media and mental health professionals have paid increasing attention to the problem. Various articles have emphasized not only the link between depression and suicide but also the fact that suicide is more prevalent than many people think.

Suicide is the 10th leading cause of death in the United States, placing just ahead of homicide (Large, 1983). Especially troublesome is the rapid increase in suicide among adolescents and young adults, the rate having nearly tripled in the past few decades. Studies have shown a link between drug abuse and the rapid rise of suicide among young people. In older individuals, depression, physical illness, and loneliness are major contributing factors (Fowler, Rich, & Young, 1986; McIntosh, 1985; Rich, Young, & Fowler, 1986; Shafil, Carrigan, Whittinghill, & Derrick, 1985; Statistical Abstract of the United States, 1983, pp. 78–86).

False Beliefs about Suicide

The following examples illustrate a few of the more prevalent myths about suicide and the evidence that contradicts them (Shneidman & Faberow, 1961; Shneidman, Faberow, & Litman, 1970; Snyder, 1980, pp. 34–35).

■ **People who threaten suicide usually don't try it.** *False:* 75 percent of the people who eventually committed suicide had attempted it previously or had threatened to do so.

■ **Improvement after a suicidal crisis is over indicates that the future risk of suicide is minimal.** *False:* Almost 50 percent of people who had undergone a suicidal crisis and subsequently committed suicide did so within 90 days after passing the crisis, while seemingly on the way to recovery.

■ **Suicides occur suddenly, with no prior warning.** *False:* People who attempt suicide often give clues of their intentions, which in many instances represent cries for help. However, such warnings may be missed by others or be too subtle for detection.

Claiming versus Self-blaming

On the basis of extensive clinical observations, Silvano Arieti and Jules Bemporad (1978) have distinguished between claiming and self-blaming types of depressed people. This distinction is highly relevant to the problem of suicide and cries for help. Claiming individuals tend to be dependent and clinging; they suffer from anguish but want people around them to be aware of that anguish. They show little feeling of self-accusation or guilt, which when present plays a secondary role in their depression. Their appetites are often normal, although they may spend a great deal of time in bed. Their pattern of depression transmits the message: "Help me; pity me. It is in your power to relieve me. If I suffer, it is because you don't give me what I need." Even expressed wishes for suicide or actual attempts at suicide emit a cry for help: "Do not abandon me" (Arieti & Bemporad, 1978, p. 72).

In contrast, depressed individuals of the self-blaming type do not share their anguish with others; instead, they withdraw and seek solitude in their misery. Their appetite is poor, insomnia is frequent, and they express strong feelings of self-accusation and guilt. Although Arieti and Bemporad do not make the matter explicit, it seems reasonable to infer that it would be more difficult to recognize the danger of suicide in self-blaming persons than in the claiming type, since the withdrawal behavior of the self-blaming individuals would obscure their cries for help.

Legal and Ethical Issues

The possibility of suicide as a consequence of depression raises crucial legal and ethical questions. In recent years, there has been a great deal of argument about the civil and moral rights of individuals who choose to kill themselves (Clum, 1987; Siegel, 1986). Most states have laws against suicide; thus, people who fail in the attempt are subject to legal prosecution. Although advocates of the right to suicide have concentrated on situations where suicide is apparently a rational act — not an aspect of an emotional disorder — more extreme supporters, including some mental health professionals, have insisted that such rights should apply in all circumstances (for example, see Szasz, 1986). In discussing the latter argument, Martin Seligman (1975) points out that even though highly depressed individuals typically view the future as hopeless, in many instances their cognitive set could change in just a few weeks and by reason of time alone: "The future would [then] seem less hopeless, even though the actual circumstances remained the same. In other words, the force of the depressive's wish to kill himself would weaken, even though his reasons might remain the same. One of the most tragic aspects of suicide is that often, if the person could be rendered inactive for a week or two, he would no longer wish to kill himself" (p. 89).

Seligman's view has direct relevance for the contributions that drug therapy and psychotherapy can make in helping the depressed individual deal with a suicidal crisis. The efforts of community mental health services such as suicide prevention centers are also significant sources of help, especially for individuals who are not receiving any kind of assistance in their crisis. The benefits and limitation of these centers, as well as other approaches to understanding and preventing suicide, are discussed in Chapter 21, where we consider suicide as a community problem.

Summary

1. Disorders of mood, also known as affective disorders, may range from abnormal excitement to maladaptive depression.

2. Although writings on mood disorders during the 17th, 18th, and 19th centuries emphasized that mania (abnormal excitement) and depression were part of a unitary disorder, modern evidence shows that such disturbances do not necessarily reflect a single disorder.

3. DSM-III-R classifies mood disorders into bipolar disorders, which involve episodes of abnormal excitement as well as depression, and major depression. The latter disorder does not include periods of abnormal excitement. Each of these broad diagnostic categories is subdivided into more specific patterns. As classified in DSM-III-R, mood disorders to not include affective abnormalities resulting from physical illnesses, such as deterioration of brain tissue, traumatic injuries, or infections or from shifts in emotions caused by drugs.

4. Both manic and depressive episodes can range from relatively moderate degrees of personal and social impairment to behavior and feelings that clearly represent a break with reality (psychosis). Relatively mild episodes of alternating manic and depressive episodes are called cyclothymia, traditionally considered to be a neurotic disorder. Mild levels of depression are called dysthymia. Recent research on cyclothymia and dysthymia suggest that they may not necessarily be self-limiting, as was once believed, but may be forerunners of more serious manic or depressive episodes.

5. Major depression is one of the most serious disorders of mood. The disorder is diagnosed more often in women than in men. Some research suggests that one reason for the discrepancy is that men are more likely to engage in various distracting behaviors that help counteract their depressed mood. In contrast, women are more likely to amplify their depressed mood. Although the former pattern seems to be more adaptive, it may also be true that social restrictions give women fewer opportunities to engage in such distracting activities.

6. Although depression can occur without the person ever having a manic episode, the two may also alternate (bipolar disorder). The more usual pattern is for a manic episode to occur prior to a depressive one. This phenomenon suggests, from a psychodynamic viewpoint, that the manic attack is a defense against depression.

7. Depression can occur in children as well as in adults. During adolescence, episodes of depression may be associated with restlessness, negativistic behavior, and antisocial activity. Depression in elderly people may often stem from or be intensified by personal loss. In contrast to the losses of younger people, this loss is often irretrievable. Thus, depression in the elderly may be more understandable than in children or other adults.

8. Some researchers and practitioners in psychopathology distinguish between endogenous and exogenous depression (also called reactive depression). Endogenous depression stems mainly from biological factors, and its occurrence is relatively

independent of precipitating life experiences. In exogenous depression, biological factors may also play a role, but the disorder is more likely to be precipitated by stressful events. It is often difficult to maintain the distinction in clinical practice.

9. Cross-cultural studies of depression have concluded that its modes of expression vary considerably across different societies. There does not appear to be a universal conception of depression. The more Westernized a culture is, the more one finds both somatic (bodily) and psychological components of depression. In non-Western societies, depression involves less expression of guilt and fewer attempts at suicide or expressed suicidal wishes.

10. A great deal of research has been carried out on the role of biochemical processes in the brain in the etiology of manic and depressive episodes. Among the main substances are biogenic amines, which act as neurotransmitters; that is, they transmit impulses from one neuron to another. The catecholamine hypothesis states that depression is associated with a deficiency and manic episodes with an excess of catecholamines in the brain. In general, researchers have agreed that biochemical levels play a part in the development of mood disorders but provide only a partial explanation.

11. The metabolites (products of metabolism) of biogenic amines have also been studied as possible etiological agents in the development of mood disorders, especially the metabolites of norepinephrine (a catecholamine). Results are suggestive but not conclusive.

12. Other efforts to obtain evidence concerning the role of biogenic amines in mood disorders have involved drugs known to reduce episodes of depression through increasing production of norepinephrine in the brain. If raising the level of norepinephrine brings about recovery from depression, one might well conclude that a norepinephrine deficiency is a cause.

13. In spite of inconsistencies and limitations of the research, the weight of evidence favors the influence of biogenic amines in the etiology of mood disorders. However, the relationship is far more complex than early research indicated. Furthermore, biochemical studies have supported the conclusion that manic or depressive episodes are not completely homogeneous disorders, biochemically or psychologically. Finally, even where the evidence of biochemical influences on the development of mood disorders is strong, one must always take into consideration the possible joint influence of other neurotransmitters not yet understood.

14. Various studies have suggested that genetic factors play an important role in the origin and expression of mood disorders. Some researchers have related the evidence on genetics to abnormal biochemical changes in the brain. Others have studied the independent influence of genetic factors.

15. The evidence on genetic factors comes from research on first-degree relatives of people diagnosed with a mood disorder, as well as studies of twins. The research on twins has yielded stronger results. Some studies have concluded that genetic factors are important in the development of bipolar and major depressive disorders, but much less so in dysthymic disorder. Even where the genetic evidence is convincing, the interaction of heredity and environment must always be considered.

16. Stressful life events can be crucial factors in the development of mood disorders, even where biological factors also play a role. Stress is not always obvious. Sometimes what looks like a minor stressful event might simply be the last link in a chain of stressful experiences.

17. According to some psychodynamic interpretations, manic episodes are defenses against depression. Other psychodynamic explanations emphasize that people who are especially susceptible to manic episodes have a deep fear of relying on other people, a fear they may only partially recognize.

18. In contrast to people experiencing a manic episode, those suffering from major depression show little overt hostility. Freud's classical psychoanalytic interpretation of this passivity is that depression is a reaction against the loss of a love object, real or imagined. The loss creates hostility that is turned inward (introjected) and then expressed in self-hatred and depression.

19. In later theorizing, Freud proposed that depression (melancholia) results from conflict between an overly harsh superego and the ego. What the depressed person fears is the loss of love—a fear that resides in the superego as the legacy of parental figures.

20. Other psychodynamic explanations of depression have invoked (a) the influence of childhood frustration and traumatic experiences, resulting in bitter disappointments; (b) low self-esteem; and (c) a sharp discrepancy between the ideal self and the real self.

21. Seligman and his colleagues have developed a theory of depression based on principles of cognitive learning. It is called learned helplessness. When individuals come to believe, through learning in a variety of situations, that highly desirable outcomes are improbable and that they can do nothing to change the situation, they feel helpless—a feeling of defeat and depression.

22. Seligman and his colleagues have applied their theory of learned helplessness to psychotherapy. The goals of this therapy include the following: (a) reducing the individual's estimates as to how frequently uncontrollable events will occur; (b) increasing expectations that a significant number of events can be controlled; (c) changing unrealistic attributions, such as always blaming oneself for failure and attributing all success to good luck; and (d) increasing self-esteem.

23. Beck and his colleagues have also developed an elaborate cognitive approach to explaining depression and how it can be reduced through therapy. A goal of therapy is to teach the individual how to correct errors in thinking that contribute to the depression. They include (a) drawing negative conclusions about oneself in the absence of evidence, (b) focusing on details taken out of context, (c) overgeneralizing, (d) magnifying negative experiences, (e) consistently relating external events to one's own deficiencies, and (f) putting all experiences in one of two opposite sets—for example, good or bad.

24. Psychotherapy for depression is often combined with drug therapy. In some instances, the use of drugs may be essential to at least start the individual toward reducing depression and becoming more amenable to psychological treatment.

25. Clinical observations have distinguished between claiming and self-blaming types of depressed people. This distinction is relevant to the potential threat of suicide, which is always a danger in major depression. Claiming individuals are dependent and clinging; they want others to know about their suffering. Self-blaming individuals do not share their anguish with others; they withdraw and seek solitude in their misery. It seems reasonable to conclude, therefore, that it would be more difficult to recognize the danger of suicide in self-blaming persons than in the claiming type.

Outline of Topics

A body seriously out of equilibrium either
with itself or with the environment perishes
outright. Not so a mind. Madness and suffering
can set themselves no limit.

GEORGE SANTAYANA
The Life of Reason (1905–1906)

What is madness? to have erroneous perceptions
and to reason correctly from them.

VOLTAIRE
"Madness," *Philosophical Dictionary* (1764)

**An Interview
with Kevin**

I: Who brought you here?

K: The police is what brought me to the hospital and that's all I know.

I: And no one's ever told you why?

K: I began seeing visions in the wall and things like that. Although it didn't prove to be mental illness, it could be religion.

I: Have you ever heard voices?

K: Yes, all the time. It started ten years ago this month, really, and I have heard voices ever since. I believe there are people really speaking to me. I believe I have extrasensory perception or something. I don't believe it is hallucinations.

I: What sort of things do you hear?

K: I hear people talking to me and I talk to other people. I hear two kinds of voices, really. I have conferences with people about religion and things like that, and then on the other hand I get beaten up by the voices of other people. I have always had this counter-balance with voices.

I: How can you be beaten up by voices?

K: Oh, it's what they say, they say horrible things.

I: About you?

K: Yes, and they ask questions. They interrogate me. Interrogation is painful. (Shean, 1978, pp. 72–73)

**A Woman Writes
to Her Physician**

Will you see that I am taken out of this hospital and returned to the equity court so I can prove to the court who I am and thereby establish my identity to the world. Possibly you do not remember or care to remember that you married me May 21, 1882, while you were in England and that I made you by that marriage the Prince of Wales, as I was born Albert Edward, Prince of Wales. I am feminine absolutely, not a double person or a hermaphrodite, so please know I am England's feminine king—the king who is a king. . . .

Sincerely,
"TANT"

Queen of Scotland, Empress of the World, Empress of China, Empress of Russia, Queen of Denmark, Empress of India, Maharajahess of Durban, "Papal authority" as a Protestant. (Kolb & Brodie, 1982, pp. 366–367)

A Man Describes His Confused Thinking

My thoughts get all jumbled up. I start thinking or talking about something but I never get there. Instead I wander off in the wrong direction and get caught up with all sorts of different things that may be connected with the things I want to say but in a way I can't explain. (McGhie & Chapman, 1961, p. 258)

All of the people quoted in the above excerpts were diagnosed as suffering from schizophrenia. Kevin focused on his **auditory hallucinations**—sensory perceptions that occurred in the absence of external stimuli. Tant concentrated on her bizarre **delusions**—beliefs obviously contrary to demonstrable facts and expressed incoherently. The third patient revealed another common symptom of schizophrenia—the inability to maintain a logical train of thought.

The term **schizophrenia** is a convenient generic label that embraces a group of related disorders. These disorders have certain basic characteristics in common, such as gross misinterpretations of external reality and confused thinking, but they differ significantly in their specific manifestation and etiology. Thus, it is technically more accurate to speak of *schizophrenic disorders*, or *disorders of the schizophrenic syndrome* (which implies patterns or subgroups of disturbances) rather than to employ the single term *schizophrenia* (American Psychiatric Association, 1987, pp. 187–190; Andreasen, 1987; Bellak, 1979). Nevertheless, because the term is well established in the literature of psychopathology, we will continue to use it.

A common symptom in certain forms of schizophrenia is an almost complete withdrawal from the person's surroundings.

Although schizophrenia does not occur as often as mood disorders (see Chapter 10), it is far from rare. According to various estimates, between 0.5 and 1 percent of people throughout the world suffer from schizophrenia, compared to 8–20 percent for mood disorders. Studies of urban populations in the United States have reported rates of schizophrenic disorders even higher than 1 percent. Furthermore, schizophrenia is usually more chronic than mood disorders and generally has more long-term disabling effects. Approximately 30 percent of patients in mental hospitals in the United States are there because of a schizophrenic disorder (American Psychiatric Association, 1987, p. 192; Andreasen, 1984a, pp. 52–53; Lickey & Gordon, 1983, p. 53).

This chapter deals primarily with schizophrenia; it also considers a related but rarer set of psychotic disturbances known as delusional, or paranoid, disorder. Their central feature is the dominating presence of delusions, usually those of persecution or jealousy.

Patterns of Schizophrenic Disorders

Historical Note

The concept of what we now call schizophrenia can be traced at least to the writings of Hippocrates. In his remarkable work *The Sacred Disease*, Hippocrates challenged the prevalent belief that mental disorders were of sacred origin. Instead, he claimed, they stemmed from natural causes—an unhealthy brain (Jones, 1923).

During the following centuries, various attempts at a rational understanding of schizophrenia continued. Nevertheless, until the 19th century, physicians and lay persons alike considered mental disorders to be products of witchcraft. Psychological abnormalities such as hallucinations and delusions, which we now know are common symptoms of schizophrenia, were often regarded as forms of evil possession that needed to be destroyed. In Königsberg, in 1636, a man was condemned to death because he claimed he was "God the Father . . . [and] that all the angels and the Son of God recognized his power" (Zilboorg & Henry, 1941, p. 259). His tongue was cut out, his head was cut off, and his body was burned.

By the 19th century, more rational approaches to diagnosing and understanding schizophrenia proliferated, at least in psychiatric circles. Schizophrenia was known as dementia praecox, a term that the psychiatrist Bénédict Augustin Morel (1809–1873) first used in his voluminous text, *Traité des Maladies Mentales* (1860). Morel claimed not only that the disorder involved a deterioration of mental ability (*démence*, dementia) but that the decline always began early in life (*précoce*, or praecox, "precocious, premature").

Morel's views greatly influenced the psychiatric writings of his time, especially in France and Germany. The German psychiatrist Emil Kraepelin (1856–1926), generally acknowledged to be the founder of modern psychiatric classification (see Chapter 2), was so impressed by the concept of dementia praecox that he incorporated it into his diagnostic system of mental disorders. He also gave it an additional interpretation. The dementia, said Kraepelin, began soon after the onset of the disorder and almost always signified a fatal ending. Toward the close of his career, Kraepelin became somewhat less pessimistic about the outcome of dementia praecox, since his later observations convinced him that at least some individuals diagnosed with the disorder actually did recover. Nevertheless, his earlier views persisted in the psychiatric profession, contributing to a fatalistic attitude toward the disorder and discouraging the provision of help to people who had received the tragic diagnosis (Arieti, 1974).

The Swiss psychiatrist Eugen Bleuler (1957–1939) countered the gloomy prognosis of

Until the nineteenth century, most physicians and lay persons believed that mental disorders were caused by the possession of demons. This late seventeenth-century illustration by Benedetto Luti shows "St. Romuald Curing a Woman Possessed."

Kraepelin and his followers. Bleuler demonstrated that dementia praecox did not necessarily begin in youth; nor did it necessarily proceed to a fatal end. In his landmark monograph *Dementia Praecox or the Group of Schizophrenias* (1911/1950), Bleuler renamed the disorder schizophrenia (from the Greek *schizo*, "split," and *phren*, "mind") and included a much wider range of disturbances. Bleuler emphasized that the symptoms of schizophrenia represented a splitting in the basic functions of an individual's personality rather than an inevitable path toward dementia. This splitting can be revealed in several ways: lack of coherence in the association of ideas; **autism**, in which the individual avoids communicating with others by becoming immersed in fantasy; and a sharp discordance between mood and thought, in which a person shows signs of inappropriate affect, such as laughing while describing a sad event.

Half the time I am talking about one thing and thinking about a half a dozen other things at the same time. It must look queer to people when I laugh about something that has got nothing to do with what I am talking about, but they don't know what's going on inside and how much of it is running round in my head. You see, I might be talking about something quite serious to you and other things come into my head at the same time that are funny and this makes me laugh. If I could only concentrate on the one thing at the one time I wouldn't look half so silly. (McGhie & Chapman, 1961, p. 258)

Diagnostic Criteria

The criteria DSM-III-R specifies for diagnosing schizophrenia include delusions, hallucinations, and incoherent communication. Other symptoms may include a marked deterioration in work habits, social relations, and self-care; inappropriate or flat affect; and catatonic behavior, such as assuming bizarre postures or refusing to speak. Symptoms must persist for at least six months to justify a diagnosis of schizophrenic disorder. Furthermore, the diagnosis should rule out the possibility that the symptoms are due to an organic mental disorder (see Chapter 13).

If the duration of the symptoms is less than six months, DSM-III-R classifies the disturbance as a separate psychosis, **schizophreniform disorder** (taking the form of schizophrenia). In general, the prognosis of the disorder is especially favorable if there is an absence of flat affect and good social and occupational adjustment prior to the episode (American Psychiatric Association, 1987, pp. 207–208).

Types of Schizophrenia

Classifying schizophrenia into types is a time-honored procedure that DSM-III-R continues. However, in clinical practice, it is sometimes difficult to find schizophrenic behavior and experience conforming to one particular type. Furthermore, some individuals may not only reveal more than one type but also change from one type to another during the course of their illness, especially if they have been hospitalized for long periods of time. Some of these shifting symptoms may result from imitation of other patients or from various adverse conditions that are inherent in any long-term confinement. Nevertheless, a knowledge of the major characteristics of the types of schizophrenia can be useful in clinical practice and research, provided they are not viewed as fixed categories to which schizophrenic individuals must always be rigidly assigned

Disorganized Type of Schizophrenia

In DSM-II (American Psychiatric Association, 1968) the **disorganized type of schizophrenia** was called *hebephrenic* (from the Greek *hebe*, "youth," and *phren*, "mind"). Thus, the term signifies immature, regressive thinking and behavior. In DSM-III and its 1987 revision, the label was changed to *disorganized* to emphasize that confused thinking, feeling, and behavior stand out as central features, especially for the cognitive processes. The following excerpt represents the kind of incoherent thought processes that typically occur in the disorganized type of schizophrenia: "Care glass *body or build* height soap long to be with him or near him. Tight slacks schooling. Albert Leonard Bruce. How can people realize which road to travel without a guide which is their consentance. When in depression think of some things you have done or something you have 3 = A Sycottic Newrow alientist" (Sinnett, 1964, p. 199).

Other characteristics of the disorganized type of schizophrenia include incongruous, flat, or silly affect, such as inappropriate giggling and other behavior highly inconsistent with the normal expectations in a situation. Delusions and hallucinations are common; but they are usually fragmentary, shifting rapidly from one kind of content to another and lacking a systematic, coherent theme.

The onset of the disorganized type of schizophrenia is often marked by a gradual loss of interest in the social environment, sometimes as early as adolescence. Unless interrupted with appropriate forms of treatment, such as medication and psychotherapy, the symptoms tend to expand and take a chronic course, eventually leading to extreme impairment of daily life. Because of its insidious nature, the disorder may not be recognized as truly serious until it has progressed to the point where psychotic breaks with reality become painfully obvious to family and friends. Unfortunately, it is often only then that some form of therapeutic intervention is sought.

Catatonic Type of Schizophrenia

Extreme psychomotor disturbances, ranging from abnormal excitement to highly withdrawn behavior, mark the **catatonic type of schizophrenia**. The German psychiatrist Karl Ludwig Kahlbaum (1828–1899), a pioneer in the classification of mental disorders, gave the first clear description of a catatonic condition (see Chapter 2). Kahlbaum was so impressed with the distinct nature of catatonia that he considered it to be a separate disease entity. In modern clinical practice, however, catatonic behavior is usually regarded as a type of schizophrenia, although certain aspects of it may also occur in other mental disorders, including those involving organic pathology (see Chapter 13).

Excited catatonic behavior typically involves excessive and sometimes violent motor activity, often manifested in a mechanical, stereotyped manner. Withdrawn catatonic behavior is characterized by general negativism, mutism (refusal to speak), and even stupor. Stereotyped and peculiar mannerisms often occur, including **waxy flexibility**. In the latter condition, the individual assumes strange poses that can be readily changed, either voluntarily or by someone else moving parts of the person's body. This kind of bizarre behavior gave rise to the diagnostic label *catatonic* (from the Greek *katatonie*, "to take or seize a position," and *tonus*, "muscle tension"). Although abnormal excitement and social withdrawal are also found in manic and major depressive episodes (see Chapter

Catatonic schizophrenia is characterized by psychomotor disturbances that may range from abnormal excitement to highly withdrawn behavior. In this photograph the patient is expressing his withdrawal by assuming a rigid posture and refusing to speak. The use of drug therapy has reduced the occurrence of catatonic symptoms.

10), they lack the stereotyped nature of catatonic reactions as well as the more basic characteristics of schizophrenia described earlier.

Catatonic individuals sometimes alternate rapidly between excited and withdrawn behavior. In both states, they require careful supervision. They may inflict injury on themselves or others during abnormal excitement or may simply become exhausted to the point of bodily harm. When they are withdrawn, they may refuse to eat and thus may develop serious problems of malnutrition.

Some clinicians have interpreted immobility and mutism of catatonic schizophrenia as an extreme defense against a physical and social environment the individual can no longer control. As one patient put it after recovering from such a state: "I did not want to move, because if I did everything changed around me, and upset me horribly, so I remained still to hold onto a sense of permanence" (Freeman, 1960, p. 932).

The expanded use of drug therapy in the last few decades has reduced the incidence of full-blown catatonic behavior, at least in hospitalized schizophrenic patients, especially in Europe and North America (American Psychiatric Association, 1987, p. 196).

Paranoid Schizophrenia

The symptoms of **paranoid schizophrenia** (from the Greek *para*, "beyond," and *nous*, "irrationality") usually begin later in life than those of other types, and they are also more consistent over time. Delusions of persecution or grandeur are prominent. Delusions involving extreme and irrational jealousy may also occur.

Although the delusions in paranoid schizophrenia tend to be more coherent than those commonly encountered in disorganized and catatonic schizophrenia, they still have a strange and implausible quality. The following case excerpt illustrates a typical delusion.

> Jim is . . . a third-year medical student. Over the last few weeks he has been noticing that older men appear to be frightened of him when he passes them on the street. Recently, he has become convinced that he is actually the director of the Central Intelligence Agency and that these men are secret agents of a hostile nation. Jim has found confirmatory evidence for his idea in the fact that a helicopter flies over his house every day at 8:00 A.M. and at 4:30 P.M. Surely, this surveillance is part of the plot to assassinate him. (Bernheim & Lewine, 1979, p. 4).

Hallucinations involving persecution, grandeur, or jealousy may occur as a central feature or, more often, in association with delusions. Hostility, argumentativeness, and even physical violence may play a noticeable part in the paranoid pattern, the mode of expression being consistent with the content of delusions or hallucinations.

Although obviously impaired in their everyday functioning, individuals suffering from paranoid schizophrenia do not usually display the gross disintegration of personality or the cognitive impairment typical of nonparanoid schizophrenics. Paranoid schizophrenics tend to score higher on standardized intelligence tests. They also have longer attention spans, and they are less distractible. Furthermore, the length of their hospitalization is usually shorter (Strauss, 1973). Treatment with neuroleptic drugs can help considerably in alleviating the hallucinations and delusions (see Chapter 18).

Undifferentiated Type of Schizophrenia

As the label implies, the **undifferentiated type of schizophrenia** includes symptoms that are definitely schizophrenic in nature but do not meet the criteria for the disorganized, catatonic, or paranoid type.

Residual Type of Schizophrenia

The diagnosis of **residual type of schizophrenia** is used when (a) the individual has experienced at least one schizophrenic episode, (b) symptoms are not currently prominent, and (c) some signs of schizophrenic disorder persist. When delusions or hallucinations are present, they tend not to be strongly expressed.

Schizophrenia as a Formal Thought Disorder

The disordered thinking of schizophrenia involves disturbances in the content and the form of thought. The latter is known as **formal thought disorder**. Various clinical researchers believe that this condition is a key symptom of schizophrenia. Schizophrenic individuals may move from one unrelated topic to another. Often, they fail to realize that the topics are unrelated. Furthermore, even within a particular discourse, the organization may be so incoherent that meaningful communication becomes impossible. The speech of manic individuals (see Chapter 10) is also incoherent, but the disorganization is mainly a matter of rapid shifts from one coherent discourse to another. In contrast, the ability of schizophrenics to maintain any coherent structure in their speech is deficient (George & Neufeld, 1985; Hoffman, Stopek, & Andreasen, 1986; Holtzman, 1986).

Theoretical Views and Clinical Observations of Formal Thought Disorder

Overinclusion and Deficits in Abstract Thinking

The concept **overinclusion** refers to the tendency of many schizophrenic individuals to include more objects in a particular class than belong there. Apparently, they are unable to filter out irrelevant information when trying to solve problems. Norman Cameron was a pioneer in systematically describing this aspect of formal thought disorder. For example, he cited the behavior of a schizophrenic patient who found it impossible to limit his attention to the blocks in a block-sorting task:

> I've got to pick it out of the whole room. I can't confine myself to the game. . . . Three blues [test block]—now, how about that green blotter? Put it in there too. (Green) peas you eat, you can't eat them unless you write on it [pointing to the green blotter]. Like that wrist watch [on experimenter's wrist]—I don't see any three meals coming off that watch . . . White and blue (blocks) is Duke's mixture. This (pulling out match box). There's a man out there [on porch] with a white tie; that's got something to do with white suits. (Cameron, 1963, pp. 613–614)

Since Cameron's work, a wide variety of studies have demonstrated the nature of overinclusive thinking (Pishkin & Williams, 1984; Rabin, Doneson, & Jentons, 1979; Shimkunas, 1978). Among the tasks were sorting cards and blocks into classes of objects, synonym tests, the number of words used to give the meaning of proverbs, and other problems involving the identification of concepts. Because the underlying thought processes used in many of the measures differed considerably, some critics have argued that overinclusion is too broad a formulation to serve as a unifying principle of schizophrenic thought (Chapman & Chapman, 1973). Nevertheless, it does seem to play an important role in at least some aspects of schizophrenic thinking.

On the basis of experiments with normal children and schizophrenic patients, the Russian psychologist Lev Semonovich Vigotsky concluded that schizophrenia involves regression to immature thinking in which concrete thought replaces abstract thought.

Like Vigotsky, psychiatrist Kurt Goldstein, who emigrated to the United States in 1935, stressed that schizophrenic individuals suffer from a deficit in abstract thinking.

Chief among the pioneering researchers who emphasized the deficits in abstract thinking that often occur in schizophrenia were Lev Semonovich Vigotsky (1896–1934), a Russian psychologist, and Kurt Goldstein (1878–1965), a German neurologist and psychiatrist who emigrated to the United States in 1935.

As the result of various experiments with normal children and schizophrenics, Vigotsky (1934, 1962) concluded that schizophrenia involves a regression to immature ways of thinking in which concrete thought increasingly replaces abstract thought. Goldstein stressed that schizophrenic individuals suffer from a deficit in abstract thinking, or, as he put it, "an impairment of the abstract attitude" (1963, p. 64). He distinguished between the impairment that accompanies certain forms of brain damage and the more temporary loss typical of schizophrenic thought disorder. A schizophrenic individual might well show an inability to think abstractly under some circumstances but not others, whereas the loss of abstract thinking in brain damage is more widespread. Goldstein concluded that the defect in schizophrenia was psychogenic rather than organic — a defense against anxiety rather than the result of physical damage to the brain.

Dissociation of Ideas

Eugen Bleuler (1911/1950, 1924/1976) called the disordered thought in schizophrenia the breaking of associative threads, an abnormal disruption in the relationship between ideas. The disruption serves a purpose, although it is maladaptive. By splitting ideas from each other, the schizophrenic can hold contradictory beliefs. For example, a schizophrenic patient may state that "he is the father and mother of his child," that he is "both a millionaire and impoverished," or that he "is a bachelor and has three wives" (Chapman & Chapman, 1973, p. 111).

Excessive Yielding to Normal Biases

Loren J. Chapman and Jean P. Chapman (1973)) agree with Bleuler that schizophrenic individuals often use inappropriate associations that might well reflect a breaking of associative threads. However, Chapman and Chapman seek to explain why some associative threads are broken and others remain intact. They stress the inappropriate use of strong association, something that normal individuals might do only occasionally. For example, they cite Bleuler's description of a schizophrenic patient enumerating the members of her family. She first said, "father, son," and then added, "and the Holy Ghost." Bleuler attributed this latter response to the breaking of associative threads, but one could interpret it as a strong association — that is, the first words that even normal individuals might call to mind when their judgment concerning the appropriateness of their response is temporarily relaxed. In contrast to such normal situations, the patient's use of the strong association was not a matter of momentarily relaxed judgment. It reflected a persistent mode of inappropriate associations, an excessive yielding to the same kinds of biases present in normal persons. The crucial difference is that schizophrenic individuals have relinquished control over their biases (Chapman & Chapman, 1973, pp. 112, 125–126).

An especially attractive feature of Chapman and Chapman's theory is that it does not relegate schizophrenic thought to a domain completely separate from normal thought. It views such thinking as part of a continuum from normality to abnormality, a concept that is consistent with modern views of abnormal psychology.

Some researchers have questioned whether this yielding occurs only in schizophrenia. In a study involving a word meaning test, Naficy and Willerman (1980) found that groups of manic patients also yielded excessively to normal biases. Nevertheless, the theory of excessive yielding does help account for a number of phenomena that appear in schizophrenic thinking, such as errors in logical reasoning, excessive use of concrete thinking (overinclusiveness), and a variety of inappropriate ways of associating ideas (breaking of associative threads).

Experimental Laboratory Studies

Emil Kraepelin not only provided the first clinical description of schizophrenic disorders but also initiated experimental research. Thus, the history of experimentation on schizophrenia goes back close to 100 years, almost as long as the history of experimental psychology itself. The German psychologist Plaum (1975) has summarized the findings under four broad principles.

1. The performance of schizophrenic individuals becomes impaired under conditions of emotional involvement. Emotional stimuli cause schizophrenics to stumble over tasks that they are perfectly able to perform under neutral (nonemotional) conditions. This impairment occurs in highly diverse tasks.

2. Schizophrenic individuals form concepts in an abnormal manner and experience disruption in their thinking when they must operate on an abstract level. The rules of logic that nonschizophrenics apply efficiently or automatically are used by schizophrenics in an erratic, unpredictable, and highly personalized manner. A schizophrenic person is more effective in dealing with concrete objects of experience than in manipulating intangible concepts and abstractions.

3. The associations in schizophrenic thinking are not only unusual but also highly maladaptive. Bleuler (1924/1976) described this lack of cognitive control as an inability to hold "the train of thought in the proper channels."

4. Schizophrenic individuals reveal a specific impairment in how they receive and process information. Although their sensory acuity remains unimpaired, their thinking is disturbed at the gateway of perception — that is, at the moment of receiving information. This disturbance continues in the subsequent operations of sorting and retrieving information. It is as though their minds operate with a highly inefficient and unusual filing system. As one patient put it: "Things are coming in too fast. I lose my grip of it and get lost. I am attending to everything at once and as a result I do not really attend to anything" (McGhie & Chapman, 1961, p. 104).

Recent laboratory studies of reactions to visual stimuli support the hypothesis that faulty information processing may be a genetically transmitted trait. For example, controlled observations of eye movements in patients diagnosed as schizophrenic revealed impairments in the ability to select and pay attention to visual stimuli. Furthermore, various family members of such patients showed similar deficiencies in their selective attention to visual stimuli, even though they did not display clinical symptoms of schizophrenia. Thus, the impairment in visual attention may be a marker for the faulty information processing found in schizophrenic individuals and may serve as a way of detecting people at high risk of developing the disorder. Additional laboratory studies involving first-degree relatives of schizophrenics are needed. Also, the tests themselves need greater standardization and refinement (Holtzman, 1987; Merritt & Balogh, 1985; Nuerchterlein & Dawson, 1984; Rosenbaum, Shore, & Chapin, 1988).

Course and Outcome of Schizophrenic Disorders

The Process-Reactive Dimension

Eugen Bleuler (1924/1976) first used the terms *process* and *reactive* to indicate what he believed were two distinct forms of schizophrenia—a distinction he based on etiology. According to Bleuler, **process schizophrenia** originates in faulty biological processes; **reactive schizophrenia** stems from maladaptive responses to life situations. In succeeding years the process–reactive dimension took on an additional meaning. Individuals who showed little or no improvement were classified as process schizophrenics. Those who showed considerable improvement or recovered were called reactive schizophrenics. Thus, the distinction came to imply that schizophrenic disorders rooted in biological errors had a poor prognosis, but those presumably caused by life experiences had a better prognosis.

Many researchers and practitioners still use the terms *process* and *reactive*, but their earlier connotations have changed. Process and reactive schizophrenia are now more likely to be considered the extreme ends of a continuum of schizophrenia. Furthermore, this bipolar dimension has a broad prognostic meaning that does not require a sharp separation between biological processes and social–psychological factors. The process end of the dimension involves symptoms and premorbid characteristics (characteristics existing prior to the onset of symptoms) that predict a relatively unfavorable course and outcome of schizophrenia. The reactive end of the dimension includes symptoms and premorbid characteristics that predict a relatively favorable course and outcome. Most studies of premorbid characteristics as predictors of schizophrenia have emphasized psychological and social variables. Some, however, have included certain biological factors, such as estimates of an individual's genetic vulnerability (Harrow & Westermeyer, 1987; Harrow, Westermeyer, Silverstein, Strauss, & Cohler, 1986; Herron, 1987; Neale & Oltmanns, 1980; Shean, 1978; Strauss & Carpenter, 1979; Strauss, Kokes, Klorman, & Sacksteder, 1977).

Development of Symptoms

A slow, insidious development of symptoms is often associated with a relatively unfavorable course and outcome (the process end of the dimension). Symptoms whose onset is relatively rapid and obvious are more likely to be associated with a favorable course and outcome (the reactive end of the dimension). Although environmental stress no doubt plays a role in both patterns of development, the rapid onset of symptoms seems more obviously related to precipitating events than in the case of insidious onset (Neale & Oltmanns, 1980). To some extent, this relationship is consistent with Bleuler's proposal that reactive schizophrenia stems mainly from the impact of life experiences rather than from biological factors. However, the fact that stressful events are not always obvious does not necessarily mean they play an unimportant part in the slow, insidious development of symptoms. Stress may build up over a long period of time; thus, precipitating events may not always be noticed.

Prognostic Rating Scales

One of the main ways of predicting the course and outcome of schizophrenic disorders is through the use of **prognostic rating scales** (Fenton & McGlashan, 1987; Kokes, Strauss, & Klorman, 1977; Moller, Schmid-Bode, & von Zerssen, 1986). These scales enable the clinician to estimate objectively how often certain premorbid characteristics have occurred. The items in these scales come from a number of sources—for example: (a) interviews with the patient and family members, (b) questionnaires filled out by the patient where this is feasible, (c) direct observations of the patient's behavior in a variety of situations, and (d) other information from case history records concerning the patient's past life, especially those involving interpersonal relationships. The items retained in a scale are those found to differentiate between patients who show significant improvement and patients who fare less well. In estimating the prognosis for a given individual, one may examine responses to specific items as well as the total score for all items.

A number of fairly consistent findings have emerged from research with prognostic rating scales, although not all investigators have phrased their predictions specifically in terms of the process–reactive dimension. In general, this research has shown that highly specific variables—for example, age of onset—do not predict the development and outcome of schizophrenia as well as more complex dimensions of premorbid adjustment, such as sexual and interpersonal adjustment, interests and skills, and various aspects of community functioning (Kokes, Strauss, & Klorman, 1977; McGlashan, 1986b; Wallace, 1984). This is to be expected, since the outcome of schizophrenia can itself be viewed along a number of different dimensions. Thus, some individuals may show a particularly favorable outcome in sexual adjustment, but for others the most favorable outcome may be in certain aspects of social adjustment (Schwartz, Myers, & Astrachan, 1975; Strauss & Carpenter, 1979). One of the best single predictors of outcome is marital status. Single individuals (especially males) are hospitalized more often than married persons and tend to remain hospitalized longer (Klorman, Strauss, & Kokes, 1977).

There are a number of plausible explanations for the predictive power of marital status. For one thing, being single probably reflects the influence of other premorbid characteristics that in themselves are predictors of outcome. For example, poor premorbid sexual adjustment and lack of competence in personal and social relationships, which may consist of a complex of characteristics, tend to go along with an unfavorable prognosis. In addition, married individuals may leave the hospital more rapidly than single people because they have more support on the outside and a more receptive environment to enter. It is also possible that length of hospitalization reflects hospital policy more than actual improvement. That is, hospital personnel may be more willing to discharge married people because they expect them to have a better support system to go to. Studies using various criteria of posthospital adjustment also found marriage to be a favorable prognostic indicator for schizophrenic patients (Harrow, Westermeyer, Silverstein, Strauss, & Cohler, 1986).

DSM-III-R Criteria

A knowledge of the various ways in which schizophrenic disorders develop is an important factor in planning appropriate treatment and predicting outcomes. Furthermore, these variations often reveal differences not always apparent when symptoms are simply classified according to type. For these reasons, DSM-III-R provides specific criteria for the clinician to follow in diagnosing the course of a schizophrenic disorder (American Psychiatric Association, 1987, p. 195).

1. Subchronic. Less than two years but at least six months have elapsed from the time the individual first showed signs of the disorder.

2. Chronic. More than two years have elapsed since signs of the disorder were first noted.

3. Subchronic with acute exacerbation. Prominent psychotic symptoms (for example, delusions and hallucinations) have reappeared in an individual whose symptoms followed a subchronic course and who has been in the residual phase.

4. Chronic with acute exacerbation. Same as for item 3, except that the symptoms followed a chronic course.

5. In remission. This category indicates the diagnostic status of an individual who has had a definite history of schizophrenia but who currently shows no signs of the disorder regardless of whether medication or other treatment is still being continued. The clinician must be careful to differentiate "in remission" from "no mental disorder." The distinction depends on such factors as how long it has been since symptoms were observed (the shorter the period, the more likely the diagnosis "in remission" is more appropriate than "no mental disorder") and how important it is for prophylactic treatment and evaluation of progress to continue. Prophylactic treatment, aimed at preventing recurrence of the disorder, may involve medication, psychotherapy, or both.

Bleuler's Research

Manfred Bleuler (1978), a professor of psychiatry at the University of Zurich and the son of Eugen Bleuler, reviewed the life histories of some 2000 individuals diagnosed as schizophrenic in Switzerland and the United States and came to the following conclusions.

■ On the average, after a five-year duration, schizophrenic symptoms do not seem to progress any further. Indeed, the tendency is for the disorder to improve. This trend is not apparent if one considers only rough indices, such as "recovered or not recovered" and "hospitalized or not." However, if one examines the individual's behavior carefully, various signs of improvement, such as gains in the ability to communicate with others, in as well as out of the hospital, become clearer. Bleuler tempered this conclusion with the observation that many schizophrenic individuals who had recovered from severe psychotic symptoms seemed to be rather inactive, lacked personal initiative, and had "somewhat apathetic, colorless personalities" (1978, p. 633). Bleuler compared this residual condi-

Manfred Bleuler, Professor of Psychiatry at the University of Zurich, and the son of Eugen Bleuler, has concluded that the prognosis for schizophrenic individuals is more hopeful than many other mental health professionals had believed.

tion to the "impoverished personality" that might result from long-term incarceration in a concentration camp or "after an uneventful, unsatisfactory life during which the person's talents and abilities had no occasion to develop" (p. 633–634). One can infer from Bleuler's observations that long-term hospitalization itself can contribute significantly to "impoverished personality." Indeed, studies have shown that the longer schizophrenic patients remain hospitalized, the less interested they become in leaving (Neale & Oltmanns, 1980, p. 424; Tsuang, 1982).

■ At least 25 percent of schizophrenic patients recover entirely and remain recovered for good. Bleuler's criteria for recovery included a lack of psychotic symptoms, a normal integration into social life, and the ability to maintain a job.

■ About 10 percent of schizophrenic individuals remain permanently hospitalized as severely psychotic. Although Bleuler viewed this as frightening, he pointed out that the percentage is relatively low when one considers that some years ago many psychiatrists thought schizophrenia a progressive disease that almost always led to lifelong invalidism.

Bleuler attributed the relatively good record of improvement in schizophrenic disorder to better hospital and outpatient care, but he did not point to any particular mode of treatment as the key to success. "Any therapeutic technique," he stated, "can be replaced by another good one, provided it includes at least one of the following: an active therapeutic community, 'tranquilizing' drugs, or confrontation with stress" (Bleuler, 1978, p. 635). This confrontation can take a variety of directions — for example, giving the patient unexpected responsibilities, discharging the patient from the hospital, changing the hospital environment, or interpreting the patient's behavior appropriately.

Psychiatrist George Vaillant supports Bleuler's optimism: "If we can spare our patients the indignity of chronic hospitalization," says Vaillant, "and if we can provide some supportive after-care, the supposed progressive deterioration of schizophrenics, originally reported by Kraepelin and still widely believed by many psychiatrists, does not, in fact, characterize the group of schizophrenics" (Vaillant, 1978, p. 637).

Recent follow-up studies on the long-term (10-to-30-year) outcomes of schizophrenic patients reinforce Vaillant's position. These studies found that at least half of the individuals showed a marked improvement in various aspects of social and psychological functioning (Harding, Brooks, Ashikaga, Strauss, & Breier, 1987a, 1987b).

Positive and Negative Symptoms

In recent years, a great deal of research and controversy has focused on the proposition that a useful distinction can be made between *positive* and *negative* symptoms of schizophrenia. Positive symptoms include the hallucinations, delusions, fluent but disorganized speech, and severe thought disorder that are typical of acute schizophrenia. Negative symptoms include emotional flattening and the inability to feel and express emotions appropriately; severe decrease in motivation, such as the constant inability to complete tasks; inability to enjoy relationships with other people; and extreme withdrawal from the social environment. These symptoms are typical of chronic schizophrenia. In recent years, a great deal of research, discussion, and controversy has centered around the distinction between positive and negative symptoms (Andreasen, 1982a, 1982b, 1983, 1984b, 1985, 1987; Berenbaum, Oltmanns, & Gottesman, 1987; Crow, 1980, 1985; Lewine, 1985; Sommers, 1985; Strauss, 1985; Zubin, 1985). Almost an entire issue of the *Schizophrenia Bulletin* (1985, vol. 11 no. 3) was devoted to the topic.

Dividing symptoms of schizophrenia into categories seems to oversimplify the problem, especially since schizophrenic patients often show a mixture of symptoms (Andreasen, 1985, pp. 365–366). Nevertheless, some researchers argue that understanding such differences can have important implications for predicting the outcome of schizophrenia and for methods of treatment, especially the use of medication. For example, negative symptoms are said to be much less amenable to drug treatment than positive symptoms. On the other hand, in a review of five large studies, Goldberg (1985) concluded that the outcome of drug treatment for negative symptoms was considerably more favorable than some researchers have claimed. Other mental health professionals suggest that the term *negative symptoms* is simply a relabeling of chronic and process schizophrenia (Lewine, 1985). Future research may well reveal that the positive–negative distinction can make a new and significant contribution to the understanding and treatment of schizophrenia. Research may eventually support the long-held belief of many clinicians that schizophrenia is a group of related but separate disorders rather than a single entity (American Psychiatric Association, 1987; Kay, Fiszbein, & Opler, 1987.

Genetic Influences on Schizophrenia

In his closing remarks at a famous research conference held in Puerto Rico during the summer of 1967, behavioral geneticist David Rosenthal stated that the conference "could be remembered as the time that it was definitely and openly agreed by our foremost students of family interaction that heredity is implicated in the development of schizophrenia" (Rosenthal, 1968, p. 415).

Research on the inheritance of schizophrenic disorders have expanded so greatly in the last few decades that a comprehensive review of the results would require going far beyond the limits of this chapter (see Barnes, 1987a; Cancro, 1979; Defries & Plomin, 1978; Goldstein, 1988; Goldstein & Tuma, 1987; Gottesman & Shields, 1982; Kessler, 1980; Neale & Oltmanns, 1980; Schulsinger, 1980). Our present discussion, therefore, is restricted primarily to studies of twins and adopted children. The data from these kinds of investigations are probably the strongest evidence for demonstrating the influence of heredity on the development of schizophrenia.

Research on Twins

Studies of schizophrenia in twins have generally employed the concordance rate to estimate the extent of genetic influence — the same strategy used to study the occurrence of mood disorders in twins. The concordance rate — the tendency for both twins to develop a particular disorder — was discussed in Chapter 10. The effect of heredity on the disorder can be inferred through a comparison of the concordance rate for MZ (identical) twins with that for DZ (fraternal) twins. If the rate is higher for MZ twins than for DZ twins, heredity can be assumed to be at least partly responsible for the difference.

The usual procedure is to find people who have a twin and who have been diagnosed as schizophrenic. These individuals are designated index cases, or probands (subjects). The researchers locate the twin of each proband, termed the *co-twin*, and determine whether the co-twin was ever diagnosed as schizophrenic. The concordance rate for schizophrenia is then calculated. The simplest method, and the one that behavioral geneticists commonly use, is based on the number of twin pairs in the sample. The degree of concordance is the percentage of all pairs in which both twins have a history of schizophrenia. For example, if a sample has 25 pairs of twins, and 5 pairs have such a history, the concordance rate is 20 percent (Gottesman & Shields, 1966, 1972; Maher, 1970, pp. 157–158).

David Rosenthal (1971, p. 73) has summarized the concordance rates reported in studies carried out in Denmark, England, Finland, Norway, and the United States. The concordance rates were consistently higher for MZ pairs than for DZ pairs. The results of the British studies (Gottesman & Shields, 1966, 1972) are especially impressive, not only because of the high degree of concordance for MZ twins (41.7 percent) but also because of the extreme care the researchers took to avoid bias in making diagnostic judgments. They obtained data for the twins from a systematic search of the records of some 45,000 patients treated at hospitals in London over a period of 16 years. Six judges representing various cultural backgrounds and professional orientations (from England, the United States, and Japan) examined the case summaries. Each judge made a diagnosis independently of the others and without knowing the relationship between one twin and another. The study clearly demonstrates the importance of heredity in the development of schizophrenia.

Leonard Heston (1970) examined data on 358 pairs of MZ twins. He concluded that given a schizophrenic individual with an MZ twin, the probability that the twin will also be schizophrenic is about .46. Heston also hypothesized that a deficit in a single dominant gene may account for the genetic contribution to schizophrenia.

The results of later studies on schizophrenia in twins are consistent with those just discussed (McGuffin, Farmer, Gottesman, Murray, & Reveley, 1984; Rosenthal, 1971). However, the concordance rate for MZ twins varies from one study to another. It can be as high as 86 percent and as low as 6 percent. Such results indicate that nonhereditary factors must also play an important part in determining whether a given individual will develop schizophrenia. On the average, however, an identical twin of a schizophrenic person is at least three times as likely as a fraternal twin to develop the disorder. Indeed, as Figure 11.1 shows, estimates of the lifetime risk of schizophrenia to the relatives of schizophrenic patients increase markedly with the degree of genetic relatedness. This is true even if the relatives have not shared a specific environment with the schizophrenic patient (Gottesman & Shields, 1982; Nicol & Gottesman, 1983).

The evidence of twin studies is often countered with the obvious fact that MZ twins have more than their identical heredity in common. For example, they are often dressed alike

Figure 11.1

Lifetime risk of developing schizophrenia as a function of genetic relatedness. (From Nicol & Gottesman, 1983, p. 399.) The lifetime risk of schizophrenia to the relatives of schizophrenic individuals increases with the degree of relatedness, even if the relatives have not shared a specific environment with the patient. Genetic relatedness cannot be expressed in a percentage in the case of an individual with two schizophrenic parents, however the estimated risk is the same as for identical twins.

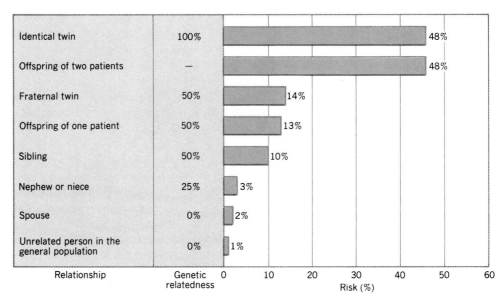

and treated alike. Their identities are frequently confused, and others often regard them as a pair rather than as two separate individuals (Cancro, 1979). In an ideal, natural experiment involving MZ twins, one would want heredity to be the only characteristic they shared. Thus, any tendency for both twins to develop schizophrenia could be attributed to heredity without question. This ideal is impossible to attain, but that is not a sufficient reason to discard the results of twin studies.

One way to address the problem of similarity in the treatment of MZ twins is to study those who have been reared apart. Such situations are rare, but Gottesman and Shields (1972) reviewed studies involving 14 pairs of MZ twins who had been separated from their biological parents by the time they were 2 years of age and reared apart from them and from each other. Of the 14 pairs, 10 were concordant for schizophrenia, a higher rate than that of MZ twins living together. Results based on only 14 pairs of twins need to be interpreted conservatively, but they do add general support to the importance of heredity in the development of schizophrenia.

Studies of Adopted Children

Probably the most powerful evidence for genetic influences on the development of schizophrenia comes from studies of individuals who were adopted early in life. One of the most extensive and carefully planned studies of this kind, involving some 5500 children, was carried out in Denmark (Kety, Rosenthal, Wender, & Schulsinger, 1968). The investigation examined the records of all children who, between 1924 and 1947, were adopted by people other than biological relatives. On the basis of information from Denmark's centralized Psychiatric Register, all of the adoptees who had been admitted to a psychiatric facility and diagnosed as schizophrenic were designated index cases. A control group was then selected from the remaining adoptees. It consisted of people with no history of psychiatric disturbance, and it was matched with people in the index group for age, sex, age when adopted, preadoption history, and socioeconomic status of the adoptive parents. In all, 33 schizophrenic adoptees and their matched controls were selected for study. In addition, the adoptive parents and the biological parents of both the index cases and the control group were identified. Researchers then consulted the Psychiatric Register to see which parents had a history of psychiatric disorder. Significantly higher rates of schizophrenic disturbances occurred among the biological parents of index cases than among the biological parents of the control group. However, there was no significant difference between adoptive parents of index cases and adoptive parents of the control group.

More refined follow-up studies in Denmark have confirmed these findings. They include interviews with about 90 percent of the biological and adoptive families of the schizophrenic individuals and the control group and an increase in the numbers of index cases and their controls (Kety, Rosenthal, Wender, Schulsinger, & Jacobsen, 1975, 1978).

More recently, an independent analysis of the Danish adoption data came to conclusions highly consistent with those of the previous studies: (a) genetic factors play an etiological role in schizophrenia, (b) the likelihood that people adopted at an early age and reared by nonrelatives will develop a schizophrenic disorder is greatly increased if at least one of their relatives is schizophrenic, (c) the genetic factors involved in schizophrenia seem to be specific — that is, they do not appear to increase vulnerability to other mental disorders (Kendler & Gruenberg, 1984).

As a whole, the evidence from studies of twins and adopted children supports the conclusion that heredity plays an important part in the development of schizophrenic disorders. However, one must also consider the interaction of heredity with environmental events. Thus, the question Is schizophrenia an inherited disorder? is a pseudoquestion. One should ask instead a more complex and meaningful question: What kinds of aversive environmental events can help induce schizophrenic disorder in people who are genetically vulnerable? (Goldstein, 1988; Hartmann, Milofsky, Vaillant, Oldfield, Falke, & Ducey, 1984; Rosenthal, 1970; Yeatman & Hirsch, 1971). Later in the chapter, we will consider some of those environmental events. Before doing so, however, we turn to another area of biological research in the development of schizophrenia—biochemical disturbances in the brain.

Biochemical Disturbances in the Brain

Although studies on twins and adopted children support the conclusion that hereditary factors influence the development of schizophrenia, they do not indicate what the underlying biological disturbances actually are. Some researchers are increasingly convinced that biochemical abnormalities in the brain, transmitted or aggravated by defective genes, play an important role in schizophrenic disorders.

Until about 1970, a great deal of the research on the biochemistry of schizophrenia was concerned primarily with discovering abnormal and often esoteric chemical substances in various bodily fluids, especially the blood and urine. Such substances were thought to reflect a biochemical disturbance in the brain that contributed to schizophrenic thinking and behavior.

The Taraxein Hypothesis

Robert Heath and his associates isolated from the blood serum of schizophrenic patients a copper–protein that they named **taraxein** (from the Greek *tarassein*, "to disturb") (Heath, 1963). They hypothesized that taraxein interacts with other chemical substances to produce a toxin that interferes with the normal functioning of the brain. One source of support for the hypothesis was the finding that when taraxein was injected into nonschizophrenic individuals (volunteer prisoners), it produced schizophrenic symptoms. Further studies of taraxein convinced Heath and his colleagues that schizophrenia is basically a biological disorder. They hypothesized that a metabolic error, yet undiscovered but probably of genetic origin, causes the body to manufacture taraxein. In turn, taraxein acts as an antibody in the brain, interfering with the normal transformation of information from one brain cell to another (Heath, Krupp, Byers, & Liljekvist, 1967; Heath & Krupp, 1968).

A number of researchers attempted to confirm the taraxein hypothesis, with little success (Boehme, Cottrell, Dohan, & Hillegass, 1974; Logan & Deodhar, 1970). Others looked for sources of antibodies other than taraxein that might influence the development of schizophrenia, but the search has not been conclusive (Durell & Archer, 1976; Van Praag, 1977).

Much of the uncertainty of the research lies in the fact that the findings often cannot be replicated. Furthermore, the presence of antibodies in the blood or urine of schizophrenics might be a result rather than a cause of the disorder.

The Dopamine Hypothesis

Amphetamine and Dopamine

Various studies have shown that amphetamine is a schizomimetic drug — that is, it mimics some of the symptoms commonly found in schizophrenia. Among these symptoms are hallucinations, delusions, and paranoid symptoms (Angrist, Lee, & Gershon, 1974; Snyder, 1973; Snyder, Banjerjee, Yamamura, & Greenberg, 1974; Wyatt, 1978). Amphetamine psychosis also involves a flattening of affect and an autistic withdrawal from reality. However, the symptoms generally disappear a few days after ingestion of the drug.

The effects of amphetamine have led to the **dopamine hypothesis**. Apparently, amphetamine causes symptoms similar to schizophrenia by stimulating excessive amounts of dopamine in the brain. Dopamine is a biochemical substance that acts as a neurotransmitter, facilitating the passage of electrochemical impulses from one nerve cell (neuron) to another. Recent biochemical research has strengthened the hypothesis that an excess of dopamine causes, in part, at least some of the forms of schizophrenia (Andreasen, 1984a, pp. 133–135; Barnes, 1987a, p. 432; Meltzer, 1987).

Dopamine, Neuroleptics, and Endorphins

Many researchers believe the best evidence to support the dopamine hypothesis is based on the effectiveness of **neuroleptic drugs**. (The term *neuroleptic* comes from the Greek words *neuron*, "nerve," and *lepsis*, "taking hold.") These drugs not only alleviate schizophrenic symptoms but also reduce dopamine activity in the brain. The question thus arises: Since neuroleptics block dopamine activity in schizophrenia, which in turn reduces schizophrenic symptoms, might not an increase in dopamine activity play a role in the development of schizophrenic symptoms? Many biochemical researchers give a tentative yes to the question. Furthermore, some researchers have found that the dopamine activity in schizophrenic patients who had not been treated with neuroleptics was higher than in a volunteer group of normal individuals. This discovery was based on the use of positron emission tomography, a newly developed imaging technique that can reveal the density of dopamine receptors in the brains of living human beings (Buchsbaum & Haier, 1987; Wong, et al., 1988).

A number of studies have considered the possible interaction between endorphins and dopamine activity (Davis, Buchsbaum, & Bunney, 1979; McGeer and McGeer, 1980; Van Kammen, 1979; Verebey, Volavka, & Clouet, 1978; Volavka, Davis, & Ehrlich, 1979). Endorphins are opiatelike substances that bind to the same sites in the brain as morphine and the other opiates. They belong to a group of biochemical compounds known as peptides, which contain amino acids and form the constituent parts of proteins.

The cerebrospinal fluid of chronic schizophrenics contains excessive levels of endorphins. These levels go down after treatment with neuroleptic drugs. The drugs block dopamine, and neurons containing endorphins regulate the activity of neurons containing dopamine as well. Thus, a decrease in endorphin activity may result in a decrease in dopamine activity (Rimon, Terenius, Kampman, 1980; Terenius, Wahlstrom, Lindstrom, & Widerlov (1976).

These findings are tentative, and some researchers doubt if there is any direct link between endorphins and dopamine (Watson & Akil, 1979). Other researchers question whether endorphins affect schizophrenic symptoms at all, because they have found instances in which this did not occur (Usdin, 1979).

The precise role of biochemical changes in producing schizophrenic symptoms is far from settled. It seems unlikely that a single biochemical factor, such as dopamine or endorphin activity in the brain, can account for all types of schizophrenic disorder (Buschsbaum & Haier, 1983; Csernansky, Holman, & Hollister, 1983; Kety, 1980). Since schizophrenia is not a single disorder but a group of disorders, the biochemical factors that underlie some forms may not necessarily be involved in others.

Additional biological possibilities must also be investigated. It may be that biochemical changes in individuals who develop schizophrenia at a young age are absent in those who develop it at later ages. Also, biochemical changes present at certain stages of the disorder may not be present at other stages (Nicol & Gottesman, 1983).

It is unlikely that biochemical changes operate in isolation. One must consider not only the interaction among the changes themselves but also the impact of the social and psychological experiences of the schizophrenic. Even if an individual is biologically vulnerable to developing a schizophrenic disorder, a benign environment may attenuate that vulnerability. On the other hand, stressful life events over a long period of time and consequent deficiencies in coping skills may increase the risk of developing a schizophrenic disorder (Lukoff, Snyder, Ventura, & Nuechterlein, 1984; Nuechterlein & Dawson, 1984). An important area of research on the impact of social and psychological experiences focuses on the family.

Family Interaction and the Development of Schizophrenia

Aversive Maternal Control

Heilbrun (1973) reviewed a large number of studies focusing on the mothers of schizophrenic patients. Such mothers are described as oversolicitous, overprotective, restrictive, dominating, autocratic, moralistic, puritanical, rigid, cold, and manipulative — reflecting what Heilbrun called **aversive maternal control**.

At one time, many mental health professionals thought that such aversive maternal characteristics were of central importance in the development of schizophrenic disorders. Indeed, the term *schizophrenogenic* (schizophrenia-producing) was coined to describe them. More recently, however, practitioners and researchers in the field of psychopathology have become increasingly skeptical about the validity of the label, and especially its implication that aversive mothers play the central role in family influences on the development of schizophrenia (Waxler, 1975). Silvano Arieti, a prolific expert on schizophrenia, argued in 1955 that the research evidence strongly supported the concept of "schizophrenogenic" mothers. Almost 20 years later, after reexamining the same evidence and considering subsequent work, Arieti concluded that even though serious family disturbances contributed to the development of schizophrenic disorders, it was misleading to focus on so-called schizophrenogenic mothers as the most important influence (Arieti, 1974, p. 81).

Aversive Attitudes of Fathers

Although most studies have focused on the mother's role in the development of schizophrenic disorders, a number of investigations have dealt with the influence of the father. A common theme runs through all the results: The fathers of schizophrenic individuals display aversive attitudes that resemble those of schizophrenogenic mothers. For example, studies have reported that the fathers of schizophrenic individuals were either overtly rejecting and cruel or expressed their rejection more subtly by being passive and aloof (Lidz, Cornelison, Fleck, & Terry, 1957). An especially extensive study involving more than 500 schizophrenic men found that about 50 percent had been severely rejected, especially by their fathers (Wahl, 1956).

Evaluation of Studies

It is misleading to form any precise conclusions about the role of parental attitudes from the kinds of studies just described, especially because of various methodological problems (Fontana, 1966; Goldstein, 1988; Neale & Oltmanns, 1980, pp. 316–318). To begin with, the studies have been retrospective — that is, they obtained a history of attitudes by questioning parents, relatives, and friends of schizophrenic patients. A serious weakness in this method is that the informants may have lapses of memory or make errors in recalling their experiences. Furthermore, they may actually distort their memories, deliberately or unconsciously, and often in accordance with what they think the inquirer wants to hear.

A second problem is that many of the studies failed to use a control group. Even though one may discover a correlation between aversive parents and the occurrence of schizophrenia in their children, one still needs to know the extent to which the children of normal parents become schizophrenic.

A third problem lies in the interpretation of the correlation. Was it aversive parental attitudes that influenced the development of schizophrenia in the children, or did the children's schizophrenic behavior result from other factors and, in turn, actually cause the aversive parental response?

Finally, the studies did not take into account the socioeconomic status of the schizophrenic individuals. Various studies have shown that relatively more people from the lower classes are hospitalized for mental disorders, including schizophrenia (Kessler, Price, & Gartrell, 1985; Neale & Oltmanns, 1980, p. 304; Turner & Gartrell, 1978). Since most of the studies on parental attitudes and schizophrenia were carried out with hospitalized patients, it is difficult to know the extent to which the results reflect socioeconomic status rather than parental attitudes as such.

Follow-Up Studies of Family Interaction

A distinct improvement over retrospective studies is the follow-up design. Follow-up studies take groups of subjects whose behavior was originally observed during childhood or adolescence, usually when they were patients in a child guidance clinic, and attempt to determine their psychological status during adulthood. The family history of those who became schizophrenic can then be compared with those who did not. Defects of long-term memory or distorted recollections do not influence the results of follow-up studies.

The Judge Baker Guidance Clinic in Boston conducted an outstanding follow-up study (Ricks & Berry, 1970). The results showed a close relationship between aversive family interaction, much of it clearly psychopathological, and the development of schizophrenia in the children. The family dynamic that most differentiated children who became schizophrenic from those who did not was one in which the child was expected to comply with a distorted view of reality imposed by one or both parents. In addition, a great deal of social isolation was enforced. This family environment was present in more than one-third of the families in which children eventually became schizophrenic. In addition, some of the schizophrenic children came from families that openly rejected them. Some were even driven from the home.

It is not advisable to generalize too broadly from the findings of the Judge Baker Center study. All of the subjects had been treated for disturbances during childhood or adolescence. Therefore, those who became schizophrenic may not have been representative of all schizophrenic individuals, especially those whose psychological problems were not noted during their formative years (Neale & Oltmanns, 1980, p. 320).

Direct Observation of Family Interaction

Some studies attempt to achieve better control by observing parents and their schizophrenic children directly as they talk with each other. A number of studies compare the observations with those of normal family sessions under similar conditions (Mishler & Waxler, 1968). Some of the results are consistent with earlier studies, in that the parents of schizophrenic children show more aversive attitudes than the parents of normal children. Again, however, the question arises: Were the aversive attitudes cause or consequence of schizophrenia in the children?

The Double-Bind Hypothesis

The double-bind hypothesis of family interaction, originated by anthropologist Gregory Bateson and colleagues, proposes that schizophrenic individuals tend to come from families in which parents consistently send them conflicting messages—*double binds*.

Gregory Bateson and his colleagues originated the **double-bind hypothesis of family interaction**. It states that schizophrenic individuals tend to come from families in which parents consistently send them conflicting messages—double binds. These messages usually take the form of contradictory demands, which the child can neither ignore nor satisfy (Bateson, Jackson, Haley, & Weakland, 1956). For example, parents may constantly complain that their child seldom shows affection, but they become cold and withdrawn when the child tries to express affection or shows it in ways of which the parents disapprove.

The conflicting messages are often ambiguous, consisting of verbal messages, nonverbal communication about attitudes, and behavior as well. According to proponents of the double-bind hypothesis, children growing up in such families learn to expect a great deal of ambiguity in their relationships with other people. Their thinking becomes confused, distorting their attempts to communicate rationally with others. They may also simply give up such attempts. Gradually, then, their thinking and behavior become schizophrenic.

The double-bind hypothesis has attracted a great deal of attention among mental health professionals and has spurred popular discussion as well. However, most of the claims supporting the hypothesis are based on investigations that lack adequate control (Waxler, 1975). The data come mainly from case histories of schizophrenics and their families or transcripts of family therapy sessions designed to help schizophrenic individuals. This information illustrates the nature of double-bind communication, but the studies do not compare communication in normal families.

Mishler and Waxler's (1968) study is an interesting exception. The researchers observed three kinds of family sessions systematically: (a) parents interacting with their schizophrenic child, (b) the same parents interacting with a nonpsychotic child in the family, and (c) control families, matched to the other two groups with respect to various socioeconomic characteristics and the sex of the children. The kinds of interactions most typical of double-bind families occurred in the sessions involving communication with a schizophrenic child. Parents showed considerably less acceptance or acknowledgment of the child's communications. However, Mishler and Waxler could not say that this lack of acknowledgment (a double-bind characteristic) actually caused schizophrenia in the child. Living with a schizophrenic child might have influenced the parents to ignore the child in order to avoid serious disruption to family life.

Double-bind patterns of and similar forms of ambiguous communication also occur in families that do not produce schizophrenics. Therefore, they must be regarded as possible contributing factors, acting in concert with others, rather than as a central cause of schizophrenia (Lewis, 1981).

Laing's Existentialist Views

Born in Glasgow in 1927 into a poor family, Robert D. Laing became one of Britain's most radical and controversial antiestablishment psychiatrists. His views of schizophrenia were shaped not only by intensive clinical observations of patients with whom he interacted closely but also by the dual influences of Jean-Paul Sartre's existentialist philosophy and radical social and political theory (Sedgwick, 1971). Laing believed that, no matter what the symptoms, schizophrenia represents "a special strategy that a person invents in order to live in an unlivable situation" (1967, pp. 78–79).

Laing is not an orthodox psychoanalyst, so he does not adhere to Freud's views on biological drives and their importance in producing psychological conflict. Nevertheless, he was greatly influenced by the psychoanalytic emphasis on family relationships and their role in psychopathology. He became convinced that family disturbances are major factors in the development of schizophrenia. Interestingly, however, his approach to therapy, like that of orthodox psychoanalysts, centers on the disturbed individual's unique experiences and does not involve other family members directly (Laing, 1967; Laing & Esterson, 1972; Siegler, Osmond, & Mann, 1971).

Laing's radical theory of schizophrenia is epitomized in his statement that schizophrenia is a voyage and a "natural way of healing our own appalling state of alienation" (1967, p. 116). According to Laing, this "voyage of madness" need not be a complete breakdown. "It is potentially liberation and renewal as well as enslavement and existential death" (1967, p. 93). Schizophrenia's potential for liberation and renewal has a crucial implication for Laing's revolutionary approach to therapy, the most controversial aspect of his views. To help schizophrenics recover, said Laing, we must allow them to explore their inner world, to descend even more into madness. The therapist guides them through that voyage with "full social encouragement and sanction" (Laing, 1967, p. 89).

Laing's views have attracted a great deal of attention and a certain amount of acceptance. However, there is little empirical evidence that a "voyage into madness" would be a positive experience for most schizophrenics. Nevertheless, Laing's focus on family relationships as factors in the development of schizophrenic disorders remains an influential aspect of his work.

Culture and Schizophrenia

Like other mental disorders, schizophrenia was identified and investigated at a specific time and place—late 19th-century and 20th-century Europe and the United States. Does schizophrenia exist in other parts of the world? If it does, is its rate of incidence uniform throughout the world? Are its manifestations, course, and outcomes identical in different cultures? A great many cross-cultural studies attempt to answer these questions. Their results show that similarities and differences exist across various cultures.

Jane Murphy (1976) demonstrated that schizophrenic behavior patterns are recognized and distinctively labeled in cultures as different from ours as those of the Eskimo of the Canadian Arctic and the Yoruba of western Nigeria. (See Chapter 4 for a detailed description of this research.) A major international study of schizophrenia under the auspices of the World Health Organization (1973) reached similar conclusions. In nine very different countries (Colombia, Czechoslovakia, Denmark, Great Britain, India, Nigeria, the Soviet Union, Taiwan, and the United States) a core syndrome of schizophrenia was identified by means of standardized interview procedures. The pattern of disorder consisted of the following symptoms: restricted affect, poor insight, thinking aloud, poor rapport, incoherent speech, unrealistic information, and bizarre delusions.

Follow-up studies revealed major differences in the nine countries (World Health Organization, 1979). Schizophrenics in developing countries, such as India and Nigeria, experienced fewer relapses than their counterparts in prosperous, technologically advanced settings, such as England, the United States, and Denmark. Certainly, these differences could not be attributed to the greater sophistication or intensity of treatment in the various Third World countries. Cooper and Sartorius (1977) have speculated that the more chronic quality of schizophrenia in technologically advanced countries is a function of the change in cultural attitudes wrought by the Industrial Revolution of the 19th century. Modern, precision-oriented, clock-regulated societies do not tolerate schizophrenic manifestations in the form of social withdrawal and autism. This pushes schizophrenics into custodial institutions and isolates them from their communities and families.

Notwithstanding the frequent assertions in the psychiatric literature (for example, Siegler & Osmond, 1976) that the rates of schizophrenia are uniform throughout the world, the transcultural psychiatrist H. B. M. Murphy (1982, 1983) identified two settings in Europe in which the incidence of schizophrenia was markedly elevated: the western regions of Ireland and the southwestern portion of Croatia in Yugoslavia. By contrast, Murphy found very low rates of schizophrenia among the Hutterites, a collectivist, pacifist Christian sect of western Canada, and in the Tonga Islands of the South Pacific. Murphy explained these variations with an expanded version of the double-bind concept. In his view, schizophrenia is promoted by conflicting and complex demands of the environment to which historically the inhabitants of the two schizophrenia-prone locations in Europe have been exposed. More generally, schizophrenia is fostered by excessive individualism and personal and financial insecurity. By contrast, low rates of schizophrenia obtain when there is a high degree of social integration and harmony and little preoccupation with questions of either social acceptance or financial security. There is, moreover, some evidence to indicate that rates of schizophrenia increase when the traditional culture, with its pattern of secure and accustomed roles, is destroyed (Murphy, 1982, 1983).

Other studies have uncovered variations in schizophrenic symptoms across ethnic and cultural lines. An early but uncommonly thorough investigation by Opler and Singer (1956) concerned differences between Irish and Italian Americans. The former expressed their symptoms in fantasy and the latter in behavioral disturbance. A host of other studies followed, comparing schizophrenics of different ethnicity in the same and different geographic settings. Almost invariably, the studies found cultural differences in the manifestation of schizophrenic symptoms (Draguns, 1980; Dunham, 1976; Murphy, 1983; Torrey, 1980).

Finally, there are studies that point to differences in schizophrenia across time. For example, catatonic stupor was at one time a prominent characteristic of schizophrenia, but advances in drug treatment have decreased it sharply in the United States and other developed Western countries. It is still prominent, however, in many countries of the Third World (Leff, 1981). Similarly, visual hallucinations have declined in the West but not in many parts of Africa and Asia.

Table 11.1 Drugs Used in the Treatment of Schizophrenia

Drug Class	Generic Name	Trade Name
Phenothiazines	Chlorpromazine	Thorazine
	Thioridazine	Mellaril
	Acetophenazine	Tindal
	Perphenazine	Trilafon
	Trifluoperazine	Stelazine
Butyrophenones	Haloperidol	Haldol
Thioxanthenes	Thiothixene	Navane

Sources: American Psychiatric Association, 1980b, pp. 63–64; Honigfeld & Howard, 1978, p. 6.

Treatment of Schizophrenia

Effectiveness of Neuroleptic Drugs

Since their first use some 30 years ago, the application of neuroleptic drugs (also known as psychoactive and antipsychotic drugs) to the treatment of schizophrenia has increased tremendously (Davis, Schaffer, Killian, Kinard, & Chan, 1980; Donaldson, Gelenberg, & Baldessarini, 1983; Friedhoff, 1983; Rebec, Centore, White, & Alloway, 1985). Chlorpromazine was one of the first neuroleptic drugs to be used successfully. It was introduced in the United States in 1954 under the trade name Thorazine (Lickey & Gordon, 1983, pp. 75–77). Chlorpromazine belongs to a class of drugs called **phenothiazines**, now among the most widely prescribed biochemical agents for treating psychotic disorders, especially schizophrenia. Table 11.1 shows the generic and trade names for some of the phenothiazines and other antipsychotic drugs used frequently in the treatment of schizophrenia.

Neuroleptic drugs have been especially effective in reducing such symptoms of schizophrenia as delusions and related paranoid beliefs, auditory and visual hallucinations, confused thinking, and loosened associations (Alford, 1983, p. 642; Honigfeld & Howard, 1978, pp. 11–12. The use of neuroleptic drugs has greatly reduced the number of schizophrenic patients in mental hospitals. Patients leave the hospital earlier and profit more from psychotherapy and positive changes in their social environments. Neuroleptic therapy also allows many patients to be treated at outpatient facilities.

It is important to remember that schizophrenia is a highly complex group of disorders. Neuroleptic therapy must be carefully tailored to individual patients, even if they display highly similar symptoms.

One of the most pressing problems in the use of neuroleptic drugs is a side effect known as **tardive dyskinesia**. This reaction involves involuntary muscle movements (dyskinesia) that may occur months and sometimes years after the drug treatment begins (tardive). Thus, it is essential to consider carefully the risk of using neuroleptic drugs, especially over long periods of time (Bohacek, 1986; Jeste & Wyatt, 1982; Shore, 1986). In Chapter 18, we discuss at greater length the various problems associated with drug treatment of schizophrenic disorders.

Modern methods of drug therapy have helped schizophrenic patients to leave the hospital much earlier than in former years. Maintaining such treatment after leaving the hospital helps the patient continue improving. In many instances optimal improvement requires combining drug therapy, psychotherapy, and changes in the environment.

Combining Drug Treatment with Psychotherapy and Social Intervention

Some studies suggest that neuroleptic drugs alone are more effective than psychotherapy alone in treating schizophrenia. However, there is also evidence that the optimal treatment is to combine the use of drugs, psychotherapy, and positive changes in the schizophrenic's social environment (Falloon & Liberman, 1983; Karon, 1986; Karon & VandenBos, 1981; Lennard, Epstein, Bernstein, & Ransom, 1970, p. 400).

Various studies have compared the effectiveness of different approaches to individual psychotherapy with schizophrenic patients. By and large, there is little evidence that one method is consistently more effective than another (Carpenter, 1984; Gunderson, Frank, Katz, Vannicelli, Frosch, & Knapp, 1984; Klerman, 1984; Stanton et al., 1984).

Delusional (Paranoid) Disorders

The symptoms of **delusional (paranoid) disorders** resemble those found in paranoid schizophrenia, especially delusions involving persecution and jealousy. Some mental health professionals doubt whether these disorders should be classified separately. However, DSM-II made the distinction, and DSM-III and DSM-III-R continued it, because paranoid disorders do not meet some of the basic diagnostic criteria of schizophrenia.

■ The essential feature of paranoid disorders is the persistence of a central delusional system involving a tightly woven pattern of irrational beliefs, especially related to persecution and jealousy. Delusions with similar themes also occur in paranoid schizophrenia, but they are usually more bizarre, illogical, and incoherent. Furthermore, they are frequently combined with prominent hallucinations.

■ Individuals suffering from a delusional disorder show far less intellectual deterioration than is typically the case in paranoid schizophrenia.

"IT'S NOT PARANOIA, GREG. EVERYONE IN PUBLISHING, ADVERTISING, IN FACT ALL THE MEDIA, DOES HATE YOU."

■ The delusions that occur in paranoid disorders usually involve a single theme or series of related themes. Typical is the belief that one is the victim of a conspiracy. Delusions may also take the form of extremely irrational jealousy, in which the paranoid individual might take quite trivial signs of evidence as conclusive proof of infidelity. The individual may develop the argument in support of the delusion quite logically, but the basic premises are false, or at least irrationally exaggerated.

■ In reaching a diagnosis of delusional disorder, it is important to rule out the possibility of a substance-induced organic mental disorder (see Chapters 14 and 15). For example, delusions of persecution may also occur in psychotic syndromes resulting from the ingestion of amphetamine.

Types of Delusional Disorders

DSM-III-R specifies the following types of delusional disorders based on the predominant delusional (paranoid) theme. When a delusional disorder does not fit any of these types, it is classified as "other type."

■ **Persecutory type.** The dominant delusion is that one is being harmed.

■ **Jealous type.** The dominant delusion is that one's sexual partner is unfaithful.

- **Erotomanic type.** The main theme is that a person of much higher status is in love with one.

- **Somatic type.** The dominant delusion is that the person has a physical disorder or an abnormal appearance.

- **Grandiose type.** The predominant theme is the delusion of inflated power, knowledge, special identity, or a special relationship to a famous person or to a deity.

The Pseudocommunity

Norman Cameron (1943, 1963) pointed out some years ago that the paranoid creates a pseudocommunity. Threats of persecution unite into a coherent system, and persecutors become organized into a recognizable group. This pseudocommunity has great functional significance for the paranoid because knowing who the persecutors are brings comfort (Day & Semrad, 1978). The existence of this pseudocommunity is based on real events that have been grossly misinterpreted. Arieti (1974, p. 678) has described three ways in which this may occur.

1. The victim becomes involved in an accident, and then becomes convinced it was not really an accident but planned. Eventually the idea of a machinery of conspiracy emerges to explain the accident.

2. The individual was actually the innocent victim of an injustice but subsequently builds up a delusional system stemming from the episode.

3. The paranoid misinterprets in a peculiar way the behavior and attitudes of a close associate and then elaborates it into a system of delusions.

Psychodynamics of Delusional Disorders

Freudian Theory   Psychodynamic explanations of delusional disorders focus mainly on psychological conflict (Day & Semrad, 1978). One of the best-known theories stems from Freud's analysis of Daniel Paul Schreber's autobiographical writings. Schreber, a German jurist, described

Norman Cameron, for many years professor at the University of Wisconsin, was trained in both clinical psychology and psychiatry. Among his significant contributions to the understanding of delusional (paranoid) disorders is his concept of the *pseudocommunity*. The paranoid individual unites supposed threats of persecution by organizing them into a coherent system. The "persecutors" become a recognizable group—a pseudocommunity.

In his autobiography, the German jurist Daniel Paul Schreber described his development of paranoid disorder. In his analysis of Schreber's writing, Freud concluded that Schreber's delusions of persecution represented repressed homosexual feelings for his supposed persecutor.

his psychotic breakdown in his *Memoirs* (1903/1955). A central belief in Schreber's delusional system was that a psychiatrist named Dr. Flescheg, who had treated him earlier for what presumably was a neurotic disorder, was waging a campaign of persecution against him. According to Schreber, Flescheg was a soul murderer who planned to transform him into a woman.

Freud concluded that Schreber's delusions represented homosexual feelings for Flescheg. He interpreted this attraction as a transference of Schreber's unconscious sexual feelings for his father, which he had maintained for many years. Essentially, Schreber's delusion that Flescheg would transform him into a woman was a projection of his conflict over homosexual desires. By accusing Flescheg of a threatening sexual act, he defended his ego against the anxiety engendered by his own homosexual feelings—a way of "warding off a homosexual wishful fantasy" (Freud, 1911/1958, p. 59).

Freud generalized from his analysis of Schreber that the center of the conflict that underlay paranoid disorders was an unconscious homosexual wish—whether the patients were men or women and regardless of "race, occupation, and social standing" (1911/1958, p. 59).

Critique of Freudian Theory

Freud never met Schreber, and his analysis is based only on a particular portion of Schreber's *Memoirs*. He ignored the fact that Schreber's father, a physician and pedagogue, used an array of harsh and confusing methods of childrearing, although the elder Schreber had written extensively about them and some were mentioned in the son's *Memoirs*.

Morton Schatzman (1976) points out that the paranoid system involved in Schreber's psychotic breakdown can more plausibly be linked to the aversive childrearing methods inflicted on him rather than to conflicts about homosexual desires: "Schreber's entire madness is an *image* of his father's war against his independence. He is never free of coercion by what he thinks are external spiritual powers. However, he never connects the coercion with his father. He cannot, possibly because his father masked (probably unawares) the source of control by defining the state of being controlled by parents as *self*-control" (1976, pp. 21–22). Thus, Schreber's belief that his therapist was persecuting him might well have been a transference to the therapist of his unconscious view of his father.

Other Psychodynamic Views

Some clinicians consider paranoia to stem from conflict over one's biological sex. Stoller (1976b, p. 285) claims that many paranoiacs, especially males, are expressing indirectly their fears over transsexual desires (see Chapter 8). If transsexual conflicts and fears are involved in paranoia, one could interpret Schreber's fear of being turned into a woman as a projection of his own unconscious desire to be one. By blaming Flescheg he defends himself against his unacceptable and threatening wish.

Writing from a broad psychodynamic position, Arieti (1974) also points to confusion over sexual identification as an important factor in the development of paranoid disorders. However, he emphasizes its context within the individual's total interpersonal network.

> My clinical experiences have not revealed that homosexual leanings are important in the psychodynamics of most paranoiacs. What is prominent, however, is either a confusion in sexual identification or a sense of deep inadequacy in sexual life. The inadequacy actually manifests

itself in all areas of interpersonal relations. The patient is almost compelled to live alone, aloof, in celibacy, and is indeed considered inadequate or bizarre. But he cannot accept this fate and lives for the time when he can manifest to the world his real worth. That time never comes; he feels more and more disappointed, to the point of desperation. Eventually a life experience occurs that he was consciously or unconsciously waiting for. He gives special meaning to the episode: this may be the beginning of an ever-expanding paranoic system. (pp. 677−678)

Treatment of Delusional Disorders

The treatment of delusional disorders and paranoid schizophrenia is often similar. It includes the use of neuroleptic drugs to reduce delusions and psychosocial methods that focus on the nature of the delusions and the social and psychological forces that help support them. Some mental health professionals believe that it is also important for the therapist to maintain a considerate and open attitude of trust. This is no easy task, for the therapist must be careful not to convey an actual acceptance of the delusions (Kolb & Brodie, 1982). The treatment of delusional disorders may vary according to the particular pattern of symptoms (Reid, 1983, pp. 124−125).

Acute Pattern of Symptoms

Especially in the early stages, acute symptoms of delusional disorders are difficult to distinguish from paranoid schizophrenia. Thus, initial treatment generally focuses on the use of neuroleptic drugs. If patients seem ready to take action on the basis of their delusions, as is often the case, immediate hospitalization may be necessary. If the threat of action is dangerous, it may warrant the assistance of a law enforcement agency.

Physical disabilities or adverse environmental circumstances may precipitate acute paranoid symptoms. For example, elderly persons with severe problems of deafness may become much more suspicious than usual, to the point of developing paranoid beliefs. This is especially likely to occur where there is a lack of social and emotional support. Thus, treating the physical ailment and improving the psychosocial environment can in themselves help reduce the paranoid symptoms.

Extreme and sudden changes in culture, as in the case of people who emigrate from a distant and very different country, can also precipitate acute paranoid symptoms. Although medication may reduce some of the symptoms, psychosocial therapy that emphasizes an understanding and sympathetic reorientation to the new environment is also important.

Chronic Pattern of Symptoms

The longer a delusional disorder persists, the more difficult it becomes to relieve it. One of the central problems in treating people with a chronic delusional disorder is that they rarely seek help and feel that they do not need it. Even when they do seek help, their motivation for dealing with the problem may be quite low. In general, the prognosis for people suffering from a chronic delusional disorder is much less favorable than for paranoid schizophrenics. Fortunately, the incidence of the disorder is lower (American Psychiatric Association, 1987, p. 201).

Summary

1. Despite the fact that Hippocrates had emphasized that mental disorders originate in disturbed conditions of the brain, until the 19th century many physicians and lay people believed that the disorder was the result of witchcraft. In the 19th century, more rational approaches emerged. The French physician Morel noted that symptoms of schizophrenia began early in life and involved a severe loss of cognitive abilities. He named the disorder dementia praecox.

2. Morel's ideas influenced a number of other psychiatrists, including Emil Kraepelin, who incorporated dementia praecox into his classification of mental disorders. Eugen Bleuler, a Swiss psychiatrist, disputed Kraeplin's notion that the disorder always began in youth and always had a fatal end. Bleuler renamed the disorder schizophrenia, to signify the split (*schiz*) in the individual's mental life (*phren*).

3. Prominent among the diagnostic criteria for schizophrenia, as described in DSM-III-R, are delusions, hallucinations, and incoherent communication.

4. DSM-III-R also classifies schizophrenia into four main types: disorganized, catatonic, paranoid, and undifferentiated. The disorganized type involves immature, regressive behavior. The catatonic type is characterized by stereotyped bodily movements or stances. The paranoid type is marked by delusions and hallucinations, of suspicion, persecution, and power. The undifferentiated type includes schizophrenic symptoms, but they do not form a consistent pattern.

5. Disordered thinking in schizophrenia affects both the form and the content of thought. The latter is called formal thought disorder, and some clinicians and researchers consider it to be a key characteristic of schizophrenia. The theoretical views of formal thought disorder focus on deficits in abstract thinking, dissociation of ideas, and excessive yielding to normal biases in thinking.

6. Experimental laboratory studies of formal thought disorder have come to these conclusions: (a) performance becomes impaired under conditions of emotional involvement, (b) schizophrenics form concepts in an abnormal manner when they must operate on an abstract level, (c) cognitive associations are highly maladaptive, and (d) schizophrenics show specific impairments in how they receive and process information. In recent years, evidence has grown suggesting that faulty information processing in schizophrenia may be a genetic trait.

7. Concepts of a process–reactive dimension in schizophrenia stem from the early work of Eugen Bleuler, who believed there were two distinct forms of schizophrenia. According to Bleuler, process schizophrenia originates in faulty biological processes and reactive schizophrenia stems more from maladaptive responses to life situations.

8. In succeeding years the process–reactive dimension took on diagnostic meaning. Individuals who showed little improvement were classified as process schizophrenics; those who showed considerable improvement or who recovered were called reactive schizophrenics. The concepts of process and reactive schizophrenia are now considered to be extreme ends of a continuum, rather than two highly distinct types.

9. Prognostic rating scales have been developed to predict the course and outcome of schizophrenic disorders. They differ in the kinds of premorbid characteristics they measure, the emphasis they give to those variables, and the power of prediction.

10. Marital status has been shown to be a predictor of outcome in schizophrenia. Single individuals (especially males) are hospitalized more often than married individuals and tend to remain hospitalized longer.

11. Manfred Bleuler, a professor of psychiatry in Zurich, reviewed the life histories of 2000 individuals in Switzerland and the United States who had been diagnosed schizophrenic. He concluded that (a) after a five-year duration, schizophrenic symptoms do not progress any further; (b) about 25 percent of schizophrenic patients recover entirely; and (c) about 10 percent remain permanently hospitalized as severely psychotic. Bleuler attributed the positive outcomes to better care and treatment in today's hospitals.

12. Bleuler's findings are relatively optimistic, and his conclusion is shared by psychiatrist George Vaillant, who argues for even greater care with dignity to allay the progressive deterioration of schizophrenic individuals once thought to be inevitable.

13. Another way of considering the diagnosis and outcome of schizophrenia is through positive and negative symptoms. Positive symptoms include hallucinations, fluent but disorganized speech, and severe thought disorder. Negative symptoms involve emotional apathy and flattening, inability to express emotion appropriately, severe loss of motivation, withdrawal from the environment, and inability to enjoy social relationships.

14. The distinction between positive and negative symptoms resembles the distinction between process and reactive concepts. Some researchers argue that the concept of positive and negative symptoms has increased the usefulness of the process – reactive concept. Negative symptoms are said to be much less amenable to drug treatment than positive symptoms. Other researchers dispute this, claiming they have found that positive and negative symptoms respond to drug treatment about as well.

15. Research on the inheritance of a predisposition toward developing schizophrenia has expanded greatly in the last several decades. Studies of twins found that the concordance rate for schizophrenia in monozygotic twins was higher than the rate for dizygotic twins. The overall findings of such studies suggest that genetic factors can play an important role in the development of schizophrenia. Even so, one must also consider joint environmental influences.

16. Other evidence for genetic influences comes from studies of adopted children. The biological parents of children who had been reared apart from them and had been diagnosed as schizophrenic have a higher rate of schizophrenia than adoptive parents or than a control group.

17. There is some convincing evidence that biochemical disturbances in the brain contribute to the development of schizophrenia. The most promising line of investigation centers around the dopamine hypothesis. Dopamine is a biochemical substance that acts as a neurotransmitter, facilitating the passage of electrochemical impulses from one nerve cell to another. Neuroleptic drugs, used to treat schizophrenia, reduce dopamine activity in the brain. Since these drugs are also effective in reducing schizophrenic symptoms, many researchers think that increased dopamine activity in the brain may possibly be related to the development of schizophrenia.

18. Some research suggests that an interaction between dopamine and endorphins may be an important influence on the development of schizophrenia. Endorphins bind to the same sites in the brain as morphine and other opiates. An abnormal increase in the level of endorphins has been found in the cerebrospinal fluid of schizophrenics, and the amounts decrease following treatment with neuroleptic drugs. Since these drugs also block dopamine activity in the brain, the blocking may in part be influenced by endorphins.

19. In the past, various studies concluded that the aversive attitudes of the mothers of schizophrenic individuals played a significant role in the development of the disorder. They were labeled schizophrenogenic. Silvano Arieti has concluded that although serious family disturbances might well contribute to the development of schizophrenia, it is misleading to focus on schizophrenogenic mothers as the most important of those influences.

20. Other studies have focused on the role of aversive attitudes of fathers in the development of schizophrenia. Although some evidence indicates that they may be influential, these studies suffer from methodological errors.

21. Follow-up investigations to assess the relationship between family interaction and the development of schizophrenia are an improvement over retrospective studies. One of the better studies found a close relationship between aversive family relationships and the later occurrence of schizophrenia in the children. The most important variable was the reality orientation of the family. Children were more likely to develop schizophrenia if they were expected to comply with a distorted view of reality imposed by the parents.

22. Another research method is the direct observation of interactions among the members of families — both those that have and those that do not have schizophrenic members. Some results have revealed aversive parental attitudes, but it is not clear whether the attitudes are the cause or the consequence of the schizophrenic behavior of the children.

23. The double-bind hypothesis states that schizophrenic individuals tend to come from families in which parents consistently send conflicting messages — double binds. Most of the data for the hypothesis come from case studies. Although the studies are valuable for illustrating family life with schizophrenic children, they usually lack a comparison with communication in normal families. It is likely that double-bind messages, in concert with other influences, play a contributing role in the development of schizophrenia, at least in some families.

24. The British psychiatrist Robert Laing developed the view that schizophrenic experiences and behavior are strategies to enable a person to live in an unlivable situation. In his approach to treatment, Laing encouraged patients to descend further into madness as a way of healing their state of alienation. Although Laing attracted considerable attention for a while, including active opposition from many psychiatrists, his views today are valuable mainly because they focused on family relationships as factors in the development of schizophrenia.

25. Cross-cultural studies have shown that schizophrenia occurs in many societies and cultures, although the specific content and mode of expression may vary considerably. This pervasiveness helps support the hypothesis that biological as well as environmental factors play a role in the development of schizophrenia.

26. Neuroleptic drugs have been effective in the treatment of schizophrenia, especially for such symptoms as delusions and paranoid beliefs. Their use has greatly reduced the number of schizophrenic patients in mental hospitals. A distressing side effect is tardive dyskinesia, which causes involuntary muscle movements. Drug treatment of schizophrenia is often combined with psychotherapy and manipulation of the social environment.

27. The symptoms of delusional (paranoid) disorders resemble those of paranoid schizophrenia. Indeed, some clinicians doubt that the disorders should be classified separately. However, delusional disorders do not have all the basic characteristics of schizophrenia. For example, they lack loose cognitive associations, incoherent thinking, prominent hallucinations, and blunted affect.

28. The essential feature of delusional disorders is the persistence of a central delusional system involving a tightly woven pattern of irrational beliefs, especially with regard to feelings of persecution and jealousy. Another distinguishing characteristic is the individual's creation of pseudocommunity — definitely known and recognizable persecutors.

29. Freudian theory postulates that the central conflict underlying paranoid disorders is an unconscious homosexual wish. The development of a paranoid system of beliefs prevents this wish from emerging into consciousness. This view has been widely criticized, even by some psychoanalytically oriented clinicians.

30. Other psychodynamic views of paranoid disorders consider them to stem from conflicts over one's biological sex — for example, the fear (especially in males) of transsexual desires. Other psychodynamic theories argue more generally that some confusion in sexual identity or a sense of sexual inadequacy can be important factors.

31. Because it is difficult to differentiate between the paranoid type of schizophrenia and paranoid disorders as such, the methods of treatment are often similar. They include the use of neuroleptic drugs to reduce delusions and psychosocial methods that focus on the nature of the delusions and the social and psychological forces that sustain them. In addition, some mental health professionals point to the importance of maintaining a considerate and open attitude of trust.

32. Methods of treatment vary according to whether the paranoid symptoms are acute or chronic. In acute forms, the initial treatment focuses on the use of neuroleptic drugs. The longer the disorder persists, the more difficult treatment becomes. A central problem in chronic delusional disorder is that the person neither seeks help nor feels the need for it. The prognosis is less favorable for chronic paranoid disorders than for acute paranoid episodes or the paranoid form of schizophrenia.

Outline of Topics

12

Personality Disorders and Disorders of Impulse Control

Perverseness is one of the primitive impulses of the human heart.

EDGAR ALLAN POE
The Black Cat (1843)

In this chapter, we discuss a broad range of abnormal behavior and experience known as **personality disorders**. Some of these disturbances resemble patterns found in schizophrenic and delusional disorders (see Chapter 11), but they are less severe. Others involve extreme egocentricity, abnormally low self-esteem, an inability to express warm and tender emotions, overdependence, chronic antisocial behavior, or maladaptive patterns of self-dramatization, such as exaggerated expression of emotions.

We also consider certain maladaptive patterns called **disorders of impulse control**. These disorders include recurrent urges to steal objects of little monetary value so as to gain pleasure and release tension, uncontrollable impulses to set fires for excitement and pleasure, and chronic preoccupation with gambling to the point where it seriously disrupts personal, family, or occupational life.

Personality Disorders: General Characteristics

DSM-III-R offers the following definition of **personality traits** and their relationship to personality disorders: "Personality traits are enduring patterns of perceiving, relating to, and thinking about the environment and oneself, and are exhibited in a wide range of important social and personal contexts. It is only when personality traits are inflexible and maladaptive and cause either significant functional impairment or subjective distress that they constitute personality disorders" (American Psychiatric Association, 1987, p. 335).

The manifestations of personality disorders are often apparent at adolescence or even earlier. Individuals with personality disorders may be well aware of the negative impact their behavior has on other people, even though they themselves do not regard it as undesirable. In other instances, they may be extremely troubled by their disturbing personality characteristics. They realize such characteristics are not desirable, but they are unable to change them despite efforts to do so.

Although individuals with personality disorders often encounter considerable problems in relating to others, they may not necessarily experience personal discomfort in doing so. When they do suffer distress, they often ascribe such reactions to a lack of consideration and understanding in other people. In general, they tend to excuse themselves from responsibility for behavior that alienates others. Thus, it becomes difficult for them to seek help for their problems. Indeed, they may often do so only under coercion.

Basic approaches to alleviating personality disorders usually include various forms of individual and group psychotherapy. In some instances, the supplementary use of therapeutic drugs may become necessary.

Personality disorders are coded on Axis II of DSM-II-R (see Chapter 2 for a discussion of the DSM coding procedures). Their specific characteristics differ; but because some show similar themes, they are organized in clusters.

Personality traits, whether normal or abnormal, vary considerably from one individual to another. They can be revealed in a variety of situations.

Cluster A
Paranoid
Schizoid
Schizotypal
Cluster B
Histrionic
Narcissistic
Antisocial
Borderline
Cluster C
Avoidant
Dependent
Obsessive compulsive
Passive aggressive

We will describe each disorder in turn. However, because the antisocial personality disorder produces exceptionally harmful behavior and has serious social implications, it will receive special consideration.

In addition to the disorders listed here, DSM-III-R has added two highly controversial categories: self-defeating personality disorder and sadistic personality disorder. Because mental health professionals disagree so strongly about these new diagnoses, the authors of DSM-III-R placed them in an appendix entitled "Proposed Diagnostic Categories Needing Further Study" (American Psychiatric Association, 1987, pp. 369–374).

When what is now called **self-defeating personality disorder** was first proposed, it was labeled masochistic personality disorder. Some psychologists strongly opposed such a term, arguing that the diagnosis might well be applied to women in relationships with abusive men and thus perpetuate a blame-the-victim pattern. Consequently, the "masochistic" part of the label was dropped, and certain aspects of the diagnosis were clarified (Fisher, 1986a, 1986b; Landers, 1986a; Widiger, Frances, Spitzer, & Williams, 1988). At least five of the following criteria must be present to warrant a diagnosis of self-defeating personality disorder.

- Chooses persons and situations that lead to disappointment, failure, or mistreatment, even when better options are clearly available.

- Rejects attempts of others to help.

- Responds to new achievements with guilt or depression.

- Invites angry or rejecting behavior from others, then feels hurt or humiliated.

- Turns down opportunities for pleasure; is reluctant to acknowledge enjoyment.

- Fails to achieve tasks consistent with objectives, in spite of the ability to do so.

- Becomes bored with or uninterested in people, even though they consistently treat the individual well.

- Engages in excessive self-sacrifice, when it is unsolicited and discouraged by the recipient.

The diagnosis is inappropriate if self-defeating behavior occurs only in response to or in anticipation of physical, sexual, or psychological abuse or only when the person is depressed.

DSM-III-R defines **sadistic personality disorder** as a "pervasive pattern of cruel, demeaning, and aggressive behavior, beginning by early adulthood" (American Psychiatric Association, 1987, p. 369). Among the specific criteria are consistently using physical cruelty or violence whose main purpose is to inflict pain and suffering, humiliating or demeaning people before others, taking pleasure in the suffering of others, and being fascinated with violence, injury, and torture. DSM-III-R also stipulates that to warrant a diagnosis of sadistic personality disorder, the sadistic behavior must be aimed at more than one person and must not be used only for the purpose of sexual arousal. If the latter is the dominant motive, the behavior is more appropriately diagnosed as sexual sadism (see Chapter 8). Among the main arguments against including sadistic personality disorder in the DSM-III-R classification is the contention that rapists and other perpetrators of violence against women might use it as a legal defense.

When an individual reveals abnormal personality characteristics and behavior that seem to justify a diagnosis of personality disorder but that do not fit any of the diagnostic categories, DSM-III-R provides a residual diagnostic category, "personality disorder NOS" (not otherwise specified). In DSM-III, this residual diagnosis was termed "mixed personality disorder" (American Psychiatric Association, 1980a, pp. 329–330).

Paranoid Personality Disorder

The central characteristic of **paranoid personality disorder** is a highly pervasive and long-standing pattern of suspiciousness and mistrust. Individuals with this disorder are hypersensitive in their relationships with other people; their feelings are easily hurt from real or imagined rebuffs. They persistently scan the environment for various clues that will support their expectation of being rejected or acted against in other ways. As a result, their emotional and social life is apt to be highly restrictive, since it is difficult for them to enter or maintain a mutually trusting relationship with others. They persist in questioning other people's motives and intentions, are quick to suspect them of trickery, and in general are ready to blame them and ascribe evil motives to their behavior.

In many respects, paranoid personality disorder is an exaggeration of certain normal patterns of behavior one can easily encounter in everyday life. Paranoid patterns have been described in writings dating back more than 2000 years. Consider, for example, these observations by the Greek philosopher and naturalist Theophrastus (371–287 B.C.), which appear in his famous character sketches.

The Suspicious Man

> Now, suspiciousness is a habit of assuming that everybody is out to cheat you. The suspicious man is the kind who sends one servant to do the marketing and then another to check on what everything cost. He insists on carrying the petty cash himself, too, stopping every few hundred feet to make sure it's all there. And he will ask his wife, after he has come to bed, whether she remembered to lock the strong-box and close up the cupboards and shut the bolt on the outside door. It makes no difference, either, if she says yes: he gets out from under the covers, takes a lamp, and makes the rounds dressed only in his nightshirt. . . .
>
> . . . If a neighbor comes over to borrow some winecups, he will do his best not to lend them. He has to say yes to a close friend or a relative, but not until he has practically weighed and tested every piece and asked for a deposit. . . . And perhaps somebody who has purchased an item from him says, "Make out the bill; and put it on my account, will you? I'm pressed for time right now." "That's perfectly all right," comes the answer. "I'll just walk along with you until you're not so pressed." (Anderson, 1970, p. 77)

Paranoid personality disorder does not as a rule involve the sharp break with reality found in the delusions of paranoid schizophrenia and other paranoid forms of psychoses. Indeed, individuals who suffer from this kind of disorder may be highly competent intellectually. Nevertheless, because their paranoid approach to personal and social life prevents their maintaining satisfactory relationships with other people, they often fail to achieve the goals that their intelligence would allow.

Concepts of defense mechanisms (see Chapter 3) are especially useful in explaining certain dynamics of personality disorders (Millon & Everly, 1985; Vaillant, 1987). A central dynamic in the paranoid personality disorder is the extreme and consistent use of projection. This defense mechanism enables individuals to avoid being conscious of their own highly suspicious nature by attributing suspiciousness to other people. They can then justify their right to behave aggressively toward others (Millon & Everly, 1985, p. 247).

People with paranoid personalities rarely seek treatment. When they do, their chief motivation seems to be to prove that other people are wrong. Psychotherapy is the basic approach to helping them with their problems. However, drugs may also be used if symptoms seem to be moving in a psychotic direction or if there is a great deal of anxiety.

More than 2000 years ago, the Greek philosopher and naturalist Theophrastus, anticipated modern concepts of personality disorders in his famous *Character Sketches*.

Schizoid Personality Disorder

Seclusiveness and lack of desire for social involvement mark **schizoid personality disorder**. Schizoid individuals tend to be cold, aloof loners. They often seem indecisive and somewhat detached from their surroundings, but their remoteness does not take the extreme form of retreat one often finds in schizophrenics.

The primary defense mechanism used by schizoid people is **intellectualization**—thinking about one's interpersonal experience in highly objective, almost mechanical terms. Such people regard displays of emotion as a sign of immaturity. In this way, they maintain their detached perspective on the human world and thus feel safe.

Traditional psychodynamic therapies, which emphasize the uncovering of deeply unconscious conflicts, are extremely difficult to manage in schizoid personality disorders. The most important goal in psychotherapy is probably the consistent use of emotional support. Medication is sometimes useful, but only as a temporary aid for reducing extreme distress.

Schizotypal Personality Disorders

People with **schizotypal personality disorders** resemble schizophrenics, but they usually do not reveal sharp breaks with reality, such as delusions and hallucinations (McGlashan, 1986c).

Research offers slight support to the possibility of genetic influences in the development of schizotypal personality disorders. For example, in Torgersen's (1984) study of co-twins, 7 out of 21 pairs of monozygotic (identical) twins were schizotypal, but only one pair out of 23 dizygotic co-twins was so diagnosed.

Schizotypal individuals have strange ways of communicating ideas, but they are not incoherent. They have great difficulty in meeting and talking with people. Because of their eccentric convictions, they often alienate other people.

> The patient is a 32-year-old unmarried, unemployed woman who complains that she feels "spacey." Her feelings of detachment have gradually become stronger and more uncomfortable. For many hours each day she feels as if she were watching herself move through life, and the world around her seems unreal. She feels especially strange when she looks into a mirror. For many years she has felt able to read people's minds by a "kind of clairvoyance I don't understand." According to her, several people in her family apparently also have this ability. She is preoccupied by the thought that she has some special mission in life, but is not sure what it is; she is not particularly religious. She is very self-conscious in public, often feels that people are paying special attention to her, and sometimes feels that strangers cross the street to avoid her. She is lonely and isolated and spends much of each day lost in fantasies or watching TV soap operas. She speaks in a vague, abstract, digressive manner, generally just missing the point, but she is never incoherent. She seems shy, suspicious, and afraid she will be criticized. She has no gross loss of reality testing, such as hallucinations or delusions. She has never had treatment for emotional problems. She has had occasional jobs, but drifts away from them because of lack of interest. (Spitzer, Skodol, Gibbon, & Williams, 1981, pp. 95–96)

Schizotypal behavior often involves the defense mechanism of **undoing**, a form of atonement in which the individual engages in various acts as repentance for undesirable and even evil motives and behavior. In its more extreme forms, undoing may include bizarre rituals or magical acts. There are similar to the behavior that often occurs in obsessive compulsive disorder (see Chapter 5). In this way, schizotypal individuals hope to be cleansed of unworthy motives and thoughts. Although they may consciously admit that their behavior is foolish, they often reach the point where they cannot control or suppress it (Millon & Everly, 1985, p. 218).

The basic approach in psychotherapy for schizotypal personality disorders is similar to that for schizoid disorder. The emphasis is on emotional support. However, symptoms are more apt to move toward a greater distortion of reality than in the case of schizoid disorder, so antipsychotic medication may become necessary (Goldberg, Schulz, Schulz, Resnick, Hamer, & Friedel, 1986).

Histrionic Personality Disorder

Traditionally, **histrionic personality disorder** has been called *hysterical personality disorder*, but *histrionic*, which means "acting," "deliberately affected," and "theatrical," is a more appropriate term. DSM-III-R specifies the following diagnostic criteria. At least four should be present to justify a diagnosis of histrionic personality disorder (American Psychiatric Association, 1987, p. 349).

- Exaggerated expression of emotion (self-dramatization).

- Overconcern with physical attractiveness.

- Constant seeking of approval, reassurance, or praise.

- Inappropriately sexual seductiveness in appearance or behavior.

- Discomfort in situations where the person is not the center of attention.

- Shallow and rapidly shifting expression of emotions.

- Extreme self-centeredness, with no tolerance for delayed gratification.

- Style of speech excessively impressionistic, lacking appropriate details.

One feature of histrionic personality disorder is the strong fear of expressing sexuality. In response, histrionic individuals may employ the defense mechanism of **reaction formation**, behaving in ways that are opposite from what they fear. This defense is illustrated in the following observations.

> Such women are fearful of their sexual drives, yet seek through seductive behavior to achieve security and power vicariously through the passionate engagement of a man to themselves. Secretly they are competitive — against men as a means of conquering them and against women as a method of exclusion. Their seductive behavior to men then covers both an aggressive element and a wish for a dependent childish relationship.
>
> The "Don Juan" character represents this personality type in men. Again there is the histrionic display. The drive for sexual conquest . . . often rests upon a hid-

den feeling of masculine inadequacy and is coupled with the need to deceive, outwit and conquer. The Don Juan makes evident through the repetition of his concepts the lack of satisfaction in each successful affair. (Kolb & Brodie, 1982, pp. 598–602)

Many victims of histrionic personality disorder respond well to supportive psychotherapy. The therapist must be alert to suicide threats, however, even though the majority of them are made for dramatic purposes. In general, medication is not recommended, except for very short periods and in low doses, as in the case of temporary depression.

Narcissistic Personality Disorder

The central features of **narcissistic personality disorder** are a consistent exaggeration of self-importance and an intense preoccupation with fantasies of power and success. Narcissistic individuals often demand a great deal of attention, provided it is completely supportive. They find it very difficult to accept criticism, often reacting with "feelings of rage, shame, humiliation, or emptiness" (American Psychiatric Association, 1987, p. 351). They frequently show a great lack of empathy. Not only do they fail to understand how others feel, but they seek special treatment from them with no thought of reciprocating. Consequently, they appear to be exploiters of other people, using them for their own personal gain. Such egocentricity is also a characteristic of antisocial personality disorder, which we discuss in detail later in the chapter. However, the narcissistic individual does not usually reveal the marked destructiveness of the antisocial person.

The exaggerated self-esteem of narcissistic individuals is reflected in their frequent use of **rationalization** to defend themselves against conflict, frustration, and anxiety. They consistently create superficially plausible but inaccurate reasons for their disappointments and failures to conceal from themselves the real reasons. This self-deception is strengthened because they always try to place themselves in the best possible light to other people. Thus, they further protect their unrealistic and inflated self-esteem (Millon & Everly, 1985, pp. 74–75; Siomopoulos, 1988).

As a practical matter, many clinicians treat narcissistic individuals for specific crises reflecting a sudden loss of self-esteem rather than for the basic disorder itself. Thus, the goals of psychotherapy are often limited, aimed mostly at bolstering self-esteem. Some patients, however, can profit from treatment that goes to deeper lengths in helping them gain insight into the origin of their problems. Some therapists have found group therapy helpful. In cases where symptoms are especially severe, hospitalization and a limited use of medication may become necessary.

Borderline Personality Disorder

Many of the features of **borderline personality disorder** overlap with other personality disturbances and with various psychotic symptoms, especially those found in schizophrenia. The concept of borderline in psychiatric diagnosis was developed to indicate serious psychopathology for which no specific diagnostic category seemed to be appropriate. Over the years, its use languished because there was little consensus as to what criteria should be used to place various symptoms in the borderline category. More recently, some clinicians have attempted to clarify the concept (Grinker & Werble, 1977;

Hartocollis, 1977; Millon, 1987; Millon & Everly, 1985; Reid, 1983, pp. 194–196), but others remain skeptical about its usefulness, since it can be applied to so many kinds of conditions (Fyer, Frances, Sullivan, Hurt, & Clarkin, 1988; Story, 1978).

DSM-III-R offers the following diagnostic criteria. At least five are required, and they must be characteristic of the individual's long-term behavior (American Psychiatric Association, 1987, p. 347).

1. Impulsivity in at least two areas of potentially self-damaging activity (for example, spending, sexual activities, gambling, drug or alcohol use, shoplifting, overeating, self-damaging behavior).

2. Unstable interpersonal relationships — for example, intense shifts in attitudes or self-concept or exploitation of other people.

3. Inappropriate expression of feelings or lack of control — for example, frequent loss of temper or chronic feelings of anger.

4. Identity problems such as self-image, gender identity, career goals, friendships, values, and loyalties.

5. Extreme shifts in mood, especially in the direction of depression, irritability, or anxiety; shifts may last from a few hours to a few days.

6. Problems with being alone — for example, extreme fear about being alone.

7. Carrying out physically self-damaging acts, such as mutilation, involvement in frequent accidents or fights, or suicidal gestures.

8. Chronic feelings of boredom or emptiness.

The patient with a borderline personality disorder often comes for treatment only in times of crisis. A central difficulty in treatment is the acting out of problems, which may disrupt the therapeutic process. Group therapy, with emphasis on group support can be helpful. The temporary use of various antipsychotic drugs may be necessary, especially when symptoms are acute (Cowdry & Gardner, 1988; Goldberg, Schulz, Schulz, Resnick, Hamer, & Friedel, 1986; Gunderson, 1986; Soloff, George, Nathan, Schulz, Ulrich, & Perel, 1986). Some clinicians believe the borderline patient with extreme symptoms but good potential for recovery can be helped in a long-term, highly structured inpatient environment, such as a residential treatment center (McGlashan, 1986a).

Avoidant Personality Disorder

The central feature of **avoidant personality disorder** is an extreme hypersensitivity to being rejected. Any slight sign of disapproval is interpreted as calamitous. Even innocuous remarks may provoke strong feelings of rejection.

Individuals with long-term feelings of rejection are often reluctant to enter relationships unless they feel sure of being completely accepted. As a defense, they may become socially withdrawn and refrain from choosing social and occupational goals that are likely to bring criticism. Typically, their fear of rejection and their social withdrawal are coupled with the feelings of low-esteem and an exaggeration of personal shortcomings.

A basic goal in helping individuals with an avoidant personality disorder is improving their self-image and increasing their positive relationships with other people. Group

People who suffer from a dependent personality may be helped through group psychotherapy by sharing their perceptions and feelings with others.

psychotherapy can be especially helpful, since the setting offers a protective environment for exploring directions that are feared in everyday life.

Dependent Personality Disorder

The chief characteristic of **dependent personality disorder** is the imputing to others a responsibility for one's own decisions and way of life. Passivity and fear of accepting responsibility are often coupled with acquiescence to other people's actions that may be detrimental. For example, the dependent person may tolerate beyond reason an extremely abusive spouse, friend, or supervisor.

By handing responsibility to others, dependent people defend themselves against conscious recognition of their negative self-image. Thus, they avoid the conflicts and anxieties that would arise if they assumed a more assertive role in relating to others.

Individuals with a dependent personality who seek psychotherapy are often reluctant to present their basic problem. More likely, they will seek help for immediate problems, such as lack of positive social relationships, vocational problems, or other failures to reach desired practical goals. They may also seek help for immediate problems of isolation that they experience when they are deprived of an important person on whom they depend a great deal. Within this context, psychotherapy can gradually aim toward helping them gain insight into the basic reasons for their immediate problems. However, the therapist should not ignore the immediate concerns, for which various techniques of behavior therapy (see

Chapter 20) can be especially appropriate. Group psychotherapy can also help dependent individuals.

Obsessive Compulsive Personality Disorder

Constricted feelings and behavior mark **obsessive compulsive personality disorder**. Individuals with this disorder find it difficult to express warm feelings. They may be unduly conventional and formal in their relationships, even stingy. They often become so preoccupied with highly trivial details in their work and social life that they see nothing but the details. They may insist that others fit in with their own compulsion, not realizing how this interferes with interpersonal relationships. plans, and goals. They may become so preoccupied with details and so fearful of making a mistake that they cannot complete important tasks.

Obsessive compulsive personality disorder resembles obsessive compulsive neurosis (see Chapter 5), but it is less all-consuming and tends to be under better control.

The disorder helps individuals protect themselves from feelings they do not wish to recognize. For example, dwelling on trivial details helps them avoid the danger of failing at more challenging tasks. Immersion in details that do not require interpersonal skills also helps people avoid unconscious feelings of hostility toward others (Kolb & Brodie, 1982, p. 613; Millon & Everly, 1985, pp. 154–155).

Psychotherapy often combines the goals of insight with direct behavior modification techniques to teach the individual to work more flexibly with others. In treatment, it often becomes necessary to uncover the defenses that serve the compulsive behavior. How intensive this uncovering should be depends on the strength of the individual's ability to deal with such disclosures.

Passive Aggressive Personality Disorder

The central feature of **passive aggressive personality disorder** is a hostile resistance to demands for adequate performance, both on the job and in general social relationships. However, the hostility is expressed through passive incompetence rather than overt aggression. Not all clinicians agree that this diagnostic category can be used with confidence, since the behavior of individuals does not always indicate that passive resistance actually conceals deep-seated hostility (Stricker, 1983b, p. 7). A central question is whether such resistance is a defensive technique used in relatively isolated social situations or whether it is actually part of a long-standing and pervasive personality pattern. DSM-III-R proposes the following criteria. At least five must be present to warrant a diagnosis, and they must be so pervasive that they result in chronic social and occupational inefficiency (American Psychiatric Association, 1987, p. 357).

- Procrastinates — delays accomplishing things that should be done so that deadlines cannot be met.

- Becomes irritable, argumentative, or sulky when asked to do undesired things.

- Deliberately works slowly or poorly on unwanted tasks.

- Protests without justification that people are making unreasonable demands.

- Avoids responsibilities by pretending to have forgotten.

- Believes he or she is doing a better job than others think is true.

- Resents useful suggestions from others for improving production.

- Interferes with work of others by not doing her or his share.

- Unreasonably criticizes people in positions of authority.

In most forms of insight-oriented psychotherapy (see Chapter 19), people resist understanding their problems and changing their behavior. This is an especially difficult obstacle in the treatment of individuals with a passive aggressive personality disorder. Rather than expressing resistance openly, the patient often disguises it by forgetting important information that would facilitate therapeutic progress (Reid, 1983, p. 198). It may therefore be necessary for the psychotherapist to be especially careful in structuring the rules of psychotherapy, including the necessity for keeping appointments and for actively participating in a therapeutic alliance. At the same time, however, the therapist should avoid placing patients in a situation where, deprived completely of the passive aggressive defense, they have no other more constructive ways of coping.

Antisocial Personality Disorder

One pattern of abnormal behavior is so injurious to others that it deserves special attention. **Antisocial personality disorder** is the most troublesome of all the personality disorders, especially in its implications for a broad range of social situations. Antisocial individuals have an almost incredible inability to maintain loyalty to others. Their attitudes and feelings are grossly callous. Such people are not only extremely irresponsible, they also have little guilt about their antisocial behavior. The harm they frequently inflict on others, and their great resistance to becoming more prosocial, justifies regarding their pattern of abnormality as the most serious of the personality disorders.

Historical Background

Pinel's Influence

Modern diagnostic concepts of antisocial personality disorder can be traced most directly to the work of Philippe Pinel (1745–1826), who is more generally known for his humanitarian reforms at the Bicêtre and Salpêtrière hospitals in Paris. In the midst of the French revolutionary regime, Pinel removed the chains from the mentally ill. He also introduced the taking of psychiatric case histories and the keeping of systematic case records (Zilboorg & Henry, 1941). Among his astute clinical observations, Pinel noted that some patients engaged in highly impulsive and antisocial behavior, although they showed no impairment in their intellectual functions and seemed to be well aware of their actions. He called the disorder *manie sans délire*, or mania without delirium (Pichot, 1978; Schulsinger, 1977; Werlinder, 1978, pp. 28–30).

Prichard's Concept of Moral Insanity

Acknowledging Pinel's contributions and expanding on them, James Cowles Prichard (1786–1848), senior physician at the Bristol Royal Infirmary in England, made extensive records of antisocial behavior, which he called moral insanity (Prichard, 1835; Smith, 1917). In his *Treatise on Insanity*, Prichard defined the disorder as a "morbid perversion of the feelings, affections, and active powers." Like Pinel, he noted that these perversions

Modern diagnostic concepts of antisocial personality disorder can be traced to the work of the French physician, Philippe Pinel. He is more generally known for his humanitarian reforms in the treatment of the mentally ill, which he carried out in hospitals during the French Revolution.

PHILIPPE ❋ PINEL ❋

could co-exist with an "apparently unimpaired state of the intellectual faculties" (Prichard, 1835, p. 12).

Prichard's observations are remarkably consistent with modern clinical information about antisocial personality disorder. Individuals suffering from "moral insanity," he said, are "continually engaging in new pursuits" and "soon relinquishing them without any other inducement than mere caprice and fickleness." They always have plausible reasons for their "wild projects and speculations," and they display "no particular mental illusion [delusion, in the modern sense], a feature which is commonly looked upon as essential to madness" (1835, p. 13). Nevertheless, concluded Prichard, in spite of their apparent lack of "madness," these individuals are unable to guide their lives according to moral principles.

Prichard's theory of the etiology of moral insanity included reverses of fortune, loss of a beloved relative, or some severe physical shock, such as paralysis, epilepsy, or inflammation. Although this view has been superseded, Prichard's view that moral insanity is a deeply ingrained personality disorder developing gradually over the years is consistent with modern concepts. "In some cases," Prichard wrote, "the alteration in temper and habits [of the morally insane] has been gradual and imperceptive, and it seems only to have consisted in an exaltation and increase of peculiarities, which were always more or less natural and habitual" (1835, p. 13).

Reflecting the views of Pinel and Prichard, the concept of moral insanity continued to appear in psychiatry textbooks for many years. The British psychiatrist Charles Mercier (1853–1910), a lecturer on insanity at the Westminister Hospital Medical School in London, had this to say about morally insane individuals (he preferred the diagnostic label *moral perversion*): "There are persons who indulge in vices with such persistence, at a cost of punishment so heavy, so certain, and so prompt, who incur this punishment for the sake of pleasure so trifling and so transient, that they are by consent considered insane, although they exhibit no other indication of insanity" (Mercier, 1902, p. 97).

Antisocial Personality as Psychopathic

Toward the end of the 19th century, moral insanity and moral perversion gave way to *constitutional psychopathic inferiority*, or, more simply, *psychopathic inferiority*. Julius L. A. Koch, director of Zwiefalten's psychiatric asylum, coined these terms (Henderson, 1939; Pichot, 1978). Koch distinguished among various types of psychopathic states. Some types were acquired defects in socialization; others were innate. Koch's conviction that certain forms of antisocial behavior were inborn had a great influence on German psychiatry and on Emil Kraepelin (Pichot, 1978). (See Chapter 2 for a discussion of Kraepelin and his psychiatric classification system.)

With the increasing influence of Freudian theory and its emphasis on the role of early experiences in the development of psychopathology, psychopathic inferiority gradually gave way to *psychopathic personality*, reflecting a greater emphasis on environmental factors than on genetic inheritance. During the first half of the 20th century, that term was widely applied in the United States and other countries. In England the Mental Health Act of 1980 adopted the term *psychopathic disorder*, defined as "a persistent disorder or disability of mind (whether or not including subnormality of intelligence) which results in

One's particular location can have a significant influence on the kinds of antisocial behavior considered to be most serious.

abnormally aggressive or seriously irresponsible conduct on the part of the patient, and requires or is susceptible to treatment" (Lewis, 1974, p. 137).

Changes in the DSM

The 1952 edition of the DSM, (DSM-I) replaced *psychopathic disorder* with *sociopathic personality disturbance* (American Psychiatric Association, 1952). Recognizing the social significance of the disorder, the DSM writers included two subtypes — dyssocial and antisocial. Dyssocial individuals showed various kinds of antisocial behavior, such as habitually following criminal pursuits, but nevertheless were able to maintain close loyalties and to show affection. Antisocial individuals were unable to maintain those kinds of relationships. They were cold and callous people whose low level of conscience was an important factor in their antisocial behavior but who may or may not have engaged in criminal activities.

DSM-II replaced *sociopathic personality disturbance* with *antisocial personality* to strengthen the distinction between antisocial and dyssocial behavior (American Psychiatric Association, 1968). The dyssocial type of personality disorder was renamed dyssocial behavior and moved to a different category, "conditions without manifest psychiatric disorder and nonspecific conditions." This change helped strengthen the idea that antisocial personality is not necessarily synonymous with criminality, although the two often coexist.

In DSM-III and DSM-III-R, *antisocial personality* was changed to *antisocial personality disorder*. The term *dyssocial* no longer appears, but a new diagnosis, **adult antisocial behavior**, maintains the distinction between criminal behavior per se and antisocial personality disorder. This diagnosis appears in a broad category, "conditions not attributable to a mental disorder." The diagnostician considers applying the adult antisocial behavior label to individuals who commit criminal or other antisocial acts but who do not meet the full criteria for antisocial personality disorder and whose antisocial behavior is apparently not due to a mental disorder (American Psychiatric Association, 1987, pp. 344, 359). For example, the diagnosis could be used for an adult whose antisocial behavior is confined to thievery.

The central feature of the DSM-III-R criteria for antisocial personality disorder is a history of continuous antisocial behavior that flagrantly violates the rights of others. The behavior begins early in life, often before age 15, and persists into adulthood. Typically, the early childhood of individuals with this diagnosis is marked by persistent lying, stealing, physical aggression, truancy, and resistance to authority. As adolescents, these individuals are often involved in aggressive sexual activity, illicit drugs, and excessive drinking.

The diagnosis of antisocial personality disorder applies only to individuals age 18 or older. When similar behavior occurs in younger people, the DSM-III-R designation is **conduct disorder**. The reason for this distinction is that antisocial behavior in childhood or adolescence does not always lead to antisocial personality disorder later in life. Antisocial behavior in children sometimes disappears spontaneously, or it may develop into other kinds of disorders, such as schizophrenia.

A Clinical Profile

In his classic work, *The Mask of Sanity*, Hervey Cleckley (1976) gave a detailed clinical profile of antisocial personality disorder. The following characteristics are derived primarily from his extensive description.

Superficial Charm. On the surface, the antisocial person is amiable, capable of making a good first impression. Charm is often coupled with superior intelligence, at least as measured by standard intelligence tests. Such a combination can be devastating when turned in antisocial directions. A good example of this pattern can be seen in the case of imposters who claim to be prestigious figures, often of a high social status.

> A penniless man posed as a peer and bought his way into high society with his Barclaycard, a court was told yesterday. He convinced titled young Englishmen that he was a member of the aristocracy and played his role so well that the society magazine, *Harper's and Queen,* used a picture of his twenty-first birthday party.
>
> But yesterday Duncan Roy, a Londoner, aged 22, was jailed for 15 months for obtaining property and services by deception. . . . Roy ran up huge bills entertaining his rich friends, and when he was arrested owed Barclaycard nearly £10,000. . . .
>
> Mr. Scott Crolla, who was pictured with Roy in *Harper's and Queen,* said after the case: . . . "He was very persuasive, a real charmer and totally believable." ("Bogus Sloanne Ranger," 1983, p. 3)

Lack of Normal Anxiety. Antisocial people show a remarkable deficiency in adaptive anxiety. Normal individuals learn to delay gratification when it is appropriate to do so and experience anxiety and guilt if they do not. Antisocial individuals insist that gratification must be immediate, regardless of the possible consequences, and experience little anxiety and guilt. Their lack of normal anxiety and appropriate guilt reflects in part an inability to recognize and express socially acceptable behavior. In psychoanalytic language, antisocial individuals have a weak superego.

Untruthfulness and Insincerity. Antisocial individuals have no trouble ignoring the truth. Since they lie with supreme ease, they can acknowledge the fault of their behavior without really meaning it.

Inadequately Motivated Behavior. Antisocial people lack reasonable goals, even in their antisocial behavior. They may commit a host of unlawful acts for amazingly small stakes and with much greater risk of discovery than the ordinary criminal. Indeed, they often seem to commit such acts without any apparent goal at all (Cleckley, 1976, p. 343). As the psychoanalyst Robert M. Lindner (1944) once put it, they are rebels without a cause.

Poor Judgment. Antisocial individuals typically show very poor judgment in their personal affairs and in social situations. They frequently waste excellent opportunities to achieve what they claim are their goals. If incarcerated for their antisocial acts, they repeat such behavior soon after release. This failure of judgment does not seem to be related to decisions about abstract or theoretical situations. Indeed, as long as it is a question of what could or should be done, they may offer quite wise advice. It is when the test of action arrives that their deficiency in judgment is manifest (Cleckley, 1976, p. 346).

Abnormal Egocentricity and Incapacity for Love. Antisocial individuals have an astonishing degree of vanity (1976, p. 346). Coupled with this abnormal self-centeredness is an inability to maintain close, affectionate relationships. They usually show only a whimsical and fleeting fondness for others but are highly proficient at pretending to love.

Lack of Insight. Antisocial individuals have virtually no ability to see themselves as others do. The following letter written by a young man who had been engaged in a long succession of thefts, truancies, and other antisocial acts clearly demonstrates this deficiency. Shortly before writing the letter, he had been expelled from college and sent back to his distant home by his aunt and uncle, with whom he had been staying, and who had hoped to reform him.

> Dear Doctor _____:
>
> Arrived home safe and sound. I really was astonished at the great change in this small, typical, midwestern town when I pulled into it on Sunday. . . . I'm getting on fine here with Mother and Father. I feel like a different fellow. Dr. _____ I don't know how I'll ever thank you for what you did for me down there. It was my chance to straighten out and I took it. I believe I can say I did a good job of it. I don't know whether I could have done it alone. But the main thing is it's done and I want you to know I appreciate your help. (Cleckley, 1976, p. 353)

In summing up his clinical profile, Cleckley points out that antisocial people rarely show the usual signs of psychotic disorder, such as delusions or hallucinations. He also acknowledges that insanity is a legal judgment rather than a psychiatric or psychological concept. Nevertheless, he insists that, in a very real sense, antisocial people are insane in that they have incomplete contact with the realities of social life. Although outwardly they present a convincing mask of sanity, says Cleckley, they lack the purposes and experiences of human relationships that bind the normal person to social reality.

The criteria used to determine the presence of antisocial characteristics inevitably reflect the attitudes and beliefs of the dominant culture in which the presumed antisocial behavior occurs. Weiss and Perry (1976) point out the following in their survey of opinions on antisocial behavior in a number of cultural settings.

> A judge or policeman in St. Louis may be much more concerned with offenses involving theft than would similar officials in Paris, although theft is considered a serious crime everywhere. A psychiatrist in Bombay may well give considerably more weight to perceived nonviolent sexual misbehavior such as promiscuity or adultery in making the diagnosis of "antisocial personality" than will one in London or many other urban areas. Neither education nor occupation nor degree of expertise, significantly changes this bias (the word is used in its nonpejorative sense). One's location substantially influences what kinds of antisocial behavior are viewed as most serious or, indeed, if certain kinds of behavior are to be considered "antisocial" at all. (p. 344)

Weiss and Perry (1976) also report considerable agreement on certain kinds of criteria for antisocial behavior even from one culture to another. This is especially true for people in urban areas, who appear to be uniformly concerned about crimes of violence (especially homicide), crimes against property, and exploitation and dishonesty in interpersonal and public dealings.

Etiological Factors

Cortical Underarousal   When the cerebral cortex and the reticular formation in the brain stem are optimally aroused, the individual's general state of awareness, feeling of pleasantness, and efficiency generally increase (see Figure 12.1). (The network of the brain stem extends into the central region of the brain. The lower part of the brain stem includes the reticular activating system (RAS), which controls arousal and alertness. Fibers from the pons and medulla connect with cells in the RAS. In turn, fibers from the RAS connect with the cerebellum, hypothalamus, and cerebral cortex — the outer covering of the cerebral hemispheres.) An arousal level that is too low reduces the reactions; too high a level produces a disorganized state of awareness, strong feelings of unpleasantness, and inefficient behavior. Various researchers have reported that a significant number of antisocial individuals consistently experience **cortical underarousal**, a condition in which the cerebral cortex and reticular formation require continuous and unusually high levels of stimulation to produce and maintain an optimum level of arousal (Hare, 1970, 1975; Hare & Cox, 1978; Satterfield, 1978; Zuckerman, 1978). This underarousal may account, at least in part, for certain characteristics of antisocial personality disorder, such as a chronic concern with seeking excitement and an inability to tolerate conventional routines of daily life. The concentration on seeking high levels of cortical stimulation may interfere with paying attention to the various subtle cues in the environment that help guide individuals toward socially acceptable behavior (Hare, 1970).

Cortical Immaturity   Another abnormality of brain functioning that may account for some of the characteristics of antisocial personality disorder is an immature development of the cerebral cortex. Various studies have reported the presence of abnormal amounts of slow-wave activity in the electroencephalograph (EEG) patterns of adults diagnosed with an antisocial personality disorder. Because this type of brain activity is also present in some normal children, it may be that **cortical immaturity** is responsible, at least in part, for the development of

Figure 12.1

Brain stem and reticular formation. (From Davison & Neale, 1986, p. 601.)

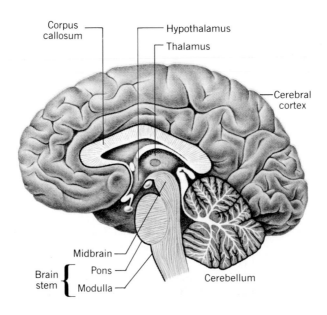

an antisocial personality (Elliott, 1978; Hare, 1970, 1975; Hare & Cox, 1978; Monroe, 1970).

At first glance, the hypothesis of cortical immaturity appears to be plausible, since certain characteristics of antisocial personality disorder are childlike. For example, antisocial people are egocentric, are unable to delay gratification, and cannot work toward long-term goals. The fact that slow-wave brain activity occurs less often in middle-aged antisocial people than in younger ones is consistent with clinical observations that the more blatant aspects of antisocial disorder often decrease after age 30 (American Psychiatric Association, 1980a, p. 318; Elliott, 1978). Nevertheless, there are serious limitations to the cortical immaturity hypothesis.

1. It fails to account for many of the characteristics of antisocial personality disorder that are not particularly childlike.

2. Studies that seem to support the hypothesis have not ruled out various environmental influences that may be greatly responsible for the antisocial behavior. For example, Monroe (1970, p. 165) points out that almost all careful studies of antisocial people whose EEG patterns are abnormal reveal highly disturbed family and social relationships during the subjects' early life, marked by parental dissension, separation, emotional deprivation, and cultural and economic privations. Monroe concludes that the ultimate expression of antisocial personality disorder may well depend on a combination of faulty brain equipment and faulty learning within an inadequate social environment.

3. At least 15 percent of adults who have EEG patterns of slow-wave activity similar to those reported for antisocial personality disorder show no signs of antisocial behavior (Hare, 1970; Monroe, 1970).

4. Explanations other than cortical immaturity have been offered for the occurrence of slow-wave activity in the antisocial person. Some kind of actual brain pathology, rather than simply a delay in development, may be present. Also, the low level of activity reflected in the patterns may be due to boredom during routine EEG examinations (Hare, 1970, 1975; Hare & Cox, 1976).

In an extensive critical review of research dealing with EEG patterns in antisocial personalities, Syndulko (1978) concluded that there is no firm empirical basis for stating that such individuals have abnormal amounts of slow-wave activity or that their behavior stems from immature development of the cerebral cortex.

Abnormal Sex Chromosomes

Each cell of the human body contains 23 pairs of chromosomes; one of these pairs determines the individual's sex. There are two kinds of sex chromosomes, X (female) and Y (male). Half of the male's sperm cells carry an X chromosome and the other half a Y chromosome, but the female reproductive cell (ovum) carries only an X chromosome. If a fertilized ovum (zygote) receives a Y chromosome from the sperm, the child will be a male (XY genotype); if the zygote receives an X chromosome, the child will be a female (XX genotype).

Some years ago, reports from a Scottish maximum security prison set off a flurry of excitement among professional mental health workers because of the finding that certain male inmates convicted of violent antisocial behavior had an extra Y chromosome. This abnormality resulted in an XYY genotype instead of the normal XY (Jacobs, Brunton, Melville, Brittain, & McClemont, 1965). Several subsequent studies claimed confirmation of the earlier data and were heralded in the popular press as the discovery of a criminal chromosome (Hook, 1973, 1975; Jacobs, 1975; Reid, 1978). The scientific reports themselves, however, were more conservative, usually interpreting the findings as an indication that the extra Y chromosome may increase aggressive tendencies, which in turn may lead to an increase in criminal behavior.

Others have seriously questioned, and in some instances completely repudiated, the notion that an XYY genotype has any significant relationship to the development of an antisocial personality disorder or to the occurrence of violent criminal behavior (Culliton, 1975; National Institute of Mental Health, 1970; Robins, 1975; Witkin et al., 1976). In perhaps the most extensive evaluation of the problem, Baker (1972) examined some 200 studies and concluded that there was no clear evidence specifically relating antisocial behavior to a chromosomal error.

Negative Family Models

In a pioneering longitudinal study of antisocial behavior, Lee N. Robins (1966, 1975) studied adults who 30 years earlier had been referred to a child guidance clinic for various behavioral and emotional problems, including conduct disorders; 75 percent of the subjects were male and 25 percent female. For purposes of comparison, the study followed into adulthood a control group of 100 normal children, with about the same proportion of males and females and similar age, race, intelligence, neighborhood, and other characteristics. As adults, the two groups differed significantly in their rates of antisocial behavior: 22 percent of the clients at the child guidance clinic, but only 2 percent of the control group, were diagnosed as sociopathic. Antisocial acts during childhood were found to be the best predictor of adult antisocial behavior. Prominent among such acts were "truancy, theft, staying out late, and refusing to obey parents. [The children] lied gratuitously, and showed little guilt over their behavior. They were generally irresponsible about where they were supposed to be or taking care of money" (Robins, 1966, p. 57). There was practically no difference between boys and girls in the antisocial behavior.

The Robins study also pointed to another important predictor of antisocial personality disorder: the presence during childhood of antisocial parents, especially the father. The father's influence was particularly negative when it was accompanied by inadequate discipline and a great deal of family strife. When antisocial fathers were strict disciplinarians, there was less likelihood of their children being diagnosed during adulthood as sociopathic.

Stewart and Leone (1978) found that the fathers of boys admitted to an outpatient unit for unsocialized aggressive behavior qualified for the diagnosis of antisocial personality disorder more often than did fathers of a control group of boys admitted to the unit for other kinds of problems. The difference even extended to uncles; those relatives of the unsocialized aggressive boys more often had a history of marked antisocial behavior than did the uncles of the control group.

Lack of opportunities to develop open relationships in the family and to disclose one's more intimate feelings may play an important role in the development of at least some forms of antisocial behavior. One study (Anchor, Sandler, and Cherones, 1977) compared highly aggressive antisocial male psychiatric patients between the ages of 23 and 32 with control groups of psychiatric patients and employees of the hospital. On the whole, the antisocial patients were the least exposed to family models for the sharing of intimate feelings and openness and the least rewarded for such self-disclosure.

Other studies suggest the importance of poor parental models in the etiology of antisocial personality disorder, especially the inability of antisocial people to delay gratification and to resist the impulsive behavior with which they so often ignore other people's feelings and rights (Lahey, et. al., 1988). Tolerating the delay of rewards depends to a significant degree on the expectations individuals develop in their families and the behavior that is reinforced. If parents always provide rewards sporadically, or if they regularly promise rewards that are never actually given, then children may well learn to get what they can while they can (Hare, 1970). Furthermore, parents may themselves demonstrate a gross inability to delay gratification, thus denying their children the opportunity to learn to delay rewards through observation of the desirable results of doing so. Parents may also avoid the responsibility by being positive models by overindulging their children.

Approaches to Treatment

Psychotherapy

The usual forms of psychotherapy have not been very effective in helping antisocial individuals change their behavior (Cleckley, 1976; Reid, 1983). For one thing, such people lack the motivation to change, especially since they do not experience the anxiety and concern for future consequences that drive other disturbed individuals to seek professional help. Furthermore, successful psychotherapy depends to a great extent on an empathic interpersonal relationship between the client and the therapist. Ordinarily, the antisocial person is unable to maintain this kind of relationship (Cleckley, 1976). Perhaps even more crucial is the fact that a significant number of antisocial people are never punished for their destructive behavior. All too often their superficial charm gains them support not only from friends and family but also from their victims. Since their antisocial behavior is positively reinforced, they see no compelling reason to change. Antisocial people who are caught and punished for their crimes may agree to participate in psychotherapy, but their purpose is to gain favorable attention from prison authorities. They have little interest in actual change (Cavanaugh, Rogers, & Wasyliw, 1981).

Residential Treatment Programs

An alternative to conventional psychotherapy is **residential treatment programs**. They include psychotherapy, but they emphasize the total environment. These programs, sometimes called therapeutic communities or milieu therapy, usually operate within special correctional institutions or in special hospitals that are part of a broader correctional system. The basic assumption of the programs is that antisocial individuals are not sufficiently socialized. They therefore require a psychosocial environment that is firm and disciplined—an environment that was missing while their personality was developing (McCord, 1982). William H. Reid (1983) has summarized the essential features of such programs as follows.

> Successful inpatient programs involve long-term, strictly structured, hierarchical settings [that] involve every aspect of the patient's life . . . [and] progress. [The patient] begins with very few privileges except that of being treated as a human being. As [the patient] slowly moves through a four- or five-step hierarchy of privileges, . . . [and] acquires more and more self-esteem and social and interpersonal competence, . . . [there is] less need for the antisocial character style. In addition to the rigorous structure there should always be time for reflection, during which, particularly in the early stages,

the patient may become "emotional" without [being exposed] completely to others, . . . although sharing one's feelings with others is a necessary later part of the treatment program. (p. 193)

Although residential treatment programs report a moderate degree of success in socializing their participants, optimism about their outcomes must be tempered. For one thing, improvement has not consistently been transferred to the outside. Successful transfer seems to depend on the condition of the patient at discharge. For example, when patients were released from the Treatment Center at Bridgewater, Massachusetts, against the advice of administrators, the recidivism rate ranged between 30 and 40 percent. On the other hand, when therapists and administrators were satisfied with the decision to release, the recidivism rate fell to about 6 percent (Carney, 1981; Kozol, Boucher, & Garofolo, 1972).

The experience of residential treatment centers suggests possible directions for the treatment of antisocial personality disorder, particularly when it involves consistent transgressions against the law. Especially if antisocial individuals are more the product of social learning than biological deficit, success in helping them should be based on a psychosocial model that focuses on group support and practice in learning how to be a contributing member of society.

Many mental health professionals are convinced that antisocial personality disorder can be traced mainly to disturbances in family relationships, the lack of adequate models in the family, and other negative psychosocial conditions. Therefore, they argue for prevention through early therapeutic intervention and positive changes in the individual's psychosocial environment designed to remedy the root conditions of the disorder. This prevention demands the resources and programs of social action as part of a wider community mental health movement (see Chapter 21).

Disorders of Impulse Control

In the broadest sense, **disorders of impulse control** encompass a number of disturbances that DSM-III-R classifies under various other diagnostic categories. Examples are sexual disorders such as paraphilias (see Chapter 8) and substance use disorders (see Chapters 14 and 15), which include the abuse of alcohol or other drugs. However, a number of impulse disorders are sufficiently distinctive to warrant separate consideration. They are classified in DSM-III-R as "disorders of impulse control not elsewhere classified." They include kleptomania, pyromania, and pathological gambling.

Traditionally, these abnormalities were regarded as forms of neurotic obsessions and compulsions, similar to obsessive compulsive disorder (see Chapter 5). However, the victim of the latter perceives the obsessions and compulsions as an unwanted invasion of consciousness. In contrast, the impulse disorders we discuss in this chapter are inherently pleasurable and consciously desired.

Kleptomania

The term **kleptomania** is derived from the Greek word *kleptein*, "to steal." The central features of the disorder are as follows (American Psychiatric Association, 1987, pp. 322–323).

- Repeated failure to resist stealing objects that are of little monetary value or immediate usefulness.

- An increasing sense of tension just prior to committing the theft.

- An intense experience of pleasure or relief at the time of committing the theft.

- Stealing for reasons other than the expression of anger or revenge.

Discussions on kleptomania sometimes claim that the disorder is more prevalent among women than men. However, the actual gender ration is not known. It is true that the majority of people caught at shoplifting are women, but only a small proportion are diagnosed as having kleptomania.

Psychoanalytic Views

Traditional psychoanalytic interpretations of kleptomania usually ascribe it to frustrated infantile desires. It may represent an attempt to compensate for emotional deprivation. Thus, the stolen article is a symbol of a desired love object. Some psychoanalytic interpretations link kleptomania with penis envy: Stealing objects represents stealing a penis. This assertion is used to explain why kleptomania is supposedly more common among women than men (Fenichel, 1945, pp. 370–371). According to another interpretation, kleptomania represents a desire to carry out in secret some forbidden sexual activity. For example: "A woman of forty, who constantly reverted to thievery, reported that she was sexually excited whenever she accomplished her theft. In sexual intercourse she was frigid; while masturbating, she would imagine that she was stealing" (Fenichel, 1945, p. 371). Psychoanalytic interpretations have not been substantiated systematically; instead, case histories have been used selectively. Nevertheless, a number of reports on the psychoanalytic treatment of kleptomania claim that such approaches can be successful in overcoming the disorder (Kaplan & Sadock, 1985, p. 483).

Kleptomania as Learned Behavior

The cognitive approach to kleptomania explains it on the basis of past experiences in the environment of the individual. For example, conditioning may form an association between stealing and some reinforcing consequence, such as praise from peers or the thrill of getting away with a forbidden act; or the kleptomaniac may have been influenced by negative models.

The positive results of therapy for the treatment of kleptomania based on principles of conditioning and learning do suggest their importance in the development of the disorder (Ullmann & Krasner, 1975, p. 282). Behavior therapy may require an individual to send money back to the store to pay for a stolen object and then visit the store without doing any shoplifting (Kraft, 1970). Applying aversive stimuli to individuals as they watch a film showing acts of shoplifting has reduced kleptomanic behavior. Some therapists have exposed individuals to situations of increasing intensity involving stealing to desensitize them (Marznagao, 1972). Thus, the necessity to reduce tension through stealing was gradually eliminated. (See Chapter 21 for the use of desensitization methods in behavior therapy.)

Pyromania

The diagnostic label **pyromania** is derived from the Greek word *pyr*, meaning "fire." DSM-III-R lists the following criteria of pyromania (American Psychiatric Association, 1987, pp. 325–326).

Pyromaniac individuals may reveal their abnormal impulses and arouse suspicion by regularly watching fires in their neighborhood, or even setting false alarms to experience the excitement of seeing the firefighters arrive.

■ Repeated failure to resist the impulse to set fires.

■ Increasing tension just prior to setting a fire.

■ Intense pleasure or relief from tension when setting a fire, witnessing a fire, or observing the results.

■ Setting fires for reasons other than monetary gain, the expression of social or political views, concealment of criminal activity, revenge, or in response to a delusion or hallucination.

Not all impulsive and chronic fire-setting necessarily indicates pyromania. Fire-setting may also accompany such disturbances as schizophrenia, antisocial personality disorder, and organic mental disorders.

Individuals often reveal their pyromanic impulses and arouse the suspicion of others by watching fires in their neighborhoods and showing extreme interest in the fire-fighting equipment, even setting off false alarms just to see the equipment arrive at the scene.

Pyromania is considerably more common in males than females. Symptoms typically begin during childhood and become more intense during adolescence and adulthood, when the fire-setting tends to be more deliberately destructive (American Psychiatric Association, 1987, p. 326).

Psychoanalytic Views   Traditional psychoanalytic explanations and treatment of pyromania emphasize a sexual motivation. Supposedly, the excitement that accompanies the setting of fires is sexual. According to some psychoanalysts, the association between sexual pleasure and fire is normal in early childhood. It represents a fusion of the sadistic (aggressive) drive, which aims to destroy objects, with pleasurable sexual sensations from the warmth of the fire. In its abnormal development, this fusion becomes perverse, so that setting fires actually becomes an indispensable condition for sexual satisfaction. The destructive force of the fire then serves as a symbol of the intensity of the sexual drive (Fenichel, 1945, p. 371).

The psychoanalytic interpretation suffers from the same limitations we pointed out earlier in connection with kleptomania: the use of selected case histories to fit a previously determined explanation.

Pyromania as Learned Behavior

Learning theories of psychopathology seek the origins of pyromania in the particular learning history of the individual. For some individuals, learned sexual motives may play a role, but they are not necessarily present for others. In general, the treatment of pyromania has been especially difficult. Many people refuse to accept responsibility for their behavior and thus resist the cooperation necessary for successful psychotherapy (Kaplan & Sadock, 1985, p. 484).

Pathological Gambling

Chronic involvement in gambling to the extent of seriously harming one's personal, family, and occupational life is **pathological gambling**. The subject has been examined more widely than kleptomania and pyromania in both professional writings and the popular press. Because gambling itself generally receives strong social support (for example, most states have legalized it in one form or another), its abnormal manifestations are especially difficult to prevent or reduce (Eadington, 1976; Herman, 1976; Lesieur, 1977). It is appropriate, therefore, to consider pathological gambling in somewhat more detail.

> "My name is Rudy R. and I am a compulsive gambler," the leadoff speaker began the other night at the chapter meeting in a loft building on East 23rd Street. "I didn't have to commit suicide, I killed everything around me. I was a walking plague. I stole, lied, cheated, connived. I'd look forward to each new sports season. All I could think about was gambling."
>
> The other men nodded understandingly as Rudy R. told of the family misery his gambling caused. "I'd pick a fight with my wife just so I could say, 'I'm going out.' 'I'm going out.' I've got a son that stutters because I'd never let him finish a sentence. I'd say, 'Not now.' I was too busy thinking about my next bet. In my crazy dream world, nothing was ever coming true. Then I surrendered. I finally accepted defeat and my life has changed." Rudy R. sat down to loud applause. (Cady, 1973, p. 7)

Rudy R.'s confession was made at a meeting of Gamblers Anonymous, a self-help organization that shares the philosophy and methods of Alcoholics Anonymous (see Chapter 15). Its goal is to help compulsive gamblers (in DSM-III-R terms, pathological gamblers) understand their maladaptive behavior and eliminate it (Stewart & Brown, 1988). Rudy R's description of his problems reflects the general tenor of the DSM-III-R criteria of pathological gambling. At least four must be present to justify that diagnosis (American Psychiatric Association, 1987, p. 325).

1. Persistent preoccupation with gambling or with obtaining money for gambling.

2. Frequent gambling of larger amounts of money than intended or gambling over a longer period of time.

3. Increasing size and frequency of bets to obtain the desired excitement of gambling.

4. Restlessness or irritability if prevented from gambling.

5. Repeated losing of money through gambling but continuation of efforts to win it back.

6. Repeated but unsuccessful attempts to cut down on gambling.

7. Giving up of important social or occupational activities for gambling.

8. Continuation of gambling in spite of inability to pay increasing debts or incurring of other social, occupational, or legal problems that the individual knows will be intensified by the gambling.

Onset and Development

The onset of pathological gambling can often be traced to adolescence, and it tends to take a chronic course. The eventual outcome is likely to be extremely incapacitating, resulting in great financial loss and the inability to provide the basic necessities for self and family. Alienation from family and friends is a common consequence. Ensuing depression may lead to attempts at suicide. Because of huge debts, the gambler may become involved in illegal attempts to get money, which may lead to arrest and imprisonment (Dielman, 1979, p. 41).

The development of pathological gambling is complex, arising from a variety of interacting events. Evidence obtained through clinical study suggests the following predisposing factors (American Psychiatric Association, 1987, p. 324).

■ Loss of parents through death, separation, divorce, or desertion prior to age 15.

■ Inadequate parental discipline — for example, inconsistency, harshness, or failure to exercise any kind of discipline.

■ Easily available gambling activities during adolescence.

■ High family value on material goods and symbols of financial success.

■ Lack of family values involving savings, planning, and budgeting.

Although individuals diagnosed with an antisocial personality disorder may also become deeply involved in problems of gambling, their motives and behavior differ from those of pathological gamblers. As a rule, pathological gamblers engage in antisocial behavior only out of a desperate need for money to pursue gambling, and only when the money can no longer be obtained from legal sources. In contrast, the criminal activities that antisocial individuals carry out in connection with gambling are usually part of a more widespread and preferred pattern of antisocial behavior. Furthermore, pathological gamblers usually have a positive work career until it is destroyed by gambling. Individuals with an antisocial personality disorder typically have erratic work histories (American Psychiatric Association, 1987, pp. 342, 345).

Psychoanalytic Interpretations

According to various followers of Freudian theory, the origins of pathological gambling can be traced to repressed memories of Oedipal conflict involving guilt about masturbation and fears of castration (Fuller, 1977). The little that Freud wrote on the psychopathology of gambling appears in an essay on Dostoevsky's creativity and its relationship to various abnormal aspects of his personality and behavior (Freud, 1928/1961). Freud concluded that, like all pathological gamblers, Dostoevsky harbored an unconscious wish to lose that represented a desire to be punished for unresolved Oedipal conflicts. Freud pointed out that Dostoevsky's literary production never went better than when he had lost all of his possessions and those of his wife as the result of gambling: "When his sense of guilt was satisfied by the punishments he had inflicted upon himself, the inhibition upon his work became less severe and he allowed himself to take a few steps along the road to success" (Freud, 1928/1961, p. 191).

Drawing on his clinical experience, Otto Fenichel, an orthodox follower of Freudian psychoanalysis, was even more explicit than Freud about the sexual motivation of pathological gambling: "The excitement of the game corresponds to sexual excitement; that of winning to orgasm . . . ; that of losing to punishment by castration. . . . [T]he gambler . . . tempts fate to declare whether it is in favor of his playing (masturbating) or whether it is going to castrate him" (Fenichel, 1945, p. 372).

Not all psychoanalytic interpretations of pathological gambling have been so specifically sexual. For example, Edmund Bergler (1977), who has devoted a great deal of attention to the psychology of gambling, emphasizes that the gambler's unconscious aggression against authority figures is basically a denial of the reality principle — the rules of logic, intelligence, and moderation transmitted by parental or other authority figures. In losing, says Bergler, the gambler engages in self-punishment, "paying the penalty for this aggression" (pp. 177–178).

Thus, according to Bergler, pathological gambling is an unconscious rejection of rationality. Fenichel thought that even more fundamental than the specific sexual aspects was the magical quality of the pathological gambler's thinking and behavior. The pathological gambler acts as if he believes in the right "to ask for special protection by fate" (Fenichel, 1945, p. 372), an irrational conviction that persists in spite of all previous losses. Dostoevsky's "The Gambler" portrays the kind of magical belief Fenichel refers to with almost clinical vividness. Here, the protagonist, Aleksei, is conversing with Polina, a young woman to whom he is greatly attracted and whose money he has just lost at the roulette table. (Polina is based on Dostoevsky's wife.)

> "I am still convinced that I am going to win, I must really admit that you have just made me ask myself a question: why is it that my failure today, muddleheaded and utterly disgraceful though it is, has not left the trace of doubt in my mind? I am still convinced that as soon as I start playing for myself I'll most certainly win."
>
> "Why are you so positive about it?"
>
> "If you insist, I just don't know. I only know that I *must* win, also that it is the only way out that's left for me. Well, maybe that's why it seems to me that I'll win for sure." (Dostoevsky, 1866/1972, pp. 39–40)

Finally, penniless, bereft of family and friends, and suffering from the shame of having been imprisoned for his debts, Aleksei is still possessed with the belief that he will ultimately win.

> As I was leaving the casino I looked, there was still one gulden in my vest pocket: "Ah, so there's money for my dinner!" I thought, but then, having walked a hundred more paces, I changed my mind and went back to the casino. I staked my gulden on *manque* [numbers 1 to 18 in roulette], and, believe me, there is something special about that feeling which you have, all alone, in a foreign country, far from home and from your friends, not knowing what you'll eat tomorrow, as you bet your last, your

very, very last gulden! I won, and left the casino twenty minutes later, with one hundred and seventy guldens in my pocket. That is a fact, yes, sir! That's what the last gulden can sometimes mean for you! And what if I had lost heart that time, if I had not dared to take that last chance? (p. 192)

Gambling and Learning

From the standpoint of reinforcement theory, especially B. F. Skinner's version (see Chapter 4), all persistent gambling is a learned pattern of behavior based on **variable-ratio schedules of reinforcement**. (Skinner and his adherents prefer the term *reinforcement* to what more ordinarily is called *reward*.) A reinforcement occurs after a given average number (a ratio) of responses. However, the particular response to be reinforced cannot be predicted and thus is variable. Therefore, according to Skinner, it is not necessary to attribute pathological gambling to certain kinds of feelings, as psychoanalytic theory does.

It has been estimated that more than 1 million persons in the United States are pathological gamblers. The disorder is apparently more common among men than women. It is especially interesting to note that the fathers of male pathological gamblers and the mothers of female pathological gamblers are more likely to have the disorder than is the population at large (Kaplan & Sadock, 1985, p. 481). This fact suggests the importance of role models in the learning of such behavior.

Summary

1. Personality disorders reflect long-standing personality traits often apparent at adolescence or even earlier. These disorders are quite pervasive, affecting many personal and social relationships.

2. Personality disorders are classified in DSM-III-R on Axis II.

3. New controversial categories of personality disorders classified in a DSM-III-R appendix are self-defeating personality disorder and sadistic personality disorder. Their placement in the appendix reflects strong disagreement among mental health professionals over their appropriateness.

4. DSM-III-R groups personality disorders into three clusters. Cluster A includes paranoid, schizoid, and schizotypal personality disorders. The central characteristic of paranoid personality disorder is a highly pervasive and long-standing pattern of maladaptive suspiciousness and mistrust. Schizoid personality disorder is marked by seclusiveness and lack of desire for social involvement. Schizotypal personality disorder shows some resemblance to schizophrenia, but it does not reveal sharp breaks with reality, such as delusions and hallucinations.

5. Cluster B includes histrionic, narcissistic, antisocial, and borderline personality disorders. Histrionic symptoms include maladaptive self-dramatization, overconcern with one's effect on others, abnormal seeking of approval, and shallow social relationships. Narcissistic disorder is marked by a consistent and abnormal exaggeration of one's self-importance and an intense preoccupation with fantasies of power and success. Antisocial personality disorder is characterized by a long history of violating other people's rights and a chronic history of poor and shifting job performance. Borderline personality disorder has a relatively ambiguous pattern; it overlaps other personality disorders. It includes such features as overimpulsive behavior, unstable personal relationships, chronic feelings of boredom, and undependable shifts in mood.

6. Cluster C includes avoidance, dependent, obsessive compulsive and passive aggressive personality disorders. A central feature of avoidant disorder is hypersensitivity to rejection by others and hesitation about entering social relationships unless one is sure of being accepted. Dependent personality disorder is characterized by the inability to assume responsibility for decisions and an extreme lack of self-confidence. Obsessive compulsive personality disorder is marked by a constant and maladaptive preoccupation with rules and details and the consequent failure to see other aspects of social situations or interpersonal relationships.

7. Personality disorders lend themselves especially well to interpretations based on defense mechanisms.

8. Of all the personality disorders, the antisocial pattern is the most troublesome, especially in its implications for a broad range of social situations.

9. Modern diagnostic concepts of antisocial personality disorder can be traced to the work of the French physician Philippe Pinel and the English physician James Cowles Prichard.

10. The most comprehensive description and analysis of antisocial personality is Cleckley's *The Mask of Sanity*. His profile of the disorder includes such characteristics as superficial charm, lack of normal anxiety, untruthfulness and insincerity, poor judgment, and a gross incapacity for love.

11. Biological factors that may contribute to the development of at least some of the characteristics of antisocial personality include cortical underarousal and immaturity and abnormal sex chromosomes. However, the evidence is support of a biological etiology is far from conclusive.

12. Chief among the social influences that contribute to antisocial personality disorders are negative family models. The evidence here is more conclusive than that for biological factors.

13. The psychotherapeutic treatment of individuals diagnosed with a personality disorders varies. For example, in working with the schizoid individual, the consistent use of emotional support is important; in narcissistic disorder, the goals often center on bolstering self-esteem. In the case of antisocial personality disorder, the strict discipline of residential treatment centers has been helpful. Unfortunately, the antisocial individual often returns to old patterns of behavior after leaving the center.

14. Many mental health professionals are convinced that antisocial personality disorder stems mainly from disturbances in family relationships. They therefore argue for early therapeutic intervention before the antisocial pattern takes firm roots.

15. Disorders of impulse control have a number of distinctive characteristics: (a) individuals are unable to resist acting out impulses that harm themselves or other people; (b) there is an increase in tension prior to committing the act; (c) after carrying out the impulse, the individual experiences release of tension or feelings of pleasure; (d) the individual sometimes expresses guilt, remorse, or self-blame upon completing the impulsive act.

16. The diagnosis of kleptomania involves the following criteria: (a) repeated impulsive stealing of objects of little monetary value or immediate use, (b) the feeling of increased tension prior to the stealing and pleasure or relief of tension following the act, and (c) stealing for reasons other than the expression of anger or revenge.

17. Traditional psychoanalytic interpretations of kleptomania ascribe it to frustrated infantile or childhood desires, especially those with a sexual motive. There is insufficient evidence to support this explanation if it is applied broadly to many cases of kleptomania. It is conceivable that in highly selected cases the psychoanalytic interpretation may apply.

18. Clinicians who focus on a learning theory of psychopathology prefer to explain kleptomania on the basis of specific contingencies in the past environment of the individual. For example, kleptomania may develop through conditioning: An association is made between stealing and a reinforcing consequence, such as admiration from peers or the thrill of accomplishing a forbidden act.

19. Psychodynamic approaches and behavior therapy are among the methods used for treating kleptomania. Behavior therapy has been particularly successful.

20. Pyromania involves the following basic characteristics: (a) repeated failure to resist impulses to set fires; (b) increase in tension prior to setting the fire and reduction of tension following the act, especially in actually observing it; and (c) setting fires for reasons other than monetary gain, the expression of political or social protest, revenge, or as a response to delusions or hallucinations.

21. Psychoanalytic interpretations of pyromania regard the relief of tension as having a basically sexual motivation. The association between fire-setting and sexual motivation begins during early childhood and is a fusion of normal aggressive and sexual drives. In its abnormal development, it becomes indispensable for sexual satisfaction. Some instances of pyromania fit this orthodox psychoanalytic explanation, but others do not.

22. From a learning viewpoint, pyromania has its origins in the particular learning history of the individual. Although that history may sometimes involve sexual motives, other motives may also be important.

23. In general, the treatment of individuals suffering from well-established pyromania is especially difficult. Many refuse to accept responsibility for their behavior and resist the cooperation vital to successful psychotherapy.

24. Compared with kleptomania and pyromania, pathological gambling has been more widely and thoroughly examined. One reason for this attention is the strong social support that gambling in general has in our society.

25. DSM-III-R lists the following criteria as guides in the diagnosis of pathological gambling: (a) persistent preoccupation with gambling; (b) frequent gambling with larger amounts of money than intended, or more often; (c) betting in larger amounts and more often to obtain increased excitement; (d) restlessness or irritability if prevented from gambling; and (e) continuation of gambling in spite of repeated losses.

26. Clinical studies have revealed a variety of predisposing factors in the development of pathological gambling. Among them are (a) loss of parents prior to age 15, (b) inadequate parental discipline, (c) gambling activities easily available during adolescence, (d) high family value on material goods and symbols of financial success, and (e) lack of family values involving savings, planning, and budgeting.

27. Some followers of Freudian theory trace the origins of pathological gambling to repressed conflicts of the phallic phase of psychosexual development. However, Freud himself wrote little concerning his clinical experiences with pathological

gamblers. Many of his interpretations were based on a literary analysis of Dostoevsky and his writings. Freud concluded that, like other pathological gamblers, Dostoevsky had an unconscious wish to lose — a wish that represented the desire to be punished for unresolved conflicts developed during childhood.

28. From the standpoint of learning theory, especially B. F. Skinner's versions, pathological gambling is a learned process of behavior based on a variable-ratio schedule of reinforcement. Under this kind of schedule, a reinforcement occurs after a given average number of responses. However, the particular response to be reinforced is variable. Therefore, gambling continues in spite of previous losses.

29. Other learning views of pathological gambling emphasize the role of models in the gambler's life as reinforcers of their behavior. For example, some research has shown that the fathers of male pathological gamblers and the mothers of female pathological gamblers are more likely to have the disorder than is the population at large.

13

**Organic
Mental
Disorders:
Syndromes,
Biophysical
Pathology,
and Problems
of Aging**

I am a very foolish fond old man,
Fourscore and upward, not an hour more nor less;
And, to deal plainly,
I fear I am not in my perfect mind.
Methinks I should know you and know this man;
Yet I am doubtful; for I am mainly ignorant
What place this is, and all the skill I have
Remembers not these garments, nor I know not
Where I did lodge last night.

SHAKESPEARE
King Lear, **Act IV, Scene 7**

This chapter and the next two deal with a large and heterogeneous group of disabilities known as organic mental disorders. The underlying causes of these disorders are various biological and physical abnormalities that interfere with the normal functioning of the central nervous system (see Figure 13.1). For example, brain tissue may gradually deteriorate during the later years of life, resulting in a progressive loss of memory and other cognitive functions. Such deficits may also result from blood clots in the brain that obstruct normal circulation, thus preventing the blood from nourishing the brain cells.

Figure 13.1

The central nervous system. (From Julien, 1981, p. 252).

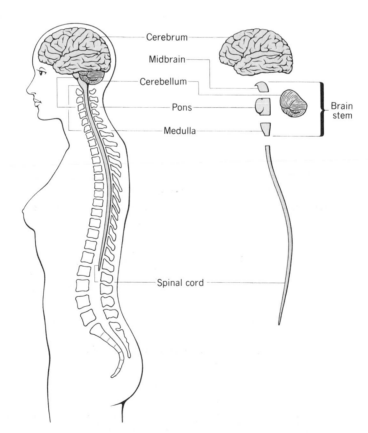

Symptoms of organic mental disorders may also result from long-term dependence on psychoactive substances such as alcohol, cocaine, and heroin.

The particular ways in which organic mental disorders are expressed depend on the specific nature of the underlying biophysical pathology, how rapidly it first appears and spreads, and such characteristics as intelligence, education, emotional state, interpersonal skills, and cultural background. Thus, although biophysical pathology is a prerequisite for organic mental syndromes, psychosocial and cultural factors may also influence their development (Lipowski, 1980a, 1980b).

DSM-III-R distinguishes between organic mental syndromes and organic mental disorders (American Psychiatric Association, 1987, pp. 97–98). **Organic mental syndrome** refers only to a specific pattern of psychological symptoms and related behavior. It does not indicate their etiology—that is, their underlying biophysical pathology. **Organic mental disorder** is a more comprehensive designation. It includes both the syndrome and its known or presumed etiology. This is an important distinction, since in some instances the same organic mental syndrome may be associated with a variety of abnormal biophysical conditions. For example, the dementia syndrome, which involves a widespread loss of intellectual functioning, can result from such diverse pathological conditions as a gradual degeneration of brain tissue, severe head injuries, blood clots that block circulation in the brain, infectious diseases, carbon monoxide poisoning, brain tumors, and vitamin B_{12} deficiency.

Diagnosing organic mental disorders requires a thorough assessment of the individual's symptoms and their etiology. Such an assessment includes a comprehensive history of the person's complaints and careful observations of other behavior, information about family background that might help explain certain aspects of the disorder, and various psychological tests, especially those that measure cognitive functioning and patterns of personality (see Chapter 2). In addition, laboratory tests and neurological and other physical examinations are necessary (Jones & Butters, 1983).

Since the syndromes are an integral part of organic mental disorders, we first consider their basic characteristics. Then we examine the more complex nature of organic mental disorders—their etiology, treatment, and sociocultural implications.

Basic Characteristics of Organic Mental Syndromes

Delirium

The central feature of **delirium** is a significant decrease in the clarity with which individuals perceive and understand their environment. Clinicians sometimes describe this confused condition as a clouded state of consciousness. The term *delirium* comes from the Latin word *delirare*, literally, "to go out of the furrow." Figuratively, *delirare* can be translated as "deranged" or "out of one's wit" (Lipowski, 1980c).

Delirious people have great difficulty paying attention to external stimuli. Their thinking often becomes fragmented and disorganized and their memory severely impaired. Perceptual misinterpretations, such as illusions and hallucinations, may occur. For example, garments hanging in the corner of a room may be perceived as living individuals (an illusion), or people may be seen in the room who are not really there (a hallucination).

Delirium often involves sleep disturbances, ranging from sleeping for unusually long periods of time to falling asleep only with great difficulty. Psychomotor disturbances are often present, sometimes shifting from hyperactivity to apathy.

Some of the symptoms of delirium resemble those of schizophrenia (see Chapter 11), especially those involving distortions of perception. Usually, however, the symptoms in delirium are more random than those in schizophrenic disorders and indeed show few signs of systematic organization. Furthermore, although schizophrenia may involve biochemical disturbances in the brain, there is still much debate about the influence of biological factors; and, in any case, they are not as specific as the organic cases of delirium.

Delirium may appear abruptly, following a head injury, for example; or it may develop slowly, especially if the cause is a chronic illness or a nutritional deficiency. As a rule, episodes of delirium are brief, lasting about a week. If the underlying organic factors are detected and treated, recovery is usually quite good. However, if the organic causes are not discovered and the condition is not adequately treated, the delirium may become stabilized and death can result.

Among the most common causes of delirium are disorders of metabolism and traumatic injuries to the head. Delirium may also occur when an addictive substance is withdrawn or its intake is sharply reduced. In long-term alcoholics, signs of delirium may appear even if the level of drinking is reduced. The decrease in the blood level of alcohol can produce symptoms of delirium just as drastic as those that occur when the use of alcohol is abruptly stopped (Rosenbaum & Beebe, 1975). Typically, the symptoms include a clouding of consciousness, tremors, and hallucinations. In their severest form, such conditions are known as **delirium tremens,** or, more popularly, the **DTs** (see Chapter 14).

Dementia

The main feature of **dementia** is a global decline in intellectual abilities that is severe enough to interfere with the individual's everyday life. Among the areas of cognitive deficit involved are memory, judgment, and abstract thinking (Joynt & Shoulson, 1979).

Memory loss may be mild, and the forgetfulness may be alleviated simply by repetition of the information. In more serious instances, the afflicted person may fail to recall the events of the day or the names of well-known individuals, regardless of prompting from others. The quotation at the beginning of the chapter is a good example of this state of mind, for King Lear was speaking to his daughter.

Judgment may be seriously impaired, especially in social situations. For example, the individual may grossly neglect personal hygiene, converse in a highly inappropriate manner, act extremely impulsively, and generally show an inability to make reasonable decisions about matters of everyday life.

Other changes in personality and behavior may also occur. For instance, a once active person may become apathetic and withdrawn; a neat person may become slovenly. It is not unusual, however, for negative changes in personality to be exaggerations of traits the individual exhibited in normal times (Bonkalo & Munro, 1980, p. 232).

Depending on the underlying organic factors causing the dementia, the course of the symptoms can vary from an abrupt beginning with a relatively stable development over many years to an insidious start with a progressive deterioration over a period of a few years. How well the dementia can be arrested or reversed depends to a great extent on the underlying organic factors.

Dementia can develop at almost any age. Most commonly, however, it is associated with a progressive deterioration of brain tissue during the late years of life.

Among the many causes of dementia are infections of the central nervous system, such as viral encephalitis (inflammation of the brain caused by a virus) and the tertiary stage of neurosyphilis. Still other causes are vascular disorders, in which blood clots form in the brain, blocking circulation and thus causing brain tissue to be destroyed; and brain damage from alcohol, heavy metal poisoning (for example, lead or arsenic), carbon monoxide, or medical drugs.

A diagnosis of dementia assumes an underlying biophysical pathology, which may or may not be clearly demonstrable. The diagnostician usually assumes the presence of dementia if there has been a widespread loss of intellectual abilities and there are no factors other than organic ones that may have produced the loss (American Psychiatric Association, 1987, p. 107).

Organic Amnestic Syndrome

More selective areas of cognitive impairment are involved in **organic amnestic syndrome.** The central characteristic of this syndrome is a significant loss in both short-term and long-term memory. Thus, it is difficult, and sometimes impossible, for the individual to learn new things (**anterograde amnesia**) and to recall material that was learned in the past (**retrograde amnesia**). People who suffer from retrograde amnesia sometimes remember events that happened many years ago much better than those of recent years. This discrepancy may reflect not only an organic disability but also an attempt to escape current unpleasantness by selectively remembering more pleasant past events.

The most common cause of an organic amnestic syndrome is the chronic and excessive use of alcohol, coupled with a deficiency in vitamin B_1 (thiamine). These two etiological factors are closely related; long-term heavy drinking often leads to severe nutritional deficiencies. An amnestic syndrome occurring under such conditions is also called Wernicke–Korsakov's syndrome (see Chapter 14). Organic amnestic syndrome may also result from traumatic injuries to the head, the formation of blood clots in cerebral arteries, and encephalitis caused by the herpes simplex virus (Kaplan & Sadock, 1985, p. 280).

Organic Hallucinosis

The main features of **organic hallucinosis** are the persistent recurrence of hallucinations in the absence of delirium and the presence of specific biophysical factors that contribute to the hallucinations. Hallucinogenic drugs such as LSD (lysergic acid diethylamide) and mescaline tend to produce visual hallucinations; chronic and excessive use of alcohol is often associated with auditory hallucinations. Physical trauma may also induce organic hallucinosis in various forms, depending on the sense organs affected. For instance, people who become blind because of cataracts may experience visual hallucinations, whereas individuals who become deaf because of the formation of spongy bone in the ear (otosclerosis) often have auditory hallucinations (Lipowski, 1980c, p. 1385).

The emotional responses of people experiencing organic hallucinosis depend to a great extent on the situation. If the surroundings are pleasant, as in the case of a group of friends sharing hallucinogenic drugs, the experience may be enjoyable. But an individual who experiences hallucinosis alone, say after a number of long-term bouts of excessive drinking, may become very frightened.

Organic Delusional Syndrome

The central feature of the **organic delusional syndrome** is the persistent occurrence of delusions that can be traced to specific biological or physical causes (American Psychiatric Association, 1987, pp. 109–110). Irrational beliefs of persecution, similar to those that occur in paranoid schizophrenia, are especially prominent (see Chapter 11).

The etiological factors in the organic delusional syndrome are diverse. Long-term and excessive use of such drugs as amphetamines and LSD can lead to persecutory delusions. These may persist even after the substances that instigated them are no longer present in the body. Excessive and habitual use of alcohol may also lead to delusions, especially those centering around irrational feelings of jealousy. And brain tumors and syphilitic infection of the brain may cause delusions. Studies of delusions in elderly people have found that sensory deficits such as deafness, poor general health, and social and economic difficulties can all be important etiological factors (Christenson & Blazer, 1984).

Organic Mood Syndrome

The main characteristics of **organic mood syndrome** are abnormal shifts in affect and behavior, similar to those that occur in manic and depressive episodes (Chapter 10). In an organic mood syndrome, however, the etiology can be traced to specific biophysical factors, such as infection, drugs, or various kinds of metabolic diseases. Viral infections as well as certain hallucinogenic drugs can lead to serious episodes of depression. Abnormal underactivity of the thyroid gland (hypothyroidism) can also cause depression, and overactivity (hyperthyroidism) can lead to maniclike behavior.

Organic Anxiety Syndrome

A new category — which does not appear in DSM-III — is **organic anxiety syndrome**. Its most prominent features are recurrent panic attacks and generalized anxiety. The specific criteria for this syndrome are the same as for panic disorders and generalized anxiety disorders (discussed in Chapter 5). However, the diagnosis of organic anxiety syndrome is made only when there is evidence that a specific organic factor is mainly responsible for the syndrome (American Psychiatric Association, 1987, pp. 113–114).

Organic Personality Syndrome

The central feature of **organic personality syndrome** is a distinct change in fundamental aspects of the individual's personality and behavior that can be traced to an abnormality in brain functioning or structure (American Psychiatric Association, 1987, pp. 115–116). The kinds of changes that most often occur include marked increases in emotional instability and severe lapses in social judgment. Fits of crying, outbursts of temper, and similar kinds of impulsive behavior may appear without provocation. Socially inappropriate behavior such as public displays of sexual impropriety is not unusual. All this may go on with little regard for the effects they have on other people or for their consequences to the individual. In other instances, an almost opposite personality pattern may emerge, with apathy and withdrawal from social situations dominating.

Among the most frequent causes of organic personality syndrome are brain tumors, especially those of the frontal lobe (see Figure 13.2); injuries to the head; and vascular disease that affects the circulation of blood in the brain. Other possible causes are neurological disorders, such as multiple sclerosis, and syphilitic infection of the brain.

Figure 13.2

Structures of the brain and spinal cord. (From *Dorland's Illustrated Medical Dictionary*, 1988, plate IX, B.)

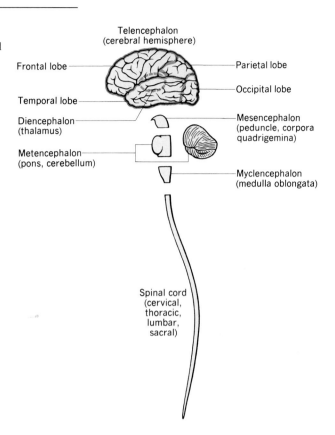

Organic Mental Disorders in the Later Years

Classification of Disorders

The organic mental disorders that typically appear during the later years of life most often involve the gradual deterioration of brain tissue. This process is sometimes referred to as abnormal aging of the brain. The central syndrome is dementia. The disorders are classified in DSM-III-R as dementias arising in the senium and presenium (American Psychiatric Association, 1987, p. 112). The word *senium*, Latin for "weakness of old age," refers to the period in life in which advanced years may bring physical or mental disabilities. *Presenium* literally means any age before the senium. However, it is generally used in psychopathology to mean the decade or so before the onset of the senium. In DSM-III-R, the senium is the period after age 65.

As classified in DSM-III-R, the most common form of dementia arising during the senium or presenium is primary degenerative dementia of the Alzheimer type. The other major form is multi-infarct dementia. DSM-III-R also includes two residual diagnostic categories: senile dementia NOS (not otherwise specified) and presenile dementia NOS. These categories are used when the clinical picture differs distinctly from that of Alzheimer's disease or multi-infarct dementia (American Psychiatric Association, 1987, p. 123). If the underlying organic pathology is known (for example, a brain tumor or a severe deficiency of vitamin B_{12}), that additional diagnosis is noted on Axis III, Physical Disorders or Conditions. (See Chapter 2 for a description of the multiaxial system in DSM-III-R.)

Primary Degenerative Dementia of the Alzheimer Type

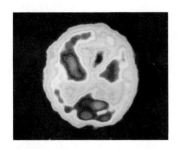

PET scan (positron emission tomography) of the brain of an individual suffering from Alzheimer's disease. Brain tissue shrinks and undergoes other degenerative changes. A short-lived radioactive tracer is injected into the bloodstream to show the reduced areas of brain tissue (at upper right).

DSM-III-R classifies **primary degenerative dementia of the Alzheimer type** (Alzheimer's disease) into two subtypes: senile onset (after age 65) and presenile (age 65 and below). The central diagnostic criteria include (a) definite signs of dementia, (b) an insidious onset, (c) a steady and progressive course of dementia, and (d) the exclusion of other possible causes of the syndrome—for example, chronic and excessive use of alcohol. The clinician excludes other causes by means of a thorough history of the individual, physical examinations, and laboratory tests (American Psychiatric Association, 1987, p. 121).

The German neurologist Alois Alzheimer (1864–1915) first described Alzheimer's disease in 1906. Postmortem examination of people diagnosed with the disease typically reveals atrophy and shrinkage of brain tissue, tangled nerve fibers, destruction of nerve cells, and rounded areas of degenerated tissue known as senile plaques. The presence of these pathologies can also be revealed through computerized axial tomography, commonly known as a CAT scan, or CT scan (Kolata, 1981b; Weinberger, 1984). The CAT scan pictures the brain on a transverse plane and shows abnormally widened sulci (grooves) on the surface of the brain and abnormal enlargement of ventricles (cavities) in the cerebrum. Positron emission tomography (PET) is another imaging technique that shows promise for detecting brain pathology. Recently, magnetic resonance imaging (MRI) has become available. This technique can image in all planes (Andreasen, 1988; Crook & Miller, 1985).

Prevalence and Course of Development

Estimates indicate that at least 5 percent of people over 65 suffer from Alzheimer's Disease. It accounts for more than one-fourth of the long-term residents of nursing homes and is the fourth leading cause of death among Americans over 65 ("Alzheimer's Disease," 1988; Heckler, 1985; Joynt & Shoulson, 1979; Katzman, 1976; Liston, 1979; Terry, 1976).

Since its onset is insidious, the disorder may not be noticed immediately. However, as the dementia increases, intellectual efficiency, judgment, and abstract thinking decrease progressively. Psychomotor activity gradually declines, and there may be a noticeable deterioration in personal habits and hygiene. Delusions resembling those of paranoid individuals sometimes occur (see Chapter 11). In the early stages of the disorder, the individual often shows signs of apathy and a lack of interest in other people and in social affairs. As deterioration continues, these signs become more marked. Eventually, the person may regress to the point were constant nursing is necessary. However, the severity of the symptoms varies from one individual to another. In many instances, the abnormal changes in behavior are simply extreme manifestations of patterns in evidence before the onset of the disorder

Etiological Factors

There is increasing evidence that the decline in cognitive functions associated with Alzheimer's disease is related to the degeneration of neurons in the brain that release acetylcholine. This biochemical substance, normally present in many parts of the body, aids in the transmission of impulses from one nerve fiber to another. Acetylcholine-releasing neurons in the brain are important for cognition, especially memory ("Alzheimer's Disease," 1988; Coyle, Price, & DeLong, 1983; Kolata, 1981a, 1982, 1983).

It is not clear why deterioration of brain tissue occurs more in some older individuals than in others. The fact that first-degree relatives are four times more likely than the general population to develop primary degenerative dementia suggests that genetic factors may play an important role (Heston & Mastri, 1977; Terry, 1976).

Recent research suggests that at least one form of Alzheimer's disease may be inherited — the type that occurs about the age of 50 (presenile dementia). The gene or genes believed to be involved are located on chromosome 21. There is some evidence that the abnormal coding of the gene or genes contributes to the formation of the plaques and tangled nerve fibers often found in the brain tissue of individuals suffering from Alzheimer's disease (Barnes, 1987b; Goldgaber, Lerman, McBride, Saffiotti, & Gajdusek, 1987).

Another important aspect of primary degenerative dementia, and one that is yet to be fully understood, is the lack of a consistent relationship between the severity of the symptoms and the degree of brain deterioration. Postmortem examinations have found that in some instances there was relatively little deterioration in people who had displayed many signs of primary degenerative dementia but severe deterioration in individuals who had shown fewer signs (Raskind & Storrie, 1980, p. 308). These findings suggest that the symptoms of primary degenerative dementia may also be influenced by psychological and social factors, such as previously learned motives, attitudes, and habits, as well as current environmental stresses (LaRue, Dessonville, & Jarvik, 1985, pp. 683–685).

Helping the Victim

In recent years, the victims of Alzheimer's disease and their families have been helped to come to terms with their problems through an organization called Alzheimer's Disease and Related Disorders Association (ADRDA). ADRDA has its national headquarters in Chicago and chapters in more than 30 states and the District of Columbia. A similar organization, Alzheimer's Disease Society, operates in some 322 localities in England and Scotland. ADRDA and its British counterpart promote research into the causes, diagnosis, and treatment of the disease (Khachaturian, 1985; Rickards, Zuckerman, & West, 1985).

People suffering from the progressive dementia of Alzheimer's disease can benefit from a sheltered environment and cues to help orient them.

Especially frustrating is the emotional and financial toll on those who must care for the victims of Alzheimer's disease (Freese, 1981; Heston & White, 1983; Zarit, Orr, & Zarit, 1985). Consider these remarks by the husband of a woman suffering from Alzheimer's disease: "My wife refused to believe I was her husband. Every day we went through the same routine: I would tell her we had been married for 30 years, that we had four children. She listened, but she still thought she lived in her hometown with her parents. Every night when I got into bed she'd say, 'Who are you?'" (Brody, 1983, p. 17). Faced with such problems, family members often become depressed to the point where they need to be helped. They may also experience guilt over their inadequacies in caring for the person or their impatience and anger (Goldman & Luchins, 1984).

Multi-infarct Dementia

The underlying organic pathology in **multi-infarct dementia** is the repeated occurrence of many small infarcts in the brain over an extended period of time. An **infarct** is an area of tissue that has been destroyed because an obstruction in a blood vessel has prevented the blood from reaching and nourishing that area.

In DSM-II, multi-infarct dementia was called psychosis with cerebral arteriosclerosis (American Psychiatric Association, 1968). This diagnosis referred to a condition of dementia caused by the abnormal thickening and hardening of the arterial walls in the brain. The term *multi-infarct dementia* is more appropriate, because the disorder is related more to the cumulative effect of repeated infarcts in the brain. Postmortem examinations of individuals diagnosed with dementia resulting from cerebral arteriosclerosis revealed multiple infarcts in the brain that had occurred at various ages (Joynt & Shoulson, 1979, p. 489).

The intellectual disability of multi-infarct dementia begins more abruptly than that of primary degenerative dementia of the Alzheimer type, and it tends to fluctuate rather than progress steadily, especially in the early stages. Some intellectual functions may remain relatively intact while others deteriorate rapidly, depending in part on which regions of the brain the infarcts have affected (Raskind & Storrie, 1980, pp. 307–308).

In addition to dementia, certain neurological problems accompany infarcts. They include weaknesses in the limbs, disturbances in speech caused by lack of muscular control, and an inability to walk except by taking small steps. People suffering from multi-infarct dementia may also reveal signs of delirium, delusions, or depression. However, those syndromes are not as central as the dementia itself.

Among the most significant predisposing factors in multi-infarct dementia is a sustained, abnormally high level of arterial blood pressure (hypertension). Thus, dementia may be prevented or at least mitigated through early diagnosis and treatment of hypertension and related vascular disorders, such as diseases of the blood vessels in the neck and defective valves in the heart (American Psychiatric Association, 1987, p. 122; Joynt & Shoulson, 1979, p. 489; Merskey, 1980, p. 283).

Interpreting Dementia in the Elderly

It is important to distinguish between symptoms of dementia in the elderly and the relatively mild slowing down of cognitive function that often appears as part of the normal process of aging (Rosen, Mohs, & Davis, 1984). It is also important to rule out other causes of dementia in the aged. For example, from 10 to 20 percent of elderly people who show signs of cognitive impairment are actually suffering from the effects of other physical

Golda Meir

George Bernard Shaw   Georgia O'Keeffe

John Dewey   George Burns   Katharine Hepburn

Martha Graham

Dementia (senility) is by no means an inevitable adjunct of old age. These notable persons were productive well into their seventies and beyond.

ailments. Among them are bacterial infections, diabetes, nutritional deficiencies, and reactions to long-term use of medications, such as the tranquilizer Valium (Johnson, 1981).

Signs of intellectual deterioration may also occur as the result of depression. Indeed, some experts have estimated that depression is one of the most common psychological disturbances occurring in the elderly (LaRue, Dessonville, & Jarvik, 1986; Roybal, 1988, p. 189). These changes in mood may so interfere with intellectual efficiency that they are mistaken for senility. The depression is often linked to threatening changes in the social environment, such as a move to a strange place, the loss of a loved one, or increased isolation from familiar social situations (Butler, 1975; Johnson, 1981; Merskey, 1980, pp. 283 – 284; Miller, 1980, p. 52; Tolliver, 1983). Proper treatment of this depression through social intervention and therapy can do much to prevent serious intellectual deterioration or reverse its progress (see Chapter 10).

The failure of diagnosticians to recognize the wide variety of disorders that can contribute to intellectual deterioration has often caused elderly people to be diagnosed as incurable and placed in nursing homes or mental hospitals, where they go untreated for ailments that could be remedied (Butler, 1975; Cohn, 1978; Select Committee on Aging, 1975a, 1975b). Gerontologist Robert N. Butler has testified that a significant percentage of the conditions of the later years that have been labeled senility are actually treatable and reversible (Select Committee on Aging, 1975a, p. 6).

Dementia is by no means an inevitable consequence of growing old. Indeed, one can easily think of outstanding individuals who continued to be productive well beyond their 70s — for example, artists Georgia O'Keeffe and Pablo Picasso; psychologist B. F. Skinner; author George Bernard Shaw (who was 94 when one of his plays was first produced); the late prime minister of Israel Golda Meir; educator, philosopher, and psychologist John Dewey; entertainer and actor George Burns; author, ambassador, and political adviser Clare Boothe Luce; actress Katharine Hepburn; and modern dance choreographer, performer, and director Martha Graham.

Social Implications

For many years, the wards of mental hospitals contained elderly people with dementia who were there mainly because they had no other place to go. Nevertheless, many such patients can, if properly diagnosed and treated, function satisfactorily outside mental institutions (Maddox, 1980).

A growing number of states have removed the aged from state mental hospitals and have placed them in nursing homes instead. In principle, this is a progressive measure, but it raises a crucial dilemma. The care in nursing homes is often inadequate. Many of the facilities are understaffed and underfunded hospitals. Even where medical treatment is satisfactory, the care provided the residents often does not include the social and emotional components that are just as necessary as medication and other attention to physical needs. Furthermore, nursing homes in the United States are to a great extent proprietary enterprises in which quality care is often sacrificed for financial profit (Gelfand, 1984, p. 213; Roybal, 1988, p. 192). Consequently, an increasing number of layperson groups, mental health professionals, and government committees have insisted that state and federal agencies not only raise the standards of nursing home care but also apply present standards more diligently (Kane & Kane, 1978; Maddox, 1980; Select Committee on Aging, 1975a, 1975b; Shadish & Bootzin, 1981, 1984; Shadish, Straw, McSweeney, Koller, & Bootzin, 1981; Townsend, 1978; Vladeck, 1980, pp. 122 – 126).

Nursing home residents can profit from a stimulating psychosocial milieu, which this barren dayroom does not provide.

It has been estimated that by 1990 the number of individuals 65 years of age and older will be almost 30 million, about 12.5 percent of the population (U.S. Bureau of the Census, 1979, 1981). How the elderly who become mentally disabled will fare depends not only on the severity of their disorder and the psychological and social resources they can marshal but also on social decisions that must be made at all levels of government. Can our society provide the necessary medical, psychological, and social care? The question cannot be separated from the larger problem of meeting the needs of all aged individuals, whether they become mentally disabled or not. Many people doubt whether our society can provide adequate services. However, at least 13 European countries with higher proportions of people 65 years of age and older have been able to provide for their aged. Among those countries are Norway (14 percent of the population), Austria (15 percent), and the German Democratic Republic (16 percent) (Palmore, 1980, pp. 225–226).

Other Biophysical Disabilities Associated with Organic Mental Disorders

Many kinds of biophysical pathology, occurring over a wide range of ages, can have negative effects on the brain and nervous system and thus lead to organic mental syndromes. The syndromes may be transitory, disappearing shortly after the physical disabilities are remedied, or even becoming permanent.

Traumatic Head Injuries, Vascular Strokes, and Aphasia

About 10 million head injuries occur each year in the United States; of these, more than 600,000 are sufficiently traumatic to produce brain damage. The most common cause is automobile accidents, although gunshot wounds, injuries suffered in professional boxing, and industrial accidents are also significant factors (Drew, 1986; Kaplan & Sadock, 1985, p. 276).

One of the earliest documented instances of cognitive and attitudinal changes resulting from traumatic injury to the brain is the case of Phineas Gage (Harlow, 1868). A railroad construction foreman, Gage was tamping dynamite into a hole with an iron rod. The dynamite exploded, driving the rod through Gage's head. Although the penetration destroyed a large part of his frontal lobes, Gage made what was apparently a full physical recovery. However, his behavior changed a great deal. He had formerly been a conscientious, reliable, and serious worker. After the accident, he became uninhibited, emotionally impulsive, unreliable, lacking in judgment, and indolent.

A great deal of research has been carried out to determine the relationships between the sites at which traumatic injuries to the brain occur and the kinds of psychological deficits that result from the injuries. The nature of the psychological deficits also depends to some extent on the size of the brain lesions — that is, on the amount of tissue destroyed (Goodglass & Kaplan, 1979).

Many of the psychological abnormalities caused by traumatic injuries to the brain involve deficits in the ability to communicate. These cognitive disabilities are known as **aphasia**, a special form of the dementia syndrome. The term is derived from the Greek word *phasis*, meaning "speech." *Aphasis* literally means "without speech." Aphasia may also involve the inability to express oneself through writing or signs and may include deficits in the comprehension of spoken or written language.

One way of classifying aphasia is to divide it into four major forms: motor, sensory, nominal, and syntactical (*Dorland's Illustrated Medical Dictionary*, 1988). In **motor aphasia**, the individual cannot speak or write, or has great difficulty doing so, but can understand written or spoken words. In **sensory aphasia**, the person cannot comprehend written or spoken words, although there is no loss in the ability to say the words. In **nominal aphasia**, the person cannot name objects correctly or recognize their names. **Syntactical aphasia** refers to the inability to arrange words in their proper sequence. In especially severe instances of aphasia, more than one of these forms — and sometimes all four of them — may be present. The extent of the aphasia depends on the area of the brain affected and the amount of tissue damage.

Victims of aphasia can recover their ability to communicate. In some instances, the recovery is spontaneous, especially where there is a great deal of emotional support for the effort. Therapy for aphasia usually focuses on traditional methods of language training, although in recent years a great many innovative techniques have been developed (Kertesz, 1979; Luria, 1970; Moss, 1972).

In 1943, Lev Zasetsky, a 23-year-old Russian soldier, had part of his head shot away during the battle of Smolensk. Zasetsky was first seen by the distinguished Russian psychologist A. R. Luria about three months after the injury. In his book *The Man with a Shattered World*, Luria (1972) describes the psychological damage done to Zasetsky and the soldier's own account of his 25-year struggle to regain at least some of his ability to read, speak, and write.

The deep wound that Zasetsky received was on the left side of his head in the parietal–occipital area (see Figure 13.2). Among the major consequences was a drastic deficit in Zasetsky's ability to use concepts and symbols — fundamental tools of thinking and reasoning. For example, when Luria first saw him, Zasetsky could not read and could write only his name. He was confused about the order of the seasons, and he could not add simple numbers or describe a simple scene or picture. His vision was so distorted that he could see only parts of objects. He could not recognize scenes from the past, such as those of his hometown; and he did not recognize the town when he returned to it. Most

The distinguished Russian psychologist Alexander Luria was a pioneer in research on aphasias resulting from head injuries and in developing methods of retraining the cognitive functions of victims.

troubling to him was his loss of memory for words. As Zasetsky explained it later: "My biggest problem was not being able to remember the right words when I wanted to talk. From the time I was wounded, as soon as I could recognize myself again, I'd repeat a word a doctor, nurse, or patient had used but a minute later I had already forgotten it. At that time, I couldn't think of a particular word when I wanted to express something; I just couldn't remember anything at will" (Luria, 1972, p. 107).

In spite of his extreme cognitive deficits, Zasetsky retained a high level of motivation, the ability to plan and carry out his intention to improve, a strong sensitivity to everyday experiences, and the ability to adjust emotionally to such events. These are qualities controlled to a significant extent by the frontal lobes of the brain, areas that were not injured (Damasio, 1979, pp. 272–274; Gardner, 1974, p. 416).

Working with Zasetsky for many months, Luria was able to help him start recovering some of his lost cognitive skills. Although Zasetsky was never able to read normally again (the pace remained torturously slow), he did begin to learn how to write once more. For some 25 years he worked on a personal journal, telling in dramatic detail how he gradually improved his vocabulary and his ability to express himself in writing.

Howard Gardner (1974) offers an explanation of the progress Zasetsky made in spite of the significant amount of brain tissue he lost. First of all, enough was left to enable some restoration of Zasetsky's ability to use language. Gardner also attributes Zasetsky's progress to previously developed psychological resources, such as high intelligence and motivation (p. 421).

Aphasia can also follow a single acute vascular stroke, in which brain tissue dies because of a sudden abnormal change in the circulatory system of the brain. A clot or other foreign material circulating in the blood may block an artery. (This blockage is called an embolism.) Or a blood vessel may be so abnormally dilated (an aneurysm) that it ruptures, so that brain tissue is destroyed because of extensive hemorrhaging.

A number of journal articles and books have been written by or about the victims of vascular stroke and their experiences with aphasia (Moss, 1972, pp. 186–198). Two accounts are about and by the well-known actress Patricia Neal (Farrell, 1969; Neal, 1988), whose stroke, resulting from a ruptured aneurysm in the brain, occurred while she was pregnant. Even after extensive surgery, her right arm and leg were paralyzed, and her vision and memory were severely impaired.

Actress Patricia Neal, who suffered aphasia after having an acute vascular stroke. Through courageous efforts she overcame the disability and resumed her career with a highly acclaimed performance in *The Subject Was Roses*.

Nonetheless, Neal had a normal baby and eventually recovered from her physical disabilities and aphasia. The central factors in her recovery were formal language therapy, support from her family and friends, and her own determination. The most difficult problems she faced were in her acting career. What had been routine in the past, learning ordinary lines, now became difficult. In making her first movie after the stroke—*The Subject Was Roses* (for which she received praise from the critics)—she required 26 takes of one simple scene, because "her traitor brain would offer old formula phrases, relics of her illness. . . . Or else a desperate, gagging silence" (Farrell, 1969, p. 43).

Brain Tumors

The brain is one of the more common areas where tumors develop. Technically, brain tumors are known as **intracranial neoplasms**—new growths (neoplasms) within the brain (intracranial). About 50 percent of such neoplasms are benign (noncancerous) and thus tend to remain more localized than cancerous growths (Solomon, 1985b).

The particular nature of the psychological impairments (syndromes) associated with brain tumors depends on complex, interacting factors. The factors include the location of the tumor, the type of tumor cells involved (for example, benign or cancerous), the extent to which the tumor infiltrates brain tissue, the rapidity with which it develops, and the stricken individual's perception of and response to the predicament.

The psychological disabilities caused by tumors include abnormalities of perception, cognition, and mood as well as general deficits in intellectual functioning, such as impaired reasoning, judgment, and problem solving. Psychological tests can be especially useful in detecting these kinds of intellectual losses, for the deficits may be so subtle in the early stages of the tumor that they go unnoticed except by those who know the individual extremely well. (See Chapter 2 for the role of tests in the clinical assessment of intellectual abilities.)

However, more definitive conclusions depend on thorough physical examinations and laboratory tests. The electroencephalograph, which measures the electrical output of the brain, can be useful in diagnosing a wide variety of tumors. Another method involves withdrawing cerebrospinal fluid intermittently through punctures in the lumbar region of the spin (lower back area). The fluid is replaced by air, oxygen, or helium; and a radiograph (film record from x-rays) is then obtained. It shows the various fluid-containing structures of the brain and can thus indicate the presence of tumors. However, the recently developed imaging techniques have proved far more accurate and safe in detecting tumors (Solomon, 1985a, p. 101).

The treatment of brain tumors depends to a great extent on the type of cell involved and the particular site of the tumor. Surgery is appropriate when the tumor is in the meninges, the membranes that envelop the brain. This type of tumor is called a meningioma. (*Oma* is the suffix used in neurological terminology to mean "tumor.") Meningiomas, which usually involve blood vessels, are benign and slow-growing. Surgery will often reduce the symptoms of the tumor and even eradicate it. When tumors are deeper in the brain, surgery becomes more problematic and may serve only as a palliative. Surgery becomes even more questionable when there is more than one kind of lesion, usually from *metastasis* of the tumor—the spread of cancerous tissue. Surgery may need to be so extensive that the patient's physical and psychological disabilities could become even greater. When surgery is not advisable, radiotherapy and chemotherapy are alternatives (Solomon, 1985b, pp. 105–110).

The American neurologist George Huntington first described in 1872 the symptoms of what is now called Huntington's disease (or Huntington's chorea), a fatal neurological disorder which is transmitted by a single dominant gene.

Huntington's Disease

In 1872, the American physician George Huntington (1850–1916) first described **Huntington's disease**, or **Huntington's chorea**. "Chorea" is used because of the choreiform bodily movements that typically occur: irregular spasms of the limbs and facial muscles, grimaces, bizarre dancing movements, jerky gait, impairment of speech, and a persistent smacking of the lips. As the disease progresses, swallowing becomes very difficult. Walking may eventually become impossible, so that the individual must be confined to a wheelchair or bed. Most prominent among the psychological impairments is the gradual and progressive development of dementia. Early signs include failing memory, poor attention, irritability, and apathy. Mental deterioration increases steadily, until the loss of cognitive abilities is totally disabling.

Huntington's disease occurs in adults between the ages of 30 and 50. It is a hereditary disease, thought to be transmitted by a dominant gene. There is a 50 percent chance that the offspring of an individual with the disorder will also develop it. Although certain tranquilizers and antipsychotic drugs, such as haloperidol, can help reduce the severity of the mental symptoms and choreiform movements for a time, Huntington's disease is

Woody Guthrie, famous American songwriter and balladeer, was a victim of Huntington's disease, a fatal neurological disorder. His former wife Marjorie founded the Committee to Combat Huntington's Disease. She is shown here describing the "ripple effect" of the disease.

inevitably fatal. Death occurs from 10 to 20 years after the onset (Comings, 1981; Kolb & Brodie, 1982, p. 339–341; Solomon, 1985b; Rainer, 1985, p. 40).

Huntington's disease involves a slow and progressive degeneration of brain cells, especially in the cerebral cortex. This thin layer of gray matter on the surface of the cerebral hemispheres (see Figure 13.2) is important for the functioning of the higher mental processes, such as reasoning and judgment. It also helps control general bodily movements, perception, and visceral reactions. (*Visceral* refers to the large interior organs in the cavities of the body, especially the abdomen.)

Huntington's disease is a relatively rare neurological disorder, estimated to occur in the Western hemisphere in about 6 people per 100,000 (Kaplan & Sadock, 1985, p. 306; Mulder, 1980, p. 1418). It received a good deal of publicity as the disease that afflicted the famous American songwriter and balladeer Woody Guthrie, who died of it in 1967 at the age of 55. His former wife, Marjorie, took care of him during much of his illness and helped found the Committee to Combat Huntington's Disease (Yurchenko, 1970). One function of the committee is to offer genetic counseling to people at risk of developing the disease and to help them decide whether they should have children. (The nature of genetic counseling in relation to inherited disorders is discussed in Chapter 17).

Syphilitic Infection of the Brain

Organic mental disorders can result from various kinds of infectious diseases involving the central nervous system. Among the most widely known and potentially most devastating of these diseases is **syphilis**.

Syphilis is caused by the spirochete *Treponema pallidum*, an unusually large, spiral-shaped bacterium. This organism's invasion of the brain initiates a progressive degeneration of nerve cells, especially in the frontal lobes. As the infection spreads, it involves nerve cells in other parts of the brain. The neurological damage typically produces psychotic thought and behavior. (See Box 3.1.)

Historical Background

Some medical historians theorize that Christopher Columbus and his crew brought syphilis to Europe when they returned from Haiti in 1493 (Zilboorg & Henry, 1941; Osler, 1908/1929). In any event syphilis spread rapidly throughout Europe shortly after 1493 and has continued to be a pandemic disease (Garrison, 1924, pp. 181–184). Syphilis was simply called the pox, and various countries gave it the name of other places to emphasize that the disease had originated elsewhere. For example, the Italians, Germans, and English all called it the French pox (Rosebury, 1971, p. 30). The present name of the disease is derived from a poem that was very popular during the Renaissance in southern Europe. Written by the Italian physician Fracastorius (1483–1533), the poem tells of a shepherd named Syphilus, who lived in the New World. Angered because of a drought that killed his cattle, Syphilus blasphemed the Sun God, who punished him by infecting the land, air, and streams. Syphilus was the first victim of the disease (Osler, 1908/1929, p. 293).

Mode and Stages of Infection

Sir William Osler, the celebrated Canadian-born physician, called syphilis the "great imitator" because its symptoms were often mistaken for those of other diseases. He traced the history of the disease and found that it was named after the shepherd Syphilus in a poem by a 16th-century Italian physician, Fracastorius.

Syphilis is most often contracted through direct contact with the moist body surfaces of infected people, especially the mucous membranes of sexual organs. It is not transmitted by sneezing or coughing or by objects that were handled by infected people. Indeed, *Treponema pallidum* is easily killed by soap, drying, and heat (Snyder, 1980, pp. 166–167).

The first physical sign of syphilitic infection is a hard ulcer (a chancre) that appears three to five weeks after infection at the point where the spirochetes initially invaded the body. The chancre disappears within a month or so, even if the individual does not receive any treatment. Thus, an infected person can have the disease without realizing it. This stage is called primary syphilis.

The secondary stage of syphilis occurs about six weeks after the chancre appears. The main physical sign is a rash that covers the body, often accompanied by glandular swelling, fever, headache, and loss of appetite—symptoms that occur in many other infectious diseases. The secondary stage can also subside spontaneously. Thus, people who have not sought treatment may think they have recovered, or they may not even realize they have contracted syphilis.

The final and potentially fatal manifestation is the tertiary stage, which may appear many years after the initial infection. During this stage, *Treponema pallidum* can cause inflammation and lesions in almost any organ of the body, especially the blood vessels and the central nervous system.

Syphilitic infection of the brain is usually slow to develop. The interval between the initial infection and the appearance of symptoms indicating that spirochetes have invaded the brain can vary from 5 to 30 or more years. When *Treponema pallidum* infiltrates the brain, the membranes (meninges) that surround the brain become inflamed. Progressive deterioration of nerve cells follows, especially in the frontal region of the brain. As the infiltration of spirochetes increases, other areas of the brain become involved in the destructive process. This general infection and destruction of brain tissue causes psychotic behavior and eventually death.

Organic Mental Syndromes

One of the most prominent syndromes associated with syphilitic infection of the brain is dementia. Marked changes in personality may also appear, and delusions may develop, especially as the destruction of brain tissue continues.

As the infection spreads, increasing signs of physical breakdown appear. Convulsions or strokes may occur, and there is often a progressive weakening and loss of control of voluntary muscles. This physical deterioration is accompanied by an increasing malfunctioning of cognitive and emotional behavior. If untreated, the disease usually runs its course in about three years, with the fatal ending being one of extreme intellectual and physical deterioration (Solomon, 1985b, p. 127).

Treatment

The usual method of treating syphilis is to administer large doses of penicillin. However, if the infection has already made extensive inroads into brain tissue, there is usually a permanent loss of intellectual and emotional functioning even though the infection is halted. The loss can be extensive enough to require continuous hospitalization. However, if penicillin treatment is initiated when symptoms of brain infection just begin to emerge, about 60 percent of patients usually improve sufficiently to return to their regular jobs. If therapy begins before the behavioral signs of infection appear, 85 percent of the victims remain free of the symptoms of brain disorder. If penicillin treatment is initiated at the chancre stage, the probability of halting further development is extremely good (Kolb & Brodie, 1982, p. 163).

Social Implications

Since penicillin has been so effective in treating syphilis during the last few decades, especially in its early states, many mental health professionals began to believe that the mental disorders associated with syphilitic infection of the central nervous system would soon become a medical curiosity. However, over the last 10 years, syphilis has been on the rise (Brandt, 1988; Centers for Disease Control, 1987) and many of its victims are not seeking professional treatment. It is possible that the lack of treatment will result in an increase in mental disorders.

A large number of individuals who acquire sexually transmitted diseases, perhaps as many as 50 percent, are young people under 25 years of age. The prevailing opinion of public health professionals is that the increase is due in part to greater sexual permissiveness and the increased use of birth control pills instead of barrier contraceptive devices such as condoms, which can prevent sexually transmitted disease. (See Chapter 9 for comments on the most dangerous disease that can be transmitted sexually — AIDS).

Hyperthyroidism

The interaction of physical pathology and previously established patterns of personality and behavior is especially clear in **hyperthyroidism** — the abnormal overactivity of the thyroid gland. Hyperthyroidism (also called Graves disease) is characterized by emotional excitement, heightened motor activity, restlessness, and supersensitivity to external stimuli — behavior that is often described simply as nervousness. Studies have shown that many people who suffer from hyperthyroidism tend to have long-standing feelings of insecurity and dependence (Kolb & Brodie, 1982, pp. 314–315).

Helping individuals with hyperthyroidism, especially in its more severe states, should be a joint task of the medical internist and the psychotherapist. The medical goal is to restore the disturbed thyroid metabolism to normal levels. The goal of the psychotherapist is to help the patient overcome the personality problems that develop from the abnormal physical condition.

Vitamin Deficiencies

Deficiencies in vitamins can lead to serious malfunctioning of the central nervous system and abnormal patterns of thought and behavior. These disorders are especially apt to occur in people who have been seriously deprived of the vitamin B complex, especially thiamine (vitamin B_1) and niacin (nicotinic acid).

In its severest manifestations, chronic deficiency in the vitamin B complex is most apt to exist in underdeveloped countries or other regions where poverty or famine prevail. However, such deprivation occurs even when adequate nutrition is available, as in the case of the chronic alcoholic who prefers to drink rather than eat. (See Chapter 14 for a discussion of the relationship between alcoholism and vitamin deficiencies.)

Epilepsy

The term **epilepsy** is derived from the Greek word *epilepsia* ("to seize or fall upon") and refers to a chronic abnormal condition in the brain whose main symptom is episodic seizures. The recurrent seizures begin with a spontaneous, transient, and excessive discharge of neurons in the cerebral cortex, indicating that the central nervous system has failed to maintain the equilibrium of certain nerve cells in the brain (Small, 1980, p. 80). This activity of neurons results in abnormal patterns of behavior.

The etiology of epilepsy varies considerably. It can be genetic, or seizures may arise from various intracranial disorders, such as tumors, damaged tissue resulting from head injuries, diseases of the blood vessels, or maldevelopment of intracranial structures during the prenatal period. In addition, seizures can result from extracranial disabilities, including diseases of metabolism and glandular functions, systemic infections, ingestion of toxins (for example, lead or arsenic), and excessive use of drugs (Small, 1980, pp. 95–101; Snyder, 1980, pp. 173–176).

In the majority of cases of epilepsy, the origins are still unknown, or at best uncertain. About 1 percent of the world's population suffers from epileptic seizures whose etiology remains in doubt (Snyder, 1980, pp. 173–174). In biomedical circles, it is customary to apply the label *idiopathic* to such seizures. The term is derived from the Greek and means "peculiar to the individual," or "arising from obscure causes." Some biomedical workers believe that all instances of idiopathic epilepsy represent an inherited predisposition to develop seizures. The evidence for this belief comes mainly from family studies, which have found that the occurrence of epileptic seizures among first-degree relatives is relatively high (Hinsie & Campbell, 1977, p. 271). Although many instances of idiopathic epilepsy may well stem from genetic factors, the fact that the cause of a seizure in a particular individual is unknown does not mean in itself that the disorder was inherited. Also, the specific genetic factors involved in epilepsy are yet to be determined.

Historical Background

The type of seizure in which an individual periodically loses consciousness, falls to the ground, foams at the mouth, and thrashes about — called a **grand mal seizure** — has been known for many centuries. In ancient Greece, during the time of Hippocrates, it was called the sacred disease because of the belief that the gods inflicted it. The specific nature of the seizure was thought to vary according to the particular god involved. Hippocrates himself deplored such beliefs: "It is not, in my opinion, any more divine or more sacred than other diseases, but has a natural cause, and its supposed divine origin is due to men's inexperience, and to their wonder at its peculiar character." Hippocrates believed that people named epilepsy the sacred disease because they knew of no treatment that would help. Therefore they "concealed and sheltered themselves behind superstition; and called this illness sacred, in order that their utter ignorance might not be manifest" (quoted in Jones, 1923, pp. 139–141).

During the Roman era, the Middle Ages, and the early modern period, epilepsy was often called "the falling sickness," a term certainly more appropriate for a grand mal seizure than "sacred disease." In the following excerpt from *Julius Caesar*, Act I, Scene 2, Shakespeare has some of the conspirators discuss Caesar's affliction with the falling sickness.

> **Cassius:** What, did Caesar swound?
>
> **Casca:** He fell down in the market-place and foamed at mouth and was speechless
>
> **Marcus Brutus:** 'Tis very like: he hath the falling-sickness. . . . What said he when he came unto himself?
>
> **Casca:** . . . When he came to himself again, he said, if he had done or said anything amiss, he desired their worships to think it was his infirmity.

Patterns of Epileptic Seizures

In his famous novel *The Idiot*, Fyodor Dostoevsky described the *aura* that precedes an epileptic convulsion, basing his account on his own experience.

The convulsions of a grand mal seizure begin with tonic movements of the body, which involve the tensing of muscles and a momentary halt in breathing. Then, as the clonic phase appears, air is forced from the lungs, resulting in what has been called the epileptic cry. The clonic phase consists of active, rhythmic movements of the arms, legs, and other parts of the body. Some individuals will repeat the tonic–clonic sequence before subsiding. When the seizure ends, the individual regains consciousness and typically experiences a period of confusion, drowsiness, and headache. Some people will fall asleep and continue to experience confusion and head pain when they awake, a state that may last several days.

Perhaps the most striking feature of grand mal seizures is the aura that precedes the tonic phase. About 50 percent of individuals who suffer such seizures report experiencing the aura (Snyder, 1980, p. 174). For some, it consists of a vague feeling of discomfort; for others, it is tingling sensations in the extremities. Still others report the aura as an altered state of consciousness, almost mystical in nature. One of the most dramatic portrayals of this aspect of the aura is found in Fyodor Dostoevsky's masterpiece *The Idiot*. Myshkin, the central character of the novel, recalls the sensations he had just prior to an epileptic seizure. Dostoevsky based the account on his own experiences with epileptic seizures.

> He remembered among other things that he always had one minute just before the epileptic fit (if it came on while he was awake), when suddenly in the midst of sadness, spiritual darkness and oppression, there seemed at moments a flash of light in his brain, and with extraordinary impetus all his vital forces suddenly began working at their highest tension. The sense of life, the consciousness of self, were multiplied ten times at these moments which passed like a flash of lightning. . . . It was not as though he saw abnormal and unreal visions of some sort at that moment, as from hashish, opium, or wine, destroying the reason and distorting the soul. He was quite capable of judging of that when the attack was over. These moments were only an extraordinary quickening of self-consciousness — if the condition was to be expressed in one word. (Dostoevsky, 1913, pp. 224–225).

Grand mal seizures represent only one pattern of epilepsy. Some seizures may involve only a partial state of unconsciousness, with bodily movements at a minimum; others may involve peculiar sensations and perceptions but no loss of consciousness, or only a momentary lapse. The nature of the seizure depends in large measure on the particular areas of the cortex in which the abnormal discharge of neurons takes place and the speed with which this excitation spreads (Small, 1980, p. 90; Snyder, 1980, p. 172).

For purposes of diagnosis and treatment, it is important to know where in the brain the epileptic seizures originate. The most widely used system for describing these locations is the *International Classification of Epileptic Seizures*. Seizures are divided into two main categories, according to the site of origin. **Focal seizures** originate within fairly localized areas of the cerebral cortex. In adults, the temporal lobes are the most common sites. These seizures account for 40 to 60 percent of all adult epilepsy. **Generalized seizures**, the other main category, are more widespread, originating in more extensive areas of the brain. They occur more often in children (Bear, Freeman, & Greenberg, 1986; Westmoreland, 1980).

The *International Classification* includes a third and much less frequent type, **unilateral seizures** (also called **hemoconvulsive seizures**). This type of seizure almost always occurs on only one side of the body. A fourth category is reserved for seizures that cannot be classified because of inadequate information.

An important diagnostic aid in determining the type of epileptic seizures is the electroencephalogram. Electrodes are attached to the scalp and transmit to the recording instrument abnormal changes in brain waves, which indicate neuron activity. This procedure shows whether the seizures are focal, generalized, or unilateral, and it points out the particular sites of the brain that are involved.

Treatment and Psychosocial Implications

The treatment of epilepsy should focus on medication designed to control the seizures and on the discovery of their causes. When specified damage in the brain is the main underlying cause, surgery may be necessary. However, it should be performed only after the alternatives are carefully considered. Westmoreland (1980, p. 148) proposes the following criteria as a guide for deciding when surgery is appropriate.

1. Medication has failed to control the seizures.

2. The seizures are so severe that they interfere with the person's lifestyle.

3. The focus of surgical intervention is a readily accessible site in the cerebral cortex.

4. The electroencephalogram shows only a single site of origin for the seizures, and other areas of the brain are not involved in any pathological process.

5. Removal of pathological material from the brain is not likely to result in any further neurological deficit.

6. The patient's intellectual ability and emotional status are such that a satisfactory psychosocial adjustment following the operation seems likely.

Even when the causes of epileptic seizures are unknown or highly uncertain, proper medication can still be effective. A wide array of drugs are now available for controlling various types of seizures.

In addition to drugs, the treatment of epileptic seizures should include appropriate forms of psychological and social intervention. People with epilepsy do not necessarily have disabling psychological and social problems. However, the seizures can be very disturbing, even for individuals who in other respects are quite normal. These problems arise not only from the fear and discomfort associated with the physical disorder but also from the negative attitudes of other people, which can cause anxiety and depression. Furthermore, victims of epileptic seizures may find themselves at a disadvantage in their work and in their social relationships, especially if they are discriminated against because of their physical condition. As a result, they often develop feelings of inadequacy that further hamper their occupational and social lives.

Psychotherapy can help people with epilepsy understand their personal and social problems and work through them. Indeed, for some individuals, psychotherapy may be necessary to reduce tension and anxiety before drug treatment can become optimally effective (Small 1980, pp. 105–111). However, social action is also important, both to reduce discrimination (through legislation, if necessary) and to help educate the general public about the nature of epilepsy.

Under federal and state programs of vocational rehabilitation, people with epilepsy are eligible for services on the same basis as individuals with other kinds of physical handicaps. Counselors in state vocational rehabilitation centers help the individual get ready for a job and remain in it. Such services include medical diagnosis and treatment, individual counseling, and job training where necessary (U.S. Department of Health, Education, and Welfare, 1972a, p. 25).

More than 2 million people in the United States have some form of epilepsy, and most of them can lead productive and satisfying lives. Through research, technical and popular publications, and other educational and scientific activities, the U.S. Public Health Service has done a great deal to add to the knowledge about epilepsy, to inform the general public about such knowledge, and to encourage volunteer organizations in similar efforts. One of the best known of these organizations is Epilepsy Foundation of America, which supplies people with the names of clinics and doctors especially interested in the treatment of epilepsy.

Summary

1. The underlying causes of organic mental disorders are various biological and physical abnormalities that interfere with the normal functioning of the brain and central nervous system. These abnormalities include the deterioration of brain tissue, blood clots in the brain, infections, traumatic injuries, and damage caused by long-term use of psychoactive substances.

2. Biophysical pathology is a necessary prerequisite for organic mental disorders. However, such factors as intelligence, education, emotional state, interpersonal skills, and cultural background may also influence their development.

3. DSM-III-R distinguishes between organic mental syndrome and organic mental disorder. Organic mental syndrome is a specific pattern of psychological symptoms, such as delirium and dementia. It does not include the underlying organic pathology. Organic mental disorder is a more comprehensive concept, including both the syndrome and its etiology.

4. Diagnosing organic mental disorders involves obtaining a history of the individual's complaints and observing other relevant behavior, gathering information about the person's family background, and using psychological, neurological, and laboratory tests.

5. The central feature of delirium is a significant decrease in the clarity with which individuals perceive and understand their environment. Clinicians sometimes describe this condition as a clouded state of consciousness. Among the most common causes of delirium are metabolic disorders, traumatic injuries to the brain, and the withdrawal or reduction of an addictive substance.

6. The main characteristic of dementia is a global decline in intellectual functioning, so severe that it interferes with the person's daily life. Changes in personality may also occur. For example, a once active person may become apathetic. Dementia can occur at almost any age, but it usually is associated with a progressive deterioration of brain tissue during the later years of life.

7. The chief characteristic of the organic amnestic syndrome is a significant loss of short-term and long-term memory. This makes it difficult for the individual to learn new tasks or recall what was learned in the past. The most common cause of this syndrome is the chronic and excessive use of alcohol, coupled with a deficiency in vitamin B_1 (thiamine). Under these two conditions, the amnestic syndrome is also called Wernicke-Korsakov's syndrome. The syndrome may also be caused by traumatic injuries to the head, blood clots in the cerebral arteries, or encephalitis.

8. Organic hallucinosis is marked by persistent recurrence of hallucinations in the absence of delirium and by evidence of specific biophysical factors that contribute to the hallucinations. Among these factors are the ingestion of LSD and the chronic, excessive use of alcohol.

9. The central characteristic of the organic delusional syndrome is the persistent occurrence of delusions that can be traced to specific biological or physical causes, including the excessive and habitual use of alcohol and the long-term abuse of such drugs as LSD and amphetamines.

10. The main feature of organic mood syndrome is an abnormal shift in mood similar to that which occurs in manic and depressive episodes. In this instance, however, the etiology can be traced to such biophysical factors as drugs, diseases of metabolism, and infections.

11. The organic anxiety syndrome is a new diagnostic category in the DSM. Its most striking features are recurrent panic attacks and generalized anxiety. The diagnosis is made only when there is evidence that specific organic factors are mainly responsible for the symptoms.

12. The central feature of the organic personality syndrome is a distinct change in the individual's personality and behavior that arises from an abnormality in brain functioning or structure. Among the most common causes of this syndrome are brain tumors, injuries to the head, and vascular diseases that interfere with the normal circulation of blood in the brain.

13. The organic mental disorders that typically occur during the later years of life involve the gradual deterioration of brain tissue. The central syndrome is dementia. Thus, the condition is called primary degenerative dementia.

14. The most common form of primary degenerative dementia is the Alzheimer type, named after the German neurologist Alois Alzheimer. Modern advances in the use of computerized axial tomography, positron emission tomography, and magnetic resonance imaging have shown plaques and tangled nerve fibers in the brain tissue of individuals suffering from this disorder.

15. The precise cause of Alzheimer's disease is unknown. However, recent research suggests that the abnormal coding of a gene or genes on chromosome 21 may be responsible for at least one form, that which occurs at about age 50.

16. Although there is as yet no cure for Alzheimer's disease, its victims and their families have been helped through various mutual support organizations that offer emotional and social guidance.

17. Multi-infarct dementia is another major form of organic mental disorder whose onset typically occurs during the later years. The underlying organic pathology is the repeated occurrence of many infarcts in the brain over an extended period of time. An infarct is an area of tissue destroyed because an obstruction in a blood vessel has prevented the blood from reaching and nourishing that area.

18. The onset of intellectual disability in multi-infarct dementia is usually more abrupt than it is in primary degenerative dementia.

19. It is important to distinguish between symptoms of dementia and the relatively mild slowing down of cognitive functions that may accompany the normal process of aging. It is also important to consider causes of intellectual deterioration other than those involved in primary degenerative dementia and multi-infarct dementia. For example, from 10 to 20 percent of elderly people who show signs of cognitive impairment are suffering from the effects of other physical ailments. In addition, depression may interfere with intellectual ability. If these kinds of problems are recognized and treated early enough, cognitive functions can be improved.

20. Dementia is not an inevitable outcome of old age. For example, there are individuals who have continued to make outstanding contributions in the arts, literature, education, and politics well beyond their 70s.

21. It has been estimated that by 1990 the number of individuals in the United States who are 65 years of age or older will be almost 30 million, about 12.5 percent of the population. How those who become mentally disabled will fare depends not only on the severity of the disability and the psychological and social resources they can marshal but also on decisions made at all levels of government.

22. Many other biophysical disabilities may result in organic mental disorders. Among them are traumatic head injuries and brain tumors; vascular strokes, in which brain tissue is damaged because of insufficient circulation of the blood; Huntington's chorea, an inherited neurological disease marked by progressive deterioration of brain tissue and of physical mobility; syphilitic infection of the brain, resulting in loss of intellectual functions and various delusions; metabolic and nutritional deficiencies that adversely affect the normal functioning of the brain and nervous system; and epileptic seizures, which may be associated with abnormal patterns of behavior.

23. A variety of organic mental syndromes may be associated with these conditions. Among them are dementia, delusions, and amnesia, as in the aphasia that may result from head injuries and vascular stroke.

24. The diagnosis and treatment of organic mental disorders requires the judicious combination of a variety of approaches: medical and psychological, educational, and social.

14

Psychoactive Substance Use Disorders: Alcohol

When the cock is drunk, he forgets
about the hawk.

ASHANTI PROVERB

The vine bears three kinds of grapes:
the first of pleasure, the next of
intoxication, and the third of disgust.

ANACHARSIS
ca. 60 B.C.

This chapter and the next deal with two broad and closely related areas of drug disorders: (1) psychoactive substance-induced organic mental disorders and (2) psychoactive substance abuse and dependence. The term *psychoactive* refers to drugs that have a significant effect on mental processes and behavior. We begin the chapter with a general description of drug disorders as classified in DSM-III-R. We then discuss in detail various disorders associated with the use of alcohol. In the following chapter, we consider other psychoactive substance use disorders.

DSM-III-R Classification of Drug Disorders

Substance-Induced Organic Mental Disorders

The disorders that DSM-III-R classifies as **psychoactive substance – induced organic mental disorders** are maladaptive patterns of behavior and experience caused by the direct action of drugs on the central nervous system. Among the psychoactive substances are alcohol and barbiturates, which depress the normal functioning of the brain and nervous system; cocaine and amphetamines, which stimulate the central nervous system; opiates such as morphine and heroin, whose main effect is to narcotize the senses (that is sedate and relieve pain); hallucinogenic drugs — for example, mescaline and LSD (lysergic acid diethylamide); and certain products of the cannabis plant, such as marijuana and hashish, whose excessive and habitual use may produce intoxication and delusions. Although some of these drugs are helpful under responsible medical direction, their unsupervised or recreational use, especially when excessive, can result in serious physical and psychological disturbances.

DSM-III-R classifies substance-induced organic mental disorders according to the kinds of drugs whose use can result in organic mental syndromes. These syndromes are abnormal patterns of symptoms directly associated with malfunctioning of the brain and nervous system, such as delirium, dementia, and hallucinosis. (See Chapter 13 for a detailed discussion of these syndromes.)

Substance Abuse and Dependence

As defined in DSM-III-R **psychoactive substance abuse** involves at least one of the following two maladaptive patterns of behavior: (a) continuous use of psychoactive drugs even though it causes or exaggerates problems; and (b) recurrent use of psychoactive drugs in situations where such use poses a definite hazard — for example, driving a car or working with power equipment.

Psychoactive substance dependence is a more severe drug disorder. DSM-III-R lists the following criteria, at least three of which should be present to warrant the diagnosis.

1. Spending a great deal of time looking forward to and arranging to get the substance.

2. Using the substance in larger amounts or over a longer period of time than originally planned.

3. Persistently trying to control the substance use but not succeeding.

4. Finding that tolerance of the substance increases.

5. Experiencing withdrawal symptoms.

6. Taking the substance often to reduce or avoid withdrawal symptoms.

7. Frequently becoming intoxicated when expected to fulfill social or occupational obligations.

8. Giving up important activities because they conflict with substance use.

9. Continuing to use the substance despite persistent problems.

These diagnostic criteria include psychosocial symptoms and the physiological signs of dependence — tolerance and withdrawal. However, physiological symptoms (also known as addiction) are not required for a diagnosis of substance dependence, since any three of the nine criteria suffice. DSM-III-R has broadened the diagnosis since DSM-III, which stipulated that withdrawal or tolerance must be present (American Psychiatric Association, 1980a, p. 165).

Absorption of Alcohol

Alcohol is absorbed into the bloodstream from the stomach and small intestine. Combining alcohol intake with food helps reduce the effect. Since food slows the digestive process that causes the contents of the stomach to move into the intestine, the alcohol remains longer in the stomach, becomes more absorbed with the food, and enters the bloodstream more gradually. Berton Roueché (1971) quotes this interesting anecdote about how the effects of alcohol can be retarded if drinking is accompanied by food.

> J. M. Nielsen, Clinical Professor of Neurology at the University of California at Los Angeles, describes a drinking bout he witnessed in a neighboring bar between two alcoholics[:] "The wager stated that he who first became unable to stand would pay the bill," he reports. "One of the contestants ordered the bartender to put a raw egg into each drink; the man who took the eggs won and was able to walk home, while the other became helpless." (p. 51)

How rapidly alcohol is absorbed also depends on the weight of the individual. The heavier the person, the more blood and the lower the concentration of alcohol. However, women generally develop a higher blood concentration of alcohol than men of the same weight when each has had the same amount to drink. That is because women have a higher proportion of fatty tissue and therefore less blood for each unit of weight.

Alcohol is very quickly metabolized and converted into energy, mainly in the liver. Since the rate is constant, if one drinks alcohol faster than it can be metabolized, the blood level rises rapidly and intoxication follows.

Adverse Physiological Effects of Alcohol

About 15 percent of all heavy drinkers develop cirrhosis of the liver, a degenerative disease in which fibrous tissue is formed. Most instances of primary liver cancer in the United States originate in livers that have become cirrhotic because of heavy use of alcohol (Cohen, 1981, pp. 240–244; Reif, 1981).

Alcohol can also have other adverse effects on the body. It can, for example, irritate the stomach lining and cause dehydration and hangover headaches, especially after heavy drinking.

Contrary to much popular opinion, alcohol is a physiological depressant. It is thought to be a stimulant because under its influence people often feel less inhibited. Although the precise physiological mechanism is not fully understood, researchers generally believe that alcohol depresses the reticular activating system in the brain stem (see Figure 12.1). This, in turn, suppresses the cerebral cortex, in which the reasoning and judgment functions of the brain are located. The decreased cognitive control presumably makes the individual feel less inhibited (Snyder, 1980, pp. 134–135).

The popular belief that alcohol enhances one's sexual abilities is also false. Alcohol may indeed motivate individuals to seek sexual activity more readily than under ordinary circumstances. However, it is apt to hinder their sexual behavior, especially when it is used excessively. As Shakespeare observed, "It provokes the desire but it takes away the performance" (*Macbeth*, Act II, Scene 3).

Alcohol-Induced Organic Mental Disorders

Alcohol Intoxication

DSM-III-R specifies the following three diagnostic criteria for **alcohol intoxication** (American Psychiatric Association, 1987, p. 128).

1. Recent ingestion of alcohol in an amount sufficient to cause intoxication in most people.

2. Maladaptive changes in behavior.

3. At least one of these signs: slurred speech, uncoordinated or unsteady gait, nystagmus (involuntary to-and-fro movement of the eyeballs), flushed face.

The change in individuals as they become increasingly intoxicated may sometimes be an exaggeration of their usual behavior rather than a completely different pattern. Occasionally, however, the change represents an opposite pattern. For example, inhibited people might become overly convivial as they approach intoxication.

Some people who become highly intoxicated suffer blackouts, although these are not inevitable. Upon recovering from their state of intoxication, they have no memory of the

Figure 14.1

Blood alcohol levels and their consequences. (Data from Mendelson & Mello, 1985, p. 11; Schuckit, 1979, p. 42.)

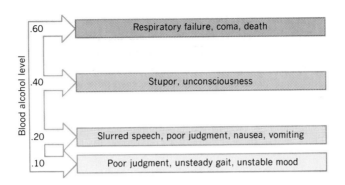

events that occurred. Blackouts are apt to increase as heavy drinking becomes more frequent, because the toxic effects of the alcohol on brain functions increase.

The behavioral signs of intoxication accelerate as the concentration of alcohol in the blood rises. Thus, **blood alcohol level** is generally a reliable indicator of the degree of intoxication. This level is determined by calculation of the percentage of blood volume accounted for by alcohol. The alcohol content of the blood is measured in milligrams (mg); blood volume is measured in milliliters (ml). Since one gram (g) of alcohol is equal in volume to one milliliter of blood, 100 grams of alcohol in 100 milliliters of blood is blood alcohol level of 100 percent (100 g/100 ml). Thus, for example, 100 milligrams of alcohol per 100 milliliters of blood is a blood alcohol level of 0.10 percent (100 mg/100 ml). Most social drinkers show definite behavioral signs of intoxication at blood alcohol levels between 100 and 150 mg/100 ml (0.10 to 0.15 percent) and will be highly intoxicated at levels of 200 mg/100 ml (0.20 percent). Stupor and unconsciousness may occur at levels between 0.40 and 0.50 percent, and death may occur between 0.60 and 0.80 percent (see Figure 14.1). In most states, blood alcohol level of 0.10 percent is considered to be legal evidence of intoxication. However, long-term abusers of alcohol who have become addicted and have developed a high tolerance for the drug may reveal blood alcohol levels about the legal limit and still not show the obvious behavioral signs of intoxication that a social drinker would with the same blood level. Thus, a standard legal definition of intoxication may not necessarily coincide with a clinical diagnosis based on overt behavior (Mendelson & Mello, 1985, p. 11).

Alcohol Idiosyncratic Intoxication

DSM-III-R distinguishes between alcohol intoxication as such and a related organic mental disorder called **alcohol idiosyncratic intoxication,** or pathological intoxication. The disorder has many similarities to alcohol intoxication but it occurs from drinking in amounts that are usually insufficient to cause intoxication in most people.

The onset of idiosyncratic intoxication is usually quite sudden, beginning while the individual is drinking or shortly afterwards. Typically, behavior during idiosyncratic intoxication is very different from that when the individual is sober. The behavior often appears to be psychotic, revealing such losses of contact with reality as confusion and disorientation. Other reactions may range from extremely inappropriate depression to equally inappropriate hostility. The attack is relatively brief. The individual usually returns to normal as the blood alcohol level is reduced — a relatively short period, since the intake of alcohol is low. After the period of intoxication is over, the person often falls into a deep sleep, and upon awakening has little memory of what occurred.

The causes of idiosyncratic intoxication are not clear. Some theories hold that it tends to occur in individuals who have some kind of brain damage that lowers their tolerance for alcohol considerably. Other theories claim that it occurs in people who are already emotionally unstable or unusually fatigued (Kaplan & Sadock, 1985, pp. 417–418).

Specialists in psychopathology tend to agree that the idiosyncratic form of intoxication is relatively rare. Some even argue that the disorder has been greatly overdiagnosed (Schuckit, 1979, p. 63). this claim deserves close attention, since the diagnosis may be introduced as part of the legal defense for individuals who have committed violent acts while under the influence of alcohol.

Alcohol Withdrawal

The immediate cause of the disorder known as **alcohol withdrawal** is the cessation of heavy and prolonged drinking or a sudden and severe reduction in the amount of alcohol habitually consumed. Symptoms typically appear from 4 to 12 hours after the intake of alcohol stops, but the interval may be as long as 48 hours (Honigfeld & Howard, 1978, p. 72; Janowsky, Addario, & Schuckit, 1978, p. 127; Korsten & Lieber, 1985, p. 51). The most obvious symptoms are coarse tremors of the hand, tongue, and eyelids, popularly known as the shakes, as well as one or more of the following signs (American Psychiatric Association, 1987, p. 130).

- Nausea and vomiting.
- General feeling of weakness.
- Hyperactivity of the autonomic nervous system, such as abnormally rapid heartbeat (tachycardia), profuse sweating, and elevated blood pressure.
- Anxiety, depressed mood, or irritability,
- Transient hallucinations or illusions.
- Headache.

People undergoing alcohol withdrawal symptoms may have great difficulty in sleeping and are often disturbed by nightmares. Occasionally they may experience fleeting hallucinations. Convulsions occur about 5 to 15 percent of the time (Schuckit, 1979, p. 60).

The first step in the treatment of alcohol withdrawal is to identify the specific physical and psychological reactions and to assess the person's general health, which is often in a state of deterioration. The goals of treatment must usually go beyond remedying the withdrawal itself.

Since withdrawal symptoms indicate that the individual has become addicted to alcohol (that is, physiologically dependent on it), detoxification must be carried out before rehabilitative measures can be successful. **Detoxification** has been defined as "taking the alcoholic safely through the period of withdrawal" (Miller & Hester, 1980, p. 15). Among the methods used is to administer alcohol or some other depressant drug in doses high enough to abolish the symptoms of withdrawal, and then decrease the dosage gradually. In the case of alcohol, for example, the decrease can be approximately 20 percent of the initial dose each day. Some practitioners prefer to use a depressant drug other than alcohol in the detoxification process—for example, a barbiturate or chlordiazepoxide (Librium). The dose needs to be monitored carefully, especially to safeguard against an addiction to the treatment drug itself (Janowsky, Addario, & Schuckit, 1980, pp. 69–72; Schuckit, 1985, pp. 310–312).

Withdrawal symptoms usually last from 3 to 10 days. Once detoxification has been accomplished, further recovery depends on proper medical care, especially to remedy the deficiencies in nutrition so often found in chronic alcoholism, such as lack of thiamine and other B complex vitamins. In addition, good nursing care and a supportive attitude toward the individual are important factors in hastening recovery. In some cases, detoxification and further treatment can be accomplished on an outpatient basis. How successful that is depends on the severity of the withdrawal symptoms and the kinds of physical, social, and emotional support the patient has outside the hospital (Pattison, 1985; Vaillant, 1983, p. 149).

Alleviating the symptoms of alcohol withdrawal is not the same as curing the person of alcoholism. That kind of progress depends on further methods of therapy, which we discuss later in the chapter.

Alcohol Withdrawal Delirium (Delirium Tremens)

Historical Background

Although certain symptoms of delirium tremens (a more severe form of alcohol withdrawal) were described many centuries ago, the term itself was not used until 1813, when the British physician Thomas Sutton published a clear account of the disorder as he had observed it in his practice. In 1832, John Ware, a professor of medical practice at Harvard University, completed an exhaustive study of the subject. Medical historians consider Sutton's clinical observations and Ware's work to be the classic accounts of delirium tremens (Garrison, 1929, p. 439; Zilboorg & Henry, 1941, pp. 554–556).

Symptoms

Delirium tremens (commonly known as the DTs) usually occur for the first time between the ages of 30 and 40, after the individual has drunk heavily for a decade or more. Unless physical illness complicates the delirium, the attack generally lasts for two or three days (American Psychiatric Association, 1980a, 134–135). The initial symptoms resemble those of ordinary alcohol withdrawal—for example, nausea, general malaise, vague

Visual hallucinations are common in delirium tremens. In this scene from the film *The Lost Weekend*, based on a novel by Charles Jackson, the alcoholic Don, who is played by Ray Milland, "sees" a bat circling the room.

feelings of anxiety, and perhaps some fragmentary hallucinations. These reactions usually begin a day or so after the drinking has stopped. Then convulsions, resembling the grand mal seizures of epileptic disorders, often appear (see Chapter 13). In another day or so, new and more terrifying reactions emerge. Hallucinations, usually visual, become more definite and vivid.

> Jim is a moderately successful lawyer, despite his chronic alcoholism. He "goes off on a bender" about once a month, disappearing for several days to a week. In the past ten years, Jim has been briefly hospitalized more than 20 times in conjunction either with delirium tremens or some other alcohol-related difficulty.
>
> In a recent episode, his "girlfriend" called the emergency ward at the local hospital because Jim was jabbing himself with a fork "to get those miserable gnats off" his body. He was screaming and delirious upon admission to the hospital, terrified not only of the hallucinated gnats, but of the "crazy shapes" and "smelly queeries" that were "coming after" him. Nothing could be done to comfort Jim for several hours; he continued to have tremors, sweated profusely, cowered in a corner, drew his blankets over his head, twisted and turned anxiously, vomited several times and kept screaming about hallucinated images which "attacked" him and "ate up his skin."
>
> After three days of delirium, with intermittent periods of fitful sleep, Jim began to regain his normal senses. He was remorseful, apologized to all for his misbehavior and assured them of his "absolute resolution never to hit the bottle again." Unfortunately, as was expected, he again was hospitalized three months later as a consequence of a similar debauche that was followed by delirium tremens. (Millon, 1969, p. 509)

Treatment

Although the immediate cause of delirium tremens is a sudden drop in the level of blood alcohol, concurrent physical illnesses can contribute significantly to the severity of reactions. A clinical study of patients with delirium tremens found that almost half had other serious disabilities, such as infections, insufficient functioning of the liver, inflammation of the pancreas, and severe vitamin deficiencies.

Estimates of the mortality rate from delirium tremens range from 1 to 15 percent. Treatment is basically the same as for ordinary alcohol withdrawal symptoms, but the greater severity of the reactions and the possibility of complications from other physical illnesses make hospitalization necessary (Ludwig, 1980, p. 285).

Alcohol Hallucinosis

Hallucinations occurring in the absence of delirium are the central feature of **alcohol hallucinosis** (American Psychiatric Association, 1987, p. 132). The hallucinations appear within about 48 hours after the individual stops drinking altogether or significantly reduces intake. As a rule, the hallucinations take the form of voices, but they may be hissing or buzzing noises.

Alcohol Amnestic Disorder

Korsakov's Psychosis

In 1887, Sergei Korsakov (1854–1900), a Russian neurologist, described in great detail a disorder involving loss of memory and defects in the association of ideas that he believed resulted directly from alcohol poisoning.

> The disorder of memory manifests itself in an extraordinarily peculiar amnesia, in which the memory of recent events, those which just happened, is chiefly disturbed, whereas the remote past is remembered fairly well. . . . At first, during conversation with such a patient it is difficult to note the presence of psychic disorder. . . . Only after a long conversation with the patient, one may note that at times he utterly confuses events and that he remembers absolutely noting of what goes on around him: he does not remember whether he had his dinner, whether he was out of bed. On occasion the patient forgets what happened to him just an instant ago. (Victor & Yakolev, 1955, pp. 397–398)

The disorder came to be known as **Korsakov's psychosis**, a label used in the second edition of DSM-II (American Psychiatric Association, 1968, p. 25). In DSM-III and DSM-III-R, Korsakov's psychosis was renamed **alcohol amnestic disorder** (American Psychiatric Association, 1980a, pp. 236–237; 1987, p. 133).

Although Korsakov emphasized that the memory loss was confined to recent events, deficits in long-term memory may also occur. In recent years, researchers have studied other disturbances associated with alcohol amnestic disorder — for example, deficits in attention, perception, and motivation. These deficits are so intertwined with memory processes that they must be considered part of the disorder, even though its central characteristic is organic amnesia (Oscar-Berman, 1980).

Korsakov believed that alcohol poisoning caused the disorder. However, it is now known that the more fundamental cause is a severe lack of the B complex vitamins, especially thiamine. Nevertheless, the etiological factors of alcohol and nutritional deficiency are linked, since long-term, excessive drinking is commonly associated with dietary neglect.

Korsakov was especially interested in a phenomenon known as **confabulation** — the filling of memory gaps with imaginary events. Confabulation is usually interpreted as an organic disability, but it may also represent an attempt (perhaps unconscious) to deny the loss of memory. This psychodynamic aspect of confabulation is well illustrated in the following example of an individual whose long-term alcoholism impaired his memory.

> When asked questions he could not answer, [he] would give responses that were patently absurd. Questioned as to where he had seen me before, he immediately replied that we had gone fishing together for many years in Canada. Queried about the name of the hospital, he replied, "Why, this is the Quincy branch of the Massachusetts General Hospital." [In actuality, it was a clinic of the Boston University Medical School.] A question about where he had been before entering the hospital elicited the answer, "Why, I'm just back from Korea, where I've been on active duty." (Gardner, 1974, pp. 185–186)

Wernicke's Encephalopathy

In 1881, the German neurologist Karl Wernicke (1848–1905) observed that chronic alcoholics sometimes suffer from a degeneration of nerve tissue, especially in the midbrain. This pathological process became known as **Wernicke's encephalopathy**, or, more simply, Wernicke's disease. It involves a state of confusion, the loss of motor coordination (ataxia), eye-movement abnormalities such as nystagumus, and other neurological abnormalities (American Psychiatric Association, 1987, p. 133). Wernicke's disease may occur independently of alcoholism, since its basic cause is a deficiency of B complex vitamins. However, it is most often associated with chronic heavy drinking, which is commonly linked to severe nutritional deficiencies. Wernicke's disease may be fatal. More often, the symptoms subside but are followed by alcohol amnestic disorder (Korsakov's psychosis). If the disease is treated early enough with massive doses of thiamine, the amnestic disorder may not occur. Once it is established, however, it tends to persist indefinitely, with permanent and extensive damage to the brain, especially in the areas of the thalamus, and the frontal lobe (see Figure 13.2). (Oscar-Berman, 1980).

Dementia Associated with Alcoholism

Long-term dependence on alcohol may lead to dementia — a global decline in cognitive abilities such as reasoning, problem solving, and judgment (see Chapter 13). Since it takes many years of heavy drinking to produce such effects, the dementia seldom appears before the age of 35. DSM-III-R lists the following diagnostic criteria (American Psychiatric Association, 1987, pp. 134).

1. Dementia follows chronic and heavy ingestion of alcohol.

2. Dementia persists at least three weeks after alcohol intake has stopped. This criterion helps distinguish the transitory cognitive deficits that may occur during withdrawal from the more lasting ones of dementia.

3. Possible causes of the dementia other than chronic and excessive use of alcohol must be ruled out.

Dementia associated with alcoholism may range from mild to severe. The mild level is the most prevalent and is most subject to reversal, provided the individual stops drinking. In its mild form, the dementia may not always be readily apparent to the casual observer. However, one can usually discern some social and occupational difficulties that reflect a decline in intellectual functioning. Psychological tests can reveal the intellectual losses more precisely. As the dementia increases form mild to moderate, impairment in social and occupational relationships becomes more obvious, so that even ordinary observers begin to notice the change. At the most severe level of impairment the individual becomes intellectually helpless and unable to function independently, either socially or occupationally. Signs of personality deterioration usually accompany the intellectual loss. At this point, the individual usually requires constant care.

Alcohol Abuse and Dependence

Thus far, we have discussed the organic mental syndromes that arise from prolonged and excessive drinking. We turn now to a group of disturbances closely related to alcohol-induced organic mental disorders: alcohol abuse and dependence. These disorders reflect problems with drinking other than physical disabilities.

Alcohol abuse is the persistent use of alcohol in spite of the problems that result. **Alcohol dependence**, commonly known as **alcoholism**, is a more extensive and severe disorder than alcohol abuse. It also involves an abnormal pattern of drinking, to the point where the drinking creates serious problems. In spite of these problems, the individual may continue to drink. Physiological dependence is likely to develop, marked by an increase in the tolerance for alcohol and, in more severe instances, symptoms of withdrawal. In **alcohol tolerance**, a substantial increase in the amount of alcohol consumed becomes necessary to achieve the same effect. Withdrawal symptoms may occur when drinking stops. the following case illustrates a pattern of alcohol dependence.

> A 45-year-old, twice-married woman has been drinking a pint of vodka daily for 13 years. . . . During the period of her first divorce she became depressed and found that alcohol made her feel better. While drinking in a bar she met her second husband, also a heavy drinker. They continued to drink at home in the evenings. She increasingly found reasons not to go to work, and was eventually dismissed from her job. She began drinking throughout the day, allowing herself an ounce of vodka per hour, interspersed with occasional beers. She hid bottles and beer cans so her husband would not know she was drinking so much. Her husband, finding her intoxicated on his return home, began complaining and threatened to leave her. She vowed to drink only beer. She kept this up for a month, drinking two or three six-packs a day. Then she became worried about her weight and decided not to drink at all except for "two" drinks before dinner. The two drinks became three, and soon she was drinking a pint of vodka again. She began having memory lapses. Once she burned a hole in the divan and did not remember it. Her husband moved out after a violent argument. Drinking alone, she cried a good deal and thought about suicide. She finally called Alcoholics Anonymous for help. (Spitzer, Skodol, Gibbon, & Williams, 1981, p. 233)

One may abuse alcohol without developing signs of dependence — that is, without developing a tolerance for alcohol or undergoing withdrawal symptoms. However, it is highly likely that long-term heavy abuse will eventually lead to such symptoms. In turn, chronic alcoholism almost always results in some manifestation of alcohol-induced organic mental disorder. Repeated episodes of intoxication and withdrawal are the most prevalent syndromes (Polich, Armor, & Braiker, 1981, pp. 46–50).

Alcohol abuse and alcoholism occur more often among the middle and upper classes in the United States than among the lower classes. Far from being homeless drifters, most people for whom drinking is a serious personal and social problem live at home with their families or maintain at least some contact. They are usually employed or have employable skills. Nevertheless, as their pathological use of alcohol increases, their occupational skills often suffer, sometimes to the point where they lose their jobs.

Although estimates vary, the consensus seems to be that the lifetime prevalence of alcohol abuse or dependence may be as high as 28 percent for men but less than 5 percent for women (Helzer, 1987). However, some reports indicate that the rate for women is rising. One reason may be that as women have entered the mainstream of social and economic life, they have taken on new values and stresses that contribute to the maladaptive use of alcohol. It may also be that the reported increase in alcohol abuse and alcoholism among women is more apparent than real. That is, women may now be more willing to seek treatment for their drinking problems, and thus the apparent rate of their misuse rises. In the past, cultural pressure caused many women to engage in hidden drinking ("Alcoholism and Women," 1974; p. 102; Gomberg, 1976, 1977; Johnson, 1984; Lex, 1985; Lindbeck, 1972; U.S. Department of Health and Human Services, 1980; Wilsnack, Wilsnack, & Klassen, 1984–1985).

A nationwide survey disclosed that drinking is highest in the 18- to 25-year-old group. About 76 percent of that group said they used alcohol, compared with 61 percent of older adults. For those under age 18, 37 percent reported the use of alcohol. If one considers only the 16- and 17-year-olds in that group, the rate increases to 55 percent (*National Survey on Drug Abuse*, 1980, p. 23). However, the overall pool of potential abusers is much smaller: 10 percent of drinkers imbibe about 50 percent of the total amount of alcohol consumed in the United States (American Psychiatric Association, 1987, p. 173).

Fetal Alcohol Syndrome

It is well established that alcohol can cross the placenta. Thus, a pregnant woman's blood alcohol level can definitely affect the unborn child. If the woman is a heavy drinker, the child may suffer a pattern of severe birth defects known as **fetal alcohol syndrome**. Often associated with mental retardation, the syndrome may also include central nervous system disorders, growth deficiencies, a specific cluster of facial abnormalities, and malformations involving the skeletal, urogenital, and cardiac systems. Even if she does not bear a child with the full syndrome, a woman who drinks heavily during pregnancy is more likely to have a child with at least one of the defects associated with it (Gallant, 1987, pp. 101–102; Lex, 1985, pp. 113–115; Smith, 1977; U.S. Department of Health and Human Services, 1981a).

Some authorities have pointed out that the average daily consumption of alcohol throughout pregnancy may not be as crucial in producing fetal alcohol syndrome as heavy drinking during the critical periods of early embryonic development (Julien, 1981, pp. 67–68). Nevertheless, physicians generally agree that pregnant women should be highly cautious in their drinking patterns at all times, and some advise abstaining altogether. Significant decreases in birth weight have been observed among the children of some women who averaged only one ounce of absolute alcohol (two standard drinks) per day during pregnancy. Studies have also shown a significant increase in spontaneous abortions when reported alcohol consumption levels during pregnancy were as low as one ounce of absolute alcohol twice a week (U.S. Department of Health and Human Services, 1981a).

A baby can be born with severe birth defects if the mother has drunk heavily during pregnancy. Some studies show that the baby's birth weight can be significantly lower even when the mother has had two standard drinks (one ounce of absolute alcohol) a day.

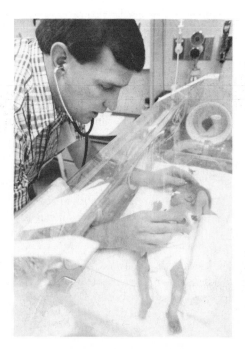

Alcoholism and the Elderly

Although the rate of alcoholism in the United States is lower among individuals 65 and older than in the general population, it has been steadily rising in recent years. The excessive use of alcohol has debilitating effects on the health of the elderly, and it also masks the symptoms of other illnesses. A variety of federal agencies are increasing the study of problem drinking among older individuals and are establishing special counseling centers. These efforts are especially important since the nation's aged population is growing steadily.

Elderly people drink excessively for the same reasons as younger people, except that social and economic problems make the elderly especially vulnerable. Loneliness and depression are among the chief factors that impel them to become problem drinkers. As one woman who lived alone in a tiny room in a New York hotel put it: "A bottle keeps you company if you're lonely. . . . It makes you feel a little better" (Collins, 1985, p. 20).

Social Consequences of Alcohol Abuse and Dependence

The personal, social, and occupational losses that result from alcohol misuse are far greater than the damage caused by such illicit substances as heroin and cocaine. Many authorities in the field of drug abuse are now convinced that alcohol is the most abused drug in the United States and that the problem is increasing (Blum, 1984, pp. 237–238; Gallant, 1987; pp. xi, xii, 24; Smith, 1986; Snyder, 1980, pp. 131–132; U.S. Department of Health and Human Services, 1980).

Although crimes committed by heroin addicts are a significant problem in American life, the misuse of alcohol is much more frequently a factor in crime. In almost 50 percent of assaults or murders, either the victim or the assailant had been drinking heavily. More than one-third of all arrests are related to the misuse of alcohol.

The abuse of alcohol is implicated in a vast number of injuries and accidents, including auto accidents. This wreck, the work of a drunken driver, was left in a Massachusetts street as a warning to other drivers.

"I USED TO NEED A REASON TO COME
HERE. NOW, I JUST SHOW UP."

From 10 to 15 million people suffer from alcohol abuse or alcoholism in the United States. However, considering the problems that the misuse of alcohol creates for families, at least 36 million people are adversely affected. Alcoholism is the third leading cause of death, and it is implicated in a vast number of injuries and accidents.

■ About 44 percent of civilian noncommercial aviation accidents in which the pilot died.

■ About 80 percent of all fire fatalities and over 60 percent of all nonfatal burns.

■ As many as 70 percent of the deaths and 63 percent of the nonfatal injuries resulting from falls.

■ Almost 70 percent of all drownings.

Estimates of annual industrial casualties in which alcohol is a contributing factor range from 12,600 deaths and more than 2 million injuries to 18,000 deaths and 10 million injuries. At least $20 billion in production is lost annually because of alcohol problems. Over all, the problem of alcohol costs our society over $100 billion a year.

The social acceptance of alcohol use may account for our failure to pay attention to its misuse. Only in recent years has alcoholism been admitted to be a public health problem. The growing recognition that alcohol abuse and dependence can be cured or at least controlled has helped increase public funds for research and thus has helped provide better knowledge for dealing with the problem (Blum, 1984, p. 238).

The general social acceptance of alcohol in our culture may help account for our failure, until recent years, to pay sufficient attention to problems of alcohol abuse.

Phases in the Development of Alcohol Abuse and Dependence: Jellinek's Analysis

In a detailed survey of 2000 alcoholics, E. M. Jellinek (1971) traced the development of their addiction from early and relatively mild abuse of alcohol to the point where dependence was so great they could no longer function adequately. Jellinek distinguished four phases in this development: prealcoholic, prodromal, crucial, and chronic.

Prealcoholic Phase. The alcoholic's drinking begins in social situations. However, alcohol reduces tension far more effectively for the potential alcoholic than for other individuals. Gradually, more alcohol becomes necessary to reduce tension, so the habit of daily drinking becomes well established. Many social drinkers never go beyond this **prealcoholic phase**, although they are vulnerable. For others, however, the gradual increase in drinking is an important first step toward alcohol dependence.

Prodromal Phase. Behavior during the **prodromal phase** begins to take on some of the characteristics of alcohol abuse. The drinker may begin to experience sudden blackouts, although behavior during the blackouts appears to be quite normal. Drinking in secret may begin. Sometimes an individual in the prodromal phase needs several drinks before going to social events where alcoholic beverages will be served. Feelings of guilt often develop, and the individual is likely to deny any suggestion that drinking is a problem. Difficulties with family, friends, and co-workers increase as the drinker moves from the abuse of alcohol to dependence on it.

Crucial Phase. Control of drinking is out of hand in the **crucial phase.** Dependence has set in, and usually it is evidenced by an increasing tolerance for alcohol or by episodes of withdrawal. Once people in the crucial phase start drinking, they cannot stop until they become intoxicated or simply too ill to continue.

Chronic Phase. Alcoholism becomes a way of life in the **chronic phase.** The drinker is more or less intoxicated most of the time. Social and occupational relationships are completely disrupted. Symptoms of an organic mental disorder become noticeable. Withdrawal symptoms inevitably follow the cessation of drinking or a sudden reduction in intake. As years go on additional organic disorders such as delirium tremens and alcohol amnestic disorder (Korsakov's psychosis) begin to take their toll.

Jellinek's analysis is useful provided one does not apply it rigidly. Some alcoholics omit a phase or do not experience a blackout until they go beyond the prodromal phase. Others may reach that stage and then enter a long period of abstinence. Suddenly they resume drinking, perhaps as the result of some traumatic event, and then they progress inexorably toward the crucial and chronic phases. Still others may control their drinking sufficiently to never reach the chronic phase, but they continue to show definite signs of the crucial phase.

Etiology of Alcohol Abuse and Dependence

The prevalent view today is that multiple etiological factors are involved in alcohol abuse and dependence. However, researchers disagree about what these factors are and about their relative importance (U.S. Department of Health and Human Services, 1980; Vaillant & Molofsky, 1982).

Physiological Abnormalities

Innate physiological abnormalities may be extremely important in the etiology of alcohol abuse and dependence (Schuckit, 1979, pp. 48–49; Schuckit & Haglund, 1977). It has been suggested that some individuals drink excessively because their tolerance for alcohol is considerably greater than that of most people. Consequently, they are more likely to eventually become dependent on alcohol.

There is little empirical evidence to support this theory. Furthermore, it does not explain why some people drink maladaptively regardless of their tolerance level, others choose not to drink at all, and still others are able to drink well within their physiological tolerance (Costin, 1976, p. 145).

Abnormalities in metabolism have also been proposed as possible factors in the development of alcohol abuse and dependence. It has been claimed that alcoholics do not metabolize alcohol as rapidly as nonalcoholics. However, studies have shown that many alcoholics actually metabolize alcohol 10 to 20 percent more rapidly, especially when drinking large amounts.

It has also been suggested that deficiencies in hormonal activity and vitamins may be important factors in the etiology of drinking problems. However, most of the hormonal and nutritional disorders associated with alcohol abuse and dependence are likely to be the result of heavy drinking rather than its cause (U.S. Department of Health and Human Services, 1980).

Genetic Factors

Sons of alcoholic fathers are at high risk for developing alcoholism, even when they are separated from their biological parents soon after birth (Goodwin, 1985a, 1985b). The strongest support for the influence of genetic factors comes from studies of Danish male and female adoptees with at least one alcoholic biological parent. These adoptees had been reared from an early age without knowing their biological parents. The studies included a control group of adoptees whose biological parents had no history of alcohol abuse or dependence. The male adoptees with at least one alcoholic biological parent had a greater rate of alcoholism than the female adoptees in their group and the control group

(Goodwin, 1985a, 1985b; Goodwin, Schulsinger, Knop, Mednick, & Guze, 1977a, 1977b; Goodwin, Schulsinger, Moller, Hermansen, Winokur, & Guze, 1974); Schulsinger, 1980).

The studies also compared the occurrence of alcoholism in the siblings and half-siblings of adoptees who had an alcoholic biological parent and who had remained with the alcoholic parent during childhood. The adopted siblings had about the same rate of alcoholism as their brothers and half-brothers who had remained at home (Goodwin, Schulsinger, Moller, Hermansen, Winokur, & Guze, 1974).

These studies suggest that genetic factors may play a part in the occurrence of alcohol abuse and dependence. However, although these factors may increase an individual's vulnerability to alcoholism, environmental influences can exacerbate that vulnerability or minimize it (Goodwin, 1976, 1985a, 1985b; Searles, 1988). The children of alcoholics may be more vulnerable to alcoholism for a number of reasons. Their parents may make it difficult for them to achieve a strong positive identity with authority figures. Also, the emotional support alcoholic parents give their children is inconsistent and unpredictable. Since children learn from their parents, they may model their drinking habits after those of their parents, and in fact, studies suggest that they are much less likely to grow up to be teetotalers than children who were influenced in the direction of abstinence. In structured interviews, most of a sample of 133 members of a large midwestern metropolitan Protestant church attributed their abstinence to the influence of parents who themselves were teetotalers. Only 2 percent ascribed their abstinence to unpleasant encounters with alcoholic relatives or friends (Goodwin, Johnson, Maher, Rappaport, & Guze, 1969).

Conflict and frustration may activate a genetic vulnerability to alcohol. These forces may become so strong that the individual starts drinking as an escape. Furthermore, one must take into account how a culture teaches people to use alcohol and the extent to which the culture sanctions the use of alcohol to escape from frustration and conflict. Drinking itself is a learned behavior (Snyder, 1980). Thus, environmental factors still play a "major and possibly overriding role" (p. 141).

Conflict and Frustration: Psychoanalytic Theory

Traditional psychoanalytic theory emphasizes the importance of conflict and frustration in the etiology of alcohol abuse and dependence. Some psychoanalysts focus on the oral phase — the first six months or so after birth. Orthodox Freudian theory claims that during this phase the child gains a primitive form of sexual pleasure in satisfying nutritional needs. Prolonged and undue frustration at this phase may result in fixation, so that later in life exaggerated oral desires persist. This pattern constitutes what orthodox psychoanalysis labels the oral character, or oral personality. Excessive drinking during adulthood is one way that individuals with an oral character satisfy their frustrated need for oral pleasure.

The retrospective data that are the traditional support of the **orality theory** are not sufficiently objective to test the theory adequately. Several empirical studies have been conducted with male alcoholic patients to see if there is any relationship between orality and alcoholism. Story (1968) asked alcoholic and nonalcoholic men to respond with free associations to various stimuli that were oral and nonoral in content. The alcoholic subjects showed more conflict and inhibition in responding to the oral stimuli. Other studies compared the reactions to inkblots of alcoholic and nonalcoholic men. The alcoholic subjects showed a higher degree of "oral imagery" (Bertrand & Masling, 1969; Weiss & Masling, 1970).

Some reviewers interpret these findings as support for the orality theory (Fisher & Greenberg, 1977; Kline, 1972, 1981). However, the studies found a correlation between current personality characteristics (orality) and alcoholism. They did not demonstrate the causal relationship postulated by Freudian theory — that alcoholism is a result of frustrated oral needs during childhood. The findings may actually show that the alcoholic's current involvement with oral activity is the factor influencing the strong oral imagery.

Other psychoanalytic views focus on the anal – sadistic phase of psychosexual development. If the child's attempts to achieve independence typical of this stage are greatly frustrated, unconscious feelings of conflict and hostility toward the parents may persist into adulthood. Since the individual's superego forbids the expression of such hostility, it is turned inward. Alcohol becomes both a means of self-destruction an indirect way of getting revenge on parental figures. This view of the origins of alcohol abuse and alcoholism is basically one of suicidal motivation, a dynamic that also plays a prominent part in the psychoanalytic theory of depression (see Chapter 10).

The notion that alcohol abuse and dependence stem from frustrated anal and sadistic needs has not been tested experimentally, so there is nothing but retrospective data to support it.

Other Views of Conflict and Frustration

Some researchers have pointed to such factors as parental neglect, harsh and rejecting treatment, and inconsistent punishment of the child as possible precursors to drinking problems. Conflicts among family members may also play an influential role. According to this view, alcoholics are likely to come from homes where they were made to feel unloved, inadequate, and insecure. Consequently, they develop personality traits that make them more vulnerable to drinking problems.

Research has failed to disclose a typical personality pattern among alcoholics. Indeed, studies have disclosed a wide variety of characteristics: immaturity, loneliness, impulsiveness, neurotic dependence, hostility, low self-esteem (sometimes masked by outward assertions of superiority), self-punishing behavior, hypersensitivity in social situations, low tolerance for frustration and conflict, and denial of obvious problems arising from drinking behavior. Studies attribute varying importance to such traits. The question also arises as to whether these characteristics are actually factors that led to alcoholism or whether they are the results of the maladaptive drinking. Furthermore, the factors may correlate with other variables as yet unknown that have a prime influence on the development of alcohol problems. Finally, the kinds of personality characteristics that studies have attributed to alcoholics may also be present in many nonalcoholics (U.S. Department of Health and Human Services, 1980).

Most abusers of alcohol realize that their drinking habits continually bring them a great deal of trouble and unhappiness. This insight causes some problem drinkers to seek help, but many others persist in drinking. A central characteristic of this disorder is impulsive, irresponsible behavior in which immediate gratification dominates social relationships (see Chapter 12).

Social Labeling and Reinforcement

Social psychologists and sociologists have pointed out that the pathological use of alcohol may persist because the drinker has been diagnosed and labeled an alcoholic and conforms to that assigned role (Roman & Trice, 1977). This behavior perpetuates the cycle of labeling and reinforcement. Others perceive the drinking unfavorably, react negatively toward the drinker, and thus reinforce the label that the drinker has now accepted.

A number of sociologists have warned against a too facile and literal acceptance of the concept of labeling to explain deviant behavior. Howard Becker (1974), an early advocate of labeling theory, has reconsidered the issue and pointed out that the degree to which labeling perpetuates deviant behavior is an empirical question. It should be settled by examination of specific cases rather than by application of a theoretical rule.

Operant Conditioning

According to some learning theorists, the maladaptive behavior characteristic of alcohol abuse and alcoholism results from the same kind of learning that produces adaptive behavior. The central process is operant conditioning — behavior that is reinforced. If the consequences of the behavior are satisfying, it will tend to be repeated. (See Chapter 4 for a detailed discussion of conditioning theory.) At least initially, alcohol usually produces feelings of well-being and seems to offer an escape from troubling experiences. Therefore, the drinking is likely to be repeated so the person can achieve the same effects again. However, this pattern also occurs in people who never misuse alcohol.

Cognitive Expectations

Cognitive social learning explanations of the development of alcoholism stress the effect of the individual's cognitive expectations concerning the use of alcohol (Cox & Klinger, 1988; Donovan & Marlatt, 1980, pp. 1159–1161). These expectations may be learned through peer and parental modeling, previous experiences with drinking, and exposure to advertising. Thus, people come to expect alcohol to reduce tension and improve negative moods. They also expect it to enhance social interaction and to heighten their perception of personal control and power. Interestingly, how they actually feel when intoxicated may not always correspond to their expectations.

Cultural Variations

Patterns of drinking differ considerably from one country to another as well as among various ethnic and racial groups within a country (Barry, 1982, pp. 323–327; Cahalan, 1978a, 1978b; Feifer, 1981; Lex, 1985; MacAndrew & Edgerton, 1969; Plant, 1975; Vaillant, 1983, pp. 58–71; World Health Organization, 1974; Zinberg & Fraser, 1985). The rates of alcohol abuse and alcoholism are extremely high in France, Ireland, Scotland, and certain parts of the Soviet Union. In contrast, they are relatively low in Finland, Japan, England, Taiwan, and Israel. Research has provided some useful insights into the reasons for such differences.

National Variations

The association of moderate drinking as part of religious rituals and in family life can be traced to antiquity. Among the Greeks, for example, occasional intoxication on festive occasions was tolerated, but chronic drunkenness was perceived as evil by most of the poets and philosophers of the time. Drinking wine as part of Jewish religious observances can be traced to biblical times. The ancient Israelites used wine in religious festivals, at funerals, as sacred libations in the temple, as medicine, and as nourishment. The immoderate and inappropriate use of wine, however, was considered a social vice and was condemned in various texts of the Old Testament (Bacon, 1973, p. 174; Barry, 1982; p. 332; Cahalan, 1978b; Raymond, 1927, pp. 22–27; Rolleston, 1927; Snyder, 1958, 1962).

The use of alcohol in China is as old as China itself. Alcohol is readily available and there are no moral prohibitions on drinking. However, traditional family and social norms are opposed to excessive and solitary drinking. In Taiwan, alcohol is consumed mostly

This shopper in Moscow is loading up in anticipation of a recently enacted law limiting the hours during which hard liquor can be sold. The law is part of a comprehensive Soviet compaign against widespread alcohol abuse.

with meals and in groups or is used on ceremonial occasions. Although occasional intoxication at a party is acceptable, chronic drunkenness is strongly disapproved of. It is considered to be a sign of weakness and deterioration. Instead of using alcohol as a means of reducing conflict, as in Western cultures, people in Taiwan use personal contact and social gambling to seek solace for their everyday problems (Singer, 1972; Sanua, 1980, p. 203).

In France, especially in rural areas, small children regularly drink wine at meals. The French government proposed a 10-year plan to reduce alcoholism, a plan that met with great resistance from the wine industry (Prial, 1980).

It has been estimated that the rate of alcoholism in Scotland is four to five times greater than in England or Wales. Plant (1975) noted widespread cultural support for heavy consumption of alcohol in Scotland. One form of this cultural support is the acceptance of drinking in public places to assert an image of male potency and domination.

In recent years, the Soviet Union renewed its efforts to deal with its perennial problems with alcoholism. New restrictions included cutting the production of vodka and banning the sale of liquor before 2 P.M. on workdays. However, public resentment and revenue losses have caused the restrictions to be eased somewhat (Schmemann, 1985; Taubman, 1988).

Cultural Variations in the United States

Certain groups in the United States, such as Mormons and Moslems, have especially low rates of alcohol abuse and dependence because their religions forbid the drinking of alcoholic beverages. Jews also have a low rate of maladaptive drinking, although one seldom finds teetotalers among them (Keller, 1970; Singer, 1972). Most research has concluded that their moderate use of alcohol is due to the fact that drinking occurs mainly within the contexts of family life and religious observance.

Alcohol dependence among persons of Irish background in the United States is relatively high, perhaps reflecting patterns of drinking in Ireland. Some researchers believe that their rate is higher because it is not associated with religious ritual except for the drinking of wine by the priest during the celebration of the Mass in Catholic churches (Muhlin, 1985; Vaillant, 1983, pp. 61–64).

Alcohol abuse and dependence are serious health problems among black Americans. Like white Americans, blacks use alcohol to escape social and economic problems, but their problems are magnified because in general they are lower in the economic scale than whites. "The adverse effects of excessive alcohol tend to have an even greater impact in the black than in the white community. Money for alcohol is more likely to be money that would otherwise go for necessities such as food or even housing. General nutritional levels tend to be somewhat lower, creating greater susceptibility to the physical effects of alcohol. Unlike the wealthy executive who can accommodate his job to his drinking habits for some time, the unskilled black is more likely to be fired for drinking on the job" (Bourne & Light, 1979, p. 85).

Among Native Americans, especially those who still live on reservations or in urban ghettos, social and economic problems contribute greatly to a high level of alcohol abuse and alcoholism (Lex, 1985, pp. 154–156). For many years, the belief persisted that Native Americans are more physiologically susceptible than whites to alcohol. (Leland, 1976; Trillin, 1971). However, the belief is false. Increasing alienation brought on by the social and economic deprivation characteristic of much reservation life is the likely explnation for the present high rate of drinking problems among North American Indians.

Therapeutic Approaches to Treatment for Alcoholics

Proper medical treatment can help alcoholics recover from the deleterious effects of intoxication and withdrawal reactions and remedy their nutritional deficiencies. Too often, however, once alcoholics have passed safely through these crises, they return to their previous patterns of abuse and dependence. A wide variety of methods have been developed to prevent this regression.

Medication

A common medical approach involves the use of drugs that interact with alcohol in the body to produce extremely adverse reactions, such as severe nausea and vomiting. One of the most frequently used medictions is disulfiram (Antabuse). This drug is excreted from the body very slowly, so that after a dose has been taken, the individual cannot drink alcohol for four or five days without becoming quite ill. To keep from returning to drinking, the individual must usually take the medication at least twice a week and in some instances every day. However, many alcoholics are not sufficiently motivated to take it regularly (Jaffe & Ciraulo, 1985; Lundwall & Baekeland, 1971; Ritchie, 1975, p. 178; Viamontes, 1972).

Medical practitioners usually consider Antabuse to be only a partial treatment. In addition, they may want the patient to receive some form of insight psychotherapy or behavior therapy, or they may urge the patient to join Alcoholics Anonymous (Goodwin, 1976, pp. 129–133; Miller & Hester, 1980; Snyder, 1980, pp. 143–144).

Treatement with drugs can also produce unfortunate side effects. In the case of Antabuse, such reactions may range from skin eruptions and headaches to sexual dysfunctions and disturbances of the central nervous system. Furthermore, Antabuse may interact with nitrites, a common meat preservative, to produce cancer of the esophagus. Certain preexisting conditions rule out the use of Antabuse: coronary and liver disease, diabetes, and hyperthyrodism. Thus, Antabuse needs to be prescribed with great caution (Jaffe & Ciraulo, 1985; Miller & Hester, 1980; Pattison, 1985; ppp. 229–230).

All forms of insight psychotherapy assume that gaining self-understanding is essential if people are to solve their problems and conflicts. In some forms of insight psychotherapy, self-understanding may be enhanced by sharing attitudes, feelings, and experiences with other victims of alcoholism. A variant of this group therapy is family therapy, in which the alcoholic and other members of the family talk about their problems and their feelings for one another (Root, 1986). The assumption in this form of psychotherapy is that the person's drinking problems cannot be separated from the context in which they have a great impact — the family. (See Chapter 20 for a discussion of group and family therapy.)

After reviewing a large number of studies, Miller and Hester (1980) concluded that insight psychotherapy in itself is not a treatment of choice for many alcoholics. They cite the high dropout rates and the fact that it is often less effective than behavior therapy.

Behavior Therapy

Modern behavior therapists enphasize that insight will not necessarily lead to actual changes in behavior. Therefore, they work with the troubled person to achieve specific changes in behavior by directly applying various principles of learning — the same principles that help explain why the maladaptive drinking began (Nathan, 1978a).

One of the techniques used in behavior therapy is aversive conditioning (Wilson, 1978). The therapist pairs the act of drinking alcohol with a painful or unpleasant stimulus, such as an electric shock. The principle here is that, after repeated pairings, the sight, smell, or taste of alcohol will arouse aversive reactions similar to those produced by the stimulus.

Aversive conditioning can also pair drugs that produce unpleasant reactions with the act of drinking alcohol. In one common procedure, emetine hydrochloride is administered intramuscularly. This drug produces nausea and vomiting. Just prior to the onset of the nausea, the patient is given alcoholic drinks to consume and to vomit afterwards. The treatment may continue for about 30 minutes for each of five sessions while the patinet is in the hospital. Reinforcers are given on an outpatient basis (Miller & Hester, 1980).

Some therapists object to using harsh physical stimuli to produce aversion to alcohol. They claim that the individual can be guided to imagine scenes involving alcohol and to associate them with unpleasant feelings such as nausea and vomiting (Cautela, 1970b; Lazarus, 1971, 1976). The procedure is called **covert sensitization**, because the desirable conditioned stimulus (alcohol) and the unconditioned stimulus (vomiting) are imagined — not actually experienced. The goal of sensitization is to develop an avoidance response to the alcohol, so that it is no longer a desirable stimulus.

Aversion therapy has mixed results. On the average, conditioning procedures involving actual aversive stimuli have produced abstinence in 50 to 60 percent of the people who stayed with the treatment. However, the droupout rate is high because of the harshness of the procedures. Covert sensitization is less successful. About 40 percent of individuals achieve complete abstinence; however, the droupout rate is lower (Miller & Hester, 1980).

Several theories have been proposed to explain why aversive therapy is less effective than its proponents expect it to be (Redd, Porterfield, & Andersen, 1979, p. 213). The aversive stimuli may not have been strong enough to overcome the gratification of drinking. Some therapists have tried increasing the strength, but there are ethical problems involved. Clearly, the positive results obtained in treatment do not generalize sufficiently to daily life outside. Many patients may realize that aversive consequences are far less likely if they drink in their everyday environment.

A wide range of other behavioral techniques have been used to help the alcoholic. Among them are the teaching of social skills as alternatives to drinking, operant conditioning methods in which drinking (or excessive drinking) is punished and non-drinking (or moderate drinking) is rewarded, and various forms of training in self-control. Such training can be carried out without the individual being confined to a hospital and may include formal classroom instruction as well as the assignment of apppropriate reading materials dealing with problem drinking (Miller, 1978; Miller & Hester, 1980).

A great deal of controversy has centered around the claims of some behavior therapists that a goal of moderate controlled drinking is feasible. Opponents argue that controlled drinking has never been achieved and that relapses are inevitable. (Caddy, 1982; Lang & Marlatt, 1982; Marlatt, 1983, 1985; Nathan, 1978b; Nathan & Niaura, 1985; Nirenberg, 1983; Polich, Armor, & Braiker, 1981; Vaillant, 1983, pp. 217–235; Wallace, 1986).

The goal of controlled drinking is not necessarily desirable for all problem drinkers. In some instances, it may be a treatment of last resort, when total abstinence appears to be impossible. Miller and Caddy (1977) have proposed a number of guidelines for determining whether the problem drinker is a reasonably good candidate for the goal of controlled drinking. The goal is approprite when the individual

- Refuses to accept abstincence as a solution.

- Has strong external support for drinking (for example, the person is expected to drink socially with customers).

- Is in a relatively early stage of problem drinking and shows signs of physiological dependence.

Abstincence is a more appropriate goal for problem drinkers who have

- Physical health problems that making drinking dangerous.

- A strong personal commitment to achieving abstinence or strong social support for doing so.

- A history of physiological dependence.

Most programs designed to help problem drinkers achieve the goal of moderate, controlled drinking combine various therapeutic techniques. The particular combinations of such multimodal approaches depends on a thorough evaluation of the individuals seeking treatment and their particular resources and goals. Multimodal methods are not necessarily more effective than single, less costly methods, such as training in self-control (Miller & Hester, 1980, pp. 81–87).

Alcoholics Anonymous

Alcoholics Anonymous (AA) was founded in 1935 by two alcoholics: William Griffith Wilson, a stockbroker from Vermont, and Dr. Robert Holbrook Smith, a surgeon from Ohio. Since its founding, AA has become the most widely known organization for helping alcoholics. It does not depend on professional expertise. Rather, all of its activities are conducted by members. They emphasize the value of self-help, the importance of spiritual guidance, and the belief that ultimately only an alcoholic can really understand and help another alcoholic (Robertson, 1988; Zinberg & Fraser, 1985, pp. 473–479).

A basic principle of AA is that alcoholism is a physical disease — a disease that can be controlled but not cured. It is impossible for a chronic alcoholic to become a social drinker. Instead, complete abstinence is necessary. Even when they have remained dry for many years, loyal members of AA still regard themselves as alcoholics whose disease has only been arrested.

Another important principle of AA is that only alcoholics can really be effective in helping other alcoholics. This conviction instills a strong sense of loyalty and commitment to AA.

Members of AA avoid terms such as *therapy* in describing their work, since such terms imply professionalism. However, many of the activities in AA meetings resemble professional group psychotherapy and behavior therapy. Such activities include testimonials from members as to how AA is helping them keep dry. New members introduce themselves (first names only), and anniversaries of keeping dry are celebrated. There is a great deal of mutual social reinforcement for staying sober, with members acting as positive models for one another.

The principles of AA — as described in the 12 steps members must accept in order to control their alcoholism — reflect a basic religious and moral orientation. For example, two of the steps include a belief "that a Power greater than ourselves could restore us to sanity" and that our "decision [was] to turn our will and our lives over to the care of God *as we understood Him*" (emphasis in original).

As Whitley (1977) pointed out in a report of the group dynamics of weekly meetings he attended, AA uses identifiably religious resources to achieve its goal. Although AA is nonsectarian, Whitely was impressed with how similar its activities were to Methodist class meetings, an approach to group process conceived by John Wesley.

Precise figures on the success rate of AA are hard to come by. The consensus of a number of studies is that about 40 percent of those who join AA never drink again after their first attendance, about 25 percent drink occasionally and then stop within a year, and another 20 percent or so are able to give up drinking after two years (Bacon, 1973; Snyder, 1980). On the face of it, this would appear to be a remarkable achievement in comparison with the success rates of other forms of help. However, AA's success rates are based only on those who stay with the organization. Many alcoholics come to one or two meetings and never return. It has been estimated that membership in the organization does not exceed more than 10 percent of the problem drinkers in the United States. There is also some evidence that AA is most successful for individuals with a middle or upper socioeconomic status who do not have other major forms of psychopathology (Snyder, 1980, p. 145).

In a comprehensive review of studies dealing with the effectiveness of AA, Paul Bebbington (1976) found that because of methodological problems all conclusions must remain highly tentative. Some studies were statistically inadequate; others failed to include data on follow-up observations, making it difficult to assess the long-term effectiveness of the program. In addition, studies obtained data about the drinking habits of members in a variety of ways: questionnaires to family members, questionnaires to the alcoholics themselves, and interviews. Thus, it was difficult to compare the results.

Many mental health professionals have been favorably impressed with AA and have often recommended it as a form of treatment, either alone or in conjunction with other methods (Curlee-Salisbury, 1977). In an extensive and critical review of research dealing with the goals, methods, and effectiveness of AA, Miller and Hester (1980) point out that professional therapists and AA members have a great deal to learn from one another.

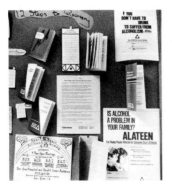

Since the founding of Alcoholics Anonymous, related programs have developed: Al-Anon, for spouses and other relatives of alcoholics, and Alateen, for teenage children of alcoholics.

Other Self-Help Organizations

Family members of alcoholics can be helped by Al-Anon, an organization of spouses and other relatives of alcoholics that offers emotional and practical support even when the alcoholic is not a member of AA or in any other rehabilitation program (Root, 1986). A parallel organization is Alateen, for the teenage children of alcoholics (Ablon, 1977; U.S. Department of Health and Human Services, 1980).

Summary

1. The term *psychocactive* refers to drugs that have a significant effect on mental processes. Two broad and closely related areas of drug disorders are (a) organic mental disorders induced by alcohol and (b) alcohol abuse and dependence.

2. The physiology of alcohol involves such factors as the rate at which alcohol is absorbed into the bloodstream under various conditions and the adverse physiological effects that may result from excessive and prolonged drinking.

3. DSM-III-R specifies the following diagnostic criteria for alcohol intoxication: (a) recent ingestion of alcohol in amounts sufficient to cause intoxication in most people, (b) maladaptive changes in behavior, and (c) slurred speech, unsteady gait, flushed face, and involuntary to-and-from movements of the eyeballs.

4. Most social drinkers show behavioral signs of intoxication when blood alcohol levels are between 0.10 and 0.15 percent. In most states, a blood alcohol level of 0.10 percent is legal evidence of intoxication.

5. Idiosyncratic intoxication occurs in certain individuals whose alcohol intake is considerably below what for most people would cause intoxication. Some theories hold that this form of intoxication tends to occur in individuals who have brain damage that lowers their tolerance for alcohol.

6. Alcohol withdrawal occurs when heavy and prolonged drinking is suddenly halted or when there is a sudden and severe reduction in the amount of alcohol that has been habitually consumed. Symptoms of withdrawal include (a) nausea and vomiting; (b) general feelings of weakness; (c) hyperactivity of the autonomic nervous system; (d) anxiety, depression, or irritability; (e) hallucinations or illusions; and (f) headache.

7. The treatment of alcohol withdrawal begins with detoxification. Further recovery depends on the proper application of special medication, the improvement of nutrition, good nursing care, and a supportive attitude. Alleviating the symptoms of alcohol withdrawal is not the same as curing alcoholism. That depends on further treatment, especially psychotherapy.

8. Delirium tremens is an especially severe form of alcohol withdrawal. It usually occurs for the first time between the ages of 30 and 40 after heavy drinking of a decade or more. Initial symptoms include nausea, anxiety, and fragmentary hallucinations. After a few days, worse symptoms, such as convulsions and terrifying hallucinations, often appear.

9. Treating delirium tremens involves treating the physical damage that heavy drinking has caused, such as infections, problems of liver functioning, inflammation of the pancreas, and severe vitamin deficiencies. Treatment is similar to that of alcohol withdrawal. Because estimates of the mortality rate from delirium tremens range from 1 to 15 percent, treatment is especially crucial.

10. Chronic alcohol hallucinosis typically involves vivid auditory hallucinations occurring after long-term and heavy drinking and in the absence of delirium.

11. Another psychological disorder resulting from long-term and heavy use of alcohol is alcohol amnestic disorder (deficits in memory), traditionally known as Korsakov's

psychosis. A distinctive characteristic of the disorder is confabulation — filling in memory gaps with imaginary events.

12. Wernicke's disease involves various pathological states, such as mental confusion and loss of motor coordination. The disease may also occur in the absence of alcoholism, since its basic cause is a deficiency of B complex vitamins. If it is treated early with massive doses of thiamine, loss of memory may be avoided. Once it is firmly established, however, its damage to the brain persists and may be fatal.

13. Long-term and heavy use of alcohol may lead to dementia — a general decline in intellectual abilities. Mild cases can be reversed, provided drinking is halted. In severe cases, intellectual deterioration may be so serious that the individual requires permanent nursing care.

14. Alcohol abuse is a continuous and maladaptive use of alcohol that persists in spite of the problems that result from its use. Alcohol dependence, commonly known as alcoholism, is more extensive and severe. Addiction (physiological dependence) is likely to develop; it is marked by an increase in tolerance for alcohol and, in more severe instances, withdrawal symptoms. Long-term alcohol abuse is very likely to result in dependence, which, in turn, almost always leads to an alcohol-induced mental disorder.

15. Alcohol abuse and dependence occur more often among the middle and upper classes in the United States than among the lower classes. About 75 percent of individuals who misuse alcohol are men and about 25 percent are women. In recent years, the proportion of women has risen.

16. About 70 percent of adults in the United States report that they use alcohol, but only 10 percent of drinkers imbibe about 50 percent of the total amount of alcohol consumed.

17. The fetal alcohol syndrome involves a cluster of disabilities found in newborn infants whose mothers drank heavily during pregnancy: mental retardation and malformations of the skeletal, urogenital, and cardiac systems. The syndrome is most apt to develop if the heavy drinking occurs during the early months of pregnancy. However, even light drinking may have adverse effects.

18. Although the rate of alcoholism is lower among individuals 65 and older, it has been rising in recent years. Loneliness, depression, and various social and economic problems make older individuals especially vulnerable.

19. Many authorities in the field of drug abuse believe that alcohol is the most abused drug in the United States and the problem is increasing. The wide range of negative social consequences includes homicide and other crimes, accidents, and disruption of family life.

20. On the basis of questionnaires involving 2000 alcoholics, Jellinek traced the development of their addiction from mild abuse to levels of dependence so severe that the people could no longer function adequately. He divided this development into four phases: prealcoholic, prodromal (development of symptoms of abuse); crucial (control of drinking out of hand); and chronic (alcohol now a way of life).

21. Many etiological factors are involved in the misuse of alcohol. Some researchers propose that innate physiological abnormalities predispose a person to be an alcohol abuser. However, the evidence for this theory remains inconclusive. Other theories point to genetic predispositions. Although family studies support the theory, they have been criticized on methodological grounds.

22. The influence of environmental events in the development of alcoholism must be considered. Social and cultural factors have an impact on biological vulnerability.

23. Traditional psychoanalytic theory proposes that alcoholism grows out of conflicts and frustrations experienced during the early years of psychosexual development, specifically the oral and anal – sadistic phases. There is little empirical evidence to support the theory.

24. Other theories hypothesize that conflict and frustration arising from a variety of sources during childhood contribute to the development of alcohol abuse and dependence. Parental neglect, harsh treatment, inconsistent punishment, and poor parental models are some of the factors involved.

25. The pathological use of alcohol may be learned through operant conditioning, with the rewards of drinking outweighing the negative consequences. If drinkers come to be labeled as alcoholics, they may increasingly try to conform to that label. Some mental health professionals and sociologists warn against a too easy acceptance of the labeling theory.

26. Learning theory often emphasizes the role of operant conditioning in the development of alcoholism. The pleasurable effects of alcohol and its ability to offer temporary escape from problems encourage the repetition of the behavior. In other words, cognitive expectations concerning the effects of alcohol arise. They may be learned through peer and parental modeling, previous experience with drinking, and exposure to advertising. Expectations develop that drinking will reduce tension and improve mood, enhance social interaction, and increase the perception of power and control.

27. Drinking patterns vary across cultures and among different ethnic groups within a country.

28. A combination of medical care and psychotherapy is common treatment for alcoholism. Behavioral therapy is often used. Aversive conditioning, a technique that is sometimes effective, involves pairing noxious stimuli with the act or thought of drinking. A wide range of other behavioral techniques have been used — for example, teaching social skills as alternatives to drinking, operant conditioning in which drinking is punished but nondrinking or moderate drinking is rewarded, and various forms of training in self-control.

29. A great deal of controversy has arisen over whether behavior therapy can teach alcoholics to become social drinkers or whether complete abstinence is essential. Some researchers and practitioners have developed guidelines for determining when the problem drinker can become a moderate drinker.

30. Many programs designed to help problem drinkers become moderate drinkers use a multimodal approach, combining various forms of psychotherapy.

31. Alcoholics Anonymous (AA) does not use mental health professionals in its program, but its methods resemble those of group therapy. AA's position is that alcoholism is a disease with no cure, and the alcoholic's only path is to abstain completely.

32. Two self-help organizations for the families of alcoholics are Al-Anon and Alateen.

15

Psychoactive Substance Use Disorders: Drugs Other than Alcohol

With genial joy to warm the soul,
Bright Helen mix'd a mirth-inspiring bowl:
Temper'd with drugs of sovereign use, t' assuage
The boiling bosom of tumultuous rage;
To clear the cloudy front of wrinkled care,
And dry the tearful sluices of despair.

ALEXANDER POPE
The Odyssey of Homer (1725)

In Chapter 14, our discussion of substance-induced organic mental disorders, substance abuse, and substance dependence focused on alcohol. We now consider various other drugs implicated in such disturbances.

Barbiturates and Other Sedatives and Hypnotics

Two of the most commonly prescribed drugs are **sedatives** and **hypnotics**. The main physiological effect is to depress the central nervous system, thus reducing excitement and agitation. The difference between sedatives and hypnotics is a matter of dosage. The drug that as a sedative has only a calming effect becomes a hypnotic in a higher dose, inducing a state similar to normal sleep. A still higher dose can produce **anesthesia** — a deep sleep from which the individual cannot be aroused until the concentration of the drug in the bloodstream drops sufficiently. Thus, **barbiturates** may be used in small doses as sedatives and in larger doses as sleeping pills. In still higher doses, they may be used as anesthetics during surgery, administered by intravenous injection (Blum, 1984, pp. 165–170).

Tolerance to sedatives and hypnotics may develop in a matter of weeks or months for individuals who have been taking them regularly. Increasing the dose as tolerance develops is highly dangerous, since the lethal dose is low. Thus, the chronic user of barbiturates is just as susceptible as the novice to taking a fatal overdose. Because barbiturates have such deadly effects in relatively small doses, they are often used to commit suicide (Jones & Jones, 1977, 99–100).

Historical Background

Barbiturates are derived from barbiturate acid, which has no sedative or hypnotic qualities. The German chemist von Bayer first obtained it from uric acid in 1862. More than 2500 synthetic barbiturates have been manufactured, but only a few are now widely used. During the early decades of the 20th century, physicians had already begun to prescribe barbiturates quite freely, even though there was some evidence that they were highly addictive. Not until the 1950s, however, did medical practitioners become convinced of their dangerous qualities. Their medical use began to decrease, but the chronic abuse of barbiturates remains a serious problem. Among the most often abused of these drugs are secobarbital (Seconal) and pentobarbital (Nembutal). Since the drugs exert their maximum effect for about four hours, they have been widely used to help people sleep. Unfortunately, they are also highly addictive (Blum, 1984, pp. 166–170; Julien, 1981, pp. 42–49; Leavitt, 1974, pp. 345–346).

Some commonly used barbiturates and their street names. In small doses, barbiturates may be used as sedatives; in larger doses, they may be used as sleeping pills. Barbiturates are highly addictive and may be lethal even in relatively small doses.

A number of nonbarbiturate sedative–hypnotics were developed with the expectation that they would be safer, for example, glutehimide (Doriden) and methaqualone (Quaalude). These drugs, however, are just as subject to abuse and addiction as the barbiturates. Quaalude has probably been the most widely abused drug in this group (Blum, 1984, pp. 169–170; Pascarelli, 1973; Schuckit, 1979, p. 22). One of the most tragic consequences of the use of these successors to the barbiturates occurred in the case of thalidomide, which had devastating effects on fetal development. Pregnant women who took the drug as a sleeping pill bore children with missing arms and legs (Snyder, 1980, p. 116).

Other drugs have been developed specifically to reduce anxiety and produce relatively mild sedation; these drugs are the so-called minor tranquilizers. (See Chapter 18 for their use in treating anxiety disorders.) For the most part, such drugs have proved to be safer than the barbiturates and their immediate successors. Among the best known are the benzodiazepines — for example, chlordiazepoxide (Librium) and diazepam (Valium). Diazepam has become one of the most widely prescribed drugs in the world. It can induce mild levels of sedation and reduce anxiety with relative safety. In higher doses, it can act as a hypnotic, inducing sleep. Like other benzodiazepines, diazepam is subject to abuse and dependence — a danger that specialists in drug therapy have recently come to appreciate (Julien, 1981). Consequently, diazepam dropped from the most highly prescribed drug in the United States to fourth place in 1983 (Baum, Kennedy, Knapp, & Faich, 1985; Molotsky, 1985).

Disorders and Treatment

The abuse of barbiturates and other sedative–hypnotics is likely to result in dependence, and sometimes organic mental disorders. The syndromes involved in such disorders include intoxication, withdrawal, delirium following withdrawal, and amnestic disorder. These syndromes are similar to those that occur in alcohol-induced organic mental disorders (see Chapter 14). The following case illustrates some of the milder symptoms of withdrawal.

> A disheveled, 27-year-old man walked into an emergency room shortly after midnight asking to be hospitalized. He stated that he was depressed and would kill himself if not admitted so that he could get a good night's rest. He was observed to be anxious and tremulous, sweaty, and had a rapid pulse. He became angry when the interviewer tried to ask him questions, denied heavy drug use, but said that he would settle for "a few pills" to help him sleep. The intern suspected drug dependence and gave a barbiturate tolerance test, which indicated daily use of 1,200–1,6000 mg. [According to the American Psychiatric Association (1980a, p. 140), the upper limit for a lethal dose of barbiturates is 3,500 to 4,000 mg.] (Spitzer, Skodol, Gibbon, & Williams, 1981, p. 72)

In treating barbiturate dependence, the drug must be withdrawn gradually so as to avoid causing severe withdrawal symptoms (Schuckit, 1979, pp. 32–34).

Cocaine

Extracted from the leaves of the shrub *Erythroxylon coca,* cocaine is an alkaloid stimulant. The shrub is cultivated mainly on the mountain slopes of Bolivia, Ecuador, Colombia, and Peru; it is also raised in abundance in Java, Mexico, and the West Indies.

Derived from the coca plant, cocaine is a powerful antifatigue drug. It is highly addictive and widely abused. The current abuse of cocaine involves a broad range of social and economic classes.

In recent years smoking cocaine instead of sniffing it has become more common. This is especially true of "crack," a cheaper, more powerful, and more dangerous form of cocaine.

Cocaine is a powerful antifatigue substance and a potent local anesthetic. It increases the heart rate and constricts the blood vessels, thus increasing blood pressure. Common psychological reactions include euphoria, excitement, hallucinations, indifference to pain, and decreased hunger (Julien, 1981, pp. 85–86; Leavitt, 1974, p. 44).

The drug is ingested in a variety of ways. Usually, it is purchased in the form of a powder or flake, which is inhaled. In recent years, smoking has become more common, especially of a cheaper and more powerful form of cocaine, known as "crack." Some researchers think smoking the drug is potentially more addictive than inhaling it. (Barnes, 1988, p. 1731)

Cocaine is also injected intravenously, especially by opiate users who mix it with heroin. As is the case for other drugs used this way, there is danger of infection from contaminated needles and syringes. The rapid spread of AIDS (acquired immune deficiency syndrome) adds a new dimension to this danger (American Psychiatric Association, 1987, p. 141; "Facts about AIDS and Drug Abuse," 1986; Gross, 1988; Kozel & Adams, 1986, p. 970; Shulman & Mantell, 1988).

The illegal production of cocaine has increased tremendously over the last decade in Peru, Bolivia, and Colombia. From time to time, open warfare erupts between law enforcement officials and those who process and sell the drug. In some instances, corrupt officials are in league with the traffickers. Some observers believe the cocaine war is being lost both at the sources of production and in the countries to which the drug is exported, especially the United States (Brinkley, 1984; Carroll, 1977; Iyer, 1985; Marshall, 1988; Riding, 1987; Sciolino, 1988; Spotts & Shontz, 1980, pp. 3–4).

Historical Background

The leaves of the coca plant have been used as mild stimulants by the Indians of South America for more than 1200 years. During the 19th century, cocaine was used medically in the United States for a variety of ailments: to cure opiate addiction, to ease stomach irritability and vomiting, to relieve depression, and as a local anesthetic.

Between 1884 and 1887, Freud wrote a series of papers on cocaine, the first of which was entitled *Uber Coca*. In these papers, he described the nature and history of the drug, his experiments with it, his own use of it, and his positive evaluation of its benefits (Byck, 1974). A number of Freud's medical colleagues who recognized the dangers of cocaine criticized his position. Although Freud defended the drug against these criticism, he discontinued all use of it shortly afterwards. In later years, he admitted that his advocacy of cocaine as a therapeutic drug had earned him serious reproaches (Roazen, 1975, p. 68).

At about the time Freud began experimenting with cocaine, the drug was beginning to receive notoriety through the works of Arthur Conan Doyle, whose master detective, Sherlock Holmes, used it avidly.

> Sherlock Holmes took his bottle from the corner of the mantelpiece and his hypodermic syringe from its neat morocco case. With his long, white, nervous fingers he adjusted the delicate needle, and rolled back his left shirt-cuff. For some little time his eyes rested thoughtfully upon the sinewy forearm and wrist, all dotted and scarred with innumerable puncturemarks. Finally, he thrust the sharp point home, pressed down the tiny piston, and sank back into the velvet-line arm-chair with a long sigh of satisfaction. . . .
>
> "Which is it today," I [Dr. Watson] asked, "morphine or cocaine?"
>
> "It is cocaine," he said, "a seven-percent solution. Would you care to try it?"
>
> "No indeed," I answered, brusquely. "My constitution has not got over the Afghan campaign yet. I cannot afford to throw any extra strain upon it." (Doyle, 1884/1900, pp. 1–2)

During the early part of the 20th century, many patent medicines and soft drinks, such as cola beverages, contained small amounts of cocaine (May, 1988). Under the U.S. Comprehensive Drug Abuse and Drug Act of 1970 (Public Law 91–513), cocaine is classified as a Schedule II drug—a substance with high abuse potential and little medical value. Its medical use is extremely limited in the United States, where it is occasionally applied as a local anesthetic. The illegal manufacture, distribution, and possession of cocaine are felonies (Blum, 1984, p. 331; Spotts & Shontz, 1980, p. 13).

For several decades in the United States, cocaine gained the reputation of being an elite drug, used mainly by well-known entertainers and the socially prominent and affluent. Because of its association with social prominence and affluence, it became the drug of choice for perhaps millions of "solid, conventional and often upwardly mobile citizens—lawyers, businessmen, students, government bureaucrats, politicians, policemen, secretaries, bankers, mechanics, real estate brokers, waitresses" (Demarest, 1981, p. 56).

As the availability of cocaine has increased, and its street price has dropped, its psychosocial and physical effects have become especially devastating. Since crack first appeared on the streets of New York, it has taken an unprecedented toll on families. This is reflected in a growing number of reports of child abuse, neglect, and the birth of children with cocaine in the bloodstream. A greater burden has thus been placed on medical centers and social service agencies dealing with drug problems (Altman, 1988; Brower, Hierholzer, & Maddahian, 1987; Kerr, 1987a, 1987b).

Disorders and Treatment

Prolonged abuse of cocaine can cause psychological and physiological dependence as well as various organic mental syndromes—for example, intoxication, withdrawal, delirium, and delusions of persecution (American Psychiatric Association, 1987, pp. 141–144).

Intoxication is probably the most immediately life-threatening. Cocaine intoxication usually runs its course in a 24-hour period. Typical physiological reactions include tachycardia (abnormal increase in heartbeat), dilation of pupils, elevated blood pressure, chills or perspiration, nausea, and vomiting. Overt behavioral reactions may include fighting, agitated psychomotor reactions, abnormally elated behavior, expressions of grandiosity, visual or tactile hallucinations, and abnormal awareness of environmental stimuli. Severe intoxication, usually resulting from large overdoses, can produce chest pains and seizures. Especially life-threatening are cardiac arrhythmia (irregular heartbeat) and paralysis of respiratory function. These are the most common causes of death in cocaine overdoses (American Psychiatric Association, 1987, p. 141; Crowley, 1987, pp. 201–202).

The immediate treatment of cocaine intoxication is aimed at supporting the cardiovascular and respiratory systems. Diazepam is often used to counteract the overstimulating effects of the cocaine. After the adverse physical effects are alleviated, the individual is usually referred to a drug treatment center for counseling to address the problem of drug abuse itself (Blum, 1984, pp. 334–337).

Amphetamines and Their Derivatives

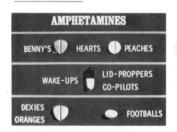

Amphetamines stimulate the central nervous system. Widely abused as a way of reducing fatigue and increasing alertness, they may lead to dependence and organic mental syndromes such as intoxication and delusions. Shown in the photo are some commonly abused amphetamines and their street names.

The main chemical action of **amphetamines** and their derivatives is to stimulate the central nervous system. They are used in a wide variety of situations to reduce fatigue and increase alertness. Some amphetamines also suppress the appetite and thus have been used, often unwisely, by individuals who wish to lose weight. Research pharmacologists have synthesized hundreds of amphetamine derivatives, many of which are readily available to physicians for prescription. Amphetamines are among the most abused drugs in our society. Those most commonly abused include amphetamine sulfate (Benzedrine), dextroamphetamine sulfate (Dexedrine), and methamphetamine hydrocholoride (Methedrine).

Habitual use of amphetamines may lead to abuse and dependence and to such organic mental syndromes as intoxication, delusions, and delirium. Physiological signs of amphetamine intoxication include tachycardia, dilation of pupils, elevated blood pressure, chills, and vomiting. Among the typical overt behavioral reactions are agitated bodily movements, unusual talkativeness, and hypervigilance (ultrasenstivity to external stimuli). Often, poor judgment and inadequate social or occupational functioning are present. Delusions usually center around suspiciousness, feelings of persecution, and similar paranoid reactions. Delirium involves a clouded state of consciousness, often manifested by difficulty in paying attention, a disordered stream of thought, disorientation as to time and place, and disturbances in perception (for example, hallucinations). Aggressive and even violent behavior may occur (American Psychiatric Association, 1987, pp. 134–138; Cohen, 1981, pp. 77–78; Jaffe, 1985, pp. 10907–1008).

Amphetamine reactions, especially those involving organic mental disorders, demand immediate medical attention and follow-up programs of psychological counseling (Schuckit, 1979, pp. 76–77). Hospitalization is necessary if the reactions clearly indicate a significant and persistent break with reality. Signs of physical pathology should be examined, and vital signs should be carefully monitored and recorded. Significantly elevated blood pressure, a prominent danger in amphetamine intoxication, should be treated immediately with appropriate drugs.

The patient should be placed in a nonthreatening, quiet atmosphere; and a careful history should be taken to determine if the person is suffering from a psychotic disorder or a major affective disorder. The person may also have been abusing drugs other than amphetamines—for example, depressants. Signs of withdrawal should therefore be checked.

Antipsychotic drugs may be used, but they should be administered cautiously and only for a brief period of time. Where anxiety is prominent, diazepam is often used. After recovery from the amphetamine crisis, the patient should be referred to a drug treatment center, which can help the person deal with drug problems. Such treatment can also disclose other psychological disorders.

Opioids

Forms of heroin, an opiate derived from morphine, which in turn comes from opium. Although now an illegal drug, some medical practitioners have argued for its legal use as a pain reducer in certain selected cases.

The **opioids**, which are narcotic drugs, include substances derived from opium as well as substances of natural or synthetic origin that have characteristics similar to those of opium derivatives. The term **opiates** is a more specific designation, referring only to drugs made from opium: morphine, heroin, and codeine (Blum, 1984, p. 53). Under certain circumstances, opioids can be valuable medical aids, especially for relieving extreme pain and related forms of distress. Unfortunately, they not only are highly addictive but can also produce severe intoxication. Our discussion of disorders involving opioids concentrates on opium derivatives, since their use generally produces the greatest physical, psychological, and social problems.

Opium is an alkaloid substance obtained from the milky juices of unripened seed capsules of the oriental poppy *Papaver somniferum*. The juices are dried and powdered into an opium base, which is used in preparing smoking opium. More often, however, the opium base is converted into a morphine base. In the United States, **morphine** has a legitimate medical use; it relieves the agonizing pain that may be suffered in highly traumatic accidents, heart attacks, or the terminal stages of cancer. The further processing of morphine yields two other opiates: heroin and codeine.

Although **heroin** is an illegal drug, some medical authorities have argued for its legal use in special circumstances, such as highly painful terminal illnesses. However, this view is very controversial (Wallis, 1984). Heroin is the most popular opiate. It produces an intense euphoria, described by some users as very much like a powerful sexual orgasm. Pure heroin is nearly 10 times as potent as morphine. **Codeine** is used in various medical prescriptions to reduce pain and in cough syrups to reduce coughing. It is most often abused in the form of cough syrup. Occasionally, however, pure codeine is used by the opiate addict. In general, the effects of codeine are milder than those of heroin and morphine.

Historical Background

The opium plant is indigenous to the Middle East and Southeast Asia. It has been used since ancient times to dull the senses, induce lethargy and sleep, and relieve pain. The Roman medical historian Cornelius Celsus, whose treatise *De rea medica* was written early in the first century A.D., described how Roman physicians used a concoction made from poppies to quiet agitated patients, especially those who suffered from insomnia (Zilboorg & Henry, 1941, pp. 68–71).

In China, for many centuries, opium was ingested as a combination of poppy juice and tea or food. This practice was apparently moderate and did not lead to addiction. During the 1600s, however, with the introduction of tobacco, the practice of smoking large quantities of opium began to spread rapidly; and serious problems of addiction developed.

During the first half of the 19th century, the Chinese government forbade the import and use of the drug. In 1840, it destroyed a store of opium that Britain had shipped to China. Britain, which was heavily involved in the profitable opium trade, then initiated what came to be known as the Opium Wars — an attempt to get China to reverse its ban on the drug. In 1842, China capitulated. By the Treaty of Nanking, it agreed to pay the costs of the wars and of the stores of British opium that had been destroyed. Britain's opium trade with China began again (Blum, 1984, pp. 56–57; Callahan, 1980, pp. 145–146).

Chinese laborers brought opium to the United States when they came West to help build the railroads. Opium smoking flourished in Chinese communities in the West, especially in San Francisco. In 1855, San Francisco passed the first law in the United States forbidding the use of opium. Over the years, a succession of federal laws, beginning with the Harrison Narcotic Act of 1914, have made the general sale and use of opiates illegal (Blum, 1984, pp. 67–68).

Patterns of Opioid Disorders

The main effect of opiates is to depress the various functions of the central nervous system and to produce a state of euphoria. Side effects include constipation, nausea, pupillary constriction (pinpoint pupils), and marked depression of the respiratory system (Leavitt, 1974, pp. 59–61).

The euphoric effects of opiates last only about four or five hours and are followed by a letdown. Thus, very early on, the user is motivated to continue taking the drug regularly, and a pattern of pathological use becomes established. As dependence increases, the body's metabolism becomes altered, requiring the user to increase the amount of the drug in order to achieve the euphoria and other desired effects. This tolerance is lost if use is discontinued for as little as one or two weeks. If the drug is then taken again at the usually large prewithdrawal dosage, the effects are that of an overdose (Blum, 1984, p. 65). This overdose may result in **opiate poisoning**, a form of acute intoxication. Signs of poisoning include shock, coma, and severely depressed respiration. Opiate poisoning often results in death. However, if it is detected promptly, the symptoms can be reversed by administration of a **narcotic antagonist**, such as naloxone. Naloxone produces reactions similar to those of withdrawal, but it also reverses respiratory depression. The use of narcotic antagonists to counter opiate poisoning is an emergency measure. The antagonists do not treat opiate addiction (Julien, 1981, p. 116).

DSM-III-R stipulates several criteria for diagnosing opiate intoxication. They apply to any opioid drug (American Psychiatric Association, 1987, p. 143).

1. Recent use of an opioid.

2. Maladaptive behavioral changes — for example, impaired social or occupational functioning, impaired judgment, feelings of general malaise, apathy, and retarded psychomotor activity.

3. Constriction of pupils, or, in cases of an overdose, dilation of pupils from a severe lack of oxygen.

4. At least one of these signs: (a) drowsiness, (b) slurred speech, and (c) impaired attention or memory.

Some fairly typical signs apply to most forms of opioid withdrawal. They include sweating, restlessness, nausea, cramps, tremors, alternating hot and cold spells, diarrhea, and fever — symptoms very similar to those of influenza. Signs of withdrawal from morphine or heroin may appear as soon as six to eight hours after the last dose. Symptoms reach a peak the second or third day, and disappear in 7 to 10 days. Withdrawal from nonopiate narcotics is different. For example, withdrawal symptoms involving meperidine, a synthetic opioid, begin more rapidly and subside sooner. In contrast, signs of withdrawal from methadone, another synthetic opioid, appear slowly, and the symptoms are often mild. Methadone is used as a substitute for opiates in the treatment of addiction.

Some mental health professionals argue that opiate dependence may be more psychosocial than physical. In the case of morphine and heroin, the most commonly abused narcotics, the majority of addicts can withdraw cold turkey. In contrast to the reactions to alcohol and barbiturate withdrawal, the reactions to heroin withdrawal are never fatal and are usually unspectacular (Weil, 1972, pp. 41–42). "It is . . . the addict's obsession with the drug experience and the expense of the habit that contribute significantly to . . . personal destruction. Some few persons have both affluence and necessary access to drugs to maintain a hidden addiction for extended periods of time. But male addicts steal and women addicts prostitute themselves when money to buy drugs is not available. . . . [This] total dependence . . . is a most destructive event" (McNeil, 1967, p. 143).

Treating Opioid Abuse and Dependence

Therapeutic Communities

The basic methods of psychotherapy for helping individuals overcome opioid abuse and dependence are essentially the same as for alcoholism (see Chapter 14). Therapeutic community programs have claimed greater success than the more conventional methods of psychotherapy. Charles Diederich, the founder of Synanon, was a pioneer in this movement (Yablonsky, 1967). Synanon communities function as communes. The residents live together, operate businesses, and share the proceeds. Vigorous encounter group sessions take place weekly; in them, members must assert again and again that they have been failures as the result of their drug-seeking behavior. Commitment to the program means a permanent dissociation from their former drug-oriented environments.

The Day Top Village is a well-known therapeutic community program designed to help individuals overcome their drug abuse and dependence. Many of the methods resemble those in conventional group therapy, but they also often include more harsh forms of intervention. In this photo one of the members is wearing a debasing sign as a "learning experience."

The Synanon program deteriorated considerably in the late 1970s because of the increasingly bizarre behavior of Diederich himself (Snyder, 1980, p. 96). However, a number of therapeutic communities have modeled themselves on the Synanon approach. Two well-known ones are Day Top Village and Phoenix House. Some of the techniques used are similar to those of conventional group psychotherapy, but the methods can also be quite harsh. People entering the community may be ridiculed and debased. Violators of the community rules face strict punishment.

Whether this therapeutic approach really cures drug addicts is debatable. Between 50 and 90 percent of the participants are rejected or quit early, and relapses are high. Indeed, many therapeutic communities have admitted that they probably cannot cure drug addiction, in the sense that residents would remain drug-free after leaving the community. Instead, residents must stay in the community to maintain abstinence. Thus, the community becomes their new life (Blum, 1984, p. 71; Brecher et al., 1972, p. 78).

Methadone Maintenance

Dole and Nyswander (1965) pioneered a therapeutic approach to controlling heroin addiction: **methadone maintenance.** Methadone is a synthetic opioid (methadone hydrochloride) that in daily doses administered orally blocks the desire to resume taking heroin after its withdrawal symptoms have disappeared. Addicts using methadone are capable of working and being self-supporting. Thus, they can leave their drug environment with its reinforcing effects, and can escape the need for performing criminal acts to obtain drugs. Requiring heroin addicts to obtain methadone treatment at legally established clinics makes it possible to monitor the dosage carefully (Cohen, 1981, p. 257).

Certain patients may have to be maintained on methadone all their lives. Others might be able to abstain from the drug eventually. Patients who have not been addicted to heroin for a long time might be able to try going without methadone for a trial period. If they relapse to the heroin habit, methadone maintenance can be reinstituted (Cohen, 1981, p. 253).

The advantages of methadone maintenance have been widely publicized. However, some mental health professionals have expressed doubts about its effectiveness in preventing the addict from returning to heroin. Others point out that since methadone itself is addictive, its use simply substitutes one undesirable habit for another and reinforces a drug-oriented approach to solving personal and social problems (Ullmann & Krasner,

Methadone is a synthetic opioid. In daily doses taken orally, it blocks the desire to resume heroin after its withdrawal symptoms have disappeared. The methadone program, carried out in special clinics, helps the heroin addict work more regularly and be self-supporting. Some critics argue that the program substitutes one undesirable habit for another.

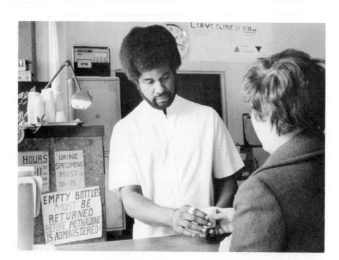

1975, pp. 467–468). Critics also argue that methadone has gradually entered illegal channels through staff members or patients of poorly managed programs (Cohen, 1981, pp. 255–257; McCarthy & Borders, 1985; Schuckit, 1979, pp. 186–187).

Recent research has produced tentative evidence that the use of another addictive drug, 1-a-acetylmethadol, (LAAM) may be successfully substituted for methadone. It has a steadier effect, its action is more delayed, and the effect lasts longer. Thus, it tends to be less reinforcing of drug-seeking behavior (Marcovici, O'Brien, McClellan, & Kacian, 1981). However, more research is needed to see if its promise can be fulfilled.

Medical and Social Issues

The controversy over methadone maintenance programs reflects differing opinions on how drug addiction should be handled medically and socially. Some mental health professionals in the United States argue for the British system, which allows physicians to administer illicit drugs regularly when prolonged attempts at cures have failed (Cohen, 1981, p. 268). Whether the British system would work in the United States is debatable, however. There is a great difference in the size of the populations and in complex social and cultural factors.

Furthermore, there is little evidence that the British system has decreased heroin use, and there are strong indications that heroin addiction has increased ("British Fight Rise in Heroin Addiction," 1985). The dropout rate from clinics is high, about 50 percent a year. Illicit sales of heroin have been traced to some of the clinics (Blum, 1984, pp. 70–71). Cohen (1981) concludes: "A large scale, open program of HM [heroin maintenance] in this country could be catastrophic. We should not be persuaded by those who think that it will solve our crime in the streets, or by those who think that we have the inalienable right to do and take what we please. Careful, small scale efforts to answer specific questions and to increase the treatment options seem worthy of consideration" (p. 272).

Phencyclidine (PCP)

Phencyclidine (PCP) was first tested in pharmacological laboratories during the 1950s for its potential use as an anesthetic, but side effects such as agitation and delirium prevented its medical acceptance (Schuckit, 1979, p. 122).

Phencyclidine is easily manufactured and has thus become one of the most commonly abused drugs (U.S. Department of Health, Education, and Welfare, 1978). Less than 5 mg typically produces a mild euphoria and a feeling of numbness; 5 to 10 mg usually results in muscular rigidity, hypertension, and a noncommunicative state; more than 20 mg generally produces conclusions and coma and can cause death (American Psychiatric Association, 1987, p. 154).

The central feature of PCP abuse is a pattern of pathological use, for at least a month, that leads to impairment in social or occupational functioning. The chronic abuse of PCP can produce dependence and various organic mental disorders, including intoxication, delirium, abnormal changes in mood, and delusions. Except for intoxication, the DSM-III-R criteria for these disorders are basically the same as for other psychoactive drugs. Guidelines for diagnosing PCP intoxication include the following (American Psychiatric Association, 1987, p. 155).

1. Recent use of PCP or similar acting substance.

2. Maladaptive behavioral changes—for example, belligerence, impulsivity, unpredictable reactions, agitated psychomotor behavior, and impaired judgment.

3. Within an hour of using PCP (less if it smoked, snorted, or injected intravenously), at least two of these signs: (a) vertical or horizontal nystagmus, (b) abnormal increase in blood pressure or heart rate, (c) numbness or diminished ability to experience pain, (d) lack of coordination in muscular movements, (e) exceptionally acute sense of hearing, and (f) impaired articulation of speech.

Treatment to alleviate the effects of PCP abuse often involves drugs that are also used to control the symptoms of other mental disorders. For example, diazepam, which is used in the treatment of anxiety disorders (see Chapter 5), is sometimes prescribed to reduce the heightened psychomotor activity and restlessness. Dilantin, a drug employed to control epileptic seizures (see Chapter 13), is sometimes used to control the convulsive reactions. When the symptoms are not severe, drug therapy may not be necessary. Instead, a quiet, nonstimulating environment may be sufficient while the reactions to PCP run their course (Cohen, 1981, p. 65; Schuckit, 1979, pp. 124–125).

Hallucinogens

Also known as psychedelic or psychomimetic drugs, **hallucinogens** can produce various forms of abnormal perceptions, especially hallucinations. Most commonly, the hallucinations are visual, but they may involve sensations of touch and hearing (Jacobs, 1987). One of the most powerful hallucinogens is LSD (lysergic acid diethylamide), a manufactured drug. Two natural hallucinogens are mescaline (from the peyote cactus) and psilocybin (from the psilocybe mushroom). (Lachter & Weisman, 1979, p. 17).

Hallucinogen Abuse and Dependence

A persistent pattern of maladaptive use of hallucinogens resulting in impaired social or occupational functioning is involved in hallucinogen abuse or dependence. Among the diagnostic signs are the inability to stop or to reduce the intake of hallucinogens. Other symptoms include recurring episodes of abnormal perceptual experiences and various abnormal emotional reactions, typically depression or anxiety that develops a day or so after the drug is ingested.

Although the chronic user of hallucinogens often develops a psychological dependence

Illicit dosage forms of lysergic acid diethylamide (LSD). The abuse of hallucinogens, such as LSD, can result in impaired social and occupational functions, as well as recurring episodes of abnormal perceptual experiences, depression, and anxiety.

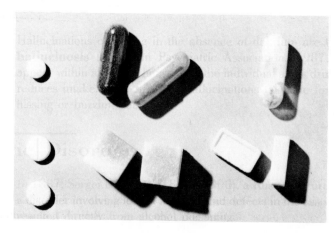

on the drugs, there is little clear-cut evidence that physiological dependence and the withdrawal syndrome occur. However, some authorities have pointed out that hallucinogens are potentially addictive, since tolerance is apt to occur after repeated use of at least some hallucinogens. Why, then, does addiction not usually occur? "Dependency . . . does not usually result because [the hallucinogenic drugs] are used sporadically and seldom on a daily basis. The impression of a powerful hallucinogenic experience lasts for several days or even months; during this time, the user rarely feels the inclination to repeat the experience. Although chemical addiction is thus avoided, marked tolerance does develop if the drug is taken as often as once a week, and the dose must then be increased to maintain the effects. When this happens most LSD users simply stop for several weeks until their capacity to respond returns" (Jones & Jones, 1977, p. 96).

DSM-III-R does not specify the withdrawal syndrome as a consequence of long-term abuse of hallucinogens. However, it does describe a number of other organic mental disorders that can occur; among them are hallucinosis, delusional and mood syndromes, and posthallucinogen perception disorder, more commonly known as flashback disorder (American Psychiatric Association, 1987, pp. 142–148).

Hallucinosis

The central feature of **hallucinogen hallucinosis** is the occurrence of abnormal perceptions. Hallucinations are usually visual, often consisting of various geometric designs, but sometimes they are auditory or tactile—all in the absence of any external stimuli. Abnormal perceptual experiences may also include illusions, such as taking the sound of the wind to be human voices; **depersonalization**—feeling detached from one's body; and **synesthesia**—the transformation of one kind of sensation into another. With synesthesia, a sound, for example, can produce the sensation of flashing lights.

Typically, various physical symptoms accompany abnormal perceptual reactions to hallucinogens. Among them are rapid heartbeat, profuse sweating, blurred vision, tremors, uncoordinated motor behavior, and abnormal dilation of pupils.

Hallucinogen Delusional Disorder

During or after hallucinosis, **hallucinogen delusional disorder** may appear. The diagnosis should not be made unless the delusions develop shortly after the ingestion of a hallucinogenic substance (American Psychiatric Association, 1987, p. 146). Typically, the delusions center around a conviction that actual events rather than drugs cause the hallucinations. For example, hallucinations may involve seeing objects or persons that the individual believes are real and dangerous. The delusions may be transitory, but sometimes they persist to the point where it becomes difficult to distinguish them from the delusions that often appear in schizophrenic and paranoid disorders (see Chapter 11). A detailed history of the individual's previous behavior and drug habits is important for making the distinction.

Hallucinogen Mood Disorder

The central feature of a **hallucinogen mood disorder** is the appearance of depression, often mingled with great anxiety, soon after the use of a hallucinogenic drug. For example, individuals may express strong feelings of self-approach and guilt, experience unpleasant tensions, become restless, and have difficulty sleeping. They may become preoccupied with thoughts of going crazy and believe that the drug has injured their brain so that they will never be normal again. Less often, their mood is similar to that of manic episodes.

DSM-III-R specifies that symptoms must persist for at least 24 hours after the individual has stopped taking a hallucinogenic drug to justify a diagnosis of hallucinogen mood disorder. In some cases the symptoms disappear within a few days, but they may last considerably longer, even to the point where the pattern is indistinguishable from that of nonorganic affective disorders. Furthermore, some individuals who already suffer from depression may take a hallucinogen in the hopes of pulling out of it, and instead make their depression more intense (American psychiatric Association, 1987, pp. 146–147). A careful report of the individual's medical and psychological history, including previously established drug habits, can help clarify the diagnosis and aid in planning proper treatment.

Posthallucinogen Perception Disorder

A particularly distressing syndrome that may develop as a result of hallucinogen use is **posthallucinogen perception disorder (flashbacks).** Heavy users of LSD are most likely to experience them, but novices may also do so. Flashbacks are recurrences of abnormal perceptions after the hallucinogen that first produced them is no longer present in the body. They can occur days or even months later. They may be spontaneous, offering no clue as to why they occur; or they may be triggered by stress, medications, or marijuana. Their spontaneousness can be a great source of anxiety (Lachter & Weisman, 1979). Reactions to hallucinogens depend not only on the specific nature of the substances themselves but also on the user's previous experience with them, the social setting in which their use occurs, and expectations concerning their effects (American Psychiatric Association, 1987, p. 179).

Helping the Victim of Hallucinogens

Various tranquilizing drugs can mitigate severe reactions to hallucinogens. Among those used most often are the phenothiazines, such as Thorazine. This treatment can relieve immediate symptoms, but it is not particularly helpful in eliminating residual effects of hallucinogens — for example, feelings of guilt and fear of recurring adverse symptoms (Jones & Jones, 1977, pp. 163–164).

In most instances, the use of tranquilizers is not necessary. Calm reassurance and a supportive environment may be sufficient to get the individual through the crisis (Snyder, 1980, p. 104). However, a program of counseling and psychotherapy is advisable to counteract residual guilt and fear and to attack the problem of drug use as a whole. Well-run drug treatment centers are usually equipped to deal with both the medical and the psychological aspects of hallucinogen disorders.

Cannabis: Marijuana, Hashish, and THC

Marijuana consists mainly of the dried leaves and flowering tops of the hemp plant, *Cannabis sativa.* **Hashish** comes from the resin produced by the flowering plant. The chemical compound responsible for the psychoactive effects of cannabis is delta−9−tetrahydrocannabinol, or simply **THC.** The Israeli chemist Raphael Mechoulam established the chemical structure of THC in 1964 (Snyder, 1980, p. 121).

Historical Background

The cannabis plant has been known for some 5000 years. It grows throughout the world, especially in Colombia, India, Jamaica, and the Middle East. It was not until the 1800s, that its use as a social drug appeared in Europe to any appreciable extent. Until the Civil War, the cannabis plant was widely cultivated in the United States for its fibers, which were used in rope and various paper products. Its psychoactive effects and intoxicating potential were practically unknown. Late in the 19th century, physicians in the United States, following the practice in Europe, began to prescribe cannabis extracts as sedatives and pain relievers. This use declined considerably early in the 20th century as the more powerful opiates and barbiturates, as well as aspirin, became available. At about the same time, marijuana preparations for recreational use began to make their way across the border from Mexico into Texas. (*Marijuana* originally referred to a cheap form of tobacco used in Mexico.)

During the 1920s, marijuana became more popular in the United States, especially in New Orleans among jazz musicians and economically marginal groups. During this period, exaggerated accounts of the dangers of marijuana began to appear in newspapers. Vivid stories described dramatically how the drug led young people to commit all sorts of crimes, including murder. In reaction, Congress passed the Marijuana Tax Act in 1937. Under the guise of being a revenue-producing measure, the act prohibited the use of cannabis as a social drug and in effect made it extremely difficult to obtain cannabis legitimately for purposes of research. In recent years, this situation has eased somewhat (Cohen, 1981, p. 15; Grinspoon, 1977, pp. 21–23; Snyder, 1980, pp. 122–123).

Cannabis Preparations

For street sales, the most commonly used parts of the marijuana plant are the leaves and flowery tops, which are ground up. Some dealers include stems and seeds, which are less potent. The flowering plant also produces a sticky resin that can be scraped away and pressed into blocks, which are called hashish, or hash, in most Western countries.

The percentage of THC in marijuana and hashish varies considerably, depending on where and how the plant is cultivated, harvested, and prepared and how pure (unadulterated) the end product is. Regardless of the THC content, the effects of cannabis occur most rapidly when the drug is smoked (Cohen, 1981, pp. 7–8; Grinspoon, 1977, pp. 200–202; Leavitt, 1974, p. 48; Snyder, 1980, pp. 121–122).

Modern pharmacological methods have produced extracts of pure THC from the cannabis plant. Chemical analogues of THC have also been developed and have been found to be especially useful in controlling the vomiting and nausea resulting from chemotherapy treatments for cancer. THC is also used with positive results to treat asthma attacks, since the drug dilates the bronchial tubes. In addition, it can help reduce the abnormal pressure in the eye associated with the most common form of glaucoma. There is some evidence that direct application of THC to the eyeball may be a better method of treatment than simply smoking marijuana, although the latter has been shown to be of value (Blum, 1984; p. 503; Julien, 1981, p. 179)

Cannabis Abuse and Dependence

In DSM-III-R, cannabis abuse is indicated by the presence of at least one of the following: repeated use in spite of persistent problems arising from that use, or recurrent use in situations that are clearly hazardous—for example driving while intoxicated from cannabis. Extreme cannabis abusers, those whose existence seems to center around using cannabis, may have difficulty holding down a job. They may lose friends, other than those in their drug circle, and get into legal difficulties involving their abuse.

Cannabis abuse, if prolonged, may lead to dependence on the drug. Among the psychosocial signs of dependence are spending a great deal of time arranging to procure the substance; taking it in increasingly larger amounts than originally intended; attempting persistently but unsuccessfully to cut down or quit; frequently being intoxicated, especially when faced with important social or occupational responsibilities; and failing repeatedly to fulfill such obligations because of its use.

Experts debate whether the abuse of cannabis can lead to tolerance, a sign of physiological dependence. The weight of professional opinion now supports the view that tolerance can occur in heavy cannabis use (Blum, 1984, pp. 495–498; Cohen, 1981, pp. 14–18; Jones & Jones, 1977, pp. 85–91).

Cannabis Intoxication and Related Effects

Some experienced smokers of marijuana, like some drinkers of alcohol, are able to monitor their intake so they stay just below the level of intoxication or at a very mild level of it. Typically, however, intoxication occurs rapidly, peaks within 30 minutes or so, and lasts about three hours. When marijuana or hashish are mixed with food or taken as a tea they become absorbed into the bloodstream more slowly and reach a lower peak blood level. However, the intoxicating effects last longer (American Psychiatric Association, 1987, p. 139; Blum, 1984, pp. 467, 474).

Among the most consistent physical effects of cannabis intoxication are increased heart rate and dilation of blood vessels in the membrane lining of the eye. Other reactions include dryness of the mouth, muscular weakness, unsteady hands, and an increased desire for sweets. There is little evidence that cannabis in itself damages bodily organs. However, smoking marijuana or hashish releases tars that over long periods may cause physical damage similar to that of cigarettes. More research is needed to see if smoking marijuana or hashish regularly and intensively may cause lung cancer (Cohen, 1981).

For moderate users who are able to monitor their intake and maintain a borderline state of intoxication, psychological symptoms of cannabis intoxication include feelings of mild euphoria, relaxation, occasional drowsiness, and increased sociability. Such effects depend not only on the potency of the drug and the amount consumed but also on one's previous experience. Novices often do not have the euphoric reactions and increased feeling of sociability, in part because they have not yet acquired the proper smoking techniques but also because they have not yet learned what to expect from using marijuana. The habitual user is able to anticipate the pleasurable effects, and the expectation itself enhances reactions to the drug.

As the level of cannabis intoxication increases, the pleasure may give way to anxiety, restlessness, confusion, and difficulty in concentrating. Some people shift rapidly from one idea to another—behavior similar to that which occurs in manic episodes (see Chapter 10). In more extreme cases, hallucinations and delusions may occur. Some individuals become paranoid in their thinking, and feelings of depersonalization may occur. Short-term memory may suffer, and individuals may develop a speech block because they cannot remember what they just said (American Psychiatric Association, 1987, p. 139; Cohen, 1981, p. 9; Leavitt, 1974, p. 48).

Cannabis Use and Driving Ability

Heavy use of cannabis may result in perceptual and cognitive impairments that can have serious consequences for driving. Among these consequences are overestimation of time intervals (events seem to occur much more slowly and last longer) and difficulty in coping with complex and rapidly changing stimuli. Although the negative effect of alcohol intoxication on driving skills has been well documented and legally established, conclusions are less firm for cannabis. The research takes two major approaches: epidemiological and experimental (U.S. Department of Transportation, 1980).

Epidemiological Studies

The focus of epidemiological studies is on determining the extent to which cannabis is implicated in traffic accidents. Information is gathered about drivers in a number of ways: (a) questionnaires on which drivers report the use of cannabis, (b) examination of driving records, (c) interviews with friends and relatives, and (d) chemical analysis of the blood to determine THC content—a technique not available until recent years. Researchers generally agree that unless the chemical analysis is included, the data are not sufficient to allow conclusions to be drawn about cannabis use and driving safety.

Chemical tests have provided more direct evidence on the relationship between marijuana use and driving safety. In one study, Reeve (1979) found that THC was in the blood specimens of 85 (5 percent) of 1792 California drivers who had been arrested because of impaired driving. However, in many instances, alcohol was also detected in the bloodstream, making it difficult to draw conclusions about the effects of marijuana alone. Furthermore, the impact of low levels of marijuana in the bloodstream is uncertain. Because of the ambiguity involved in interpreting chemical data, a report to the U.S. Congress interprets epidemiological studies conservatively: Between 1 and 5 percent of drivers using marijuana alone are likely to get into trouble when driving (U.S. Department of Transportation, 1980, p. 10).

Experimental Studies

A study under actual road conditions found that marijuana had an adverse effect on driving performance, although some of the subjects were less influenced than others (Klonoff, 1974). Hansteen and his colleagues (Hansteen, Miller, Lonero, Reid, & Jones, 1976) used objective tests of car handling on a closed driving course to assess the effects of marijuana. They found that the higher of two dosage levels did result in poorer driving.

A number of studies used driving simulators to measure the effects of marijuana on the kinds of responses necessary for adequate driving. The consensus of these studies was that marijuana interfered significantly with performance on some measures but not others (Moskowitz, Hulbert, & McGlothlin, 1976; Rafaelsen, Bech, Christiansen, Christrup, Nyboe, & Rafaelsen, 1973). In the Moskowitz study, marijuana did not have any effect on such variables as the ability to reverse steering and the use of the brake and accelerator, but it did have a negative effect on visual search tasks and recognition tasks. Some laboratory tests have found that, in sufficient doses, marijuana can affect various psychomotor and sensory elements important for driving, such as sense of time, reaction time, perceptual–motor coordination, and detection of auditory and visual signals (Jones & Jones, 1977).

Some studies have found an interesting difference between the ability of cannabis users and that of alcohol consumers to evaluate the adequacy of their driving. Dott (1972) reported that marijuana users seemed to be more cautious about deciding to pass another car.

A number of laboratory studies have examined differences in the effects of alcohol or marijuana alone and combined. As one would expect, they found greater psychological impairment when the two drugs were used together (Burford, French, & LeBlanc, 1974; Chesher et al., 1976; Julien, 1981, p. 181).

In general, laboratory studies of the effects of cannabis on driving ability show that the use of marijuana can affect the tracking and perceptual tasks called for in safe driving and that perceptual and complex mental tasks are more affected than are relatively simple motor or sensory tasks. Thus, the greater the demand for information processing, the greater the negative effect of marijuana.

Far fewer studies have tested the effects of cannabis on driving under actual road conditions, but those few support the conclusions of laboratory studies: Marijuana use by drivers, can increase the probability of traffic accidents (U.S. Department of Transportation, 1980, p. 12).

Issues of Legalization and Decriminalization

The trend in recent years has been to reduce penalties for the possession of small amounts of cannabis but to retain the severe penalties against dealers. In a number of states, the penalty for possession is now similar to that for traffic violations. This practice, called decriminalization (Cohen, 1981, p. 15; Julien, 1981, pp. 185–189; National Commission on Marijuana and Drug Abuse, 1972, p. 68), differs from legalization, a change that would place the use and sale of marijuana on the same regulated basis as alcohol (Brecher et al., 1972, pp. 535–539).

Whether cannabis should continue to be an illegal drug is strongly debated in the United States. In support of legalization, some experts point out that the enforcement of laws against the use of cannabis forces the police to abuse constitutional rights through illegal entries, searches, and seizures (Hellman, 1975). Lester Grinspoon (1977), a psychiatrist whose work centers on drug abuse, argues that making the possession and use of marijuana a criminal offense is hypocritical when one considers the harm that comes from the legal use of alcohol.

Other authorities on drug abuse, however, remain unconvinced that cannabis is safe enough to be legalized. Some prefer to emphasize educational programs that would deter use, especially in young people (Jones & Jones, 1977, pp. 275–296). Sidney Cohen (1981) concludes that just as the dangers of cannabis have been exaggerated in the past, today its possible dangers are being minimized. He predicts that legalization is likely to produce the following consequences (pp. 16–17).

1. The number of marijuana users, including daily users, will increase markedly.

2. The potency of cannabis preparations will increase.

3. Children will become increasingly involved in smoking marijuana at an early age—a trend that is already in motion.

Marijuana consists mainly of the dried leaves and flowering tops of the hemp plant, *cannabis sativa*. This plant has been known for its intoxicating effects some 5000 years. Whether it should continue to be an illegal substance is currently a subject of debate in the United States.

4. The use of alcoholic beverages will not decrease.

5. Tobacco smoking will not be affected significantly.

6. Federal and state revenues will increase tremendously. At the same time, a $2 billion legal industry of cannabis production and sales would emerge, and thousands of acres in this country would be devoted to the cultivation of cannabis.

Inhalants

In recent years, a form of substance abuse involving the habitual inhaling of commercial solvents, glues, aerosol sprays, and gases has increased. Most users are young people (aged 7 to 17) who are economically and socially deprived. Typical users also include prisoners and employees in factories where violatile solvents are available (Blum, 1984, pp. 212–213, 217; Jaffe, 1985, p. 1012).

Inhalants damage the brain, liver, kidneys, and bone marrow and cause serious irregularities in the heartbeat. In extreme instances, death may result, especially from abnormal heart functioning (Kaplan & Sadock, 1985, p. 410).

The abuse of inhalants can cause organic brain syndromes, such as intoxication and delirium. Early signs of intoxication include slurred speech and unsteady gait. As the level of intoxication increases, various signs of delirium may appear: hallucinations, mental confusion, and illusions. In some instances, the individual may become excited to the point of violence. These reactions may be relatively brief, or they may persist for several hours. There are few withdrawal reactions when inhalant use is stopped or severely reduced. However, tolerance may develop quickly (Kaplan & Sadock, 1985, p. 410).

Most teenagers abandon the use of inhalants as they grow older. Those who continue usually suffer from the same sorts of personal problems that influence the abuse of other substances.

> The treatment of the solvent-dependent youngster is difficult, and relapse is frequent despite knowledge of the physical dangers and the possibility of punitive action. The child, the family, the school, and the "gang" may have to be dealt with if any definitive gains are to be made. The patient's self image must be changed from that of a "loser" and a "loner" to that of a person who is respected and loved. Every effort should be made to reduce the youngster's demoralization. As confidence and self-respect increase, his ability to cope with the problems of everyday life begins to improve. (Cohen, 1981, p. 45)

Nicotine

The physical damage from dependence on **nicotine** that tobacco can inflict or intensify has been well documented and widely publicized. Nicotine—the main alkaloid of tobacco—is responsible for tobacco's addictive effect. Tobacco smoke releases coal tars, whose primary ingredients contribute to the development of lung cancer, bronchitis, and pulmonary emphysema—a pathological accumulation of air in the lung tissues that interferes with normal respiration. The nicotine and carbon monoxide released in tobacco smoke are important factors in causing or exacerbating coronary heart disease (American Psychiatric Association, 1980a, p. 177; American Thoracic Society, 1985; Lichtenstein & Brown, 1980. pp. 169–170; U.S. Department of Health, Education and Welfare, 1972b; U.S. Department of Health and Human Services, 1981b, 1986, p. 7). A recent report by the Surgeon General has also emphasized the addictive quality of nicotine, likening it to the addictive quality of heroin and cocaine (Byrne, 1988; Tolchin, 1988).

Nicotine Withdrawal

Typical symptoms of nicotine withdrawal include a persistent craving for the substance, difficulty in concentrating, anxiety, restlessness, irritability, and decreased heart rate. Some individuals report having gastrointestinal upsets and headaches. It is difficult to determine the extent to which the symptoms result from the physiological deprivation of nicotine and how much they are due to frustration at giving up a pleasant and psychologi-

"Does anyone mind if I smoke?"

cally reinforcing habit (Hughes & Hatsukami, 1986; U.S. Department of Health and Human Services, 1986, pp. 27–29).

Withdrawal symptoms are not inevitable, although they are highly likely to appear in long-term heavy cigarette smokers. In many instances, the symptoms begin to appear only hours after the last cigarette has been consumed. The intense craving for tobacco tends to reach a peak within the first 24 hours after smoking is stopped and then tapers off. The intensity usually diminishes greatly after several weeks. Nevertheless, the recall of pleasure associated with smoking and the inability to compensate for the psychological utility of smoking can be extremely powerful. Some smokers report that after stopping they did not feel as much at ease in social situations. Thus, smokers often return to the habit even though the physical effects of withdrawal are over.

Treatment and Prevention of Nicotine Dependence

Some people spend years periodically stopping smoking and returning to it; others stop once and never resume. Formal methods of treatment include individual and group counseling, hypnosis, and behavior modification techniques. The relapse rate is estimated to be about 50 percent in the first 6 months after the cessation of smoking and approximately 70 percent within the first 21 months. Abstention for one year is a good predictor of continuing success. (U.S. Department of Health and Human Services, 1986, pp. 33–34).

Numerous educational campaigns attempt to convince people to quit or not to start smoking at all. These programs have had some success, but many dedicated smokers do not allow disagreeable facts about physical damage to dissuade them from continuing their practice. Consequently, some mental health authorities as well as some members of the tobacco industry itself have argued for the production of low-tar and low-nicotine cigarettes. Unfortunately, heavy smokers often consume more of such cigarettes and inhale more deeply, thus defeating the purpose (Cohen, 1981, pp. 158–161).

Caffeine

During the two centuries following Columbus's first voyage, explorers, traders, and travelers discovered a variety of sources of **caffeine** and introduced them to Europe, from which they spread to other parts of the Western world. Coffee was found in Turkey and Arabia, having been brought there from Ethiopia. Tea was found in China. The kola nut was discovered in West Africa (and eventually was widely used in Western countries in cola drinks). The cacao tree (*Theobroma cacao*) was found in Central and South America, the West Indies, and Mexico. In those areas, chocolate, made from the ground roasted kernels of the cacao bean, had been a favorite drink for centuries (Brecher et al., 1972, pp. 195–196).

The main physiological effect of caffeine is the stimulation of the central nervous system and the skeletal muscles. The most immediate action is on the cerebral cortex, reducing feelings of fatigue and increasing mental alertness. The increase in alertness allows sustained intellectual efforts to be made over extended periods of time, but without the disruptive effects of such stimulants as cocaine and amphetamines. As the dosage is increased, the stimulation spreads to the brain stem and then to the spinal cord (Julien, 1981, p. 91).

Caffeine Abuse

The continual and heavy use of caffeinated beverages or caffeinated over-the-counter stimulants even after suffering toxic effects from their use is caffeine abuse. Persisting in the use of caffeine in spite of medical advice to the contrary is also caffeine abuse.

DSM-III-R does not include a diagnostic category of caffeine dependence, because there is little evidence that the drug is addictive (producing physiological dependence, tolerance, and withdrawal symptoms). However, individuals who gradually increase their intake to the point where they regularly ingest large quantities of caffeine (10 to 12 cups of strong coffee a day, for example) may experience a mild degree of tolerance (Julien, 1981, pp. 92–93).

Individuals whose use of caffeine is long term and excessive may experience a form of withdrawal syndrome, although it is unlike that experienced by users of alcohol, amphetamines, barbiturates, and the like. What they may experience is irritability, nervousness, and an inability to work as effectively as before. Some authorities on drug abuse consider such reactions signs of a withdrawal syndrome (Brecher et al., 1972, p. 203; Leavitt, 1974, p. 79). However, it is possible that these reactions are the result of frustration of psychological needs rather than changes in physiological systems.

Caffeine Intoxication

The excessive use of caffeine can produce toxic reactions known as **caffeinism**, or caffeine intoxication. Symptoms of mild intoxication include flushed face, gastrointestinal upsets, and an increased flow of urine, as well as psychological reactions such as restlessness, tenseness and nervousness, hyperactivity, and insomnia.

As with other drugs, the amount of caffeine necessary to produce adverse effects may vary significantly from person to person. However, if the levels increase to beyond a gram a day (about 10 to 12 cups of strong coffee), more serious physiological reactions may occur. Among them are muscle twitching, agitated psychomotor activity, irregularities in heartbeat, rambling thoughts and speech, ringing in the ears, and visions of flashing lights

(American Psychiatric Association, 1987, p. 138; Julien, 1981, p. 91; Leavitt, 1974, p. 79; Schuckit, 1979, p. 148).

Polysubstance Abuse

The problem of **polysubstance abuse** is increasing. As defined in DSM-III-R, the term *polysubstance* refers to the simultaneous or sequential nonmedical use of at least three psychoactive substances, excluding tobacco (and caffeine) (American Psychiatric Association, 1987, p. 185). *Nonmedical* means the recreational or social use of drugs or their use for self-medication without professional guidance. By convention, some researchers and practitioners have excluded opioids from their definition of polysubstance abuse and dependence. However, since opioids are often used with other drugs, other researchers use the terms *polysubstance*, *polydrug*, and *multidrug* less restrictively.

Cohen (1981) describes five basic patterns of polydrug abuse.

1. Depending mainly on one drug but using other drugs when they are available.

2. Changing from one type of psychoactive drug to another either to experiment with different combinations or to counter the negative effects of a particular drug. Thus, for example, some individuals may use a sedative–hypnotic to counter the effects of amphetamines or cocaine.

Table 15.1 Some Dangers of Drug Interactions

Type of Interaction	Example	Danger
Depressant–depressant	Combining alcohol with barbiturates or other sedative–hypnotics	Increased respiratory depression; possible death
Depressant–opiate	Combining alcohol with heroin	Overdosing, since both drugs depress the central nervous system; increased likelihood of death
Depressant–stimulant	Combining opiates with cocaine	Unpredictability, since the central nervous system and the metabolic systems attempt to maintain equilibrium in the presence of opposing physiological effects
Hallucinogen–stimulant	Combining LSD with amphetamine	Increased adverse reactions, since both drugs have similar chemical structures and physiological effects
Cannabis–other drugs	Combining marijuana with alcohol or hallucinogens	Increase in the depressing effects of alcohol on the central nervous system and reduction in motor coordination; also, increased liklihood of flashbacks

Sources: Schuckit, 1979, pp. 155–156; Kosten, Rounsaville, & Kleber, 1987.

3. Cycling the use of drugs. For example, some people regularly take sedatives at night and stimulants on awakening.

4. Trying another drug when the basic drug is in short supply or unavailable.

5. Consuming anything at hand

Polysubstance abuse is especially hazardous because of the possible adverse interactions between one drug and another. A particularly risky pattern is combining drugs that depress the central nervous system — for example, alcohol — with narcotics or sedative–hypnotics, such as barbiturates. (See Table 15.1 for some typical hazardous combinations).

A recent analysis of heroin deaths in Washington, D.C., illustrates the danger of combining drugs. The study was carried out between April 1979 and December 1982. The mortality rate for 1981 was the highest ever recorded. The epidemic was attributed largely to the use of heroin in combination with alcohol. In addition, heroin that was adulterated with quinine, which depresses the action of heart muscle, was also thought to be a factor (Ruttenber & Luke, 1984)

Summary

1. Sedatives and hypnotics, such as the barbiturates, are among the most commonly prescribed drugs. Their regular and excessive use may easily result in abuse and dependence. In some instances, organic mental syndromes occur — for example, intoxication, delirium, and amnestic disorder.

2. The main physiological effect of barbiturates is to depress the central nervous system. Tolerance to barbiturates can occur in a relatively short period of time. Since the lethal dose is low, the chronic user of barbiturates is just as susceptible as the novice to a fatal overdose.

3. During the 1950s, physicians became aware of the dangers of barbiturates and wrote fewer prescriptions for them. In addition, federal control increased. Nevertheless, barbiturates continue to be a danger.

4. After the dangers of barbiturates became well known, a number of nonbarbiturates sedative–hypnotics were developed with the expectation that they would be safer. One is diazepam (Valium), which has become one of the most widely prescribed drugs in the world. All the barbiturate substitutes are as prone to abuse and dependence as the barbiturates themselves.

5. The treatment of barbiturate dependence requires that the substance be withdrawn gradually to avoid severe withdrawal symptoms. Medical treatment for well-established abusers should be combined with a program of counseling and psychotherapy.

6. Cocaine is an alkaloid stimulant that is a powerful antifatigue substance and a potent local anesthetic. It increases the heart rate and constricts the blood vessels. Psychological reactions include euphoria, excitement, indifference to pain, and decreased hunger. It can be inhaled, smoked, or injected. It illegal production has increased tremendously over the last decade.

7. In the 19th century, cocaine was used medically for a variety of ailments. Freud experimented with it and used it himself but was criticized by his colleague for doing so and discontinued all use of the drug.

8. In the United States, cocaine is now classified by federal regulations as a drug with high abuse potential and small recognized medical use. A new danger is the appearance of crack, a cheaper and more potent form of the drug.

9. Prolonged abuse of cocaine often results not only in dependence (addiction) but also in various organic mental syndromes. They may include intoxication, withdrawal, delirium, and delusions of persecution. The most common causes of death in cocaine overdose are cardiac arrhythmia (irregular heartbeat) and paralysis of respiratory functions.

10. Medical treatment aims first to reduce immediate symptoms—for example, through support of the cardiovascular and respiratory systems. Once the physical effects have been alleviated, the individual can then be referred to a treatment center for counseling and psychotherapy.

11. The main chemical action of amphetamines and their derivatives is to stimulate the central nervous system. Since some amphetamines suppress the appetite, people have used them to lose weight.

12. Amphetamines rank among the most widely abused drugs in the United States, usually through overprescription or unsupervised use.

13. Habitual and excessive use of amphetamines may lead not only to abuse and dependence but also to such organic mental syndromes as intoxication, delusions, and delirium. Amphetamine reactions, especially those involving organic mental syndromes, require immediate medical attention as well as follow-up programs of psychological counseling.

14. Opioids include drugs derived from opium and also substances of natural or synthetic origin that have characteristics similar to those of opium derivatives. The term *opiates* is a more specific designation. It refers to drugs made only from opium: morphine, heroin, and codeine.

15. Even though it is highly addictive, morphine has a legitimate medical use, especially in relieving the agonizing pain that may occur as the result of traumatic accidents, heart attacks, or the terminal stages of cancer.

16. Further processing of morphine yields heroin and codeine. Heroin is highly addictive. It is the most popular abused opiate, producing a powerful euphoria.

17. Codeine is used in medical prescriptions to reduce pain and coughing. It is most often abused in the form of cough syrup. In general, the effects of codeine are milder than those of morphine and heroin. However, codeine is also addictive.

18. The opium plant is indigenous to the Middle East and Southeast Asia. Its use goes back to at least the third century B.C. in Greece. Early in the first century A.D., Roman medical historians wrote about its effectiveness in quieting agitated patients. For many centuries it was used in China to induce relaxation.

19. The main effect of the opiates on the central nervous system is to depress its various functions and produce euphoria. This pleasant effect lasts only four or five hours and is followed by a letdown. Thus, the opiate abuser is motivated to continue taking the drug regularly.

20. Withdrawal from the use of opiates results in such symptoms as sweating, restlessness, nausea, cramps, diarrhea, and other reactions similar to the symptoms of flue. Some mental health professionals have claimed that withdrawal is as much a psychosocial problem as a physical one, and that if the addict can receive sufficient emotional support, the symptoms can be tolerated. Opiate intoxication is more serious, requiring immediate medical treatment.

21. Methods of psychotherapy for helping individuals overcome opiate abuse and dependence are essentially the same as for alcoholism. Among the approaches are therapeutic community programs, which use some methods of group psychotherapy, but in a strictly controlled residential setting. Some mental health professionals are skeptical about the lasting results of these approaches. Indeed, many therapeutic community program leaders admit that once addicts are drug-free and leave the community, they often return to drug use.

22. Methadone maintenance is another method of controlling heroin addiction. Methadone is a synthetic opioid that blocks the desire to return to heroin after withdrawal symptoms have disappeared. Methadone enables the addict to be self-supporting and to leave the environment that reinforced the heroin habit. Critics of methadone maintenance programs argue that they simply replace one form of addiction with another. Methadone has also entered the illicit traffic in drugs.

23. Pehencyclidine (PCP) was first tested in pharmacological laboratories during the 1950s for its potential usefulness as a human anesthetic, but various side effects prevented it from becoming medically acceptable.

24. Small doses of PCP produce mild euphoria; increased dosages typically result in muscular rigidity, hypertension, and a noncommunicative state. Very high dosages produce convulsions, coma, and possibly death.

25. Chronic use of PCP can result in dependence and various organic mental disorders. The latter may involve such syndromes as intoxication, delirium, abnormal changes in mood, and delusions.

26. Medical treatment to allieviate the effects of PCP abuse often use diazepam. Dilantin is sometimes used to control convulsions. In many instances, however, drug treatment may not be necessary. A quiet, nonstimulating environment may be sufficient while reactions to PCP run their course.

27. Hallucinogens, also known as psychedelic and psychomimetic drugs, can produce various forms of abnormal perceptions, especially visual hallucinations. Hallucinogens can also produce anxiety and depression, especially a day or two after they are taken. Delusions and flashbacks can also occur.

28. When adverse reactions to hallucinogens are severe, various tranquilizing drugs may be used. Chief among these drugs are the phenothiazines, such as Thorazine. However, their use must be monitored carefully, since what some users think is LSD may actually be STP, a form of amphetamine. The interaction of STP with Thorazine can be fatal.

29. In many instances, the use of tranquilizers in helping the victim of hallucinogens is not necessary. Calm reassurance and a supportive environment may be sufficient. In addition, psychological counseling is advisable. In well-run drug treatment centers, both medical and psychological treatment are available.

30. The cannabis plant and its use as a psychoactive drug has been known for some 5000 years. However, it was not until the 1800s that its use as a social drug appeared in Europe to any appreciable extent. In 1937, Congress passed an act prohibiting the use of cannabis as a social drug and making it difficult for legitimate purposes of research. In recent years, this restriction has eased somewhat.

31. The criteria for cannabis abuse and dependence include repeated use in spite of persistent problems that arise from that use and recurrent use in situations that are clearly hazardous — for example, deriving while intoxicated from cannabis.

32. Although prolonged cannabis abuse can lead to psychosocial dependence, there is some debate among researchers as to whether it can result in tolerance, a prime characteristics of addiction. However, the weight of professional opinion today is that especially heavy use can result in tolerance.

33. Among the most consistent physical effects of cannabis intoxication are increased heart rate, dilation of blood vessels in the eye, mouth dryness, muscle weakness, unsteady hands, and an increased desire for sweets. The tars in marijuana may also damage the lungs.

34. Psychological symptoms of cannabis intoxication include euphoria, relaxation, occasional drowsiness, and an increased feeling of sociability. These reactions depend on how much experience an individual has had with the drug, the amount ingested, and the social setting in which its use occurs.

35. Experimental evidence supports the conclusion that cannabis can interfere seriously with driving ability. In many cases, the driver who is under the influence of marijuana has also been drinking alcoholic beverages, thus exacerbating driving problems.

36. In some areas, cannabis has been decriminalized, but some legal experts argue that it should be legalized and then licensed and regulated like alcohol. Some mental health professionals agree, but the weight of opinion is in the other direction. Some experts in the field of drug abuse argue that legalization will increase the daily use of marijuana and the potency of cannabis preparations and that children will become more involved in smoking marijuana.

37. Most teenagers who use inhalants give up the practice as they grow older. Those who continue usually have some deep personality problems that lead them to continue focusing on these easily available substances.

38. Nicotine dependence usually begins in later adolescence or early adulthood. Methods of treatment include individual and group psychotherapy, hypnosis, and behavior modification techniques. Despite the numerous educational campaigns to convince people to stop smoking, studies have shown that the relapse rate is about 50 percent.

39. Caffeine comes from a variety of sources: coffee, tea, the kola nut, and the cacao bean. Its main physiological effect is the stimulation of the central nervous system and the skeletal muscles. It reduces feelings of fatigue and increases alertness.

40. The continual and heavy use of caffeine even after suffering toxic effects from it is caffeine abuse. Also, persisting in its use in spite of medical advice to the contrary is caffeine abuse.

41. DSM-III-R does not include caffeine dependence as a diagnostic category, but heavy users may experience a mild degree of tolerance and a form of withdrawal syndrome that includes irritability, nervousness, and an inability to work as effectively as before.

42. The excessive use of caffeine can result in toxic reactions known as caffeinism, or caffeine intoxication. Symptoms include flushed face, gastrointestinal upsets, and an increased flow of urine, as well as restlessness, tenseness and nervousness, hyperactivity, and insomnia.

43. Polysubstance (multidrug) abuse and dependence has been a focus of researchers and practitioners in the field of psychoactive substance use disorders. One of the greatest dangers is the deadly interactions of certain combinations of drugs.

16

Disorders
of Childhood
and Adolescence

Children need models rather than critics

JOSEPH JOUBERT
Pensées (1842)

In previous chapters, our focus has been primarily on the abnormal behavior and experience of adults; children and adolescents also undergo psychological distress and disability. Moreover, the way they perceive their psychological problems may be quite different from how adults regard theirs. The study of mental disorders in children and adolescents is a fairly recent development. A generation ago, relatively few textbooks in abnormal psychology and psychiatry contained separate chapters dealing with those age periods. Now almost all of them do. Apart from rather isolated early contributions, such special fields of research and practice as child clinical psychology and child psychiatry can be traced mainly to the past 40 or 50 years (Eisenberg, 1969).

Initially, the various patterns of mental disorders occurring during childhood and adolescence were regarded mainly as younger versions of adult disturbances. More recently, however, mental health professionals have recognized that childhood and adolescent disorders are qualitatively different from adult syndromes, and often unique (Children's Defense Fund, 1982; Phillips, Draguns, & Bartlett, 1974; Wenar, 1982).

Identifying and Diagnosing Disorders

We start with an obvious but important observation: The situation of disturbed children and adolescents is different from that of equally troubled adults. Adults by no means always take the initiative in seeking professional help, but they often do. In contrast, children usually have neither the ability nor the inclination to do so. The identification of their disorders is inevitably filtered through the eyes of adults (Gibbs, 1982, pp. 6–7).

In recent years, the situation has changed slightly in the case of adolescents. In some communities, special services such as hot lines are available for those who need immediate help. Nevertheless, adolescents must ultimately depend on adults for the availability of professional services.

Perceptions of Parents

Although teachers, school social workers, psychologists, and law enforcement officers may on occasion serve as important figures in the process of identifying mental disorders of children and adolescents, parents usually play the paramount part (Achenbach & Edelbrock, 1984, p. 232). The judgments of parents, however, do not necessarily correspond to the children's actual disturbances.

The parents' understanding of and attitudes toward the child, their feelings about seeking professional help, and their own psychological states all shape their assessments. Consequently, there can be considerable overlap between the symptoms of children whose parents think they need psychological services and the symptoms of other children. Nonetheless, parents notice certain symptoms more readily than others do. A number of studies have demonstrated the importance of parental perceptions in identifying children's mental disorders.

Parents' understanding of their child and their own psychological state help determine whether they seek professional help for their child's problems.

Piers (1972) compared the self-concepts of children who had been referred to mental health clinics with those of children who had not. The self-concepts of the referred children were not significantly lower than those of the comparison group. However, there were differences in how parents perceived their children's self-concepts. Mothers of referred children rated their children's self-concepts more negatively than did mothers of the control group children. "Differences between the two groups of parents [were] much wider than between the two groups of children" (Piers, 1972, p. 432).

The nature of the child's symptoms may also determine whether parents seek the help of mental health professionals. Violent or destructive behavior is much more likely to be identified as requiring professional treatment than are less conspicuous expressions of personal distress (Campbell & Steinert, 1978). As a result, children's treatment agencies serve a disproportionate number of clients with grossly visible behavior problems, frequently in the form of aggression. In contrast, children who are hurting internally and suffer quietly are much more likely to be overlooked. Related to this observation is the well-known and consistent preponderance of boys over girls in treatment settings. Sometimes the ratio is as high as three to one. Although this discrepancy cannot be traced to a single cause, a searching review of the sources of these gender differences concluded that one reason for them was the more upsetting nature of boys' problem behavior from the point of view of parents, especially mothers (Eme, 1979).

The educational level of parents and related socioeconomic factors can also make a difference in parental perceptions of children's psychological problems. Some studies have demonstrated that college-educated mothers are more likely to use psychological services than are mothers with less education (Langner, Gersten, Greene, Eisenberg, Herson, & McCarthy, 1974).

Finally, the parents' own problems must be considered. Some research has demonstrated that mothers who rated their children as maladjusted also tended to express symptoms of depression. In contrast, trained observers' reports of the children's symptoms, observed in the home environment, failed to correlate significantly with the mothers' ratings (Griest, Wells, & Forehand, 1979).

The relationship between a child's behavior and the parent's perception of that behavior is complex. However, mental health professionals often overlook this complexity and instead rely on parents' accounts of their children's behavior as though they necessarily reflected objective reality. In a study by McCoy (1976), clinicians examined film clips of normal children's behavior and the parents' reports of the behavior. The clinicians relied almost exclusively on what the parents said rather than on what they themselves observed.

The clinicians (in this study), however, were doctoral students in clinical and counseling psychology and thus were relatively inexperienced. There is some evidence that experienced mental health professionals view parents' reports about their children's abnormal behavior more skeptically (Steinhausen & Göbel, 1987).

Developments in Diagnostic Classification

DSM-I to DSM-III-R   In DSM-I, psychological disturbances of childhood were hardly differentiated from adult mental disorders (American Psychiatric Association, 1952). DSM-II designated 10 diagnostic categories as disorders of infancy, childhood, or adolescence (American Psychiatric Association, 1968, p. 12). DSM-III-R listed more than 40 specific categories under the broad rubric of disorders usually first evident in infancy, childhood, or adolescence (American Psychiatric Association, 1987). (See Chapter 2 for a detailed listing of the disorders.)

A trend toward a greater differentiation of diagnostic concepts has paralleled the increase in the number of diagnostic categories. For example, the DSM-II diagnosis of schizophrenia, childhood type, is incorporated into a new classification in DSM-III and DSM-III-R: pervasive developmental disorders. Although the symptoms are similar, they do not simply represent a milder childhood version of adult schizophrenia. Rather, they are serious disorders in their own right, with their own etiology and dynamics.

Mental retardation is also included in the DSM-III-R classification of childhood and adolescent disorders. It is an abnormal deficiency in cognitive skills that begins early in life and persists throughout adulthood. Because of its complex nature and widespread social and economic ramifications, we devote Chapter 17 to this disorder.

Dimensions of Symptoms   Another important trend in classifying mental disorders of childhood and adolescence has developed out of empirical research on the interrelationship of symptoms. What types of symptoms can be observed? What types seem to occur together? What are the dimensions to which the various symptoms can be reduced? These are some of the questions such research has attempted to answer.

Some studies have shown that psychological disorders of childhood and adolescence can be placed along a continuum from internalization to externalization. Examples of **internalized symptoms** are abnormal anxiety, depression, and social withdrawal. **Externalized symptoms** include maladaptive aggression, hyperactivity, and abnormal sexual behavior. Achenbach and Edelbrock (1981), who identified this continuum, found that it accounts for more variance in childhood and adolescent disorders than does any other factor. Troubled children and adolescents tend either to suffer internally or to reveal their psychological disorders through highly visible, often aggressive behavior. Both the DSM-III and the DSM-III-R classifications recognize this distinction.

In addition to the internalization–externalization dimension, a number of other broad dimensions of symptoms have been identified: overcontrolled behavior, undercontrolled behavior, and abnormal withdrawal from the social environment (Achenbach, 1982). These dimensions form the basis for the specific disorders considered in this chapter.

Hyperactivity and Attention Deficits

In practically every grade school classroom, there are children who have trouble sitting still, whose attention jumps in momentary spurts from one object to another, and whose behavior disrupts their teacher and their classmates. In DSM-III-R, this condition is called **attention deficit disorder with hyperactivity** (American Psychiatric Association, 1987, pp. 41–43). This rather awkward label reflects the shift of focus in psychiatry and clinical psychology from the obviously disruptive nature of children's excessive movement to the presumably more basic problem of shifting attention.

Etiological Views

The consensus of investigations into hyperactive behavior is that its source is more biological than psychological. Early research hypothesized that the jumpiness and flightiness of hyperactive children was caused by minute brain damage that was difficult to detect by the available neurological techniques. This hypothesis was rather widely, if hastily, accepted, and the disorder came to be viewed as one of the several manifestations of minimal brain damage. This diagnostic category is no longer used, but the view prevails that hyperactivity and attention deficit originate in some kind of neurological abnormality. However, there is no general agreement on its nature or location (August & Steward, 1982, p. 311; Kolb & Brodie, 1982, p. 681; Quay, Routh, & Shapiro, 1987, p. 497).

Educational and Social Implications

Some children manifest an attention deficit without hyperactivity. They have trouble listening and concentrating, even though their behavior lacks the visible features of jumpiness and dramatic motor activity. They may experience learning difficulties but present fewer disciplinary problems. Consequently, their problems are somewhat less readily detected and diagnosed, and they loom less large in the professional literature.

The problems of hyperactive children affect the children's relationships with adults in and out of the classroom. Parents become exhausted and frustrated trying to keep up with the unceasing torrent of their child's activity. Teachers regard hyperactive youngsters as troublemakers and rule breakers. Confrontations with adult authority figures recur, and the children make poor progress in school subjects. All of these experiences may set the pattern for later conflict with established authorities. For example, some researchers have found that the persistence of hyperactivity and attention deficit in childhood may lead to serious antisocial behavior in adolescence (de Haas, 1986; Gittelman, Mannuzza, Shenker, & Bonagura, 1985).

On the other hand, follow-up studies seem to justify a more complex and less pessimistic set of conclusions. One team of researchers found that formerly hyperactive children still showed signs of maladaptive impulsivity during young adulthood, for example, they often moved from one locality to another without much foresight (Weiss, Hechtman, Perlman, Hopkins, & Wener, 1979). However, their jobs were comparable to those of their normal peers. A later follow-up study of young adults (aged 17–24 years) found that those who had been diagnosed hyperactive as children were not involved in a greater number of antisocial acts than a control group (Hechtman, Weiss, & Perlman, 1984). Other studies of hyperactivity in childhood found an increased activity level in adolescence, but not more antisocial behavior. Furthermore, problems that accompany the hyperactivity, rather than the disorder itself, may predict future problems. For example, hyperactivity is often associated with poor relationships with peers (Thorley, 1984). Thus, maladaptive behavior that results from hyperactivity may place the child at risk in future psychological and social development.

Issues in Diagnosis and Treatment

Diagnosis and Drugs

Some mental health professionals argue that hyperactivity and attention deficit serve as convenient but misleading labels. They allow adults to transform an interpersonal problem into a medical problem and thus to control the behavior of a heterogeneous group of children by coercive means, often drugs, that otherwise would not be tolerated. (Cápèra, Côté, & Thivierge, 1985; Salholz, Washington, & Drew, 1987; Sandberg, 1985).

Paradoxically, amphetamines, especially methylphenidate (Ritalin), rather than tranquilizers, are effective in treating hyperactive children. These stimulants substantially quiet down such youngsters and at the same time make them more alert and attentive. As a result, their schoolwork often improves (Pelham, Bender, Caddell, Booth, & Moorer, 1985).

To explain this paradox, some researchers argue that amphetamines act differently on hyperactive and nonhyperactive children (Wender, 1987, p. 60). They soothe rather than stimulate. Closer examination has shown that Ritalin produces the same effect in both groups (Loney, 1980; Whalen, 1982). It sharpens attention and enhances alertness. Therefore, random activity declines, and attention focuses on the task at hand. The tranquilizing effect is secondary to the enhancement of attention. Normal people do not need such enhancement and thus do not benefit from amphetamines, but hyperactive children do. The reduction of their abnormal motor activity is a by-product.

Critics contend that Ritalin is indiscriminately used in many situations where educational and psychological approaches would be more appropriate. Moreover, they claim that it may subtly promote the use of drugs as a cure for all kinds of problems and thereby start its users on the road toward drug abuse. Even some supporters of Ritalin concede that its use is seductive. "It is difficult to imagine feasible nonchemical interventions that can be applied at the cost of approximately 20 cents and five minutes per day and generate short-term success rates of 60 to 90 percent. As cost effectiveness increases, long-term hazards become less salient and evaluations of alternative solutions less probable" (Whalen, 1982, p. 394).

Opponents of medication emphasize that it is a unilateral solution to a multifaceted problem. Hyperactivity tends to be specific to a situation and a time. a child who is hyperactive in school may not be at home, and vice versa. Similarly, estimates of hyperactivity vary widely from observer to observer (Gittelman-Klein & Klein, 1975; Whalen, 1982). In actual situations, it is inevitable that truly hyperactive children are confounded to some extent with normal youngsters whose behavior appears to an adult observer to be excessively rambunctious.

Behavior Therapy

An increasing number of health professionals find behavior therapy a more acceptable alternative. Ayllon, Layman, and Kandel (1975) demonstrated that positive reinforcement of schoolwork greatly improved the academic performance of three hyperactive youngsters, 8 to 10 years old. At the same time, hyperactivity, which was neither rewarded nor punished, declined dramatically. Subsequent research found that positive reinforcement decreased abnormal fidgeting in school and increased compliance with instructions (O'Leary, 1980). It remains to be demonstrated whether these beneficial effects can be made to last. Furthermore, some researchers have found that cognitive–behavioral training has not been sufficiently effective in the absence of medication (Abikoff & Gittelman, 1985). Thus, more studies are needed before definitive conclusions can be drawn about the treatment of hyperactivity and attention deficit disorder (Dulcan, 1986).

Conduct Disorder

As described in DSM-III-R, **conduct disorder** is a recurrent and persistent pattern of behavior in which age-appropriate social norms are violated. In particular, the rights of other people are openly disregarded. Such behavior may involve a variety of specific antisocial acts—for example, injurious and destructive behavior, stealing, lying, and cheating. A single transgression, no matter how serious, is not sufficient for a diagnosis of conduct disorder.

Conduct disorder corresponds in certain respects to antisocial personality disorder, but it does not entail the lack of enduring emotional ties of the adult syndrome. This difference can be seen in the DSM-III-R subtypes of conduct disorder: solitary aggressive type and group type (American Psychiatric Association, 1987, p. 56). In the first type, the individual initiates aggressive behavior. It is not part of a group activity, and the perpetrator is often socially isolated. In the second type, the problem behavior occurs primarily as a group activity.

In a now classic study, Lee Robins (1966) followed a large number of children treated at a St. Louis child guidance clinic. She found that in well over half of the cases, a pattern of antisocial behavior during childhood predicted trouble with the law and subsequent incarceration during adulthood. These findings point to the importance of early therapeutic intervention to help prevent a continuing pattern of antisocial behavior.

Conduct disorders are among the most difficult conditions to treat. One of the more promising approaches has been in residential treatment settings (Van Evra, 1983, p. 323). In a Lawrence, Kansas, residential treatment center called Achievement Place, small groups of boys are placed with professionally trained parent surrogates. These adults systematically reinforce all kinds of socially appropriate behavior that many of the boys had failed to learn. With modeling of prosocial responses, intense social interaction, and opportunities for cooperative decision making with peers, Achievement Place provides a full-time therapeutic environment. The results have been encouraging (Kirigin, Wolf, Braukmann, & Fixsen, 1979).

Achievement Place, in Lawrence, Kansas, is a residential treatment center for boys. Professionally trained surrogate parents systematically reinforce socially appropriate behavior, which the boys had previously failed to acquire.

Anxiety Disorders

Under the broad rubric of anxiety disorders of childhood, DSM-III-R specifies three diagnostic categories: separation anxiety disorder, avoidant disorder, and overanxious disorder (American Psychiatric Association, 1987, pp. 58–65). The common denominator of these disorders is excessive and inappropriate anxiety and fear.

Separation Anxiety Disorder

Symptoms

According to DSM-III-R, at least three of the following symptoms must be present to justify a diagnosis of **separation anxiety disorder** (American Psychiatric Association, 1987, pp. 60–61).

A child's fear of temporarily leaving a major attachment figure may sometimes be a sign of separation anxiety disorder but does not in itself justify that diagnosis. See the text for other criteria.

1. Unrealistic fear that harm will come to major attachment figures, usually parents, or fear that they will leave and never return.

2. Unrealistic worry that some terrible event will separate the child from major attachment figures — for example, fear of being kidnapped or of being the victim of an accident.

3. Persistent reluctance or refusal to go to school in order to stay with major attachment figures.

4. Persistent reluctance or refusal to go to sleep without being close to a major attachment figure.

5. Persistent avoidance of being alone in the home; emotional upset if unable to follow the major attachment figure around the home.

6. Repeated nightmares dealing with separation.

7. Complaints of physical distress on school days.

8. Excessive stress when separated temporarily from major attachment figure or when anticipating such separation.

9. Repeated instances of social withdrawal, sadness, apathy, or difficulty in concentrating on play or work in the absence of the major attachment figure.

DSM-III-R further stipulates that the disturbance must be of at least two weeks' duration. In addition to these symptoms, children suffering from separation anxiety disorder may reveal a variety of phobias — irrational fears directed toward specific objects or situations. (See Chapter 5 for a detailed discussion of phobic disorders.) These reactions are exaggerations of fears that many children normally experience. In diagnosing them as a form of anxiety disorder, one must consider the intensity of the fears, the disabling consequences, and their appropriateness for the child of a given age.

School Phobia

Refusal to go to school is only one possible sign of separation anxiety disorder. However, because of its social and legal implications, it is usually of central importance in many cultures. Although some children may dread school and refuse to attend it without necessarily being afraid of separation from home, the overlap with separation anxiety is considerable. That overlap is reflected in the wide use of the term **school phobia** in contemporary clinical and research literature to include both conditions. We follow that practice here.

School phobia afflicts boys and girls with about equal frequency. There is no clear relationship to socioeconomic status or intelligence. Children with school phobia do not appear to be particularly unusual in other respects (Graziano, DeGiovanni, & Garcia, 1979). Moreover, not all such children are alike. Two types have been noted (Lachen-meyer, 1982, pp. 63–64). In one type, the disturbance is reasonably circumscribed, is not preceded by a history of other psychological disturbance, tends to occur in the lower grades, and diminishes gradually. In the other type, the disturbance is more pervasive and generalized. Communication between the parents and the child is disrupted, and there is a lack of understanding of the child's problem in the family. Children of this type have a poorer prognosis. Their fear and avoidance of school spill beyond the first few grades and continue to disrupt attendance and performance. As with adult phobias, the child is intensely aware of the fear but experiences difficulty in justifying or explaining it.

Some explanations of school phobia have focused on the learning of anxiety and fear. Such learning may originate in the home and be an integral part of a broader pattern of separation anxiety. For example, parental fears and insecurities may spread as the child models the parents' behavior and feelings. However, the learning may be even more direct. For example, the child may have a frightening experience at school or on the way to school and therefore may connect school with fear. Once this conditioning has been established, it may be maintained through avoidance behavior. That is, the child's refusal to attend school becomes reinforced because it helps to reduce fear and anxiety. (See Chapter 5 for the role of avoidance behavior in maintaining phobias.)

Many psychodynamic therapists who work with children suffering from separation anxiety prefer to see the entire family, although they focus on the child's unconscious wishes and fears. For example, the therapist may interpret the child's worries about the parents' health as unconscious hostile impulses and fantasies. The therapist then works through with the family the nature of the child's feelings and the parents' role in producing them. Supposedly, as insights are gained and conflicts eventually overcome, the symptoms of separation anxiety diminish by themselves.

Proponents of behavior therapy favor a more direct approach to treatment. Techniques used with adults are also applied to children. For example, desensitization procedures, in which the child pairs anxiety and fear with states of relaxation, have been successful. Behavior therapists have also used operant conditioning approaches. These approaches often incorporate a program of therapy in which going to school is rewarded with attention and expressions of care and love. Furthermore, these kinds of reinforcers are withdrawn as responses to the refusal to go to school and are redirected at responses to school attendance (Doleys & Williams, 1977; Lachenmeyer, 1982, pp. 67–69).

Overanxious Disorder

The manifestations of **overanxious disorder** closely parallel those of generalized anxiety disorder in adults (see Chapter 5). Children and adolescents with this disorder are chronically tense and beset by a multitude of fears. For example, they are worried about the future, uncertain of their behavior in the past, insecure about their present abilities, and self-conscious in a wide variety of situations. Because they often lack self-esteem, they ask for reassurance; yet it seldom comforts them. Somatic complaints may accompany this wide range of psychological distress. Overanxiety can be highly disabling, interfering with progress in school and with positive social relationships.

"Oh, to dream once more the untroubled dreams of childhood!"

Bob was a fourteen-year-old boy referred because of occasional bizarre and odd behavior in school, difficulties in learning, fearfulness, and low self-esteem. He was very guarded and tense and extremely concerned with how well he was doing. He attempted to use an extensive vocabulary in highly intellectualized discussions of various news events, seemingly to impress the examiner with his intellect and knowledge. The overall impression was of someone attempting to appear self-assured and competent to cover thinly veiled insecurity.

As soon as it became clear that he would be unable to answer many of the items or do some of the tasks, he became increasingly anxious. His speech became more rapid, he became visibly agitated, and he soon began to pace up and down. He was no longer able to concentrate, and quickly left the room, perspiring and trembling. His anxiety level had very quickly gone from barely controlled to completely out of control and disrupted entirely his capacity to function. The threat of being made to look "stupid" or inadequate was so great for him that the only way he could handle the situation was to leave entirely.

After being in treatment for a year, however, Bob had had more frequent success experiences, and his self-esteem had improved significantly. He could tolerate making some mistakes, and he was able to function for much longer periods of time.

He appeared to use obsessive-compulsive behaviors initially to maintain very precarious control of his anxiety. When stress and the level of perceived threat became too high, the behaviors were ineffectual and the anxiety surfaced. Treatment focused on efforts to reduce stress where possible and to reinforce behaviors which were adaptive for him in the face of stress.

Follow-up studies of overanxious children have established that they rarely become overanxious adults (Robins, 1966). It is not clear whether these findings attest to the effectiveness of treatment or whether they indicate spontaneous remission. At any rate, overanxiety in childhood does not mean that the individual will necessarily be burdened with it in adulthood.

Depression

DSM-III-R does not list depression as a distinct diagnostic category of childhood disorders. Yet many clinicians are impressed with the prominence of depressive symptoms in children. The past two decades have seen an upsurge in the number of writings on depression in children. As a result, a lively controversy has developed about the very existence of depression as a specific syndrome of that age period (Achenbach, 1982; Achenbach & Edelbrock, 1984, p. 228; Mullins, 1985; Petti, 1983; Wetzel, 1984, pp. 54–54). We begin by reviewing the historical development of this argument.

The traditional psychiatric view, going back to the great systematizers of the late 19th century, was that depression was exclusively a problem of adults. In fact, Emil Kraepelin thought that age of onset was one of the major differences between manic–depressive psychosis and dementia praecox (that is, schizophrenia). He asserted that depression as a psychotic syndrome typically occurred later than schizophrenia, even though children and adolescents experience feelings of depression from time to time.

Some contemporary researchers have agreed with the older view that depression does not occur before adulthood as a syndrome—an independent pattern of symptoms (Lefkowitz & Burton, 1978). Other researchers disagree. Kovacs and Beck (1977) found that depression was extremely difficult to identify in children younger than age 6, probably because the researchers relied mainly on verbal methods of assessment. However, beyond that age, they were able to increase the reliability and validity of their judgments. They concluded that, in many respects, depression in those children resembled depression found in adults (see Chapter 10). Moreover, they found teachers' judgments of depression in children were consistent with the children's self-ratings. Gittelman-Klein (1977) identified four varieties of depression in children. One of them closely resembled endogenous depression in adults—that is, it appeared without a readily identifiable environmental stimulus. The second variety was clearly linked to situations involving loss or disappointment. The third appeared in children with disproportionately wide mood swings. In the fourth variety, depression occurred together with, or as a result of, behavior problems. Further support for the validity of depression in children comes from the finding of recent studies that children of depressed parents are at greater risk of developing depression than are children of normal parents (Orvaschel, Walsh-Allis, & Ye, 1988; Weissman, Gammon, John, & Merikangas, 1987).

Various clinicians suggest that other symptoms can mask depression in childhood and adolescence (Rosenstock, Kraft, Rosenstock, Mendell, & Stubblefield, 1986; Seagull & Weinshank 1984; Wetzel, 1984, pp. 54–55). **Masked depression** includes a host of indirect symptoms, such as loss of appetite, delinquent behavior, obsessions, restlessness, passive response to praise or blame, lethargy, flat affect, and unpredictable school performance. Yet all of these complaints can occur independently. When are we justified in postulating underlying depression, supposedly masked by this baffling variety of surface manifestations? Proponents of the concept of masked depression have not always provided objective and rigorous criteria that would enable us to identify it. Nevertheless, some clinicians are convinced that indirect expressions of depression ('masked depression') deserve increasing attention (Quay, Routh, & Shapiro, 1987, pp. 518–519).

Eating Disorders of Infancy and Childhood

Pica

The persistent eating of a nonnutritive substance, such as dirt, clay, paper, or plaster is called **pica**. DSM-III-R stipulates that the behavior should continue for at least one month to justify a diagnosis. Also, other conditions that may involve the chronic ingestion of nonnutritive substances, such as autism or a physical disorder, should be ruled out. (American Psychiatric Association, 1987, p. 69).

Pica in children occurs most frequently before the age of 6. One of its greatest physical hazards is lead poisoning, especially when plaster is eaten regularly. Parasitic infestation may also occur when contaminated soil is eaten. Therge are two main theories about the origin of pica. One states that the basic cause lies in a nutritional deficiency and that this deficiency causes the child to eat indiscriminately. The other theory points to an inadequate relationship between the child and the parents, resulting in frustrated oral needs. This frustration is expressed in a chronic search for oral satisfaction. Not cited as often, but another possible cause, is chronic neglect of the child, which allows the habit to become established. In more extreme cases, sheer hunger caused by economic deprivation may be a factor (Kolb & Brodie, 1982, p. 697).

The treatment of pica involves a number of approaches. To eliminate the hazards involved in ingesting injurious substances, the physical environment should be altered and nutritional deficiencies should be corrected. Behavioral methods have also been successful. All of this, of course, requires a great deal of supervision, which may be lacking in situations of economic and cultural deprivation.

Rumination Disorder

The central characteristic of **rumination disorder**, which occurs in infants, is the repeated regurgitation of food for at least a month in the absence of nausea or gastrointestinal illness. The rumination usually begins after a period of normal eating. Associated with this behavior is weight loss or the failure to make expected gains in weight (American Psychiatric Association, 1987, p. 70).

The abnormal regurgitation usually begins between 3 and 12 months of age. At first, it may be difficult to distinguish from the normal regurgitation of food that occurs in infants. However, as the disorder progresses, its symptoms become more obvious. The infant repeatedly brings up partially digested food and seems to enjoy the activity.

The abnormal pattern of regurgitation may become complicated by the caretaker's discouragement about feeding the infant successfully. This discouragement, together with the noxious odor of the regurgitated food, can lead to the caretaker's avoidance of the child. As a result, understimulation and malnutrition may further complicate the infant's life (American Psychiatric Association, 1987, p. 70). Thus, some forms of treatment focus directly on the caretaker's attitudes and attempt to foster a more positive relationship to the infant (Kaplan & Sadock, 1985, p. 783).

Eating Disorders Usually First Evident in Adolescence

The mass media have sensitized the American public to eating disorders among adolescents and young adults. It is debatable, however, whether these disorders have actually increased over the last few decades. Eating disorders in adolescence come in two major forms: anorexia nervosa and bulimia nervosa. For a variety of reasons, adolescent girls and women in their early 20s are particularly vulnerable. Most come from upper socioeconomic groups (Fairburn, Cooper, & Cooper, 1986; Strober, 1986).

Anorexia Nervosa

In **anorexia nervosa**, food intake is severely reduced, major weight loss occurs, and various health problems result. Individuals continue to experience a desire for food, but counteract it with unrealistic and excessive dieting. They are often preoccupied with food and with an exaggerated concern about slimness. As a result, they skip meals, avoid whole categories of nutrients, and develop elaborate subterfuges to justify not eating. As one diagnostic criterion, DSM-III-R stipulates a weight loss of at least 15 percent of the original body weight. People with anorexia continue to starve past all sorts of danger points, sometimes to death.

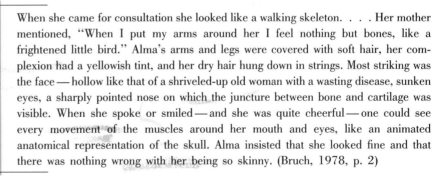

> When she came for consultation she looked like a walking skeleton. . . . Her mother mentioned, "When I put my arms around her I feel nothing but bones, like a frightened little bird." Alma's arms and legs were covered with soft hair, her complexion had a yellowish tint, and her dry hair hung down in strings. Most striking was the face — hollow like that of a shriveled-up old woman with a wasting disease, sunken eyes, a sharply pointed nose on which the juncture between bone and cartilage was visible. When she spoke or smiled — and she was quite cheerful — one could see every movement of the muscles around her mouth and eyes, like an animated anatomical representation of the skull. Alma insisted that she looked fine and that there was nothing wrong with her being so skinny. (Bruch, 1978, p. 2)

Interpretation

Clinicians assert that patients with anorexia fail to see the unattractiveness or the consequences of their dieting. What may look emaciated to others is to them pleasantly slim. So described, anorexia nervosa appears to be dieting gone wild in a culture that promotes both immoderate food consumption and the ideal of fatless beauty. Yet anorexia nervosa is not just an eating disorder. It is deeply embedded in the person's formative relationships, self-image, goals, and aspirations (Schwarz, Thompson, & Johnson, 1982).

Hilde Bruch, in her early writings (1973), capitalized on the regressive aspects of anorexia nervosa as a central dynamic. Girls who suffer from the disorder are often precocious and ambitious in all spheres but one — relationships with boys. Moreover, the cessation of menstruation (amenorrhea) often accompanies anorexia. From a psychoana-

This painting was made by an anorexic adolescent during treatment for her disorder.

lytic perspective, the disorder represents a defensive recoiling from adolescent and adult female sexuality. In her later work, however, Bruch (1986) concluded that anorexia nervosa was related primarily to developmental deficits and only secondarily to sexual conflicts. In addition to severe weight loss and amenorrhea, typical symptoms include severe disturbances in body image and disturbances in the perception and interpretation of stimuli arising in the body, especially hunger. In addition, Bruch pointed to a paralyzing sense of ineffectiveness that pervades the thinking and behavior of anorexic individuals (Bruch, 1986, p. 329).

Treatment

Psychodynamically oriented therapy has had mixed results with anorexic individuals. At its worst, it promotes insight that does not result in behavioral change. Even its proponents recognize that in anorexia nervosa the techniques must be modified to bring about desired results. These modifications all focus on the eating problem, and they involve the family and its interactions in a meal setting. The pioneering work of Minuchin and his co-workers (Minuchin, Rosman, & Baker, 1978) is an outstanding contribution to this approach. The researchers consider the family of an anorexic patient to have certain basic problems. Among them are rigidity, recourse to the same behavior patterns regardless of whether they work; enmeshment, excessive involvement in other family members' problems; and lack of conflict resolution. These problems are resolved in family sessions. In combination with reinforcement for weight gain, this procedure has produced positive results.

Behavior therapists concentrate on finding effective reinforcers to promote more normal eating and to help recover the weight lost (Garner, 1986). Direct reward for weight gain in the form of luxuries and privileges has achieved the best results. The treatment plan should not be unilaterally imposed. Instead, the therapist and the patient should negotiate a contract. These procedures are in some instances important components of a more comprehensive treatment program that includes (a) hospitalization and treatment with weight-inducing drugs, (b) behavior and insight-oriented therapy, and (c) recognition of the patient's interaction with the family as a significant factor in the development and cure of the disorder (Agras, 1984, p. 517; Brady & Rieger, 1975; Halmi, Eckert, LaDu, & Cohen, 1986; Hsu, 1986; Strober & Bowen, 1986).

Bulimia Nervosa

The central feature of **bulimia nervosa** is repeated episodes of gross overeating, often terminated by self-induced vomiting or the use of laxatives. The bulimic individual is aware that such behavior is abnormal and fears that the urge is uncontrollable. Depression and feelings of unworthiness often follow binges. Bulimia may result in serious physical problems, such as dehydration and imbalances in the chemical composition of the body's fluids. In addition, suicide is a persistent risk (American Psychiatric Association, 1980a, p. 67; Fairburn & Cooper, 1982; Fairburn, Cooper, & Cooper, 1986); Mitchell, 1986; Pope & Hudson, 1984; Russell, 1979).

The psychological aspects of bulimia are similar to those of anorexia nervosa. The bulimic individual would like to be thinner, entertains excessive and unrealistic ideals of slimness, is often anxious or depressed, and has low self-esteem. There are also differences. The bulimic individual's weight is more variable and less extreme. Often, bulimic people are only slightly underweight, although there is a great deal of variance among them. Some may be grossly overweight; others may be emaciated (Johnson & Holloway, 1988; Striegel-Moore, Silberstein, & Rodin, 1986).

Bulimia has been the focus of research and clinical attention for a relatively short period of time, so we know much less about it than about anorexia (Polivy & Herman, 1985). Like anorexia, it is typically a disorder of young women. However, it usually begins a little later than anorexia, in later rather than middle or early adolescence or even in young adulthood (Boskind-White & White, 1986). Less is known about the family situation of bulimics or about their formative relationships.

Recent developments in cognitive-behavior therapy hold promise for treatment (Fairburn, 1980, 1981, 1983; Garner, 1986; Wilson, 1986). One goal is to help bulimic individuals increase their self-control by providing them with methods of monitoring their food intake. Another goal is changing their maladaptive attitudes toward eating. The use of drugs has been effective in certain instances (Hughes, Wells, Cunningham, & Ilstrup, 1986; Walsh, Stewart, Roose, Gladis, & Glassman, 1984).

Tic Disorders

An involuntary motor movement or vocal sound that occurs repeatedly in a sudden, rapid, and stereotyped manner is a **tic**. It is usually uncontrollable.

One of the most disturbing patterns of complex tics is **Tourette's disorder,** first described in detail by the French physician Georges de la Tourette (1857–1904). It is characterized by various motor and vocal tics, although they do not necessarily occur at the same time. To warrant a diagnosis of Tourette's disorder, the tics should be well established for more than a year and repeated many times each day. The disorder begins before age 21 (American Psychiatric Association, 1987, p. 179–180). One of its most embarrassing and bizarre symptoms is the uncontrollable shouting of obscenities.

A number of plausible theories have been advanced to explain the etiology of Tourette's disorder (Grossman, Mostofsky, & Harrison, 1986). Biological explanations focus on brain dysfunction, possibly occurring in groups of nerve cell bodies (ganglia) at the base of the brain. Proponents of such theories rely mainly on drugs (for example, haloperidol) to treat the disorder.

Other theories emphasize learned anxiety and conflict, similar to that involved in simpler tics and in stuttering. Still other views suggest that Tourette's disorder involves the interaction between neurological defects — possibly genetic — and sociopsychological influences (Price, Kidd, Cohen, Pauls, & Leckman, 1985). Supporters of these theories argue that even if biological factors cause the disorder, its treatment should include psychotherapy, since individuals undergo considerable psychological distress because of their symptoms (Grossman, Mostofsky, & Harrison, 1986).

Elimination Disorders

The persistent failure to control urination is classified in DSM-III-R as **functional enuresis**. More unusual is the lack of bowel control, called **functional encopresis**. DSM-III-R lists the following diagnostic criteria for each disorder (American Psychiatric Association, 1987, pp. 83–85).

Functional Enuresis	Functional Encopresis
Repeated voluntary or involuntary voiding of urine by day or night into bed or clothing.	Repeated voluntary or involuntary passage of feces of normal or near normal consistency into inappropriate places.
At least two such events per month for children between the ages of 5 and 6, and at least one event per month for older children.	At least one such event a month for at least six months.
Chronological age at least 5 and mental age at least 4.	Chronological and mental age at least 4.
Not caused by a physical disorder such as bladder infection or seizure.	Not caused by a physical disorder such as an abnormally large or dilated colon.

Psychoanalytic Approach

Psychoanalytic theorists were the first to call attention to the long-term effects of toilet training. It is therefore not surprising that the Freudian explanation of enuresis held sway for a long time. The traditional psychoanalytic view regards enuresis and encopresis as symptoms of a more general disturbance in the parent–child relationship, especially with respect to sexual and aggressive impulses (Fenichel, 1945). Consequently, the recommended mode of treatment is intense psychotherapy. In practice, such treatment is lengthy, costly, and uncertain in its outcome.

Behavorial Approach

Mowrer and Mowrer (1938) proposed that enuresis could be eliminated by means of classical Pavlovian conditioning (see Chapter 4). They developed a procedure that would automatically awaken children every time they wet the bed. The child wore a special pad, the Mowrer blanket, that completed an electric circuit whenever it became wet. At that point, a bell would ring, and the child would wake up and presumably rush to the bathroom.

All recently developed techniques to treat enuresis assume that it results from the failure to acquire a classical conditioned response. Behavior therapy procedures aim to develop this response. In the simplest cases, this is accomplished mechanically as in the Mowrer treatment, but a more complex procedure requiring a trainer may be necessary. In general, behavioral techniques have been moderately successful (Doleys, 1977; Doleys, Weiler, & Pegram, 1982, p. 93).

Similar techniques are used to treat encopresis, except that operant conditioning techniques are more prominent (Azrin & Foxx, 1976; Doleys, Weiler, & Pegram, 1982, p. 96). These procedures entail positive reinforcement for appropriate behavior, punishment for soiling, or a combination of several other learning procedures. Rewards must predominate over punishment, and the role of punishment should be temporary and limited. Punishment may result in disruptive complications when it is used to the exclusion of rewards or when it clearly overshadows positive reinforcements.

Pervasive Developmental Disorders

Symptoms

Although DSM-III-R does not use the term *psychosis* in its classification of childhood disorders, the broad diagnostic category of **pervasive developmental disorders** includes symptoms that resemble various characteristics of psychosis in adults, especially schizophrenia (Tsiantis, Macri, & Maratos, 1986) (see Chapter 11). More than two decades ago, Creak (1963) proposed a set of nine basic symptoms that he thought were characteristic of childhood psychosis.

1. Serious disturbance of personal relationships, extending over a considerable period of time.

2. Disruption in the sense of personal identity, illustrated by grotesque posturing and self-mutilation.

3. Unusual interest in certain inanimate objects.

4. Resistance to change in the environment, and behaviors and rituals designed to maintain and promote monotony.

5. Exaggerated, diminished, or distorted sensory reactions and perceptual experiences.

6. Unrealistic and irrational fears reaching panic proportions.

7. Disruption or disturbance in normal speech development.

8. Distortion of motor behavior in the form of contortions, prolonged immobility, and the repetition of unusual motions.

9. Lag in the development of age-appropriate scholastic skills, sometimes accompanied by unusually proficient intellectual functioning in a narrow area of accomplishment.

DSM-III-R classifies pervasive developmental disorders into two groups: autistic disorder and a residual category labeled "pervasive developmental disorder not otherwise specified." Our focus is on autistic disorder.

Autistic Disorder

Leo Kanner, for many years a child psychiatrist at Johns Hopkins School of Medicine, was one of the first researchers on autism in children. He called the disorder *early infantile autism* to indicate that it was one of the earliest occurring psychological disturbances in human beings.

Leo Kanner (1894–1981), for many years a prominent child psychiatrist at the Johns Hopkins University School of Medicine, first used the term *infantile autism* to describe what DSM-III-R calls **autistic disorder.** On the basis of his clinical observations and intensive study of a small number of autistic children, Kanner reported a puzzling and dramatically deviant pattern of behavior with three central features: (a) social isolation and an inability to relate to people, (b) an unusual and intense need for preventing change in the environment, and (c) mutism (lack of communicative speech). Thus, these children shrank from social interaction, variety, and communication—experiences that normal children respond to and actively seek. Another puzzling aspect of the disorder was its age of onset. Unlike other disturbed youngsters, these children had barely experienced a period of normal development. On the basis of these symptoms, Kanner coined the term *early infantile autism* to represent one of the earliest occurring psychological disturbances in human beings (Kanner, 1943, 1949, 1962).

The DSM-III-R criteria for diagnosing autistic disorder include the symptoms reported by Kanner. However, as Table 16.1 shows, they are far more extensive. In addition, DSM-III-R specifies the following categories for when the disorder begins: infantile onset (before 36 months of age), childhood onset (after 36 months of age), and age of onset unknown.

Various studies estimate that autistic disorder occurs in about 2 to 5 children out of every 10,000. it is three to four times more prevalent in males than in females (American Psychiatric Association, 1986, p. 36; Schopler, 1982).

Mental health professionals have generated a formidable body of writing on autistic disorder. Their preoccupation with the subject is understandable, because it is so puzzling. How does a disorder so dramatic and pervasive develop in children so young? What could be responsible for so thorough a disruption of functioning at such an early age? How can this condition be reversed? Although Kanner described some of its manifestations in meticulous detail, much about the disorder continues to be shrouded in mystery.

Theories of Etiology

Kanner's original idea (1943) was that early infantile autism developed in response to a major disruption in the relationship between infants and their parents. In particular, he felt that the bond of warmth and closeness between the mother and child was deficient from the earliest period of life. Kanner used the term *refrigerated parents*—so cold and unfeeling they cast a frigid spell upon their children.

Kanner's observations were inappropriately generalized to the entire population of autistic children. Data collected since then (DeMyer, Pontius, Norton, Barton, Allen, & Steele, 1972; Rutter, Bartak, & Newman, 1971) show no significant differences between parents of autistic children and parents of normal children. Most experts on childhood autism now agree that it is not caused by a pernicious distortion of the parent–child interaction. Thus, there is no basis for blaming parents for the disorder in their children.

Additional lines of evidence support this conclusion. If parents were the agents of autistic disorder, it would run in families; however, it does not (Coleman & Rimland, 1976; Rimland, 1971). This evidence also argues against the possibility of genetic transmission and once again highlights the mysterious character of the disorder.

Some investigators of autistic disorder have sought biochemical and neurological explanations. Studies report elevated levels of serotonin, a neurotransmitter, in the brains of autistic children (Russo & Newsom, 1982). However, it is not clear that the elevation is

Table 16.1 Diagnostic Criteria for Childhood Autistic Disorder

Qualitative impairment in social interaction as manifested by

  Marked lack of awareness of the feelings of other people.

  No or abnormal seeking of comfort when distressed.

  No or impaired imitative behavior.

  No or abnormal social play.

  Gross impairment in the ability to make peer friendships.

Qualitative impairment in verbal and nonverbal communication and in imagination as manifested by

  No mode of communication.

  Abnormal nonverbal communication (for example, abnormal eye-to-eye gaze and facial expression).

Marked restriction of activities and interests as manifested by

  Stereotyped bodily movements.

  Persistent occupation with parts of objects.

  Marked distress over trivial changes in environment.

  Unreasonable insistence on following routines in precise detail.

  Markedly restricted range of interests (for example, constant preoccupation with lining up objects).

Onset during infancy or childhood as manifested by

  Absence of imaginative activity (for example, playacting of adult roles).

  Marked abnormality in production of speech (for example, volume or pitch).

  Marked abnormality in form or content of speech (for example, stereotyped use of speech).

  Marked impairment in ability to initiate or sustain a conversation with others.

At least 8 of the 16 items listed must be present, with at least 2 items from the first group and 1 each from the second and third groups. The behavior must be abnormal for the child's developmental level.

Source: American Psychiatric Association, 1987, p. 38.

unique to this group, and this uncertainty casts doubt on whether the serotonin could be responsible for the disturbance. Other hypotheses focus on genetic abnormalities that impair the functioning of the thalamus, a complex cluster of neurons (nerve cells) buried deep in the center of the brain (see Figure 12.1). Impairment of this sort disrupts the regulation of arousal mechanisms in the brain and normal responses to incoming stimuli. Another possible genetic abnormality is a failure to develop a sheath (myelin) around certain nerve fibers. In the absence of myelin, the proper transmission of stimuli is reduced. Such hypotheses imply that autism is basically a gatekeeping disorder of the brain, producing an inability to attend and to respond adaptively to the stimuli of the external world (Ornitz, 1983; Ornitz & Ritvo, 1976; Reiss, Feinstein, & Rosenbaum, 1986; Rimland, 1964).

Biological explanations tend to prevail among mental health professionals today, but support for them is certainly not unanimous. For example, Sanua (1981) argues that the biological evidence is contradictory and inconclusive. He proposes that we reopen the social and psychological avenues for explaining the disorder, suggesting that cultural and social factors deserve closer scrutiny. Sanua finds it noteworthy that in several cultural settings — for example, Latin America, the collective agricultural settlements in Israel (kibbutzim), and Africa — autism is virtually unknown. He therefore proposes that it may occur in families that are traumatized by the processes of cultural change. In his view, autism thrives in periods of rapid social transformation; it declines during periods of social stability. Sanua's formulation is certainly controversial, and he would be the first to admit that it is a hypothesis, not a demonstrated fact. Nonetheless, it deserves to be taken seriously, especially since the avenues of explanation pursued so far have not yielded definitive results.

Approaches to Treatment

For a long time, there seemed to be no effective treatment for the massive resistance to interaction with people that constitutes the crux of autistic disorder. Operant behavior therapy, first applied in the 1960s, appeared to promise a breakthrough. Lovaas (1977) concentrated on teaching autistic children first words, then phrases, and then sentences. In an immediate, practical sense, his attempts were successful. In response to positive reinforcement, usually in the form of candy, autistic children learned to emit words and phrases intelligibly and to use them appropriately. However, Lovaas's project failed to achieve its more general objectives. His autistic children did not acquire speech in the same way normal children do; nor did their acquisition of words and sentences flourish. Lovaas found that a major stumbling block was the autistic children's lack of motivation to practice speech on their own and for its own sake. The verbal communication that normal toddlers enjoy remained aversive. The children talked when they were rewarded for it, but not spontaneously (Quay, Routh, & Shapiro, 1987, pp. 516–517).

Operant behavior approaches have been used to teach self-help and social skills, with successful but limited results. Behavioral techniques have also been applied to suppress injurious and self-mutilating behavior — the scratching and the head banging that are so conspicuous and baffling in the behavior of some autistic children. Suppressing the undesirable behavior is accomplished by quickly dispensing moderate doses of physical punishment every time the injurious behavior occurs. The benefit gained may ethically justify the imposition of temporary suffering. Moreover, as with other techniques that include punishment, effectiveness in the long run depends on what follows. The effects of punishment are temporary; they can be made more permanent if desired behavior is

Ivor Lovaas is a pioneer in the use of operant conditioning to teach autistic children to speak. Here he is helping a mother learn how to work with her autistic child.

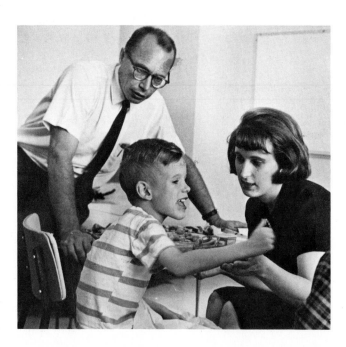

positively reinforced. Autistic children need to acquire new responses, not just shed their old ones (Rutter, 1985).

The prominence and success of behavioral approaches in the treatment of autism is something of a paradox. Not even the most outspoken advocates of behavioral explanations of abnormal behavior maintain that autism results from a deprivation in opportunities to learn or a deficit in reinforcement provided. Agreeing for the moment with the majority view that autism is an organic disorder, we must acknowledge that some of the most promising approaches to its remediation have nothing to do with its etiology.

Other forms of psychotherapy have been attempted with autistic children, despite the obvious difficulties of establishing a therapeutic relationship with them. Wenar and Ruttenberg (1976) have concluded that psychotherapy can bring about higher rates of improvement than those produced with just custodial care, but the gains are modest. The sooner treatment begins, the better the results. Preschool autistic children have a better prognosis than those in middle and late childhood.

What happens to autistic children when they grow up? Approximately one-sixth of them achieve a reasonable degree of social adjustment and manage to obtain employment, even though residual symptoms remain. Another one-sixth can live independently, but the members of this group remain socially isolated, living according to a rigid set of rules, rarely marrying or being active sexually. They lack playfulness and spontaneity and rarely display normal emotion or show evidence of experiencing pleasure. Unfortunately, approximately two-thirds remain more severely handicapped, usually unable to live independently; in some cases, they are institutionalized permanently (American Psychiatric Association, 1987, p. 36; Rutter, 1985; Sahakian, Sahakian, & Nunn, 1986, p. 285; Shapiro & Sherman, 1983).

Treatment of Childhood and Adolescent Disorders

Play Therapy

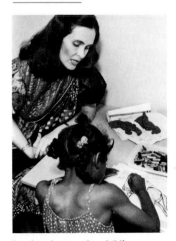

In play therapy the child's feelings may be expressed through a variety of media. In this scene at Children's Hospital in Washington, D.C., the therapist is interacting with a young girl as she makes a crayon drawing.

Therapists who work intensively with children realized early in their endeavors that it was important to go beyond words. Pioneering play therapists all agreed that a child's play is neither random nor trivial. The child's wishes, fears, conflicts, and concerns are expressed through play, sometimes directly but often indirectly or symbolically.

Person-centered therapists (see Chapter 19) observe the child at play and reflect the child's feelings through interaction in play and in speech. They put the child's feelings into words without adding their own interpretations (Axeline, 1964, 1969). With young children, the medium of this interaction is toys, supplemented by building blocks, clay, paints, puppets, and other aids to self-expression. With adolescents and preadolescents, words assume greater importance. Even then, however, psychotherapy is still less stationary than it is with adults. The client and the therapist might take a walk together, or play a game of ping-pong, or visit a video arcade in addition to talking about the client's experiences and feelings.

In child psychoanalysis, play is a substitute for the process of free association, the basic avenue for reaching the unconscious (see Chapter 19). When psychoanalysts observe and interpret play, they are concerned with the fantasies — wishful impulse representations — that the child expresses. They question, probe, and, on the basis of the information obtained, imbue these seemingly momentary and fleeting products of the child's imagination with meaning. They then convey this understanding by means of simple statements attuned to the child's level of development (Egan & Vandersall, 1982, p. 331).

In the process of understanding, the child's relationship with the analyst is explored. However, in contrast to analysis with adults, it is not assumed that most of this relationship reflects transference — the replay of the child's relationship with the parents. Rather, as Anna Freud (1966) discovered, a new experience and bond have come to the fore in the child's life by virtue of the intensive and long-term relationship with an adult, the psychoanalyst. Consequently, child psychoanalysts cannot be as shadowy and ambiguous as their colleagues who analyze adults (Egan & Vandersall, 1982).

Behavior Therapy

Behavior therapy for children and adolescents is similar to that for adults. The same principles of classical and operant conditioning constitute its historical and conceptual points of departure (Ayllon & Simon, 1982). Thus, for example, desensitization techniques are applicable in reducing children's fears. Operant learning is prominently used in developing various adaptive responses. A variant of this technique, **shaping by successive approximations**, has yielded results with children who have no meaningful speech responses. By starting with the best available approximation of meaningful speech sounds, such as ma-ma and da-da, and following them with an effective reinforcer — for example, small pieces of candy — therapists have enabled these children to take their initial steps toward the effective use of language in communication.

For children with phobic disorders or other patterns of anxiety, **observational learning** (Bandura, 1977) has been used to model positive, anxiety-free behavior. For example, the therapist who plays with a frightening dog and gives every indication of enjoying it sets the stage for the child's initial tentative approach (Ayllon & Simon, 1982, p. 285; Van Evra, 1983, p. 130).

Cognitive-Behavior Therapy

In recent years, techniques of therapeutic intervention have shifted from the control of externally visible behavior to the influencing of internal, subjective processes. This development has affected work with children and adolescents as well as adults. Proponents claim that it closely approximates the natural process of acquiring a great many cognitive skills in the course of development (Kendall & Urbain, 1982). Role playing and rehearsing responses in the environment prior to their actual application are two of the cognitive techniques used successfully with children. **Perspective taking** — learning to look at a situation from another person's point of view — is another promising approach, especially with older children and adolescents.

Involvement of Parents and Other Adults

The traditional mode of contact between therapist and parents involves regular meetings with an ancillary therapist, who is different from the person working with the child. The object of these meetings is to listen to the parents, to respond to their concerns, and to keep them informed. Most therapists take care not to violate the child's confidentiality, which is an important feature of the therapy process. Thus, they carefully refrain from divulging specific statements and expressions of feelings by the child. This approach draws a careful line between the child's problems and any personal problems of the

In family therapy with disturbed children a child's problems must be understood in the context of the family system as various members of the family express their feelings.

parents. The parents are not pressed to bring up any of their private concerns or difficulties except as they intertwine with those of the child.

Many modern child therapists believe that such carefully circumscribed participation is not enough. The most outspoken among them assert that it is futile to treat the child's problem as though it were an independent entity (Nichols, 1984). Instead, they look at the family as a system within which one or more members, often children, are chosen to express family problems. These members are designated as disturbed or sick so that the rest of the family can go about its business seemingly unaffected. The mode of intervention to counteract this state of affairs is **family therapy** (see Chapter 20). All members of the family are seen as a group. The central objective is to adjust the balance of forces in the family so as to make the disturbed behaviors of some of its members unnecessary. This objective is accomplished by opening lines of communication, by recognizing and reflecting group feelings, by interpreting particular defensive maneuvers by some or all members of the family, and by relating them to the symptomatic behaviors of the disturbed members. Beyond that, there is considerable variation in the conceptions that guide the interventions of family therapists and in the interventions themselves. Family therapy is a diverse and dynamic field (see Chapter 20). It now includes many highly articulate and persuasive proponents and is used increasingly to treat a wide range of disorders (Foley, 1984; Harris, 1984; Levant, 1987; Minuchin & Fishman, 1981; Schultz, 1984).

Effectiveness of Therapies

How well do all of these therapeutic approaches work? Which of them, if any, is demonstrably superior to others? Hundreds of research studies have addressed these questions (Levitt, 1971; Barrett, Hampe, & Miller, 1978; Ollendick, 1986). Earlier reviews found it difficult to discern any difference between children who had received therapy and those (with matching characteristics) who had not. Levitt (1971), for example, could not see any obvious advantages of play therapy over other therapeutic approaches with children. Interestingly, this result came about because such a large proportion of children with psychological disorders improved spontaneously. According to Levitt's appraisal, the outcomes of psychotherapy could not beat the high percentages of spontaneous improvement.

Casey and Berman (1985) conducted an analysis of 75 studies comparing children under 13 who had received psychotherapy with children who had not. These researchers found that therapy generally produced a significantly greater improvement than was observed in the absence of therapy. However, Casey and Berman were hard put to identify the relative effectiveness of the various therapies. Behavior therapy appeared to hold the edge over psychodynamic and person-centered approaches. This advantage, however, was explained by the fact that the objectives of behavioral interventions tend to be closely tailored to outcome measures. Therefore, it is not surprising that they achieve a higher degree of success. By the same token, the proportion of positive outcomes is understandably lower when such general criteria as relationships with peers or an improved sense of self-esteem are involved.

Research has answered the first question we posed at the beginning of the section: Therapy with children makes a difference for the better. However, we cannot state conclusively which therapy is better than the others; nor can we specify the optimal combinations of problems and modes of therapy. In this respect, the situation with children is no different from the adult situation (see Chapter 20).

Summary

1. The study of mental disorders in children and adolescents is a fairly recent development, beginning mainly in the 1920s and 1930s.

2. Referral of children and adolescents to mental health professionals depends a great deal on how parents perceive the problems. Some symptoms of psychological disturbance may be readily noticed, while others may be overlooked. The parents' own problems can also play a role in determining whether children and adolescents are referred for help.

3. Mental health professionals increasingly view the mental disorders of children and adolescents as distinct from adult disorders — not simply younger versions. DSM-III-R reflects that view.

4. The prevailing view of mental health professionals is that attention deficit disorder with hyperactivity originates in some kind of neurological abnormality. However, there is no general agreement on the precise nature and location of this malfunctioning.

5. Not all children who manifest an attention deficit are hyperactive. The ones who aren't may suffer from learning problems too, but they generally present fewer disciplinary problems that hyperactive children.

6. Follow-up studies show that some people who were hyperactive as children showed signs of the disorder in adulthood, but they were not at a significant occupational disadvantage; nor were they involved in more antisocial behavior than other adults.

7. It may be the problems that accompany hyperactivity, rather than the disorder itself, that predict later problems.

8. Some mental health professionals claim that the diagnosis of hyperactivity and attention deficit may often be made because of poor management by teachers and parents. The blanket diagnosis of a disorder then permits transforming an interpersonal problem into a medical one. This argument is tied to the use of drugs to control hyperactive behavior.

9. The most widely used drug is Ritalin, a stimulant that paradoxically reduces hyperactivity. Critics claim that it is used indiscriminately when educational and psychological approaches to the problem would be preferable. Reports of side effects have reinforced the criticism.

10. An alternative to drug therapy is behavior therapy emphasizing positive reinforcement. More research is needed to evaluate its effectiveness.

11. Conduct disorders are recurrent and persistent patterns of behavior in which age-appropriate social norms are violated. In particular, the rights of other people are openly disregarded. The pattern corresponds to certain aspects of antisocial personality disorder.

12. Conduct disorders are more difficult to treat and have a much poorer prognosis than disorders of attention deficit and hyperactivity. One of the more promising therapeutic approaches has been the programs of residential treatment centers.

13. Anxiety disorders of childhood include separation anxiety, avoidant disorder, and overanxious disorder. The common denominator of these disorders is excessive and inappropriate fear and anxiety.

14. The central feature of separation anxiety disorder is abnormal worry and fear concerning separation from those to whom the child is attached, usually the parents. The main characteristic of avoidant disorder is an excessive shrinking from being with unfamiliar people. Overanxious disorder involves a more generalized form of anxiety not related to separation from parents.

15. School phobia is one of the more familiar forms of separation anxiety disorders. It affects boys and girls with about equal frequency and occurs in various social and economic classes. Some explanations of its etiology focus on overindulgent mothers and passive fathers, both dominated by a controlling child. Others point to controlling mothers, passive fathers, and a child who is obedient at home and fearful away from home. However, some families of children with school phobia do not fit any of these patterns. Furthermore, it is not clear why these two different patterns should both result in school phobia.

16. Other explanations of school phobia focus on the role of learning in the development of anxiety and fear. The anxiety may originate at home, or it may come from fearsome situations connected with school attendance. Once the fear conditioning has been established, it is maintained through avoidance behavior.

17. Some mental health professionals focus on family relationships in the treatment of school phobia, often working with the entire family, or at least with the parents and the child. Therapists with a psychodynamic approach emphasize the child's unconscious motivations as they relate to the fears of attending school. As insight develops, the fear is presumably resolved.

18. Behavior therapy is more direct in its approach. Techniques such as desensitization have been successfully applied to children. Behavior therapists also employ operant conditioning and the positive reinforcement of school attendance.

19. Overanxious disorder is characterized by chronic tension. Children suffering from this disorder constantly seek reassurance, but it seldom comforts them.

20. Children tend to outgrow overanxious disorder and become reasonably normal adults.

21. Depression is not listed in DSM-III-R as a distinct diagnostic category of childhood disorders. However, clinicians have become increasingly impressed with the prominence of depressive symptoms in children.

22. Some clinicians suggest that the reason depression is sometimes not recognized as a childhood disorder is because it is masked by other symptoms — for example, loss of appetite, lack of interest in school, restlessness, and passive response to praise.

23. Eating disorders in infancy and childhood include pica, the persistent eating of a nonnutritive substance, and rumination disorder, repeated regurgitation of food. The treatment of pica may involve altering the physical environment so that harmful substances will not be around; using behavioral methods, including rewards for not eating harmful substances; and using parental modeling to show the proper choices of substances to be eaten.

24. Anorexia nervosa and bulimia nervosa occur most often in adolescent girls and women in their early 20s. In anorexia, food intake is severely reduced, major weight loss occurs, and various health problems result. In bulimia, excessive food intake in the form of binges, followed by self-induced vomiting, is a typical characteristic.

25. People suffering from anorexia have an exaggerated concern with slimness through unrealistic dieting. Self-perception of the body is often at great variance with what others see. Anorexia nervosa is deeply embedded in the person's formative relationships, self-image, goals, aspirations, and cultural expectations.

26. Psychoanalytic perspectives emphasize that anorexia represents a defensive retreat from adolescent and adult sexuality. Treatment based on psychoanalytic theories emphasizes the attainment of self-understanding.

27. Modifications of traditional psychoanalytic approaches consider the family of the anorexic patient as part of the therapeutic effort. The basic problems the patient and the family must explore are the persistence of behavioral patterns regardless of whether they work (rigidity), excessive involvement in one another's problems (enmeshment), and lack of conflict resolution. Resolution of these problems has been successful in helping people overcome anorexia nervosa.

28. Behavior therapy concentrates on changing the anorexic's behavior by finding reinforcers that promote normal eating and help the individual recover the weight loss. Such procedures can be components of a more comprehensive treatment program: hospitalization and treatment with weigh-inducing drugs, behavioral and insight-oriented therapy, and recognition that the patient's interaction with the family as a significant factor in the development and cure of the disorder.

29. The psychological aspects of bulimia are similar to those of anorexia: the desire to be thin, unrealistic concepts of slimness, anxiety, social and cultural pressures, depression, and low self-esteem. However, bulimic individuals are often only slightly underweight and in some cases may be overweight. Bulimia is typically a disorder of young women, but it usually begins somewhat later than anorexia.

30. Treatment of bulimia is similar to that of anorexia. Behavioral and cognitive methods have been successful, and combining them with insight therapy has been effective as well. Therapeutic goals include changing maladaptive attitudes toward food and increasing self-control by monitoring food intake. In certain instances drugs are used.

31. Tics are involuntary motor movements or vocal sounds that occur repeatedly in a sudden, rapid, and stereotyped manner. One of the most disturbing patterns of complex tics is Tourette's disorder. Explanations of its etiology include brain dysfunction as a primary cause. Learning anxiety and conflict, anger and guilt, and social alienation are possible psychosocial factors that may interact with biological causes. Treatment focuses on these psychological and social influences.

32. DSM-III-R classifies the persistent failure of children to control urination as functional enuresis. The disorder of bowel control is called functional encopresis. Traditional psychoanalytic theory explains such disorders as symptoms of a more general disturbance in parent–child relationships. Psychotherapy aims at improving this relationship.

33. The earliest approach of behavior therapy to elimination disorder used Pavlovian (classical) conditioning. Behavior therapy now includes positive reinforcement for appropriate behavior, as well as other operant conditioning techniques. The prevailing view of behavior therapists is that rewards must predominate over punishment, and that punishment must be temporary and limited if it is used at all. Punishment may result in disruptive complications and actually may intensify disorder.

34. As classified in DSM-III-R, pervasive developmental disorders represent what in more traditional terms was called childhood psychosis. The most prominent and troubling of these disturbances is autistic disorder.

35. Autistic disorder was first called early infantile autism, a term invented by child psychiatrist Leo Kanner in his pioneering work on the disorder. DSM-III-R includes the following symptoms of autistic disorder: social isolation and inability to relate to people, unusual and intense need to prevent change in the environment, and lack of communicative speech. Typically, such symptoms appear very early in life after a brief period of normal development.

36. Kanner theorized that early infantile autism developed because the bond of warmth and closeness between the mother and child was deficient early in life. Kanner's observations were inappropriately generalized to the entire population of autistic children.

37. Some investigators have explained the disorder on the basis of abnormal biochemical and neurological processes in the brain. This explanation prevails today.

38. The most successful therapeutic approach to autistic disorder uses operant conditioning. This approach emphasizes the shaping of verbal behavior and related normal reactions through rewards for the right responses. Operant conditioning has also been used to teach self-help and social skills. Another goal of therapy has been to eliminate self-injurious behavior, such as head banging. Outcomes have been successful but limited.

39. What happens to autistic children when they grow up? About one-sixth achieve a reasonable degree of social adjustment; another one-sixth can live independently but remain socially isolated; and the remaining two-thirds remain severely handicapped, often needing institutional care.

40. Recent research indicates that therapy for children and adolescents generally results in a significantly greater improvement than no therapy. There are no conclusive answers to the question of whether one method is superior to another. However, most therapists agree that for many children it is important to go beyond words, as in play therapy.

17

**Mental
Retardation**

The final phases of this "century
of decision" for those who are
mentally retarded will depend on
what image, in the end, is the guide
to public action.

KEVIN PACKARD AND BART LAVECK
"Public Attitudes" **(1976)**

The various patterns of abnormal behavior and experience we have discussed in previous chapters are often marked by a distinct departure from the quality of intellectual performance displayed prior to the onset of the disorder. In contrast, the subject of this chapter — mental retardation — does not represent a decline in previously established cognitive skills. Rather, it reflects an abnormal deficiency that begins very early in life.

The term **mental retardation** is simply a convenient, all-embracing designation for particular patterns of subaverage intellectual functioning that have certain features in common. The patterns may vary widely in their specific manifestations and etiology. Taken as a whole, however, mental retardation is probably the single largest category of lifelong handicaps affecting the populations of developed countries (Baird & Sadovnick, 1985).

Mentally retarded individuals are especially vulnerable to emotional and social problems stemming from the frustration and conflict they encounter in their experiences with people who not only perform so much better intellectually but who also fail to understand them or give them social and emotional support. Depression, loneliness, humiliation, and poor self-esteem accompany those experiences (Benson, Reiss, Smith, & Laman, 1985; Luftig, 1988; Reiss & Benson, 1985; Reynolds & Baker, 1988). Appropriate forms of education, training, and personal attention, including psychotherapy, can do much to help many mentally retarded individuals handle such problems adaptively and live useful lives in spite of their cognitive limitations.

Defining and Classifying Mental Retardation

As defined in DSM-III-R, the criteria for diagnosing mental retardation are (a) subaverage general intellectual functioning; (b) concurrent defects or other impairments in adaptive behavior, taking into consideration the individual's age; and (c) onset before the age of 18 (American Psychiatric Association, 1987, pp. 31–32). These criteria agree essentially with those adopted by the American Association on Mental Deficiency (AAMD), the most widely known professional organization devoted primarily to the study of mental retardation (Grossman, 1983).

Subaverage Intellectual Functioning

DSM-III-R defines **subnormal general intellectual functioning** as an IQ score of approximately 70 or less on a standardized individual (clinical) intelligence test, such as the Stanford–Binet scale or the Wechsler scales (Matarazzo, 1972; Thorndike, Hagen, &

| Table 17.1 Degrees of Severity of Mental Retardation |||
Degree of Severity	IQ	Frequency (Approximate Percentage)
Mild	50–55 to approximately 70	85
Moderate	35–40 to 50–55	10
Severe	20–25 to 35–40	3–4
Profound	Below 20 or 25	1–2

The fourth edition (1986) of the Stanford–Binet Intelligence Scale uses a numerical index called standard age score (SAS) rather than IQ to designate levels of intellectual ability. The SAS distribution corresponds closely to the distributions of IQs derived from such individual intelligence tests as the Wechsler Adult Intelligence Scale–Revised (WAIS-R) and the revised Wechsler Intelligence Scale for Children (WISC). For example, in the Stanford–Binet scale, the SAS level for mental retardation is 67 and below; in the WAIS-R the IQ level is 69 and below. The range of IQs shown in the table (from DSM-III-R) allows for differences in distributions among various individual intelligence tests.

Sources: American Psychiatric Association, 1987, pp. 32–33; Thorndike, Hagen, & Sattler, 1986; Wechsler, 1974, 1981.

Sattler, 1986; Wechsler, 1974, 1975, 1981). (See Chapter 2 for a discussion of these scales.) Since infant tests of intelligence do not yield IQs or similar numerical values, other clinical judgments derived from the tests must be made in defining *subaverage general intellectual functioning* (American Psychiatric Association, 1987, p. 31). From 2 to 3 percent of the general population have IQs that classify them as mentally retarded. Table 17.1 shows the degree of severity of mental retardation according to IQ scores, as listed in DSM-III-R. By far the greatest proportion of mentally retarded individuals are classified at the mild level of severity.

The terminology employed to designate degrees of mental retardation conforms to that used by the AAMD (Grossman, 1977, 1983). The labels are a decided improvement over the stigmatizing designations of moron, imbecile, and idiot, introduced in the United States by psychologist Henry Goddard (1914) and widely used for many years in the professional literature to designate various types of feebleminded individuals.

An IQ or equivalent score should be interpreted flexibly. A common practice in clinical diagnosis is to accept a measurement error of approximately five points in either direction for such scales as the Stanford–Binet and the Wechsler. For example, an IQ of 70 represents a band of possible scores that may range from 65 to 75.

Impaired Adaptive Behavior

Adaptive behavior is "the effectiveness with which an individual meets the standards of personal independence and social responsibility expected of his or her age and cultural group" (American Psychiatric Association, 1987, pp. 28–29). The assessment of defects or impairments in adaptive behavior depends ultimately on clinical judgments. A number of scales can aid the clinician in making those judgments (Haywood, Meyers, & Switzky, 1982, p. 327; Meyers, Nihira, & Zeitlin, 1979; Sparrow, Balla, & Cicchetti, 1984). They are based on such information as a history of the individual's adaptive behavior other than that shown in a formal testing situation. For example, information about developmental

Table 17.2 Social—Adaptive Behavior of Mentally Retarded Individuals	
Degree of Mental Retardation	**Social—Adaptive Behavior**
Preschool (First Five Years): Maturation and Development	
Mild (IQ 50–70)	Can develop social and communication skills; minimal impairment in sensorimotor areas; often not distinguished from normal until later age
Moderate (IQ 35–49)	Can talk or learn to communicate; poor awareness of social conventions; fair motor development; may profit from training in self-help; can take care of themselves with moderate supervision
Severe (IQ 20–34)	Poor motor development; minimal speech; generally unable to profit from training in self-help; little or no communication skills
Profound (IQ below 20)	Gross retardation; minimal ability to function in sensorimotor areas; in need of nursing care
School (Age 6–20): Training and Education	
Mild (IQ 50–70)	Can learn academic skills up to approximately sixth-grade level by late teens; can be guided toward social conformity
Moderate (IQ 35–49)	Can profit from training in social and occupational skills; can learn functional academic skills to approximately fourth-grade level if given special education; may learn to travel alone to unfamiliar places
Severe (IQ 20–34)	Can talk or learn to communicate; can be trained in elementary health habits; can profit from systematic habit training; cannot learn functional academic skills
Profound (IQ below 20)	Some motor development present; cannot profit from training in self-help; in need of total care
Adult (Age 21 and Over): Social and Vocational Adequacy	
Mild (IQ 59–70)	With proper education and training, can usually achieve social and vocational skills adequate to maintain minimal self-support; may need guidance under unusual social or economic stress
Moderate (IQ 35–49)	May achieve self-maintenance in unskilled or semiskilled work under sheltered conditions (e.g., sheltered workshops); will need supervision and guidance when under mild social stress
Severe (IQ 20–34)	May contribute partially to self-maintenance under complete supervision; can develop self-protection skills to a minimal useful level in controlled environment; generally unable to profit from vocational training
Profound (IQ below 20)	Some motor and speech development; usually incapable of self-care; must have constant care and supervision in a highly structured environment

Source: American Psychiatric Association, 1987, pp. 32–33.

School achievement is an important criterion of adaptive behavior in the assessment of mental retardation. This mentally retarded girl is learning to read in a public school class for exceptional children.

This mentally retarded boy is learning to play a miniature piano to the delight of his normal sister.

history, school or occupational achievement, sensorimotor skills, social behavior, and emotional maturity are useful (Grossman, 1983). Table 17.2 shows the kinds of social–adaptive behavior one can reasonably expect for each level of mental retardation. However, these criteria are average characteristics based on large numbers of individuals. People in the same IQ range may differ significantly in the level of their attainments, depending on the nature of the retardation, the resources available for remedial action, and the attitudes and values of those with whom they have close contact.

Although the concept of social–adaptive behavior is useful in diagnosing mental retardation, it does not, in the opinion of many psychologists, lessen the importance of intelligence tests. For example, Edward Zigler and his colleagues point to these advantages of the IQ as an estimate of cognitive ability: (a) the IQ is probably the most theoretically important measure of cognitive functioning yet developed, (b) it has more correlates than other measures of such functioning, (c) it predicts behavior in many situations, (d) it is more stable than measures of adaptive behavior, and (e) there is a higher degree of consensus as to what it is measuring than with other estimates (Hodapp & Zigler, 1986; Zigler, Balla, & Hodapp, 1984).

On the other hand, applying the criterion of defects or impairments in adaptive behavior increases flexibility in the use of IQ scores for diagnosing mental retardation. For example, an individual might score 65 on an IQ test but not be diagnosed as mentally retarded because there is insufficient evidence of significant defects or other impairments in adaptive behavior. That is, given the limitations of cognitive ability, the person seems to be getting along reasonably well in social and occupational life. Conversely, an individual might attain an IQ slightly above 70 but still be diagnosed as mentally retarded because observations of adaptive behavior show significant defects or other impairments. The diagnosis might benefit the person by permitting special education or training (Barnett, 1986).

Onset before Age 18

The third criterion for diagnosing mental retardation — onset before the age of 18 — is used to distinguish mental retardation from the subaverage intelligence and impaired adaptive behavior that occurs in individuals who suffer from other kinds of mental disorders and who have not previously shown significant signs of abnormally low intelligence. However, this distinction does not mean that a diagnosis of mental retardation rules out the possibility of a coexisting mental disorder. If a prominent clinical syndrome in addition to mental retardation is observed in a particular individual, both diagnoses should be made.

Prevalence of Mental Retardation

If one considers only the results of standardized intelligence tests, the prevalence of mental retardation in the United States is about 3 percent. However, if one also uses the criterion "defects or impairment in adaptive behavior," the prevalence is more like 1 percent (American Psychiatric Association, 1987, p. 31; Crandall, 1977; Mercer, 1973; Tarjan, Wright, Eyman, & Keernan, 1978).

■ Intelligence tests do not measure the full scope of cognitive abilities and achievements that many societies regard as useful and rewarding. Thus, an individual may score at the mentally retarded level on a standardized achievement test but show sufficient adaptive behavior in cognitive tasks of everyday life to be considered normal.

■ Individuals who were labeled mildly retarded as children may not be so regarded when they become adults. That is mainly because the school tasks that their retardation prevented them from performing are not the same as the tasks they need to perform to meet the ordinary demands of adult life. They become part of a large, unidentified group of adults who could profit from help in making better use of their limited intellectual resources. However, they are usually more neglected by society as adults than they were as children because their handicaps are less obvious. Consequently, they seldom show up in statistics on mental retardation (Haywood, Meyers, & Switzky, 1982, p. 324).

Biological and Physical Causes of Mental Retardation

At least 50 percent of the time, abnormal biological and physical conditions cause mental retardation. Among the most common causes are abnormalities in chromosomes and disorders of metabolism. Another important cause is damage to the brain and nervous system of the developing fetus. This damage may result from infections of the uterus and toxic agents such as alcohol and radiation. In addition, postnatal brain disease and traumatic injuries can be crucial factors (American Psychiatric Association, 1987, pp. 30–31; McClaren & Bryson, 1987).

Chromosomal Defects

Prominent among the chromosomal abnormalities resulting in mental retardation are the presence of an extra chromosome, the absence of a chromosome, and the fusion of one

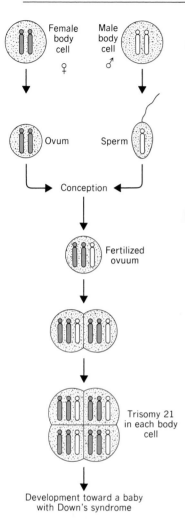

Figure 17.1

Trisomy 21 and Down's syndrome as a result of nondisjunction in the cell division of the ovum. (Adapted from MacMillan, 1982, p. 120).

chromosome with another. Probably the best-known pattern of mental retardation caused by chromosomal defects is **Down's syndrome**, which accounts for more than one-third of the severely to moderately retarded population of the United States. Occasionally, some individuals attain an IQ at the mildly retarded level.

The incidence of Down's syndrome in the United States is about 1 in every 700 live births (Kaplan & Sadock, 1985, p. 718). It has been estimated that for every infant born alive with Down's syndrome, from two to three fetuses are miscarried because their physical abnormalities are not compatible with survival (Smith & Berg, 1976).

A number of chromosomal errors result in Down's syndrome (Kolb & Brodie, 1982, p. 735). Normally, each body cell has 46 chromosomes: one pair of sex chromosomes and 22 pairs of autosomal (nonsex) chromosomes. The French scientist Jerome Lejeune and his colleagues (1959) demonstrated the existence of an extra number 21 chromosome in people afflicted with Down's syndrome. This condition, called **regular trisomy 21**, is the most common cause of Down's syndrome. Unlike other forms of trisomy 21, especially those that are directly inherited (de la Cruz & Gerald, 1981; Krompotic, 1978), regular trisomy 21 is not transmitted from parent to child through specific defective genes. It usually results from the number 21 pair of chromosomes failing to separate during the ovum's early stage of cell division. This error is called **nondisjunction**. The two chromosomes then combine with the single number 21 chromosome from the father, and the child receives three number 21 chromosomes instead of the normal two. Figure 17.1 shows how the error occurs.

Down's syndrome is more likely to occur in a child who is born when the mother is over 40. The aging of the mother's egg cells may be an important factor in producing the nondisjunction. The eggs become fewer over the years and more exposed to environmental damage, such as toxic chemicals (Koch, 1976).

A number of studies indicate that the father may contribute the extra number 21 chromosome. Magenis and his colleagues at the University of Oregon (Magenis, Overton, Chamberlin, Brady, & Lourien, 1977) found that in about 20 percent of the cases they investigated, the father's sperm contained the extra chromosome. There is little evidence that the abnormality is related to the father's age (Edgerton, 1979, p. 25).

Down's syndrome is named after the British physician John Langdon Haydon Down (1828–1896), who provided the first systematic and detailed description of the disorder in an article entitled "Observations on Ethnic Classification of Idiots" (Down, 1866; Vollman, 1969). A number of other clinical reports soon followed. By 1973, the medical researcher Gerhard Koch had amassed an international bibliography on the subject numbering more than 1700 entries.

Down's syndrome is also known as mongolism. This unfortunate label stems from Down's use of the term *mongolian idiot,* which derived from the theory that the disability was an evolutionary retrogression to the Mongolian race, a theory that one specialist in mental retardation has called a "scientific nightmare" (Gibson, 1978, p. 2).

Down based his theory on what he took to be a mongolian appearance in some of the mentally retarded patients he observed. He noted especially their slanting eyelids with vertical folds covering the end of each eye nearest the nose. These features, called **epicanthal folds,** do occur in some Asian peoples. However, the use of such terms as *mongolism* and *mongoloid* has demeaning racial connotations, and it makes a misleading physical comparison. Children with Down's syndrome are found in all races and ethnic groups. Indeed, a Japanese child (for example) with Down's syndrome looks as different from other Japanese children as an affected European child does from normal Europeans (Gath, 1978). Most mental health professionals rejected the term *mongoloid* some years ago. Unfortunately, it persists in popular comments on the subject and occasionally in professional writings as well. (See Box 17.1)

**BOX 17.1 Mongolism or Down's Syndrome?
A Historic Appeal for a Change**

Nineteen internationally known geneticists published this letter in the British journal *Lancet* more than 25 years ago. It is a notable effort to eliminate the pejorative term *mongolism* and suggest more acceptable substitutes. One of the signers of the letter, J. Lejeune, discovered a chromosomal cause of the syndrome.

Mongolism Sir—It has long been recognized that the terms "mongolian idiocy," "mongolism," "mongoloid," etc., as applied to a specific type of mental deficiency, have misleading connotations. The occurrence of this anomaly among Europeans and their descendants is not related to the segregation of genes derived from Asians; its appearance among members of Asian populations suggests such ambiguous designations as "mongolin and Mongoloid;" and the increasing participation of Chinese and Japanese investigators in the study of the condition imposes on them the use of an embarrassing term. We urge, therefore, that the expressions which imply a racial aspect of the condition be no longer used.

Some of the undersigned are inclined to replace the term "mongolism" by such designations as "Langdon-Down anomaly," or "Down's syndrome or anomaly," or "congenital acromicria." Several others believe that this is an appropriate time to introduce the term "trisomy 21 anomaly," which would include cases of simple trisomy as well as translocations. It is hoped that agreement on a specific phrase will soon crystallize if once the term "mongolism" has been abandoned.

Source: Letters to the Editor, *Lancet*, April 8, 1961, p. 775.

Various physical signs associated with Down's syndrome have been observed, although only a few may appear in any one person. In addition to the epicanthal folds, physical characteristics may include a small round head; a large fissured tongue protruding from a rather small mouth (the tongue appears unusually large mainly because of the small mouth); a short, flat nasal bridge; and a white speckled iris (first described in 1924 by Thomas Brushfield and known as Brushfield spots). Other typical signs are low-set,

The facial appearance of this girl with Down's syndrome belies the long-held stereotype that such children have a "mongoloid" look.

misshapen earlobes; short hands with curved fifth fingers; and abnormally small external genitalia. These characteristics can provide a valuable guide for early diagnosis of the syndrome. However, when physical signs are minimal, diagnosis depends on careful observation of the child's intellectual development and a laboratory analysis of chromosomes.

Children with Down's syndrome are often born with heart and respiratory defects (Chaney, Eyman, & Miller, 1985). Consequently, their life expectancy is significantly lower than average. They are especially at risk during the early years. However, medical advances have increased the survival rate, so that if the child can progress satisfactorily during the early months of life, the chances of living into adulthood are quite good.

Disorders of Metabolism

Phenylketonuria

The basic metabolic error in **phenylketonuria (PKU)** is a deficiency in the liver enzyme phenylalanine hydroxylase. This enzyme is necessary for converting phenylalanine, an amino acid, into another essential amino acid, tyrosine. The failure to metabolize phenylalanine, which is found in many dietary sources of protein, causes it to accumulate in the blood and eventually to be converted into phenylpyruvic acid. Excessive levels of this acid eventually cause serious damage to the nerve cells of the brain, resulting in mental retardation (Berman, 1978). Phenylpyruvic acid belongs to a group of biochemical compounds known as phenylketones; *Phenylketonuria* means "phenylketones in the urine" (Centerwall & Centerwall, 1972, p. 1).

The Norwegian physician and biochemist Asbjorn Fölling discovered PKU in 1934 after a mother had fruitlessly consulted other physicians to learn the cause of the peculiar and persistent musty odor of her two retarded children. When Fölling added ferric acid to a urine specimen from each child, the solution turned an unusual green color. He later demonstrated that phenylpyruvic acid in the urine caused the chemical reaction. Fölling hypothesized that the acid was an important cause of the children's mental retardation. Subsequent examinations of other mentally retarded children strengthened his supposition (Centerwall & Centerwall, 1961, 1972).

PKU is transmitted from parents to child by a recessive gene. If both parents are carriers of the defective gene but do not themselves have PKU, each child will have one chance in four of inheriting the disorder (see Figure 17.2). It is also possible for a child to

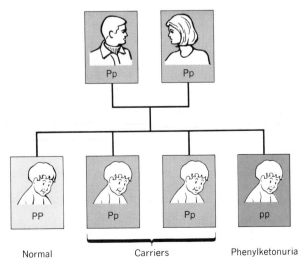

Figure 17.2

Inheritance pattern for phenylketonuria (PKU). The two clinically normal parents are both carriers (Pp) of the defective gene for PKU. The children can be noncarriers and normal (PP), they can be carriers but clinically normal (Pp), or they can have two abnormal genes and thus have PKU (pp). (From Centerwall & Centerwall, 1972, p. 2.)

Pp   Pp

PP   Pp   Pp   pp

Normal   Carriers   Phenylketonuria

acquire PKU from the intrauterine environment, since phenylalanine can penetrate the placenta. A high maternal level of phenylalanine can be reduced by a low-protein diet.

PKU occurs in both females and males in many different national, ethnic, and racial groups; but its incidence is extremely low in blacks (Centerwall & Centerwall, 1972). Estimates of the incidence of PKU in the United States during the last two decades have ranged from 1 in 10,000 to 1 in 25,000 live births (Kaplan & Sadock, 1985, p. 711).

Screening programs designed to detect the disease in newborn infants have increased steadily. Texas initiated one of the earliest of these programs in 1964. Over an 11-year period, almost a million and a half screening tests were performed. During the last two decades, more than 40 states have passed legislation requiring PKU screening. As a result, more than 90 percent of babies now born in hospitals are screened before they leave the hospital (Kaplan & Sadock, 1985, pp. 711–714).

Abnormal levels of phenylalanine can be detected in the infant's blood serum within a day after birth. However, since infants who do not have PKU sometimes have elevated levels of phenylalanine in their blood serum, medical authorities emphasize that urine tests should also be used. These tests can detect abnormal levels of phenylalanine within three to nine weeks after birth (Kolb & Brodie, 1982, p. 730).

Follow-up tests are always essential to confirm the diagnosis and plan treatment if it is indicated. Repeated tests are important, since a child without the disease may show an initial positive reaction, and children who do not have PKU can be harmed by the highly regulated diet prescribed for treating the disease. (President's Committee on Mental Retardation, 1975).

Although not all infants with abnormally high phenylalanine levels develop PKU, it has become standard medical practice to place such children on a special low-phenylalanine diet for at least a trial period. This period may be as little as three months, although some authorities recommend that it last a year. If dietary treatment is started during the first few months of life and continued for a sufficient length of time, the negative consequences of PKU can usually be avoided.

Tay–Sachs Disease

The genetic error in metabolism that causes **Tay–Sachs disease** leads not only to profound mental retardation but also to tragic physical deterioration early in life. The English ophthalmologist Warren Tay (1843–1927) identified the disease in 1881, and the American neurologist Bernard Sachs (1858–1944) discovered it independently in 1887.

Tay–Sachs disease results from a lack of the enzyme hexosaminidase-A. This deficiency prevents the normal metabolism of lipids, a group of organic compounds that includes fats and waxes. Lipids build up in the brain and nerve cells, resulting in a progressive deterioration of physical and mental development. Between six months and one year, a characteristic triad of clinical signs is usually apparent: (a) a cherry red spot (macula) on the retina, resulting from the degradation of cells at the site, bordered by fluffy white cells containing excessive lipids; (b) exaggerated responses to sounds; and (c) retarded psychomotor activity. Deterioration steadily increases; severe mental retardation, blindness, and convulsions are all common symptoms. There is no known cure for the disease. Death usually occurs by the time the child is 3 or 4 years of age (Volk, Adachi, & Schneck, 1978).

Because Tay–Sachs disease is transmitted by a single recessive gene, it can occur only when two carriers of the defect have children. As Figure 17.3 shows, the probability that Tay–Sachs disease will affect a child born to such parents is 25 percent.

Tay–Sachs disease occurs in Jews of East European origin (Ashkenazic) more often

Figure 17.3

Possible outcomes for children born to Tay-Sachs carriers. (From President's Committee on Mental Retardation, 1975, p. 26).

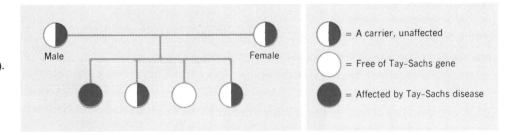

than in any other ethnic group. Various estimates indicate that 1 out of 30 are carriers. For Sephardic Jews (Spanish or Portuguese origin), the rate is about 1 in 200; for Yemenite Jews and other ethnic groups, the rate is about 1 in 300 (Edgerton, 1979).

Although Tay–Sachs disease is fatal, it can be prevented. If the genetic history of a family suggests that both spouses are carriers, professional counseling can help them decide whether they should risk a pregnancy. Blood tests for the enzyme hexosaminidase-A can determine more precisely whether the parents are actually carriers. In the event that pregnancy has already occurred, the probability of Tay–Sachs disease can be determined by amniocentesis (which will be discussed in the next section of the chapter). If analysis of the amniotic fluid indicates a marked reduction in or absence of the enzyme hexosaminidase-A, the fetus is at high risk for Tay–Sachs disease. The couple can then discuss these findings with a genetic counselor — and a religious adviser, if appropriate.

Genetic Counseling

When there are grounds to suspect genetic defects, **genetic counseling** can be extremely important in helping individuals decide whether pregnancy is advisable (Applewhite, Busbee, & Borgaonkar, 1981; Culliton, 1976a; Edgerton, 1979, pp. 9–12; Gath, 1978, pp. 91–94; Kabach & Leisti, 1975; Massarik & Kabach, 1981; Omenn, 1978; President's Committee on Mental Retardation, 1975, 1980, pp. 10–12).

Although physicians, sometimes engage in genetic counseling, it usually involves other specialists as well, including research geneticists, clinical psychologists, clinical social workers, public health nurses, and members of the clergy.

Genetic counseling usually begins with detailed interviews to obtain a family history that might reveal a risk of genetic defects. Laboratory examinations of chromosomes from skin and blood samples can determine whether prospective parents are carriers of such defects. If pregnancy has already begun and there are reasons to suspect an increased risk of mental retardation or other problems caused by genetic defects, **amniocentesis** can be carried out (Omenn, 1978). In this surgical procedure, a small amount of amniotic fluid is drawn from the amniotic sac with a needle and analyzed to determine the chromosomal composition of the fetus. The accuracy of the test is greater than 99 percent. Amniocentesis is a valuable technique in determining the probability of mental retardation, especially in the following circumstances (Gath, 1978): (a) the mother is 40 years of age or older; (b) either parent has had a child with Down's syndrome, is a suspected carrier of a genetic defect associated with mental retardation, or has had a child with a chromosomal abnormality; and (c) the woman has had multiple miscarriages for no apparent reason (Crandall, 1977; Smith & Berg, 1976, pp. 272–273).

The procedure cannot be performed until about 15 weeks after conception; and results

A genetic counselor discusses the meaning of chromosome analysis with a pregnant patient prior to chorionic villi sampling. This procedure can reveal chromosomal abnormalities in the fetus.

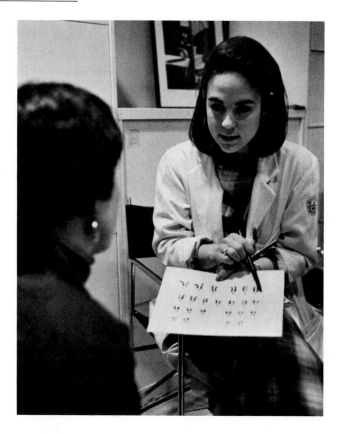

are not usually available for another 3 weeks. At this point, termination of pregnancy is still relatively safe, but more difficult than it would have been earlier.

A newer alternative to amniocentesis, called **chorionic villi sampling**, has promising advantages over amniocentesis, especially in that it can often be carried out as early as the 9th and 10th week of pregnancy, with preliminary results obtained in one or two days and a more thorough analysis in about two weeks. A catheter guided by ultrasound is inserted into the uterus to withdraw a small amount of chorionic villi tissue (the villi envelop the fetus and later become the placenta). The sample contains fetal tissue and therefore provides genetic information.

Intrauterine Infections

Infections acquired by the mother during pregnancy may cause serious harm to the developing fetus, resulting in physical disabilities and mental retardation. Among the major intrauterine infections are rubella (German measles) and congenital syphilis.

Rubella

Although rubella is a relatively mild disease in children and adults, intrauterine infection with the rubella virus can have damaging effects on fetal development. The effects include brain lesions associated with mental retardation, congenital heart disease, hearing loss, and glaucoma. The most crucial time for rubella infection is during the first trimester of pregnancy; and the earlier infection occurs during that trimester, the more likely it will be to cause defects (Wright, 1976). With the licensing of rubella vaccine in 1969, it is now possible to virtually eliminate rubella as a cause of mental retardation. In pursuit of this goal, the Centers for Disease Control in Atlanta recommend that all children under the age of puberty be immunized if they do not have a history of rubella infection, which results in immunity (President's Committee on Mental Retardation, 1980). There is already evidence of the protection mass immunization with rubella vaccine can offer. For example, an expected epidemic between 1970 and 1973 did not materialize, mainly because of increased efforts to immunize children (Gotoff, 1973). The importance of such immunization is crucial. Although gamma globulin has been somewhat useful in preventing rubella in pregnant women who have been exposed to the disease, it is not as effective as a systematic program of early immunization.

Congential Syphilis

The spirochete *Treponema pallidum*, which causes syphilis, is spread through sexual contact. A pregnant woman who is infected with the disease can transmit it to the fetus, since the spirochete is capable of crossing the placental barrier. Infection of the fetus is most likely to occur after the fifth month of gestation and may result in considerable damage to the nervous and circulatory systems of the newborn. In some instances, the infection may cause a miscarriage or stillbirth.

Children who are born with a syphilitic infection (congenital syphilis) may not show any signs of the disease until later childhood. However, serious symptoms may appear in infancy, especially those involving the central nervous system. Among such symptoms is **meningitis** — inflammation of the *meninges*, the membranes that envelop the brain and spinal cord — which appears during the fourth or fifth month. Later symptoms, which may not appear until the first or second year, include **hydrocephaly**, an abnormal accumulation of fluid in the cranium, with consequent brain damage; blindness; paralysis; speech disorders; and mental retardation. In other instances, obvious signs of congenital syphilis are not noticeable until the affected children are of school age. Typically, they perform poorly at school, become apathetic, and neglect personal hygiene. Speech and writing may deteriorate, deafness often develops, gait is unsteady, and coarse tremors appear.

Physical damage and mental retardation can generally be prevented or considerably reduced if penicillin therapy is initiated early. Thus, early diagnosis is crucial. The diagnosis is usually based not only on clinically observed overt symptoms but also on the results of laboratory tests of blood serum. The latter are especially important when congenital syphilis is suspected but obvious clinical signs of the disease are absent. Some of these tests depend on the detection of antibodies produced as a specific reaction to the syphilitic infection (Sparling, 1971). Even more desirable is prevention. Since infection of the fetus is not likely to occur before the fifth month of pregnancy, prompt treatment of the infected mother with penicillin can keep the fetus from acquiring the disease.

Other Diseases Related to Mental Retardation

Postnatal Infections

Infections transmitted during the birth process or shortly afterwards may also lead to mental retardation and related physical disabilities. One of the most serious of these infections is meningitis (defined in the previous section of the chapter). It can cause damage to the central nervous system at any time of life; however, it is especially serious during the first three months (Gotoff, 1973; Szymanski, & Crocker, 1985, p. 1649).

Other Postnatal Brain Diseases

Brain diseases that are not associated with any known infection can also damage the central nervous system and cause mental retardation. Some of these disorders involve **neoplasms** — new and abnormal growths of tissues (tumors) that serve no special physiological function. Others involve such degenerative processes as the destruction of myelin, the soft white matter that forms a sheath around the nerve fibers in the brain. Genetic defects seem to be involved in some of these disorders. In other cases, however, the etiology is puzzling.

The Rh Factor

In 1940, Karl Landsteiner, who had already won the Nobel prize in medicine in 1930 for his discovery of blood groups, and his colleague Alexander Wiener reported on research with Rhesus monkeys that had led to their discovery of a new blood factor. Weiner named it the **Rh factor** because humans possess it in common with Rhesus monkeys (Zimmerman, 1973, p. 19). About 85 percent of individuals have the Rh factor in their red blood cells and thus are Rh-positive. Individuals who lack the factor are Rh-negative.

The year following the discovery, Philip Levine and his co-workers (Levine, Katzin, & Burnham, 1941) published their theory that Rh incompatibility between mother and fetus could produce a disorder called **erythroblastosis fetalis**. Since then, the theory has been thoroughly substantiated. In erythroblastosis, the hemoglobin becomes separated from the red blood cells (erythrocytes), causing severe oxygen deficiency, neurological damage, and mental retardation in the fetus and the newborn infant. Erythroblastosis can occur only if the father is Rh-positive and the mother is Rh-negative. The Rh-positive factor is a dominant genetic trait. Suppose an Rh-positive male and an Rh-negative female conceive a child. If the male is homozygous (pure) for the Rh-positive factor, all the fetuses of the Rh-negative women he impregnates will be Rh-positive. If he is heterozygous (partial), half of her fetuses will be Rh-positive and half Rh-negative.

If the fetus of an Rh-negative mother is Rh-positive, the blood cells of the fetus can sensitize the mother if they leak into her circulatory system. This is most likely to happen with the separation and delivery of the placenta during the birth process (Guttmacher, 1973, p. 268). The mother's immune system responds by producing antibodies, whose function is to destroy the Rh-positive blood cells from the fetus. Although no damage is usually done to the fetus in the first pregnancy, in future pregnancies the antibodies the mother has developed can be transmitted to the fetus through the placenta and can destroy its red blood cells.

Among the symptoms of erythroblastosis are anemia; hydrops (dropsy) — an accumulation of fluids in body cells or cavities; and severe jaundice. Brain damage eventually results because bilirubin, a bile pigment, is released from the mother's blood in reaction to antibodies and enters the fetal circulatory system through the placenta. The bilirubin reaches toxic levels that cause brain damage because the liver of the fetus is too immature to metabolize it (Chinn, Drew, & Logan, 1979; Chinn & Mueller, 1971; MacMillan, 1982).

Various remedies have been developed to treat erythroblastosis. The most successful is partial or complete blood transfusion shortly after birth, or, more recently, before birth. However, even more effective is a method for preventing the disorder. Injection of a substance called Rh gamma globulin into the bloodstream of an Rh-negative mother within 72 hours after the birth of her first Rh-positive child will prevent her from becoming sensitized and producing antibodies that could harm subsequent children. Successful treatment with Rh gamma globulin depends to a great extent on the susceptible mother receiving competent prenatal and postnatal care and advice, so that she will not miss being immunized if that becomes necessary.

Other Adverse Physical Conditions

Mental retardation sometimes results from physical trauma and other aversive physical conditions. These may occur prenatally, during the birth process itself, or after birth, especially in the early months.

Irradiation

A particularly important source of prenatal damage is excessive irradiation. It has been known for some time that therapeutic doses of x-rays or radium administered to pregnant women can cause brain defects in the developing fetus and subsequent mental retardation. The danger is particularly great during early pregnancy. However, irradiation during the later months can also be harmful (Norris, 1978). In recent years medical practitioners have become increasingly aware of such dangers. There is as yet no conclusive evidence that environmental radiation (from nuclear power plants or industrial waste) plays a significant role in producing mental retardation. Nevertheless, exposure to these sources should be kept as minimal as possible, especially during pregnancy.

Trauma during Birth

Cerebral damage and subsequent mental retardation may occur because of complications during the mother's labor and the delivery of her baby (Schwartz, 1978). The fetus may be in an abnormal position, creating hazardous conditions for proper delivery. Brain damage during the birth process may occur because of insufficient oxygen resulting from interference with circulation in the placenta. Physical damage to the baby's skull or various kinds of cerebrospinal lesions may occur during the birth process. This type of damage can have negative consequences for the child's future intellectual development.

Lead Poisoning

Lead can cause serious damage to the central nervous system, the kidneys, and the various blood-forming elements in the body. Abnormally elevated levels of lead in the blood may cause sterility in men, spontaneous abortion (miscarriage), stillbirth, and birth defects. Children who ingest toxic levels of lead may suffer recurrent seizures, cerebral palsy, mental retardation, and, in some instances, death. It has been estimated that 3 to 5 percent of children in the United States have an elevated level of lead in the blood that potentially poses serious threats to their physical and mental development (Machol, 1980; President's Committee on Mental Retardation, 1980). Lead poisoning is a particular hazard for children living in old dwellings that have been painted with lead-based paint. If they eat flakes of this paint or inhale plaster dust containing the paint, they are in danger of suffering brain damage. Screening has shown that 10 percent of children living in poor, inner-city neighborhoods have toxic levels of lead in their systems (MacMillan, 1982).

Industrial workers in plants using large quantities of lead may also be at special risk. Some studies have shown that newborns of women who work in plants where lead is a crucial part of production have blood levels of lead that correspond closely to those of the mother. Evidence also indicates that male lead workers may incur significant damage to sperm (Machol, 1980).

Lead poisoning is a hazard for children living in old, deteriorated housing where walls have been covered with lead-based paints. Ingestion of paint flakes or dust can contribute to brain damage.

There is a growing danger of lead poisoning from air pollution, especially in neighborhoods with heavy industrial production and traffic congestion. Lead-free gasoline may help reduce the hazard, but it by no means will eliminate it.

Adverse Effects of Drugs

The thalidomide tragedy of the 1960s, in which 3600 babies were born with grossly deformed limbs because their mothers took the drug during pregnancy, stimulated interest in the adverse effects of various drugs on fetal development (Edgerton, 1979; Koch, 1976). Researchers and practitioners in the health sciences recognize the danger of taking drugs during pregnancy. Drugs available through prescription and over the counter, as well as illegal drugs, can all cause harm. Among the more commonly prescribed drugs that can harm the fetus are various anticonvulsants (for example, Dilantin), quinine, antibiotics, and antihistamines.

In addition to drugs, the use of alcohol during pregnancy can cause serious damage to the fetus. Heavy use can result in fetal alcohol syndrome. Among its consequences for the child are abnormally low birth weight, deformities of the face and skull, malformations of the limbs, cardiac defects, and retarded physical and mental development (Edgerton, 1979; Green, 1974; Jones & Smith, 1973; Machol, 1980; U.S. Department of Health and Human Services, 1981a). It has been estimated that more than 15,000 children are born in the United States each year with definite signs of the syndrome. (See Chapter 14 for a detailed account of fetal alcohol syndrome.)

This pregnant woman is drinking wine while she reads a book on baby names. The use of alcohol during pregnancy can cause serious damage to the fetus. The heavy use of alcohol can result in fetal alcohol syndrome, which includes abnormalities such as low birth weight and retarded physical and mental development.

Social and Cultural Causes of Mental Retardation

Mental Retardation and Social Systems

Whether or not individuals are judged to be mentally retarded depends a great deal on the criteria their social systems use to determine mental retardation (Kurtz, 1977; Mercer, 1973; President's Committee on Mental Retardation, 1975). In complex and heterogeneous cultures such as the United States, criteria may differ from one group (or social system) to another. Since a person often operates in different social groups, decisions as to whether or not the individual is mentally retarded may vary. In some instances, such decisions may depend mainly on clinical judgments derived from IQ tests. In other situations, however, different criteria may be more salient. For example, children defined as mentally retarded at school may be regarded quite differently by their friends in the neighborhood, perhaps because of social skills, unusual physical ability, or mechanical proficiency.

Sociocultural views of mental retardation generally emphasize these basic principles:

■ The definition of intelligence is not formed apart from a particular and cultural setting.

■ Whether an individual is labeled mentally retarded depends to a great extent on the expectations and levels of tolerance within a particular social system. Labeling can have adverse consequences, since people may behave negatively toward the labeled individual even when the basis for the labeling is not justifiable (see Chapter 4).

Sociocultural definitions of mental retardation have had their greatest impact on a particular social system—the school. Various social critics have pointed out that in the United States the public schools have been the prime labelers of the mentally retarded. They have based their labeling almost completely on intelligence test scores, ignoring the cultural and social factors that can influence those scores. Significant numbers of children have been unable to benefit educationally as much as they might have if a broader appraisal of their cognitive abilities and potentialities had been used (Mercer, 1973). Such findings helped lay the groundwork for federal legislation mandating more flexibility in the schools for determining who is mentally retarded. Insofar as possible, this approach is expected to bring within the mainstream of the educational process children who formerly were more isolated.

The Meaning of Sociocultural Mental Retardation

Adverse sociocultural conditions can greatly impede the acquisition of knowledge and skills necessary for adequate intellectual functioning. Environmental deficits include (a) severe poverty, (b) lack of perceptual and social stimulation during early developmental years, and (c) cultural values that place an individual at a disadvantage in learning how to achieve intellectual, educational, and occupational goals. These are the kinds of conditions that underlie **sociocultural mental retardation**. The majority of mentally retarded persons show this form of cognitive deficit (Edgerton, 1979).

Sociocultural mental retardation is usually at a mild level of intellectual impairment (see Tables 17.1 and 17.2) and tends to run in families. As a rule, it does not involve detectable organic pathology. When it does, the role of organic pathology is minor or is closely connected with conditions of cultural and social deprivation.

The *Manual on Terminology and Classification of Mental Retardation* published by the AAMD initially labeled sociocultural mental retardation as cultural–familial (Heber, 1961). The label conveyed that the condition resulted from adverse cultural circumstances and that it tended to occur in more than one family member.

Later editions of the manual replaced cultural–familial with the label "environmental influences," although the diagnostic criteria remained the same. The criteria include (a) a mild level of retardation, (b) no evidence of significant organic pathology related to mental retardation, (c) subnormal intellectual functioning in other members of the family, and (d) adverse social and cultural conditions. Our use of the term *sociocultural retardation* corresponds to the manual's category "environmental influences," an inclusive term that points directly to the basic conditions that underlie the retardation (Edgerton, 1979; Grossman, 1983).

Sociocultural mental retardation is concentrated in the most marginal groups of individuals — those whose social and economic life tends to be at a bare subsistence level. Such individuals are concentrated in deteriorated inner-city neighborhoods or poor and isolated rural areas (President's Committee on Mental Retardation, 1980).

At the present time, the possible role of hereditary influences in sociocultural retarda-

These children live in poverty surrounded by water pollution and other unsanitary conditions. These are the kinds of conditions that may lead to sociocultural mental retardation.

tion is speculative. Future research may reveal more definite evidence. In the meantime, there is sufficient information at hand that social and cultural conditions are of central importance in producing mild mental retardation. Such knowledge can strengthen our ability to remedy and even prevent it.

Sociocultural Mental Retardation and Poverty

The adverse sociocultural conditions most often associated with mild mental retardation are fundamentally those of poverty: (a) severe economic deprivation; (b) deficiencies in nutrition and general health; (c) inadequate medical care; (d) poor housing, frequently in slums; and (e) unusually large families, which place an added burden on already limited resources. Conditions such as these are frequently associated with low parental education, little motivation for children to advance educationally, unskilled laboring occupations, and membership in ethnic and racial groups that perennially suffer from prejudice and discrimination (Edgerton, 1979; Miller, 1970; Scott & Carran, 1987).

Conditions of poverty are often reflected in various forms of bodily deprivation and neglect known to be correlated with mental retardation and physical disability. For example, poor and socially disadvantaged mothers frequently suffer from inadequate nutrition and prenatal care. In turn, these deficiencies can lead to their having premature babies with dangerously low birth weights (Costin & Rapp, 1984, p. 149). Under such circumstances, the risk of mental retardation and physical disability increases significantly.

Deficiency in Sensory Stimulation

Children whose social environment lacks a sufficient variety of visual, tactile, kinesthetic, and other sensory stimulation can become retarded in their intellectual development. A pioneering observer of such deprivation was John Bowlby (1969, 1973), who studied the development of children reared from infancy in orphanages, where the kinds of opportunities for stimulation ordinarily supplied by mothering were drastically limited. Later investigations supported Bowlby's findings. For example, a lack of sensory experiences can impair visual–spatial abilities and verbal intelligence, as expressed in reading, writing, speaking, and calculating. This deprivation is not confined to children reared in institutions. It may also occur in homes, especially those of disadvantaged social and economic status, and with just as devastating effects (Rutter, 1972).

Although these findings have been the subject of some controversy, mainly with respect to the methodology of certain studies, the overall conclusion that perceptual deprivation can impede intellectual development has met with fairly wide agreement (Hunt, 1979). Among interpretations that have needed correction, however, is Bowlby's belief that the bond between mother and child is the most essential factor in adequate perceptual stimulation. Ordinarily, the mother is a central source of stimulation during infancy and childhood, but there are other important sources as well as various stages of the child's development. Michael Rutter (1972) emphasized that it is the quality of the relationship the infant and child has to human sources of stimulation that is crucial for adequate intellectual development, rather than a bonding per se to the mother alone. "The father, the mother, brothers and sisters, friends, school-teachers and others all have an impact on development, but their influence and importance differ for different aspects of development" (Rutter, 1972, p. 125).

Social Ecology of Mental Retardation

One of the most crucial problems facing mentally retarded people is where they will live, go to school, work, and in general carry on their daily activities. The wide range of individual differences among them means that appropriate social settings are likely to change considerably over time and at different stages of development (Eyman & Borthwick, 1980); Haywood, Meyers, & Switsky, 1982).

The great majority of mentally retarded people live in their own homes or in special community-based residential homes. Many of them go to school during their school-age years, either in regular classes or in special education settings, especially if they are mildly or moderately retarded. They often interact freely in their community, marry, and hold jobs. Because they gradually blend in with the general population, they are often difficult to locate after they leave school.

Noninstitutional placement settings include foster homes and special residential homes in which a small group of mentally retarded people live independently, usually with a counselor–supervisor. In most instances, they have full- or part-time jobs, either in sheltered workshops and developmental centers or in ordinary work settings. In general, these settings are quite successful. One of the greatest problems is that of neighborhood resistance. Some people harbor stereotyped notions of mentally retarded people, viewing them as undesirable neighbors. Such prejudice needs to be countered through educational programs and community action (Borthwick, Meyers, & Eyman, 1981; Eyman, Borthwick, & Miller, 1981; Flynn & Nitsch, 1980; Haywood & Newbrough, 1981; Lei, Nihira, Sheehy, & Meyers, 1981; Meyer, R.J., 1980; Schalock & Harper, 1981).

A recent advance in this area is the 1985 decision of the Supreme Court that under certain conditions the denial of a zoning permit for a noninstitutional residence for mentally retarded people may be so irrational as to be unconstitutional. Although the Court did not give the mentally retarded special protection against official discrimination, it did establish a legal basis for seeking housing rights for them. The Court affirmed that mere negative attitudes, vague fears, and irrational prejudice may not form the basis for official action that places the retarded at a disadvantage. For example, if a particular neighborhood is already zoned for apartments, it cannot deny a housing permit to a group of mentally retarded people who wish to live in similar arrangements ("Court Denies", 1985).

In this community-based group residence for mentally retarded adults, a social worker supervises the planning of a weekly budget. Here the supervisor is reading some suggestions while the two residents make notes and calculations.

Early Environmental Intervention

Special programs to enrich the early environment of children who are at high risk for sociocultural mental retardation have developed in recent years. Prominent among them is the Head Start program supported by federal funds (Hechinger, 1984; Lynch, Simms, von Hippel, & Schuchat, 1980; Sontag, 1985). Head Start is a comprehensive child development program designed for low-income preschool children, handicapped and nonhandicapped. It emphasizes experiences in the classroom; medical, dental, nutrition, and mental health services; parental involvement; and social services. The Head Start program works in close cooperation with other programs and agencies that serve children (Lynch, Simms, von Hippel, & Schuchat, 1980, pp. 104–105). In general, this program seems to have improved the current intellectual skills of preschoolers. However, the long-term effects are difficult to assess (Woodhead, 1988).

The most common method of assessing the outcomes of early intervention programs has been to use the results of intelligence tests as an indication of success or failure. However, as we discussed early in the chapter, the IQ is only one measure of intelligence. A broader approach to assessing the effectiveness of early intervention programs is to consider goals involved in achieving social competence. This criterion goes much beyond the skills measured by standardized intelligence tests. Such competencies include (a) measures of physical health and well-being, (b) formal cognitive ability as measured by a standard IQ test or some similar device, (c) school achievement, and (d) motivational and emotional variables.

The inclusion of physical health and well-being in the criteria of social competence is of special importance because of the close relationship between biological deprivation and the sociocultural factors that can contribute to mild mental retardation. An example of this relationship can be seen in a project carried out with chronically undernourished children in Cali, Colombia. This city of nearly 1 million people has many problems characteristic of rapidly expanding cities in developing countries (McKay, Sinisterra, McKay, Gomez, & Lloreda, 1978). The problems are basically no different from those of many families living in marginal social and economic conditions in the deteriorated inner cities of the United States and other developed countries. Approximately 300 children were involved, all of them from families of extremely low socioeconomic status. Beginning at different

Special programs such as Head Start have improved the cognitive skills of low-income preschool children at risk for sociocultural mental retardation. This scene shows work and play areas of a Head Start program for 3- to 4-year-olds.

ages during their preshcool years, the children participated in a program that combined improved nutritional and health care with special educational features. By school age, the gap in cognitive abilities between these children and a group of economically and socially privileged children in Cali had narrowed significantly. The younger the children were when they entered the program, the more beneficial it was and the narrower the gap. Among the cognitive abilities measured were language usage, immediate memory, information and vocabulary, quantitative concepts, spatial relations, and logical thinking. The gains in these abilities were maintained by the end of the first grade in primary school, a year after the experimental program had ended.

Counseling and Psychotherapy

Mentally retarded people are often especially vulnerable to emotional and social problems. Their intellectual deficits help create special problems of adjustment at the same time that they limit the ability to solve those problems. One of the most neglected areas for mentally retarded people has been the use of counseling and psychotherapy to help them solve their personal and social problems within their limited intellectual resources. In fact, they may well be one of the most underserved populations in the United States (Reiss, Levitan, & McNally, 1982).

There are a number of reasons that mentally retarded people seldom receive adequate professional attention for their emotional problems (Reiss, Levitan, & McNally, 1982). In the first place, mentally retarded people with emotional problems often fall through a gap that seems to exist between mental health centers that serve emotionally disturbed people and developmental centers that serve mentally retarded people. There is frequent disagreement as to whose function it is to provide psychotherapy and counseling for them. Secondly, cognitive deficit in mentally retarded people is such a salient characteristic that the possibility of emotional problems is often overlooked. Finally, clinical psychologists and psychiatrists are not especially interested in the mentally retarded population.

There is a growing movement toward community-based living facilities for mentally retarded people as a substitute for institutional care (Landesman & Butterfield, 1987). Such relocation can in itself be a stressful experience, making psychotherapy and counseling services even more necessary. Reiss, Levitan, and McNally (1982) have suggested a multidimensional approach involving clinicians, researchers, and administrators. Among the components of this approach are the following.

1. Mental health professionals need to be made aware of the serious lack of attention paid to providing psychotherapy and counseling for mentally retarded people.

2. More research is needed to build knowledge about effective psychotherapy and counseling for the mentally retarded.

3. University programs on mental retardation should increasingly sponsor demonstration projects to illustrate how clinical services can help mentally retarded people. Universities should also train professionals and paraprofessionals to provide such services and pursue research to evaluate their methods and outcomes.

4. Psychotherapy and counseling for the mentally retarded must be cost-effective, with an emphasis on short-term therapy. Such efforts should include social learning programs aimed toward managing stress, increasing self-confidence and adaptive assertiveness, and developing social skills.

5. Families often need help in understanding and relating mentally retarded people. The frequent lack of such help, especially on the part of mental health professionals, goes along with neglect in the provision of psychotherapy and counseling for mentally retarded people. This kind of help should be provided.

A Bill of Rights for Mentally Retarded People

The Special Olympics has helped support a "bill of rights" for mentally retarded individuals (see the text for details of these rights). Here a 10-year-old boy gets a pep-talk from his teacher as he gets ready for the 50-meter dash.

In a foreword to *The Mentally Retarded Citizen and the Law* (Kindred, Cohen, Penrod, & Shaffer, 1976), a series of papers sponsored by the President's Committee on Mental Retardation, Eunice Kennedy Shriver pointed out that mentally retarded persons have always been among the first to have their human rights denied. She went on to emphasize the importance of a comprehensive bill of rights for these people. One of the tasks of the President's Committee on Mental Retardation was to delineate those personal and civil rights and propose how they should be guaranteed (President's Committee on Mental Retardation, 1976, pp. 58–67; Wald, 1976). To a great extent, the presentation was modeled after the United Nations 1971 declaration on the rights of the mentally retarded, which includes legislative procedures to bring full citizenship to mentally retarded people. The declaration includes the following major principles (Friedman, 1976, pp. 175–177).

1. Mentally retarded people have, to the maximum degree of feasibility, the same rights as other human beings.

2. Mentally retarded people have a right to proper medical care and to such education, training, and guidance that will enable them to develop their abilities and potentialities.

3. Mentally retarded people have the right to economic security, the right to perform productive work, and the right to engage in a meaningful occupation consistent with their capabilities.

4. Whenever possible, mentally retarded children (and, if appropriate, mentally retarded adults) should live with their own parents or with foster parents and participate in community life. If it is necessary for them to live in an institution (not more than 4 or 5 percent need do so), it should be in a setting that is as close as possible to normal life.

5. Mentally retarded people have a right to a legally appointed and qualified guardian if that is necessary for their well-being and interests.

6. Mentally retarded people have a right to legal protection against exploitation, abuse, and degrading treatment. If prosecuted for breaking the law, they have a right to the same due process accorded other citizens, with full regard for the degree to which they are mentally responsible.

7. In some instances, mentally retarded people may be so severely handicapped as to be unable to exercise all their rights, or it may become necessary to restrict or deny such rights. In such instances, they must be afforded proper legal safeguards against abuse and violation of due process. These procedures must include an evaluation of the social competence of the individual by qualified experts and must be subject to periodic review and to the right of appeal to higher authorities.

The second goal in this bill of rights, concerning the education, training, and guidance of mentally retarded people, has received the greatest impetus from federal legislation.

One of the points in the "bill of rights" for mentally retarded persons states that such individuals have the right to economic security and the right to engage in a meaningful occupation consistent with their abilities. These two persons are exercising that right.

Public Law 94–142, which deals broadly with the education of all handicapped children, sets forth regulations that are intended to safeguard their rights to education and training consistent with their particular handicap. They can no longer be excluded from a public education simply on the basis of the degree of their handicap, whether it is physical, emotional, or intellectual. The regulations set forth in the law govern the provision of grant funds to state and local educational agencies to help them educate handicapped children. Since all school systems in the United States depend in one way or another on such funds, the regulations have a sweeping effect on virtually all education for handicapped children. The regulations are specifically designed to assure that all handicapped children, including those who are mentally retarded, have a free and appropriate public education consistent with their abilities. In addition, the regulations are designed to help state and local educational systems provide for this education and to assess their own effort (*Education of Handicapped Children*, 1977; Lynch, Simms, von Hippel, & Schuchat, 1980; Schroeder, Schroeder, & Landesman, 1987).

Summary

1. Mental retardation reflects an abnormal deficiency in the development of cognitive skills that usually begins soon after birth. The term is a convenient, comprehensive designation for particular patterns of subaverage intellectual functioning that have certain features in common.

2. Mentally retarded individuals are especially vulnerable to emotional and social problems, such as depression, loneliness, poor self-esteem, and the negative reactions of others.

3. DSM-III-R cites the following criteria for diagnosing mental retardation: (a) subaverage intellectual functioning; (b) concurrent defects or other impairments in adaptive behavior, taking into consideration the individual's age; and (c) onset prior to age 18.

4. Scores obtained from standardized intelligence tests, such as the IQ test, are routinely used to assess average intellectual functioning. If one considers only their results, the prevalence of mental retardation in the United States is about 3 percent. However, if the criterion "defects or impairments in adaptive behavior" is also used, the prevalence is more like 1 percent.

5. At least 50 percent of the time, mental retardation is caused primarily by abnormal biological and physical conditions. They include (a) abnormalities in chromosomes, (b) disorders of metabolism, and (c) damage to the brain and nervous system of the developing fetus.

6. Down's syndrome is the best known and most widely researched pattern of mental retardation caused by chromosomal abnormality. More than one-third of the severely to moderately retarded population in the United States has Down's syndrome.

7. The most common chromosomal error causing Down's syndrome is the presence of an extra chromosome: three number 21 chromosomes instead of the normal two. This condition is called trisomy 21.

8. The discoverer of Down's syndrome, the British physician John Langdon Haydon Down, gave the name *mongolism* to the disorder, because he thought the syndrome was an evolutionary regression to the Mongolian race. Down based his theory on the facial resemblance he perceived between mentally retarded individuals and Asian people — for example, the epicanthal folds of the eye. Modern viewpoints reject Down's theory.

9. A large number of metabolic disorders may result in abnormal brain development and mental retardation. The most widely known and researched are phenylketonuria (PKU) and Tay–Sachs disease.

10. The basic metabolic error in PKU is a deficiency in the liver enzyme phenylalanine hydroxylase. The body's failure to metabolize phenylalanine causes the enzyme to accumulate in the blood and eventually to be converted into phenylpyruvic acid. Excessive levels of this acid can cause brain damage.

11. PKU is primarily a hereditary disease transmitted by a recessive gene, but a child can acquire it from the intrauterine environment. PKU occurs in a wide range of ethnic and racial groups, but its prevalence is very low among black people.

12. During the last two decades, more than 40 states have passed legislation requiring PKU screening for newborns. Although not all infants with abnormally high phenylalanine levels develop PKU, a standard medical practice is to place such children on a special low-phenylalanine (low-protein) diet. Systematic screening and preventive treatment should reduce the occurrence of mental retardation related to PKU.

13. Tay–Sachs disease is caused by a genetic error in metabolism that leads not only to profound mental retardation but also to tragic physical deterioration early in life. The disease results from a lack of the enzyme hexosaminidase-A, which prevents the normal metabolism of lipids (fats, waxes, and related substances). Consequently, abnormal levels of lipids become stored in the brain and nerve cells, resulting in progressive physical and mental deterioration.

14. Tay–Sachs is transmitted by a single recessive gene. Thus, it occurs only when two carriers of the defect have children. The probability that a child born to such parents will be affected by Tay–Sachs disease is 25 percent. The disease occurs most often in Jews of East European (Ashkenazic) origin. Although it is fatal, the disease can be prevented. The genetic history of a family thought to be at risk needs to be studied. If both parents are carriers, professional counseling should be sought so they can decide whether they should risk having a child. Blood tests can also determine the risk. In the event a pregnancy has already begun, the probability of

Tay–Sachs disease can be determined through amniocentesis. An alternative to amniocentesis is chorionic villi sampling (ultrasound). It can be carried out earlier in pregnancy than can amniocentesis.

15. Intrauterine infections acquired by the mother during pregnancy may cause serious harm to the development of the fetus, resulting in physical disabilities and mental retardation. Among these infections are rubella (German measles) and congenital syphilis.

16. Various infections transmitted during the birth process or shortly afterwards can also lead to mental retardation and related physical disabilities. One of the most serious is bacterial meningitis. Other causes of mental retardation include tumors and destruction of blood cells in the fetus.

17. In 1940, Landsteiner and Wiener reported their research with Rhesus monkeys, leading to the discovery of a new blood factor that they named Rh. On the average about 85 percent of individuals have this factor; they are Rh-positive. Individuals lacking the factor are Rh-negative. Levine and his colleagues published their theory, now conclusively supported, that Rh incompatibility between mother and fetus causes physical and mental defects in the child. The disease is called erythroblastosis fetalis.

18. In erythroblastosis, the hemoglobin becomes separated from the red blood cells (erythrocytes). This destruction can cause severe oxygen deficiency, neurological damage, and mental retardation. Erythroblastosis occurs in the fetus and newborn only if the father is Rh-positive and the mother is Rh-negative. This incompatibility is genetically determined.

19. If the fetus of an Rh-negative mother is Rh-positive, the mother can become sensitized by the blood cells of the fetus if they leak into her circulatory system. The mother's immune system responds by producing antibodies, which destroy the Rh-positive blood cells of the fetus. Usually, no damage is done during a first pregnancy, but in future pregnancies the mother's antibodies can be transmitted to the fetus through the placenta and can destroy its red blood cells.

20. Prevention is the most effective treatment for erythroblastosis. A substance called Rh gamma globulin is injected into the bloodstream of an Rh-negative mother after the birth of her first Rh-positive child. This prevents the mother from becoming sensitized and producing antibodies that could harm subsequent children.

21. Other aversive physical conditions that can affect physical and mental development in the womb, during birth, or shortly after birth include (a) excessive irradiation, (b) trauma during delivery, and (c) lead poisoning.

22. The use of drugs during pregnancy can lead to abnormal development of the fetus, resulting in physical and mental damage. The drugs include prescription and over-the-counter medication as well as illegal psychoactive substances. Alcohol can also have deleterious effects. If its use during pregnancy is heavy, it can cause the fetal alcohol syndrome.

23. Whether or not an individual is judged to be mentally retarded depends a great deal on the criteria used for judging mental retardation.

24. A great deal of controversy has centered around the concept of mental retardation as applied to placement in public schools. In the past, school officials emphasized intelligence test scores and slighted the many social and cultural factors that influenced those scores. Some children were inappropriately labeled and placed in educational situations that kept them out of the mainstream of the educational process, to their disadvantage. Newer approaches have attempted to correct those errors.

25. Adverse sociocultural conditions can impede cognitive development. Sociocultural retardation tends to be at a mild level. Among the aversive environmental factors that contribute to it are (a) severe economic deprivation; (b) deficiencies in nutrition; (c) inadequate medical care; (d) poor housing, often in slums; and (e) lack of sensory stimulation.

26. Special programs have been developed to enrich the early environment of children who are at high risk for sociocultural mental retardation. Such programs do seem to improve the intellectual levels of preschoolers.

27. One of the most neglected areas in helping the mentally retarded is the use of counseling and psychotherapy. A growing movement now recognizes the value of such treatment and the importance of community-based living facilities.

28. Under the auspices of the President's Committee on Mental Retardation, a bill of rights for the mentally retarded has been developed. It makes the following provisions: (a) mentally retarded individuals, insofar as feasible, have the same rights as other human beings; (b) they have a right to proper medical care and education and training that will help them develop their potential; (c) they have the right to economic security; (d) they should live with parents, in foster homes, in group homes, or independently, with supervision where necessary, rather than in institutions; insofar as possible; and (e) they have a right to legal protection against exploitation and degrading treatment.

29. Under Public Law 94–142, mentally retarded children can no longer be excluded from a public education simply on the basis of physical, emotional, or intellectual deficiencies. All are entitled to a free and appropriate public education consistent with their abilities.

In previous parts, we discussed various methods of treating mental disorders. In Part 3 (Chapters 18–21), we consider therapeutic intervention more broadly, including biomedical, psychodynamic, humanistic, existential, behavioral, and cognitive approaches. In addition, we deal with legal issues of mental disorders, principles and methods of community mental health programs, and social action.

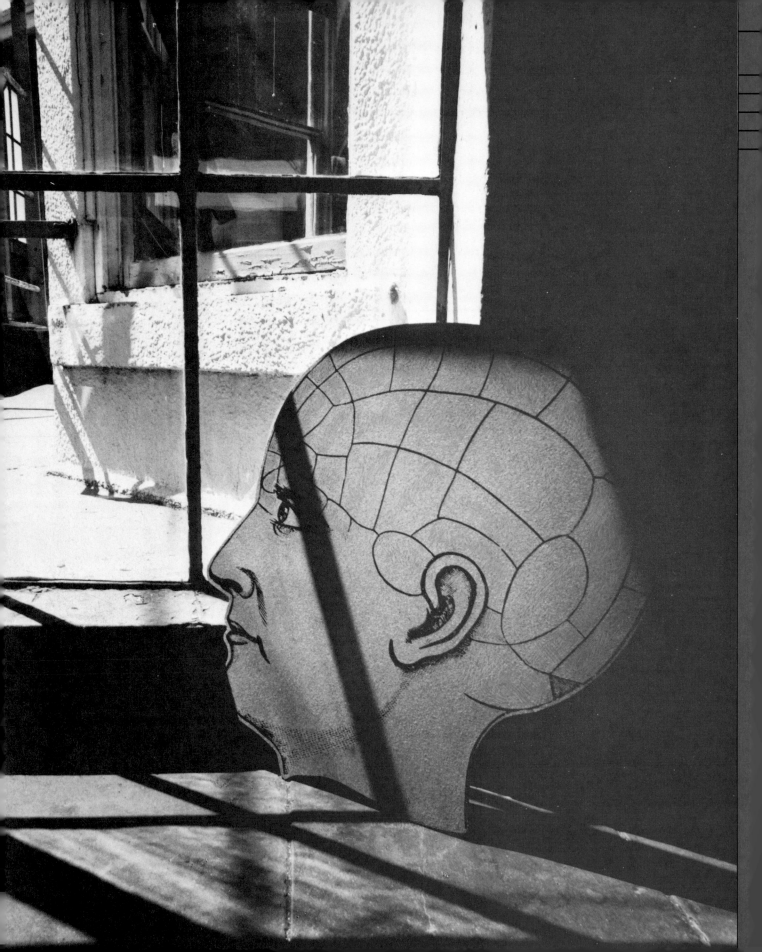

18

Biomedical Therapy

Canst thou not minister to a mind diseased,
Pluck from the memory a rooted sorrow;
Raze out the written troubles of the brain,
And with some sweet oblivious antidote
Cleanse the stuff'd bosom of that perilous stuff
Which weighs upon the heart?

SHAKESPEARE
Macbeth, Act V, Scene 3

In Chapter 3, we discussed various biomedical approaches to understanding abnormal behavior and experiences. We emphasized the biomedical view that mental disorders can ultimately be traced to abnormal structures and functions of the brain and nervous system. This perspective has stimulated a great deal of neuroscience research, especially studies that attempt to discover the biological basis of major depression and schizophrenic disorders (see Chapters 10 and 11). The application of this research to the treatment of mental disorders is a more recent development. The purpose of this chapter is to examine the origins, current use, and effectiveness of such therapy. The kinds of treatment we discuss are the province of psychiatrists and allied medical practitioners. In the next two chapters, we will consider various modes of psychotherapy, whose methods are used by nonmedical mental health professionals, such as clinical psychologists and clinical social workers, as well as by psychiatrists.

We begin our discussion of the biomedical treatment of mental disorders with insulin coma therapy, an instructive example of an early and wrong approach. We then deal with convulsive therapies and psychosurgery, both highly controversial. We conclude our discussion with the most advanced methods of biomedical treatment—the use of psychoactive drugs.

Insulin Coma Therapy: A Historical Note

Although it has now fallen into disrepute, **insulin coma therapy** is worth considering because it illustrates an early wrong path taken by biomedical therapists. Its very failure helped stimulate the search for better methods of biological treatment.

The Polish psychiatrist Manfred Sakel (1900–1957) introduced insulin coma therapy in 1933. In Vienna, Sakel developed a method for using insulin to produce coma in highly excited schizophrenic patients. He based his technique on the theory that an excess of adrenaline caused the brain cells of those patients to become oversensitive to external stimulation, which led to abnormally excited behavior. Sakel concluded that insulin was an effective treatment since it decreased the production of adrenaline and would therefore counteract the excessive stimulation. Sakel's theory proved to be wrong. Subsequent research found that schizophrenic patients did not have an excess of adrenaline prior to treatment. Indeed, the adrenaline levels of many of the patients increased rather than decreased during the insulin coma (Costin, 1976, p. 184).

Sakel eventually acknowledged the error of his theory, but he continued to insist that the use of insulin reduced schizophrenic excitement. Other practitioners disputed that claim. The use of Sakel's method rapidly declined, not only because of its questionable theoretical basis and effectiveness but also because of the dangerous physical complications that often occurred after treatment. The failure of insulin coma therapy, however, encouraged the quest for safer and more effective biomedical methods of treatment.

Convulsive Therapies

Drug-Induced Convulsions

In 1935, the Hungarian-born psychiatrist Lazlo Joseph Meduna (1896–1964), who later practiced in the United States, claimed he had successfully reduced the symptoms of schizophrenic patients by inducing convulsions with intravenous injections of a synthetic camphor preparation. Known in Europe as Cardiazol and in the United States as Metrazol, the drug produced violent convulsions that often resulted in bone fractures or dislocations. In addition, the treatment was frightening for patients, since they were conscious during the early stages of the convulsions.

Meduna based his treatment on observations he had made of schizophrenic patients undergoing epilepticlike convulsions. He claimed that their schizophrenic symptoms had decreased following those convulsions. Meduna theorized that the biochemical factors (actually unknown) that produced the epileptic convulsions were antagonistic to those that produced the schizophrenic symptoms. Thus, he concluded, by deliberately inducing convulsions in schizophrenic patients, he could reduce their symptoms (Costin, 1976, pp. 194–195).

Although research evidence did not support Meduna's theory or replicate his results, the use of other drugs to produce convulsions in psychotic patients continued. During the 1950s one of the most widely used drugs was an anesthetic gas known as Indoklon, applied by means of a mask and vaporizer. The advantage of Indoklon over Metrazol was that it produced unconsciousness before the convulsions began.

The use of drugs in convulsive therapy has all but disappeared and has been replaced by electric techniques. In addition, clinical work has found that convulsive therapy is more appropriate for major depression than for schizophrenic disorders (U.S. Department of Health and Human Services, 1985).

Electroconvulsive Therapy

In 1937, the Italian psychiatrists Ugo Cerletti (1877–1963) and Lucio Bini (1908–1964) introduced **electroconvulsive therapy (ECT),** more popularly known as electroshock therapy. Although they were favorably impressed by Meduna's work, they thought electric stimulation of the brain would be a more controlled and efficient procedure for producing convulsions. Cerletti and Bini's theory about why convulsive therapy was effective also differed from Meduna's. They hypothesized that the convulsions brought on a state similar to death, and therefore acted as a biological defense mechanism, which they called agonine. They were not able to describe the exact nature of agonine, but they speculated that it strengthened the adaptive capacities of the patient and thus aided recovery (Cerletti & Bini, 1938).

Although ECT was widely adopted in the treatment of major depression, Cerletti and Bini's theory of agonine has never been empirically verified. However, there has been no lack of other theories to explain the therapeutic effects (Miller, 1967). It has been proposed that the spasms produced by ECT destroy pathological nerve cells responsible for depression. Various psychoanalysts have hypothesized that the convulsions represent a

Italian psychiatrists Ugo Cerletti and Lucio Bini introduced electroconvulsive therapy in 1937. Although their theory explaining why it was effective failed to gain empirical support, the therapy became widely used in treating depression.

punishment that the patient unconsciously desires. This supposition is based on the observation that highly depressed people often express strong feelings of guilt and self-condemnation. Conditioning theory (see Chapter 4) also considers the possibility that the patient perceives ECT as a punishment. The aversive effect of the electric shock may become associated with the depression. Thus, the patient becomes conditioned to avoid such feelings and behavior (Costin, 1976, p. 195).

A more recent theory, and one better supported by evidence, is based on the activity of catecholamines in the brain. As we discussed in Chapter 11, catecholamines are biochemical substances that help transmit information between nerve cells, including those involved in arousal and emotion. Major depression is often accompanied by a reduction in this activity. Since studies have shown that ECT produces a massive increase in catecholamines, it may well be that this biochemical change alleviates the depression (Leavitt, 1974; Wetzel, 1984, p. 259). More research is needed to confirm this theory.

Techniques of Electroconvulsive Therapy

Currently ECT is used mainly in the treatment of major depression—deep, psychotic depression that removes sufferers from contact with their environment and makes them resistant to human communication (see Chapter 10). One of the main advantages of ECT is its prompt effect. Thus, it is often used when the depression is accompanied by preoccupation with suicide or by anguish so intense and unbearable that the patient welcomes prompt relief.

Electroconvulsive therapy was first used in the United States in 1940 (Schuyler, 1974, p. 127). Its early application often resulted in bone fractures and cerebrovascular problems and occasionally in death. One of the central reasons for these tragic consequences was improper preparation of the patient for the treatment. Since then, ECT has undergone considerable modification, making it safer and less frightening.

In the standard ECT procedure, the patient is given an intravenous injection of a fast-acting barbiturate, such as Pentothol. Once the anesthetic begins to take effect, usually within a minute, a muscle relaxant is injected intravenously. One of the most widely used drugs is succinylcholine chloride (Anectine). The patient lies on a well-padded table or bed while electrodes are attached above each temple. This is called the bilateral method. In the unilateral method, the electrodes are placed only on the right temple area. A button is pressed, sending an alternating current of 70 to 130 volts (200 to 1600 milliamperes) through the brain for a fraction of a second, causing a **convulsive seizure**.

The seizure consists of two phases. During the **clonic phase**, which begins immediately after the current is applied, the voluntary muscles contract for about 10 seconds. The **tonic phase** follows; in it, the voluntary muscles alternately contract and relax for about 30 seconds, producing mild twitching and jerking movements. Since the muscle relaxant also affects respiration, an oxygen mask is applied during the seizure until breathing becomes spontaneous. Upon awakening, the patient has no memory of the convulsive period, is usually confused for a few hours, has difficulty in concentrating, and often cannot remember events that occurred just before or after the treatment. In some instances, the mental confusion and loss of memory persist for several months, although that is not typical (Kolb & Brodie, 1982, pp. 836–837; Wetzel, 1984, pp. 257–258).

**Evaluation of
Electroconvulsive
Therapy**

Studies of the effectiveness of ECT have generally focused on the extent to which it alleviates symptoms of major depression and on the side effects of the treatment. Reviews of the evidence conclude that ECT can be an effective means of treating major depression, especially for people who have not responded to antidepressant drugs (Royal College of Psychiatrists, 1977; U.S. Department of Health and Human Services, 1985).

Since loss of memory immediately after ECT is common, a number of studies have examined the extent to which such loss persists. Generally, the disability does not extend beyond six months. However, some patients continue to complain of memory impairment even though objective memory tests do not show a loss. Possibly, they expect and fear sensory loss and therefore use normal instances of forgetting to substantiate their apprehensions (Squire & Chase, 1975).

In spite of the many refinements in ECT over the years, and in spite of evidence that its use has increased in the United States, there is still considerable debate over the value of the procedure. Its proponents point out that 80 to 90 percent of depressed patients who undergo ECT are greatly improved (Andreasen, 1984a, pp. 208–209). An evaluation of the side effects of ECT in California over a seven-year period (1977–1983) cites the following results (Kramer, 1985).

This patient is being prepared for electroconvulsive therapy. The current consensus among psychiatrists in the United States is that ECT should be used only when drug therapy is not effective or in an extreme emergency.

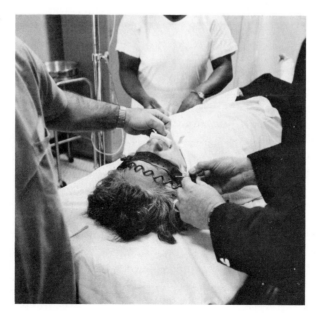

■ No cases of fracture were reported.

■ Two deaths were associated with the treatment — an incidence of 0.2 deaths per 10,000 treatments. The mortality rate of childbirth in the United States is six times greater.

■ Thirty-five cases of cardiac arrest occurred, and all patients were successfully resuscitated.

Mental health professionals who support the use of ECT generally do so with certain reservations. They emphasize that the treatment must be used with discretion and carefully monitored. Also, the total number and frequency of treatment sessions must be limited (U.S. Department of Health and Human Services, 1985).

Although some opponents of ECT concede that it is a relatively safe and effective method of treating severe depression, they still have serious ethical and social–psychological objections.

> Fear of loss of control or even fear of dying is readily understandable in the case of electroshock patients and should be addressed by the clinician. Less likely to be acknowledged is the damage done to an already fragile sense of self-esteem. ECT can be a humiliating experience, a procedure that is subjectively dehumanizing. Rather than fear death, the patient may fear waking from the seizure and facing those who have witnessed it. . . . ECT also plays directly into "justifiable" punishment fantasies for those already riddled with self-blame. For these reasons alone, I believe the treatment is contraindicated. Should a physician decide in favor of ECT, time should be taken to gently explore these feelings that are so congruent with the depressed person's sense of self. To ignore them or to be superficial in regard to them is destructive to the patient and will hinder the progress of treatment. (Wetzel, 1984, p. 258).

Psychosurgery

As the name suggests, **psychosurgery** produces changes in thinking and behavior by destroying or removing brain tissue or by severing brain tissue so as to disconnect one area of the brain from another. In contrast to neurosurgery (for example, removing a brain tumor), psychosurgery is usually carried out in the absence of any direct knowledge that a particular area of the brain is diseased or injured.

In labeling psychosurgical procedures, the suffix "otomy" is used when brain tissues are destroyed or nerve fibers in the brain are cut. The suffix "ectomy" is used when tissue is actually removed from the brain. For example, a **prefrontal lobotomy** is the destruction of tissue in the anterior lobes of the cerebral hemispheres or the severing of nerve fibers that connect those lobes to the rest of the brain. A **prefrontal lobectomy** involves the actual removal of prefrontal lobes or parts of them (Brown, Wienckowski, & Bivens, 1973).

Development of Surgical Procedures

Psychosurgery for reducing the emotional distress involved in severe psychotic disorders was initially developed by the Portuguese neurologist Egas Moniz (1874–1953) and performed in 1935 by his colleague Almeida Lima, a neurosurgeon. The operation was called prefrontal leucotomy, because it involved the use of a leucotome, a hollow needle containing a steel wire loop. The leucotome was inserted into the brain through a burr hole drilled into the skull. When the leucotome was in the desired location of the prefrontal lobes, the steel wire loop was extended from the needle and then rotated. In this way, the nerve fibers in the frontal lobes of the cerebral hemisphere, a center of thought, were disconnected from the thalamus, a center of emotion. Moniz theorized that the severing of those fibers would eliminate certain abnormal pathways in the brain that contributed to the psychotic patient's violent or unmanageable behavior. In a preliminary report, Moniz described the results of the prefrontal leucotomy. Of 20 patients who had undergone the operation, all had survived, 7 had recovered, and 7 had improved. Subsequently, Moniz supervised operations on some 100 patients. He then concluded that the procedure was generally successful in reducing the severity of psychotic symptoms, especially those that involved violent and irrational emotional behavior. In 1949, Moniz received the Nobel prize in physiology and medicine for having discovered "the therapeutic value of prefrontal leucotomy in certain psychoses" (Valenstein, 1973, p. 54).

Several years after Moniz reported his work, neurosurgeons Walter Freeman and James Watts developed a similar operation in the United States, using more precise techniques. They called their procedure prefrontal lobotomy. Like the Moniz operation, the Freeman and Watts method involved the severing of subcortical connections in the prefrontal lobes. However, the theory underlying the operation differed from that of Moniz. Freeman and Watts believed that in psychotic disorders, especially those involving unmanageable behavior and painful emotional distress, the thought processes controlled by the prefrontal lobes intensified the emotions controlled by the thalamus (see Figure 18.1). Thus, severing the neural connections between those two areas would reduce the patient's abnormal behavior and distress. According to their reports, that theory was confirmed (Freeman & Watts, 1942; Miller, 1972).

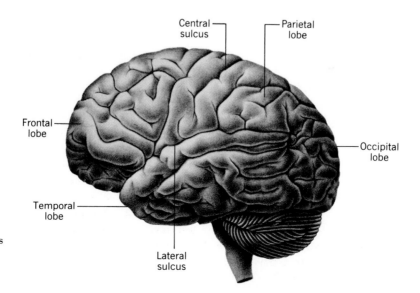

Figure 18.1

Surface of the left cerebral hemisphere. Shown are the lobes and two main fissures (sulci). (From Davison & Neale, 1986, p. 600).

During the late 1940s and early 1950s, the use of psychosurgical techniques spread considerably, especially in the United States and England. Operations were carried out not only on the frontal lobes but also on other areas of the brain — for example, the parietal (upper), the temporal (side), and the occipital (rear) lobes of the cerebral hemisphere. In some instances even more radical operations were performed, such as prefrontal lobectomy, in which an entire area was removed from the frontal lobes. In addition, the operation was extended from the treatment of schizophrenic patients to those who were highly depressed and those who suffered from severe obsessions and compulsions.

Although the operations did seem to produce a calming effect, so that the patient's behavior became more manageable, various critics noted that the change was accompanied by a pronounced flattening of emotional experience. Although the patients now appeared on the surface to react more appropriately to their environment, they seemed to be only going through the motions of responding to other people and expressing their feelings. Whatever they had felt deeply before the operation now seemed barely to excite their concern. Indeed, the pendulum had swung back from their previous emotional excess to an equally abnormal diminished emotional state.

As the use of psychosurgery increased, mental health professionals and the public in general began to react with revulsion. Critics pointed out that the methods were crude, that excessively large amounts of frontal white matter were cut, and that patients showed losses in social judgment, creativity, and motivation (Andreasen, 1984a, p. 214). As a result, the number of operations subsided considerably. At the same time, drugs for the treatment of mental disorders began to gain a great deal of attention from mental health professionals. These drugs produced beneficial results without the damaging and irreversible effects of psychosurgery.

In the early 1970s, psychosurgery began to show a revival. However, the procedures were cautiously introduced on a small scale, subject to carefully specified and individualized conditions. The techniques became more sophisticated and precise, involving a more controlled and minimal alteration of brain tissue (Brown, Wienckowski, & Bivens, 1973; Culliton, 1976b). The lobotomy was discarded in favor of operations on areas deeper in the brain to avoid the extreme intellectual and emotional deficits that the older procedures had often produced. Surgeons now concentrated on cutting away highly selected portions of the limbic system. Located in the cerebral hemisphere below the cortex (see Figure 3.1), the limbic system plays an important role in the arousal of emotion (Kimble, 1988, p. 79). Numerous nerve fibers connect the structures within the system and the system as a whole with other areas of the cerebral hemispheres.

During the 1970s, **stereotaxic procedures** were developed to operate on the limbic system. Guided by geometric coordinates and x-rays, the surgeon places an electrode in a precise location in the brain. The surgeon then excises the tissue at the tip of the electrode by passing a current through the electrode. Thus, highly selected portions of the limbic system can be cut away, as well as portions of other structures involved in emotional behavior, such as the thalamus and hypothalamus. Current techniques have concentrated on specific cutting of very tiny portions of tracts connecting the cingulate gyrus to the remainder of the limbic system. Presumably, this method breaks up certain circuits of the limbic system and thus helps stop the cycle of adverse emotional stimulation. The cingulate gyrus was selected because it is one of the most accessible parts of the limbic system. The procedure is called **cingulotomy**. Although these newer procedures are far more precise than the earlier and cruder prefrontal lobotomy operations, there still remain important ethical issues, as well as questions about how the specific structures in the limbic system are related to specific disturbances in emotional behavior (Andreason, 1984a, pp. 214–215; Holden, 1973; Older, 1974).

Ethical Issues and Current Status of Psychosurgery

Critics questioned both the usefulness and the justification of the new surgical techniques. Why resort to them, they asked, when a wide range of other treatments — biochemical, behavioral, and psychotherapeutic — are available? More fundamentally, critics raised issues concerning the ethical justification of psychosurgery (Breggin, 1972, 1974). In response to these criticisms, the National Association on Mental Health published a position paper on psychosurgery, emphasizing that it "should not be used except in those instances where the patient is in such great personal distress due to his mental disorder that he, by his own choice, would prefer psychosurgery rather than remain with his existing condition." In addition, the association emphasized that all other alternatives must first be considered "or have been given an adequate trial as defined by consensus of the patient, [the] family, and at least two reputable physicians, one of whom should be a psychiatrist" ("Psychosurgery: An NAMH Position Statement," 1974, p. 22).

Also in response to the increasing controversy, the U.S. Department of Health, Education, and Welfare (now the Department of Health and Human Services) issued specific guidelines to regulate the use of psychosurgery in medical research and services supported by grants or contracts from the department. These guidelines were designed to safeguard the rights and welfare of patients, to ensure that the potential benefits of psychosurgery outweighed the risks, and to ensure that the patient's informed consent was obtained in an appropriate manner. The department also outlined the correct procedures to follow in obtaining informed consent (Brown, Wienckowski, & Bivens, 1973, pp. 9 – 10).

1. A fair explanation of the procedures to be followed, including identifying those that are experimental.

2. A description of the possible discomforts and risks.

3. A description of the possible benefits.

4. An explanation of appropriate alternative therapeutic procedures that might help the patient.

5. An offer to answer any questions concerning the procedures to be used.

6. A statement that the patient is free to withdraw consent at any time prior to the proposed operation.

Psychiatrists Kaplan and Sadock (1985) estimate that well under 100 operations are now being performed in the United States each year, and that those operations represent a treatment of last resort. They conclude that "in spite of the recent advances in the therapeutic modalities for psychiatric disorders, a relatively small number of severely distressed patients, totally incapacitated both socially and vocationally, are not responsive to any of the currently available forms of treatment. . . . [F]or them, psychosurgery is the only alternative hope" (p. 687).

Although the use of psychosurgery has waned considerably, ethical issues remain. Nobody would contend that neurosurgery is unjustifiable for remedying physical disabilities — for example, removing a brain tumor. However, critics continue to maintain that the situation is qualitatively different when neural pathways are interrupted and brain tissue is destroyed solely to achieve a predetermined behavioral end. In addition, many people feel a natural revulsion at the thought of cutting up people's brains in order to achieve social and behavioral control. Given the prevailing social and political climate, it is unlikely that a resurgence of psychosurgery is imminent (Valenstein, 1986).

Psychoactive Drug Therapy

Over the past four decades, various biochemical substances have been developed that produce marked effects on psychological states. They can affect the way in which one perceives the environment, experiences emotions, solves problems, organizes information, and stores in memory various impressions of external reality. Collectively, these substances are known as **psychoactive drugs**. Researchers and clinicians in the field of **psychopharmacology** — the science that deals with the effects of drugs on behavior and experience — have developed a wide range of psychoactive agents for the treatment of mental disorders. Many of these drugs have proved to be very beneficial. Others were promising at first but turned out to be of little value, and others are still being tested.

Psychoactive drugs have greatly reduced the number of patients in mental hospitals. People leave the hospital much earlier and are also in a better position to profit from psychotherapy and changes in their social environment. The drugs have enabled many people to be helped as outpatients instead of being hospitalized.

In the early flush of success with psychoactive drugs, some biomedical researchers and clinicians believed that they would eliminate the need for psychotherapy. Others remained less optimistic because psychoactive drugs do not in themselves change the aversive social and personal circumstances that contribute to psychological disorders. "Real permanent improvement of symptoms results from favorable experience with the environment which shapes behavior so that it can persist in the absence of drugs. The benefit of a drug which temporarily permits normal functioning by relieving anxiety or facilitating communicativeness, is that it may indirectly lead to long-range improvement" (Leavitt, 1974, p. 148).

The majority of psychoactive drugs used today for the treatment of mental disorders fall into four broad categories: antipsychotic, antidepressant, antianxiety, and antimanic. Table 18.1 shows some of the more commonly used drugs in each of these categories.

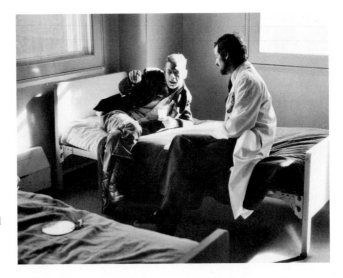

In this scene in a mental hospital the therapist is combining drug treatment with an informal psychotherapy session.

Table 18.1 Some Psychoactive Drugs Commonly Used in Therapy

Use in Therapy	Class of Drugs	Generic Name	Trade Name
Antipsychotic	Soporific (sedating) phenothiazines	Chlorpromazine	Thorazine
		Thioridazine	Mellaril
	Nonsoporific phenothiazines	Acetophenazine	Tindal
		Fluphenazine	Permitil
		Trifluoperazine	Stelazine
		Perphenazine	Trilafon
	Butyrophenones	Haloperidol	Haldol
Antidepressant	Tricyclics	Imipramine	Tofranil
		Amitriptyline	Elavil
	Monoamine oxidase inhibitors	Phenelzine	Nardil
		Tranylcypromine	Parnate
Antianxiety	Propanediols	Meprobamate	Equanil, Miltown
	Benzodiazepines	Chlordiazepoxide	Librium
		Diazepam	Valium
Antimanic	Lithium salts	Lithium carbonate	Eskalith
			Lithane

Antimanic drugs are also antipsychotics, since manic episodes are a form of psychosis. The separate category "antimanic" is listed here because lithium is used almost exclusively in the treatment of manic disorder.

Sources: American Psychiatric Association, 1980b; Honigfeld & Howard, 1978; Lickey & Gordon, 1983.

Antipsychotic Drugs

Also known as major tranquilizers, psychotropics, and neuroleptics, **antipsychotic drugs** have been extremely effective in treating various psychotic disorders, especially schizophrenia (see Chapter 11). Unfortunately, they have also been misused. To some extent, the label *tranquilizer*, which drug manufacturers used when the medications were first put on the market, fostered this misuse. For many practitioners, the label implied that the principal use of such drugs was for anxiety disorders. However, they are effective mainly for treating schizophrenia (Honigfeld & Howard, 1978, pp. 4–5). They have also been helpful in alleviating the symptoms of agitated depression, manic episodes, emotionally unstable personalities, and toxic psychoses induced by LSD or other recreational drugs.

The first of the antipsychotic drugs to be used successfully was chlorpromazine (Thorazine), which was introduced into the United States from France in 1954 and released for marketing in 1955. Chlorpromazine belongs to a class of drugs called phenothiazines. These drugs have become the most widely prescribed and best researched biochemical agents for treating psychotic disorders, especially schizophrenia (Julien, 1981, p. 126).

Effectiveness of Phenothiazines

Within a few years after its introduction in France, chlorpromazine was adopted on a large scale in a great many countries, including the United States. It continued to be effective in reducing the stress and cognitive confusion that are especially characteristic of acute phases of certain psychoses, schizophrenia in particular. The administration of chlorpromazine to large numbers of severely disturbed patients produced a dramatic change in the social climate of the typical ward in public psychiatric hospitals. The disruptive atmosphere of former years, punctuated by crises with which the nurses and attendants barely managed to cope, began to disappear. The noise level on the ward decreased noticeably, the stench so characteristic of the old-time psychiatric hospital vanished, and the state hospital ward became a more tolerable place to stay. More important, the reduction of impulsive, violent, and unpredictable behavior made it possible to develop a variety of occupational, recreational, and group psychotherapy programs. Liberated from a large share of their custodial and policelike functions, nurses and attendants could now spend a greater share of their time interacting socially with the patients, relating to them, and meeting their psychological needs.

The use of chlorpromazine and other phenothiazines has been a major factor in shortening the average hospital stay of psychiatric patients. During the first half of the 20th century, the number of patients in mental hospitals in the United States increased from 150,000 to about 500,000. Some patients spent their entire lives in the hospital. In 1956, the first year antipsychotic drugs were used extensively, the upward trend in the hospitalized population began to reverse. By 1975, the number of patients had declined to about 200,000, and the downward trend has continued (Berger, 1978; Lickey & Gordon, 1983, p. 4).

Side Effects of Phenothiazines

Phenothiazines can produce troublesome and even highly noxious symptoms. Short-term and relatively minor reactions include dry mouth, blurred vision, and various allergic reactions. These side effects usually occur shortly after treatment has begun. As a rule, they can be controlled through regulating dosage or changing medication. Other short-term but more distressing side effects include symptoms similar to those found in Parkinson's disease — stiff shuffling gait, tremor, and fixed facial expression. Fortunately, these reactions can usually be decreased or even eliminated by such medications as biperiden (Akineton). Some therapists prescribe the drug as soon as treatment begins (Baldessarini, 1977; Hollister, 1977, p. 144; Honigfeld & Howard, 1978, pp. 23 – 26, 92 – 98).

A more long-term and highly distressing effect of antipsychotic drug treatment is **tardive dyskinesia,** which involves stereotyped and involuntary muscular activity that may occur months or even years after drug treatment has begun and may persist long after treatment has ended. The precise frequency of tardive dyskinesia is difficult to estimate. Reported prevalence rates among hospitalized patients range as high as 56 percent, with an overall rate of about 25 percent. Unfortunately, reliable methods of countering tardive dyskinesia have not yet been discovered. Therefore, experts in psychopharmacology have increasingly warned psychiatrists and other medical practitioners to prescribe antipsychotic drugs very cautiously, especially for long-term treatment (Berger & Rexroth, 1980; Davis, Schaffer, Killian, Kinard, & Chan, 1980; Jeste & Wyatt, 1982; Kucharski & Unterwald, 1981; Mukherjee, Rosen, Caracci, & Shukla, 1986; Munnetz & Roth, 1985; Slaw & Kalachnik, 1985; Toenniessen, Casey, & McFarland, 1985).

Other Antipsychotic Medications

In addition to the phenothiazines, a class of drugs known as butyrophenones has been effective in the treatment of psychotic disorders, especially schizophrenia. One of the most widely used drugs in this class is haloperidol (Haldol). Some reports indicate that the butyrophenones cause less drowsiness and general sedation than do the soporific type of phenothiazines. In addition, butyrophenones work faster—a particular advantage in cases of highly distraught and disruptive behavior, as in acute schizophrenic episodes (Kolb & Brodie, 1982, p. 822).

Antidepressant Drugs

Clinicians prescribe **antidepressant drugs** for a broad spectrum of depressive disorders, ranging from depressive neurosis (classified in DSM-III-R as dysthymia) to depression of psychotic proportions (major depression in DSM-III-R). Because of this wide application, the drugs are called antidepressant rather than antipsychotic, even though their greatest importance is in the treatment of major (psychotic) depression (see Chapter 10).

In general, drugs are quite effective in treating depression. However, an analysis of studies published during a 10-year period (1974–1984) suggests that combining drugs with psychotherapy is more effective than either treatment is alone (Conte, Plutchik, Wild, & Karasu, 1986).

Tricyclics

A number of chemically related compounds have entered psychopharmacological treatment in the last few decades. The general name for this group of drugs is tricyclics, because their chemical structure is in the form of two benzene rings joined to a central ring. All of the tricyclics produce similar effects, and all of them are useful primarily in the treatment of major depression (Andreasen, 1984a, pp. 194–196).

The earliest tricyclic to be introduced into biochemical therapy was imipramine (Tofranil), developed in Switzerland. The most immediate effect of this chemical agent is to reduce such symptoms of depression as chronic fatigue, slowness of thought and action, and the inability to experience pleasure or maintain interests. As these symptoms diminish, other indications of major depression—including feelings of guilt, unworthiness, and helplessness—also recede (Andreason, 1984a, p. 195; Berger, 1977, p. 175). Imipramine seems to be most effective in cases of endogenous depression (see Chapter 10)—that is, depression that has no identifiable external causes (Kaplan & Sadock, 1985, p. 653).

Undesirable consequences of imipramine treatment include a fine, high-frequency tremor of the hands, arms, and head, distinct from the Parkinsonlike symptoms associated with the phenothiazines. The patient may have difficulty forming speech sounds and may feel tingling sensations in the arms and legs. Less frequently, inability to walk and visual hallucinations have been observed; these symptoms are more likely to occur with very high doses. Imipramine also affects the functioning of the autonomic nervous system; for example, it induces heart palpitations, rapid heartbeat, profuse sweating, urinary retention, and a marked lowering of blood pressure. These complications require careful and continuous monitoring, so that dosages may be decreased, drugs substituted, or treatment discontinued as side effects appear (Honigfeld & Howard, 1978).

Clinicians hoped that the tricyclics would be workable substitutes for the other major somatic treatment of depression, ECT, and to some extent they are. However, tricyclics work slowly; often two or more weeks must elapse before their benefits become apparent. For that reason, strong psychological support and direct social intervention may be crucial from the very outset in helping the depressed person. Furthermore, some biomedical therapists argue that ECT may still be necessary in cases of extremely severe depression, especially when it is accompanied by suicidal intentions (Andreasen, 1984a, pp. 207–209).

Monoamine Oxidase Inhibitors

Another major group of antidepressant drugs are the monoamine oxidase inhibitors (MAOIs). As the acronym suggests, MAOIs inhibit the production of monoamine oxidase (MAO), an enzyme that reduces the level of catecholamines in the brain. Thus, administering MAOIs can increase the production of catecholamines. Since depression, especially that of psychotic proportions, may be associated with a reduction of catecholamines, increasing them may alleviate the depression. (See Chapter 10 for a discussion of theories concerning the role of catecholamines in the development of mood disorders.)

During the 1960s, MAOIs were used extensively in the United States and were reported to be highly effective. Since then, however, their use has been curtailed considerably because their side effects have been more severe than those of any other class of drugs used in treating depression. Certain MAOIs damaged the liver, and they were withdrawn from the market (Raskin, 1974). However, MAOIs in current use still have serious side effects. For example, they interact with other drugs, such as stimulants, cold tablets, and pills used in reducing diets. MAOIs also interact with foods containing tyramine, including beer, chocolate, coffee, chicken livers, aged cheese, pickled herring, lox, and wine, especially Chianti. Such interactions can result in sudden attacks of dangerously high blood pressure. For these reasons, MAOIs are prescribed only when a wide range of tricyclics have failed (Baldessarini, 1977, pp. 114–121; Leavitt, 1974, p. 34; Lickey & Gordon, 1983, pp. 202–203).

Antianxiety Drugs

As their label suggests, **antianxiety drugs** are used mainly to alleviate a variety of disturbances that DSM-III-R classifies under the broad heading of anxiety disorders: phobias, panic attacks, obsessions and compulsions, and posttraumatic stress disorder. (See Chapter 5 for a detailed discussion of these disorders.) They are also used in the treatment of conversion (hysterical) disorders (see Chapter 6).

Barbiturates

Before the 1950s, the main drugs used to control anxiety disorders were the barbiturates. Barbiturates depress the central nervous system, and thus have a sedative effect, but they are dangerously addictive. (See Chapter 15 for a detailed discussion of drug tolerance and addiction.)

Other Antianxiety Drugs

Since the late 1950s and early 1960s, various alternatives to barbiturates have been developed. These drugs are more selective in their effects and are generally less dangerous than the barbiturates. For example, the propanediols, such as meprobamate (Equanil, Miltown), when properly applied, can reduce the panic that occurs in certain forms of anxiety disorders without seriously disturbing perceptual and intellectual behavior. When inability to sleep is a crucial problem in anxiety behaviors, the benzodiazepines (Librium, Valium) can be just as effective as barbiturates but are less likely to lead to addiction or produce toxic effects. Modern antianxiety drugs are more difficult to use in suicide attempts than the barbiturates. This is especially true of the benzodiazepines, which depress the central nervous system less severely than the barbiturates (Honigfeld & Howard, 1978, p. 46).

Studies comparing the relative effectiveness of antianxiety drugs have reported few marked differences. However, the propanediols carry a greater risk of withdrawal symptoms and toxic effects than the benzodiazepines. The most common side effect of all antianxiety drugs is drowsiness. However, this usually disappears early in the treatment regimen. Less common and usually rather mild reactions include tremors, skin eruptions, and abdominal pain.

Dangers and Limitations

THE WALL STREET JOURNAL

"That's life. Just take your Valium."

The danger of abuse and dependence is always present in the use of antianxiety drugs, especially if high dosage levels are maintained over a long time. Although these drugs were originally intended for the control of anxieties and fears so intense that they significantly impair normal functioning, they have often been prescribed to cushion people against everyday stresses and frustrations. By 1981, more than 65 million prescriptions for diazepam (Valium) were being filled each year, making it the most highly prescribed drug in the United States. Some observers became convinced that antianxiety drugs were grossly overprescribed. By 1983, Valium had declined to fourth place, mainly because the medical profession realized that the drug had an extremely high potential for abuse (Baum, Kennedy, Knapp, Faich, 1985; Julien, 1981, pp. 53, 83; Molotsky, 1985).

Problems of dependence still exist with the antianxiety drugs. What limits their effectiveness in the long run is that people build up a tolerance for a given dosage. To maintain the same effect, the dosage must be increased. Abrupt discontinuation of the drug has produced physiological dependence and significant withdrawal symptoms, which means that addiction has developed. In the case of benzodiazepines, the withdrawal symptoms are less severe and dangerous than with the barbiturates. Moreover, it is unlikely that any withdrawal symptoms will be experienced if the drug has been used less than two months. Their legitimate and helpful use, then, is primarily in short-range treatment. However, they are not in themselves a cure for anxiety or for the stresses, frustrations, and disappointments that we inevitably encounter in our daily lives (Baldessarini, 1977).

Antianxiety drugs are best used as adjuncts to treatment. Their greatest value lies in reducing the most obvious and disturbing symptoms of maladaptive anxiety and hysterical disorders. In that way, they can facilitate the use of psychotherapy and the manipulation of the social environment to overcome such disorders (Beitman & Klerman, 1984) (see Chapters 19 and 20).

Lithium Carbonate: An Antimanic Drug

The salt **lithium carbonate** was introduced into American psychiatric practice during the 1960s. Its therapeutic effects had already been studied in Australia (Cade, 1949), but the report that it markedly reduced manic episodes (see Chapter 10) evoked little response from psychiatric practitioners in the United States and Europe. Later reports, however, demonstrated more thoroughly that lithium carbonate was directly responsible for reducing manic symptoms (Johnson, 1975; Schou, 1968). Currently, lithium is used to reduce the symptoms of manic episodes and prevent their recurrence, especially when the episodes occur in cycles that presumably have a biological basis (see Chapter 10 for a discussion of bipolar mood disorder).

Unfortunately, lithium treatment poses a considerable toxic risk if the dosage is not controlled precisely. The effectiveness and safety of the drug have a much narrower margin of error than most of the other psychoactive drugs. For that reason, the dosage must be carefully monitored until the proper maintenance level is safely established. In this procedure, special attention is focused on the patient's blood lithium level. This level must be kept within a narrow range, not only to achieve positive results but also to prevent undesirable side effects, including gastrointestinal disturbances, such as diarrhea, loss of appetite, nausea, and vomiting; dizziness, tremor, and blurred vision; and difficulty in walking. These reactions can serve not only as a warning that the level of lithium is too high but also that the patient is not able to adapt satisfactorily to that particular form of treatment (Fieve, 1976; Honigfeld & Howard, 1978, pp. 40–44; Lickey & Gordon, 1983). A possible side effect of long-term use of lithium is "permanent impairment of kidney function" (Honigfeld & Howard, 1978, p. 43).

How and Why Psychoactive Drugs Work

Researchers in the area of drug therapy have long been aware that expectation and suggestion can color the patient's experience and the observer's perceptions of drug effects. To show that the drug itself produces the effects observed, it is necessary to demonstrate that they exceed the results of suggestion and expectation. This is accomplished by the use of **placebo drugs** — pharmaceutically inert compounds whose effects are entirely attributable to suggestion or expectation. In research on psychoactive drugs, the drugs are administered under **double-blind conditions**. In this procedure, each drug is coded; neither the physician nor the patient knows whether it is the real thing or the placebo.

The major drugs we have described in this chapter have all been tested under double-blind conditions with a variety of clinical populations. Our knowledge of their effects is not confounded by suggestion and expectation, and the changes they produce are genuine. We turn, then, to the question of how these agents work and what their impact is on the disorders they are intended to counteract.

The traditional position is that psychoactive drugs eliminate the symptoms of a disorder without affecting its causes. Moreover, their effects are more general than specific — that is, they do not directly attack schizophrenia, depression, anxiety, or mania.

> Regrettably, pharmacotherapy has not proven itself to be a cure for the schizophrenic syndrome. In most instances it affects primarily what Eugen Bleuler called the secondary symptoms — that is, delusions, hallucinations, and possibly thought disorders — but it does not affect the personality structure of schizophrenics. In fact, recent research suggests that neuroleptics may affect neurotransmitters and neuroreceptors involved in hallucinations and delusions, but that they may not significantly affect the schizophrenic personality at all. The patient often remains withdrawn, peculiar, etc., or what we might call a "silent schizophrenic." (Bellak, 1979, pp. 17–18)

Bellak's comments can be extended to other disturbances, notably anxiety and mood disorders (see Chapters 5 and 10).

Other researchers take a different point of view, asserting that the development of a wide variety of psychoactive drugs has made it possible in many instances, to prescribe the right drug for the right patient (Wender & Klein, 1981). Moreover, the proponents of the new biological psychiatry relate the effectiveness of drug treatment to the growing state of knowledge concerning biochemical disturbances of the central nervous system, especially in such disorders as depression and schizophrenia (Andreasen, 1984a, pp. 150–151).

That psychoactive drugs work is a matter of wide agreement. How they work, and whether in effect they actually "cure" mental disorders, remains a topic of controversy. Few practitioners are prepared to abandon the use of psychoactive drugs, especially in treating the most serious and incapacitating psychological conditions. It is undeniable that these drugs have radically changed the nature of treatment and the experience of psychological disorder in the second half of the 20th century. Nevertheless, their effectiveness does not lessen the importance of psychotherapy and social intervention for the treatment of mental disorders.

Summary

1. Although it has fallen into disrepute, insulin coma therapy is a good illustration of an early wrong path that biomedical therapists took in the treatment of mental disorders. Polish psychiatrist Manfred Sakel first used insulin to produce coma in highly excited schizophrenic patients in 1933. Use of the method rapidly declined because of its questionable theoretical basis and the dangerous physical complications it caused.

2. In 1935, the Hungarian-born psychiatrist Lazlo Meduna claimed he had successfully reduced the symptoms of schizophrenic patients by inducing convulsions with intravenous injections of a synthetic camphor preparation. Research did not support Meduna's claims. Electroconvulsive therapy (ECT) has replaced the use of convulsive drugs to treat psychotic patients, and it is applied to the treatment of major depression rather than schizophrenia.

3. ECT was introduced in 1937 by the Italian psychiatrists Ugo Cerletti and Lucio Bini. They hypothesized that the convulsions the shock produced acted as a biological defense mechanism, strengthening the adaptive capacities of the patient and thus aiding recovery.

4. Although ECT was widely adopted for the treatment of major depression, Cerletti and Bini's theory was never verified. Other theories have been advanced as to why ECT is sometimes effective, but none have been conclusively supported by empirical evidence.

5. ECT was first used in the United States in 1940. For some time, it was a standard treatment for severe depression, but in recent years its use has declined. Even mental health professionals who support its use have reservations. They point out that it must be used with discretion and carefully monitored. Also, the number and spacing of treatments must be limited.

6. Opponents of ECT argue that, even though it is effective in treating some cases of deep depression, it raises important ethical and social–psychological questions that cannot be ignored. For example, it lowers self-esteem in patients who already have a poor self-image, and it is subjectively dehumanizing.

7. A more radical treatment for severe psychotic disorders is the use of psychosurgery: destroying or removing brain tissue, or severing the tissue so as to disconnect one area of the brain from another. Even the surgeons who developed the techniques have stated that psychosurgery is a treatment of last resort.

8. During the 1940s and early 1950s, the use of psychosurgery for treating psychotic disorders spread considerably. Even though methods have been improved, its use has decreased considerably in recent years. The treatment may reduce severe

psychotic symptoms, but its negative effects are irreversible, since brain tissue cannot be restored. Side effects such as deadening emotional life, are a frequent consequence, so the treatment raises a host of social and ethical issues.

9. In response to the rising controversy, the U.S. Department of Health, Education, and Welfare (now the Department of Health and Human Services) issued guidelines to regulate the use of psychosurgery in medical research and treatment supported by federal grants and contracts. These guidelines are designed to safeguard the rights and welfare of patients, to ensure that the benefits of the treatment outweigh the risks, and to make sure that the patient's informed consent is obtained ethically.

10. A survey of the use of psychosurgery during the 1980s shows that well under 100 psychosurgery procedures were performed in the United States each year and that, in general, the operations were considered to be treatments of last resort.

11. During the last four decades, various biochemical substances have been developed that markedly improve the perception of the environment, the intellectual performance, and the emotional life of mentally disturbed people. These substances are known as psychoactive drugs.

12. The use of psychoactive drugs has greatly reduced the number of patients in mental hospitals. Many are now able to leave the hospital earlier and to derive more benefit from psychotherapy and from changes in their social environment. Psychoactive drugs have enabled many people to be helped as outpatients who would formerly have entered the hospital.

13. The majority of psychoactive drugs used today for the treatment of mental disorders fall into four broad categories: antipsychotic, antidepressant, antianxiety, and antimanic. Antipsychotic drugs are also known as major tranquilizers and neuroleptics. The earliest of them to be used successfully was chlorpromazine (Thorazine). It belongs to a class of drugs called phenothiazines. These drugs have become the most widely prescribed and best researched biochemical agents for treating psychotic disorders, especially schizophrenia.

14. One of the greatest dangers in the long-term use of antipsychotic drugs is tardive dyskinesia, which involves stereotyped and involuntary muscular activity that may occur months or even years after drug treatment has begun. It may even persist after drug treatment has ended.

15. No reliable methods exist for countering tardive dyskinesia. As a result, experts in psychopharmacology have increasingly warned psychiatrists and other medical practitioners to prescribe antipsychotic drugs cautiously, especially in long-term treatment.

16. Antidepressant drugs are used for a broad spectrum of depressive disorders. In general their use has been quite effective. An analysis of studies over a 10-year period suggests that combining drug treatment with psychotherapy in the treatment of depression is more effective than either is alone.

17. A number of chemically related compounds have been used to treat major depression. These drugs are called tricyclics, because their chemical structure is in the form of two benzene rings joining a central ring. The earliest tricyclic to be introduced into biochemical therapy was imipramine. Tricyclics have side effects, and they work slowly. Often, two or three weeks must elapse before the benefits of the treatment become apparent.

18. Another group of antidepressant drugs are the monoamine oxidase inhibitors (MAOIs). These drugs inhibit the production of monoamine oxidase, an enzyme that reduces the level of catecholamines in the brain. Thus, administering MAOIs

can increase the concentration of catecholamines. Since low levels of catecholamines may be associated with depression, increasing their concentration can be a factor in lifting depression.

19. During the 1960s, MAOIs were used extensively in the United States, with reported success; but their use has been curtailed in recent years because of side effects that are potentially more dangerous than those of other antidepressant drugs. For example, they may interact with common over-the-counter drugs used in treating colds or for reducing diets, and they may also interact with a wide range of foods. For these reasons, MAOIs are usually used only when a wide range of tricyclics have failed.

20. Antianxiety drugs are used mainly to alleviate phobias, panic attacks, generalized states of anxiety, and conversion (hysterical) disorders. Until the early 1950s, barbiturates were commonly used to control anxiety disorders. However, as their dangers began to be more widely understood, their use declined.

21. Since the late 1950s, various antianxiety drugs that are less addictive than barbiturates have been developed. These drugs include meprobamate (Equanil, Miltown) and the benzodiazepines (Librium, Valium). The drugs are equally effective, but in recent years the medical use of benzodiazepines has increased in comparison with meprobamate. Meprobamate is more likely to cause withdrawal symptoms and toxic effects.

22. In spite of their relative safety compared with barbiturates, the newer antianxiety drugs must still be used with caution. The dangers of abuse and dependence are always present, especially when high dosages are administered over a long time. In the last decade or so, Valium became the most highly prescribed drug in the United States and also was highly abused. However, its use has declined somewhat because of the increasing awareness of the medical profession that the drug has an extremely high potential for abuse.

23. As with other psychoactive drugs, antianxiety drugs are best used as adjuncts to treatment. Their greatest value lies to reducing the most obvious and disturbing symptoms of maladaptive anxiety and hysterical disorders. They can help facilitate a more effective use of psychotherapy and manipulation of the social environment.

24. The use of lithium carbonate in the treatment of manic episodes was introduced into American psychiatric practice during the 1960s. The drug is most effective as a specific treatment for manic episodes, especially when they occur as part of a bipolar cycle.

25. Unfortunately, lithium carbonate treatment poses considerable toxic risk. For that reason, the dosage must be monitored with particular care. The patient's blood lithium level must be kept within a narrow range. Various side effects, such as nausea, dizziness, tremor, blurred vision, and difficulty in walking serve as warning signs that the level of lithium is too high or that the patient is not able to adapt satisfactorily to the treatment.

26. To investigate how and why psychoactive drugs work, researchers use double-blind conditions — conditions in which neither the patient nor the therapist knows which drug is the psychoactive substance and which is the placebo (a pharmaceutically inert substance). This procedure controls the effect of suggestion.

27. Some mental health professionals have argued that psychoactive drugs may remove the surface symptoms of a disorder but do not get at the underlying causes. Other experts argue that psychoactive drugs do get at certain underlying causes that have biological roots. In any case, the effectiveness of such drugs does not diminish the importance of psychotherapy and social intervention for the treatment of mental disorders.

19

Psychodynamic, Humanistic, and Existentialist Therapy

It is not enough to understand
what we ought to be, unless we know
what we are; and we do not understand
what we are, unless we know what we
ought to be.

                                                    T. S. Eliot
                                        Religion and Literature **(1935)**

In Chapter 18 we examined such biomedical methods of treating mental disorders as psychoactive drugs, electroshock, and surgery. In this chapter and the next, we focus on psychological approaches to alleviating distress and changing maladaptive patterns of thinking and behavior.

Psychotherapy and Biomedical Therapy

Psychotherapy literally means treatment by psychological means. The essence of psychotherapy is a human relationship whose goal is to bring about positive changes in thinking, feeling, and acting. Put another way, the aim of the psychotherapist is to help troubled people move away from maladaptive modes of living and develop more adaptive ways. Because words such as *treatment*, *doctor*, *patient*, and *cure* are traditional medical terms that one also encounters in discussions of psychotherapy, it is easy to conclude that psychotherapy is solely a form of medical practice. That view, however, is erroneous. Many different kinds of mental health professionals provide psychotherapy. They may differ considerably not only in the particular techniques they use but also in the theories and values that underlie their methods (Strupp, 1978; Garfield & Bergin, 1986).

There are a number of important differences between biomedical methods of treating mental disorders and psychotherapy. In biomedical treatment, the main task of the patient is to comply with the therapist's instructions; hence the term *patient*. In contrast, the person undergoing psychotherapy is expected to be more active in achieving the outcome (Johnson & Matress, 1977).

Another difference is in the objectives of the two forms of treatment. Biomedical procedures are usually highly specific and concrete. Their purpose is to eliminate particular symptoms directly. In psychotherapy, the objectives are generally more open-ended. The therapeutic process may include such goals as developing self-understanding and a more accepting attitude without specifying the exact nature of those changes. This is especially true of psychodynamic and humanistic approaches to psychotherapy, which we consider in this chapter. Behavioral and cognitive therapies, which we deal with in the next chapter, usually involve more concrete goals specified at the outset of treatment. Nevertheless, the individual is still expected to assume a greater degree of responsibility and to participate more actively in the therapeutic process than is typically in biomedical treatment.

Biomedical therapy and psychotherapy are not mutually exclusive. Treatment with psychoactive drugs may sometimes be necessary to enable an individual to profit from psychotherapy, especially in the case of disorders that involve loss of contact with reality and severe withdrawal from others. In other instances, psychotherapy may be the principal or even the sole method of choice.

Although all forms of psychotherapy share certain basic characteristics, their specific methods and settings vary.

Defining Psychotherapy

For further information see the collected works of Sigmund Freud, vol. 17, p. 423.

Psychotherapy is a term more easily used than defined. One of the most straightforward definitions is that offered by Raymond Prince, professor of psychiatry at McGill University: "'I suffer.' Psychotherapy is any psychological procedure whose purpose is to relieve an individual with such a complaint. However, how individuals experience such suffering, how they interpret its meaning and causes, and methods of relieving it may vary greatly from one culture to another" (Prince, 1980, p. 292).

Although theories and methods of psychotherapy vary, all psychotherapists emphasize verbal communication. Equally important is the relationship between the therapist and the person seeking help (Garfield & Bergin, 1986; Hamilton, 1988; Kahn, 1981; Strupp, 1986, pp. 1123–1124). On the one side is the professional helper, trained and experienced in aiding people with burdensome, difficult problems. On the other side are the people who are faced with problems that are beyond their ability to solve alone. One notable authority, William Schofield (1986), has called this situation the "purchase of friendship." Schofield's concept has merit but needs to be qualified. What people expect from their personal friends is usually quite different from what they expect from professional psychotherapists. From their friends they usually want specific suggestions and advice; from the therapist they expect more general encouragement and the sharing of feelings (Reisman & Yamakoski, 1974). Schofield points out that the "notion that all psychotherapy is *nothing more* than exchange of friendship for a few is *not* the major thesis." Nevertheless, he continues, psychotherapy does provide "a very special, perhaps ideal, form of friendship" (Schofield, 1986, p. 109).

The goals of psychotherapy are inevitably tied to the personal experiences and characteristics of the individual who undergoes treatment. Psychotherapy is designed to either strengthen the patterns of personality and behavior by making them more adequate in coping with life's challenges or to help the individual develop different and more constructive patterns. It follows, then, that the various ways of conducting psychotherapy are closely related to certain concepts and theories of personality and behavior. A large number of these approaches are actively practiced today. We will direct our discussion around four broadly conceived and widely used approaches to psychotherapy: psychodynamic and humanistic methods, which we take up in this chapter, and behavioral and cognitive methods, which we treat in the next chapter.

One of the goals of professional societies whose members practice psychotherapy — indeed their official code — is the rejection of any sexual contact with clients. Nevertheless, such behavior is a serious problem. In surveys of psychologists engaged in psychotherapy, approximately 2 to 8 percent admitted that they had been involved sexually with their clients (Pope, Levenson, & Schover, 1979; Pope, Tabachnick, & Keith-Spiegel, 1987).

A national survey of psychiatrists found that about 6 percent acknowledge sexual contacts with clients (Gartrell, 1986). Generally, female therapists are much less likely than males to engage in sexual intimacies with their clients.

Some therapists have claimed that their sexual intimacies with clients were helpful to the therapeutic process. In contrast, many clients report that the experience was exploitive and harmful (Pope & Bouhoutsos, 1986). In recent years, professional associations have stressed the importance of improving the training of therapists so as to sensitize them to the problem and to work toward reducing it (Pope, 1987). This point was underscored in a recent report by the American Psychological Association (Ethics Committee of the American Psychological Association, 1988).

Psychodynamic Therapies

Traditional Psychoanalysis: Methods and Goals

Psychoanalytic practice as originally developed by Freud is based on the conviction that it is of paramount importance to bring to consciousness thoughts and motives that lie buried in the unconscious. To that end, Freud developed a number of techniques for bridging the gap between the conscious and subconscious. The professional literature refers to the process variously as **Freudian psychoanalysis**, **classical psychoanalysis**, **traditional psychoanalysis**, and **orthodox psychoanalysis**. We will use these terms interchangeably (Arlow, 1984).

The Pact

According to Freudian theory, the ego of the neurotic individual is anxious because of its awareness of id impulses — sexual and aggressive drives that an overly severe superego forbids the ego to express. (See Chapter 3 for psychoanalytic theories of development and behavior.) To resolve the conflict and defend itself against anxiety, the ego represses these impulses — banishing them into the unconscious. The ego may also employ various other defense mechanisms, such as projection and denial (see Chapter 3).

To facilitate free association, Freud initiated the custom of having the patient recline while the analyst sat beyond the patient's view. This practice is still followed in traditional psychoanalysis.

Since the ego has been weakened by the struggle between the id and the superego, the psychoanalyst and the patient (the analysand in psychoanalytic language) must form a pact. The patient's sick ego must promise the psychoanalyst the most complete frankness. In turn, the analyst promises the patient the strictest confidence and puts at the patient's service the analyst's expertise in understanding and interpreting thoughts and motives that have been relegated to the unconscious.

The Fundamental Rule

At the outset of treatment, the psychoanalyst imposes on the patient the fundamental rule to be used in bridging the gap between the conscious and the unconscious. In Freud's own words, the patient "must tell us not only what he can say intentionally and willingly, what will give him relief like a confession, but must also tell us everything else — everything that comes into his head, even if it is *disagreeable* to say it, even if it seems *unimportant* or positively *meaningless*" (Freud, 1940/1949, p. 65). Thus, said Freud, the patient transmits to the analyst "a mass of material" — thoughts, ideas, memories — that has been influenced by unconscious anxieties, conflicts, and feelings of guilt. The analyst is then in a position to understand and interpret this material and to convey that interpretation to the patient.

Free Association

To carry out the fundamental rule, the patient must learn and practice **free association** — the skill of putting thoughts into words as they occur. This is more easily said than done. As people in psychoanalysis from Freud's time to our own day have discovered, free association runs counter to one's massive experience and training in being logical, controlled, and socially appropriate in speech. Psychoanalysts ask that patients cancel the powerful effects of this training. The process requires time and takes up the initial stage of psychoanalysis. Once the person has learned to free associate, the actual process of analysis can begin.

To facilitate free association, Freud initiated a procedure that has become standard in traditional psychoanalysis. The patient lies on a couch while the analyst sits at the head, outside the patient's view. Freud thought that the reclining position would help stimulate the flow of free association. By not seeing the psychoanalyst, reasoned Freud, the patient would free associate with fewer inhibitions caused by the analyst's facial expression, whether real or imagined. Moreover, as Freud in a frank moment confessed to his biographer Ernest Jones (1955), "he did not like being stared at for many hours of the day at close quarters" (p. 236). Mental health professionals who do psychotherapy full time may well agree that such close encounters are stressful and tiring.

As psychoanalysis proceeds, patients soon find that their train of free associations leads them from the present to the past, and especially to the formative experiences of childhood that loom so large in Freudian theory (see Chapter 3). At the same time, many of these associations are traced to their unconscious sources, usually aggressive and sexual in nature. Thus, for example, patients may find out why they are so strongly aroused every time they make a risky investment, or why they get especially angry whenever they argue with a person they admire.

In practice, the completion of traditional psychoanalysis takes years. Why does it take so long, and what are the factors that stand in the way of its completion?

Resistance and the Therapeutic Alliance

Freud discovered some of the factors that complicate and prolong the course of psychoanalytic treatment early in his experience. The foremost factor is **resistance**. The behavior of some of his patients puzzled Freud considerably. They sincerely sought treatment, but they appeared to go out of their way to sabotage it. Instead of free associating, they discussed trivialities. They forgot appointments or arrived late and sat in silence. Such behavior deliberately counteracts the objectives of psychoanalysis. Instead of free associating, the patient represses. Instead of dipping into the unconscious, the patient remains on the surface.

Dewald (1964) has identified three sources of resistance. One is the wish to avoid full awareness of the nature of unconscious drives and conflicts because such awareness inevitably produces anxiety. The avoidance is accomplished with the help of such defense mechanisms as repression and denial.

The second source of resistance can be traced to the dual nature of neurotic symptoms. Undeniably, symptoms involve suffering, but they also entail wish fulfillment and gratification—a fact that stands as a powerful obstacle in the path of psychoanalysis.

The third source of resistance is fear of change. Even if it involves suffering, the known is preferable to the unknown.

Although resistance complicates and prolongs the psychoanalytic process, it does not, as a rule, prevail in the sense of causing the patient to terminate treatment prematurely. In opposition to resistance is the **therapeutic alliance**, which unites in its goals at least portions of the patient's ego with the ego of the analyst. Freud did not emphasize this concept, but other psychoanalysts have given it more prominence (Sandler, Dare, & Holder, 1973). The therapeutic alliance means that part of the patient's adaptive organization is committed to seeing analysis through. In the absence of such a commitment, there is nothing to counterbalance resistance, and analysis becomes almost impossible.

Transference

Another major complicating factor in psychoanalysis is **transference**. Freud discovered transference in the conduct of some of his early patients and those handled by his senior associate, Joseph Breuer (Breuer & Freud, 1936). These patients developed an intense and often erotic emotional involvement with the analyst that was not justified by anything he had done. These observations led Breuer to withdraw from psychoanalysis, but Freud persevered in untangling the sources of the feelings. He concluded that they were transferred to the analyst from significant people in the patient's past life, usually parents. Further experiences in psychoanalysis led Freud to the realization that not all transference reactions are positive. The analyst may be perceived as a loving and lovable parent or a hateful, indifferent parent. In the course of psychoanalysis, positive transference alternates with negative transference; the analyst may be praised at one time and derogated at another. Often, negative and positive feelings coexist despite their contradictory nature.

Traditional psychoanalysts hold that transference is an indispensable part of the treatment that must be worked through and resolved. At the beginning of analysis, the patient sees the analyst as a potentially helpful expert who is a stranger. During analysis, the analyst acquires many of the features of people who have been important in the patient's life, especially parents. At the end of analysis, the patient once again sees the analyst as a trained professional who has performed a useful service for a fee.

The physical conditions of psychoanalysis powerfully stimulate the experience of transference. The analyst, out of sight and interacting with the patient sparingly, remains a neutral, shadowy figure upon whom a number of fantasies can be focused.

Countertransference

Freud was well aware that the analyst might develop a personal involvement with patients—becoming variously fascinated, bored, irritated, worried, and even personally and sexually attracted to them. The name for the experience of such feelings, presumably rooted in the analyst's past, is **countertransference**. Analysts encourage the experience of transference, but they attempt to minimize countertransference. Beyond a professional commitment to the patient's welfare, the analyst is supposed to remain detached, quickly resolving any positive or negative feelings that are activated during analysis. This detachment is maintained through the analyst's own self-understanding. To enable the analyst to develop such understanding, training in psychoanalytic therapy includes a personal analysis.

Interpretation and Working Through

The basic tool of the analyst is **interpretation**—communication of the unconscious meanings of the patient's various experiences and acts. Interpretation may take several forms. The patient's behavior in a number of different situations may be linked as expressions of the same drive, motive, or conflict. The past and the present may be connected. Sandor Ferenczi (1951), an early follower of Freud, admonished psychoanalysts to take patients to the past when they are talking about the present and to bring them to the present when they are talking about the past.

Interpretation also involves the deciphering of symbols that occur in dreams and, to a lesser extent, in waking experience. Symbols are concrete, usually visual representations of unconscious drives in camouflaged form. Freudians believe that the meaning of symbols is sexual or aggressive. These two basic drives are transformed into symbolic images to protect the individual from the anxiety that is inherent in sudden confrontation with unconscious impulses. For example, a young woman who desires yet fears sexual intercourse may dream of a beautiful church being desecrated. A man doubtful of his masculinity may see in his dream a fencing match in which his sword is bent or broken. Of course, not all symbols are that transparent. The analyst's raw material in interpreting symbols is the patient's free associations. Dreams, because of their special role as disguised messages from the unconscious, occupy a particularly prominent place in psychoanalysis. One of Freud's most important works (1900/1938) deals with dream interpretations; the principles he formulated continue to guide psychoanalysts in linking the unconscious with the conscious.

A crucial consideration in interpretation is timing. A premature interpretation, even if correct, serves only to strengthen resistance. On the other hand, an interpretation that has been inordinately delayed loses its punch; the patient learns nothing new from it, or at least nothing surprising. An important part of the analyst's skill is timing interpretations sensitively yet realistically.

The concept **working through** refers to interpretation extended over time. An interpretation does not remove resistance or resolve transference once and for all. Interpretations must be presented time and again, and the patient needs time to assimilate them (Arlow, 1984, pp. 33 – 34). The same considerations apply to the interpretation of important events and relationships in the patient's everyday life.

A common misconception of psychoanalysis, as embodied in certain plays, novels, and short stories, is that it discloses a critical and forgotten event. Once that event is brought to consciousness and interpreted, everything falls into place and analysis is completed. This view is an oversimplification. Interpretation is not a one-shot affair. Working through requires time and implies not only learning about but emotionally reexperiencing the events and behavior brought into consciousness.

Goals of Psychoanalysis

Freud believed that a central goal of psychoanalysis was to help the patient develop an undisturbed capacity to experience pleasure while at the same time adapting to reality. Traditional psychoanalysis represents a very indirect approach to achieving this goal and overcoming psychological problems. Individuals may come into psychoanalysis with anxiety attacks, phobias, counting and checking compulsions, or problems of pervasive passivity in the face of life's difficulties. They are asked to put such problems aside — at least for a period of time — in order to undertake a systematic review of the interconnections of motives and behavior patterns throughout their life. Psychoanalysts assume that once this reexamination is successfully completed, symptoms will lose their purpose and disappear by themselves. Hans Strupp (1975) provided a succinct statement of the broader objectives of psychoanalysis when he said, "Analytic therapy is an education for optimal personal freedom in the context of social living" (p. 135).

Limitations of Traditional Psychoanalysis

As a method of treating psychological disorders, psychoanalysis has distinct limitations. It works best with a rather limited range of disorders, the neuroses to which Freud first applied it — that is, anxiety, dissociative, and somatoform disorders (see Chapter 5 & 6). Psychoanalysts generally agree with their critics that psychoanalysis in its traditional form is exceedingly difficult and unpredictable when applied to individuals with personality disorders (Chapter 12). Furthermore, it is of little value in treating psychotic people, and may even be harmful. Freud himself pointed out that the ego of the psychotic individual is too divorced from reality to carry out the necessary pact with the analyst. Thus, he said, "we must renounce the idea of trying our plan of cure upon psychotics — renounce it forever, perhaps, or only for the moment, until we have discovered some other plan better suited for that purpose" (Freud, 1940/1949, p. 64).

Traditional psychoanalysis is also restricted by considerations of cost, time, availability, and relevance. As of 1987, there were only 2,768 full members of the American Psychoanalytic Association, the bastion of orthodox psychoanalysis (Koek & Martin, 1987). Psychoanalysts are unevenly distributed, clustering around major metropolitan centers. Vast stretches of the country have none. Furthermore, because traditional psychoanalysis is time-consuming and costly, it is restricted to the affluent segments of the population, although others may undergo it on a reduced-fee basis or with the help of third-party payments. Last, psychoanalysis requires a long-term commitment to the difficult and laborious task of acquiring self-understanding and knowledge. Readiness to embark upon such an undertaking is linked to a number of socioeconomic and cultural factors. To a number of people, traditional psychoanalysis does not make sense; they demand a more direct and less costly means of alleviating their distress.

Modified Forms of Psychoanalysis

Over the years, various changes have occurred in the theory and practice of psychoanalysis, and many more people have been exposed to one of its modified forms. Like traditional psychoanalysis, these modifications are based on Freudian principles. However, they do not entail the entire range of Freudian procedures and their theoretical underpinnings. For example, although modified forms of psychoanalysis use free association and dream analysis, their interpretation is more flexible than that of traditional psychoanalysis. They also explain resistance and transference differently. Working through tends to be briefer. In short, modified forms of psychoanalysis do not aim toward a complete reorganization of personality, as orthodox procedures demand. Instead, the goals tend to center more on immediate problems. Unlike traditional psychoanalysis, which involves a year or more of continuous treatment, modified forms of psychoanalytic therapy may vary considerably in length, depending on the goals that are set and the kinds of problems encountered.

Influence of Ego Psychology

Although Freud continued throughout his career to focus on the importance of the sexual and aggressive drives in the development of psychological disorders, he did not neglect the role of the ego in mediating conflicts between those drives (id impulses) and the restrictions of the superego. As we discussed in Chapter 3, the ego psychology movement within psychoanalysis extended and clarified Freud's concepts of the ego and its role in psychological disorders. It also expanded concepts of the defenses the ego uses in protecting itself against conflict and anxiety. These changes were stimulated to a great extent by new knowledge from the fields of psychology, sociology, and anthropology. Among the leading theoreticians in the development of ego psychology were Freud's daughter, Anna Freud (1946), Erik Erikson (1963, 1964, 1968), Heinz Hartmann (1958, 1964), and David Rapaport (1951, 1958, 1967).

Ego psychology emphasizes not only the crucial role and power of the ego but also its autonomy from the id. This emphasis implies that pleasure can be derived from our senses and muscles, as directly experienced by the ego. For example, we need not express sexual impulses in a game of tennis or touch football, as some orthodox psychoanalysts might have it. Nor does interest in visual arts necessarily imply the gratification of infantile voyeuristic impulses. Rather, activities controlled by the ego, such as seeing, hearing, touching, moving, exercising our masculature, and using our problem-solving powers, are enjoyable in and of themselves. In more technical terms, ego psychoanalysts would say that the ego has its own source of energy and does not simply act as a mediator of biological drives.

Ego psychology shifts attention from childhood sources of present experiences to the analysis of the individual's current ways of adapting and using the ego's resources in solving current problems of living. Practitioners tend to emphasize the social and cultural origins of psychological disturbances. They agree with Freud that symptoms of psychological disorder reflect unconscious conflicts, but they usually focus more on how those conflicts arise from the ego's frustrated attempts to satisfy social needs and to maintain positive relationships with other people. They also agree that the individual's history is important for explaining current psychological problems, but they usually focus more on current events in the person's life and how they contribute to maladaptive thinking and behavior. The term *neo-Freudian* is sometimes applied to psychoanalysts who not only reflect the influence of ego psychology but also focus more on the influence of the social environment in the development of normal and abnormal behavior (see Chapter 3).

Centers of Training

A number of psychoanalytic centers in the United States concentrate on teaching various modifications in psychoanalytic theory and techniques, especially those reflecting the influence of ego psychology and the neo-Freudian emphasis on social and cultural sources of unconscious conflict and frustration. Among these centers are the William Alanson White Institute and Psychoanalytic Society, whose development has been greatly influenced by the work of Harry Stack Sullivan (1892–1949); the American Institute of Psychoanalysis, which for many years was under the direction of Karen Horney (1885–1952); and the Chicago Institute of Psychoanalysis, whose early innovations were under the leadership of Franz Alexander (1891–1964) and Thomas French (1892–1976) (Alexander & French, 1946). More recently, the concepts and practices of Heinz Kohut (1971, 1977), who worked at the Chicago Institute and the University of Chicago, have attracted a great deal of attention among psychoanalytic professionals and have dismayed some orthodox ones (Malcolm, 1981, p. 120).

Sullivan and Interpersonal Relations

Harry Stack Sullivan, an American psychiatrist, modified traditional psychoanalytic methods by emphasizing the interpersonal nature of emotional problems.

Harry Stack Sullivan pioneered a number of sensitive techniques in the treatment of mentally disturbed persons, including those who suffered from schizophrenic disorders. He was born into an Irish Catholic family in Norwich, New York, a small town some 200 miles northeast of New York City. All four of his grandparents had emigrated from Ireland during the famine that followed the potato crop failure in the late 1840s. He completed his medical school training at the Chicago College of Medicine and Surgery. After serving in various medical capacities, including work as a physician in a Chicago steel plant and with the United States Veterans Bureau's rehabilitation services, he joined the staff of St. Elizabeth's Hospital in Washington, D.C., as a liaison medical officer. There he launched his career as a psychiatrist, making up for his lack of formal psychiatric education through his intense study of the patients he served. He later became the central figure of the William Alanson White Foundation and the Washington School of Psychiatry. For the last several years of his life, Sullivan suffered from repeated episodes of cardiac illness. He died in Paris of a brain hemorrhage while returning from a conference in Amsterdam where he had outlined how his ideas of psychiatry and interpersonal relationships could be applied to public education and the shaping of social attitudes (Chapman, 1976).

Sullivan focused his approach to psychiatry on the relationship between the therapist and the patient. His concept of this relationship extended well beyond Freud's, which had cast the analyst in a remote and shadowy role. Depending on the patient's personality and needs, the therapist might appear inquisitive or passive, aggressive or gentle, detached or actively involved. Sullivan's recasting of the psychoanalytic relationship is consistent with his view that the personality is the characteristic way an individual deals with other people (Chapman, 1976, p. 69; Rioch, 1985; Sullivan, 1953a, 1953b).

At times, Sullivan could be extremely frank and informal with his patients. For example, during a discussion with his students on the subject of fees, Sullivan related this anecdote about a patient who had complained about his fee: "Oh, I agree. But, you see, it is this way: If my work does not help you it is not worth two cents. If it does help, money can't pay its value to you. I simply have decided that I want to live at a certain level of comfort and I have to charge enough to pay for that. I do not know any other way to put it" (Rioch, 1985, pp. 150–151).

In a similar vein, Sullivan offered this formula for therapists to use when informing a patient that they were going away for awhile: "Never say . . . 'I *have* to go.' The patient knows you don't *have* to. Always say, 'I will . . . ,' 'I plan . . . ,' 'I want to go . . . ,' and so on. Never say where you are going or what you propose to do — those things are irrelevant to the patient" (Rioch, 1985, p. 151).

Sullivan emphasized that psychotherapy could damage patients as well as help them. Probing extreme anxieties can exacerbate symptoms, even to the point of a psychotic break with reality. Thus, he offered the following rule of therapy: "Never undermine a patient's security (emotional comfort) unless you can offer something that will be promptly constructive" (Chapman, 1976, p. 239).

Sullivan extended his views on psychiatry from the patient–therapist relationship to questions of race and ethnic prejudice, education, and how our society contributes to mental disorder. Ultimately, said Sullivan, improving the mental health of people must go beyond the one-to-one therapeutic relationship. It must involve the gradual reform of the ills of our society that lead to mental disorder (Chapman, 1976, p. 240).

Horney's Approach to Psychotherapy

Originally trained in classical psychoanalysis, Karen Horney eventually stressed the significance of cultural and social factors in causing mental disorders and their applicability in devising therapies.

The views of Margaret Mead, distinguished cultural anthropologist, were an important influence on Karen Horney's thinking. Thus, the psychoanalyst emphasized social and cultural factors in the development of social disorders.

Karen Horney was born in Hamburg into an upper-middle-class family. She received her medical degree in 1913. As part of her training in psychoanalysis, she was first analyzed by Karl Abraham and then by Hanns Sachs, both of whom were loyal disciples of Freud. She joined the Berlin Psychoanalytic Institute in 1918 and remained there as a training analyst and lecturer for some 14 years.

In spite of the orthodox orientation of the institute and her training in classical psychoanalysis, Horney gradually moved away from some of those views. In 1932, she immigrated to the United States at the invitation of Franz Alexander, who was instrumental in having her appointed associate director of the Chicago Psychoanalytic Institute. Two years later, she moved to New York City, where she practiced psychoanalysis and became a training analyst at the New York Psychoanalytic Institute. Her growing disagreement with orthodox psychoanalysis flourished in the culture of America. She became a close friend of the neo-Freudian psychologist and psychoanalyst Erich Fromm and anthropologist Margaret Mead. Their social orientation toward problems of human existence greatly influenced her thinking.

Increasingly, her views, especially her rejection of Freud's theories concerning femininity and penis envy, began to clash with those of the traditional New York Psychoanalytic Institute. In 1941, together with other psychoanalysts, she established the Association for the Advancement of Psychoanalysis and the American Institute for Psychoanalysis, both in New York City, Subsequently, she became dean of the institute and founding editor of the *American Journal of Psychoanalysis*, which continues to reflect the basic orientation of the Horney school of thought. These views also prevail in the training of psychoanalysts at the American Institute and the practice of therapy at the Karen Horney Clinic in New York City (Clemmons, 1984; Horney, 1937, 1939, 1945, 1946, 1967, 1970; Kelman, 1965; Ogara, 1984; Rendon, 1984; Rubins, 1978).

Horney and her disciples focused on the social sources of an individual's conflicts and frustrations and their importance in psychotherapy. Horney stressed the importance of human relationships, especially the early emotional relationship between mother and child. According to Horney, the basic origin of neurotic disorders lies in the failure of the child to satisfy psychological needs. In early life, these needs include love, affection, and reliable care. Later in childhood, needs for understanding and self-esteem emerge. When these needs go unsatisfied, a core of neurotic disorder becomes established. Horney called this core **basic anxiety**, revealed through loneliness, helplessness, and hostility.

According to Horney, the development of basic anxiety into psychological disorders represents a distortion of normal needs in everyday relationships. The first of these — the need to move toward other people — is normally revealed in friendliness, consideration, trusting others, and seeking and giving help. The second normal pattern is the need to move against others. It is expressed by standing up for one's legitimate rights, protesting when attacked, and being alert to possible attack. The third normal pattern is the need to

According to Karen Horney, psychological disorders represent a distortion of normal needs. These normal needs are to move toward people (trust, friendliness, helping), against people (standing up for one's legitimate rights), and away from people (self-sufficiency, privacy).

move away from other people, reflected in self-sufficiency, independence, and the maintenance of one's privacy. Mentally healthy people, Horney said, maintain a reasonable balance among these three normal patterns. Neurotic people, however, exaggerate and rigidify them, becoming overly dependent, excessively hostile, or inappropriately withdrawn from others. At the same time, their self-image is unrealistic, linked to rigid and false ideals.

The ultimate goal of the Horney system of therapy is to help neurotic individuals overcome their unrealistic, idealized self-image and their distortion of normal needs. To accomplish this goal, they must attain insight into the nature of their self-image and to recognize the kinds of conflicts that are involved in their maladaptive use of normal needs.

The Horney approach uses many of the same techniques as classical psychoanalysis, such as interpretation of the patient's free associations and dreams. The main goal here is to show the individual how these associations and dreams illustrate contradictions between the real self and the false, neurotic, idealized self-image the patient has developed. The interaction between the patient and the analyst is more flexible and conversational than in orthodox psychoanalysis. The therapist is often more directive, actively suggesting to the patient the path that thoughts might take and sometimes probing with such phrases as "Why did you say that?" and "Tell me more about that."

Similarly, Horney advocated more active and frequent interpretation than Freud. Her guiding principle was to save time, even though it meant risking a wrong interpretation. That risk, she concluded, was better than being too passive and noninterfering.

This direct involvement still looms large among current followers of Horney's approach. As one analyst has put it, "Far from being an impersonal mirror in which the patient [is] reflected, the analyst becomes [emotionally] involved with [the] patient, and at the same time avoids manipulating him" (Clemmons, 1984, p. 314).

Although Horney acknowledged the importance of resistance during therapy, she said it consisted mainly of the patient wanting to defend a false self-image and inappropriate ways of relating to others. The task of the analyst, therefore, was to help the patient understand this resistance. Horney was not as concerned with negative resistance as Freud was: thus, she moved faster and more directly in interpreting what the patient did.

Like traditional psychoanalysts, Horney also accepted the importance of transference, but she did not think it necessarily represented childhood attitudes toward parental or other authority figures. Rather, she regarded transference as the emotional relationship between the therapist and the patient regardless of what content was involved. As the therapist shows understanding of the patient, and conveys that understanding, **positive transference** occurs. This enables the patient to make use of the inherent constructive forces that aid recovery. When **negative transference** inevitably occurs, the therapist continues to show understanding and explains what is happening to the patient.

Horney had an interesting view of countertransference, which the analyst usually experiences when analysis is faltering. Freud believed that in countertransference the analyst reflected attitudes formerly held toward a father or other authority figure during childhood — negative reactions to being defeated or overpowered. Horney argued that countertransference — a term she disliked — represented the analyst's direct reactions to the patient's behavior during therapy. Thus, analysts become irritated at the patient's failure to progress in spite of their efforts because of their unrealistic expectation that every patient must succeed.

Along with other modifiers of psychoanalysis, Horney often shortened the time required for therapy. In contrast to the traditional four or six sessions a week, spanning at least a year and often more, she emphasized having fewer sessions, setting time limits, and in general speeding up the process. In recent years, this emphasis on accelerating the rate of psychoanalysis has become increasingly prominent (Davanloo, 1979, 1980).

Kohut and Self-Psychology

Heinz Kohut (1913 – 1981) was born in Vienna. Trained in medicine and psychoanalysis at the University of Vienna, he received his M.D. degree in 1938. Because his father was Jewish, he fled the Nazis in 1939, a year after Freud. He went first to Britain and then, in 1940, to the United States, where he was appointed resident in neurology at the University of Chicago. He then went on to teach and practice psychoanalysis at the University of Chicago and the Chicago Institute of Psychoanalysis, where he developed an approach that differed in significant ways from classical psychoanalysis (Kohut, 1971, 1977; Lawner, 1985; Socarides & Stolorow, 1986).

Kohut called his version of psychoanalysis **self-psychology**. His focus was on individuals whose problems stem from narcissism — excessive self-love. Kohut believed that narcissism begins very early in childhood and is more important in the development of maladaptive behavior than is the Oedipus complex. Consistent with many other neo-Freudians, Kohut emphasized that social conditions, especially family relationships, are crucial in the development of mental disorders. Under normal circumstances, children internalize parental love and thus form a basis for developing a sense of self-worth. In the absence of parental love, children may develop a narcissistic personality disorder, characterized by an inability to form deep relationships and a generalized alienation from other people. Kohut believed that narcissistic disorders are becoming more frequent than the neurotic disorders described by Freud.

One of the most crucial differences between Kohut's views and classical psychoanalytic theory can be seen in this description by an orthodox psychoanalyst of a speech given by Kohut at a meeting of the American Psychoanalytic Association.

Trained in psychoanalysis and medicine in Vienna, Heinz Kohut taught at the University of Chicago, practiced at the Chicago Institute of Psychoanalysis, and established a variant therapy known as self psychology. His basic idea is that children not accorded warmth and empathy by their parents may have trouble acquiring a sense of self-worth. They may then become narcissistic, unable to form intimate relationships.

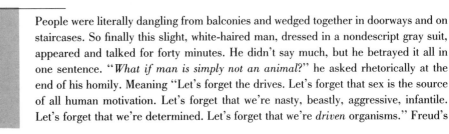

People were literally dangling from balconies and wedged together in doorways and on staircases. So finally this slight, white-haired man, dressed in a nondescript gray suit, appeared and talked for forty minutes. He didn't say much, but he betrayed it all in one sentence. "*What if man is simply not an animal?*" he asked rhetorically at the end of his homily. Meaning "Let's forget the drives. Let's forget that sex is the source of all human motivation. Let's forget that we're nasty, beastly, aggressive, infantile. Let's forget that we're determined. Let's forget that we're *driven* organisms." Freud's hypothesis of the drives has never been acceptable to the public, or palatable even to many within psychoanalysis itself. There has been a persistent attempt to whittle away at the radicalism of psychoanalytic theory — to make it less harsh and less damaging to man's traditional sentimental idea of his nature. (Malcolm, 1981, p. 120)

Although for Kohut, psychotherapy had the same basic goal as classical psychoanalysis — the achievement of insight — his relationship to patients was much less neutral. It involved more warmth, explicit understanding, kindliness, and friendliness. The response of classical psychoanalysts was to uphold the traditional neutrality of psychoanalysis because "it . . . paradoxically gives the patient more freedom than he has under the more relaxed analytic techniques. Ruthless and authoritarian though it seems, strict analytic neutrality is the libertarian alternative. When you temper the rigors of analysis with judicious doses of kindliness and friendliness, you are taking away some of the patient's freedom, because *you* are deciding what is best for him" (Malcolm, 1981, p. 77).

Defectors from Psychoanalysis

Freud attracted a number of promising and creative disciples and then broke sharply with them. Prominent among those he rejected were Alfred Adler (1870–1937) and Carl Gustav Jung (1875–1961), both of whom developed their own independent approaches.

Adlerian Psychotherapy

Alfred Adler, originally a participant in Freud's psychoanalytic circle, defected and formed his own approach, which he named individual psychology. He exported this theory and method to the United States.

Adler was born in Vienna and received his medical degree from the University of Vienna. In 1902, Freud invited him to join the Vienna Psychoanalytic Society. During the weekly discussion meetings of the society, Adler often argued against Freud's views, especially those that emphasized sexual drives as sources of maladaptive conflict and anxiety. Although Adler became president of the society in 1910, he resigned a year later, taking with him a small group of other dissenters. Initially, they called their movement the Society of Free Psychoanalytic Research. Later, in order to make their break with Freudian thought more distinct, they changed its name to Individual Psychology, a puzzling choice in view of Adler's social emphasis (Ansbacher, 1977; p. 3; Mosak, 1984).

Freud considered Adler to be a disciple who went astray. Adler, however, went to great lengths to dissociate himself from Freud's movement and to avoid labeling himself with any term that suggested psychoanalysis. Nevertheless, Adler argued that he was sufficiently familiar with Freud's view to recognize Freud's mistakes and criticize him (Adler, 1964).

In 1926, Adler began lecturing in the United States, and he made it his home in 1934, settling in New York City. Adler's views have been less influential in the United States than Freud's, but their impact has spread through Adlerian training institutes in New York City, Chicago, Minneapolis, Berkeley, and other cities. The institutes award certificates in psychotherapy, counseling, and child guidance. The International Association of Individual Psychology and special summer institutes in the United States and other countries help maintain the influence of the Adlerian movement. Other important avenues of influence are the *Journal of Individual Psychology*, the *Individual Psychologist*, and the *Individual Psychology Newsletter*. The North American Society of Adlerian Psychology, with headquarters in Chicago, is also an important source of information about the Adlerian movement (Ansbacher, 1977; Mosak, 1984).

Adlerian psychotherapy recognized the significance of the unconscious and of early childhood determinants of behavior. However, Adler attached paramount importance to the inevitable experience of weakness and inferiority throughout infancy and childhood. According to Adler, people compensate in a variety of ways for this experience, with far-reaching results. For example, to counter their self-perceptions of inadequacy, they unconsciously strive for superiority by reaching for unrealistic goals. Other people stimulate this overcompensation by encouraging the unrealistic ambition. Adler gave the name **inferiority complex** to these psychodynamics, a term that, like *Oedipus complex*, has passed into popular language (Adler, 1964, pp. 96–126, 1973).

According to Adler, symptoms of neurotic disorders are used to conceal feelings of inferiority. These symptoms include anxiety, fear, bodily discomfort, or hostile and dominating attitudes toward people. In general they isolate the individual from positive social relationships (Adler, 1964, pp. 156–181).

Adlerian therapists use much more direct techniques than those of classical psychoanalysis. They believe that psychotherapy is an educative process in which the therapist explains to the patient how unrealistic goals and neurotic (maladaptive) ways of achieving superiority cause such problems as self-defeating competitiveness, domination, overdependence, or undue hostility. The Adlerian therapist makes great use of dreams, which are seen as problem-solving activities. Since the neurotic dreamer uses dreams to engage in self-deception and avoid problems, dreams provide clues about the patient's neurotic disorder. The therapist interprets these clues to the patient (Adler, 1964; Mosak, 1984).

A central goal of Adlerian therapy is to strengthen social interests. This is a cooperative effort. The therapist discovers which social interests are already present, then works with the patient toward extending self-understanding and positive relationships with other people. The ultimate purpose of this endeavor is to help the individual develop healthier and more realistic goals that will be socially useful. The therapist guides patients toward an understanding of their true motivations and their particular style of life. This style includes specific problems and symptoms as well as the ways these symptoms are used to conceal overcompensation.

Adler strongly believed that the earliest memories are not accidental but reveal the major themes of a person's life. He was convinced that birth order is associated with distinctive personality patterns and symptom constellations. Similarly, childhood problems are relevant to the understanding of current conflicts.

As Adler's theories of social interest and family relationships developed, he began to extend his activities beyond psychotherapy. He became an educator and social reformer, founding family education centers in the community so that parents and teachers could benefit from information on childrearing. He also wrote on many social issues, including crime, war, religion, political radicalism, and nationalism.

Jungian Psychotherapy

Carl Gustav Jung (1875–1961) was born in Kesswell, a small village in Switzerland. His father was a poor country pastor in the Swiss Reformed Church. Jung differed sharply with his father, whom he regarded as too conventional.

Jung received his medical training in Basel, Switzerland. Early in his career, Freud's psychoanalytic theories impressed him, and he participated actively in the Viennese Freudian circle. Freud was strongly attracted to Jung's energy and imagination and appointed him the first president of the International Psychoanalytic Association. In 1909, Jung accompanied Freud to the United States to lecture on psychoanalysis at Clark University. By this time, he was internationally known. He lectured extensively on psychoanalysis and taught courses at the University of Zurich, Switzerland.

Like Adler, Jung developed some of his own ideas on psychology before becoming

Carl Gustav Jung, Freud's most cherished pupil, broke with him early in his career and established his own analytic psychology.

associated with Freud. Over the years, he differed more and more with Freud, especially with the emphasis on sexual drives. With the publication of his book *Symbols of Transformation* (Jung, 1911/1956), the break with Freud became definite. In 1912, when Jung lectured on psychoanalysis in New York, he still described his views as extensions of Freud's ideas. However, by 1914, he considered his version of psychoanalysis so different that he gave it a new name — **analytical psychology** (Maduro & Wheelwright, 1977).

In 1948, the C. G. Jung Institute opened in Zurich to teach Jungian principles and to train psychotherapists in their application. Since then, other training centers have been established in Britain, France, Germany, Israel, and Italy. In the last two decades, the movement has attracted increasing attention in the United States. There are training centers in New York, Los Angeles, and San Francisco. Prospective analysts come from a variety of fields, including psychology, medicine, social work, and theology. Prospective therapists are accepted in a training center only after a minimum of 100 hours of personal analysis by a qualified Jungian therapist, recommendation from the therapist, and interviews by three Jungian analysts on the training board (Kaufmann, 1984).

Jung believed that Freud overemphasized sexual drives in his theory of the unconscious. For Jung, the unconscious was only partially rooted in personal childhood experience. To a much greater extent, it was the repository of the accumulated wisdom of humanity, the **collective unconscious**. Freud aimed at making the unconscious conscious, but Jung' approach was to reconcile patients to the unconscious and to enable them to learn to trust it (Jung, 1968).

Jung's theory of the unconscious centered on his concept of **archetypes**, the original patterns or models of ideas and beliefs. For example, an archetype that men have universally is the *anima* — the archetype of the woman — which shapes their perception of what women are. Women have a corresponding archetype of the man, which Jung called the *animus*. Other archetypes are the great mother, the hero, the wise old man, birth, and death. All of them reflect the collective beliefs of the cultural group the individual belongs to and, at an even deeper level, unconscious images common to all human beings. Jung emphasized that archetypes are not directly accessible to consciousness. However, we can observe them indirectly in myths, fairy tales, works of art, and folklore. Archetypes, said Jung, are the main carriers of creative energy. However, overpossession by a certain archetype, such as the great mother, the hero, or the wise old man, may produce delusions of grandeur. Analytical psychology views the symptoms of neurotic disorders as clues to what is missing in the life of the patient. To overcome psychological problems, the individual must be put in touch with the collective unconscious (Jung, 1928/1953; 1936/1959).

Jung's concept of the collective unconscious clearly distinguishes him from Freud. Unfortunately, there is no way to test the concept empirically. Furthermore, the notion that the unconscious contains ancestral roots implies a genetic notion that contradicts modern science. One could interpret the collective unconscious as a form of cultural learning, but Jung implied that it was genetic.

Inherent in Jung's approach to therapy is the belief that neurotic disorders occur when the individual's emotional and intellectual potentialities are unable to develop in a positive direction. This inhibition is especially likely when problems stem from potentialities within the collective unconscious. Therefore, the ultimate goal of Jung's "analytical" psychotherapy is to help patients release their creative potentialities by putting them in touch with their collective unconscious. Since this layer of the unconscious is not directly accessible to the conscious ego, the contact must be indirect, through the use of symbols.

Jung's universal archetypes included the great mother and the wise old man, reflected in these famous works of art by Picasso, *Mother and Child*, and Ghirlandaio, *St. Jerome*.

In Jungian therapy, the symbolic products of the collective unconscious serve as guides in helping the patient overcome neurotic thinking and behavior. By understanding these symbols, the individual discovers the conflict that underlies neurotic problems. For example, a patient found himself constantly attracted to deformed or mutilated women. The Jungian interpretation was that the patient's own woman, his feminine side, was mutilated. Through interpretation, the therapist helps patients become aware of feelings buried in the unconscious so they can heal that area of life and accept that aspect of their personality (Whitmont & Kaufmann, 1973, p. 90).

Jung's techniques in therapy tend to be more flexible and less formal than Freud's (Fordham, 1978). Free association is supplemented with graphic techniques, for example, drawing a recurrent symbol in a dream. In contrast to Freudians, Jungians interpret dreams in reference to the future rather than the past; they consider them to be expressions of intentions that the person has not yet consciously perceived.

Jungian therapy usually begins with an investigation of the patient's conscious state and current problems. Inquiries are made into the patient's past history, attitudes, ideals, and values. The analyst points out inconsistencies that seem to get the patient into trouble. Then the unconscious is explored, especially the collective unconscious. The focus here is on the analysis of the patient's dreams and what their symbols reveal. For example, if the symbolic content of the dreams contradicts the patient's conscious perceptions of problems, the analyst points this out, emphasizing that the content of the dreams is a more dependable index of the problems (Kaufmann, 1984).

Since the main elements of the collective unconscious are archetypes, a purpose of therapy is to help the individual get in touch with these archetypes indirectly and thus gain creative energy (Goleman, 1985, p. 22; Kaufmann, 1984).

In Jungian analysis the patient and analyst face each other directly. Jungian analysts believe such contact makes it less likely that the patient will lapse into passivity or that a void will develop between patient and analyst.

Humanistic and Existentialist Approaches to Psychotherapy

Humanistic therapists shift their emphasis from the influence of the unconscious on present behavior to the problems of alienation from present potentialities for personal growth and strength. Because of this emphasis on the present, humanistic approaches to psychotherapy are often called existentialist, and they are linked to the philosophical movement of existentialism.

As applied to psychotherapy, the existentialist viewpoint is a broad approach to understanding human behavior and experience rather than a special set of techniques that differ completely from other forms of therapy (May, 1969, p. 15). Any therapeutic technique can have an existentialist operation, provided it focuses on the world of troubled people as they presently perceive it.

All of the currently prominent systems of humanistic psychotherapy see human beings as seekers of truth and meaning in their own lives. Abnormal behavior obstructs that quest. Therefore, the task of the therapist is to help clients find their own meanings and to integrate and accept their experiences in that quest.

Person-Centered Therapy

Carl Rogers (1902–1987) and his followers developed **person-centered therapy**, formerly known as nondirective therapy and client-centered therapy, over a span of some 50 years. Person-centered therapy differs from psychodynamic therapy, and especially from psychoanalysis, in both style and substance. Freud's formulations are complex, elaborate, and often speculative. In contrast, Rogers's views rest upon a minimal number of key concepts (Cain, 1986; Meador & Rogers, 1973, 1979; Rogers, 1942, 1951, 1974, 1980, 1986a, 1986b).

The development of Rogers's ideas falls into three periods: nondirective, 1940–1950; reflective, 1950–1957; and experiential, 1957 to the present (Hart, 1970).

Nondirective Period

Carl Rogers, pioneer exponent of humanistic and existentialist approaches to psychotherapy. He was the founder of person-centered therapy.

During the nondirective period, Rogers focused on techniques and their role in helping the person achieve insight. He became convinced that psychodynamic therapists interfered with the spontaneous expression of the client's feelings and experiences. Nothing should be done, said Rogers, to hamper the person from this process of self-expression. Everything should be aimed at facilitating and cultivating it. In Rogers's view, the therapist is like a catalyst in a chemical reaction — there to make a change possible without producing it directly. To this end, Rogers recommended that therapists limit themselves to accepting, recognizing, and clarifying what clients said and their underlying feelings. Hence, Rogers applied the label **nondirective therapy** to his evolving set of therapeutic techniques (Rogers, 1942). The therapist deals with the client's experience here and now and is little concerned with understanding it intellectually in light of the formative experiences of the client's past. The therapist does not step out of the client's **phenomenal field** — that is, the actual pattern of experience at the time. To accept, recognize, and clarify feelings, the therapist rephrases what the client says, with a special emphasis on feelings. The following excerpt illustrates this emphasis (Rogers, 1942, p. 338).

Client: The actual involvement in a battle I think, odd as it may seem, would be more agreeable to me than army life in camp.

Therapist: M-hm. In other words, the thing that strikes you worst about it is the possible regimentation and having somebody else order your life.

In his nondirective period, Rogers was emphatic about what a therapist should not do: no questions, no bringing up of new topics, no interpretation, and no expression of the therapist's personal feelings.

Reflective Period

During the reflective period, Rogers gradually began to move away from a preoccupation with specific techniques to a concern with global issues of the therapeutic process. The goals and methods of therapy developed during this period are described in the book *Client-Centered Therapy* (Rogers, 1951). Rogers emphasized that a goal of therapy was not only for clients to gain insight into their specific problems but also for them to reorganize and integrate their self-perceptions. In this way, they would gradually come to understand who they were and what they wanted to become. Their concept of self would become more congruent with their personal experiences. For example, as therapy progresses, the client may discover that "one aspect of his experience . . . [is] hatred for his father; another [is] . . . strong homosexual desires. He reorganizes the concept he holds of himself to include those characteristics, which would previously have been inconsistent with self" (Meador & Rogers, 1973, p. 135).

Thus, the goal of client-centered therapy was to develop a more inclusive self-perception and a greater degree of self-acceptance. On the therapist's part, clarification of the client's responses became more focused, with emphasis on reflecting the client's self-perceptions and feelings. The following example illustrates the technique of **reflection** (Rogers, 1951, p. 211).

Client: I've never told anyone they were the most wonderful person I've ever known, but I've told you that. It's not just sex. It's more than that.

Therapist: You really feel very deeply attached to me.

Rogers also faced more squarely the problem of transference, which he had previously ignored. He accepted the fact that transference occurred during psychotherapy, but he minimized its importance. He concluded that the therapist should handle transference like other attitudes and feelings expressed by the client: reflecting feeling, showing understanding, and conveying acceptance.

Experiential Period

In the experiential period, which is still evolving, Rogers and his colleagues broadened their methods. For example, they emphasized that the therapist should respond not only to the client's verbal statements and questions but also to nonverbal behavior, such as facial expressions, gestures, and even silences. Person-centered therapists now began to intervene more directly by expressing their personal feelings and opinions when appropriate and on occasion asking leading questions. Rogerian methods were also extended to a wider range of clients, including schizophrenics (Rogers, Gendlin, Kiesler, & Truax, 1967).

In 1974, Rogers and his colleagues changed the name of their approach from client-centered to person-centered therapy, believing that this name described more adequately the human values that their work represented (Meador & Rogers, 1979, p. 131).

Early in the experiential phase, Rogers began to concentrate on the therapeutic relationship as the core of his approach. Over a 20-year period, he delineated the necessary and sufficient conditions for successful psychotherapy (Rogers, 1957, 1962, 1980, pp. 115–118).

1. Positive regard. The therapist values and respects the client. This does not necessarily mean personally liking the client, although Rogers did believe that such liking was apt to result if positive regard was truly present.

2. Unconditional acceptance. The therapist avoids judging behavior or attaching worth to the client. Unconditional acceptance does not imply agreement, however. One can show understanding through acceptance without endorsing the rightness of the views.

3. Genuineness. The therapist is a genuine person, without facade, willing to acknowledge private feelings when that seems to be appropriate. Rogers's emphasis on authenticity was greatly influenced by his interest in existential philosophy and its application to psychology (May, 1969). To Rogers, being a therapist was incompatible with pretense, role-playing, or insincerity.

4. Empathy. To empathize with the client, the therapist perceives the client's behavior as if it were personal experience. The therapist shares the person's phenomenal (experienced) world. This empathy is then communicated to the client, as in the following interchange from one of Rogers's therapy sessions (Rogers, 1986a, p. 201).

> **Jan:** When I look at my mother's life — and she had many talents — she unfortunately, toward the end, became a bitter woman. The world owed her a living. Now I don't want ever to be in that situation. And, at this point in time, I'm not. I've had a very full life — both very exciting and very sad at times. I've learned a lot and I've a lot to learn. But — I *do* feel that what happened to my mother is happening to me.
>
> **Carl:** So that remains sort of a specter. Part of your fear is: "Look what happened to my mother, and I am following along in the same path. [*Jan:* Right] and will I feel that same fruitlessness, perhaps?"

According to Rogers, the more successfully the four necessary and sufficient conditions of therapy are met, the more the client will perceive their presence and thus experience the positive regard, unconditional acceptance, and emotional understanding of the therapist. As the client relates this experience and the therapist responds, the client becomes increasingly able to move toward self-understanding, self-acceptance, and more positive relationships with others. The therapist need not be concerned with the correctness of highly specific techniques as long as the necessary and sufficient conditions are met.

Rogers's basic view of human nature is more optimistic than Freud's. Rogers emphasized a natural tendency toward growth and development. This tendency can be temporarily obstructed but is seldom completely submerged. The task of the person-centered therapist is to create conditions that enable the client to grow again.

A number of psychologists have noted similarities between the views of Rogers and Kohut. One writer has suggested that the similarities represent a bridge between psychoanalytic and humanistic therapy (Kahn, 1985). Both Rogers and Kohut are very much concerned with the subjective, experiential life of individuals and the importance of understanding their phenomenal world. Both derived the data for their concepts of personality from active therapeutic work. Both emphasize the concept of self as a central element in understanding and helping individuals. Both perceive people as experiencing entities, able to make choices and control their destiny. The individual's self-enhancement is a central goal of psychotherapy for each of them. Finally, both reject the traditional psychoanalytic view that the therapist must be neutral. In an article published a year before his death, Rogers himself pointed to these similarities (Rogers, 1986c).

Training and Research

Training in the theory and practice of person-centered therapy has for the most part been carried out in university settings, where the emphasis has been on empirical research involving intensive analysis of interviews with clients. A year before his death, Rogers warned that the person-centered approach was in danger of becoming dogmatic and restrictive. This could be avoided, he said, only through continuing research that would "challenge our hypotheses, enrich our theory, and expand our knowledge . . . of human beings" (Rogers, 1986b, p. 259).

Frankl's Logotherapy: An Existentialist Approach

Viktor Frankl, a Viennese psychiatrist, established logotherapy. Frankl's experiences in a Nazi concentration camp influenced his conceptions of therapy. He helps individuals to find some meaning in suffering, by placing it in a larger context, and to integrate their understanding of life and death.

Viktor Frankl (1905–   ), a psychiatrist in Vienna and a survivor of Nazi concentration camps, originated what is sometimes called the third Viennese school of psychotherapy. Frankl believes that understanding the events of childhood may be necessary, but it is certainly not sufficient to help a person attain optimal functioning. Frankl was impressed with the extent to which problems of spiritual meaning and existence permeated the lives of his patients. He concluded, therefore, that psychotherapy should facilitate this personal quest for meaning and should help people integrate the various elements of their existence. For example, people often shrink from thoughts about suffering and death. Yet both are an inevitable part of human existence. **Logotherapy,** as Frankl named his approach (from the Greek *logos*, the "word" or "reason"), helps the troubled individual find meaning in suffering and integrate life and death rather than mindlessly avoiding the thought of death's inevitability. Absence of meaning and lack of purpose in life are painful states, and, according to Frankl, they produce a variety of mental disorders. Finding meaning often leads to the disappearance of these disorders (Frankl, 1959, 1963, 1975b).

Two techniques of logotherapy are paradoxical intention and dereflection (Frankl, 1975a). **Paradoxical intention** is designed to counteract the anticipatory anxiety associated with the prospective appearance of a symptom. For example, individuals who suffer from insomnia may become so anxious about their condition that the worry itself contributes to the insomnia. In such a case, and in a great many instances of phobias and of obsessive compulsive disorders, the instruction of the logotherapist is simple and to the point: Do whatever you are worried about doing to your heart's content. Instead of running away from the object of your fear, as in phobia, or fighting against it, as in obsessions and compulsions, give in to the symptoms and thereby ridicule them.

Dereflection is designed to counteract what Frankl called "a compulsive inclination to self-observation." Patients are instructed to do two things: shift from their worry and concentrate on something else. In practice, Frankl (1975b) has successfully shifted some of his patients from petty, exaggerated, neurotic concerns to the more fundamental problems of existence and meaning. Thus, logotherapy relieves symptoms and enables people to confront the basic problems of life that can be avoided only by the disturbance of serenity and well-being.

Gestalt Therapy

Trained in psychoanalysis, Frederick [Fritz] Perls, in collaboration with his wife Laura, founded a humanistic and present-oriented form of treatment, which he called Gestalt therapy.

The originator of **Gestalt therapy** was Frederick S. Perls (1894–1970), a German-born psychoanalyst. Out of his dissatisfaction with orthodox psychoanalytic theory, Perls worked with his wife, Laura, to apply Gestalt theory to psychotherapy.

Gestalt psychology arose in Germany early in this century. Gestalt psychologists maintained that our perceptual and cognitive experience cannot be broken down into elementary sensations because we experience the world as organized into patterns, wholes, or configurations (the German word *Gestalt* is a rough synonym for those terms). The pioneering Gestalt psychologists had little to say about abnormal behavior and less about psychotherapy. However, on the basis of his experience as a therapist and his reading of Gestalt theory, Perls (1973) aimed to fill that gap.

The basic premise of Gestalt therapy is that our experience is organized according to the **figure–ground principle**. Some of our experiences are in the focus (figure) of our awareness, and others are at the periphery (ground), less directly and intensely perceived. The figure–ground relationship may be reversed—that is, we may focus on the peripheral and trivial and not perceive what is truly at the core of our experience. Also, our figures may be broken up so that we are unaware of the interrelationships of our experiences.

Gestalt therapy aspires to restore the lost unity and connectedness of personal experience. To this end, the Gestalt therapist may foster a dialogue between the various parts of the patient's personality. Just as the couch is a mainstay of Freudian psychoanalysis, the empty chair has become an important prop for some Gestalt therapists. Clients are encouraged to converse with a part of themselves in the empty chair.

Gestalt therapy strives to intensify self-awareness by focusing on the client's body language and the emotions that are expressed nonverbally. With the help of the therapist, clients put these feelings into words and eventually integrate them into their figures. Some Gestalt therapists replay a videotape of the session to help the client express the meaning of body language, as in this example.

Florence: I have been crying a lot. I know at times my eyes are puffed up or look very angry.

Jim: Does either of those feel right for you at this moment?

Florence: Uh-huh.

Jim: That you are angry or crying a lot?

Florence: Uh-huh. I haven't been as in touch with my anger as my sadness this week.

Jim: Just hold that pose a moment. See if you can get in touch with how you are. [Videotape is again played back.] What is that posture like for you?

Florence: Cold. I've got my feet up like I am starting to run a race. I brace myself with my hands, and my head is on the side, like balancing myself.

Jim: So, if your posture could talk, what would it say?

Florence: My feet would say I better stay on my toes. [Looks to her left.]

Jim: And you looked over there. Did something attract you over there?

Florence: I'm worried—get away from you—worried—get away from you.

Jim: All right. I better stay on my toes away from you.

Florence: I'm hanging on to the chair like it might be a rocky landing.

Jim: And you're smiling. Are you pleased? I'd like to understand your smile.

Florence: Not pleased with the idea of the rocky landing as so much pleased at — oh, stepping aside and watching myself, maybe come up with the right-bright answers or something like that. (Simkin, Simkin, Brien, & Sheldon, 1986, pp. 210–211)

Like psychoanalysts, Gestalt therapists assign an important value to dreams, although they deal with them quite differently.

In Gestalt therapy we don't interpret dreams. We do something much more interesting with them. Instead of analyzing and further cutting up the dream, we want to bring it back to life. And the way to bring it back to life is to re-live the dream as if it were happening now. Instead of telling the dream as if it were a story in the past, act it out in the present, so that it becomes part of yourself, so that you are really involved. (Perls, 1969, p. 27)

Gestalt therapy emphasizes the here and now rather than the reconstruction of the past. Enactment of an experience or event is preferred to its cognitive and narrative reconstruction. In the process, Gestalt therapists assume a highly directive role. They are outspoken, expressive, and dramatic, sometimes to the point of flamboyance. Intensity, spontaneity, and immediacy are highly valued and practiced.

There are now more than 50 Gestalt training centers in the United States and other parts of the world. In recent years, newer modes of practice have developed at some centers, with an increased emphasis on a softer demeanor on the part of the therapist, a greater degree of self-acceptance, and an increased trust of the patient's perceptions of the world (Simkin & Yontef, 1984). Like many other methods of psychotherapy, Gestalt therapy continues to evolve. This development can be seen in the two journals dealing specifically with the method: *Gestalt Theory* and the *Gestalt Journal*.

Practitioners of Psychotherapy

In Chapter 1, we identified briefly various kinds of mental health professionals whose work to varying degrees involves the use of psychotherapy. As a further guide to understanding this involvement, we now consider their professional roles in more depth.

Clinical Psychologists

Clinical psychologists have usually earned a doctoral degree in psychology, the desirable level of training officially recognized by the American Psychological Association (1986, 1988). In addition to carrying out their practice and research in mental hospitals, outpatient clinics, and community mental health centers, clinical psychologists teach and do research in universities, colleges, and public health services. Some also engage in independent practice (Bernstein & Nietzel, 1980).

The graduate education of clinical psychologists has traditionally emphasized not only methods of practice, such as diagnosis, psychotherapy, and social intervention, but also research on problems of mental and behavioral disorders. In recent years, however, the number of clinical psychology programs that concentrate mainly on practice has risen

(Strickland, 1988). Some universities now award two kinds of degrees in clinical psychology: the traditional Ph.D (doctor of philosophy), which combines training, research, and practice; and the Psy.D. (doctor of psychology), which emphasizes practice. Doctor of psychology degrees are also awarded by free-standing schools of professional psychology —institutions of recent development that are not part of a university.

Practitioner programs in clinical psychology that virtually exclude training in research are controversial. Some psychologists are convinced that the traditional mode of training graduate students to be both productive scholars and practitioners is still the most desirable pattern. Others support a two-track system: one track for students who want to combine research and practice, the other for students whose main interest is practice. Various psychologists oppose the rapid rise of free-standing professional schools. They argue that such institutions are too academically isolated and thus lack the broad intellectual stimulation and other educational resources that come from being part of a university (McNett, 1982; Peterson, 1985).

Counseling Psychologists

In settings where the main purpose is to help people solve their educational and vocational problems or other relatively normal problems of living, **counseling psychologists** are likely to be found (American Psychological Association, 1986, 1988). College and university counseling centers often employ counseling psychologists. Of course, normal problems sometimes merge with more serious psychological disturbances. Thus, the roles of counseling psychologists are often very similar to those of clinical psychologists. Furthermore, both clinical and counseling psychologists engage in independent practice, so that it becomes even more difficult to make clear distinctions between their roles. Nevertheless, universities that offer training in both professions usually have separate programs, with counseling psychology often located in colleges of education. Such programs offer the Ed.D. (doctor of education), a degree that emphasizes clinical practice.

Psychiatrists

Psychiatry is a specialty in the field of medical practice and research. **Psychiatrists**, therefore, are mental health professionals with a medical degree (M.D.). In addition to their residency in psychiatry, they receive other specialized postgraduate training, including methods of diagnosis, psychotherapy, and somatic (biomedical) treatment. The American Psychiatric Association controls the education and training of psychiatrists in the United States.

The work of psychiatrists overlaps with that of clinical and counseling psychologists. However, psychiatrists are the only mental health professionals who are legally qualified by virtue of their medical training to provide biomedical treatment—for example, prescribing drugs and administering electroconvulsive therapy (ECT). (See Chapter 18.)

Psychiatric Nurses and Nurse Practitioners

For many years **psychiatric nurses** acted mainly as assistants to psychiatrists in mental hospitals and psychiatric wards of general hospitals. More recently, however, they have taken on greater responsibility for direct treatment, especially in psychotherapy. For example, psychiatric nurses often conduct group psychotherapy sessions (see Chapter 20). Like some nurses in other medical specialties, many psychiatric nurses are now taking advanced training leading to the professional status of nurse practitioner.

Psychoanalysts

Mental health professionals who derive their principles and methods of psychotherapy primarily from Freudian theory are called **psychoanalysts**. Until recently, almost all psychoanalysts were medical doctors who completed a residency in psychiatry before specializing in psychoanalysis. Training in psychoanalysis is carried out in institutes sponsored by various psychoanalytic associations. The most traditional is the American Psychoanalytic Association, the largest psychoanalytic society in the United States. With some exceptions, admission to the association and to the institutes it controls is restricted to members of the medical profession. However, a number of psychoanalytic institutes are considerably less restrictive and accept clinical psychologists and clinical social workers. The largest of these is the National Psychological Association for Psychoanalysis, founded by psychologist Theodor Reik (Arlow, 1984).

Freud himself did not believe it was necessary to become a physician in order to practice the methods of psychoanalysis, even though he had his initial training in medicine. In his provocative book *The Question of Lay Analysis*, Freud declared, "The important question is not whether an analyst possesses a medical diploma but whether he has the special training necessary for the practice of analysis" (Freud, 1927/1969, p. 102).

School Psychologists

The training of **school psychologists** overlaps with that of clinical and counseling psychologists. However, school psychologists also complete various courses in education to prepare them to understand the nature of school systems and the educational process and to work better in schools. At least a master's degree and certification by a state board of education are required of school psychologists.

The main task of school psychologists is to increase the effectiveness of schools by improving the intellectual, social, and emotional behavior of children. This task sometimes involves direct treatment of children with psychological and educational problems. School psychologists often act as consultants in improving the education of mentally and physically handicapped children. They also develop in-service training programs to help school personnel improve their understanding of children's problems and how they can interfere with learning.

Clinical Social Workers

The training of **clinical social workers** usually leads to an M.S.W. (master of social work) degree, although a degree at the doctoral level may also be earned. The M.S.W. is the standard practitioner degree. Doctoral degrees, such as the Ph.D. and D.S.W. (doctor of social work), are designed for professionals who wish to emphasize research and teaching or who wish to combine research with direct service to clients. In their therapeutic work, clinical social workers stress the relationship between mental and behavioral disorders and the social conditions that underlie or aggravate them. Some clinical social workers concentrate on the nature of family life and how it can contribute to psychological disturbances. Clinical social workers work in mental health clinics, hospitals, family service agencies, and private practice (Mishne, 1980; Northern, 1982).

School Social Workers

Like clinical social workers, **school social workers** represent a specialty in the field of social work. School social workers attempt to help individual children who have personal problems that are affecting their schoolwork, to enable parents to better understand and support their children's school learning, and to increase teacher sensitivity to home and societal conditions. School social workers and school psychologists often collaborate to help individual children or to modify school conditions that adversely affect groups of children (Allen-Meares, Washington, & Welsh, 1986; Costin, 1987).

Marriage and Family Therapists

Mental health professionals who specialize in marital and family problems are called **marriage and family therapists**. They come from a variety of professional backgrounds — clinical and counseling psychology, psychiatry, clinical social work, and special graduate programs that center on problems of marriage and the family as well as methods of counseling and psychotherapy (Freeman, 1982; Perez, 1979, Sholevar, 1981). Their major professional associations are the American Association of Marriage Counselors and the American Association for Marriage and Family Therapy.

In some instances, conflicts that people present to marriage and family therapists may involve much more serious psychosocial problems. Depending on their training, experience, and personal preferences, counselors either continue working with such individuals or refer them to other mental health professionals.

Pastoral Counselors

Professional **pastoral counselors** complete specialized programs in schools of theology that include studies in psychology, psychiatry, and social work. They often complete postgraduate training in those areas as well. The counselors are trained to recognize psychosocial problems that go beyond their professional resources, so that they can refer individuals to the appropriate mental health professional or agency. They may also work concurrently with other mental health professionals — for example, providing religious counseling to hospital patients who are undergoing psychiatric treatment (Mollica, Boscarino, & Redlich, 1986).

Pastoral counselors can perform valuable services even with highly disturbed individuals. Indeed, some people with serious disorders may choose to see a pastoral counselor. The counselor is then in a position to refer them to an appropriate professional or agency and thus help them get treatment. Whether or not they offer specialized programs in pastoral counseling, some schools of theology now require all of their students to complete at least a minimum of training designed to increase their sensitivity to serious psychosocial problems so that they can make appropriate referrals when necessary.

Summary

1. **Psychotherapy** means treatment by psychological means. It is a human relationship whose goal is to help bring about positive changes in thinking, feeling, and acting.

2. In biomedical treatment, the main task of the patient is to comply with the therapist's instructions. In contrast, the person undergoing psychotherapy (the client) is expected to be more active in achieving the outcome. Another difference is that the objectives of psychotherapy tend to be more open-ended. For example, psychotherapy may include such goals as self-understanding and changes in attitude toward oneself and others. This is especially true of psychodynamic and humanistic methods of therapy.

3. Behavioral and cognitive therapies, like biomedical therapy, involve concrete goals that are specified at the very outset of treatment. However, the individual is still expected to assume a greater degree of responsibility and to participate more actively than in biomedical therapy.

4. The major hallmark of psychotherapy is communication, often but not necessarily verbal. The goals of psychotherapy are tied to the experiences and characteristics of the individuals undergoing treatment. A goal of organizations whose members practice psychotherapy is to prevent therapists from having sexual contact with their clients.

5. A core characteristic of psychodynamic therapies is the central importance they assign to the unconscious. Therefore, bringing the unconscious into consciousness is a prime goal of psychodynamic therapies.

6. The ultimate source of psychodynamic approaches to psychotherapy lies in the theory and practice of Sigmund Freud, the founder of psychoanalysis. A prime goal is to help the individual resolve conflicts that arise between the ego, the id, and the superego. At the same time, conflicts between those intrapsychic events and external reality must be considered. Analysis of how the ego defends itself is also important.

7. Freud developed a number of techniques to help the patient achieve insight and understanding and to resolve conflicts and a number of concepts with which to explain the process. They include the fundamental rule (a pact between patient and therapist), free association, resistance, the therapeutic alliance, transference and countertransference, interpretation, and working through.

8. Traditional psychoanalysis has a number of limitations. It works best with a limited range of disorders, such as neuroses (anxiety, dissociative, and somatoform disorders). It is of less value when applied to individuals with personality disorders or psychotic individuals. It is also a prolonged and expensive procedure.

9. Modified forms of psychoanalysis, such as neo-Freudian approaches and methods based on ego psychology, have gained a great deal of prominence within the broad psychoanalytic movement. Neo-Freudian methods retain many concepts and techniques of orthodox psychoanalysis but emphasize more current problems and social forces in the development of psychological problems. Ego psychology focuses on the analysis of defense mechanisms and the autonomy of the ego to a greater extent than traditional psychoanalysis. These two orientations overlap considerably and often merge in modern practice.

10. Among those prominent in the development of modified forms of psychoanalysis are Harry Stack Sullivan, who strongly influenced the development of the William Alanson White Institute and Psychoanalytic Society; Karen Horney, founding editor of the *American Journal of Psychoanalysis* and the American Institute for Psychoanalysis; and Franz Alexander and Thomas French of the Chicago Institute of Psychoanalysis.

11. Sullivan developed a number of sensitive techniques in the treatment of mentally disturbed people, including those suffering from schizophrenia. He focused on the relationship between patient and therapist, going beyond Freud's concepts of transference. He also extended his views of psychiatry to deal with issues of race, ethnic prejudice, education, and how our society contributes to mental disorders.

12. Karen Horney and her followers emphasize that the origin of anxiety disorders and related psychological problems stems from a distortion of normal needs in everyday relationships. These needs involve moving toward, away from, and against others. Mentally healthy people maintain a reasonable balance among these normal needs. The neurotic individual exaggerates and rigidifies them. Horney's goals of therapy focus on helping patients overcome their unrealistic self-image and their distortion of normal needs. Her approach uses many of the same techniques as orthodox psychoanalysis, such as free association and interpretation. However, the interaction between patient and therapist is more flexible and less distant. Horney also differs from Freud in concepts and methods of handling such events as transference and countertransference.

13. Heinz Kohut, late professor and practitioner of psychoanalysis at the University of Chicago and the Chicago Institute of Psychoanalysis, gradually switched from orthodox psychoanalysis to a version he calls self-psychology. He emphasizes narcissism in early childhood as a source of neurotic disorders and is concerned with conditions. Kohut deemphasizes the importance of biological drives in the development of neuroses and focuses more on the relevance of sociocultural forces and ego analysis. In general, Kohut's techniques are more flexible than the traditional Freudian methods.

14. Alfred Adler and Carl Gustav Jung were early members of Freud's inner circle. However, they became disenchanted with psychoanalysis. Not content to modify it, they broke away completely and established their own independent approaches.

15. Adler named his concepts and methods of therapy individual psychology. Although his influence in the United States has not been as great as that of Freud, a number of centers in various cities are highly active in training Adlerian therapists. Several journals have been founded to communicate the Adlerian approach.

16. Adler recognized the importance of unconscious motivations established in early childhood as determiners of psychological disturbances. However, he departed from Freudian psychoanalysis in focusing on concepts of weakness and inferiority. Individuals who have self-perceptions of inadequacy unconsciously strive for unrealistic goals of superiority, which Adler called the inferiority complex. Symptoms of neurotic disorders are used to conceal that complex, resulting in abnormal anxiety, fears, bodily discomfort, and hostile attitudes toward others.

17. Adlerian techniques of therapy are more direct than those of psychoanalysis, especially the Freudian versions. Psychotherapy is more of an educational process in which the therapist explains to the patient how unrealistic goals and maladaptive ways of achieving superiority are causing trouble. A central goal is to strengthen social interests — a cooperative effort between client and therapist. Position in the family constellation is also an important focus of inquiry and explanation. Adler extended his concepts and methods of therapy to education, social reform, and community action.

18. Originally trained in medicine in Switzerland, Jung departed from the Viennese Freudian circle to found his own therapeutic movement, which he named analytical psychology. The C. G. Jung Institute was opened in Zurich in 1948 to teach Jungian principles and techniques. Since then, training centers have been established in a number of countries.

19. Jung believed that Freud had overemphasized the sexual component of the unconscious. He emphasized that the unconscious is only partly rooted in childhood experiences. To a greater extent, it stems from the accumulated wisdom of humanity—the collective unconscious. Jung aimed to reconcile troubled patients to their unconscious and to enable them to learn to trust it.

20. An important aspect of the collective unconscious is the concept of archetypes, which Jung believed represented the original collective patterns or ideals of ideas and beliefs. All reflect the beliefs of the cultural group to which the individual belongs as well as the universal unconscious images common to all human beings. Archetypes can be understood through myths, fairy tales, works of art, folklore, and other creative works.

21. According to Jung, symptoms of neurotic disorders are messages representing clues from the unconscious about what is missing in the life of the patient and what must be done to overcome psychological problems. Therefore, the individual must be brought in touch with the collective unconscious, in order to achieve self-understanding.

22. Jungian techniques in therapy are more flexible and less formal than Freudian methods. Free association might be used, but it is supplemented by graphic techniques, such as drawing current symbols in a dream.

23. Jungian therapy usually begins with an investigation of the patient's conscious state and common problems. Inquiries are made as to the patient's past history, attitudes, ideas, and values. Inconsistencies are pointed out. The unconscious is then explored, with emphasis on the patient's dreams and their symbols. In this way, the therapist helps the patient get in touch indirectly with archetypes, the creative energy they represent, and their relationship to the person's current psychological problems.

24. Humanistic therapies emphasize that the goal of psychotherapy is to help distressed individuals realize their potential and grow toward self-realization. The focus is on the person's current existence and its significance. Thus, humanistic psychology is often called existential.

25. The most prominent approach to humanistic and existential psychotherapy is that developed by Carl Rogers and extended by his followers. Now called person-centered therapy, the approach differs from psychodynamic approaches in both style and substance. For example, Rogers's views rest upon far less detailed and speculative concepts. His goal was to develop a set of therapeutic techniques and a formulation of how personality changes during psychotherapy.

26. Rogers's work can be divided into three periods: nondirective, reflective, and experiential. During the experiential period, Rogers and his colleagues shed their concern about such specific techniques as clarification and reflection of the feelings exercised by the client and broadened their approach. The change included a focus

on nonverbal as well as verbal statements. Intervention became more direct, including the therapist's willingness to ask leading questions. It was during this period that the label *client-centered* was changed to *person-centered*, because it reflected the basic approach more accurately.

27. During the experiential period, Rogers defined the necessary and sufficient conditions for successful psychotherapy. These conditions, which remain a cornerstone of person-centered therapy, include positive regard for the client, unconditional acceptance, genuineness on the part of the therapist, and perceiving the client with empathy. According to Rogers, the more successfully these conditions are met, the more the client will perceive their presence and experience them. Thus, the client is enabled to move toward self-understanding, self-acceptance, and positive relationships with others. The therapist need not be concerned with highly specific techniques as long as the necessary and sufficient conditions are met.

28. In general, the views of person-centered therapists are more optimistic than the views of psychoanalysts, especially orthodox psychoanalysts. Some researchers and practitioners have noted a similarity between the person-centered view of Rogers and the views of Heinz Kohut, a modern modifier of psychoanalysis. For example, both Rogers and Kohut are concerned about the experiential life of individuals and the importance of exploring their phenomenal (subjectively experienced) world. Individuals can make choices and to some extent control their destiny. The therapist need not be neutral, as in classical psychoanalysis.

29. One of Rogers's greatest contributions to psychotherapy was his insistence that what goes on in therapy must be studied directly through the intensive analysis of interviews with the client.

30. Victor Frankl, a psychiatrist in Vienna and a survivor of Nazi concentration camps, has developed a therapy method called logotherapy. Logotherapy is not as well known or influential as various other methods, but it does have its adherents, especially those who are philosophically and spiritually concerned with the meaning of existence. Two techniques emphasized in logotherapy are paradoxical attention and dereflection. Paradoxical attention is designed to counteract anticipatory anxiety associated with the appearance of a symptom — for example, worrying about a condition to the extent that the worry actually intensifies the symptom. Dereflection is designed to counteract what Frankl calls a compulsive inclination to self-observation. Patients are instructed to shift from petty concerns to focus on more fundamental problems on existence and meaning.

31. The originator of Gestalt therapy was Frederick Perls, a German-born psychoanalyst who gradually became disenchanted with the theory and practice of psychoanalysis. In collaboration with his wife, Laura, he applied concepts and theories of Gestalt psychology to psychotherapy.

32. Gestalt psychology, developed in Germany and now absorbed into general psychology, maintains that our perceptual and cognitive experiences are not simply the sum of separate elementary sensations. We normally perceive and experience the world as organized into patterns, wholes, or configurations.

33. The basic premise of Gestalt therapy is that our experience is organized according to figure–ground relationships. Experiences that are the focus of our attention are the figure; those at the periphery are the ground configurations may become so fractured that we fail to be conscious of figure–ground relationships. Gestalt therapy aspires to restore the lost unity and connectedness of personal experience.

34. Gestalt therapy also attempts to intensify self-awareness by focusing on body language feelings that are expressed nonverbally. With the help of the therapist, these feelings are then translated into words and put into the person's figure. Videotape replays of therapeutic interviews may be used in this process.

35. Dreams are important in Gestalt therapy, but they are used as a vehicle for the person to act out the present. This use of dreams emphasizes the here and now.

36. The Gestalt therapist usually assumes a highly directive role — outspoken, self-expressive, and dramatic. Intensity, spontaneity, and immediacy are highly valued and practiced by both therapist and client.

37. There are more than 50 Gestalt therapy training centers in the United States and other parts of the world. In recent years, newer modes of practice have developed at these centers, with an increased focus on a somewhat softer approach and an increased trust in the patient's perceptions of the world.

38. Practitioners of psychotherapy include clinical psychologists, counseling psychologists, school psychologists, psychiatrists, psychiatric nurses and nurse practitioners, psychoanalysts, clinical and school social workers, marriage and family therapists, and pastoral counselors.

20

**Behavior
Therapy,
Effectiveness
of Individual
Psychotherapy,
and Group
Therapy**

Learning without thought is labor lost; thought without learning is perilous.

CONFUCIUS
(551–479 B.C.)

With three or more people there is something bold in the air: direct things get said which would frighten two people alone and conscious of each inch of their nearness to one another.

ELIZABETH BOWEN
The House of Paris **(1938)**

In this chapter, we extend our discussion of psychotherapy to behavior therapy, which aims to change more specific aspects of behavior and thinking than do psychodynamic and humanistic therapies. Behavior therapy is based on the assumption that the same principles of learning can be used to explain how abnormal as well as normal patterns of behavior and thinking are acquired. Therefore, these forms of psychotherapy focus on unlearning maladaptive patterns and learning more adaptive ones. In recent years, many behavior therapists have expanded their approach by incorporating principles of cognitive psychology. They focus on maladaptive patterns of thinking and how new, more adaptive patterns can be learned.

Following our discussion of behavior therapy, we consider such crucial questions as: What does research reveal about the outcomes of individual psychotherapy? To what extent does it actually help individuals overcome their psychological problems? Do certain approaches to psychotherapy have advantages over others?

Finally, we describe methods of psychological treatment in group settings. We discuss the development of these methods and their effectiveness.

Behavior Therapy

Historical Background

The Problem of Symptom Substitution

In the last 25 years, behavior therapy has become an increasingly important approach to the treatment of psychological disorders. Although its antecedents go back to the first two decades of this century, the few isolated attempts to change specific responses of abnormally distressed people continued to be overshadowed for many years by psychodynamic therapies (Kazdin, 1978a, 1978b). Under the influence of psychodynamic theory, mental health professionals believed that to help people overcome their psychological problems it was necessary to go far beyond the relief of specific symptoms. Removing symptoms without dealing with their hidden causes brought only temporary and illusory relief, for the symptoms would return in a different form. This belief in **symptom substitution** became so deeply embedded in psychodynamic therapy that for many years it inhibited a systematic search for techniques that would attack the symptoms of psychological disabilities directly.

Psychiatrist Joseph Wolpe emigrated from South Africa to the United States. The set of therapy techniques that he developed, known as systematic desensitization, apply classical conditioning to eliminate maladaptive fears and anxieties.

Wolpe's Work on Classical Conditioning

In the late 1950s, behavioral approaches to psychotherapy began to gain prominence. Of special importance was the pioneering work of Joseph Wolpe (1958, 1961). Originally trained in medicine at the University of Witwatersrand in Johannesburg, South Africa, he later engaged in teaching and research in the Department of Psychiatry at Temple University. He developed a set of techniques based on principles of classical conditioning previously demonstrated by the Russian physiologist Ivan Pavlov (see Chapter 4). Wolpe first called these methods *psychotherapy by reciprocal inhibition* and subsequently renamed them **systematic desensitization therapy.** They were designed to eliminate behavioral excesses, such as unreasonable fears and other maladaptive anxieties. Wolpe's contributions soon alerted other mental health professionals to the possibility of efficiently removing certain patterns of maladaptive behavior by the direct application of principles of learning. In addition, Wolpe pointed to the lack of evidence for symptom substitution, thus weakening the psychodynamic claim that the hidden causes of symptoms must be understood before psychotherapy can be successful. Later studies have substantiated Wolpe's early claims that no clear evidence supports symptom substitution and that the removal of symptoms through behavior therapy has a lasting effect (Kazdin & Wilson, 1978; Marks, 1978a).

The value of Wolpe's pioneering work went beyond direct treatment. It offered a new challenge to psychodynamic therapy.

Skinner and Operant Conditioning

While Wolpe was developing the use of classical conditioning techniques in psychotherapy, B. F. Skinner (1938/1966, 1953) took the first steps toward applying principles of operant conditioning to the changing of maladaptive behavior. Skinner's contributions to theories of learning began in the 1930s, but their application to psychotherapy did not gain momentum until the 1950s and 1960s. (See Chapter 4 for a detailed description of Skinner's theories of conditioning.)

Operant conditioning techniques focus on correcting behavior deficits — that is, it seeks to impart desirable patterns of behavior that are absent from an individual's repertoire. For example, operant techniques have been used to help abnormally shy people develop better social skills, to increase the ability of schizophrenics to achieve more positive interpersonal relations, to teach basic self-help skills to mentally retarded individuals, and to help autistic children learn to speak.

Some therapists have restricted the term *behavior therapy* to procedures based on classical conditioning and the term *behavior modification* to methods that focus on operant conditioning (Chambless & Goldstein, 1979). Increasingly, however, the terms have come to be used synonymously, a practice we will follow.

Basic Characteristics of Behavior Therapy

Although it is a relatively new field, behavior therapy now includes a wide array of techniques. Before considering them, however, we will describe some of the basic characteristics that underlie all behavioral approaches to psychotherapy (Franks & Barbrack, 1983, pp. 507–511; Kazdin, 1978a, 1978b).

Unlike psychoanalysts, behavior therapists focus on current rather than historical determinants of behavior. They do not deny that past experience may have caused present behavior, but they focus on the factors that are currently sustaining it.

For behavior therapists, changes in behavior are the essential criterion for evaluating the effectiveness of their intervention. Unlike humanistic therapy, behavior therapy does not aim to provide a greater sense of self-fulfillment. Instead, its objectives focus on changing the probabilities of particular patterns of behavior — that is, increasing or decreasing the likelihood of their occurrence.

Behavior therapists insist upon specifying goals and techniques of treatment in objective terms readily understood by the client. Their reports of the therapeutic process typically include what they did, how they did it, and the client's behavior before and after their intervention. Behavior therapy defines and measures problems and symptoms very specifically. For example, it is not sufficient simply to know that a client suffers from agoraphobia. The behavior therapist wants to know how often, when, where, and under what circumstances the fear of open spaces occurs and how it varies under different environmental circumstances.

The source of hypotheses about the treatment of psychological disorders for behavior therapists is experimental laboratory research, not clinical practice. Basic models of learning that have grown out of this research have been especially influential in the development of therapeutic techniques.

Behavior therapists do not usually assume that the symptoms of a psychological disorder reflect unconscious conflicts that must be understood before the disorder can be alleviated. The problem behavior itself constitutes the disorder. Thus, for example, behavior therapists have little interest in such psychoanalytic conclusions as "the patient's obsession is symbolic of an unresolved Oedipal conflict." Rather, they seek information that is directly related to their therapeutic interventions.

Behavior therapists do not reject inferences about underlying mediators of disordered behavior, such as motives, thoughts, and intentions. They insist, however, that these inferences be directly tied to observable stimuli and behavior. They are well aware that psychological disturbances may go beyond observable behavior and be revealed in more subtle ways. Nevertheless, they believe that the causes of these deeper problems also lie in the learning history of the individual, and thus are amenable to treatment with the techniques of behavior therapy.

In recent years, a strong cognitive orientation has developed within behavior therapy. Here, the focus is on the individual's patterns of thinking and how they can be changed to take a more adaptive and realistic direction. Some psychotherapists have called this emphasis cognitive-behavior therapy, to distinguish it from older forms of behavior therapy.

Classical Conditioning Techniques

In classical conditioning, responses to one stimulus situation become transferred to another (see Chapter 4). Thus, attitudes and feelings may become attached to various situations that had not previously elicited those responses. Techniques of behavior therapy based on classical conditioning are designed mainly to eliminate behavioral excesses, such as unreasonable fears and maladaptive anxieties. Prominent among these methods are systematic desensitization therapy, implosive therapy, covert sensitization, and aversion therapy.

Systematic Desensitization

Problems centering around maladaptive conditioned anxiety are the ones most often treated with systematic desensitization therapy. Among such problems are (a) generalized anxiety in the absence of objective dangers or threats; (b) failure to perform cognitive or motor tasks adequately because of anxiety that interferes with performance or the readiness to perform; (c) disruption of normal behavior in order to avoid or escape anxiety; and (d) the continual maintenance of a specific pattern of maladaptive behavior, such as obsessions and compulsions, in order to ward off an anxiety-provoking situation (see Chapter 5).

Wolpe (1958, 1961, 1969) pioneered techniques of systematic desensitization therapy to eliminate maladaptive behavior that had originally been acquired through classical conditioning. The basic therapeutic principle was that if a response incompatible with anxiety can be made to occur in the presence of the anxiety-producing stimuli, the bond between these stimuli and anxiety will be weakened (Wolpe, 1958; Wolpe & Lazarus, 1966).

Systematic desensitization usually involves the following three steps: (a) training in deep relaxation to produce a state that is incompatible with anxiety; (b) construction of hierarchies of anxiety-producing stimuli, ranging from weak to strong, that the client can visualize under controlled conditions; and (c) desensitization of anxiety by gradual presentation of the anxiety-eliciting stimuli while the client is in a state of deep relaxation (Costin, 1976, p. 168; Paul & Bernstein, 1973; Wolpe, 1975, 1985).

A number of techniques exist to train clients in deep relaxation. The method most often used is some form of **progressive relaxation**, as developed by Edmund Jacobson (1957, 1964). This method involves teaching the client how to alternately tense and relax various groups of muscles. The sudden releasing of muscles after tensing them produces a sensation of warmth and relaxation, accompanied by a reduction in the arousal of the autonomic nervous system. Some therapists also instruct the client to hold a deep breath while tensing the muscles and then to release it for normal breathing when the muscles are relaxed. To help induce relaxation, therapists may also use direct suggestion, including light hypnosis. This training takes place while the client reclines in a comfortable chair. Once training in relaxation is completed, deep relaxation can be produced on demand.

In the second step, the client and therapist work together to determine the kinds of situations that produce maladaptive anxiety. Then they develop a hierarchy of stimuli ranging from those that elicit the least amount of anxiety to those that elicit the most.

There are two main types of hierarchies: thematic and spatial–temporal. In a **thematic hierarchy**, the stimuli are arranged in order of intensity, but they all have a thematic similarity. For example, a thematic hierarchy dealing with fears of closed places might include a small room, an elevator, and a closet. In a **spatial–temporal hierarchy**, the stimuli are arranged along a physical or time dimension. An example of this arrangement

Edmund Jacobson, a physician and for many years a professor of physiology at the University of Chicago, developed a method of inducing deep muscular relaxation, called progressive relaxation. Various forms of the technique are widely used as an integral part of systematic desensitization therapy.

In systematic desensitization of maladaptive anxiety about speaking in public, a hierarchy of anxiety-producing stimuli are developed by the client and therapist. They may range from reading about speeches a week before delivery to the actual presentation of the speech.

is the following hierarchy used in desensitizing excessive anxiety about presenting a speech. The lower the number preceding the item the less anxiety it provokes (Costin, 1976, p. 169; Paul 1966, pp. 117–118).

1. Reading about speeches alone in school one or two weeks before it is time to give the speech.

2. Discussing the speech a week before it is due.

3. Listening to someone else give a speech a week before.

4. Writing the speech in a study area, room, or library.

5. Practicing the speech alone in a room.

6. Getting dressed the morning of the speech.

7. Practicing just prior to leaving for the speech.

8. Walking to the room where the speech will be given on the day of the speech.

9. Waiting while another person gives a speech.

10. Walking in front of the audience.

11. Presenting the speech before the audience.

The development of hierarchies is not a mechanical procedure. It involves accurate clinical perceptions of the client's anxieties and the ability of the therapist to work cooperatively with the client. It is a difficult clinical skill requiring expert training.

In the third step of systematic desensitization, the therapist presents the various stimuli in the hierarchy one by one. The client is instructed to relax deeply, visualize the lowest item in the hierarchy, and then signal the therapist if there is any feeling of anxiety. If there is no signal, the client continues the visualization for 10 to 15 seconds, stops, and continues deep relaxation for 15 to 30 seconds. The therapist presents the item several more times. If the client reports no discomfort, the therapist proceeds with the next item. If the client signals anxiety, visualization stops and the therapist asks the client to concentrate on relaxing. The therapist repeats the stimulus until it elicits no anxiety for several successive presentations, then introduces the next item in the hierarchy. If the client continues to indicate anxiety toward an item, the therapist repeats an item lower in the hierarchy until the client no longer signals anxiety. Systematic desensitization is complete when the client progresses through the entire hierarchy without experiencing anxiety. Typically, the entire procedure can be completed in a month or so.

Research has shown that generalization from the treatment procedures to the everyday world is usually quite successful. However, some people have great difficulty imagining the various stimuli (Foa, Stekettee, & Ascher, 1980). For them, the therapist can present slide projections or use **in vivo** (real-life) **desensitization** by instructing clients in the kinds of carefully graded situations they should deliberately encounter outside the office.

In vivo desensitization is complicated, but properly handled it can be quite effective. It usually begins after training in deep relaxation is complete. The client is instructed to approach the anxiety-producing situation until a mild increase in anxiety occurs. At that point, the client stops and relaxes, rests a few minutes, and then continues the approach–relaxation cycle until no anxiety is experienced. The client follows the same procedure throughout the hierarchy of anxiety-eliciting items (Paul & Bernstein, 1973).

When an unreasonable fear results from misconceptions rather than conditioned anxiety, the best response may be to supply the client with corrective information. For instance, a person may fear getting stuck in an elevator and suffocating, being unaware that ventilation devices are mandatory in all elevators. The anxiety is usually alleviated when correct information is supplied. On the other hand, people who fear closed spaces even though they acknowledge that the fear is irrational are excellent candidates for systematic desensitization therapy (Wolpe, 1985).

Systematic desensitization is efficient as well as effective (Kazdin & Wilcoxon, 1976; Sloane, Staples, Cristol, Yorkston, & Whipple, 1975). Typically, it takes several weeks, rather than months, to complete. Nevertheless, we don't know why it works. Conditioning is no doubt part of the reason, but other factors may contribute. For example, the therapist's suggestion that the technique will work may lead the client to expect success, and this expectation may shape the outcome. Sorting out the variables that contribute to successful desensitization remains a challenge to research on behavior therapy. Nevertheless, practitioners are rightly encouraged by its demonstrated effectiveness.

Implosive Therapy

The obverse of systematic desensitization, **implosive therapy** (also termed *flooding*) confronts clients with frightening situations in all their intensity. For example, clients may be asked to imagine that they are precariously perched on the rim of a pit full of snakes. Stampfl and Levis (1967), the originators of implosive therapy, reasoned that an experience of intense anxiety not followed by its anticipated consequences could be a powerful aid in extinguishing phobias. Practitioners of implosive therapy have become adept in producing vivid, even lurid, word pictures designed to arouse their clients' anxieties. Where systematic desensitization procedures may strike the outside observer as monotonous, there is no denying that implosive therapy is dramatic. In Stampfl and Levis's view (1967), elaborate avoidance behavior governs the life of the person suffering from irrational anxieties. Once avoidance is replaced with confrontation and the feared situation is experienced, the basis for the maladaptive reactions disappears.

Like systematic desensitization, implosive therapy works in a great many situations with many clients. Several reviewers of the accumulated research on its outcomes, however, found that it had no particular advantage over systematic desensitization. Morganstern (1973) concluded that there is no reason to prefer implosive therapy over desensitization. Furthermore, desensitization is more humane because it inflicts less suffering on the client. On the other hand, certain long-term, hard-to-treat anxieties — for example, agoraphobia — respond especially well to implosion techniques (Levis, 1974).

Covert Sensitization

In contrast to systematic desensitization, which is designed to eliminate conditioned anxieties, **covert sensitization** attempts to induce them. Normal fears are adaptive in that they help us avoid dangerous or undesirable stimuli. In some people, these adaptive signals are absent or they operate improperly. Covert sensitization helps check undesirable behavior by conditioning it to fear and anxiety (Cautela, 1969, 1970a).

Covert sensitization takes place in the individual's imagination. For example, the therapist asks a client being treated for alcohol abuse to imagine passing by a bar, having an urge to drink, experiencing discomfort, and then immediately losing the feeling of discomfort: "You are walking near the bar and you say to yourself, 'I think I'll have a drink.' As soon as you say that to yourself you get a pain and feeling of nausea and then you say, 'The hell with it; I'm not going to drink.' As soon as you think that you immediately feel better and walk away from the bar. You feel proud of yourself because you were able to lick the temptation" (Cautela, 1970b, p. 88).

Although covert desensitization has been successful, its use raises important ethical questions. Who is to decide which behaviors are undesirable and ought to be eliminated?

On what behalf is covert sensitization conducted? One solution—which does not do justice to the complexity of all the issues involved—is to insist that these procedures be conducted only with informed voluntary consent. The other precaution is for therapists to refrain from using the technique unless its objectives are in harmony with their ethics. For example, few behavior therapists would agree to covertly sensitize homosexuals at the request of some external authority (Goldfried & Davison, 1976).

Aversion Therapy

In **aversion therapy**, classical conditioning is used to inhibit unwanted, maladaptive behavior; but the stimuli used to induce avoidance are physically aversive rather than imaginary. Indeed, the stimuli are often quite painful. For example, the therapist may give an alcoholic client a favorite drink (a conditioned stimulus) and then immediately administer a painful electric shock (an unconditioned stimulus). After repeated pairings of the two stimuli, the therapist presents only the alcoholic beverage. If conditioning has been successful, the client will respond with aversion. A conditioned aversive response to alcohol has now replaced a liking for it.

In the past, the unconditioned stimuli most widely used in aversion therapy for alcoholics were drugs that produce a great deal of nausea, such as emetine and apomorphine. Giving the drug was timed to induce vomiting when alcohol was consumed. As a result, nausea became conditioned to the ingestion of alcoholic beverages.

Aversive conditioning is among the least popular and most controversial techniques of behavior therapy. it is difficult to time the pairing of the emetic drug with the conditioned stimulus of alcohol, and the procedure requires close medical supervision. Many of the procedures of aversion therapy fit the coercive and manipulative image that behavior therapy has in the minds of at least part of the public. In addition, it raises the same sort of ethical questions as covert sensitization. Under what circumstances can the use of such harsh methods be justified? Arnold Lazarus (1971, 1976) a former student and associate of Wolpe, claims that the use of aversive physical stimuli often amounts to torture. Equally

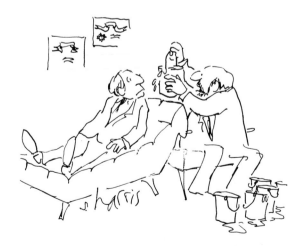

"Today we'll try aversion-therapy. Every time you say something stupid, I'll spill a bucket of water on your head."

effective results can be gained with milder physical stimuli. For example, Lazarus found that the use of an ammonia inhalant as the aversive unconditioned stimulus was more effective than electric shock in treating alcoholics. Finally, aversion therapy is less effective than other modes of behavior therapy (Marks, 1978a).

Operant Conditioning Techniques

Teaching individuals various patterns of behavior that are socially desirable but missing from the person's repertoire is the focus of **operant conditioning techniques**. The specific techniques we now consider include shaping behavior, token economies, contingency contracting, and assertiveness training.

Shaping Behavior

In laboratory work with animals, B. F. Skinner originally demonstrated the use of shaping in developing new patterns of behavior (see Chapter 4). Shaping has now been widely applied in behavior therapy, especially in programs designed to teach individuals new and more adaptive patterns of behavior. To carry out a program of **behavioral shaping**, the therapist must consider three basic questions: What are the current active responses in the person's behavioral repertoire? What are effective reinforcers (rewards) for that person? What is the target behavior? At the beginning of the procedure, the therapist reinforces a response even if it barely resembles the desired behavior. By rewarding successively closer approximations to the desired behavior, the therapist can maintain a schedule of reinforcement that gradually helps the individual move in a positive direction. Under some circumstances, a great deal of trial and error may occur before the client gives even a reasonably correct response. One way the therapist can speed up the procedure is to model the desired response and then reinforce the individual when that response is given. Each response that brings the person nearer the goal is reinforced.

One of the best-known applications of shaping is the work of Ivor Lovaas and his colleagues in the treatment of autistic children (Lovaas, 1977). These children withdraw from their social environment and show a great deal of bizarre behavior. They do not learn to speak, but they do emit sounds (see Chapter 16). Some of the sounds resemble English words—for example, ma-ma and da-da. The therapist reinforces these crude approximations to actual words with a treat to which the child naturally responds. Setting directly in front of the child and maintaining constant eye contact, the therapist models a desired response. When the child imitates the model correctly, the therapist immediately gives an appropriate reward as well as words of praise and affection. Gradually, the modeling becomes more complex, moving from words to sentences. Throughout the process, it is necessary for the therapist to maintain strict attention, discouraging bizarre behavior and other forms of distraction from the task of modeling and shaping. Successive approximations of the modeling, followed by appropriate rewards, gradually extend to carrying on a conversation and even playing games with others. Under the guidance of the therapist, parents and teachers may also learn to take over the procedures, thus broadening the child's growing ability to communicate with others.

Token Economy Methods

What is attempted with individuals through behavioral shaping is carried out on a large scale in a **token economy**. Positive reinforcement is used to influence the behavior of a group of people—a class in school, a hospital ward, a cell block in a correctional institution. To begin with, the various kinds of desired behaviors are listed. Each target behavior is then rewarded with varying numbers of tokens that can be exchanged for goods and services. The token economy also establishes a limited schedule of responses that cannot be tolerated in a social setting, such as stealing and physical aggression. Such acts are subject to fines. Thus, the token economy consists of punishments as well as rewards. However, many more acts should be rewarded than punished. When punishment outweighs reward, a token economy may come to resemble a totalitarian society that obtains compliance mainly through coercion.

Since the pioneering work of Teodoro Ayllon and his colleagues at the Anna State Hospital in Illinois (Ayllon & Azrin, 1968), token economies have been extended to many other mental hospitals (Karoly & Harris, 1986; Kazdin, 1982). They have also been applied to schools for delinquent youth and community halfway houses for the social rehabilitation of people just discharged from mental hospitals. The token economy system has been adapted to teach mentally retarded children to read, write, and do simple computations, as well as to reduce their emotional problems (Bijou, 1972, 1973).

Not everyone achieves behavioral change in token economies. After reviewing the research literature, some mental health professionals have concluded that approximately 10 percent of the participants in token economy programs remained unresponsive to the reinforcers that were offered (Kazdin, 1977, 1983). The proportion of unresponsive individuals was higher among psychotic and mentally retarded people. The tokens were simply not effective reinforcers for some people because the people were not interested in the particular goods and services that the tokens could buy. Token economies might be more effective if the tokens bought a wider range of goods. Token economies also failed because they could be circumvented. In some institutions, a black market flourished so the token economy collapsed (Kazdin, 1982, 1983).

Some mental health professionals question whether the token economy system generalizes to behavior outside the institution once the participants depart (Karoly & Harris, 1986, p. 136). It is important, they argue, to incorporate into the program various natural reinforcers, such as intrinsic interest in an activity, rather than depending completely on tokens that bring material goods. In this way, the participants will learn the greater use of psychological reinforcers that will help achieve self-control. Indeed, an increasing number of well-run token economies emphasize the attainment of self-control as a goal (Paul & Lentz, 1977).

Contingency Contracting

The principle on which token economies are based can be implemented with individuals and small groups. Participants agree to a contract in which a variety of rewards are made contingent on the achievement of desirable behavior. (Kanfer & Gaelick, 1986, pp. 308–310). Sometimes the contracts are bilateral, as in the example of a husband and wife who trade behaviors that each of them wants the other to perform. **Contingency contracting** uses a feature of everyday life: All of us both receive and dispense reinforcement. Our behavior controls that of others and theirs controls ours.

Assertiveness Training

Many individuals are afraid to express themselves appropriately in their everyday relationships with others. They may be overly submissive when it is to their benefit to be assertive and stand up for their legitimate rights. Consequently, they let others take advantage of them, while silently resenting it. They may be unable to express anger when it is appropriate, or they may react to rebuffs with maladaptive outbursts of anger. Such behavior is typical of the kinds of problems that Karen Horney has labeled neurotic trends (see Chapters 3 and 19). The purpose of **assertiveness training** is to teach such individuals how to express themselves in adaptive ways and how to better understand the effects their assertive behavior has on others. As therapy reinforces their assertiveness, it competes with their anxiety and eventually helps extinguish it (Greenburg, 1985; Lazarus, 1971; pp. 30–31).

The techniques of assertiveness training sometimes combine elements of systematic desensitization with operant methods of modeling and shaping. The training may be carried out with one individual at a time or with groups. The latter approach has become very popular in recent years.

In individual assertiveness training, the therapist works closely with the client to develop a hierarchical list of carefully graded situations in which assertive behavior is appropriate. During the sessions, the client rehearses these situations, gradually moving up the hierarchy as soon as anxiety decreases for a given situation. The therapist assumes the role of significant figures in the client's life toward whom the client is afraid to be more assertive and reinforces the client's assertive responses as they gradually move up the hierarchy. After the client has learned to respond appropriately in the therapist's office, the process continues in real-life situations. The client keeps notes in order to report to the therapist those situations in which anxiety blocked assertiveness and those in which assertiveness was successful. The therapist evaluates the effectiveness of the procedure and makes productive suggestions. The therapist not only models the client's target for expressing assertiveness but also demonstrates appropriate assertive behavior. The client practices that behavior with the therapist, who assumes the role of the target.

Cognitive-Behavior Therapy

As behavior therapists ventured into new areas of application, they encountered complex problems of living for which classical and operant conditioning were inadequate. Many contemporary behavior therapists have stopped relying on traditional conditioning techniques as universal tools of intervention. One of the most significant developments in this direction is the recent emphasis on cognition.

Cognitive-behavior therapy reflects a pervasive trend in contemporary psychology: the rediscovery of cognition as a fundamental area of research. (*Cognition* is the acquiring and storing of information about the self and the world.)

Among behavior therapists, the recognition of the importance of cognitive factors in the control and change of maladaptive behavior has developed gradually. Its proponents assert that internal mechanisms as well as external influences change and maintain our behavior. In agreement with the Greek philosopher Epictetus (ca. A.D. 55–135), the advocates of cognition as a basic avenue of behavior therapy maintain that people are disturbed "not by things, but by the views they take of them." The Roman emperor and philosopher Marcus Aurelius Antonius (A.D. 121–180) put the same idea into different words: "If thou art pained by an external thing, it is not this thing that disturbs thee, but thine own judgment about it. And it is in thy power to wipe out this judgment now" (Mahoney, 1980, p. 127). An important implication of these statements, reemphasized in the writings of cognitive-behavior therapists, is that a great deal of human suffering is self-inflicted and avoidable. It can be reversed by changing our ways of thinking (Beck, 1976; Beck, Emery, & Greenberg, 1985; Mahoney, 1977; Meichenbaum, 1977, 1986).

Cognitive factors play an important role in even the simplest forms of human learning. How much more, then, is this true for complex patterns of behavior — those involved in discovery and problem solving? Proponents of cognitive-behavior therapy capitalize on the peculiarly human ability to reason.

Another central characteristic of cognitive-behavior therapy is the concept of **reciprocal influence**: linking the person with the environment. In traditional views of classical and operant conditioning, the person is at the receiving end of a variety of environmental influences — just like the salivating dog in Pavlov's laboratory or the rat in the Skinner box. Cognitive therapists argue that even though much of our behavior is externally controlled, at the same time we act upon our environment and change it. We may do so overtly, as we remove various obstacles in our path and change our environments through agricultural, industrial, and commercial activity. We may also do so covertly through our perceptions and cognitions. Thus, we have the capacity to make an objectively innocuous situation appear threatening to us. Conversely, we may make an objectively threatening situation appear harmless. Cognitive-behavior therapy relies a great deal on this interaction in its methods for changing maladaptive patterns of behavior (Bandura, 1978, 1982; Meichenbaum, 1986, pp. 347–350).

Modeling and Cognition

From its very early development, cognitive-behavior therapy made use of modeling. Indeed, interest in imitation as an avenue toward making behavior more adaptive helped bring cognitive-behavior therapy into being. More than two decades ago, Albert Bandura (1962) called attention to a type of modeling he called **observational learning**. In contrast to the older and better-known forms of modeling based on operant procedures that worked gradually, observational learning is faster. It does not require extensive and repetitive practice, and it does not depend on external positive reinforcement. A related concept is **modeling**, which involves imitating people of greater status and power. By modeling the behavior of people we admire, we experience the pleasure of being like them. Modeling and observational learning tend to carry their own intrinsic satisfactions (Bandura, 1962, 1982). They also have been especially successful in the treatment of phobias and the development of social skills (Perry & Furukawa, 1986; Rachman, Marks, & Hodgson, 1973; Rosenthal & Bandura, 1978; Sarason, 1976). For example, in treating individuals who have an irrational fear of heights, the therapist overtly enjoys the view from a high observation tower, showing no signs of fear. In many of the treatment programs, practice supplements modeling. The client does not just observe the therapist's behavior but actively attempts to emulate it. However, less practice is generally required than in the traditional operant procedures, since much has already been learned through observing and cognitively tracing the skills of the therapist–model.

Beyond their immediate therapeutic value, modeling and observational learning contributed to a greater recognition and acceptance of cognitive factors in behavior therapy. Since there is an observable gap in modeling procedure between acquiring information and using it, attention began to focus on the mediating mechanism. What happens between the stimulus and the observer's response? Some sort of cognitive activity takes place, during which information is not just passively stored but actively transformed. Similar operations occur in cognitive activities not involving therapy. It is these operations, which became a central focus of cognitive psychology, that the exponents of cognitive-behavior therapy attempt to influence.

Cognitive Restructuring

A number of therapeutic techniques attempt to alter deeply established and maladaptive ways of thinking. Cognitive therapists — for example, Aaron Beck and Albert Ellis (who calls his approach rational emotive therapy) — hold that various emotional disorders can be traced to irrational and illogical ways of thinking, often involving persistent anxiety, depression, and low self-esteem. (Beck, 1976; Beck, Emery, & Greenberg, 1985; Beck & Young, 1985; Ellis, 1987a, 1987b,; Ellis & Bernard, 1985; Marzillier, 1987; McMullin, 1986).

A common problem is **faulty generalizing**. For instance, a person may interpret a slight social rejection to mean "I am an unlovable person" or "Everybody rejects me." Annoyance and disappointment that seem only mildly upsetting to other people are magnified to catastrophic proportions.

Cognitive therapists often deal with **polarized thinking**. The individual rigidly classifies actions into mutually exclusive categories — for example, good or bad, strong or weak, right or wrong. No provision is made for shades of difference.

Another problem is the individual's incorrect assumptions about what is threatening and what is safe. For example, the person acts upon such inflexible formulas as "It is always dangerous to express my views forcefully" or "Showing my anger openly will always lead to violence."

Some individuals harbor maladaptive attitudes toward pleasure and pain. For example, they may believe that whatever they enjoy must be bad or sinful or that painful experiences must be avoided at all cost.

Cognitive therapists must often deal with the **tyranny of shoulds**, as some express it. In this instance, the client holds dogmatically to self-directed commands of thinking and behavior that must always be obeyed unquestioningly.

Following are illustrations of some of the more common approaches that cognitive-behavior therapists use to help clients restructure their maladaptive patterns of thinking (Beck, 1976; Beck, Emery, & Greenberg, 1985; Bedrosian & Beck, 1980; Ellis, 1987a, 1987b; Ellis & Bernard, 1985; McMullin, 1986).

Psychologist Albert Ellis has developed rational-emotive therapy, techniques based on the theory that many emotional disorders stem from irrational and illogical ways of thinking.

Aaron Beck, professor of psychiatry at the University of Pennsylvania, has developed various techniques for altering deeply established maladaptive ways of thinking. He is especially well known for his cognitive theory of depression.

1. Distancing and hypothesis testing. Clients are encouraged to draw back from and look at their problems as outsiders. The process helps them learn how to formulate the probable consequences of their acts.

2. Decentering and altering personalization of events. Clients are encouraged to consider their own subjective reactions to problematic events and to separate them from a more objective appraisal.

3. Changing attribution of responsibility. The therapist helps clients question the habitual practice of blaming others or blaming themselves for failures in everyday events. The goal is to be more flexible and realistic in attributing responsibility to oneself and others.

4. Decatastrophizing. The therapist introduces the what-if technique by restructuring the events that the client always perceives as catastrophic. Clients come to see that the result may not be nearly as awful as they originally thought, and they eventually come to understand how maladaptive anxiety represents catastrophizing. Thus, clients can see events that were always threatening in a new and more manageable light.

Critique of Cognitive-Behavior Therapy

The methods of cognitive-behavior therapy are still too new to be thoroughly and conclusively evaluated. It is clear, however, that they have expanded the scope of behavior therapy and have made it applicable to conditions on which conditioning approaches had little impact. Depression, for example, has been difficult to counteract with conditioning techniques. Very positive results, however, have been attained by attacking the cognitive foundation of depressive experience, providing depressed people with new ways of thinking about themselves and their world, and enabling them to draw different conclusions from their experiences. Systematic research studies have substantiated these results (Hollon & Beck, 1986; Meichenbaum, 1986; Rush, Beck, Kovacs, & Hollon, 1977; Shaw, 1977). According to these studies, cognitive-behavior therapy is either equal or superior to drug therapy in helping people overcome depression.

The advocates of traditional behavior therapy have responded to the new cognitive emphasis with skepticism (Ledwidge, 1978). Joseph Wolpe has been one of its most outspoken critics. He argues that this development eliminates much of what is valid and valuable in behavior therapy: "Thinking is behavior and is as unfree as any other behavior. Our perceptual responses keep us constantly in touch with the world around us. Learning connects the sequences of our experience. . . . The view that the psychotherapeutic task is exclusively a matter of cognitive correction seems mistaken both because it is contrary to established facts about autonomic responses and because it is not supported by clinical data" (Wolpe, 1978, p. 444).

Other critics claim that cognitive-behavior therapists have not gone far enough — that is, they have not done full justice to the central importance of cognitive factors in causing and maintaining maladaptive behavior. For example, Mahoney (1980), a major contributor to the development of cognitive-behavior therapy, points to the following limitations.

1. Cognitive therapists tend to deemphasize or disregard the potential importance of unconscious processes.

2. They tend to take a narrow view of feelings, as something to be controlled rather than experienced.

3. Contributions from basic theories of cognitive psychology are not well integrated with the techniques of cognitive therapy.

4. Cognitive therapists overemphasize the correspondence between words and beliefs.

5. They also overemphasize the role of human rationality in adaptation; thus, their view of human nature errs in the direction of reasonableness.

6. They tend to make a normative distinction between the therapist and the client by assuming that for the most part the therapist is rational and the client is irrational.

7. Cognitive therapists are in danger of developing a potentially narrow orthodoxy and defensiveness.

Self-control and Behavior Therapy

The use of self-control in behavior therapy involves helping clients to become their own therapists, or at least to assume some of the therapist's functions. It rests on the recognition that to a considerable extent all of us are agents of our own control and dispensers of reinforcers. To be sure, as Skinner rightly emphasizes, external physical reinforcers control and maintain much of our behavior. Few of us, for example, would remain on our jobs without a paycheck. Not many students would continue studying if grades were suddenly eliminated. However, it is still true that we are both the originators and the recipients of our own reinforcement. Typically, we reinforce and punish ourselves continuously by dispensing and withdrawing self-approval. We feel good about our accomplishments and feel bad when we fail. This state of affairs constitutes the point of departure for the development of **self-management behavior therapy** (Kanfer & Gaelick, 1986; Karoly & Kanfer, 1982).

The link between self-management behavior therapy and cognitive-behavior therapy is quite close. In order to practice systematic self-management, people must be able to monitor, evaluate, and record their responses. Not everybody is capable of systematically exercising such self-control; motivational as well as cognitive limitations have to be taken into account. Yet there is no denying that a great many people have the resources to apply self-management techniques.

Current applications of self-management behavior therapy focus on relatively mild disturbances — for example, problems of weight control, smoking, and test anxiety. It is not yet known how far these techniques can be extended and to what degree self-management behavior therapy can be successful with such serious symptoms as hallucinations and delusions.

Self-management behavior therapy emphasizes (a) the self-administration of rewards and punishments related to the behavior that is to be reinforced and (b) the control of external and internal environments. Individuals may reward themselves for losing weight or for not smoking by buying especially desirable objects with the money they save. They can avoid places where smoking or eating are likely to occur. Individuals who are anxious about tests may make reassuring statements to themselves during preparation for and performance at examinations.

Multimodal Therapy

Psychologist Arnold Lazarus, former disciple of Joseph Wolpe, has helped broaden the scope of traditional behavior therapy. His multi-modal approach, incorporating a variety of methods, constitutes a total treatment package for many different kinds of disturbances.

Traditional behavior therapy generally focused on one symptom at a time. As the scope of behavior therapy expanded to treat more complex behaviors, therapists recognized the need to revise their traditional approach. Arnold Lazarus (1971, 1976, 1981), a former disciple of Wolpe, initiated a movement that in his words represented "behavior therapy and beyond." Lazarus now calls this approach **multimodal therapy**, because, in addition to the well-established behavior therapy techniques, it uses a variety of other methods and deals with a multiplicity of problems—all within an entire treatment package. The modalities in this package are *b*ehavior, *a*ffective processes, *s*ensations, *i*mages, *c*ognitions, *i*nterpersonal relationships, *d*rugs (Lazarus, 1981, 1984, 1985). The first letter of each of the modalities forms the acronym BASIC ID (ID as in identity). Lazarus (1985, pp. 1–2) cautions that the letter D (for drugs) stands for the biological modality. *D* is used instead of *B* to generate a more compelling acronym. Lazarus emphasizes that the *D* stands for more than drug treatment. It also includes biological causes of psychological disorders as well as the entire range of somatic intervention.

Following is an example of multimodal assessment of a client. The assessment suggests the broad spectrum of modalities the therapist dealt with in helping the client (Greenburg, 1985, pp. 20–23).

Behavior: "P's most salient behavioral deficit was her passivity in both work and interpersonal areas of her life."

Affect: "P's primary negative feelings were depression and anxiety."

Sensations: "P's withdrawal behavior was accompanied at times by a distortion of depth perceptions."

Images: "Imagery played an important role in triggering P's anxiety and fears. She would picture herself twitching in situations in which she felt evaluated."

Cognitions: "P held numerous dysfunctional beliefs that were primary precipitants of her problems. She believed that any objectionable behavior or mistake would cause to reject her completely. At the same time she believed it catastrophic if others did not like or approve of her."

Interpersonal relationship: "P was generally unassertive and guarded with people whom she admired. . . . She seemed to expect that others would find her boring. She also expected that others would not trust her."

Drugs/Biology: "P was in good health both in childhood and adolescence. Several years ago, when treated by a psychiatrist for her anxiety attacks, she had used tranquilizers. Her current health was excellent."

Current Issues in Behavior Therapy

Removing Specific Symptoms

Research results show that behavior therapy has been quite successful in eliminating specific symptoms, especially those related to disabling anxiety. Furthermore, it has helped individuals develop new, more adaptive responses to replace the maladaptive ones. Not only have older methods been successful; recent variations have as well.

Studies have found that removing symptoms does not require the lengthy process usually involved in psychodynamic and humanistic therapies, where a central goal is the reorganization of personality. In addition, the psychodynamic argument that rapid removal of symptoms simply means that others will be substituted has generally not been confirmed. Thus, behavior therapy would seem to be the treatment of choice if one desires to reduce or eliminate specific patterns of maladaptive behavior and thinking in a relatively short time. Similarly, behavior therapy is advantageous for developing new and relatively specific social skills.

Relationship to Other Therapies

To some extent, behavior therapy is an overt rejection of psychodynamic and humanistic approaches. However, the latter approaches may have more in common with behavior therapy than is readily apparent (Martin, 1972; Murray, 1976; Silverman, 1974; Wachtel, 1977).

Consider such central features of person-centered therapy (Chapter 19) as unconditional positive regard, acceptance and clarification of feelings, and empathic understanding. The therapist who responds to a client in this manner reinforces certain aspects of the client's behavior and thinking, even thought that is not an explicit goal. To illustrate how this can happen, David Martin (1972) cites the following instance of a hypothetical client whose partially conscious hostility toward his father resulted in his making numerous mistakes in his father's business (p. 107).

Client: I usually feel that I love my father so much that there's almost nothing I wouldn't do for him . . . (voice trails off uncertainly).

Therapist: I guess it"'s sort of a mixed thing for you.. . . . Usually you feel that way, and sometimes your feeling is less strong. I sense some feelings of puzzlement over that.

According to Martin, the therapist's response rewarded the client for expressing a painful conflict. In Skinnerian language, the response reinforced the client's behavior — that is, it increased the likelihood that he would begin taking the initiative to deal with his conflicts. By consistently responding to the client's region of conflict, as Martin puts it, the therapist uses positive reinforcement to help the client become aware of conflicts at an acceptable pace. Gradually, then, the client can learn to be strong enough to continue facing and solving those conflicts and the anxieties that accompany them.

Critics of behavior therapy point out that it underestimates the importance of attitudes and feelings that a client may have difficulty expressing. (Mahoney, 1980; Wachtel, 1977). Behavior therapists could therefore profit by integrating concepts of unconscious motivation and conflict. On the other hand, psychodynamic and humanistic therapists might benefit from applying some of the specific and productive techniques of behavior therapy — methods that directly produce specific changes in behavior. This approach would not necessarily rule out more long-term objectives, such as self-insight and deep-seated changes in personality.

Ethics and Control

Paradoxically, some critics have attacked behavior therapy because of its effectiveness. Since the techniques of behavior therapy work so dramatically, they are a powerful tool in the hands of experts in behavioral technology, and they can be used to manipulate or coerce. Many people are afraid that behavior therapy will be used for unethical ends or that the ethical issues involved in its application will be disregarded.

Practitioners of behavior therapy recommend that therapists refuse to apply such methods for unethical ends and that they insist upon the voluntary and informed consent of clients. Still, ambiguous situations arise. What about the application of behavior therapy in institutional settings that severely circumscribe the client's freedom of choice? Can a prisoner in a correctional institution or a mentally retarded person in a state school effectively refuse to participate in a token economy (Stolz, Wienckowski, & Brown, 1975)? What about the modification of behaviors that are subject to massive social disapproval? How do we really know whether homosexuals want to change their sexual orientation or whether they are just responding to massive social pressure to conform (Davison, 1976)? Behavior therapists are aware of these issues, and none of them would claim that they operate in an ethical vacuum. However, these questions are easier to raise than they are to answer.

Effectiveness of Individual Psychotherapy

Since the range of approaches to psychotherapy is so wide, it is understandable that an individual in trouble may wonder whether psychotherapy really helps. In this section of the chapter, we consider three basic questions: How well does psychotherapy work? What processes seem to be responsible for its beneficial results? To what extent are those processes common to successful psychotherapy regardless of the particular school it represents?

Outcomes of Psychotherapy

Eysenck's Analysis

In 1952, Hans J. Eysenck, a prominent British psychologist, analyzed various studies on the outcomes of psychotherapy and concluded that about two-thirds of neurotics who entered individual psychotherapy improved significantly. However, he also found that about an equal proportion of troubled individuals who did not undergo psychotherapy also improved. In later reports Eysenck (1966) came to essentially the same conclusion, except that the results of behavior therapy favored treatment over nontreatment. Eysenck concluded, "Whatever effects psychotherapy may have are likely to be extremely small. . . . [P]sychologists and psychiatrists will have to acknowledge the fact that current psychotherapeutic procedures have not lived up to the hopes which greeted their emergence fifty years ago" (1966, p. 40).

Eysenck's conclusions caused a great deal of consternation among psychotherapists. Various researchers attempted to clarify the issues he raised by examining more extensively and in more detail a wide range of studies on the outcomes of psychotherapy, including the studies that Eysenck had examined.

Meltzoff and Kornreich's Evaluation

Julian Meltzoff and Melvin Kornreich reviewed a large number of controlled studies dealing with the outcomes of psychotherapy. They divided the studies into three groups: (a) adequate studies that reported positive results, (b) questionable studies that reported positive results, and (c) studies with negative outcomes. After considering the evidence, they found that "reviews of the literature that have concluded that psychotherapy has, on the average, no demonstrable effect are based on an incomplete survey of the existing body of research and an insufficiently stringent appraisal of the data. . . . [C]ontrolled research has been notably successful in demonstrating significantly more behavioral change in treated patients than in untreated controls. In general, the better the quality of the research, the more positive the results obtained" (Meltzoff & Kornreich, 1970, p. 177).

Bergin, Lambert, and Shapiro's Analyses

Allen Bergin (1971) reanalyzed the studies that Eysenck had reviewed in 1953 and examined a large number of other studies dealing with outcomes of psychotherapy. He pointed to a number of factors that called Eysenck's conclusions into question.

1. The various disorders were not always defined well enough to allow for adequate comparison of outcomes.

2. There were marked differences between time of onset and duration of the disorders.

3. The criteria for judging improvement varied from one study to another.

4. There were significant variations in both the quantity and the quality of therapy the patients received.

5. Follow-up of patients after therapy varied in thoroughness and duration.

Bergin and Michael Lambert (1978) have argued that a growing number of controlled studies suggest that treatment is more beneficial than no treatment. These studies include more experienced and competent therapists. Bergin and Lambert have concluded that psychotherapy is definitely worthwhile when carried out by wise and stable therapists. These conclusions are consistent with those of a number of other studies of psychotherapy reporting positive outcomes (Lambert, 1979, 1981; Luborsky, Singer, & Luborsky, 1975; Strupp & Hadley, 1977).

A more recent assessment of studies dealing with outcomes of psychotherapy (Lambert, Shapiro, & Bergin, 1986) came to even more positive and extensive conclusions.

1. Empirical studies have shown that many psychotherapists had positive effects on a variety of clients.

2. The effects of therapy tend to be lasting.

3. Psychotherapy patients show gains that surpass those resulting from placebo control groups.

4. Interpersonal, social, and affective factors common to many therapies are highly important in the improvement of clients.

5. Paraprofessionals, who are often selected, trained, and supervised by professional therapists, are sometimes as helpful as professional clinicians.

6. Although research supports the conclusion that psychotherapy has positive effects, additional research using more valid and sensitive modes of assessment is needed.

7. The use of meta-analysis (explained in the next section of the chapter) in assessing outcomes of psychotherapy is a definite advance in research methodology.

The research team emphasized that positive effects averaged across many studies can mask significant variations in the outcomes of therapy. Some therapists appear to be unusually effective, others less so. Thus, we need more research on the relationship between what actually goes on in psychotherapy and its outcomes.

Meta-analysis of Outcomes

Mary Lee Smith and her colleagues conducted one of the most extensive investigations of psychotherapy outcomes in recent years (Smith & Glass, 1977; Smith, Glass, & Miller, 1980). The outcomes, based on 375 studies, were subjected to a quantitative technique called **meta-analysis**. The method involves a statistical averaging of the standardized results of a large number of studies. Meta-analysis, which is presumed to be a more objective method than other methods of analysis, indicates not only whether a treatment made a difference but also how much of a difference it made.

Smith and her colleagues concluded: "Psychotherapy is beneficial, consistently so and in many different ways. Its benefits are on a par with other expensive and ambitious interventions, such as school and medicine" (Smith, Glass, & Miller, 1980, p. 183). Smith also stated that one of the greatest contributions of psychotherapy is the improvement it makes in the client's inner experiences.

Soon after Smith's initial investigation was published (Smith & Glass, 1977), a number of researchers criticized its findings, mainly on methodological grounds. They pointed, for example, to a lack of information on what proportion of the studies had included a control group (Frank, 1979; Gallo, 1978; Mansfield & Busse, 1977). In an attempt to resolve these issues, Janet Landman and Robyn Dawes (1982) reanalyzed 65 studies randomly selected from the original sample of 375 and from a list of 93 additional studies that Smith and Glass (1977) provided. Although they were not able to resolve all the methodological issues, Landman and Dawes found that the results generally supported the conclusions of Smith and her co-workers.

Relative Effectiveness of Different Therapies

A number of researchers have compared the relative effectiveness of different approaches to psychotherapy. In one such study, clients were assigned randomly either to psychodynamic or to behavioral therapists (Sloane, Staples, Cristol, Yorkston, & Whipple, 1975). Successful outcomes occurred at about the same rate — 80 percent for each group. Several other studies have found similar results. There is no clear pattern of superiority for any particular approach — including behavior therapy (Luborsky, Singer, & Luborsky, 1975; Smith, Glass, & Miller, 1980; Stiles, Shapiro, & Elliott, 1986). On the other hand, Kazdin and Wilson (1978) arrived at a different set of conclusions after analyzing various studies of therapy outcomes. In nine of these studies, behavior therapy produced superior results; in seven studies, behavior and psychodynamic therapies were equally effective.

How can such contradictory findings be reconciled? Perhaps the results of these studies are discrepant because they did not take into account whether the fit between the nature of the client's problems and the particular therapeutic method applied was appropriate. For example, when clients seek help for specific symptoms, behavioral techniques may well hold the advantage. When problems are more diffuse and people seek to attain better understanding or a more satisfying sense of meaning and purpose in their lives, psychodynamic therapies may be more effective. If studies about outcomes do not try to match psychological problems with therapeutic methods before they evaluate outcomes, they are likely to produce inconclusive results.

Outcomes of psychotherapy depend on more than the choice of technique. In an analysis of studies on outcomes, Lambert (1981) estimated that techniques accounted for only 5 percent of the variance. Another 5 percent was due to the experience of the therapist, 15 percent could be traced to the relationship between client and therapist, and 25 percent came from characteristics of the client — for example, the nature of the client's problems and the motivation to solve them.

Facilitative Processes in Psychotherapy

A number of researchers have attempted to delineate the basic processes that facilitate successful psychotherapy, regardless of its particular methods or theoretical orientation. They postulate the following underlying processes: (a) persuasion, (b) encouragement of honesty and self-scrutiny, (c) interpretation of behavior and ideas, (d) provision of personal examples of maturity, (e) manipulation of rewards (reinforcers), (f) presence of a relationship modeled in some respects on parental roles, and (g) behavioral regulation — the modification and control of behavior (Strupp, 1973a, 1973b; Karasu, 1986).

Group Therapy: Psychological Intervention as a Social Process

Historical Background

Group therapy began with the work of physician, Joseph Hersey Pratt (1872–1956). As early as 1905, Pratt held weekly group meetings with his tuberculosis patients. The patients talked about their progress in following their medical instructions and lent support to one another in their efforts to get well. Pratt discovered that this mutual encouragement helped ward off the depression and feelings of isolation he had so often seen in tuberculosis patients (Yalom, 1985, p. 503).

During the 1920s, the Viennese psychiatrist Jacob L. Moreno (1890–1974) brought to the United States one of the earliest and most influential systems of group therapy, which he called **psychodrama**. This system used dramatic techniques to explore "interpersonal relations and private worlds," as Moreno put it (1953, p. 81). In Vienna, psychodrama was performed in Moreno's Theater of Spontaneity. Here, in a specially constructed stage before an audience, members of the psychodrama group acted out the crucial conflicts and problems they had experienced in their past life. Certain members acted out the particularly troubling feelings and conflicts they had observed in group members who had experienced a great deal of difficulty in expressing their problems. Presumably, those individuals saw how "auxiliary egos" had viewed them and thus gained more insight into their own problems (Kaplan & Sadock, 1985, pp. 619–620; Moreno, 1947, 1953; Moreno & Kipper, 1968). Psychodrama continues to be used as a form of group therapy, although changes in techniques have been made (Greenberg, 1986). For example, current practitioners are not bound to use a specially constructed stage, as in Moreno's original procedure. Instead, they may use a small area in a room, the entire room, a theater, or an auditorium. Videotapes are often made of the sessions, so that participants can later observe their behavior and discuss it. Furthermore, practitioners of psychodrama no longer find it necessary to require an audience other than the group members themselves.

S. R. Slavson (1891–1981) made another significant contribution to the development of group therapy. For many years, he directed the group therapy program at the Jewish

Board of Guardians in New York City, where he helped disturbed children and adolescents. Slavson applied Freudian psychoanalysis to group therapy (Slavson, 1940, 1947, 1964).

During World War II, group therapy gained considerable momentum, mainly because the number of psychiatric patients in military hospitals was too great for psychotherapy to retain the traditional one-to-one relationship. Since then, the therapy has continued to expand among mental health professionals. Practically all of the basic approaches used in individual psychotherapy have been adapted for group therapy (Kaplan & Sadock, 1985, p. 612).

Basic Characteristics of Group Therapy

Although group therapy is based on a variety of theoretical viewpoints and is carried out in a variety of ways, certain broad characteristics are common to all of its procedures: There is usually one therapist who meets with several clients on a regular basis for the purpose of helping them solve their psychological and social problems.

The most obvious advantage of group therapy is its economy; more people can be treated in less time and at a lower cost. However, the pioneers of group therapy insisted from the very beginning that its distinctive features could help participants in ways that individual therapy could not (Kaul & Bednar, 1986; Yalom, 1985).

By sharing their experiences, participants in group therapy learn that their problems are not unique.

First, members of the group learn that their problems are not unique. As they share their experiences they discover that they are not alone in their discomfort, alienation, and maladaptive behavior. This knowledge is not only therapeutic in itself but can also motivate people to move toward more positive goals.

Second, feelings of belonging and mutual support develop in the group setting. The participants find that they can help each other by expressing mutual acceptance, positive regard, and reassurance. They learn to share their problems and the insights they have gained. Such mutual help can become a strong therapeutic force.

Third, the therapy group provides an opportunity for the correction of family experiences. As members of the group interact with the therapist and one another, they perceive certain characteristics of the group that resemble family life. They now have the opportunity to correct problems that arose from their own family relationships.

Fourth, group therapy can help individuals develop or enhance basic social skills more effectively than individual therapy. Learning social skills can be especially helpful for individuals who have undergone long-term hospitalization for psychological problems. It eases their transition to the broader society. This is one of the main reasons that group therapy is used in mental hospitals.

Fifth, the therapy group promotes positive imitative behavior. In group therapy, as in individual psychotherapy, the therapist serves as a model for the participants. However, the group setting provides additional models for members to imitate—one another. Yalom (1985) points out that members of the group may "try on . . . bits and pieces of other people and then relinquish them as illfitting" (p. 18). In discovering what they do not want to be, members can make progress in deciding what they do want to be.

Sixth, group therapy is especially useful in helping individuals become more adaptive in their interpersonal relationships. It has an advantage over individual therapy in that the learning situation more closely resembles the situation of the outside society. Among the interpersonal learning experiences especially important in group therapy is learning to see oneself as others do. Group therapy also offers an opportunity for individuals to test gains in interpersonal relations that they have achieved in individual therapy.

Seventh, as group cohesiveness develops, it enhances the other advantages of group therapy. **Group cohesiveness** includes not only the relationship between the therapist and other members of the group but also the relationship of all members to one another. As cohesiveness increases, feelings of solidarity and mutual acceptance increase and feelings of isolation and alienation from other people diminish.

Group therapy can be thought of as a social laboratory in which relationships with others can be developed, experienced, understood, and modified. The group benefits not only from the sensitivity and skill of the therapist but also from the shared experiences of the other members. Proponents of group therapy claim that progress can often be faster than in individual therapy because the emotional experiences are more intense and the results of group learning are more directly applicable to everyday situations.

A central feature of group therapy is the **group process**: the continuous change in attitudes, perceptions, and relationships that the group shares. It may be trite to say that the group is more than the sum of its members. Yet, it does possess its own characteristics, and this has implications for the therapist's role and technique. Doing group therapy is more than just working with so many individuals in a group. Typically, the therapist's interventions are addressed to the whole group and are designed to stimulate the group process. It is the group as a whole that contributes to self-understanding and clarifies the feelings of specific individuals. The therapist's role is more catalytic than directive. The main task is to see that the group process takes place (Hogan, 1980; Levine, 1979; Yalom, 1985).

Family (and Marital) Therapy

The principle that group therapy is an interpersonal experience that goes beyond individual therapy makes it useful for treating families and couples (Bockus, 1980; Freeman, 1982; Gurman, Kniskern, & Pinsof, 1986; Minuchin, 1974; Perez, 1979; *Psychotherapy*, 1987; Sager & Kaplan, 1972; Sholevar, 1981).

Family and marital therapists emphasize that psychological problems are between people, not merely within people. To a family therapist, a disturbed child's symptoms are but the visible focus of problems that encompass the entire family. Therefore, the disturbance needs to be considered within the context of the family.

Family therapy has some of the characteristics of group therapy. Family therapists never forget that they are addressing themselves to a unit — a family or couple — rather than to separate individuals who just happen to be members of the unit. The central emphasis in the process is to facilitate interaction among the members of the group, even when a particular individual happens to be the focus of attention. To prepare for this interaction, therapists establish a connection early in the initial interview — that is, they encourage each member of the group to describe the problem. The following excerpt from a therapist's description illustrates the approach.

"Ted, your father has told quite a story. I wonder if you'd like to tell me something of what's been happening, as you see it."

"No."

"You know, your input is important here. Parents and children don't always see eye to eye on things that happen — like parties and ground rules and stuff like that. Could you say a few words about how you see things at home?"

Marital therapists point out that conflicts in marriage must be considered as the joint product of the couple's attitudes and behavior, and not simply as the problem of one or the other spouse.

"Why should I? So you can dump on me too? Another nosey—"

"Ted," said Frank [the father] warningly.

"No—." I stopped him. Turning to Ted again, I said, "Please go on, Ted. I really want to hear what you have to say." (Taylor, 1986, p. 442)

In commenting on this interaction, the therapist explained why she interrupted the father and how that blocking was an integral part of her effort to facilitate communication.

One of the things a family therapist does is to provide, by blocking, a boundary. I wanted to make a connection, of any kind, between Ted and me, as I had with the other family members, and Frank was stopping it. The therapy would see me again and again acting as a boundary regulator. Where people were separated I would actively encourage their communication. When communication between two persons was stopped by the action of a third person, I would block that person. When decisions could not be made because too many people were speaking, I would direct who could speak, when, and to whom. This action in stopping Frank was the first of many in which I tried out my power to direct the flow of family communication. (Taylor, 1986, pp. 442–443).

Encounter Groups and Self-enhancement

An especially active movement in group therapy today emphasizes the goal of self-enhancement. The group experience is intended not so much to alleviate psychological distress as to provide a means of self-actualization—that is, to strengthen members' ability to fulfill their potential to the widest extent possible. This objective is prominent in the encounter group movement. **Encounter groups** have been especially attractive to group therapists with humanistic approach to psychotherapy (Schutz, 1986).

Self-enhancement and the development of a person's potentials are a central goal of encounter groups, a form of group therapy especially attractive to humanistic–existentialist therapists. In this encounter session at the Western Behavioral Sciences Institute, La Jolla, California, Carl Rogers (far right) was the therapist.

A variation on encounter groups is the **marathon group**, which involves an intensive group encounter carried on continuously for 12 to 36 hours, with time out only for absolute essentials (Mintz, 1986). A basic assumption of this method is that fatigue will hasten the breakdown of psychological defenses and group members will become more open in exploring problems and interpersonal relationships.

A modified version of the marathon group is the **weekend encounter program**. Each group encounter session is several hours long and occurs a number of times each day. There is time out for meals, recreation, and informal meetings with other members of the group. Therapists (they prefer the term *facilitators*) who work in weekend encounter programs believe this approach maintains the advantages of the marathon group but is less threatening to the participants. They also believe the informal sessions can help promote relationships and progress in solving problems because they impose less pressure on participants (Yalom, 1985, pp. 279–285).

Encounter groups do not focus on serious psychological disturbances. Therefore, ethical group leaders warn people who are suffering from such disorders against participating in the group (Shapiro, 1978, pp. 11–12).

Effectiveness of Group Therapy

A number of studies have found that group therapy is effective in a variety of situations and for different kinds of problems. Its benefits include a decrease in anxiety and depression and more positive interpersonal relationships (Hoberman, Lewinsohn, & Tilson, 1988; Kaul & Bednar, 1986). However, other studies have not found group therapy particularly effective in reducing problems.

Given the complexity of research involving group therapy, the inconsistency in evaluation of outcomes is not unexpected. What is needed in future research is more than a study of outcomes. Even more crucial is a determination of the specific elements in the therapeutic process that are associated with positive outcomes (Kaul & Bednar, 1986).

Summary

1. Behavior therapy has become an increasingly important approach to the treatment of psychological disorders. Its roots go back to Pavlov's concepts of classical conditioning and B. F. Skinner's principles of operant conditioning.

2. In the late 1950s, behavior therapy gained momentum through the work of Joseph Wolpe, a psychiatrist from South Africa who immigrated to the United States. Wolpe developed a set of techniques called reciprocal inhibition, which he later renamed systematic desensitization therapy. These methods were designed to eliminate behavioral excesses, such as unreasonable fears, by pairing them with incompatible responses, such as states of deep relaxation.

3. Skinner's principles of operant conditioning correct behavioral deficits through reinforcement of desirable responses. The method has been used to help abnormally shy people develop better social skills, to increase the ability of schizophrenics to form more positive interpersonal relationships, and to teach basic self-help skills to mentally retarded individuals.

4. The various techniques of behavior therapy all reflect the following basic characteristics. Behavior therapy focuses on current determinants of maladaptive behav-

ior. Change in behavior is the essential criterion for evaluating the effectiveness of therapeutic intervention. Behavior therapists specify the goals and techniques of treatment in objective terms. The source of hypotheses about the treatment of psychological disorders is experimental laboratory research rather than clinical practice. Behavior therapists do not assume that the symptoms of a psychological disorder necessarily reflect unconscious conflicts that must be understood before the disorder can be alleviated.

5. During the last decade or so, a strong cognitive orientation has developed within behavior therapy. The focus is on the individual's patterns of thinking and how they can be changed in a more adaptive and realistic direction.

6. Systematic desensitization uses classical conditioning to eliminate maladaptive conditioned anxiety. The procedures include (a) training the client in deep relaxation to produce a state that is incompatible with anxiety (b) constructing hierarchies of anxiety-producing stimuli, and (c) desensitizing anxiety by gradually presenting these stimuli while the client is in a state of deep relaxation.

7. Research has shown that generalization from systematic desensitization treatment to the everyday world is usually quite successful. When people have a difficult time imagining anxiety-producing stimuli, the therapist furnishes more concrete stimuli with slide projections. In addition, the treatment procedures can be amplified by having a client encounter carefully graded situations outside the treatment room.

8. Implosive therapy deliberately exposes the individual to the stimuli that promote maladaptive responses. The theory is that forcing the person to confront those situations will eliminate the maladaptive responses. Implosive therapy has worked for some clients, although its overall effectiveness is still inconclusive.

9. Covert sensitization attempts to induce conditioned fears and anxieties in order to establish desirable patterns of behavior that are missing from a person's repertoire. First, the therapist has the individual imagine unpleasant reactions to situations that formerly provided pleasure. Then the individual imagines relief from the reactions, and the therapist suggests that the person has overcome temptation and can now face such scenes without succumbing to undesirable behavior. This method has been used successfully to treat a wide range of problems, including alcoholism and sexual disorders. However, it raises a number of ethical questions.

10. Aversion therapy uses classical conditioning techniques to inhibit maladaptive behavior. This method involves pairing the unwanted response with a noxious stimulus — for example shock or a drug that produces nausea. It has been used to treat a variety of disorders, especially alcoholism. Some therapists argue against its use because the aversive stimuli are painful. All in all, such methods are used less today.

11. A great many operant conditioning techniques are in use. They include shaping behavior, token economies, contingency contracting, and assertiveness training. All depend on supplying reinforcers when responses that fulfill, or begin to fulfill, the desired goal are made.

12. Operant conditioning has been used in a wide variety of situations — for example, teaching autistic children to speak, improving the behavior of patients in hospital wards or correctional institutions, alleviating marital problems, and building up patterns of assertive behavior in abnormally shy people.

13. Cognitive-behavior therapy expands the theoretical foundation of traditional methods based on classical and operant conditioning. Its proponents assert that

internal cognitive processes as well as external influences change and maintain behavior. Cognitive behavior therapy capitalizes on the ability of human beings to reason.

14. Research on observational learning supports certain aspects of cognitive-behavior therapy. For example, Bandura and his colleagues showed that people can eliminate undesirable behavior if they watch and imitate models carrying out the desirable behavior.

15. The cognitive restructuring approach is used to counter self-defeating thinking that interferes with adaptive behavior. Forms of self-defeating thinking include (a) faulty generalizing, (b) polarized thinking, (c) incorrect assumptions about what is threatening and what is safe, (d) maladaptive attitudes toward pleasure and pain, and (e) dogmatic positions on thinking and behavior that must be maintained in all circumstances.

16. Cognitive techniques to help clients reconstruct their maladaptive patterns of thinking include (a) distancing and hypothesis testing, (b) decentering and altering excessive personalization of events, and (c) changing the attribution of responsibility.

17. Critics have argued that cognitive versions of behavior therapy do not represent a new discovery because thinking is a form of behavior. Other critics say that cognitive therapists have not gone far enough. For example, one critic argues that they disregard the potential importance of unconscious processes and they take a narrow view of feelings.

18. A promising development in behavior therapy in recent years has been the development of procedures to enhance self-control. In a sense, this involves helping clients become their own therapists. It rests on the recognition that in our daily lives all of us are agents of our own control and dispensers of self-administered reinforcers.

19. Self-control approaches to behavior therapy are closely linked to cognitive behavior. For example, in order to practice systematic self-management of behavior, people must be able to monitor, evaluate, and record their responses. This is a cognitive enterprise.

20. Multimodal therapy, pioneered by Arnold Lazarus, combines behavioral methods of therapy with insight-oriented procedures. It specifies the modalities (BASIC ID) that need to be considered in therapy. They include behavior, affective processes, sensations, images, cognitions, interpersonal relations, and drugs (biological factors influencing maladaptive behavior).

21. Behavior therapy raises a number of ethical concerns. Some critics fear that the methods of behavioral technology will be used to manipulate or coerce. They also fear that behavior therapy may be used for unethical purposes.

22. Many studies evaluate the outcomes of psychotherapy. They show that on the whole psychotherapy is beneficial, but they do not show whether one method is superior to another. The relative effectiveness depends on the fit between the client's problem and the technique. When the problem is highly specific and easily targeted, behavior therapy techniques are effective. Where the problem is more diffuse, psychodynamic or humanistic approaches are more appropriate.

23. All psychotherapy shares certain facilitative processes: persuasion, encouragement of honesty and self-scrutiny, interpretation of behavior and ideas, the provision of personal examples of maturity, manipulation of reinforcers, a relationship modeled in some respects on parental or similar kinds of supportive roles, and behavior regulation.

24. Group therapy began with the work of a Boston physician, Joseph Pratt. As early as 1905, Pratt held weekly meetings for tuberculosis patients to talk about their progress. He discovered that their mutual encouragement helped ward off the depression and feelings of isolation that he often encountered in patients.

25. During the 1920s, Jacob Moreno, a Viennese psychiatrist, brought to the United States a form of group therapy called psychodrama, in which patients acted out their conflicts and interpersonal relationships.

26. Another pioneer in group therapy was S. R. Slavson, who directed a program at the Jewish Board of Guardians in New York City. His approach was greatly influenced by Freudian psychoanalysis.

27. During World War II, group therapy gained considerable momentum because of the number of psychiatric patients in military hospitals and the shortage of therapists trained in individual psychotherapy. Since then, group therapy has expanded tremendously. A wide range of mental health professionals practice group therapy using all the basic approaches of individual psychotherapy.

28. All forms of group therapy share the following characteristics. There is usually one therapist who meets with several clients at the same time on a regular basis for the purpose of helping them solve their psychological and social problems.

29. Proponents of group therapy believe that it has certain advantages over individual psychotherapy. Members of the group learn that their problems are not unique. Feelings of belonging and mutual support develop in the group setting. The group provides an opportunity for the correction of family experiences. Group therapy helps participants develop or enhance basic social skills more effectively than individual therapy. The therapy group provides more models for limitative behavior. Group therapy is especially useful in helping individuals become more adaptive in their interpersonal relationships. As group cohesiveness develops, it enhances the other advantages of group therapy.

30. Family therapy applies group therapy processes to problems that arise within the family. Family therapists tend to emphasize that psychological problems are between people, not merely within people.

31. Encounter groups are designed to achieve self-enhancement rather than to alleviate psychological distress. The encounter group movement has been greatly influenced by the tenets of humanistic psychology.

32. A variation on encounter groups is the marathon group—an intensive group encounter that continues for 12 to 35 hours. A basic assumption is that fatigue will promote the breakdown of psychological defenses. A modified version of the marathon group is the weekend encounter program, where there is time out for meals, recreation, and informal meetings with other members of the group. Leaders of encounter groups are usually called facilitators rather than therapists.

33. Ethically responsible encounter group leaders warn people who are suffering from serious psychological disturbances that they should not participate.

34. A number of studies on the outcomes of group therapy have concluded that it is effective in a variety of situations and for different kinds of problems. Not all studies have obtained such positive results, however. Future studies need to consider not only the outcomes of group therapy but the processes associated with them.

21

Legal
Intervention
and Community
Mental
Health

Logic — history — custom — utility, and the accepted standards of right conduct are the forces which singly and in combination shape the progress of the law.

BENJAMIN N. CARDOZO
The Nature of the Judicial Process (1921)

Rain does not fall on one roof alone.
CAMEROONIAN PROVERB

In this chapter, we consider two broad aspects of abnormality that directly or indirectly affect all of us: (a) legal decisions that have developed over the years in society's attempts to regulate the behavior of people judged to be mentally disabled and (b) programs of community action to alleviate psychological disturbances and promote positive mental health.

Abnormal Behavior and Criminal Responsibility

For many years, the term insanity has been generally applied to psychotic disorders. Derived from the Latin word *sanus* ("healthy"), **insanity** literally means "not mentally healthy." As properly used today, however, *insanity* is a legal rather than a psychological or psychiatric term. It refers to the fact that a court of law has judged that a defendant was so mentally disturbed when committing a crime that the person is not legally responsible for the act. Usually the verdict reads, "Not guilty by reason of insanity" (Rosenhan, 1983).

The legal judgment of insanity relies on various tests that have been accepted by the court. In recent years, these tests, or rules, as they are also called, have been greatly influenced by advances in psychological and psychiatric knowledge.

The Expert Witness

The verdict not guilty by reason of insanity ordinarily depends on whether expert witnesses for the defense have successfully answered questions that fit the particular test of insanity that the court accepts. The experts must convince the judge and jury that the defendant suffered from a major mental disorder at the time of the crime. Expert witnesses have a special status, for they are permitted to testify to conclusions as well as to facts. For example, the expert witness who says, "The defendant showed definite signs of delusions," is making a conclusion. Ordinarily, witnesses may testify only to facts, such as, "I heard the defendant say he had the right to kill." Thus, the expert witness must truly be expert if tests of insanity are to be applied judiciously. Expert witnesses are not asked to state whether or not they believe a defendant is insane. That decision lies with the judge and jury after they carefully consider the opinions of the experts as well as other evidence (Bazelon, 1974, pp. 19–20; Brakel & Rock, 1971, p. 403; Dix, 1983, pp. 172–173).

Until recently, only psychiatrists served as expert witnesses in trials involving a plea of insanity. However, in the case of *Jenkins v. United States* (1962), the United States Court of Appeals for the District of Columbia Circuit ruled that qualified psychologists could also testify as experts.

Vincent E. Jenkins had been convicted of housebreaking with intent to commit an assault and assault with intent to rape. In arguing a plea of insanity, the defense had been forced to rely on expert testimony from psychiatrists only, since the judge would not permit clinical psychologists to testify. During the appeal, the American Psychiatric Association supported the lower court's decision, claiming that medical training was necessary for expert witnesses in cases involving the insanity plea. Judge David Bazelon of the appeals court overturned the verdict, stating that the critical factor in determinations of insanity should be the relevant professional training and experience of the expert witnesses, regardless of whether they had been trained in medicine (Bazelon, 1974, pp. 21–22). Since that decision, clinical psychologists have become increasingly active as expert witnesses (Blau, 1984; Nietzel & Dillehay, 1986, pp. 97–115).

Judge Bazelon also specified what is expected of the expert witness in cases involving the insanity plea: "While the expert may testify as to the existence or not of mental disease, and the causal relationships between such disease and the defendant's capacity to control and appreciate the wrongfulness of his conduct, he will be required to present the basis underlying his conclusions" (Bazelon, 1974, p. 23).

More recently, Judge Bazelon reemphasized his belief that the conclusions of expert witnesses must be backed by insightful observations and explanations. In an address at a convention of the American Psychological Association, he said: "Behavioral scientists who appear in the public arenas all too often focus on little more than making conclusory pronouncements. . . . To paraphrase Lewis Carroll, they use 'labels as shrouds rather than guides.' . . . What the public needs most from any expert, including the psychologist, is a wealth of intermediate observations and conceptual insights that are adequately explained" (Bazelon, 1982, p. 116).

In a yet more recent review of research on expert witnesses in psychology and psychiatry, David Faust and Jay Ziskin (1988, p. 35) find data to support Judge Bazelon's observations. They conclude that mental health professionals who serve as expert witnesses often fail to reach reliable or valid conclusions, and they argue that psychological research will eventually yield more certain knowledge and methods that will improve the accuracy of expert witnesses. In the meantime, they suggest, courts should continue to admit testimony based on useful knowledge and methods — testimony that can be supported by empirical studies.

Legal Tests of Insanity

Historical Background

The belief that a person must be mentally capable of making a free choice to be legally responsible for a criminal act has ancient roots. The Talmud — the authoritative body of Jewish tradition that has been in effect for some 1500 years — states that "a deaf-mute, an idiot, and a minor are awkward to deal with, as he who injures them is liable, whereas if they injure others they are exempt" (Platt & Diamond, 1978, p. 81). Both Greek and Roman law held that responsibility for criminal behavior required the presence of a **guilty mind** (in legal terms, **mens rea**). The offender must be aware that such behavior was morally and legally wrong. In particular, Roman law stipulated that mentally disturbed violators of the law were not able to act voluntarily and therefore must be judged differently from other individuals. Concepts such as the guilty mind and freedom of choice have played crucial roles in the development of modern tests of insanity (Halleck, 1980, p. 209; Weiner, 1985b, pp. 708–709).

For many years, the prevailing opinion in English courts was that *insanity* meant a total deprivation of memory and understanding — in short, complete madness (Quen, 1978). In 1800, this view was challenged for the first time.

James Hadfield was indicted for attempting to assassinate King George III. Evidence showed that Hadfield harbored the delusion that if he sacrificed his life he could save the world. Comparing himself to Jesus Christ, he avowed that his death must come through execution. By killing the king, he hoped to achieve that end. Hadfield's barrister acknowledged that Hadfield was not completely mad, since he had been able to plan and carry out his plot. Nevertheless, he was sufficiently insane to justify the defense plea of insanity, since it was his mental condition that had induced his crime. The jury found Hadfield not guilty, "being under the influence of insanity at the time the act was committed" (Ray, 1853, pp. 21–22). The Hadfield decision set a precedent for a later test of insanity that affected Anglo–American law for many years — the M'Naghten Rule.

The M'Naghten Rule

This portrait of Daniel M'Naghten, who attempted to assassinate Sir Robert Peel, prime minister of England, appeared in the official summary of a report in 1843 by the 15 criminal judges of England. The summary set forth the inability to understand "right from wrong" as the basis for the insanity plea in criminal trials. Known as the M'Naghten rule, it has been used throughout the English-speaking world.

In 1843, Daniel M'Naghten, a woodturner from Glasgow, fatally shot Edward Drummond, principal secretary to the prime minister of England, Sir Robert Peel. The defense at M'Naghten's trial was insanity, based on evidence showing that he was suffering from morbid delusions. Among these delusions were the beliefs that he was pursued by spies and that Peel and the Tories were persecuting him because he had voted against the Tories in the last election.

In his charge to the jury, the Lord Chief Justice did not specifically mention the testimony concerning M'Naghten's delusions. Instead, his guiding words emphasized concepts of right and wrong: "If he was *not sensible* at the time that it was a violation of the law of God or man, undoubtedly he was not responsible . . . or liable to any punishment flowing from that act . . . but if on balancing the evidence in your minds, you think the prisoner capable of *distinguishing between right and wrong*, then he was a responsible agent and liable to all the penalties the law imposes [emphasis added]" (Quen, 1978, pp. 94–95).

M'Naghten was acquitted and committed to a criminal wing of Bethlehem Hospital in Southward, where he languished for some 20 years. As a physician during that time described Bethlehem's criminal wings: "It is not a modern prison, for there is no corrective discipline; it is not a hospital, for suitable treatment is impossible; it is not an asylum for the relief and protection of the unfortunate, for it is one of the most gloomy abodes to be found in the metropolis. It is simply a [place] into which the waifs of criminal laws are swept, out of sight and out of mind" (Rieber & Gundlach, 1981, p. 119). In 1863, M'Naghten was transferred to the newly completed Broadmoor Institution for the Criminally Insane, where he died a year later (Smith, 1981, p. 23).

M'Naghten's acquittal created a great stir among the ruling classes in Great Britain. Much shaken by the verdict, Queen Victoria asked the House of Lords to put a series of questions before the 125 criminal judges — questions for them to use in proposing rules for the relationship between criminal responsibility and insanity. Their response is now known as the **M'Naghten Rule**.

To establish a defence on the ground of insanity, it must clearly be proved that at the time of committing the act the party accused was labouring under such a defect of reason, from disease of the mind, as not to know the nature and quality of the act he was doing, or as not to know that what he was doing was wrong. . . .

> . . . Where an accused person is supposed to be insane, a medical man, who has been present in Court and heard the evidence, may be asked, as a matter of science, whether the facts stated by the witnesses, supposing them to be true, show a state of mind incapable of distinguishing between right and wrong. (Bazelon, 1974, p. 19)

The M'Naghten Rule has had a great influence on criminal trials involving the issue of insanity, not only in Great Britain but also in the United States and throughout the English-speaking world. By the beginning of the 20th century, practically every state and federal court in the United States had adopted the test (Slicker, 1985). However, because of problems in applying the rule, it is now the sole test of insanity in fewer than 25 states. Much of the criticism of the M'Naghten Rule, from both legal specialists and mental health professionals, points to its ambiguities (Rieber & Vetter, 1978, pp. 48–49; Smith, 1981, pp. 15–18). For example, courts have given various interpretations to the phrase "not to know that what he was doing was wrong." Does *know* refer to cognition only, or can it also refer to emotion? Does *wrong* mean moral wrong or only legal wrong? In spite of its deficiencies, the M'Naghten Rule is still in effect in some states. Furthermore, the language that defines *insanity* in the 1984 Comprehensive Crime Control Act is basically the same as that used in the M'Naghten Rule (Slicker, 1985, p. 30).

The Irresistible Impulse Test

The **irresistible impulse test** of insanity argues that it is possible to know the nature and quality of a criminal act, know that it is wrong, and yet be driven to commit it by an irresistible (or uncontrollable) impulse resulting from a mental condition. The irresistible impulse test probably originated in Ohio in 1834, thus preceding the M'Naghten Rule by nine years (Brakel & Rock, 1971, p. 380).

An early attempt to apply the test in England can be seen in the following exchange between the judge and an expert medical witness. The defendant, Charles Fooks, was being tried for murder at Dorchester in 1863. Evidence was introduced to show that Fooks suffered from delusions of persecution.

> **The Judge:** From what you have heard of this case and seen, can you, as a professional man, with due regard to the solemnity of your oath say that, in your opinion, at the time he fired that gun, he did not know that what he was doing was wrong?
>
> **Witness:** I have the greatest difficulty in answering that question. He certainly knows it is wrong now. But, on my oath, whether he then knew it to be right or wrong or not, he was under an uncontrollable impulse. (Smith, 1981, p. 141)

Obviously, the judge wished to apply the M'Naghten Rule, but the witness was trying to reconcile the rule with the concept of irresistible impulse as a defense. The M'Naghten Rule prevailed, and Fooks was found guilty, for the court judged that "at the time of the act he knew the nature of the act and its consequences" (Smith, 1981, p. 140).

The irresistible impulse test makes explicit the possibility that lack of emotional control can excuse an individual from criminal responsibility. However, many legal experts and mental health professionals point out that it is extremely difficult to distinguish between an irresistible impulse and an unresisted impulse. Furthermore, how can one determine the relationship between the irresistible impulse and the mental condition that presumably caused it? Indeed, the term *mental condition* is itself too vague. Legal specialists have also argued that concentrating on just one element — the irresistible impulse — unduly restricts the scope of expert testimony during the trial. For these reasons, the irresistible impulse test is generally used in conjunction with the M'Naghten Rule (Fingarette & Hasse, 1979, pp. 60–61; Weiner, 1985a, p. 710).

The Durham Rule

When Monte Durham was convicted of burglary, his lawyers appealed on the grounds that the trial court had incorrectly applied the rules that governed the plea of insanity. In 1954, Judge David L. Bazelon of the U.S. Court of Appeals for the District of Columbia Circuit reversed the verdict and adopted a new test of criminal responsibility — the **Durham Rule** (*Durham v. United States*).

The rule states that an accused person is not criminally responsible if the unlawful act is the product of mental disease or mental defect. Thus, in applying the rule, juries do not need to be concerned with determining the meaning of right or wrong, as in the case of the M'Naghten Rule, or with the ambiguities of the irresistible impulse test.

Many psychiatrists reacted favorably to the Durham Rule and its various clarifications, since they thought the rule would give their expert testimony more weight. Nevertheless, the Durham Rule has not been wisely used. Many legal experts deny that it is actually an improvement over the M'Naghten Rule. Furthermore, along with various mental health professionals, they argued that a criminal act is an integral part of an individual's total behavior and should not be regarded as an isolated product of an entity called mental disease. Nevertheless, the Durham Rule helped stimulate a nationwide debate about criminal responsibility and mental illness that has far outlasted the rule itself (Gerber, 1984, pp. 47–48; Taylor, 1985; Weiner, 1985b, pp. 710–711).

The Model Penal Code Rule

In 1957, Vermont adopted an insanity rule recommended by the American Law Institute. The **Model Penal Code Rule** stated: "A person is not responsible for criminal conduct if at the time of such conduct as a result of mental disease or defect he lacks substantial capacity to appreciate the wrongfulness of his conduct or to conform his conduct to the requirements of the law" (Weiner, 1985b, p. 711).

Tests of insanity based on the Model Penal Code Rule have now been adopted by all 11 circuits of the United States Court of Appeals and also in a number of states. Many critics agree that these tests are a decided improvement. The phrasing is more precise and permits the court to judge various degrees of intellectual and emotional capacity rather than forcing it to make a decision about insanity on an absolute basis. Testimony in a court using the Model Penal Code Rule usually deals with the question of whether the defendant was psychotic when committing the crime. Testimony under the M'Naghten Rule focused on whether defendants could be said to know that they were committing crimes. If they were capable of such knowledge, they could not be acquitted even if they were seriously mentally disturbed.

Some critics argue that the Model Penal Code Rule still contains ambiguities that can confuse juries. One of their main objections centers around the terms *mental disease* and *mental defect*. Some mental health professionals would prefer such labels as *mental disorder* or *behavior disorder*, which they believe have broader meaning and can be applied more flexibly to the insanity plea.

Consequences of Acquittal on Grounds of Insanity

When a defendant is found not guilty by reason of insanity, the court may then order the person to be hospitalized. The hospitalization might be brief, mainly to decide if the individual is still insane. If so, the person can be required to remain in a mental institution until legally discharged as sane.

In some jurisdictions, hospitalization is automatic, but the trend has been to move toward more flexible procedures (Morris, 1983; Weiner, 1985b, pp. 725–734; Wexler, 1981, pp. 122–127, 141–154). In some states, for instance, the court must say specifically that the individual is still insane and therefore requires hospitalization. Increasingly, this decision is made in a separate hearing following the acquittal. In other states, the courts exercise broad discretionary powers. They may commit the individual to the care of a relative or friend, with the provision that treatment be sought if necessary.

The decision to release a person requires evidence that the individual is no longer insane. As a rule, the kinds of questions that must be answered are these: Is the individual likely to repeat the offense that resulted in trial and commitment? Is it safe for the person to be released and allowed to live again in the broader society? Technically, the answers to these questions are legal ones. However, the testimony of mental health professionals is extremely important in helping legal authorities develop the answers.

Criticisms of the Insanity Plea

Views of Thomas Szasz

Probably the most persistent and outspoken critic of the insanity plea is psychiatrist Thomas S. Szasz (1963, 1965, 1970, 1974, 1977a, 1977b). For many years, Szasz has argued that criminals, like everyone else, should bear responsibility for their acts. Therefore, a defendant should be found guilty even though suffering from a mental illness. Then, if treatment is necessary, it can be carried out in a treatment center connected with the prison system. According to Szasz, conviction for a crime is a separate issue from treatment for a mental illness.

Szasz emphasizes that in many instances defendants who are found not guilty by reason of insanity would actually be better off with a prison sentence. At least convicted criminals know the length of a sentence. Defendants who are committed to a hospital are not allowed to return to society unless they are cured or at least improved. Thus, they may well spend more time in the hospital than they would have spent in prison. Szasz claims that when defendants realize that a successful insanity plea will result in commitment to a hospital, they rarely feel that the plea has served their best interests (Szasz, 1970).

Other Criticisms

Some opponents of the insanity plea claim that juries are too easily persuaded to accept such a defense. However, little evidence supports this assertion. Other critics claim that the insanity plea results in expensive trials that accomplish very little, since a verdict of not guilty by reason of insanity usually results in the offender being institutionalized anyway. It is extremely difficult for indigent defendants to make use of the insanity defense, since they cannot afford psychiatrists. When questions of insanity arise in such cases, court-appointed psychiatrists handle them. A private psychiatrist might well present a different opinion from that of the state-employed psychiatrist (Becker, 1973; Dershowitz, 1973; Gerber, 1984, pp. 81–85; Halleck, 1980; Steadman & Braff, 1983; Weiner, 1985a).

John Hinckley, Jr. was found not guilty by reason of insanity for his attempted assassination of President Reagan. He was then committed to St. Elizabeth's Hospital in Washington, D.C. The verdict reinforced criticisms of the insanity plea.

An additional criticism of the insanity plea has wide appeal. Many people fear that the defense can too easily be used as a means to escape deserved punishment. The Hinckley case, in which John Hinckley was acquitted of shooting President Reagan on the basis of an insanity plea, has reinforced these fears (Rogers, 1987; Rosenhan, 1983, pp. 97–99).

Hinckley offered to plead guilty on all counts if he could serve his sentences concurrently and be eligible for parole in 15 years. The Justice Department refused to plea bargain because it wanted to win the case and imprison Hinckley for life. It also believed that Hinckley's offer to plead guilty cast doubt on his insanity defense. However, the Justice Department lost the case, and Hinckley was, in fact, acquitted and committed to a mental hospital. By law, he will be released as soon as he can prove that he is no longer dangerous. It is conceivable that his release could occur well before he would have been paroled even under the terms he offered. Thus, successful use of the insanity defense might significantly reduce the penalty for criminal acts (Caplan, 1984, p. 77).

In reaction to Hinckley's acquittal, both the American Psychiatric Association (1983) and the American Bar Association (1984) urged that the Model Penal Code test of insanity be modified to delete the **volitional prong** (lacks substantial capacity to conform his conduct to the requirements of the law) while retaining the **cognitive prong** (lacks substantial capacity to appreciate the wrongfulness of his conduct). The argument for the change was twofold: The volitional prong cannot be measured as reliably as the cognitive prong, and the cognitive–volitional combination makes the rule less specific than the cognitive prong alone (Rogers, 1987). In 1984, in *United States v. Lyons*, the court rejected the volitional prong; and that year, Congress passed the Insanity Reform Act, establishing the cognitive-only prong for all federal jurisdictions.

The American Psychological Association has objected to the change. One appraisal of the situation (Rogers, 1987) points out that empirical research does not support the position that judgments regarding the volitional prong are less reliable than those regarding the cognitive prong (p. 842). Lack of reliability was one of the arguments the American Bar Association used to support the change.

One effort for circumvent problems arising from the defense of insanity has been the recent change in state laws shifting the burden of proof of insanity from the prosecution to the defense. More than 25 states now require defendants to prove that they were insane when they committed the crime. Trial lawyers have objected to the change, but prosecutors agree with it. As a district attorney put it: "Shifting the burden makes it much more feasible for the prosecution to be successful. I think this will protect the public" (Gargan, 1984, p. 1).

Arguments Supporting the Insanity Defense

The jurist J. Skelly Wright criticized Szasz's assertion that a defendant committed to a mental hospital is really receiving an indeterminate sentence. Most jurisdictions provide for a periodic review of individuals who have been committed to hospitals, and legislation to protect the rights of such people is increasing.

Wright also argued that Szasz did not understand the legal, social, and moral structure underlying the insanity plea and its consequences. Before a defendant can be labeled a criminal, it must be proved that the crime had two elements: first, the defendant actually committed the antisocial act, and second, the defendant had a guilty mind (*mens rea*). There can be no guilty mind where the criminal act results from mental disability. "The finding 'not guilty by reason of insanity' means that the defendant committed the act, . . . is therefore subject to custody and control, but . . . did not have a guilty mind and should not be branded a criminal. Thus the law has the jury, as the social consensus, sit in judgment" (Wright, 1964, pp. 24–25).

The concept of the guilty mind as a basis for the insanity defense has a long historical tradition and still persists in the view of many legal authorities (Biggs, 1955; Fingarette, 1972, pp. 128–129; Gerber, 1984, p. 7; Smith, 1981, p. 71). Those who favor the concept generally argue that it is morally sound not to punish offenders who are mentally ill, since they lack the ability to make reasonable choices. Thus, punishment in the form of a prison sentence cannot serve as a deterrent to crime (Halleck, 1980, p. 222; Pollack, 1976).

In response to the many critics of the insanity defense who claim that defendants use it to escape punishment, supporters argue that most individuals who plead insanity are not acquitted, even though they may be psychologically disturbed. Thus, the plea does not destabilize the criminal justice system. Furthermore, the insanity defense diverts at least some criminal offenders from an overburdened prison system (Monahan, 1973; Morris, 1983; Steadman & Braff, 1983).

A 1985 Supreme Court decision mitigates the problem of indigent defendants being compelled to rely on court-appointed psychiatrists in preparing an insanity defense. The decision requires free psychiatric assistance to be provided as a constitutional right. Most states had already provided some form of assistance, but the Court established a broader right (Greenhouse, 1985). Associate Justice Thurgood Marshall prepared the 8–1 majority opinion: "Without the assistance of a psychiatrist, the risk of inaccurate resolution of sanity issues is extremely high. . . . We therefore hold that when a defendant demonstrates to the trial judge that his sanity at the time of the offense is to be a significant factor at the trial, the state must, at a minimum, assure the defendant access to a competent psychiatrist" ("Excerpts from Court Opinion," 1985).

Guilty but Mentally Ill: A Compromise

Several states now provide for an alternate verdict in the case of insanity pleas — **guilty but mentally ill**. The first state to do so was Michigan, and it was followed by Illinois and Indiana. The verdict means that the individual was suffering from a substantial disorder of thought, mood, or behavior at the time of the crime, but not to the extent of being absolved of criminal responsibility. The defendant receives the same sentence as in an ordinary guilty verdict, but as much of the sentence as necessary is used to treat the mental disorder. The rest of the sentence is served in prison. This procedure represents a compromise between the verdict of not guilty by reason of insanity and a verdict of guilty (Blunt & Stock, 1985; Gerber, 1984, 79–81).

California courts consider the guilty but mentally ill verdict in a two-stage trial. The first stage of the trial determines whether the defendant actually committed the crime. If so, the second stage of the trial determines the sentence. If insanity is not established during the second stage, the offender is sentenced to prison, although the term may be reduced. If insanity is established, the offender is committed to a hospital. An important advantage of this two-stage procedure is that evidence concerning the defendant's mental state can be introduced during the first stage of the trial, while the court is deciding whether the defendant actually committed the crime. This evidence can then be reinforced during the second stage of the trial.

Diminished Responsibility

The defense of **diminished responsibility** (also called *diminished capacity*) is an alternative to the insanity defense. It has been used in the United States since the 1880s.

The defense of diminished responsibility serves two main functions in a trial. First, it permits evidence of abnormal behavior to be introduced even though it may not be sufficient to prove legal insanity according to the tests accepted by the court. The purpose of such evidence is to demonstrate that the defendant did not possess a state of mind commensurate with the charge. Thus, if the diminished responsibility defense is successful, the defendant can be convicted, but only of a lesser crime — for example, manslaughter rather than first degree murder. Second, the defense allows evidence of abnormality to be presented in order to reduce the severity of a sentence, even though the original charge remains.

The diminished responsibility defense is used most frequently in California under the Wells–Gorshen doctrine (Halleck, 1980, pp. 220–221; *People v. Wells*, 1949; *People v. Gorshen*, 1959; Weiner, 1985b, p. 711). This doctrine allows mental illness to be introduced as a defense against criminal intent, which is a necessary component in many charges resulting from serious crimes, such as homicide. Essentially, the defendant can be found not guilty of intent to commit a crime without relying on the insanity plea.

Competence to Stand Trial

The question of **competence to stand trial** affects a far greater number of individuals accused of a crime than the insanity defense does (Halleck, 1980, p. 225; Roesch & Golding, 1980; Stone, 1975, pp. 195–217; Weiner, 1985b, pp. 694–707; Winick, 1983). As interpreted by the U.S. Supreme Court in *Pate v. Robinson* (1966), the defense attorney, the prosecutor, and the judge must raise the question of mental illness whenever they believe that it may interfere with a defendant's ability to participate in the trial. The law demands that a defendant be sufficiently competent to exercise the right to choose and assist the defense counsel, to confront opposing witnesses, and to give testimony. If an individual is mentally incapable of exercising those rights but is nevertheless brought to trial, the rights have been denied.

A defendant may actually suffer from a mental illness but nevertheless be found competent to stand trial. The finding of competence does not preclude an insanity defense during the trial.

The court's determination of a defendant's competence to stand trial depends to a great extent on the results of examinations made by mental health professionals. These examinations address a variety of questions (Halleck, 1980; Roesch & Golding, 1980).

1. How capable is the defendant of understanding the nature of the charges and their seriousness?

2. How aware is the defendant of the various legal defenses that could be used?

3. Does the defendant's present behavior indicate that the trial can be conducted without undue disruption?

4. Can the accused understand and cooperate in the planning of legal strategy — for example, pleading guilty to a lesser charge (plea bargaining)?

5. Does the defendant have at least a minimal understanding of the adversarial process — for example, the role of the prosecuting attorney and prosecution witnesses and the role of defense counsel as friend, the judge as impartial, and the jury as the determiner of guilt or innocence?

6. Can the defendant understand the various procedures that will occur, such as the nature and purpose of direct examination and cross-examination?

7. How realistically does the accused understand the possible outcomes of the trial?

8. To what extent is the defendant capable of helping defense counsel challenge the testimony of prosecution witnesses?

9. Is the defendant capable of testifying in a coherent and relevant way?

A number of problems arise when defendants are found to be incompetent to stand trial. Should they be given treatment and then brought to trial when they are competent? Would commitment to a mental hospital be a better solution, especially if evidence indicates that a defendant is dangerous? In actual practice, the latter choice is usually made, with the commitment lasting until the person can stand trial. Regular reviews are required to avoid unnecessarily prolonged stays in the hospital.

In recent years, determinations of competence have increased. Indeed, the procedure has become almost routine when the crime is unusually spectacular or bizarre (Roesch & Golding, 1980; Steadman, 1979, p. 115; Steadman & Hartstone, 1983; Winick, 1983).

Involuntary Hospitalization

Civil Law and Social Issues

Involuntary hospitalization can occur under circumstances that involve civil rather than criminal proceedings. This form of hospitalization has been defined legally as "the removal of a person judged to be mentally ill from his normal surroundings to a hospital authorized to detain him" (Brakel & Rock, 1971, p. 35). In only a few states are laws phrased so loosely that people can be hospitalized simply because they are a nuisance to others. "There is never any moral, medical, or legal justification for committing a patient whose behavior is merely offensive to others unless the patient is also mentally ill" (Halleck, 1980, p. 140).

In order for involuntary hospitalization to occur, (a) individuals must pose a danger to themselves or to others as a result of a mental disorder, (b) they must need treatment for the mental disorder, and (c) there must be no reasonable alternative to hospitalization that is less restrictive (Rozovsky, 1984, p. 343).

Improving Hospitalization Procedures

Legal specialists in the field of mental disability have made a number of recommendations that jurisdictions should adopt in their procedures for civil involuntary hospitalization (Brakel, 1985a).

Joyce Brown, flanked by attorneys from the American Civil Liberties Union, shortly after being released in January 1988 from Bellevue Hospital in New York City. She had been committed involuntarily as part of a plan to remove from the streets of New York homeless mentally ill individuals. The case aroused national attention, not only to the problem of homelessness, but also to issues of involuntary commitment.

1. Efforts should continue to develop clearer and more workable definitions of the degree of mental illness that justifies involuntary hospitalization. These definitions should be incorporated into the statutes governing hospitalization.

2. Terms used in criminal proceedings, such as *insanity*, *committed*, and *arrested*, should be eliminated from statues governing involuntary hospitalization.

3. Emergency detention of individuals alleged to be mentally ill should take place in special facilities. Such detention should avoid the use of jails or police vehicles except under the most extreme emergencies.

4. Provisions should be adopted to ensure that there is enough time to diagnose the mental status and consider the social conditions of all individuals before a final decision is made concerning extended hospitalization.

5. All people being considered for involuntary hospitalization are entitled to be notified of that possibility, to be given an opportunity to respond, and to be represented by legal counsel.

6. The property rights of patients who have been hospitalized involuntarily should be carefully observed.

7. Before an order for involuntary hospitalization is issued, the alternative of voluntary hospitalization should be carefully explored. A person should be permitted to choose voluntary action if it is judged to be appropriate.

Kenneth Donaldson, a former mental hospital patient, was the central figure in the landmark 1975 decision of the United States Supreme Court protecting nondangerous mentally ill persons from involuntary commitment. The court held that mental illness in itself does not disqualify a person from remaining at home rather than being sent to an institution, provided the person can live safely at home.

Some of these recommendations have been incorporated into the statutes of various jurisdictions. In 1975, the Supreme Court handed down an opinion that has become a landmark in protecting nondangerous mentally ill people from involuntary confinement. The decision stemmed from a malpractice suit that Kenneth Donaldson, a patient in a Florida state hospital, brought against the hospital superintendent. The suit maintained that because Donaldson had received only custodial care in spite of his requests for treatment, he should have been released. In upholding the lower court's decision to award damages to Donaldson, the Supreme Court set forth new rights for mentally disabled people (*O'Connor v. Donaldson*, 1975; Halleck, 1980, pp. 158–159). Justice Potter Stewart wrote the opinion stating that the mere presence of mental illness does not disqualify a person from preferring his home to an institution, provided the person can live safely in freedom, either alone or with the help of willing and responsible family members or friends.

The Right to Treatment

In 1960, the physician Morton Birnbaum first made explicit the **right to treatment principle** as applied to involuntary hospitalization. Attempting to improve the standard of treatment in public mental hospitals, Birnbaum argued that if the state confines someone to a mental hospital, it has an obligation to provide adequate treatment. Birnbaum's position was fundamentally a moral one. Although he tried to develop a constitutional basis for his argument, he was not successful (Halleck, 1980, p. 157).

The first major case based explicitly on a constitutional right to treatment was *Wyatt v. Stickney* (1972). The case was a class action suit brought against the state of Alabama, charging that it was not providing adequate treatment to patients confined to Alabama's mental hospitals and institutions for the mentally retarded. This was the first time a right to treatment suit had been filed on behalf of individuals not committed because of criminal behavior. Federal Judge Frank Johnson, presiding in the United States District Court for the Middle District of Alabama, ruled that involuntarily hospitalized mental patients have a constitutional right to treatment. If such treatment is not provided, they must be released. The court also required all of Alabama's mental hospitals and institutions for the mentally retarded to provide a constitutionally adequate level of treatment and care. Patients could no longer be required to perform labor involving the operation and maintenance of the institutions in which they were confined, because work assignments not specifically designed as therapeutic were dehumanizing and lowered the patients' self-esteem (Weiner, 1985c, pp. 251–252, 283, 311–321).

Wyatt v. Stickney relied on the due process clause of the Fourteenth Amendment of the Constitution. However, the court could also have involved the Eighth Amendment, which protects every citizen against cruel and unusual punishment, because forcing mental patients to be hospitalized without the provision of adequate treatment could be considered equivalent to punishment (Ennis & Siegel, 1973, p. 50). Since the *Wyatt v. Stickney* decision, therapeutic services in mental hospitals have been expanded (Weiner, 1985c, pp. 296–297).

The Supreme Court did not address the right to treatment issue directly until the case of *Youngberg v. Romeo* in 1982. Nicholas Romeo was a resident of a state institution for the mentally retarded in Pennsylvania. Romeo had suffered injuries on many occasions from his own violent behavior as well as that of other residents. As a result, he had been placed in physical restraints a number of times. The Supreme Court held that mentally retarded people have a constitutional right to reasonable care and safety, reasonably nonrestrictive conditions of confinement and adequate training. Although the decision was directed to the mentally retarded, it could be applied to a wide range of mentally disabled people. In making its decision, the Court pointed out that the right to treatment still left judgment about the nature of that treatment to mental health professionals.

Right to Refuse Treatment

The recent idea that institutionalized mentally disabled people have the right to refuse treatment has become one of the most controversial issues facing mental health professionals during the 1980s. Court decisions upholding at least a limited right to refuse treatment have been based on such constitutional rights as freedom of religion (for example, in the case of Christian Scientists) and the individual's right to liberty as protected by the due process clause of the Fourteenth Amendment (Bonnie, 1982; Weiner, 1985d). These decisions have involved such treatments as electroconvulsive therapy (ECT), psychosurgery, and medication (see Chapter 18). Since medication is now the most frequent form of treatment for mentally disabled persons in institutions, the refusal to accept such treatment has attracted the greatest attention.

At least 20 states have enacted provisions relating to the administration of drugs. A few states specifically grant the patient the right to refuse, although in some instances the refusal can be overruled if mental health professionals state that the treatment is necessary to protect the patient from self-injury. Other states have required simply that no excessive or unnecessary medication be given, and still others have forbidden only the use of medication as a form of punishment (Weiner, 1985d, pp. 342–350).

In spite of the trend toward granting the institutionalized mentally disabled patient at least a limited right to refuse treatment, the question arises as to whether a complete restriction would be good for the patient. For example, some mental health professionals have pointed out that a patient may not be sufficiently competent to make a rational decision. The problem then arises as to whether an absolute right to refuse treatment would necessarily be in the patient's best interests.

Considering various aspects of the problem, Barbara Weiner (1985d, p. 351) has stated the issues as follows: (a) Full autonomy for persons whose decision-making competence is questionable may conflict with their right to treatment. Thus refusal may not be in their best interests. (b) There needs to be a careful balance between the right to refuse treatment and the right of the state to care and protect. However, this balance at the very least must grant the right to refuse treatment for individuals whose decision is "knowing and rational."

Voluntary Hospitalization

When a patient seeks admission to a hospital for the treatment of mental disorders, it is termed voluntary hospitalization. The procedures for voluntary admission are similar to those used for physical illnesses (Rozovsky, 1984, pp. 339–340). Both require that the patient understand the consequences involved in accepting treatment. Both also require that the patient give up certain everyday liberties.

Voluntary admission has a number of advantages. It has fewer of the traumatic effects that often result from compulsory hospitalization. It encourages mentally disturbed patients and their families to seek help earlier. And patients are more likely to participate actively in therapy. Consequently, in recent years, private and public mental health agencies have increased their efforts to make voluntary admission more available so that compulsory hospitalization does not become necessary.

As a rule, the voluntary patient in a mental hospital must make a written application when seeking release. In most states, there is a designated waiting period after the application is submitted. It can be as short as 48 hours or as long as 15 days. The waiting period allows patients time to reconsider the request and decide whether it is in their best interests. It also allows time for a physical and psychological examination whose results can help patients decide whether release is desirable. Some hospital authorities uphold the importance of the waiting period on the grounds that a voluntary patient's mental condition may be such that release should be denied, thus making it necessary to initiate involuntary hospitalization proceedings. They argue that in some instances the patient may not recognize that a serious disability still exists and that further treatment is necessary.

The legality of unreasonable delays in releasing voluntary patients has been challenged in courts on the grounds that they violate the constitutional right of due process. In New Mexico, a statutory requirement that 10 days must elapse between application and release was overruled as an unreasonable delay. In other jurisdictions, however, courts have upheld longer periods of delay.

A number of legal specialists and mental health professionals argue that there should be no bar to immediate release on request of a voluntary patient whose condition would not have justified involuntary hospitalization. Furthermore, they insist that it is not enough to have a statute that permits immediate release. Patients who admit themselves should be fully informed about the steps necessary to secure release. Otherwise, the statutory right becomes meaningless. In spite of growing support for this position, a majority of the states still do not specifically require that voluntary patients be fully informed of their rights to release (Brakel, 1985b, pp. 185–189).

Legal Incompetence and Mental Disorder

In civil law, the purpose of determining *incompetence* is to safeguard the assets of individuals whose mental disability makes them incapable of handling their business and financial affairs. Usually, the court appoints a guardian (or conservator) to handle transactions for such individuals. If later evidence indicates that they have recovered the capacity to handle their own affairs, proceedings can be initiated to allow them to do so.

There is no necessary relationship between the finding of incompetence and the need for hospitalization. People in mental institutions may continue to handle their own finances, and people who are incompetent to do so may be sufficiently functional in other areas to not require hospitalization.

Thus, there are important differences between the purpose of involuntary hospitalization and the finding of incompetence. Unfortunately, in some states, rules concerning involuntary hospitalization merge with those for finding incompetence. Judicial orders committing an individual to the hospital are sometimes equivalent to finding that person incompetent. Some jurisdictions simply order the appointment of a guardian whenever a person suffers form a mental disorder requiring hospitalization — whether or not the person is actually incompetent.

Legal Limits to Confidentiality: The Tarasoff Case

Thus far in the chapter, we have focused on the treatment of mentally disabled individuals after they have committed a crime or have indicated to those who know them that they pose a danger to themselves or others. Usually, mentally health professionals become involved in such problems at the behest of the court — in the absence of a psychotherapeutic relationship with the individual who is the subject of the legal proceedings. However, another legal issue of increasing importance involves therapists and their clients and arises when a client's confidential disclosures in treatment give the therapist reason to believe that the client poses a serious threat to someone else.

Freud made privileged communication an integral part of the psychoanalytic process, and mental health professionals have upheld the client's right to confidentiality for many years (Rosenhan, 1983, p. 105). Legal tradition has generally respected the confidential nature of the therapist–client relationship, but there are exceptions. One exception especially disturbing to mental health professionals is the Tarasoff decisions of 1974 and 1976. The case involved Prosenjit Poddar, a student at the University of California at Berkeley, and Tatiana Tarasoff, whom he had met at folk-dancing classes. Tarasoff rejected him, causing him (according to his account) to become depressed. Poddar sought help at the university's health center, where he confided to a therapist that he intended to kill Tarasoff. The therapist notified the police, recommending that Poddar be committed to the hospital for further observation. He was confined briefly but was released because he seemed to be rational and he promised to stay away from Tarasoff. He failed to return for treatment, although required to do so. Two months later, he went to Tarasoff's house and killed her (Stone, 1976, p. 358).

Tarasoff's parents brought suit against several defendants, including the therapists at the university health center, for failing to warn them or Tarasoff of the danger posed by Poddar's threats. Eventually, the suit came before the California Supreme Court, which ruled that when a therapist is convinced that a patient presents a serious danger to another person, the therapist is obligated to use "reasonable care to protect the intended victim against such danger" (*Tarasoff v. Regents*, 1976).

A major concern of mental health professionals is that the Tarasoff decision may undermine the therapeutic alliance by causing aggressive patients to resist confiding in their therapists. It also increases the perennial problem of how well a therapist can predict danger, aside from threats. On the other hand, the decision has also alerted therapists that individual psychotherapy has its limits. Not all problems can be handled in the consulting room, especially where violence is concerned. Other intervention may be required (Rosenhan, 1983, p. 111).

Community Mental Health: Problems, Services, and Issues

Community mental health programs involve a wide variety of disciplines and professions, including psychology, social work, psychiatry and other medical specialties, law, and sociology.

Community mental health professionals emphasize a seeking mode of delivering services. That is, they seek to intervene in the lives of troubled people considerably earlier than do the more traditional mental health professionals, who usually wait for clients to come to them with their problems. The seeking mode also differs from the waiting mode in another important way. it focuses not only on the disordered behavior and thinking of individuals but also on the various environmental conditions that contribute to their problems — for example, chronic unemployment, inadequate housing, limited educational opportunities, and the social structure of the neighborhood.

Community mental health workers do not maintain a benign neutrality when it comes to social, economic, and political issues, because these issues are virtually inseparable from the problems their clients face. In contrast to traditional psychotherapists, the community therapist is also a social activist, intervening in areas that traditional therapists often consider out of bounds (Iscoe & Harris, 1984; Rappaport, 1977; Rappaport & Chinsky, 1974; Rappaport & Seidman, 1983).

The ultimate goal of community mental health programs is primary prevention of

Community mental health programs encompass a wide variety of disciplines, professions, and problems. Here a social worker is counseling a client at a shelter for battered women.

The day hospital program is an important alternative to the traditional mental hospital. The patient comes to the hospital during the day, receives various kinds of therapy, and returns home at night.

mental and behavioral disorders. This goal involves three main functions: (a) intervening as early as possible in the crises that affect people's adaptive thinking and behavior, (b) helping clients to recognize their strengths, and (c) seeking to make changes in the social organization of the community and the broader society to alleviate the conditions that contribute to mental and behavioral disorders (Bloom, 1980).

The community mental health movement is more of an attitude toward mental health (adaptive ways of living) than a fixed set of principles and techniques. This attitude is reflected in the importance that community mental health programs place on such activities as developing new ways of reaching and helping people in trouble, delivering services to people who are often neglected by more traditional mental health services, and focusing on the prevention of mental and behavioral disorders (Rappaport, 1977; Rappaport & Chinsky, 1974; Rappaport & Seidman, 1983).

Alternatives to Traditional Mental Hospitals

Halfway Houses

People who have just been discharged from mental hospitals can live for a time in **halfway houses**, which are generally located in urban communities. Halfway houses provide a bridge between the restrictive society of the mental hospital and the broader society. One of their goals is to reduce the necessity of a return to the hospital (Rappaport & Seidman, 1983; Rog & Raush, 1975).

Halfway houses provide systematic programs in an informal atmosphere resembling that of a boarding house. Residents can begin to adapt to social rules and customs more like those of the society they will be entering than the ones they had encountered in the hospital. Halfway houses also provide employment training as residents begin to be able to make use of it.

It is difficult to tell how effective halfway houses are, because many of the studies assessing them have lacked uniform research designs and quantitative measures of community adjustment (Cometa, Morrison, & Ziskoven, 1979). Thus, it is not yet clear which elements in the program actually contribute to the success of halfway houses and which are less important.

Partial Hospitalization

In day hospital programs, the patients come to the hospital during the day, receive various kinds of therapy, and go home at night (Baker, Gardiner, Perez-Gill, & Wood, 1986; Neffinger, 1981; Vidalis & Baker, 1986). In night hospitalization programs, patients spend the day at a job or pursue other activities outside the hospital. At the end of the day, they return to the hospital, where therapy can be carried out. This kind of program, which was pioneered at the Montreal General Hospital, is especially helpful for people whose evenings have been highly stressful, usually at home with their families. It is also more economical than full-time hospital residence.

Evaluation of partial hospitalization programs show that they are often just as effective in improving patients' adaptive behavior as traditional full-time hospitalization. Patients are also less subject to the dangers of institutionalization — that is, of becoming so adapted to the routines of institutional life that it becomes increasingly difficult to get along in the world outside. In addition, there is an obvious economic advantage to part-time programs (Rappaport & Seidman, 1983).

Home Treatment

The central purpose of home treatment is to provide an alternative to situations in which hospitalization might well retard recovery (Fenton, Tessler, & Struening, 1979). An essential ingredient of home treatment is the availability of mental health workers who are always on call to respond to emergencies at the patient's home. This form of support was first developed in the United States at Boston State Hospital, where in 1962 it became a permanent part of the hospital program (Weiner, Becker, & Friedman, 1967).

Ordinarily, home treatment is carried out in conjunction with treatment at a clinic. Psychologists, psychiatrists, and social workers all join forces in the endeavor. For example, social workers maintain a constant relationship with the patients and their families and thus are able to help the psychologists and psychiatrists at the clinic better understand the individuals they are trying to help. In addition, the home treatment service cooperates closely with other social agencies in the community.

General Hospital Wards

An increasing number of general hospitals now provide regular services for mentally disturbed patients. As a rule, programs are short term, with treatment lasting several weeks. After treatment, patients usually convalesce at home. In many instances, patients receive home treatment after they have been discharged, or they continue treatment at an outpatient clinic.

An advantage of treatment in a general hospital is that it tends to reduce the stigma attached to confinement in a mental hospital. Furthermore, length of the stay tends to be shorter.

Social Issues

In some communities where large mental hospitals were about to close, organized labor groups exerted pressure to keep them open because the hospitals were one of the major sources of employment in the communities. This conflict between economic necessity and innovative ways of helping people illustrates that problems of community mental health cannot be separated from problems of the large social system. One of the tasks facing community mental health professionals, including psychologists, is to find ways of making the social changes necessary to resolve the conflicts as they arise.

Many community mental health professionals now realize that the great shift away from treatment in large mental hospitals has not been without its social cost. For example, seriously disturbed people who at one time in mental hospitals but who now live at home and receive treatment at outpatient facilities can have adverse effects on other family members. Indeed, sometimes these effects may be greater than those that full-time residence in an institution would have had on the patient.

How to balance the advantages and disadvantages of removing mentally ill patients who still need treatment from institutions is a complex problem, and the social costs of the policy should not be ignored (Arnhoff, 1975; Brown, 1980, 1982). It is essential to have various supportive programs, such as halfway houses and outpatient clinics, so that the community does not become a dumping ground for seriously disturbed people who need help with the activities of everyday life. Studies of the urban homeless in the United States suggest that a significant proportion, at least 20 percent, suffer from mental disorders (Rossi, Wright, Fisher, & Willis, 1987). Many of them were discharged from mental hospitals under the assumption that treatment would continue in the community. Unfortunately, all too often the resources for such treatment have not been sufficient.

Suicide Prevention Centers

The Los Angeles Suicide Prevention Center, founded by two psychologists, Norman L. Faberow and Edwin S. Shneidman, was a pioneering effort to create a community service to combat suicide. Most of the suicide prevention centers now in operation are modeled after the Los Angeles center (Shneidman & Faberow, 1961; Shneidman, Faberow, & Litman, 1970).

Usually, the first contact with a potential suicide victim is by telephone. The telephone workers are often nonprofessionals who have been trained in techniques of relationship counseling for crises. They communicate empathy to the client, transmit the feeling that they understand the problem, explain where the caller can get help, try to move the caller away from suicidal plans, arrange for an appointment at the center, and instill in the caller a measure of optimism that the suicidal crisis will pass and that the future is not hopeless (Speer, 1972).

Studies on the effectiveness of suicide prevention centers are inconclusive, because it is difficult to interpret the available data. One study reported that most callers who threaten suicide do not call again (Speer, 1971). Does this mean that the prevention service was

The first contact that a potential suicide victim has with a suicide prevention center is usually by telephone. This suicide hotline is on a bridge in Poughkeepsie, New York, where there have been numerous suicides.

effective or that the people who called actually committed suicide? It is impossible to know, but other data do indicate that a significant number of people who call suicide prevention centers recover from their crises. Thus, since no firm conclusions can be drawn, most community mental health workers believe that from a humanistic viewpoint alone the centers should continue to be supported. (McGee, 1974; Muñoz & Kelly, 1975; Shneidman, Faberow, & Litman, 1970; Dew, Bromet, Brent, & Greenhouse, 1987).

Helping Victims of Rape

The development of special counseling centers for rape victims is a good example of how community mental health programs represent the interdependence of different approaches: psychological, medical, sociological, and legal. They are generally part of a wider service that deals with other problems of abuse as well.

Rape counseling centers have a number of goals (Costin, 1976, pp. 216–217). First, they provide immediate medical and psychological help. Most workers at these centers believe that the first counselor to see the victim should be a woman.

Second, they seek improvement in hospital treatment. For many years, victims of rape have complained about the callous attitudes they encountered in hospital professionals.

Third, they attempt to improve police attitudes. Rape victims commonly complain about the behavior of police. In the past, the police simply dismissed a large number of complaints—sometimes as many as 30 percent—without any systematic investigation. As a response to pressure from female activists, some police departments have improved their policies and practices. They now hire female officers and give them special training in dealing with problems of sexual assault; social workers and psychologists may also form part of the police team.

Many rape counseling centers, especially those in college and university settings, have become increasingly aware of date rape—sexual assault in which a woman's date forces her to have sexual intercourse against her will (Kanin, 1984; Koss, Gidycz, & Wisniewski, 1987). Such acts go counter to the popular stereotypes people have of the rapist. "Women are hesitant to think that someone they met in an English class or at a [college] party might assault them. . . . We tend to visualize rapists as wearing stocking masks and jumping out at women from dark alleys" (Sherman, 1985, p. 15). As a result, the

Rape counseling centers provide immediate medical and psychological help. Most workers at these centers believe that the first counselor to see the victim should be a woman.

woman is apt to feel guiltier, or distrust her judgment more, than if she is raped by a stranger.

Legal Aspects of Rape

Some states have changed their laws to reduce the widespread practice of placing the blame for rape on the victim. For example, new rulings have eliminated the judge's charge to juries that they regard the uncorroborated testimony of an alleged victim with caution. That prejudicial statement has a long history, going back 300 years to a ruling made by Sir Matthew Hale, Lord Chief Justice of England. It has been a major obstacle for women who sought to press charges against their attackers.

Another change that has helped reduce women's reluctance to enter formal charges of rape concerns the kinds of testimony permitted during the trial. At one time, practically all states permitted the defense attorney to probe into the victim's sexual history in an effort to persuade the jury that the woman was at fault. Now, at least 41 states have passed legislation of some sort limiting the admissibility of evidence concerning the victim's sexual conduct with persons other than the defendant. Usually, a pretrial hearing is held to determine the relevance of such information (Deckard, 1983, p. 146).

One of the most recent changes in law deals with the question of whether a husband can be accused of raping his wife. Traditionally, jurisdictions have taken the position that the act of rape cannot legally take place within a marriage. The notion stems from the idea, still prevalent in our society implicitly if not explicitly, that the woman belongs to the man. Thus, in accepting her marriage vows, she accepts her husband's right to her body. Attitudes such as these are changing. At least 18 states now have laws that enable a man to be charged with raping his wife (Margolick, 1984).

The legal profession did not initiate these changes in the law. They resulted primarily from social action on the part of women's groups and their supporters, and they demonstrate an important aspect of the direction that community mental health can take.

Feminist Analysis of Rape

A basic feminist view of rape emphasizes that it reflects much more than the mental disorder of the perpetrator. Rape is inevitable in societies that continually reinforce the belief that women are fair sexual game. This attitude is all too prevalent among many men who in other respects would not be considered abnormal or pathological. Furthermore, it is supported by a belief that women should occupy an inferior position in society. Thus, rape is less a sexual act than a crime of violence aimed toward dominating, humiliating, and debasing the victim. The sexual act itself is secondary. Rapists, then, are a danger to society not because they are sexually perverted but because they are criminally aggressive and violent (Amir, 1971; Brownmiller, 1975; Groth & Birnbaum, 1981; Hilberman, 1976; Koerper, 1980; Rapaport & Burkhart, 1984; Russell, 1975; Sanday, 1981).

If these views of rape are correct, it is reasonable to hypothesize that people who believe that women must be kept in their place would also endorse myths about rape. Studies in four countries (the United States, England, Israel, and West Germany) have confirmed that hypothesis (Costin, 1985; Costin & Schwarz, 1987). They found that people who accepted such myths as "Many women really want to get raped" also hold restrictive beliefs about women's social roles, such as "Women should not have as much sexual freedom as men." The correlation was consistent for all the groups tested, including male and female college students, employed women and men in different occupations, and homemakers. Similar results emerged in a study of the attitudes of college students toward date rape (Fischer, 1986). Positive attitudes toward such behavior correlated significantly with traditional restrictive attitudes towards women's social roles.

Indigenous Workers and Self-Help Groups

The community mental health movement emphasizes programs that respond to the cultural idiom of clients, especially those whose way of life lies outside the mainstream of the dominant culture. (Cowen, 1973, pp. 453–459; Kelly, Snowden, & Muñoz, 1977, p. 329–330; Muñoz & Kelly, 1975, pp. 36–42; Rappaport, 1977; Rappaport & Seidman, 1983; Sue & Zane, 1987). As a result, it has pioneered in the use of paraprofessional and nonprofessional workers. These individuals are trained in specific helping techniques important for community programs—for example, telephone counseling services or rape counseling—but do not have the education and training required of professional mental health workers. **Paraprofessional workers** receive formal training in an educational institution, although at a level significantly below that of the professional. **Nonprofessional workers** usually receive their training on the job or in crash courses sponsored by the agency where they will be working. (Zax & Specter, 1974, pp. 369–393).

The central emphasis in the use of paraprofessionals and nonprofessionals is the special reliance on **indigenous workers**—individuals who share and understand their clients' cultural heritage and practices. Indigenous workers can be especially important in developing and delivering mental health services for people whose cultural background may be very different from that of the professionals who are trying to help them. They maintain an atmosphere of cultural familiarity and acceptance that can do a great deal to bridge the cultural gap between minority clients and professionals, who are often from the dominant culture. The contributions of indigenous workers underscore the importance of continuing to recruit professional mental health workers from minority groups.

Indigenous workers may also collaborate with mental health professionals in helping to establish and guide self-help groups—for example, of racial and ethnic minorities who share common problems and of former mental patients (Bobo, Gilchrist, Cvetkovich, Trimble & Schinke, 1988; Gesten & Jason, 1987; Lefley, 1986; Rappaport, 1987; Riessman, 1985; Spiegel & Papajohn, 1986).

Summary

1. The term *insanity* is a legal designation that refers to the fact that a court of law has judged a defendant to be so mentally disturbed when committing a crime that the person is not legally responsible for the act. This judgment rests on various tests that have been accepted by the court.

2. The verdict not guilty by reason of insanity ordinarily depends on whether expert witnesses for the defense have successfully answered questions that fit the court's acceptance of a particular test of insanity. Unlike other witnesses, the expert witness is permitted to testify to conclusions as well as to facts.

3. As the result of various legal decisions, qualified psychologists are now permitted to be expert witnesses in cases involving a plea of insanity.

4. The belief that a person must be mentally capable of making a free choice in order to be legally responsible for a criminal act has ancient roots, going back to the Talmud.

5. In 1843, Daniel M'Naghten was acquitted of the murder of Edward Drummond because, in the judgment of the court, he could not distinguish right from wrong. Following the trial, the House of Lords formalized an insanity rule, which came to

be known as the M'Naghten Rule. It stated that, for an accused person to be judged insane, the person must show a "state of mind incapable of distinguishing between right and wrong."

6. Legal experts in the United States have criticized the M'Naghten Rule, arguing that the concepts of right and wrong are too vague. Nevertheless, the rule prevails in several states.

7. The irresistible impulse test of insanity states that it is possible to know the nature and quality of one's criminal behavior, know that it is wrong, and yet be driven to commit a criminal act by an irresistible impulse resulting from an abnormal mental condition. This test has been used in the United States, but usually in conjunction with the M'Naghten Rule.

8. The Durham Rule, adopted by the United States Court of Appeals some 35 years ago, states that "an accused is not criminally responsible if his unlawful act is the product of mental disease or mental defect." Psychiatrists reacted favorably to the rule, since it made their diagnoses and opinions more important. However, it was never widely used, because many legal experts and mental health professionals did not think it was a significant improvement over the M'Naghten Rule.

9. The Model Penal Code Rule is now the standard test of insanity in United States federal courts and is also used in some state jurisdictions. It states that a person is not responsible for criminal conduct if at the time of that conduct, and as the result of a mental disease or mental defect, the person did not have the capacity to appreciate the wrongfulness of the conduct or conform that conduct to the requirements of the law. Most critics agree that this rule is an improvement over earlier tests of insanity. Testimony usually deals directly with whether the defendant was psychotic when committing the crime.

10. Subsequent to acquittal on the grounds of insanity, the court may order the defendant to be committed to a mental institution until recovered. Important questions to answer in deciding the question of hospitalization include: Is the individual likely to repeat the offense? Is it safe for the person to be released? Does the individual show signs of being so mentally ill that release is not wise? Mental health professionals play an important role in answering such questions.

11. Thomas Szasz, a major critic of the insanity plea, argues that all individuals mentally disturbed or not should bear responsibility for their crimes.

12. Criticisms of the insanity plea have intensified in recent years, spurred to some extent by John Hinckley's successful insanity defense. Also, statutes have been passed to make the plea more difficult to use. In 1984, Congress passed the Insanity Reform Act. The act deleted the volitional prong of the Model Penal Code Rule, which dealt with the lack of substantial capacity to conform conduct to requirements of the law. The rule now uses only the cognitive prong: lacking substantial capacity to appreciate the wrongfulness of conduct. In addition, more than 25 states now place the burden of proof of insanity on the defendant.

13. Several states now provide for an alternate verdict in the case of the insanity plea: guilty but mentally ill. This verdict means that defendants suffered from a substantial disorder of thought, mood, or action, but not to the extent that it absolves them of criminal responsibility. The defendant receives the same sentence as in an ordinary verdict of guilty but serves as much of the sentence as necessary in treatment for the mental disorder. The rest of the sentence is served in prison.

14. Over the years, the plea of diminished responsibility has developed as an alternative to the insanity defense. If diminished responsibility is demonstrated, a murder charge can be reduced to manslaughter, which carries a less severe penalty.

15. The issue of competence to stand trail affects far more individuals than the insanity plea. The defense attorney, prosecutor, and judge are bound to raise the question of mental illness whenever they believe it may interfere with a defendant's ability to participate in the trial.

16. Involuntary hospitalization involves the civil procedure of removing individuals judged to be mentally ill from their normal surroundings and placing them in a hospital for further examination and treatment. An important principle that has been established in connection with this procedure is the right to treatment.

17. Another important principle is the right of patients to refuse treatment. In some states, the refusal can be overruled if mental health professionals state that the treatment is required to protect the patient from self-injury. Some mental health professionals have pointed out that a patient might not be competent to make a rational decision in regard to treatment, so the absolute right to refuse treatment might not be in the patient's best interests.

18. In voluntary hospitalization, the individual can request release more readily. Opinions vary in states as to whether the release should be automatic when requested, what the waiting period should be, and whether the request can be denied if examinations show the individual to be mentally ill. A growing number of legal experts and mental health professionals argue that people who have volunteered to be committed to a mental hospital should be released upon request if their condition would not have resulted in an involuntary hospitalization.

19. Legal incompetence means that mentally ill people are unable to manage their business and financial affairs. The purpose of an incompetence ruling is to safeguard a person's material assets. The court appoints a guardian (or conservator) to handle the various transactions of individuals found to be legally incompetent.

20. Legal tradition has generally upheld the confidential nature of the client–therapist relationship. However, the Tarasoff decision, which states that the therapist is obliged to warn a possible victim of violence threatened by a client, has placed limits on confidentiality.

21. Community mental health is a movement that involves a wide variety of disciplines and professions, and it has pioneered in the use of paraprofessional and nonprofessional workers.

22. Community mental health workers emphasize a seeking mode of delivering services. Thus, they intervene in the lives of troubled people earlier than do more traditional mental health professionals. The ultimate goal of community mental health programs is primary prevention of mental disorders. This goal involves (a) intervening in crises as soon as possible, (b) helping clients recognize their strengths, and (c) making changes in social factors that contribute to mental disorders.

23. In recent years, as part of community mental health actions, there have been various alternatives proposed to traditional mental hospitals. They include halfway houses, partial hospitalization, home treatment, and the use of general hospital wards rather than the more stigmatizing mental hospital.

24. Suicide prevention centers are an important aspect of community mental health programs. The pioneer in such efforts is the Los Angeles Suicide Prevention Center, founded by psychologists Normal Faberow and Edwin Schneidman. Most of the centers now operating in the United States are modeled after the Los Angeles center.

25. It is difficult to demonstrate conclusively how effective suicide prevention centers are. However, data do indicate that a significant number of people who call such centers recover from their crises.

26. Rape counseling centers have developed rapidly over the last several years. These are often part of a wider service that deals with other problems of abuse.

27. The development of rape counseling centers illustrates the interdependence of various approaches: psychological, medial, sociological, and legal. Among the goals of these centers are (a) to provide immediate medical and psychological help, (b) to seek improvement in hospital treatment and (c) to improve police attitudes.

28. Many rape counseling centers, especially those in college and university settings, have become increasingly aware of date rape. This mode of assault goes counter to many popular conceptions of the rapist as a stranger who jumps out at women from a secluded place. Consequently, victims of date rape tend to feel guiltier or distrust their judgment more than they do when they are raped by a stranger.

29. In recent years, a number of changes in state law have helped reduce the widespread practice of placing the blame for rape on the victim herself. Some states have eliminated the judge's charge to juries that they should consider uncorroborated testimony with caution. At least 41 states now prohibit testimony about the victim's sexual history unless the defense can demonstrate clearly that it is relevant to the case. Another recent change in law deals with the question of whether a husband can be accused of raping his wife. At least 18 states now have laws acknowledging the validity of this charge.

30. For the most part, these changes in the law have come about through the efforts of women's groups and their supporters. Underlying this movement is the perception that rape is a criminal act that does not necessarily involve a mentally ill perpetrator. Rather, it is an act of violence. Sexual motives are secondary to those of violence.

31. People who accept myths about rape, such as that many women want to be raped, also tend to hold restrictive beliefs about women's social roles and rights. Thus, empirical data support feminist views that rape is a way of keeping women in their place.

32. The use of paraprofessionals and nonprofessionals in community mental health programs increases the response of these programs to the cultural idiom of clients whose way of life lies outside the cultural mainstream. Paraprofessionals and nonprofessionals are trained at various levels of expertise. A central emphasis in the use of paraprofessionals and nonprofessionals is on indigenous workers — people who share and understand the clients' cultural heritage and practices. Indigenous workers also collaborate with mental health professionals in setting up self-help groups for racial and ethnic minorities and for former mental patients.

Glossary

The glossary defines important terms and concepts that are discussed in the text. Many of the entries have cross-references to help you locate related terms and concepts.

adaptive anxiety. Anxiety that is appropriate to the situation and that may enhance efficiency and achievement.

adult antisocial behavior. A pattern of antisocial behavior that does not represent a mental disorder as defined in DSM-III-R. (see also *antisocial personality disorder*.)

affect. Feeling, tone, or mood.

agoraphobia. Irrational fear of leaving home or being in public places.

alarm reaction stage (of GAS). (See *general adaptation syndrome*.)

alcohol abuse. The persistent use of alcohol in spite of the problems that result.

alcohol amnestic disorder (Korsakov's psychosis). A syndrome resulting from long-term heavy drinking; central features are a loss of memory and defects in the association of ideas.

alcohol dependence (alcoholism). A more extensive and severe disorder than alcohol abuse that involves an abnormal pattern of drinking to the point where it creates severe psychosocial problems. Alcohol tolerance usually occurs.

alcohol hallucinosis. Hallucinations caused by long-term heavy drinking that occur in the absence of delirium. (See also *delirium tremens; hallucinations*.)

alcohol idiosyncratic intoxication. Intoxication that occurs from drinking amounts that are usually insufficient to cause intoxication in most people; sometimes called *pathological intoxication*.

alcohol intoxication. Ingestion of alcohol to the point where toxic (poisonous) effects appear, including maladaptive social behavior and abnormal changes in physical behavior.

alcohol tolerance. A substantial increase in the amount of alcohol consumed to achieve the same effect, a prime sign of increased dependence.

alcohol withdrawal. Various psychological and physical symptoms that appear when heavy and prolonged drinking ceases or when the amount of alcohol regularly consumed is suddenly reduced.

amniocentesis. A surgical procedure involving the withdrawal of a small amount of amniotic fluid from the amniotic sac to determine the chromosomal composition of the fetus. (See also *genetic counseling*.)

amphetamines. A group of psychoactive drugs that stimulate the central nervous system and reduce fatigue.

anal–sadistic phase. In Freudian theory, the phase of development lasting from six months of age to the end of the second year and characterized by the child's discovery that sexual satisfaction can be gained from anal functions and that it can be combined with aggressiveness in an attempt to control the parents.

analogue observations. The use of contrived situations that simulate natural (real-life) settings when it is not feasible to observe actual behavior — for example, role-playing of parent–child interactions in a clinic. (See also *naturalistic observation*.)

analytical psychology. A system of psychotherapy started by Carl Jung and involving Jung's theory that the symptoms of psychopathology represent clues as to what is missing from an individual's collective unconscious. (See also *collective unconscious*.)

anesthesia. A deep sleep induced by sedative and hypnotic drugs administered in high doses.

anorexia nervosa. A disorder in which individuals counteract the desire for food with unrealistic and excessive dieting; they are usually preoccupied with food and have an exaggerated concern about their weight. (See also *bulimia nervosa*.)

anterograde amnesia. Loss of memory to the extent that it becomes highly difficult to learn new things.

antianxiety drugs. A group of drugs mainly used to treat anxiety disorders and conversion disorders.

antidepressant drugs. A group of drugs used to treat a wide variety of conditions, but mainly major depression.

antipsychotic drugs. A groups of drugs useful mainly in the treatment of schizophrenia but also in the treatment of the symptoms of agitated depression, manic episodes, emotional instability, and toxic psychoses induced by recreational drugs.

antisocial personality disorder. The personality disorder whose central characteristic is persistent antisocial behavior, irresponsibility, and a low level of conscience; older terms sometimes used for this disorder are *psychopathic personality* and *sociopathic personality*.

anxiety. Feeling of apprehension or fear, accompanied by physiological changes — for example, tension, increased heart rate, and gastrointestinal stress; anxiety may be appropriate to the situation (normal, adaptive) or inappropriate (abnormal, maladaptive).

aphasia. A special form of the dementia syndrome resulting from various organic disabilities in the brain, especially traumatic injuries. (See also *motor aphasia; nominal aphasia; sensory aphasia; and syntactical aphasia*.)

archetypes. (See *collective unconscious*.)

assertiveness training. The use of behavioral techniques to teach individuals who are unduly submissive how to become more assertive. (See also *behavior therapy*.)

assessment of mental disorder. A complex process whose aim is to diagnose and classify mental disorders, predict their outcome, and recommend treatment.

atherosclerosis. A circulatory disease in which deposits of plaque containing cholesterol and other fatty substances are deposited in arteries, causing the arterial walls to thicken and lose elasticity.

attention deficit disorder with hyperactivity. A condition in which the child has trouble sitting still, has a short attention span, and is generally disruptive to others.

auditory hallucinations. The hearing of voices or other sounds in the absence of stimuli that ordinarily produce such perceptions.

autism. An abnormal condition in which an individual becomes immersed in fantasy to avoid communicating with others.

austistic disorder. A disorder in which the child avoids normal childhood activities, such as social interaction and speech communication, and tries to prevent change in the environment.

aversion therapy. The elimination of undesired behavior by the application of aversive stimuli when such behavior occurs, either in actual situations or in imagined ones. (See also *covert sensitization; implosive therapy.*)

aversive maternal control. An inclusive term referring to maternal characteristics that were once thought to contribute to the development of schizophrenia in children, such as restrictive, rigid, and manipulative behaviors.

avoidant personality disorder. The personality disorder marked by an extreme hypersensitivity to rejection that interferes with positive interpersonal relationships.

barbiturates. A group of sedatives that have a calming effect in relatively low doses and that induce sleep in larger doses; continuous use may lead to addiction.

basic anxiety. According to Karen Horney, the core of neurotic disorders formed early in life, when needs for love, affection, caring, and self-esteem are not sufficiently satisfied.

behavior–genetic analysis. The study of individual differences in behavior that can be traced, at least in part, to differences in genetic makeup.

behavior therapy. Techniques of psychotherapy based directly on principles of classical and operant conditioning.

behavioral medicine. The field of therapy that applies various behavioral techniques to the treatment of psychosomatic disorders.

behavioral shaping. A technique used in behavior therapy to produce desired responses. (See also *shaping.*)

biofeedback. The use of behavioral techniques to provide patients with information about the physiological processes creating psychosomatic or physical problems.

biogenic amines. Chemical compounds in the brain and nervous system that play an important part in various biological functions.

biopolar disorders. A group of mood disorders involving cycles of manic episodes and major depressive episodes.

bipolar disorders, depressed. A syndrome of mood disorders in which an individual undergoes a major depressive episode, having previously experienced one or more manic episodes.

bipolar disorders, mixed. A syndrome of mood disorders in which manic and major depressive episodes intermingle or alternate rapidly every few days.

blood alcohol level. The percentage of blood volume accounted for by alcohol; in most states .10 percent is legal evidence of

intoxication, and death is likely to occur at levels between .60 and .80 percent.

borderline personality disorder. Personality disorder characterized by maladaptive impulsivity, unstable interpersonal relationships, poor emotional control, problems with self-image, and chronic feelings of boredom or emptiness.

bronchial asthma. Recurrent attacks of breathing difficulty and wheezing caused by spasmodic contractions of the air passages of the lungs (bronchi).

bulimia nervosa. A disorder, mainly of adolescence and young adulthood, including repeated episodes of gross overeating, often terminated by self-induced vomiting or the use of laxatives. (See also *anorexia nervosa.*)

caffeine intoxication. Intoxication resulting from the excessive use of caffeine (symptoms include gastrointestinal distress, restlessness, nervousness, hyperactivity, and insomnia); especially high intake of caffeine can produce more serious symptoms, including irregular heartbeat and rambling thoughts and speech.

castration complex. (See *Oedipus complex.*)

catatonic schizophrenia. A form of schizophrenic disorder characterized by abnormal psychomotor disturbances, ranging from excitement to withdrawal.

catecholamine hypothesis. The theory that major depression is associated with a deficiency of catecholamines in the brain and that abnormal elation (manic states) is associated with an excess.

catecholamines. Biogenic amines derived from the amino acid tyrosine and produced mainly in the adrenal glands, the brain, and the autonomic nervous system. (See also *biogenic amines.*)

chorionic villi sampling. A procedure involving the withdrawal of a small amount of chorionic villi tissue in order to determine genetic information about the fetus. (See also *genetic counseling.*)

chronic phase (of alcoholism). The level of alcohol dependence in which social and occupational relations are completely disrupted because the drinker is intoxicated most of the time; organic mental syndromes become noticeable.

cingulotomy. A method of psychosurgery that involves cutting tiny portions of the tracts that connect the cingulate gyrus to the remainder of the limbic system in order to break up certain circuits of the limbic system and thus help to stop the cycle of adverse emotional stimulation.

classical conditioning. A pattern of learning in which a neutral stimulus is repeatedly paired with another stimulus, the unconditioned stimulus, that ordinarily elicits a certain response, the unconditioned response. Under proper conditions, this repetition can cause the neutral stimulus to become a conditioned stimulus and to elicit the conditioned response, which is a reaction similar to the unconditioned response.

client-centered therapy. (See *person-centered therapy.*)

clinical psychologists. Mental health professionals who diagnose mental disorders, conduct psychotherapy and research, and often teach in universities and colleges; doctoral degrees in psychology are usually required.

clinical social workers. Mental health professionals (typically with masters' degrees in social work) who emphasize the relationship between psychological problems and the social conditions that contribute to them. They conduct psychotherapy in mental health agencies, engage in independent practice, and may also teach in schools of social work.

clonic phase. (See *convulsive seizure*.)

cocaine. An alkaloid stimulant derived from the shrub *Erythroxylon coca* and used as a highly addictive drug. (See also *crack*.)

codeine. A potentially addictive drug derived from opium that is contained in certain prescription medications. (See also *opiates*.)

cognition. The internal processing of information that includes acquiring, storing, and applying knowledge.

cognitive–behavior therapy. An approach to therapy that combines techniques of learning and the modification of thinking processes; sometimes referred to as *cognitive therapy*.

cognitive prong (of the Model Penal Code Rule). The portion of the rule that includes the phrase, "lacks substantial capacity to appreciate the wrongfulness of his conduct." Federal jurisdictions have retained this prong. (See also *Model Penal Code Rule; volitional prong*).

cognitive structuring. A cognitive–behavioral method of treating anxiety disorders in which the anxious person learns to develop new ways of thinking about the problem.

cognitive triad. A triad that includes negative self-perceptions, a persistent tendency to perceive external events negatively, and a negative view of the future—all of which play a role in the development of depression.

colitis. Inflammation of the colon.

collective unconscious. An important concept in Jungian psychotherapy that centers on the concept of archetypes: the perceptions and collective beliefs of the cultural group to which a person belongs. These exist at various levels, from conscious to deeply unconscious. (See also *analytical psychology*.)

community psychologists. Mental health professionals who emphasize the relationship between community problems (e.g., poverty and crime) and individual psychological problems; the approach overlaps that of social workers.

competence to stand trial. The ability of individuals to participate adequately in their own defense when standing trial for a criminal act.

complaints. (See symptoms.)

conditioned response. (See *classical conditioning*.)

conditioned stimulus. (See *classical conditioning*.)

conduct disorder. A diagnostic category reserved for individuals under the age of 18 who show signs similar to those seen in antisocial personality disorder.

confabulation. A phenomenon often observed in alcohol amnestic syndrome, in which the individual fills in gaps of memory with imaginary events. (See also *alcohol amnestic disorder*.)

contiguity. The close association in time of the conditioned stimulus and the neutral unconditioned stimulus.

contingency contracting. The application of token economy principles to small groups or to an individual; participants agree to achieve certain goals in exchange for a variety of rewards. (See also *token economy*.)

continuous amnesia. A form of psychogenic amnesia in which the individual remembers some events that occurred before the onset of the amnesia but not others; Similar to localization amnesia except that the memory loss covers a longer span of time.

control group. In an experiment, those individuals who do not experience the conditions under investigation. (See also *criterion group*.)

conversion disorder. Disorder marked by a loss of or alteration in physical function—for example, paralysis of the arm—that occurs in the absence of an organic disability that could explain the change; also called *hysterical neurosis, conversion type*.

convulsive seizure. In electroconvulsive therapy, a seizure caused by the sending of an alternating current through the brain. The seizure consists of two phases: The clonic phase, in which the voluntary muscles contract, and the tonic phase, in which the voluntary muscles alternately contract and relax. Both phases produce mild twitching and jerking movements.

coprophilia. Sexual pleasure associated with defecating on one's sex partner, being defecated on, or handling and eating feces.

cortical immaturity. An explanation of antisocial personality disorder based on the hypothesis that the cerebral cortex is not sufficiently developed.

cortical underarousal. An explanation of antisocial personality disorder based on the assumption that the cerebral cortex and reticular activating system of the brain require abnormally high levels of stimulation to sustain sufficient arousal.

counseling psychologists. Mental health professionals who most often help people with their educational and vocational problems or with relatively normal problems of living.

countertransference. The process by which therapists transfer to the patient the feelings that they have toward significant people in their own lives; Freud emphasized that well-trained analysts avoid countertransference. (See also *transference*.)

covert sensitization. A method of inducing anxiety through the imagining of frightening situations and then relieving it through the imagining of relaxing situations; the ultimate goal is to replace undesirable behavior with desirable behavior.

crack. A cheap and particularly dangerous form of cocaine. (See also *cocaine*.)

criterion group. In the development of the Minnesota Multiphasic Personality Inventory (MMPI), the group that included patients whom clinicians had diagnosed with various kinds of psychological disturbances before the tests were completed. The items were also administered to a control group, a normal group of individuals. Thus, the responses of people taking the test later could be compared to the responses of the criterion group and the control group.

crucial phase (in the development of alcoholism). The phase of alcohol dependence in which drinking is out of control and dependence sets in, marked by increasing tolerance and signs of withdrawal when drinking stops or is reduced. (See also *alcohol dependence.*)

cultural relativism. A theory emphasizing that criteria defining psychopathology have meaning only when considered in the context of a particular social and cultural setting.

culture. The total way of life of a people, including their ways of thinking, feeling, and believing.

cyclothymia. Mood disorders involving numerous periods of depression and maniclike (hypomanic) behavior that are significantly briefer and less severe than full-fledged manic and major depressive episodes.

defense mechanisms. In Freudian theory, the distortions and denials made by the ego about the true meaning of its conflicts and anxieties.

delirium. An organic mental syndrome whose central feature is a significant decrease in the clarity with which individuals perceive their environment; clinicians sometimes describe the condition as a clouding of consciousness.

delirium tremens. Commonly known as the DTs, a syndrome that may appear in individuals who have drunk heavily for a decade or so; convulsions and hallucinations often occur.

delusional (paranoid) disorders. A disorder whose essential feature is the persistence of a central delusion system involving a tightly woven pattern of irrational beliefs that often reflect themes of jealousy and persecution.

delusions. False beliefs that persist in spite of obvious contradictory evidence. Most common are delusions of grandeur (exaggerated self-importance), delusions of control (the belief that other people have power over one's thoughts and behavior), delusions of reference (the belief that other people's motives and behavior are always directed toward oneself), paranoid delusions (persistent and unrealistic suspicion of others), and delusions of persecution (the belief that one is constantly being harmed by others).

dementia. An organic mental syndrome marked by a global decline in intellectual abilities that interferes with the individual's everyday life.

dementia praecox. An outmoded designation for the disorder that is now called schizophrenia. The French psychiatrist Augustin Morel introduced the term during the 19th century to indicate a disorder marked by mental deterioration that occurred only in youth and that always had a fatal end. (See also *schizophrenic disorders.*)

denial. A basic process that underlies all defense mechanisms, in which the ego suppresses impulses from the id that are in conflict with what external reality permits the ego to express.

dependent personality disorder. A disorder that involves imputing to others the responsibility for one's own decisions and way of life.

depersonalization. An effect of hallucinogens, marked by the feeling of detachment from one's body.

depersonalization disorder. A dissociative disorder involving a drastic change in self-perception in which the individual's usual experiences are greatly distorted.

depression. Dejected mood, accompanied by retarded psychomotor

activity and feelings of sadness; depression may be appropriate to the situation (normal, adaptive) or inappropriate (abnormal, maladaptive). (See also *dysthymia; major depression, recurrent; major depression, single episode.*)

dereflection. A technique in logotherapy designed to counteract what therapist Viktor Frankl calls a compulsive inclination to self-observation, especially petty, exaggerated, and neurotic concerns. (See also *logotherapy.*)

descriptive validity. The extent to which people who have been diagnosed with a particular mental disorder actually reveal behavior typical of that diagnostic category.

destructive (death) drive (Thanatos). In Freudian theory, one of the two drives that form the id, incorporating destructive impulses, which may be directed toward the external world or focused inward, resulting in self-destructive behavior.

detoxification. A medical process in which an individual is treated for physiological dependence on alcohol.

deviant behavior. Acts that violate social norms and bring a strong negative reaction from others.

deviation IQ. An index of intelligence used in various revisions of the Standford–Binet Intelligence Scale to overcome technical problems in the formula. The deviation IQ is determined by the relationship of the test score to its deviation from the mean of scores in the standardized population. The mean IQ is set at 100. (See also *intelligence quotient.*)

diagnosis. The art and science of determining the nature of a disorder and differentiating the disorder from other disorders.

diathesis–stress concept. An approach to understanding body–environment interaction in the development of mental disorders; genetic predispositions, stressful events, and attitudes are studied in their relationship to the development and onset of mental disorders.

diathesis–stress theory (in psychosomatic disorders). Individuals possess a predisposition (diathesis) to developing certain biophysical disorders; this predisposition, coupled with appropriate stressors and the failure to cope adequately with them, can result in various psychosomatic disorders.

diminished responsibility. A defense used in criminal proceedings that is based on evidence not sufficient for the usual tests of insanity but that demonstrates a diminished ability to behave legally; used more often to obtain a lighter sentence than to obtain acquittal.

directed masturbation. A relatively recent innovation in the treatment of inhibited sexual excitement and chronic failure to reach an orgasm; following directions from the therapist, the person learns how to focus on stimulating and experiencing sexual pleasure without the anxiety of working with a sexual partner.

discriminative stimuli. Environmental stimuli that act as signals to indicate when and where operant behavior is likely to be reinforced. (See also *operant behavior.*)

diseases of adaptation. Psychosomatic symptoms that result from prolonged defensive reactions to aversive stressors.

disorders of impulse control. Maladaptive urges producing behavior that disrupts personal, family, or occupational life. (See also *kleptomania*; *pathological gambling*.)

disorganized type of schizophrenia. A form of schizophrenia characterized by confused thinking, feeling, and behavior; inappropriate giggling and other peculiar mannerisms; hallucinations; and fragmentary delusions.

disorientation. A state of mental confusion as to time, place, or identity.

displacement. In Freudian theory, a defense mechanism in which the ego shifts various id impulses or demands of the superego and external reality from one situation to another.

dissociative disorders. A sudden alteration in the normal integration of consciousness and identity, occurring in the absence of organic disease that could explain the alteration.

dopamine hypothesis. A chemical substance that acts as a neurotransmitter, facilitating the passage of electrochemical impulses from one nerve cell (neuron) to another; research strongly suggests that dopamine plays a causal role in the development of schizophrenia.

double-bind hypothesis of family interaction. The theory that schizophrenic individuals tend to come from families in which parents consistently send them conflicting messages.

double-blind conditions. A method of testing drug effectiveness in which neither the physician nor the patient knows whether the drug is real or a placebo.

Down's syndrome. A pattern of mental retardation caused by chromosomal defects that accounts for about one-third of the severely to moderately retarded population of the United States.

drive. In Freudian theory, the biological forces that motivate and form the structures of personality.

Durham rule. A legal test of insanity stating that an accused person is not criminally responsible for an unlawful act if it was the product of mental defect or mental disease.

dyspareunia. A sexual dysfunction marked by painful intercourse or coital discomfort; may occur in men as well as women.

dysthymia. A chronic disturbance involving a series of depressed moods, but considerably less severe than major depressive episodes.

ego. In Freudian theory, the agency of personality that develops from the id and acts as an intermediary between the id and external reality; the ego initiates all voluntary actions and controls the demands of the id.

ego-dystonic homosexuality. A diagnostic category in DSM III that focuses on the conflict of homosexual individuals about their sexual preference and their desire to acquire or increase their heterosexual relations. (See also *sexual orientation disturbance*.)

ego psychology. A development in psychoanalytic theory that clarified and extended classical Freudian psychoanalysis by shifting Freud's emphasis on the primacy of the id to a greater recognition of the ego's role in human action.

Electra complex. In Freudian theory, the part of the phallic phase in which the female child becomes a rival of her mother in order to gain her father as a sexual partner. (See also *Oedipus complex*.)

electroconvulsive therapy (ECT) (electroshock therapy). A form of therapy used to treat depression by electrically stimulating the brain to produce controlled convulsions.

electroencephalograph. A laboratory device that measures the electrical output of the brain.

encopresis (functional). A childhood disorder involving persistent failure to control bowel movement.

encounter group. A form of group therapy that grew out of the humanistic movement in psychology, in which the chief goal is to provide a means of self-actualization — strengthening the ability to fulfill one's potential. (See also *humanistic psychology*.)

endogenous depression. Episodes of major depression whose onset seems to be relatively independent of a precipitating life experience.

endorphins. Opiatelike biochemical substances in the brain thought by some researchers to play an important part in producing schizophrenic disorders.

enuresis (functional). A childhood mental disorder involving persistent failure to control urination.

epicanthal folds. A feature of the face characterized by slanting eyelids with vertical folds covering the end of each eye, nearest the nose; this feature is common in some Asian peoples and was once thought to be an essential characteristic of Down's syndrome.

epilepsy. A chronic abnormal condition of the brain marked by episodic seizures.

equipotentiality premise of conditioning. The assumption that all environmental events have an equal potential for becoming conditioned fear stimuli.

erectile disorder. (See *sexual arousal disorders*.)

Eros. In Freudian theory, one of the two drives that form the id; uses a form of energy known as libido, which is the source of all pleasurable behavior.

erythroblastosis fetalis. (See *Rh factor*.)

exhaustion stage (of GAS). (See *general adaptation syndrome*.)

exhibitionism. Compulsive desire to obtain sexual stimulation and gratification by exposing one's sexual organs to an unsuspecting stranger; apparently a disorder confined to men, who usually exhibit to female adults or children.

existentialism. A movement in philosophy and psychology that focuses on the current existence of individuals and their present motives, self-perceptions, and psychological problems.

exogenous depression. Episodes of major depression apparently preceded by highly stressful experiences; also called *reactive depression*.

externalized symptoms. A classification of symptoms in mental disorders of childhood and adolescence — including, for example, maladaptive aggression, hyperactivity, and abnormal sexual behavior.

extinction. The process through which a conditioned response is gradually extinguished if the conditioned stimulus is repeated alone.

family therapy. A form of therapy emphasizing that psychological problems arise between people, not simply internally; consequently, the family members meet as a group with the therapist in order for the therapist to help them.

faulty information processing (faulty generalizing). A theory about the causes of depression that holds that depressed individuals process information ineffectively; for example, they make arbitrary and illogical conclusions, they take information out of context, and they overgeneralize from isolated incidents.

fetal alcohol syndrome. Severe birth defects caused by a pregnant woman's drinking, especially when the alcohol intake is heavy and prolonged.

fetishism. The use of nonliving objects (for example, articles of clothing) as the preferred or exclusive way of obtaining sexual arousal and satisfaction.

figure–ground principle. (See *Gestalt therapy*.)

focal seizures. Epileptic seizures that originate within fairly localized areas of the brain, especially the temporal lobes.

forcible rape. Sexual relations of an adult with a nonconsenting partner; may be a heterosexual or homosexual assault. (See also *statutory rape*.)

formal thought disorder. Characteristic symptoms of schizophrenia that focus on disturbed forms of thinking, such as overinclusion and deficits in the ability to think abstractly. (See also *overinclusion*.)

free association. A technique in psychoanalysis that requires the patient to put thoughts into words spontaneously as they occur.

freudian (classical, traditional, orthodox) psychoanalysis. Psychodynamic concepts and methods developed by Freud and his followers to help the individual bridge the gap between the conscious and the unconscious.

frigidity. (See *sexual arousal disorders*.)

frotteurism. The habitual compulsion (confined primarily to males) to become sexually aroused by touching or rubbing against a nonconsenting person, usually a stranger in a public place.

gender. The degree of masculinity or femininity in a person, as defined psychologically and culturally. (See also *sex*.)

gender identity. The sense of belonging to one biological sex, not to the other.

gender role. The social behavior individuals display in accordance with their gender identity, revealing how they evaluate their identity how they want others to evaluate it.

general adaptation syndrome (GAS). The syndrome consisting of three stages involving the effects of stressors on behavior: alarm reaction (organism prepares for sudden action), resistance (response to stress begins to deplete the body of resources), and exhaustion (resources are depleted, exhaustion sets in, and death may occur).

general paralysis (general paresis). The psychological disability that results from syphilitic infection of the brain.

generalization (of a conditioned response). A phenomenon that occurs when variations of a conditioned stimulus also elicit the previously established conditioned response; the closer the similarity between the original stimulus and the later stimuli, the more likely that generalization will occur.

generalized amnesia. One of the least common types of psychogenic amnesia, in which the loss of memory is for the person's entire life.

generalized anxiety disorders. Chronic states of vague apprehension that persist without any objective evidence to support them.

generalized reinforcer. A reinforcer that promotes a wide variety of operant behaviors.

generalized seizures. Epileptic seizures originating in extensive areas of the brain.

genetic counseling. A series of tests and detailed interviews intended to determine the probability of genetic defects in an unborn child.

genital phase. In Freudian theory, the final phase of psychosexual development, normally beginning at puberty and extending through adulthood and consolidating all of the psychosexual tasks accomplished during previous phases of development.

Gestalt therapy. A humanistic–existentialist approach to therapy emphasizing that experiences are organized according to the figure–ground principle of Gestalt psychology and aiming to restore the lost unit and figure–ground relations of individuals suffering from psychological problems.

grand mal seizure. A severe form of epileptic seizure in which the individual loses consciousness, falls, and foams at the mouth. (See also *epilepsy*.)

group cohesiveness. The feeling of belonging to a group; it develops in successful group therapy and helps participants share problems and overcome them.

group process. A central feature of group therapy constituting the continuous change in attitudes, perceptions, and relationships that the group shares.

group therapy. The use of a group process to foster the overcoming of maladaptive patterns of thinking and behavior; group therapy involves a variety of techniques and may be based on different theoretical approaches.

guilty but mentally ill verdict. An alternative to the verdict of guilty by reason of insanity now used by some states; requires the guilty person to serve a prison term if recovery in a mental hospital occurs before the lapse of the sentence.

guilty mind (mens rea). A concept originating in ancient Greek and Roman law and emphasizing that responsibility for criminal behavior requires the awareness that the act is morally and legally wrong; underlies a long tradition in legal tests of insanity.

hallucinations. Sensory perceptions that occur in the absence of identifiable external stimuli.

hallucinogen. A psychoactive drug that produces various forms of abnormal perceptions, especially hallucinations; may be manufactured or obtained from certain plants, such as the peyote cactus.

Hallucinogen delusional disorder. Disorders involving delusions that result from the ingestion of hallucinogens; symptoms may resemble those found in schizophrenia and paranoid disorders. (See also *delusions*.)

hallucinogen hallucinosis. The occurrence of hallucinations caused primarily by the ingestion of hallucinogens.

hallucinogen mood disorders. The appearance of depression soon after the use of a hallucinogenic drug.

Halstead–Reitan Neuropsychological Battery (HRB). A research instrument to evaluate brain–behavior relationships, also useful in the diagnosis of brain damage.

hashish. (See *marijuana*.)

heroin. An illegal and a highly addictive psychoactive drug synthesized from opium. (See also *opiates*.)

histrionic personality disorder. A maladaptive pattern involving unusual self-dramatization, overconcern with one's physical appearance, a shallow expression of emotions, and extreme self-centeredness; traditionally known as *hysterical personality disorder*.

humanistic psychology. A movement in psychology that focuses on human values for both the individual and the group; closely allied to the philosophy and psychology of existentialism. (See also *existentialism*.)

Huntington's disease (chorea). An inherited neurological disorder involving spasms of the limbs, impairment of speech, progressive dementia, and death.

hypertension. Abnormal and persistent elevation of arterial blood pressure; *essential hypertension* occurs in the absence of known organic disabilities.

hyperthyroidism. Excessive activity of the thyroid gland, manifested by emotional excitement, heightened motor behavior, restlessness, and supersensitivity to external stimuli.

hypnotics. (See *sedatives*.)

hypochondriasis. An exaggerated and chronic concern with bodily functions and a chronic fear that one has a serious undetected disease; also known as *hypochondriacal neurosis*.

hypoglycemia. Abnormally low level of glucose in the blood.

hypomania. Abnormalities of mood that fall between normal elation and excitement and the extreme state of euphoria found in manic episodes.

hysteria. Diagnostic term first used by Hippocrates to indicate a disorder believed to occur only in women and marked by agitation, pain, and convulsions caused by an upward movement of the uterus.

hysterical neurosis, conversion type. Loss of physical functioning resembling a physical disorder but resulting from psychological conflict rather than organic causes.

id. In Freudian theory, the agency of personality that contains everything present at birth, including instincts (drives) and other biological forces.

identification. In Freudian theory, a defense mechanism in which the ego defends itself by identifying with a powerful figure, sometimes one that is feared.

illusions. Perceptual misinterpretations of actual external stimuli.

imipramine. A drug ordinarily used in the treatment of depression but also useful for alleviating symptoms of anxiety disorders.

implosive therapy. A behavioral technique to reduce anxiety that requires the individual to imagine a highly intense version of the frightening situation.

impotence. (See *sexual arousal disorders*.)

in vivo desensitization. The application of conditioning techniques for reducing anxiety in real-life situations instead of imagined ones. (See also *systematic desensitization*.)

incompetence (legal). A civil law ruling based on evidence that an individual is so mentally disabled as to be incapable of handling business and financial affairs.

indigenous workers. Nonprofessional or paraprofessional workers who share their client's cultural heritage and practices; employed most often in community mental health programs.

individual psychology. A system of psychotherapy started by Alfred Adler and based on his theory that neurotic individuals avoid their overwhelming feelings of helplessness and inferiority by relegating them to the unconscious and striving for unrealistic goals.

infarct. (See *multi-infarct dementia*.)

inferiority complex. A central concept of Adlerian theory and therapy emphasizing that symptoms of neurotic disorders are used to conceal and deny strongly embedded feelings of inferiority.

inhalants. A form of substance abuse in which commercial solvents, glues, and aerosol gases are inhaled.

inhibited female orgasm. The persistent and distressful absence or delay of orgasm following an adequate phase of sexual arousal. (See also *sexual response cycle*.)

inhibited male orgasm. The persistent delay or absence of ejaculation following an adequate phase of sexual arousal. (See also *sexual response cycle*.)

insanity. A legal concept applied to individuals who have been judged in a court of law to be so psychologically disabled that they are not responsible for their criminal behavior and are therefore not subject to the usual rules and penalties of criminal justice.

insulin coma therapy. An early and obsolete method of biomedical treatment that included the use of insulin-induced comas to treat schizophrenic patients.

intellectualization (in schizoid personality disorder). A primary defense mechanism employed by schizoid personalities, enabling them to think about their interpersonal relationships in an abnormally detached manner.

intelligence quotient (IQ). An index of intelligence originally obtained by dividing the mental age (MA) an individual achieved on the intelligence test by the chronological age (CA): $IQ = MA/CA \times 100$. Although the term *IQ* is still used in some current intelligence tests, the formula is not. (See also *deviation IQ*; *mental age*.)

intermittent reinforcement (partial reinforcement). A schedule of reinforcement that does not reinforce the behavior on a continuous basis.

internalized symptoms. A classification of symptoms in mental disorders of childhood and adolescence—including, for example, abnormal anxiety, depression, and social withdrawal.

interpretation. A central technique in psychoanalysis and other psychodynamic therapies in which the analyst explains to the patient the meaning of the free associations, dreams, and other expressions of motives, feelings, and significant life events. (See also *free association*.)

intersexuality. A condition in which faulty prenatal development results in a baby being born with anatomical characteristics of both sexes.

interview schedule. A printed list of procedures to be followed in carrying out an interview. (See also *semistructured interviews*; *structured interviews*.)

intracranial neoplasm. A new growth within the brain that may be benign or cancerous.

intrapsychic conflict (and anxiety). As defined by Freud, the conflict and anxiety that arise when biological impulses of sex and aggression (the id) oppose the demands of conscience and ideals (superego).

intrapsychic events. In classical psychoanalytic theory, events that occur in the mind rather than through physical and biochemical processes.

introjection. In Freudian theory, the child's assimilation of new values and beliefs resulting from the process of identifying with the parent of the same sex.

introspection. The self-description of one's own cognition.

irresistible impulse test. A test of insanity based on the argument that it is possible to know the criminal nature of one's act and yet be driven to commit the act by an irresistible impulse resulting from an abnormal mental condition.

isolation. In psychoanalytic theory, a defense mechanism in which the ego defends itself by separating an idea, motive, or act from its emotional component.

kleptomania. A personality disorder marked by persistent stealing of objects that are of little monetary value or use.

Korsakov's psychosis. (See *alcohol amnestic disorder*.)

latency phase. In Freudian theory, the stage of psychosexual development that lasts from about the age of 6 to the age of 12. It is characterized by an end to the overt rivalry between the father and the male child and the end of the female child's wish for the father as a sexual partner.

learned helplessness. A theory developed to explain the cause of depression, emphasizing that repeated exposure to uncontrollable events can produce feelings of helplessness and depression.

learned reinforcers. Stimuli that, through learning, have become discriminative stimuli and promote further operant behavior and reinforcement.

libido. (See *Eros*.)

lithium carbonate. A drug that is useful in the treatment of manic episodes.

live modeling with participation. A form of treatment for anxiety that progresses from the subject's observation of a live model involved in a frightening act or situation to the subject eventually engaging in the act.

localized amnesia. A form of psychogenic amnesia often following a highly traumatic incident where the individual fails to recall events that occurred during a relatively brief period.

logotherapy. An approach to psychotherapy closely allied with existentialism and focusing on the problems of spiritual meaning and existence that seem to permeate the client's life.

Luria–Nebraska Neuropsychological Battery. A series of tests covering a large variety of tasks that are relatively easy for normal individuals but that may present difficulties for people with brain disorders.

major depression, recurrent. A mood disorder in which the individual undergoes a major depressive episode after previously experiencing such an episode.

major depression, single episode. A mood disorder in which the individual undergoes a major depressive episode for the first time.

maladaptive anxiety. Inappropriate, self-defeating anxiety that interferes with efficiency and achievement.

maladaptive behavior. Persistent failure to respond effectively to environmental demands and to reach desired goals; may also involve interference with other people's responses to environmental demands and their attempts to reach goals.

mania. An abnormal state of excitement.

manic episode. An abnormal state of excitement, often involving euphoria and maladaptive physical activity. (See also *mood disorders*.)

marathon group. A variation of the encounter group involving an intensive encounter carried on continuously for 12 to 36 hours. (See also *encounter group*.)

marijuana. A psychoactive drug consisting mainly of the dried leaves and flowering tops of the hemp plant, *Cannabis sativa*. Hashish comes from the resin produced by the flowering plant.

marriage and family therapists. Mental health professionals who work primarily with couples and families in the treatment of marriage and family problems.

masked depression. A form of depression including a host of indirect symptoms, such as loss of appetite, delinquent behavior, obsessions, restlessness, passive response to praise or blame, lethargy, and unpredictable school performance.

melancholia. A type of major depressive episode characterized by loss of interest in practically all activities.

mental age (MA). As used in the original Binet–Simon Intelligence Scale and some of its revisions, the highest age level the child achieves on the test before failing tasks at the next highest level. (See also *intelligence quotient*.)

mental retardation. Markedly deficient intellectual development and functioning noticeable at birth or soon after or during early childhood.

meprobamate. A sedative often used in alleviating panic attacks.

meta-analysis. A statistical technique that averages the standardized results of a large number of studies; has been used in analyzing studies that evaluate the effects of psychotherapy.

metabolites. Products of biogenic amines that result from the metabolism of those amines.

methadone maintenance. A controversial method of controlling heroin addiction through the use of methadone, which blocks the desire for heroin but which is itself addictive.

methodological behaviorism. A type of behaviorism that rejects the study of private events.

migraine. A disorder involving severe one-sided headaches, often accompanied by nausea and disturbed vision.

Minnesota Multiphasic Personality Inventory (MMPI). One of the most widely used personality inventories for the assessment of mental disorders.

M'Naghten Rule. A test of insanity, stemming from British legal tradition, indicating that to be found not guilty of a crime by reason of insanity one must be unable to distinguish right from wrong.

Model Penal Code Rule. The most widely used test of insanity, stating that people are not responsible for criminal acts if at the time they committed such acts they lacked the capacity to appreciate that the acts were wrong or the capacity to conform their conduct to the requirements of the law because of mental disease or mental defect.

modeling. (See *observational learning.*)

monoamine oxidase inhibitors (MAOIs). A group of drugs used to treat depression that block the production of monoamine oxidase, a brain enzyme that reduces the availability of biogenic amines.

mood disorders. A group of disorders involving abnormal and persistent changes in mood (affect), ranging from extreme excitement and elation (manic episodes) to highly maladaptive depression; also known as *affective disorders.*

moral anxiety. In Freudian theory, a response to the fact that the conscience incorporates the threats of punishment that parents or other authority figures make for the childhood transgression of moral rules.

morphine. A highly addictive drug derived from opium that can be used legally under strict medical procedures to relieve extreme pain. (See also *opiates.*)

motor aphasia. A form of dementia in which the individual cannot speak or write, or has difficulty doing so, but can understand written or spoken words. (See also *aphasia.*)

multi-infarct dementia. A syndrome of intellectual deterioration resulting from repeated infarcts in the brain—i.e., the destruction of tissue caused by obstructions in blood vessels.

multimodal therapy. An extension of traditional behavior therapy that uses not only conditioning techniques but a wide variety of other modalities, all within an entire treatment package.

multiple personality disorder. A relatively rare form of dissociative disorder in which the individual has two or more distinct personalities, each with its own pattern of perceiving and relating to the environment and each alternately taking full control of the individual's behavior.

narcissistic personality disorder. A maladaptive pattern marked by a consistent exaggeration of self-importance and an intense preoccupation with fantasies of power and control.

naturalistic observation. The systematic monitoring and recording of behavior in a person's natural (real-life) environment.

necrophilia. Sexual arousal at the sight of a corpse or sexual intercourse with a corpse.

negative reinforcer. An environmental stimulus that strengthens the behavior that reduces or terminates the stimulus. In contrast to punishment, whose purpose is to remove behavior, negative reinforcement generates behavior.

negative transference. (See *transference.*)

neoplasm. The development of new and abnormal growths of tissues (tumors) that serve no useful physiological function.

nervous breakdown. A catchall term sometimes used in popular speech and writings to indicate a mental disorder; often used to avoid the stigma some people associate with such labels as *mental disorder* and *mental illness.*

neuroleptic drugs. A group of drugs that have been effective in alleviating schizophrenic symptoms.

neuroscience. A broad field of knowledge that integrates various disciplines whose common goal is to discover how functions and structures of the brain are related to behavior and experience.

neurotic anxiety. According to Freud, a form of anxiety that arises from unconscious fears and conflicts; it may represent an inappropriate exaggeration of dangerous situations.

neurotransmitters. Biochemical substances in the brain that transmit impulses from one nerve cell to another. (See also *norepinephrine; serotonin.*)

nicotine. The psychoactive and addictive ingredient in tobacco.

nominal aphasia. A form of aphasia in which a person cannot name objects correctly or recognize their name. (See also *aphasia.*)

nondirective therapy. (See *person-centered therapy.*)

nondisjunction. The failure of the number 21 chromosome pair to separate during the ovum's early stage of cell division, possibly causing regular trisomy in the infant. (See also *Down's syndrome.*)

nonprofessional workers. Community mental health workers who do not have formal professional training but who can provide valuable help in certain community mental health programs—for example, telephone hot lines.

norepinephrine. A biogenic amine that occurs in various parts of the brain and transmits impulses from one nerve cell to another. (See also *biogenic amines.*)

nosology. The science of classifying abnormal patterns of behavior and experience.

objective anxiety. Defined by Freud as anxiety that arises when one is faced with a realistic danger in the environment, either actual or anticipated.

observational learning. A technique used in cognitive behavior therapy based on the fact that people learn positive behavior by observing that of others (models).

observational treatment of phobic disorders. A behavior therapy technique in which the therapist participates in the frightening act or situation with signs of enjoyment so that the individual can observe this and gradually become unafraid.

obsessive compulsive disorder. A subtle form of anxiety disorder, marked by distressing preoccupation with certain thoughts (obsessions) and uncontrollable repetition of certain acts (compulsions); the compulsions help reduce the anxiety aroused by the obsessions.

obsession compulsive personality disorder. A personality disorder marked by constricted feelings and behavior as well as extreme difficulty in expressing warm feelings; undue conventionality, formality, and even stinginess in relationships.

Oedipus complex. In Freudian theory, the part of the phallic phase in which the male child wishes to seduce his mother, is a sexual rival with the father, and fears castration from him. The reaction to the fear of castration from the father is referred to as the castration complex.

operant behavior. Behavior that operates on the environment to produce changes that may lead to new patterns of behavior.

operant conditioning. A process of learning in which the learner operates on an environmental stimulus or situation, referred to as a reinforcer, thus making the behavior (operation) more likely to be repeated; also called instrumental learning.

opiate poisoning. A form of acute intoxication caused by an overdose of an opiate drug, such as morphine or heroin.

opiates. A form of opioid drugs derived from opium. (See also *codeine; morphine.*)

opioids. Highly addictive narcotic drugs derived from opium, produced synthetically, or derived from natural substances similar to opium.

opium. An alkaloid substance obtained from the milk juices of the unripened seed capsules of the oriental poppy, *Papaver somniferum.*

oral–dependent phase. In Freudian theory, the phase of psychosexual development that lasts from birth to about six months and is characterized by the need for dependence on another person, usually the mother, and sexual satisfaction through feeding.

orality theory (of alcohol abuse and dependence). A traditional psychoanalytic explanation that focuses on fixation on the oral phase of psychosexual development.

organic amnestic syndrome. An organic mental syndrome whose central characteristic is a significant loss in short-term and long-term memory.

organic anxiety syndrome. A new diagnostic category marked by recurrent panic attacks or generalized anxiety that can be traced to specific organic disabilities.

organic delusional syndrome. A syndrome whose central characteristic is the persistent occurrence of delusions that can be traced to specific biological or physical factors.

organic hallucinosis. An organic mental syndrome characterized by the persistent recurrence of hallucinations in the absence of delirium; may be the result of various kinds of biophysical pathology.

organic mental disorder. A broad diagnostic category including both the organic mental syndrome (pattern of symptoms) and the underlying biophysical pathology.

organic mental syndrome. A syndrome referring to a specific pattern of psychological symptoms and related behavior stemming from an organic disability but not specifying the nature of the underlying organic pathology. (See also *organic mental disorder.*)

organic mood syndrome. A syndrome whose main feature is abnormal shifts in mood and related behavior that stem from specific biophysical causes, such as infections or diseases of metabolism.

organic personality syndrome. A syndrome involving a definite change in fundamental aspects of an individual's personality that can be traced to an abnormality in the brain's functioning or structure; common causes include brain tumors, infections of the brain, and vascular disease.

overanxious disorder. A childhood disorder in which the individual is chronically tense and beset by a multitude of fears.

overinclusion. The tendency of schizophrenic individuals to include more objects in a particular class than belong there; the inability to filter out irrelevant information in solving problems.

panic disorders. Disorders marked by recurrent attacks of panic anxiety that are apparently unrelated to any kind of life-threatening situation.

paradoxical intention. A technique in logotherapy designed to counteract the anticipatory anxiety associated with the prospective appearance of a symptom. (See also *logotherapy.*)

paranoid personality disorder. A disorder whose central feature is a highly pervasive and long-standing pattern of suspiciousness and mistrust that is not manifested at a psychotic level.

paranoid schizophrenia. A form of schizophrenia marked by delusions, especially those of persecution or grandeur.

paraphilias. Disorders involving intense sexual urges and fantasies focusing on at least one of these: (a) nonhuman objects, (b) real or pretended humiliation by oneself or one's sexual partner, (c) children or nonconsenting people.

paraprofessional workers. Workers in community mental health programs who have received some formal professional training in educational institutions, but not at a level that meets the requirements for full professional status.

parasympathetic division (of the autonomic nervous system). The division of the autonomic nervous system that controls such physiological responses as bladder and bowel activity; responses may intensify during anxiety.

passive aggressive personality disorder. Personality disorder marked by a subtle but hostile resistance to demands for adequate performance on the job or in general social relationships.

pastoral counselors. Mental health workers who complete special program in schools of theology, designed to train them to help individuals resolve religious conflicts and related problems; they often collaborate with other mental health professionals.

pathological gambling. A chronic involvement in gambling to the extent of seriously harming personal, family, and occupational life.

pathology. A biomedical concept referring to the underlying nature of a physical disease process, such as abnormal changes in bodily cells and tissues.

pedophilia. A disorder whose central feature is the persistent attempt of an adult or adolescent to obtain sexual excitement and satisfaction with children.

peptic ulcers. Ulcers that form in the mucous membrane of the esophagus, stomach, or duodenum, caused by excessive secretion of gastric juices.

person-centered therapy. A humanistic–existentialist approach to psychotherapy emphasizing human values and the emotional–attitudinal relationship between the therapist and the client; formerly called *nondirective therapy* and *client-centered therapy*. (See also *existentialism*; *humanistic psychology*.)

personality disorders. Enduring patterns of personality traits that are inflexible and maladaptive, causing impaired behavior and significant distress. (See also *personality traits*.)

personality inventories. Highly objective methods of assessing self-reported aspects of behavior and experience.

personality traits. Distinguishable, relatively enduring ways in which an individual differs from others, including highly general characteristics as well as narrow and specific habits.

perspective taking. A form of cognitive–behavior therapy involving role playing, in which the subject learns to look at a situation from another person's viewpoint.

pervasive development disorders. A diagnostic category of symptoms of childhood disorders that resemble symptoms of adult psychosis.

phallic phase. In Freudian theory, the phase of development lasting from about the third to the sixth year of childhood, in which children begin to gain excitement from their genital organs.

phencyclidine (PCP). An easily manufactured and illegal drug that produces euphoria in small doses but hypertension, convulsions, and even death in high doses.

phenomenal field. The individual's pattern of experiences at a given time.

phenothiazines. A class of drugs that are effective in reducing the symptoms of schizophrenia.

phenylketonuria (PKU). A genetic condition that causes the accumulation of excessive levels of phenylpyruvic acid in the blood, resulting in mental retardation.

phobias (phobic disorders). Persistent, irrational fears and avoidance of objects and situations, despite the realization that the fears are unrealistic.

pica. A disorder involving persistent eating of nonnutritive substances such as dirt, clay, or paper.

placebo drugs. Pharmaceutically inert compounds whose effects are entirely attributable to suggestion or expectation.

placebo effects. Effects of therapy that are caused by factors not explicitly part of the therapeutic procedures.

polarized thinking. A problem delineated by practitioners of cognitive–behavior therapy, involving the tendency to think in terms of mutually exclusive categories. (See also *cognitive–behavior therapy*.)

polysubstance abuse. The simultaneous or sequential nonmedical use of at least three psychoactive substances.

positive reinforcer. An environmental stimulus that strengthens the behavior that produces the stimulus; also called a *reward*. (See also *operant conditioning*.)

positive symptoms of schizophrenia. (See *prognostic rating scales*.)

positive transference. (See *transference*.)

posthallucinogen perception disorder (flashbacks). Recurrences of abnormal perceptions after the hallucinogen that produced them is no longer in the body; may be spontaneous or triggered by stress. (See also *hallucinogen*.)

posttraumatic stress disorder. Repeated attacks of anxiety that follow severe, emotionally damaging experiences.

prealcoholic phase. The first phase in the development of alcoholism, in which increasing amounts of alcohol become necessary to reduce tension.

preconscious. In Freudian theory, an intermediate part of the mind between the conscious and unconscious; the preconscious can become conscious relatively easily, but the transformation from unconscious to conscious is much more difficult.

predictive validity. The effectiveness of diagnostic categories in assisting mental health professionals to (a) choose the most appropriate treatment, (b) maximize the chances of successful treatment, and (c) predict how well the patient will respond to the treatment.

prefrontal lobectomy. A method of psychosurgery involving the removal of part or all of the prefrontal lobes.

prefrontal lobotomy. A method of psychosurgery involving the destruction of tissue in the anterior lobes of the cerebral hemispheres or the severing of nerve fibers that connect those lobes to the rest of the brain.

premature ejaculation. A form of sexual dysfunction in males marked by excessively rapid ejaculation during sexual activity.

primary degenerative dementia of the Alzheimer type. Dementia resulting from Alzheimer's disease, in which brain cells and fibers degenerate. (See also *dementia*.)

primary gain. A psychoanalytic concept explaining the use of conversion symptoms to help the individual repress the underlying conflicts aroused by a situation. (See also *conversion disorder*; *repression*; *secondary gain*.)

primary orgasmic dysfunction. Inability of a woman to have an orgasm under any condition. (See also *inhibited female orgasm*.)

primary reinforcers. Reinforcers that are innately useful to the learner, such as food or bodily comfort. (See also *operant conditioning*.)

process schizophrenia. Patterns of schizophrenic symptoms and premorbid characteristics that are presumably due to faulty biological processes; thought to have a poorer prognosis than reactive schizophrenia. (See also *reactive schizophrenia*.)

prodromal phase (of alcoholism). The second phase of alcoholism, in which the drinker begins to experience blackouts, needs several drinks before going to a party where alcoholic beverages will be served, and begins to feel guilty about excessive drinking.

prognostic rating scales (schizophrenia). Scales to enable the clinician to predict the course and outcome of schizophrenic disorders (prognosis); they include negative symptoms (for example, emotional flattening), positive symptoms (for example, hallucinations), and premorbid characteristics.

progressive relaxation. A method of teaching deep relaxation as part of a therapy program to replace undesirable responses to a situation with desirable ones. (See also *systematic desensitization.*)

projection. In psychoanalytic theory, a defense mechanism in which the ego defends itself against conflict, anxiety, and guilt by projecting to others motives and feelings that the superego has forbidden.

projective tests. Personality tests consisting of ambiguous stimuli that presumably allow respondents to project onto the stimuli their own personality characteristics, including those that they may not be aware of. (See also *Rorschach test; Thematic Apperception Test.*)

pseudohermaphroditism. Condition in which genitalia in a newborn appear sexually ambiguous although the gonads are of one sex.

psychiatric nurses. Mental health professionals increasingly engaged in the direct treatment of mental disorders in hospital settings, especially group psychotherapy.

psychiatrists. Medical doctors with advanced training in the treatment of mental disorders; the only mental health professionals who can legally prescribe drugs and use other medical forms of therapy.

psychoactive drugs. Biochemical substances that produce marked effects on psychological states.

psychoactive substance abuse. Continuous use of psychoactive drugs even though it causes or exaggerates problems; recurrent use in situations posing definite hazards.

psychoactive substance dependence. Using drugs to the point where daily life is extremely disrupted; physiological dependence (tolerance and addiction) often occur.

psychoactive substance-induced organic mental disorder. Maladaptive patterns of behavior and experience caused by the direct action of drugs on the central nervous system.

psychoanalysis. The theories and methods of treatment originated by Sigmund Freud; based on the assumption that abnormal behavior and experience can ultimately be traced to internal conflicts.

psychoanalysts. Mental health professionals who derive their principles and methods of psychotherapy from Freudian theory and its variants.

psychobiology. A term reflecting the belief that psychological and biological factors are necessary in explaining the nature of mental disorders.

psychodrama. A form of group therapy that uses dramatic techniques to explore psychological problems, especially conflicts in interpersonal relations. (See also *group therapy.*)

psychogenic amnesia. A dissociative disorder whose central feature is a sudden and serious loss of memory in the absence of any organic damage that could account for the loss.

psychogenic fugue. A complex form of memory loss in which the individual travels away from home or work and takes on a new or partly new identity, forgetting the previous identity.

psychopathic personality. (See *antisocial personality disorder.*)

psychopathology. A concept derived from biomedical science, whose literal meaning is disease (pathology) of the mind (psycho).

psychopharmacology. The science that deals with the effects of drugs on behavior and experience.

psychosocial abnormality. Maladaptive characteristics of experience and behavior that indicate psychological and social impairment.

psychosomatic disorders. Physical illnesses whose development and manifestation are significantly influenced by psychosocial factors.

psychosurgery. A form of treatment that produces changes in thinking and behavior by destroying or removing brain tissue or by severing brain tissue to disconnect one area of the brain from another.

psychotherapy. The use of psychological techniques, especially verbal, in the context of a human relationship whose goal is to help bring about more positive ways of thinking, feeling, and acting.

psychotic disorders. Serious impairments in the ability to recognize and deal with reality, to communicate meaningfully with others, and to maintain adequate emotional stability.

punishment. The use of a stimulus or stimulus situation whose purpose is to remove behavior.

radical behaviorism. A variant of behaviorism that accepts the study of private events, provided they can be tied to observable behavior.

rationalization. According to psychoanalytic theory, a form of denial in which the ego invents intellectually reasonable excuses for the way it handles feelings of anxiety, conflict, and guilt.

reaction formation. In Freudian theory, a defense mechanism in which the ego avoids the conflict and anxiety produced by the demands of the id, superego, or external reality by expressing the opposite of the demands.

reactive schizophrenia. Patterns of schizophrenic symptoms and premorbid characteristics that stem mainly from maladaptive responses to life situations; thought to have a better prognosis than process schizophrenia. (See also *process schizophrenia.*)

realistic anxiety. In Freudian theory, a response to a known or real danger in the external world.

reciprocal influence. A concept of cognitive behavior therapy that links the person with the environment, both as a receiver and as an activator of stimuli. (See also *cognitive behavior therapy.*)

reflection. A technique in person-centered therapy in which the therapist clarifies the client's responses by reflecting their essence, especially the feelings they reveal.

regression. In Freudian theory, attempts by the ego to reduce or avoid conflict and anxiety by resuming earlier, less mature forms of thought and behavior.

regular trisomy. A condition in which an extra number 21 chromosome is present in the genetic structure, causing Down's syndrome.

reinforcement. Any event whose occurrence after a response increases the probability of that response. (See also *negative reinforcer*; *positive reinforcer*.)

reliability. In diagnostic procedures, the extent to which diagnosticians agree in their assessment of an individual's problems. (See also *assessment of mental disorder*; *diagnosis*.)

repression. In Freudian theory, the movement of painful memories from the conscious to the unconscious.

residential treatment program (for antisocial personality disorder). An alternative to psychotherapy that involves the total environment, emphasizing firmness, discipline, and an opportunity to learn more adaptive ways of living.

residual deviance. The violation of standards of behavior for which social agreement is so great that members of a society take them for granted.

residual type of schizophrenia. A diagnosis used when the individual has experienced at least one schizophrenic episode but the symptoms are no longer prominent.

resistance stage (of GAS). (See *general adaptation syndrome*.)

respondent behavior. Involuntary behavior elicited directly by a stimulus.

retrograde amnesia. Inability to recall material that was learned in the past, especially the recent past.

Rh factor. A factor in the red blood cells of 85 percent of the population. Incompatibility between the blood of those with the factor and those without causes problems in transfusion and a birth disorder called erythroblastosis fetalis.

right to refuse treatment. State laws giving the hospitalized mentally ill patient the right to refuse treatment under certain circumstances.

right to treatment principle. The legal principle that a mental patient has the right to expect adequate treatment when confined to a hospital.

Rorschach test. A projective test developed to measure abnormal and normal patterns of personality through the subject's description of inkblots. (See also *projective tests*.)

rumination disorder. A disorder in which infants repeatedly regurgitate their food in the absence of nausea or gastrointestinal illness.

sadistic personality disorder. A disorder involving a pervasive pattern of cruel, demeaning, and aggressive behavior.

schemas. Cognitive patterns with which individuals select and interpret the many different stimuli they encounter in everyday life.

schizoid personality disorder. A maladaptive pattern marked by seclusiveness and lack of desire for social involvement but lacking key characteristics of schizophrenia.

schizophrenic disorders (schizophrenia). A severely disabling group of mental disorders typically marked by a lack of integration between thought and emotion, distorted communication, delusions, and hallucinations.

schizophreniform disorder. A psychotic disorder in which the individual displays some of the basic symptoms of a schizophrenic disorder but in which the duration of these symptoms is less than six months.

schizotypal personality disorder. Disorder whose symptoms resemble those of schizophrenia in some respects but without the sharp break with reality; central features include odd behavior and strange ways of communicating.

school phobia. A condition, whose symptoms closely resemble those of separation anxiety disorder, in which the child refuses to go to school.

school psychologists. Psychologists who also complete courses in education to help them work with students and their problems and to understand the school system and the nature of learning in school.

school social workers. Mental health professionals who help students with personal problems and work with teachers and parents to help them understand the nature of students' problems and how they are related to school life.

secondary gain. A psychoanalytic concept used to explain how conversion symptoms can be used to avoid a threatening situation. (See also *conversion disorder*; *primary gain*.)

sedatives. Psychoactive drugs whose main physiological effect is to depress the central nervous system. At higher doses, sedatives produce deeper sleep; at this level they are called *hypnotics*.

selective amnesia. A form of psychogenic amnesia in which the memory loss covers events that occurred during a relatively brief time and in a more narrow range than in localized amnesia.

self-defeating personality disorder. A controversial diagnostic category that includes a wide variety of behaviors that interfere with positive interpersonal relationships and achievement.

self-management behavior therapy. The use of self-monitoring techniques to solve problems of maladaptive behavior, including the self-administration of rewards (reinforcers) or punishments.

self-psychology. A version of psychoanalysis that focuses on the belief that psychological problems stem primarily from narcissism —excessive self-love.

semistructured interviews. Interviews designed to be more flexible than structured interviews, using suggested guidelines rather than strict rules. (See also *structured interviews*.)

sensate focus. A technique used to treat sexual dysfunctions in which the sexual partners learn to pleasure (caress) each other without an immediate expectation of engaging in coitus or having an orgasm.

sensory aphasia. A form of dementia in which the person cannot comprehend written or spoken words, although there is no loss in the ability to say the words. (See also *aphasia*.)

separation anxiety disorder. A disorder characterized by unrealistic fear and excessive stress when the person is separated from major attachment figures, usually parents.

serotonin. A biogenic amine that occurs in various parts of the brain and transmits impulses from one nerve cell to another. (See also *biogenic amines*.)

sex. The biological characteristics that differentiate females from males. (See also *gender*.)

sexual arousal disorders. The recurrent and persistent failure to maintain the psychophysiological changes of sexual arousal (excitement).

sexual desire disorders. Significant and chronic lack of sexual appetite or drive not caused by an organic factor or other mental disorder.

sexual dysfunctions. Disorders involving disturbances in the psychological and physiological functions of normal sexual response.

sexual masochism. The habitual desire to obtain sexual excitement and gratification by being mistreated, either physically or psychologically.

sexual orientation disturbance. A diagnostic label applied to homosexual individuals who are in conflict about their sexual orientation and want to change it or learn how to live with it more adaptively.

sexual response cycle. Stages of psychophysiological changes in normal sexual response: excitement (arousal), plateau (a more intense continuation of arousal, orgasm (climax and release of sexual tension), and resolution (return to the unaroused state).

sexual sadism. The habitual desire to obtain sexual arousal and gratification by abusing the sexual partner, physically or verbally.

shaping. The creation of an operant behavior by positive reinforcement of a response when it first resembles the desired behavior and the continuation of the response as the behavior comes closer to the goal.

shaping by successive approximations. A type of behavior therapy that has been successful in developing speech in children. The children start with the best available approximation of meaningful speech sounds and are given effective reinforcers as they get closer to correct word usage.

signs. (See *symptoms*.)

simple phobia. A persistent fear of an object or situation other than the fear of having a panic attack; also called *specific phobia*.

sleepwalking (somnambulism). A form of dissociative disorder in which the individual carries out various activities while still asleep.

social deviance. Behavior that departs markedly from social standards and rules as defined by a particular society.

social phobia. An irrational and persistent fear and avoidance of situations where the individual may be exposed to the scrutiny of others.

society. A group of people who are related to each other in specific ways. (See also *culture*.)

sociocultural mental retardation. A form of cognitive defect resulting from adverse sociocultural conditions, such as severe poverty or lack of perceptual stimulation during development, that impede the acquisition of knowledge and skills necessary for adequate intellectual functioning.

sociopathic personality. (See *antisocial personality disorder*.)

somatic weakness theory. The theory that a psychosomatic disorder is most likely to occur in a bodily organ or organ system that was already biologically vulnerable.

somatization disorder. A pattern of somatoform disorders in-

volving chronic and multiple complaints of bodily discomfort that persist even though repeated medical examinations disclose no evidence of physical disease.

somatoform disorders. Disorders involving somatic (bodily) symptoms that take the form of physical disease but cannot be traced to actual organic disability.

somatoform pain disorder. A disorder characterized by a preoccupation with pain that persists for at least six months and cannot be explained on the basis of physical pathology.

spatial–temporal hierarchy. The arrangement of levels of anxiety-producing situations according to the distance one is from the situation or the time that elapses before one faces the situation.

squeeze technique. A variation of the stop–start method in the treatment of premature ejaculation in which the woman squeezes the man's penis for several seconds when he has the urge to ejaculate. (See also *stop–start technique*.)

state anxiety. Anxiety that varies according to specific situations.

statistical abnormality. A quantitative deviation from the average—the normal frequency of an event; may or may not connote psychological and social abnormality. (See also *psychosocial abnormality*.)

statutory rape. Sexual relations of an adult with a minor, even if that person consents. (See also *forcible rape*.)

stereotaxic procedures. A method of psychosurgery in which the surgeon removes tissue in a precise location by passing current through an electrode.

stop–start technique. A method used in the treatment of premature ejaculation in which the woman stimulates her partner until he approaches orgasm, then stops until his urge to ejaculate diminishes.

stressors. The various life situations that may provide stress, some of which may be particularly threatening to an individual and thus have the greatest implications for psychosomatic disorders.

structured interviews. Interviews designed to follow specific rules.

subliminal psychodynamic activation. A procedure used in experiments involving the exposure of stimuli for such a brief period of time that the subjects cannot consciously recognize them.

subnormal general intellectual functioning. An IQ score (or comparable score) of approximately 70 or less on a standardized individual intelligence test.

superego. In Freudian theory, the agency of personality that contains the conscience and ideals deriving from the moral ideals absorbed from the parents during childhood; it is the last agency to emerge.

symbolic modeling. A form of psychological treatment in which the subject observes others involved in an act or situation.

sympathetic division (of the autonomic nervous system). The division of the autonomic nervous system that controls such physiological responses as increases in heart rate; dilation of the arteries, skeletal muscles, and heart; and the increase in perspiration.

symptom. An observed psychological or physiological manifestation of a disorder. Patterns of symptoms are called syndromes. Symptoms that an individual reveals directly are known as complaints; symptoms that can be observed without the individual stating them directly are called signs.

symptom substitution. A psychodynamic view that simply removing symptoms without dealing with their underlying causes is temporary, since the symptoms will return in a different form.

syndromes. (See *symptoms*.)

synesthesia. A hallucination marked by sensations of flashing lights; may occur as the result of ingesting hallucinogens.

syntactical aphasia. A form of dementia marked by the inability to arrange words in their proper sequence.

syphilis. A disease caused by the spirochete *Treponema palidum*; symptoms involve a gradual development of dementia and general physical deterioration.

systematic desensitization (therapy). A form of treatment involving the pairing of two incompatible stimuli, such as muscular relaxation and a fearful situation, in order to reduce avoidance and eventually eliminate the fear. (See also *spatial–temporal hierarchy*; *thematic hierarchy*.)

systemic diseases. A biomedical concept referring to physical disorders not caused by infectious organisms but manifested by a malfunction of a bodily organ or system of organs.

Tarasoff decision. A court ruling that has significantly limited the right of a psychotherapist to keep completely confidential the information learned from a client that is potentially dangerous to another person.

taraxein. A copper–protein that is isolated from the blood serum of schizophrenic patients; some researchers believe it to be a cause of schizophrenia, but this has not been confirmed.

tardive dyskinesia. A serious side-effect involving involuntary muscular movement that sometimes results from the use of neuroleptic drugs in the treatment of schizophrenia and may occur months or even years after treatment begins.

Tay–Sachs disease. A genetic condition in which lipids build up in the brain and nerve cells, resulting in progressive physical and mental deterioration.

telephone scatology. Preoccupation with being sexually aroused by making obscene phone calls.

THC. Delta-9-tetrahydrocannabinol, the chemical compound responsible for the psychoactive effects of cannabis (marijuana and hashish).

Thematic Apperception Test (TAT). A projective test consisting of a series of pictures presented individually about which the subject is instructed to tell a story. (See also *projective tests*.)

thematic hierarchy. The arrangement of various anxiety-producing situations in the order of their influence; used in systematic desensitization, where relaxation is opposed to visualization of the anxiety-producing situation.

therapeutic alliance. In psychoanalysis, the goal of uniting at least portions of the patient's ego with the ego of the analyst. (See also *ego*.)

tic. An involuntary motor movement or vocal sound that occurs repeatedly in a sudden, rapid, and stereotyped manner.

token economy. The use of positive reinforcement to change the behavior of a group of people, in which the tokens that are used as rewards can be exchanged for more concrete things. (See also *positive reinforcer*.)

tonic phase. (See *convulsive seizure*.)

Tourette's disorder. A disorder involving a pattern of complex motor and vocal tics, occurring together or at different times, that persist daily for more than one year.

trait anxiety. A person's usual state of anxiety.

transference. A central concept in psychoanalysis and other psychodynamic therapies in which the patient transfers to the analyst positive and negative feelings about significant persons in the patient's life.

transsexualism. A disorder whose basic characteristic is one's deep sense of discomfort with one's sexual anatomy and a strong desire to change it to that of the other sex.

transvestism. Habitual cross-dressing by a heterosexual male to achieve sexual arousal and satisfaction.

tricyclics. A group of drugs often used, especially in the United States, to alleviate episodes of depression.

true hermaphroditism. A form of intersexuality in which an individual is born with ovaries as well as testes. (See also *intersexuality*.)

Type A behavior. Coronary-prone behavior characterized by extreme competitiveness, hostility, and a pervasive sense of urgency.

Type B behavior. The opposite of Type A behavior; behavior that is more relaxed, less hostile, and less impatient.

tyranny of shoulds. A maladaptive form of thinking that involves the dogmatic holding of self-imposed commands that must always be obeyed unquestioningly. (See also *cognitive–behavior therapy*.)

unconditioned stimulus. (See *classical conditioning*.)

unconscious. In Freudian theory, the part of the mind containing all memories and drives that, through repression or other defense mechanisms, have been removed from the conscious mind.

unconscious motivation. In Freudian theory, the proposition that experiences and motives affect behavior even though the person may not be aware of their influence or their origin.

unconventional sexual preference (homosexuality). Sexual relationships between mutually consenting members of the same sex.

undifferentiated type of schizophrenia. A disorder involving symptoms that are definitely schizophrenic but that do not meet the criteria for the disorganized, catatonic, or paranoid type of schizophrenia.

undoing. In Freudian theory, a defense mechanism involving a shift of feelings from one extreme to another so that the second attitude contradicts the first.

unilateral (hemoconvulsive) seizures. Epileptic seizures that almost always occur on one side of the body.

urolagnia. Sexual gratification associated with urinating on one's sex partner or being urinated on.

vaginismus. Recurrent and persistent muscular spasms of the outer third of the vagina that interfere seriously with coitus.

variable-ratio schedules of reinforcement. A pattern of behavior in which reinforcement (reward) occurs after a given average number (a ratio) of responses. (See also *intermittent reinforcement; reinforcement.*)

vicarious reinforcement. Reinforcement of behavior through the observation of the reinforcement experiences of others.

Visual Motor Gestalt Test. A psychological test for the appraisal of possible brain damage; it consists of a series of cards with geometric designs that the subject copies.

volitional prong (of Model Penal Code Rule). The part of the MPC rule that includes the phrase "lacks substantial capacity to conform" conduct to the requirement of the law. (See also *cognitive prong; Model Penal Code Rule.*)

voyeurism. Compulsive desire to gain sexual satisfaction by viewing the sexual organs or sexual acts of others, especially unsuspecting strangers.

waxy flexibility. A pattern that may occur in catatonic schizophrenia, marked by strange poses that can change voluntarily or by someone else moving parts of the person's body.

weekend encounter program. A briefer version of the marathon group in which sessions are several hours long and occur a number of times each day. (See also *Marathon groups.*)

Wernicke's encephalopathy. Degeneration of nerve tissue in the brain, caused primarily by a severe deficiency in vitamin B complex; often associated with prolonged and heavy drinking.

working through. In psychoanalysis, the technique involving the use of interpretation over an extended period of time so that the patient can assimilate the understanding gained in therapy sessions.

zoophilia (bestiality). The habitual desire for sexual arousal and gratification through physical contacts with animals even when opportunities for human relationships are available.

References

ABARBANEL, A. R. (1978). Diagnosis and treatment of coital discomfort. In J. LoPiccolo & L. LoPiccolo (Eds.), *Handbook of sex therapy*. New York: Plenum.

ABIKOFF, H., & GITTELMAN, R. (1985). Hyperactive children treated with stimulants: Is cognitive training a useful adjunct? *Archives of General Psychiatry, 42,* 953–961.

ABLER, G. (1980). A treatment framework for adult patients with borderline and narcissistic personality disorders. *Bulletin of the Menninger Clinic, 44,* 171–180.

ABLON, J. (1977). Perspectives on Al-Anon family groups. In N. J. Estes & M. E. Heinemann (Eds.), *Alcoholism: Development, consequences, and interventions*. St. Louis: Mosby.

ABRAHAM, K. (1927). Ejaculatio praecox. In K. Abraham, *Selected papers of Karl Abraham, M.D.* (E. Jones, Ed.; D. Bryan & A. Strachey, Trans.) (The International Psycho-Analytical Library, No. 13). London: Hogarth. (Original work published 1917)

ABRAHAM, K. (1948). A short study of the development of libido, viewed in the light of mental disorders. In K. Abraham, *Selected papers on psychoanalysis*. London: Hogarth. (Original work published 1924)

ABRAHAM, K. (1960). Note on the psychoanalytic treatment of manic–depressive insanity and allied conditions. In K. Abraham, *Selected papers on psychoanalysis*. New York: Basic Books. (Original work published 1911)

ABRAMOWITZ, S. L. (1986). Psychosocial outcomes of sex reassignment surgery. *Journal of Consulting and Clinical Psychology, 54,* 183–189.

ABRAMSON, L. Y., GARBER, J., & SELIGMAN, M. E. P. (1980). Learned helplessness in humans: An attributional analysis. In J. Garber & M. E. P. Seligman (Eds.), *Human helplessness: Theory and applications*. New York: Academic Press.

ABRAMSON, L. Y., SELIGMAN, M. E. P., & TEASDALE, J. D. (1978). Learned helplessness in humans: Critique and reformulation. *Journal of Abnormal Psychology, 87,* 49–74.

ACHENBACH, T. M. (1982). Empirical approaches to the classification of child psychopathology. In J. R. Lachenmeyer & M. G. Gibbs (Eds.), *Psychopathology in childhood*. New York: Gardner Press.

ACHENBACH, T. M. (1984). Developmental psychopathology. In M. E. Lamb & M. H. Bornstein (Eds.), *Developmental psychopathology: An advanced textbook*. Hillsdale, NJ: Erlbaum.

ACHENBACH, T. M., & EDELBROCK, C. S. (1981). Behavioral problems and competencies reported by parents of normal and disturbed children aged 4 through 16. *Monographs of the Society for Research in Child Development, 46*(Serial No. 188).

ACHENBACH, T. M., & EDELBROCK, C. S. (1984). Psychopathology of childhood. *Annual Review of Psychology, 35,* 227–256.

ADAMS, H. W., FEUERSTEIN, M., & FOWLER, J. L. (1980). Migraine headache: Review of parameters, etiology, and intervention. *Psychological Bulletin, 87,* 217–237.

ADAMS, K. M. (1980). In search of Luria's battery: A false start. *Journal of Consulting and Clinical Psychology, 48,* 511–516.

ADER, R. (1981). *Psychoneuroimmunology*. New York: Academic Press.

ADER, R., & COHEN, N. (1984). Behavior and the immune system. In W. D. Gentry (Ed.), *Handbook of behavioral medicine*. New York: Guilford Press.

ADLER, A. (1964). *Problems of neurosis: A book of case histories* (P. Mairet, Ed.). New York: Harper & Row. (Original work published 1929)

ADLER, A. (1964). *Social interest: A challenge to mankind* (J. Linton & R. Vaughan, Trans.). New York: Capricorn Books.

ADLER, A. (1973). *The practice and theory of individual psychology*. Totowa, NJ: Littlefield, Adams.

AGRAS, W. S. (1984). The behavioral treatment of somatic disorders. In W. D. Gentry (Ed.), *Handbook of behavioral medicine*. New York: Guilford Press.

AGRAS, S., SYLVESTER, D., & OLIVEAU, D. (1969). The epidemiology of common fears and phobias. *Comprehensive Psychiatry, 10,* 151–156.

AIDS ALARMS, AND FALSE ALARMS. (1987, February 4). *New York Times,* p. 22.

AKISKAL, H. S., & MCKINNEY, W. T. (1975). Overview of recent research in depression. *Archives of General Psychiatry, 32,* 285–305.

ALBEE, G. W. (1977). Does including psychotherapy in health insurance represent a subsidy to the rich from the poor? *American Psychologist, 32,* 719–721.

ALCOHOLISM AND WOMEN. (1974, Summer). *Alcohol Health and Research World,* pp. 2–7.

ALEXANDER, F. (1950). *Psychosomatic medicine: Its principles and applications*. New York: Norton.

ALEXANDER, F., & FRENCH, T. M. (1946). *Psychoanalytic therapy*. New York: Ronald Press.

ALEXANDER, F., FRENCH, T. M., & POLLACK, G. H. (Eds.). (1968). *Psychosomatic specificity* (Vol. 1). Chicago: University of Chicago Press.

ALFORD, G. S. (1983). Pharmacotherapy. In M. Hersen, A. E. Kazdin, & A. S. Bellack (Eds.), *The clinical psychology handbook*. New York: Pergamon Press.

AL-ISSA, I. (1980). *Psychopathology of women*. Englewood Cliffs, NJ: Prentice–Hall.

AL-ISSA, I. (1982). Sex differences in psychopathology. In I. Al-Issa (Ed.), *Culture and psychopathology*. Baltimore: University Park Press.

ALLEN, H. (1934). *Israfel: The life and times of Edgar Allan Poe*. New York: Farrar & Rinehart.

ALLEN-MEARES, P., WASHINGTON, R. O., & WELSH, B. L. (1986).

Social work services in schools. Englewood Cliffs, NJ: Prentice–Hall.

ALLPORT, G. W. (1937). *Personality: A psychological interpretation.* New York: Holt, Rinehart & Winston.

ALTMAN, L. K. (1988, January 26). Cocaine's many dangers: The evidence mounts. *New York Times,* p. 18.

ALZHEIMER'S DISEASE. (1988, April). *Harvard Medical School Health Letter,* pp. 1–5.

AMERICAN BAR ASSOCIATION, STANDING COMMITTEE ON ASSOCIATION STANDARDS FOR CRIMINAL JUSTICE. (1984). *Criminal justice and mental health standards.* Chicago: Author.

AMERICAN PSYCHIATRIC ASSOCIATION. (1952). *Diagnostic and statistical manual of mental disorders.* Washington, DC: Author.

AMERICAN PSYCHIATRIC ASSOCIATION. (1968). *Diagnostic and statistical manual of mental disorders* (2nd ed.). Washington, DC: Author.

AMERICAN PSYCHIATRIC ASSOCIATION. (1973, December 15). *Press release.* (Available from American Psychiatric Association, Division of Public Affairs, 1700 18th Street, NW, Washington, DC.)

AMERICAN PSYCHIATRIC ASSOCIATION. (1980a). *Diagnostic and statistical manual of mental disorders* (3rd ed.). Washington, DC: Author.

AMERICAN PSYCHIATRIC ASSOCIATION. (1980b). *A psychiatric glossary* (5th ed.). Washington, DC: Author.

AMERICAN PSYCHIATRIC ASSOCIATION. (1983). American Psychiatric Association statement on the insanity defense. *American Journal of Psychiatry, 140,* 681–688.

AMERICAN PSYCHIATRIC ASSOCIATION. (1987). *Diagnostic and statistical manual of mental disorders* (3rd ed. rev.). Washington, DC: Author.

AMERICAN PSYCHOLOGICAL ASSOCIATION. (1981). Ethical principles of psychologists. Washington, DC: Author.

AMERICAN PSYCHOLOGICAL ASSOCIATION. (1985). Ethical standards of psychologists. *Biographical Directory of the American Psychological Association, XXVIII–XXXI.* Washington, DC: Author.

AMERICAN PSYCHOLOGICAL ASSOCIATION. (1986). *Careers in psychology.* Washington, DC: Author.

AMERICAN PSYCHOLOGICAL ASSOCIATION. (1988). *Graduate study in psychology and associated fields.* Washington, DC: Author.

AMERICAN THORACIC SOCIETY. (1985). Cigarette smoking and health. *American Review of Respiratory Disease, 132,* 1133–1136.

AMIR, M. (1971). *Patterns in forcible rape.* Chicago: University of Chicago Press.

ANACHARSIS (ca. 60 B.C.). In R. T. Tripp (1970), *International thesaurus of quotations.* New York: Crowell.

ANASTASI, A. (1988). *Psychological testing* (6th ed.). New York: Macmillan.

ANCHOR, K. N., SANDLER, H. M., & CHERONES, J. H. (1977). Maladaptive antisocial aggressive behavior and outlets for intimacy. *Journal of Clinical Psychology, 33,* 947–949.

ANDERSEN, B. L. (1983). Primary orgasmic dysfunction: Diagnostic considerations and review of treatment. *Psychological Bulletin, 93,* 105–136.

ANDERSON, J. C., WILLIAMS, S., McGEE, R., & SILVA, P. A. (1987). DSM-III disorders in preadolescent children. *Archives of General Psychiatry, 44,* 69–76.

ANDERSON, W. (Trans.). (1970). *Theophrastus: The character sketches.* Kent, OH: Kent State University Press.

ANDREASEN, N. C. (1982a). Negative symptoms in schizophrenia: Definition and reliability. *Archives of General Psychiatry, 39,* 784–788.

ANDREASEN, N. C. (1982b). Negative vs. positive schizophrenia: Definition and validation. *Archives of General Psychiatry, 39,* 789–794.

ANDREASEN, N. C. (1983). The Scale for the Assessment of Negative Symptoms (SANS). Iowa City: University of Iowa.

ANDREASEN, N. C. (1984a). *The broken brain: The biological revolution in psychiatry.* New York: Harper & Row.

ANDREASEN, N. C. (1984b). The Scale for the Assessment of Positive Symptoms (SAPS). Iowa City: University of Iowa.

ANDREASEN, N. C. (1985). Positive vs. negative schizophrenia: A critical evaluation. *Schizophrenia Bulletin, 11,* 380–389.

ANDREASEN, N. C. (1987). The diagnosis of schizophrenia. *Schizophrenia Bulletin, 13,* 9–22.

ANDREASEN, N. C. (1988). Brain imaging: Applications in psychiatry. *Science, 239,* 1381–1388.

ANDREASEN, N. C., RICE, J., ENDICOTT, J., REICH, T., & CORYELL, W. (1986). The family history approach to diagnosis: How useful is it? *Archives of General Psychiatry, 43,* 421–429.

ANGRIST, B., LEE, H. K., & GERSHON, S. (1974). The antagonism of amphetamine-induced symtomatology by a neuroleptic. *American Journal of Psychiatry, 131,* 817–819.

ANSBACHER, H. L. (1977). Individual psychology. In R. J. Corsini (Ed.), *Current personality theories* (2nd ed.). Itasca, IL: Peacock.

APFELBAUM, B. (1980). The diagnosis and treatment of retarded ejaculation. In S. R. Leiblum & L. A. Pervin (Eds.), *Principles and practice of sex therapy.* New York: Guilford Press.

APPELS, A., JENKINS, C. D., & ROSENMAN, R. H. (1982). Coronary-prone behavior in the Netherlands: A cross-cultural validation study. *Archives of Behavioral Medicine, 5,* 83–90.

APPLEBOME, P. (1988, April 25). With inmates at record high sentence policy is reassessed. *New York Times,* pp. 1, 11.

APPLEWHITE, S. R., BUSBEE, D. L., & BORGAONKAR, D. S. (EDS.). (1981). Genetic screening and counseling: A multidisciplinary perspective. *Proceedings of a Conference on Genetic Screening and Counseling.* Springfield, IL: Charles C Thomas.

ARIETI, S. (1955). *Interpretation of schizophrenia.* New York: Brunner.

ARIETI, S. (1974). *Interpretation of schizophrenia* (2nd ed. rev.). New York: Basic Books.

ARIETI, S. (1980). Psychotherapy of schizophrenia: New or revised procedures. *American Journal of Psychotherapy, 34,* 464–486.

ARIETI, S., & BEMPORAD, J. R. (1978). *Severe and mild depression: The psychotherapeutic approach.* New York: Basic Books.

ARIETI, S., & BEMPORAD, J. R. (1980). The psychological organization of depression. *American Journal of Psychiatry, 137,* 1360–1365.

ARLOW, J. A. (1984). Psychoanalysis. In R. J. Corsini (Ed.), *Current psychotherapies* (3rd ed.). Itasca, IL: Peacock.

ARNHOFF, F. N. (1975). Social consequences of policy toward mental illness. *Science, 188,* 1277–1281.

ATKINSON, R. L., ATKINSON, R. C., & HILGARD, E. R. (1983). *Introduction to Psychology* (8th ed.). New York: Harcourt Brace Jovanovich.

AUGUST, G. J., & STEWARD, M. A. (1982). Is there a syndrome of pure hyperactivity? *British Journal of Psychiatry, 140,* 305–311.

AXELINE, V. (1964). *Dibbs in search of self.* New York: Ballantine.

AXELINE, V. (1969). *Play therapy.* New York: Ballantine.

AXELROD, J. (1984). Neuroscience advances. *Science, 225,* 1253.

AYLLON, T., & AZRIN, N. H. (1968). *The token economy: A motivational system for therapy and rehabilitation.* New York: Appleton–Century–Crofts.

AYLLON, T., LAYMAN, D., & KANDEL, H. J. (1975). A behavioral–educational alternative to drug control of hyperactive children. *Journal of Applied Behavior Analysis, 8,* 137–146.

AYLLON, T., & SIMON, J. S. (1982). Behavior therapy with children. In J. R. Lachenmeyer & M. S. Gibbs (Eds.), *Psychopathology in children.* New York: Gardner Press.

AZRIN, N. H., & FOXX, R. M. (1976). *Toilet training in less than a day.* New York: Pocket Books.

BAARS, B. J. (1986). *The cognitive revolution in psychology.* New York: Guilford Press.

BACON, M. K. (1973). Cross-cultural studies in drinking. In P. G. Bourne & R. Fox (Eds.). *Alcoholism: Progress in research and treatment.* New York: Academic Press.

BAIRD, P. A., & SADOVNICK, A. D. (1985). Mental retardation in over half-a-million consecutive live births: An epidemiological study. *American Journal of Mental Deficiency, 89,* 323–330.

BAKAL, D. A. (1979). *Psychology and medicine: Psychobiological dimensions of health and illness.* New York: Springer.

BAKER, D. (1972). Chromosome errors and antisocial behavior. *CRC Critical Reviews in Clinical Laboratory Sciences, 3,* 41–101.

BAKER, G. H. B., GARDINER, B. M., PEREZ-GIL, J., & WOOD, R. J. (1986). Psychiatric day hospitals: The patients and their preference in treatment. *International Journal of Psychiatry, 32*(3), 64–72.

BALAY, J., & SHEVRIN, H. (1988). The subliminal activation method: A critical review. *American Psychologist, 43,* 161–174.

BALDESSARINI, R. J. (1975). An overview of the basis for anine hypotheses in affective illness. In J. Mendels (Ed.), *The psychobiology of depression.* New York: Spectrum.

BALDESSARINI, R. J. (1977). *Chemotherapy in psychiatry.* Cambridge, MA: Harvard University Press.

BAMMER, K., & NEWBERRY, B. H. (1981). *Stress and cancer.* Toronto: Hogrefe.

BANCROFT, J. (1983). *Human sexuality and its problems.* Edinburgh: Churchill Livingstone.

BANDURA, A. (1962). Social learning through imitation. In M. R. Jones (Ed.), *Nebraska Symposium on Motivation,* Lincoln: University of Nebraska Press.

BANDURA, A. (1969). *Principles of behavior modification.* New York: Holt, Rinehart & Winston.

BANDURA, A. (1974). Behavior theory and the models of man. *American Psychologist, 29,* 859–869.

BANDURA, A. (1977). *Social learning theory.* Englewood Cliffs, NJ: Prentice–Hall.

BANDURA, A. (1978). The self system is reciprocal determinism. *American Psychologist, 33,* 344–358.

BANDURA, A. (1982). Self-efficacy mechanism in human agency. *American Psychologist, 37,* 122–147.

BANDURA, A., BLANCHARD, E. B., & RITTER, B. (1968). *The relative efficacy of desensitization and modeling approaches for inducing behavioral, affective, and attitudinal changes.* Unpublished manuscript, Stanford University.

BARBACH, L. G. (1975). *For yourself: The fulfillment of female sexuality.* New York: Doubleday.

BARLOW, D. H., O'BRIEN, G. T., & LAST, C. G. (1984). Couples treatment of agoraphobia. *Behavior Therapy, 15,* 41–58.

BARNES, D. M. (1986). Grim projections for AIDS epidemic. *Science, 232,* 1589–1590.

BARNES, D. M. (1987a). Biological issues in schizophrenia. *Science, 235,* 430–433.

BARNES, D. M. (1987b). Defect in Alzheimer's is on chromosome 21. *Science, 235,* 846–847.

BARNES, D. M. (1988). Drugs: Running the numbers—addiction. *Science, 240,* 1729–1731.

BARNETT, W. S. (1986). Definition and classification of mental retardation: A reply to Zigler, Balla, & Hodapp. *American Journal of Mental Deficiency, 91,* 111–116.

BARRETT, C. L., HAMPE, I. E., & MILLER, L. C. (1978). Research on child psychotherapy. In S. L. Garfield & A. E. Bergin (Eds.), *Handbook of psychotherapy and behavior change: An empirical analysis* (2nd ed.). New York: Wiley.

BARRINGER, F. (1987, October 21). Soviet abuse of psychiatry said to linger. *New York Times,* pp. 1–2.

BARRY, H. (1982). Cultural variations in alcohol abuse. In I. Al-Issa (Ed.), *Culture and psychopathology.* Baltimore: University Park Press.

BARRY, H., JR., & BARRY, H., III. (1972). Homosexuality and testosterone. *New England Journal of Medicine, 286,* 380–381.

BARSKY, A. J., & KLERMAN, G. L. (1983). Hyopchondriasis, bodily complaints, and somatic styles. *American Journal of Psychiatry, 140,* 273–283.

BARSKY, A. J., WYSHAK, G., & KLERMAN, G. L. (1986). Hypochondriasis: An evaluation of the DSM-III criteria in medical outpatients. *Archives of General Psychiatry, 43,* 493–500.

BASMAJIAN, J. V. (ED.). (1979). *Biofeedback—principles and practice for clinicians.* Baltimore: Williams & Wilkins.

BATESON, G., JACKSON, D. D., HALEY, J., & WEAKLAND, J. (1956). Toward a theory of schizophrenia. *Behavioral Science, 1,* 251–264.

BAUM, C., KENNEDY, D. L., KNAPP, D. E., & FAICH, G. A. (1985). *Drug utilization in the United States.* Washington, DC: Food and Drug Administration.

BAUM, A., SINGER, J. E., & BAUM, C. S. (1981). Stress and the environment. *Journal of Social Issues, 37,* 4–35.

BAYER, R., & SPITZER, R. L. (1982). Edited correspondence on the status of homosexuality in DSM-III. *Journal of the History of the Behavioral Sciences, 18,* 32–52.

BAZELON, D. L. (1974, June). Psychiatrists and the adversary process. *Scientific American, 230*(6), 18–23.

BAZELON, D. L. (1982). Veils, values and social responsibility. *American Psychologist, 37,* 115–121.

BEAR, D., FREEMAN, R., & GREENBERG, M. (1986, December). Temporal lobe epilepsy. *Harvard Medical School Mental Health Letter,* pp. 4–6.

BEBBINGTON, P. E. (1976). The efficacy of Alcoholics Anonymous: The elusiveness of hard data. *British Journal of Psychiatry, 128,* 572–580.

BECK, A. T. (1970). *Depression: Causes and treatment.* Philadelphia: University of Pennsylvania Press.

BECK, A. T. (1976). *Cognitive therapy and the emotional disorders.* New York: International Universities Press.

BECK, A. T. (1978). *Beck Depression Inventory* (rev. ed.). Philadelphia: Center for Cognitive Therapy.

BECK, A.T., EMERY, G., & GREENBERG, R. L. (1985). *Anxiety disorders and phobias.* New York: Basic Books.

BECK, A. T., RUSH, A. J., SHAW, B. F., & EMERY, G. (1979). *Cognitive therapy of depression.* New York: Guilford Press.

BECK, A. T., STEER, R. A., & GARBIN, M. G. (1988). Psychometric properties of the Beck Depression Inventory: Twenty-five years of evaluation. *Clinical Psychology Review, 8,* 77–100.

BECK, A. T., & YOUNG, J. E. (1985). Depression. In D. H. Barlow (Eds.), *Clinical handbook of psychological disorders: A step-by-step treatment manual.* New York: Guilford Press.

BECK, S. J. (1944). *Rorschach's test: I. Basic processes.* New York: Grune & Stratton.

BECK, S. J. (1945). *Rorschach's test: II. A variety of personality pictures.* New York: Grune & Stratton.

BECK, S. J. (1952). *Rorschach's test: III. Advances in interpretation.* New York: Grune & Stratton.

BECK, S. J., BECK, A. G., LEVITT, E., & MOLISH, H. B. (1961). *Rorschach's test: I. Basic processes* (3rd ed.). New York: Grune & Stratton.

BECK, S. J., & MOLISH, H. B. (1967). *Rorschach's test: II. A variety of personality pictures.* New York: Grune & Stratton.

BECKER, H. S. (1974). Labeling theory reconsidered. In P. Rock & M. McIntosh (Eds.), *Deviance and social control.* London: Tavistock.

BECKER, J. (1977). *Affective disorders.* Morriston, NJ: General Learning Press.

BECKER, J. V., & SKINNER, L. L. (1983). Assessment and treatment of rape-related sexual dysfunctions. *Clinical Psychologist, 36*(4), 102–105.

BECKER, J. V., SKINNER, L. L., ABEL, G. G., & CICHON, J. (1986). Levels of postassault sexual functioning in rape and incest victims. *Archives of Sexual Behavior, 15,* 37–49.

BECKER, L. E. (1973, August). Durham revisited: Psychiatry and the problem of crime. *Psychiatric Annals, 3*(8), 17–21, 25, 28–29, 33–34, 38–39, 44–45, 48–49.

BECKMAN, E. E. (1984). The comparative efficacy of psychotherapy and pharmacotherapy in treating depression. *Psychotherapy in Private Practice, 2,* 31–37.

BEDROSIAN, R. C., & BECK, A. T. (1980). Principles of cognitive therapy. In M. J. Mahoney (Ed.), *Psychotherapy process: Current issues and future directions.* New York: Plenum.

BEERS, C. W. (1937). *A mind that found itself: An autobiography* (5th ed. rev.). Garden City, NY: Doubleday, Doran. (Original work published 1908)

BEITMAN, B. D., & KLERMAN, G. L. (1984). Combining psychotherapy and drug therapy in clinical practice. Jamaica, NY: Spectrum.

BELL, A. P., & HALL, C. S. (1976). The personality of a child molester. In M. S. Weinberg (Ed.), *Sex research: Studies from the Kinsey Institute.* New York: Oxford University Press.

BELL, A. P., WEINBERG, M. S., & HAMMERSMITH, S. K. (1981). *Sexual preference: Its development in men and women.* Bloomington: Indiana University Press.

BELLACK, A. S., HERSEN, M., & HIMMELHOCH, J. (1981). Social skills training compared with pharmacotherapy and psychotherapy in the treatment of unipolar depression. *American Journal of Psychiatry, 138,* 1562–1567.

BELLAK, L. (1979). An idiosyncratic overview. In L. Bellak (Ed.), *Disorders of the schizophrenic syndrome.* New York: Basic Books.

BELLACK, L., & BELLAK, S. S. (1973). *Senior appreciation technique.* New York: CPS.

BEMPORAD, J. (1978). Manifest symptomatology in children and adolescents. In S. Arieti & J. Bemporad, *Severe and mild depression.* New York: Basic Books.

BENDER, L. (1938). *A visual motor gestalt test and its clinical use* (American Orthopsychiatric Association Research Monograph No. 3).

BENDER, L. (1946). Instructions for the use of the "Visual Motor Gestalt Test." New York: American Orthopsychiatric Association.

BENDER, L. (1974). Childhood schizophrenia. *American Journal of Orthopsychiatry, 17,* 40–56.

BENEDICT, R. (1950). *Patterns of culture.* New York: New American Library. (Original work published 1934)

BENNER, D. G., & JOSCELYNE, G. (1984). Multiple personality as a borderline disorder. *Journal of Nervous and Mental Disease, 172,* 98–104.

BENSON, B. A., REISS, S., SMITH, D. C., & LAMAN, D. S. (1985). Psychosocial correlates of depression in mentally retarded adults: II. Poor social skills. *American Journal of Mental Deficiency, 89,* 657–659.

BERENBAUM, H., OLTMANNS, T. F., & GOTTESMAN, I. I. (1987). A twin study perspective on positive and negative symptoms of schizophrenia. In P. D. Harvey & E. F. Walker (Eds.), *Positive and negative symptoms of psychoses: Description, research, and future directions.* Hillsdale, NJ: Erlbaum.

BERGER, P. A. (1977). Antidepressant medications and the treatment of depression. In J. D. Barchas, P. A. Berger, R. D. Ciaranello, & G. R. Elliott (Eds.), *Psychopharmacology: From theory to practice.* New York: Oxford University Press.

BERGER, P. A. (1978). Medical treatment of mental illness. *Science, 200,* 974–981.

BERGER, P. A., & BARCHAS, J. D. (1977). *Biochemical hypotheses of affective disorders.* In J. D. Barchas, P. A. Berger, R. D. Ciaranello, & G. R. Elliott (Eds.), *Psychopharmacology: From theory to practice.* New York: Oxford University Press.

BERGER, P. A., & REXROTH, K. (1980). Tardive dyskinesia: Clinical, biological, and pharmacological perspectives. *Schizophrenia Bulletin, 6,* 102–116.

BERGIN, A. E. (1971). The evaluation of therapeutic outcomes. In A. E. Bergin & S. L. Garfield (Eds.), *Handbook of psychotherapy and behavior change: An empirical analysis.* New York: Wiley.

BERGIN, A. E., & LAMBERT, M. J. (1978). The evaluation of therapeutic outcomes. In S. L. Garfield & A. E. Bergin (Eds.), *Handbook of psychotherapy and behavior change: An empirical analysis* (2nd ed.). New York: Wiley.

BERGLAS, A. (1986). *The success syndrome.* New York: Plenum.

BERGLER, E. (1977). The psychology of gambling. In J. Halliday & P. Fuller (Eds.), *The psychology of gambling.* New York: Penguin.

BERMAN, J. L. (1978). Inborn errors of metabolism, variation, and mental retardation in phenylalanine metabolis. In C. H. Carter (Ed.), *Medical aspects of mental retardation* (2nd ed.). Springfield, IL: Charles C Thomas.

BERNHEIM, K. F., & LEWINE, R. R. J. (1979). *Schizophrenia: Symptoms, causes, treatments.* New York: Norton.

BERNSTEIN, D. A., & NIETZEL, M. T. (1980). *Introduction to clinical psychology.* New York: Mcgraw-Hill.

BERTRAND, S., & MASLING, J. (1969). Oral imagery and alcoholism. *Journal of Abnormal Psychology, 74,* 50–53.

BESCHNER, G., ADAMS, K., WESSON, D., CARLIN, A., & FARLEY, E. (1978). Introduction. In D. R. Wesson, A. S. Carlin, K. M. Adams, & G. Beschner (Eds.), *Polydrug abuse: The results of a national collaborative study.* New York: Academic Press.

BESS, B. E., & WARREN, F. Z. (1982, November). Some mistaken ideas men have about women's sexuality. *Medical Aspects of Human Sexuality, 16*(11), 101–102, 109, 113–114, 117.

BETTELHEIM, B. (1943). Individual and mass behavior in extreme situations. *Journal of Abnormal and Social Psychology, 38,* 417–452.

BETTELHEIM, B. (1982, March 1). Freud and the soul. *New Yorker,* pp. 52–93.

BIEBER, I., DAIN, H. J., DINCE, P. R., DRELLICH, M. G., GRAND, H. C., GUNDLACH, R. H., KREMER, M. W., RIFKIN, A. H., WILBUR, C. B., & BIEBER, T. B. (1962). *Homosexuality: A psychoanalytic study.* New York: Basic Books.

BIGGS, J. JR. (1955). *The guilty mind: Psychiatry and the law.* New York: Harcourt, Brace.

BIJOU, S. W. (1952). The technology of teaching young handicapped children. In S. W. Bijou & E. Ribes-Inesta (Eds.), *Behavior modification: Issues and extensions.* New York: Academic Press.

BIJOU, S. W. (1973). Behavior modification in teaching the retarded child. In C. E. Thoresen (Ed), *72nd Yearbook of the National Society for the Study of Education.* Chicago: University of Chicago Press.

BINET, A., & SIMON, T. (1905). Méthodes nouvelles pour le diagnostic du niveau intellectual des anormaux [New methods for diagnosing the intellectual level of the retarded]. *L'Année Psychologique, 11,* 191–244.

BINET, A., & SIMON, T. (1916). *The development of intelligence in children: The Binet–Simon scale* (E. S. Kite, Trans.). Baltimore: Williams & Wilkins.

BINITIE, A. (1975). A factor-analytical study of depression across cultures (African and European). *British Journal of Psychiatry, 127,* 559–563.

BIRK, L., WILLIAMS, G. H., CHASIN, M., & ROSE, L. L. (1973). Serum testosterone levels in homosexual men. *New England Journal of Medicine, 287,* 1236–1238.

BIRNS, H., & LEVIEN, J. S. (1980). Dangerousness: Legal determinations and clinical speculations. *Psychiatric Quarterly, 52,* 108–131.

BLANCHARD, E. B., & YOUNG, L. D. (1974). Clinical applications of biofeedback training. *Archives of General Psychiatry, 30,* 573–589.

BLASHFIELD, R. K., & DRAGUNS, J. G. (1976a). Evaluative criteria for psychiatric classification. *Journal of Abnormal Psychology, 85,* 140–150.).

BLASHFIELD, R. K., & DRAGUNS, J. G. (1976b). Toward a taxonomy of psychopathology: The purpose of psychiatric classification. *British Journal of Psychiatry, 129,* 574–583.

BLAU, T. H. (1984). *The psychologist as expert witness.* New York: Wiley.

BLEULER, E. (1950). *Dementia praecox or the group of schizophrenias* (J. Zinkin, Trans.) (Monograph Series on Schizophrenia No. 1). New York: International Universities Press. (Original work published 1911).

BLEULER, E. (1976). *Textbook of psychiatry* (A. A. Brill, Trans.). New York: Arno Press. (Original work published 1924)

BLEULER, M. E. (1978). The long-term course of schizophrenic psychoses. In L. C. Wynne, R. L. Cromwell, & S. Matthysse (Eds.),

The nature of schizophrenia: New approaches to research and treatment. New York: Wiley.

BLISS, E. L. (1984). A symptom profile of patients with multiple personality, including MMPI results. *Journal of Nervous and Mental Disease, 172,* 197–202.

BLISS, E. L., & JEPPSEN, E. A. (1985). Prevalence of multiple personality among inpatients and outpatients. *American Journal of Psychiatry, 142,* 250–251.

BLOCH, S., & REDDAWAY, P. (1977). *Psychiatric terror: How Soviet psychiatry is used to suppress dissent.* New York: Basic Books.

BLOOM, B. L. (1980). Social and community interventions. *Annual Review of Psychology, 31,* 111–142.

BLUM, K. (1984). *Handbook of abusable drugs.* New York: Gardner Press.).

BLUMENTHAL, J. A., WILLIAMS, R. B., JR., KONG, Y., SCHANBERG, M., & THOMPSON, L. W. (1978). Type A behavior pattern and coronary atherosclerosis. *Circulation, 58,* 634–639.

BLUNT, L. W., & STOCK, H. V. (1985). Guilty but mentally ill: An alternative verdict. *Behavioral Sciences and the Law, 3,* 49–68.

BOARD ON MENTAL HEALTH AND BEHAVIORAL MEDICINE, INSTITUTE OF MEDICINE (1985). Research on mental illness and addictive disorders: Progress and prospects. *American Journal of Psychiatry, 142*(Suppl.).

BOBO, J. K., GILCHRIST, L. D., CVETKOVICH, G. T., TRIMBLE, J. E., & SCHINKE, S. P. (1988). Cross-cultural service: Delivery to minority communities. *Journal of Community Psychology, 16,* 263–272.

BOCKUS, F. (1980). *Couple Therapy.* New York: Aronson.

BOEHME, D. H., COTTRELL, J. C., DOHAN, F. C., & HILLEGASS, L. M. (1974). Demonstration of nuclear and cytoplasmic fluorescence in brain tissues of schizophrenic and non-schizophrenic patients. *Biological Psychiatry, 8,* 89–94.

BOFFEY, P. M. (1986, July 2). Three new psychiatric categories accepted. *New York Times,* p. 11.

BOGGAN, E. C., HAFT, M. G., LISTER, G., & RUPP, J. P. (1975). *The rights of gay people: The basic ACLU guide to a gay person's rights.* New York: Avon.

BOGUS SLOANE RANGER LIVED LIKE A LORD ON BARCLAYCARD. (1983, April 10). *The Times,* London, p. 3.

BOHACEK, N. (1986). Psychopharmacology of schizophrenia: European view. *Schizophrenia Bulletin, 12,* 20–25.

BOHLEN, J. G., HELD, J. P., & SANDERSON, M. O. (1980). The male orgasm: pelvic contractions measured by anal probe. *Archives of Sexual Behavior, 9,* 503–521.

BOLL, T. J. (1981). The Halstead–Reitan Neuropsychology Battery. In S. B. Fisher & T. J. Boll (Eds.), *Handbook of clinical neuropsychology.* New York: Wiley–Interscience.

BOND, P. A., JENNER, F. A., & SAMPSON, G. A. (1972). Daily variations of the urine content of 3-methoxy-4-hydroxyphenylglycol in two manic–depressive patients. *Psychological Medicine, 2,* 81–85.

BONKALO, A., & MUNRO, A. (1980). Organic disorders (intracere-

bral). In S. E. Greben, R. Pos, V. M. Rakoff, A. Bonkalo, F. H. Lowy, & G. Voineskos (Eds.), *A method of psychiatry.* Philadelphia: Lea & Febiger.

BONN, J. A., READHEAD, C., & TIMMONS, B. (1984). Enhanced adaptive behavioural responses in agoraphobic patients. *Lancet, 8404,* 665–669.

BONNIE, R. J. (1982). The psychiatric patient's right to refuse medication: A survey of the legal issues. In A. E. Doudera & J. P. Swazey (Eds.), *Refusing treatment in mental health institutions—values in conflict.* Ann Arbor, MI: AUPHA Press.

BOOTH, W. (1988). AIDS and drug abuse: No quick fix. *Science, 239,* 717–719.

BORSKY, P. N. (1980). Research on community response to noise since 1973. In J. V. Tobias (Ed.), *The Proceedings of the Third International Congress on Noise as a Public Health Problem.* Washing, DC: American Speech and Hearing Association.

BORTHWICK, S., MEYERS, C. S., & EYMAN, R. K. (1981). Comparative adaptive and maladaptive behavior of mentally retarded clients of five residential settings in three western states. In R. H. Bruininks, C. E. Meyers, B. B. Sigford, & K. C. Lakin (Eds.), *Deinstitutionalization and community adjustment of mentally retarded people.* Washington, DC: American Association of Mental Deficiency.

BOSKIND-WHITE, M., & WHITE, W. C., JR. (1986). Bulimarexia: A historical–sociocultural perspective. In K. D. Brownell & J. P. Foreyt (Eds.), *Handbook of eating disorders: Physiology, psychology, and treatment of obesity, anorexia, and bulimia.* New York: Basic Books.

BOURNE, P. G., & LIGHT, E. (1979). Alcohol problems in blacks and women. In J. H. Mendelson & N. K. Mellow (Eds.), *The diagnosis and treatment of alcoholism.* New York: McGraw-Hill.

BOUSFIELD, W. A. (1955). Lope de Vega on early conditioning. *American Psychologist, 10,* 828.

BOWEN, E. (1935). *The house in Paris.* New York: Vintage Press.

BOWERS, M. B., JR. (1981). Biochemical processes in schizophrenia: An update. In U.S. Department of Health and Human Services, Public Health Service, *Schizophrenia 1980: Special report.* Washington, DC: U.S. Government Printing Office.

BOWLBY, J. (1969). *Attachment and loss* (Vol. 1). New York: Basic Books.

BOWLBY, J. (1973). *Attachment and loss* (Vol. 2). New York: Basic Books.

BRADY, J. P., & RIEGER, W. (1975). Behavioral treatments of anorexia nervosa. In T. Thompson & W. S. Duckens (Eds.), *Applications of behavior modification.* New York: Academic Press.

BRAKEL, S. J. (1985a). Involuntary institutionalization. In S. J. Brakel, J. Parry, & B. A. Weiner (Eds.), *The mentally disabled and the law* (3rd ed.). Chicago: American Bar Foundation.

BRAKEL, S. J. (1985b). Voluntary institutionalization. In S. J. Brakel, J. Parry, & B. A. Weiner (Eds.), *The mentally disabled and the law* (3rd ed.). Chicago: American Bar Foundation.

BRAKEL, S. J., & ROCK, R. S. (EDS.). (1971). *The mentally disabled and the law* (rev. ed.). Chicago: University of Chicago Press.

BRANDT, A. M. (1988). The syphilis epidemic and its relation to AIDS. *Science, 239,* 375–380.

BRECHER, E. M., & THE EDITORS OF CONSUMER REPORTS. (1972). *Licit and illicit drugs.* Boston: Little, Brown.

BREGGIN, P. R. (1972). Lobotomies: An alert. *American Journal of Psychiatry, 129,* 97–98.

BREGGIN, P. R. (1974). Underlying a method. *Mental Hygiene, 58,* 19–21.

BREGMAN, E. (1934). An attempt to modify the emotional attitudes of infants by the conditioned response technique. *Journal of Genetic Psychology, 45,* 169–196.

BREIER, A., CHARNEY, D. S., & HENINGER, G. R. (1986). Agoraphobia with panic attacks: Development, diagnostic stability, and course of illness. *Archives of General Psychiatry, 43,* 1029–1036.

BRENNER, C. (1973). *An elementary textbook of psychoanalysis* (rev. ed.). New York: International Universities Press.

BREUER, J., & FREUD, S. (1936). *Studies in hysteria* (A. A. Brill, Trans.) (Nervous and Mental Disease Monograph No. 61). New York & Washington, DC: Nervous and Mental Disease Publishing. (Original work published 1893)

BRINKLEY, J. (1984, September 14). The war on narcotics: Can it be won? *New York Times,* pp. 1, 6.

BRIQUET, P. (1859). *Traité clinique et therapeutique de l'hystérie* [Clinical and therapeutic treatise on hysteria]. Paris: Baillière.

BRITISH FIGHT RISE IN HEROIN ADDICTION. (1985, April 11). *New York Times,* p. 6.

BRODY, J. E. (1983, November 30). Guidance in the care of patients with Alzheimer's disease. *New York Times,* p. 17.

BRODY, J. E. (1984, October 19). Panic attacks: The terror is treatable. *New York Times,* p. 18.

BROVERMAN, I. K., BROVERMAN, D. M., CLARKSON, F. E., ROSENKRANTZ, P. S., & VOGEL, S. R. (1970). Sex-role stereotypes and clinical judgments of mental health. *Journal of Consulting and Clinical Psychology, 34,* 1–7.

BROWER, K. J., HIERHOLZER, R., & MADDAHIAN, E. (1986). Recent trends in cocaine abuse in a VA psychiatric population. *Hospital and Community Psychiatry, 37,* 1229–1234.

BROWN, B. S., WIENCKOWSKI, L. A., & BIVENS, L. W. (1973). *Psychosurgery: Perspectives on a current issue.* Washington, DC: U.S. Department of Health, Education, and Welfare, Public Health Service.

BROWN, G. W., BHROLCHAIN, M. N., & HARRIS, T. O. (1975). Social class and psychiatric disturbance among women in an urban population. *Sociology, 9,* 225–254.

BROWN, P. (1980). Social implications of deinstitutionalization. *Journal of Community Psychology, 8,* 314–322.

BROWN, P. (1982). Public policy failure in deinstitutionalization: A response to critics. *Journal of Community Psychology, 10,* 90–94.

BROWNMILLER, S. (1975). *Against our will: Men, women, and rape.* New York: Simon & Schuster.

BRUCH, H. (1973). *Eating disorders: Obesity, anorexia nervosa, and the person within.* New York: Basic Books.

BRUCH, H. (1978). *The golden cage: The enigma of anorexia nervosa.* Cambridge, MA: Harvard University Press.

BRUCH, H. (1986). Anorexia nervosa: The therapeutic task. In K. D. Brownell & J. P. Foreyt (Eds.), *Handbook of eating disorders.* New York: Basic Books.

BUCHSBAUM, M. S., & HAIER, R. J. (1983). Psychopathology: Biological approaches. *Annual Review of Psychology, 34,* 401–430.

BUCHSBAUM, M. S., & HAIER, R. J. (1987). Functional and anatomical brain imaging: Impact on schizophrenia research. *Schizophrenia Bulletin, 13,* 115–132.

BULLOUGH, V. L. (1987). A nineteenth-century transsexual. *Archives of Sexual Behavior, 16,* 81–84.

BUNNEY, W. E., JR., & DAVIS, J. M. (1965). Norepinephrine in depressive reactions: A review. *Archives of General Psychiatry, 13,* 483–494.

BURFORD, R., FRENCH, I. W., & LEBLANC, A. E. (1974). The combined effects of alcohol and common psychoactive drugs: I. Studies on human pursuit tracking capability. In S. Israelstam & S. Lambert (Eds.), *Alcohol, Drugs, and Traffic Safety: Proceedings of the Sixth International Conference on Alcohol, Drugs, and Traffic Safety.* Toronto: Addiction Research Foundation of Ontario.

BURGESS, A. W., & HOLMSTROM, L. L. (1977). *Rape trauma syndrome.* In D. Chappell, R. Geis, & G. Geis (Eds.), *Forcible rape: The crime, the victim, and the offender.* New York: Columbia University Press.

BUROS, O. K. (ED.). (1978). *The eighth mental measurement yearbook* (Vol. 1). Highland Park, NJ: Gryphon Press.

BURTLE, V. (ED.). (1979). *Women who drink: Alcoholic experience and psychotherapy.* Springfield, IL: Charles C Thomas.

BUSS, A. H. (1966). *Psychopathology.* New York: Wiley.

BUTCHER, J. N., & FINN, S. (1983). Objective personality assessment in clinical settings. In M. Hersen, A. E. Kazdin, & A. S. Bellack (Eds.), *The clinical psychology handbook.* New York: Pergamon Press.

BUTCHER, J. N., & KELLER, L. S. (1984). Objective personality assessment. In G. Goldst & M. Hersen (Eds.), *Handbook of psychological assessment.* New York: Pergamon Press.

BUTLER, R. N. (1975). *Why survive? Being old in America.* New York: Harper & Row.

BYCK, R. (ED.). (1974). *Cocaine papers by Sigmund Freud.* New York: Stonehill.

BYRNE, D. G., & ROSENMAN, R. H. (1986). The type A behaviour pattern as a precursor to stressful life-events: A confluence of coronary risks. *British Journal of Medical Psychology, 59,* 75–82.

BYRNE, G. (1988). Nicotine likened to cocaine, heroin. *Science, 240,* 1143.

CADDY, G. R. (1982). A multivariate approach to restricted drinking. In W. M. Hay & P. E. Nathan (Eds.), *Clinical case studies in the behavioral treatment of alcoholism.* New York: Plenum.

CADE, J. F. J. (1949). Lithium salts in the treatment of psychotic excitement. *Medical Journal of Australia, 36,* 349–352.

CADORET, R. J., & TANNA, V. L. (1977). Genetics of affective disorders. In G. Usdin (Ed.), *Depression: Clinical, biological, and psychological perspectives*. New York: Brunner/Mazel.

CADORET, R. J., & WINOKUR, G. (1975). Genetic studies of affective disorders. In F. F. Flach & S. C. Draghi (Eds.), *The nature and treatment of depression*. New York: Wiley.

CADY, S. (1973, January 21). Twenty-three men on life raft, one bet from disaster. *New York Times*, p. 7.

CAHALAN, D. (1978a). Implications of American drinking practices and attitudes for prevention and treatment of alcoholism. In G. A. Marlatt & P. E. Nathan (Eds.), *Behavioral approaches to alcoholism*. New Brunswick, NJ: Rutgers Center for Alcohol Studies.

CAHALAN, D. (1978b). Subcultural differences in drinking behavior in U.S. national surveys and selected European studies. In P. E. Nathan, G. A. Marlatt, & T. Liberg (Eds.), *Alcoholism: New directions in behavioral research and treatment*. New York: Plenum.

CAHOON, D. D. (1968). Symptom substitution and the behavior therapies: A reappraisal. *Psychological Bulletin, 69*, 149–156.

CAIN, D. J. (1986). What does it mean to be "person-centered"? *Person-centered Review, 1*, 251–255.

CALDER, N. (1971). *The mind of man*. New York: Viking Press.

CALLAHAN, E. J. (1980). Alternative strategies in the treatment of narcotic addiction: A review. In W. R. Miller (Ed.), *The addictive behaviors: Treatment of alcoholism, drug abuse, smoking, and obesity*. Oxford: Pergamon Press.

CAMERON, N. A. (1943). The paranoid pseudo-community. *American Journal of Sociology, 49*, 32–38.

CAMERON, N. A. (1963). *Personality development and psychopathology: A dynamic approach*. Boston: Houghton Mifflin.

CAMPBELL, S. B., & STEINERT, Y. (1978). Comparisons of rating scales of child psychopathology in clinical and nonclinical samples. *Journal of Consulting and Clinical Psychology, 46*, 358–359.

CANCRO, R. (1979). The genetic studies of the schizophrenic syndrome: A review of their clinical implications. In L. Bellak (Ed.), *Disorders of the Schizophrenic syndrome*. New York: Basic Books.

CANCRO, R. (1985). Overview of affective disorders. In H. I. Kaplan & B. J. Sadock (Eds.), *Comprehensive textbook of psychiatry* (Vol. 1) (4th ed.). Baltimore: Williams & Wilkins.

CANNON, W. (1915). *Bodily changes in pain, hunger, fear, and rage*. New York: Appleton–Century.

CANNON, W. (1963). *Bodily changes in pain, hunger, fear, and rage* (2nd ed.). New York: Harper & Row.

CAPÉRAÀ, P., CÔTE, R., & THIVIERGE, J. (1985). Hyperactivity: Comment on Trites' article. *Journal of Child Psychology and Psychiatry and Allied Disciplines, 26*, 485–486.

CAPLAN, L. (1984, July 2). Annals of law: The insanity defense. *New Yorker*, pp. 45–46, 48–52, 54–78.

CAPRIO, F. (1961). Fetishism. In A. Ellis & A. Abarbanel (Eds.), *Encyclopedia of sexual behavior* (Vol. 1). New York: Hawthorn.

CARDOZO, B. (1921). *The nature of the judicial process*. New Haven: Yale University Press.

CARNEY, F. L. (1981). Residential treatment programs for antisocial personality disorders. In W. H. Reid (Ed.), *The treatment of antisocial syndromes*. New York: Van Nostrand Reinhold.

CARPENTER, W. T., JR. (1984). A perspective on the psychotherapy of schizophrenia project. *Schizophrenia Bulletin, 10*, 599–603.

CARPENTER, W. T., STRAUSS, J. S., & BARTKO, J. J. (1973). Flexible system for the diagnosis of schizophrenia: Report from the WHO International Pilot Study of Schizophrenia, *Science, 179*, 1275–1278.

CARROLL, E. (1977). The plant and its use. In R. C. Petersen & R. C. Stillman (Eds.), *Cocaine: 1977* (NIDA Research Monograph No. 13). Washington, DC: U.S. Government Printing Office.

CASEY, R. J., & BERMAN, J. S. (1985). The outcome of psychotherapy with children. *Psychological Bulletin, 98*, 388–400.

CATTELL, J. McK. (1890). Mental tests and measurement. *Mind, 15*, 373–380.

CAULDWELL, D. O. (1949). Psychopathia transsexualis. *Sexology, 16*, 274–280.

CAUTELA, J. R. (1967). Covert sensitization. *Psychological Record, 20*, 459–468.

CAUTELA, J. R. (1969). Behavior therapy and self-control: Technique and implications. In C. M. Franks (Ed.), *Behavior therapy: Appraisal and status*. New York: McGraw–Hill.

CAUTELA, J. R. (1970a). Covert reinforcement. *Behavior, 1*, 35–40.

CAUTELA, J. R. (1970b). The treatment of alcoholism by covert sensitization. *Psychotherapy: Theory, Research, and Practice, 7*, 86–90.

CAUTELA, J. R. (1977). The use of covert conditioning in modifying pain behavior. *Journal of Behaviour Therapy and Experimental Psychiatry, 8*, 45–52.

CAVANAUGH, J. L., JR., ROGERS, R., & WASYLIW, O. E. (1981). Mental illness and antisocial behavior: Treatment approaches. In W. H. Reid (Ed.), *The treatment of antisocial syndromes*. New York: Van Nostrand Reinhold.

CENTERS FOR DISEASE CONTROL (1987). *Morbidity, Mortality Weekly Report, 36*, 393.

CENTERWALL, W. R., & CENTERWALL, S. A. (1961). Phenylketonuria (Folling's disease): The story of its discovery. *Journal of the History of Medicine and Allied Sciences, 16*, 292–296.

CENTERWALL, W. R., & CENTERWALL, S. A. (1972). *Phenylketonuria: An inherited metabolic disorder associated with mental retardation* (rev. ed.). Washington, DC: U.S. Government Printing Office.

CERLETTI, U., & BINI, L. (1938). L'elettroshock [Electric shock]. *Archivio Generale di Neurologia, 19*, 266–268.

CHAMBERS, W. J., PUIG-ANTICH, J., HIRSCH, M., PAEZ, P., AMBROSINI, P. J., TABRIZI, M. A., & DAVIES, M. (1986). The assessment of affective disorders in children and adolescents by semi-structured interview. *Archives of General Psychiatry, 42*, 696–702.

CHAMBLESS, D. K., & GOLDSTEIN, A. J. (1979). Behavioral psychotherapy. In R. J. Corsini (Ed.), *Current psychotherapies* (2nd ed.). Itasca, IL: Peacock.

CHANEY, R. H., EYMAN, R. K., & MILLER, C. R. (1985). The relationship of congenital heart disease and respiratory infection mortality in patients with Down's syndrome. *Journal of Mental Deficiency Research, 29,* 23–27.

CHAPMAN, A. H. (1976). *Harry Stack Sullivan: The man and his work.* New York: Putnam.

CHAPMAN, L. J., & CHAPMAN, J. P. (1973). *Disordered thought in schizophrenia.* Englewood Cliffs, NJ: Prentice–Hall.

CHESHER, G. B., FRANKS, H. M., HENSLEY, V. R., HENSLEY, W. J., JACKSON, D. M., STARMER, G. A., & TEO, R. K. C. (1976). The interaction of ethanol and delta-9-tetrahydrocannabinol in man. Effects on perceptual, cognitive, and motor functions. *Medical Journal of Australia, 2,* 159–163.

CHESLER, P. (1972). *Women and madness.* New York: Avon.

CHESSER, E. (1971). *The human aspects of sexual deviation.* London: Jarrolas.

CHILDREN'S DEFENSE FUND (1982). Unclaimed children: The failure of public responsibility to children and adolescents in need of mental health services. Washington, DC: U.S. Government Printing Office.

CHILMAN, C. S. (1980). Social and psychological research concerning adolescent children. *Journal of Marriage and the Family, 42,* 793–805.

CHINN, P. C., DREW, C. J., & LOGAN, D. R. (1979). *Mental retardation: A life cycle approach.* St. Louis: Mosby.

CHINN, P. C., & MUELLER, J. M. (1971). Advances in treatment of Rh negative incompatibility of mothers and infants. *Mental Retardation, 9*(1), 12–15.

CHODOFF, P. (1982). Hysteria and women. *American Journal of Psychiatry, 139,* 545–551.

CHRISTENSON, R., & BLAZER, D. (1984). Epidemiology of persecutory ideation in an elderly population in the community. *American Journal of Psychiatry, 141,* 1088–1091.

CIARANELLO, R. D., & PATRICK, R. L. (1977). Catecholamine neuroregulators. In J. D. Barchas, P. A. Berger, R. D. Ciaranello, & G. R. Elliott (Eds.), *Psychopharmacology: From theory to practice.* New York: Oxford University Press.

CLANCY, K., & GOVE, W. (1975). Sex differences in mental illness: An analysis of response bias in self-reports. *American Journal of Sociology, 80,* 205–215.

CLECKLEY, H. (1976). *The mask of sanity* (5th ed.). St. Louis: Mosby.

CLEMMONS, E. R. (1984). The work of Karen Horney. *American Journal of Psychoanalysis, 44,* 242–253.

CLUM, G. A. (1987). Abandon the suicidal: A reply to Szasz. *American Psychologist, 42,* 883–885.

COATES, S., & PERSON, E. S. (1985). Extreme boyhood femininity: Isolated behavior or pervasive disorder? *Journal of the American Academy of Child Psychiatry, 24,* 702–709.

COHEN, A. (1949). *Everyman's Talmud.* New York: Dutton.

COHEN, E. A. (1954). *Human behaviour in the concentration camp.* London: Jonathan Cape.

COHEN, L., & ROTH, S. (1987). The psychological aftermath of rape: Long-term effects and individual differences in recovery. *Journal of Social and Clinical Psychology, 5,* 525–534.

COHEN, S. (1980). Cognitive processes as determinants of environmental stress. In I. Sarason & C. Speilberger (Eds.), *Stress and anxiety* (Vol. 3). Washington, DC: Hemisphere Press.

COHEN, S. (1981). *The substance abuse problems.* New York: Haworth Press.

COHEN, S., GLASS, D. C., & PHILLIPS, S. (1979). Environment and health. In H. E. Freeman, S. Levine, & L. G. Reeder (Eds.), *Handbook of medical sociology.* Englewood Cliffs, NJ: Prentice–Hall.

COHEN, S., & WEINSTEIN, N. (1981). Nonauditory effects of noise on behavior and health. *Journal of Social Issues, 37*(1), 36–70.

COHN, V. (1978, July 19). Many elderly mistakenly labeled "senile," experts say. *Chicago Sun-Times,* p. 20.

COLEMAN, M., & RIMLAND, B. (1976). Familial autism. In M. Coleman (Ed.), *The autistic syndromes.* Amsterdam: North Holland.

COLLINS, G. (1985, June 17). For aged, problem drinking is on the rise. *New York Times,* p. 20.

COMETA, M. S., MORRISON, J. K., & ZISKOVEN, M. (1979). Halfway to where? A critique of research on psychiatric halfway houses. *Journal of Community Psychology, 7,* 23–27.

COMINGS, D. E. (1981). The ups and downs of Huntington disease research. *American Journal of Human Genetics, 33,* 314–317.

CONTE, H. R., PLUTCHIK, R., WILD, K. V., & KARASU, T. B. (1986). Combined psychotherapy and pharmacotherapy for depression. *Archives of General Psychiatry, 43,* 471–479.

COOPER, C. L. (1984). The social–psychological precursors to cancer. *Journal of Human Stress, 10,* 4–11.

COOPER, J. E., & SARTORIUS, N. (1977). Cultural and temporal variations in schizophrenia. *British Journal of Psychiatry, 130,* 50–55.

CORYWELL, W. (1980). A blind family history study of Briquet's syndrome: Further validity of the diagnosis. *Archives of General Psychiatry, 37,* 1266–1269.

CORYWELL, W. (1981). Diagnosis-specific mortality, primary unipolar depression and Briquet's syndrome (somatization disorder). *Archives of General Psychiatry, 38,* 939–942.

COSTELLO, A. J., EDELBROCK, C., KALAS, R., KESSLER, M. S., & KLARIC, S. (1982). *The NIMH diagnostic interview schedule for children.* Pittsburgh: Author.

COSTIN, F. (1976). *Abnormal psychology: A programmed learning aid.* Homewood, IL: Learning Systems–Irwin.

COSTIN, F. (1985). Beliefs about rape and women's social roles. *Archives of Sexual Behavior, 14,* 319–325.

COSTIN, F., & SCHWARZ, N. (1987). Beliefs about rape and women's social roles: A four nations study. *Journal of Interpersonal Violence, 2,* 46–56.

COSTIN, L. B. (1979). *Child welfare: Policies and practice* (2nd ed.). New York: McGraw–Hill.

COSTIN, L. B. (1987). School social work. *Encyclopedia of social work*

(Vol. 2) (18th ed.). Silver Spring, MD: National Association of Social Workers.

COSTIN, L. B., & RAPP, C. R. (1984). *Child welfare: Policies and practice* (3rd ed.). New York: McGraw-Hill.

COURT DENIES RETARDED SPECIAL LEGAL PROTECTION (1985, July 2). *New York Times*, p. 13.

COWDRY, R. W., & GARDNER, D. L. (1988). Pharmacotherapy of borderline personality disorder. *Archives of General Psychiatry, 45,* 111–119.

COWEN, E. L. (1973). Social and community interventions. *Annual Review of Psychology, 24,* 423–472.

COX, W. M., & KLINGER, E. A. (1988). A motivational model of alcoholism. *Journal of Abnormal Psychology, 97,* 168–170.

COYLE, J. T., PRICE, D. L., & DeLONG, M. R. (1983). Alzheimer's disease: A disorder of cortical cholinergic innervation. *Science, 219,* 1184–1190.

COYNE, J. C., ALDWIN, C., & LAZARUS, R. S. (1981). Depression and coping in stressful episodes. *Journal of Abnormal Psychology, 90,* 439–447.

CRANDALL, B. F. (1977). Genetic disorders and mental retardation. *Journal of the American Academy of Child Psychiatry, 16,* 88–108.

CRANDALL, J. W. (1981). A study in pathological nurturance: The marriage of Gustav Mahler. *Clinical Social Work Journal, 9,* 91–100.

CREAK, E. M. (1963). Childhood psychosis: A review of 100 cases. *British Journal of Psychiatry, 109,* 84–89.

CREWDSON, J. (1988). *By silence betrayed: Sexual abuse of children in America.* Boston: Little, Brown.

CROOK, T. H., & MILLER, N. E. (1985). The challenge of Alzheimer's disease. *American Psychologist, 40,* 1245–1250.

CROW, T. J. (1980). Molecular pathology of schizophrenia: More than one disease process? *British Medical Journal, 280,* 66–68.

CROW, T. J. (1985). The two-syndrome concept: Origins and current status. *Schizophrenia Bulletin, 11,* 471–486.

CROWLEY, T. J. (1987). Clinical issues in cocaine abuse. In S. Fisher, A. Raskin, & E. H. Uhlenhuth (Eds.), *Cocaine: Clinical and biobehavioral aspects.* New York: Oxford University Press.

CROWN, S. (1975). "On being sane in insane places": A comment from England. *Journal of Abnormal Psychology, 84,* 453–455.

CSERNANSKY, J. G., HOLMAN, C. A., & HOLLISTER, L. E. (1983). Variability and the dopamine hypothesis. *Schizophrenia Bulletin, 9,* 325–328.

CULLITON, B. J. (1975). XYY: Harvard researcher under fire stops newborn screening. *Science, 188,* 1284–1285.

CULLITON, B. J. (1976a). Genetic screening: States may be writing the wrong kinds of laws. *Science, 191,* 926–929.

CULLITON, B. J. (1976b). Psychosurgery: National commission issues surprisingly favorable report. *Science, 194,* 299–301.

CUMMINGS. J. (1987, October 6). An earthquake aftershock: Calls to mental health triple. *New York Times,* p. 6.

CURLEE-SALISBURY, J. (1977). Perspectives on Alcoholics Anony-

mous. In N. J. Estes & M. E. Hermann (Eds.), *Alcoholism; Development, consequences and interventions.* St. Louis: Mosby.

DAMASIO, A. (1979). The frontal lobes. In K. M. Heilman & E. Valenstein (Eds.), *Clinical neuropsychology.* New York: Oxford University Press.

D'ATRI, D. A. (1975). Psychophysiological responses to crowding. *Environment and Behavior, 7,* 237–250.

DAVANLOO, H. (1979). Techniques of short-term dynamic psychotherapy. *Psychiatric Clinics of North America, 2*(1), 11–22.

DAVANLOO, H. (1980). *Short-term dynamic psychotherapy.* New York: Aronson.

DAVENPORT, C. W. (1986). A follow-up of 10 feminine boys. *Archives of Sexual Behavior, 15,* 511–517.

DAVIS, G. C., BUCHSBAUM, M. S., & BUNNEY, W. E., JR. (1979). Research in endorphins and schizophrenia. *Schizophrenia Bulletin, 9,* 244–250.

DAVIS, J. M., SCHAFFER, C. B., KILLIAN, G. A., KINARD, C., & CHAN, C. (1980). Important issues in the treatment of schizophrenia. *Schizophrenia Bulletin, 6,* 70–87.

DAVIS. L. J. (1980). Rape and older women. In C. G. Warner (Ed.), *Rape and sexual assault: Management and intervention.* Germantown, MD: Aspen Systems.

DAVISON, G. C. (1976). Homosexuality: The ethical challenge. *Journal of Consulting and Clinical Psychology, 44,* 157–162.

DAVISON, G. C. (1978). Not can but ought: The treatment of homosexuality. *Journal of Counseling and Clinical Psychology, 46,* 170–172.

DAVISON, G C., & NEALE, J. M. (1986). *Abnormal psychology: An experimental clinical approach.* New York: Wiley.

DAY, M., & SEMRAD, E. V. (1978). Paranoia and paranoid states. In A. M. Nicholi, Jr. (Ed.), *The Harvard guide to modern psychiatry.* Cambridge, MA: Harvard University Press.

DECKARD, B. S. (1983). *The women's movement: Political, socioeconomic, and psychological issues.* New York: Harper & Row.

DEFENDORF, A. R. (TRANS.). (1902). *Clinical psychiatry: A textbook for students and physicians* (adapted from E. Kraepelin, *Lehrbuch der Psychiatrie,* 6th ed.). New York: Macmillan.

DeFRIES, J. C., & PLOMIN, R. (1978). Behavioral genetics. *Annual Review of Psychology, 29,* 473–515.

deHAAS, P. A. (1986). Attention styles and peer relationships of hyperactive and normal boys and girls. *Journal of Abnormal Child Psychology, 14,* 457–467.

DE LA CRUZ, F., & GERALD, P. S. (EDS.). (1981). *Trisomy 21 (Down's syndrome): Research perspectives.* Baltimore: University Park Press.

DE LA FUENTE, J. R., & ALARCON-SEGOVIA, D. (1980). Depression as expressed in pre-Columbian Mexican art. *American Journal of Psychiatry, 137,* 1095–1098.

DEMAREST, M. (1981, July 6). Cocaine: Middle class high. *Time,* pp. 56–63.

DeMYER, M., PONTIUS, W., NORTON, J., BARTON, S., ALLEN, J., & STEELE, R. (1972). Parental practices and innate activity in autistic and brain damaged infants. *Journal of Autism and Childhood Schizophrenia, 2,* 49–66.

DERSHOWITZ, A. (1973). Abolishing the insanity defense: The most significant feature of the administration's proposed code—an essay. *Criminal Law Bulletin, 9,* 435.

DEW, M. A., BROMET, E. J., BRENT, D., & GREENHOUSE, J. B. (1987). A quantitative literature review of the effectiveness of suicide prevention centers. *Journal of Consulting and Clinical Psychology, 55,* 239–244.

DEWALD, P. A. (1964). *Psychotherapy: A dynamic approach.* New York: Basic Books.

DIELMAN, T. E. (1979). Gambling: A social problem? *Journal of Social Issues, 35,* 36–42.

DIX, G. E. (1983). Special dispositional alternatives for abnormal offenders: Developments in the law. In J. Monahan & H. J. Steadman (Eds.), *Mentally disordered offenders: Perspectives from law and social science.* New York: Plenum.

DIXON, N. F. (1971). *Subliminal perception: The nature of a controversy.* London: McGraw–Hill.

DOHRENWEND, B. P., & DOHRENWEND, B. S. (1974). Social and cultural influences on psychopathology. *Annual Review of Psychology, 25,* 417–452.

DOHRENWEND, B. P., & DOHRENWEND, B. S. (1976). Sex differences in psychiatric disorders. *American Journal of Sociology, 81,* 1447–1471.

DOLE, V. P., NYSWABDER, M. A. (1965). Medical treatment for diacetylmorphine (heroin) addiction—a clinical test with methadone hydrochloride. *Journal of the American Medical Association, 198,* 646–650.

DOLEYS, D. M. (1977). Behavioral treatments for nocturnal enuresis in children: A review of the recent literature. *Psychological Bulletin, 84,* 30–54.

DOLEYS, D. M., WEILER, D., & PEGRAM, V. V. (1982). Special disorders of childhood: Enuresis, encopresis, and sleep disorders. In J. R. Lachenmeyer & M. S. Gibbs (Eds.), *Psychopathology in children.* New York: Gardner Press.

DOLEYS, D. M., & WILLIAMS, S. C. (1977). The use of natural consequences and a make-up period to eliminate school phobic behavior: A case study. *Journal of School Psychology, 15,* 44–50.

DOLLARD, J., & MILLER, N. E. (1950). *Personality and psychotherapy: An analysis in terms of learning, thinking, and culture.* New York: McGraw–Hill.

DONALDSON, S. R., GELENBERG, A. J., & BALDESSARINI, R. J. (1983). The pharmacologic treatment of schizophrenia: A progress report. *Schizophrenia Bulletin, 9,* 504–527.

DONOVAN, D. W., & MARLATT, G. A. (1980). Assessment of expectancies and behaviors associated with alcohol consumption: A cognitive–behavioral approach. *Journal of Studies on Alcohol, 41,* 1153–1185.

Dorland's illustrated medical dictionary (27th ed.). (1988). Philadelphia: Saunders.

DOSTOEVSKY, F. (1913). *The idiot* (C. Garnett, Trans.). London: Heinemann.

DOSTOEVSKY, F. (1972). *The gambler* (V. Teras., Trans., E. Wasiolek, Ed.). Chicago: University of Chicago Press. (Original work published 1866)

DOTT, A. B. (1972). *Effect of marijuana on risk acceptance in a simulated passing task* (Public Health Service Report No. ICRL–RR–71–3). Washington, DC: U.S. Government Printing Office.

DOWN, J. L. H. (1866). Observations on an ethnic classification of idiots. *London Hospital: Clinical Lectures and Reports, 3,* 259–262.

DOYLE, A. C. (1900). The sign of the four. In *Works of A. Conan Doyle* (Vol. 2). New York: Collier. (Original work published 1884)

DRAGUNS, J. G. (1973). Resocialization into culture: The complexities of taking a worldwide view of psychotherapy. In R. W. Brislin, S. Bochner, & W. J. Lonner (Eds.), *Cross-cultural perspectives on learning.* New York: Halstead.

DRAGUNS, J. G. (1980). Psychological disorders of clinical severity. In H. C. Triandis & J. G. Draguns (Eds.), *Handbook of cross-cultural psychology: Vol. 6. Psychopathology.* Boston: Allyn & Bacon.

DRAGUNS, J. G. (1981). Cross-cultural counseling and psychotherapy: History, issues, current status. In A. J. Marsella & P. B. Pedersen (Eds.), *Cross-cultural counseling and psychotherapy.* New York: Pergamon Press.

DRAGUNS, J. G., & PHILLIPS, L. (1971). *Psychiatric classification and diagnosis: An overview and critique.* Morristown, NJ: General Learning Press.

DREW, R. H. (1986). Neuropsychological deficits in active licensed professional boxers. *Journal of Clinical Psychology, 42,* 520–525.

DRUGS THAT CAUSE SEXUAL DYSFUNCTION. (1983). *Medical Letter on Drugs and Therapeutics, 25*(64), 73–76.

DRYER, P. I., & CHURCH, R. W. (1970). Reinforcement of shock induced fighting. *Psychonomic Science, 18,* 147–148.

DUGAS, L., & MOUTIER, F. (1911). *La dépersonnalisation* [Depersonalization]. Paris: Felix Alcan.

DULCAN, M. K. (1986). Comprehensive treatment of children and adolescents with attention deficit disorders: The state of the art. *Clinical Psychology Review, 6,* 539–569.

DUNBAR, H. F. (1935). *Emotions and bodily changes.* New York: Columbia University Press.

DUNBAR, H. F. (1938). *Emotions and bodily changes* (2nd ed.). New York: Columbia University Press.

DUNBAR, H. F. (1943). *Psychosomatic diagnosis.* New York: Hoeber.

DUNBAR, H. F. (1946). *Emotions and bodily changes* (3rd ed.). New York: Columbia University Press.

DUNHAM, H. W. (1976). Society, culture, and mental disorder. *Archives of General Psychiatry, 33,* 147–156.

DUNN, M. (1984, February 28). Social phobia: Fear of embarrassment debilitates sufferers. *Champaign–Urbana News-Gazette,* p. B–7.

DURATION OF PENILE INTROMISSION AND FEMALE ORGASM RATES (1982). *Medical Aspects of Human Sexuality, 16*(2), p. 32.

DURELL, J., & ARCHER, E. G. (1976). Plasma proteins in schizophrenia: A review. *Schizophrenia Bulletin, 2,* 147–159.

DURHAM V. UNITED STATES. (1954). 214 F.2d 862 (D.C. Cir.).

EADINGTON, W. R. (ED.). (1976). *Gambling and society: Interdisciplinary studies on the subject of gambling.* Springfield, IL: Charles C Thomas.

EATON, W. W., SIGAL, J. J., & WEINFELD, M. (1982). Impairment in Holocaust survivors after 33 years: Data from an unbiased community sample. *American Journal of Psychiatry, 139,* 773–777.

EBER, M. (1980). Gender identity conflicts in male transsexualism. *Bulletin of the Menninger Clinic, 1,* 31–38.

ECKERT, E. D., BOUCHARD, T. J., BOHLEN, J., & HESTON, L. L. (1986). Homosexuality in monozygotic twins reared apart. *British Journal of Psychiatry, 148,* 421–425.

ECKHOLM, E. (1986, October 18). Heterosexuals and AIDS: The concern is growing. *New York Times,* pp. 25, 30.

EDELBROCK, C., & COSTELLO, A. J. (1984). Structured psychiatric interviews for children and adolescents. In G. Goldstein & M. Hersen (Eds.), *Handbook of psychological assessment.* New York: Pergamon Press.

EDGERTON, R. B. (1979). *Mental retardation.* Cambridge, MA: Harvard University Press.

EDUCATION OF HANDICAPPED CHILDREN: IMPLEMENTATION OF PART B OF THE EDUCATION OF THE HANDICAPPED ACT. (1977, August 23). *Federal Register, 42*(163), Part II.

EGAN, J. H., & VANDERSALL, T. A. (1982). Psychoanalytic psychotherapies with children. In J. R. Lachenmeyer & M. S. Gibbs (Eds.). *Psychopathology in children.* New York: Gardner Press.

EISDORFER, C. (1977). Intelligence and cognition in the aged. In E. W. Busse & E. Pfeiffer (Eds.), *Behavior and adaptation in late life.* Boston: Little, Brown.

EISENBERG, L. (1969). Child psychiatry: The past quarter century. *American Journal of Orthopsychiatry, 39,* 369–401.

ELIOT, T. (1935). *Religion and literature.* In R. T. Tripp (1970), *International thesaurus of quotations.* New York: Crowell.

ELLENBERGER, H. F. (1970). *The discovery of the unconscious: The history and evolution of dynamic psychiatry.* New York: Basic Books.

ELLIOTT, F. A. (1978). Neurological aspects of antisocial behavior. In W. H. Reid (Ed.), *The psychopath: A comprehensive study of antisocial disorders and behavior.* New York: Brunner/Mazel.

ELLIS, A. (1987a). A sadly neglected cognitive element in depression. *Cognitive Therapy and Research, 11,* 121–145.

ELLIS, A. (1987b). The impossibility of achieving consistently good mental health. *American Psychologist, 42,* 364–375.

ELLIS, A. (1980). Treatment of erectile dysfunction. In R. Leiblum & L. A. Pervin (Eds.), *Principles and practice of sex therapy.* New York: Guilford Press.

ELLIS, A., & BERNARD, M. E. (EDS.). (1985). *Clinical applications of rational–emotive therapy.* New York: Plenum.

ELLIS, L., & AMES, M. A. (1987). Neurohormonal functioning and sexual orientation: A theory of homosexuality–heterosexuality. *Psychological Bulletin, 101,* 233–258.

EME, R. F. (1979). Sex differences in childhood psychopathology: A review. *Psychological Bulletin, 86,* 574–595.

EMMELKAMP, P. M. G. (1986). Behavior therapy with adults. In S. L. Garfield & A. E. Bergin (Eds.), *Handbook of psychotherapy and behavior change* (3rd ed.). New York: Wiley.

ENDICOTT, J., & SPITZER, R. L. (1978). A diagnostic interview: The schedule for affective disorders and schizophrenia. *Archives of General Psychiatry, 35,* 837–844.

ENGELS, W. D., & WITTKOWER, E. D. (1980). Skin disorders. In H. I. Kaplan, A. M. Freedman, & B. J. Sadock (Eds.), *Comprehensive textbook of psychiatry* (Vol. 2) (3rd ed.). Baltimore: Williams & Wilkins.

ENGELSMANN, P. (1982). Culture and depression. In I. Al-Issa (Ed.), *Culture and psychopathology.* Baltimore: University Park Press.

ENGLISH, H. B. (1929). Three cases of the "conditioned fear response." *Journal of Abnormal and Social Psychology, 34,* 221–225,

ENNIS, B., & SIEGEL, L. (1973). *The rights of mental patients: The basic ACLU guide to a mental patient's rights.* New York: Avon.

ENNIS, J., & EMBRY, R. D. (1978). *The rights of mental patients.* New York: Avon.

EPHRON, H. D. (1957). *Re* early conditioning. *American Psychologist, 12,* 158.

EPSTEIN, Y. M. (1981). Crowding, stress, and human behavior. *Journal of Social Issues, 37,* 126–144.

ERDBERG, P., & EXNER, J. E. (1984). *Rorschach assessment.* In G. Goldstein & M. Hersen (Eds.). *Handbook of psychological assessment.* New York: Pergamon Press.

ERDMAN, H. P., KLEIN, M. H., & GREIST, J. H. (1985). Direct computer interviewing. *Journal of Consulting and Clinical Psychology, 53,* 760–773.

ERIKSON, E. H. (1959). Identity and the life cycle: Selected papers. *Psychological Issues, 1,* 50–100.

ERIKSON, E. H. (1963). *Childhood and society* (rev. ed.). New York: Norton.

ERIKSON, E. H. (1964). *Insight and responsibility.* New York: Norton.

ERIKSON, E. H. (1968). *Identity: Youth and crisis.* New York: Norton.

ERRERA, P. (1962). Some historical aspects of the concept, phobia. *Psychiatric Quarterly, 36,* 325–336.

ETHICS COMMITTEE OF THE AMERICAN PSYCHOLOGICAL ASSOCIATION (1988). Trends in ethics cases, common pitfalls, and published resources. *American Psychologist, 43,* 564–572.

EVANS, D. R. (1970). Exhibitionism. In C. G. Costello (Ed.), *Symptoms of psychopathology: A handbook.* New York: Wiley.

EVANS, R. B. (1969). Childhood parental relationships of homosexual men. *Journal of Consulting and Clinical Psychology, 33,* 129–135.

EVERLY, G. S. (1986). A biopsychosocial analysis of psychosomatic disease. In T. Millon & G. L. Klerman (Eds.), *Contemporary directions in psychopathology: Toward the DSM-IV.* New York: Guilford Press.

EXCERPTS FROM COURT OPINION. (1985, February 27). *New York Times*, p. 10.

EXNER, J. E. (1974). *The Rorschach: A comprehensive system* (Vol. 1). New York: Wiley.

EXNER, J. E. (1978). *The Rorschach, a comprehensive system: Vol. 2. Current research and advanced interpretation.* New York: Wiley.

EXNER, J. E. (1980). But it's only an inkblot. *Journal of Personality Assessment, 44,* 563–577.

EYMAN, R. K., & BORTHWICK, S. A. (1980). Patterns of care for mentally retarded persons. *Mental Retardation, 18,* 63–66.

EYMAN, R. K., BORTHWICK, S. A., & MILLER, C. (1981). Trends in maladaptive behavior of mentally retarded persons placed in community and institutional settings. *American Journal of Mental Deficiency, 85,* 473–477.

EYSENCK, H. J. (1952). The effects of psychotherapy: An evaluation. *Journal of Consulting Psychology, 16,* 319–324.

EYSENCK, H. J. (1966). *The effects of psychotherapy.* New York: International Science Press.

EYSENCK, H. J. (1970). A dimensional system of psychodiagnosis. In A. R. Mahrer (Ed.), *New approaches to personality classification.* New York: Columbia University Press.

EYSENCK, H. J. (1986). A critique of contemporary classification and diagnosis. In T. Millon & G. L. Klerman (Eds.), *Contemporary directions in psychopathology: Toward the DSM–IV.* New York: Guilford Press.

EYSENCK, H. J., & RACHMAN, S. (1965). *The causes and cures of neurosis: An introduction to modern behavior therapy based on learning theory and the principles of conditioning.* San Diego: Robert R. Knapp.

EYSENCK, H. J., & WILSON, G. D. (1973). *The experimental study of Freudian theories.* London: Methuen.

FACTS ABOUT AIDS AND DRUG ABUSE. (1986). Washington, DC: American Red Cross & U.S. Public Health Service.

FAIRBURN, C. G. (1980). Self-induced vomiting. *Journal of Psychosomatic Research, 24,* 193–197.

FAIRBURN, C. G. (1981). A cognitive behavioural approach to the treatment of bulimia. *Psychological Medicine, 11,* 707–711.

FAIRBURN, C. G. (1983). The place of a cognitive–behavioral approach in the management of bulimia. In P. L. Darby (Ed.), *Anorexia nervosa: Recent developments in research.* New York: Alan R. Liss.

FAIRBURN, C. G., & COOPER, P. J. (1982). Self-induced vomiting and bulimia nervosa: An undetected problem. *British Medical Journal, 284,* 1153–1155.

FAIRBURN, C. G., COOPER, Z., & COOPER, P. J. (1986). The clinical features and maintenance of bulimia nervosa. In K. D. Brownell & J. P. Forcyt (Eds.), *Handbook of eating disorders.* New York: Basic Books.

FALLOON, I. R. H., & LIBERMAN, R. P. (1983). Interactions between drug and psychosocial therapy in schizophrenia. *Schizophrenia Bulletin, 9,* 543–554.

FANCHER, R. E. (1973). *Psychoanalytic psychology: The development of Freud's thought.* New York: Norton.

FARAONE, S. (1982). Psychiatry and political repression in the Soviet Union. *American Psychologist, 37,* 1105–1112.

FARRELL, B. (1969). *Pat and Roald.* New York: Random House.

FAUST, D., & ZISKIN, J. (1988). The expert witness in psychology and psychiatry. *Science, 241,* 31–35.

FAWCETT, J., MAAS, J. W., & DEKIRMENJIAN, H. (1972). Depression and MHPG excretion: Response to dextroamphetamine and tricyclic antidepressants. *Archives of General Psychiatry, 26,* 246–251.

FEIFER, G. (1981, February). Russian disorders. *Harper's,* pp. 41–55.

FELDMAN, G. M. (1976). The effect of biofeedback training on respiratory resistance of asthmatic children. *Psychosomatic Medicine, 38,* 27–34.

FENICHEL, O. (1945). *The psychoanalytic theory of neurosis.* New York: Norton.

FENTON, F. R., TESSLER, L., & STRUENING, E. L. (1979). A comparative trial of home and hospital psychiatric care. One-year follow-up. *Archives of General Psychiatry, 36,* 1073–1079.

FENTON, W. S., & MCGLASHAN, T. H. (1987). Prognostic scales for chronic schizophrenia. *Schizophrenia Bulletin, 13,* 277–286.

FERENCZI, S. (1951). *Further contribution to the theory and techniques of psychoanalysis.* New York: Basic Books.

FESBACH, S. (1971). Dynamics of morality of violence and aggression: Some psychological considerations. *American Psychologist, 26,* 281–291.

FIEVE, R. R. (1976). Therapeutic uses of lithium and rubidium. In L. L. Simpson (Ed.), *Drug treatment of mental disorders.* New York: Raven Press.

FINGARETTE, H. (1972). *The meaning of criminal insanity.* Berkeley: University of California Press.

FIGLEY, C. R. (ED.). (1985). *Trauma and its wake: The study and treatment of post-traumatic stress disorder.* New York: Brunner/Mazel.

FINGARETTE, H., & HASSE, A. F. (1979). *Mental disabilities and criminal responsibility.* Berkeley: University of California Press.

FISCHER, G. J. (1986). College student attitudes toward forcible date rape: I. Cognitive predictors. *Archives of Sexual Behavior, 15,* 457–466.

FISHER, K. (1986a, February). DSM-III-R. *APA Monitor,* pp. 17, 18, 24.

FISHER, K. (1986b, August). DSM-III-R protest. *APA Monitor,* pp. 15–16.

FISHER, S., & GREENBERG, R. P. (1977). *The scientific credibility of Freud's theories and therapy.* New York: Basic Books.

FLYNN, R. J., & NITSCH, K. E. (EDS.) (1980). *Normalization, social integration, and community services.* Baltimore: University Park Press.

FOA, E. B., STEKETEE, G. S., & ASCHER, M. (1980). Systematic desensitization. In E. B. Foa & A. Goldstein (Eds.), *Handbook of behavioral interventions: A clinical guide*. New York: Wiley.

FONTANA, A. F. (1966). Familial etiology of schizophrenia: Is a scientific methodology possible? *Psychological Bulletin, 66,* 214–227.

FORDHAM, M. (1978). *Jungian psychotherapy: A study of analytical psychology*. New York: Wiley.

FOWLER, R. C., RICH, C. L., & YOUNG, D. (1986). San Diego suicide study: II. Substance abuses in young cases. *Archives of General Psychiatry, 43,* 962–965.

FOY, D. W., SIPPRELLE, R. C., RUEGER, D. B., & CARROLL, E. M. (1984). Etiology of postraumatic stress disorder in Vietnam veterans: Analysis of premilitary, military, and combat exposure influences. *Journal of Consulting and Clinical Psychology, 52,* 79–87.

FRAMPTON, M. (1974). *Overcoming agoraphobia: Coping with the world outside*. New York: St. Martin's Press.

FRANK, J. D. (1972). The bewildering world of psychotherapy. *Journal of Social Issues, 28,* 27–43.

FRANK, J. (1979). The present status of outcome studies. *Journal of Consulting and Clinical Psychology, 47,* 310–316.

FRANKL, V. E. (1959). *From death camp to existentialism: A psychiatrist's path to new therapy*. Boston: Beacon Press.

FRANKL, V. E. (1963). *Man's search for meaning: An introduction to logotherapy*. New York: Washington Square Press.

FRANKL, V. E. (1975a). Paradoxical intention and dereflection. *Psychotherapy: Theory, Research, and Practice, 12,* 226–237.

FRANKL, V. E. (1975b). *The unconscious god: Psychotherapy and theology*. New York: Simon & Schuster.

FRANKS, C. M., & BARBRACK, C. R. (1983). Behavior therapy with adults: An integrative perspective. In M. Hersen, A. E. Kazdin, & A. S. Bellack (Eds.), *The clinical psychology handbook*. New York: Pergamon Press.

FRAZER, A. (1975). Adrenergic responses in depression: Implications for a receptor defect. In J. Mendels (Ed.), *The psychobiology of depression*. New York: Spectrum.

FREEDMAN, A. M., KAPLAN, H. I., & SADOCK, B. J. (1976). *Modern synopsis of comprehensive textbook of psychiatry* (2nd ed.). Baltimore: Williams & Wilkins.

FREEDMAN, J. L., HESHKA, S., & LEVY, A. (1975). Population density and pathology: Is there a relationship? *Journal of Experimental Social Psychology, 11,* 539–552.

FREEMAN, D. R. (1982). *Marital crisis and short-term counseling: A casebook*. New York: Free Press.

FREEMAN, T. (1960). On the psychopathology of schizophrenia. *Journal of Mental Science, 106,* 925–937.

FREEMAN, W., & WATTS, J. (1942). *Psychosurgery*. Springfield, IL: Charles C Thomas.

FREESE, A. (1981, May–June). How to cope with Alzheimer's disease. *NRTA Journal,* p. 8.

FREUD, A. (1946). *The ego and the mechanisms of defence* (C. Baines, Trans.). New York: International Universities Press.

FREUD, A. (1966). *Normality and pathology in childhood: Assessments of development* (International Psycho-analytic Library, No. 69). London: Hogarth Press and the Institute of Psychoanalysis.

FREUD, S. (1936). *The problem of anxiety* (H. A. Bunker, Trans.). New York: Psychoanalytic Quarterly Press and Norton.

FREUD, S. (1938). The interpretation of dreams. In A. A. Brill (Ed. and Trans.), *The basic writings of Sigmund Freud*. New York: Modern Library. (Original work published 1900)

FREUD, S. (1949). *An outline of psychoanalysis* (J. Strachey, Trans.). New York: Norton. (Original work published 1940)

FREUD, S. (1955). Analysis of a phobia in a five-year-old-boy. In J. Strachey (Ed. and Trans.), *The standard edition of the complete psychological works of Sigmund Freud* (Vol. 10). London: Hogarth Press. (Original work published 1909)

FREUD, S. (1955). On transformations of instinct as exemplified in anal erotism. In J. Strachey (Ed. and Trans.), *The standard edition of the complete psychological works of Sigmund Freud* (Vol. 17). London: Hogarth Press. (Original work published 1917)

FREUD, S. (1957). Narcissism, an introduction: Part II. Narcissism in organic disease, hypochondria, and erotic life. In J. Strachey (Ed. and Trans.), *The standard edition of the complete psychological works of Sigmund Freud* (Vol. 17). London: Hogarth Press. (Original work published 1914)

FREUD, S. (1957). Mourning and melancholia. In J. Strachey (Ed. and Trans.), *The standard edition of the complete psychological works of Sigmund Freud* (Vol. 14). London: Hogarth Press. (Original work published 1917)

FREUD, S. (1958). Psychoanalytic notes on an autobiographical account of a case of paranoia (dementia paranoides). In J. Strachey (Ed. and Trans.), *The standard edition of the complete psychological works of Sigmund Freud* (Vol. 12). London: Hogarth Press. (Original work published 1911)

FREUD, S. (1958). The disposition to obsessional neurosis: A contribution to the problem of choice of neurosis. In J. Strachey (Ed. and Trans.), *The standard edition of the complete psychological works of Sigmund Freud* (Vol. 12). London: Hogarth Press. (Original work published 1913)

FREUD, S. (1959). Character and anal erotism. In J. Strachey (Ed. and Trans.), *The standard edition of the complete psychological works of Sigmund Freud* (Vol. 9). London: Hogarth Press. (Original work published 1908)

FREUD, S. (1960). *The psychopathology of everyday life* (J. Strachey, Ed., A. Tyson, Trans.). New York: Norton. (Original work published 1901)

FREUD, S. (1961a). The dissolution of the Oedipus complex. In J. Strachey (Ed. and Trans.), *The standard edition of the complete psychological works of Sigmund Freud* (Vol. 19). London: Hogarth Press. (Original work published 1924)

FREUD, S. (1961b). The economic problem of masochism. In J. Strachey (Ed. and Trans.), *The standard edition of the complete psychological works of Sigmund Freud* (Vol. 19). London: Hogarth Press. (Original work published 1924)

FREUD, S. (1961). Some psychical consequences of the anatomical distinction between the sexes. In J. Strachey (Ed. and Trans.), *The* standard edition of the complete psychological works of Sigmund Freud (Vol. 19). London: Hogarth Press. (Original work published 1925)

FREUD, S. (1961). The future of an illusion. In J. Strachey (Ed. and Trans.), The standard edition of the complete psychological works of Sigmund Freud (Vol. 21). London: Hogarth Press. (Original work published 1927)

FREUD, S. (1961). Dostoevsky and parricide. In J. Strachey (Ed. and Trans.), The standard edition of the complete psychological works of Sigmund Freud (Vol. 21). London: Hogarth Press. (Original work published 1928)

FREUD, S. (1962). Early psycho-analytic publications: Further remarks on the neuro-psychoses of defense. In J. Strachey (Ed. and Trans.), The standard edition of the complete psychological works of Sigmund Freud (Vol. 3). London: Hogarth Press. (Original work published 1894)

FREUD, S. (1962). The ego and the id (J. Strachey, Ed., J. Riviere, Trans.). New York: Norton. (Original work published 1923)

FREUD, S. (1962). Civilization and its discontents. (J. Strachey, Ed. and Trans.). New York: Norton. (Original work published 1930)

FREUD, S. (1965). New introductory lectures on psychoanalysis. (J. Strachey, Ed. and Trans.). New York: Norton. (Original work published 1933)

FREUD, S. (1967). A general introduction to psychoanalysis. New York: Washington Square Press. (Original work published 1920)

FREUD, S. (1969). The question of lay analysis. (J. Strachey, Ed. and Trans.). New York: Norton. (Original work published 1927)

FRIEDHOFF, A. J. (1983). A strategy for developing novel drugs for the treatment of schizophrenia. Schizophrenia Bulletin, 9, 555–562.

FRIEDMAN, H. S., & BOOTH-KEWLEY, S. (1987). The "disease-prone" personality: A meta-analytic view of the construct. American Psychologist, 42, 539–555.

FRIEDMAN, M., & ROSENMAN, R. H. (1959). Association of specific overt behavior pattern with blood and cardiovascular findings: Blood cholesterol level, blood clotting time, incidence of arcus senilus, and clinical coronary artery disease. Journal of the American Medical Association, 169, 1286–1296.

FRIEDMAN, M., & ROSENMAN, R. H. (1960). Overt behavior pattern in coronary disease: Detection of overt behavior pattern A in patients with coronary disease by a new psychophysiological procedure. Journal of the American Medical Association, 173, 1320–1325.

FRIEDMAN, P. R. (1976). The rights of mentally retarded persons: The basic ACLU guide for the mentally retarded persons' rights. New York: Avon.

FROMM, E. (1947). Man for himself. New York: Holt, Rinehart & Winston.

FROMM, E. (1955). The sane society. New York: Holt, Rinehart & Winston.

FULLER, G. D. (1978). Current status of biofeedback in clinical practice. American Psychologist, 33, 38–48.

FULLER, P. (1977). Gambling: A secular "religion" for the obses-sional neurotic? In J. Halliday & P. Fuller (Eds.), The psychology of gambling. New York: Penguin.

FURNHAM, A., BOROVOY, A. & HENLEY, S. (1986). Type A behaviour pattern, the recall of positive personality information, and self-evaluation. British Journal of Medical Psychology, 59, 365–374.

FYER, M. R., FRANCES, A. J., SULLIVAN, T., HURT, S. W., & CLARKIN, J. (1988). Comorbidity of borderline personality disorder. Archives of General Psychiatry, 45, 348–352.

GAGNON, J. H. (1977). Human sexualities. Glenview, IL: Scott, Foresman.

GAGNON, J. H., & SIMON, W. (1973). Sexual conduct: The social origins of human sexuality. Chicago: Aldine.

GALLANT, D. M. (1987). Alcoholism: A guide to diagnosis, intervention, and treatment. New York: Norton.

GALLO, P. S. (1978). Meta-analysis—A mixed meta-phor? [Comment]. American Psychologist, 33, 515–517.

GALTON, F. (1883). Inquiries into human faculty and its development. London: Dent.

GARDNER, H. (1974). The shattered mind: The person after brain damage. New York: Random House.

GARFIELD, S. L., & BERGIN, A. E. (1986). Introduction and historical overview. In S. L. Garfield & A. E. Bergin (Eds.), Handbook of psychotherapy and behavior change (3rd ed.). New York: Wiley.

GARGAN, E. A. (1984, June 13). Limit on insanity defense is voted in Albany. New York Times, pp. 1, 47.

GARNER, D. M. (1986). Cognitive–behavior therapy for eating disorders. Clinical Psychologist, 39, 36–39.

GARRISON, F. H. (1924). An introduction to the history of medicine (3rd ed.). Philadelphia: Saunders.

GARRISON, F. H. (1929). An introduction to the history of medicine (4th ed.). Philadelphia: Saunders.

GARTRELL, N. (1986). Psychiatrist–patient sexual contact: Results of a national survey: I. Prevalence. American Journal of Psychiatry, 143, 1126–1131.

GATH, A. (1978). Down's syndrome and the family: The early years. London: Academic Press.

GAY, P. (1988). Freud: A life for our time. New York: Norton.

GEBHARD, P. H. (1976). Fetishism and sadomasochism. In M. S. Weinberg (Ed.), Sex research: Studies from the Kinsey Institute. New York: Oxford University Press.

GEEN, R. G., & PIGG, R (1970). Acquisition of aggressive response and its generalization to verbal behavior. Journal of Personality and Social Psychology, 15, 165–170.

GEIS, G. (1977). Forcible rape: An introduction. In D. Chappell, R. Geis, and G. Geis (Eds.), Forcible rape: The crime, the victim, and the offender. New York: Columbia University Press.

GELFAND, D. E. (1984). The aging network: Programs and services (2nd ed.). New York: Springer.

GENTRY, W. D. (1984). Behavioral medicine. In W. D. Gentry (Ed.), Handbook of behavioral medicine. New York: Guilford Press.

GEORGE, L., & NEUFELD, R. W. J. (1985). Cognition and symptomatology in schizophrenia. *Schizophrenia Bulletin, 11,* 264–285.

GERBER, R. J. (1984). *The insanity defense.* Port Washington, NY: Associated Faculty Press.

GESTEN, E. L., & JASON, L. A. (1987). Social and community intervention. *Annual Review of Psychology, 38,* 427–460.

GIBBS, M. S. (1982). Identification and classification of child psychopathology: A pragmatic analysis of traditional approaches. In J. R. Lachenmeyer & M. G. Gibbs (Eds.), *Psychopathology in childhood.* New York: Gardner Press.

GIBSON, D. (1978). *Down's syndrome: The psychology of mongolism.* Cambridge: Cambridge University Press.

GITTELMAN, R., MANNUZZA, S., SHENKER, R., & BONAGURA, N. (1985). Hyperactive boys almost grown up. *Archives of General Psychiatry, 42,* 937–947.

GITTELMAN-KLEIN, R. (1977). Definition and methodology concerning depressive illness in children. In J. G. Schulterbrandt & A. Raskin (Eds.), *Depression in childhood: Diagnosis, treatment, and conceptual models.* New York: Raven Press.

GITTELMAN-KLEIN, R., & KLEIN, D. F. (1975). Are behavioral and psychometric changes related in methylphenidate-treated, hyperactive children? *International Journal of Mental Health, 4,* 182–198.

GLANZER, M., & CLARK, E. O. (1979). Cerebral mechanisms of information storage: The problem of memory. In H. S. Gazzaniga (Ed.), *Handbook of behavioral neurobiology: Vol. 2. Neuropsychology.* New York: Plenum.

GLASS, A. L., & HOLYOAK, K. J. (1986). *Cognition* (2nd ed.). New York: Random House.

GLASS, D. C., CONTRADA, R., & SNOW, B. (1980). Stress, type A behavior, and coronary disease. *Weekly Psychology Update, 1,* 2–6.

GLASS, D. C., & SINGER, J. E. (1972). *Urban stress: Experiments on noise and social stressors.* New York: Academic Press.

GODDARD, H. H. (1914). *Feeble mindedness—its causes and consequences.* New York: Macmillan.

GOFFMAN, E. (1963). *Behavior in public places: Notes on the social organization of gatherings.* New York: Free Press.

GOLDBERG, D. C. (1983). The treatment of sexual dysfunctions. In C. E. Walker (Ed.), *The handbook of clinical psychology: Theory, research, and practice.* Homewood, IL: Dow Jones–Irwin.

GOLDBERG, S. C. (1985). Negative and deficit symptoms in schizophrenia do respond to neuroleptics. *Schizophrenia Bulletin, 11,* 453–456.

GOLDBERG, S. C., SCHULZ, S. C., SCHULZ, P. M., RESNICK, R. J., HAMER, R. M., & FRIEDEL, R. O. (1986). Borderline and schizotypal personality disorders treated with low-dose thiothixene vs. placebo. *Archives of General Psychiatry, 43,* 680–686.

GOLDBERGER, L. (1982). Sensory deprivation and overload. In L. Goldberger & S. Bresnitz (Eds.), *Handbook of stress: Theoretical and clinical aspects.* New York: Free Press.

GOLDEN, C. J. (1980). In reply to Adams' "In search of Luria battery: A false start." *Journal of Consulting and Clinical Psychology, 48,* 517–521.

GOLDEN, C. J. (1981). A standardized version of Luria's neuropsychological tests: A quantitative and qualitative approach to neuropsychological evaluation. In S. B. Filskov & T. J. Boll (Eds.), *Handbook of clinical neuropsychology.* New York: Wiley–Interscience.

GOLDEN, C. J., HAMMEKE, T., & PURISCH, A. (1978). Diagnostic validity of the Luria neuropsychological battery. *Journal of Consulting and Clinical Psychology, 46,* 1258–1265.

GOLDEN, C. J., HAMMEKE, T., & PURISCH, A. (1980). *The Luria–Nebraska battery manual.* Los Angeles: Western Psychological Services.

GOLDFRIED, M. R., & DAVISON, G. C. (1976). *Clinical behavior therapy.* New York: Holt, Rinehart & Winston.

GOLDGABER, D., LERMAN, M. I., McBRIDE, O. W., SAFFIOTTI, U., & GAJDUSEK, D. C. (1987). Characterization and chromosomal localization of DNA encoding brain amyloid of Alzheimer's disease. *Science, 235,* 877–884.

GOLDMAN, L. S., & LUCHINS, D. J. (1984). Depression in the spouses of demented patients. *American Journal of Psychiatry, 141,* 1467–1468.

GOLDSTEIN, A. P. (1981). Evaluating expectancy effects in cross-cultural counseling and psychotherapy. In A. J. Marsella & P. B. Pedersen (Eds.), *Cross-cultural counseling and psychotherapy.* New York: Pergamon Press.

GOLDSTEIN, A. P., & STEIN, N. (1978). *Prescriptive psychotherapies.* New York: Pergamon Press.

GOLDSTEIN, G. (1984). Comprehensive neuropsychological assessment batteries. In G. Goldstein & M. Hersen (Eds.), *Handbook of psychological assessment.* New York: Pergamon Press.

GOLDSTEIN, K. (1963). *Human nature in the light of psychopathology.* New York: Schocken.

GOLDSTEIN, M. J. (1984). Schizophrenia: The interaction of family and neuroleptic therapy. In B. D. Beitman & G. L. Klerman (Eds.), *Combining psychotherapy and drug therapy in clinical practice.* Jamaica, NY: Spectrum.

GOLDSTEIN, M. J. (1987). Psychosocial issues. *Schizophrenia Bulletin, 13,* 157–171.

GOLDSTEIN, M. J. (1988). The family and psychopathology. *Annual Review of Psychology, 39,* 283–299.

GOLDSTEIN, M. J., & TUMA, A. H. (EDS.). (1987). High risk research [Special issue]. *Schizophrenia Bulletin, 13*(3).

GOLEMAN, D. (1985, July 2). In the spirit of Jung, analyst seeks therapy nearer art than science. *New York Times,* pp. 19, 22.

GOLEMAN, D. (1987, August 25). Embattled giant of psychology speaks his mind. *New York Times,* p. 17.

GOLIN, S., SWEENEY, P. D., & SCHAEFFER, D. E. (1981). The causality of caused attributions to depression: A cross-lagged panel correlational analysis. *Journal of Abnormal Psychology, 90,* 14–22.

GOMBERG, E. S. (1976). Alcoholism in women. In B. Kissin & H. Begleiter (Eds.), *Social aspects of alcoholism.* New York: Plenum.

GOMBERG, E. W. (1977). Women with alcohol problems. In N. J.

Estes & M. E. Heinemann (Eds.), *Alcoholism: Development, consequences and interventions.* St. Louis: Mosby.

GOODLGLASS, H., & KAPLAN, E. (1979). Assessment of cognitive deficit in the brain-inured patient. In M. S. Gazzaniga (Ed.), *Handbook of behavioral neurobiology: Vol. 2. Neuropsychology.* New York: Plenum.

GOODMAN, P. (1964). *Compulsory mid-education.* New York: Horizon Press.

GOODMAN, P. (1976). *Is alcoholism hereditary?* New York: Oxford University Press.

GOODWIN, D. W. (1985a). Genetic determinants of alcoholism. In J. H. Mendelson & N. K. Mellow (Eds.), *The diagnosis and treatment of alcoholism.* New York: McGraw–Hill.

GOODWIN, D. W. (1985b). Alcoholism and genetics. *Archives of General Psychiatry, 42,* 171–174.

GOODWIN, D. W., JOHNSON, J., MAHER, C., RAPPAPORT, A., & GUZE, S. B. (1969). Why people do not drink: A study of teetotalers. *Comprehensive Psychiatry, 10,* 209–214.

GOODWIN, D. W., SCHULSINGER, F., HERMANSEN, L., GUZE, S. B., & WINOKUR, G. (1975). Alcoholism and the hyperactive child syndrome. *Journal of Nervous and Mental Disease, 160,* 349–353.

GOODWIN, D. W., SCHULSINGER, F., KNOP, J., MEDNICK, S., & GUZE, S. B. (1977a). Alcoholism and depression in adopted-out daughters of alcoholics. *Archives of General Psychiatry, 34,* 751–755.

GOODWIN, D. W., SCHULSINGER, F., KNOP, J., MEDNICK, S., & GUZE, S. B. (1977b). Psychopathology in adopted and nonadopted daughters of alcoholics. *Archives of General Psychiatry, 34,* 1005–1009.

GOODWIN, D. W., SCHULSINGER, F., MOLLER, N., HERMANSEN, L., WINOKUR, G., & GUZE, S. B. (1974). Drinking problems in adopted and nonadopted sons of alcoholics. *Archives of General Psychiatry, 31,* 164–169.

GOODWIN, F. K., & POTTER, W. Z. (1978). The biology of affective illness: Amine neurotransmitters and drug response. In J. O. Cole, A. F. Schatzberg, & S. H. Frazier (Eds.), *Depression: Biology, psychodynamics, and treatment.* New York: Plenum.

GOTOFF, S. P. (1973). Infections. In R. E. Behrhman (Ed.), *Neonatology: Diseases of the fetus and infant.* St. Louis: Mosby.

GOTTESMAN, I. I., & SHIELDS, J. (1966). Schizophrenia in twins: 16 years consecutive admissions to a psychiatric clinic. *British Journal of Psychiatry, 112,* 809–818.

GOTTESMAN, I. I., & SHIELDS, J. (1972). *Schizophrenia and genetics: A twin study vintage point.* New York: Academic Press.

GOTTESMAN, I. I., & SHIELDS, J. (1982). *Schizophrenia: The epigenetic puzzle.* Cambridge: Cambridge University Press.

GOTTSCHALK, L. A., HAER, J. L., & BATES, D. E. (1972). Changes in social alienation, personal disorganization and cognitive–intellectual impairment produced by sensory overload. *Archives of General Psychiatry, 27,* 451–457.

GOVE, W. R. (1970). Societal reaction as an explanation of mental illness: An evaluation. *American Sociological Review, 35,* 873–884.

GOVE, W. R. (1975). Labeling and mental illness: A critque. In W. R. Gove (Ed.), *The labeling of deviance: Evaluating a perspective.* New York: Sage.

GOVE, W. R. (1987). Mental illness and psychiatric treatment among women. In M. R. Walsh (Ed.), *The psychology of women: Ongoing debates.* New Haven: Yale University Press. (Original work published 1980)

GOVE, W. R., & TUDOR, J. F. (1973). Adult sex roles and mental illness. *American Journal of Sociology, 77,* 812–835.

GOVE, W. R., & TUDOR, J. F. (1977). Sex differences in mental illness: A comment on Dohrenwend and Dohrenwend. *American Journal of Sociology, 82,* 1327–1336.

GRAZIANO, A. M., DEGIOVANNI, I. S., & GARCIA, K. A. (1979). Behavioral treatment of children's fears: A review. *Psychological Bulletin, 86,* 804–830.

GREAVES, G. B. (1980). Multiple personality 164 years after Mary Reynolds. *Journal of Mental and Nervous Disease, 168,* 577–596.

GREEN, A. R., & COSTAIN, D. W. (1979). The biochemistry of depression. In E. S. Paykel & A. Coppen (Eds.), *Psychopharmacology of affective disorders.* (British Association for Psychopharmacology Monograph). Oxford: Oxford University Press.

GREEN, H. B. (1974). Infants of alcoholic mothers. *American Journal of Obstetrics and Gynecology, 118,* 713–716.

GREEN, J. A., & SHELLENBERGER, R. D. (1986). Biofeedback research and the ghost in the box: A reply to Roberts. *American Psychologist, 41,* 1003–1005.

GREEN, R. (1975). *Sexual identity conflict in children and adults.* Baltimore: Penguin.

GREEN, R. (1986). *The sissy boy syndrome and the development of homosexuality.* New Haven: Yale University Press.

GREENBERG, I. A. (1986). Psychodrama. In I. L. Kutash & A. Wolff (Eds.), *Psychotherapist's casebook.* San Francisco: Jossey–Bass.

GREENBURG, S. L. (1985). The case of P. In A. A. Lazarus (Ed.), *Casebook of multimodal therapy.* New York: Guilford Press.

GREENHOUSE, L. (1985, February 27). High court gives indigent on trial added safeguard: Issue is plea of insanity. *New York Times,* pp. 1, 10.

GREENSPAN, K., SCHILDKRAUT, J., GORDON, E., BAER, L., ARONOFF, M. S., & DURELL, J. (1970). Catecholamine metabolism in affective disorders: III. MHPG and other catecholamine metabolites in patients treated with lithium carbonate. *Journal of Psychiatric Research, 7,* 171–183.

GREER, S. (1964). Study of parental loss in neurotics and sociopaths. *Archives of General Psychiatry, 11,* 177–180.

GREER, S. (1979). Psychological inquiry: A contribution to cancer research. *Psychological Medicine, 9,* 81–89.

GRIER, W., & COBBS, P. M. (1969). *Black rage.* New York: Bantam.

GRIEST, D., WELLS, K. C., & FOREHAND, R. (1979). Examination of predictors of maternal perceptions of maladjustment in clinic-referred children. *Journal of Abnormal Psychology, 88,* 277–281.

GRINKER, R. R., SR. (1953). *Psychosomatic research.* New York: Norton.

GRINKER, R. R., SR., & WERBLE, B. (1977). *The borderline patient.* New York: Aronson.

GRINSPOON, L. (1977). *Marijuana reconsidered* (2nd ed.). Cambridge, MA: Harvard University Press.

GRINSPOON, L., & BAKALAR, J. B. (1976). *Cocaine: A drug and its social evolution.* New York: Basic Books.

GRODDECK, G. (1961). *The book of the it.* New York: New American Library. (Original work published 1923)

GROSS, J. (1988, February 13). Cocaine and AIDS in New York cause rise in infant death. *New York Times,* pp. 1, 10.

GROSSMAN, H. J. (ED.). (1983). *Classification in mental retardation* (rev. ed.). Washington, DC: American Association on Mental Deficiency.

GROSSMAN, H. Y., MOSTOFSKY, D. I., & HARRISON, R. H. (1986). Psychological aspects of Gilles de la Tourette Syndrome. *Journal of Clinical Psychology, 42,* 228–235.

GROTH, A. N., & BIRNBAUM, H. J. (1981). *Men who rape: The psychology of the offender.* New York: Plenum.

GROTH, A. N., HOBSON, W., & GARY, T. (1982). The child molester: Clinical observations. In J. Conte & D. Shore (Eds.), *Social work and child sexual abuse.* New York: Haworth.

GUILFORD, J. P. (1959). *Personality.* New York: McGraw–Hill.

GUNDERSON, J. G. (1986). Pharmacotherapy for patients with borderline personality disorder. *Archives of General Psychiatry, 43,* 698–700.

GUNDERSON, J. G., FRANK, A. F., KATZ, H. M., VANNICELLI, M. L., FROSCH, J. P., & KNAPP, P. H. (1984). Effects of psychotherapy in schizophrenia: II. Comparative outcome of two forms of treatment. *Schizophrenia Bulletin, 10,* 564–598.

GURMAN, A. S., KNISKERN, D. P., & PINSOF, W. M. (1986). Research on marital and family therapies. In S. L. Garfield & A. E. Bergin (Eds.), *Handbook of psychotherapy and behavior change* (3rd ed.). New York: Wiley.

GUSTAVSON, K. H. (1964). *Down's syndrome: A clinical and cytogenetical investigation.* Uppsala: Institute for Medical Genetics, University of Uppsala.

GUTHRIE, G. M., VERSTRAETE, A., DEINES, M. M., & STERN, R. M. (1975). Symptoms of stress in four societies. *Journal of Social Psychology, 95,* 165–172.

GUTTMACHER, A. F. (1973). *Pregnancy, birth, and family planning.* New York: New American Library.

HAAGA, D. A., & DAVISON, G. C. (1986). *Cognitive change methods.* In F. H. Kanfer & A. P. Goldstein (Eds.), *Helping people change* (3rd ed.). New York: Pergamon Press.

HALE, R. L. (1983). Intellectual assessment. In M. Hersen, A. E. Kazdin, & A. S. Bellack (Eds.), *The clinical psychology handbook.* New York: Pergamon Press.

HALL, C. S., & LINDZEY, G. (1978). *Theories of personality* (3rd ed). New York: Wiley.

HALL, H. R. (1983). Hypnosis and the immune system: A review with implications for cancer and the psychology of healing. *American Journal of Clinical Hypnosis, 25,* 92–103.

HALLAM, R. S., & RACHMAN, S. (1976). Current status of aversion therapy. In M. Hersen, R. Eisler, & P. Miller (Eds.), *Progress in behavior modification* (Vol. 2). New York: Academic Press.

HALLAM, R. S., RACHMAN, S., & FALKOWSKI, W. (1972). Subjective, attitudinal, and physiological effects of electrical aversion therapy. *Behaviour Research and Therapy, 10,* 1–14.

HALLECK, S. L. (1980). *Law in the practice of psychiatry: A handbook for clinicians.* New York: Plenum Medical Book.

HALLIDAY, J. L. (1948). *Psychosocial medicine.* New York: Norton.

HALMI, A., ECKERT, E., LADU, T. J., & COHEN, J. (1986). Anorexia nervosa. Treatment efficacy of cyproheptadine and amitriptyline. *Archives of General Psychiatry, 43,* 177–181.

HAMILTON, M. (1982). Symptoms and assessment of depression. In E. S. Paykel (Ed.), *Handbook of affective disorders.* Boston: Little, Brown.

HAMILTON, S. A. (1988). Behavioral formulations of verbal behavior in psychotherapy. *Clinical Psychology Review, 8,* 181–193.

HAMSHER, K. DES. (1984). Neuropsychological assessment of children. In G. Goldstein & M. Hersen (Eds.), *Handbook of psychological assessment.* New York: Pergamon Press.

HANKOFF, L. D. (1972). Ancient descriptions of organic brain syndrome: The "kordiakos" of the *Talmud. American Journal of Psychiatry, 129,* 233–236.

HANKOFF, L. D. (1982). Suicide and attempted suicide. In E. S. Paykel (Ed.), *Handbook of affective disorders.* New York: Guilford Press.

HANSTEEN, R. W., MILLER, R. D., LONERO, L., REID, L. D., & JONES, B. (1976). Effects of cannabis and alcohol on automobile driving and psychomotor tracking. *Annals of the New York Academy of Sciences, 282,* 240–256.

HARDING, C. M., BROOKS, G. W., ASHIKAGA, T., STRAUSS, J. S., & BREIER, A. (1978a) The Vermont longitudinal study of persons with severe mental illness: I. Methodology, study sample, and overall status 32 years later. *American Journal of Psychiatry, 144,* 718–726.

HARDING, C. M., BROOKS, G. W., ASHIKAGA, T., STRAUSS, J. S., & BREIER, A. (1978b) The Vermont longitudinal study of persons with severe mental illness: II. Long-term outcome of subjects who retrospectively met DSM-III criteria for schizophrenia. *American Journal of Psychiatry, 144,* 727–735.

HARE, R. D. (1970). *Psychopathy: Theory and research.* New York: Wiley.

HARE, R. D. (1975). *Psychopathy.* In P. H. Venables & M. J. Christie (Eds.), *Research in psychophysiology.* London: Wiley.

HARE, R. D., & COX, D. N. (1978). Psychophysiological research on psychopathy. In W. H. Reid (Ed.), *The psychopath: A comprehensive study of antisocial disorders and behavior.* New York: Brunner/Mazel.

HARLOW, J. M. (1868). Recovery from the passage of an iron bar through the head. *Publications of the Massachusetts Medical Society, 2,* 327–346.

HARRELL, J. P. (1980). Psychological factors and hypertension: A status report. *Psychological Bulletin, 87,* 482–501.

HARRIS, B. (1979). Whatever happened to little Albert? *American Psychologist, 34,* 151–160.

HARRIS, S. (1984). The family of the autistic child: A behavioral-systems view. *Clinical Psychology Review, 4,* 227–239.

HARROW, M., & WESTERMEYER, J. F. (1987). Process–reactive dimension and outcome for narrow concepts of schizophrenia. *Schizophrenia Bulletin, 13,* 361–368.

HARROW, M., WESTERMEYER, J. F., SILVERSTEIN, M., STRAUSS, B. S., & COHLER, B. J. (1986). Predictors of outcome in schizophrenia: The process–reactive dimension. *Schizophrenia Bulletin, 12,* 195–207.

HART, J. T. (1970). The development of client-centered therapy. In J. T. Hart & T. M. Tomlinson (Eds.), *New directions in client-centered therapy.* Boston: Houghton Mifflin.

HARTMANN, E., MILOFSKY, E., VAILLANT, G., OLDFIELD, M., FALKE, R., & DUCEY, C. (1984). Vulnerability to schizophrenia. *Archives of General Psychiatry, 41,* 1050–1056.

HARTMANN, H. (1958). *Ego psychology and the problem of adaptation.* New York: International Universities Press.

HARTMANN, H. (1964). *Essays on ego psychology.* New York: International Universities Press.

HARTOCOLLIS, P. (ED.). (1977). *Borderline personality disorders: The concept, the syndrome, the patient.* New York: International Universities Press.

HASEGAWA, K. (1985). The epidemiological study of depression in late life. *Journal of Affective Disorders* (Suppl. 1), S3–S6.

HASSETT, J. (1978). *A primer of psychophysiology.* San Francisco: Freeman.

HATCH, J. P., GATCHEL, R. J., & HARRINGTON, R. (1982). Biofeedback: Clinical applications in medicine. In R. J. Gatchel, A. W. Baum, & J. F. Singer (Eds.), *Handbook of psychology and health: Vol. 1. Clinical psychology and behavioral medicine, overlapping disciplines.* Hillside, NJ: Erlbaum.

HATHAWAY, S. R., & MCKINLEY, J. C. (1943). *MMPI Manual.* New York: Psychological Corp.

HAYNES, S. N. (1983). Behavioral assessment. In M. Hersen, A. E. Kazdin, & A. S. Bellack (Eds.), *The clinical psychology handbook.* New York: Pergamon Press.

HAYWOOD, H. C., MEYERS, C. E., & SWITZKY, H. N. (1982). Mental retardation. *Annual Review of Psychology, 33,* 309–342.

HAYWOOD, H. C., & NEWBROUGH, J. R. (EDS.). (1981). *Living environments for developmentally retarded persons.* Baltimore: University Park Press.

HEATH, R. G. (ED.). (1963). *Seriological fractions in schizophrenia.* New York: Harper & Row.

HEATH, R. G., & KRUPP, I. M. (1968). Schizophrenia as a specific biologic disease. *American Journal of Psychiatry, 124,* 27–45.

HEATH, R. G., KRUPP, I. M., BYERS, L. W., & LILJEKVIST, J. I. (1967). Schizophrenia as an immunologic disorder. *Archives of General Psychiatry, 16,* 1–33.

HEBER, R. A. (1961). A manual on terminology and classification in mental retardation. *American Journal of Mental Deficiency* (Monograph Suppl., 2nd ed.).

HECKINGER, F. M. (1984, September 11). Preschool found to benefit blacks. *New York Times,* p. 20.

HECKLER, M. M. (1985). The fight against Alzheimer's disease. *American Psychologist, 40,* 1240–1244.

HECKTMAN, L., WEISS, G., & PERLMAN, T. (1984). Hyperactive as young adults: Past and current substance abuse and antisocial behavior. *American Journal of Orthopsychiatry, 54,* 415–425.

HEILBRUN, A. B., JR. (1973). *Aversive maternal control: A theory of schizophrenic development.* New York: Wiley.

HEIMAN, J., LoPICCOLO, L., & LoPICCOLO, J. (1976). *Becoming orgasmic: A sexual growth program for women.* Englewood Cliffs, NJ: Prentice–Hall.

HEIMAN, J. R., LoPICCOLO, L., & LoPICCOLO, J. (1981). The treatment of sexual dysfunctions. In A. S. Gurman & D. P. Kniskern (Eds.), *Handbook of family therapy.* New York: Brunner/Mazel.

HEINRICH, A., & PRICE, S. (1977). *Group treatment of men and women without partners.* Paper presented at the 85th annual convention of the American Psychological Association, San Francisco, CA.

HEINROTH, J. C. (1975). *Textbook of disturbances of mental life: Vol. I. Theory, Vol. II. Practice* (J. Shmorak, Trans.). Baltimore: Johns Hopkins University Press. (Original work published 1818)

HELLMAN, A. D. (1975). *Laws against marijuana: The price we pay.* Urbana: University of Illinois Press.

HELZER, J. E. (1987). Epidemiology of alcoholism. *Journal of Consulting and Clinical Psychology, 55,* 284–292.

HENAHAN, D. (1984, January 29). In the end Mahler's torments won out. *New York Times,* pp. 17–18.

HENDERSON, D. K. (1939). *Psychopathic states.* New York: Norton.

HENDERSON, D., & BATCHELOR, I. R. C. (1962). *Henderson and Gillespie's textbook of psychiatry for students and practitioners* (9th ed.). London: Oxford University Press.

HENRY, G. W. (1967). Quoted in *Contemporary Psychology, 12,* 438.

HERMAN, R. D. (1976). *Gamblers and gambling.* Lexington, MA: Heath.

HERRON, W. G. (1987). Evaluating the process–reactive dimension. *Schizophrenia Bulletin, 13,* 357–359.

HESTON, L. L. (1970). The genetics of schizophrenic and schizoid disease. *Science, 167,* 249–256.

HESTON, L. L., & MASTRI, A. R. (1977). The genetics of Alzheimer's disease: Association with hematologic malignancy and Down's disease. *Archives of General Psychiatry, 34,* 976–981.

HESTON, L. L., & WHITE, J. A. (1983). *Dementia: A practical guide to Alzheimer's disease and related illnesses.* New York: Freeman.

HESTON, P. L., & DYCK, D. G. (1986). Perfectionism, stress, and vulnerability to depression. *Cognitive Therapy and Research, 10,* 137–142.

HILBERMAN, E. (1976). *The rape victim.* New York: Basic Books.

HILGARD, E. R. (1973). The domain of hypnosis, with some comments on alternative paradigms. *American Psychologist, 28,* 972–982.

HILGARD, E. R. (1987). *Psychology in America.* New York: Harcourt Brace Jovanovich.

HILGARD, E. R., & BOWER, G. H. (1966). *Theories of learning* (3rd ed.). New York: Appleton–Century–Crofts.

HINKLE, L. E. (1961). Ecological observations of the relation of physical illness, mental illness, and the social environment. *Psychosomatic Medicine, 23,* 289–296.

HINSIE, L. E., & CAMPBELL, R. J. (1977). *Psychiatric dictionary* (4th ed.). New York: Oxford University Press.

HIROTO, D. S., & SELIGMAN, M. E. P. (1975). Generality of learned helplessness in man. *Journal of Personality and Social Psychology, 31,* 311–327.

HIRSCH, J. (ED.). (1967). *Behavior–genetic analysis.* New York: McGraw–Hill.

HIRSCH, J. (1986). Behavior–genetic analysis. In J. Medioni & G. Vaysse (Eds.), *Genetic approaches to behaviour.* Toulouse: Centre de Recherches en Biologie du Comportement, Editions Privat.

HIRSCH, J., McGUIRE, T. R., & VETTA, A. (1988). Concepts of behavior genetics and misapplications to humans. In J. S. Lockard (Ed.), *The evolution of human social behavior.* New York: Elsevier.

HISTORICAL NOTES. (1951). A letter from Freud. *American Journal of Psychiatry, 107,* 786–787.

HITE, S. (1976). *The Hite report: A nationwide study on female sexuality.* New York: Macmillan.

HOBERMAN, H. M., LEWINSOHN, P. M., & TILSON, M. (1988). Group treatment of depression. Individual predictors of outcome. *Journal of Consulting and Clinical Psychology, 56,* 393–398.

HODAPP, R. M., & ZIGLER, E. (1986). Reply to Barnett's comments on the definition and classification of mental retardation. *American Journal of Mental Deficiency, 91,* 117–119.

HODGES, K., KLINE, J., STERN, L., CYTRYN, L., & McKNEW, D. (1982). The development of a child assessment interview for research and clinical use. *Journal of Abnormal Child Psychology, 10,* 173–189.

HODGES, K., McKNEW, D., CYTRYN, L., STERN, L., & KLINE, J. (1982). The Child Assessment Schedule (CAS) diagnostic interview: A report on reliability and validity. *Journal of the American Academy of Child Psychiatry, 21,* 468–473.

HOFFMAN, R. E., STOPEK, S., & ANDREASEN, N. C. (1986). A comparative study of manic vs. schizophrenic speech disorganization. *Archives of General Psychiatry, 43,* 831–838.

HOGAN, D. R. (1978). The effectiveness of sex therapy: A review of the literature. In J. LoPiccolo & L. LoPiccolo (Eds.), *Handbook of sex therapy.* New York: Plenum.

HOGAN, R. A. (1980). *Group psychotherapy: A peer-focused approach.* New York: Holt, Rinehart & Winston.

HOIBERG, A., & McCAUGHEY, B. G. (1984). The traumatic after effects of collision at sea. *American Journal of Psychiatry, 14,* 70–73.

HOLBOROW, P., & BERRY, P. (1985). Is there an independent syndrome of hyperactivity? A comment on Trites and Laprade. *Journal of Child Psychology & Psychiatry & Allied Disciplines, 26,* 491–493.

HOLDEN, C. (1973). Psychosurgery: Legitimate therapy or laundered lobotomy? *Science, 179,* 1109–1112.

HOLDEN, C. (1978). Cancer and the mind: How are they connected? *Science, 200,* 1363–1369.

HOLDEN, C. (1986a). Giving mental illness its research due. *Science, 232,* 1084–1085.

HOLDEN, C. (1986b). Depression research advances, treatment lags. *Science, 233,* 723–726.

HOLDEN, C. (1986c). Proposed new psychiatric diagnoses raise charges of gender bias. *Science, 231,* 327–328.

HOLDEN, C. (1987). Alcoholism and the medical cost crunch. *Science, 235,* 1132–1133.

HOLDEN, C. (1988). Politics and Soviet psychiatry. *Science, 239,* 551–553.

HOLLISTER, L. E. (1977). Antipsychotic medications and the treatment of schizophrenia. In J. D. Barchas, P. A. Berger, R. D. Ciaranello, & G. R. Elliott (Eds.), *Psychopharmacology: From theory to practice.* New York: Oxford University Press.

HOLLON, S., & BECK, A. T. (1986). Cognitive therapies. In S. L. Garfield & A. E. Bergin (Eds.), *Handbook of psychotherapy and behavior change* (3rd ed.). New York: Wiley.

HOLROYD, J. C., & BRODKSY, A. M. (1977). Psychologists' attitudes and practices regarding erotic and nonerotic physical contact with patients. *American Psychologist, 11,* 807–811.

HOLSTROM, L. L., & BURGESS, A. W. (1980). Sexual behavior of assailants during reported rapes. *Archives of Sexual Behavior, 9,* 427–439.

HOLT, R. R. (1982). Occupational stress. In L. Goldberger & S. Breznitz (Eds.), *Handbook of stress: Theoretical and clinical aspects.* New York: Free Press.

HOLTZMAN, P. S. (1986). Thought disorder in schizophrenia: Editor's introduction. *Schizophrenia Bulletin, 12,* 342–347.

HOLTZMAN, P. S. (1987). Recent studies of psychophysiology in schizophrenia. *Schizophrenia Bulletin, 13,* 49–75.

HOLTZMAN, W. H., THORPE, J. S., SWARTZ, J. D., & HERRON, E. W. (1961). *Inkblot perception and personality.* Austin: University of Texas Press.

HOMOSEXUALITY DROPPED AS A MENTAL DISORDER. (1974, February). *APA Monitor,* p. 1.

HONIGFELD, G., & HOWARD, A. (1978). *Psychiatric drugs: A desk reference* (2nd ed.). New York: Academic Press.

HOOD, T. (1827). *Ode to melancholy.* In J. Bartlett (1965), *Familiar quotations* (14th ed.). Boston: Little, Brown.

HOOK, E. B. (1973). Behavioral implications of the human XYY genotype. *Science, 179,* 139–150.

HOOK, E. B. (1975). XYY genotype. *Science, 189,* 1004.

HORNEY, K. (1937). *The neurotic personality of our time.* New York: Norton.

HORNEY, K. (1939). *New ways in psychoanalysis.* New York: Norton.

HORNEY, K. (1945). *Our inner conflicts: A constructive theory of neurosis.* New York: Norton.

HORNEY, K. (ED.). (1946). *Are you considering psychoanalysis?* New York: Norton.

HORNEY, K. (1967). *Feminine psychology* (H. Kelman, Ed.). New York: Norton.

HORNEY, K. (1970). *Neurosis and human growth: The struggle toward self-realization.* New York: Norton.

HORTON, P., & MILLER, D. (1972). The etiology of multiple personality. *Comprehensive Psychiatry, 13,* 151–159.

HSU, L. G. (1986). The treatment of anorexia nervosa. *American Journal of Psychiatry, 143,* 573–581.

HUGHES, J. R., & HATSUKAMI, D. (1986). Signs and symptoms of tobacco withdrawal. *Archives of General Psychiatry, 43,* 289–294.

HUGHES, P. L., WELLS, L. A., CUNNINGHAM, C. J., & ILSTRUP, D. M. (1986). Treating bulimia with desipramine. *Archives of General Psychiatry, 43,* 182–186.

HUGHES, W. (1970). Alzheimer's disease. *Generontologia Clinica, 12,* 129–148.

HUMPHREYS, L. (1975). *Tearoom trade: Impersonal sex in public places.* Chicago: Aldine.

HUNT, J. McV. (1979). Psychological development: Early experience. *Annual Review of Psychology, 30,* 103–143.

HUNT, S. M., SINGER, K., & COBB, S. (1967). Components of depression. *Archives of General Psychiatry, 16,* 441–447.

HURLEY, R. L. (1969). *Poverty and mental retardation: A causal relationship.* New York: Random House.

International Classification of Diseases, Clinical Modification (9th rev. ed.). (1979). Ann Arbor, MI: Edwards Bros.

ISAACS, W., THOMAS, J., & GOLDIAMOND, I. (1960). Application of operant conditioning to reinstate verbal behavior in psychotics. *Journal of Speech and Hearing Disorders, 25,* 8–12.

ISCOE, I., & HARRIS, L. C. (1984). Social and community interventions. *Annual Review of Psychology, 35,* 333–360.

IVANCEVICH, J. M., & MATTESON, M. T. (1988). Type A behaviour and the healthy individual. *British Journal of Medical Psychology, 61,* 37–56.

IYER, P. (1985, February 25). Fighting the cocaine wars. *Time,* pp. 26–35.

JACOBS, B. L. (1987). How hallucinogenic drugs work. *American Scientist, 75,* 386–392.

JACOBS, P. A. (1975). XYY genotype. *Science, 189,* 1004.

JACOBS, P. A., BRUNTON, M., MELVILLE, M. M., BRITTAIN, R. P., & McCLEMONT, W. F. (1965). Aggressive behavior, mental subnormality, and the XYY male. *Nature, 208,* 1351–1352.

JACOBSON, A., KALES, J. D., & KALES, A. (1969). Clinical and electrophysiological correlates of sleep disorders in children. In A. Kales (Ed.), *Sleep: Physiology and pathology—a symposium.* Philadelphia: Lippincott.

JACOBSON, E. (1957). *You must relax: A practical method of reducing the strains of modern living* (4th ed.). New York: McGraw–Hill.

JACOBSON, E. (1964). *Anxiety and tension control.* Philadelphia: Lippincott.

JACOBSON, E. (1975). The psychoanalytic treatment of depressive patients. In E. J. Anthony & T. Benedek (Eds.), *Depression and human existence.* Boston: Little, Brown.

JACOBSON, N. S., & BUSSOD, M. (1983). Marital and family therapy. In M. Hersen, A. E. Kazdin, & A. S. Bellack (Eds.), *The clinical psychology handbook.* New York: Pergamon Press.

JAFFE, J. H. (1985). Drug dependence. In H. I. Kaplan & B. J. Sadock (Eds.), *Comprehensive textbook of psychiatry* (Vol. 2) (4th ed.). Baltimore: Williams & Wilkins.

JAFFE, J. H., & CIRAULO, D. A. (1985). Drugs used in the treatment of alcoholism. In J. H. Mendelson & N. K. Mello (Eds.), *The diagnosis and treatment of alcoholism* (2nd ed.). New York: McGraw–Hill.

JANET, P. (1907). *The major symptoms of hysteria: Fifteen lectures given in the Medical School of Harvard University.* New York: Macmillan.

JANIS, I. L. (1958). *Psychological stress.* New York: Macmillan.

JANIS, I. L. (1971). *Stress and frustration.* New York: Harcourt Brace Jovanovich

JANOFF-BULMAN, R. (1985). The aftermath of victimization: Rebuilding shattered assumptions. In C. R. Figley (Ed.), *Trauma and its wake: The study and treatment of post-traumatic stress disorder.* New York: Brunner/Mazel.

JANOWSKY, D. S., ADDARIO, D., & SCHUCKIT, M. A. (1978). *Psychopharmacology case studies: A compilation of 53 case histories.* Garden City, NY: Medical Examination Publishing.

JANOWSKY, D. S., EL-YOUSEF, M. K., & DAVIS, J. M. (1974). Interpersonal maneuvers of manic patients. *American Journal of Psychiatry, 131,* 250–255.

JANSEN, G. (1969). Effects of noise on physiological state. In W. D. Ward & J. E. Fricke (Eds.), *Noise as a public health problem.* Washington, DC: American Speech and Hearing Association.

JELLINEK, E. M. (1971). Phases of alcohol addiction. In G. D. Shean (Ed.), *Studies in abnormal behavior.* Chicago: Rand McNally.

JENKINS, C. D., ROSENMAN, R. H., & FRIEDMAN, M. (1967). Development of an objective psychological test for the determination of the coronary-prone behavior pattern in employed men. *Journal of Chronic Diseases, 20,* 371–379.

JENKINS, C. D., ZYZANSKI, S., & ROSENMAN, R. (1971). Progress toward validation of a computer-scored test for the Type A coronary-prone behavior pattern. *Psychosomatic Medicine, 33,* 193–202.

JENKINS, C. D., ZYZANSKI, S. J., & ROSENMAN, R. H. (1979). *Jenkins activity survey for health prediction.* New York: Psychological Corporation.

JENKINS, E. D. (1985). New horizons for psychosomatic medicine. *Psychosomatic Medicine, 47,* 1–24.

JENKINS V. UNITED STATES. (1962). 307 F.2d 637 (D.C. Cir.).

JENSEN, A. R. (1980). *Bias in mental testing.* New York: Free Press.

JESTE, D. V., & WYATT, R. J. (1982). *Understanding and treating tardive dyskinesia.* New York: Guilford Press.

JOHNSON, D., & MATRESS, R. (1977). Interpersonal influence in psychotherapy: A social psychological view. In A. Gurman & A. Razin (Eds.), *Effective psychotherapy: A handbook of research.* New York: Pergamon Press.

JOHNSON, F. N. (1975). *Lithium research and therapy.* London: Academic Press.

JOHNSON, G. T. (ED.). (1981, May). Senility. *Harvard Medical School Health Letter*, pp. 1–2, 5.

JOHNSON, M. (1987). Mental illness and psychiatric treatment among women: A response. In M. R. Walsh (Ed.), *The psychology of women: Ongoing debates.* New Haven: Yale University Press.

JOHNSON, N. S. & HOLLOWAY, E. L. (1988). Conceptual complexity and obsessionality in bulimic college women. *Journal of Counseling Psychology, 35,* 251–257.

JOHNSON, R. D. (1972). *Aggression in man and animals.* Philadelphia: Saunders.

JOHNSON, S. (1984, November 12). Alcoholism in women under 30. *New York Times,* p. 12.

JONES, B. P., & BUTTERS, N. (1983). Neuropsychological assessment. In M. Hersen, A. E. Kazdin, & A. S. Bellack (Eds.), *The clinical psychology handbook.* New York: Pergamon Press.

JONES, E. (1923). *Papers on psycho-analysis* (5th ed.). London: Ballière, Tindall and Cox.

JONES, E. (1964). *Hamlet and Oedipus.* Garden City, NY: Doubleday. (Original work published 1949)

JONES, E. (1955). *The life and work of Sigmund Freud* (Vol. 2). New York: Basic Books.

JONES, E. (1957). *The life and work of Sigmund Freud* (Vol. 3). New York: Basic Books.

JONES, H. B., & JONES, H. C. (1977). *Sensual drugs: Deprivation and rehabilitation of the mind.* Cambridge: Cambridge University Press.

JONES, K. L., & SMITH, D. W. (1973). Recognition of the fetal alcohol syndrome in early infancy. *Lancet, 2,* 999–1101.

JONES, M. M. (1980). Conversion reaction: Anachronism or evolutionary form? A review of the neurologic, behavior, and psychoanalytic literature. *Psychological Bulletin, 87,* 427–441.

JONES, R. T. (1977). Human effects. In R. C. Petersen (Ed.), *Marijuana Research Findings: 1976.* (NIDA Research Monograph No. 14, HEW Publication No. ADM 77–501). Washington, DC: U.S. Government Printing Office.

JONES, W. H. S. (TRANS.). (1923). *Hippocrates: Vol. 2. The sacred disease.* London: Heinemann.

JOUBERT, J. (1842). *Pensées* (Katherine Lyttleton, Trans.). In R. T. Tripp (1970). *International thesaurus of quotations.* New York: Crowell.

JOYCE, J. (1961). *Ulysses.* New York: Random House. (Original work published 1922)

JOYNT, R. J., & SHOULSON, I. (1979). Dementia. In K. M. Heilman & E. Valenstein (Eds.), *Clinical neuropsychology.* New York: Oxford University Press.

JULIEN, R. M. (1981). *A primer of drug action* (3rd ed.). New York: Freeman.

JUNG, C. G. (1953). The relations between the ego and the unconscious. In C. G. Jung, *Collected works: Vol. 7. Two essays on analytical psychology.* Princeton, NJ: Princeton University Press. (Original work published 1928)

JUNG, C. G. (1956). *Collected works: Vol. 5. Symbols of transformation.* Princeton, NJ: Princeton University Press. (Original work published 1911)

JUNG, C. G. (1959). The concept of the collective unconscious. In C. G. Jung, *Collected works: Vol. 9, Part 1. The archetypes and the collective unconscious.* Princeton, NJ: Princeton University Press (Original work published 1936)

JUNG, C. G. (1968). *Analytical psychology: Its theory and practice.* New York: Pantheon Press.

JURY FINDS DRIVE GUILTY OF MURDER. (1985, February 9). *New York Times,* p. 7.

KABACH, M. M., & LEISTI, J. (1975). Prenatal detection of Down's syndrome: Technical and ethical considerations. In R. Koch & F. C. de la Cruz (Eds.), *Down's syndrome (mongolism): Research, prevention and management.* New York: Brunner/Mazel.

KAHN, E. (1985). Heinz Kohut and Carl Rogers: A timely comparison. *American Psychologist, 40,* 893–904.

KAHN, J. P., KRONFELD, D. S., BLOOD, D. K., LYNN, R. B., HELLER, S. S., & FRANK, K. A. (1982). Type A behavior and the thallium stress test. *Psychosomatic Medicine, 44,* 431–436.

KAHN, M. W. (1981). *Basic methods for mental health practitioners.* Cambridge, MA: Winthrop.

KAHN, R. J., MCNAIR, D. M., LIPMAN, R. S., COVI, L., RICKELS, K., DOWNING, R., FISHER, S., & FRANKENTHALER, L. (1986). Imipramine and chlordiazepoxide in depressive and anxiety disorders: II. Efficacy in anxious outpatients. *Archives of General Psychiatry, 43,* 79–85.

KAMINOFF, R. D., & PROSHANSKY, H. M. (1982). Stress as a consequence of the urban physical environment. In L. Goldberger & S. Breznitz (Eds.), *Handbook of stress: Theoretical and clinical aspects.* New York: Free Press.

KAMPMAN, R. (1976). Hypnotically induced multiple personality: An experimental study. *International Journal of Clinical and Experimental Hypnosis, 24,* 215–227.

KANE, J. M. (1987). Treatment of schizophrenia. *Schizophrenia Bulletin, 13,* 133–156.

KANE, R. L., & KANE, R. A. (1978). Care of the aged: Old problems in need of new solutions. *Science, 200,* 913–918.

KANFER, F. H., & GAELICK, L. (1986). Self-management methods. In F. H. Kanfer & A. P. Goldstein (Eds.), *Helping people change: A textbook of methods* (3rd ed.). New York: Pergamon Press.

KANFER, F. H., & PHILLIPS, S. (1970). *Learning foundations of behavior therapy.* New York: Wiley.

KANIN, E. (1984). Date rape: Unofficial criminals and victims. *Victimology, 9,* 95–108.

KANNER, L. (1943). Autistic disturbances of affective contact. *Nervous Child, 2,* 181–197.

KANNER, L. (1949). Problems of nosology and psychodynamics of early infantile autism. *American Journal of Orthopsychiatry, 19,* 416.

KANNER, L. (1962). Emotionally disturbed children: A historical review. *Child Development, 33,* 97–102.

KAPLAN, H. I., & SADOCK, B. J. (1985). *Modern synopsis of comprehensive textbook of psychiatry* (4th ed.). Baltimore: Williams & Wilkins.

KAPLAN, H. S. (1974). *The new sex therapy: Active treatment of sexual dysfunction.* New York: Brunner/Mazel.

KAPLAN, H. S. (1975). *The illustrated manual of sex therapy.* New York: Quadrangle/New York Times Book.

KAPLAN, H. S. (1977). Hypoactive sexual desire. *Journal of Sex and Marital Therapy, 3*(1), 3–9.

KAPLAN, H. S. (1979). *Disorders of sexual desire and other new concepts and techniques in sex therapy: Vol. 2. The new sex therapy.* New York: Brunner/Mazel.

KAPLAN, H. S. (1983). *The evaluation of sexual disorders: Psychological and medical aspects.* New York: Brunner/Mazel.

KAPLAN, H. S. (1987). *The illustrated manual of sex therapy* (2nd ed.). New York: Quadrangle/New York Times Book.

KAPLAN, M. (1983a). A woman's view of DSM-III. *American Psychologist, 38,* 786–792.

KAPLAN, M. (1983b). The issue of sex bias in DSM-II: Comments on the articles by Spitzer, Williams, & Kass. *American Psychologist, 38,* 802–803.

KARAFIN, L. (1982, May). Myths about the penis. *Medical Aspects of Human Sexuality, 16*(5), 48R–48RR.

KARASU, T. B. (1986). The specificity versus nonspecificity dilemma: Toward identifying therapeutic change agents. *American Journal of Psychiatry, 143,* 687–695.

KAROLY, P., & HARRIS, A. (1986). Operant methods. In F. H. Kanfer & A. P. Goldstein (Eds.), *Helping people change: A textbook of methods.* New York: Pergamon Press.

KAROLY, P., & KANFER, F. H. (EDS.). (1982). *Self-management and behavior change: From theory to practice.* New York: Pergamon Press.

KARON, B. P. (1986). Psychiatrists, psychologists, medication, and psychotherapy. *Psychotherapy Bulletin, 20,* 7–8.

KARON, B. P., & VANDENBOS, G. E. (1981). *Psychotherapy of schizophrenia: The treatment of choice.* New York: Aronson.

KASS, F., SPITZER, R. L., & WILLIAMS, J. B. W. (1983). A study of the issue of sex bias in the diagnosis criteria of DSM-III: Axis II personality disorders. *American Psychologist, 38,* 799–801.

KATZMAN, R. (1976). The prevalence and malignancy of Alzheimer's disease: A major killer. *Archives of Neurology, 33,* 217–218.

KAUFMANN, Y. (1984). Analytical psychotherapy. In R. J. Corsini & D. Wedding (Eds.), *Current psychotherapies* (3rd ed.). Itasca, IL: Peacock.

KAUL, T. J., & BEDNAR, R. L. (1986). Research on group and related therapies. Experiential group research: Results, questions, and suggestions. In S. L. Garfield & A. E. Bergin (Eds.), *Handbook of psychotherapy and behavior change* (3rd ed.). New York: Wiley.

KAY, S. R., FIZBEIN, A., & OPLER, L. A. (1987). The positive and negative syndrome scale (PANSS) for schizophrenia. *Schizophrenia Bulletin, 13,* 261–276.

KAZDIN, A. E. (1977). *The token economy: A review of evaluation.* New York: Plenum.

KAZDIN, A. E. (1978a) *History of behavior modification: Experimental foundations of contemporary research.* Baltimore: University Park Press.

KAZDIN, A. E. (1978b) Behavior therapy: Evolution and expansion. *Counseling Psychologist, 7,* 34–37.

KAZDIN, A. E. (1982). The token economy: A decade later. *Journal of Applied Behavior Analysis, 15,* 431–443.

KAZDIN, A. E. (1983). Failure of persons to respond to the token economy. In E. B. Foa & P. M. G. Emmelkamp (Eds.), *Failures in behavior therapy.* New York: Wiley.

KAZDIN, A. E., & WILCOXON, L. A. (1976). Systematic desensitization and nonspecific treatment effects: A methodological evaluation. *Psychological Bulletin, 83,* 729–758.

KAZDIN, A. E., & WILSON, G. T. (1978). *Evaluation of behavior therapy: Issues, evidence, and research strategies.* Cambridge, MA: Ballinger.

KELLAM, A. M. F. (1969). Shoplifting treated by aversion to a film. *Behaviour Research and Therapy, 7,* 125–127.

KELLER, B. (1987, February 2). Russian back from bedlam still hears shrieks at night. *New York Times,* pp. 1, 6.

KELLER, B. (1988, January 5). Mental patients in Soviet Union to get new legal rights. *New York Times,* pp. 1, 6.

KELLER, M. (1970). The great Jewish drink mystery. *British Journal of Addiction, 64,* 289–296.

KELLNER, R. (1982). Psychotherapeutic strategies in hypochondriasis: A clinical study. *American Journal of Psychotherapy, 36,* 146–147.

KELLY, J. G., SNOWDEN, L. R., & MUÑOZ, R. F. (1977). Social and community interventions. *Annual Review of Psychology, 28,* 323–361.

KELMAN, H. (ED.). (1965). *New perspectives in psychoanalysis: Contributions to Karen Horney's holistic approach.* New York: Norton.

KEMPE, R. S., & KEMPE, C. H. (1984). *The common secret: Sexual abuse of children and adolescents.* New York: Freeman.

KENDALL, P. C., & KRISS, M. R. (1983). Cognitive–behavioral interventions. In C. E. Walker (Ed.), *The handbook of clinical psychology: Theory, research and practice* (Vol. 2). Homewood, IL: Dow Jones–Irwin.

KENDALL, P. C., & URBAIN, E. (1982). Social–cognitive approaches to therapy with children. In J. R. Lachenmeyer & M. S. Gibbs (Eds.), *Psychopathology in children.* New York: Gardner Press.

KENDELL, R. E. (1973). Psychiatric diagnoses: A study of how they are made. *British Journal of Psychiatry, 122,* 437–445.

KENDELL, R. E. (1975). *The role of diagnosis in psychiatry.* Oxford: Blackwell.

KENDLER, K. S., & GRUENBERG, A. M. (1984). And independent analysis of the Danish adoption study of schizophrenia: VI. The relationship between psychiatric disorder as defined by DSM-III in the relatives and adoptees. *Archives of General Psychiatry, 41,* 555–546.

KENNEDY, J. G. (1973). Cultural psychiatry. In J. J. Honigmann (Ed.), *Handbook of social and cultural anthropology.* Chicago: Rand McNally.

KENNEDY, S., THOMPSON, R., STANCER, H. C., ROY, A., & PERSAD, E. (1983). Life events precipitating mania. *British Journal of Psychiatry, 142,* 398–403.

KENNEDY, W. A. (1965). School phobia: Rapid treatment of fifty cases. *Journal of Abnormal Psychology, 70,* 285–289.

KENT, F. (1977). *Nothing to fear: Coping with phobias.* Garden City, NY: Doubleday.

KENYON, F. E. (1976). Hypochondriacal states. *British Journal of Psychiatry, 129,* 1–14.

KERR, P. (1987a, February 9). Crack addiction: The tragic impact on women and children in New York. *New York Times,* p. 14.

KERR, P. (1987b, March 7). Rise in violence is seen among users of cocaine. *New York Times,* p. 10

KERTESZ, A. (1979). Recovery and treatment. In K. M. Heilman & E. Valenstein (Eds.), *Clinical neuropsychology.* New York: Oxford University Press.

KESSEN, W., & CAHAN, E. D. (1986). A century of psychology: From subject to object to agent. *American Scientist, 74,* 640–649.

KESSLER, R. C., PRICE, R. H., & WORTMAN, C. B. (1985). Social factors in psychopathology: Stress, social support, and coping processes. *Annual Review of Psychology, 36,* 531–572.

KESSLER, S. (1980). The genetics of schizophrenia: A review. *Schizophrenia Bulletin, 6,* 404–416.

KESSLER, S. (1981). The genetics of schizophrenia: A review. In U.S. Department of Health and Human Services, *Schizophrenia 1980: Special report.* Washington, DC: U.S. Government Printing Office.

KETY, S.S. (1969). Biomedical hypotheses and studies. In L. Bellak & L. Loeb (Eds.), *The schizophrenic syndrome.* New York: Grune and Stratton.

KETY, S. S. (1974). From rationalization to reason. *American Journal of Psychiatry, 131,* 957–963.

KETY, S. S. (1975). Mental illness in the biological and adoptive families of adopted individuals who have become schizophrenic. In H. M. van Praag (Ed.), *On the origin of schizophrenic psychoses.* Amsterdam: Erven Bohn.

KETY, S. S. (1980). The syndrome of schizophrenia: Unresolved questions and opportunities for research. *British Journal of Psychiatry, 136,* 421–436.

KETY, S. S., ROSENTHAL, D., WENDER, P. H., & SCHULSINGER, F. (1968). The types and prevalence of mental illness in the biological and adoptive families of adopted schizophrenics. In D. Rosenthal & S. S. Kety (Eds.), *The transmission of schizophrenia.* Oxford: Pergamon Press.

KETY, S. S., ROSENTHAL, D., WENDER, P. H., SCHULSINGER, F., & JACOBSEN, B. (1975). Mental illness in the biological and adoptive families of adopted individuals who have become schizophrenic: A preliminary report based on psychiatric interviews. In R. R. Fieve, D. Rosenthal, & H. Brill (Eds.), *Genetic research in psychiatry.* Baltimore: Johns Hopkins University Press.

KETY, S. S., ROSENTHAL, D., WENDER, P. H., SCHULSINGER, F., & JACOBSEN, B. (1978). The biologic and adoptive families of adopted individuals who became schizophrenic: Prevalence of mental illness and other characteristics. In L. C. Wynne, R. L. Cromwell, & S. Matthysse (Eds.), *The nature of schizophrenia: New approaches to research and treatment.* New York: Wiley.

KHACHATURIAN, Z. S. (1985). Progress of research on Alzheimer's disease: Research opportunities for behavioral scientists. *American Psychologist, 40,* 1251–1255.

KIELHOLZ, P. (1973). *Masked depression.* Bern: Hans Huber.

KIERKEGAARD, S. (1944). *The concept of dread* (W. Lowrie, Trans.). Princeton, NJ: Princeton University Press. (Original work published 1844)

KIEV, A. (1972). *Transcultural psychiatry.* New York: Free Press.

KILMANN, P. R. & AUERBACH, R. (1979). Treatment of premature ejaculation and psychogenic impotence: A critical review of the literature. *Archives of Sexual Behavior, 8,* 81–100.

KILOH, L. G., & OSSELTON, J. W. (1970). *Clinical electroencephalography* (2nd ed.). London: Butterworth.

KIMBLE, D. P. (1988). *Biological psychology.* New York: Holt, Rinehart & Winston.

KINDRED, M., COHEN, J., PENROD, D., & SHAFFER, T. (EDS.). (1976). *The mentally retarded and the law.* New York: Free Press.

KING, L. M. (1978). Social and cultural influences on psychopathology. *Annual Review of Psychology, 29,* 405–433.

KINSBOURNE, M. (1988). Review of B. Kissin, *Conscious and unconscious programs in the brain. Contemporary Psychology, 33,* 415–416.

KINSEY, A. C., POMEROY, W. B., & MARTIN, C. E. (1948). *Sexual behavior in the human male.* Philadelphia: Saunders.

KINSEY, A. C., POMEROY, W. B., MARTIN, C. E., & GEBBARD, P. H. (1965). *Sexual behavior in the human female.* New York: Pocket Books. (Original work published 1953)

KIRIGIN, K., WOLF, M. M., BRAUKMANN, C. J., FIXSEN, D. L., & PHILLIPS, E. L. (1979). Achievement place: A preliminary outcome evaluation. In J. S. Stumphauzer (Ed.), *Progress in behavior therapy with delinquents.* Springfield, IL: Charles C Thomas.

KIRKPATRICK, M., & FRIEDMANN, C. T. H. (1976). Treatment of requests for sex-change surgery with psychotherapy. *American Journal of Psychiatry, 133,* 1194–1196.

KITANO, H. L. L. (1970). Mental illness in four cultures. *Journal of Social Psychology, 80,* 121–134.

KLEIN, D. N., CLARK, D. C., DANSKY, L., & MARGOLIS, E. T. (1988). Dysthymia in the offspring of parents with primary unipolar affective disorder. *Journal of Abnormal Psychology, 97,* 265–274.

KLEIN, D. N., DEPUE, R. A., & SLATER, J. F. (1986). Inventory identification of cyclothymia: IX. Validation in offspring of bipolar I patients. *Archives of General Psychiatry, 43,* 441–445.

KLEIN, D. N., TAYLOR, E. B., DICKSTEIN, S., & HARDING, K.

(1988). The early–late onset distinction in DSM-III-R dysthymia. *Journal of Affective Disorders, 14,* 25–33.

KLEIN, D. N., TAYLOR, E. B., DICKSTEIN, S., & HARDING, K. (in press). Primary early-onset dysthymia: Comparison with primary non-polar non-chronic major depressives on demographic, clinical, familial, personality, and socioenvironmental characteristics and short-term outcome. *Journal of Abnormal Psychology.*

KLERMAN, G. L. (1978). Psychopharmacologic treatment of depression. In J. G. Bernstein (Ed.), *Clinical psychopharmacology.* Littleton, MA: PSG.

KLERMAN, G. L. (1980). Overview of affective disorders. In H. I. Kaplan, A. M. Freeman, & B. J. Sadock (Eds.), *Comprehensive textbook of psychiatry* (3rd ed.). Baltimore: Williams & Wilkins.

KLERMAN, G. L. (1982). Practical issues in the treatment of depression and mania. In E. S. Paykel (Ed.), *Handbook of affective disorders.* New York: Guilford Press.

KLERMAN, G. L. (1984). Ideology and science in the individual psychotherapy of schizophrenia. *Schizophrenia Bulletin, 10,* 608–612.

KLERMAN, G. L. (1986). Historical perspectives on contemporary schools of psychopathology. In T. Millon & G. W. Klerman (Eds.), *Contemporary directions in psychopathology: Toward the DSM-IV.* New York: Guilford Press.

KLINE, N. S. (1975). *From sad to glad. Kline on depression.* New York: Ballantine.

KLINE, P. (1972). *Fact and fantasy in Freudian theory.* London: Methuen.

KLINE, P. (1981). *Fact and fantasy in Freudian theory* (2nd ed.). London: Methuen.

KLONOFF. H. (1974). Marijuana and driving in real-life situations. *Science, 186,* 317–324.

KLOPFER, B., AINSWORTH, M. D., KLOPFER, W. G., & HOLT, R. R. (1954). *Developments in the Rorschach technique: Vol. I. Technique and theory.* Yonkers, NY: World Book.

KLOPFER, B., AINSWORTH, M. D., KLOPFER, W. G., & HOLT, R. R. (1956). *Developments in the Rorschsch technique: Vol. II. Fields of application.* Yonkers, NY: World Book.

KLOPFER, B., & KELLEY, D. (1942). The *Rorschach technique.* Yonkers, NY: World Book.

KLOPFER, B., MEYER, M. M., & BRAWER, F. (1970). *Developments in the Rorschach technique: Vol. III. Aspects of personality structure.* New York: Harcourt Brace Jovanovich.

KLORMAN, R., STRAUSS, J. S., & KOKES, R. F. (1977). Premorbid adjustment in schizophrenia: Concepts, measures and implications: Part III. The relationship of demographic and diagnostic factors to measures of premorbid adjustment in schizophrenia. *Schizophrenia Bulletin, 3,* 214–225.

KOCH, G. (1973). Down-syndrome. *Mongolisms: Vol. 1. Bibliographica Genetica Medica.* Erlangen: Hogl.

KOCH, R. (1976). Prenatal factors in causation (general). In R. Koch & J. C. Dobson (Eds.), *The mentally retarded child and his family: A multidisciplinary handbook* (rev. ed.). New York: Brunner/Mazel.

KOEK, K. E., & MARTIN, S. (EDS.). (1987). *Encyclopedia of Associations: Vol. 1. National Organizations of the U.S., Part 2* (22nd ed.). Detroit: Gale Research.

KOERPER, J. (1980). Rape prevention—whose responsibility? In C. G. Warner (Ed.), *Rape and sexual assault: Management and intervention.* Germantown, MD: Aspen Systems.

KOHUT, H. (1971). *The analysis of the self: A systematic approach to the psychoanalytic treatment of narcissistic personality disorders.* New York: International Universities Press.

KOHUT, H. (1977). *The restoration of the self.* New York: International Universities Press.

KOKES, R., STRAUSS, J., & KLORMAN, R. (1977). Premorbid adjustment in schizophrenia: Concepts, measures and implications: Part II. Measuring premorbid adjustment: The instruments and their development. *Schizophrenia Bulletin, 3(2),* 186–213.

KOLATA, G. B. (1981a). Clues to the cause of senile dementia. *Science, 211,* 1032–1033.

KOLATA, G. B. (1981b). Consensus on CT scans. *Science, 214,* 1327–1328.

KOLATA, G. B. (1982). Alzheimer's research poses dilemma. *Science, 215,* 47–48.

KOLATA, G. B. (1983). Clues to Alzheimer's disease emerge. *Science, 219,* 941–942.

KOLATA, G. (1986). Manic–depression: Is it inherited? *Science, 232,* 575–576.

KOLB, L. G., & BRODIE, H. K. H. (1982). *Modern clinical psychiatry* (10th ed.). Philadelphia: Saunders.

KOLODNY, R. C., MASTERS, W. H., HENDRIX, J., & TORO, G. (1971). Plasma testosterone and semen analysis in male homosexuals. *New England Journal of Medicine, 285,* 1170–1178.

KOPPITZ, E. M. (1964). *The Bender–Gestalt test for young children.* New York: Grune & Stratton.

KORSTEN, M. A., & LIEBER, C. S. (1985). Medical complications of alcoholism. In J. H. Mendelson & N. K. Mello (Eds.), *The diagnosis and treatment of alcoholism* (2nd ed.). New York: McGraw-Hill.

KOSS, M. P., GIDYCZ, C. A., & WISNIEWSKI, N. (1987). The scope of rape: Incidence and prevalence of sexual aggression and victimization in a national sample of higher education students. *Journal of Consulting and Clinical Psychology, 55,* 162–170.

KOSTEN, T. R., ROUNSAVILLE, B. J., & KLEBER, H. D. (1977). A 2.5-year follow-up of cocaine use among treated opioid addicts. *Archives of General Psychiatry, 44,* 281–284.

KOVACS, M. (1986). A developmental perspective on methods and measures in the assessment of depressive disorders: The clinical interview. In M. Rutter, C. E. Izard, & P. B. Read (Eds.), *Depression in young people: Developmental and clinical perspectives.* New York: Guilford Press.

KOVACS, M., & BECK, A. T. (1977). An empirical–clinical approach toward the definition of childhood depression. In J. G. Schulterbrand & A. Raskin (Eds.), *Depression in childhood: Diagnosis, treatment, and conceptual models.* New York: Raven Press.

KOVACS, M., FEINBERG, T. L., CROUSE-NOVAK, M. A., PAULAUSKAS, S. L., POLLOCK, M., & FEINSTEN, R. (1984). Depressive disorders in childhood: II. A longitudinal study of the risk for a subsequent major depression. *Archives of General Psychiatry, 41*, 643–649.

KOZEL, N. J., & ADAMS, E. H. (1986). Epidemiology of drug abuse: An overview. *Science, 234*, 970–974.

KOZOL, H. L., BOUCHER, R. J., & GAROFOLO, R. F. (1972). The diagnosis and treatment of dangerousness. *Crime and Delinquency, 18*, 371–392.

KRAEPELIN, E. (1923). *Textbook of psychiatry* (8th ed.). New York: Macmillan. (Original work published 1915)

KRAEPELIN, E. (1977). Manic–depressive insanity. In E. A. Wolpert (Ed.), *Manic–depressive illness: History of a syndrome.* New York: International Universities Press. (Original work published 1921)

KRAFT, T. (1970) Treatment of compulsive shoplifting by altering social contingencies. *Behavior Research and Therapy, 8*, 393–394.

KRAMER, B. A. (1985). Use of ECT in California, 1977–1983. *American Journal of Psychiatry, 142*, 1190–1192.

KRANTZ, D. S., CONTRADA, R. J., HILL, D. R., & FRIEDLER, E. (1988). Environmental stress and biobehavioral antecedents of coronary heart disease. *Journal of Consulting and Clinical Psychology, 56*, 333–341.

KRANTZ, D. S., GLASS, D. C., SCHAEFFER, M., & DAVIS, J. (1982). Behavior patterns and coronary disease. A critical evaluation. In J. Cacioppo & R. Petty (Eds.), *Focus on cardiovascular psychopathology.* New York: Guilford Press.

KRANTZ, D. S., & MAANUCK, S. B. (1984). Acute physiologic reactivity and risk of cardiovascular disease: A review and methodological critique. *Psychological Bulletin, 96*, 435–464.

KRASNER, W., & ISENSTEIN, V. R. (1977). *The switch process in manic–depressive illness.* Washington, DC: U.S. Government Printing Office.

KRISHABER, M. (1873). *De la neuropathie cérébro-cardiaque.* Paris: Masson.

KROMPOTIC, E. (1978). Cytogenetic counseling in mental retardation. In C. H. Carter (Ed.), *Medical aspects of mental retardation* (2nd ed.). Springfield, IL: Charles C Thomas.

KRYTER, K. D. (1970). *The effects of noise on man.* New York: Academic Press.

KUCHARSKI, L. T., & UNTERWALD, E. M. (1981). Symptomatic treatment of tardive dyskinesia: A word of caution. *Schizophrenia Bulletin, 7*, 571–573.

KURTZ, R. A. (1977). *Social aspects of mental retardation.* Lexington, MA: Heath.

LACHENMEYER, J. R. (1982). Special disorders of childhood: Depression, school phobia and anorexia nervosa. In J. R. Lachenmeyer & M. S. Gibbs (Eds.), *Psychopathology in childhood.* New York: Gardner Press.

LACHMAN, S. J. (1972). *Psychosomatic disorders: A behavioristic interpretation.* New York: Wiley.

LACHTER, S. B., & WEISMAN, R. (1979). *Let's talk about drug abuse: Some questions and answers.* Washington, DC: U.S. Government Printing Office.

LAHEY, B. B., ET AL. (1988). Psychopathology in the parents of children with conduct disorder and hyperactivity. *Journal of the American Academy of Child and Adolescent Psychiatry, 27*, 163–170.

LAHRER, P. M., & WOOLFOLK, R. L. (1982). Self-report assessment of anxiety: Somatic, cognitive, and behavioral modalities. *Behavior Assessment, 4*, 167–177.

LAING, R. D. (1967). *The politics of experience.* New York: Pantheon.

LAING, R. D., & ESTERSON, A. (1972). *Sanity, madness, and the family: Families of schizophrenics* (2nd ed.). Baltimore: Penguin.

LAMBERT, M. L. (1979). *The effects of psychotherapy.* Montreal: Eden Press.

LAMBERT, M. L. (1981). Evaluating outcome variables in cross-cultural counseling and psychotherapy. In A. J. Marsella & P. B. Pedersen (Eds.), *Cross-cultural counseling and psychotherapy.* New York: Pergamon Press.

LAMBERT, M. L., SHAPIRO, D. A., & BERGIN, A. E. (1986). The effectiveness of psychotherapy. In S. L. Garfield & A. E. Bergin (Eds.), *Handbook of psychotherapy and behavior change* (3rd ed.). New York: Wiley.

LANDERS, S. (1986a, August). Semi-final DSM vote both delights, dismays. *APA Monitor,* p. 15.

LANDERS, S. (1986b, December). Violence in the wake of AIDS. *APA Monitor,* pp. 8–9.

LANDMAN, J. T., & DAWES, R. M. (1982). Psychotherapy outcome. Smith and Glass' conclusions stand up under scrutiny. *American Psychologist, 37*, 504–516.

LANDSMAN, S. & BUTTERFIELD, E. C. (1987). Normalization and deinstitutionalization of mentally retarded individuals: Controversy and facts. *American Psychologist, 42*, 809–816.

LANG, A. R., & MARLATT, G. A. (1982). Problem drinking: A social learning perspective. In R. J. Gatchel, A. Baum, & J. E. Sinfer (Eds.), *Handbook of psychology and health: Vol. 1. Clinical psychology and behavioral medicine: Overlapping disciplines.* Hillsdale, NJ: Erlbaum.

LANGNER, T. S., GERSTEN, J. C., GREENE, E. L., EISENBERG, J. G., HERSON, J. H., & MCCARTHY, E. D. (1974). Treatment of psychological disorders among urban children. *Journal of Consulting and Clinical Psychology, 42*, 170–179.

LANYON, R. I. (1986). Theory and treatment in child molestation. *Journal of Consulting and Clinical Psychology, 54*, 176–182.

LARGE, A. J. (1983, August 10). Preventive action: Suicide research gains as curbing depression becomes more feasible. *Wall Street Journal,* pp. 1, 19.

LARUE, A., DESSONVILLE, C., & JARVIK, L. F. (1985). Aging and mental disorders. In J. E. Birren & K. W. Schaie (Eds.), *Handbook of the psychology of aging* (2nd ed.). New York: Van Nostrand Reinhold.

LAWNER, P. (1985). Recent sociohistorical trends and the ascent of Kohutian "self-psychology." *American Journal of Psychoanalysis, 45*(2), 152–159.

LAZARE, A. (1981). Conversion symptoms. *New England Journal of Medicine, 305,* 745–748.

LAZARUS, A. A. (1963). The treatment of chronic frigidity by systematic desensitization. *Journal of Nervous and Mental Disease, 136,* 272–278.

LAZARUS, A. A. (1971). *Behavior therapy and beyond.* New York: McGraw–Hill.

LAZARUS, A. A. (1976). Multimodal behavior therapy: Treating the BASIC ID. In A. A. Lazarus (Ed.), *Multimodal behavior therapy.* New York: Springer.

LAZARUS, A. A. (1980). Psychological treatment of dyspareunia. In S. R. Leiblum & L. A. Pervin (Eds.), *Principles and practice of sex therapy.* New York: Guilford Press.

LAZARUS, A. A. (1981). *The practice of multimodal therapy: Systematic, comprehensive, and effective psychotherapy.* New York: McGraw–Hill.

LAZARUS, A. A. (1984). Multimodal therapy. In R. J. Corsini & D. Wedding (Eds.), *Current psychotherapies* (3rd ed.). Itasca, IL: Peacock.

LAZARUS, A. A. (1985). A brief overview of multimodal therapy. In A. A. Lazarus (Ed.), *Casebook of multimodal therapy.* New York: Guilford Press.

LEAVITT, F. (1974). *Drugs and behavior.* Philadelphia: Saunders.

LEBOVITZ, P. S. (1972). Feminine behavior in boys: Aspects of its outcomes. *American Journal of Psychiatry, 128,* 1283–1289.

LEDWIDGE, B. (1978). Cognitive behavior modification: A step in the wrong direction. *Psychological Bulletin, 85,* 353–375.

LEFF, J. (1981). *Psychiatry around the globe: A transcultural view.* New York: Dekker.

LEFKOWITZ, M. M., & BURTON, N. (1978). Childhood depression: A critique of the concept. *Psychological Bulletin, 85,* 716–726.

LEFLEY, H. P. (1986). The cross-cultural training institute for mental health professionals. In H. P. Lefley & P. B. Pedersen, *Cross-cultural training for mental health professionals.* Springfield, IL: Charles C Thomas.

LEHRER, P. M., & WOOLFOLK, R. L. (1982). Self-report assessment of anxiety: Somatic, cognitive, and behavioral modalities. *Behavior Assessment, 4,* 167–177.

LEI, T., NIHIRA, L., SHEEHY, N., & MEYERS, C. E. (1981). A study of small family care for mentally retarded people. In R. H. Bruininks, C. E. Meyers, B. B. Sigford, & K. C. Lakin. *Deinstitutionalization and community adjustment of mentally retarded people.* Washington, DC: American Association on Mental Deficiency.

LEJEUNE, J., TURPIN, R., & GAUTIER, M. (1959). Le mongolisme: Premier exemple d'aberration autosomique humaine. *Annals de Génétique, 1,* 41–49.

LELAND, J. (1976). *Firewater myths: North American Indian drinking and alcohol addiction.* New Brunswick, NJ: Rutgers Center of Alcohol Studies.

LENNARD, H. L., EPSTEIN, L. J., BERNSTEIN, A., & RANSOM, D. C. (1970). Hazards implicit in prescribing psychoactive drugs. *Science, 169,* 438–441.

LEON, G. R. (1974). *Case histories of deviant behavior: A social learning analysis.* Boston: Holbrook Press.

LEONARD, W. E. (1928). *The locomotive-god.* London: Chapman and Hall.

LESIEUR, H. R. (1977). *The chase: Career of the compulsive gambler.* Garden City, NY: Anchor Press/Doubleday.

LETTERS TO THE EDITOR. (1961). Mongolism. *Lancet, 1,* 775.

LEVANT, R. F. (1987). Foreword: Psychotherapy with families [Special issue]. *Psychotherapy, 24*(3S), 453–454.

LEVINE, B. (1979). *Group psychotherapy: Practice and development.* Englewood Cliffs, NJ: Prentice–Hall.

LEVINE, P., KATZIN, E., & BURNHAM, L. (1941). Immunization in pregnancy. *Journal of the American Medical Association, 116,* 825–827.

LEVIS, D. J. (1974). Implosive therapy: A critical analysis of Morganstern's review. *Psychological Bulletin, 81,* 155–158.

LEVITT, E. E. (1971). Research on psychotherapy with children. In A. E. Bergin & S. Garfield (Eds.), *Handbook of psychotherapy and behavior change: An empirical analysis.* New York: Wiley.

LEVY, L. H. (1983). Trait approaches. In M. Hersen, A. E. Kazdin, & A. S. Bellack (Eds.), *The clinical psychology handbook.* New York: Pergamon Press.

LEWINE, R. R. J. (1985). Editor's introduction: Negative symptoms in schizophrenia. *Schizophrenia Bulletin, 11,* 361–363.

LEWINSOHN, P. M. (1975). The behavioral study and treatment of depression. In M. Hersen, R. M. Eisler, & P. M. Miller (Eds.), *Progress in behavior modification* (Vol. 1). New York: Academic Press.

LEWIS, A. (1974). Psychopathic personality: A most elusive category. *Psychological Medicine, 4,* 133–140.

LEWIS, A. J. (1934). Melancholia: A historical review. *Journal of Mental Science, 80,* 1–42.

LEWIS, J. M., RODNICK, E. H., & GOLDMAN, M. J. (1981). Intrafamilial interactive behavior, parental communication deviance, and risk for schizophrenia. *Journal of Abnormal Psychology, 90,* 448–457.

LEX, B. W. (1985). Alcohol problems in special populations. In J. H. Mendelson & N. K. Mello (Eds.), *The diagnosis and treatment of alcoholism* (2nd ed.). New York: McGraw–Hill.

LEY, R. (1987). Panic disorder: A hyperventilation interpretation. In L. Michelson & L. M. Ascher (Eds.), *Anxiety and stress disorder: Cognitive–behavioral assessment and treatment.* New York: Guilford Press.

LICHTENSTEIN, E., & BROWN, R. A. (1980). Smoking cessation methods: Review and recommendation. In W. R. Miller (Ed.), *The addictive behaviors: Treatment of alcoholism, drug abuse, smoking, and obesity.* Oxford: Pergamon Press.

LICKEY, M. E., & GORDON, B. (1983). *Drugs for mental illness: A revolution in psychiatry.* San Francisco: Freeman.

LIDZ, T., CORNELISON, A. R., FLECK, S., & TERRY, D. (1957). The intrafamilial environment of the schizophrenic patient: I. The father. *Psychiatry, 20,* 329–342.

LIEF, H. (1977). What's new in sex research? Inhibited sex desire. *Medical Aspects of Human Sexuality, 11*(7), 94–95.

LINDBECK, V. (1972). The woman alcoholic: A review of the literature. *International Journal of the Addictions, 7,* 567–580.

LINDEMALM, G., KORLIN, D., & UDDENBERG, N. (1986). Long-term follow-up of "sex change" in 13 male-to-female transsexuals. *Archives of Sexual Behavior, 15,* 187–210.

LINDEMAN, E. C. (1967). Quoted in *Contemporary Psychology, 12,* 262.

LINDNER, R. M. (1944). *Rebel without a cause.* New York: Grove Press.

LINN, E. L. (1961). Agents, timing, and events leading to mental hospitalization. *Human Organization, 20,* 90–98.

LIPOWSKI, Z. J. (1973). Psychosomatic medicine in a changing society: Some current trends in theory and research. *Comprehensive Psychiatry, 14,* 203–215.

LIPOWSKI, Z. J. (1977). Introduction. In Z. J. Lipowski, D. R. Lipsitt, & P. C. Whybrow (Eds.), *Psychosomatic medicine: Current trends and clinical applications.* New York: Oxford University Press.

LIPOWSKI, Z. J. (1980a). A new look at organic brain syndromes. *American Journal of Psychiatry, 137,* 674–678.

LIPOWSKI, Z. J. (1980b). Organic mental disorders: Introduction and review of syndromes. In H. I. Kaplan, A. M. Freedman, & B. J. Sadock (Eds.), *Comprehensive textbook of psychiatry* (Vol. 2) (3rd ed.). Baltimore: Williams & Wilkins.

LIPOWSKI, Z. J. (1980c). *Delirium: Acute brain failure in man.* Springfield, IL: Charles C Thomas.

LIPOWSKI, Z. J. (1984). What does the word "psychosomatic" really mean? A historical and semantic inquiry. *Psychosomatic Medicine, 46,* 153–171.

LIPSITT, P. (1980). Emergency admission of civil involuntary patients to mental hospitals following statutory modification. In P. D. Lipsitt & B. D. Sales (Eds.), *New directions in psycholegal research.* New York: Van Nostrand Reinhold.

LISTON, E. H. (1979). The clinical phenomenology of presenile dementia: A critical review of the literature. *Journal of Nervous and Mental Disease, 167,* 329–336.

LLOYD, C. (1980). Life events and depressive disorder reviewed: II. Events as precipitant factors. *Archives of General Psychiatry, 37,* 529–535.

LOBITZ, W. C., & BAKER, E. L. (1979). Group treatment of single males with erectile dysfunction. *Archives of Sexual Behavior, 8,* 127–138.

LOEHLIN, J. C., WILLERMAN, L., & HORN, J. M. (1988). Human behavior genetics. *Annual Review of Psychology, 39,* 101–133.

LOGAN, D. G., & DEODHAR, S. D. (1970). Schizophrenia, an immunologic disorder. *Journal of the American Medical Association, 212,* 1703–1704.

LOH, W. D. (1981). Q: What has reform of rape legislation wrought? A: Truth in criminal labelling. *Journal of Social Issues, 37,* 28–52.

LONEY, J. (1980). Hyperkinesis comes of age: What do we know and where should we go? *American Journal of Orthopsychiatry, 50,* 28–42.

LoPICCOLO, J., HEIMAN, J. R., HOGAN, D. R., & ROBERTS, C. W. (1985). Effectiveness of single therapists versus cotherapy teams in sex therapy. *Journal of Consulting and Clinical Psychology, 53,* 287–294.

LoPICCOLO, J., & LOBITZ, W. C. (1972). The role of masturbation in the treatment of orgasmic dysfunction. *Archives of Sexual Behavior, 2,* 163–171.

LoPICCOLO, J., & MILLER, V. H. (1975). A program for enhancing the sexual relationship of normal couples. *Counseling Psychologist, 5,* 41–45.

LoPICCOLO, J., & STOCK, W. E. (1986). Treatment of sexual dysfunction. *Journal of Consulting and Clinical Psychology, 54,* 158–167.

LoPICCOLO, L. (1980). Low sexual desire. In S. R. Leiblum & L. A. Pervin (Eds.), *Principles and practice of sex therapy.* New York: Guilford Press.

LORAINE, J. A., ADAMOPOULOS, D. A., KIRKHAM, E. E., ISMAIL, A. A., & DOVE, G. A. (1971). Patterns of hormone excretion in male and female homosexuals. *Nature, 234,* 552–555.

LOTHSTEIN, L. M. (1980). The post-surgical transsexual: Empirical and theoretical considerations. *Archives of Sexual Behavior, 9,* 547–564.

LOTHSTEIN, L. (1982). Sex reassignment surgery: Historical, bioethical, and theoretical issues. *American Journal of Psychiatry, 139,* 417–426.

LOTHSTEIN, L. M., & LEVINE, S. B. (1981). Expressive psychotherapy with gender dysphoric patients. *Archives of General Psychiatry, 38,* 924–929.

LOVAAS, O. I. (1977). *The autistic child: Language development through behavior modification.* New York: Irvington.

LUBORSKY, L., DOCHERTY, J. P., & PENICK, S. (1973). Onset conditions for psychosomatic symptoms: A comparative review of immediate observation with retrospective research. *Psychosomatic Medicine, 35,* 187–203.

LUBORSKY, L., SINGER, B., & LUBORSKY, L. (1975). Comparative studies of psychotherapies. *Archives of General Psychiatry, 32,* 995–1008.

LUBORSKY, L., & SPENCE, D. P. (1978). Quantitative research on psychoanalytic therapy. In S. L. Garfield & A. E. Bergin (Eds.), *Handbook of psychotherapy and behavior change: An empirical analysis* (2nd ed.). New York: Wiley.

LUDOLPH, P. S. (1985). How prevalent is multiple personality? *American Journal of Psychiatry, 142,* 1526–1527.

LUDWIG, A. M. (1980). *Principles of clinical psychiatry.* New York: Free Press.

LUFTIG, R. L. (1988). Assessment of the perceived school loneliness and isolation of mentally retarded and nonretarded students. *American Journal of Mental Retardation, 93,* 472–475.

LUKOFF, D., SNYDER, K., VENTURA, J., & NUECHTERLEIN, K. H. (1984). Life events, familial stress, and coping in the developmental course of schizophrenia. *Schizophrenia Bulletin, 10,* 258–292.

LUNDWALL, L., & BAEKELAND, F. (1971). Disulfiram treatment of alcoholism: A review. *Journal of Nervous and Mental Disease, 153,* 381–384.

LURIA, A. R. (1970). *Traumatic aphasia: Its syndromes, psychology, and treatment.* The Hague: Mouton.

LURIA, A. R. (1972). *The man with a shattered world: The history of a brain wound* (L. Solotaroff, Trans.). New York: Basic Books.

LURIA, Z., & OSGOOD, C. E. (1976). The three faces of Evelyn—a case report: IV. A postscript to "The Three Faces of Evelyn." *Journal of Abnormal Psychology, 85,* 276–286.

LUTHER, S. L., & PRICE, J. H. (1980). Child sexual abuse: A review. *Journal of School Health, 30,* 161–165.

LYNCH, E. W., SIMMS, B. H., VON HIPPEL, C. A., & SCHUCHAT, J. (1980). *Mainstreaming preschoolers: Children with mental retardation.* Washington, DC: U.S. Government Printing Office.

LYONS, R. D. (1983, December 27). Migraine headaches: Promising treatment investigated. *New York Times,* pp. 19, 21.

MAAS, J. W. (1975). Biogenic amines and depression. *Archives of General Psychiatry, 32,* 1357–1365.

MAAS, J. W., KOSLOW, S. H., DAVIS, J., KATZ, M., FRAZER, A., BOWDEN, C. L., BERMAN, N., GIBBONS, R., STOKES, P., & LANDIS, H. (1987). Catecholamine metabolism and disposition in healthy and depressed subjects. *Archives of General Psychiatry, 44,* 337–344.

MACANDREW, C., & EDGERTON, R. B. (1969). *Drunken comportment: A social explanation.* Chicago: Aldine.

MACHOL, L. (1980). Environmental hazards: What they'll mean to your patients in the 1980s. *Contemporary Ob/Gyn, 15,* 22–43.

MACMILLAN, D. L. (1982). *Mental retardation in school and society* (2nd ed.). Boston: Little, Brown.

MADDOX, G. L. (1980). The continuum of care: Movement toward the community. In E. W. Busse & D. G. Blazer (Eds.), *Handbook of geriatric psychiatry.* New York: Van Nostrand Reinhold.

MADURO, R. J., & WHEELWRIGHT, J. E. (1977). Analytical psychology. In R. J. Corsini (Ed.), *Current personality theories.* Itasca, IL: Peacock.

MAGENIS, R. E., OVERTON, K. M., CHAMBERLIN, J., BRADY, T., & LOURIEN, E. (1977). Parental origin of the extra chromosome in Down's syndrome. *Human Genetics, 36,* 7–16.

MAHER, B. A. (1966). *Principles of psychopathology: An experimental approach.* New York: McGraw–Hill.

MAHER, B. (1970). Introduction to research in psychopathology. New York: McGraw–Hill.

MAHLER, A. (1968). *Gustav Mahler: Memories and letters.* Seattle: University of Washington Press.

MAHONEY, M. J. (1977). Reflections on the cognitive learning trend in psychotherapy. *American Psychologist, 32,* 5–13.

MAHONEY, M. J. (1980). Psychotherapy and the structures of personal revolutions. In M. J. Mahoney (Ed.), *Psychotherapy process: Current issues and future directions.* New York: Plenum.

MALCOLM, J. (1981). *Psychoanalysis: The impossible profession.* New York: Knopf.

MALMQUIST, C. P. (1983). Major depression in childhood: Why don't we know more? *American Journal of Orthopsychiatry, 53,* 262–268.

MANN, T. (1939). *The magic mountain.* New York: Knopf.

MANSFIELD, R. S., & BUSSE, T. V. (1977). Meta-analysis of research: A rejoinder to Glass. *Educational Researcher, 6,* 3.

MARCOVICI, M., O'BRIEN, C. P., McCLELLAN, A. T., & KACIAN, J. (1981). A clinical controlled study of l-a-acetylmethadol in the treatment of narcotic addiction. *American Journal of Psychiatry, 138,* 234–236.

MARGOLICK, D. (1984, December 21). Top court in New York rules men can be charged in rape of wives. *New York Times,* pp. 1, 14.

MARGOLICK, D. (1985, May 11). Many veterans cite trauma of Vietnam in trials. *New York Times,* pp. 1, 11.

MARKS, I. M. (1969). *Fears and phobias.* New York: Academic Press.

MARKS, I. M. (1978a). *Living with fear: Understanding and coping with anxiety.* New York: McGraw–Hill.

MARKS, I. M. (1978b). Behavioral psychotherapy of adult neurosis. In S. L. Garfield & A. E. Bergin (Eds.), *Handbook of psychotherapy and behavior change: An empirical analysis* (2nd ed.). New York: Wiley.

MARLATT, G. A. (1983). The controlled-drinking controversy: A commentary. *American Psychologist, 38,* 1097–1110.

MARLATT, G. A. (1985). Controlled drinking: The controversy rages on. *American Psychologist, 40,* 372–373.

MARSELLA, A. J. (1980). Depressive experience and disorder across cultures. In H. C. Triandis & J. G. Draguns (Eds.), *Handbook of cross-cultural psychology: Vol. 6. Psychopathology.* Boston: Allyn & Bacon.

MARSHALL, E. (1988). Flying blind in the war on drugs. *Science, 240,* 1605–1607.

MARTIN, D. G. (1972). *Learning-based client-centered therapy.* Monterey, CA: Brooks/Cole.

MARZILLIER, J. (1987). A sadly neglected element in depression: A reply to Ellis. *Cognitive Therapy and Research, 11,* 147–151.

MARZNAGAO, L. R. (1972). Systematic desensitization treatment of kleptomania. *Journal of Behavior Therapy and Experimental Psychiatry, 3,* 327–328.

MASLOW, A. (1954). *Motivation and personality.* New York: Harper & Bros.

MASSARIK, R., & KABACH, M. M. (1981). Genetic disease control: A social psychological approach. *Sage Library of Social Research* (Vol. 116). Beverly Hills, CA: Sage.

MASSERMAN, J. H. (1973). *Theory and therapy in dynamic psychiatry.* New York: Aronson.

MASTERS, W. H., & JOHNSON, V. E. (1966). *Human sexual response.* Boston: Little, Brown.

MASTERS, W. H., & JOHNSON, V. E. (1970). *Human sexual inadequacy.* Boston: Little, Brown.

MASTERS, W. H., & JOHNSON, V. E. (1982). Sex and the aging process. *Medical Aspects of Human Sexuality, 16*(6), 40, 53–57.

MASTERS, W. H., JOHNSON, V. E., & KOLODNY, R. C. (1986). *Masters and Johnson on sex and human loving.* Boston: Little, Brown.

MASTERS, W. H., JOHNSON, V. E., & KOLODNY, R. C. (1988). *Human sexuality* (3rd ed.). Glenview, IL: Scott, Foresman.

MATARAZZO, J. D. (1972). *Wechsler's measurement and appraisal of adult intelligence* (5th ed.). Baltimore: Williams & Wilkins.

MATSUNGA, E., TONOMURA, A., OISHI, H., & YASUMOTO, K. (1978). Reexamination of parental age effect in Down's syndrome. *Human Genetics, 40,* 259–268.

MATTHEWS, K. A. (1982). Psychological perspectives in the Type A behavior pattern. *Psychological Bulletin, 91,* 293–323.

MAY, C. D. (1988, January 25). Coca-Cola discloses an old secret. *New York Times,* pp. 25, 29.

MAY, R. (1969). The emergence of existentialist psychology. In R. May (Ed.), *Existentialist psychology* (2nd ed.). New York: Random House.

MAY, R. (1977). *The meaning of anxiety* (rev. ed.). New York: Norton.

MCANDREW, C., & EDGERTON, R. B. (1969). *Drunken comportment: A social explanation.* Chicago: Aldine.

MCCAIN, G., COX, V. C., & PAULUS, P. B. (1976). The relationship between illness, complaints and degree of crowding in a prison environment. *Environment and Behavior, 8,* 283–290.

MCCARTHY, J., & BORDERS, O. T. (1985). Limit setting on drug abuse in methadone maintenance patients. *American Journal of Psychiatry, 142,* 1419–1423.

MCCARY, J. L. (1979). *Human sexuality* (2nd ed.). New York: Van Nostrand Reinhold.

MCCLAREN, J., & BRYSON, S. E. (1987). Review of recent epidemiological studies of mental retardation: Prevalence, associated disorders, and etiology. *American Journal of Mental Retardation, 92,* 243–254.

MCCORD, W. M. (1982). *The psychopath and milieu therapy: A longitudinal study.* New York: Academic Press.

MCCOY, S. A. (1976). Clinical judgments of normal childhood behavior. *Journal of Consulting and Clinical Psychology, 44,* 710–714.

MCCRAINIE, E. J. (1979). Hypochondriacal neurosis. *Psychosomatics, 20,* 11–15.

MCCURDY, H. G. (1941). A note on the dissociation of a personality. *Character and Personality, 10,* 33–41.

MCGEE, R. K. (1974). *Crisis intervention in the community.* Baltimore: University Park Press.

MCGEER, P. L., & MCGEER, E. G. (1980). Chemistry of mood and emotion. *Annual Review of Psychology, 31,* 273–307.

MCGHIE, A., & CHAPMAN, H. (1961). Disorders of attention and perception in early schizophrenia. *British Journal of Medical Psychology, 34,* 103–116.

MCGLASHAN, T. H. (1986a). The Chestnut Lodge follow-up study: III. Long-term outcome of borderline personalities. *Archives of General Psychiatry, 45,* 20–30.

MCGLASHAN, T. H. (1986b). The prediction of outcome in chronic schizophrenia: IV. The Chestnut Lodge follow-up study. *Archives of General Psychiatry, 43,* 167–176.

MCGLASHAN, T. H. (1986c). Schizotypal personality disorder. Chestnut Lodge follow-up study: VI. Long-term follow-up perspectives. *Archives of General Psychiatry, 43,* 329–334.

MCGUFFIN, R., FARMER, A. E., GOTTESMAN, I. I., MURRAY, R. M., & REVELEY, A. M. (1984). Twin concordance for operationally defined schizophrenia. *Archives of General Psychiatry, 41,* 541–545.

MCINTOSH, J. L. (1985). Suicide among the elderly: Levels and trends. *American Journal of Orthopsychiatry, 55,* 288–293.

MCKAY, H., SINISTERRA, L., MCKAY, A., GOMEZ, H., & LLOREDA, P. (1978). Improving cognitive ability in chronically deprived children. *Science, 200,* 270–278.

MCLEAN, E. K., & TARNOPOLSKY, A. (1977). Noise, discomfort, and mental health: A review of the socio-medical implications of disturbance by noise. *Psychological Medicine, 7,* 19–62.

MCMULLIN, R. E. (1986). *Handbook of cognitive therapy techniques.* New York: Norton.

MCNALLY, R. J. (1987). Preparedness in phobias: A review. *Psychological Bulletin, 101,* 283–303.

MCNEIL, E. B. (1967). *The quiet furies: Man and disorder.* Englewood Cliffs, NJ: Prentice–Hall.

MCNETT, I. (1982, January). Psy.D. fills demand for practitioners. *APA Monitor,* pp. 10–11.

MCREYNOLDS, W. T. (1976). Anxiety as a fear: A behavioral approach to one emotion. In M. Zuckerman & C. D. Speilberger (Eds.), *Emotions and anxiety: New concepts, methods, and applications.* Hillside, NJ: Erlbaum.

MEAD, M. (1979). On Freud's view of female psychology. In J. H. Williams (Ed.), *Psychology of women: Selected readings.* New York: Norton.

MEADOR, B. D., & ROGERS, C. R. (1973). Client-centered therapy. In R. Corsini (Ed.), *Current psychotherapies.* Itasca, IL: Peacock.

MEADOR, B. D., & ROGERS, C. R. (1979). Person-centered therapy. In R. J. Corsini (Ed.), *Current psychotherapies* (2nd ed.). Itasca, IL: Peacock.

MEADOR, B. D., & ROGERS, C. R. (1984). Person-centered therapy. In R. J. Corsini & D. Wedding (Eds.), *Current psychotherapies* (3rd ed.). Itasca, IL: Peacock.

MECHANIC, D. (1974a). *Politics, medicine, and social science.* New York: Wiley.

MECHANIC, D. (1974b). Discussion of research programs on relations between stressful life events and episodes of physical illness. In B. S. Dohrenwend & B. P. Dohrenwend (Eds.), *Stressful life events: Their nature and effects.* New York: Wiley.

MEEHL, P. E. (1986). Diagnostic taxa as open concepts: Metatheoretical and statistical questions about reliability and construct validity in the grand strategy of nosological revision. In T. Millon & G. L. Klerman (Eds.), *Contemporary directions in psychopathology: Toward the DSM-IV.* New York: Guilford Press.

MEHLMAN, S. K., BAUCOM, D. H., & ANDERSON, D. (1983). Effectiveness of cotherapists versus single therapists and immediate versus delayed treatment in behavioral marital therapy. *Journal of Consulting and Clinical Psychology, 51,* 258–266.

MEICHENBAUM, D. (1977). *Cognitive behavior modification.* New York: Plenum.

MEICHENBAUM, D. (1986). *Cognitive behavior modification*. In F. H. Kanfer & A. P. Goldstein (Eds.), *Helping people change* (3rd ed.). New York: Pergamon Press.

MELCHER, J. (1988). Keeping our elderly out of institutions by putting them back in their homes. *American Psychologist, 43*, 643–647.

MELTZER, H. Y. (1987). Biological studies in schizophrenia. *Schizophrenia Bulletin, 13*, 77–111.

MELTZOFF, J., & KORNREICH, M. (1970). *Research in psychotherapy*. Chicago: Aldine.

MELZACK, R. (1975). The promise of biofeedback: Don't hold the party yet. *Psychology Today, 9*(2), 18–22, 80–81.

MEMORY IS A BLANK FOR YOUTH WALKING ONTO KEY WEST BEACH (1972, June 2), *New York Times*, p. 70.

MENDELS, J. (1970). *Concepts of depression*. New York: Wiley.

MENDELS, J. (1974). Biological aspects of affective illness. In S. Arieti (Ed.), *American handbook of psychiatry* (Vol. 3) (2nd ed.). New York: Basic Books.

MENDELS, J. (1975). Postscript. In J. Mendels (Ed.), *The psychology of depression*. New York: Spectrum.

MENDELS, J., STERN, S., & FRAZER, A. (1976). Biological concepts of depression. In D. M. Gallant & G. M. Simpson (Eds.), *Depression: Behavioral, biochemical, diagnostic and treatment concepts*. New York: Spectrum.

MENDELSON, J. H., & MELLO, N. K. (1985). Diagnostic criteria for alcoholism and alcohol abuse. In J. H. Mendelson & N. K. Mello (Eds.), *The diagnosis and treatment of alcoholism* (2nd ed.). McGraw–Hill.

MENNINGER, K., MAYMAN, M., & PRUYSER, P. (1963). *The vital balance: The life process in mental health and illness*. New York: Viking Press.

MENTAL HEALTH ASSOCIATION. (No date). *Facts about mental illness*. Arlington, VA: Author.

MENTAL HEALTH ASSOCIATION. (No date). *How to deal with mental problems*. Arlington, VA: Author.

MENTAL HEALTH ASSOCIATION. (No date). *How to deal with your tensions*. Arlington, VA: Author.

MENTAL HEALTH ASSOCIATION. (No date). *Mental illness can be prevented*. Arlington, VA: Author.

MERCER, J. R. (1973). *Labeling the mentally retarded: Clinical and social system perspectives on mental retardation*. Berkeley: University of California Press.

MERCIER, C. (1902). *Textbook of insanity*. London: Macmillan.

MERRITT, R. D., & BALOGH, D. W. (1985). Critical stimulus duration: Schizophrenic trait or state? *Schizophrenia Bulletin, 11*, 341–343.

MERSKEY, H. (1980). *Psychiatric illness: Diagnosis, management, and treatment for general practitioners and students*. London: Baillière, Tindall.

MERSKEY, H., & SHAFRAN, B. (1986). Political hazards in the diagnosis of "sluggish schizophrenia." *British Journal of Psychiatry, 148*, 247–256.

MERVIS, J. (1986, July). NIMH data points way to effective treatment. *APA Monitor*, pp. 1, 13.

METCALF, S., & WILLIAMS, W. (1977). A case of childhood transsexualism and its management. *Australian and New Zealand Journal of Psychiatry, 11*, 53–59.

MEYER, A. (1934). The psychobiological point of view. In M. Bentley & E. V. Cowdry (Eds.), *The problem of mental disorder*. New York: McGraw–Hill.

MEYER, A. (1935). The birth and development of the mental hygiene movement. *Mental Hygiene, 19*, 29–37.

MEYER, J. K. (1980). Paraphilias. In H. I. Kaplan, A. M. Freedman, & B. J. Sadock (Eds.), *Comprehensive textbook of psychiatry* (Vol. 2) (3rd ed.). Baltimore: Williams & Wilkins.

MEYER, J. K. (1985). Paraphilias. In H. J. Kaplan & B. J. Sadock (Eds.), *Comprehensive textbook of psychiatry* (4th ed.). Baltimore: Williams & Wilkins.

MEYER, R. J. (1980). Attitudes of parents of institutionalized mentally retarded individuals toward deinstitutionalization. *American Journal of Mental Deficiency, 85*, 184–187.

MEYER, C. E., NIHIRA, K., & ZEITLIN, A. (1979). The measurement of adaptive behavior. In N. R. Ellis (Ed.), *Handbook of mental deficiency: Psychological theory and research* (2nd ed.). Hillside, NJ: Erlbaum.

MEYERS, D. H., & GRANT, C. (1972). A study of depersonalization in students. *British Journal of Psychiatry, 121*, 59–65.

MILLER, E. (1967). Psychological theories of E.C.T.: A review. *British Journal of Psychiatry, 113*, 301–311.

MILLER, E. (1972). *Clinical neuropsychology*. Baltimore: Penguin.

MILLER, J. O. (1970). Cultural deprivation and its modification: Effect of intervention. In H. C. Haywood (Ed.), *Socio-cultural Aspects of Mental Retardation: Proceedings of the Peabody NIMH Conference*. New York: Appleton–Century–Crofts.

MILLER, M. E. (1980). Middle age and maturity (old age). In S. E. Greben, R. Pos, V. M. Rakoff, A. Bonkalo, F. H. Lowy, & G. Voinseskos (Eds.), *A method of psychiatry*. Philadelphia: Lea & Febiger.

MILLER, N. E. (1969). Learning of visceral and glandular responses. *Science, 163*, 434–445.

MILLER, N. E. (1974). Biofeedback: Evaluation of a new technique. *New England Journal of Medicine, 290*, 684–685.

MILLER, N. E. (1978). Biofeedback and visceral learning. *Annual Review of Psychology, 29*, 373–404.

MILLER, N. E., & DWORKIN, B. R. (1977). Critical issues in therapeutic applications of biofeedback. In G. E. Schwartz & J. Beatty (Eds.), *Biofeedback: Theory and research*. New York: Academic Press.

MILLER, P. M., & EISLER, R. M. (1975). Alcohol and drug abuse. In W. E. Craighead, A. E. Kazdin, & M. J. Mahoney (Eds.), *Behavior modification: Principles, issues and applications*. Boston: Houghton Mifflin.

MILLER, W. R. (1978). Behavioral treatment of problem drinkers: A comparative outcome study of three controlled drinking therapies. *Journal of Consulting and Clinical Psychology, 46*, 74–86.

MILLER, W. R., & CADDY, G. R. (1977). Abstinence and controlled drinking in the treatment of problem drinkers. *Journal of Studies on Alcohol, 38,* 986–1003.

MILLER, W. R., & HESTER, R. K. (1980). Treating the problem drinker: Modern approaches. In W. R. Miller (Ed.), *The addictive behaviors: Treatment of alcoholism, drug abuse, smoking and obesity.* Oxford: Pergamon Press.

MILLER, W. R., ROSELLINI, R. A., & SELIGMAN, M. E. P. (1977). Learned helplessness and depression. In J. D. Maser & M. E. P. Seligman (Eds.), *Psychopathology: Experimental models.* San Francisco: Freeman.

MILLER, W. R., & SELIGMAN, M. E. P. (1975). Depression and learned helplessness. *Journal of Abnormal Psychology, 84,* 228–238.

MILLETT, K. (1970). *Sexual politics.* Garden City, NY: Doubleday.

MILLIC, J. H., & CROWNE, D. P. (1986). Recalled parent–child relationships and need for approval of homosexual and heterosexual men. *Archives of Sexual Behavior, 15,* 239–246.

MILLON, T. (1969). *Modern psychopathology: A biosocial approach to maladaptive learning and functioning.* Philadelphia: Saunders.

MILLON, T. (1975). Reflections on Rosenhan's "On being sane in insane places." *Journal of Abnormal Psychology, 84,* 456–461.

MILLON, T. (1986). On the past and future of the DSM-III: Personal recollections. In T. Millon & G. L. Klerman (Eds.), *Contemporary directions in psychopathology: Toward the DSM-IV.* New York: Guilford Press.

MILLON, T. (1987). On the genesis and prevalence of the borderline personality disorder: A social learning thesis. *Journal of Personality Disorders, 1,* 64–82.

MILLON, T. & EVERLY, G. S., JR. (1985). *Personality and its disorders: A biosocial learning approach.* New York: Wiley.

MILLON, T., & KLERMAN, G. L. (EDS.). (1986). *Contemporary directions in psychopathology: Toward the DSM-IV.* New York: Guilford Press.

MILLON, T., & MILLON, R. (1974). *Abnormal behavior and personality: A biosocial learning approach.* Philadelphia: Saunders.

MILNE, A. A. (1961). *When we were very young.* New York: Dutton. (Original work published 1924)

MINTZ, E. E. (1986). Marathon groups. In I. L. Kutash & A. A. Wolff (Eds.), *Psychotherapists' casebook.* San Francisco: Jossey–Bass.

MINUCHIN, S. (1974). *Families and family therapy.* Cambridge, MA: Harvard University Press.

MINUCHIN, S., & FISHMAN, H. C. (1981). *Family therapy techniques.* Cambridge, MA: Harvard University Press.

MINUCHIN, S., ROSMAN, B. L., & BAKER, L. (1978). *Psychosomatic families.* Cambridge, MA: Harvard University Press.

MISHLER, E. G., & WAXLER, N. E. (1968). *Interaction in families: An experimental study of family processes and schizophrenia.* New York: Wiley.

MISHNE, J. (ED.). (1980). *Psychotherapy and training in clinical social work.* New York: Gardner Press.

MITCHELL, J. E. (1986). Laxative abuse complicating bulimia: Medical and treatment implications. *International Journal of Eating Disorders, 5,* 325–333.

MOLLER, H-J., SCHMID-BODE, W., & VON ZERSSEN, D. (1986). Prediction of long-term outcome in schizophrenia by prognostic scales. *Schizophrenia Bulletin, 12,* 225–234.

MOLLICA, R. F., BOSCARINO, J., & REDLICH, F. C. (1986). A community study of formal pastoral counseling activities of the clergy. *The American Journal of Psychiatry, 143,* 323–328.

MOLOTSKY, I. (1985, March 16). Changing patterns of use in prescriptions in U.S. *New York Times,* p. 18.

MONAHAN, J. (1973). Abolish the insanity defense?—not yet. *Rutgers Law Review, 26,* 719–740.

MONEY, J. (1987). Sin, sickness, or status? Homosexual gender identity and psychoneuroendocrinology. *American Psychologist, 42,* 384–399.

MONEY, J., & ERHARDT, A. A. (1972). *Man and woman, boy and girl: The differentiation and dimorphism of gender identity from conception to maturity.* Baltimore: Johns Hopkins University Press.

MONROE, R. R. (1970). *Episodic behavioral disorders.* Cambridge, MA: Harvard University Press.

MORA, G. (1975). Introduction: Heinroth's contribution to psychiatry. In J. C. Heinroth, *Textbook of disturbances of mental life* (Vol. 1) (J. Schmorak, Trans.). Baltimore, MD: Johns Hopkins University Press.

MOREL, B. A. (1860). *Traité des maladies mentales* [Treatise on mental illness]. Paris: Baillière.

MORENO, J. L. (1947). *Psychodrama.* Beacon, NY: Beacon House.

MORENO, J. L. (1953). *Who shall survive?* (rev. ed.). Beacon, NY: Beacon House.

MORENO, J. L., & KIPPER, D. A. (1968). Group psychodrama and community-centered counseling. In G. M. Gazada (Ed.), *Basic approaches to group psychotherapy and group counseling.* Springfield, IL: Charles C Thomas.

MORGANSTERN, K. P. (1973). Implosive therapy and flooding procedures: A critical review. *Psychological Bulletin, 79,* 328–334.

MORRIS, G. (1983). Acquittal by reason of insanity: Developments in the law. In J. Monahan & H. J. Steadman (Eds.), *Mentally disordered offenders. Perspectives from law and science.* New York: Plenum.

MORRIS, J. (1986, July). DART program (depression, awareness, recognition, treatment) takes aim at depression. *APA Monitor,* pp. 1, 13.

MORRIS, R. J., & KRATOCHWILL, T. R. (1983). *Treating children's fear and phobias.* New York: Pergamon Press.

MOSAK, H. H. (1984). Adlerian psychotherapy. In R. J. Corsini & D. Wedding (Eds.), *Current psychotherapies* (3rd ed.). Itasca, IL: Peacock.

MOSKOWITZ, H., HULBERT, S., & McGLOTHLIN, W. H. (1976). Marijuana: Effects on simulated driving performance. *Accident Analysis and Prevention, 8,* 45–50.

Moss, C. Scott. (1972). *Recovery with aphasia: The aftermath of my stroke*. Urbana: University of Illinois Press.

Mostofsky, D. I. (1985). Behavioral medicine: What the books say. *Professional Psychology: Research and Practice, 16,* 448–454.

Mowrer, O. H. (1965, Fall). Stage-fright and self-regard. *Western Speech*, pp. 197–201.

Mowrer, O. H., & Mowrer, W. M. (1938). Enuresis: A method for its study and treatment. *American Journal of Orthopsychiatry, 8,* 436–459.

Muhlin, G. L. (1985). Ethnic differences in alcohol misuse: A striking reaffirmation. *Journal of Studies on Alcohol, 46,* 172–173.

Mukherjee, S., Rosen, A. M., Caracci, G., & Shukla, S. (1986). Persistent tardive dyskinesia in bipolar patients. *Archives of General Psychiatry, 43,* 342–346.

Mullins, L. L. (1985). Cognitive problem-solving and life events correlates of depressive symptoms in children. *Journal of Abnormal Child Psychology, 13,* 305–314.

Munoz, R. F., & Kelly, J. G. (1975). *The prevention of mental disorders*. Homewood, IL: Learning Systems–Irwin.

Munnetz, M. R., & Roth, L. H. (1985). Informing patients about tardive dyskinesia. *Archives of General Psychiatry, 42,* 866–871.

Murphy, D. L., Goodwin, F. K., & Bunney, W. E., Jr. (1975). The psychobiology of mania. In S. Arieti (Ed.), *American Handbook of Psychiatry* (Vol. 2). New York: Basic Books.

Murphy, H. B. M. (1982). Culture and schizophrenia. In I. Al-Issa (Ed.), *Culture and psychopathology*. Baltimore: University Park Press.

Murphy, H. B. M. (1983). *Comparative psychiatry*. Berlin: Springer–Verlag.

Murphy, H. B. M., Wittkower, E. D., & Chance, N. A. (1967). Cross-cultural inquiry into the symptomatology of depression: A preliminary report. *International Journal of Psychiatry, 3,* 6–15.

Murphy, H. B. M., Wittkower, E. D., & Chance, N. W. (1970). The symptoms of depression–a cross-cultural survey. In I. Al-Issa & W. Dennis (Eds.), *Cross-cultural studies of behavior*. New York: Holt, Rinehart & Winston.

Murphy, J. M. (1976). Psychiatric labeling in cross-cultural perspective. *Science, 191,* 1019–1028.

Murray, H. A., and collaborators. (1938). *Explorations in personality*. New York: Oxford University Press.

Murray, H. A. (1943). *A Manual of the Thematic Apperception Test*. Cambridge, MA: Harvard University Press.

Murray, M. E. (1976). A dynamic synthesis of analytic and behavioral approaches to symptoms. *American Journal of Psychotherapy, 30,* 561–569.

Murstein, B. I. (1973). *Theory and research in projective techniques emphasizing the T.A.T.* New York: Wiley.

Naficy, A., & Willerman, L. (1980). Excessive yielding to normal biases is not a distinctive sign of schizophrenia. *Journal of Abnormal Psychology, 89,* 697–703.

Nathan, P. E. (1978a). Behavioral therapy and behavioral theories of alcoholism. In G. A. Marlatt & P. E. Nathan (Eds.), *Behavioral approaches to alcoholism*. New Brunswick, NJ: Rutgers Center of Alcohol Studies.

Nathan, P. E. (1978b). Overview of behavioral treatment approaches. In G. A. Marlatt & P. E. Nathan (Eds.), *Behavioral approaches to alcoholism*. New Brunswick, NJ: Rutgers Center of Alcohol Studies.

Nathan, P., & Niaura, R. S. (1985). Behavioral assessment and treatment of alcoholism. In J. H. Mendelson & N. K. Mello (Eds.), *The diagnosis and treatment of alcoholism* (2nd ed.). New York: McGraw–Hill.

Nathanson, C. (1975). Illness and the feminine role: A theoretical review. *Social Science Medicine, 9,* 57–62.

National Commission on Marijuana and Drug Abuse. (1972). *Marijuana: A signal of misunderstanding*. New York: New American Library.

National Institute of Mental Health. (1970). Study says XYY males not proved violence prone. *Psychiatric News, 5,* 19.

National Institute of Mental Health. (1983). *Depressive disorders: Causes and treatment* (DHHS Publication No. ADM 83–1081). Rockville, MD: U.S. Department of Health and Human Services.

National Institute on Alcohol Abuse and Alcoholism (1987). *Sixth special report to the U.S. Congress on alcohol and health*. Washington, DC: U.S. Government Printing Office.

National Survey on Drug Abuse — Main Findings: AIDS. (1980). (Report No. ADM 80–976). Washington, DC: U.S. Government Printing Office.

Neal, P. (1988). *As I am: An autobiography*. New York: Simon & Schuster.

Neale, J. M., & Oltmanns, T. F. (1980). *Schizophrenia*. New York: Wiley.

Neffinger, G. G. (1981). Partial hospitalization: An overview. *Journal of Community Psychology, 9,* 262–269.

Nelson, J. C., & Charney, D. C. (1981). The symptoms of major depressive illness. *American Journal of Psychiatry, 138,* 1–13.

Nemiah, J. C. (1973). *Foundations of psychopathology*. New York: Aronson.

Nemiah, J. C. (1985a). Obsessive–compulsive disorders (obsessive–compulsive neurosis). In H. I. Kaplan & B. J. Sadock (Eds.), *Comprehensive textbook of psychiatry* (Vol. 1) (4th ed.). Baltimore: Williams & Wilkins.

Nemiah, J. C. (1985b). Dissociative disorders (hysterical neuroses, dissociative types). In H. I. Kaplan & B. J. Sadock (Eds.), *Comprehensive textbook of psychiatry* (Vol. 1) (4th ed.). Baltimore: Williams & Wilkins.

Nemiah, J. C. (1985c). *Somatoform disorders*. In H. I. Kaplan & B. J. Sadock (Eds.), *Comprehensive textbook of psychiatry* (Vol. 1) (4th ed.). Baltimore: Williams & Wilkins.

Newcombe, F., & Ratcliff, G. (1979). Long-term psychological consequences of cerebral lesions. In M. S. Gassaniga (Ed.), *Hand-*

book of behavioral neurobiology: Vol. 2. Neuropsychology. New York: Plenum.

NICHOLS, M. (1984). *Family therapy: Concepts and methods*. New York: Gardner Press.

NICOL, S. E., & GOTTESMAN, I. I. (1983). Clues to the genetics and neurobiology of schizophrenia. *American Scientist, 71*, 398–404.

NIETZEL, M. T., & DILLEHAY, R. C. (1986). *Psychological consultation in the courtroom*. New York: Pergamon Press.

NIRENBERG, T. D. (1983). Treatment of substance abuse. In C. E. Walker (Ed.), *The handbook of clinical psychology: Theory, research and practice* (Vol. 2). Homewood, IL: Dow Jones–Irwin.

NOLEN-HOEKSEMA, S. (1987). Sex differences in unipolar depression: Evidence and theory. *Psychological Bulletin, 101*, 259–282.

NORDHEIMER, J. (1987, April 3). AIDS specter for women: The bisexual man. *New York Times*, pp. 1, 10.

NORRIS, A. S. (1978). Mental retardation associated with conditions due to trauma or physical agents in the prenatal period. In C. H. Carter (Ed.), *Medical aspects of mental retardation* (2nd ed.). Springfield, IL: Charles C Thomas.

NORRIS, P. A. (1986). On the status of biofeedback and clinical practice. *American Psychologist, 41*, 1009–1010.

NORTHERN, H. (1982). *Clinical social work*. New York: Columbia University Press.

NOVACO, R. W., STOKOLS, D., CAMPBELL, J., & STOKOLS, J. (1979). Transportation, stress, and community psychology. *American Journal of Community Psychology, 7*, 361–380.

NOWLIN, J. B., & BUSSE, E. W. (1977). Psychosomatic problems in the older person. In E. D. Wittkower & H. Warnes (Eds.), *Psychosomatic medicine: Its clinical applications*. New York: Harper & Row.

NUECHTERLEIN, K. H., & DAWSON, M. E. (1984). A heuristic vulnerability/stress model of schizophrenic episodes. *Schizophrenic Bulletin, 10*, 300–312.

NURNBERGER, J. I., & GERSHON, E. S. (1982). Genetics. In E. S. Paykel (Ed.), *Handbook of affective disorders*. New York: Guilford Press.

OAKES, R. (1984). Sex patterns in DSM-III: Bias or basis for theory development. *American Psychologist, 39*, 1320–1322.

O'CONNOR V. DONALDSON. (1975). 442 U.S. 563.

O'CONNOR, J. J. (1988, April 21). The life of Sylvia Plath: In painful retrospect. *New York Times*, p. 19.

OFFIR, C. W. (1982). *Human sexuality*. New York: Harcourt Brace Jovanovich.

OGARA, C. R. (1984). The concept of neurosis in Karne Horney. *American Journal of Psychoanalysis, 44*, 314–318.

OHMAN, A., ERIXON, G., & LOFBERG, I. (1975). Phobia preparedness: Phobic versus neutral pictures as conditioned stimuli for human autonomic responses. *Journal of Abnormal Psychology, 84*, 41–45.

OLDER, J. (1974). Psychosurgery: Ethical issues and a proposal for control. *American Journal of Orthopsychiatry, 44*, 661–674.

O'LEARY, K. D. (1980). Pills or skills for hyperactive children? *Journal of Applied Behavior Analysis, 13*, 191–204.

OLLENDICK, T. H. (1986). Child and adolescent behavior therapy. In S. L. Garfield & A. E. Bergin (Eds.), *Handbook of psychotherapy and behavior change* (3rd ed.). New York: Wiley.

OLLENDICK, T. H., & MEADOR, A. E. (1984). Behavioral assessment of children. In G. Goldstein & M. Hersen (Eds.), *Handbook of psychological assessment*. New York: Pergamon Press.

OMENN, G. S. (1978). Prenatal diagnosis of genetic disorders. *Science, 200*, 952–958.

OPLER, M. K., & SINGER, J. L. (1956). Ethnic differences in behavior and psychopathology: Italian and Irish. *International Journal of Social Psychiatry, 2*, 11–23.

ORNITZ, E. M. (1983). The functional neuroanatomy of infantile autism. *International Journal of Neuroscience, 19*, 85–124.

ORNITZ, E. M., & RITVO, E. R. (1976). The syndrome of autism: A critical review. *American Journal of Psychiatry, 133*, 609–621.

ORVASCHEL, H., WALSH-ALLIS, G., & YE, W. (1988). Psychopathology in children of parents with recurrent depression. *Journal of Abnormal Child Psychology, 16*, 17–28.

OSCAR-BERMAN, M. (1980). Neuropsychological consequences of long-term chronic alcoholism. *American Scientist, 68*, 410–419.

OSGOOD, C. E., & LURIA, Z. (1954). A blind analysis of a case of multiple personality using the semantic differential. *Journal of Abnormal and Social Psychology, 49*, 579–591.

OSLER, W. (1929). *An Alabama student and other biographical essays*. London: Oxford University Press. (Original work published 1908)

OST, L-G., & HUGDAHL, K. (1983). Acquisition of agoraphobia, mode of onset and anxiety response patterns. *Behavior Research and Therapy, 21*, 623–631.

PACKARD, K., & LAVECK, B. (1976). Public attitudes. In President's Committee on Mental Retardation, *Report to the President: Mental retardation—century of decision*. Washington, DC: U.S. Government Printing Office.

PAGE, I. H. (1954). Serotonin (5-hydroxytryptamine). *Physiological Review, 64*, 563–588.

PALMORE, E. (1980). The social factors in aging. In E. W. Busse & D. G. Blazer (Eds.), *Handbook of geriatric psychiatry*. New York: Van Nostrand Reinhold.

PARISI, T. (1987). Why Freud failed: Some implications for neurophysiology and sociobiology. *American Psychologist, 42*, 235–245.

PARKER, T. (1972). *The twisting lane: The hidden world of sex offenders*. London: Hutchinson.

PASCARELLI, E. F. (1973). Methaqualone abuse, the quiet epidemic. *Journal of the American Medical Association, 224*, 1512–1514.

PATE V. ROBINSON. (1966). 383 U.S. 375.

PATTISON, E. M. (1985). The selection of treatment modalities for the alcoholic patient. In J. H. Mendelson & N. K. Mello (Eds.), *The diagnosis and treatment of alcoholism* (2nd ed.). New York: McGraw–Hill.

PATTISON, E. M., SOBELL, M. B., & SOBELL, L. C. (EDS.). (1977). *Emerging concepts of alcohol dependence.* New York: Springer.

PAUL, G. L. (1966). *Insight vs. desensitization in psychotherapy.* Stanford, CA: Stanford University Press.

PAUL, G. L., & BERNSTEIN, D. A. (1973). *Anxiety and clinical problems: Systematic desensitization and related techniques.* Morristown, NJ: General Learning Press.

PAUL, G. L., & LENTZ, R. J. (1977). *Psychosocial treatment of chronic mental patients: Milieu versus social learning programs.* Cambridge, MA: Harvard University Press.

PAUL, S. M. (1977). Movement and madness. Towards a biological model of schizophrenia. In J. D. Maser & M. E. P. Seligman (Eds.), *Psychopathology: Experimental models.* San Francisco: Freeman.

PAULUS, P., McCAIN, G., & COX, V. (1978). Death rates, psychiatric commitments, blood pressure, and perceived crowding as a function of institutional crowding. *Environmental Psychology and Nonverbal Behavior, 3,* 998–999.

PAULY, I. B., & EDGERTON, M. T. (1986). The gender identity movement: A growing surgical-psychiatric liaison. *Archives of General Psychiatry, 15,* 315–329.

PAVLOV, I. P. (1927). *Conditioned reflexes: An investigation of the physiological activity of the cerebral cortex* (G. V. Andrep, Ed. and Trans.). London: Oxford University Press/Humphrey Milford.

PAVLOV, I. P. (1928). *Lectures on conditioned reflexes: Twenty-five years of objective study of the higher nervous activity (behaviour) of animals* (Vol. 1). (W. H. Gantt, Ed. and Trans.). New York: International Publishers.

PAYKEL, E. S. (1975). Environmental variables in the etiology of depression. In F. F. Flach & S. C. Draghi (Eds.), *The nature and treatment of depression.* New York: Wiley.

PAYKEL, E. S. (1979a). Management of acute depression. In E. S. Paykel & A. Coppem (Eds.), *Psychopharmacology of affective disorders* (A British Association for Psychopharmacology Monograph). Oxford: Oxford University Press.

PAYKEL, E. S. (1979b). Recent life events in the development of the depressive disorders. In R. Depue (Ed.), *The psychobiology of the depressive disorders: Implications for the effects of stress.* New York: Academic Press.

PAYKEL, E. S. (1982). Life events and early environment. In E. S. Paykel (Ed.), *Handbook of affective disorders.* New York: Guilford Press.

PEARLIN, L. I. (1982). The social contexts of stress. In L. Goldberger & S. Breznitz (Eds.), *Handbook of stress: Theoretical and clinical aspects.* New York: Free Press.

PEDERSEN, P. B. (1986). Developing interculturally skilled counselors: A prototype for training. In H. P. Lefley & P. B. Pedersen (Eds.), *Cross-cultural training for mental health professionals.* Springfield, IL: Charles C Thomas.

PELHAM, W. E., BENDER, M. E., CADDELL, J., BOOTH, S., & MOORER, S. H. (1985). Methylphenidate and children with attention deficit disorder. *Archives of General Psychiatry, 42,* 948–952.

PEOPLE V. GORSHEN. (1959). 336 P.2d 492, 503.

PEOPLE V. WELLS. (1949). 202 P.2d 53, 62–63. *Cert. denied* 337 U.S. 919.

PEPPARD, T. A. (1949). Mistakes in diagnosis. *Minnesota Medicine, 32,* 510–511.

PEREZ, J. F. (1979). *Family counseling: Theory and practice.* New York: Van Nostrand Reinhold.

PERLS, F. S. (1969). *Gestalt therapy verbatim.* Lafayette, CA: Real People Press.

PERLS, F. S. (1973). *The Gestalt approach: Eye witness to therapy.* Palo Alto, CA: Science and Behavior Books.

PERRY, M. A., & FURUKAWA, J. J. (1986). Modeling methods. In F. H. Kanfer & A. P. Goldstein (Eds.), *Helping people change: A textbook of methods* (3rd ed.). Elmsford, NY: Pergamon Press.

PETERSON, D. R. (1985). Twenty years of practitioner training in psychology. *American Psychologist, 40,* 441–451.

PETTI, T. A. (1983). Depression and withdrawal in children. In T. H. Ollendick & M. Hersen (Eds.), *Handbook of child psychopathology.* New York: Plenum.

PHILLIPS, D. L. (1963). Rejection: A possible consequence of seeking help for mental disorders. *American Sociological Review, 28,* 963–972.

PHILLIPS, L. (1968). *Human adaptation and its failures.* New York: Academic Press.

PHILLIPS, L., & DRAGUNS, J. G. (1971). Classification of the behavior disorders. *Annual Review of Psychology, 22,* 447–482.

PHILLIPS, L., DRAGUNS, J. G., & BARTLETT, D. P. (1974). Classification of behavior disorders: Issues and trends. In N. Hobbs (Ed.), *Handbook of classification of exceptional children* (Vol. 1). San Francisco: Jossey–Bass.

PICHOT, P. (1978). Psychopathic behaviour: A historical overview. In R. D. Hare & D. Schalling (Eds.), *Psychopathic behaviour: Approaches to research.* London: Wiley.

PIERS, E. V. (1972). Parent prediction of children's self-concepts. *Journal of Consulting and Clinical Psychology, 38,* 428–433.

PISHKIN, V., & WILLIAMS, W. V. (1984). Redundancy and complexity of information in cognitive performances of schizophrenic and normal individuals. *Journal of Clinical Psychology, 40,* 648–654.

PLANT, M. (1975). Alcoholism in Scotland. *New Psychiatry, 2,* 12–13.

PLATT, A., & DIAMOND, B. L. (1978). The origins of the "right and wrong" test of criminal responsibility and its subsequent development in the United States: An historical survey. In R. W. Rieber & H. J. Vetter (Eds.), *The psychological foundations of criminal justice: Vol. 1. Historical perspectives on forensic psychology.* New York: John Jay Press.

PLAUM, E. (1975). Theories of cognitive disorder in schizophrenia based on psychological experiments (English translation). *Fortschritte der Neurologie Psychiatrie und ihrer Grenzgebiete, 43*(1), 1–41.

POE, E. A. (1843). *The black cat*. In J. Bartlett (1968). *Familiar quotations* (14th ed.). Boston: Little, Brown.

POE, E. A. (1978). Fall of the house of Usher. In *Collected works of Edgar Allan Poe* (Vol. 2). Cambridge, MA: Harvard University Press (originally published 1839).

POLICH, J. M., ARMOR, D. J., & BRAIKER, H. B. (1981). *The course of alcoholism: Four years after treatment*. New York: Wiley.

POLIVY, J., & HERMAN, C. (1985). Dieting and binging: A causal analysis. *American Psychologist, 40*, 193–201.

POLLACK, S. (1976). The insanity defense as defined by the proposed Federal Criminal Code. *Bulletin of the American Academy of Psychiatry and the Law, 4*(1), 11–23.

POMEROY, W. B. (1972). *Dr. Kinsey and the Institute for Sex Research*. New York: Harper & Row.

POPE, A. (1725). *The Odyssey of Homer*. London: Barnard Lintot.

POPE, H. G., & HUDSON, J. I. (1984). *New hope for binge eaters: Advances in the understanding and treatment of bulimia*. Hagerstown, MD: Harper & Row.

POPE, K. S. (1987). Preventing therapist–patient sexual intimacy: Therapy for a therapist at risk. *Professional Psychology: Research and Practice, 18*, 624–628.

POPE, K. S., & BOUHOUTSOS, J. (1986). *Sexual intimacy between therapists and patients*. New York: Praeger.

POPE, K. S., LEVONSON, H., & SCHOVER, L. R. (1979). Sexual intimacy in psychology training: Results and implications of a national survey. *American Psychologist, 34*, 682–689.

POPE, K. S., TABACHNICK, B. G., & KEITH-SPIEGEL, P. (1987). Ethics of practice: The beliefs and behaviors of psychologists as therapists. *American Psychologist, 42*, 993–1006.

POST, R. M., & GOODWIN, F. K. (1975). Studies of cerebrospinal fluid amine metabolites in depressed patients: Conceptual problems and theoretical implications. In J. Mendels (Ed.), *The psychobiology of depression*. New York: Spectrum.

POST, R. M., GORDON, E. K., GOODWIN, F. K., & BUNNEY, W. E., JR. (1973). Central norepinephrine metabolism in affective illness: MHPG in the cerebrospinal fluid. *Science, 177*, 1002–1003.

POST, R., KOTIN, J., GOODWIN, F. K., & GORDON, E. K. (1973). Psychomotor activity and cerebrospinal fluid amine metabolites in affective illness. *American Journal of Psychiatry, 130*, 67–72.

POWELL, L. H., FRIEDMAN, M., THORESEN, C. E., GILL, J. J., & ULMER, D. K. (1984). Can the Type A behavior pattern be altered after myocardial infarction? A second year report from the recurrent coronary prevention project. *Psychosomatic Medicine, 46*, 293–313.

PRESIDENT'S COMMITTEE ON MENTAL RETARDATION. (1975). *Mental retardation: The known and the unknown*. Washington, DC: U.S. Government Printing Office.

PRESIDENT'S COMMITTEE ON MENTAL RETARDATION. (1976). *Report to the President: Mental retardation — century of decision*. Washington, DC: U.S. Government Printing Office.

PRESIDENT'S COMMITTEE ON MENTAL RETARDATION. (1980). *Report to the President: Mental retardation — prevention strategies that work*. Washington, DC: U.S. Government Printing Office.

PRIAL, F. J. (1980, December 16). France opens drive against alcoholism. *New York Times*, p. 11.

PRIBRAM, K. H. (1986). The cognitive revolution and mind/brain issues. *American Psychologist, 41*, 507–520.

PRICE, K. P., TRYON, W. W., & RAPS, C. S. (1978). Learned helplessness and depression in a clinical population: A test of two behavioral hypotheses. *Journal of Abnormal Psychology, 87*, 113–121.

PRICE, R. A., KIDD, K. K., COHEN, D. J., PAULS, D. L., & LECKMAN, J. F. (1985). A twin study of Tourette syndrome. *Archives of General Psychiatry, 42*, 815–820.

PRICE, R. H. (1978). *Abnormal behavior: Perspectives in conflict* (2nd ed.). New York: Holt, Rinehart & Winston.

PRICE, S. C., REYNOLDS, B. S., COHEN, B. D., ANDERSON, A. J., & SCHOCHET, B. V. (1981). Group treatment of erectile dysfunction for men without partners: A controlled evaluation. *Archives of Sexual Behavior, 10*, 253–267.

PRICHARD, J. C. (1835). *A treatise on insanity and other disorders affecting the mind*. London: Sherwood, Gilbert & Piper.

PRINCE, M. (1908). *The dissociation of a personality: A biographical study in abnormal psychology* (2nd ed.). New York: Longmans, Green.

PRINCE, M. (1939). *Clinical and experimental studies in personality*. Cambridge, MA: Sci–Art.

PRINCE, R. H. (1980). Variations in psychotherapeutic experience. In H. C. Triandis & J. G. Draguns (Eds.), *Handbook of cross-cultural psychology: Vol. 6. Psychopathology*. Boston: Allyn & Bacon.

PSYCHOSURGERY: AN NAMH POSITION STATEMENT (1974). *Mental Hygiene, 58*, 22–24.

Psychotherapy, 24, No. 35, Fall 1987, pp 453–659

PUIG-ANTIOCH, J., & CHAMBERS, W. (1978). *The Schedule for affective disorders and schizophrenia for school-aged children*. New York: New York State Psychiatric Institute.

QUAY, H. C., ROUTH, D. K., & SHAPIRO, S. K. (1987). Psychopathology of childhood: From description to validation. *Annual Review of Psychology, 38*, 491–532.

QUEN, J. M. (1978). An historical view of the M'Naghten trial. In R. W. Rieber & H. J. Vetter (Eds.), *The psychological foundations of criminal justice: Vol. 1. Historical perspectives on forensic psychology*. New York: John Jay Press.

RABIN, A. I., DONESON, S. L., & JENTONS, R. L. (1979). Studies of psychological functions in schizophrenia. In L. Bellak (Ed.), *Disorders of the schizophrenic syndrome*. New York: Basic Books.

RACHMAN, S. J. (1978). *Fear and courage*. San Francisco: Freeman.

RACHMAN, S. (1979). The conditioning theory of fear-acquisition. *Behavior Research and Therapy, 15*, 375–387.

RACHMAN, S. (1988). Panics and their consequences. In S. Rachman & J. Maser (Eds.), *Panic: Psychological perspectives*. Hillsdale, NJ: Erlbaum.

RACHMAN, S., & HODGSON, R. J. (1968). Experimentally-induced "sexual fetishism" replication and development. *Psychological Record, 18*, 25–27.

RACHMAN, S., MARKS, I., & HODGSON, R. (1973). The treatment of obsessive–compulsive neurotics by modeling and flooding *in vivo*. *Behavior Research and Therapy, 11,* 463–471.

RAFAELSEN, O. L., BECH, P., CHRISTIANSEN, J., CHRISTRUP, J., NYBOE, J., & RAFAELSON, L. (1973). Cannabis and alcohol: Effects on simulated car driving. *Science, 179,* 920–923.

RAGLAND, D. R., & BRAND, R. J. (1988). Type A behavior and mortality from coronary heart disease. *New England Journal of Medicine, 318*(2), 65–69.

RAIMY, V. (1975). *Misunderstandings of the self: Cognitive psychotherapy and the misconception hypothesis.* San Francisco: Jossey–Bass.

RAINER, J. D. (1985). Genetics and psychiatry. In H. J. Kaplan & B. J. Sadock (Eds.), *Comprehensive textbook in psychiatry* (Vol. 1) (4th ed.). Baltimore: Williams & Wilkins.

RAPAPORT, D. (1951). *The organization and pathology of thought.* New York: Columbia University Press.

RAPAPORT, D. (1958). The theory of ego-autonomy: A generalization. *Bulletin of the Menninger Clinic, 22,* 13–15.

RAPAPORT, D. (1967). *The collected papers of David Rapaport* (M. M. Gil, Ed.). New York: Basic Books.

RAPAPORT, K., & BURKHART, B. R. (1984). Personality and attitudinal characteristics of sexually coercive college males. *Journal of Abnormal Psychology, 93,* 216–221.

RAPPAPORT, J. (1977). *Community psychology: Values, research, and action.* New York: Holt, Rinehart & Winston.

RAPPAPORT, J. (1987). The power of empowerment language. *Social Policy, 16,* 15–21.

RAPPAPORT, J., & CHINSKY, J. M. (1974). Models for delivery of service from a historical and conceptual perspective. *Professional Psychology, 5,* 42–50.

RAPPAPORT, J., & SEIDMAN, E. (1983). *Social and community interventions.* In C. E. Walker (Ed.), *Handbook of clinical psychology* (Vol. 2). Homewood, IL: Dow Jones–Irwin.

RASKIN, A. (1974). A guide for drug use in depressive disorders. *American Journal of Psychiatry, 131,* 181–185.

RASKIND, M. A., & STORRIE, M. C. (1980). The organic mental disorders. In E. W. Busse, & D. G. Blazer (Eds.), *Handbook of geriatric psychiatry.* New York: Van Nostrand Reinhold.

RAY, I. (1853). *Treatise on the medical jurisprudence of insanity* (3rd ed.). Boston: Little, Brown.

RAYMOND, I. W. (1927). *The teaching of the early church on the use of wine and strong drink.* New York: Columbia University Press.

REBEC, G. V., CENTORE, J. M., WHITE, L. K., & ALLOWAY, K. D. (1985). Ascorbic acid and the behavioral response to haloperidol: Implications for the action of antipsychotic drugs. *Science, 227,* 438–439.

RECKLER, J. M. (1983). The urologic evaluation of male dyspareunia. In H. S. Kaplan (Ed.), *The evaluation of sexual disorders: Psychological and medical aspects.* New York: Brunner/Mazel.

REDD, W. H., PORTERFIELD, A. L., & ANDERSEN, B. (1979). *Behavior modification: Behavioral approaches to human problems.* New York: Random House.

REED, S. D., KATKIN, E. S., & GOLDBAND, S. (1986). Biofeedback and behavioral medicine. In F. H. Kanfer & A. P. Goldstein (Eds.), *Helping people change: A textbook of methods* (3rd ed.). New York: Pergamon Press.

REES, L. (1964). The importance of psychological, allergic and infective factors in childhood asthma. *Journal of Psychosomatic Research, 7,* 253–262.

REEVE, V. C. (1979). *Incidence of marijuana in a California impaired driving population* (Office of Highway Safety, National Highway Traffic Safety Administration Contract No. OTS 087705). Sacramento: California State Department of Justice, Division of Law Enforcement.

REID, H. C. (1978). The psychopath in rural areas: Special considerations. In W. H. Reid (Ed.), *The psychopath: A comprehensive study of antisocial disorders and behaviors.* New York: Brunner/Mazel.

REID, W. H. (1978). Genetic correlates of antisocial syndromes. In W. H. Reid (Ed.), *The psychopath: A comprehensive study of antisocial disorders and behaviors.* New York: Brunner/Mazel.

REID, W. H. (ED.). (1981). *The treatment of antisocial syndromes.* New York: Van Nostrand Reinhold.

REID, W. H. (1983). *Treatment of the DSM-III psychiatric disorders.* New York: Brunner/Mazel.

REIF, A. E. (1981). The causes of cancer. *American Scientist, 69,* 437–447.

REISMAN, J. M., & YAMAKOSKI, T. (1974). Psychotherapy and friendship: An analysis of the communication of friends. *Journal of Counseling Psychology, 21,* 269–273.

REISS, A. L., FEINSTEIN, C., & ROSENBAUM, K. N. (1986). Autism and genetic disorders. *Schizophrenia Bulletin, 12,* 724–738.

REISS, S., & BENSON, B. A. (1985). Psychosocial correlates of depression in mentally retarded adults: I. Minimal social support and stigmatization. *American Journal of Mental Deficiency, 89,* 331–337.

REISS, S., LEVITAN, G. W., & MCNALLY, R. J. (1982). Emotionally disturbed mentally retarded people: An underserved population. *American Psychologist, 37,* 361–367.

REITAN, R. M., & WOLFSON, D. (1985). *The Halstead–Reitan Neuropsychological Test Battery: Theory and clinical interpretation.* Tucson, AZ: Neuropsychology Press.

RENDON, M. (1984). Clinical work in the Horney tradition. *American Journal of Psychoanalysis, 44,* 319–333.

RENSHAW, D. C. (1982, January). Sex and older women. *Medical Aspects of Human Sexuality, 16*(1), 132–134, 139.

RESCORLA, R. (1988). Pavlovian conditioning: It's not what you think it is. *American Psychologist, 43,* 151–160.

REYNOLDS, B. S. (1977). Psychological treatment models and outcome results for erectile dysfunction: A critical review. *Psychological Bulletin, 84,* 1218–1238.

REYNOLDS, C. R., & PAGET, K. D. (1981). Factor analysis of the Revised Children's Manifest Anxiety Scale for blacks, whites, males, and females with a national normative sample. *Journal of Consulting Clinical Psychology, 49,* 306–307.

REYNOLDS, W. M., & BAKER, J. A. (1988). Assessment of depression in persons with mental retardation. *American Journal of Mental Retardation, 93,* 93–103.

RHODEWALT, F., & COMER, R. (1982). Coronary-prone behavior and reactance: The attractiveness of an eliminated choice. *Personality and Social Psychology Bulletin, 8,* 152–158.

RHODEWALT, F., HAYS, R. B., CHEMERS, M. M., & WYSOCKI, J. (1984). Type A behavior, perceived stress, and illness: A person–situation analysis. *Personality and Social Psychology Bulletin, 10,* 149–159.

RICH, C. L., YOUNG, D., & FOWLER, R. C. (1986). San Diego suicide study: I. Young vs. old subjects. *Archives of General Psychiatry, 43,* 577–582.

RICKARDS, L. D., ZUCKERMAN, D. M., & WEST, P. R. (1985). Alzheimer's disease: Current congressional response. *American Psychologist, 40,* 1256–1261.

RICKS, D. F., & BERRY, J. C. (1970). Family and symptom patterns that precede schizophrenia. In M. Roff and D. Ricks (Eds.), *Life history research in psychopathology.* Minneapolis: University of Minnesota Press.

RIDING, A. (1987, March 8). Cocaine billionaires: The men who hold Colombia hostage. *New York Times Magazine,* pp. 27–32, 36, 95.

RIEBER, R. W., & GUNDLACH, H. (1981). *Insanity and the law.* New York: De Capo Press.

RIEBER, R. W., & VETTER, H. J. (1978). Introduction. In R. W. Rieber & H. J. Vetter (Eds.), *The psychological foundations of criminal justice: Vol. 1. Historical perspectives on forensic psychology.* New York: John Jay Press.

RIESSMAN, F. (1985). New dimensions in self-help. *Social Policy, 15,* 2–5.

RIMLAND, B. (1964). *Infantile autism: The syndrome and its implications for a neural theory of behavior.* New York: Appleton–Century–Crofts.

RIMLAND, B. (1971). The differentiation of childhood psychosis: An analysis of checklists for 2218 psychotic children. *Journal of Autism and Childhood Schizophrenia, 1,* 161–174.

RIMON, R., TERENIUS, L., & KAMPMAN, R. (1980). Cerebrospinal fluid endorphins in schizophrenia. *Acta Psychiatrica Scandinavica, 61,* 395–403.

RIOCH, D. McK. (1985). Recollections of Harry Stack Sullivan and the development of his interpersonal psychiatry. *Psychiatry: Journal for the Study of Interpersonal Processes, 48,* 141–158.

RITCHIE, J. M. (1975). The aliphatic alcohols. In L. S. Goodman (Ed.), *The pharmacological basis of therapeutics.* New York: Macmillan.

ROAZEN, P. (1975). *Freud and his followers.* New York: Knopf.

ROBBINS, M. B., & JENSEN, G. D. (1977). Multiple orgasm in males. In R. G. Gemme & C. C. Wheeler (Eds.), *Progress in sexology.* New York: Plenum.

ROBERTS, A. H. (1985). Biofeedback: Research, training, and clinical roles. *American Psychologist, 40,* 938–941.

ROBERTS, A. H. (1986). Biofeedback, science, and training. *American Psychologist, 41,* 1010.

ROBERTS, L. (1988). Vietnam's psychological toll. *Science, 241,* 159–161.

ROBERTSON, N. (1988). *Getting better: Inside Alcoholics Anonymous.* New York: Morrow.

ROBINS, E., & HARTMAN, B. K. (1972). Biochemical theories of mental disorders. In F. Ablers, G. J. Siegel, R. Katzman, & B. W. Agranoff (Eds.), *Basic neurochemistry.* Boston: Little, Brown.

ROBINS, L. N. (1966). *Deviant children grown up: A sociological and psychiatric study of sociopathic personality.* Baltimore: Williams & Wilkins.

ROBINS, L. N. (1975). Discussion of genetic studies of criminality and psychopathy. *Proceedings of the American Psychopathological Association, 63,* 117–122.

ROBINS, L. N., & HELZER, J. E. (1986). Diagnosis and clinical assessment: The current state of psychiatric diagnosis. *Annual Review of Psychology, 37,* 409–432.

ROEN, P. R. (1983). When ejaculation is painful. *Medical Aspects of Human Sexuality, 17*(10), 199–202.

ROESCH, R., & GOLDING, S. L. (1980). *Competency to stand trial.* Urbana: University of Illinois Press.

ROG, D. J., & RAUSH, H. L. (1975). The psychiatric halfway house. How is it measuring up? *Community Mental Health Journal, 11,* 155–162.

ROGERS, C. R. (1942). *Counseling and psychotherapy: Newer concepts in practice.* Boston: Houghton Mifflin.

ROGERS, C. R. (1951). *Client-centered therapy: Its current practice, implication, and theory.* Boston: Houghton Mifflin.

ROGERS, C. R. (1957). The necessary and sufficient conditions of therapeutic personality change. *Journal of Consulting Psychology, 21,* 95–103.

ROGERS, C. R. (1962). The interpersonal relationships: The core of guidance. *Harvard Educational Review, 2,* 416–429.

ROGERS, C. R. (1974). In retrospect: Forty-six years. *American Psychologist, 29,* 115–123.

ROGERS, C. R. (1980). *A way of being.* Boston: Houghton Mifflin.

ROGERS, C. R. (1986a). Client-centered therapy. In I. L. Kutash and A. Wolf (Eds.), *Psychotherapist's casebook.* San Francisco: Jossey–Bass.

ROGERS, C. R. (1986b). Carl Rogers on the development of the person-centered approach. *Person-centered Review, 1,* 257–259.

ROGERS, C. R. (1986c). Rogers, Kohut, and Erickson. *Person-centered Review, 1,* 125–140.

ROGERS, C. R. (1987). APA's position on the insanity defense: Empiricism versus emotionalism. *American Psychologist, 42,* 840–848.

ROGERS, C. R., GENDLIN, E. T., KIESLER, D. J., & TRUAX, C. B. (1967). *The therapeutic relationship and its impact: A study of psychotherapy with schizophrenics.* Madison: University of Wisconsin Press.

ROGERS, R. (1987). APA's position on the insanity defense. Empiricism versus emotionalism. *American Psychologist, 42,* 840–848.

ROLLESTON, J. D. (1927). Alcoholism in classical antiquity. *British*

Journal of Inebrity (Alcoholism and Drug Addiction), *24*, 101–124.

ROMAN, P. M., & TRICE, H. M. (1977). The sick role, labeling theory, and the deviant drinker. In E. M. Pattison, M. B. Sobell, & L. C. Sobell (Eds.), *Emerging concepts of alcohol dependence*. New York: Springer.

ROOK, K. S., & HAMMEN, C. L. (1977). A cognitive perspective on the experience of sexual arousal. *Journal of Social Issues*, *33*(2), 7–29.

ROOT, L. E. (1986). Treatment of the alcoholic family. *Journal of Psychoactive Drugs*, *18*, 51–56.

RORSCHACH, H. (1921a). *Psychodiagnostics*. Bern: Hans Huber.

RORSCHACH, H. (1921b). *Psychodiagnostics: A diagnostic test based on perception* (P. Lemkau and B. Kronenberg, Eds. and Trans.) (9th ed., 1981). New York: Grune & Stratton.

ROSE, F. C., & GAWEL, M. (1979). *Migraine: The facts*. Oxford: Oxford University Press.

ROSEBURY, T. (1971). *Microbes and morals: The strange story of venereal disease*. New York: Viking Press.

ROSEN, W. G., MOHS, R. C., & DAVIS, K. L. (1984). A new rating scale for Alzheimer's disease. *American Journal of Psychiatry*, *141*, 1356–1364.

ROSENBAUM, A. H., MARUTA, T., SHATZBERG, A. F., ORSULAK, P. J., JIANG, N-S, COLE, J. O., & SCHILDKRAUT, J. J. (1983). Toward a biochemical classification of depressive disorders: VII. Urinary free cortisol and urinary MHPG in depression. *American Journal of Psychiatry*, *140*, 314–318.

ROSENBAUM, C. P., & BEEBE, J. E., III. (1975). *Psychiatric treatment: Crisis/clinic/consultation*. New York: McGraw–Hill.

ROSENBAUM, G., SHORE, D. L., & CHAPIN, K. (1988). Attention deficit in schizophrenia and schizotypy: Marker versus symptom variables. *Journal of Abnormal Psychology*, *97*, 41–47.

ROSENBAUM, J. (1979, March 25). Are you a workaholic? *Family Weekly*, p. 11.

ROSENBERG, S. D. (1970). The disculturation hypothesis and the chronic patient syndrome. *Social Psychiatry*, *5*, 155–165.

ROSENHAN, D. L. (1973). On being sane in insane places. *Science*, *179*, 250–258.

ROSENHAN, D. L. (1983). Psychological abnormality and law. In C. J. Scheirer & B. L. Hammonds (Eds.), *Psychology and the law: The Master Lecture Series* (Vol. 2). Washington, DC: American Psychological Association.

ROSENMAN, R. H. (1978). The interview method of assessment of the coronary prone behavior pattern. In T. M. Dembroski, S. M. Weiss, J. J. Shields, S. G. Haynes, & M. Feinleib (Eds.), *Coronary-prone behavior*. New York: Springer.

ROSENMAN, R. H., & CHESNEY, M. A. (1982). Stress, Type A behavior, and coronary disease. In L. Goldberger & S. Breznitz (Eds.), *Handbook of stress: Theoretical and clinical aspects*. New York: Free Press.

ROSENSTOCK, H. A., KRAFT, I., ROSENSTOCK, J. D., MENDELL, D., & STUBBLEFIELD, R. (1986). Depression in childhood. *Medical aspects of human sexuality*, *20*(10), 18–19, 23–24, 25, 27, 31.

ROSENTHAL, D. (1968). The heredity–environment issue in schizophrenia: Summary of the conference and present status of our knowledge. In D. Rosenberg & S. S. Kety (Eds.), *The transmission of schizophrenia*. Oxford: Pergamon Press.

ROSENTHAL, D. (1970). *Genetic theory and abnormal behavior*. New York: McGraw–Hill.

ROSENTHAL, D. (1971). *Genetics of psychopathology*. New York: McGraw–Hill.

ROSENTHAL, R. H., & AKISKAL, H. S. (1985). Mental status examination. In M. Hersen & S. M. Turner (Eds.), *Diagnostic interviewing*. New York: Plenum.

ROSENTHAL, T. L., AKISKAL, H. S., SCOTT-STRAUSS, A., ROSENTHAL, R. H., & DAVID, N. (1981). Familial and developmental factors in characterologic depression. *Journal of Affective Disorders*, *3*, 183–192.

ROSENTHAL, T. L., & BANDURA, A. (1978). Psychological modeling: Theory and practice. In S. L. Garfield & A. E. Bergin (Eds.), *Handbook of psychotherapy and behavior change*. New York: Wiley.

ROSENZWEIG, S. (1988). The identity and idiodynamics of the multiple personality "Sally Beauchamp": A confirmatory supplement. *American Psychologist*, *43*, 45–48.

ROSSI, P. H., WRIGHT, J. D., FISHER, G. A., & WILLIS, G. (1987). The urban homeless: Estimating composition and size. *Science*, *235*, 1336–1341.

ROTH, S., DYE, E., & LEBOWITZ, L. (1988). Group therapy for sexual assault victims. *Psychotherapy: Theory, practice, and research*, *25*, 82–93.

ROTHBLUM, E. D., SOLOMON, S. J., & ALBEE, G. W. (1986). A sociopolitical perspective of DSM-III. In T. Millon & H. L. Klerman (Eds.), *Contemporary directions in psychopathology: Toward the DSM-IV*. New York: Guilford Press.

ROUECHÉ, B. (1971). *Alcohol: The neutral spirit*. New York: Berkley Publishing Co.

ROWAN, R. L. (1982). Irrelevance of penis size. *Medical Aspects of Human Sexuality*, *16*(7), 153, 156.

ROYAL COLLEGE OF PSYCHIATRISTS. (1977). Memorandum on the use of electroconvulsive therapy. *British Journal of Psychiatry*, *131*, 261–272.

ROYBAL, E. R. (1988). Mental health and aging: The need for an expanded federal response. *American Psychologist*, *43*, 189–194.

ROZOVSKY, F. A. (1984). *Consent to treatment: A practical guide*. Boston: Little, Brown.

RUBIN, E. H., ZORUMSKI, C., & GUZE, S. B. (1986). Somatoform disorders. In T. Millon & G. L. Klerman (Eds.), *Contemporary directions in psychopathology: Toward the DSM-IV*. New York: Guilford Press.

RUBINS, J. L. (1978). *Karen Horney*. New York: Dial.

RUSH, A. J., BECK, A. T., KOVACS, M., & HOLLON, S. (1977). Comparative efficacy of cognitive therapy and imipramine in the treatment of depressive outpatients. *Cognitive Therapy and Research*, *1*, 17–37.

RUSH, A. J., & FULTON, C. (1982). Affective disorders. In R. J. Gatchel, A. Baum, & J. E. Singer (Eds.), *Handbook of psychology and health: Vol. 1. Clinical psychology and behavioral medicine: Overlapping disciplines.* Hillside, NJ: Erlbaum.

RUSSELL, D. E. H. (1975). *The politics of rape: The victim's perspective.* New York: Stein and Day.

RUSSELL, G. (1979). Bulimia nervosa: An ominous variant of anorexia nervosa. *Psychological Medicine, 9,* 429–448.

RUSSO, D. C., & NEWSOM, C. D. (1982). Psychotic disorders of childhood. In J. R. Lachenmeyer & M. S. Gibbs (Eds.), *Psychopathology in childhood.* New York: Gardner Press.

RUTTENBER, A. J., & LUKE, J. L. (1984). Heroin-related deaths: New epidemiological insights. *Science, 226,* 14–20.

RUTTER, M. (1972). *Maternal deprivation reassessed.* Middlesex: Penguin.

RUTTER, M. (1985). The treatment of autistic children. *Journal of Child Psychology and Psychiatry and Allied Disciplines, 26,* 193–214.

RUTTER, M. (1986). Myerian psychobiology, personality development, and the role of life experience. *American Journal of Psychiatry, 143,* 1077–1087.

RUTTER, M., BARTAK, L., & NEWMAN, S. (1971). Autism—a central disorder of cognition and language? In M. Rutter (Ed.), *Infantile autism: Concepts, characteristics, and treatment.* London: Churchill–Livingstone.

SADOCK, B. J., & SPITZ, H. I. (1976). Group psychotherapy of sexual disorders. In B. J. Sadock, H. I. Kaplan, & A. M. Freedman (Eds.), *The sexual experience.* Baltimore: Williams & Wilkins.

SADOCK, V. A., & SADOCK, B. J. (1976). Dual-sex therapy. In B. J. Sadock, H. I. Kaplan, & A. M. Freedman (Eds.), *The sexual experience.* Baltimore: Williams & Wilkins.

SADOFF, R. L. (1976). Other sexual deviations. In B. J. Sadock, H. I. Kaplan, & A. M. Freedman (Eds.), *The sexual experience.* Baltimore: Williams & Wilkins.

SAGER, C. J., & KAPLAN, H. S. (EDS.). (1972). *Progress in group and family therapy.* New York: Brunner/Mazel.

SAGHIR, M. T., & ROBINS, E. (1969). Homosexuality: I. Sexual behavior of the female homosexual. *Archives of General Psychiatry, 20,* 192–201.

SAGHIR, M. R, ROBINS, R., & WALBRAN, B. (1969). Homosexuality: II. Sexual behavior of the male homosexual. *Archives of General Psychiatry, 21,* 219–229.

SAHAKIAN, W. S., SAHAKIAN, B. J., & NUNN, P. L. S. (1986). *Psychopathology today: The current status of abnormal psychology.* Itasca, IL: Peacock.

ST. GEORGE-HYSLOP, P. H., ET AL. (1987). The genetic defect causing familial Alzheimer's disease maps on chromosome 21. *Science, 235,* 885–890.

SALHOLZ, E., WASHINGTON, F. S., & DREW, L. (1987, April 20). Behavior pills. *Newsweek,* p. 76.

SANDAY, P. R. (1981). The socio-cultural context of rape: A cross-cultural study. *Journal of Social Issues, 37,* 5–27.

SANDBERG, S. (1985). Comment on "Hyperactivity: Nature of the syndrome and its natural history." *Journal of Autism and Developmental Disorders, 15,* 229–231.

SANDBURG, C. (1926). *Abraham Lincoln: Vol. 1. The prairie years.* New York: Harcourt, Brace, & World.

SANDLER, J., DARE, C., & HOLDER, A. (1973). *The patient and the analyst: The basis of the psychoanalytic process.* New York: International Universities Press.

SANTAYANA, G. (1905–1906). *The life of reason: Reason in common sense.* In R. T. Tripp (1970). *International thesaurus of quotations.* New York: Crowell.

SANUA, V. D. (1980). Familial and sociocultural antecedents of psychopathology. In H. C. Triandis and J. G. Draguns (Eds.), *Handbook of cross-cultural psychopathology: Vol. 6. Psychopathology.* Boston: Allyn & Bacon.

SANUA, V. D. (1981). Cultural changes and psychopathology in children: With special reference to infantile autism. *Acta Paedopsychiatrica, 47,* 133–142.

SARASON, I. G. (1976). A modeling and informational approach to delinquency. In E. Ribes-Inesta & A. Bandura (Eds.), *Analysis of delinquency and aggression.* Hillsdale, NJ: Erlbaum.

SARBIN, T. R., & JUHASZ, J. B. (1978). The social psychology of hallucinations. *Journal of Mental Imagery, 2,* 117–144.

SARGENT, J. D. (1977). Biofeedback and biocybernetics. In E. D. Wittkower & H. Warners (Eds.), *Psychosomatic medicine: Its clinical applications.* Hagerstown, MD: Harper & Row.

SARTRE, J. P. (1947). *Existentialism.* New York: Philosophical Library.

SATTERFIELD, J. H. (1978). The hyperactive child syndrome: A precursor of adult psychopathy? In R. D. Hare & D. Schalling (Eds.), *Psychopathic behaviour: Approaches to research.* London: Wiley.

SATTLER, J. M. (1982). *Assessment of children's intelligence and special abilities* (2nd ed.). Boston: Allyn & Bacon.

SCHALOCK, R. L., & HARPER, R. S. (1981). A systems approach to community living skills training. In R. H. Bruininks, C. E. Meyers, B. B. Sigford, & K. C. Lakin. *Deinstitutionalization and community adjustment of mentally retarded people.* Washington, DC: American Association on Mental Deficiency.

SCHATZMAN, M. (1976). *Soul murder: Persecution in the family.* Middlesex: Penguin.

SCHEFF, T. J. (1975). The labeling theory of mental illness. In T. J. Scheff (Ed.), *Labeling madness.* Englewood Cliffs, NJ: Prentice–Hall.

SCHEFF, T. J. (1984). *Being mentally ill: A sociological theory* (2nd ed.). New York: Aldine.

SCHILDKRAUT, J. J. (1965). The catecholamine hypothesis of affective disorders: A review of supportive evidence. *American Journal of Psychiatry, 122,* 509–522.

SCHILDKRAUT, J. J. (1969). Biogenic amine metabolism in depressive illnesses: Basic and clinical studies. In T. A. Williams, M. M. Katz, & J. A. Shields, Jr. (Eds.), *Recent Advances in the Psychobiology of the Depressive Illnesses: Proceedings of a Workshop Sponsored by the*

National Institute of Mental Health. Washington, DC: U.S. Government Printing Office.

SCHILDKRAUT, J. J. (1970). *Neuropsychopharmacology and the affective disorders.* Boston: Little, Brown.

SCHILDKRAUT, J. J. (1975). Depression and biogenic amines. In D. Hamburg & H. K. H. Brodie (Eds.), *American handbook of psychiatry* (Vol. 6). New York: Basic Books.

SCHILDKRAUT, J. J. (1977). Biochemical research in affective disorders. In G. Usdin (Ed.), *Depression: Clinical, biological, and psychological perspectives.* New York: Brunner/Mazel.

SCHILDKRAUT, J. J., GREEN, A. I., & MOONEY, J. J. (1985). Affective disorders: Biochemical aspects. In H. I. Kaplan & B. J. Sadock (Eds.), *Comprehensive textbook of psychiatry* (Vol. 1) (4th ed.). Baltimore: Williams & Wilkins.

SCHILDKRAUT, J. J., & KETY, S. S. (1967). Biogenic amines and emotion. *Science, 156,* 21–30.

SCHMEMANN, S. (1985, May 17). Soviet Union, once again, proclaims measures against alcoholism. *New York Times,* pp. 1, 4.

SCHOFIELD, W. (1986). *Psychotherapy: The purchase of friendship.* New Brunswick, NJ: Transaction Books.

SCHOPLER, E. (1982). Evolution in understanding and treatment of autism. *Triangle, 21,* 51–57.

SCHOU, M. (1968). Special review: Lithium in psychiatric therapy and prophylaxis. *Journal of Psychiatric Research, 6,* 67–95.

SCHREBER, D. P. (1955). *Memoirs of my nervous illness* (I. Macalpine & R. A. Hunter, Eds. and Trans.). London: Dawson. (Original work published 1903)

SCHROEDER, C. S., & BUTTERFIELD, E. C. (1987). Normalization and deinstitutionalization of mentally retarded individuals. *American Psychologist, 42,* 809–816.

SCHROEDER, S. R., SCHROEDER, C. S., & LANDESMAN, S. (1987). Psychological services in educational settings to persons with mental retardation. *American Psychologist, 42,* 805–808.

SCHUCKIT, M. A. (1979). *Drug and alcohol abuse: A clinical guide to diagnosis and treatment.* New York: Plenum.

SCHUCKIT, M. A. (1985). Treatment of alcoholism in office and outpatient settings. In J. H. Mendelson & N. K. Mello (Eds.), *The diagnosis and treatment of alcoholism* (2nd ed.). New York: McGraw–Hill.

SCHUCKIT, M. A., & HAGLUND, R. M. J. (1977). An overview of the etiologic theories on alcoholism. In N. J. Estes & M. E. Heinemann (Eds.), *Alcoholism: Development, consequences and interventions.* St. Louis: Mosby.

SCHULSINGER, F. (1977). Psychopathy: Heredity and environment. In S. A. Mednick & K. O. Christiansen (Eds.), *Biosocial bases of criminal behavior.* New York: Gardner Press.

SCHULSINGER, F. (1980). Biological psychopathology. *Annual Review of Psychology, 31,* 583–606.

SCHULTZ, S. (1984). *Family systems therapy: An integration.* New York: Aronson.

SCHUTZ, W. (1986). Encounter groups. In I. L. Kutash & A. A. Wolff (Eds.), *Psychotherapist's casebook.* San Francisco: Jossey–Bass.

SCHUYLER. D. (1974). *The depressive spectrum.* New York: Aronson.

SCHWARTZ, F., & LAZAR, Z. (1979). The scientific status of the Rorschach. *Journal of Personality Assessment, 43,* 3–11.

SCHWARTZ, C. C., MYERS, J. K., & ASTRACHAN, B. M. (1975). Concordance of multiple assessments of the outcome of schizophrenia. *Archives of General Psychiatry, 32,* 1221–1227.

SCHWARTZ, D. M., THOMPSON, M. G., & JOHNSON, C. L. (1982). Anorexia nervosa and bulimia: The socio-cultural context. *International Journal of Eating Disorders, 1*(3), 20–36.

SCHWARTZ, P. (1978). Parturitional injury of the newborn as a cause of mental deficiency and allied conditions. In C. H. Carter (Ed.), *Medical aspects of mental retardation.* Springfield, IL: Charles C Thomas.

SCHWITZGEEL, R. K. (1979). *Legal aspects of the enforced treatment of offenders.* Washington, DC: U.S. Government Printing Office.

SCIOLINO, E. (1988, March 20). U.S. finds output of drugs growing sharply. *New York Times,* pp. 1, 6.

SCOTT, K. G., & CARRAN, D. T. (1987). The epidemiology and prevention of mental retardation. *American Psychologist, 42,* 801–808.

SEAGULL, E. A., & WEINSHANK, A. R. (1984). *Journal of Clinical Child Psychology, 13,* 134–140.

SEARLES, J. S. (1988). The role of genetics in the pathogenesis of alcoholism. *Journal of Abnormal Psychology, 97,* 153–167.

SEDGWICK, P. (1971). R. D. Laing: Self, symptom, and society. In R. Boyers (Ed.), *R. D. Laing and anti-psychiatry.* New York: Harper & Row.

SEIFERT, J. A., DRAGUNS, J. G., & CAUDILL, W. (1971). Role orientation, sphere dominance, and social competence as bases of psychiatric diagnosis in Japan: A replication and extension of American findings. *Journal of Abnormal Psychology, 78,* 101–106.

SELECT COMMITTEE ON AGING, HOUSE OF REPRESENTATIVES, NINETY-FOURTH CONGRESS, FIRST SESSION. (1975a, June 9). *The state of aging.* Washington, DC: U.S. Government Printing Office.

SELECT COMMITTEE ON AGING, HOUSE OF REPRESENTATIVES, NINETY-FOURTH CONGRESS, FIRST SESSION. (1975b, November 11). *Society's responsibilities to the elderly.* Washington, DC: U.S. Government Printing Office.

SELIGMAN, M. E. P. (1970). *On the generality of the laws of learning. Psychological Review, 77,* 406–418.

SELIGMAN, M. E. P. (1971). Phobias and preparedness. *Behavior Therapy, 2,* 307–320.

SELIGMAN, M. E. P. (1974). Depression and learned helplessness. In R. J. Friedman & M. M. Katz (Eds.), *The psychology depression: Contemporary theory and research.* Washington, DC: Winston.

SELIGMAN, M. E. P. (1975). *Helplessness: On depression, development, and death.* San Francisco: Freeman.

SELIGMAN, M. E. P., ABRAMSON, L. Y., SEMMEL, A., & VON BAEYER, C. (1979). Depressive attributional style. *Journal of Abnormal Psychology, 88,* 242–247.

SELYE, H. (1950). *The psychology and pathology of exposure to stress.* Montreal: Acta.

SELYE, H. (1956). *The stress of life*. New York: McGraw–Hill.

SELYE, H. (1976). *The stress of life* (rev. ed.). New York: McGraw–Hill.

SELYE, H. (ED.) (1980). *Selye's guide to stress research* (Vol. 1). New York: Van Nostrand Reinhold.

SELYE, H. (1982). History and present status of the stress concept. In L. Goldberger & S. Bresnitz (Eds.), *Handbook of stress: Theoretical and clinical aspects*. New York: Free Press.

SEMANS, J. H. (1956). Premature ejaculation: A new approach. *Journal of Southern Medicine, 49,* 353–361.

SEQUIN, E. (1866). *Idiocy and its treatment by the physiological method*. New York: William Wood.

SHADISH, W. R., JR., & BOOTZIN, R. R. (1981). Nursing homes and chronic mental patients: A challenge to the community-based care movement. *Schizophrenia Bulletin, 7,* 580–585.

SHADISH, W. R., & BOOTZIN, R. R. (1984). The social integration of psychiatric patients in nursing homes. *American Journal of Psychiatry, 141,* 1203–1207.

SHADISH, W. R., JR., STRAW, R. B., McSWEENEY, A. J., KOLLER, D. L., & BOOTZIN, R. R. (1981). Nursing home care for mental patients: Descriptive data and some propositions. *American Journal of Community Psychology, 9,* 617–633.

SHAFFER, J. W., DUSZYNSKI, K. R., & THOMAS, C. B. (1981). Orthogonal dimensions of individual and group forms of the Rorschach. *Journal of Personality Assessment, 45,* 230–239.

SHAFII, M., CARRIGAN, S., WHITTINGHILL, J. R., & DERRICK, S. (1985). Psychological autopsy of completed suicide in children and adolescents. *American Journal of Psychiatry, 142,* 1061–1064.

SHAPIRO, A. K., & MORRIS, L. A. (1978). The placebo effect in medical and psychological therapies. In S. L. Garfield & A. E. Bergin (Eds.), *Handbook of psychotherapy and behavior changes: An empirical analysis* (2nd ed.). New York: Wiley.

SHAPIRO, D. (1981). Biofeedback and behavioral medicine in perspective. In D. Shapiro, J. Stoyva, J. Kamiya, T. X. Barber, N. E. Miller, & G. E. Schwartz (Eds.), *Biofeedback and behavioral medicine, 1979/1980: Therapeutic applications and experimental foundations*. New York: Aldine.

SHAPIRO, D., & SURWIT, R. S. (1976). Learned control of physiological function and disease. In H. Leitenberg (Ed.), *Handbook of behavior modification and behavior therapy*. Englewood Cliffs, NJ: Prentice–Hall.

SHAPIRO, J. L. (1978). *Methods of group psychotherapy and encounter: A tradition of innovation*. Itasca, IL: Peacock.

SHAPIRO, T., & SHERMAN, M. (1983). Long-term follow-up of children with psychiatric disorders. *Hospital and Community Psychiatry, 34,* 522–527.

SHATAN, C. F. (1978). Stress disorders among Vietnam veterans: The emotional content of combat continues. In C. F. Figley (Ed.), *Stress disorders among Vietnam veterans*. New York: Brunner/Mazel.

SHAW, B. F. (1977). Comparison of cognitive therapy and behavior therapy in the treatment of depression. *Journal of Consulting and Clinical Psychology, 45,* 543–551.

SHEAN, G. (1978). *Schizophrenia: An introduction to research and theory*. Cambridge, MA: Winthrop.

SHEEHAN, S. (1982). *Is there no place on earth for me?* Boston: Houghton Mifflin.

SHERMAN, B. (1985, October 23). The new realities of "date rape." *New York Times,* pp. 1, 15.

SHIELDS, J. (1968). Summary of the genetic evidence. In D. Rosenthal & S. S. Kety (Eds.), *The transmission of schizophrenia*. Oxford: Pergamon Press.

SHIELDS, J., & GOTTESMAN, I. I. (1972). Cross-national diagnosis of schizophrenia in twins. *Archives of General Psychiatry, 27,* 725–730.

SHIMKUNAS, A. (1978). Hemispheric asymmetry and schizophrenic thought disorder. In S. Schwartz (Ed.), *Language and cognition in schizophrenia*. Hillsdale, NJ: Erlbaum.

SHNEIDMAN, E. S., & FABEROW, N. C. (EDS.). (1961). *The cry for help*. New York: Mcgraw–Hill.

SHNEIDMAN, E. S., FABEROW, N. L., & LITMAN, R. E. (1970). *The psychology of suicide*. New York: Science House.

SHOLEVAR, G. P. (ED.). (1981). *The handbook of marriage and marital therapy*. Jamaica, NY: Spectrum.

SHOPSIN, B., WILK, S., SATHANANTHAN, G., GERSHON, S., & DAVIS, K. (1974). Catecholamines and affective disorders revised: A critical assessment. *Journal of Nervous and Mental Disease, 158,* 369–383.

SHORE, D. (ED.). (1986). *Schizophrenia: Questions and answers* (DHHS Publication No. ADM 86–1457). Rockville, MD: National Institute of Mental Health.

SHULMAN, L. C., & MANTELL, J. E. (1988). The AIDS crisis: A united health care perspective. *Social Science and Medicine, 26,* 979–988.

SIEGEL, J. M., & LEITCH, C. J. (1981). Type A in adolescents. *Psychosomatic Medicine, 43,* 45–56.

SIEGEL, K. (1986). Psychosocial aspects of rational suicide. *American Journal of Psychotherapy, 40,* 405–418.

SIEGLER, M., & OSMOND, H. (1976). *Models of madness, models of medicine*. New York: Harper & Row.

SIEGLER, M., OSMOND, H., & MANN, H. (1971). Laing's models of madness. In R. Boyers (Ed.), *R. D. Laing and antipsychiatry*. New York: Harper & Row.

SILVERMAN, L. H. (1974). Some psychoanalytic considerations of non-psychoanalytic therapies: On the possibility of integrating treatment approaches and related issues. *Psychotherapy: Theory, Research, and Therapy, 11,* 298–305.

SILVERMAN, L. H. (1976). Psychoanalytic theory. "The reports of my death are greatly exaggerated." *American Psychologist, 32,* 621–637.

SILVERMAN, L. H., & WEINBERGER, J. (1985). Mommy and I are one: Implications for psychotherapy. *American Psychologist, 40,* 1296–1308.

SIMKIN, J. S., SIMKIN, A. N., BRIEN, L., & SHELDON, C. (1986).

Gestalt therapy. In I. L. Kutash & A. Wolf (Eds.), *Psychotherapist's casebook*. San Francisco: Jossey–Bass.

SIMKIN, J. S., & YONTEF, G. M. (1984). Gestalt therapy. In R. J. Corsini & D. Wedding (Eds.), *Current psychotherapies* (3rd ed.). Itasca, IL: Peacock.

SINGER, K. (1972). Drinking patterns and alcoholism in the Chinese. *British Journal of Addiction, 67,* 3–14.

SINNETT, E. R. (1964). The diary of a schizophrenic man. In B. Kaplan (Ed.), *The inner world of mental illness: A series of first-person accounts of what it was like*. New York: Harper & Row.

SIOMOPOULOS, V. (1988). Narcissistic personality disorder: Clinical features. *American Journal of Psychotherapy, 42,* 240–259.

SIZEMORE, C. S., & PITTILLO, E. S. (1977). *I'm Eve*. Garden City, NY: Doubleday.

SKINNER, B. F. (1953). *Science and human behavior*. New York: Macmillan.

SKINNER, B. F. (1966). *The behavior of organisms*. New York: Appleton–Century–Crofts. (Original work published 1938)

SKINNER, B. F. (1968). *The technology of teaching*. New York: Appleton–Century–Crofts.

SKINNER, B. F. (1974). *About behaviorism*. New York: Knopf.

SKINNER, B. F. (1975). The steep and thorny way to a science of behavior. *American Psychologist, 30,* 42–49.

SKINNER, B. F. (1987). Whatever happened to psychology as the science of behavior? *American Psychologist, 42,* 780–786.

SLAVIN, B. (1976, March 25). Compulsive gambling—a disease affects many lives. *Champaign–Urbana News-Gazette*, p. 23–B.

SLAVSON, S. R. (ED.). (1940). Group therapy. *Mental Hygiene, 24,* 36–49.

SLAVSON, S. R. (ED.). (1947). *The practice of group therapy*. New York: International Universities Press.

SLAVSON, S. R. (1964). *A textbook in analytical group psychotherapy*. New York: International Universities Press.

SLAW, K. M., & KALACHNIK, J. E. (1985). Tardive dyskinesia: Facts the mental health administrator may not know. *Journal of Mental Health Administration, 12*(2), 22–27.

SLICKER, W. D. (1985). Current perspectives on the insanity defense. *Case and Comment, 91*(6), 22–30.

SLOANE, R. B., STAPLES, F. R., CRISTOL, A. H., YORKSTON, N. J., & WHIPPLE, K. (1975). *Psychoanalysis and behavior therapy*. Cambridge, MA: Harvard University Press.

SMALL, L. (1980). *Neuropsychodiagnosis in psychotherapy* (rev. ed.). New York: Brunner/Mazel.

SMART, C. (1977). *Women, crime, and criminality: A feminist critique*. London: Routledge & Kegan Paul.

SMITH, D. E. (1986). Cocaine–alcohol abuse: Epidemiological, diagnostic and treatment considerations. *Journal of Psychoactive Drugs, 18,* 117–129.

SMITH, D. W. (1977). Fetal alcohol syndrome: A tragic and preventable disorder. In N. J. Estes & M. E. Heinemann (Eds.), *Alcohol-*

ism: Development, consequences, and interventions. St. Louis: Mosby.

SMITH, G. F., & BERG, J. M. (1976). *Down's anomaly* (2nd ed.). Edinburgh: Churchill Livingstone.

SMITH, G. M. (1917). *A history of the Bristol Royal Infirmary*. Bristol: Arrowsmith.

SMITH, M. B. (1982). Psychology and humanism. *Journal of Humanistic Psychology, 22*(2), 44–45.

SMITH, M. L., & GLASS, G. V. (1977). Meta-analysis of psychotherapy outcome studies. *American Psychologist, 32,* 752–760.

SMITH, M. L., GLASS, G. V., & MILLER, T. I. (1980). *The benefits of psychotherapy*. Baltimore: Johns Hopkins University Press.

SMITH, R. (1981). *Trial by medicine: Insanity and responsibility in Victorian trials*. Edinburgh: Edinburgh University Press.

SNYDER, C. R. (1958). *Alcohol and the Jews: A cultural study of drinking and sobriety*. New Brunswick, NJ: Rutgers Center of Alcohol Studies.

SNYDER, C. R. (1962). Culture and Jewish sobriety: The ingroup–outgroup factor. In D. J. Pittman & C. R. Snyder (Eds.), *Society, culture, and drinking patterns*. New York: Wiley.

SNYDER, S. H. (1972, August). The true speed trip: Schizophrenia. *Psychology Today*, pp. 42–46, 74–75.

SNYDER, S. H. (1973). Amphetamine psychosis: A "model" schizophrenia medicated by catecholamines. *American Journal of Psychiatry, 130,* 61–67.

SNYDER, S. H. (1978). Dopamine and schizophrenia. In L. C. Wynne, R. L. Cromwell, & S. Matthysse (Eds.), *The nature of schizophrenia: New approaches to research and treatment*. New York: Wiley.

SNYDER, S. H. (1980). *Biological aspects of mental disorder*. New York: Oxford University Press.

SNYDER, S. H. (1984). Neurosciences: An integrative discipline. *Science, 225,* 1255–1257.

SNYDER, S. H., BANJERJEE, S. P., YAMAMURA, H. I., & GREENBERG, D. (1974). Drugs, neurotransmitters, and schizophrenia. *Science, 184,* 1243–1253.

SOCARIDES, D. D., & STOLOROW, R. D. (1986). Self psychology and psychoanalytic phenomenology. In I. L. Kutash & A. Wolf (Eds.), *Psychotherapist's casebook*. San Francisco: Jossey–Bass.

SOLLOD, R. N., & KAPLAN, H. S. (1976). The new sex therapy: An integration of behavioral, psychodynamic, and interpersonal approaches. In J. L. Claghorn (Ed.), *Successful psychotherapy*. New York: Brunner/Mazel.

SOLOFF, P. H., GEORGE, A., NATHAN, S., SCHULZ, P. M., ULRICH, R. F., & PEREL, J. M. (1986). Progress in pharmacotherapy of borderline disorders. A double-blind study of amitriptyline, haloperidol, and placebo. *Archives of General Psychiatry, 43,* 691–697.

SOLOMON, S. (1985a). Neurological evaluation. In H. J. Kaplan & B. J. Sadock (Eds.), *Comprehensive textbook of psychiatry* (Vol. 1) (4th ed.). Baltimore: Williams & Wilkins.

SOLOMON, S. (1985b). Clinical neurology and neuropathology. In

H. J. Kaplan & B. J. Sadock (Eds.), *Comprehensive textbook of psychiatry* (Vol. 1) (4th ed.). Baltimore: Williams & Wilkins.

SOMMERS, A. (1985). "Negative symptoms": Conceptual and methodological problems. *Schizophrenia Bulletin, 11,* 364–379.

SONTAG, S. (1985, July 4). Head Start's incentives for parents. *New York Times,* pp. 15–16.

SOUTHAM, M. A., AGRAS, W. S., TAYLOR, C. B., & KRAEMER, H. D. (1982). Relaxation training: Blood pressure lowering during the working day. *Archives of General Psychiatry, 39,* 715–717.

SPARLING, P. F. (1971). Diagnosis and treatment of syphilis. *New England Journal of Medicine, 284,* 652–653.

SPARROW, S. S., BALLA, D. A., & CICCHETTI, D. V. (1984). *Vineland Adaptive Behavior Scales: A revision of the Vineland Social Maturity Scale by Edgar A. Doll.* Circle Pines, MN: American Guidance Service.

SPEARMAN, C. (1904). "General intelligence": Objectively determined and measured. *American Journal of Psychology, 15,* 210–292.

SPECIAL ISSUE ON THE FOUNDATIONS OF COGNITIVE SCIENCE. (1980). *Behavioral and Brain Sciences, 3*(1).

SPEER, D. C. (1971). Rate of caller re-use of a telephone crisis service. *Crisis Intervention, 3,* 83–86.

SPEER, D. C. (1972). An evaluation of a telephone crisis service. Paper presented at the meeting of the Midwestern Psychological Association, Cleveland, OH.

SPIEGEL, J. P., & PAPAJOHN, J. (1986). Training program in ethnicity and mental health. In H. P. Lefley & P. B. Pedersen (Eds.), *Cross-cultural training for mental health professionals.* Springfield, IL: Charles C Thomas.

SPIKER, D. G., & EHLER, J. G. (1984). Structured psychiatric interviews for adults. In G. Goldstein & M. Hersen (Eds.), *Handbook of psychological assessment.* New York: Pergamon Press.

SPITZER, R. L. (1973, June 7). *A proposal about homosexuality as one form of sexual behavior and sexual orientation disturbance as a psychiatric disorder.* Washington, DC: American Psychiatric Association, Task Force on Nomenclature and Statistics.

SPITZER, R. L. (1976). More on pseudoscience in science and the case for psychiatric diagnosis: A critique of D. L. Rosenhan's "On being sane in insane places" and "The contextual nature of psychiatric diagnosis." *Archives of General Psychiatry, 33,* 459–470.

SPITZER, R. L. (1981). The diagnostic status of homosexuality in DSM-III: A reformulation of the issues. *American Journal of Psychiatry, 138,* 210–215.

SPITZER, R. L., & FLEISS, J. L. (1974). A reanalysis of the reliability of psychiatric diagnosis. *British Journal of Psychiatry, 125,* 341–347.

SPITZER, R. L., SKODOL, A. E., GIBBON, M., & WILLIAMS, J. B. W. (1981). *DSM-III case book: A learning companion to the diagnostic and statistical manual of mental disorders* (3rd ed.). Washington, DC: American Psychiatric Association.

SPITZER, R. L., & WILLIAMS, J. B. W. (1980). Classification of mental illness and DSM-III. In H. I. Kaplan, A. M. Freedman, &

B. J. Sadock (Eds.), *Comprehensive textbook of psychiatry* (Vol. 3). Baltimore: Williams & Wilkins.

SPOTTS, J. V., & SHONTZ, F. C. (1980). *Cocaine users: A representative case approach.* New York: Free Press.

SQUIRE, L. R., & CHASE, P. M. (1975). Memory functions six to nine months after electroconvulsive therapy. *Archives of General Psychiatry, 32,* 1557–1564.

STAMPFL, T. G., & LEVIS, D. J. (1967). Essentials of implosive therapy: A learning-theory based psychodynamic behavior therapy. *Journal of Abnormal Psychology, 72,* 496–503.

STANTON, A. H., GUNDERSON, J. G., KNAPP, P. H., FRANK, A. F., VANNICELLI, M. L., SCHNIZTER, R., & ROSENTHAL, R. (1984). Effects of psychotherapy in schizophrenia: I. Design and implementation of a controlled study. *Schizophrenia Bulletin, 10,* 520–583.

Statistical Abstract of the United States (104th ed.). (1983). Washington, DC: U.S. Bureau of the Census.

STEADMAN, H. J. (1979). *Beating a rap? Defendants found incompetent to stand trial.* Chicago: University of Chicago Press.

STEADMAN, H. J., & BRAFF, J. (1983). Defendants not guilty by reason of insanity. In J. Monahan, & H. J. Steadman, (Eds.), *Mentally disordered offenders: Perspectives from law and social science.* New York: Plenum.

STEADMAN, H. J., & HARTSTONE, E. (1983). Defendants incompetent to stand trial. In J. Monahan & H. J. Steadman (Eds.), *Mentally disordered offenders: Perspectives from law and social science.* New York: Plenum.

STEIN, M. (1986). A reconsideration of specificity in psychosomatic medicine: From olfaction to the lymphocyte. *Psychosomatic Medicine, 48,* 3–22.

STEINBRUECK, S. M., MAXWELL, S. E., & HOWARD, G. S. (1983). A meta-analysis of psychotherapy and drug therapy in the treatment of unipolar depression with adults. *Journal of Consulting and Clinical Psychology, 51,* 856–863.

STEINHAUSEN, H.-C., & GOEBEL, D. (1987). Convergence of parent check lists and child psychiatric diagnoses. *Journal of Abnormal Child Psychology, 15,* 147–151.

STEINMETZ, P. L., LEWINSOHN, P. M., & ANTONUCCIO, D. O. (1983). Prediction of individual outcome in a group intervention for depression. *Journal of Consulting and Clinical Psychology, 51,* 331–337.

STEKETTEE, G., & FOA, E. B. (1987). Rape victims: Post-traumatic stress responses and their treatment—a review of the literature. *Journal of Anxiety Disorders, 1,* 69–86.

STENSTEDT, A. (1952). A study in manic-depressive psychosis: Clinical, social and genetic investigations. *Acta Psychiatrica Scandinavica* (Suppl. 79).

STEPHENS, J. H., & KAMP, M. (1962). On some aspects of hysteria: A clinical study. *Journal of Nervous and Mental Disease, 134,* 305–315.

STERN, W. (1914). *The psychological methods of testing intelligence* (G. M. Whipple, Trans.) (Education Psychological Monograph No. 13). Baltimore: Warwick & York.

STEVENS, J. H., TURNER, C. W., RHODEWALT, F., & TALBOT, S. (1984). The Type A behavior pattern and carotid artery artheros-clerosis. *Psychosomatic Medicine, 4,* 105–113.

STEVENSON, R. L. (1974). *The strange case of Dr. Jekyll and Mr. Hyde.* London: Folio Press & J. M. Dent. (Original work published 1886)

STEWART, M. A., & LEONE, L. (1978). A family study of unsocia-lized aggressive boys. *Biological Psychiatry, 13,* 107–117.

STEWART, R. M., & BROWN, R. I. F. (1988). An outcome study of Gamblers Anonymous. *British Journal of Psychiatry, 152,* 284–288.

STILES, W. B., SHAPIRO, D. A., & ELLIOTT, R. (1986). Are all psychotherapies equivalent? *American Psychologist, 41,* 165–180.

STOLLER, R. J. (1967). Transvestites' women. *American Journal of Psychiatry, 124,* 333–339.

STOLLER, R. J. (1974). *Sex and gender: Vol. 1. The development of masculinity and femininity.* New York: Aronson.

STOLLER, R. J. (1976a). Gender identity. In B. J. Sadock, H. I. Kaplan, & A. M. Freedman (Eds.), *The sexual experience.* Balti-more: Williams & Wilkins.

STOLLER, R. J. (1976b). *Sex and gender: Vol. 2. The transsexual experiment.* New York: Aronson.

STOLLER, R. J. (1977). Psychoanalytic diagnosis. In V. M. Rakoff, H. C. Stancer, & H. B. Kedward (Eds.), *Psychiatric diagnosis.* New York: Brunner/Mazel.

STOLLER, R. J. (1985). Gender identity disorders in children and adults. In H. I. Kaplan, A. M. Freedman, & B. J. Sadock (Eds.), *Comprehensive textbook of psychiatry* (Vol. 1) (4th ed.). Baltimore: Williams & Wilkins.

STOLZ, S. B., WIENCKOWSKI, L. A., & BROWN, B. S. (1975). Behavior modification: A perspective on critical issues. *American Psychologist, 30,* 1027–1048.

STONE, A. A. (1975). *Mental health and law: A system in transition.* Washington, DC: U.S. Government Printing Office.

STONE, A. A. (1976). The *Tarasoff* decisions: Suing psychotherapists to safeguard society. *Harvard Law Review, 90,* 358–378.

STONE, A. A., & NEALE, J. M. (1981). Hypochondriasis and tend-ency to adopt the sick role as moderators of the relationship be-tween life-events and somatic symptomatology. *British Journal of Medical Psychology, 54,* 75–81.

STORR, A. (1974). *Sexual deviance.* London: Heinemann.

STORY, I. (1978). Review of *The Borderline Patient* by R. G. Grinker, Sr., and B. Werble. *Contemporary Psychology, 23,* 945–946.

STORY, R. I. (1968). Effects on thinking of relationships between conflict arousal and oral fixation. *Journal of Abnormal Psychology, 73,* 440–448.

STRAUSS, J. S. (1985). Negative symptoms: Future developments of the concept. *Schizophrenia Bulletin, 11,* 457–460.

STRAUSS, J. S., & CARPENTER, W. T., JR. (1979). The prognosis of schizophrenia. In L. Bellak (Ed.), *Disorders of the schizophrenic syndrome.* New York: Basic Books.

STRAUSS, J. S., KOKES, R. F., KLORMAN, R., & SACKSTEDER, J. L. (1977). Premorbid adjustment in schizophrenia—concepts, mea-sures and implications: Part I. The concept of premorbid adjust-ment. *Schizophrenia Bulletin, 3,* 182–185.

STRAUSS, M. E. (1973). Behavioral differences between acute and chronic schizophrenics: Course of psychosis, effects of institution-alization, or sampling biases? *Psychological Bulletin, 79,* 271–279.

STRETCH, R. H. (1985). Posttraumatic stress disorder among U.S. Army reserve Vietnam and Vietnam-era veterans. *Journal of Con-sulting and Clinical Psychology, 53,* 935–936.

STRICKER, G. (1983a). Some issues in the psychodynamic treatment of the depressed patient. *Professional Psychology: Research and Practice, 14,* 209–217.

STRICKER, G. (1983b). Passive–aggressiveness. A condition espe-cially suited to the psychodynamic approach. In R. C. Parsons & R. J. Wicks (Eds.), *Passive-aggressiveness: Theory and practice.* New York: Brunner-Mazel.

STRICKLAND, B. R. (1988). Clinical psychology comes of age. *Ameri-can Psychologist, 43,* 104–107.

STRIEGEL-MOORE, R. H., SILBERSTEIN, L. R., & RODIN, J. (1986). Toward an understanding of risk factors in bulimia. *American Psychologist, 41,* 246–263.

STROBER, M (1986). Anorexia nervosa: History and psychological concepts. In K. D. Brownell, & J. P. Foreyt, (Eds.), *Handbook of eating disorders.* New York: Basic Books.

STROBER, M., & BOWEN, E. (1986). Hospital management of the adolescent with anorexia nervosa. *Clinical Psychologist, 39,* 46–48.

STRUPP, H. H. (1972). *Psychotherapy.* Morristown, NJ: General Learning Press.

STRUPP, H. H. (1973a). On the basic ingredients of psychotherapy. *Journal of Consulting and Clinical Psychology, 41,* 1–8.

STRUPP, H. H. (1973b). Toward a reformulation of the psychothera-peutic influence. *International Journal of Psychiatry, 32,* 127–135.

STRUPP, H. H. (1975). Psychoanalysis, "focal psychotherapy," and the nature of the therapeutic influence. *Archives of General Psychia-try, 32,* 127–135.

STRUPP, H. H. (1978). Psychotherapy research and practice: An overview. In S. L. Garfield and A. E. Bergin (Eds.) *Handbook of psychotherapy and behavior change: An empirical analysis* (2nd ed.). New York: Wiley.

STRUPP, H. H. (1986). Psychotherapy: Research, practice, and pub-lic policy (how to avoid dead ends). *American Psychologist, 41,* 120–130.

STRUPP, H. H., & HADLEY, S. W. (1977). A tripartite model of mental health and therapeutic outcomes: With special reference to negative effects in psychotherapy. *American Psychologist, 32,* 187–196.

STUART, F. M., HAMMOND, D. C., & PETT, M. A. (1987). Inhibited sexual desire in women. *Archives of Sexual Behavior, 16,* 91–106.

STURT, E., KUMAKURA, N., & DER, G. (1984). How depressing life is—life-long morbidity risk for depressive disorder in the general population. *Journal of Affective Disorders, 7,* 109–122.

SUE, S., & ZANE, N. (1987). The role of culture and cultural techniques in psychotherapy: A critique and reformulation. *American Psychologist, 42,* 37–45.

SULLIVAN, H. S. (1953a). *The interpersonal theory of psychiatry* (H. S. Perry & M. L. Gawel, Eds.). New York: Norton.

SULLIVAN, H. S. (1953b). *Conceptions of modern psychiatry: The first William Alanson White memorial lectures* (2nd ed.). New York: Norton.

SULLIVAN, R. (1987, October 22). New York finds more drug addicts than homosexuals killed by AIDS. *New York Times,* p. 13.

SULLOWAY, F. J. (1979). *Freud, biologist of the mind: Beyond the psychoanalytic legend.* New York: Basic Books.

SURWIT, R. S., FEINGLOS, M. N., & SCOVERN, A. W. (1983). Diabetes and behavior: A paradigm for health psychology. *American Psychologist, 38,* 255–262.

SWETS, J. A. (1988). Measuring the accuracy of diagnostic systems. *Science, 140,* 1285–1293.

SYNDULKO, K. (1978). Electrocortical investigations of sociopathy. In R. D. Hare & D. Schalling (Eds.), *Psychopathic behavior: Approaches to research.* London: Wiley.

SYZMANSKI, L., & CROCKER, A. C. (1985). Mental retardation. In H. I. Kaplan & B. J. Sadock (Eds.), *Comprehensive textbook of psychiatry* (Vol. 2) (4th ed.). Baltimore: Williams & Wilkins.

SZASZ, T. S. (1961). *The myth of mental illness: Foundations of a theory of personal conduct.* New York: Harper & Row.

SZASZ, T. S. (1963). *Law, liberty, and psychiatry: An inquiry into the social uses of mental health practices.* New York: Macmillan.

SZASZ, T. S. (1965). *Psychiatric justice.* Westport, CT: Greenwood Press.

SZASZ, T. S. (1970). *Ideology and insanity: Essays on the psychiatric dehumanization of man.* New York: Doubleday.

SZASZ, T. S. (1974). *The myth of mental illness: Foundations of a theory of personal conduct* (rev. ed.). New York: Harper & Row.

SZASZ, T. S. (1977a). *Psychiatric slavery: When confinement and coercion masquerade as cure.* New York: Free Press.

SZASZ, T. S. (1977b). *The theology of medicine: The political philosophical foundations of medical ethics.* Baton Rouge: Louisiana State University Press.

SZASZ, T. S. (1986). The case against suicide prevention. *American Psychologist, 41,* 806–812.

SZYMANSKI, H. V., & KEILL, S. L. (1985). Schizophrenia. In M. Hersen & S. M. Turner (Eds.), *Diagnostic interviewing.* New York: Plenum.

TACHE, J., SELYE, H., & DAY, S. B. (1979). *Cancer, stress, and death.* New York: Plenum.

TARASOFF V. REGENTS OF UNIVERSITY OF CALIFORNIA. (1976). 17 Cal.3d. 425. 131 Cal. Rptr. 14. 551 P.2d. 334.

TARJAN, G., WRIGHT, S. W., EYMAN, R. K., & KEERNAN, C. V. (1978). Natural history of mental retardation: Some aspects of epidemiology. *American Journal of Mental Deficiency, 77,* 369–379.

TARNOPOLSKY, A., WATKINS, G., & HAND, D. J. (1980). Aircraft noise and mental health: I. Prevalence of individual symptoms. *Psychological Medicine, 10,* 683–698.

TAUBMAN, P. (1988, September 20). Soviets ease drinking curbs in a setback for Gorbachev, *The New York Times,* September 20, 1–2.

TAYLOR, F. G., & MARSHALL, W. L. (1977). Experimental analysis of a cognitive–behavior therapy for depression. *Cognitive Therapy and Research, 1,* 59–72.

TAYLOR, F. K. (1982). Depersonalization in the light of Brentano's phenomenology. *British Journal of Medical Psychology, 55*(4), 297–306.

TAYLOR, G. J. (1980). Psychosomatic disorders. In S. E. Greben, R. Pos, V. M. Ratoff, A. Bonkalo, F. H. Lowry, & G. Voineskos (Eds.), *A method of psychiatry.* Philadelphia: Lea & Febiger.

TAYLOR, H. G., FLETCHER, J. M., & SATZ, P. (1984). Specialized neuropsychological methods. In G. Goldstein & M. Herdsen (Eds.), *Handbook of psychological assessment.* New York: Pergamon Press.

TAYLOR, J. K. (1986). Family therapy. In I. L. Kutash and A. Wolf (Eds.), *Psychotherapist's casebook.* San Francisco: Jossey–Bass.

TAYLOR, M. A., & HEISER, J. F. (1971). Phenomenology: An alternative approach to diagnosis of mental disease. *Comprehensive Psychiatry, 12,* 480–486.

TAYLOR, S., JR. (1985, June 11). Spokesman for liberals watches tide flow out. *New York Times,* p. 9.

TAYLOR, W. S., & MARTIN, M. F. (1944). Multiple personality. *Journal of Abnormal and Social Psychology, 39,* 281–300.

TERENIUS, L., WAHLSTROM, A., LINDSTROM, L., & WIDERLOV, E. (1976). Increased CSF levels of endorphins in chronic psychosis. *Neuroscience Letters, 3,* 157–162.

TERKEL, S. (1974). *Working.* New York: Random House.

TERMAN, L. M. (1916). *The measurement of intelligence.* Boston: Houghton Mifflin.

TERMAN, L. M., & MERRILL, M. A. (1937). *Measuring intelligence.* Boston: Houghton Mifflin.

TERMAN, L. M., & MERRILL, M. A. (1960). *Stanford–Binet intelligence scale: Manual for the third revision, Form L–M.* Boston: Houghton Mifflin.

TERMAN, L. M., & MERRILL, M. A. (1973). *Stanford–Binet Scale: 1972 Norms Edition.* Boston: Houghton Mifflin.

TERRY, R. D. (1976). Dementia: A brief and selective review. *Archives of Neurology, 33,* 1–4.

THIGPEN, C. H., & CLECKLEY, H. (1954). A case of multiple personality. *Journal of Abnormal and Social Psychology, 49,* 135–151.

THIGPEN, C. H., & CLECKLEY, H. M. (1957). *The three faces of Eve.* New York: Macmillan.

THIGPEN, C. H., & CLECKLEY, H. M. (1984). On the incidence of multiple personality disorder: A brief communication. *International Journal of Clinical and Experimental Hypnosis, 32,* 63–66.

THOMAS, H. (1980). Personality and adjustment to aging. In J. E. Birren & R. B. Sloane (Eds.), *Handbook of the psychology of aging.* New York: Van Nostrand Reinhold.

THOMAS, L. (1974). *The lives of a cell.* New York: Bantam.

THORLEY, G. (1984). Review of follow-up and follow-back studies of childhood hyperactivity. *Psychological Bulletin, 96,* 116–132.

THORNDIKE, E. L. (1898). Animal intelligence: An experimental study of the associative process in animals. *Psychological Review Monograph Supplement* (4, Whole No. 8).

THORNDIKE, E. L. (1935). *The psychology of wants, interests and attitudes.* New York: Appleton–Century.

THORNDIKE, R. L., HAGEN, E. P., & SATTLER, J. M. (1986). *The Stanford–Binet Intelligence Scale* (4th ed.). Chicago: Riverside.

THORNE, F. C. (1966). An analysis of Szasz "Myth of mental illness." *American Journal of Psychiatry, 123,* 652–656.

TILLICH, P. (1952). *The courage to be.* New Haven: Yale University Press.

TOENNIESSEN, L. M., CASEY, D. E., & MCFARLAND, B. H. (1985). Tardive dyskinesia in the aged: Duration of treatment relationships. *Archives of General Psychiatry, 42,* 278–284.

TOLCHIN, M. (1988, May 15). Surgeon General asserts smoking is an addiction. *New York Times,* pp. 1, 26.

TOLLISON, C. D., & ADAMS, H. E. (1979). *Sexual disorders: Treatment, theory, research.* New York: Gardner Press.

TOLLIVER, L. M. (1983). Social and mental health needs of the aged. *American Psychologist, 38,* 316–318.

TORGERSEN, S. (1984). Genetic and nosological aspects of schizotypal and borderline personality disorders. *Archives of General Psychiatry, 41,* 546–554.

TORGERSEN, S. (1986). Genetic factors in moderately severe and mild affective disorders. *Archives of General Psychiatry, 43,* 222–226.

TORREY, E. F. (1972). *The mind game: Witchdoctors and psychiatrists.* New York: Emerson Hall.

TORREY, E. F. (1980). *Schizophrenia and civilization.* New York: Aronson.

TORREY, E. F., & PETERSON, M. R. (1974). Schizophrenia and the limbic system. *Lancet, 2,* 942–946.

TOWNSEND, J. M. (1978). *Cultural conceptions and mental illness: A comparison of Germany and America.* Chicago: University of Chicago Press.

TRIANDIS, H. C., & BRISLIN, R. W. (1984). Cross-cultural psychology. *American Psychologist, 39,* 1006–1016.

TRIANDIS, H. C., & DRAGUNS, J. G. (EDS.). (1980). *Handbook of cross-cultural psychology: Vol. 6. Psychopathology.* Boston: Allyn & Bacon.

TRIANDIS, H. C., MALPASS, R. S., & DAVIDSON, A. R. (1973). Psychology and culture. *Annual Review of Psychology, 24,* 355–371.

TRILLIN, C. (1971, September 25). U.S. Journal: Gallup, New Mexico—drunken Indians. *New Yorker,* pp. 110–114.

TRIMBLE, M. R. (1985). Post-traumatic stress disorder: History of a concept. In C. R. Figley (Ed.), *Trauma and its wake: The study and treatment of post-traumatic stress disorder.* New York: Brunner/Mazel.

TRIMMER, E. (1978). *Basic sexual medicine: A textbook of sexual medicine and an introduction to sex counseling techniques.* London: Heinemann.

TRIPP, C. A. (1976). *The homosexual matrix.* New York: New American Library.

TRIPP, R. T. (1970). *International thesaurus of quotations.* New York: Crowell.

TSIANTIS, J., MACRI, I., & MARATOS, O. (1986). Schizophrenia in children: A review of European research. *Schizophrenia Bulletin, 12,* 101–119.

TSUANG, M. T. (1976). Schizophrenia around the world. *Comprehensive Psychiatry, 17,* 477–481.

TSUANG, M. T. (1982). Long-term outcome in schizophrenia. *Trends in Neuroscience, 5,* 203–207.

TUDOR, W., TUDOR, J., & GOVE, W. R. (1977). The effect of sex role differences on the social control of mental illness. *Journal of Health and Social Behavior, 18,* 98–112.

TURKINGTON, C. (1982, April). PTSD: New name for condition old as war. *APA Monitor,* p. 15.

TURKINGTON, C. (1985, February). Stress found to play major role in onset, treatment of diabetes. *APA Monitor,* pp. 28, 37.

TURNER, R. J., & GARTRELL, J. W. (1978). Social factors in psychiatric outcome: Toward the resolution of interpretive controversies. *American Sociology Review, 43,* 368–382.

TURNER, S. M., & HERSEN, M. (1985). The interviewing process. In M. Hersen & S. M. Turner (Eds.), *Diagnostic interviewing.* New York: Plenum.

TURNS, D. M. (1985). Epidemiology of phobic and obsessive–compulsive disorders among adults. *American Journal of Psychotherapy, 39,* 360–370.

ULLMANN, L. P., & KRASNER, L. (1975). *A psychological approach to abnormal behavior* (2nd ed.). Englewood Cliffs, NJ: Prentice–Hall.

UNIFORM LAW COMMISSIONERS. (1984, August 3). *Model Insanity Defense and Post-Trial Disposition Act.* Model legislation approved at the National Conference of Commissioners on Uniform State Laws, Keystone, CO.

UNITED STATES V. LYONS. (1984). 704 F.2d 743 (5th Cir.).

USDIN, E. (1979). "Endorphins, dopamine, and schizophrenia": Two discussions. *Schizophrenia Bulletin, 5,* 242–243.

U.S. BUREAU OF THE CENSUS. (1979). *Illustrative projections of world populations to the 21st century: Current population reports* (Special Studies Series P–23, No. 79). Washington, DC: U.S. Government Printing Office.

U.S. BUREAU OF THE CENSUS. (1981). *Age, sex, race, and Spanish origin of the population by regions, divisions, and states: 1980* (1980 Census of Population Supplementary Reports, PC80–81–1). Washington, DC: U.S. Government Printing Office.

U.S. DEPARTMENT OF HEALTH, EDUCATION, AND WELFARE. (1972a). *Epilepsy: Hope through research* (rev. ed.). Washington, DC: U.S. Government Printing Office.

U.S. DEPARTMENT OF HEALTH, EDUCATION, AND WELFARE. (1972b).

The health consequences of smoking: A report of the Surgeon General. Washington, DC: U.S. Government Printing Office.

U.S. DEPARTMENT OF HEALTH, EDUCATION, AND WELFARE. (1978). *Phencyclidine use among youths in drug abuse treatment.* Washington, DC: U.S. Government Printing Office.

U.S. DEPARTMENT OF HEALTH AND HUMAN SERVICES. (1980). *Facts about alcohol and alcoholism.* Washington, DC: U.S. Government Printing Office.

U.S. DEPARTMENT OF HEALTH AND HUMAN SERVICES. (1981a, July). Surgeon General's advisory on alcohol and pregnancy. *FDA Drug Bulletin,* pp. 9–10.

U.S. DEPARTMENT OF HEALTH AND HUMAN SERVICES. (1981b). *The health consequences of smoking—the changing cigarette: A report of the Surgeon General.* Washington, DC: U.S. Government Printing Office.

U.S. DEPARTMENT OF HEALTH AND HUMAN SERVICES. (1985). *Electroconvulsive Therapy* (Consensus Development Conference Statement, Vol. 5, No. 1). Washington, DC: U.S. Government Printing Office.

U.S. DEPARTMENT OF HEALTH AND HUMAN SERVICES (1986). *Smoking and health—a national status report: A report to Congress* (OHHS Publication No. CDC 87–8396). Washington, DC: U.S. Government Printing Office.

U.S. DEPARTMENT OF HEALTH AND HUMAN SERVICES. (1987). *Bibliography on smoking and health* (DDHS Public Health Service Bibliography Series No. 45). Bethesda, MD: Office of Smoking and Health.

U.S. DEPARTMENT OF JUSTICE. (1972). *Drugs of abuse.* Washington, DC: U.S. Government Printing Office.

U.S. DEPARTMENT OF TRANSPORTATION. (1980). *Marijuana, other drugs, and their relation to highway safety: A report to Congress* (No. DOT HS 805 229). Washington, DC: National Highway Traffic Safety Administration.

U.S. WILDS HIDE SCARS OF VIETNAM. (1983, December 31). *New York Times,* p. 6.

VAGINITIS, PART TWO (1984, March). *Harvard Medical School Health Letter,* pp. 1–2.

VAILLANT, G. E. (1978). The distinction between prognosis and diagnosis in schizophrenia: A discussion of Manfred Bleuler's paper. In L. C. Wynne, R. L. Cromwell, & S. Matthysse (Eds.), *The nature of schizophrenia: New approaches to research and treatment.* New York: Wiley.

VAILLANT, G. E. (1983). *The natural history of alcoholism: Causes, patterns, and paths to recovery.* Cambridge, MA: Harvard University Press.

VAILLANT, G. E. (1986, July). Adaptation and ego mechanisms of defense. *Harvard Medical School Mental Health Letter,* pp. 4–6.

VAILLANT, G. E. (1987). A developmental view of old and new perspectives of personality disorders. *Journal of Personality Disorders, 1,* 146–156.

VAILLANT, G. E., & MILOFSKY, E. S. (1982). The etiology of alcoholism: A prospective viewpoint. *American Psychologist, 37,* 494–503.

VALENSTEIN, E. S. (1973). *Brain control: A critical examination of brain stimulation and psychosurgery.* New York: Wiley.

VALENSTEIN, E. S. (1986). *Great and desperate cures: The rise and decline of psychosurgery and other radical treatment for mental illness.* New York: Basic Books.

VAN, J. (1978, October 8). Doctors find rape suspect has 10 lives. *Chicago Tribune,* pp. 1, 20.

VAN BUREN, A. (1978, August 12). Dear Abby. *Champaign – Urbana News Gazette,* p. B–6.

VANCE, E. B., & WAGNER, N. N. (1976). Written descriptions of orgasm: A study of sex differences. *Archives of Sexual Behavior, 5,* 87–98.

VAN EVRA, J. P. (1983). *Psychological disorders of children and adolescents.* Boston: Little, Brown.

VAN KAMMEN, D. P. (1979). The dopamine hypothesis of schizophrenia revisited. *Psychoneuroendocrinology, 4,* 37–46.

VAN PRAAG, H. M. (1977). *Depression and schizophrenia: A contribution to their clinical pathologies.* New York: Spectrum.

VEITH, I. (1977). Four thousand years of hysteria. In M. J. Horowitz (Ed.), *Hysterical personality.* New York: Aronson.

VEREBEY, K., VOLAVKA, J., & CLOUET, D. (1978). Endorphins in psychiatry: An overview and a hypothesis. *Archives of General Psychiatry, 35,* 877–888.

VIAMONTES, J. A. (1972). A review of drug effectiveness in the treatment of alcoholism. *American Journal of Psychiatry, 128,* 1570–1571.

VICKERS, R. R., HERVIG, L. K., RAHE, R. H., & ROSENMAN, R. H. (1981). Type A behavior pattern and coping and defense. *Psychosomatic Medicine, 43,* 381–396.

VICTOR, M., & YAKOLEV, P. I. (1955). S. S. Karsakoff's psychic disorder in conjunction with peripheral neuritis: A translation of Karsakoff's original article with brief comments on the author and his contribution to clinical medicine. *Neurology, 5,* 394–406.

VIDALIS, A. A., & BAKER, G. H. B. (1986). Factors influencing effectiveness of day hospital treatment. *International Journal of Psychiatry, 32*(3), 3–8.

VIGOTSKY, L. S. (1934). Thought in schizophrenia (J. Kasanin, Trans.). *Archives of Neurology and Psychiatry, 31,* 1063–1077.

VIGOTSKY, L. S. (1962). *Thought and language* (E. Hanfmann & G. Vakar, Eds. and Trans.). Cambridge, MA: MIT Press and Wiley.

VINEY, L. L. (1985). Patterns of psychological reaction to asthma in children. *Journal of Abnormal Child Psychology, 13,* 477–484.

VLADECK, B. C. (1980). *Unloving care: The nursing home tragedy.* New York: Basic Books.

VOLAVKA. J., DAVIS, L. G., & EHRLICH, Y. H. (1979). Endorphins, dopamine, and schizophrenia. *Schizophrenia Bulletin, 5,* 227–239.

VOLK, B. W., ADACHI, M., & SCHNECK, L. (1978). The sphingolipidoses. In C. H. Carter (Ed.), *Medical aspects of mental retardation* (2nd ed.). Springfield, IL: Charles C Thomas.

VOLLMAN, R. F. (ED.). (1969). *Down's syndrome (mongolism): A reference bibliography*. Washington, DC: U.S. Government Printing Office.

VOLTAIRE, FRANÇOIS-MARIE AROUET. (1764). *Philosophical dictionary*. In R. T. Tripp (1970). *The international thesaurus of quotations*. New York: Crowell.

WACHTEL, P. L. (1977). *Psychoanalysis and behavior therapy: Toward an integration*. New York: Basic Books.

WAHL, C. W. (1956). Some antecedent factors in the family histories of 568 male schizophrenics of the United States Navy. *American Journal of Psychiatry, 113*, 201–210.

WAKEFIELD, J. C. (1987). Sex bias in the diagnosis of primary orgasmic dysfunction. *American Psychologist, 42*, 464–471.

WALD, P. M. (1976). Personal and civil rights of mentally retarded citizens. In M. Kindred, J. Cohen, D. Penrod, & T. Shaffer (Eds.), *The mentally retarded citizen and the law*. New York: Free Press.

WALDORF, D., MURPHY, S., REINARMAN, C., & JOYCE, B. (1977). *Doing coke: An ethnography of cocaine users and sellers*. Washington, DC: Drug Abuse Council.

WALKER, J. I., & BRODIE, H. K. H. (1985). Paranoid disorders. In H. I. Kaplan & B. J. Sadock (Eds.), *Comprehensive textbook of psychiatry* (4th ed.). Baltimore: Williams & Wilkins.

WALLACE, C. J. (1984). Community and interpersonal functioning in the course of schizophrenic disorders. *Schizophrenia Bulletin, 10*, 233–257.

WALLACE, J. (1986). The alcoholism controversy revisited. *American Psychologist, 41*, 479.

WALLIS, C. (1984, June 11). Heroin, a doctors' dilemma. *Time*, p. 62.

WALSH, B. T., STEWART, J. W., ROOSE, S. P., GLADIS, M., & GLASSMAN, A. H. (1984). Treatment of bulimia with phenelzine. *Archives of General Psychiatry, 41*, 1105–1108.

WARREN, L., & MCEACHREN, L. (1983). Psychosocial correlates of depressive symptomatology in adult women. *Journal of Abnormal Psychology, 92*, 151–160.

WASYLENKI, D., & FREEMAN, S. J. (1980). Life events and illness. In S. E. Greben, R. Pos, V. M. Rakoff, A. Bonkalo, F. H. Lowy, & G. Voineskos (Eds.), *A method of psychiatry*. Philadelphia: Lea & Febiger.

WATSON, J. B. (1913). Psychology at the behaviorist views it. *Psychological Review, 20*, 158–177.

WATSON, J. B. (1924). *Psychology from the standpoint of a behaviorist*. Philadelphia: Lippincott.

WATSON, J. B., & RAYNER, R. (1920). Conditioned emotional reactions. *Journal of Experimental Psychology, 3*, 1–14.

WATSON, S. J., & AKIL, H. (1979). "Endorphins, dopamine, and schizophrenia": Two discussions. *Schizophrenia Bulletin, 5*, 240–241.

WAXLER, N. (1975). The normality of deviance: An alternate explanation of schizophrenia in the family. *Schizophrenia Bulletin, 14*, 38–47.

WECHSLER, D. (1974). *Manual for the Wechsler Intelligence Scale for Children – Revised*. New York: Psychological Corporation.

WECHSLER, D. (1975). Intelligence defined and undefined: A relativistic appraisal. *American Psychologist, 30*, 135–139.

WECHSLER, D. (1981). *WAIS-R Manual: Wechsler Adult Intelligence Scale – Revised*. New York: Psychological Corporation.

WEIL, A. (1972). *The natural mind: A new way of looking at drugs and the higher consciousness*. Boston: Houghton Mifflin.

WEINBERGER, D. R. (1984). Brain disease and psychiatric illness: When should a psychiatrist order a CAT scan? *American Journal of Psychiatry, 141*, 1521–1527.

WEINER, B. A. (1985a). The insanity defense: Historical development and present status. *Behavioral Sciences and the Law, 3*, 3–35.

WEINER, B. A. (1985b). Mental disability and the criminal law. In S. J. Brakel, J. Parry, & B. A. Weiner, *The mentally disabled and the law*. Chicago: American Bar Foundation.

WEINER, B. A. (1985c). Rights of institutionalized persons. In S. J. Brakel, J. Parry, & B. A. Weiner, *The mentally disabled and the law*. Chicago: American Bar Foundation.

WEINER, B. A. (1985d). Treatment rights. In S. J. Brakel, J. Parry, & B. A. Weiner, *The mentally disabled and the law* (3rd ed.). Chicago: American Bar Foundation.

WEINER, L., BECKER, A., & FRIEDMAN, T. T. (1967). *Home treatment: Spearhead of community psychiatry*. Pittsburgh: University of Pittsburgh Press.

WEINGER, B. (1975). "On being sane in insane places": A process (attributional) analysis and critique. *Journal of Abnormal Psychology, 84*, 433–451.

WEISS, E., & ENGLISH, O. S. (1943). *Psychosomatic medicine*. Philadelphia: Saunders.

WEISS, E., & ENGLISH, O. S. (1949). *Psychosomatic medicine* (2nd ed.). Philadelphia: Saunders.

WEISS, G., HECHTMAN, L., PERLMAN, T., HOPKINS, J., & WENER, A. (1979). Hyperactives as young adults. *Archives of General Psychiatry, 36*, 675–681.

WEISS, J. M. A., & PERRY, M. E. (1976). Transcultural attitudes toward antisocial behavior: The "worst" crimes. *Social Science and Medicine, 10*, 541–545.

WEISS, L., & MASLING, J. (1970). Further validation of a Rorschach measure of oral imagery: A study of six clinical groups. *Journal of Abnormal Psychology, 76*, 83–87.

WEISSMAN, M. M., & BOYD, J. H. (1985). Affective disorders: Epidemiology. In H. I. Kaplan & B. J. Sadock (Eds.), *Comprehensive textbook of psychiatry* (Vol. 1) (4th ed.). Baltimore: Williams & Wilkins.

WEISSMAN, M. M., GAMMON, G. D., JOHN, K., MERIKANGAS, K., WARNER, V., PRUSOFF, B. A., & SHOLOMSKAS, D. (1987). Children of depressed parents: Increased psychopathology and early onset of major depression. *Archives of General Psychiatry, 44*, 847–853.

WEISSMAN, M. M., MERIKANGAS, K. R., JOHN, K., WICKRAMARATNE, P., PRUSOFF, B. A., & KIDD, K. K. (1986). Family–genetic studies of psychiatric disorders. *Archives of General Psychiatry, 43*, 1104–1116.

WENAR, C. (1982). *Psychopathology from infancy through adolescence*. New York: Random House.

WENAR, C., & RUTTENBERG, B. A. (1976). The use of BRIACC to evaluate therapeutic effectiveness. *Journal of Autism and Childhood Schizophrenia, 6,* 175–191.

WENDER, P. H. (1987). *The hyperactive child, adolescent, and adult: Attention deficit disorder through the lifespan.* New York: Oxford University Press.

WENDER, P. H., KETY, S. S., ROSENTHAL, D., SCHULSINGER, F., ORTMANN, J., & LUNDE, I. (1984). Psychiatric disorders in the biological and adoptive families of adopted individuals with affective disorders. *Archives of General Psychiatry, 43,* 923–929.

WENDER, P. H., & KLEIN, D. F. (1981). *Mind, mood, and medicine: A guide to the new biological psychiatry.* New York: Farrar, Straus, & Giroux.

WERLINDER, H. (1978). *Psychopathy: A history of the concepts—analysis of the origin and development of a family of concepts in psychopathology* (Uppsala Studies in Education, No. 6). Stockholm: Almquist & Wiksell.

WESTMORELAND, B. F. (1980). Organic mental disorders associated with epilepsy. In H. I. Kaplan, A. M. Freedman, & B. J. Sadock (Eds.), *Comprehensive textbook of psychiatry* (Vol. 2) (3rd ed.). Baltimore: Williams & Wilkins.

WETZEL, J. W. (1984). *Clinical handbook of depression.* New York: Gardner Press.

WEXLER, D. B. (1981). *Mental health law: Major issues.* New York: Plenum.

WHALEN, C. K. (1982). Hyperactivity and psychostimulant treatment. In J. R. Lachenmeyer & M. S. Gibbs (Eds.), *Psychopathology in childhood.* New York: Gardner Press.

WHITE, L., & TURSKY, B. (1986). Commentary on Roberts. *American Psychologist, 41,* 1003–1007.

WHITE, R. W., & WATT, N. F. (1973). *The abnormal personality* (4th ed.). New York: Ronald Press.

WHITE, R. W., & WATT, N. F. (1981). *The abnormal personality* (5th ed.). New York: Wiley.

WHITEHEAD, T. (1983). Mental illness and the law (rev. ed.). Oxford: Blackwell.

WHITLEY, O. R. (1977). Life with Alcoholics Anonymous: The Methodist class meeting as a paradigm. *Journal of Studies on Alcohol, 38,* 831–848.

WHITMONT, E. C., & KAUFMANN, Y. (1973). Analytical psychotherapy. In R. Corsini (Ed.), *Current psychotherapies.* Itasca, IL: Peacock.

WHITWELL, J. R. (1936). *Historical notes on psychiatry.* London: Lewis.

WIDIGER, T. A., FRANCES, A., SPITZER, R. L., & WILLIAMS, J. B. W. (1988). The DSM-III-R personality disorders: An overview. *American Journal of Psychiatry, 145,* 786–795.

WIDIGER, T. A., & NIETZEL, M. T. (1984). Kaplan's view of DSM-III: The data revisited. *American Psychologist, 39,* 1319–1320.

WILLIAMS, J. B. W., & SPITZER, R. L. (1983). The issue of sex bias in DSM-III: A critique of "A woman's view of DSM-III" by Marcia Kaplan. *American Psychologist, 38,* 793–798.

WILSNACK, S. C., WILSNACK, R. W., & KLASSEN, A. D. (1984/1985). *Alcohol Health and Research World, 9*(2), 5–13.

WILSON, G. T. (1978). Alcoholism and aversion therapy: Issues, ethics, and evidence. In G. A. Marlatt & P. E. Nathan (Eds.), *Behavioral approaches to alcoholism.* New Brunswick, NJ: Rutgers Center of Alcohol Studies.

WILSON, G. T. (1986). Cognitive–behavioral and pharmacological therapies for bulimia. In K. D. Brownell & J. P. Foreyt (Eds.), *Handbook of eating disorders: Physiology, psychology, and treatment of obesity, anorexia, and bulimia.* New York: Basic Books.

WILSON, J. R., & EDITORS OF TIME–LIFE BOOKS. (1969). *The mind.* New York: Time–Life Books.

WING, J. K. (1978). *Reasoning about madness.* Oxford: Oxford University Press.

WING, J. K., & BROWN, G. W. (1970). Institutionalism and schizophrenia. London: Cambridge University Press.

WING, J. K., COOPER, J. E., & SARTORIUS, N. (1974). The measurement and classification of psychiatric symptoms: Cambridge: Cambridge University Press.

WINICK, B. J. (1983). Incompetency to stand trial: Developments in the law. In J. Monahan & H. J. Steadman (Eds.), *Mentally disordered offenders: Perspectives from law and social science.* New York: Plenum.

WITKIN, H. A., MEDNICK, S. A., SCHULSINGER, F., BAKKESTROM, E., CHRISTIANSEN, K. O., GOODENOUGH, D. R., HIRSCHORN, K., LUNDSTEEN, C., OWEN, D. R., PHILLIP, J., RUBIN, D. B., & STOCKING, M. (1976). Criminality in XYY and XXY men. *Science, 193,* 547–555.

WITTKOWER, E. D. (1969). Perspectives of transcultural psychiatry. *International Journal of Psychiatry, 8,* 811–824.

WITTKOWER, E. D. (1974). Historical perspective of contemporary psychosomatic medicine. *International Journal of Psychiatry in Medicine, 5,* 309–319.

WITTKOWER, E. D. (1977). Historical perspective of contemporary psychosomatic medicine. In Z. L. Lipowski, D. R. Lipsit, & P. C. Whybrow (Eds.), *Psychosomatic medicine: Current trends and clinical applications.* New York: Oxford University Press.

WITZIG, J. S. (1970). The group treatment of male exhibitionists. *American Journal of Psychiatry, 125,* 179–185.

WOLPE, J. (1958). *Psychotherapy by reciprocal inhibition.* Stanford, CA: Stanford University Press.

WOLPE, J. (1961). The systematic desensitization treatment of neuroses. *Journal of Nervous and Mental Disease, 132,* 189–203.

WOLPE, J. (1969). *The practice of behavior therapy.* New York: Pergamon Press.

WOLPE, J. (1975). *The practice of behavior therapy* (2nd ed.). New York: Pergamon Press.

WOLPE, J. (1978). Cognition and causation in human behavior and its therapy. *American Psychologist, 33,* 437–446.

WOLPE, J. (1985). *The practice of behavior therapy* (3rd ed.). New York: Pergamon Press.

WOLPE, J., & LAZARUS, A. A. (1966). *Behavior therapy techniques: A guide to the treatment of neuroses.* New York: Pergamon Press.

WOLPERT, E. A. (1980). Major affective disorders. In H. I. Kaplan & B. J. Sadock (Eds.), *Comprehensive textbook in psychiatry* (3rd ed.). Baltimore: Williams & Wilkins.

WONG, D. F., ET AL. (1986). Positron emission tomography reveals elevated D$_2$ dopamine receptors in drug-naive schizophrenics. *Science, 234,* 1558–1563.

WOOD, G. (1983). *Cognitive psychology: A skills approach.* Monterey, CA: Brooks–Cole.

WOODHEAD, M. (1988). When psychology informs public policy. The case of early childhood intervention. *American Psychologist, 43,* 443–454.

WOODRUFF, R. A., JR., GOODWIN, D. W., & GUZE, S. B. (1974). *Psychiatric diagnosis.* New York: Oxford University Press.

WOODS, P. J., MORGAN, B. T., DAY, B. W., JEFFERSON, T., & HARRIS, C. (1984). Findings on a relationship between Type A behavior and headaches. *Journal of Behavioral Medicine, 7,* 277–286.

WORLD HEALTH ORGANIZATION. (1968). *International classification of diseases* (8th rev. ed.). Geneva: Author.

WORLD HEALTH ORGANIZATION. (1973). *Report of the international pilot study of schizophrenia.* Geneva: Author.

WORLD HEALTH ORGANIZATION. (1974). *Problems and programmes related to alcohol and drug dependence in 33 countries* (Publication No. 6). Geneva: Author.

WORLD HEALTH ORGANIZATION. (1979). *Schizophrenia: An international follow-up study.* New York: Wiley.

WORTMAN, C. B., & DINTZER, L. (1978). Is an attributional analysis of the learned helplessness phenomenon viable? A critique of the Abramson–Seligman–Teasdale reformulation. *Journal of Abnormal Psychology, 87,* 75–90.

WRIGHT, H. T., JR. (1976). Prenatal factors in causation (viral). In R. Koch & J. C. Dobson (Eds.), *The mentally retarded child and his family: A multi-disciplinary handbook* (rev. ed.). New York: Brunner/Mazel.

WRIGHT, J., PERRAULT, R., & MATHIEU, M. (1977). Treatment of sexual dysfunction: A review. *Archives of General Psychiatry, 34,* 881–890.

WRIGHT, J. S. (1964, May 9). The mentally disabled: Stepchildren of the law. *New Republic,* pp. 24, 26–27.

WRIGHT, L. (1988). The Type A behavior pattern and coronary artery disease: Quest for the active ingredients and the elusive mechanism. *American Psychologist, 43,* 2–14.

WYATT, R. J. (1978). Is there an endogenous amphetamine? A testable hypothesis of schizophrenia. In L. C. Wynne, R. L. Cromwell, & S. Matthysse (Eds.), *The nature of schizophrenia: New approaches to research and treatment.* New York: Wiley.

WYATT V. STICKNEY. (1972). 344 F.Supp. 373 (M.D. Ala.).

YABLONSKY, L. (1967). *Synanon: The tunnel back.* Baltimore: Penguin.

YAHRAES, H. (1978). *Causes, detection and treatment of childhood depression.* Washington, DC: U.S. Government Printing Office.

YALOM, I. (1985). *The theory and practice of group psychotherapy* (3rd ed.). New York: Basic Books.

YATES, A. J. (1980). *Biofeedback and the modification of behavior.* New York: Plenum.

YEATMAN, P., & HIRSCH, J. (1971). Review of D. Rosenthal & S. Kety (Eds.), *The transmission of schizophrenia. Psychiatry, 34,* 103–105.

YERKES, R. M., & MORGULIS, S. (1909). The method of Pavlov in animal psychology. *Psychological Bulletin, 6,* 257–273.

YOUNGBERG V. ROMEO. (1982). 102 S.Ct. 2452.

YURCHENCO, H. (1970). *A mighty high road: The Woody Guthrie Story.* New York: McGraw–Hill.

ZARIT, S. H., ORR, N. K., & ZARIT, J. M. (1985). *The hidden victims of Alzheimer's disease: Families under stress.* New York: New York University Press.

ZAX, M., & SPECTER, G. A. (1974). *An introduction to community psychology.* New York: Wiley.

ZIGLER, E., BALLA, D., & HODAPP, R. (1984). On the definition and classification of mental retardation. *American Journal of Mental Deficiency, 89,* 215–230.

ZIGLER, E., & PHILLIPS, L. (1961). Psychiatric diagnosis: A critique. *Journal of Abnormal and Social Psychology, 63,* 607–618.

ZILBERGELD, B. (1975). Group treatment of sexual dysfunction in men without partners. *Journal of Sex and Marital Therapy, 1,* 204–214.

ZILBERGELD, B. (1978). *Male sexuality: A guide to sexual fulfillment.* Boston: Little, Brown.

ZILBERGELD, B. (1980). Alternatives to couples counseling for sex problems: Group and individual therapy. *Journal of Sex and Marital Therapy, 6,* 3–18.

ZILBOORG, G., & HENRY, G. W. (1941). *A history of medical psychology.* New York: Norton.

ZIMMERMAN, D. R. (1973). *RH: The intimate history of a disease and its conquest.* New York: Macmillan.

ZIMMERMAN, M., CORYELL, W., CORENTHAL, C., & WILSON, S. (1986). A self-report scale to diagnose major depressive disorder. *Archives of General Psychiatry, 43,* 1076–1081.

ZINBERG, N. E., & FRASER, K. M. (1985). The role of the social setting in the prevention and treatment of alcoholism. In J. H. Mendelson & N. K. Mello (Eds.), *The diagnosis and treatment of alcoholism* (2nd ed.). New York: McGraw–Hill.

ZIS, A. P., & GOODWIN, F. K. (1982). The amine hypothesis. In E. S. Paykel (Ed.), *Handbook of affective disorders.* New York: Little, Brown.

ZUBIN, J. (1972). Discussion of symposium on newer approaches to personality assessment. *Journal of Personality Assessment, 36,* 427–434.

ZUBIN, J. (1985). Negative symptoms: Are they indigenous to schizophrenia? *Schizophrenia Bulletin, 11,* 461–469.

ZUCKERMAN, M. (1978). Sensation seeking and psychopathy. In R. D. Hare & D. Schalling (Eds.), *Psychopathic behaviour: Approaches to research.* London: Wiley.

Credits

Chapter 1

Case excerpt "Mr. and Mrs. A." reprinted by permission from R. L. Spitzer, A. E. Skodol, M. Gibbon, and J. B. W. Williams, *DMS-III Casebook*, First Edition, pp. 108–109. Copyright 1981 American Psychiatric Association. Table 1.1 reproduced by permission from D. Wechsler, *WAIS-R Manual: Wechsler Adult Intelligence Scale – Revised*, p. 28. Copyright © 1981 by the Psychological Corporation. All rights reserved.

Chapter 2

Figure 2.1 adapted by permission from *Assessment of Children's Intelligence and Special Abilities* (2nd edition) by J. M. Sattler, p. 16. Copyright © 1982 by J. M. Sattler, Publisher. Figure 2.2 adapted by permission from L. Bender, *Visual Motor Gestalt Test*, published by American Orthopsychiatric Association, 1938 ©. Box 2.1 adapted by permission from the *Diagnostic and Statistical Manual of Mental Disorders*, Third Edition Revised, pp. 3–10. Copyright 1987 American Psychiatric Association. Table 2.1 adapted by permission from the *Diagnostic and Statistical Manual of Mental Disorders*, Third Edition Revised, p. 12. Copyright 1987 American Psychiatric Association. Description of Luteal Phase Dysphoric Disorder quoted by permission from the *Diagnostic and Statistical Manual of Mental Disorders*, Third Edition Revised, p. 367. Copyright 1987 American Psychiatric Association. Box 2.3, *Minnesota Multiphasic Personality Inventory*, copyright © 1943, renewed 1950, this report 1982. From J. M. Butcher and L. S. Keller, *Objective Personality Assessment*. In G. Goldstein and M. Hersen (Eds.), *Handbook of Psychological Assessment*, Pergamon Press, Copyright 1987. Reprinted by permission of University of Minnesota and Pergamon Press.

Chapter 3

Figure 3.1 from *Biological Psychology*, D. P. Kimble, Figure 3–14. Copyright © 1988, Holt, Rinehart and Winston. Reprinted by permission of the publisher. Figure 3.2 adapted from H. M. van Praag, *Depression and Schizophrenia*, p. 13. Copyright 1977 Spectrum Publications, adapted by permission of H. M. van Praag.

Chapter 4

Figure 4.1 from R. M. Yerkes and S. Morgulis, "The Method of Pavlov in Animal Psychology," *Psychological Bulletin*, vol. 6, 257–273. Copyright 1909 American Psychological Association. Figure 4.2 from *Principles of Behavior Modification*, by Albert Bandura, Figure 3–14, Copyright © 1969, Holt, Rinehart and Winston. Reprinted by permission of the publisher.

Chapter 5

Figure 5.1 from *Introduction to Psychology – Eighth Edition*, by Rita L. Atkinson, R. C. Atkinson, & E. R. Hilgard, Figure 2–14, Copyright © 1983 by Harcourt Brace Jovanovich. Reprinted by permission of the publisher. Figure 5.2 from *Personality* by Irving L. Janis,

Figure 6–2, Copyright © 1969 by Harcourt Brace Javanovich. Also in *Stress and Frustration* by Irving L. Janis, 1971, Harcourt Brace Jovanovich. Reprinted by permission of the publisher. Lines of poem "Affliction of Margaret" from William Wordsworth, *The Complete Poetical Works of Wordsworth*, p. 312, Copyright 1904 and 1932, Houghton Mifflin Company. Reprinted courtesy of the publisher. Case excerpt, "Heart Attack," reprinted by permission from R. L. Spitzer, A. E. Skodol, M. Gibbon, and J. B. W. Williams, *DSM-III Casebook*, First Edition, p. 35. Copyright 1981 American Psychiatric Association. First 12 lines of poem "Lines and Squares" from A. A. Milne, *When We Were Very Young*. Copyright 1924 by E. P. Dutton, renewed 1932 by A. A. Milne. Reprinted by permission of the publisher, a division of NAL Penguin, Inc.

Chapter 6

"Memory Is a Blank for Youth Walking onto Key West Beach," Copyright © 1972 by the New York Times Company. Reprinted by permission.

Chapter 7

Figure 7.1 from *A Primer of Psychophysiology* by James Hassett. Copyright © 1978 W. H. Freeman and Company. Reprinted with permission.

Chapter 9

Figure 9.1 from *Sexual Behavior in the Human Male* by A. C. Kinsey, W. B. Pomeroy, and C. E. Martin, p. 638. Copyright 1948 by The Kinsey Institute for Research in Sex, Gender, and Reproduction. Reprinted by permission of the Institute. Case excerpt, "Professor," reprinted by permission from R. L. Spitzer, A. E. Skodol, M. Gibbon, and J. B. W. Williams, *DSM-III Casebook*, First Edition, p. 48. Copyright 1981 American Psychiatric Association. "A Letter from Freud," *American Journal of Psychiatry*, Volume 107, pp. 786–787. Copyright 1951. Reprinted courtesy of American Psychiatric Association.

Chapter 11

Figure 11.1 reprinted by permission from S. E. Nicol and I. I. Gottesman, "Clues to the Genetics and Neurobiology of Schizophrenia," *American Scientist*, volume 71, p. 399. Copyright 1983, Sigma Xi, The Scientific Research Society.

Chapter 12

Figure 12.1 reprinted from G. C. Davison and J. M. Neale, *Abnormal Psychology: An Experimental Clinical Approach*, Fifth Edition, p. 601. Copyright 1986 John Wiley & Sons. Excerpt from "23 Men on Life Raft, One Bet from Disaster," by S. Cady. Copyright © 1973 by the New York Times Company. Reprinted by permission. "The Suspicious Man" excerpt from W. Anderson (translator), *Theophrastus — The Character Sketches*, p. 77, Kent State University Press, 1970.

Chapter 13

Chapter 14

Chapter 15

Chapter 16

Chapter 17

Chapter 18

Photo Credits

Chapter 1

Opener: Andre Kertesz/Archive Pictures. Page 7: (left and center right) Culver Pictures, (center left) AP/Wide World Photos, (right) Reproduced from the Collection of The Library of Congress. Page 8: Edvard Munch. "The Scream." Courtesy Collection of Philip and Lynn Straus. Page 13: Michael O'Brien/Archive Pictures.

Chapter 2

Opener: Mike Mazzaschi/Stock, Boston. Page 23: Topham/The Image Works. Page 24: (left) Culver Pictures, (right) BBC Hulton/The Bettmann Archive. Page 25: (left) Courtesy The National Library of Medicine, (right) The Bettmann Archive. Page 36: Courtesy University of Minnesota Psychiatric Residential Unit. Page 42: (top) Frank Siteman/Picture Cube, (bottom left) From *The Life, Letters and Labours of Francis Galton* by K. Pearson, 1930, Vol. IIIA, (bottom right) Courtesy James McKeen Cattell. Page 43: (left) The Bettmann Archive, (right) Courtesy News & Publications Service, Stanford University. Page 44: Hayes/Monkmeyer Press. Page 46: (top left) Courtesy David Wechsler, (top right) Ken Robert Buck/The Picture Cube, (bottom) Nancy Hayes/Monkmeyer Press. Page 52: Courtesy Hans Huber, Bern, Switzerland. Page 53: (left) Courtesy Dr. Henri F. Ellenberger, University of Montreal, (right) Barbara Ries/Photo Researchers. Page 55: Courtesy Harvard University News Office. Page 56: Ellan Young/Photo Researchers. Page 60: Ulrike Welsch.

Chapter 3

Opener: Manfred Kage/Peter Arnold. Page 68: (top) M. Abbey/Photo Researchers, (bottom) The Bettmann Archive. Page 71: Courtesy Dr. Monte Buchsbaum, University of California at Irvine. Page 72: Lawrence Fried. Page 73: Edward A. Hubbard. Page 76: (top) Mary Evans/Sigmund Freud Copyrights/Photo Researchers, (center) Courtesy Weidenfeld and Nicolson, (bottom) Courtesy The National Library of Medicine. Page 77: (top left) Culver Pictures, (top right) Edmund Engelman, (bottom) The Bettmann Archive. Page 78: (top) Edmund Engelman, (bottom left) AP/Wide World Photos, (bottom right) The Bettmann Archive. Page 90: (left) Ergy Randall/Rapho/Photo Researchers, (right) Jon Erikson.

Chapter 4

Opener: Andre Kertesz/Archive Pictures. Page 101: Courtesy Archives of The History of American Psychology, University of Akron. Page 103: The Bettmann Archive. Page 104: Kathy Bendo. Page 106: Erika Stone/Peter Arnold. Page 107: Elizabeth Crews. Page 108: Courtesy Albert Bandura. Page 113: Owen Franken/Stock, Boston. Page 117: (left) Courtesy Price M. Cobbs, Pacific Management Systems, (right) The Bettmann Archive. Page 122: Ted Polumbaum. Page 123: (top) Henri Cartier Bresson/Magnum Photos, (bottom) Bernard Gotfryd.

Chapter 5

Opener: Arthur Tress/Photo Researchers. Page 133: Culver Pictures. Page 136: Richard Hutchings/Photo Researchers. Page 138: From

Phobia by John Vassos, Friede Covici, Inc., 1931, Special Collections, The Research Libraries, The New York Public Library. Page 145: UPI/Bettmann Newsphotos. Pages 148 and 149: Sidney Harris. Page 153: Martin Gershen/Photo Researchers.

Chapter 6

Opener: Charles Harbutt/Archive Pictures. Page 163: The Bettmann Archive. Page 166: Courtesy Museum of Modern Art/Film Stills Archive. Page 167: Courtesy Wisconsin Center for Film and Theatre Research. Page 169: Movie Star News. Page 170: Gerald Martineau/*The Washington Post*. Page 171: Joe Corello/Black Star. Page 175: Culver Pictures. Page 181: Ray Ellis/Photo Researchers.

Chapter 7

Opener: Erich Hartmann/Magnum Photos. Page 191: The Bettmann Archive. Page 192: Jeff Dunn/Stock, Boston. Page 195: George Mars Cassidy/The Picture Cube. Page 197: Elliot Erwitt/Magnum Photos. Page 204: Mark Antman/The Image Works. Page 205: (top) Owen Franken/Stock, Boston, (bottom) Mark Antman/The Image Works. Page 207: Lew Merrim/Monkmeyer Press.

Chapter 8

Opener: Fredrik D. Bodin/Stock, Boston. Page 215: Abigail Heyman/Archive Pictures. Page 217: Wide World Photos. Page 221: copyright © Punch-Spencer/Rothco. Page 224: Culver Pictures. Page 225: Historical Pictures Service, Chicago. Page 226: Tequila Minsky. Page 230: (left) Mary Ellen Mark/Archive Pictures, (right) Topham/The Image Works. Page 231: copyright © 1982 Columbia Pictures Industries, Inc.

Chapter 9

Opener: Christopher S. Johnson/Stock, Boston. Page 242: Wallace Kirkland/Time-Life Picture Agency. Page 245: Jason Aronson, Inc. Page 248: Rafael Macia/Photo Researchers. Page 251: Robert Levin/Black Star. Page 253: Courtesy Helen Singer Kaplan. Page 255: Sidney Harris.

Chapter 10

Opener: Eugene Richards/Magnum Photos. Page 270: Taken from "Depression as Expressed in Pre-Columbian Mexican Art" by Juan-Ramon de la Fuente, M.D., and Donato Alarcón-Segovia, M.D., *The American Journal of Psychiatry*, volume 137, number 9, page 1096. Copyright © 1980 The American Psychiatric Association. Reprinted with permission. Page 272: Sidney Harris. Page 273: Frances M. Cox/Stock, Boston. Page 276: Tony Mendoza/The Picture Cube. Page 278: Freda Leinwand/Monkmeyer Press. Page 292: Rob Nelson/Picture Group.

Chapter 11

Opener: Arthur Tress/Magnum Photos. Page 303: Raymond Depardon/Magnum Photos. Page 305: Courtesy National Museum, Stockholm. Page 307: Bill Bridges/Globe Photos. Page 310: (left) Courtesy Dr. Michael Cole, Laboratory of Comparative Human Cognition, (right)

Courtesy The National Library of Medicine. Page 315: Courtesy Manfred Bleuler. Page 323: AP/Wide World Photos. Page 327: Louis Fernandez/Black Star. Page 328: Sidney Harris. Page 329: (left) Courtesy Alburtus-Yale News Bureau, (right) Keystone/The Image Works.

Chapter 12

Opener: Erich Hartmann/Magnum Photos. Page 339: Ulrike Welsch. Page 341: The Bettmann Archive. Page 346: Bohdan Hrynewych/Stock, Boston. Page 349: Culver Pictures. Page 350: Bettye Lane/Photo Researchers. Page 360: Greenberg/Photo Researchers.

Chapter 13

Opener: Lynn McLaren/Photo Researchers. Page 376: CEA-ORSAY/CNRI/Science Photo Library/Photo Researchers. Page 377: Abigail Heyman/Archive Pictures. Page 379: (top left) UPI/Bettmann Newsphotos, (top center) Dan Budnik/Woodfin Camp, (top right) Jason Laure/Woodfin Camp, (center left and center) Culver Pictures, (center right) UPI/Bettmann Newsphotos, (bottom) Steve Kagan/Photo Researchers. Page 381: Sepp Seitz/Woodfin Camp. Page 382: Dr. M. Cole/Sovfoto. Page 383: Courtesy The Museum of Modern Art/Film Stills Archive. Page 384: Courtesy The National Library of Medicine. Page 385: (left) Culver Pictures, (right) AP/Wide World Photos. Page 386: The Bettmann Archive. Page 389: Culver Pictures.

Chapter 14

Opener: Arthur Tress/Photo Researchers. Page 401: Courtesy The Museum of Modern Art/Film Stills Archive. Page 406: Ethan Hoffman/Archive Pictures. Page 407: Paul Conklin. Page 408: Sidney Harris. Page 409: Howard Dratch/The Image Works. Page 414: AP/Wide World Photos. Page 418: Suzanne Arms/Jeroboam.

Chapter 15

Opener: Henriques/Magnum Photos. Page 425: Courtesy U.S. Department of Justice/National Archives. Page 426: (left) Courtesy U.S. Department of Justice/National Archives, (right) James Prince/Photo Researchers. Pages 428 and 429: Courtesy U.S. Department of Justice/National Archives. Page 431: Mark Antman/The Image Works. Page 432: Robert Goldstein/Photo Researchers. Page 434: Courtesy U.S. Department of Justice/National Archives. Page 441: Jeff Albertson/Stock, Boston.

Chapter 16

Opener: Cary Wolinsky/Stock, Boston. Page 453: Cary Wolinsky/Stock, Boston. Page 457: Tom Plambeck. Page 458: Gale Zucker/Stock, Boston. Page 464: Susan Rosenberg/Photo Researchers. Page 468: Courtesy The Alan Mason Chesney Medical Archives of The Johns Hopkins Medical Institutions. Page 470: Allan Grant. Page 471: Al Stephenson/Woodfin Camp. Page 473: Linda Ferrer/Woodfin Camp.

Chapter 17

Opener: From Jerry Uelsmann, *Uelsmann: Process and Perception*, essay by John Ames (Gainesville, FL: University of Florida Press,

1985), by permission. Page 483: (left) Sybil Shelton/Peter Arnold, (right) Ray Solomon/Monkmeyer Press. Page 486: Hank Lebo/Jeroboam. Page 490: Alan Carey/The Image Works. Page 494: Jeff Albertson/Stock, Boston. Page 495: Melissa Hayes English/Photo Researchers. Page 496: Philip J. Griffiths/Magnum Photos. Page 498: Hazel Hankin/Stock, Boston. Page 499: Elizabeth Crews. Page 501: Evan Johnson/Feroboam. Page 502: Anestis Diakopoulos/Stock, Boston.

Chapter 18

Opener: Arthur Tress/Woodfin Camp. Page 512: From *Comprehensive Textbook of Psychiatry* by Kaplan and Sadock, Courtesy The New York Academy of Medicine Library. Page 513: Paul Fusco/Magnum Photos. Page 518: Michael O'Brien/Archive Pictures. Page 523: From The Wall Street Journal-Permission, Cartoon Features Syndicate.

Chapter 19

Opener: From Jerry Uelsmann, *Uelsmann: Process and Perception*, essay by John Ames (Gainesville, FL: University of Florida Press, 1985), by permission. Page 531: (top left) Joan Menschenfreund, (top right) Sybil Shelton/Peter Arnold, (center left) Paul Fusco/Magnum Photos, (center right) Ken Robert Buck/Stock, Boston, (bottom) Sidney Harris. Page 533: Stella Kupferberg. Page 538: Historical Pictures Service, Chicago. Page 539: (top) The Bettmann Archive, (bottom) Cornell Capa/Magnum Photos. Page 540: (top) Jean-Claude Lejeune, (center) Daniel S. Brody/Stock, Boston, (right) Hazel Hankin. Page 541: Courtesy Institute of Psychoanalysis, Chicago. Photo by Bachrack. Page 542: Courtesy Alfred Adler Consultation Center. Page 544: UPI/Bettmann Newsphotos. Page 545: (left) Courtesy The Art Institute of Chicago, (right) North Wind Picture Archives. Page 546: The Bettmann Archive. Page 549: Inge Morath/Magnum Photos. Page 550: Real People Press.

Chapter 20

Opener: Benjamin Porter/Archive Pictures. Page 563: Courtesy Temple University Health Sciences Center. Page 565: UPI/Bettmann Newsphotos. Page 566: Alan Carey/The Image Works. Pages 568 and 571: Sidney Harris. Page 573: Historical Pictures Service, Chicago. Page 574: Dan Miller/*The New York Times*. Page 576: Van Bucher/Photo Researchers. Pages 582 and 584: Bohdan Hrynewych/Stock, Boston. Page 585: Michael Rougier, Life Magazine. Copyright © 1968 Time, Inc.

Chapter 21

Opener 21

Opener: Jeff Albertson/Stock, Boston. Page 594: Culver Pictures. Page 598: UPI/Bettmann Newsphotos. Pages 602 and 603: AP/Wide World Photos. Page 607: Mark ANtman/The Image Works. Page 608: M. E. Warren/Photo Researchers. Page 610: Mark Antman/The Image Works. Page 611: Bettye Lane/Photo Researchers Color Plates: Courtesy Adamson Collection, 16 Hollywood Rd., London SW10, 9 HY, England.

Author Index

Bhrolchain, M. N., 114
Bieber, Irving, 245
Biggs, J., Jr., 599
Bijou, S. W., 570
Binet, Alfred, 43
Bini, Lucio, 511, 525
Binitie, A., 120
Birk, L., 244
Birnbaum, H. J., 72, 155, 224, 612
Birnbaum, Morton, 603
Bivens, L. W., 514, 516, 517
Blanchard, E. B., 108, 208
Blashfield, R. K., 34, 36
Blau, T. H., 593
Blazer, D., 374
Bleuler, Eugen, 25, 62, 304–305, 310, 311, 312, 313, 314, 332, 524
Bleuler, Manfred, E., 314–315, 333
Bliss, E. L., 169
Bloch, S., 38
Bloom, B. L., 608
Blum, K., 407, 408, 424, 425, 427, 428, 429, 430, 432, 433, 437, 438, 441
Blumenthal, J. A., 198
Blunt, L. W., 600
Board on Mental Health and Behavioral Medicine, 295
Bobo, J. K., 613
Bockus, F., 584
Boehme, D. H., 319
Boffey, P. M., 33
Boggan, E. C., 248
Bohacek, N., 326
Bohlen, J., 244
Boll, T. J., 58
Bonagura, N., 455
Bonaparte, Marie, 78
Bonaparte, Napoleon, 85
Bond, P. A., 285
Bonet, Theophile, 271
Bonkalo, A., 372
Bonn, J. A., 156
Bonnie, R. J., 604
Booth, S., 456
Booth Luce, Clare, 380
Booth-Kewley, S., 209
Bootzin, R. R., 380
Borders, O. T., 433
Borgaonkar, D. S., 489
Borovoy, A., 197
Borsky, P. N., 203
Borthwick, S., 498
Boscarino, J., 554
Boskind-White, M., 465
Bouchard, T. J., 244
Boucher, R. J., 358
Bouhoutsos, J., 532
Bourne, P. G., 415
Bousfield, W. A., 101
Bowen, E., 464
Bowen, Elizabeth, 562
Bower, G. H., 101
Bowers, M. B., Jr., 70
Bowlby, John, 497
Boyd, J. H., 280
Brady, J. P., 464
Brady, T., 485

Braff, J., 597, 599
Braiker, H. B., 405, 417
Brakel, S. J., 592, 595, 602, 605
Brand, R. J., 198
Brandt, A. M., 387
Braukmann, C. J., 457
Brawer, F., 53
Brecher, E. M., 432, 440, 443, 444
Breggin, P. R., 517
Breier, A., 140, 315
Brenner, C., 222
Brent, D., 611
Breuer, Joseph, 163, 534
Brien, L., 551
Brill, A. A., 77
Brinkley, J., 426
Briquet, Paul, 176
Brittain, R. P., 355
Brodie, H. K. H., 10, 177, 228, 284, 303, 331, 344, 347, 385, 387, 455, 462, 485, 488, 513, 521
Brody, J. E., 137, 378
Bromet, E. J., 610
Brooks, G. W., 315
Broverman, D. M., 114, 115
Broverman, I. K., 114, 115
Brower, K. J., 427
Brown, B. S., 514, 516, 517, 578
Brown, G. W., 114
Brown, P., 610
Brown, R. A., 442
Brown, R. I. F., 361
Brownmiller, S., 225, 612
Bruch, Hilde, 463, 464
Brunton, M., 355
Brushfield, Thomas, 486
Bryson, S. E., 484
Buchsbaum, M. S., 69, 320, 321
Bullitt, William, 78
Bullough, V. L., 217
Bunney, W. E., Jr., 284, 285, 320
Burford, R., 440
Burgess, A. W., 155
Burkhart, B. R., 612
Burnham, L., 492
Burns, George, 380
Buros, O. K., 48
Burton, N., 461
Busbee, D. L., 489
Buss, Arnold H., 34, 67, 117, 118
Busse, E. W., 183
Busse, T. V., 580
Bussod, M., 263
Butcher, J. N., 49, 50, 51
Butler, Robert N., 380
Butterfield, E. C., 500
Butters, N., 57, 58, 371
Byck, R., 426
Byers, L. W., 319
Byrne, D. G., 199
Byrne, G., 442

Caddell, J., 456
Caddy, G. R., 417
Cade, J. F. J., 523
Cadoret, R. J., 287
Cady, S., 361

Cahalan, D., 413
Cahan, E. D., 104
Cain, D. J., 546
Callahan, E. J., 430
Cameron, Norman A., 10, 309, 329
Campbell, J., 203
Campbell, R. J., 68, 388
Campbell, S. B., 453
Cancro, R., 273, 316, 318
Cannon, Walter Bradford, 191, 209, 283
Capéraà, P., 456
Caplan, L., 598
Caprio, F., 229
Caracci, G., 520
Cardozo, Benjamin, N., 592
Carney, F. L., 358
Carpenter, W. T., Jr., 121, 312, 313, 327
Carran, D. T., 497
Carrigan, S., 295
Carroll, E., 426
Carroll, E. M., 154
Carroll, Lewis, 593
Casey, D. E., 520
Casey, R. J., 474
Cattell, James McKeen, 42, 43
Cautela, J. R., 180–181, 416, 567
Cavanaugh, J. L., Jr., 357
Celsus, Cornelius, 429
Centers for Disease Control, 387, 491
Centerwall, S. A., 487, 488
Centerwall, W. R., 487, 488
Centore, J. M., 326
Cerletti, Ugo, 511, 525
Chamberlin, J., 485
Chambers, W. J., 40
Chambless, D. K., 564
Chan, C., 326, 520
Chance, N. A., 120
Chaney, R. H., 487
Chapin, K., 312
Chapman, A. H., 538, 539
Chapman, H., 303, 305, 311
Chapman, Jean P., 309, 310–311
Chapman, Loren J., 309, 310–311
Charcot, Jean Martin, 76, 77, 178
Charney, D. C., 279
Charney, D. S., 140
Chase, P. M., 513
Chasin, M., 244
Chemers, M. M., 199
Cherones, J. H., 356
Chesher, G. B., 440
Chesler, P., 114
Chesney, M. A., 197, 198
Chesser, E., 220
Children's Defense Fund, 452
Chinn, P. C., 492
Chinsky, J. M., 607, 608
Chodoff, P., 162
Christenson, R., 374
Christiansen, J., 439
Christrup, J., 439
Church, R. W., 224
Ciaranello, R. D., 284
Cicchetti, D. V., 481
Ciraulo, D. A., 415
Clancy, K., 114

Subject Index